Freedom in the
2017

The findings of *Freedom in the World 2017* include events
From January 1, 2016, through December 31, 2016

Freedom in the World 2017
The Annual Survey of
Political Rights and Civil Liberties

Arch Puddington
General Editor

Jennifer Dunham
Managing Editor

Elen Aghekyan, Shannon O'Toole, Tyler Roylance, Sarah Repucci
Associate Editors

Freedom House • New York, NY and Washington, DC

ROWMAN & LITTLEFIELD PUBLISHERS, INC.
Lanham • Boulder • New York • Toronto • Oxford

Published by Rowman & Littlefield
A wholly owned subsidiary of The Rowman & Littlefield Publishing Group, Inc.
4501 Forbes Boulevard, Suite 200, Lanham, Maryland 20706
www.rowman.com

Unit A, Whitacre Mews, 26–34 Stannary Street, London SE11 4AB

British Library Cataloguing in Publication Information Available

Library of Congress Cataloging-in-Publication Data

978-1-5381-0007-3 (paper)
978-1-5381-0008-0 (electronic)

♾ ™ The paper used in this publication meets the minimum requirements of American National Standard for Information Sciences—Permanence of Paper for Printed Library Materials, ANSI/NISO Z39.48–1992.

Printed in the United States of America

Contents

Acknowledgments

Freedom in the World 2017 could not have been completed without the contributions of numerous Freedom House staff members and consultants. The section titled "The Survey Team" contains a detailed list of the writers and advisers without whose efforts this project would not have been possible.

Sarah Repucci served as the project director for this year's survey and Jennifer Dunham served as director of research. Elen Aghekyan, Bret Nelson, Shannon O'Toole, and Tyler Roylance provided extensive research, analytical, editorial, and administrative assistance. Joshua Adamson, Valentina Duhanaj, Jacqueline Laks Gorman, Anne Kosseff-Jones, M.L. Liu, Janet Olson, Jake Palmer, Peter Schmidtke, Amy Slipowitz, and Matthew Thomas served as additional country report editors. Rebeka Foley, Marian Jones, Sara Rosales, and Aliyah Salim provided additional support. Overall guidance for the project was provided by Daniel Calingaert, acting president of Freedom House, Arch Puddington, distinguished fellow for democracy studies, and Vanessa Tucker, vice president for analysis. A number of Freedom House staff offered valuable additional input on the country reports and/or ratings process.

Freedom House would like to acknowledge the generous financial support for *Freedom in the World* by the Smith Richardson Foundation, the Lilly Endowment, the Schloss Family Foundation, and Kim G. Davis. Freedom House also gratefully acknowledges the contributions of the 21st Century ILGWU Heritage Fund, the Reed Foundation, and other private contributors. Freedom House is solely responsible for the report's content.

Populists and Autocrats
The Dual Threat to Global Democracy

Arch Puddington and Tyler Roylance

In 2016, populist and nationalist political forces made astonishing gains in democratic states, while authoritarian powers engaged in brazen acts of aggression, and grave atrocities went unanswered in war zones across two continents.

All of these developments point to a growing danger that the international order of the past quarter-century—rooted in the principles of democracy, human rights, and the rule of law—will give way to a world in which individual leaders and nations pursue their own narrow interests without meaningful constraints, and without regard for the shared benefits of global peace, freedom, and prosperity.

The troubling impression created by the year's headline events is supported by the latest findings of *Freedom in the World*. A total of 67 countries suffered net declines in political rights and civil liberties in 2016, compared with 36 that registered gains. This marked the 11th consecutive year in which declines outnumbered improvements.

While in past years the declines in freedom were generally concentrated among autocracies and dictatorships that simply went from bad to worse, in 2016 it was established democracies—countries rated Free in the report's ranking system—that dominated the list of countries suffering setbacks. In fact, Free countries accounted for a larger share of the countries with declines than at any time in the past decade, and nearly one-quarter of the countries registering declines in 2016 were in Europe.

As the year drew to a conclusion, the major democracies were mired in anxiety and indecision after a series of destabilizing events. In the United States, the presidential victory of Donald Trump, a mercurial figure with unconventional views on foreign policy and other matters, raised questions about the country's future role in the world. Britain's vote to leave the European Union, the collapse of the Italian government after a failed referendum on constitutional reform, a series of antidemocratic moves by the new government in Poland, and gains by xenophobic nationalist parties elsewhere in Europe similarly cast doubt on the strength of the alliances that shaped the institutions of global democracy.

At the same time, Russia, in stunning displays of hubris and hostility, interfered in the political processes of the United States and other democracies, escalated its military support for the Assad dictatorship in Syria, and solidified its illegal occupation of Ukrainian territory. China also flouted international law, ignoring a tribunal's ruling against its expansive claims of sovereignty over the South China Sea and intensifying its repression of dissent within its borders. And unscrupulous leaders from South Sudan and Ethiopia to Thailand and the Philippines engaged in human rights violations of varying scale with impunity.

In the wake of last year's developments, it is no longer possible to speak with confidence about the long-term durability of the EU; the incorporation of democracy and human rights priorities into American foreign policy; the resilience of democratic institutions in Central Europe, Brazil, or South Africa; or even the expectation that actions like the assault on Myanmar's Rohingya minority or indiscriminate bombing in Yemen will draw international criticism from democratic governments and UN human rights bodies. No such assumption, it seems, is entirely safe.

SYRIA'S IMPACT ON DEMOCRACIES

While the democratic world stood aside throughout the year, a coalition of repressive dictatorships bombed and shelled Aleppo and other Syrian cities where opponents of President Bashar al-Assad had gained footholds. Assad, with crucial assistance from Russia, Iran, and a multinational array of Iranian-backed Shiite militias, clearly regained the initiative in the five-year civil war, whose grinding violence has killed hundreds of thousands of people and displaced millions more. A U.S.-led coalition pounded the Islamic State (IS) militant group in the east, but left the pro-Assad alliance undisturbed as it focused its military might on non-IS rebels and civilians.

Since the war began, each new horror has appeared to deter rather than motivate a coordinated international response. The conflict has only grown more complex and intractable, however, and democratic governments continue to reap the consequences of their hesitation.

The enormous refugee flows and IS-inspired terrorism generated by the Syrian conflict have played an important role in the weakening of democratic standards in Europe and the United States. Arrivals of asylum seekers in Europe declined in 2016, largely due to the hardening of borders in the Balkans and an agreement between the EU and Turkey in which Ankara pledged to block irregular departures. But the drop in numbers failed to stem anti-refugee rhetoric, as European political leaders routinely smeared those fleeing conflict zones as criminals, rapists, and terrorists.

Moreover, the agreement with Turkey—an already dubious haven for refugees given its raging Kurdish insurgency and regular terrorist attacks—became a deeper source of embarrassment after Turkish president Recep Tayyip Erdoğan embraced an unvarnished form of authoritarianism in response to a failed coup attempt in July. Having put down the coup, the government imposed emergency rule that resulted in the arrest of nearly 40,000 civilians, the imprisonment of dozens of journalists for their work, the shuttering of hundreds of media outlets and nongovernmental organizations (NGOs), the arrest of the leaders and hundreds of officials from the third-largest party in the parliament, and the firing of more than a hundred thousand civil servants.

Terrorism continued to fuel political upheaval in Europe and the United States despite major territorial losses suffered by IS and other extremist groups such as Boko Haram. France, Belgium, and Germany endured high-profile terrorist attacks, an IS-inspired mass shooting struck the U.S. state of Florida, and smaller assaults elsewhere in Europe were foiled or interrupted by the authorities.

Several European governments reacted by adopting laws that gave enhanced powers to security forces and eased constraints on surveillance. More ominously, persistent fears over the upsurge in terrorist attacks stoked public hostility toward Muslim minorities and immigrants, deepening existing social rifts and threatening civil liberties. During the American presidential campaign, Donald Trump at various times promised to prevent all Muslims from entering the United States, deport Syrians already in the country, and carry out "extreme vetting" of the beliefs of refugees and immigrants.

RADICALIZING AUTHORITARIAN STATES

The conflicts in the Middle East and political upheavals in the democracies often deflected the world's attention from worsening domestic repression in China, Russia, and other authoritarian countries, which stand to gain from a breakdown in democratic norms at the international level. In fact, both Beijing and Moscow stepped up efforts to reshape the world in their own image.

In China, the Communist Party regime led by President Xi Jinping tightened its grip with the adoption of new laws and regulations on cybersecurity, foreign nonprofits, and religious affairs. Heavy sentences handed down to human rights lawyers, microbloggers, grassroots activists, and religious believers dealt an additional blow to those seeking to improve conditions in the country.

As Xi consolidated his personal power, moving rapidly away from the existing pattern of collective leadership within the party elite, he sought to enforce greater ideological discipline through a propaganda campaign that forbade intraparty dissent and relentlessly criticized "Western" democratic values. The regime also advanced plans to introduce a "social credit" system that would connect each citizen's financial, social, political, and legal data to produce a single numerical rating of his or her behavior and trustworthiness. A misstep in one area would presumably have repercussions in every other aspect of an individual's life.

Beijing's growing intolerance for individual autonomy at home was mirrored by its intrusions into the affairs of neighboring societies. The leadership issued an unprecedented ruling on Hong Kong's Basic Law with the aim of preventing pro-independence and pro-democracy politicians from taking their seats in the self-governing territory's legislature. The Chinese government similarly adopted a hostile attitude toward Taiwan after the local opposition party, which opposes unification with China, swept to victory in presidential and parliamentary elections. And Beijing has intensified its pressure on governments in the region to return those who have fled China to escape persecution, especially members of the Uighur Muslim minority.

Russia followed a comparable pattern, combining domestic repression with an ambitious program of regional intimidation and long-distance political sabotage. The regime of President Vladimir Putin stage-managed Russia's parliamentary and regional elections, leading to record low turnout and the total extinction of liberal opposition in the legislature. The Kremlin also added to its blacklists of "extremist" websites and NGOs that it considers "foreign agents" or "undesirable."

Outside its borders, Russia radically accelerated its indiscriminate bombing campaign against population centers held by anti-Assad rebels in Syria, contributing little to the fight against IS elsewhere in the country. Moscow also deepened its interference in elections in established democracies through a strategy that combined support for populist and nationalist parties, theft and publication of the internal documents of mainstream parties and candidates, and the aggressive dissemination of fake news and propaganda. Russia's efforts to influence the Italian constitutional referendum and the presidential election in the United States represented a major leap forward in Putin's bid to undermine the integrity and even change the outcome of democratic processes.

THE AMERICAN ELECTION

The success of Donald Trump, an outsider candidate who challenged the mainstream forces of both major parties, demonstrated the continued openness and dynamism of the American system. It also demonstrated that the United States is not immune to the kind of populist appeals that have resonated across the Atlantic in recent years. The campaign featured a series of disturbing events, stemming mainly from Trump's own remarks and the actions of his supporters, and punctuated by Trump's insistence, without evidence and even after he won, that the election results were marred by massive fraud.

Trump's statements and actions during the postelection transition period suggested that he had abandoned or softened a number of his more contentious campaign promises, including mass deportations of immigrants, lowering the legal bar for libel suits, and the prosecution of his Democratic opponent, Hillary Clinton—something he had frequently vowed to pursue during the campaign. At the same time, Trump did not immediately make clear the guiding principles of his foreign policy or his vision for America's role in the world. Before the election, he belittled the country's treaty alliances and was critical of the EU. He repeatedly praised Vladimir Putin, spoke dismissively of broadly accepted evidence that Russia had interfered in the campaign, and indicated a willingness to accept Russia's occupation of Crimea.

After eight years as president, Barack Obama left office with America's global presence reduced and its role as a beacon of world freedom less certain. Trump's positions during 2016 raised fears of a foreign policy divorced from America's traditional strategic commitments to democracy, human rights, and the rules-based international order that it helped to construct beginning in 1945.

THE MENACE OF COUNTER-DEMOCRATIC TRANSITIONS

Recent developments in Central Europe have raised the possibility that some of the most remarkable transitions from dictatorship to democracy in the 1980s and '90s will be substantially reversed by elected populist leaders.

After little more than a year in power, the right-wing Law and Justice (PiS) party has already delivered several serious blows to Poland's democratic institutions. The government passed legislation that has politicized public media, neutered the constitutional court, handed the security services sweeping powers of surveillance, and restricted the right of public protest. It has also proposed worrisome regulations on NGOs.

Observers have described the PiS's actions as an accelerated and condensed version of what the ruling Fidesz party has accomplished in Hungary since 2010. Both governments have repudiated liberal values, attacked the institutions of pluralism, and sought to use the economic power of the state for partisan political ends. While the PiS has focused on providing economic benefits to its core constituents, Fidesz has manipulated laws and state contracts to enrich an affiliated business elite that can buttress its future political dominance.

The system pioneered by Hungarian prime minister Viktor Orbán stands as an appealing model for elected political leaders with authoritarian leanings. A further spread of such "illiberal democracy" in Central Europe and the Balkans seems likely given the orientation of major figures in Slovakia, the Czech Republic, and Serbia, among others.

While none of these leaders have moved their countries entirely outside the democratic sphere as of yet, the record in places like Venezuela and Turkey suggests that elected populists who initially limit their authoritarian impulses can graduate to political purges and prosecutions, the militarization of government, sweeping controls on journalism, and politicized wrecking of the economy.

A POPULIST-AUTHORITARIAN NEXUS

Over the past decade or more, authoritarian powers have formed loose coalitions to counter the influence of the United States and its democratic allies. Initially, they focused on neutralizing efforts at the United Nations and other transnational bodies to enforce global standards on democracy and human rights. They also worked to mobilize support for fellow dictators facing domestic or international pressure, like Syria's Assad.

More recently, however, the authoritarian regimes have reached out to sympathetic parties, movements, and political figures from democracies in Europe and elsewhere. Marine Le Pen, the leader of France's National Front, frequently praises Vladimir Putin, has received financial assistance from Russian sources, and has called for France to align with Russia as a counterweight to the United States. Populist politicians in the Netherlands, Britain, Italy, and Austria meet regularly with Russian officials, criticize the sanctions imposed by the EU after the Kremlin's invasion of Ukraine, and support Russia's interests in votes at the European Parliament.

This affection for authoritarians like Putin probably represents a minority view in Europe. Polls still show that Europeans regard Russia as repressive and dangerous. But many have come to have doubts about certain core values that underpin the European idea. They are increasingly inclined to question the economic and social benefits of European integration and democratic solidarity in general. They tend to regard sovereign states rather than supranational entities as best equipped to address problems like economic inequality and displacement, surging rates of immigration, and humanitarian crises. And they are less likely to support a foreign policy that requires their nation to assist others for the greater good.

For all of these reasons, citizens of democracies may look to Putin, Xi, and other authoritarian rulers as proof that nation-states can and should buck international commitments and do what they must to protect their own interests. Partnering with such leaders is equated with an embrace of hard-nosed national opportunism.

History shows that this strategy leads to ruin. When universal values and international law are cast aside, global affairs are governed by force. Small-state nationalists who admire foreign dictators today could find their countries subjugated by the same leaders tomorrow. Worse still, they could simply be trampled amid the lawless competition of great powers.

Orphaned Democrats

Citizens in many vulnerable democracies, such as Taiwan and the Baltic states, are alert to these threats. Others in places like Hong Kong, Tunisia, and Ukraine understand that the survival of their freedoms depends on international democratic solidarity. Protesters, activists, refugees, and besieged civilians around the world rely on the promise of international aid and advocacy backed by democratic governments.

The question is whether the United States and Europe will ignore their own long-term interests and retreat from their responsibilities as global leaders. If they do, Russia, China, Iran, and their ilk can be expected to fill the void.

REGIONAL TRENDS

Sub-Saharan Africa: Entrenched Autocrats, Fragile Institutions

Several major countries in sub-Saharan Africa faced critical tests in the form of elections, popular protests, or surges in political violence during 2016.

Ethiopia experienced its worst political upheaval in many years, when protests by the Oromo people over ethnic and land rights broadened into a general eruption of popular discontent after decades of ethnicity-based political marginalization by the authoritarian ruling party, the Ethiopian People's Revolutionary Democratic Front (EPRDF). Security forces used disproportionate and lethal force against protesters in the Oromia and Amhara regions, killing hundreds of people over the course of the year. Tens of thousands were detained, the internet and social media were periodically blocked, and a state of emergency imposed in October further expanded the government's already vast powers to crack down on the rights to expression, assembly, and movement.

In the Democratic Republic of Congo, unpopular president Joseph Kabila successfully maneuvered to delay constitutionally mandated elections, reaching a fragile "consensus" deal to extend his term beyond its scheduled December 2016 expiration; while the deal is supported by the main opposition coalition and much of civil society, skepticism remains over implementation. Kabila's regime violently suppressed protests against the election delay, and blocked social media in an effort to thwart protest organizers—taking a page from the playbook of the EPRDF and other repressive regimes around the world.

Some of the stronger democracies in Southern and East Africa exhibited worrying signs of dysfunction during the year. In South Africa, revelations about the vast political influence of the wealthy Gupta family placed even greater pressure on President Jacob Zuma, who was also contending with protests over service delivery and university governance and the ruling African National Congress's unprecedented losses in subnational elections. Meanwhile, Zuma's administration moved to withdraw South Africa from the International Criminal Court, tarnishing the country's commitment to the rule of law.

Political violence in Mozambique reached dangerous new levels, as supporters of the opposition Mozambique National Resistance (RENAMO) and ruling Front for the Liberation of Mozambique (FRELIMO) engaged in assassinations. Clashes erupted between the army and RENAMO fighters, and security forces' abuse of civilian populations in the country's central region forced thousands to flee to Malawi.

In Zimbabwe, citizens increasingly frustrated with an inept and corrupt government vented their dissatisfaction through social protest movements, prompting violence, arrests, and demonstration bans. The protests, combined with factional rivalries in the ruling Zimbabwe African National Union–Patriotic Front (ZANU-PF) and a self-inflicted economic crisis, have further weakened the regime of 92-year-old president Robert Mugabe.

In a bright spot at year's end, Ghana consolidated its position as one of the most stable democracies on the continent when opposition candidate Nana Akufo-Addo defeated incumbent John Mahama in the December presidential election.

Also that month, the Gambia seemed poised to deliver a major democratic breakthrough when authoritarian president Yahya Jammeh initially conceded defeat to opposition candidate Adama Barrow in a shock election result. However, Jammeh later reneged, and at year's end he continued to dispute Barrow's victory despite intense pressure from domestic, regional, and international officials to turn over power on schedule in January 2017.

Asia-Pacific: Silencing Critics of Arbitrary Rule

A number of repressive rulers in Asia reined in free speech and assembly during 2016 to smother public criticism of their own crimes and abuses.

Thailand's military junta, which seized power in a 2014 coup, maintained its grip on power by prosecuting even the slightest criticism under an array of restrictive laws. In this constrained atmosphere, voters approved a draft constitution that guaranteed the military outsized influence over civilian politics even after general elections scheduled for 2017. In China, an intrusive new cybersecurity law made it easier for authorities to monitor and prosecute online criticism of President Xi Jinping's Communist Party regime, while authorities in both Malaysia and the Maldives cracked down on demonstrators responding to allegations that top politicians had embezzled vast amounts of money from state coffers.

In the Philippines, newly elected president Rodrigo Duterte won widespread support for his policy of extrajudicial killings of suspected drug dealers and addicts, which by some counts claimed as many as 6,000 lives. Duterte admitted to shooting suspected criminals himself as mayor of Davao, and his aggressive public admonitions of his critics contributed to a climate of fear among activists in the country.

However, in a demonstration of democratic strength, enormous protests calling for the ouster of President Park Geun-hye in response to corruption allegations went forward peacefully in South Korea. The hundreds of thousands of citizens who took to the streets demanded an end to cronyism and opacity among political and business elites, and the protest movement ultimately led to Park's impeachment.

Americas: Political Turmoil and the Promise of Peace

Venezuelan president Nicolás Maduro's combination of strong-arm rule and dire economic mismanagement pushed his country to a status of Not Free for the first time in 2016. Venezuela had served as a model for populist regimes in the region, but today it epitomizes the suffering that can ensue when citizens are unable to hold their leaders to account.

The like-minded regime of President Daniel Ortega brought Nicaragua to its lowest point in more than 20 years. Having stacked the judiciary in his favor and whittled away the independent media, Ortega was able to nearly eliminate the opposition in presidential and legislative elections. With Venezuela, Nicaragua is one of the few countries in the Americas on an extended downward trajectory.

In Brazil, the ouster of President Dilma Rousseff dominated the political scene in 2016. However history may judge the impeachment itself, the process impeded government functions by absorbing executive and legislative attention for months, and it did little to resolve a broader corruption crisis in which virtually the entire political class faced allegations of bribery, influence peddling, and embezzlement. The year's events only increased public frustration, as elected officials seemed more concerned with their own fates than with the country's severe economic recession and soaring unemployment.

The peace deal in Colombia offered a welcome counterpoint to the economic and political breakdown in neighboring Venezuela. The agreement, which was rejected in a popular referendum but then revised and passed into law, augurs well for a democracy that has long been crippled by violence. However, a political opening in Cuba, which helped broker the peace, still seemed far off despite the death of Fidel Castro and two years of warming relations with the United States.

Middle East and North Africa: The Open Wounds of Civil Conflict

The Middle East and North Africa (MENA) has long been one of the world's two worst-performing regions. In 2016, it demonstrated the depths to which human freedom can fall after decades of authoritarian misrule, corruption, and erratic foreign interventions.

Libya was further plagued by political and security crises during the year. Despite a UN-brokered political agreement and the formation of a presidential council, the country's governance remained crippled by the existence of multiple, competing state authorities, autonomous militias, and the presence of IS fighters opposed to all sides. The humanitarian situation and conditions for human rights have worsened as a result of insecurity and widespread impunity, and prospects for improvement are dim.

The war in Yemen continued to devastate what was already the poorest country in the region. The Houthi rebels occupying the capital and most of the north sought to form their own government given the failure of peace talks with the recognized government, which holds territory in the south. In the process they have made no guarantee that they will restore the country's past political pluralism. Media independence has been all but eliminated as a result of the conflict, and civil liberties in general have effectively been suspended.

Syria remained the world's least free country. Most of those living behind the front lines were governed by a dictatorship, IS extremists, or Kurdish militants, and many others were trapped in the middle of appalling violence. The humanitarian crisis reached a nadir toward the end of the year as regime forces bombarded and finally recaptured eastern Aleppo from rebel militias.

Eurasia: Incumbents Armored against the Future

Eurasia was divided between a more European-oriented fringe and a core of rigid autocracies in 2016. While Ukraine, Georgia, and Moldova struggled to build on fragile democratic gains, several leaders to the east took steps to shore up their power in the face of economic and political uncertainty.

Apparently unnerved by the repercussions of a lengthy slump in oil prices, the rulers of Azerbaijan and the Central Asian states used tightly controlled constitutional referendums to extend their rule into the future. In Azerbaijan, the authorities declared voter approval for a longer presidential term, among dozens of other changes. As a result, President Ilham Aliyev, who already enjoyed freedom from term limits, will not need to seek reelection again until 2020.

In Tajikistan, a referendum cleared the way for President Emomali Rahmon to run for an unlimited number of terms and lowered the age of eligibility for the presidency—a move likely meant to allow Rahmon's son to succeed him.

The Kyrgyz political elite also turned to a plebiscite to serve its own interests, rushing through a constitutional overhaul that will shift power from the presidency to the prime minister. The amendments drew allegations that President Almazbek Atambayev, whose single term is set to expire in 2017, aimed to retain power by moving to the premiership.

Europe: Cracks in a Pillar of Global Freedom

From the Brexit vote to antidemocratic reforms by Poland's new government, the many internal strains within Europe exposed vulnerabilities that were previously hidden or ignored. Combined with external pressures like Russian interference and the migrant crisis, these problems made it clear that the continent can no longer be taken for granted as a bastion of democratic stability.

The rise of antiestablishment parties in Poland, France, Germany, and elsewhere is changing Europe's political landscape. It is also shifting the debate in ways that undermined the fundamental values of democracy. Xenophobia, religious intolerance, and in some cases the neutering of democratic institutions for partisan ends are gaining acceptance among both voters and government officials. Even German chancellor Angela Merkel seemed to pander to anti-Muslim sentiment by calling for a ban on the full-face veil toward the end of the year.

The Czech Republic's October 2017 elections could make it the next Central European domino to fall to a populist leader, and France's upcoming presidential race was already being closely watched in 2016 as a potential watershed for Europe as a whole. However, these trends are not inexorable. Austrian voters made it clear that a far-right head of state was unacceptable to them, choosing the Green Party's Alexander van der Bellen over Freedom Party candidate Norbert Hofer by a solid margin.

In the Balkans, meanwhile, fair election processes and the rule of law further deteriorated as the EU neglected its role in promoting democracy among aspiring member states. While there might have been deference to EU norms in the past, leaders in Bosnia and Herzegovina (BiH), Serbia, Montenegro, and Macedonia harassed civil society critics, obstructed investigations of government wrongdoing, and ignored constitutional procedures even as EU accession talks went on, largely unfazed. Observers expressed concerns that progress toward democratic standards was being replaced by a toxic mix of nationalism, corruption, governmental dysfunction, and Russian interference.

The following people were instrumental in the writing of this essay: Elen Aghekyan, Jennifer Dunham, Shannon O'Toole, Sarah Repucci, and Vanessa Tucker.

Introduction

The *Freedom in the World 2017* survey contains reports on 195 countries and 14 related and disputed territories. Each country report begins with a section containing the following information: **population, capital, political rights rating** (numerical rating), **civil liberties rating** (numerical rating), **freedom rating** (the average of the political rights and civil liberties ratings), **freedom status** (Free, Partly Free, or Not Free), **"electoral democracy" designation**, and a **10-year ratings timeline**. Each territory report begins with a section containing the same information, except for the capital and the electoral democracy designation. The population figures are drawn primarily from the *2016 World Population Data Sheet* of the Population Reference Bureau.

The **political rights** and **civil liberties** ratings range from 1 to 7, with 1 representing the most free and 7 the least free. The **status** designation of Free, Partly Free, or Not Free, which is determined by the average of the political rights and civil liberties ratings, indicates the general state of freedom in a country or territory. Any improvements or declines in the ratings since the previous survey are noted next to the relevant number in each report. Positive or negative trends that were not sufficient to trigger a ratings change may be highlighted by upward or downward **trend arrows**, which are located next to the name of the country or territory. A brief explanation of ratings changes or trend arrows is provided for each country or territory as required. For a full description of the methods used to determine the survey's ratings, please see the chapter on the survey's methodology.

The **10-year ratings time line** lists the political rights and civil liberties ratings and status for each of the last 10 years. Each year that is included in the timeline refers to the year under review, *not* the edition of the survey. Thus, the ratings and status from the *Freedom in the World 2017* edition are listed under "2016" (the year that was under review for the 2017 survey edition).

Following the section described above, each country and territory report is composed of four parts: an **overview**, bullets on **key developments**, an **executive summary**, and an analysis of **political rights and civil liberties**. The overview provides a succinct, general description that explains the country or territory's place on the 0–7 rating scale; bullets on key developments summarize key events that took place in 2017; the executive summary analyzes the year's major developments and why they are significant for the country or territory's state of freedom; and the section on political rights and civil liberties analyzes the degree of respect for the rights and liberties that Freedom House uses to evaluate freedom in the world. This section is composed of seven parts that correspond to the seven main subcategories in the methodology and justify a country or territory's score for each indicator. The scores for each indicator, subcategory, and category, along with any changes from the previous year, are noted next to the relevant subheading.

Afghanistan

Political Rights Rating: 6
Civil Liberties Rating: 6
Freedom Rating: 6.0
Freedom Status: Not Free
Electoral Democracy: No

Population: 33,400,000
Capital: Kabul

Ten-Year Ratings Time-line For Year Under Review (Political Rights, Civil Liberties, Status)

Year Under Review	2007	2008	2009	2010	2011	2012	2013	2014	2015	2016
Rating	5,5,PF	5,6,PF	6,6,NF	6,6,NF	6,6,NF	6,6,NF	6,6,NF	6,6,NF	6,6,NF	6,6,NF

Overview: Afghanistan has a progressive constitution marrying its Islamic identity with commitment to a wide range of internationally recognized rights, within the framework of an electoral democracy. In practice, citizens have never enjoyed the full range of political and civic rights promised to them. Successive disputed elections and a tendency toward bargains between elites have weakened democratic accountability. High levels of violence, limited state authority, endemic corruption, and contested ideas of Muslim identity all limit political rights and civil liberties.

KEY DEVELOPMENTS IN 2016:

- In September, it was announced that the current National Unity Government (NUG), led by President Ashraf Ghani and Chief Executive Abdullah Abdullah, intended to serve Ghani's full, five-year presidential term, but without convening a loya jirga, or grand council, to discuss constitutional reform.
- Also in September, a new electoral law was passed by presidential decree, and in November, new members were appointed to the election commission. However, no date was set for the overdue parliamentary elections.
- Members of the Hazara ethnic group led mass demonstrations in Kabul in the spring and summer, and authorities for the most part took a permissive stance toward the protests. However, one such demonstration was attacked by suicide bombers, killing some 80 people.
- Around 700,000 refugees returned to Afghanistan, most of whom had been pushed out of Pakistan.

EXECUTIVE SUMMARY

The National Unity Government, established to address a dispute over the result of the 2014 presidential election, survived its second year. Some elements of an emergent opposition had propagated the idea that the political agreement that had established the coalition government was to last only for two years, and that upon its expiration the NUG must convene a loya jirga to discuss constitutional reforms that would better define who was to hold executive power. Instead, it was announced that their NUG would operate for Ghani's full five-year presidential term.

In September, the president issued a decree containing provisions of long-awaited electoral reforms, and in November, new members were appointed to the election commission. However, no date was set for parliamentary elections, nor was it clear how elections would be possible in the prevailing insecurity. The parliament elected in 2010 continued to govern, well past its original term.

The Taliban increased their control over Afghan territory, while violence against civilians continued at levels comparable to the previous year.

A highly competent attorney general was appointed, but faced a major challenge in terms of restoring the rule of law. The most prominent example of the entrenched impunity in Afghanistan came when the first vice president was accused of ordering assault and unlawful detention, and efforts to investigate the claims stalled.

A pattern of mass forced migration became even more complex in 2016. The Afghan exodus to Europe continued, though on a smaller scale than in 2015. Meanwhile, harassment of Afghans in Pakistan prompted some 700,000 people to return to Afghanistan, with the needs of returnees severely straining public infrastructure.

POLITICAL RIGHTS: 10 / 40

A. Electoral Process: 2 / 12

Afghanistan's president is directly elected for up to two five-year terms and has the power to appoint ministers, subject to parliamentary approval. In the directly elected lower house of the National Assembly, the 249-seat Wolesi Jirga (House of the People), members stand for five-year terms. In the 102-seat Meshrano Jirga (House of Elders), the upper house, the provincial councils elect two-thirds of members for three- or four-year terms, and the president appoints the remaining one-third for five-year terms. The constitution envisages the election of district councils, which would also send members to the Meshrano Jirga, though these have not been established. Ten Wolesi Jirga seats are reserved for the nomadic Kuchi community, including at least three women, and 65 of the chamber's general seats are reserved for women.

In the 2014 presidential election, the two first-round winners—Abdullah, a former foreign minister, who received 45 percent of the vote, and Ghani, a former finance minister, who took 32 percent—faced off in a final round held that June, with a high reported turnout. After the Independent Election Commission (IEC) published preliminary results showing Ghani leading by more than 10 percentage points, the Abdullah camp alleged voter fraud, claimed victory, and threatened to overthrow the government. The United States brokered an agreement calling for an internationally supervised audit and the formation of the National Unity Government. Ghani became president, and Abdullah became chief executive, a new post resembling that of a prime minister. The final vote tallies for the two candidates were not officially announced.

The April 2014 provincial council elections were also drawn out due to complaints over irregularities and a large quantity of fraudulent votes. It was not until October 2014 that the election commission announced the winners of the 458 council seats.

The most recent parliamentary elections, held in September 2010, were characterized by widespread fraud. The parliament's term expired in 2015, with the NUG and current lawmakers unable to agree on reforms that would pave the way for the next elections. The parliament elected in 2010 was still seated throughout 2016, with a presidential decree allowing members to serve until fresh elections were held. In September 2016, after two unsuccessful attempts, a new electoral law was passed by presidential decree, amid some confusion about its content and the legality of its various provisions. In November, new IEC members were appointed. However, at year's end no date had been set for the overdue elections; there is no clarity on how redrawing constituency boundaries would be achieved; and some leading politicians had expressed concern over the lack of progress toward issuing reliable digital identification for voters. Widespread insecurity also made it impossible to guarantee conditions for free and fair elections across the country.

B. Political Pluralism and Participation: 6 / 16

Afghanistan's electoral system uses the single nontransferable vote, with most candidates for elected office running as independents and participating in fluid alliances linked to local and regional patronage networks. Political parties, many of them operating within coalitions, played an active role in backing candidates for the 2014 presidential election. However, parties lack a formal role within the legislature, weakening their ability to contribute to stable policymaking and legislative processes. Despite their limited relevance in Afghanistan's government, parties have been free to seek registration since 2005, and dozens have completed the process.

The Taliban have consistently opposed the holding of elections. Although their calls to boycott the 2014 election were widely ignored, the presence of various armed groups and local strongmen, including those enlisted by the government as anti-Taliban militias, poses a major obstacle to free public participation in the political process, especially outside major urban centers. Government officials and politicians at all levels are regularly targeted for assassination.

The United States maintained about 8,400 military personnel in Afghanistan through the end of 2016. In July, U.S. president Barack Obama slowed the pace of troop withdrawal in response to the intensification of Taliban violence. The United States covers the bulk of the operating costs of the Afghan security forces. Although the NUG was formed on the basis of an agreement brokered by a U.S. envoy, both the United States and the Kabul government insist that the latter enjoys full sovereignty and control over political decisions.

The constitution recognizes multiple ethnic and linguistic minorities and provides more guarantees of equal status to minorities than historically have been available in Afghanistan. Since 2001, the traditionally marginalized Shiite Muslim minority, which includes most ethnic Hazaras, have enjoyed increased levels of political representation and participation in national institutions. Nevertheless, participation is curtailed for all segments of the population by lack of security, flawed elections, and the dominance of local patronage networks.

C. Functioning of Government: 2 / 12

The NUG struggled to field a full cabinet in 2016. During the first half of the year, the parliament finally approved nominees for attorney general, defense and interior ministers, and intelligence chief. But later in the year, the cabinet started to unravel. In November, the parliament summoned various ministers to account for their failure to spend the development budgets allocated to their ministries, and promptly passed votes of no confidence against several deemed to have managed their budgets poorly.

Corruption remains a key concern in national life. In addition to depressing state revenues, endemic corruption reduces military effectiveness and undermines government legitimacy, and plays into Taliban claims that the Kabul government and ruling elite are inherently corrupt. In a December 2016 report, Integrity Watch Afghanistan estimated that Afghans paid approximately $3 billion in bribes to public officials during the year; 71 percent of Afghans believed that corruption was worse in 2016 than in 2014 and 2015.

The NUG has made efforts to address corruption in the public procurement program. Corrupt political appointments remain problematic, with some lucrative postings in the interior ministry in effect being bought and sold. Major corruption prosecutions are uncommon, and during 2016 no further progress was reported on recovering assets of the failed Kabul Bank.

CIVIL LIBERTIES: 14 / 60

D. Freedom of Expression and Belief: 6 / 16

Afghanistan hosts a vibrant media sector, with multiple outlets in print, radio, and television that collectively carry a wide range of views and are generally uncensored. Media providers include independent and commercial firms, as well as a state broadcaster and outlets tied to specific political interests. The rapid expansion in access to mobile phones, the internet, and social media has allowed many Afghans greater access to diverse views. Facebook alone is estimated to have a million users. The NUG has taken a public position in support of media freedom and has cooperated with initiatives to counter security threats to the media. However, amid the ongoing insurgency, media have faced both direct targeting and collateral damage. One local watchdog reported 415 violent attacks on the media in 2016, with 14 journalists killed.

While religious freedom has improved since 2001, it is still hampered by violence and discrimination aimed at religious minorities and reformist Muslims. The constitution established Islam as the official religion and guaranteed freedom of worship to other religions. Blasphemy and apostasy by Muslims are considered capital crimes, and non-Muslim proselytizing is strongly discouraged. Militant groups have targeted mosques and clerics as part of the larger civil conflict. Hindus, Sikhs, and Shiite Muslims, particularly those from the Hazara ethnic group, face official obstacles and discrimination by the Sunni Muslim majority. Moreover, conservative social attitudes, intolerance, and the inability or unwillingness of law enforcement officials to defend individual freedoms mean that those perceived as violating religious and social norms are highly vulnerable to abuse.

Academic freedom is largely tolerated in government-controlled areas. In addition to public schooling, there has been a growth in private education, with new universities enjoying full autonomy from the government. Government security forces and the Taliban have both taken over schools to use as military posts, which creates a sense of insecurity even after the forces withdraw. The expansion of Taliban control in rural areas has left an increasing number of public schools outside of government control. The Taliban operate an education commission in parallel to the official ministry of education. Although their practices vary between areas, some schools under Taliban control reportedly allowed teachers to continue teaching, but banned certain subjects and replaced them with Islamic studies. In August 2016, the Taliban kidnapped two university professors at the American University of Afghanistan in Kabul, and a fortnight later sent gunmen into the campus, where they killed 13 students and staff.

Although private discussion in government-held areas is largely free and unrestrained, discussion of a political nature is more dangerous for Afghans living in contested or Taliban-controlled areas. The government is not known to illegally restrict or monitor the internet.

E. Associational and Organizational Rights: 4 / 12

The constitution guarantees the rights to assembly and association, subject to some restrictions, but they are upheld erratically from region to region. The largest demonstrations to take place in 2016 focused on the routing of a major electricity transmission line that would deliver energy from Turkmenistan to Afghanistan. A new activist group, the Enlightenment Movement, with a base in the Hazara community, staged major rallies in Kabul in May and July in connection with concerns about the project. Although authorities took extensive security precautions to exclude demonstrators from the city center, overall the government response to the civic mobilization was permissive. However, the July demonstration ended in a massacre, when suicide bombers killed some 80 participants. The Islamic State militant group claimed responsibility for the attack, which was widely understood as a sectarian act, as the demonstrators were largely Shia and the march presented Islamic State with an opportunity to hit back at the assertiveness of this traditionally oppressed minority sect.

The constitution guarantees the right to form associations and there is a relatively enabling legal framework and supportive attitude from the national authorities. Nongovernmental organizations (NGOs) play an important role in the country, particularly in urban areas, where thousands of cultural, welfare, and sports associations operate with little interference from authorities. During 2016, the Economy Ministry counted as active 1,971 local NGOs and 279 international NGOs, although periodically organizations are deregistered when the ministry considers them noncompliant with reporting requirements. Threats and violence by the Taliban and other actors, especially a pattern of kidnappings, have curbed the activities of many NGOs and have hampered recruitment of foreign aid workers.

Despite broad constitutional protections for workers, labor rights are not well defined, and currently no effective enforcement or dispute-resolution mechanisms are in place.

F. Rule of Law: 2 / 16

The judicial system operates haphazardly, and justice in many places is administered on the basis of a mixture of legal codes by inadequately trained judges. Corruption in the judiciary is extensive, with judges and lawyers often subject to threats and bribes from local leaders or armed groups. Informal justice systems, employing variants of both customary law and Sharia (Islamic law), are widely used to arbitrate disputes, especially in rural areas. The Taliban have installed their own judiciary in areas they control, but also conduct summary executions.

In April 2016, the parliament approved appointment of a new attorney general who has a strong track record of commitment to legality and human rights. However, he faces massive challenges in promoting the rule of law.

Prosecutions and trials suffer from a number of weaknesses, including lack of proper representation, excess reliance on uncorroborated witness testimony, lack of reliable forensics evidence, arbitrary decision-making, and failure to publish court decisions. Furthermore, there is a well-ensconced culture of impunity for the country's political and military power brokers. In December 2016, the former governor of Jowzjan Province accused First Vice President Abdul Rashid Dostum of having him detained and assaulted, and at year's end it was unclear whether the attorney general could compel the vice president to cooperate with an investigation.

The police force is heavily militarized and primarily focused on its role as a first line of defense against insurgents in administrative centers. There are high levels of corruption and complicity in organized crime among police, particularly near key smuggling routes. The torture of detainees by Afghan police, military, and intelligence services reportedly remains common. Government-aligned strongmen and powerful figures within the security forces operate illegal detention centers.

The conflict in Afghanistan continued at a high intensity in 2016, with a heavy toll on civilians. The United Nations Assistance Mission in Afghanistan (UNAMA) recorded 11,418 conflict-related civilian casualties in 2016 (3,498 deaths and 7,920 injuries), almost the same level as had occurred in 2015. UNAMA attributed 61 percent of the casualties to the Taliban and other insurgents and 24 percent to Afghan security and other progovernment forces. The figures reveal a trend toward the Afghan national security forces causing an increased proportion of civilian casualties, mainly from aerial and ground-based bombard-ment. During the year, the Taliban expanded their campaign of attacks on provincial centers and their control of rural areas. They sustained a campaign of high-profile suicide bombings and complex attacks against civilian targets, such as restaurants and hotels, and targets where civilian casualties could be anticipated, such as military convoys moving through populated urban areas. The local branch of the Islamic State faced pressure from both the government and Taliban, but managed to hold onto an enclave in eastern Nangarhar Prov-ince. Although the Taliban were responsible for most insurgent violence, the Islamic State fighters also took responsibility for a string of attacks, mostly targeting Shia civilians.

Historically, Afghanistan has been home to small communities of Hindus and Sikhs, though in 2016 there were thought to be fewer than 7,000 Hindus and Sikhs in the country compared to hundreds of thousands in the 1970s. Despite some legal protections, these religious minorities remain subject to harassment and discrimination, including in employ-ment and education. In December 2016, unknown gunmen shot and killed a Sikh commu-nity leader in Kunduz.

There is no legal protection for LGBT (lesbian, gay, bisexual and transgender) people, who face societal disapproval and abuse by police. Same-sex sexual activity is considered illegal under the penal code and Sharia.

G. Personal Autonomy and Individual Rights: 2 / 16

The government does not restrict the right of travel within the country or abroad, though insecurity and other obstacles hamper freedom of movement in practice. In 2016, Afghani-stan was embroiled in a multidimensional crisis of forced migration. First, the conflict at home continued to displace Afghans within the country, and more than 580,000 people newly displaced during the year brought the cumulative total of internally displaced people to 1.6 million. Secondly, Afghans remained the second largest group of migrants or refu-gees arriving in southern Europe, with some 42,000 Afghans arriving by sea in the first eleven months of the year. However, the biggest new development concerned Afghans returning to the country. In the wake of Pakistan's campaign of harassment against Afghans during the summer of 2016 and Pakistani authorities' foot-dragging over the extension of refugee documentation, there was a surge in Afghans returning to the country from Paki-stan. Many of the arrivals had not previously planned to leave Pakistan and were ill-prepared for the move. European countries also started to deport Afghan asylum seekers whose applications were rejected, and the European Union countries effectively made their renewed aid commitments to Afghanistan conditional on the government cooperating with the deportations. An estimated 700,000 returnees, most of them from Pakistan, crossed into Afghanistan during 2016. The mass movements, happening in conditions of conflict, put severe strain on public infrastructure.

Citizens are formally free to own property, buy and sell land, and establish businesses. There has also been a trend away from government monopolies. Economic freedoms, how-ever, are constrained by patronage, corruption, and the dominant economic role of a narrow, politically connected elite. Over the past decade the most profitable activities available to Afghans have been government and defense contracting, narcotics trafficking, and property and minerals development. Investors in all of these sectors have depended on connections to those in power. A combination of harassment, extortion, and arbitrary taxation make for a highly unfavorable business climate for any investor hoping to operate within the law.

Although women have formal rights to education and employment, and some partici-pate in public life, discrimination and domestic violence remain pervasive, with the latter often going unreported because of social acceptance of the practice. Women's choices regarding marriage and divorce remain circumscribed by custom and discriminatory laws. On some issues, customary practices withhold even rights that are guaranteed to women by Sharia. The forced marriage of young girls to older men or widows to their husbands' male relations is a problem, and many girls continue to be married before the legal age of 16. The courts and the detention system have been used to enforce social control of women, for example by jailing those who defy their families' wishes regarding marriage.

Women in urban areas typically enjoy greater access to education and formal employment, and are better able to participate in national politics. Women accounted for about 16 percent of the candidates in the 2010 parliamentary elections, and roughly 41 percent of registered voters were women; 69 female candidates were elected. While no women candidates ran in the 2014 presidential election, 273 women ran for provincial council seats, securing 97 of them. Female electoral participation has been limited by threats, harassment, and social restrictions on traveling alone and appearing in public.

Most victims of human trafficking in Afghanistan are children trafficked internally to work in various industries, become domestic servants, settle debts, or be subjected to commercial sexual exploitation. Victims of trafficking are frequently prosecuted for moral crimes.

Albania

Political Rights Rating: 3
Civil Liberties Rating: 3
Freedom Rating: 3.0
Freedom Status: Partly Free
Electoral Democracy: Yes

Population: 2,900,000
Capital: Tirana

Ten-Year Ratings Timeline For Year Under Review (Political Rights, Civil Liberties, Status)

Year Under Review	2007	2008	2009	2010	2011	2012	2013	2014	2015	2016
Rating	3,3,PF	3,3,PF	3,3,PF	3,3,PF	3,3,PF	3,3,PF	3,3,PF	3,3,PF	3,3,PF	3,3,PF

Overview: Albania has a built a record of competitive elections, though political parties are highly polarized and often focused on leading personalities. Civil liberties such as religious freedom and freedom of assembly are respected. Corruption and organized crime remain serious problems despite recent government efforts to address them, and the intermingling of powerful business, political, and media interests inhibits the development of truly independent news outlets. The Romany minority continues to face discrimination in education, health care, employment, and housing.

KEY DEVELOPMENTS IN 2016:

- Beginning in July, the parliament passed a series of laws and constitutional amendments designed to reform the judicial system. The most controversial law, under which judges and prosecutors will be vetted for possible corruption and links to organized crime, was upheld by the Constitutional Court in December after a challenge by the opposition Democratic Party (PD).
- In November, the European Commission recommended that the European Union (EU) formally open accession negotiations with Albania once it has made tangible

progress in implementing the judicial reforms, particularly the vetting process. The European Council accepted the recommendation in December.

EXECUTIVE SUMMARY

In July, Albania's parliament passed the first in a series of laws and constitutional amendments aimed at overhauling the courts and justice system. The ruling Socialist Party (PD) pressed ahead with the reforms through the end of the year, as the effort was a key condition set by the EU for the opening of membership talks with Albania. However, the opposition PD sought to block many of the changes, arguing that they were unconstitutional. The most controversial law called for the evaluation of current and prospective judges and prosecutors based on their professionalism, moral integrity, and independence from the influences of organized crime, corruption, and politics. The PD and the union of judges challenged the so-called vetting law before the Constitutional Court, but the court upheld it in December, citing in part an endorsement from the Council of Europe's Venice Commission.

The current government has taken some steps to improve politicians' accountability for corruption and other abuses. A law passed in December 2015 banned individuals with criminal records from holding office, and officials submitted self-declaration forms in 2016. The Central Electoral Commission voted in December to dismiss two members of parliament and one mayor for hiding their past criminal convictions. Another lawmaker had been removed by the Constitutional Court in May due to a conflict of interest, and a whistle-blower protection law was adopted in June. According to a 2016 survey on corruption, while the general perception of corruption in state institutions remains high, the share of those reporting an actual experience with corruption—being asked to pay a bribe—decreased from 57 percent in 2010 to 44 percent in 2015.

POLITICAL RIGHTS: 28 / 40 (+ 1)

A. Electoral Process: 8 / 12

B. Political Pluralism and Participation: 13 / 16

C. Functioning of Government: 7 / 12 (+ 1)

CIVIL LIBERTIES: 40 / 60

D. Freedom of Expression and Belief: 13 / 16

E. Associational and Organizational Rights: 9 / 12

F. Rule of Law: 9 / 16

G. Personal Autonomy and Individual Rights: 9 / 16

This country report has been abridged for *Freedom in the World 2017*. For background information on political rights and civil liberties in Albania, see *Freedom in the World 2016*.

Algeria

Political Rights Rating: 6
Civil Liberties Rating: 5
Freedom Rating: 5.5
Freedom Status: Not Free
Electoral Democracy: No

Population: 40,800,000
Capital: Algiers

Ten-Year Ratings Timeline For Year Under Review (Political Rights, Civil Liberties, Status)

Year Under Review	2007	2008	2009	2010	2011	2012	2013	2014	2015	2016
Rating	6,5,NF	6,5,NF	6,5,NF	6,5,NF	6,5,NF	6,5,NF	6,5,NF	6,5,NF	6,5,NF	6,5,NF

Overview: Political affairs in Algeria are dominated by a closed elite based in the military and the ruling party, the National Liberation Front (FLN). President Abdelaziz Bouteflika has been in office since 1999, and while there are multiple opposition parties in the parliament, elections are distorted by fraud and other forms of manipulation. Authorities use restrictive laws to curb criticism in the media and suppress street protests. Other concerns include rampant corruption, the threat of terrorist attacks, and occasional violence between Arabs and Berbers as well as between Algerians and migrants from sub-Saharan Africa.

KEY DEVELOPMENTS IN 2016:

- A presidential decree in January dissolved the military's powerful Intelligence and Security Department (DRS) and replaced it with three directorates that would report directly to the presidency and focus on internal security, external security, and technical intelligence, respectively.
- In February, the parliament passed constitutional revisions that reintroduced a two-term limit for the presidency and bolstered the legislature's modest powers, among other changes.
- In March, the terrorist group Al-Qaeda in the Islamic Maghreb (AQIM) claimed responsibility for an attack in which rockets were fired at a gas facility near Ain Salah. No casualties were reported.
- In June, the authorities arrested two journalists from the television channel KBC and an official with the Culture Ministry in connection with satirical programming. Two television programs were shut down, and the defendants received suspended prison sentences in July.

EXECUTIVE SUMMARY

The government in February 2016 pushed through a number of constitutional revisions that were apparently designed to improve its popular support and lay the foundation for a smooth presidential transition in light of growing concerns about President Abdelaziz Bouteflika's health and possible successors. Amendments approved by the parliament reintroduced a two-term limit for the presidency, though Bouteflika would be able to seek reelection in 2019; enlarged the role and powers of the legislature relative to the executive, for example by requiring the president to consult the parliamentary majority on the appointment of a prime minister; made Tamazight, the language of the Berber population, an official language, meaning it could be used on administrative documents; and set the goal of gender equality in the labor market and public institutions.

However, the authorities also worked to ensure control over the media and suppress dissent. In July, the government secured a court ruling that prevented businessman and Bouteflika critic Issad Rebrab from purchasing El-Khabar media group, the parent company of television station KBC. Also that month, two KBC journalists received suspended prison sentences connected to satirical television programming, and the programs in question were shut down; the government said the journalists had violated licensing rules. Journalist and blogger Mohamed Tamalt, who had been arrested in June and sentenced to two years in prison in July for insulting the president on Facebook, died in December after engaging in a hunger strike and reporting beatings by prison guards.

Security forces regularly restricted the freedom of assembly. Among other incidents during the year, January protests against the relocation of a power plant in the town of Oued El Ma led to violent clashes between demonstrators and police after the latter used tear gas, and a demonstration by teachers seeking greater job security in Algiers in March was violently dispersed by police. The authorities also used aggressive tactics to cope with migration from sub-Saharan Africa. In December, following clashes between Algerians and migrants in an Algiers neighborhood, police rounded up some 1,400 sub-Saharan Africans and moved them to a remote camp near Tamanrasset before arbitrarily expelling many of them from the country.

POLITICAL RIGHTS: 11 / 40

A. Electoral Process: 4 / 12

B. Political Pluralism and Participation: 4 / 16

C. Functioning of Government: 3 / 12

CIVIL LIBERTIES: 24 / 60

D. Freedom of Expression and Belief: 7 / 16

E. Associational and Organizational Rights: 5 / 12

F. Rule of Law: 5 / 16

G. Personal Autonomy and Individual Rights: 7 / 16

This country report has been abridged for *Freedom in the World 2017*. For background information on political rights and civil liberties in Algeria, see *Freedom in the World 2016*.

Andorra

Political Rights Rating: 1
Civil Liberties Rating: 1
Freedom Rating: 1.0
Freedom Status: Free
Electoral Democracy: Yes

Population: 80,000
Capital: Andorra la Vella

Ten-Year Ratings Timeline For Year Under Review (Political Rights, Civil Liberties, Status)

Year Under Review	2007	2008	2009	2010	2011	2012	2013	2014	2015	2016
Rating	1,1,F	1,1,F	1,1,F	1,1,F	1,1,F	1,1,F	1,1,F	1,1,F	1,1,F	1,1,F

The country or territory displayed here received scores but no narrative report for this edition of *Freedom in the World*.

Angola

Political Rights Rating: 6
Civil Liberties Rating: 6
Freedom Rating: 6.0
Freedom Status: Not Free
Electoral Democracy: No

Population: 25,800,000
Capital: Luanda

Ten-Year Ratings Timeline For Year Under Review (Political Rights, Civil Liberties, Status)

Year Under Review	2007	2008	2009	2010	2011	2012	2013	2014	2 015	2016
Rating	6,5,NF	6,5,NF	6,5,NF	6,5,NF	6,5,NF	6,5,NF	6,5,NF	6,5,NF	6,6,NF	6,6,NF

Overview: Angola has been ruled by the same party and just two presidents since independence, and authorities have repressed political dissent and maintained restrictions on freedom of speech and assembly. Corruption, political imprisonment, and abuses by security forces all remain common.

KEY DEVELOPMENTS IN 2016:

- The 17 activists known as the Luanda book club, who were imprisoned in 2015 for discussing a book on civil disobedience, were conditionally released in June. However, their convictions on charges of sedition were not overturned.
- Police violently suppressed several protests during the year. In August, military police killed a teenage boy during a demonstration against housing demolitions.
- The national assembly passed several new laws restricting freedom of the press and free expression online, though dos Santos had yet to sign them at year's end.
- Rebels associated with separatists in the exclave of Cabinda increased attacks against government forces, with deaths on both sides reported.

EXECUTIVE SUMMARY

President José Eduardo dos Santos and his party, the Popular Movement for the Liberation of Angola (MPLA), retained tight control over the political system and significantly restricted civil liberties during 2016. Dos Santos, who has been in power for 37 years, in March announced that he would step down in 2018, though he has made and broken similar pledges before. In the meantime, he reportedly named the defense minister as his preferred successor, and in June appointed his daughter to lead the national oil company.

The drop in global oil prices continued to damage Angola's oil-dependent economy and state budget in 2016. Delays in workers' pay have led to strikes. Amid popular frustrations with economic decline, corruption, and dos Santos' continued rule, authorities have harshly suppressed protests and worked to increase restrictions on freedom of speech and the press. Meanwhile, separatists stepped up attacks on government forces in the restive exclave of Cabinda.

POLITICAL RIGHTS: 10 / 40

A. Electoral Process: 3 / 12

The 2010 constitution abolished direct presidential elections, stipulating instead that the leader of the largest party in the parliament would become president. The 220-seat unicameral National Assembly, whose members serve five-year terms, has little power, and 90 percent of legislation originates in the executive branch. The constitution permits the president to serve a maximum of two five-year terms, and to directly appoint the vice president, cabinet, and provincial governors. President dos Santos has been in power for 37 years, making him one of the longest-serving heads of state in Africa. Dos Santos' first full term under the current constitution began in 2012, and he announced in March 2016 that he would step down in 2018. Angola's scheduled August 2017 parliamentary elections are thus key to determining the next president if dos Santos follows through on his pledge. Dos Santos has reportedly named Defense Minister João Lourenço as his preferred successor.

The parliamentary elections held in 2012 were deeply flawed and followed a number of delays. The MPLA captured 72 percent of the vote, a notable decline from its 82 percent showing in 2008. Still, the party maintained its overwhelming dominance in the National Assembly, garnering 175 of 220 seats. The opposition National Union for the Total Independence of Angola (UNITA) won 32 seats; the Broad Convergence for the Salvation of Angola–Electoral Coalition (CASA–CE) won 8 seats, the Social Renewal Party (PRS) won 3, and the National Front for Angolan Liberation (FNLA) won 2.

In October 2014, dos Santos confirmed that already-delayed municipal elections, called for in the constitution, would again be postponed until after the 2017 general elections. The president justified this unilateral decision by citing the difficulties experienced in organizing the 2012 elections and those anticipated in replacing existing local government institutions with new municipal governments. The opposition vehemently protested the decision.

B. Political Pluralism and Participation: 6 / 16

Although five political parties are represented in the National Assembly, the ruling MPLA dominates Angola's party system. Mutual mistrust, the inability to agree on common strategy, and enticements from the more powerful and better-funded MPLA prevent opposition parties from coordinating their efforts. In 2015 the four opposition parties represented in the National Assembly held their first joint parliamentary meetings to promote dialogue and discuss the state of the country with civil society leaders. Human rights and democracy activists allege that opposition parties fail to challenge government efforts to suppress civil resistance.

Throughout 2014, opposition members had criticized the government's delay in establishing the Council of the Republic, a presidential advisory body that is constitutionally required to include members of the opposition. President dos Santos finally swore council members into office in February 2015, though their influence remains limited.

Political activism in the exclave of Cabinda, home to a long-standing movement for independence or autonomy, is regarded with suspicion by the government and can draw criminal charges. Rebels associated with the separatist Front for the Liberation of Cabinda (FLEC) increased attacks against government forces in 2016, with deaths on both sides reported. The clashes led to a corresponding troop build-up in the territory.

C. Functioning of Government: 1 / 12

Corruption and patronage are endemic in Angola's entrenched political elite, which is largely unaccountable to the public. Allegations of corruption continued throughout 2016, with controversy continuing to swirl around the dos Santos family's business interests. The naming of the president's daughter, Isabel dos Santos, widely thought to be the wealthiest woman in Africa, as head of national oil company Sonangol in June was a source of widespread anger in the country.

A freedom of information law ostensibly meant to allow citizens access to government-generated documents was approved in 2002. However, in practice accessing information remains extremely difficult.

CIVIL LIBERTIES: 14 / 60
D. Freedom of Expression and Belief: 5 / 16

Despite constitutional guarantees of freedom of expression, the state owns Angola's only daily newspaper, all national radio stations, and all but one national television station. These outlets, along with private media owned by senior officials and members of the dos Santos family, act as mouthpieces for the MPLA. Censorship and self-censorship are common.

In 2016, the legislature approved several restrictive new laws that would allow greater government control over online and traditional media, and raise barriers to the creation of new media outlets. Dos Santos was expected to sign the legislation in 2017. Additionally, a new MPLA-controlled regulatory body, the Angolan Social Communications Regulatory Body (ERCA), was established. Independent news outlets remain active online, but it remains to be seen how the government may use the new laws against them.

Angolan authorities have consistently prevented independent journalists from reporting the news, denying them access to official information and events, preventing them from broadcasting, and threatening them with detention and prosecution, frequently abusing libel and defamation laws. In January and June 2016, journalists Francisco Rasgado and José Manuel Alberto were charged with defamation in two separate cases for covering corruption and misuse of state funds; Rasgado had received death threats for his coverage of provincial government corruption in Benguela. In May, police in Luanda detained Voice of America journalist Coque Mukuta for recording them beating a suspect, while *Washington Post* journalists were detained for reporting on a hospital in Luanda in June. In December, journalists Rafael Marques de Morais of *Maka Angola* and Mariano Brás of *O Crime*, both longtime targets of government persecution, faced defamation-related charges for publishing reports on alleged corruption by the attorney general.

The constitution guarantees religious freedom, but the government requires religious groups to meet rigorous criteria in order to receive legal recognition. Legal approval was last granted to a new religious group in 2004. Roughly 1,200 religious groups operate illegally in Angola. All of those that have been officially recognized are Christian, despite the presence of tens of thousands of Muslims in the country. The government maintains that it has no bias against the practice of Islam, though Muslims have complained of discrimination.

In April 2016, José Kalupeteka, leader of the Light of the World religious sect, was sentenced to 28 years in prison in connection with an April 2015 clash between security forces and sect members in Huambo province, in which the government reported that 13 civilians and 9 policemen were killed. Nonstate sources reported a much higher death toll, accusing the government of a massacre, while the government blocked independent investigation of the incident, and President dos Santos declared the Light of the World to be a threat to peace and national unity. New deadly confrontations between police and group members occurred in August 2016, with allegations that over 30 sect members were massacred.

There are no formal restrictions on academic freedom, though professors avoid politically sensitive topics for fear of repercussions.

While internet access is increasing in Angola, the government actively monitors internet activity and, in some instances, uses the data collected to crack down on dissidents, while newly approved social communication laws are designed to chill free speech on social media. Offline communication is also subject to monitoring and punishment. In March 2016, 17 young activists were convicted on charges of state security crimes, including sedition, in connection with their participation in a 2015 book club discussion on civil resistance. The Supreme Court ordered the conditional release of the 17 activists in June, though their convictions have not yet been overturned.

E. Associational and Organizational Rights: 3 / 12

The constitution guarantees limited freedoms of assembly and association. In recent years, police and security forces have prohibited demonstrations, violently dispersed peaceful political gatherings, and intimidated and arrested protesters in provinces including Luanda, Malanje, and Benguela. In April 2016, police detained and assaulted protestors in Luanda demonstrating in support of the jailed Luanda book club members, while in August, police violently suppressed protests in the capital at which demonstrators called for President dos Santos's resignation; police beat protestors and attacked them with dogs. In November, authorities prohibited demonstrations against Isabel dos Santos taking control of the national oil company.

Several hundred nongovernmental organizations (NGOs) operate in Angola, and many advocate for transparency, human rights protections, and political reform. Organizations that are critical of the government have frequently faced state interference and been threatened with closure. NGOs are required to register with the government and the Ministry of Foreign Affairs to operate and must obtain further authorizations to receive donations. Once registered, NGOs are required to submit to government supervision and audits.

The constitution includes the right to strike and to form unions, but the MPLA dominates the labor movement, and only a few weak independent unions exist. Still, strikes do occur: transit workers in Luanda began 2016 on strike, while port workers in Lobito and teachers in Bengo went on strike in August and September, respectively, over grievances including unpaid wages.

F. Rule of Law: 3 / 16

The courts are hampered by a lack of trained legal professionals, as well as insufficient infrastructure, a large backlog of cases, corruption, and extensive political influence, particularly from the executive. Many areas lack functional municipal courts, thus leaving crimes and conflicts to be adjudicated by informal tribunals, or by local police.

The president appoints Supreme Court judges to life terms without legislative input. Several examples of judicial abuse and lack of due process arose in 2016, including the convictions of the 17 activists of the Luanda book club, and prosecution of human rights defenders and journalists covering corruption. However, courts in 2016 issued two promising decisions regarding the activities of Cabindan human rights activists. In May, a court overturned a dubious conviction against José Marcos Mavungo for purportedly plotting rebellion. Similar charges against Arão Bula Tempo, another Cabindan rights activist, were dismissed in July.

There is no effective protection against unjustified imprisonment, lengthy pretrial detention, extortion, or torture. Angolan jails are reported to be overcrowded, unhygienic, lacking basic necessities, and plagued by sexual abuse. They also contain a number of political prisoners, advocates of the Cabindan autonomy movement, and members of peaceful activist groups. In September 2016, police at the Rangel station in Luanda allegedly tortured and killed suspect José Padrão Loureiro, an attack for which five officers were arrested.

In diamond mining regions, private security forces have taken the law into their own hands, and frequently abuse it. In April 2016, reports emerged that such forces had beaten local miners in Lunda-Norte with machetes, while in August, private security forces in the same region killed 17-year-old Gabriel Mufugueno, sparking protests.

Tensions in Cabinda remain high. The secessionist FLEC movement and its supporters —many of whom live in exile—continue to call for talks on independence amidst sporadic violence. Activists have alleged that Cabinda residents are not permitted to voice their opinions and are under constant risk of persecution and discrimination.

Security forces allegedly harass and abuse African immigrant communities, against a backdrop of the government's failure to adequately protect refugees and asylum seekers. Nevertheless, immigration from countries including Brazil, China, and Portugal remains high, and migrants from neighboring countries also continue to enter Angola in large numbers.

National law criminalizes "acts against nature," though there have been no recent cases of this provision being applied to same-sex sexual activity. LGBT (lesbian, gay, bisexual, and transgender) people sometimes suffer harassment, and few formal LGBT organizations exist.

G. Personal Autonomy and Individual Rights: 3 / 16

Several organizations have been working to remove land mines that were placed during Angola's decades-long civil war. Land mines inhibit agriculture, construction, and freedom of movement, particularly in rural areas.

The process for securing entry and exit visas remains difficult and mired in corruption. Individuals who are critical of the government have faced problems when attempting to leave or enter the country.

Access to quality education is limited to Angola's elite and the expatriate community. Literacy rates remain low, due to the shortage of qualified teachers and the lack of school facilities, especially in rural districts. Corruption and absenteeism among some teachers continues to be a problem.

In 2016, the government continued a campaign of forced evictions in Luanda and other cities. In the Zango II area of Luanda in August, residents protesting the demolition of their homes were attacked by soldiers firing live ammunition, with 14-year-old Rufino Antonio killed by a military police officer.

Bribery often underpins business activity, and high-level corruption ensures that wealth and economic influence remain concentrated among those with political connections. Despite years of abundant oil revenues, Angola has one of the lowest life-expectancy rates in the world at 52 years, and a large share of the population still lives below the international poverty line.

Women enjoy legal protections and occupy cabinet positions and multiple seats in the National Assembly. However, de facto discrimination and violence against women continues. Child labor is a major problem, and foreign workers are vulnerable to sex trafficking and forced labor in the construction and mining industries. The authorities have failed to effectively investigate human trafficking or prosecute offenders.

Antigua and Barbuda

Political Rights Rating: 2
Civil Liberties Rating: 2
Freedom Rating: 2.0
Freedom Status: Free
Electoral Democracy: Yes

Population: 90,000
Capital: St. John's

Ten-Year Ratings Timeline For Year Under Review (Political Rights, Civil Liberties, Status)

Year Under Review	2007	2008	2009	2010	2011	2012	2013	2014	2015	2016
Rating	2,2,F	2,2,F	3,2,F	3,2,F	3,2,F	2,2,F	2,2,F	2,2,F	2,2,F	2,2,F

The country or territory displayed here received scores but no narrative report for this edition of *Freedom in the World*.

Argentina

Political Rights Rating: 2
Civil Liberties Rating: 2
Freedom Rating: 2.0
Freedom Status: Free
Electoral Democracy: Yes

Population: 43,600,000
Capital: Buenos Aires

Ten-Year Ratings Timeline For Year Under Review (Political Rights, Civil Liberties, Status)

Year Under Review	2007	2008	2009	2010	2011	2012	2013	2014	2015	2016
Rating	2,2,F	2,2,F	2,2,F	2,2,F	2,2,F	2,2,F	2,2,F	2,2,F	2,2,F	2,2,

Overview: Argentina is a vibrant representative democracy, with competitive elections and lively public debate. Corruption and violent crime are the country's most serious challenges.

KEY DEVELOPMENTS IN 2016:

- Former president Cristina Fernández de Kirchner and several members of her administration faced corruption investigations for their actions while in office. President Mauricio Macri, who was elected in 2015, cooperated with a corruption investigation into his own affairs.
- Macri's government held regular press conferences, and has been more open about policy than past administrations.
- The government instituted reforms at the previously discredited national statistics agency, and in September passed an access to information law.
- In October, a UN panel called on Argentina to release prominent community activist Milagro Sala, who had been in pretrial detention since January on charges the panel called unclear.

EXECUTIVE SUMMARY

The new government of President Macri, which took office in December 2015, made efforts in 2016 to improve government transparency. Its initiatives included an overhaul of the country's discredited statistics agency, and the approval of a freedom of information law. Macri's government also has a much more open relationship with the press than the previous administrations of Cristina Fernández de Kirchner and her late husband, Néstor Kirchner, who held the presidency before her. And while corruption remains endemic, a number of high-profile corruption investigations were ongoing in 2016, including a number that targeted Cristina Kirchner and members of her former administration. Additionally, the Panama Papers—a trove of leaked legal documents that revealed potentially corrupt business activities by powerful individuals around the world—showed that Macri held directorships of offshore companies that he had not declared to tax authorities. Macri was cooperating with an investigation into the matter.

Macri's government faced a difficult year as it sought to restore macroeconomic credibility and investor confidence in the country, following a dozen years of rule by the Kirchners. This has entailed undoing several of the Kirchners' populist policies, including reducing energy subsidies and easing restrictions on foreign currency purchases; the latter has dramatically facilitated Argentines' access to foreign currency and made travel abroad more accessible. However, public-spending cuts by the Macri government also resulted in the elimination of thousands of public-sector jobs. Cuts to the Kirchners' massive state advertising budget—which had propped up a number of outlets that were supportive of their respective administrations—resulted in job losses in the media sector.

The economic adjustment has tested the patience of ordinary Argentines, many of whom have so far failed to see its benefit as their purchasing power has been eroded by high inflation and increased prices for public services. Workers staged various strikes calling for wage increases and firing freezes in 2016.

POLITICAL RIGHTS: 33 / 40 (+ 2)

A. Electoral Process: 11 / 12

As amended in 1994, the constitution provides for a president to be elected for a four-year term, with the option of reelection for one additional term. Presidential candidates must win 45 percent of the vote to avoid a runoff. Macri won the 2015 presidential election in the second round with 51 percent of the vote, in a competitive and credible poll.

The National Congress consists of the 257-member Chamber of Deputies, whose representatives are directly elected for four-year terms, with half of the seats up for election every two years; and the 72-member Senate, whose representatives are directly elected for six-year terms, with one-third of the seats up for election every two years.

In the 2015 legislative elections, the Kirchner's Frente para la Victoria (FPV), a faction of the Justicialist (Peronist) Party, lost 26 seats compared to the previous legislature, bringing its total to 70 seats. This makes it the largest party, even though it does not have an outright majority. However, other Peronist factions hold enough seats for Peronist parties to hold an absolute majority. Macri's Cambiemos coalition gained 29 seats in the Chamber of Deputies in the elections. The FPV maintained its absolute majority in the Senate with 38 seats.

Mid-term elections will be held in October 2017, and the next presidential elections in 2019.

B. Political Pluralism and Participation: 14 / 16

The right to organize political parties is respected. Argentina's multiparty political system affords opposition candidates the realistic opportunity to compete for political power.

The Peronists have been a dominant force in politics since 1946, although they have been ideologically flexible over their existence. The Justicialist (Peronist) Party has two opposing factions: the center-left FPV and the center-right Federal Peronism faction. Other parties include Macri's center-right Republican Proposal (PRO), the Radical Civic Union (UCR), and the Civic Coalition (CC), which together comprise the Cambiemos coalition. A third important force in Argentine politics is the United for a New Alternative (UNA) coalition, which includes the Renewal Front, a breakaway faction of Justicialist Party members not aligned with the FPV.

Argentines' political choices are generally free from intimidation or harassment. Ethnic minorities have full political rights.

C. Functioning of Government: 8 / 12 (+2)

Corruption plagues Argentine society, and scandals are common. Since leaving office at the end of 2015, former president Cristina Kirchner has faced corruption indictments, as have a number of high-ranking officials who served in her administration. In May 2016, Kirchner was charged with state fraud in connection with allegations of involvement in the central bank's sale of dollars on the futures market at a below-market rate, in an alleged bid to inflate the value of the peso before the 2015 election. In December, she was indicted alongside two former members of her administration for fraud and corruption in connection with an alleged scheme to improperly direct public-works projects to certain companies. Kirchner's transport secretary, Ricardo Jaime, was arrested in April and charged with embezzlement involving the purchase of train cars. In December, it was revealed that a Brazilian construction conglomerate, Odebrecht, had paid millions of dollars in bribes in Argentina to win favorable state contracts during Kirchner's time in office. Kirchner's former chief of staff, Aníbal Fernández, in 2016 was under investigation for running an ephedrine trafficking scheme. And a former vice president, Amado Boudou, remained under investigation during the year on allegations of bribery and influence-peddling.

Meanwhile, documents released as part of the Panama Papers leak revealed that Macri held the directorship of two offshore companies that he had failed to publicly disclose. He was cooperating with an investigation, and has denied wrongdoing.

Government transparency has improved under Macri's administration. In September 2016, the Argentine Congress approved an access to information law expected to be enacted within a year. The law establishes a Public Information Agency that will permit citizens to request information from state agencies, except for information deemed restricted. Citizens must receive a response to their request within 15 business days, and will have the right to appeal a denial within 40 days. Macri's government has also revamped the country's statistics agency, which had been censured by the International Monetary Fund (IMF) since 2013 for misrepresenting data. In November 2016, the IMF lifted its censure after the agency released data on inflation and gross domestic product (GDP) that the IMF described as consistent with its obligations. The new government has held regular press conferences to explain its policies.

CIVIL LIBERTIES: 49 / 60 (+1)

D. Freedom of Expression and Belief: 14 / 16

Argentine law guarantees freedom of expression, and Congress decriminalized libel and slander in 2009. The Macri government's open relationship with the media represents a notable improvement from past years, which were characterized by the Kirchners' hostile attitude toward the media, including verbal and written attacks of critical outlets and persecution of specific journalists.

The Macri government has also faced challenges in reversing the media policies of the Kirchner years, which were characterized by the proliferation of pro-Kirchner print and broadcasting media that were largely supported by state advertising. The Macri government has made efforts to rein in the state advertising budget, which amounted to some $1.4 billion in 2015. However, the reduction in spending, combined with the country's difficult economic situation, affected media businesses' financial sustainability, and journalists have protested layoffs that followed the closing and downsizing of outlets.

Other actions by the Macri government involving the media have been controversial. In December 2015, while the FPV-dominated legislature was on recess, the newly elected president Macri issued a decree that effectively overturned a 2009 media law designed to discourage monopolies. This prompted criticism that the president was disregarding democratic processes and undermining regulatory structures established by the 2009 law. In addition, in June 2016 the government suspended the signal of Telesur, a Venezuelan-backed, left-wing media venture, and of RT, a Russian-backed channel, from free-to-air digital television, arguing that the suspension was part of government austerity measures and that the signals were needed for provincial channels. The move prompted allegations that the government was silencing critical voices.

While Argentina is a relatively safe country for journalists, they can face attack in response to reporting on sensitive issues including corruption in provincial governments, or organized crime.

The government does not restrict access to the internet, which is widely used in Argentina. Argentina's constitution guarantees freedom of religion. Academic freedom is a cherished Argentine tradition and is largely observed in practice. Private discussion is vibrant and unrestricted.

E. Associational and Organizational Rights: 11 / 12

Freedoms of assembly and association are generally respected, and citizens organize protests to make their voices heard. Civic organizations, especially those focused on human rights and abuses committed under the 1976–83 dictatorship, are robust and play a major role in society, although some fall victim to Argentina's pervasive corruption.

Organized labor remains dominated by Peronist unions, and union influence has decreased in recent years. Several labor groups called nationwide strikes in 2016, largely in protest of the austerity measures, job losses, and real wage cuts that have resulted from the Macri government's economic adjustment plan. Strikes are common at the time of annual salary renegotiations, with strikers seeking to keep wages up with inflation.

F. Rule of Law: 10 / 16

Inefficiencies and delays plague the judicial system, which can be subject to political manipulation. The Supreme Court, however, maintains relative independence. In December 2015, with the legislature on recess, Macri appointed two Supreme Court justices by decree. However, facing opposition, he later reversed course and used the legal process requiring Senate confirmation; they were both sworn in during 2016. Argentine law allows for fair trials, a right that is generally enforced by the judiciary. Police misconduct—including torture and brutality against suspects in custody—is endemic. Prisons are overcrowded, and conditions remain substandard throughout the country. Arbitrary arrests and abuse by police are rarely punished in the courts, and police collusion with drug traffickers is common. In October 2016, the UN Working Group on Arbitrary Detention called on Argentina to release prominent community activist Milagro Sala, who was detained in January in connection with a protest she had led, and was later charged with embezzlement; the UN panel said the charges against her were unclear and that her pretrial dentition was unjustified.

Drug-related violence remained a serious issue in 2016 as international criminal organizations used the country as both an operational base and a transit route; the country's northern and central regions are particularly affected.

In 2005, the Supreme Court declared that laws passed in the 1980s to safeguard the military from prosecution were unconstitutional, laying the foundation for the prosecution of past military crimes. Following the ruling, then president Néstor Kirchner initiated proceedings against former officials involved in Argentina's so-called dirty war (1976–83), during which right-wing military rulers utilized brutal tactics to silence dissent. Such prosecutions continued under Cristina Kirchner's administration, and under the current government, with dozens of military and police officers convicted of torture, murder, and forced disappearance and sentenced to life in prison.

Argentina's indigenous peoples, who represent approximately 2.4 percent of the population, are largely neglected by the government and suffer disproportionately from extreme poverty and illness. Only 11 of Argentina's 23 provinces have constitutions recognizing the rights of indigenous peoples.

Argentina's LGBT (lesbian, gay, bisexual, and transgender) population enjoys full legal rights, including the right to serve in the military. However, LGBT people face some degree of societal discrimination, and occasionally police brutality. A number of killings of transgender women that took place in fall 2015 remain unsolved.

G. Personal Autonomy and Individual Rights: 14 / 16 (+ 1)

The government respects citizens' constitutional right to free travel both inside and outside of Argentina. Harsh government restrictions on foreign currency transactions limited citizens' ability to travel and conduct business during the Kirchner years. The Macri government lifted the capital controls in late 2015, and allowed the peso to float freely. Doing so dramatically increased ordinary people's access to foreign currency, making travel abroad more accessible.

Citizens generally enjoy the right to own property and establish private businesses. However, approximately 70 percent of the country's rural indigenous communities lack titles to their lands, and forced evictions, while technically illegal, still occur. Indigenous communities increasingly struggled to defend their land rights in 2016 against oil and gas prospectors.

Women actively participate in politics in Argentina, and the law requires that 30 percent of political parties' nominees to the national legislators be women. Around 40 percent of both houses of Congress are held by women. Although abortion remains illegal, in 2012 the Supreme Court outlawed the prosecution of women who have had an abortion after being raped. An estimated 500,000 illegal abortions are performed each year, with a few resulting in death. Domestic violence against women is a serious problem, and women continue to face economic discrimination and gender-based wage gaps.

Same-sex marriage has been legal nationwide since 2010. A 2012 gender identity law allows people to legally change their gender.

Some sectors of the charcoal and brick-producing industries profit from the forced labor of men, women, and children from Argentina as well as from neighboring countries; forced labor is also present in the agriculture sector and among domestic workers and street vendors. Men, women, and children are subject to sex trafficking. Government funding for programs to assist victims of human trafficking is insufficient.

Armenia

Political Rights Rating: 5
Civil Liberties Rating: 4
Freedom Rating: 4.5
Freedom Status: Partly Free
Electoral Democracy: No

Population: 3,000,000
Capital: Yerevan

Note: The numerical ratings and status listed above do not reflect conditions in Nagorno-Karabakh, which is examined in a separate report.

Ten-Year Ratings Timeline For Year Under Review (Political Rights, Civil Liberties, Status)

Year Under Review	2007	2008	2009	2010	2011	2012	2013	2014	2015	2016
Rating	5,4,PF	6,4,PF	6,4,PF	6,4,PF	6,4,PF	5,4,PF	5,4,PF	5,4,PF	5,4,PF	5,4,PF

Overview: Armenia is ruled by a government with a history of soft authoritarian tendencies. People's ability to influence government decisions is limited, and formal political opposition is weak. High levels of corruption and political influence over the media environment also remain concerns.

KEY DEVELOPMENTS IN 2016:

- In April, a spike in hostilities between the Armenian-backed Nagorno-Karabakh territory and Azerbaijan led to a significant spike in security concerns within Armenia.
- In July, a group of armed opposition activists seized a police building in Yerevan and issued a list of political demands, including the resignation of the president.
- The July crisis sparked street protests, which the police met with a violent crackdown; dozens, including members of the media, were injured in the violence.
- A cabinet reshuffle took place in September, and the new prime minister took office amid promises of economic reform and anticorruption efforts.

EXECUTIVE SUMMARY

Political and social turbulence marked the year in Armenia. Significant uncertainty about the country's political structure lingered following a referendum in late 2015 in which voters approved constitutional changes that, among other things, will transform the country from a semipresidential to a parliamentary republic. The referendum had been marred by reports of pervasive fraud and manipulation, and public awareness of the constitutional changes' technical implications remained limited in 2016.

In April, an outbreak of fighting took place along the borders of Nagorno-Karabakh, an Armenian-majority territory that gained de facto independence from Azerbaijan following the breakup of the Soviet Union. The violence represented the fiercest escalation in the territory since the signing of a ceasefire agreement in 1994, sparking fears in Armenia about a full-blown military confrontation.

In July, a group of armed men associated with a fringe opposition party, among them veterans of the 1992–94 Nagorno-Karabakh war, seized a police building in the Erebuni district of Yerevan, killing three officers and taking a number hostage. They criticized the government's handling of the April violence and issued demands, including the resignation of President Serzh Sargsyan. Their actions led to a mixed reaction from Armenian society: while many condemned the use of violence to advance political aims, a small group of protesters gathered by the police station to show their support. They were met with harsh police violence, which in turn led to larger protests expressing grievances with Armenia's political and security apparatus. The gunmen surrendered after two weeks.

In September, the cabinet resigned. A new cabinet, headed by a former executive from the Russian gas giant Gazprom, took office with promises to implement economic reforms and anticorruption measures.

POLITICAL RIGHTS: 16 / 40

A. Electoral Process: 5 / 12

B. Political Pluralism and Participation: 7 / 16

C. Functioning of Government: 4 / 12

CIVIL LIBERTIES: 29 / 60 (-1)

D. Freedom of Expression and Belief: 9 / 16

E. Associational and Organizational Rights: 6 / 12

F. Rule of Law: 5 / 16 (-1)

G. Personal Autonomy and Individual Rights: 9 / 16

This country report has been abridged for *Freedom in the World 2017*. For background information on political rights and civil liberties in Armenia, see *Freedom in the World 2016*.

Australia

Political Rights Rating: 1
Civil Liberties Rating: 1
Freedom Rating: 1.0
Freedom Status: Free
Electoral Democracy: Yes

Population: 24,100,000
Capital: Canberra

Ten-Year Ratings Timeline For Year Under Review (Political Rights, Civil Liberties, Status)

Year Under Review	2007	2008	2009	2010	2011	2012	2013	2014	2015	2016
Rating	1,1,F	1,1,F	1,1,F	1,1,F	1,1,F	1,1,F	1,1,F	1,1,F	1,1,F	1,1,F

Overview: Australia has a long history of respect for political rights and civil liberties. However, recent years have seen some concern about laws that permit government surveillance of online communications, as well as about the country's harsh policies toward asylum seekers.

KEY DEVELOPMENTS IN 2016

- The governing Liberal Party/National Party coalition narrowly won federal elections held in July.

- Linda Burney of the Australian Labor Party (ALP) became the first indigenous woman elected to the House of Representatives.
- In April, media reports revealed that the police had admitted that they lawfully sought—without a warrant—communications metadata for a journalist who reported that an Australian ship had ventured into Indonesian waters to turn back a boat carrying asylum seekers.
- In September, health professionals were exempted from secrecy and nondisclosure provisions in Australia's controversial Border Force Act, thus permitting them to speak openly about medical treatment in immigration detention centers abroad.

EXECUTIVE SUMMARY

Australia has a strong record of protecting political rights and civil liberties. However, 2016 saw the introduction of curbs on demonstrations in New South Wales, revelations of warrantless collection of a journalist's metadata, and continued criticism of harsh conditions in the country's offshore centers for asylum seekers.

In March, the New South Wales state government passed laws intended to discourage a protest movement targeting mining operations. The measures introduced criminal penalties and increased fines for interfering with commercial operations; fines may now reach as much as $5,500, up from $550 previously. The approval of the laws prompted protests and drew denunciations from lawyers' associations.

Australia's immigration and asylum policies continued to draw domestic and international condemnation in 2016, particularly in regard to the housing and vetting of asylum seekers at processing centers in Papua New Guinea and Nauru. Reports of poor living conditions, inadequate safety for women and children, delays in processing applications, detainees attempting suicide, and lack of sufficient healthcare and education services at the centers persisted. A section of the 2015 Border Force Act known as the Secrecy Provision threatens a prison sentence of up to two years for "entrusted persons" working in the centers—including social workers, lawyers, and teachers—who disclose unauthorized information about activities or conditions within. In September 2016, the head of Australia's customs and border protection agency signed an amendment exempting "health professionals" from the Secrecy Provisions.

In April 2016, media reports revealed that the Australian Federal Police admitted that they had lawfully sought—without a warrant—communications metadata on journalist Paul Farrell in the wake of his report that an Australian ship had ventured far into Indonesian waters in order to turn back a boat carrying asylum seekers.

Voting is compulsory in Australia, and citizens participate in free and fair multiparty elections to choose representatives for the bicameral Parliament. In 2016 federal elections, the Liberal Party/National Party coalition won a slim majority of 76 seats in the 150-seat House of Representatives, down from 90 previously. Linda Burney of the ALP became the first indigenous woman elected to the House of Representatives.

POLITICAL RIGHTS: 40 / 40

A. Electoral Process: 12 / 12

B. Political Pluralism and Participation: 16 / 16

C. Functioning of Government: 12 / 12

CIVIL LIBERTIES: 58 / 60

D. Freedom of Expression and Belief: 16 / 16

E. Associational and Organizational Rights: 12 / 12

F. Rule of Law: 15 / 16

G. Personal Autonomy and Individual Rights: 15 / 16

This country report has been abridged for *Freedom in the World 2017*. For background information on political rights and civil liberties in Australia, see *Freedom in the World 2016*.

Austria

Political Rights Rating: 1
Civil Liberties Rating: 1
Freedom Rating: 1.0
Freedom Status: Free
Electoral Democracy: Yes

Population: 8,000,000
Capital: Vienna

Ten-Year Ratings Timeline For Year Under Review (Political Rights, Civil Liberties, Status)

Year Under Review	2007	2008	2009	2010	2011	2012	2013	2014	2015	2016
Rating	1,1,F	1,1,F	1,1,F	1,1,F	1,1,F	1,1,F	1,1,F	1,1,F	1,1,F	1,1,F

Overview: Austria has a democratic system of government that guarantees both political rights and civil liberties. It is frequently governed by a grand coalition of the center-left Social Democratic Party of Austria (SPÖ) and the center-right Austrian People's Party (ÖCP). In recent years, the political system has faced pressure from the Free Party of Austria (ÖVP), a rightwing populist party that openly entertains nationalist and xenophobic sentiments.

KEY DEVELOPMENTS IN 2016:
- In December, Alexander Van der Bellen was elected president after a close and controversial election that featured a repeat of the run-off between Van der Bellen and FPÖ candidate Norbert Hofer.
- The government further limited access to asylum seekers, introducing a ceiling for the number of people that can apply for asylum in Austria in one year.
- Rightwing violence and race-based hate speech remained major concerns.

EXECUTIVE SUMMARY

Political debate in 2016 was dominated by the presidential election and refugee policies, the latter issue being at the forefront of conversation since the spike in the flow of asylum seekers to Europe in 2015. Following a number of previous moves to counter migration flows to the country, the government further restricted access to asylum seekers and introduced an annual cap of 35,000 for asylum applications—a limit that will be in effect as of 2017. A number of legislators announced intentions to try to reduce this cap even further.

The Austrian presidential election was highly contested and divisive. Van der Bellen, the candidate of the Green Party, initially won the runoff against Hofer, the candidate of the FPÖ. The vote was later declared invalid, however, as the Constitutional Court established that there had been irregularities in the handling of postal ballots. A repeat of the runoff, held in December, confirmed the election of Van der Bellen.

POLITICAL RIGHTS: 37 / 40
A. Electoral Process: 12 / 12
B. Political Pluralism and Participation: 15 / 16
C. Functioning of Government: 10 / 12

CIVIL LIBERTIES: 58 / 60
D. Freedom of Expression and Belief: 16 / 16
E. Associational and Organizational Rights: 12 / 12
F. Rule of Law: 15 / 16
G. Personal Autonomy and Individual Rights: 15 / 16

This country report has been abridged for *Freedom in the World 2017.* For background information on political rights and civil liberties in Austria, see *Freedom in the World 2016.*

Azerbaijan

Political Rights Rating: 7
Civil Liberties Rating: 6
Freedom Rating: 6.5
Freedom Status: Not Free
Electoral Democracy: No

Population: 9,800,000
Capital: Baku

Note: The numerical ratings and status listed above do not reflect conditions in Nagorno-Karabakh, which is examined in a separate report.

Ten-Year Ratings Timeline For Year Under Review (Political Rights, Civil Liberties, Status)

Year Under Review	2007	2008	2009	2010	2011	2012	2013	2014	2015	2016
Rating	6,5,NF	6,5,NF	6,5,NF	6,5,NF	6,5,NF	6,5,NF	6,6,NF	6,6,NF	7,6,NF	7,6,NF

Overview: In Azerbaijan's authoritarian government, power is heavily concentrated in the hands of President Ilham Aliyev, who has ruled the country since 2003. Corruption is rampant, and following years of persecution, formal political opposition is weak. The Aliyev regime has overseen an extensive crackdown on civil liberties in recent years, leaving little room for independent expression or activism in the country. Journalists, civil society leaders, human rights advocates, and religious leaders who are deemed threatening to the government routinely face harassment, detention, and violence.

KEY DEVELOPMENTS IN 2016:
- In a September referendum, voters approved a package of constitutional changes that were pushed through without meaningful parliamentary debate or public consultation; among other changes, the legislation widely expanded presidential powers.
- Opposition groups were prevented from campaigning against the changes, and security forces detained dozens of civil society leaders in an effort to disperse protests or discourage them from taking place.

- In January, security forces violently repressed protests against price hikes and growing unemployment.
- The government pardoned and released several high-profile political prisoners, but its repressive campaign against civil society and independent media continued apace, with a number of arrests and incidents of violence and harassment.

EXECUTIVE SUMMARY

The Aliyev regime continued to aggressively consolidate power at the expense of citizens' political rights and civil liberties. In a highly flawed September referendum, voters approved a set of 29 constitutional amendments that were proposed by Aliyev and rushed to the vote without meaningful parliamentary or public consultation. Authorities prevented opposition groups from campaigning against the proposals, and security forces rounded up dozens of activists during and in advance of protests against the changes. The vote itself was marred by electoral violations, including ballot stuffing. Among other things, the amendments extended the presidential term from five years to seven, empowered the president to dissolve the legislature and call elections, abolished the minimum age for presidential candidates, and lowered the age for parliamentary candidates to 18. Overall, the legislation further concentrated power within the president's office while eroding the country's already weak checks on executive authority. The age requirement changes led to speculation that Aliyev is grooming his son for succession.

While the release of several high-profile political prisoners during the year was welcomed by both the domestic and international communities, prospects of genuine change for civil liberties were dimmed by the government's unceasing repression of human rights defenders, opposition members, civil society activists, journalists, and religious communities. The amendments approved in September also imposed new limitations on civil rights, including freedom of assembly and land ownership.

Plunged into economic crisis following the drop in global oil prices in 2014, the government has made efforts to improve budgetary planning and economic policy during, but faced public discontent in 2016 due to rising prices and unemployment. In January, these concerns sparked protests across the country. Security forces swiftly dispersed them using tear gas and water cannons and detained dozens of participants.

POLITICAL RIGHTS: 4 / 40 (− 1)

A. Electoral Process: 1 / 12

Azerbaijan's constitution provides for a strong presidency, and the 125-member Milli Majlis (National Assembly) exercises little or no independence from the executive branch.

Since the early 1990s, elections have been considered neither free nor fair by international observers. The 2013 presidential election, marred by widespread irregularities and electoral fraud, saw incumbent Aliyev—who succeeded his father, Heydar, in 2003— reelected to a controversial third term in office. Parliamentary elections were held in 2015 amid an intensifying government campaign against criticism and dissent; the main opposition parties boycotted the vote. According to official results, the ruling Yeni Azerbaijan Party (YAP) won 71 seats, with 41 going to independent candidates who tend to support the ruling party, and the remaining 12 split among small progovernment parties.

Constitutional amendments approved in a referendum in September 2016 empowered the president to dissolve the Milli Majlis in certain situations, call snap presidential elections, and appoint multiple vice presidents. The amendments also extended presidential terms from five years to seven; term limits had already been eliminated in a 2009 referendum. The changes also included the removal of age requirements for presidential candidates and the lowering of the minimum age for parliamentary candidates to 18 years, leading some analysts to warn that Aliyev could be setting the stage for his 19-year-old son to enter the political arena.

The legitimacy of the September referendum was undermined by a lack of public and parliamentary consultation, restrictions on opposition campaigning, harassment of opposition members, and electoral fraud. Neither the Organization for Security and Co-operation in Europe's Office for Democratic Institutions and Human Rights (OSCE/ODIHR) nor the OSCE Parliamentary Assembly sent observers. A small mission deployed by the Parliamentary Assembly of the Council of Europe (PACE) applauded the transparency of proceedings, but several local and international rights groups heavily criticized the PACE report and questioned the observers' reliability. Several human rights groups had also questioned the independence of the PACE observers who reported that the 2015 parliamentary elections met international standards; three of that delegation's members subsequently issued a dissenting opinion.

The electoral laws and framework do not ensure the free and fair conduct of elections. The nomination process for members of electoral commissions places the bodies under the influence of the ruling party, and commission members have been known to unlawfully interfere with the election process and obstruct the activities of observers. Complaints of electoral violations do not receive adequate or impartial treatment by the commissions or the judiciary.

B. Political Pluralism and Participation: 2 / 16 (− 1)

The political environment in Azerbaijan is neither pluralistic nor competitive, and mechanisms for public participation in political processes are limited. YAP has dominated national politics since its founding in 1995, and nominal opposition groups and independents in the parliament tend to support the government.

Amendments to the electoral code in 2009 limited candidates' access to public campaign funding and reduced the official campaign period from 28 to 22 days. Changes made to laws on freedom of assembly and association in 2012, 2013, and 2016 further restricted candidates' ability to organize and hold rallies. The political opposition has virtually no access to coverage on television, which remains the most popular news source in Azerbaijan.

In the lead-up to the September 2016 constitutional referendum, limitations on opposition parties' freedoms of association and assembly were intensified. The UN Special Rapporteur on the situation of human rights defenders, in a statement issued days before the vote, documented at least 45 cases in which authorities arrested, detained, or issued warnings to human rights defenders and others before a peaceful rally organized by the National Council of Democratic Forces, a coalition of opposition groups.

Opposition politicians and party officials are subject to arbitrary arrest on dubious charges as well as physical violence and other forms of intimidation, and have also reported widespread targeting of their relatives, some of whom have faced job dismissal and harassment by police. Ilgar Mammadov, leader of the Republican Alternative (REAL) movement, remained behind bars at year's end on politically motivated charges of involvement in mass disorder, in breach of a 2014 European Court of Human Rights decision calling for his release.

Some members of the opposition youth movement NIDA (Exclamation), behind bars since their arrest in 2013 in connection with antigovernment protests, were released as part of a presidential pardon in March, but other opposition activists, including from NIDA and REAL, were rounded up in May, August, and September.

The dominance of the ruling party limits the freedom of political parties to represent a diversity of interests and views, and there are no meaningful mechanisms to promote representation of minorities.

C. Functioning of Government: 1 / 12

The head of government and national legislative representatives are not elected in a free or fair manner. Aliyev and the YAP determine and implement the policies of the government with little opposition. The 2016 constitutional changes increased presidential power at the expense of parliamentary sovereignty.

Corruption is widespread and pervasive. Because critical institutions, including the media and judiciary, are largely subservient to the president and ruling party, government officials are rarely held accountable for corruption. Investigative reports published by foreign media in recent years have revealed evidence that Aliyev and his family control prodigious private assets, including monopolies in the Azerbaijani economy's most lucrative sectors, and had even benefitted financially from the currency devaluation in 2015.

Despite the lack of safeguards against systemic corruption, the establishment of one-stop public service centers and investment in e-government services in recent years may have contributed to improved public perceptions regarding petty corruption.

Under legislation passed in 2012, companies can keep their organizational structures and ownership secret, which severely limits journalists' ability to uncover corruption. Although public officials are nominally required to submit financial disclosure reports, disclosure procedures and compliance remain unclear, and the reports are not publicly accessible. In 2015, the Extractive Industries Transparency Initiative (EITI), an international platform that promotes good governance and transparency in resource-rich countries, demoted Azerbaijan from membership to candidate status due to noncompliance with EITI human rights standards. The country retained this downgraded status following the EITI's October 2016 review. In May, the Open Government Partnership (OGP) Steering Committee suspended Azerbaijan's participation for one year due to concerns about threats to civil society.

CIVIL LIBERTIES: 10 / 60 (− 1)

D. Freedom of Expression and Belief: 2 / 16 (− 1)

Constitutional guarantees for press freedom are routinely and systematically violated. Broadcast outlets generally reflect pro-government views. Most television stations are controlled by the government, which also controls approval of broadcast licenses. Although there is more pluralism in the print media, the majority of newspapers are owned by the state, and circulation and readership are small. Independent and opposition papers struggle financially and have faced heavy fines and other pressures as retaliation for critical coverage. Journalists are threatened, harassed, intimidated, and assaulted with impunity, and many have been detained or imprisoned on fabricated charges. An increasing number of journalists face travel bans.

In July, following a coup attempt in Turkey, the National Television and Radio Council (NTRC) terminated the license of the private, progovernment television channel ANS after it ran a preview of an interview with Muslim cleric Fethullah Gülen. The NTRC claimed that the content was damaging to Azerbaijan's strategic relations with Turkey and constituted "terrorist propaganda." The Gülen-linked *Zaman-Azerbaijan* newspaper and its website were also shut down. In September, *Azadliq* suspended operations after its state-run publishing house terminated the newspaper's contract due to outstanding debts. Local radio broadcasts of international news services, including the British Broadcasting Corporation (BBC) and Voice of America (VOA), have been banned since 2009, though they are available online. The authorities shuttered the Baku office of Radio Free Europe/Radio Liberty (RFE/RL) in 2014. During two separate periods in November and December 2016, the websites of RFE/RL and VOA were not accessible inside Azerbaijan; as of late December, the website of the independent online media outlet Meydan TV was also blocked.

The few critical outlets that are still able to disseminate information in the country—including Meydan TV, which operates from Germany—face constant pressure and risk. Authorities opened a criminal investigation into Meydan TV in April on charges that include illegal entrepreneurship, tax evasion, and abuse of power. Throughout the year, representatives of Meydan TV and other critical outlets reported that contributors and family members in Azerbaijan received death threats and were subject to interrogations and arbitrary detentions.

Defamation remains a criminal offense. In November, legislators expanded an existing ban on insulting the president to include online content, and made it illegal to disseminate libelous or insulting content using false user information or accounts.

Five journalists were released from prison in 2016. Hilal Mammadov, Tofiq Yaqublu, and Parviz Hashimli were released following a presidential pardon in March, the same day as a court commuted *Zerkalo* journalist Rauf Mirkadirov's sentence. In May, a court conditionally released investigative journalist Khadija Ismayilova. Nevertheless, a number of other media professionals were detained, arrested, or convicted in politically motivated cases during the year. According to the Committee to Protect Journalists, there were five journalists behind bars as of December, though local source gave higher estimates.

The government restricts the practice of minority and "nontraditional" religions and denominations, largely through burdensome registration requirements and interference with the importation and distribution of printed religious materials. Among other restrictive laws, a 2011 measure prescribed prison sentences for leaders of unsanctioned religious services. A number of mosques have been closed in recent years, ostensibly for registration or safety violations. Dozens of individuals faced legal repercussions due to their beliefs in 2016.

More than a dozen members of the Muslim Unity Movement, a conservative Shiite group, went on trial in August for charges including conspiracy to overthrow the government. In 2015, police had raided the conservative Shiite town of Nardaran and rounded up over 70 people, including members of the group, in an operation that left at least four residents and two officers dead. A number of defendants in the case have claimed that their confessions were obtained through torture.

Several meetings of Jehovah's Witnesses were raided during the year, and its members of continued to be detained for allegedly violating state restrictions on the practice of religion.

The authorities have long linked academic freedom to political activity. Some educators have reported being dismissed for links to opposition groups, and students have faced expulsion and other punishments for similar reasons. In July, the Education Ministry announced that Baku's Qafqaz University, founded by Gülenists, would be closed and that its management would be transferred to the state-run Baku Higher Oil School. The contracts of fifty Turkish academics from the institution were not renewed.

Law enforcement bodies are suspected of monitoring private telephone and online communications—particularly of activists, political figures, and foreign nationals—without judicial oversight. The escalation of government persecution of critics and their families has undermined the assumption of privacy and eroded the openness of private discussion.

E. Associational and Organizational Rights: 1 / 12

The government restricts freedom of assembly. Legal amendments increasing fines for organizing or participating in unauthorized protests came into effect in 2013, and changes adopted later that year extended the maximum periods of administrative detention for certain assembly-related offenses. Under the amendments approved in the September 2016 referendum, the right to free assembly is contingent on not violating "public order and morals."

Amid the rising prices and unemployment that have characterized Azerbaijan's economic crisis since the 2014 drop in oil prices, a wave of protests erupted across six regions in January. In Fizuli and Quba, security forces dispersed demonstrators using tear gas and water cannons. Scores of people were detained.

In September, opposition groups obtained authorization to hold rallies against the constitutional referendum. Police intervened during one rally in Baku, making a number of arrests. Security forces rounded up dozens of activists, opposition party members, and journalists in the days before the demonstrations in order to discourage participation.

Regressive laws require nongovernmental organizations (NGOs) to register all grants and donations with the Ministry of Justice, and to inform authorities of all donations over $250. The rules have been used to pressure both local and foreign organizations, many of which have suspended operations when their bank accounts were frozen or their offices raided and closed.

In March, a number of civil society activists received presidential pardons. Local activists linked the amnesty to the Aliyev's attendance at the Nuclear Security Summit in the United States two weeks later. In his post-mission statement in September 2016, the UN special rapporteur on the situation of human rights defenders condemned the widespread persecution of both international and Azerbaijani NGOs, calling the situation for civil society a "total crisis."

Although the law permits the formation of trade unions and the right to strike, the majority of unions remain closely affiliated with the government, and most major industries are dominated by state-owned enterprises.

F. Rule of Law: 2 / 16

The judiciary is corrupt, inefficient, and subservient to the executive. The pattern of presidential pardons for political prisoners followed by more arrests is one example of the arbitrary nature of the judicial system. A local coalition of NGOs estimated that there were 118 political prisoners in the country as of late November 2016. Arbitrary arrest and detention are common, and detainees are often held for long periods before trial. Opposition figures, journalists, and activists who were arrested or sentenced in recent years have reported many due process violations, including restricted access to legal counsel, fabrication and withholding of evidence, and physical abuse.

Medical care in prisons is generally inadequate, and overcrowding is common. The European Court of Human Rights ruled in June that the state's failure to provide human rights defenders Leyla and Arif Yunus with adequate medical care in prison constituted inhuman or degrading treatment. Torture is sometimes used to extract confessions.

Some members of ethnic minority groups have complained of discrimination in areas including education, employment, and housing. Although same-sex sexual activity is not a criminal offense, antidiscrimination laws do not specifically protect LGBT (lesbian, gay, bisexual, and transgender) people, who have reported harassment and other forms of bias or abuse, including violence.

G. Personal Autonomy and Individual Rights: 5 / 16

The government has increasingly restricted freedom of movement, particularly foreign travel, for opposition politicians, journalists, and civil society activists. Courts denied several appeals by such individuals against their travel bans in 2016.

Property rights and free choice of residence are affected by government-backed development projects that often entail forced evictions, unlawful expropriations, and demolitions with little or no notice. The authorities often violate the right of individuals to receive adequate compensation for expropriated property. The constitutional changes approved in September include a provision allowing the right to land ownership to be restricted in the interests of social justice and the effective use of the land.

Traditional societal norms and poor economic conditions restrict women's professional roles, and they remain underrepresented in both national and local government. Domestic violence remains a problem, and Azerbaijan is a source, transit point, and destination for men, women, and children subjected to forced labor and sex trafficking.

Bahamas

Political Rights Rating: 1
Civil Liberties Rating: 1
Freedom Rating: 1.0
Freedom Status: Free
Electoral Democracy: Yes

Population: 400,000
Capital: Nassau

Ten-Year Ratings Timeline For Year Under Review (Political Rights, Civil Liberties, Status)

Year Under Review	2007	2008	2009	2010	2011	2012	2013	2014	2015	2016
Rating	1,1,F	1,1,F	1,1,F	1,1,F	1,1,F	1,1,F	1,1,F	1,1,F	1,1,F	1,1,F

The country or territory displayed here received scores but no narrative report for this edition of *Freedom in the World*.

Bahrain

Political Rights Rating: 7
Civil Liberties Rating: 6
Freedom Rating: 6.5
Freedom Status: Not Free
Electoral Democracy: No

Population: 1,400,000
Capital: Manama

Ten-Year Ratings Timeline For Year Under Review (Political Rights, Civil Liberties, Status)

Year Under Review	2007	2008	2009	2010	2011	2012	2013	2014	2015	2016
Rating	5,5,PF	5,5,PF	6,5,NF	6,5,NF	6,6,NF	6,6,NF	6,6,NF	7,6,NF	7,6,NF	7,6,NF

Overview: Once a promising model for political reform and democratic transition, Bahrain has become one of the Middle East's most repressive states. Since violently crushing a popular prodemocracy protest movement in 2011, the Sunni-led monarchy has systematically eliminated a broad range of political rights and civil liberties, dismantled the political opposition, and cracked down harshly on persistent dissent in the Shiite population.

KEY DEVELOPMENTS IN 2016:

- In July, the courts approved a government request to formally disband Al-Wefaq, the country's largest opposition group, which draws its support from the Shiite Muslim majority.
- The authorities continued to harass and detain leading political and human rights activists, including Nabeel Rajab, Ibrahim Sharif, and Ghada Jamsheer.
- In June, the government revoked the citizenship of Isa Qassim, the country's most important Shiite cleric, and charged him with money laundering.
- Regular clashes between police and mostly Shiite protesters occurred throughout the year, and dozens of people were arrested or questioned for participating in a sit-in to show support for Qassim.

EXECUTIVE SUMMARY

The Bahraini authorities' drive to outlaw peaceful political opposition intensified in 2016. In June, a court acting on a motion from the government suspended Al-Wefaq, a largely Shiite group that had long been the kingdom's main opposition political society, and its assets were seized. The organization was accused of encouraging terrorism, extremism, and violence, as well as foreign interference in Bahraini affairs. A second court ruling formally dissolved Al-Wefaq in July. Its leader, Ali Salman, was sentenced by an appellate court in May to nine years in prison on charges including incitement of sectarian hatred. He had been arrested in 2014 and initially sentenced to four years in prison in 2015. The harsher penalty was confirmed after another appeal in December.

The government also took aim at the country's highest-ranking Shiite cleric, Isa Qassim. In June, the Interior Ministry announced that Qassim had been stripped of his Bahraini nationality, adding to a growing list of regime critics whose citizenship has been revoked in recent years. Authorities claimed that Qassim had incited sectarianism and served foreign interests, alluding to long-standing state allegations that the Bahraini Shiite community is politically aligned with Iran. Qassim was also charged with money laundering. His supporters gathered outside his home and maintained a vigil through the end of the year to prevent his arrest, at times clashing with police in the area.

Other violent confrontations between protesters and security forces continued in 2016, leading to widespread arrests and a militarized police presence in predominantly Shiite villages and neighborhoods.

Bahraini authorities maintained legal pressure on outspoken activists during the year. Zaynab al-Khawaja was ordered to prison in March to serve a sentence of three years and one month for various convictions related to her criticism of the regime. She was released early in May, partly as a result of pressure from the United States, but she then left the country for Denmark, where she holds dual citizenship. Prominent activists including Nabeel Rajab and Ghada Jamsheer were also imprisoned during the year. Others, including Abdulnabi al-Ekry and the journalist Nazeha Saeed, were forbidden from traveling.

In July, the minister of information issued strict new guidelines for newspapers use of internet or social media to disseminate content, further limiting the presss freedom to operate.

POLITICAL RIGHTS: 2 / 40 (− 2)

A. Electoral Process: 2 / 12

The National Action Charter of Bahrain was approved by referendum in 2001, and the country was proclaimed a constitutional kingdom the following year. The 2002 constitution gives the king power over the executive, legislative, and judicial authorities. He appoints cabinet ministers and members of the 40-seat Consultative Council, the upper house of the National Assembly. The lower house, or Council of Representatives, consists of 40 elected members serving four-year terms. The National Assembly may propose legislation to the government, but it is the government that drafts and submits the bills for consideration by the legislature.

Al-Wefaq withdrew its 18 members from the Council of Representatives in 2011—and boycotted elections to fill the vacancies—to protest the government's crackdown on that year's prodemocracy demonstrations. The group boycotted the 2014 legislative elections as well, allowing progovernment candidates to dominate the legislature once more. Largely progovernment independents won 37 of the 40 lower house seats, and the remaining seats went to two Sunni Muslim political societies.

The government reported voter turnout of more than 50 percent, while the opposition estimated that less than 30 percent of eligible voters participated. The two sides also accused each other of engaging in voter intimidation, and the government allegedly redrew electoral districts to disfavor potentially populist political networks, including leftist and Sunni Islamist groups.

B. Political Pluralism and Participation: 0 / 16 (− 2)

While formal political parties are illegal, the government has generally allowed political societies or groupings to operate after registering with the Ministry of Justice. A 2005 law makes it illegal to form political associations based on class, profession, or religion, and an amendment adopted in May 2016 bans serving religious clerics from engaging in political activity. The majority Shiite population remains underrepresented in government.

Bahrain has been in political crisis since 2011, when local activists, mostly from economically disadvantaged Shiite communities, galvanized widespread support for political reform and against sectarian discrimination. The government declared martial law in response to the uprising and instituted a prolonged and violent crackdown.

After years of failed attempts to reconcile with the opposition, the authorities have imprisoned key political leaders and taken formal steps to shutter opposition societies permanently. Al-Wefaq general secretary Ali Salman was arrested on various incitement charges in 2014, and after a trial judge imposed a four-year prison sentence in 2015, an appellate court sentenced Salman to nine years in prison in May 2016. Although the Court of Cassation overturned the decision and returned the case for reconsideration in October, the harsher sentence was confirmed in December. Meanwhile, Al-Wefaq itself was formally dissolved by the courts in July after the Justice Ministry moved to shut it down for allegedly encouraging violence.

Ibrahim Sharif, former leader of the leftist National Democratic Action Society (Wa'ad), was sentenced in February 2016 to a year in prison for "inciting hatred against the regime." Although he was released in July, he was summoned by authorities in November and threatened with new criminal charges for his remarks to foreign media. Sharif had already spent four years in prison after the 2011 crackdown and was pardoned in 2015.

C. Functioning of Government: 3 / 12

The king and other unelected officials hold most authority over the drafting and implementation of laws and government policies in Bahrain, and with the main opposition group no longer participating in the legislature, the body has become increasingly moribund. In February 2016, the Consultative Council announced that it was suspending its planned sessions for the first time since 1993 due to a lack of bills referred from the lower chamber, which in turn had frequently adjourned early because members' poor attendance denied it a quorum. The council reportedly resumed its operations in March, though both chambers closed for a five-month summer recess in May.

Bahrain has some anticorruption laws, but enforcement is weak, and high-ranking officials suspected of corruption are rarely punished. A source of frustration for many citizens is the perception that Khalifa bin Salman al-Khalifa, the king's uncle and Bahrain's prime minister since its independence from Britain in 1971, is both corrupt and a key opponent of reform.

DISCRETIONARY POLITICAL RIGHTS QUESTION B: − 3 / 0

The government has made concerted efforts to erode Bahrain's Shiite majority, mostly by recruiting foreign-born Sunnis to become citizens and serve in the countrys security forces. Since 2011, the government has maintained a heavy security presence in primarily Shiite villages. These personnel restrict the movements of Shiite citizens, periodically destroy their property, and arrest critics and activists.

CIVIL LIBERTIES: 10 / 60

D. Freedom of Expression and Belief: 2 / 16

The government owns all broadcast media outlets, and the private owners of Bahrain's main newspapers have close ties to the state. Self-censorship is encouraged by the vaguely worded 2002 Press Law, which allows the state to imprison journalists for criticizing the king or Islam or for threatening national security. A 2014 amendment to the penal code prescribes prison terms of up to seven years for insulting the king. The government continues to block a number of opposition websites. In July 2016, the information minister issued an edict regulating newspapers' use of the internet and social media to disseminate content. Among other restrictions, the outlets must apply for a one-year renewable license and are barred from live streaming, and their online content must match or "reflect" printed material.

Journalists continued to face obstacles including prosecution and deportation in 2016. In February, four U.S. journalists were arrested and subsequently deported for entering the country on tourist visas and covering unrest linked to the five-year anniversary of the 2011 protests. France 24 correspondent Nazeha Saeed received a travel ban in June, and in July she was charged with working for foreign outlets without a license, as her annual renewal had been rejected earlier in the year. In December, a military officer and member of the royal family shot and killed sports journalist Eman Salehi, a Shiite woman; the motive remained unclear. Seven journalists were behind bars in Bahrain as of December, according to the Committee to Protect Journalists.

Islam is the state religion. However, non-Muslim minorities are generally free to practice their faiths. Muslim religious groups require a license from the Ministry of Justice and Islamic Affairs to operate legally, and non-Muslim groups must register with a different ministry, though the government has not actively punished groups that operate without permits. The Islamic Ulema Council, a Shiite group, was banned in 2014, and Shiite clerics and community leaders have often faced harassment, interrogation, prosecution, and imprisonment in recent years, typically due to allegations that they had incited sectarian hatred or violence. Some Sunnis have also been charged with such offenses. The government's moves in June 2016 to revoke the citizenship of senior cleric Isa Qassim and charge with him money laundering prompted a sustained sit-in protest around his home, and other Shiite clergy were among those detained or questioned for allegedly participating in the action. Protests and police restrictions periodically obstruct access to mosques.

Academic freedom is not formally restricted, but scholars who criticize the government are subject to dismissal. In 2011, a number of faculty members and administrators were fired for supporting the call for democracy, and hundreds of students and some faculty were expelled. Those who remained were forced to sign loyalty pledges.

There are strong suspicions that security forces use networks of informers, and that the government monitors the telephone and online communications of activists, critics, and opposition members. Users of social media have faced criminal charges for their online activity. In March 2016, Ibrahim Karimi, a man whose citizenship was revoked in 2012, was sentenced to two years in prison for allegedly insulting the king on Twitter; despite being stateless, he faced deportation after completing his sentence.

E. Associational and Organizational Rights: 1 / 12

Citizens must obtain a permit to hold demonstrations, and a variety of onerous restrictions make it difficult to organize a legal gathering in practice. Police regularly use force to break up political protests, most of which occur in Shiite villages, and participants can face long jail terms, particularly if the demonstrations involve clashes with security personnel.

The 1989 Societies Law prohibits any nongovernmental organization (NGO) from operating without a permit, and authorities have broad discretion to deny or revoke permits. Bahraini human rights defenders continued to face harassment, intimidation, and prosecution on dubious grounds in 2016. Zainab al-Khawaja, daughter of the imprisoned activist Abdulhadi al-Khawaja, began a prison sentence of three years and one month in March for a series of convictions linked to her criticism of the regime. She was released early in May, though after years of activism and arrests, she left the country to live in Denmark. In June, Nabeel Rajab, head of the Bahrain Center for Human Rights, was arrested for criticizing the government and alleging the torture of political prisoners on Twitter. His trial was repeatedly delayed through the end of December, and he remained in custody at year's end. After returning from a trip abroad in August, women's rights and political activist Ghada Jamsheer was imprisoned to serve a series of sentences linked to her Twitter posts about alleged corruption at a local hospital. She was released in December due to poor health and would serve the remaining four months of her sentences doing community work. She continued to face additional charges at the end of the year.

Bahrainis have the right to establish independent labor unions, but workers must give two weeks' notice before a strike, and strikes are banned in a variety of economic sectors. Trade unions cannot operate in the public sector, and collective-bargaining rights are limited even in the private sector. Harassment and firing of unionist workers occurs in practice. Household servants, agricultural workers, and temporary workers do not have the right to join or form unions.

F. Rule of Law: 1 / 16

The king appoints all judges, and courts are subject to government pressure. The country's judicial system is seen as corrupt and biased in favor of the royal family and its allies.

Although the government has criminalized torture and claims it does not hold political prisoners, scores of opposition figures, human rights and democracy advocates, and ordinary citizens have been jailed for their political views and activities. While some detainees are periodically denied access to family and lawyers, others enjoy limited opportunities for phone calls and other amenities. Detainees report frequent mistreatment by prison officials, who are rarely held accountable for abuse. A police ombudsman's office began operating in 2013, but human rights organizations report that it has failed to investigate torture allegations, and that citizens fear retribution for filing complaints.

Police have been targeted in small bomb attacks in recent years. In April 2016, assailants reportedly threw firebombs at a patrol near Manama, killing one officer and injuring two. In December, a court upheld death sentences for three defendants and life prison terms for seven others accused of a 2014 bombing that killed an Emirati officer and two Bahraini policemen. Human rights groups argued that the defendants were denied due process and that their confessions were extracted under torture. As of 2016, Bahrain had not carried out an execution since 2010.

The government uses revocation of citizenship as a punitive measure, particularly against critics and dissidents. While not all individuals who lose their citizenship are deported, many are forced to face the difficulties arising from a stateless status. More than 200 Bahrainis have been stripped of their citizenship since 2014.

Discrimination based on sexual orientation is common, and most LGBT (lesbian, gay, bisexual, and transgender) people hide their status. Same-sex sexual activity is not illegal, but individuals have reportedly been punished for "obscene" or "indecent" acts.

G. Personal Autonomy and Individual Rights: 6 / 16

The government continued to obstruct foreign travel by key opposition figures and activists in 2016. Authorities also restricted movement inside the country, particularly for residents of largely Shiite villages outside Manama. Security forces maintained a heavy presence around Diraz, the home village of Isa Qassim, in the months after he was stripped of his citizenship and supporters gathered to protect him from arrest.

Although registered businesses are largely free to operate, obtaining approval can be difficult in practice. Legal reforms in recent years have sought to lower the capital requirements and other obstacles to registering and operating businesses. For the wealthy elites who dominate the business sector, property rights are generally respected and expropriation is rare. However, Shiite citizens encounter difficulties obtaining affordable housing and in some cases bans on purchasing land.

Although women have the right to vote and participate in elections, they are underrepresented politically. Women won three parliamentary seats in the 2014 elections, and nine women were appointed to the upper chamber. Women are generally not afforded equal protection under the law. The government drafted a personal status law in 2008, but withdrew it in 2009 under pressure from Shiite clergy; the Sunni portion was later passed by the parliament. Personal status and family law issues for Shiite Bahrainis are consequently still governed by Sharia (Islamic law) court rulings based on the interpretations of predominantly male religious scholars, rather than by any formal statute.

According to the U.S. State Department's 2016 *Trafficking in Persons Report*, Bahrain is a destination for victims of human trafficking for forced labor and sexual exploitation. Some employers subject migrant workers to forced labor, and there are reports that abusers withhold workers' documentation in order to prevent them from leaving or reporting abuse to the authorities. The government has taken steps to combat trafficking in recent years, but efforts to investigate and prosecute perpetrators remain weak.

Bangladesh

Political Rights Rating: 4
Civil Liberties Rating: 4
Freedom Rating: 4.0
Freedom Status: Partly Free
Electoral Democracy: Yes

Population: 162,900,000
Capital: Dhaka

Ten-Year Ratings Timeline For Year Under Review (Political Rights, Civil Liberties, Status)

Year Under Review	2007	2008	2009	2010	2011	2012	2013	2014	2015	2016
Rating	5,4,PF	4,4,PF	3,4,PF	3,4,PF	3,4,PF	3,4,PF	3,4,PF	4,4,PF	4,4,PF	4,4,PF

Overview: Bangladesh is an electoral democracy, though the opposition boycotted the 2014 elections, ensuring the dominance of the ruling Awami League. Official harassment of the political opposition, as well as of critical media and civil society voices, is on the rise. Security forces carry out a range of human right abuses, including extrajudicial executions, disappearances, and torture, with near impunity. Meanwhile, those with dissident views—including secularists, academics, religious minorities, and LGBT (lesbian, gay, bisexual, and transgender) activists—are subject to attacks by Islamist extremist groups.

KEY DEVELOPMENTS IN 2016:

- The ruling Awami League (AL) further consolidated power during the year, including through the arrest and harassment of leading figures in the opposition Bangladesh Nationalist Party (BNP) and those perceived to be allied with it.
- In July, 20 hostages and two police officers were killed in an attack on a bakery in Dhaka that was popular with foreigners. The Islamic State claimed responsibility for the attack.
- The Foreign Donations (Voluntary Activities) Regulation Act, which took effect in October, made it more difficult for nongovernmental organizations (NGOs) to obtain foreign funds and gave officials broad authority to deregister NGOs that make "derogatory" comments about government bodies or the constitution.
- Some 15,000 people were arrested in a government crackdown authorities said was intended to curb a spate of extremist violence. Rights groups said the initiative involved widespread human rights abuses by authorities, including arbitrary arrests, enforced disappearances, and custodial deaths.

EXECUTIVE SUMMARY

Bangladesh continued to experience political and social unrest in 2016. The opposition BNP was hampered by arrests and harassment of key party officials and activists, while the Islamist Jamaat-e-Islami (JI) party faced similar restrictive moves by the authorities, in addition to ongoing proceedings against its leaders by the International Crimes Tribunal (ICT), which was formed to try war crimes and other atrocities committed during the 1971 war of independence. Several high-ranking JI members were executed during the year after their appeals of earlier ICT rulings were dismissed.

As in 2015, attacks on religious minorities, as well as secular and dissident voices and activists, by Islamist extremist groups occurred regularly. Of particular note was the murder of writer and LGBT activist Xulhaz Mannan in April 2016; his killing left a widespread climate of fear within the LGBT community. Although the government denied the presence of international terrorist groups such as the Islamic State throughout the first half of 2016, the dramatic July terrorist attack on the Holey Artisan Bakery, in the heart of Dhaka's elite Gulshan district—in which 22 people, including foreigners, were murdered in a hostage standoff—led to a broad crackdown on extremist groups. While attacks decreased in its wake, the security forces executing it engaged in a range of human rights abuses.

The space for freedom of expression and association was further circumscribed by the use of existing laws to prosecute media and online expression, as well as by the provisions of a new law on NGOs that placed restrictions on funding from abroad and expanded authorities' power to deregister them.

POLITICAL RIGHTS: 20 / 40 (− 1)

A. Electoral Process: 7 / 12

Members of the unicameral National Parliament and the largely ceremonial president serve for five years. The National Parliament is composed of 350 members, 300 of whom are directly elected. Political parties elect a total of 50 female members based on their share of elected seats. The president is elected by the legislature.

In the 2014 national elections, the BNP and 17 allied parties boycotted the vote to protest what they said were unfair circumstances. This left the majority of elected seats (153) uncontested, ensuring an AL victory. The AL won 234 parliamentary seats, the Jatiya Party (JP) won 34, and independents and minority parties captured the remainder. Western monitoring groups declined to send election observers and criticized the conditions under which the polls were held. The elections were also marred by extensive violence—Human Rights Watch termed them the bloodiest since the country's independence—and intimidation by a range of political parties. As a result, voter turnout was low, at 22 percent, compared to 87 percent in 2008. A number of attacks specifically targeted members of the country's Hindu and Christian minority groups, affecting around 700 people. The environment surrounding local government elections held between March and June of 2016 was similarly violent, with more than 140 deaths reported.

B. Political Pluralism and Participation: 8 / 16 (− 1)

Bangladesh has a two-party system in which power alternates between political coalitions led by the AL and BNP; third parties have traditionally had difficulty achieving traction. Following a series of parliamentary boycotts in 2013, the BNP boycotted the 2014 elections and has continued to engage in street action with the aim of forcing a change in government. The JI party was banned from taking part in the 2014 elections because of its overtly Islamist charter; the constitution bans religiously based political parties. The level of political violence remains high; in 2016, the human rights group Odhikar registered 215 deaths and more than 9,050 people injured as a result of inter- or intraparty clashes.

Ruling party harassment of the opposition BNP and JI remained widespread in 2016, further weakening both parties. Many BNP party leaders were imprisoned, under house arrest, living in hiding or exile, or facing serious legal charges that could bar them from office, including BNP head Khaleda Zia. In August 2016, Mir Ahmed Bin Quasem and Hummam Quader Chowdhury, the sons of prominent figures in the JI and BNP, respectively, were forcibly disappeared and detained without charge, in an ongoing pattern of harassment. Meanwhile, authorities continued to implement death sentences ordered by the ICT, including against JI chief Motiur Rahman Nizami, who was hanged in May, and JI financier Mir Quasem Ali, who was hanged in September; both were executed after their respective appeals were rejected at the Supreme Court.

Religious minorities remain underrepresented in politics and state agencies, though the AL government has appointed several members of such groups to leadership positions.

C. Functioning of Government: 5 / 12

Endemic corruption and criminality, weak rule of law, limited bureaucratic transparency, and political polarization have long undermined government accountability. Moreover, regular opposition boycotts of the National Parliament have significantly hampered the legislature's role in providing thorough scrutiny of government policies, budgets, and proposed legislation.

Under the AL government, anticorruption efforts have been weakened by politicized enforcement and subversion of the judicial process. In particular, the Anti-Corruption Commission (ACC) has become ineffective and subject to overt political interference. The government continues to bring or pursue corruption cases against the BNP; proceedings against Zia, among others, were ongoing in 2016.

The 2009 Right to Information Act mandates public access to all information held by public bodies and overrides secrecy legislation. Although it has been unevenly implemented, journalists and civil society activists have had some success in using it to obtain information from local governing authorities.

CIVIL LIBERTIES: 27 / 60 (− 1)

D. Freedom of Expression and Belief: 7 / 16

Bangladesh's media faced continuing pressure in 2016, including through the use of legal and regulatory restrictions, and via increasing harassment of and physical attacks against reporters and bloggers. The use of criminal defamation lawsuits by ruling party loyalists against independent and opposition news outlets and journalists escalated dramatically in 2016; notably, Mahfuz Anam, editor of the *Daily Star*, and Matiur Rahman, editor of *Prothom Alo*, each faced dozens of cases. In another case of legal harassment, 81-year-old editor Shafik Rehman was accused in April of involvement in a plot to kidnap and murder the prime minister's son; he was detained without being charged until he was released on bail in September, following a Supreme Court ruling. The 2014 National Broadcasting Policy allows for restrictions on coverage that is critical of the government or security forces or that is determined to threaten national security. A draft Distortion of the History of Bangladesh Liberation War Crimes Act would restrict discussion of the 1971 war of independence by mandating imprisonment or fines for those deemed to have misrepresented the conflict; it had not yet been adopted at the end of 2016.

The threat of physical reprisals against members of the media, bloggers, and publishers in connection with their work remained at a high level in 2016. Islamist militant groups linked to either Al-Qaeda or the Islamic State were frequently behind the threats. Although several militants have been arrested in connection with attacks against journalists, a climate of impunity remained the norm, with little progress made on ensuring justice for the string of killings that has taken place since 2015. Dozens of bloggers remain on an Islamist "hit list," and many have fled or gone into hiding due to threats.

Censorship of digital content and surveillance of telecommunications and social media have become increasingly common. The Information and Communication Technology (ICT) Act was used to arrest and charge several dozen individuals for exercising freedom of expression online in 2016; for example, student activist Dilip Roy was detained in August under the ICT Act for Facebook posts criticizing the prime minister, and spent two months in jail. Mithun Chakma, an indigenous rights activist, in July was arrested in connection with material in a 2007 blog post, and spent more than three months behind bars. Various forms of artistic expression, including books and films, are occasionally banned or censored.

As reaffirmed by a 2011 constitutional amendment, Bangladesh is a secular state, but Islam is designated as the official religion. Although religious minorities have the right to worship freely, they face societal discrimination as well as harassment and legal repercussions for proselytizing. Members of minority groups—including Hindus, Christians, and Shiite and Ahmadiyya Muslims—and their houses of worship are occasionally the targets of harassment and violent attacks. There was an uptick in such attacks during 2016. In October, more than 100 Hindu homes, temples, and shrines were targeted in Brahmanbaria District.

While authorities largely respect academic freedom, research on sensitive political and religious topics is reportedly discouraged. Political polarization at many universities, including occasional clashes involving the armed student wings of the three main parties, inhibits education and access to services. Open private discussion of sensitive religious and political issues is restrained by fear of harassment.

E. Associational and Organizational Rights: 6 / 12

The constitution provides for the rights of assembly and association, but the government regularly bans gatherings of more than five people. Many demonstrations took place in 2016, though authorities sometimes try to prevent rallies by arresting party activists, and protesters are frequently injured and occasionally killed during clashes in which police use excessive force.

Many NGOs operate in Bangladesh. While most are able to function without onerous restrictions, the use of foreign funds must be cleared by the NGO Affairs Bureau, which can also approve or reject individual projects. The Foreign Donations (Voluntary Activities) Regulation Act, which took effect in October 2016, made it more difficult for NGOs to obtain foreign funds and gave officials broad authority to deregister NGOs that make "derogatory" comments about government bodies or the constitution. Groups that are seen as overly critical of the government, particularly on issues concerning human rights, are already regularly denied permission for proposed projects and have been subject to escalating harassment and surveillance. Leading human rights NGO Odhikar continued to experience significant harassment by authorities in 2016.

The formation of labor unions became easier in 2015 due to legislative reforms. However, union leaders who attempted to organize or unionize workers continued to face dismissal or physical intimidation. Organizations that advocate for labor rights, such as the Bangladesh Center for Workers' Solidarity, have also faced increased harassment over the past several years. Worker grievances fuel unrest at factories, particularly in the rapidly expanding garment industry, where strikes and protests against low wages and unsafe working conditions are common. A week-long strike in December 2016 led to the dismissal of at least 1,500 garment workers and the arrest of union leaders.

F. Rule of Law: 5 / 16 (− 1)

Politicization of the judiciary remains an issue despite a 1999 Supreme Court directive ordering the separation of the judiciary from the executive. Political authorities have continued to make appointments to the higher judiciary, in some cases demonstrating an overt political bias. Harassment of witnesses and the dismissal of cases following political pressure are also of concern.

The court system is prone to corruption and is severely backlogged, with as many as 3.1 million pending cases in December 2016. Pretrial detention is often lengthy, and many defendants lack counsel. The indigent have little access to justice through the courts. Prison conditions are extremely poor; severe overcrowding is common, and juveniles are often incarcerated with adults. Suspects are routinely subject to arbitrary arrest and detention, demands for bribes, and physical abuse by police. Torture is often used to extract confessions and intimidate detainees. In 2016, Human Rights Watch documented a disturbing trend of "kneecapping," whereby security forces deliberately shot detainees, many of them supporters of opposition parties, in the knee or leg. The incidence of custodial deaths has remained high. Odhikar reported a total of 178 extrajudicial killings perpetrated by law enforcement agencies in 2016, in addition to 90 enforced disappearances. Criminal cases against ruling party activists are regularly withdrawn on the grounds of "political consideration," undermining the judicial process and entrenching a culture of impunity.

The 1974 Special Powers Act permits arbitrary detention without charge, and the criminal procedure code allows detention without a warrant. A 2009 counterterrorism law includes a broad definition of terrorism and generally does not meet international standards. Concerns have repeatedly been raised that the current International War Crimes Tribunal's procedures and verdicts do not meet international standards on issues such as victim and witness protection, the presumption of innocence, defendant access to counsel, and the right to bail.

Violence by Islamist political parties and other pressure groups has increased in the past several years, and larger-scale terrorist attacks by Islamist militant groups escalated in 2016; the South Asia Terrorism Portal counted 47 civilian and security-personnel fatalities related to Islamist extremism, roughly double the number of the previous year. A crackdown on extremist groups in response to a spate of attacks in the spring and early summer of 2016 led to the arrests of more than 15,000 people. Rights groups said the initiative involved widespread human rights abuses by authorities, including enforced disappearances, custodial deaths, and arbitrary arrests.

Members of ethnic and religious minority groups face some discrimination under law as well as harassment and violations of their rights in practice. Indigenous people in the Chittagong Hill Tracts remain subject to physical attacks, property destruction, and land grabs by Bengali settlers, and occasional abuses by security forces.

Roughly 270,000 ethnic Rohingyas who fled to Bangladesh from Myanmar beginning in the 1990s are subject to substantial harassment. The vast majority do not have official refugee status and suffer from a complete lack of access to health care, employment, and education. The government has attempted to discourage a more recent influx, in late 2016, of some 66,000 Rohingya refugees by sealing the border. In November 2016, authorities forcibly returned hundreds of Rohingya fleeing grave abuses in Myanmar, in violation of international law.

A criminal ban on same-sex sexual acts is rarely enforced, but societal discrimination remains the norm, and dozens of attacks on LGBT individuals are reported every year. In April 2016, Xulhaz Mannan, a prominent LGBT activist, was murdered alongside a friend by suspected Islamist militants; as a result, a number of other members of the community went into hiding or fled the country. Transgender people face persecution. Although since 2013 they can be legally classified as a "third gender" if they desire, a December 2016 report by Human Rights Watch found that implementation procedures to make this change were arbitrary and inadequate.

G. Personal Autonomy and Individual Rights: 9 / 16

The ability to move within the country is relatively unrestricted, as is foreign travel. Property rights are unevenly enforced, and the ability to engage freely in private economic activity is somewhat constrained. Corruption and bribery, inadequate infrastructure, and official bureaucratic and regulatory hurdles hinder business activities throughout the country. State involvement and interference in the economy is considerable.

The 2011 Vested Properties Return Act allows Hindus to reclaim land that the government or other individuals seized, but it has been unevenly implemented. Tribal minorities have little control over land decisions affecting them, and Bengali-speaking settlers continue to illegally encroach on tribal lands in the Chittagong Hill Tracts. A commission set up in 2009 to allocate land to indigenous tribes has suffered from delays. Since 2015, the ability of foreign nationals, journalists, and human rights activists to visit the Chittagong Hill Tracts has been tightened.

Under the personal status laws affecting communities of all religions, women have fewer marriage, divorce, and inheritance rights than men. In rural areas, religious leaders sometimes impose flogging and other extrajudicial punishments on women accused of violating strict moral codes, despite Supreme Court orders calling for an end to such practices. Women also face discrimination in social services and employment.

Rape, acid throwing, and other forms of violence against women occur regularly despite laws offering some level of protection. A law requiring rape victims to file police reports and obtain medical certificates within 24 hours of the crime in order to press charges prevents most cases from reaching the courts. Giving or receiving dowry is a criminal offense, but coercive requests remain a problem; Odhikar reported more than 200 cases of dowry-related violence against women in 2016. A high rate of early marriage persists, with 52 percent of girls married by age 18, according to UNICEF statistics for 2016. Despite a stated government commitment in 2014 to abolish the practice by 2041, in November the cabinet approved a draft law that would grant exceptions to the current ban on marriage below the age of 18 for girls.

Bangladesh remains both a major supplier of and transit point for trafficking victims, with tens of thousands of people trafficked each year. Women and children are trafficked both overseas and within the country for the purposes of domestic servitude and sexual exploitation, while men are trafficked primarily for labor abroad. A comprehensive 2013 antitrafficking law provides protection to victims and increased penalties for traffickers, but enforcement remains inadequate.

Following the 2013 Rana Plaza factory collapse, increased inspections and safeguards instigated by Western apparel companies led to the closure of around 200 of a total of 4,500 factories, and ongoing safety inspections at others, according to industry representatives. In July 2016, 41 people were indicted for murder for their role in the Rana Plaza disaster. However, working conditions in the garment industry remain extremely unsafe; a fire at a packaging factory in September 2016 claimed at least two dozen lives. Comprehensive reforms of the industry are hampered by the fact that a growing number of factory owners are also legislators or influential businesspeople.

Barbados

Political Rights Rating: 1
Civil Liberties Rating: 1
Freedom Rating: 1.0
Freedom Status: Free
Electoral Democracy: Yes

Population: 300,000
Capital: Bridgetown

Ten-Year Ratings Timeline For Year Under Review (Political Rights, Civil Liberties, Status)

Year Under Review	2007	2008	2009	2010	2011	2012	2013	2014	2015	2016
Rating	1,1,F	1,1,F	1,1,F	1,1,F	1,1,F	1,1,F	1,1,F	1,1,F	1,1,F	1,1,F

The country or territory displayed here received scores but no narrative report for this edition of *Freedom in the World*.

Belarus

Political Rights Rating: 7
Civil Liberties Rating: 6
Freedom Rating: 6.5
Freedom Status: Not Free
Electoral Democracy: No

Population: 9,500,000
Capital: Minsk

Ten-Year Ratings Timeline For Year Under Review (Political Rights, Civil Liberties, Status)

Year Under Review	2007	2008	2009	2010	2011	2012	2013	2014	2015	2016
Rating	7,6,NF	7,6,NF	7,6,NF	7,6,NF	7,6,NF	7,6,NF	7,6,NF	7,6,NF	7,6,NF	7,6,NF

Overview: Belarus is an authoritarian state in which elections are carefully managed and civil liberties are minimal. Limited displays of dissent have been permitted in recent years, as the war in neighboring Ukraine, growing regional tensions, and a struggling economy motivate the government to seek better relations with the European Union (EU) and the United States.

KEY DEVELOPMENTS IN 2016:

- Parliamentary polls held in September failed to meet international standards for democratic elections. However, two opposition candidates won representation.
- The European Union (EU) lifted most sanctions against Belarus in February.
- The government permitted several street demonstrations.
- Authorities continued to hold a number of political prisoners.

EXECUTIVE SUMMARY

As the government continued hosting consultations on the implementation of Minsk Agreement to end the conflict in Ukraine, the EU and United States muted their criticism of human rights abuses and the authoritarian political system in Belarus. The Belarusian government, meanwhile, worked to develop economically beneficial partnerships with both. The EU lifted most of its sanctions against the country in February.

Parliamentary elections were held in September. Like previous elections, they failed to meet international standards. However, two independent candidates were admitted to the parliament for the first time since 2000.

POLITICAL RIGHTS: 5 / 40 (+ 1)

A. Electoral Process: 0 / 12

The president is elected for five-year terms without limits. The 110 members of the Chamber of Representatives, the lower house of the rubber-stamp National Assembly, are popularly elected for four years from single-mandate constituencies. The upper chamber, the Council of the Republic, consists of 64 members serving four-year terms; 56 are elected by regional councils, and 8 are appointed by the president.

Since Alyaksandr Lukashenka was democratically elected to his first presidential term in 1994, all elections and referenda in Belarus have been marred by systemic violations that undermined the legitimacy of their outcomes.

In 2015, Lukashenka secured his fifth term in a noncompetitive presidential race. Organization for Security and Co-operation in Europe (OSCE) observers concluded that the elections fell considerably short of fell considerably short the group's standards for democratic elections, citing significant violations in the counting of the results. The observers did take note of several positive developments, including the participation of the first-ever female presidential candidate and the peaceful pre- and postelection environment; the latter was welcomed as an improvement given the brutal crackdown on protests surrounding the 2010 election. However, key opposition figures refused to recognize the results of the 2015 election, citing in part a series of irregularities related to early voting.

The OSCE observation mission similarly assessed the September 2016 parliamentary elections, saying they took place in a restrictive environment and that electoral procedures lacked transparency. However, there was less pressure on independent candidates, the general atmosphere was calm, and two candidates not associated with Lukashenka gained seats in the lower chamber.

The legal framework for elections fails to meet democratic standards. Among other problems, electoral commission members of all levels are politically aligned with and dependent on the government, and independent observers have no access to the ballot-counting process. The access of the opposition to state-run media has improved somewhat, but it remains under tight control while heavily favoring Lukashenka.

B. Political Pluralism and Participation: 4 / 16 (+ 1)

There is no official progovernment political party, and very few lawmakers are affiliated with any party. Two candidates not considered allies of Lukashenka, Hanna Kanapatskaya of the United Civil Party and Alena Anisim of the Belarusian Language Society, gained seats in the Chamber of Representatives in the 2016 legislative elections, ending a long period without opposition in the parliament.

Lukashenka employs various tools to weaken and divide the opposition, with some suggesting that permitting the two opposition candidates entry to the parliament was an example of this strategy. For example, some dismissed their election as immaterial and designed to placate the opposition, though others nevertheless consider their representation an opportunity to advance a democratic agenda on the institutional level. Their activity in the parliament may create stronger incentives for people to exercise independent political activity aimed at gaining power through elections.

Political parties encounter difficulties when seeking official registration. In 2016, the Ministry of Justice continued denying the registration to the Belarusian Christian Democracy party and the Tell the Truth movement, limiting the space of their political activities.

Six political prisoners were released in 2015 before their prison terms expired. However, according to human rights defenders, there are still political prisoners in the country, including activist Aliaksandr Lapitski, who was undergoing forced treatment in a mental institution, and Mikhail Zhamchuzhny, founder of the human rights organization Platform Innovation. Andrey Bandarenka, former leader of the associated group Platforma, was sentenced in 2014 to four years in prison on the basis of disputed charges.

For his role in 2010 protests, activist Uladzimir Kondrus was put on trial in November 2016; after attempting to cut his wrists in the courtroom, he was sent to a psychiatric facility for observation before being released in December on an 18-month suspended sentence, during which he was to undergo psychiatric treatment.

C. Functioning of Government: 1 / 12

The constitution vests most power in the president, giving him control over the government, the judiciary, and the legislative process by stating that presidential decrees have a higher legal force than ordinary legislation.

The state controls 70 percent of the Belarusian economy, feeding widespread corruption. In addition, graft is encouraged by an overall lack of transparency and accountability in government. Information on the work of about 60 government ministries and state-controlled companies, including the Ministry of Information and the state broadcaster, is classified.

There are no independent bodies to investigate corruption cases. Graft trials are held in a closed format isolated from the public, raising questions about the fairness of the process.

CIVIL LIBERTIES: 15 / 60 (+2)

D. Freedom of Expression and Belief: 3 / 16

The government exercises almost total control over mainstream media. The 2008 media law secures a state monopoly over information about political, social, and economic affairs. Libel is both a civil and criminal offense, and the criminal code contains provisions protecting the "honor and dignity" of high-ranking officials, including greater penalties in cases of defamation or insult. In October 2016, a court convicted Eduard Palchys—the founder and author of the blog 1863x, which publishes political analysis—of inciting ethnic hatred and publishing pornography, but ruled not to imprison him.

Belarusian national television is under complete control of the state. The state-run press distribution monopoly limits the availability of private newspapers. Freelance journalists working for foreign, unaccredited news outlets continue to be harassed and persecuted.

In 2016, in an attempt to reduce the influence of pervasive Russian propaganda and to reach out to a broader domestic audience, state-run media started inviting nongovernmental experts, opposition politicians, and independent journalists to talk shows, bringing alternative opinions into the discussion. The state also limited the outright pressure on independent media.

The government owns the only internet service provider, and maintains control over the internet through legal and technical means. Amendments to the media law approved in 2015 further expanded the definition of mass media to include all websites and blogs, placing them under the supervision of the Ministry of Information. A July 2016 report by Amnesty International noted that the state engaged telecommunications companies in its efforts to control and curtail freedom of expression, and concluded that the dissemination of communications technology had "increased the risk of repression" in Belarus.

Despite the constitutional guarantees of religious equality, government decrees and registration requirements maintained some restrictions on religious activity. Legal amendments in 2002 provided for government censorship of religious publications and barred foreigners from leading religious groups. The amendments also placed strict limitations on religious groups active in Belarus for less than 20 years. In 2003, the government signed a concordat with the Belarusian Orthodox Church, which is controlled by the Russian Orthodox Church, giving it a privileged position.

Academic freedom remains subject to intense state ideological pressures, and academic personnel face harassment and dismissal if they use liberal curriculum or are suspected of disloyalty. Regulations stipulate immediate dismissal and revocation of degrees for students and professors who join opposition protests. In 2015, Belarus was admitted to the Bologna Process on European standards for higher education under the condition that by 2018 it implement reforms to bring it into compliance with the process's principles.

The use of wiretapping and other surveillance by state security agencies limits the right to free private discussion.

E. Associational and Organizational Rights: 3 / 12 (+ 2)

The government restricts freedom of assembly for critical independent groups. Protests require authorization from local authorities, who can arbitrarily deny such permission. In the past, police would routinely break up public demonstrations and arrest participants. However, moves toward a rapprochement with the EU and United States motivated the government to ease such practices in 2016. Mostly, police refrained from beatings and arrests, but selectively imposed hefty fines on participants. Many street events were held without the usual rough treatment by police, including during the parliamentary election campaign.

Freedom of association is restricted. The participation in unregistered or liquidated political parties or organizations was criminalized in 2005. Their registration remains selective, and most human rights activists face potential jail terms ranging from six months to two years. Regulations introduced in 2005 ban foreign assistance to entities and individuals deemed to promote foreign "meddling in the internal affairs" of Belarus. In 2013, officials introduced legislation simplifying registration requirements for nongovernmental organizations (NGOs), but arbitrary denials of registration have not abated. Numerous unregistered NGOs operate despite the risk of prosecution.

Independent trade unions are under pressure, and their leaders are frequently fired and prosecuted for engaging in peaceful protests. No independent trade unions have been registered since 1999, when Lukashenka issued a decree setting extremely restrictive registration requirements. At the same time, in 2016, for the second year in row, authorities allowed independent trade unions to hold demonstrations on the global World Day for Decent Work, in October. The International Labor Organization continues to call on the government to implement a series of steps to improve the conditions for independent trade unions' operation.

F. Rule of Law: 2 / 16

Although the constitution calls for judicial independence, courts are open to significant executive influence. The right to a fair trial is often not respected in cases with political overtones. Human rights groups documented instances of beatings, torture, and psychological pressure during detention. In violation of international norms, the power to extend pretrial detention lies with a prosecutor rather than a judge. Separately, recent years have seen several instances in which former executives from state-run enterprises who have been convicted or are awaiting trial on corruption charges received clemency from the president, and were then immediately assigned to new senior positions.

Conditions in prisons and in pretrial detention facilities are dangerous. Shortages of food and warm clothing have been reported and medical facilities are inadequate.

Authorities deliberately create advantageous conditions for the Russian language to increase its dominance, while UNESCO recognizes Belarusian as a "vulnerable" language. Ethnic Poles and Roma often face pressure from the authorities and discrimination.

LGBT (lesbian, gay, bisexual, and transgender) individuals are subject to discrimination and regular harassment. The constitution explicitly bans same-sex marriage. The Belarusian government led an effort in 2016 to block LGBT rights from being part of a UN international initiative focused on urban areas.

Since 2014, thousands of people have fled to Belarus from the conflict in Ukraine, with many seeking asylum there. Belarus coordinates efforts to provide them with schooling and medical treatment with the Office of the UN High Commissioner for Refugees (UNHCR) and the International Organization for Migration (IOM).

G. Personal Autonomy and Individual Rights: 7 / 16

While an internal registration system complicates freedom of movement and choice of residence, restrictions have been eased in practice in recent years, leaving few obstacles to domestic and international travel.

The state continues to dominate the economy, but limits on economic freedom have gradually decreased in recent years, allowing for greater property ownership, commercial activity, and small business operations.

There are significant discrepancies in income between men and women, and women are poorly represented in leading government positions. However, in December 2016, Natallya Kachanava was appointed the head of the presidential administration. Domestic and sexual violence against women are considered to be persistent and underreported. Sexual violence is addressed in the criminal code, and a 2008 law addresses the prosecution of domestic violence, but no effective legislative measures are aimed at preventing these problems.

Mandatory unpaid national work days, postgraduate employment allocation, compulsory labor for inmates in state rehabilitation facilities, and restrictions on leaving employment in specific industries have led labor activists to conclude that all Belarusian citizens experience forced labor at some stage of their life. Presidential Decree No. 3, adopted in 2015 and widely known as the "parasite tax," introduced taxation on people who work fewer than 183 days per year. The lack of economic opportunities led many women to become victims of the international sex trade.

Belgium

Political Rights Rating: 1
Civil Liberties Rating: 1
Freedom Rating: 1.0
Freedom Status: Free
Electoral Democracy: Yes

Population: 11,300,000
Capital: Brussels

Ten-Year Ratings Timeline For Year Under Review (Political Rights, Civil Liberties, Status)

Year Under Review	2007	2008	2009	2010	2011	2012	2013	2014	2015	2016
Rating	1,1,F	1,1,F	1,1,F	1,1,F	1,1,F	1,1,F	1,1,F	1,1,F	1,1,F	1,1,F

Overview: Belgium is a stable electoral democracy, with political rights and civil liberties legally guaranteed and largely respected in practice. Security concerns have dominated public dialogue in recent years, driven by attacks in both Belgium and neighboring states.

KEY DEVELOPMENTS IN 2016:

* In March, three coordinated terrorist bombings—two at the Brussels Airport and one at the capital's Maalbeek metro station—led to the deaths of 32 civilians and injured more than 300; the Islamic State (IS) terrorist group claimed responsibility.
* Although the March attacks deeply shook the political establishment, the governing coalition remained relatively stable during the year.
* In May, approximately 60,000 demonstrators, primarily union workers, marched in Brussels to protest labor market reforms planned by the government of Prime Minister Charles Michel.

EXECUTIVE SUMMARY

Security and economic concerns dominated public debate in 2016. In the first months of the year, national security and intelligence forces focused on searching for the perpetrators of terrorist attacks that had targeted Paris in November 2015, as intelligence reports indicated that the attacks had been planned in Belgium. The search gave rise to public debate about the divided nature of administration in Belgium, and whether these divisions create vulnerabilities for the country's security. In March, a series of coordinated bombings occurred at Brussels Airport and a metro station in the center of the capital, killing 32 civilians and injuring hundreds. The bombings were the deadliest terrorist incident in Belgium's history. They deeply shook Belgian society as well as the country's political arena, with multiple officials offering their resignations, but the governing coalition led by Prime Minister Michel remained stable. A string of stabbings targeting police officers took place in the latter half of the year, including one in Charleroi in which the perpetrator attacked two policewomen with a machete.

A set of economic reforms proposed by the Michel government—including extending maximum workweek hours, raising the retirement age, and temporarily suspending automatic wage hikes—provoked strong opposition from unions, who claimed that the reforms would weaken workers' rights as well as Belgium's welfare state. Approximately 60,000 individuals—primarily union members—marched in Brussels in May to protest the planned changes. After a group of participants broke away from the demonstration and turned violent, police responded with water cannons.

POLITICAL RIGHTS: 40 / 40
A. Electoral Process: 12 / 12
B. Political Pluralism and Participation: 16 / 16
C. Functioning of Government: 12 / 12

CIVIL LIBERTIES: 55 / 60 (− 1)
D. Freedom of Expression and Belief: 15 / 16
E. Associational and Organizational Rights: 12 / 12
F. Rule of Law: 13 / 16 (− 1)
G. Personal Autonomy and Individual Rights: 15 / 16

This country report has been abridged for *Freedom in the World 2017.* For background information on political rights and civil liberties in Belgium, see *Freedom in the World 2016.*

Belize

Political Rights Rating: 1
Civil Liberties Rating: 2
Freedom Rating: 1.5
Freedom Status: Free
Electoral Democracy: Yes

Population: 400,000
Capital: Belmopan

Ten-Year Ratings Timeline For Year Under Review (Political Rights, Civil Liberties, Status)

Year Under Review	2007	2008	2009	2010	2011	2012	2013	2014	2005	2016
Rating	1,2,F	1,2,F	1,2,F	1,2,F	1,2,F	1,2,F	1,2,F	1,2,F	1,2,F	1,2,F

The country or territory displayed here received scores but no narrative report for this edition of *Freedom in the World.*

Benin

Political Rights Rating: 2
Civil Liberties Rating: 2
Freedom Rating: 2.0
Freedom Status: Free
Electoral Democracy: Yes

Population: 10,800,000
Capital: Porto-Novo

Ten-Year Ratings Timeline For Year Under Review (Political Rights, Civil Liberties, Status)

Year Under Review	2007	2008	2009	2010	2011	2012	2013	2014	2015	2016
Rating	2,2,F	2,2,F	2,2,F	2,2,F	2,2,F	2,2,F	2,2,F	2,2,F	2,2,F	2,2,F

Overview: Benin remains among the most stable democracies in sub-Saharan Africa, having witnessed multiple free and fair elections and peaceful transfers of power since its transition to democracy in 1991. Freedom of expression and association are generally respected, but corruption remains a challenge, particularly within the courts.

KEY DEVELOPMENTS IN 2016:

- Businessman Patrice Talon was elected president in March, and took office in April. Talon, an independent candidate, has pledged not to seek a second term.
- A 35-member commission appointed by President Talon to propose political and institutional reforms issued recommendations in June, which were primarily aimed at reducing presidential influence in the judiciary and the media.
- Upon taking office, Talon took steps to reduce bonus payments for top officials and remove allegedly corrupt mayors, though there are questions over whether the mayors' removals were politically motivated.

EXECUTIVE SUMMARY

Benin is among the most stable democracies in sub-Saharan Africa, and in 2016 saw a peaceful transfer of power after Talon was elected, and President Thomas Boni Yayi stepped down upon completing his second term, as mandated by the constitution.

In the first round of the presidential election, 33 candidates competed, and no candidate won a majority of votes. A second round was subsequently held between the top two candidates: Prime Minister Lionel Zinsou, of Yayi's party, the Cowry Forces for an Emerging Benin (FCBE); and Talon, a businessman and independent candidate. Talon, endorsed by 24 of the presidential candidates from the first round, won the second round and the presidency with 65 percent of the vote. Apart from minor delays, there were few problems with the election process. Several presidential candidates who supported Talon in the second round were rewarded with cabinet positions when the new government was formed.

President Talon has pledged to serve a single term, and followed through on a campaign promise to appoint a commission to recommend political and institutional reforms. In June, the commission recommended that the president should no longer appoint the country's chief justice or head of the national audio-visual authority; an increase in the number of justices on the constitutional court; and an extension of their mandate from five to nine years. However, Talon's lack of a majority in the legislature may pose a challenge to the recommendations' implementation; Yayi's FCBE holds the most seats.

The commission considered but did not make a recommendation on a proposal to replace the two five-year term limit for the president with a single seven-year term. Talon has announced a plan to hold a national referendum on the issue—though the constitutional court in 2011 ruled that the constitutional article regarding presidential term limits could not be changed in a referendum.

Once in office, Talon repealed some 20 decrees adopted under Yayi, including those on bonus payments to high-level public officials. Steps were also taken to remove a number of mayors from office based on accusations of mismanagement, although because of the mayors' support for Yayi, there are questions of political motivation.

POLITICAL RIGHTS: 33 / 40

A. Electoral Process: 9 / 12

B. Political Pluralism and Participation: 16 / 16

C. Functioning of Government: 8 / 12

CIVIL LIBERTIES: 49 / 60

D. Freedom of Expression and Belief: 15 / 16

E. Associational and Organizational Rights: 12 / 12

F. Rule of Law: 12 / 16

G. Personal Autonomy and Individual Rights: 10 / 16

This country report has been abridged for *Freedom in the World 2017*. For background information on political rights and civil liberties in Benin, see *Freedom in the World 2016*.

Bhutan

Political Rights Rating: 3
Civil Liberties Rating: 4
Freedom Rating: 3.5
Freedom Status: Partly Free
Electoral Democracy: Yes

Population: 800,000
Capital: Thimphu

Ten-Year Ratings Timeline For Year Under Review (Political Rights, Civil Liberties, Status)

Year Under Review	2007	2008	2009	2010	2011	2012	2013	2014	2015	2016
Rating	6,5,NF	4,5,PF	4,5,PF	4,5,PF	4,5,PF	4,5,PF	3,4,PF	3,4,PF	3,4,PF	3,4,PF

The country or territory displayed here received scores but no narrative report for this edition of *Freedom in the World*.

Bolivia

Political Rights Rating: 3
Civil Liberties Rating: 3
Freedom Rating: 3.0
Freedom Status: Partly Free
Electoral Democracy: Yes

Population: 11,000,000
Capital: La Paz (administrative), Sucre (judicial)

Ten-Year Ratings Timeline For Year Under Review (Political Rights, Civil Liberties, Status)

Year Under Review	2007	2008	2009	2010	2011	2012	2013	2014	2015	2016
Rating	3,3,PF	3,3,PF	3,3,PF	3,3,PF	3,3,PF	3,3,PF	3,3,PF	3,3,PF	3,3,PF	3,3,PF

Overview: Bolivia is a democracy where credible elections are held regularly. However, respect for freedom of expression and the rights of indigenous peoples and women remain issues, as does corruption, particularly within the judicial system.

KEY DEVELOPMENTS IN 2016:

- In February, voters rejected a referendum that would have permitted President Evo Morales to run for a fourth term.

- Despite the referendum's defeat, Morales's Movement for Socialism (MAS) voted in December to approve him as its candidate for the 2019 presidential election.
- In August, Vice Minister of Interior Rodolfo Illanes was kidnapped and murdered by protesting miners.

EXECUTIVE SUMMARY

In February 2016, voters rejected a referendum that would have permitted Morales to run for a fourth term, in what was seen as a major defeat for the president. Nevertheless, in December, the MAS voted to approve Morales as its candidate for the presidential election set for 2019, and signaled that it might undertake legal reforms order to permit him to do so.

Bolivia has a vibrant civil society, but occasional outbursts of violence at demonstrations remain a concern. In August 2016, Vice Minister of the Interior Rodolfo Illanes was abducted while traveling to speak with a group of miners who were protesting environmental and labor regulations. The government announced later that he had been killed.

POLITICAL RIGHTS: 29 / 40

A. Electoral Process: 11 / 12

Bolivia's president is directly elected, and presidential and legislative terms are both five years. The Plurinational Legislative Assembly consists of a 130-member Chamber of Deputies and a 36-member Senate. All senators and 53 deputies are elected by proportional representation, and 70 deputies are elected in individual districts. Seven seats in the Chamber of Deputies are reserved for indigenous representatives. The 2009 constitution introduced a presidential runoff provision.

In the 2014 general elections, Morales was reelected president with 61 percent of the vote. Samuel Doria Medina of the Democratic Union Front (UD) obtained 24 percent of votes, and the three remaining candidates shared less than 15 percent of votes. In concurrent legislative elections, Morales's MAS party maintained a two-thirds majority in the Plurinational Legislative Assembly, the share necessary to pass constitutional reforms. The MAS took 89 seats in the lower house and 25 seats in the Senate, while the opposition UD won 31 deputies and 9 senators, followed by the Christian Democratic Party (PDC) with 10 deputies and 2 senators. The Organization of American States (OAS) electoral observation mission stated that the elections reflected the will of the people, but recommended that Bolivia strengthen its electoral institutions and campaign finance system.

In March 2015 subnational elections, the MAS won control of more departments and municipalities across the country than any other party. However, the opposition won key mayoralties and governorships, including those of La Paz and Santa Cruz. The OAS electoral observation mission reported overwhelming citizen participation in the elections, but lamented the last-minute disqualification and substitution of candidates, which occurred after the ballots had been printed. As a result of these changes, voters had incorrect information on election day. Six out of seven Supreme Electoral Tribunal members resigned after the elections. In July 2015, new members of the tribunal were elected with the support of the MAS majority in the Plurinational Legislative Assembly.

Presidential term limits are the subject of controversy. A 2013 Plurinational Constitutional Tribunal ruling allowed Morales to run for a third term in 2014, stating that his first term in office did not count toward the constitutionally mandated two-term limit since it had begun before the current constitution was adopted. In 2015, the Plurinational Legislative Assembly voted to amend the constitution in order to allow presidents to run for three consecutive terms instead of two. In February 2016, a referendum to ratify the decision took place. Official results, released after an unusually slow vote-count process, revealed that 51.3 percent of voters had rejected the amendment, with about 88 percent of eligible voters participating in the poll. The OAS electoral observation mission applauded the high turnout, but noted unequal access to the media and acts of vandalism in Santa Cruz that prompted officials to reschedule voting at 24 polling stations.

B. Political Pluralism and Participation: 11 / 16

Citizens have the right to organize political parties. Since Morales's election in 2005, the formerly dominant parties have all but collapsed, giving way to a series of new political groupings and short-lived opposition coalitions. The MAS draws support from a diverse range of social movements, unions, and civil society actors.

Opposition politicians have claimed that the Morales administration persecutes them through the judiciary, and have recently claimed that only opposition leaders were prosecuted in connection with a scandal involving irregularities in the country's Indigenous Fund. According to a report by New Democracy, a Bolivian rights organization, there were 75 cases of politically motivated judicial cases in the first six months of 2016.

People are free to make their own political decisions without undue influence from the military, foreign powers, or other influential groups. The constitution recognizes 36 indigenous nationalities, declares Bolivia a plurinational state, and formalizes local political and judicial control within indigenous territories. Although they are well represented in government, the interests of indigenous groups are often overlooked by politicians.

C. Functioning of Government: 7 / 12

Corruption affects a range of government entities and economic sectors, including law-enforcement bodies and extractive industries. Anticorruption legislation enacted in 2010 has been criticized for permitting retroactive enforcement. The government has established an Anti-Corruption Ministry, outlined policies to combat corruption, and opened investigations into official corruption cases. In 2011, legislators voted to prosecute former presidents Gonzalo Sánchez de Lozada and Jorge Quiroga for approving hydrocarbon contracts alleged to have contravened national interests. In February 2016, the U.S. government accepted an extradition request for Sánchez de Lozada, who is also facing genocide charges in Bolivia for his role in the killing of dozens of indigenous protesters in 2003. In February, Gabriela Zapata—a former manager of the Chinese company CAMC who at one point had been in a romantic relationship with Morales—was imprisoned on corruption charges linking CAMC with contracts with state institutions.

Bolivia has no law guaranteeing access to public information, but a Transparency and Access to Public Information bill was under consideration at the end of 2016. The bill has drawn criticism from transparency advocates for allowing government agencies to establish exceptions on what information would be publicly available.

CIVIL LIBERTIES: 39 / 60

D. Freedom of Expression and Belief: 14 / 16

Although the constitution guarantees freedom of expression, in practice the media are subject to some limitations. A Ministry of Communications exists, but no implementing regulation for the constitution's "right to communication" has been passed. Most media outlets are privately owned, and ownership in the print sector has become consolidated. Radio is the leading source of information, but online media are growing in importance as a source of news. Many private newspapers and television stations feature opinion pieces that favor the opposition; the opposite holds true in state media. A 2011 telecommunications law allocated 33 percent of all broadcast licenses to state-run media, another 33 percent to commercial broadcasters, and 17 percent each to local communities and indigenous groups.

Journalists and independent media frequently encounter harassment in connection with critical or investigative reporting, including from public officials. In March 2016, Minister of the Presidency Juan Ramon Quintana threatened that media outlets that that disseminated false information would be closed. In June, the Bolivian National Press Association denounced before the United Nations threats against Bolivian journalists by government officials, noting among other incidents a threat by vice president Alvaro García Linera to imprison reporters for purportedly conspiring against Morales.

Freedom of religion is guaranteed by the constitution. The 2009 constitution ended the Roman Catholic Church's official status and created a secular state. The government does not restrict academic freedom. Private discussion is free from surveillance or other interference by authorities. The government is not known to restrict or monitor the internet.

E. Associational and Organizational Rights: 9 / 12

Bolivian law provides for the rights of peaceful assembly and freedom of association. However, protests sometimes become violent. In May 2016, several people involved with a sustained protest aimed at increasing government disability stipends were attacked while traveling to La Paz to meet with officials. Police reportedly employed an irritant spray against similar protests in April and again in June. At least two protesters were killed in August amid unclear circumstances as demonstrating miners clashed with police.

In July 2016, the Constitutional Court dismissed a petition arguing that two statues in the country's law on nongovernmental organizations (NGOs) gave the government license to improperly dissolve such groups. In October, a coalition of NGOs filed a petition against the law with the Inter American Commission for Human Rights, though Bolivia's minister of autonomies, Hugo Siles, noted that any decision by the body would not be binding.

Labor and peasant unions are an active force in society and wield significant political influence.

F. Rule of Law: 6 / 16

The judiciary is politicized and overburdened, and the justice system is beset by corruption. Police are poorly paid and receive inadequate training, and corruption within the police force too remains a problem. Police officers who attempted to expose corruption often face repercussions.

Bolivian prisons are overcrowded, and conditions for prisoners are extremely poor. An increase in urban crime rates and a 1988 law that substantially lengthened prison sentences for drug-related crimes have contributed to prison overcrowding, as has the frequent use of pretrial detention. Several pardon programs enacted in recent years, as well as fast-track trial procedures, have decreased the number of people in detention, though some critics contend that fast-track trials push innocent people to plead guilty in exchange for reduced sentences and less time spent in court. A 2016 report by the Ombudsman stated that 69 percent of inmates had not received a final sentence, and that prisons were filled to 302 percent of capacity. Assaults in prisons continue to pose a significant problem.

While the constitution and jurisdictional law recognize indigenous customary law on conflict resolution, reform efforts have not fully resolved questions regarding its jurisdiction and proper application. This lack of clarity has allowed some perpetrators of vigilante crimes, including lynching, to misrepresent their actions as a form of indigenous justice.

In late August 2016, amid a protest of mining sector workers in Panduro, a mob abducted and murdered Rodolfo Illanes, the vice minister of interior, as he was traveling to speak with the demonstrators. Five people were arrested in connection with his killing, including Carlos Mamani, president of the National Federation of Mining Cooperatives.

In general, racism is rife in the country, especially against indigenous groups. The 2010 antiracism law contains measures to combat discrimination and impose criminal penalties for discriminatory acts. Bolivia has laws in place that prohibit discrimination against LGBT (lesbian, gay, bisexual, and transgender) people. However, these laws are rarely enforced, and LGBT people experience widespread societal discrimination. Transgender individuals by law can change their name and gender identity on government forms, but judicial discrimination makes the process very difficult. Additionally, no laws condemn hate crimes against LGBT people. The Bolivian Coalition of LGBT Organizations (COALIBOL) reported that six LGBT people were murdered in 2016. Transgender people often resort to sex work in dangerous conditions due to employment discrimination and groundless rejection of their credentials.

G. Personal Autonomy and Individual Rights: 10 / 16

While the law protects freedom of movement, protesters often disrupt internal travel by blocking highways and city streets. Women enjoy the same formal rights to property ownership as men, but discrimination is pervasive, leading to disparities in property ownership and access to resources.

Two controversial Supreme Decrees in 2015 threaten the right to prior consultation in cases of natural resource extraction, which is established in international legal provisions recognized by Bolivian law. In March 2015, the government enacted Supreme Decree 2298, which establishes a 45-day limit on prior consultations regarding hydrocarbon activities and allows for the subsequent approval of land exploitation, even if the indigenous peoples involved did not participate. Supreme Decree 2366, issued that May, allows for oil and gas extraction in national parks provided that companies contribute 1 percent of their investments to poverty reduction and helping to prevent negative environmental consequences. Opposition leaders and human rights organizations have criticized the decrees, saying authorities failed to adequately consult with indigenous groups before issuing them. The Bolivian Center for Documentation and Information reported in March 2016 that related consultations with 59 communities in Amazonia were not free and informed. Observers also expressed concern after the president of the National Electricity Company in October announced that prior consultation did not apply to hydrocarbon exploitations, such as the El Bala dam project.

The constitution prohibits discrimination based on gender and sexual orientation, but it reserves marriage as a bond between a man and a woman, and makes no provision for same-sex civil unions.

The 2014 general elections were the first in which half of the candidates were women. As a result, 47 percent of senators and 53 percent of deputies are women. Nevertheless, the justice system does not effectively safeguard women's broader legal rights. A 2014 law increased the penalties for rape and abuse, and included the recognition of spousal rape; created a specialized police force for crimes against women; and categorized violence against women as a public health issue. More than half of Bolivian women are believed to experience domestic violence at some point during their lives. A 2012 law is intended to protect women from harassment and political violence; however only 20 out of the 316 cases reported since the law's approval have been resolved, according to an October 2016 editorial published by *La Razón*. The lack of enforcement and allocation of resources for the implementation of legislation protecting women continue to be a concern.

Child labor and forced labor are ongoing problems. A law approved in 2014 allows children aged 12 to 14 to enter work contracts as long as they do not work for longer than six hours a day. Children as young as 10 are permitted to work in independent jobs such as shoe shining as long as they are under parental supervision. Human rights organizations and the International Labor Organization have condemned these provisions.

Bolivia is a source country for the trafficking of men, women, and children for forced labor and prostitution, and the government's efforts to address and document the problem have been inadequate, according to the U.S. State Department's 2016 Trafficking in Persons report.

Bosnia and Herzegovina

Political Rights Rating: 4
Civil Liberties Rating: 4 ↓
Freedom Rating: 4.0
Freedom Status: Partly Free
Electoral Democracy: Yes

Population: 3,500,000
Capital: Sarajevo

Ratings Change: Bosnia and Herzegovina's civil liberties rating declined from 3 to 4 due to officials' failure to comply with Constitutional Court decisions, including one prohibiting a referendum in the Republika Srpska.

Ten-Year Ratings Timeline For Year Under Review (Political Rights, Civil Liberties, Status)

Year Under Review	2007	2008	2009	2010	2011	2012	2013	2014	2015	2016
Rating	4,3,PF	4,3,PF	4,3,PF	4,3,PF	4,3,PF	3,3,PF	3,3,PF	4,3,PF	4,3,PF	4,4,PF

Overview: Bosnia and Herzegovina (BiH) is a parliamentary republic distinguished by a fragmented and inefficient constitutional regime embedded within the Dayton Peace Agreement, which ended the 1992–95 Bosnian War. Politics are characterized by severe partisan gridlock among nationalist leaders from the country's Bosniak, Serb, and Croat communities. Corruption remains a serious problem.

KEY DEVELOPMENTS IN 2016:

- The country formally submitted its European Union (EU) candidacy application in February, which was accepted by the European Commission (EC) in September.
- In September, leaders in the ethnically Serb–dominated Republika Srpska entity held an illegal referendum concerning a holiday marking the entity's founding. The vote took place in defiance of both a Constitutional Court ruling, and international leaders' repeated warnings against holding it.
- A week after the Republika Srpska referendum, BiH held its sixth municipal elections since the conclusion of the Bosnian War. The polls were marred by irregularities and several attacks against poll workers. Nationalist candidates posted strong performances.

- The results of the 2013 census were finally released in June. Officials in the Republika Srpska disputed the count and pledged to issue their own numbers.

EXECUTIVE SUMMARY

In February 2016, BiH submitted its long-awaited application for EU candidacy. The application's submission came after the country's leaders had agreed, outside of traditional legislative processes, to establish a key mechanism necessary for BiH's application to move forward. The mechanism's existence came to light two weeks after the fact, when media outlets reported on its quiet publication in the country's Official Gazette. The EC accepted the application in September, and in December, the country received the formal EU Questionnaire, the completion of which would constitute a significant step toward EU membership.

However, 2016 also saw the emergence of a political crisis in which the Republika Srpska, one of the two entities comprising BiH, held an unlawful plebiscite concerning a holiday commemorating the entity's founding in 1992. The hard-line, nationalist president of the Republika Srpska, Milorad Dodik, spearheaded efforts to hold the referendum, which was widely seen as a move to undermine central institutions and which took place in defiance of both a Constitutional Court ruling banning the poll, and international leaders' repeated warnings against holding it. While Dodik has repeatedly teased similar referenda over the last decade, and while dozens of Constitutional Court decisions have been disregarded in the past, the holding of the controversial vote marked a significant deterioration of constitutional governance in BiH. Moreover, the referendum's dubious final result—with 99.81 percent of voters supporting continued commemorations of the holiday, and 0.19 percent against on a turnout of 55.77 percent—suggested a turn toward illiberal, managed democracy in BiH.

The referendum and charged political rhetoric accompanying it overshadowed statewide municipal elections that took place a week later. The elections saw overwhelming victories by nationalist candidates. Independent monitors, during the run-up to the polls, cited issues including inaccurate voter rolls; pressure on public-sector workers to vote for particular candidates; and politicized manipulation of the commissions tasked with oversight of polling stations. Authorities generally ignored complaints about these issues. No elections were held in the country's fourth-largest city, Mostar, owing to a partisan dispute dating back to 2008. Voting was also suspended in nearby Stolac after a candidate physically assaulted an election official, while similar scenes also occurred in Prnjavor, Ilijaš, Visoko, and a number of other locales. Independent monitors noted significant instances of apparent fraud or electoral interference across the country.

Journalists risk threats and attacks in response to critical political coverage and coverage of sensitive topics, and at least two journalists fled the country after receiving death threats in 2016. Separately, an attack on an LGBT (lesbian, gay, bisexual, and transgender) youth center in March led to a high-profile and well-organized civil society response, though the police response to the incident was criticized as inadequate.

The results of the 2013 census—the first since 1991—were finally released in June, and showed a population of about 3.5 million, compared to 4.3 million in 1991. Authorities in the Republika Srpska had attempted to obstruct the release of the data, citing issues with tabulation methodology that primarily concerned the number of non-Serb returnees counted in the entity. The data that was eventually published was deemed valid by the primary EU statistics agency, but authorities in the Republika Srpska have promised to release a competing set of figures. The delays in the census data's publication, and politicization of the process, have nevertheless led to concerns about the accuracy of the information.

POLITICAL RIGHTS: 21 / 40 (− 1)

A. Electoral Process: 7 / 12 (− 1)

B. Political Pluralism and Participation: 10 / 16

C. Functioning of Government: 4 / 12

CIVIL LIBERTIES: 34 / 60 (− 1)

D. Freedom of Expression and Belief: 10 / 16

E. Associational and Organizational Rights: 7 / 12

F. Rule of Law: 7 / 16 (− 1)

G. Personal Autonomy and Individual Rights: 10 / 16

This country report has been abridged for *Freedom in the World 2017.* For background information on political rights and civil liberties in Bosnia and Herzegovina, see *Freedom in the World 2016.*

Botswana

Political Rights Rating: 3
Civil Liberties Rating: 2
Freedom Rating: 2.5
Freedom Status: Free
Electoral Democracy: Yes

Population: 2,200,000
Capital: Gaborone

Ten-Year Ratings Timeline For Year Under Review (Political Rights, Civil Liberties, Status)

Year Under Review Rating	2007	2008	2009	2010	2011	2012	2013	2014	2 015	2016
	2,2,F	2,2,F	3,2,F	3,2,F	3,2,F	3,2,F	3,2,F	3,2,F	3,2,F	3,2,F

Overview: While considered one of the most stable democracies in Africa, Botswana has been dominated by a single party since independence, and critics of President Seretse Khama Ian Khama have expressed concerns about creeping authoritarianism. Journalists covering corruption or the activities of the opposition face pressure from authorities. The indigenous San people, as well as migrants and refugees from neighboring countries and LGBT (lesbian, gay, bisexual, and transgender) people face discrimination.

KEY DEVELOPMENTS IN 2016:

- The parliament approved a constitutional amendment creating two additional seats in the legislature for "specially elected" lawmakers, who are appointed by the executive and confirmed by the parliament. The two new lawmakers entered the parliament in October. Opposition members criticized the amendment as a means of strengthening executive power.
- In February, the government confirmed that state media outlets had been ordered not to report on some opposition activities.
- In August, nine ethnic San were shot at by an aerial antipoaching unit as they were hunting antelope. They were then arrested on charges of poaching and detained for several days, during which time they were reportedly beaten.

- President Seretse Khama Ian Khama ordered the arrest and deportation of U.S. pastor Steven Anderson, characterizing Anderson's virulent antigay views as hate speech.

EXECUTIVE SUMMARY

President Khama, the son of Botswana's first president, holds significant power, including the authority to prolong or dismiss the legislature, which cannot impeach him. Democracy advocates have alleged that power has become increasingly centralized around Khama, with many top jobs going to military officers and family members. The Botswana Democratic Party (BDP), now headed by Khama, has dominated the political scene with little substantive opposition since independence in 1966. In October 2016, in preparation for general elections to be held in 2019, the opposition Umbrella for Democratic Change (UDC) and the Botswana Congress Party (BCP) entered negotiations, with a formal coalition announcement expected in 2017.

In July 2016, the parliament began to debate a constitutional amendment that would increase the number of "specially elected" members of parliament from four to six; the specially elected members are appointed by the president and approved by a simple majority in the parliament, and are intended to serve as experts to support parliamentary operations. Opposition members criticized the proposed amendment as a means of strengthening executive power. Nevertheless, the amendment was approved, and two specially elected members entered the parliament in October.

While Botswana has a robust media sector, authorities in 2016 sought to suppress reporting on the opposition and on issues related to corruption. In February, the government confirmed that state media outlets had been ordered not to report on some opposition activities, which officials described as failing to meet editorial policies; in one instance, reporters had covered an opposition rally but did not broadcast it after being told by superiors that it was not newsworthy. Separately, in March, freelance journalist Sonny Serite was arrested and held overnight at a police station in Gaborone, where he was denied access to a lawyer; Serite had recently published a series of stories about corrupt contracts involving the national railway. His detention was one of a number of cases during the year in which investigative journalists were detained briefly before being released without charge.

The rights of the indigenous San people have eroded in recent years. In 2014, the San lost rights to hunt in Botswana, effectively denying them a way of life. In August 2016, nine San were shot at by an aerial antipoaching unit as they were hunting antelope. Soon after they were arrested on charges of poaching, stripped naked, beaten and detained for several days.

LGBT (lesbian, gay, bisexual, and transgender) people face discrimination in Botswana. However, in September, Khama ordered the arrest and deportation of U.S. pastor Steven Anderson, characterizing Anderson's virulent antigay views as hate speech.

POLITICAL RIGHTS: 28 / 40

A. Electoral Process: 10 / 12

B. Political Pluralism and Participation: 10 / 16

C. Functioning of Government: 8 / 12

CIVIL LIBERTIES: 44 / 60 (−1)

D. Freedom of Expression and Belief: 12 / 16

E. Associational and Organizational Rights: 10 / 12

F. Rule of Law: 11 / 16 (− 1)

G. Personal Autonomy and Individual Rights: 11 / 16

This country report has been abridged for *Freedom in the World 2017*. For background information on political rights and civil liberties in Botswana, see *Freedom in the World 2016.*

Brazil

Political Rights Rating: 2
Civil Liberties Rating: 2
Freedom Rating: 2.0
Freedom Status: Free
Electoral Democracy: Yes

Population: 206,100,000
Capital: Brasília

Ten-Year Ratings Timeline For Year Under Review (Political Rights, Civil Liberties, Status)

Year Under Review	2006	2007	2008	2009	2010	2011	2012	2013	2014	2015
Rating	2,2,F	2,2,F	2,2,F	2,2,F	2,2,F	2,2,F	2,2,F	2,2,F	2,2,F	2,2,F

Overview: Brazil is a democracy with competitive elections and vibrant civil society engagement. However, a severe economic and political crisis has significantly challenged the functioning of government. Corruption, crime, and economic exclusion of minorities are among the country's most serious difficulties.

KEY DEVELOPMENTS IN 2016:

- Brazil faced its worst economic recession in recent history as well as a political crisis that included the impeachment of President Dilma Rousseff in August.
- Large demonstrations took place on several occasions, with participants marching for or against Rousseff's impeachment and expressing dissatisfaction with pervasive corruption, among other issues.
- A major investigation into a multibillion-dollar bribery scandal at the state-controlled oil company Petrobrás continued, with prosecutors pursuing several active court cases and continuing to file charges against public servants and officials from private.
- Rousseff's impeachment prompted heightened scrutiny over judicial independence and the country's checks and balances.

EXECUTIVE SUMMARY

Serious political and economic challenges marked the year in Brazil. Since 2014, a high inflation rate and growing unemployment have characterized what has become Brazil's worst economic recession in more than two decades. The situation was further exacerbated in 2016 by paralyzing disagreement between opposing parliamentary parties as well as the controversial Petrobrás bribery investigation, so-called Operation Car Wash. The investigation, which began in 2014, focuses on bribery, money-laundering, and bid-rigging involving the state-controlled oil giant and private construction companies. Its findings have implicated former Petrobrás executives, heads of major construction firms, and elected officials from across the political spectrum. In December, approximately 80 employees of Odebrecht, a conglomerate involved in the scandal, accepted plea deals. Their testimony is expected to inform prosecutors about dozens of politicians who took kickbacks as part of the scheme.

Rousseff, who faced low approval ratings in 2016, proved unable to sustain her political coalition or to meaningfully address the country's economic challenges. Ongoing efforts to impeach her for manipulating the country's budget, initiated in late 2015, further frayed her position. In May, legislators suspended Rousseff's presidential powers ahead of the commencement of her trial and appointed Michel Temer, Rousseff's vice president, to be interim president. Temer's party had departed from its coalition with Rousseff's in March, and upon his appointment, the new president fully withdrew from the leftist platform that had led to his and Rousseff's reelection in 2014 and installed a right-of-center, all-male cabinet. In August, the Senate voted to impeach Rousseff on charges of budgetary manipulation, and confirmed Temer to serve out the remainder of her term. Temer himself faced allegations of past involvement in corruption, and at the time of the impeachment vote, more than half of all members of the National Congress had been charged or were under investigation for serious crimes, including corruption, kidnapping, and murder.

Rousseff's ouster heightened scrutiny over the reach and strength of Brazil's judicial bodies and processes, with promoters and detractors weighing in on the constitutionality of the impeachment process and judicial independence. Some legal scholars pointed to the political implications of prosecuting officials in a system where corruption reaches most of the ruling class, and others raised questions about Judge Sergio Moro's use of pretrial detention and treatment of sensitive wiretap recordings.

Large, mostly peaceful protests took place throughout the year. Protesters marched for or against Rousseff's impeachment, as well as against the National Congress, corruption in general, and controversial preparations for the Rio de Janeiro Olympics.

POLITICAL RIGHTS: 31 / 40 (− 2)

A. Electoral Process: 11 / 12

Brazil is a federal republic governed under a presidential system. Elections are generally free and fair. The president is elected by popular vote for a four-year term and is eligible for reelection to a second term. Rousseff, the Workers' Party (PT) candidate, won the 2014 presidential election by a slim margin, taking 51.6 percent of the vote in a runoff against Aécio Neves of the centrist Brazilian Social Democratic Party (PSDB), who received 48.4 percent. In August 2016, the Senate impeached Rousseff on charges of budgetary manipulation, finding that she had committed the offense in an effort to hide Brazil's economic problems. Temer, Rousseff's vice president and one of the leading figures in the Brazilian Democratic Movement Party (PMDB), was installed as interim president at the outset of the impeachment trial in May, and was confirmed in August to serve for the remainder of her term, which ends in 2018.

The bicameral National Congress is composed of an 81-member Senate and a 513-member Chamber of Deputies. Senators serve staggered eight-year terms, with one- to two-thirds coming up for election every four years. Members of the Chamber of Deputies serve four-year terms. In the 2014 legislative elections, the PT remained the largest party in the lower house with 70 deputies, followed by the centrist, PT-allied PMDB with 66 seats and the opposition PSDB with 54 seats. The PMDB maintained its lead in the Senate with 18 seats, while the PT captured 12 seats and the PSDB took 10. Numerous smaller parties made up the remainder. The PT lost a considerable number of seats in municipal elections held in October 2016.

B. Political Pluralism and Participation: 14 / 16

Brazil has an unfettered multiparty system marked by vigorous competition between rival parties. The electoral framework encourages the proliferation of parties. Some parties display little ideological consistency, and the frequent emergence of new parties poses challenges for voters and governance alike. The sheer number of parties means that the executive branch must piece together diverse coalitions to pass legislation, which may encourage corruption. No single party has been able to dominate the executive and legislative branches in recent years. Rousseff was unable to sustain her party's legislative coalition with the PMDB, which left it in March 2016.

Afro-Brazilians and women remain underrepresented in politics. The Senate has one self-identified black representative. Temer's cabinet does not include any women or Afro-Brazilians.

C. Functioning of Government: 6 / 12 (− 2)

Corruption and graft remain endemic in Brazil, especially among elected officials. This undermines the ability of the government to make and implement policy without undue influence from private or criminal interests.

While regular government operations continued in 2016, overall functioning was weakened by a political standoff between Rousseff and her pro-impeachment opponents, and major legislative initiatives stalled amid the standoff and subsequent impeachment trial. After months of disagreement and public protest, legislators passed a controversial austerity package in December. Temer's own low approval ratings and divisive politics may further hinder efforts to ease parliamentary tensions and garner support for much-needed reforms in the face of the economic crisis.

Brazilians were deeply divided over Rousseff's impeachment proceedings. In March, millions took to the streets in antigovernment protests throughout the country, while Rousseff supporters rallied in June. Rousseff argued that impeachment constituted a coup d'état, claiming that the charges against her did not rise to the standard of "crime of responsibility," as required by the constitution.

In March, Judge Moro leaked wiretaps of conversations between Rousseff and former president Luíz Inácio Lula da Silva, who was under investigation for his involvement in the Petrobrás case. In the recordings, the two discussed a plan for Lula's appointment as presidential chief of staff, which would offer protection against prosecution in the courts. Both the conversation and the leak raised concerns about the integrity and independence of the impeachment process and the Petrobrás investigation, as well as about executive and judicial overreach in general.

Operation Car Wash, as the Petrobrás investigation has come to be known, continued throughout the year. As investigators have so far confirmed, for at least the last decade, some of the country's largest construction companies paid billions of dollars in bribes and kickbacks to politicians, political parties, and Petrobrás executives in order to land lucrative contracts with the oil producer at inflated prices. Rousseff, who had served as head of the Petrobrás board when much of the alleged corruption took place, faced allegations of involvement, but her impeachment charges did not ultimately include offenses related to the Petrobrás case. Many other current and former elected officials have been investigated or charged. Former president Lula was charged with corruption and money laundering in December. In October, the former speaker of the lower legislative house, Eduardo Cunha, was arrested and detained on the same charges. Cunha had been one of the most vocal proponents of Rousseff's impeachment. In December, the Supreme Court removed the president of the Senate, Renan Calheiros, from the presidential line of succession after he was indicted on embezzlement charges.

Brazil is a cofounder of the Open Government Partnership, a multinational initiative seeking to increase governmental transparency and democratic ideals while decreasing corruption. As part of its pledge to support these goals, Brazil enacted an Access to Information Law in 2012. In June 2016, Temer converted the National Controller's Office (CGU), an important resource for appealing denials of information requests, into a new Ministry of Transparency, Monitoring, and Oversight. Watchdogs considered this move detrimental to the independence of the country's freedom of information mechanism.

CIVIL LIBERTIES: 48 / 60

D. Freedom of Expression and Belief: 15 / 16

The constitution guarantees freedom of expression, but politicians and influential businessmen continued to make use of existing laws to curtail critical reporting in 2016. Defamation, for example, remains a crime and carries a minimum sentence of three months in prison.

Journalists, especially those who focus on organized crime or corruption, are frequently victims of violence. According to local press watchdogs, several journalists were killed in 2016, including radio host João Valdecir de Borba, shot during a live broadcast; website owner and reporter João Miranda do Carmo, shot outside his home; and blogger Manoel Messias Pereira, gunned down while driving his motorcycle. At year's end, police had not been able to confirm work-related motives in all of the cases. When the newspaper *Gazeta do Povo* published a report in February alleging that the salaries of judges, magistrates, and district attorneys in the state of Paraná were above the pay ceiling that is enshrined in the constitution, the paper and its five reporters were served with 46 individual civil suits, which press freedom advocates decried as harassment.

The news media are privately owned, and there are dozens of independent papers and broadcast stations across the country. Financial dependence on state advertising, however, sometimes renders the press vulnerable to manipulation.

Brazil has been praised as a champion of internet user rights. The 2014 Marco Civil da Internet, a so-called bill of rights for the internet, guarantees universal internet access and establishes strong privacy protections for Brazilian users.

The constitution guarantees freedom of religion, and the government generally respects this right in practice. Academic freedom and private discussion are likewise unrestricted.

E. Associational and Organizational Rights: 10 / 12

Freedom of assembly is generally respected. A series of largely peaceful demonstrations took place during the year over Rousseff's impeachment, corruption, the economic crisis, and the 2016 Summer Olympics in Rio de Janeiro. Alarmingly, police met some protests with violence, using tear gas and rubber bullets. Police conduct at public assemblies has been of concern for several years; in São Paulo, for example, police responses to protests have led to four participants being blinded in recent years. A 19-year old woman was hit in the eye with shrapnel during a demonstration in August, and two photojournalists were blinded by rubber bullets in 2013.

Although protest activity in Olympic venues was initially banned, a judge ruled in August that the government and the International Olympic Committee could not remove protesters from the sites.

There are no significant restrictions on freedom of association, and nongovernmental organizations (NGOs) are able to operate in a variety of fields. Industrial labor unions are well organized. Although they are politically connected, Brazilian unions tend to be freer from political party control than their counterparts in other Latin American countries. Labor issues are adjudicated in a system of special labor courts. Officials and employers sometimes engage in antiunion activity, including dismissal of organizers, and a number of labor activists have been threatened or murdered in recent years, particularly in rural areas.

F. Rule of Law: 10 / 16

The judiciary, though largely independent, is overburdened, inefficient, and often subject to intimidation and other external influences, especially in rural areas. Access to justice also varies greatly due to Brazil's high level of income inequality. Despite these shortcomings, the country's progressive constitution has resulted in an active judiciary that often rules in favor of citizens over the state.

In November 2016, the lower legislative house gutted an anticorruption bill, passing it with changes that would protect legislators from prosecution and allow prosecutors and judges to be punished for abuse of authority. The bill passed by 450 votes to 1, and was awaiting a vote in the Senate at year's end. Prosecutors involved in the year's major corruption scandals threatened to resign from their posts in protest. In December, a Supreme Court justice ordered the bill to be reassessed in the lower house.

Brazil has a relatively high homicide rate; approximately 60,000 homicides occurred in 2014, the majority of them involving firearms. This high level of violence is perpetuated by impunity and corruption, as well as the illegal drug trade. Highly organized and well-armed drug gangs frequently clash with military police or with private militias composed of off-duty police officers, prison guards, and firefighters. In recent years, violence has decreased in the larger and more affluent cities but increased in Brazil's poorer northeastern regions.

Brazil's police force remains mired in allegations of corruption as well as excessive and extrajudicial violence. Victims of police violence are predominantly young, black, and poor, and are often bystanders caught in crossfire between police and suspected gang members. Police use torture to extract confessions from suspects, and often portray extrajudicial killings as shootouts with dangerous criminals. Police officers are rarely prosecuted for such abuses, and those charged are almost never convicted. The long-term presence of special Pacifying Police Units (UPP) has apparently reduced crime in several urban *favelas*, or slums, though allegations of excessive or extrajudicial violence by the UPP continue to raise concerns.

A 2013 law created a watchdog body known as the National Mechanism to Prevent and Combat Torture. It consists of 11 experts with unprecedented power to visit any civilian or military facility where torture or ill-treatment has been documented. Despite this positive step, torture remained a serious problem in 2016. Brazilian law does not require that detainees be brought before a judge promptly after arrest, which increases opportunities for abuse in custody.

Brazil's prison system, known for its appalling living conditions, holds a population far above capacity. From 2000 to 2014, the prison population increased by 164 percent, due principally to an increase in drug arrests. Approximately 40 percent of inmates in Brazil's prisons are awaiting trial, and they are often held with convicted criminals, which violates international law. Pretrial detention can last for months or even years, as a chronic backlog in the court system routinely results in substantial trial delays. Some legal experts have cautioned that the multitude of pretrial detentions and plea bargains used in the Petrobrás investigation runs counter to the defendants' presumption of innocence.

Brazilian law prohibits discrimination on the basis of race, gender, disability, or social status, but the country continues to struggle with discrimination. Just over half of Brazil's population identify themselves as black or of mixed race. However, Afro-Brazilians suffer from higher rates of homicide, poverty, and illiteracy; almost 70 percent of Brazilians living in extreme poverty are black. Government attempts to address this issue include the 2010 Statute of Racial Equality, which granted land rights to inhabitants of *quilombos*— communities of descendants of escaped slaves. A 2012 affirmative action law requires public universities to reserve 50 percent of admission spots for students coming from public schools, and dictates that the number of students of African descent at public universities must change in accordance with the racial composition of each state. In 2014, the National Congress passed a law requiring that at least 20 percent of its civil service employees be of African descent.

Indigenous peoples make up less than 1 percent of the population. Many indigenous communities suffer from poverty and lack adequate sanitation and education services. Unresolved and often violent land disputes between indigenous communities and farmers continued to be a problem in 2016. In the face of court cases that further delay already lengthy disagreements, tribes occasionally resort to forcible removal of those inhabiting their protected lands. In January, a court suspended the construction of the Belo Monte hydroelectric dam in the Amazon due to the lack of adequate support for the indigenous families that the construction would affect. In August, the government withdrew plans to build the Tapajós dam, which had also faced indigenous opposition.

Although Brazil has a largely tolerant society, it reportedly has one of the world's highest levels of violence against members of the LGBT (lesbian, gay, bisexual, and transgender) community. According to Grupo Gay da Bahia, a domestic LGBT advocacy group, a gay or transgender person is killed almost every day in Brazil.

G. Personal Autonomy and Individual Rights: 13 / 16

Brazilians enjoy freedom to travel within and outside of the country, and to make decisions about their places of residence and employment. Property rights are enforced, though requirements for starting new businesses are often onerous, and corruption and organized crime sometimes pose obstacles to private business activity.

A 2003 update to the legal code granted women rights equal to those of men. In 2013, the National Congress approved a constitutional amendment extending equal labor rights to household workers, many of whom are women. Upon taking up the office of president, Rousseff had pledged to make women's rights a priority for her government, and appointed a number of women to each of her cabinets. President Temer did not appoint any women to his cabinet in 2016; Brazil had not seen an all-male cabinet since the end of its 1964–85 military dictatorship. Women hold fewer than 10 percent of seats in the Chamber of Deputies, and roughly 16 percent in the Senate.

While contraception is available, abortion is legal only in the case of rape, a threat to the mother's life, or a rare and usually fatal brain deformity in the fetus. The spread of the Zika virus in 2015 and 2016, along with related complications like microcephaly, raised awareness of women's restricted access to abortion. Abortion in cases of microcephaly, a condition in which an infant's head is underdeveloped, remains illegal. Many women turn to illegal providers, and those who undergo clandestine abortions are often hospitalized due to complications. Illegal abortions are a leading cause of maternal mortality in Brazil.

A 2013 law legalized same-sex marriage.

Slavery-like working conditions pose a significant problem in rural zones, and increasingly in urban ones as well. A 2012 constitutional amendment allows the government to confiscate all property of landholders found to be using slave labor. A report published in February 2016 by a domestic NGO showed that from May 2013 to May 2015, the Ministry of Labor fined 340 companies for using slave labor, which in Brazil is defined as forced labor, unpaid work in exchange for debt forgiveness, or working in degrading conditions.

The government has sought to address the problem of child labor by cooperating with various NGOs, increasing inspections, and offering cash grants to keep children in school.

Brunei

Political Rights Rating: 6
Civil Liberties Rating: 5
Freedom Rating: 5.5
Freedom Status: Not Free
Electoral Democracy: No

Population: 400,000
Capital: Bandar Seri Begawan

Ten-Year Ratings Timeline For Year Under Review (Political Rights, Civil Liberties, Status)

Year Under Review	2007	2008	2009	2010	2011	2012	2013	2014	2015	2016
Rating	6,5,NF	6,5,NF	6,5,NF	6,5,NF	6,5,NF	6,5,NF	6,5,NF	6,5,NF	6,5,NF	6,5,NF

The country or territory displayed here received scores but no narrative report for this edition of *Freedom in the World*.

Bulgaria

Political Rights Rating: 2
Civil Liberties Rating: 2
Freedom Rating: 2.0
Freedom Status: Free
Electoral Democracy: Yes

Population: 7,100,000
Capital: Sofia

Ten-Year Ratings Timeline For Year Under Review (Political Rights, Civil Liberties, Status)

Year Under Review	2007	2008	2009	2010	2011	2012	2013	2014	2015	2016
Rating	1,2,F	2,2,F	2,2,F	2,2,F	2,2,F	2,2,F	2,2,F	2,2,F	2,2,F	2,2,F

Overview: Multiple parties compete in Bulgaria's democratic electoral system, and there have been several transfers of power between rival parties in recent decades. The country continues to struggle with political corruption and organized crime, and the political discourse is marred by hate speech against minority groups and foreigners, especially from smaller right-wing parties. While the media sector remains pluralistic, ownership concentration is a growing problem, and news outlets often tailor coverage to suit the interests of their owners. Journalists sometimes encounter threats or violence in the course of their work. Ethnic minorities, particularly Roma, face discrimination. Despite funding shortages and other obstacles, civil society groups have been active and influential.

KEY DEVELOPMENTS IN 2016:

- Rumen Radev, a candidate endorsed by the center-left opposition, defeated a government-backed rival in the November presidential election. Incumbent Rosen Plevneliev had decided not to seek reelection.
- Following the election, the right-leaning prime minister resigned, meaning snap parliamentary elections would likely be held in early 2017.
- In September, amid growing nationalist hostility toward Muslim migrants, the parliament passed a nationwide ban on face-covering clothing in public places.

EXECUTIVE SUMMARY

A coalition government led by Prime Minister Boyko Borisov and his center-right party, Citizens for European Development of Bulgaria (GERB), held power for most of 2016. However, it began to weaken in May, when the left-leaning Alternative for Bulgarian Revival (ABV) party withdrew its support.

One of the reasons for ABV's withdrawal was disagreement over electoral reforms ahead of the November presidential election. In April, the parliament had adopted a series of changes, including the introduction of mandatory voting and the limitation of voting sites abroad to embassies and consulates. Individuals who failed to vote in two successive elections of the same type would be removed from the registry, meaning they would have to reregister to vote again. The national ombudsman appealed the mandatory voting provision to the Constitutional Court, which was considering it at year's end. Meanwhile, President Plevneliev, responding to objections from civil society and the ombudsman, vetoed the provision on voting abroad in May, and in July lawmakers adopted a new version allowing up to 35 polling sites per country. The rule was modified again in October, authorizing more than 35 sites in European Union (EU) member states.

The presidential election was held in two rounds in early November. After leading in the first round, former air force commander Rumen Radev—an independent supported by the opposition Bulgarian Socialist Party (BSP)—defeated GERB parliament speaker Tsetska Tsacheva, taking more than 59 percent of the vote. In light of his candidate's upset defeat, Borisov resigned as prime minister, meaning snap parliamentary elections were likely to be called in early 2017.

Voters in the presidential election also cast ballots for a referendum on electoral reforms initiated by a popular television personality. Although turnout fell short of a threshold that would have made the referendum binding, participants overwhelmingly supported cutting state subsidies to political parties and switching from a party-list system to a two-round majoritarian system for parliamentary elections.

Separately during the year, the parliament continued to work on judicial reform, adopting two packages of legal amendments in March and July that were designed to help improve transparency and independence among judges and prosecutors.

In September, lawmakers approved a ban on face-covering clothing in public places, with escalating fines for repeat offenses. The measure was introduced by the nationalist Patriotic Front, part of the ruling coalition. In December, the parliament adopted counterterrorism legislation that allows the president to declare an emergency and empower authorities to curb civil liberties following a broadly defined terrorist act. The law also permits officials to limit the movement of terrorism suspects as a preventive measure.

The flow of migrants into Bulgaria appeared to ebb slightly in 2016, with some 19,400 asylum applications reported, compared with about 20,400 in 2015. A new EU border agency began assisting the country in patrolling its frontier with Turkey in October. Human rights groups noted continued reports of mistreatment of migrants and refugees by both security forces and highly publicized vigilante groups that conducted their own border patrols. Some vigilante figures faced criminal charges at year's end. In November, police clashed with migrants who rioted after their reception center was sealed off in response to false media reports about infectious disease at the site.

POLITICAL RIGHTS: 33 / 40
A. Electoral Process: 11 / 12
B. Political Pluralism and Participation: 14 / 16
C. Functioning of Government: 8 / 12

CIVIL LIBERTIES: 47 / 60
D. Freedom of Expression and Belief: 14 / 16
E. Associational and Organizational Rights: 11 / 12
F. Rule of Law: 10 / 16
G. Personal Autonomy and Individual Rights: 12 / 16

This country report has been abridged for *Freedom in the World 2017*. For background information on political rights and civil liberties in Bulgaria, see *Freedom in the World 2016*.

Burkina Faso

Political Rights Rating: 4
Civil Liberties Rating: 3
Freedom Rating: 3.5
Freedom Status: Partly Free
Electoral Democracy: Yes

Population: 19,000,000
Capital: Ouagadougou

Ten-Year Ratings Timeline For Year Under Review (Political Rights, Civil Liberties, Status)

Year Under Review	2007	2008	2009	2010	2011	2012	2013	2014	2015	2016
Rating	5,3,PF	5,3,PF	5,3,PF	5,3,PF	5,3,PF	5,3,PF	5,3,PF	6,3,PF	4,3,PF	4,3,PF

Overview: Political instability in 2014 and 2015 came to an end following multiparty presidential and legislative elections held in late 2015. The elections ushered in a new regime and laid a foundation for the continued development of democratic institutions. Despite extreme poverty, terrorism, and corruption, civil society and the media remain strong forces for democracy and for the respect of civil liberties.

KEY DEVELOPMENTS IN 2016:
- In January, an unprecedented terrorist attack in the capital, Ouagadougou, killed at least 20 people. Terrorist attacks also increased throughout the year in the northern regions of the country, near the borders with Mali and Niger, where security forces were targeted.

- Municipal elections were held in May, and won praise from election monitors. The new ruling party, the People's Movement for Progress (MPP), won a majority of the municipal seats.
- The new MPP government pursued a number of policies outlined in its 2015 electoral campaign. One such proposal aimed to establish a new constitution marking the end of former president Blaise Compaoré's 27-year regime. The government established a Constitutional Commission to draft the new text.

EXECUTIVE SUMMARY

Burkina Faso's new government in 2016 worked to implement many of its promised reforms, and ones that had been adopted by the transitional government in 2015. In September, new president Roch Mark Christian Kaboré, who was inaugurated in late 2015, launched a commission responsible for writing a new constitution that would usher in the Fifth Republic of Burkina Faso, and represent a break from the former regime.

Municipal elections held in May 2016 reflected continuing erosion of support for the Congress for Democracy and Progress (CDP), the former ruling party, and increased support for the MPP. Election observers from local civil society groups and international missions noted only minor irregularities in the polls. Separately, in July, new members were appointed to the Independent National Electoral Commission (CENI) after previous commissioners' terms expired, reflecting the functionality of the country's electoral framework.

Also during the year, some high-profile members of the former regime were arrested for their involvement in the repression of demonstrations that took place during the popular uprising of 2014. The arrests suggest that the culture of impunity that existed under the former regime may be subsiding; however, police abuses and a disregard for the accused's right to due process remain problematic. Meanwhile, space for demonstrations and protests has opened under the new government; a number of demonstrations took place peacefully in 2016, and public venues previously closed in 2015 ahead of presidential and legislative elections remained open during the municipal elections.

The overall security situation in Burkina Faso deteriorated following a January terrorist attack in Ouagadougou, which left at least 20 people dead. Several smaller attacks, some of which targeted security forces, occurred in the north of the country near the borders with Niger and Mali, both of which were struggling with the presence of extremist insurgent groups.

Women's associations and movements play an important role in Burkinabe politics and society, as evidenced by their involvement in recent civil society activities and elections. Separately, a 2016 study demonstrated that a 1996 law that banned female genital mutilation has prevented over 200,000 girls from being cut.

POLITICAL RIGHTS: 23 / 40 (+ 2)

A. Electoral Process: 7 / 12 (+ 1)

B. Political Pluralism and Participation: 10 / 16 (+ 1)

C. Functioning of Government: 6 / 12

CIVIL LIBERTIES: 40 / 60 (+ 2)

D. Freedom of Expression and Belief: 14 / 16

E. Associational and Organizational Rights: 9 / 12 (+ 1)

F. Rule of Law: 8 / 16

G. Personal Autonomy and Individual Rights: 9 / 16 (+ 1)

This country report has been abridged for *Freedom in the World 2017*. For background information on political rights and civil liberties in Burkina Faso, see *Freedom in the World 2016*.

Burundi

Political Rights Rating: 7
Civil Liberties Rating: 6
Freedom Rating: 6.5
Freedom Status: Not Free
Electoral Democracy: No

Population: 11,100,000
Capital: Bujumbura

Ten-Year Ratings Timeline For Year Under Review (Political Rights, Civil Liberties, Status)

Year Under Review	2007	2008	2009	2010	2011	2012	2013	2014	2015	2016
Rating	4,5,PF	4,5,PF	4,5,PF	5,5,PF	5,5,PF	5,5,PF	5,5,PF	6,5,NF	7,6,NF	7,6,NF

Overview: Democratic gains made after the 12-year civil war ended in 2005 are rapidly being undone by a shift toward authoritarian politics and ongoing repression of and violence against the opposition and those perceived to support it.

KEY DEVELOPMENTS IN 2016:
- Repression and persecution of those suspected of opposing President Pierre Nkurunziza continued.
- At the end of the year, over 300,000 people had fled Burundi as refugees due to the ongoing crisis.
- In March, the European Union (EU) suspended direct aid to Burundi over the government's refusal to engage in peace talks.
- In October, the government announced that it would withdraw from the International Criminal Court (ICC), six months after the ICC prosecutor's office had initiated a preliminary examination of the crisis.

EXECUTIVE SUMMARY

Burundi's political crisis began in April 2015, when President Nkurunziza announced his intention to run for a constitutionally dubious third term, which he won in disputed elections held later that year. Nkurunziza's move sparked violence including assassinations, arrests, torture of government critics, and escalating attacks by antigovernment forces in 2015. The violence continued in 2016, though at a lower rate. Many opposition figures and journalists who fled the country in 2015 continued to operate in exile. At the end of 2016, over 300,000 people had fled Burundi as refugees due to the crisis.

The government has shown little interest in mediators' attempts to help negotiate a resolution to the crisis, and in March 2016, the EU suspended direct aid to Burundi over the government's refusal to engage in peace talks. The government's hard-line stance, combined with its stated intention to withdraw from the ICC, reflect a worrying disengagement from the international community.

Meanwhile, Nkurunziza's ruling National Council for the Defense of Democracy–Forces for the Defense of Democracy (CNDD–FDD) maintained near-total control of the executive, judiciary, and legislative branches, as well as the security forces.

POLITICAL RIGHTS: 5 / 40

A. Electoral Process: 1 / 12

A new constitution was adopted in 2005 after a series of agreements ended Burundi's 12-year civil war. According to the charter, the president, who is directly elected for up to two five-year terms, appoints two vice presidents, one Tutsi and one Hutu, who must be approved separately by a two-thirds majority in both the lower and upper houses of parliament.

The lower house, the National Assembly, has 100 members directly elected by proportional representation for five-year terms. The constitution requires the National Assembly to be no more than 60 percent Hutu and no less than 40 percent Tutsi, with at least 30 percent of the seats held by women, and three deputies from the Twa ethnic minority. Additional members can be added, or "co-opted," from the respective party lists to meet these requirements. The upper house, the Senate, consists of 36 members chosen by locally elected officials for five-year terms. Each of Burundi's 18 provinces chooses two senators—one Tutsi and one Hutu. As in the National Assembly, the Twa are guaranteed three seats in the Senate, and additional members can be co-opted to meet the 30 percent quota for women.

In April 2015, the CNDD–FDD announced that President Pierre Nkurunziza would seek a third presidential term in elections scheduled for later that year. Critics charged that the move contravened the constitution and would jeopardize the country's fragile peace. Nkurunziza and his supporters argued that he was eligible to run again because he had been elected by parliament rather than through a popular vote for his first term in office. Despite widespread public protests and international condemnation of the move, the Constitutional Court in May 2015 ruled in favor of Nkurunziza, even as one of the court's justices fled abroad. Days later, a group of military leaders led a coup attempt against Nkurunziza while he was in Tanzania. Government forces quickly reasserted control and began a harsh crackdown on those suspected of involvement in the plot or opposition to the president. Due to ongoing unrest in the country, the electoral commission postponed National Assembly elections until June 2015, and the presidential poll until that July. Indirect Senatorial elections were also held in July.

Despite having boycotted the vote, the opposition coalition remained on the ballot; Amizero y'Abarundi (Hope for Burundi) secured 11 percent of the vote (21 seats), while the Union for National Progress (UPRONA) captured 2 percent (2 seats). Subsequent reallocations and co-opting to meet constitutional quotas resulted in a full seating of 121 deputies. In indirect elections for the Senate, the CNDD–FDD took 33 of 36 elected seats; an additional seven seats were co-opted. In the presidential poll, Nkurunziza defeated National Forces of Liberation (FNL) leader Agathon Rwasa, 69 percent to 19 percent. Rwasa had pulled out of the race, but his name—like those of other opposition candidates—had remained on the ballot.

International observers from some organizations, including the EU and African Union (AU), refused to monitor the elections, saying they could not be free or fair given the growing violence and climate of intimidation. A UN mission observing the presidential poll stated that the overall environment had not been conducive to a free and fair electoral process, saying that while not as violent as the previous month's legislative polls, that violence had "remained an unfortunate feature of the entire process."

In August 2016, Parliament was sent a report that had been drafted by a national commission, assembled by Nkurunziza, supporting the elimination of term limits. In December, Nkurunziza suggested that he could run for a fourth term if this constitutional change were enacted.

B. Political Pluralism and Participation: 4 / 16

More than two dozen political parties are active in Burundi. The current legislature consists of members of the CNDD–FDD, a largely Hutu party associated with a former rebel group; the Tutsi-led UPRONA; and Amizero y'Abarundi, which includes members of the FNL, a former Hutu rebel movement. Many political parties include youth branches that intimidate and attack opponents.

Opposition parties, politicians, and their supporters faced harassment, intimidation, and violence throughout 2016, following the failed coup attempt in May 2015 that triggered a crackdown on those suspected of involvement. Security forces loyal to the president played a key role in the repression, as did the Imbonerakure, the ruling party's youth wing.

Many opposition politicians and groups were operating in exile in 2016, including the National Council for the Restoration of the Arusha Accords and Restoration of the State of Rights (CNARED), which accused Nkurunziza of violating the agreements that ended the civil war. Even some leading regime figures, such as Vice President Gervais Rufyikiri and National Assembly speaker Pie Ntavyohanyuma, fled the country in 2015 after voicing opposition to Nkurunziza's third-term bid. Hafsa Mossi, a former minister and member of the East African Legislative Assembly, was shot and killed in July 2016; the motive for her murder was unclear.

C. Functioning of Government: 0 / 12

The 2015 polls fell far short of international standards for democratic elections, and in the absence of freely elected leaders, the government is accountable only to the ruling CNDD-FDD party. Corruption and nontransparent government practices are significant problems in Burundi. The country does not have a freedom of information law.

CIVIL LIBERTIES: 14 / 60

D. Freedom of Expression and Belief: 6 / 16

Freedom of expression is constitutionally guaranteed, but press laws restrict journalists through broad, vaguely written provisions, and key independent news outlets were destroyed in the political violence of 2015. A 2013 media law has been widely criticized for limiting the protection of journalistic sources, requiring journalists to meet certain educational and professional standards, and banning content related to national defense, security, public safety, and the state currency. The law empowers the media regulatory body to issue press cards to journalists, suspend or withdraw cards as a result of defamation cases, and impose financial penalties for media offenses. The 15-member regulatory council is controlled by presidential appointees and journalists from state broadcasters.

The government dominates the media through its ownership of the public television and radio stations; it also runs *Le Renouveau*, the only daily newspaper. Radio is the primary source of information for the majority of the population. Some international radio broadcasts are available in the capital. Print runs of most newspapers remain small, and readership is limited by low literacy levels and availability.

Throughout 2016, the government continued to pressure outlets carrying unfavorable coverage, with some such outlets being forced to close. Additionally, in October the Burundian Union of Journalists (UBJ) was indefinitely suspended alongside several civil society groups. Journalists are frequently subject to arbitrary arrest, harassment, or threats by police and the Imbonerakure. In July, journalist Jean Bigirimana, who worked as a reporter with the independent weekly newspaper *Iwacu*, disappeared after receiving a phone call from intelligence services. He remained missing at year's end. Also in 2016, police arrested several foreign journalists, as well as their Burundian colleagues, and other foreign journalists were barred from the country. More than 100 journalists had fled into exile since April 2015, according to an October 2016 report by the Committee to Protect Journalists (CPJ).

Access to the internet remains largely confined to urban areas. As antigovernment protests began in 2015, the government attempted to cut off access to social-media sites used by the demonstrators. Many were able to circumvent the restrictions through the use of VPNs (virtual private networks).

Freedom of religion is generally observed.

For many years, civil strife and Tutsi social and institutional dominance impeded academic freedom by limiting educational opportunities for the Hutu, but this situation has improved since 2005.

The ability to engage in open and free private discussion, particularly on opposition to the ruling party, is hindered by a fear of harassment by government supporters. Private citizens, including students and youth activists, continued to face surveillance by the National Intelligence Service (SNR) and the Imbonerakure in 2016.

E. Associational and Organizational Rights: 2 / 12

The constitution provides for freedoms of assembly and association, but a 2013 law on public gatherings imposes restrictions on the right to assemble, including a one-day limit on the duration of demonstrations. The law holds the organizers of public gatherings liable for any legal infractions by participants and allows authorities to interrupt or cancel gatherings that pose a risk to public order.

Onerous and costly registration requirements prevent many local nongovernmental organizations (NGOs) from receiving official legal recognition. Registration must be completed in person at the Ministry of Interior in Bujumbura, which is difficult for NGOs based in remote areas, and extensive documentation is required. Crackdowns against Burundi's civil society sector sharply intensified during 2015 and continued into 2016. Members of human rights groups that criticized the government faced surveillance, intimidation, threats, and arrest, leading many to seek refuge abroad. Authorities continued to issue bans and suspensions against NGOs in 2016, though some groups focusing on apolitical causes continued to function.

The constitution provides protections for organized labor, and the labor code guarantees the right to strike. However, it is unlikely that union members would feel free to exercise the collective bargaining rights guaranteed by the law in the current political climate. In late December 2016, the chairman of the Confederation of Burundi Trade Unions was arrested by intelligence agents on unclear charges along with several other union leaders with whom he was meeting.

F. Rule of Law: 1 / 16

Burundi's judiciary is hindered by corruption, a lack of resources and training, and executive interference in legal matters. In 2015, justices on the Constitutional Court were reportedly intimidated into ruling in favor of Nkurunziza's decision to stand for a third term. The court's vice president, Sylvere Nimpagaritse, fled the country rather than approve the president's candidacy, which he deemed unlawful; he alleged that he and his fellow justices had come under enormous pressure, including death threats, to vote in favor of the proposal. The current judicial system struggles to function effectively or independently and cannot handle the large number of pending cases, many of which are politically sensitive. Crimes, especially those related to political violence, often go unreported or uninvestigated.

In 2014, parliament passed a law creating a truth and reconciliation commission to provide accountability for abuses committed between 1962 and 2008, though opposition members boycotted the vote due to concerns about the commission's lack of independence, claiming that most members were affiliates of the ruling party. The body began its work in March 2016.

Separately, in October 2016, the government announced that it would withdraw from the ICC. The announcement came six months after the ICC prosecutor's office had opened a preliminary examination into the current crisis.

Impunity for police brutality remains widespread. The police and the SNR increasingly engaged in torture and other ill-treatment of detainees suspected of participating in the 2015 protests or subsequent antigovernment violence. Victims described being beaten with iron bars, burned with acid, and having their heads forced under dirty water. Detainees did not have access to lawyers and were forced to make false confessions under threat of death. In April 2016, the UN High Commission for Human Rights warned that there had been a sharp increase in the use of torture during detention, noting that UN personnel had documented 345 new cases of torture in the first three months of the year. Many of those tortured were held by the intelligence services, but the UN found torture and detainee mistreatment at police stations and sometimes at army facilities. The UN also noted reports of secret detention facilities across the country.

The general security situation remained poor in 2016. Over 300,000 refugees had fled Burundi since the current crisis began, according to year-end statistics released by the United Nations refugee agency. According to a May 2016 report from the Armed Conflict Location and Event Dataset, 1,155 people were killed between April 2015 and April 2016 amid attacks against civilians, battles, protests, and other unrest, with perpetrators including security forces, ex-soldiers and opposition groups. Of the dead, according to the report, at least 690 were civilians. Because researchers and international organizations have difficulty collecting such data, the death toll could be higher. In July 2016, Human Rights Watch published a report detailing rapes by Imbonerakure of women and men suspected of being opposition supporters.

Albinos face a particular threat from discrimination and violence in Burundi. Since 2008, at least 18 albinos—whose body parts are believed by some to have magical properties—have been murdered. In February 2016, a child with albinism was murdered and dismembered, the first such killing in four years.

LGBT (lesbian, gay, bisexual, and transgender) people face official and societal discrimination. The 2009 penal code criminalizes same-sex sexual activity, and punishments include up to two years in prison.

G. Personal Autonomy and Individual Rights: 5 / 16

The constitution provides for freedom of movement, though citizens are restricted from traveling outside their communities without a special permit on Saturday mornings as part of a government effort to encourage participation in local service projects. Since 2015, concerns for personal safety further have restricted free movement, particularly in neighborhoods regarded as opposition strongholds where security forces conducted search operations. The deteriorating security situation hampers private business activity in the country.

Women have limited opportunities for advancement in the economic and political spheres, especially in rural areas. Sexual and domestic violence are serious problems but are rarely reported to law enforcement agencies. Rights monitors continue to report sexual violence against women in refugee camps, and by security forces and Imbonerakure.

The U.S. State Department's 2016 *Trafficking in Persons Report* noted that children in Burundi are often subject to forced labor and sex trafficking. In some cases they are sold into servitude by family members, or recruited and deceived by friends and neighbors. Government officials have largely failed to combat domestic child trafficking.

Cambodia

Political Rights Rating: 6
Civil Liberties Rating: 5
Freedom Rating: 5.5
Freedom Status: Not Free
Electoral Democracy: No

Population: 15,800,000
Capital: Phnom Penh

Ten-Year Ratings Timeline For Year Under Review (Political Rights, Civil Liberties, Status)

Year Under Review	2007	2008	2009	2010	2011	2012	2013	2014	2015	2016
Rating	6,5,NF	6,5,NF	6,5,NF	6,5,NF	6,5,NF	6,5,NF	6,5,NF	6,5,NF	6,5,NF	6,5,NF

Overview: Cambodia's political system has been dominated by Prime Minister Hun Sen and his Cambodian People's Party (CPP) for more than three decades. The country has held semicompetitive elections, and the opposition has a significant presence in parliament, but opposition figures are routinely beaten, arrested, and imprisoned. While civil society is relatively strong, activists working on environmental, land, labor, and civil rights issues face severe intimidation. Social media and independent news outlets have begun to challenge the control of progovernment media, though journalists and social media users who criticize the authorities risk prosecution or extralegal violence. A climate of impunity remains a serious obstacle to criminal cases of any type against powerful Cambodians.

KEY DEVELOPMENTS IN 2016:

- In July, prominent political commentator and activist Kem Ley was assassinated in the capital. Human rights groups criticized major flaws in the subsequent police investigation.
- Throughout the spring and summer, the government pursued criminal investigations against opposition leader Kem Sokha and other members of his Cambodia National Rescue Party (CNRP). Kem Sokha received a five-month jail term in September for failing to appear in court as a witness in one of the cases, which centered on his alleged extramarital affair. He remained holed up in the CNRP headquarters to avoid arrest, but received a royal pardon at the prime minister's request in December.
- Opposition leader Sam Rainsy, who remained in exile throughout the year and faced multiple criminal cases, was convicted in November in a defamation case involving criticism of the prime minister and ordered to pay fines and compensation. He was also sentenced to five years in prison in December over a post to his Facebook page regarding a border dispute with Vietnam.

- In July, the nongovernmental organization Global Witness released a report suggesting that Prime Minister Hun Sen and his family had amassed at least $200 million in assets since he took office, noting that the true total could be much larger.

EXECUTIVE SUMMARY

Cambodia's political situation deteriorated in 2016, undermining compromises made between the opposition and the ruling CPP in 2014. The authorities secured criminal convictions against both major leaders of the opposition, but CNRP president Sam Rainsy remained in exile, and his deputy, Kem Sokha, received a royal pardon in December. Meanwhile, the government pursued charges against many other opposition figures and civil society activists, several of whom remained in detention at year's end. CNRP lawmakers protested the government pressure by boycotting parliament sessions from May through November. Hun Sen publicly warned the opposition that he planned a tough approach to dissent ahead of local elections in 2017 and national elections in 2018.

Some critics of the government faced extralegal violence in 2016. Prominent activist Kem Ley was murdered at a gas station in broad daylight in July. His family later fled the country. The authorities quickly arrested the alleged gunman, but suspicions grew over who was really behind the murder, with human rights groups and other observers pointing to serious gaps in the official investigation. The government rejected calls for an independent probe into Kem Ley's death.

Beginning in May, human rights activists held a series of "Black Monday" demonstrations in Phnom Penh and other locations, protesting state abuses and seeking justice for those detained on politically motivated charges. Participants were regularly arrested, and at least one foreigner involved with the protests was deported.

A telecommunications law that took effect in December 2015 granted state authorities unchecked power to monitor personal communications during the year, potentially exposing individuals to criminal prosecution for their comments. No arrests under the new law were reported, though prosecutions for public comments on social media remained common. Separately, a law adopted in April imposed new restrictions on trade unions, but it had yet to take full effect at year's end.

In July, Global Witness released a report indicating that the family of Hun Sen, who receives a government salary of less than $15,000 a year, had created a vast network of private companies linked to government patronage and contracts. The report found that the prime minister's family had amassed holdings of at least $200 million, with higher estimates ranging into the billions. Several members of the family have also been placed in key political and security positions.

POLITICAL RIGHTS: 11 / 40

A. Electoral Process: 4 / 12

B. Political Pluralism and Participation: 4 / 16

C. Functioning of Government: 3 / 12

CIVIL LIBERTIES: 20 / 60 (− 1)

D. Freedom of Expression and Belief: 8 / 16 (− 1)

E. Associational and Organizational Rights: 3 / 12

F. Rule of Law: 3 / 16

G. Personal Autonomy and Individual Rights: 6 / 16

This country report has been abridged for *Freedom in the World 2017*. For background information on political rights and civil liberties in Cambodia, see *Freedom in the World 2016*.

Cameroon

Political Rights Rating: 6
Civil Liberties Rating: 6
Freedom Rating: 6.0
Freedom Status: Not Free
Electoral Democracy: No

Population: 24,400,000
Capital: Yaoundé

Ten-Year Ratings Timeline For Year Under Review (Political Rights, Civil Liberties, Status)

Year Under Review	2007	2008	2009	2010	2011	2012	2013	2014	2015	2016
Rating	6,6 NF	6,6 NF	6,6 NF	6,6 NF	6,6 NF	6,6 NF	6,6 NF	6,6 NF	6,6,NF	6,6,NF

Overview: President Paul Biya has ruled Cameroon since 1982. His Cameroon People's Democratic Movement (CPDM) has maintained power by rigging elections, using state resources for political patronage, and limiting the activities of opposition parties. The Boko Haram insurgent group, based in northeast Nigeria, continues to attack civilians in northern Cameroon. Cameroonian state security forces responding to the insurgency have been accused of committing human rights violations against civilians.

KEY DEVELOPMENTS IN 2016:
- The Boko Haram conflict continues to affect northern Cameroon. Boko Haram insurgents use suicide bombings and other tactics to kill civilians. State security forces in the region have been accused of carrying out arbitrary detentions and torture.
- A new penal code was approved and enacted in July. It banned genital mutilation, but also prohibited political protests on university campuses, and left intact the country's ban on same-sex relationships.
- Protests in late November and early December linked to a teachers' strike in the country's Anglophone regions were violently repressed by security forces.

EXECUTIVE SUMMARY

In 2016, Cameroon's government continued to grapple with a persistent Boko Haram insurgency in the north. Meanwhile, authorities continued to suppress the political opposition, including by banning some opposition meetings and arresting members of opposition political parties. The country lacks an obvious successor to the 83-year-old Biya, whose presidential term is scheduled to end in 2018.

Although Boko Haram has been weakened since 2014 by the combined military efforts of Cameroon, Nigeria, and several other countries in the region, the insurgent group's attacks continued to affect Cameroon's Far North region, particularly the areas around Mora and Fotokol. As of September 2016, Cameroon was hosting some 350,000 refugees who had fled the Boko Haram insurgency or Central African Republic conflict, with an additional 100,000 people displaced internally. State security services and local defense militias have carried out abuses against civilians as they fight against Boko Haram. In July 2016, Amnesty International reported that hundreds of people suspected of aiding Boko Haram had been arrested arbitrarily by security forces, that detainees had been tortured while in custody and denied access to legal representation, and that some suspects had been sentenced to death in military courts after being convicted in flawed trials.

Despite the limitations on citizens' ability to protest or organize opposition movements, strikes are regularly organized by workers' unions. Strikes in 2016 included those by some public workers, and by truck and taxi drivers. In November and December, a strike by teachers in the country's Anglophone Northwest and Southwest regions gave way to protests that were violently repressed by state security forces. Four protesters were reportedly killed.

Journalists face pressure and the possibility of being detained or arrested while working. Ahmed Abba—a Nigerian reporter who was arrested in the Far North region in 2015 in connection with his reporting on Boko Haram—remained in jail at the end of 2016. In June, a radio reporter in Douala was reporting on problems at a public hospital when she was forced by officials to strip off her clothes in a public place, supposedly as part of a search.

Biya approved a new penal code in July 2016. The new code bans political protests at public buildings, schools, and universities, and forbids same-sex sexual relations and includes prison sentences of up to five years for those convicted. It also banned genital mutilation.

POLITICAL RIGHTS: 9 / 40

A. Electoral Process: 3 / 12

B. Political Pluralism and Participation: 3 / 16

C. Functioning of Government: 3 / 12

CIVIL LIBERTIES: 15 / 60

D. Freedom of Expression and Belief: 7 / 16

E. Associational and Organizational Rights: 3 / 12

F. Rule of Law: 1 / 16

G. Personal Autonomy and Individual Rights: 4 / 16

This country report has been abridged for *Freedom in the World 2017*. For background information on political rights and civil liberties in Cameroon, see *Freedom in the World 2016*.

Canada

Political Rights Rating: 1
Civil Liberties Rating: 1
Freedom Rating: 1.0
Freedom Status: Free
Electoral Democracy: Yes

Population: 36,200,000
Capital: Ottawa

Ten-Year Ratings Timeline For Year Under Review (Political Rights, Civil Liberties, Status)

Year Under Review	2007	2008	2009	2010	2011	2012	2013	2014	2015	2016
Rating	1,1,F	1,1,F	1,1F	1,1,F	1,1,F	1,1,F	1,1,F	1,1,F	1,1,F	1,1,F

Overview: Canada has a strong history of respect for political rights and civil liberties, and has espoused a broad conception of social welfare. While indigenous peoples still face discrimination and other social and political problems, the government has acknowledged and made some moves to address these issues.

KEY DEVELOPMENTS IN 2016:

- Prime Minister Justin Trudeau's government established a commission tasked with consulting with voters and issuing recommendations on reforming the country's majoritarian electoral system. While Trudeau's Liberal Party had campaigned on ushering in such reforms, the party appeared to step back from that pledge when the commission's recommendations were issued.
- In March, a court upheld a police order that a *Vice News* reporter disclose information about their source for a story about a man suspected of harboring links to the Islamic State (IS) militant group.
- A new government body tasked with investigating cases of missing and murdered indigenous women and girls faced criticism for slow progress and a lack of transparency.

EXECUTIVE SUMMARY

The Liberal Party, led by Prime Minister Trudeau, has generally governed transparently and in consultation with the public since rising to power after winning 2015 federal elections. As part of his electoral campaign, Trudeau had promised to reform the oft-criticized first-past-the-post, or majoritarian, electoral system, before the next federal elections. In May 2016, Trudeau formed an all-party committee to consult with voters on alternatives to the current system—in which the candidate with the most votes wins, regardless of whether they capture an absolute majority of 50 percent of votes cast. In December, the committee issued a recommendation that the Liberal Party design a proportional voting system, to be put to a national referendum. However, Liberal Party representatives on the committee—who were outnumbered by opposition representatives—backed away from Trudeau's reform pledges in a dissenting statement calling the majority's recommendation "too radical" to implement and stating that reforms should not be "rushed" ahead of the 2019 polls.

In 2014, the Fair Elections Act—a broad and controversial set of provisions meant to address voter fraud and update campaign finance laws—came into force. Critics have expressed concerns that the legislation, ushered in by the previous Conservative government, could place indigenous peoples at a disadvantage due to its stringent requirements about voter identification and addresses. The government in November 2016 introduced legislation that would relax those and other regulations if approved. Separately, Trudeau's administration made little progress on pledges to roll back provisions of a controversial antiterrorism law granting the Canadian Security Intelligence Service (CSIS) broad authority to conduct surveillance and share information about individuals with other agencies.

Canada's media are generally free; journalists are mostly protected from violence and harassment in their work and are able to express diverse views. However, defamation remains a criminal offense punishable by up to five years in prison, and no statutory laws protect confidential sources. In March 2016, the Ontario Superior Court upheld a Royal Canadian Mounted Police (RCMP) order that *Vice News* hand over correspondence between its reporter and a former Canadian resident facing terrorism charges over alleged links to IS.

Indigenous women and girls face racial and economic discrimination, high rates of gender-based violence, and mistreatment by police. In August 2016, the government announced plans to establish a National Inquiry into Missing and Murdered Indigenous

Women and Girls, though the program has since faced criticism for slow progress and a lack of transparency. Separately, in October, the head of RCMP formally apologized to hundreds of women who had been sexually harassed or discriminated against while working for the force. The apology was part of a $100 million settlement of two class-actions lawsuits involving complaints dating back to the 1970s, when women were first permitted to become police officers.

POLITICAL RIGHTS: 40 / 40

A. Electoral Process: 12 / 12

B. Political Pluralism and Participation: 16 / 16

C. Functioning of Government: 12 / 12

CIVIL LIBERTIES: 59 / 60

D. Freedom of Expression and Belief: 16 / 16

E. Associational and Organizational Rights: 12 / 12

F. Rule of Law: 15 / 16

G. Personal Autonomy and Individual Rights: 16 / 16

This country report has been abridged for *Freedom in the World 2017*. For background information on political rights and civil liberties in Canada, see *Freedom in the World 2016*.

Cape Verde

Political Rights Rating: 1
Civil Liberties Rating: 1
Freedom Rating: 1.0
Freedom Status: Free
Electoral Democracy: Yes

Population: 500,000
Capital: Praia

Ten-Year Ratings Timeline For Year Under Review (Political Rights, Civil Liberties, Status)

Year Under Review	2007	2008	2009	2010	2011	2012	2013	2014	2015	2016
Rating	1,1,F	1,1,F	1,1,F	1,1,F	1,1,F	1,1,F	1,1,F	1,1,F	1,1,F	1,1,F

The country or territory displayed here received scores but no narrative report for this edition of *Freedom in the World*.

Central African Republic

Political Rights Rating: 7
Civil Liberties Rating: 7
Freedom Rating: 7.0
Freedom Status: Not Free
Electoral Democracy: No

Population: 5,000,000
Capital: Bangui

Ten-Year Ratings Timeline For Year Under Review (Political Rights, Civil Liberties, Status)

Year Under Review	2007	2008	2009	2010	2011	2012	2013	2014	2015	2016
Rating	5,5,PF	5,5,PF	5,5,PF	5,5,PF	5,5,PF	5,5,PF	7,7,NF	7,7,NF	7,7,NF	7,7,NF

Overview: The Central African Republic suffers from pervasive insecurity, intercommunal violence, and an absence of government authority across much of its territory. A new government—elected in early 2016 after more than two years of a transitional administration—does not have authority beyond the capital. As a result of ongoing attacks on civilians by a range of armed groups, the country faces a humanitarian crisis.

KEY DEVELOPMENTS IN 2016:

- Central African Republic (CAR) held peaceful presidential and parliamentary elections in February and March, resulting in the election of Faustin-Archange Touadéra as the country's new president and the seating of a new National Assembly.
- In October, a high-ranking military officer was assassinated in Bangui, the capital, setting off a new round of intercommunal clashes in the city.
- Throughout the year, self-defense militias and irregular armed groups continued to operate with impunity across much of the country, carrying out violent attacks against civilians and inhibiting the ability of humanitarian organizations to access populations in need.

EXECUTIVE SUMMARY

CAR held presidential and parliamentary elections in early 2016, leading to a peaceful transfer of power from the National Transitional Council to an elected government. Former prime minister Touadéra, an independent candidate, was elected president in February with 63 percent of the vote in a run-off, defeating Anicet-Georges Dologuélé of the Central African Union for Renewal (URCA), who received 37 percent. A rerun of December 2015 legislative elections was held concurrent to the presidential run-off, after the initial vote was annulled by the Transitional Constitutional Court due to widespread irregularities. Independent candidates took 55 of the 140 seats, and the National Union for Democracy and Progress (UNDP) became the party with the most seats, with 13. Results from the new elections were validated by the Transitional Constitutional Court, and the new National Assembly was seated in May. The elections were regarded as generally successful and peaceful. International observers expressed hope that the country's first national elections since the outbreak of armed conflict in late 2012 would be an important step toward stabilization in CAR.

However, armed groups—including those formerly part of the largely Muslim Séléka coalition and Christian militias known as the anti-Balaka—continued to operate with impunity across large sections of the country's territory. These groups—which do not answer to any single political authority—are responsible for recurrent human rights violations, sexual violence, and targeted attacks against civilians on the basis of ethnic and religious identity. In October, the assassination of a high-ranking military officer in Bangui threatened to further strain the country's fragile political situation, and a new round of interfactional violence in northwestern CAR was ignited in late November. This general environment of insecurity curtailed free expression of political views, as well as the movement of people and organizations across the country's territory.

The UN Multidimensional Integrated Mission in Central African Republic (MINUSCA)—the UN peacekeeping force in the country—had been unable to stem the violence, and has itself faced allegations of sexually abusing and exploiting members of the population.

An estimated 2.2 million people—more than a third of the country's population—remain in need of humanitarian assistance, but access is limited. Operations by nongovernmental organizations (NGOs) across different regions of the country are restricted by poor security conditions along main transportation routes. According to the United Nations, at least 336 attacks against humanitarian workers occurred throughout the year.

POLITICAL RIGHTS: 4 / 40 (+ 3)

A. Electoral Process: 3 / 12 (+ 2)

B. Political Pluralism and Participation: 2 / 16 (+ 1)

C. Functioning of Government: 0 / 12

Discretionary Political Rights Question B: − 1 / 0

CIVIL LIBERTIES: 6 / 60

D. Freedom of Expression and Belief: 4 / 16

E. Associational and Organizational Rights: 1 / 12

F. Rule of Law: 0 / 16

G. Personal Autonomy and Individual Rights: 1 / 16

This country report has been abridged for *Freedom in the World 2017*. For background information on political rights and civil liberties in Central African Republic, see *Freedom in the World 2016.*

Chad

Political Rights Rating: 7
Civil Liberties Rating: 6
Freedom Rating: 6.5
Freedom Status: Not Free
Electoral Democracy: No

Population: 14,500,000
Capital: N'Djamena

Ten-Year Ratings Timeline For Year Under Review (Political Rights, Civil Liberties, Status)

Year Under Review	2007	2008	2009	2010	2011	2012	2013	2014	2015	2016
Rating	7,6,NF	7,6,NF	7,6,NF	7,6,NF	7,6,NF	7,6,NF	7,6,NF	7,6,NF	7,6,NF	7,6,NF

Overview: Chad has held regular presidential elections since 1996, but no election has ever produced a change in power. Legislative elections are routinely delayed, and opposition leaders risk arrest and severe mistreatment while in detention. The state typically represses antigovernment protests.

KEY DEVELOPMENTS IN 2016:

- In February, a video of an opposition leader's teenage daughter being gang-raped by attackers that included the sons of Chadian officials sparked a public outcry among ordinary citizens frustrated with impunity and violence against women.
- Incumbent president Idriss Déby Itno won April's presidential election with just under 60 percent of the vote, and was sworn in to his fifth term. There were reports that several members of the military disappeared after the election, allegedly for voting against Déby.
- Opposition figures rejected the election's results and convened antigovernment demonstrations, which were repressed and saw their organizers arrested.
- In the fall, the government sought to address its increasingly poor fiscal situation by reducing public-sector salaries and eliminating scholarships for students, resulting in strikes and demonstrations throughout the country. In response, authorities repressed or banned some such actions and Déby threatened to dissolve public sector unions.

EXECUTIVE SUMMARY

Incumbent president Déby won April's presidential election with just under 60 percent of the vote, defeating opposition leader Saleh Kebzabo, who took 13 percent. The opposition rejected the result, citing a variety of electoral irregularities and other incidents, including reports that members of the military who voted against Déby had subsequently disappeared. The Constitutional Court upheld the election's result in May, though the opposition continued to reject it. Antigovernment protests were repressed and demonstration leaders arrested on several occasions during the year. Separately, parliamentary elections set for 2015 had not been held by year's end.

Two months of social protest and turmoil preceded Déby's reelection. The protests, aimed at drawing attention to impunity for members of the ruling party and violence against women, were triggered by the emergence of a video on social media of an opposition leader's teenage daughter being gang-raped by assailants that included the sons of high-level Chadian officials; while officials during the year dispersed opposition-led protests, the demonstrations that came in response to the video were largely permitted. Seven accused rapists were later arrested, tried, and convicted by the courts, though two of the convicts escaped from prison.

Due to a fiscal crisis brought on by plummeting oil prices and, presumably, state corruption, the state in 2016 adopted severe austerity measures to address budgetary constraints; these included significant cuts to public-sector salaries and benefits, and the elimination of state-funded stipends for students. The actions increased the already tense sociopolitical situation and resulted in student and public-sector strikes and demonstrations, and opposition criticism over a lack of transparency in the government's budget. At times these activities were met with repression and violence by the regime, and on instances the government forbid union and other organizations from holding public protests.

The strikes placed additional burdens on the country's already struggling economy, and in December, Déby threatened to dissolve public sector unions completely. The budgetary crisis, accompanying austerity measures, and subsequent student strikes also severely disrupted the operations of schools and universities in Chad.

POLITICAL RIGHTS: 4 / 40
A. Electoral Process: 2 / 12
B. Political Pluralism and Participation: 1 / 16
C. Functioning of Government: 1 / 12

CIVIL LIBERTIES: 14 / 60 (− 2)
D. Freedom of Expression and Belief: 6 / 16 (− 1)
E. Associational and Organizational Rights: 4 / 12 (− 1)
F. Rule of Law: 1 / 16
G. Personal Autonomy and Individual Rights: 3 / 16

This country report has been abridged for *Freedom in the World 2017*. For background information on political rights and civil liberties in Chad, see *Freedom in the World 2016*.

Chile

Political Rights Rating: 1
Civil Liberties Rating: 1
Freedom Rating: 1.0
Freedom Status: Free
Electoral Democracy: Yes

Population: 18,200,000
Capital: Santiago

Ten-Year Ratings Timeline For Year Under Review (Political Rights, Civil Liberties, Status)

Year Under Review	2007	2008	2009	20010	2011	2012	2013	2014	2015	2016
Rating	1,1,F	1,1,F	1,1,F	1,1,F	1,1,F	1,1,F	1,1,F	1,1,F	1,1,F	1,1,F

Overview: Chile is a stable presidential democracy that has experienced an expansion of political rights and civil liberties since the return of civilian rule in 1990. Ongoing concerns include corruption, physical abuse by police, and unrest linked to land disputes with the indigenous Mapuche population.

KEY DEVELOPMENTS IN 2016:
- Voter turnout in the October municipal elections reached a historic low of 34.9 percent. The process was also marred by an error in which the electoral authority wrongly changed the addresses of 485,000 people, or 3.4 percent of registered voters. The center-right opposition coalition Chile Vamos won 145 mayoralties and 916 council seats, while the ruling center-left New Majority won 141 mayoralties and 1,208 council seats.
- Also that month, Chile's national children's service released a report revealing that 865 minors had died under its care between 2005 and 2016. The government pledged additional funding and reforms at the service.

- In May, President Michelle Bachelet filed a defamation suit against the magazine *Qué Pasa* over its coverage of a case involving suspected influence peddling by her daughter-in-law. Bachelet withdrew the lawsuit in September after a professional ethics organization sanctioned the publication.

EXECUTIVE SUMMARY

In 2016 the government faced low public approval ratings amid a series of setbacks, including high-profile corruption scandals. Cases that emerged during the year involved unjustified pay and pension increases within Chile's gendarmerie and a January audit report showing that six lawmakers had received interest-free loans from the National Congress, among other revelations. In February, charges were filed against military officers accused of misappropriating funds in a scandal that broke in 2015. In June, Senator Jaime Orpis of the conservative Independent Democratic Union (UDI) party was placed in detention on suspicion of bribery and tax fraud, and a former senator and cabinet minister from the same party, Pablo Longueira, was placed under nighttime house arrest as part of a similar investigation.

Broader concerns about lack of transparency stem from the legislature's limited ability under the constitution to supervise or alter the executive budget, and from a provision that reserves 10 percent of copper export revenues for the military, with little independent oversight.

Mapuche activists seeking control over ancestral lands continued to engage in street protests and arson attacks throughout the year. In July, Bachelet announced a new 21-member dialogue panel to address the long-standing dispute. Separately in August, hundreds of thousands of people protested in the capital and other cities to call for an overhaul of the country's system of private pension funds. Despite these and other protests, there were few complaints of police brutality compared with previous years.

POLITICAL RIGHTS: 37 / 40 (-1)

A. Electoral Process: 12 / 12

B. Political Pluralism and Participation: 15 / 16

C. Functioning of Government: 10 / 12 (-1)

CIVIL LIBERTIES: 57 / 60

D. Freedom of Expression and Belief: 16 / 16

E. Associational and Organizational Rights: 12 / 12

F. Rule of Law: 14 / 16

G. Personal Autonomy and Individual Rights: 15 / 16

This country report has been abridged for *Freedom in the World 2017*. For background information on political rights and civil liberties in Chile, see *Freedom in the World 2016*.

⬇ China

Political Rights Rating: 7
Civil Liberties Rating: 6
Freedom Rating: 6.5
Freedom Status: Not Free
Electoral Democracy: No

Population: 1,378,000,000
Capital: Beijing

Trend Arrow: China received a downward trend arrow due to the chilling effect on private and public discussion, particularly online, generated by cybersecurity and foreign NGO laws, increased internet surveillance, and heavy sentences handed down to human rights lawyers, microbloggers, grassroots activists, and religious believers.

Note: The numerical ratings and status listed above do not reflect conditions in Hong Kong or Tibet, which are examined in separate reports.

Ten-Year Ratings Timeline For Year Under Review (Political Rights, Civil Liberties, Status)

Year Under Review	2007	2008	2009	2010	2011	2012	2013	2014	2015	2016
Rating	7,6,NF	7,6,NF	7,6,NF	7,6,NF	7,6,NF	7,6,NF	7,6,NF	7,6,NF	7,6,NF	7,6,NF

Overview: The ruling Chinese Communist Party (CCP) has tightened its control over the media, religious groups, and civil society associations in recent years. A renewed push for party supremacy and ideological conformity has undermined rule of law reforms and curtailed civil and political rights. The state president and CCP leader, Xi Jinping, is consolidating personal power to a degree not seen in China for decades. Faced with a slowing economy, the leadership continues to cultivate nationalism, including hostile anti-Western rhetoric, as a pillar of legitimacy. China's budding civil society and human rights movements have struggled in the midst of a multiyear crackdown.

KEY DEVELOPMENTS in 2016:
- In February, Xi Jinping held a series of meetings in which he demanded renewed loyalty to the CCP and ideological conformity from both official and commercial media outlets, and challenged them to take more innovative approaches to shaping public opinion.
- A new law on foreign nongovernmental organizations (NGOs), adopted in April, was expected to significantly constrict the activities of groups working on politically sensitive issues by imposing stringent registration requirements and granting supervisory authority to public security agencies, though it also helped clarify the nebulous regulatory system for NGOs.
- A party work conference on religion held in April, the first since 2001, laid out the leadership's plans to tighten control over religious organizations and activities.
- The authorities' crackdown on civil society continued throughout the year, with arrests and criminal prosecutions of bloggers, activists, and human rights lawyers.

EXECUTIVE SUMMARY

Xi Jinping, who took office as general secretary of the CCP in November 2012, continued to concentrate personal power in 2016 to an extent not seen in China for decades. The slowing economy made the leadership's promotion of nationalism, with an increasingly hostile anti-Western tone, a key CCP strategy for continued legitimacy. The authorities also stepped up efforts to suppress growing independent labor activism linked to the country's economic situation.

Official rhetoric and propaganda presented party supremacy as essential to the "rejuvenation of the Chinese nation" and to China's national security. The latter was increasingly cited to justify criminal prosecutions of civil society and democracy activists, human rights lawyers, and bloggers. Xi took his vision of ideological conformity to new heights during the year, demanding that cadres demonstrate absolute loyalty to the party line and doubling down on media censorship. Online speech deemed politically sensitive by the authorities was punished with imprisonment.

Prominent human rights lawyers and democracy proponents arrested in a sweeping crackdown that began in July 2015 received especially harsh prison terms in 2016, signaling the leadership's intolerance for their activism. Limited reforms to prevent miscarriages of justice continued to be implemented, but they were critically undermined by the CCP's intensified efforts to retain political control over the judiciary.

A plan for "comprehensive management" of all religious activity and organizations and the "Sinicization" of religion in China, laid out at an April party conference, further restricted the scope for religious freedoms. The government continued to impose conditions approaching martial law in Tibetan- and Uighur-populated regions of the country, refusing to reassess failed policies of repression for these ethnic minority groups.

POLITICAL RIGHTS: 1 / 40

A. Electoral Process: 0 / 12

The CCP has a monopoly on political power, and its Politburo Standing Committee (PSC) sets government and party policy. At the 18th Party Congress in 2012, a new PSC—headed by Xi Jinping—was announced, the outcome of opaque intraparty politics. Xi, the CCP general secretary, also holds the position of state president, and serves as chairman of the state and party military commissions. He heads an unusually large number of "leading groups" that give him direct supervision over domestic security, economic reform, internet management, ethnic relations, and other policy areas. Xi was expected to consolidate his power further at a party congress planned for 2017, when five of the PSC's seven incumbent members were due to retire.

The 3,000 members of the National People's Congress (NPC) are formally elected for five-year terms by subnational congresses, but in practice candidates are vetted by the CCP. The NPC formally elects the state president for up to two five-year terms, and confirms the premier after they are nominated by the president. However, only the NPC standing committee meets regularly, with the full congress convening for just two weeks a year to approve proposed legislation; party organs and the executive State Council effectively control lawmaking. The current NPC was seated in March 2013 and named Xi as state president that month.

Although independent candidates who obtain the signatures of 10 supporters are by law allowed to run for seats on the lowest, county-level people's congresses, in practice they are prevented from getting their names on the ballot through intimidation, harassment, and in some cases detention, and only a very small number of independent candidates have actually gained office in elections. Nevertheless, dozens of individuals sought office as independent candidates in 2016. Elections for village committees are also supposed to give residents the chance to choose their representatives, but in practice they are frequently undermined by fraud, corruption, and attacks on independent candidates and their supporters. Lin Zuluan—who was popularly elected in 2012 as head of the Guangdong Province village of Wukan after leading widely publicized protests against land grabs by local officials—was sentenced in September 2016 to three years in prison on corruption charges that were seen as retaliation for his continued activism.

B. Political Pluralism and Participation: 1 / 16

The CCP seeks to monopolize all forms of political organization and harshly punishes democracy activists. Democracy advocate and 2010 Nobel Peace Prize winner Liu Xiaobo remained behind bars in 2016, having been sentenced in 2009 to 11 years in prison for his role in organizing the prodemocracy manifesto Charter 08. His wife, Liu Xia, has been under strict extralegal house arrest since 2010.

The scope for political participation narrowed further in 2016 as NGOs came under intensified pressure, particularly policy advocacy groups, including those working in areas that were previously not considered sensitive, such as the environment and women's rights. The continued imprisonment of Xu Zhiyong and others associated with his New Citizens Movement—a loosely affiliated network of individuals seeking to promote the rule of law, transparency, and human rights that was targeted in a 2013 crackdown—signaled the leadership's persistent intolerance of autonomous civic initiatives.

Restrictions on political activity remain especially harsh for ethnic minorities, including Tibetans, Uighurs, and Mongolians. Even the organization of seemingly benign social activities among such groups is perceived as threatening by the authorities. Hada, a prominent Mongolian activist, remains under de facto house arrest after 15 years in prison and four years of extralegal detention; he had been imprisoned on "separatism" and "espionage" charges in apparent retaliation for his advocacy for the rights of ethnic Mongolians. Ilham Tohti, a peaceful advocate for Uighur human rights now serving a life sentence following a 2014 separatism conviction, has been denied family visits; his wife reports that he has been held in solitary confinement, and supporters have expressed concern about his health.

C. Functioning of Government: 2 / 12

The continuing concentration of power in Xi Jinping's hands, an emerging Mao-like cult of personality, and Xi's calls for greater ideological conformity and party supremacy have elicited criticism, even from within the establishment.

Since becoming CCP leader in 2012, Xi has pursued one of the most extensive and relentless anticorruption campaigns since the beginning of the reform era. Scores of senior state and party officials had been investigated and punished by the end of 2016, including from the security apparatus, the military, the Foreign Ministry, state-owned enterprises, and state media. Former high-ranking general Guo Boxiong was sentenced to life in prison in July, and General Wang Jianping, deputy chief of the Central Military Commission's Joint Staff Department, was put under investigation in December. However, the anticorruption effort remains selective and opaque, and authorities have failed to adopt basic reforms that would address corruption more comprehensively, such as requiring officials to publicly disclose their assets, creating genuinely independent oversight bodies, and allowing independent media and civic activists to function as watchdogs.

Since open-government regulations took effect in 2008, more official documents and information have been made available to the public. However, resistance on the part of government organs to providing specific information requested by citizens has dampened initial optimism. Local experiments aimed at increasing the transparency of budget-making processes have remained limited in scope, and officials have yet to disclose budgets at all levels of government. Citizens who were part of the movement to make officials disclose their assets have been arrested and monitored.

DISCRETIONARY POLITICAL RIGHTS QUESTION B: − 2 / 0

The government continued to pursue policies, including large-scale resettlement and work-transfer programs, that have altered the demography of ethnic minority regions, especially the Xinjiang Uighur Autonomous Region, Tibet, and Inner Mongolia, contributing to a steady increase of Han Chinese as a proportion of the regional populations. Cash incentives encourage Uighur families to have fewer children than the permitted three-child limit for ethnic minorities, and in some locales authorities have intensified crackdowns on "unauthorized births." Marriages between Uighurs and Han Chinese are also supported with cash rewards. Ostensibly bilingual education programs promote the use of Mandarin Chinese as the language of instruction and discourage the use of the Uighur language, with the result that increasing numbers of Uighur children are unable to speak Uighur fluently. [Note: Tibet is examined in a separate report.]

CIVIL LIBERTIES: 14 / 60 (− 1)

D. Freedom of Expression and Belief: 3 / 16 (− 1)

Citizens continued to be punished, often harshly, for publicizing critical views of the authorities online or to foreign media in 2016. Writer and activist Zhang Haitao was sentenced in January to 19 years in prison on charges of "incitement to subvert state power" for criticizing the government's record in Xinjiang in online articles and interviews with overseas media. Citizen journalists are routinely detained, harassed, and in some cases criminally charged. Wang Jing, a citizen reporter for the human rights website 64 Tianwang, was sentenced in April in Jilin Province to four years and 10 months in prison. The founder of 64 Tianwang, Huang Qi, was formally arrested in December on the charge of "illegally supplying state secrets overseas." Also that month, a citizen journalist and founder of Civil Rights and Livelihood Watch, Liu Feiyue, was formally arrested for "incitement to subvert state power." Lu Yuyu and Li Tingyu, who had documented tens of thousands of protests throughout China, were criminally detained in June and remained behind bars at year's end. The Committee to Protect Journalists identified 38 journalists in prison in China, the second-largest figure worldwide after Turkey's, as of December 2016.

Harassment of foreign journalists continued during the year, including physical abuse, detention to prevent meetings with certain individuals, intimidation of Chinese sources and staff, withholding or threatening to withhold visas, surveillance, and hostile editorials in state media. Whole regions of the country, including Tibet and Xinjiang, remain virtually off-limits to foreign journalists except through officially controlled visits.

Internet service providers are required to block websites and delete content as instructed by censors. Thousands of websites have been blocked, many for years, including major news and social media hubs like the *New York Times*, *Le Monde*, Flickr, YouTube, Twitter, Instagram, and Facebook.

Xi Jinping increased pressure on official and commercial media to ramp up censorship efforts and strictly adhere to party directives in 2016. During February visits to the headquarters of the *People's Daily*, Xinhua news agency, and China Central Television (CCTV)—the main party mouthpieces—he called on the media to demonstrate absolute loyalty to the CCP, and on other occasions he stressed that the media must serve as a tool of the party. Xi also exhorted state media workers to produce more dynamic, technologically sophisticated media products that would shape public opinion.

In June, a prohibition against the independent gathering or dissemination of original news was extended to all social media applications, while in July the Beijing branch of the Cyberspace Administration of China (CAC) reinforced rules to prevent Chinese internet portals from producing any original news content, restricting them to repackaging content provided by a small number of authorized sources. In August the CAC imposed tough new censorship requirements on internet providers, including continuous monitoring of news content and a provision holding editors in chief personally responsible for content.

Additional regulations that took effect in August required all mobile applications to use real-name user registration and to store 60 days of activity, preventing anonymous online postings, and the NPC in November adopted a cybersecurity law that will require companies to store user data in China and submit to potentially intrusive security reviews.

A new rule called the "Regulation on Collecting and Using Electronic Data as Evidence," which went into effect in October, allows authorities to collect and use private digital messaging information, text messages, e-mail, personal photos, videos, text documents, and online blog and forum posts to prosecute an individual for criminal wrongdoing, including speech-related offenses. Authorities had already begun engaging in such practices prior to the new regulation, and closed group chats on the popular messaging app WeChat have regularly been shut down by censors for discussion of topics deemed sensitive by authorities.

The space for autonomous religious practice narrowed further during the year as the government restricted and harassed a wide range of religious communities and laid out plans for tighter management of religion during the first National Conference on Religious Work in 15 years. At the April meeting, authorities asserted that religion must serve as an instrument for national unity and social stability, and called on religious groups to "Sinicize" by "endorsing the political system, conforming to Chinese society, and embodying Chinese culture."

The regime's 17-year campaign against the Falun Gong spiritual group continued in 2016, marking one of the longest and harshest campaigns of religious persecution since the CCP took power. While Falun Gong practitioners are no longer sent in large numbers to "reeducation through labor" camps, which were abolished in 2013, many are still criminally prosecuted, in some cases receiving long prison terms, or arbitrarily detained in "legal education centers," where they can face torture to force them to abandon their beliefs. Once released, they typically experience constant monitoring and harassment.

Curbs on the practice of Islam among the Uighur population of Xinjiang remained intense, affecting the wearing of religious attire, attendance at mosques, fasting during Ramadan, and other basic religious activities. Separately, an ongoing campaign against Protestant churches in Zhejiang Province, considered the heartland of Christianity in China, has resulted in the demolition of over 1,200 crosses and numerous churches in recent years, and congregations across the region remain under pressure. In August 2016, Hu Shigen, who led a number of underground churches, was sentenced to seven and a half years in prison in Tianjin for supposedly spreading subversive ideas.

Academic freedom is restricted with respect to politically sensitive issues. The CCP controls the appointment of top university officials, and many scholars practice self-censorship to protect their careers. Political indoctrination is a required component of the curriculum at all levels of education. The space for academic discussion of democratic concepts has shrunk further since 2015 amid top-down pressure on universities to shun "Western" ideals.

E. Associational and Organizational Rights: 3 / 12

China's constitution protects the right of citizens to demonstrate, but in practice protesters rarely obtain approval and risk punishment for assembling without permission. Spontaneous demonstrations have thus become a common form of protest, with a state-affiliated research center counting around 100,000 "mass incidents" annually in recent years, some of which are met with police violence. In September 2016, police used force to end protests in the village of Wukan against the prison sentence of elected leader Lin Zuluan. Separately, according to the NGO Chinese Human Rights Defenders, 118 people around China were detained, jailed, or charged between September 2014 and September 2016 for "picking quarrels and provoking trouble" or "inciting subversion of state power" by expressing support for prodemocracy protesters in Hong Kong.

Hundreds of thousands of NGOs are formally registered, often as companies due to gaps in the relevant laws, though many operate more as government-sponsored organizations. A large number of NGOs operate without formal registration. A government crackdown on civil society that began several years ago has focused on NGOs working on policy advocacy, which are considered more politically sensitive than those dedicated to various types of service delivery. In January 2016, the Beijing Zhongze Women's Legal Counseling and Service Center, founded by Guo Jianmei in 1995, was shut down after experiencing increased harassment in recent years. Also during the year, the authorities drafted revisions of a number of laws that would further strengthen party oversight of domestic social organizations.

A new law on management of foreign NGOs was adopted in April, to take effect in 2017. It was expected to bring about the closure of some foreign NGOs and significantly impede the activities of others that work on sensitive topics. The law prohibits foreign NGO activities that the government deems to "endanger China's national unity, security, or ethnic unity" or "harm China's national interests and the public interest." Foreign NGOs operating in China would be required to register with the Ministry of Public Security (MPS) and to find a "professional supervisory unit"—a government or state organ willing to act as sponsor. The new law also vests authority for foreign NGO management in the MPS, rather than the Ministry of Civil Affairs, which has historically been tasked with managing civil society organizations in China. The changes give the police the authority to enter an NGO's premises at any time to conduct searches without a court warrant, to seize property, to detain personnel, and to initiate criminal procedures.

While workers in China are afforded many protections under existing laws, violations of labor and employment regulations are widespread. Local CCP cadres have long been incentivized to prioritize economic growth over the enforcement of labor rights. The authorities have increasingly cracked down on labor activists and NGOs. Three prominent activists who were detained in December 2015 received suspended prison sentences ranging from 18 months to three years in September 2016; one of them, Zeng Feiyang, is the director of the well-known labor NGO Panyu Migrant Workers Center, which operates in Guangdong Province. The only legal labor union is the government-controlled All-China Federation of Trade Unions, which has long been criticized for failing to properly defend workers' rights. A rise in strike incidents has coincided with slowing economic growth in recent years, and nearly 2,700 were documented in 2016 by the China Labour Bulletin.

F. Rule of Law: 2 / 16

The crackdown on human rights lawyers that was launched in July 2015 continued in 2016, further calling into question the government's professed commitment to move toward the rule of law. Judicial reforms introduced over the past decade or more have sought to exclude evidence obtained through torture, guarantee better access to lawyers, allow witnesses to be cross-examined, and establish other safeguards to prevent wrongful convictions and miscarriages of justice.

However, the CCP still dominates the judicial system, with courts at all levels supervised by party political-legal committees that have influence in the appointment of judges, court operations, and verdicts and sentences. While citizens can expect a degree of fair adjudication in nonpolitical cases, those that touch on politically sensitive issues or the interests of powerful groups are subject to decisive "guidance" from political-legal committees.

Close to 300 lawyers and activists have been detained or interrogated since mid-2015 as part of the government's campaign to quash the "rights defense" movement. Some were held in secret detention for months, without access to legal counsel or their families. The first trials of those detained in 2015 were held in August 2016. Zhou Shifeng—head of the Fengrui Law Firm, which employed a large number of lawyers working on politically sensitive cases—received a seven-year prison sentence. In September, Xia Lin, who had represented high-profile clients such as the dissident artist Ai Weiwei and the human rights lawyer Pu Zhiqiang, was sentenced to 12 years in prison, having already spent nearly two years in pretrial detention. Among other pending cases against prominent human rights lawyers, Li Heping was formally arrested in January and remained in incommunicado detention under unknown charges at the end of the year, while Jiang Tianyong was held in an unknown location while police investigated him for "incitement to subvert state power." As in previous years under Xi, various human rights lawyers and activists were shown on television giving what are widely assumed to be forced confessions, drawing comparisons to tactics employed during the Mao era.

Police and public security agents generally enjoy impunity for abuses. In December 2016, a court decided not to press charges against five policemen involved in the May death in custody of Lei Yang, who worked at a state-sponsored environmental NGO. This was despite the court's conclusion that the policemen had broken the law by misusing force, delaying medical treatment, and lying about the circumstances of Lei's death. Torture is widely used to extract confessions or force political and religious dissidents to recant their beliefs. Despite the abolition of "reeducation through labor" camps at the end of 2013, tens of thousands of people are still held in other forms of arbitrary detention. In February 2016, an official recanted his confession and claimed torture under "*shuanggui*" detention, an extrajudicial system for party members that has been used extensively during Xi's anticorruption campaign.

Conditions in places of detention, which are estimated to hold three to five million people in total, are harsh, with reports of inadequate food, regular beatings, and deprivation of medical care. While the government has gradually reduced the number of crimes carrying the death penalty, currently at 46, it is estimated that thousands of inmates are executed each year; the government treats the true figure as a state secret. While the government stated that it would end the use of organs from executed prisoners by January 2015, the number of transplanted organs has apparently not diminished, despite the virtual absence of voluntary organ donations from citizens. Allegations of involuntary organ harvesting, including from prisoners of conscience, remained a matter of international concern during 2016.

Chinese laws formally prohibit discrimination based on nationality, ethnicity, race, gender, religion, or health condition, but these protections are often violated in practice. Ethnic and religious minorities, LGBT (lesbian, gay, bisexual, and transgender) people, the disabled, and people with HIV/AIDS, hepatitis B, or other illnesses face widespread discrimination in employment and access to education. Legal remedies remain weak, though a court ruled in favor of a transgender man in a landmark wrongful-dismissal case in December 2016.

Despite China's international legal obligation to protect the rights of asylum seekers and refugees, Chinese law enforcement agencies continue to seek out and repatriate North Korean defectors, who face imprisonment or execution upon return.

G. Personal Autonomy and Individual Rights: 6 / 16

In early 2016, Premier Li Keqiang reiterated a government plan to gradually reform China's *hukou* system—the personal registration rules that restrict China's roughly 270 million internal migrants from enjoying full legal status as residents in the cities where they work. The approach is to gradually expand the benefits of urban residency to 100 million migrants based on their education, employment record, and housing status, with the most stringent requirements in major cities like Shanghai and Beijing. The plan will still leave a large majority of migrants without equal rights or full access to social services such as education for their children in local schools.

Millions of people are affected by restrictions on foreign travel and passports, many of them Uighurs and Tibetans, and overseas Chinese nationals who engage in sensitive activities are at risk of being prevented by the authorities from returning to China, or choose not to return for fear of being arrested. In October 2016, the government announced that all residents of Xinjiang are required to hand in their travel documents to police for "safekeeping" and to apply for permission to leave the country. Many Chinese citizens also face restrictions on internal freedom of movement. While China's constitution gives individuals the right to petition the government concerning a grievance or injustice, in practice petitioners are routinely intercepted in their efforts to reach Beijing, forcefully returned to their hometowns, or extralegally detained in "black jails," psychiatric institutions, and other sites, where they are at risk of beatings, psychological abuse, or sexual violence.

The authorities dominate the economy through state-owned enterprises in key sectors such as banking and energy, and through state ownership of land. Chinese citizens are legally permitted to establish and operate private businesses. However, those without strong informal ties to powerful officials can find themselves at a disadvantage in legal disputes with competitors or in dealings with regulators. Foreign companies can similarly face arbitrary regulatory obstacles, demands for bribes and other inducements, or negative media campaigns.

Property rights protection remains weak. Urban land is owned by the state, with only the buildings themselves in private hands. Rural land is collectively owned by villages. Farmers enjoy long-term lease rights to the land they work, but they have been restricted in their ability to transfer, sell, or develop it. Low compensation standards and weak legal protections have facilitated land seizures by local officials, who often evict the residents and transfer the land rights to developers. Corruption is endemic in such projects, and local governments rely on land development as a key source of revenue. In October 2016, authorities eased limits on the transfer of land-use rights by farmers in an effort to facilitate more efficient agricultural enterprises.

A legal amendment allowing all families to have two children—effectively abolishing the long-standing one-child policy—took effect in January 2016. Ethnic minorities are still permitted to have up to three children. While the authorities will continue to regulate reproduction, the change means that fewer families are likely to encounter the punitive aspects of the system, such as high fines, job dismissal, reduced government benefits, and occasionally detention. Abuses such as forced abortions and sterilizations are less common than in the past.

Despite passage of the country's first law designed to combat domestic violence in 2015, domestic violence continues to be a serious problem, affecting one-quarter of Chinese women, according to official figures. Several laws bar gender discrimination in the workplace, and gender equality has reportedly improved over the past decade, but bias remains widespread, including in job recruitment and college admissions. Women remain severely underrepresented in important CCP and government positions.

Exploitative employment practices such as wage theft, excessive overtime, student labor, and unsafe working conditions are pervasive in many industries. Forced labor and trafficking are also common, frequently affecting rural migrants, and Chinese nationals are similarly trafficked abroad. Forced labor is the norm in prisons and other forms of administrative detention.

⬇ Colombia

Political Rights Rating: 3
Civil Liberties Rating: 3 ↑
Freedom Rating: 3
Freedom Status: Partly Free
Electoral Democracy: Yes

Population: 48,800,000
Capital: Bogotá

Ratings Change, Trend Arrow: Colombia's civil liberties rating improved from 4 to 3, and it received an upward trend arrow, due to the historic reduction in violence resulting from the peace process between the government and left-wing FARC guerrillas.

Ten-Year Ratings Timeline For Year Under Review (Political Rights, Civil Liberties, Status)

Year Under Review	2007	2008	2009	2010	2011	2012	2013	2014	2015	2016
Rating	3,3,PF	3,4,PF	3,4,PF	3,4,PF	3,4,PF	3,4,PF	3,4,PF	3,4,PF	3,4,PF	3,3,PF

Overview: Colombia is one of the longest-standing democracies in Latin America, and its foundational institutions serve an effective role in checking executive power. However, a low-intensity internal conflict has afflicted the country since the 1960s and greatly affected both political rights and civil liberties. A peace process between the government and Colombia's main left-wing guerilla group, launched in 2012, led to the ratification of a peace accord in 2016 and has contributed to a significant decline in violence.

KEY DEVELOPMENTS IN 2016:
- The government and left-wing guerrillas from the Revolutionary Armed Forces of Colombia (FARC) reached a deal on a peace accord in August. Although it was narrowly rejected in an October referendum, renegotiations yielded a revised accord in November, which the legislature ratified without an additional plebiscite.
- In March, the government agreed to initiate formal negotiations with another left-wing guerrilla group, the Army of National Liberation (ELN).

- In February, the chief of Colombia's National Police resigned amid a deepening scandal involving a prostitution ring within police ranks; in response to this and other revelations of malfeasance, his successor initiated an extensive purge of the force as part of a crackdown on corruption.
- A wave of lethal attacks against human rights defenders and other social activists occurred during the year—including dozens in the months after the signing of the first peace accord.

EXECUTIVE SUMMARY

The peace process between the government and the FARC dominated the political environment in 2016. Although domestic opposition created a tense negotiating environment, the two sides announced in August that they had reached a final accord, including an agreement on ceasefire and disarmament as well as provisions for UN monitoring. The agreement was formally signed in September and put to a referendum in October. While most polling suggested an advantage for the "yes" vote, the accord was rejected by roughly 53,000 votes—a margin of less than 0.5 percent—amid a 37 percent turnout.

In the aftermath of the plebiscite, the two sides relaunched talks amid a fragile calm. Following six weeks of discussions, as well as a series of large pro-peace demonstrations throughout the country, the government and the FARC produced a new accord in November. The deal contained some changes requested by opponents of the initial document, including revisions to the transitional justice system and stricter terms regarding the confinement of guerrillas convicted of war crimes under the system. Colombia's Congress subsequently ratified the agreement, and demobilization officially commenced on December 1. Later that month, the Constitutional Court confirmed Congress's ability to fast-track many laws required for implementing the accord; absent such a mechanism, legislative delays could diminish confidence in the government's ability to uphold its responsibilities.

Although UN monitors and other observers expressed concern about delays in the movement of guerrillas into demobilization and disarmament zones, implementation appeared stable at year's end. Both supporters and skeptics of the accord expressed concern that some members of the FARC would migrate to the ELN or paramilitary successor groups, and members of several FARC fronts were reported to have broken with guerrilla leadership and rejected the accords during the year. ELN activity has indeed increased in recent years, but the group agreed in March to hold formal peace talks with the government.

The peace process contributed to a significant decline in the level of violence. The homicide rate dropped to its lowest point in 40 years, and the FARC maintained a ceasefire through the year, resulting in the lowest number of conflict-related victims in over five decades. However, significant rule of law challenges—including a compromised judiciary, corrupt military, and climate of impunity—persisted. Human rights defenders and other social activists were again the targets of violent attack during the year. According to the We Are Defenders coalition, 77 activists had been killed as of mid-December.

POLITICAL RIGHTS: 29 / 40

A. Electoral Process: 10 / 12

The president is directly elected to a four-year term. As part of a series of 2015 constitutional amendments known as the Balance of Power reform, immediate presidential re-election was eliminated. Congress is composed of the Senate and the Chamber of Representatives, with all seats up for election every four years. The nation at large selects

100 Senate members using a closed-list system; indigenous communities choose two additional members. The Chamber of Representatives consists of 166 members elected by closed-list proportional representation in multimember districts. The final peace accord between the government and the FARC, ratified in November 2016, included a provision guaranteeing former guerrillas five seats in each chamber in the 2018 and 2022 elections.

The 2014 legislative and presidential elections were relatively peaceful, although the former was plagued by accusations of fraud, vote buying, and connections with criminals. President Juan Manuel Santos's main allies, the Liberal Party, the Social National Unity Party (U Party), and Radical Change, won a substantial majority in the Chamber of Representatives, taking 92 seats. In the Senate, however, the coalition won only 47 seats. Former president Álvaro Uribe's Democratic Center took 20 seats in the Senate and 19 in the Chamber of Representatives, becoming the primary opposition force.

President Santos won the second round of the 2014 election with 51 percent of the vote against Óscar Iván Zuluaga, who had won the first round with 29 percent to Santos's 26 percent. The balloting was considered relatively free and fair; the most dramatic scandal involved allegations that Andrés Sepúlveda, arrested in 2014 and sentenced to ten years' imprisonment on charges of cyberespionage, had shared illegally intercepted intelligence with Uribe and members of the Zuluaga campaign.

Regional elections in 2015 fortified parties allied with the government, which won gubernatorial races in 23 of the 32 departments. In the most closely followed race, independent former mayor Enrique Peñalosa won the seat again in Bogotá, ending 12 years of rule by the left-wing Democratic Pole. The polls were characterized by accusations of improper influence by illegal groups, irregularities in voter registration, and insufficient candidate vetting by the major parties.

The nine members of the National Electoral Council—elected by Congress for four-year terms based on party nominations—oversee the conduct of the country's elections, including the financing of political campaigns and the counting of votes.

B. Political Pluralism and Participation: 11 / 16

The traditional Liberal-Conservative partisan duopoly in Congress has been supplanted in recent years by a newer party system that is still evolving. The system consists of the traditional parties—which are often characterized by factionalism—as well as regional movements, ideological groups from both the right and the left, and technocratic or issue-oriented parties. Santos's centrist National Unity coalition, which enjoyed dominance in both chambers during his first term, maintained the loose support of a significant majority of legislators following the 2014 elections, despite the vocal and cohesive presence of the Uribe-led right.

In 2016, the ELN and criminal gangs subjected government officials to sporadic threats, harassment, and violence. Police forces and the National Protection Unit, a body under the Ministry of Interior, provided protection to hundreds of public officials during the year.

While general progress remains slow, the government has undertaken a series of steps to incorporate indigenous and Afro-Colombian voices into national political debates in recent years, including training programs to increase Afro-Colombian communities' capacity for governance and awareness of their broader political rights. The peace accord ratified in November 2016 included provisions for improving consultation mechanisms for marginalized groups.

C. Functioning of Government: 8 / 12

Corruption occurs at multiple levels of public administration. Graft scandals have emerged in recent years within an array of federal government agencies. The "parapolitics" scandal, which linked scores of politicians to illegal paramilitary groups, resulted in the investigation, arrest, or conviction of more than 90 legislators by the close of the 2006–10 Congress.

Part of the responsibility for combating corruption rests with the inspector general, who is charged with monitoring the actions of elected officials. Inspector General Alejandro Ordóñez, who removed multiple mayors and bureaucratic officials from office or suspended their right to stand for election, was forced out in September 2016—just months before his term was scheduled to end—due to alleged ethics violations during his reelection bid in 2012. Numerous officials from the Uribe administration have been convicted of corruption, trading favors, and spying on political opponents. In February 2016, the national chief of police resigned following renewed revelations of a prostitution ring within police ranks that had been used by both officers and legislators between 2004 and 2008. His successor carried out a far-reaching crackdown on corruption within the force, with more than 1,400 officers dismissed by year's close. Colombia was ranked 90 out of 176 countries and territories surveyed in Transparency International's 2016 Corruption Perceptions Index.

Public access to government information is generally available for a reasonable fee, though some lower-level officials have reportedly required bribes to expedite access. Congress maintains an online platform on which legislators can voluntarily publish financial disclosures.

CIVIL LIBERTIES: 35 / 60 (+ 1)

D. Freedom of Expression and Belief: 12 / 16

The constitution guarantees freedom of expression, and opposition views are commonly expressed in the media. However, journalists face intimidation, kidnapping, and violence both in the course of reporting and as retaliation for their work. Dozens of journalists have been murdered since the mid-1990s, many of them targeted for reporting on drug trafficking and corruption. Although no journalists were killed in 2016, a local media watchdog recorded at least 216 threats and other abuses against the press, a sharp rise from 2015. Among other cases during the year, members of the ELN kidnapped six reporters in May, holding them for nearly a week before releasing them unharmed. The government has prosecuted several notorious cases of murdered journalists in recent years, but convictions have been made in fewer than 15 percent of killings since 1977. In December 2015, evidence emerged that police had spied on journalists investigating the prostitution ring within its own ranks.

Self-censorship is common, and slander and defamation remain criminal offenses. The government does not restrict access to the internet, nor does it censor websites. Twitter and other social-media platforms have become important arenas for political discourse.

The constitution provides for freedom of religion, and the government generally respects this right in practice. The authorities also uphold academic freedom. University debates are often vigorous, though armed groups maintain a presence on some campuses to generate political support and intimidate opponents.

Human rights groups have criticized the government's use of civilian informants to gather information about suspected criminal and terrorist activities, warning that the practice threatens civil liberties, including the right to privacy.

E. Associational and Organizational Rights: 5 / 12

Although provided for in the constitution, freedoms of assembly and association are restricted in practice by violence. From May to June 2016, indigenous and peasant farmer groups across the country held a coordinated strike to demand government action on agrarian and mining policies, human rights concerns, and other issues, and to request inclusion in deliberations on such questions. The strikes, which included road blockades, led to a heavy police response. At least three participants died and more than 100 people were injured in the ensuing clashes.

The government provides protection to hundreds of threatened human rights workers, but trust in the service varies widely. Scores of activists have been murdered in recent years, mostly by the criminal organizations that succeeded paramilitary groups following a government-backed demobilization process in 2005. Although the Santos administration has reiterated its respect for nongovernmental organizations (NGOs), violations against activists have continued. In 2016, despite an overall decline in the level of violence through the country, fatal attacks against human rights defenders and other activists increased. According to We Are Defenders, a coalition of local and international organizations, 77 activists had been murdered as of mid-December, a dramatic increase compared with the previous two years. Land rights and victims' rights campaigners in particular are threatened by former paramilitaries and other local actors seeking to silence criticism of assets acquired during the conflict and halt the implementation of rural development programs. Observers noted that a significant number of the 2016 killings occurred after the signing of the first peace accord with the FARC, and that many victims were affiliated with the Patriotic March, a rural political movement expected to absorb former FARC members.

Workers may form and join trade unions, bargain collectively, and strike, and antiunion discrimination is prohibited. Over the past two decades, Colombia's illegal armed groups have killed more than 2,600 labor union activists and leaders. Killings have declined substantially from their peak in the early 2000s but still occur regularly. Although a special prosecutorial unit has substantially increased prosecutions for such assassinations since 2007, few investigations have targeted those who ordered the killings.

F. Rule of Law: 8 / 16 (+ 1)

The justice system remains compromised by corruption and extortion, although the Constitutional Court and the Supreme Court have demonstrated independence from the executive in recent years. In 2015, however, the Constitutional Court's reputation was severely damaged by allegations that its president had solicited a $200,000 bribe to rule in favor of an oil company; in August 2016, he was formally suspended from the court.

Many soldiers operate with limited civilian oversight, though the government has in recent years increased human rights training and investigated a greater number of violations by military as well as police personnel. In 2016, these efforts included an investigation of corruption within the National Police following revelations about a prostitution ring within its ranks. Collaboration between security forces and illegal armed groups has declined since the 2005 demobilization, but rights groups report official toleration of paramilitary successor groups in some regions. Primary responsibility for combating these groups rests with the police, who lack the resources of the military, are frequently accused of colluding with criminals, and are largely absent from many rural areas where the groups are active. In late March and early April, the Úsuga Clan, a paramilitary group involved in drug trafficking, announced an "armed strike" in the northeast of the country. The group forced residents of some towns to cease work and public activities, and engaged security forces in armed combat. The clashes resulted in six deaths and temporarily paralyzed economic activity in some areas.

The systematic killing of civilians to fraudulently inflate guerrilla death tolls has declined substantially since a 2008 scandal over the practice led to the firing of dozens of senior army officers. More than 3,000 people may have been killed for such reasons. As of early 2016, more than 900 soldiers had been convicted of these crimes, and thousands of security personnel remained under investigation during the year. However, rights groups have claimed that high-ranking officers largely escape punishment. The military continued to lobby for the maximal inclusion of these crimes under the transitional justice umbrella.

Civil-military relations have been a source of significant tension in recent years. A multiyear project to expand the jurisdiction of the military justice system has prompted sustained domestic and international outcry during much of Santos's time in office. Legislation passed in 2015 omitted many of the most controversial provisions regarding jurisdiction for human rights violations. In 2016, a portion of the armed forces opposed the peace process, and there was public uncertainty regarding the ability of accused human rights violators within the military to receive benefits under the transitional justice system.

Some areas, particularly resource-rich zones and drug-trafficking corridors, remain highly insecure. Guerrillas and paramilitary successor groups regularly extort payments from business owners and engage in forced recruitment, including of minors. The use of landmines in the internal conflict has added to casualties among both civilians and the military. Impunity for crime in general is rampant, with convictions achieved in only 10 percent of murders. Most massacres during the conflict have gone unpunished. In October 2016, prosecutors indicted Santiago Uribe, the former president's brother, for allegedly leading a paramilitary group responsible for dozens of deaths in the 1990s.

Nevertheless, violence has significantly subsided since the early 2000s. In 2016, the homicide rate declined to its lowest point in four decades. The peace process specifically has contributed to a significant reduction in violence. The FARC maintained a ceasefire through much of 2015 and all of 2016, resulting in the lowest number of conflict-related victims in over 50 years.

Colombians' experience of the conflict played a role in voting patterns during the October referendum. In many regions most directly afflicted by the conflict, the "yes" vote garnered a significant majority, but the "no" campaign triumphed in areas characterized by lower violence and a greater state presence. The local media and public attributed the referendum result to several factors, including the depth of negativity toward the FARC among many Colombians, Santos's low approval ratings, low mobilization of "yes" supporters, and a vigorous "no" campaign led by former president Uribe. Pro-accord observers accused the "no" campaign of distorting perceptions of the agreement by suggesting that it would grant FARC members large payouts and by creating controversy around its provisions on women's and LGBT (lesbian, gay, bisexual, and transgender) rights.

Afro-Colombians, who account for approximately 25 percent of the population, make up the largest segment of Colombia's more than five million displaced people, and 80 percent of Afro-Colombians fall below the poverty line. Areas with concentrated Afro-Colombian populations continue to suffer from abuses by the FARC, security forces, and paramilitary successors. In 2016, territorial clashes among militant groups in Chocó department displaced more than 6,000 people–largely Afro-Colombian and indigenous residents of the area—between March and May alone.

Most of Colombia's more than 1.7 million indigenous inhabitants live on approximately 34 million hectares granted to them by the government, often in resource-rich, strategic regions that are increasingly contested by various armed groups. Indigenous people have been targeted by all sides in the country's various conflicts. In October 2015, the Constitutional Court upheld the validity of a decree issued by the government in 2014 that satisfies a commitment to increased autonomy for indigenous territories.

LGBT people suffer societal discrimination and abuse, as well as high levels of impunity for crimes committed against them. According to the local NGO Colombia Diversa, more than 110 LGBT individuals were murdered in 2015. Members of the transgender community have experienced difficulties changing their gender designations on national identity documents and have been denied medical care when health care providers have refused to accept their government identification cards. In August 2016, tens of thousands of Colombians marched to protest Education Minister Gina Parody's proposals to de-emphasize gender in school policies and create a student manual about sexual orientation, which the protesters claimed would lead to pro-LGBT indoctrination. The controversy prompted Parody—who is openly lesbian and managed the "yes" campaign before the October referendum—to resign.

G. Personal Autonomy and Individual Rights: 10 / 16

Freedom of movement, choice of residence, and property rights are restricted by violence, particularly for vulnerable minority groups. Travel in rural areas is further limited by illegal checkpoints operated by criminal and guerrilla groups. Progress remains uneven on the implementation of the landmark 2011 Victims and Land Law, which recognized the legitimacy of claims by victims of conflict-related abuses, including those committed by government forces. While affected citizens continue receiving compensation, the legal process for land restitution is heavily backlogged, and the resettlement of those who were displaced during the conflict continues to move slowly.

Sexual harassment, gender-based violence, and the trafficking of women for sexual exploitation remain major concerns. Thousands of rapes have occurred as part of the conflict, generally with impunity. The country has restrictive abortion laws, though a 2006 Constitutional Court ruling allowed abortion in cases of rape or incest or to protect the life of the mother. In 2015, Congress adopted legislation specifically criminalizing femicide, the killing of a woman because of her gender or gender identity or as part of a campaign of violence. In October 2016, a unit within the prosecutor general's office reported a sharp rise in reports of gender violence in the first nine months of 2016.

In April 2016, after several years of contradictory judicial and administrative decisions regarding same-sex unions, the Constitutional Court voted to legalize them. The court legalized adoptions by same-sex couples in 2015.

Child labor, the recruitment of children by illegal armed groups, and related sexual abuse are serious problems in Colombia. A 2011 free trade agreement with the United States and a subsequent Labor Action Plan called for enhanced investigation of abusive labor practices and rights violations, but progress remains deficient in several areas.

Comoros

Political Rights Rating: 3
Civil Liberties Rating: 4
Freedom Rating: 3.5
Freedom Status: Partly Free
Electoral Democracy: Yes

Population: 800,000
Capital: Moroni

Ten-Year Ratings Timeline For Year Under Review (Political Rights, Civil Liberties, Status)

Year Under Review	2007	2008	2009	2010	2011	2012	2013	2014	2015	2016
Rating	4,4,PF	3,4,PF	3,4,PF	3,4,PF	3,4,PF	3,4,PF	3,4,PF	3,4,PF	3,4,PF	3,4,PF

The country or territory displayed here received scores but no narrative report for this edition of *Freedom in the World.*

Congo, Republic of (Brazzaville)

Political Rights Rating: 7 ↑   **Population:** 4,900,000
Civil Liberties Rating: 5   **Capital:** Brazzaville
Freedom Rating: 6.0
Freedom Status: Not Free
Electoral Democracy: No

Ratings Change: The Republic of Congo's political rights rating declined from 6 to 7 due to the election of President Denis Sassou-Nguesso to a third term through a deeply flawed process, after a 2015 constitutional referendum lifted presidential term and age limits.

Ten-Year Ratings Timeline For Year Under Review (Political Rights, Civil Liberties, Status)

Year Under Review	2007	2008	2009	2010	2011	2012	2013	2014	2015	2016
Rating	6,5,NF	6,5,NF	6,5,NF	6,5,NF	6,5,NF	6,5,NF	6,5,NF	6,5,NF	6,5,NF	7,5,NF

Overview: President Sassou-Nguesso has maintained power for more than three decades by severely repressing the opposition. Corruption and decades of political instability have contributed to extreme poverty for most of the population. Abuses by security forces are frequently reported.

KEY DEVELOPMENTS IN 2016:

- President Denis Sassou-Nguesso secured a third term in a March poll marked by the intimidation of opposition figures and journalists, an election-day shutdown of mobile and internet services, and claims of electoral fraud.
- The government responded to violent protests against the election results with air strikes in the southeast of the country, which targeted the leader of a militant group authorities blamed for the violence. The attacks killed more than two dozen people and damaged churches, schools, and medical facilities.

EXECUTIVE SUMMARY

In March 2016, President Sassou-Nguesso won a third term in the first round of presidential polling, with 60 percent of the vote. Sassou-Nguesso's candidacy had been enabled by the approval of a controversial 2015 constitutional referendum that removed age and term-limit restrictions on the presidency. The referendum had been marred by deadly violence and intimidation.

Opposition figures dismissed the subsequent 2016 presidential election as fraudulent, and the European Union (EU) and U.S. echoed concerns about the poll's credibility. In addition to allegations of widespread vote rigging, police had repeatedly summoned the main opposition candidate, retired General Jean-Marie Michel Mokoko, for questioning ahead of the election. Additionally, mobile phone and internet services were cut off the day of the poll in what observers described as a means of preventing the spread of information about voter turnout and suspected electoral fraud. There were multiple reports of the intimidation of journalists by authorities during the election period.

In early April, after the results were released, antigovernment protests erupted in Brazzaville, during which some participants barricaded certain neighborhoods and set several government buildings on fire. Armed actors eventually clashed with government forces, and more than dozen people were killed in the unrest. In response, the government launched airstrikes in the southeastern Pool region in an attempt to attack the leader of an armed group known as the Ninjas, which had fought against the government in the country's 1997–99 civil war and which was blamed for the Brazzaville violence. Some 30 people were reportedly killed and schools, churches, and medical facilities were damaged.

Opposition figures faced repression following the polls. In April, security forces surrounded Mokoko's home, preventing him from leaving, and in June he was charged with jeopardizing national security and possessing weapons illegally. In July, opposition leader Paulin Makaya of the United for Congo (UPC) party was sentenced to two years in prison following his arrest on charges of inciting disorder over his participation in protests against the 2015 constitutional referendum.

The president's family and advisers effectively control the state oil company. The Panama Papers, a trove of documents leaked from a Panama-based law firm and unveiled by media organizations in April 2016, revealed the existence of offshore companies controlled by close associates of the president allegedly used to embezzle public funds from the company. Despite being one of sub-Saharan Africa's largest oil producers, corruption and decades of political instability have contributed to extreme poverty for most of the population.

POLITICAL RIGHTS: 5 / 40 (− 1)
A. Electoral Process: 1 / 12
B. Political Pluralism and Participation: 2 / 16
C. Functioning of Government: 2 / 12 (− 1)

CIVIL LIBERTIES: 22 / 60
D. Freedom of Expression and Belief: 7 / 16
E. Associational and Organizational Rights: 6 / 12
F. Rule of Law: 2 / 16
G. Personal Autonomy and Individual Rights: 7 / 16

This country report has been abridged for *Freedom in the World 2017*. For background information on political rights and civil liberties in the Republic of Congo, see *Freedom in the World 2016*.

Congo, Democratic Republic of (Kinshasa)

Political Rights Rating: 7 ↓
Civil Liberties Rating: 6
Freedom Rating: 6.5
Freedom Status: Not Free
Electoral Democracy: No

Population: 79,800,000
Capital: Kinshasa

Rating change: The Democratic Republic of Congo's political rights rating declined from 6 to 7 due to the authorities' failure to hold constitutionally mandated elections before President Joseph Kabila's term expired in December, a flawed "consensus" deal to extend Kabila's term, and human rights violations perpetrated by security forces while putting down opposition protests.

Ten-Year Ratings Timeline For Year Under Review (Political Rights, Civil Liberties, Status)

Year Under Review	2007	2008	2009	2010	2011	2012	2013	2014	2015	2016
Rating	5,6,NF	6,6,NF	6,6,NF	6,6,NF	6,6,NF	6,6,NF	6,6,NF	6,6,NF	6,6,NF	7,6,NF

Overview: Civilians and opposition politicians are increasingly unable to influence politics by participating in elections. Civil liberties are limited, but the population continues to exercise rights to association and freedom of expression despite growing state repression. Armed groups and insecurity are prominent in the country's east, and state security forces have also been implicated in abuses.

KEY DEVELOPMENTS IN 2016:

- Constitutionally mandated national elections were not held, and President Joseph Kabila overstayed his term limit.
- In December, Kabila's administration and the opposition came to a fragile agreement that revised the expected date for elections to December 2017.
- There were several fatal attacks by state security forces against civilian protesters.
- Various militia groups carried out acts of violence against civilians in the eastern part of the country. Security forces were also implicated in abuses.

EXECUTIVE SUMMARY

Political rights constricted in the Democratic Republic of Congo (DRC) in 2016, as authorities failed to hold constitutionally mandated national elections and President Kabila overstayed his term limit. Civilian influence in politics declined as the government cracked down on Kabila's political opponents and antigovernment demonstrators. Journalists and human rights advocates faced escalating harassment, abuse, and unlawful detention at the hands of state security forces. In December, Kabila's administration and the opposition came to a fragile agreement that revised the expected date for elections to December 2017.

Armed groups remained active in the country's eastern provinces, committing human rights abuses and contributing to large-scale internal displacement. Officers affiliated with the Armed Forces of the Democratic Republic of Congo (FARDC) remained implicated in human rights violations, with little effective civilian control over their activities.

POLITICAL RIGHTS: 4 / 40 (− 5)

A. Electoral Process: 0 / 12 (− 3)

Article 70 of the DRC's 2006 constitution stipulates that the president is elected for up to two five-year terms, and Article 220 prohibits amendments to key elements of the state's political framework, including the number and length of presidential terms.

Joseph Kabila was declared the winner of the 2011 presidential election amid widespread criticism of the poll by international observers; he defeated Étienne Tshisekedi, 49 percent to 32 percent, according to the Independent National Electoral Commission (CENI). Elections to the 500-seat National Assembly, held concurrently, were also criticized as deeply flawed. Kabila's People's Party for Reconstruction and Democracy (PPRD) won 62 seats, down from the 111 seats it held previously, while Tshisekedi's Union for Democracy and Social Progress (UDPS) took 41. The AMP, Kabila's parliamentary coalition, took a total of 260 seats.

The subsequent presidential election was scheduled for November 2016, and while Kabila was constitutionally barred from seeking a third term in office, many suspected that he would attempt to extend his rule. In August, the CENI announced that the presidential election would be postponed due to a lack of necessary funding, and due to difficulties in registering new voters.

The move sparked outrage from Kabila's opponents, and the government agreed to engage in a national dialogue with a group of opposition parties, which lasted from September to October 2016 under the mediation of the African Union. The parties initially agreed to postpone the election until April 2018; however, few mainstream opposition forces had participated in the dialogue. Most chose to boycott the proceedings and formed a joint bloc to represent their interests—the Rassemblement des Forces Sociales et Politiques Acquises au Changement—led by longtime opposition figure Tshisekedi. Under the mediation of the Roman Catholic Church, representatives of the government agreed to a new round of negotiations with the Rassemblement bloc and reached an agreement in December that revised the expected date for elections to December 2017. Under the deal, Kabila would remain president until that date while sharing power with the opposition, though critics were skeptical of his level of commitment to genuinely inclusive government.

Normally, the president nominates a prime minister from the leading party or coalition in the National Assembly, whose members are popularly elected to serve five-year terms. However, under the terms of the new power-sharing arrangement, the Rassemblement will choose a prime minister to serve until a new president is elected in 2017. Provincial assemblies elect the 108-seat Senate, as well as provincial governors, for five-year terms. A long-neglected decentralization program was implemented in 2015, splitting the DRC's 11 provinces into 26, and the CENI scheduled local and provincial elections to take place between late 2015 and early 2016. However, those elections were seriously delayed. In March 2016, the government held unusual direct gubernatorial elections to select interim governors until provincial elections take place, and the assemblies are seated and able to choose permanent governors. Supporters of Kabila won elections in 14 out of the 19 seats up for election.

The country's electoral framework does not ensure transparent conduct of elections, and opposition parties and civil society groups frequently criticize the CENI for lacking independence.

B. Political Pluralism and Participation: 3 / 16 (− 1)

People have the right to organize political parties. Hundreds of parties exist, with many organized along ethnic, communal, or regional lines; most lack national reach. In addition to the PPRD and UDPS, other key parties in the country include the Union for the Congolese Nation (UNC) and the Movement for the Liberation of Congo (MLC). Nearly 100 parties and many independent candidates hold seats in the parliament.

Despite the existence of numerous parties, political pluralism remains limited in practice, and opposition members do not have a realistic opportunity to increase support through elections. A new transitional government, headed by Prime Minister Samy Badibanga and intended to serve through the remainder of Kabila's presidency, was announced in late December 2016 with an expansive cabinet of 67 ministers that incorporated some opposition members. However, aspects of the consensus government deal had yet to be implemented at year's end, and it remained to be seen how much influence the opposition had within the interim administration.

Opposition party members and leaders are often intimidated and face restrictions on their movement and organizing. Authorities in 2016 made efforts to interfere with the activities of the Rassemblement bloc and others. In August, police prevented a meeting of the bloc in Lubumbashi. In October, police used tear gas to break up a meeting at the home of opposition leader Gabriel Kyungu wa Kumwanza, in Lubumbashi, that was comprised largely of members of Tshisekedi's opposition party and the Rassemblement platform.

Congo's most popular opposition figure—Moïse Katumbi, a businessman and former governor of Katanga Province who left Kabila's majority coalition in 2015—left Congo in May 2016. Katumbi, who was widely expected to run for the presidency, said he was seeking medical treatment abroad, but left shortly after being formally charged with illegally hiring mercenaries.

C. Functioning of Government: 1 / 12 (− 1)

Due to the political crisis, there was no freely elected government to determine state policies at the end of 2016.

Massive corruption in the government, security forces, and mineral extraction industries continues to paralyze the functioning of the government and development efforts intended to raise living standards. Recruitment for government posts is often determined by nepotism. Accountability mechanisms are weak, and impunity remains a problem. Clandestine trade in minerals and other natural resources by rebels and elements of the FARDC helps finance violence and depletes government revenues. In October 2016, a former banker provided evidence that state authorities close to Kabila had embezzled millions of dollars from the public treasury. The national electoral commission, CENI, is implicated in the corruption. The same documents provided by the whistleblower indicated that the Central Bank also diverted millions of dollars to the state-owned mining company, Gecamines, which is run by individuals close to President Kabila.

Despite previous incremental improvements in revenue reporting, there is little transparency in the state's financial affairs. The law does not provide for public access to government information, and citizens often lack the practical ability to obtain information about state operations.

CIVIL LIBERTIES: 15 / 60 (− 1)
D. Freedom of Expression and Belief: 8 / 16

Although constitutionally guaranteed, freedoms of speech and the press are limited. Radio is the dominant medium in the country, and newspapers are found mainly in large cities. While the media frequently criticize Kabila and his government, political harassment of outlets and reporters is common, and outlets face pressure to carry progovernment content. Journalists risk criminal defamation suits as well as threats, detentions, arbitrary arrests, and attacks.

In recent years, the government has closed media outlets linked to the political opposition. In January 2016, two outlets owned by Katumbi—Nyota TV and Radiotélévision Mapendo—were abruptly shuttered for alleged nonpayment of taxes. And in March, the radio and television outlet La Voix du Katanga, owned by Kyungu wa Kumwanza, was closed after it allegedly failed to pay its annual fee and renew its operating license, a charge rejected by its management. Separately, a number of Congolese and foreign reporters were detained during the September 2016 street protests in Kinshasa.

The constitution guarantees freedom of religion, and authorities generally respect this right in practice. Although religious groups must register with the government to be recognized, unregistered groups operate unhindered.

There are no formal restrictions on academic freedom. Primary and secondary school curriculums are regulated but not strongly politicized.

Private discussion of politically sensitive topics can be open among close associates, though discussions of such topics in public places are sometimes limited by fears of potential reprisal. Social media usage is expanding among urban youth. The government does not frequently restrict internet access or monitor online communications, but has suspended internet access and text messaging temporarily during times of political unrest.

E. Associational and Organizational Rights: 3 / 12

The constitution guarantees freedoms of assembly and association. Demonstrations are held regularly despite limits on these rights in practice, including the violent dispersal of protests, including through the use of deadly force, as well as the arbitrary arrest of participants. In the second half of 2016, there was a wave of arrests and fatalities in the capital as demonstrators protested Kabila's move to delay elections. At least 48 street protesters were killed by state agents during one three-day protest in September organized by the Rassemblement opposition coalition, and many others were arrested. According to Human Rights Watch, police removed some of the bodies of protestors killed to eliminate evidence of political repression. The UN Joint Human Rights Office (UNJHRO), in its assessment of the violence, documented human rights abuses by state agents against 422 civilians, including the arbitrary arrests of at least 299 individuals, and counted 143 persons injured. According to the UNJHRO, the human rights violations during this three-day period of protest in the capital outnumbered the total number of abuses it documented over the whole electoral cycle in 2011. That month, the government banned demonstrations in Kinshasa, but street actions continued. In December, 26 people were shot dead by security forces at a protest in the capital marking what should have been the end of Kabila's constitutional mandate.

Nongovernmental organizations (NGOs) and professional organizations are generally able to operate, though domestic human rights advocates are subject to harassment, arbitrary arrest, and detention. There are approximately 5,000 registered NGOs in the DRC, though many have narrow scopes devoted to ethnic, partisan, and local concerns.

Congolese who fulfill a residency requirement of 20 years can form and join trade unions, though government employees and members of state security forces are not permitted to unionize. It is against the law for employers to retaliate against strikers. Unions organize strikes regularly. Some labor leaders and activists face harassment.

F. Rule of Law: 0 / 16

President Kabila appoints members of the judiciary, which remains corrupt and subject to political manipulation. Courts are concentrated in urban areas; the majority of the country relies on customary courts. Civilian cases are often tried in military courts, which are subject to interference from high-ranking military personnel. The judiciary often exhibits bias against opposition and civil society members, while government and government-allied forces often enjoy impunity for even the most heinous crimes. Prison conditions are life-threatening, and long periods of pretrial detention are common.

Civilian authorities do not maintain effective control of security forces. The FARDC are largely undisciplined, and soldiers and police regularly commit serious human rights abuses, including rape and torture. Low pay and inadequate provisions commonly lead soldiers to seize goods from civilians. In September 2016, the United States announced sanctions against Gabriel Amisi, the army commander for the country's western region, and the former national police inspector, John Numbi, over their involvement in a series of human rights abuses. This followed similar sanctions imposed in June on Célestin Kanyama, Kinshasa's police commissioner, on similar grounds.

Peace and the rule of law remain obstructed by active rebel groups, primarily concentrated in the country's eastern and southern provinces. Although armed group activity declined slightly in 2016, civilian security did not improve. The impact of years of fighting on civilians has been catastrophic, with over five million conflict-related deaths since 1998. The population of the affected regions is subject to displacement and violence due to rebel activity and poor discipline among members of the armed forces. Continuing fragmentation and changing coalitions among armed groups, as well as between armed groups and the FARDC, obstruct the deescalation of conflict.

A wave of brutal mass killings in Beni territory of North Kivu begun in October 2014 and continued in 2016; Human Rights Watch estimated in October that around 700 people have been killed in the conflict since it began. The DRC government attributed the attacks to the Uganda-based Allied Democratic Forces (ADF) rebel group, but local human rights organizations and other researchers report that local militias as well as members of the Congolese armed forces have also facilitated the violence. In August, at least 40 people were killed and multiple dwellings were set on fire by militants in the town of Beni, despite the heavy presence of Congolese and international peacekeeping forces.

Ongoing clashes between ethnic Luba fighters and the ethnic Twa continued in 2016 in Katanga province, resulting in over a dozen deaths in October. Clashes in southern Lubero Territory of North Kivu province in January also deepened displacement, with more than 21,000 people forced to flee from Miriki village following a raid by militants thought to belong to the Democratic Liberation Forces of Rwanda (FDLR).

Kidnappings for ransom are common, particularly in the Rutshuru and Lubero Territories of North Kivu province, where 22 abductions were reported in just the two months leading into October.

Ethnic discrimination, including against Kinyarwanda-speaking minority populations, remains a significant problem in some areas of the country. The constitution prohibits discrimination against people with disabilities, but they often find it difficult to find employment, attend school, or access government services. Although discrimination based on HIV status is also prohibited, people with HIV face stigma as well as difficulty accessing health care and education. No law specifically prohibits same-sex sexual relations, but legislators have made efforts to criminalize same-sex sexual activity, and individuals can still be prosecuted for such activity under public decency laws.

G. Personal Autonomy and Individual Rights: 4 / 16 (− 1)

Freedom of movement is protected by law, but is frequently restricted in practice. Armed conflict, primarily concentrated in Beni territory of North Kivu and in Central Kasai, has resulted in 1.7 million internally displaced persons in eastern Congo who are unable to return to their homes. Additionally, UNJHRO investigators were repeatedly denied access to sites of interest in 2016, as they attempted to investigate rights abuses. In April, American researcher Jason Stearns was deported after publishing a report that challenged the government's narrative of ADF rebels behind massacres in Beni and suggesting a broader range of perpetrators including military officers. In August, Human Rights Watch researcher Ida Sawyer was denied a renewed work permit and forced to leave the country.

Individuals have the right to own property and establish private businesses. In conflict zones, armed groups and FARDC soldiers have seized private property and destroyed homes. The country's economy, reliant on the extraction of natural resources, has grown in recent years, though most Congolese are not employed in the formal economy. Minerals, timber, and gold are components of a broader economy of extraction in which the national army, rebel groups, and political interests are involved. A complicated system of taxation and regulation has made bribery a regular aspect of business dealings, and embezzlement is pervasive. The country was recognized as a compliant member of the Extractive Industries

Transparency Initiative (EITI) in 2014. Some progress has been made in the internal management of natural resources, but tracking systems remain inefficient.

Women face discrimination in nearly every aspect of their lives, especially in rural areas. Although the Constitution prohibits discrimination against women in any domain, the Family Code prescribes more restrictive roles, requiring that women obey their husbands and obtain their permission to seek employment and engage in legal transactions. Nevertheless, young women are increasingly seeking professional work outside the home and engaging in commercial activities, particularly in towns and urban centers. Women are greatly underrepresented in government, making up only 9 percent of the National Assembly and 6 percent of the Senate.

Violence against women and girls, including sexual and gender-based violence, has soared since fighting began in 1994; sex crimes often affect men and boys as well. Rebels and FARDC soldiers have been implicated in kidnappings, killings, and rape. Convictions for offenses such as mass rape remain rare. Abortion is prohibited, and women's access to contraception is extremely low; many health care providers require that women obtain permission from their husbands to access family planning services.

The DRC is both a source and destination country for the trafficking of men, women, and children for the purposes of labor and sexual exploitation. Although the law prohibits all forced or compulsory labor, the practice remains common and includes forced child labor in mining, street vending, and agriculture. Various rebel groups reportedly forced civilians to work for them and at times impose tolls on vehicles passing through territory held by the groups. The recruitment and use of child soldiers by armed groups is widespread.

Costa Rica

Political Rights Rating: 1
Civil Liberties Rating: 1
Freedom Rating: 1.0
Freedom Status: Free
Electoral Democracy: Yes

Population: 4,900,000
Capital: San José

Ten-Year Ratings Timeline For Year Under Review (Political Rights, Civil Liberties, Status)

Year Under Review	2007	2008	2009	2010	2011	2012	2013	2014	2015	2016
Rating	1,1,F	1,1,F	1,1,F	1,1,F	1,1,F	1,1,F	1,1,F	1,1,F	1,1,F	1,1,F

Overview: Costa Rica has a long history of democratic stability, with a multiparty political system and regular rotations of power through free and fair elections. Freedoms of expression and association are robust. The rule of law is generally strong, though past presidents have often been implicated in corruption scandals, and prisons remain overcrowded. Among other ongoing concerns, indigenous people and other ethnic minorities face some forms of discrimination, and land disputes involving indigenous communities persist.

KEY DEVELOPMENTS IN 2016:

- The opposition National Liberation Party (PLN) won a majority of municipalities in February local elections, while the president's Citizens' Action Party placed a distant third.

- In May, the Legislative Assembly elected Antonio Álvarez Desanti of the PLN as its president, confirming opposition control over the body for another year.
- In an October ruling, the Supreme Court rebuked a state-owned bank for withdrawing advertising from a major newspaper over its critical reporting.

EXECUTIVE SUMMARY

Opposition parties maintained control over the Legislative Assembly during 2016, complicating President Luis Guillermo Solís's attempts to pass legislation that would address the country's annual fiscal deficits. The deficit for the year was about 5.2 percent of gross domestic product, slightly better than expected, but significant tax and spending reform bills stalled in the legislature.

In a positive sign for transparency and accountability, President Solís compelled Labor Minister Víctor Morales to resign in March, just a day after the newspaper *La Nación* reported that the minister's niece had been hired by the ministry in violation of an ethics code adopted the previous year.

In July, *La Nación* accused the state-owned Banco Nacional of withdrawing official advertising as a means of penalizing the paper for a series of investigative reports on alleged irregularities at the bank. An October ruling by the Supreme Court confirmed the newspaper's claims, ordering the bank to adhere to its previous media spending plan and refrain from future attempts at indirect censorship.

The homicide rate continued to increase in 2016, reaching 11.8 per 100,000 residents; the figure was comparable to those in Costa Rica's immediate neighbors, but still far below the rates in the region's worst performers. A total of 579 murders were reported, compared with 566 in 2015. Overcrowding in prisons has been a chronic problem, and the courts intervened on several occasions during 2016 to force the government to ease crowding at specific facilities. Pretrial detainees account for less than a fifth of the prison population.

POLITICAL RIGHTS: 38 / 40 (+ 1)

A. Electoral Process: 12 / 12

B. Political Pluralism and Participation: 15 / 16

C. Functioning of Government: 11 / 12 (+ 1)

CIVIL LIBERTIES: 53 / 60

D. Freedom of Expression and Belief: 16 / 16

E. Associational and Organizational Rights: 11 / 12

F. Rule of Law: 13 / 16

G. Personal Autonomy and Individual Rights: 13 / 16

This country report has been abridged for *Freedom in the World 2017*. For background information on political rights and civil liberties in Costa Rica, see *Freedom in the World 2016*.

Côte d'Ivoire

Political Rights Rating: 4
Civil Liberties Rating: 4
Freedom Rating: 4.0
Freedom Status: Partly Free
Electoral Democracy: Yes

Population: 23,900,000
Capital: Yamoussoukro (official), Abidjan (de facto)

Ten-Year Ratings Timeline For Year Under Review (Political Rights, Civil Liberties, Status)

Year Under Review	2007	2008	2009	2010	2011	2012	2013	2014	2015	2016
Rating	7,5,N	F6,5,NF	6,5,NF	7,6,NF	6,6,NF	5,5,PF	5,4,PF	5,4,PF	4,4,PF	4,4,PF

Overview: Côte d'Ivoire continues to recover from over a decade of political turbulence and civil war. However, many of the war's root causes—including questions of national identity, access to land, corruption, and impunity—remain. The administration of President Alassane Ouattara has done little to address persistent concerns that pro-Ouattara actors have not been prosecuted for crimes committed during the 2010–11 conflict.

KEY DEVELOPMENTS IN 2016:

- In January, the International Criminal Court (ICC) began a long-awaited trial against former president Laurent Gbagbo and Charles Blé Goudé, both of whom stand accused of crimes against humanity relating to the 2010–11 conflict.
- In May, the trial of former first lady Simone Gbagbo for crimes against humanity began in Abidjan, amid concerns raised by human rights watchdogs regarding the fairness of the proceedings.
- In October, voters approved a new constitution that created the post of vice president as well as a Senate, and formally removed a provision that had once barred President Alassane Ouattara from office due to mixed-nationality parentage.

EXECUTIVE SUMMARY

In 2016, Côte d'Ivoire continued its progress toward peace and stability after some 15 years of political turbulence and civil war that peaked in a 2010–11 postelection crisis. In a sign of the return to normalcy, international sanctions, including an arms embargo, were formally lifted, and the United Nations is scheduled to withdraw its peacekeeping mission by mid-2017. President Ouattara has presided over four years of economic growth, though there are serious concerns that the boom has not benefited ordinary Ivorians.

Longstanding concerns about impunity, victor's justice, and reconciliation persist. To date, only a handful of individuals have been put on trial for crimes committed during the 2010–11 crisis.

POLITICAL RIGHTS: 20 / 40

A. Electoral Process: 7 / 12

Côte d'Ivoire's new constitution, approved in an October 2016 referendum and promulgated in November, provides for the direct popular election of a president and members of a National Assembly. It further established a second house of parliament, a Senate, with one-third of its members to be chosen by the president and the remaining two-thirds to be elected indirectly. It also abolished a rule that had required both of the president's parents to be Ivorian, instead mandating that only one parent be Ivorian. Turnout for the poll was low, at about 42 percent, though 93 percent of participants backed the new charter. The constitutional referendum was boycotted by the opposition, and marred by violence at about 100 polling stations.

Ouattara won the 2015 presidential election in the first round. Despite tensions and some government crackdowns on opposition rallies in the lead-up, the election itself was found by international and domestic observers to be credible. It was the first presidential poll since the 2010 vote, which had occurred after years of delays and triggered widespread postelection violence that left 3,000 dead and another million people displaced when Gbagbo, the incumbent, refused to concede the internationally recognized victory of Ouattara. Gbagbo was ultimately arrested with the assistance of French and UN peacekeeping troops and taken into the custody of the International Criminal Court (ICC).

Credible, largely peaceful elections to the National Assembly were held in December 2016. The presidential coalition, consisting of Ouattara's Rally of the Republicans (RDR) party in alliance with the Democratic Party of Côte d'Ivoire–African Democratic Rally (PDCI-RDA) and several smaller parties won a solid majority, taking 167 of 255 seats. Independent candidates took the majority of remaining seats. Former president Gbagbo's Ivorian Popular Front (FPI) party, which boycotted the 2011 parliamentary elections, won 3 seats. Senate elections were expected to take place in 2017.

In November 2016, the African Court on Human and People's Rights ruled that Côte d'Ivoire's Independent Electoral Commission (CEI) is imbalanced in favor of the government, undermining independence and impartiality, and ordered that the electoral law be amended.

B. Political Pluralism and Participation: 8 / 16

The RDR and the PDCI-RDA, plus several smaller parties, comprise the country's dominant coalition, which holds a virtual lock on national political power. The FPI remains weak and disorganized, marked by deep divisions and infighting since Gbagbo's arrest, with supporters split between hardliners who insist on Gbagbo's release, and moderates who support Pascal Affi N'Guessan. National reconciliation has continued to be a challenge, but tensions have been mitigated somewhat by the release of dozens of FPI prisoners who were being held in conjunction with the 2010–11 crisis, the unfreezing of several FPI partisans' bank accounts, and the return of several high-level FPI members from exile.

Citizenship has been a perennial source of conflict since Ivorian nationalists adopted former president Henri Bédié's concept of "Ivoirité" to exclude perceived foreigners (including Ouattara) from the political process. A new nationality law relaxing some conditions for citizenship went into effect in 2014. However, its application remains challenging, and hundreds of thousands of individuals remain effectively stateless.

C. Functioning of Government: 5 / 12

Côte d'Ivoire's acute crisis phase continues to recede, and UN peacekeepers are expected to withdraw from the country in mid-2017. Though defense and security forces are increasingly under civilian control as a result of legislation increasing oversight, problems of parallel command and control systems within the armed forces, known as the Republican Forces of Côte d'Ivoire (FRCI) remain a challenge, and former rebel commanders of a particular faction, the Forces Nouvelles, dominate FRCI leadership.

Corruption remains endemic, and perpetrators seldom face prosecution. Illegal checkpoints and extortion outside of Abidjan are a continuing problem and are rarely prosecuted.

In January and March 2016, protestors clashed with soldiers over the soldiers' persistent extortion practices, resulting in three deaths and one injury.

In 2013, the National Assembly passed an access to information law. In 2016, the Commission on Access to Information, established to monitor the law's application, conducted training sessions for officials and established a website, among other activities.

CIVIL LIBERTIES: 32 / 40 (+ 1)

D. Freedom of Expression and Belief: 11 / 16

Freedoms of speech and of the press are protected by the constitution, though there are prohibitions on speech that incites violence, hatred, or rebellion. These prohibitions are enforced by the government media regulatory body, the Conseil National de la Presse (CNP). In 2016, the CNP frequently reprimanded journalists and suspended outlets, most of them pro-Gbagbo, for allegedly spreading false information. In April, the government banned the sale of a book written by Charles Blé Goudé, a former youth minister and leader of a pro-Gbagbo militia on trial before the ICC. Nevertheless, conditions for the press have improved since the end of the 2010–11 conflict, and incidents of violence and intimidation against journalists are relatively rare. In August, the government announced plans to submit a draft law that would strengthen freedom of the press by eliminating the possibility of pretrial detention and prison sentences for press-related offenses. There were no credible reports that the government restricted access to the internet or illegally monitored online communications.

Legal guarantees of religious freedom are typically upheld, though political and religious identities tend to overlap with ethnicity and geography. A north-south, Christian-Muslim schism has been a salient feature of Ivorian life since the civil war started in 2002, and was brought to a head in the crisis of 2010–11. However, the schism has receded since then, and the current government is a center-north coalition that includes Muslims and Christians.

Academic freedom suffered severely during the 2010–11 conflict, as public universities throughout the country were closed, occupied by armed forces, and used as military bases and training grounds. They reopened to students in 2012, and are slowly recovering. For the most part, residents can freely engage in private discussion.

E. Associational and Organizational Rights: 8 / 12 (+ 1)

The constitution protects the right to free assembly, but this right is often denied in practice. The government took action on several occasions in 2016 to interfere with opposition protests against the draft constitution. In October, authorities dispersed at least two such demonstrations, and temporarily detained several opposition leaders in attendance. Protests can escalate into violence, as was the case in July demonstrations over electricity prices in Bouaké, which gave way to looting and clashes between police and protesters. One man was killed after being shot and a number of others were injured during the unrest.

Freedom of association is constitutionally protected, and both domestic and international nongovernmental organizations (NGOs) generally operate freely.

The right to organize and join labor unions is constitutionally guaranteed. Workers have the right to bargain collectively, and Côte d'Ivoire typically has various professional strikes every year, though sometimes strikes become violent. Strikes by student unions have been more likely to involve violence than those by industry professionals. In July 2016, the government briefly suspended all student union activity after student demonstrators at Félix

Houphouët-Boigny University in Abidjan clashed with police, resulting in at least 30 injuries and several dozen arrests.

F. Rule of Law: 6 / 16

The judiciary is not independent, and judges are highly susceptible to external interference and bribes. Prisons are severely overcrowded, and prolonged pretrial detention is a serious problem for both adults and minors, with some detainees spending years in prison without trial. Incarcerated adults and minors are not always separated.

Reports of extortion, sexual violence, and killings by members of the FRCI and other security forces continued, though they have decreased since the height of the political crisis, and the government has developed an action plan to combat FRCI-related sexual violence. In some instances, abuses by security forces have resulted in deadly clashes with civilians. In 2016, human rights watchdogs expressed concern that government forestry agents had evicted tens of thousands of illegal squatters from protected forests without adequate warning, in processes marred by violence and extortion.

The security situation was stable but subject to volatility in 2016. In March, 22 people were killed and 33 were injured in a terrorist attack at a beach resort perpetrated by Al-Qaida in the Islamic Maghreb. That same month, an episode of intercommunal violence between pastoralists and farmers in the northeast resulted in at least 17 deaths. In Abidjan, youths that fought in the 2010–11 conflict have regrouped into machete-wielding gangs known as "enfant microbes," which continue to be implicated in armed robberies and assaults in the city. This has led some citizens to form "self-defense" groups, and in 2016 these vigilantes killed a number of alleged criminals.

In January 2016, the government created new ministries of human rights and public liberties, solidarity, social cohesion, and victims' compensation.

The same month, the ICC began a long-awaited trial against Laurent Gbagbo and Charles Blé Goudé, both of whom stand accused of crimes against humanity relating to the 2010–11 conflict. Although the ICC has said it is investigating pro-Ouattara actors, it has filed charges only against pro-Gbagbo defendants so far.

In May, the trial of former first lady Simone Gbagbo for crimes against humanity in connection with the 2010–11 conflict began in Abidjan, following the Ivorian government's refusal to surrender her to the ICC. Rights groups representing victims refused to take part in the new trial, expressing concerns about its fairness and raising questions as to why Simone Gbagbo was the only person on trial on charges of large-scale human rights violations. Gbagbo was previously sentenced to 20 years in prison in 2015 for undermining state security.

The work of the Special Investigative and Examination Cell, created in 2011 to investigate crimes committed during and after the 2010 postelection crisis, has suffered from inconsistent support over the years. In mid-2015, it charged more than 20 people, including high-level commanders from both sides of the conflict, though a number of them continue to occupy important positions in the state security apparatus. In February 2016, the Abidjan military tribunal handed down life sentences to three people following convictions relating to the assassination of General Robert Guéï, a former military ruler who was killed in 2002 at the outset of the civil war.

The Dialogue, Truth, and Reconciliation Commission (CDVR), established in 2011, submitted its final report to Ouattara in December 2014, and the report was finally made public in 2016. In April, the National Commission for Reconciliation and Compensation for Victims (CONARIV), conceived as the successor to the CDVR, presented Ouattara with a list of 316,954 individuals to receive reparations for crimes committed between 1990 and 2011.

Same-sex sexual conduct is not specifically criminalized in Côte d'Ivoire, but LGBT (lesbian, gay, bisexual, and transgender) people can face criminal prosecution for "public indecency." In November 2016, two gay men were each sentenced to three months in prison on such charges, in what local activists said it was the first case of its kind. No law prohibits discrimination on the basis of sexual orientation. LGBT people face societal prejudice as well as violence and harassment by state security forces. In June 2016, several gay men reported that they had been forced to flee their homes, and that two of them had been assaulted by a mob, after a photo published by the U.S. embassy depicted them signing a condolence book for a deadly attack in Orlando, Florida, in which LGBT people were targeted.

G. Personal Autonomy and Individual Rights: 7 / 16

Freedom of movement has improved in Abidjan and along major roads. However, illegal roadblocks and acts of extortion by state security forces remain a problem elsewhere, and the government's efforts to combat these practices have been undermined by inconsistent financial support and a failure to investigate and prosecute perpetrators. In the west and north of the country, highway robbery is a persistent problem.

Property rights are weak and poorly regulated, especially in the west of the country, and remain an ongoing source of conflict between migrants and "natives" who claim customary rights to land use and inheritance. Citizens have the right to own and establish private businesses, and in general economic opportunities for migrants have continued to improve compared to previous years, but obstacles abound.

Despite constitutional protections, women suffer significant legal and economic discrimination, and sexual and gender-based violence are widespread. Rape was common during the 2011 crisis, and remains a serious issue; many rapes are committed against children. Impunity for perpetrators remains a problem and when it is prosecuted, rape is routinely reclassified as indecent assault. Costly medical certificates are often essential for convictions, yet are beyond the means of impoverished victims.

Most identified trafficking victims are children, and child labor, particularly in the cocoa industry, is a serious problem. Government programs for victims of trafficking are inadequate, and most such services are supplied by NGOs.

Crimea

Population: 2,300,000
Capital: Simferopol

Political Rights Rating: 7
Civil Liberties Rating: 6
Freedom Rating: 6.5
Freedom Status: Not Free

Ten-Year Ratings Timeline For Year Under Review (Political Rights, Civil Liberties, Status)

Year Under Review Rating	2007	2008	2009	2010	2011	2012	2013	2014	2015	2016
	—	—	—	—	—	—	—	7,6,NF	7,6,NF	7,6,NF

Overview: In early 2014, Russian forces invaded the autonomous Ukrainian region of Crimea, which was then quickly incorporated into the Russian Federation through a referendum that was widely condemned as having been conducted in violation of international law. The occupation government severely limits political and civil rights, has silenced independent media, and employs antiterrorism and other laws against political dissidents. Some members of the peninsula's indigenous Tatar minority continue to vocally oppose the annexation, despite the risk of imprisonment.

KEY DEVELOPMENTS IN 2016:

- In November, the International Criminal Court stated in preliminary findings that the annexation of Crimea constituted a violation of Ukraine's territorial integrity and was "equivalent to an international armed conflict between Ukraine and the Russian Federation."
- In September, elections for the Russian State Duma were held in Crimea. Local rights activists reported that some residents were threatened with dismissal from their jobs if they failed to vote, or were pressured to attend a preelection rally for Russian president Vladimir Putin's United Russia party.
- Crimean Tatar activist Ervin Ibragimov was abducted in May, and his whereabouts were unknown at year's end.

EXECUTIVE SUMMARY

Russian occupation authorities enforced their control over Crimea for a third year in 2016, notably repressing Crimean Tatar activists, further limiting the media available to Crimean residents, and pressuring local voters to participate in Russia's State Duma elections in September. In August, President Putin claimed that Russia had thwarted an incursion into the territory by Ukrainian saboteurs planning terrorist acts, though he provided little evidence to support the allegations, which Ukrainian authorities said were fabricated. The following day, Putin accused Ukraine of attempting to provoke violence in Crimea, and Russian officials announced naval exercises in the Black Sea. Separately, Russian authorities banned the Mejlis, the official but nongovernmental representative body of the Crimean Tatar people, purportedly because its members engaged in "extremist activity." Both episodes reflected Russian authorities' strategy of pointing to the alleged presence of extremists as justification for tightening their grip on the territory.

In addition to the Mejlis closure, occupation authorities—whose leadership was largely imposed by Moscow and included individuals with ties to organized crime—continued to harass members of the Crimean Tatar minority, with the most outspoken activists facing political persecution. Since the 2014 invasion, Tatar media outlets have been shuttered and many Tatar-owned businesses arbitrarily closed.

While some Crimeans hoped that the Russian occupation would improve their standard of living, prices for many goods have soared, wages and pensions have not kept pace, and the important tourism and agriculture industries are under heavy strain.

The international community continues to oppose the Russian occupation of Crimea. In late 2016, the United States imposed new sanctions against Russian firms and individuals doing business in Crimea—particularly those involved in the construction of a bridge connecting the peninsula to the Russian mainland—and against a number of officials in the occupation government.

POLITICAL RIGHTS: − 1 / 40

A. Electoral Process: 0 / 12

Under the administrative system established by Russia, the Crimean Peninsula is divided into the Republic of Crimea and the federal city of Sevastopol, a port of roughly 380,000 residents that had also been governed separately under Ukrainian control. Sevastopol's political institutions largely mirror those of Crimea proper.

The head of the Republic of Crimea is elected by its legislature, the State Council of Crimea, for up to two consecutive five-year terms. Lawmakers choose the leader based on a list of nominees prepared by the Russian president. In October 2014, they unanimously elected Sergey Aksyonov as the head of the republic, and he simultaneously served as prime minister. Aksyonov had been the acting leader of Crimea since February 2014, when a group of armed men forced legislators to elect him prime minister at gunpoint. He had reputedly been involved in organized crime during the 1990s.

The State Council consists of 75 members elected for a term of five years. Two-thirds of the members are elected by party list and one-third in single-member districts. Legislative elections under the Russian-organized Crimean constitution took place in September 2014, on the same day as Russia's regional elections. All of the parties allowed to participate supported the annexation, pro-Ukraine parties were excluded, and the Tatar minority boycotted the voting. The ruling party in Russia, United Russia, took 70 seats, while the ultranationalist LDPR (formerly known as the Liberal Democratic Party of Russia) secured the remaining five seats. No other parties crossed the 5 percent vote threshold to enter the legislature. The elections received little international recognition.

In September 2016, the occupation authorities conducted elections for the Russian State Duma in Crimea. Local rights activists reported that public- and private-sector workers were threatened with dismissal from their jobs if they failed to vote, and some municipal officials were pressured to attend a preelection rally for United Russia.

B. Political Pluralism and Participation: 0 / 16

The occupation authorities use intimidation and harassment to eliminate any public opposition to Russia's annexation of Crimea and to the current government. Russia's Federal Security Service (FSB), the local police, and "self-defense" units made up of pro-Russian residents enforce this political order. Ukrainian political parties are not able to operate, and the Crimean Tatars—the only group that has continued to openly oppose the Russian occupation—have faced considerable political persecution. The headquarters of the 33-member Mejlis, the Tatars' representative body, was seized and closed by the authorities in 2014. The incumbent chairman of the body, Refat Chubarov, and Tatar leader Mustafa Dzhemilev have been banned from the territory since then. In April 2016, the Russian Justice Ministry suspended the Mejlis for "extremist activity." A week later, Crimea's Supreme Court formally banned the Mejlis, and the Russian Supreme Court confirmed the decision in September.

Political dissidents are subject to harassment, arrest, and persecution. Tatar activist Ervin Ibragimov was abducted in May 2016, and his whereabouts were unknown at year's end. Ilmi Umerov, a former Mejlis deputy chairman who has vocally rejected the annexation, was forced into a psychiatric hospital in August. He was released three weeks later, but faced charges under a section of the Russian criminal code allowing authorities to prosecute public opposition to the annexation. Several Tatar activists were arrested in October and charged with belonging to the Islamist group Hizb ut-Tahrir, which is banned in Russia.

C. Functioning of Government: 0 / 12

All major policy decisions are made in Moscow and executed by Putin's representatives in Crimea or the local authorities, who were not freely elected and are beholden to Moscow. The collapse of the territory's key tourism and agricultural sectors following the occupation has left Crimea heavily reliant on Russian subsidies. International sanctions and the lack of a land connection to Russia put the region under severe logistical stress.

Bureaucratic infighting, corruption scandals, and tensions between federal and local authorities interfered with governance in 2016, particularly as various Russian companies sought access to Crimea's assets. The FSB has arrested a number of Crimean officials as part of an ostensible campaign against the territory's widespread corruption. Many of the arrests were related to allegations that local authorities embezzled Russian funds meant to support the occupation.

Discretionary Political Rights Question B: − 1 / 0

Russian and local pro-Russian officials' policies and actions in Crimea have led to an influx of 30,000 to 35,000 Russian troops and additional civilian personnel, an outflow of many ethnic Ukrainians, and the persecution of ethnic Tatars. The Russian occupation also represents a major setback to Tatars' long-term campaign to reestablish property and other rights that were lost in a Soviet-era mass deportation of the group.

CIVIL LIBERTIES: 9 / 60

D. Freedom of Expression and Belief: 3 / 16

Free speech is severely limited in Crimea. In addition to other restrictive Russian laws, an amendment to the Russian criminal code that took effect in 2014 banned public calls for action aimed at violating Russia's territorial integrity, meaning statements against the annexation, including in the media, can be punished with up to five years in prison.

The Russian telecommunications agency Roskomnadzor required all media outlets to seek registration under Russian regulations by April 2015. Before the annexation, there were approximately 3,000 outlets in Crimea. After the 2015 deadline, Roskomnadzor reported that 232 outlets were registered and authorized to operate. The occupation authorities have essentially cut the territory off from access to Ukrainian television, with armed men seizing the transmission centers in 2014 and imposing Russian broadcasts. Independent and pro-Ukraine media no longer function in Crimea, nor do outlets serving the Tatar community.

Crimea's internet service providers must operate under Russia's draconian media laws. In April 2016, journalist Mykola Semena of the news website Krym.Realii, the Crimean service of Radio Free Europe/Radio Liberty (RFE/RL), was taken into custody in connection with an article in which he expressed support for a civic blockade of the peninsula imposed by Ukrainian activists. He faced a possible five-year prison sentence for extremism. Also during the year, the authorities took steps to block online news outlets including Krym.Realii, Sobytiya Kryma, ATR, and Chernomorskaya TRC.

The occupation authorities have forced religious organizations to reregister. At the time of annexation, there were approximately 1,400 registered religious groups in Crimea and 674 additional communities operating without registration. As of August 2015, there were only 53 locally registered religious organizations, in addition to a few groups registered through an alternative procedure in Moscow. Mosques associated with Crimean Tatars have been denied permission to register. Followers of the Ukrainian Orthodox Church, which has not been banned, face pressure from occupation authorities. In October 2016, a Ukrainian

Orthodox official was briefly detained upon returning to Crimea after attending a session of the Parliamentary Assembly of the Council of Europe (PACE), at which he condemned the repression of Ukrainian Orthodox Christians and of the Ukrainian language in Crimea.

Schools must use the Russian state curriculum. Instruction in the Ukrainian language has been almost completely eliminated, and authorities have also drastically reduced the availability of education in the Tatar language.

The FSB reportedly encourages residents to inform on individuals who express opposition to the annexation, and a climate of fear and intimidation seriously inhibits private discussion of political matters.

E. Associational and Organizational Rights: 1 / 12

Freedoms of assembly and association are restricted. The de facto authorities, including the FSB, repress all independent political and civic organizations. Nongovernmental organizations (NGOs) are subject to harsh Russian laws that enable state interference and obstruct foreign funding.

Trade union rights are formally protected under Russian law, but limited in practice. As in both Ukraine and Russia, employers are often able to engage in antiunion discrimination and violate collective-bargaining rights. Pro-Russian authorities have threatened to nationalize property owned by labor unions in Crimea.

F. Rule of Law: 0 / 16

Under Moscow's rule, Crimea is subject to the Russian judicial system, which lacks independence and is effectively dominated by the executive branch. Russian laws bar dual citizenship for public officials, and Crimean judges were required to receive Russian citizenship in order to return to their positions after the annexation.

Crimes attributed to "self-defense" units and other pro-Russian forces since 2014—including the alleged murder of some activists, abductions and disappearances, and arbitrary expropriations—have gone unpunished. Russia continues to imprison prominent dissidents such as Ukrainian film director Oleh Sentsov, who actively opposed Russia's annexation of Crimea, and his codefendant, activist Oleksandr Kolchenko, both of whom received lengthy prison sentences in 2015. Sentsov has reported abuse in custody, and many international leaders and human rights organizations designated the two as political prisoners.

After the annexation, Crimea became subject to Russia's 2013 law banning dissemination of information that promotes "nontraditional sexual relationships," which tightly restricts the activities of LGBT (lesbian, gay, bisexual, and transgender) people and organizations.

G. Personal Autonomy and Individual Rights: 6 / 16

The occupation authorities have sought to compel Crimea's residents to accept Russian citizenship and surrender their Ukrainian passports. Those who fail to do so face the threat of dismissal from employment, loss of property rights, inability to travel to mainland Ukraine and elsewhere, and eventual deportation as foreigners.

Property rights are poorly protected, and the Russian invasion has resulted in a redistribution of assets in favor of Russian and pro-Russian entities. The occupation authorities have seized Ukrainian state property, and a law passed by the Crimean legislature in 2014 allows the government to condemn and purchase "strategic" assets.

Same-sex marriage is not legal under Russian law. Government officials demonstrate little interest in or understanding of gender-equality issues. Domestic violence against women remains a serious problem in Crimea, and Russian laws do not offer strong protections. Discrimination on the basis of gender, physical appearance, and age is not uncommon. Women hold 14 of the 75 seats in the State Council of Crimea.

As in both Ukraine and Russia, migrant workers, women, and children are vulnerable to trafficking for the purposes of forced labor or sexual exploitation.

Croatia

Political Rights Rating: 1
Civil Liberties Rating: 2
Freedom Rating: 1.5
Freedom Status: Free
Electoral Democracy: Yes

Population: 4,200,000
Capital: Zagreb

Ten-Year Ratings Timeline For Year Under Review (Political Rights, Civil Liberties, Status)

Year Under Review	2007	2008	2009	2010	2011	2012	2013	2014	2015	2016
Rating	2,2,F	2,2,F	1,2,	1,2,F	1,2,F	1,2,F	1,2,F	1,2,F	1,2,F	1,2,F

Overview: Croatia is a parliamentary republic that regularly holds free elections. Civil and political rights are generally respected, though there are serious problems with corruption in the public sector. Minority rights have improved over the last two decades, though the Roma minority faces discrimination, and tensions between the members of the ethnic Croat majority and ethnic Serb minority persist.

KEY DEVELOPMENTS IN 2016:

- Snap parliamentary elections held in September saw low turnout.
- Corruption and bribery cases against prominent figures proceeded during the year, but key verdicts have yet to be handed down.
- The interior minister threatened to remove "false Serb" residents of Vukovar from population lists, amid tensions related to the ethnic Serb minority's use of the Cyrillic alphabet. The remarks drew criticism from officials in both Croatia and Serbia.

EXECUTIVE SUMMARY

Snap parliamentary elections in September 2016—which were held after the previous prime minister lost a confidence vote, and were the second legislative polls in less than a year—were marked by low turnout, with just over 52 percent of eligible voters casting ballots, compared to 61 percent in the last elections. The conservative Croatian Democratic Union (HDZ) won the most seats. Andrej Plenković became the new prime minister after the party formed a coalition with the reformist Most party, whose popularity in recent years is seen as reflecting growing dissatisfaction with the mainstream HDZ and center-left Social Democratic Party (SDP).

Corruption and bribery proceedings against former president Ivo Sanader continued in 2016. Corruption proceedings also continued against Zagreb mayor Milan Bandić, while new proceedings were opened against Ðuro Gavrilović, the owner of one of Croatia's largest companies, on allegations of abuse of office and war profiteering during the early 1990s. Such proceedings have been slow, due in part to multiple levels of appeals processes.

Relations between members of Croatia's ethnic Croat majority and ethnic Serb minority are sometimes fraught due to the sensitive legacy of the 1991–95 war in Croatia. In August 2016, amid increasing tensions over the use of the Cyrillic alphabet by ethnic Serbs in Vukovar, Interior Minister Vlaho Orepić announced that following a survey of Vukovar residents' ethnicities, "false Serbs" would be deleted from population lists. Under Croatian law, minority populations have the right to signage in their own language in towns and cities where they comprise at least 30 percent of the population, and thus the removal of Serbs from population lists could permit the removal of Cyrillic signage from the city. Other Croatian officials condemned the comments, as did figures in Serbia.

Croatia experienced an unprecedented wave of migration in 2015, with hundreds of thousands of people—primarily asylum seekers—arriving in the country, mostly with the intent of continuing on to other European Union (EU) countries. It is expected that thousands of those asylum seekers subsequently denied asylum in other countries will be returned to Croatia—which under treaty obligations is responsible for their registration, but lacks housing and other infrastructure to support them.

POLITICAL RIGHTS: 37 / 40

A. Electoral Process: 12 / 12

B. Political Pluralism and Participation: 15 / 16

C. Functioning of Government: 10 / 12

CIVIL LIBERTIES: 50 / 60

D. Freedom of Expression and Belief: 14 / 16

E. Associational and Organizational Rights: 12 / 12

F. Rule of Law: 11 / 16

G. Personal Autonomy and Individual Rights: 13 / 16

This country report has been abridged for *Freedom in the World 2017*. For background information on political rights and civil liberties in Croatia, see *Freedom in the World 2016*.

Cuba

Political Rights Rating: 7
Civil Liberties Rating: 6
Freedom Rating: 6.5
Freedom Status: Not Free
Electoral Democracy: No

Population: 11,200,000
Capital: Havana

Ten-Year Ratings Timeline For Year Under Review (Political Rights, Civil Liberties, Status)

Year Under Review	2007	2008	2009	2010	2011	2012	2013	2014	2 015	2016
Rating	7,7,NF	7,6,NF	7,6,NF	7,6,NF	7,6,NF	7,6,NF	7,6,NF	7,6,NF	7,6,NF	7,6,NF

Overview: Cuba is a one-party communist state that outlaws political pluralism, represses dissent, and severely restricts freedoms of the press, assembly, speech, and association. The government of Raúl Castro, who succeeded his brother Fidel as president in 2008, monopolizes the bulk of economic activity within centralized and inefficient state enterprises. Increased engagement with the United States under the administration of President Barack Obama did not result in the lifting of restrictions.

KEY DEVELOPMENTS IN 2016

- President Barack Obama made the first state visit to Cuba by a sitting U.S. president in more than 80 years in March. A month later, Communist Party of Cuba (PCC) leaders, at the Seventh Party Congress, portrayed the United States as an enemy that sought to dismantle the country's communist system through its engagement efforts.
- Arbitrary detentions reached more than 9,000 during the first 10 months of 2016, the highest level in seven years. Government repression of the island's increasingly dynamic independent digital press also increased.
- Long-time Cuban leader Fidel Castro died in November, eight years after ceding power to his younger brother Raúl.
- Though still among the least connected countries in the world, Cuba saw greater internet access via an expansion of Wi-Fi hotspots, a deal with Google, and a limited pilot project to allow home-based internet access in Havana.

EXECUTIVE SUMMARY

After more than a year of progress toward the normalization of relations between Cuba and the United States, in March 2016 U.S. president Obama made an historic state visit to Cuba during which he met with President Raúl Castro, and separately with a cross-section of independent civil society activists. Obama also delivered a speech carried live on national television in which he sought to "bury the last remnant of the Cold War in the Americas," and condemned the U.S. embargo against Cuba. Obama advocated for greater access to the internet for Cuban citizens, called for authorities to permit free speech and assembly, rejected "arbitrary detentions of people who exercise those rights," and called for democratic elections in Cuba.

In April, the (PCC) held its Seventh Party Congress. Dashing hopes that the gathering would be used to usher in a generational transition within the party leadership or liberalize the country's nascent private sector, officials instead pushed back forcefully against Obama's message, and reminded Cubans that U.S. policies continued to threaten Cuban socialism.

In 2016, arbitrary detentions reached a seven-year high, with the Cuban Committee for Human Rights and National Reconciliation (CCDHRN) reporting 9,125 such detentions in the first 10 months of the year. Authorities also cracked down on the island's emergent and increasingly diverse independent digital media, and attempted to rein in the burgeoning private sector by temporarily halting the issuance of business licenses for new private restaurants in Havana. In a positive development, the 65 public Wi-Fi hotspots first set up in the second half of 2015 grew to a total of 200, and the price of access in many cases was reduced. Google signed an agreement with state telecom monopoly Etecsa in December to set up company servers on the island to enable faster access to its content and services for Cuban internet users. Separately, a pilot program allowing home-based internet access in 2,000 homes in downtown Havana was launched.

In a historic move in October, the United States decided to abstain from a UN vote condemning its embargo against Cuba. Also that month, the Obama administration issued its sixth and final set of regulatory reforms aimed at softening the embargo and enabling greater people-to-people and economic engagement, attempting to make such changes permanent by issuing them under a rare presidential directive. However, the election of Republican candidate Donald Trump as U.S. president in November threatened to undo these changes, given that he had publicly pledged to "cancel Obama's one-sided Cuban deal" unless concessions in the areas of human rights and religious freedom were made. Ironically, Fidel Castro's death on November 25 was followed days later by the beginning of the first direct commercial flights from the United States to Havana in more than 50 years, signaling the potential opening his absence may provide for deeper commercial ties between Cuba and the United States.

POLITICAL RIGHTS: 1 / 40

A. Electoral Process: 0 / 12

The Castro brothers have long dominated Cuba's one-party political system, in which the PCC controls all government offices and most civil institutions. Every five years, Cubans go to the polls to elect delegates to the island's National Assembly, which then designates the members of the Council of State. This body in turn appoints the Council of Ministers in consultation with its president, who serves as chief of state and head of government. Raúl Castro replaced his brother Fidel as president in 2008. Neither that nor Fidel Castro's death in November 2016 prompted significant changes to Cuba's electoral system.

In 2013 National Assembly elections, voters were asked to either support or reject a single PCC-approved candidate for each of the 612 seats. All candidates were elected. The new National Assembly reelected Raúl Castro to a second five-year term. A 2012 law imposed a limit of two five-year terms on all senior officials, making Castro's current term his last. However, at the PCC's Seventh Congress in April 2016, he was reelected to a new five-year term as party leader, a more powerful position than that of president. Dimming hopes of a generational transition to a younger group of leaders, the Congress also ratified the leadership positions of two historic hardliners, José Ramón Machado Ventura and Ramiro Valdés, both of whom are in their 80s.

B. Political Pluralism and Participation: 0 / 16

All political organizing outside the PCC is illegal, and independent campaigning is not permitted. Political dissent, whether spoken or written, is a punishable offense, and dissidents are systematically harassed, detained, physically assaulted, and frequently sentenced to years of imprisonment for seemingly minor infractions. The regime has called on its neighborhood-watch groups, known as Committees for the Defense of the Revolution, to strengthen vigilance against "antisocial behavior," a euphemism for opposition activity. This has led to the use of "acts of repudiation," or supposedly spontaneous mob attacks, to intimidate and silence political dissidents. In recent years, dissident leaders have reported an increase in intimidation and harassment by state-sponsored groups as well as in short-term detentions by state security forces. In 2016, the CCDHRN reported 9,125 arbitrary arrests of "peaceful opponents" in the first 10 months of the year, the highest level in seven years.

The Cuban government relies heavily on the military as well as on members of the Castro family for control of both business and politics. However, as President Castro has gradually consolidated power since his appointment as interim president in 2006, the portion of PCC leadership represented by the military has shrunk. Meanwhile, President Castro's son, Alejandro—a former member of the army—plays a key role in the administration, serving as both chief of intelligence and top negotiator in the secret talks with the United States that yielded mutual prisoner releases and the reopening of diplomatic relations 2015. The president's son-in-law, Luis Alberto Rodríguez López-Callejas, is chief executive of Gaesa, the sector of the military that controls Cuban business operations. Castro's daughter Mariela Castro Espín has served as de facto first lady since her mother's death in 2007, and also serves in the legislature. Thus far, Raúl Castro has not made any public nod toward a potential Castro family political dynasty, and both Alejandro and Mariela Castro were left off the selections to the Central Committee during the Seventh Party Congress in April 2016. Also at the Seventh Party Congress, President Castro proposed that a maximum age limit be set for entry to the Central Committee and for the assumption of a leadership position, saying limits should be 60 and 70, respectively.

While only 2 of the 14 members of the previous PCC Political Bureau were removed by the Central Committee at the Seventh Party Congress, 5 younger members were added. Three were from the health, biotechnology, and information technology sectors, respectively; the remaining two were the leaders of the country's trade union federation, and the women's federation. The Central Committee saw significant changes; while a quarter of its members were released, total membership increased from 116 to 142, and included 55 new members younger than 60. The proportion of women also rose from 41.7 percent in 2011, to 44.4 percent. Afro-Cubans comprised 35.9 percent of the committee, compared to 31.3 percent in 2011.

C. Functioning of Government: 1 / 12

Though the 1976 constitution provides for the election of a National Assembly, which is vested with legal power to rule the country, in practice the assembly has little legislative power, meeting only twice a year for less than a week each time. Day-to-day executive power is wielded by Cuba's Council of State along with the Council of Ministers. The head of the Council of State acts as president and prime minister.

Corruption remains a serious problem in Cuba, with widespread illegality permeating everyday life. The state holds a monopoly on most business transactions and cannot be challenged or held accountable for wrongdoing. Raúl Castro's regime has made the fight against corruption a central priority, and long sentences have been imposed in corruption cases involving both high-placed Cuban officials and foreign business figures. However, it is not clear whether the government has enacted any internal reforms to make corruption less frequent or easier to identify. Cuba lacks a freedom of information law.

CIVIL LIBERTIES: 14 / 60

D. Freedom of Expression and Belief: 5 / 16

The Cuban news media are owned and controlled by the state. The independent press is considered illegal and its publications are classified as "enemy propaganda." Government agents routinely infiltrate the ranks of independent journalists, often accusing them of being mercenaries. Independent journalists, particularly those associated with the island's small independent news agencies or human rights groups, are subject to harassment.

Some state media have begun to cover previously taboo topics, such as corruption in the health and education sectors. A number of publications, especially those associated with the Catholic Church, have engaged in debates about the country's future. Additionally, in recent years Cuba has witnessed the growth of citizen journalism, an increase in the number of independent bloggers, and the appearance of a small number of independent, island-based news outlets. These include the "webzines" *Vistar*, which focuses on music and culture; *Garbos*, concentrating on fashion; and *Play-Off*, which covers sports. There are also a variety of new digital projects, some of which cover politics without necessarily being voices of dissent; these include *El Estornudo*, *Cachivache*, *El Toque*, the *Havana Times*, *Periodismo de Barrio*, and *14ymedio*. In October 2016, government agents arrested a group of independent journalists working for *Periodismo de Barrio* that had traveled to the city of Baracoa to report on the aftermath of Hurricane Matthew, and sent them to the city of Guantanamo, where they were released. Separately, a journalist with the state-run Radio Holguín was fired after publishing on his personal blog a speech on the economic crisis in Cuba given by an official with the state newspaper *Granma*. In July, a group of journalists circulated a protest letter after the official Union of Journalists of Cuba (UPEC) directed members to stop contributing to the independent digital outlet *OnCuba*, which the UPEC characterized as counterrevolutionary.

While political censorship, high costs, slow speeds, and limited access continue to characterize the internet in Cuba, the past five years have seen increases in web access via state channels like cybercafés and Wi-Fi hotspots, as well as through inventive workarounds that Cubans have designed to produce and distribute digital content. The most recent official Cuban statistics indicate that 34.8 percent of the island's population had access to the internet in 2015, up from 15.9 percent in 2010. In December 2016, the hourly connection rate dropped from $2 to $1.50, and as of September 2016, the island counted some 200 Wi-Fi hotspots. Together with about 200 state-run cybercafés and more than 600 public internet access points in places such as hotels and airports, Cuba is now home to over 1,000 access points. E-mail has been accessible via mobile phone since 2014. Still, the island is among the least connected nations in the Western Hemisphere. Indeed, even with the surge in public Wi-Fi hotspots, the vast majority of Cubans only have intermittent internet access.

In December 2016, Etecsa, the state telecommunications company, launched a pilot program providing 2,000 residents of Old Havana with home internet access. However, critical blogs and websites are often blocked. Activists have reported that the state mobile provider has blocked the delivery of SMS messages containing terms like "democracy," "human rights," and "hunger strike."

While it remains illegal to print or distribute independent media, both journalists and Cuba's new media start-ups have used innovative methods to share information online via e-mail subscription services or weekly news digests. A sophisticated data packet distribution system uses flash drives to circulate digital information, and Cuba's new private mobile phone repair shops often double as independent media and phone app distribution points. Various apps like Feedly and Pocket allow Cubans to maximize their limited time online by quickly downloading articles to read later, offline. Another app called Psiphon creates a virtual private network (VPN) that lets users access blocked sites anonymously.

Official obstacles hamper religious freedom in Cuba. Churches may not conduct ordinary educational activities, and many church-based publications are plagued by state as well as self-censorship. However, the Roman Catholic Church has played an important role in civil society, enabling discussion of topics of public concern. Partly as a result of Pope Francis's positive role in diplomatic negotiations between Cuba and the United States, Cuba's Catholic Church has enjoyed a recent expansion in its pastoral rights, including periodic access to state media and public spaces, as well as the ability to build new churches and print and distribute its own publications. On the other hand, the church has systematically refused to side with dissidents and has been accused of being too close to the state.

Academic freedom is restricted in Cuba. Teaching materials commonly contain ideological content, and affiliation with PCC structures is generally needed to gain access and advancement in educational institutions. On numerous occasions, university students have been expelled for dissident behavior, a harsh punishment that effectively prevents them from pursuing higher education. Despite the elimination of exit visas in 2013, university faculty, especially those in the social sciences, must still obtain permission from their superiors to travel to academic conferences abroad. It is also common for Cuban officials to periodically prevent dissident intellectuals from traveling abroad and to deny academic visas to prominent exiles who have been critical of the regime.

While Cubans do often engage in robust private discussions regarding everyday issues such as the economic reform process, food prices, foreign travel, and increasingly, the lack of open internet access, they tend to self-censor when referring to more political issues such as human rights and civil liberties.

E. Associational and Organizational Rights: 0 / 12

Restrictions on freedom of association remain a key political form of governmental control in Cuba. According to the constitution, citizens' limited rights of assembly and association may not be "exercised against the existence and objectives of the Socialist State." In addition, based on the 1985 Law on Associations no. 54, the government will not register any new association or organization that is not supervised by the state. Nearly all politically motivated short-term detentions in recent years have targeted members of independent associations, think tanks, human rights groups, political parties, or trade unions. Systematic repression has continued against the peaceful public activities of civil and human rights groups such as the Ladies in White, Estado de Sats, and the Patriotic Union of Cuba (UNPACU).

Two other groups specifically targeted for harassment and repression during 2016 are the Center for Legal Information, a pro-bono, public-interest legal consultancy also known as CubaLex; and the newly inaugurated, independent think tank Centro de Estudios Convivencia, or Center for Coexistence Studies. In September, CubaLex's office was raided by government authorities, and property—including laptops, mobile phones, and documents—was seized. Officials threatened to charge the organization's leaders with conducting "illicit economic activity." Its director has been interrogated at the airport ahead of international flights, and suspects that the organization is under constant surveillance. Separately, in September 2016, nine members of Centro de Estudios Convivencia were interrogated by the police. The same month, a workshop organized by the center was shut down by state security officials, as was a meeting in November.

Independent racial advocacy or civil rights organizations are illegal, and no autonomous women's or LGBT (lesbian, gay, bisexual, and transgender) organizations are recognized by the state. In February 2016, *Proyecto Arcoiris*, or Rainbow Project—a group blog defending sexual diversity that is hosted on the government-sponsored blogging platform Reflejos—was censored for a paragraph that "slandered the Revolution."

Cuban workers do not have the right to strike or bargain collectively, and independent labor unions are illegal.

F. Rule of Law: 3 / 16

The Council of State has total control over the courts and the judiciary. Laws on "public disorder," "contempt," disrespect for authority," "pre-criminal dangerousness," and "aggression" are frequently used to prosecute political opponents. From December 2014 to October 2015, graffiti artist Danilo "El Sexto" Maldonado was imprisoned, though never formally charged, for "disrespecting the leaders of the Revolution" by painting the words "Fidel" and "Raúl" on a pair of pigs. In November 2016, following Fidel Castro's death, Maldonado was arrested for spray-painting "se fue" (he's gone) on the wall of a hotel in Havana. The following month, he was transferred to the maximum-security prison Combinado del Este; his family has said they believe he was charged with damaging state property. He is considered a prisoner of conscience by Amnesty International and is represented by the U.S. lawyer Kimberly Motley, who was herself detained, interrogated, and deported from Cuba while trying to visit Maldonado in December.

The Cuban government claims it holds no political prisoners or prisoners of conscience, but various rights groups claimed there were dozens in 2016. At an impromptu and unprecedented joint press conference with Presidents Raúl Castro and Barack Obama during the latter's state visit to Cuba in March 2016, an American journalist asked Castro why Cuba held political prisoners. Castro angrily denied holding any such prisoners and demanded a list of them saying, "If there are political prisoners, they'll be free before nightfall." The CCDHRN subsequently produced a list of 93 prisoners but no releases were made.

While racial discrimination has long been outlawed as state policy, Cubans of African descent have reported widespread discrimination and profiling by law enforcement officials (many of them of African descent themselves). Many of these Cubans have only limited access to the dollar-earning sectors of the economy.

Cuba has made important strides in redressing discrimination against the LGBT community, thanks in part to the advocacy work of Mariela Castro Espín, President Castro's daughter and director of the National Center for Sexual Education (CENESEX). However, a bill proposing the legalization of same-sex marriage has been stalled in the National Assembly since 2008, even with the support of Castro Espín. The efforts of grassroots LGBT groups are largely ignored by the authorities. The government has paid for gender reassignment surgery since 2008.

G. Personal Autonomy and Individual Rights: 6 / 16

Freedom of movement and the right to choose one's residence and place of employment are restricted. The Internal Migratory Regulations for the City of Havana and its Contraventions stipulates that Cubans who move to Havana without state authorization risk losing housing and are subject to deportation back to their provincial cities. Separately, some political prisoners released on conditional freedom have complained that they are at times prevented from traveling outside of their home provinces, with occasional round-ups followed by deportations back to their homes when they are found attending dissident meetings elsewhere on the island. In addition, some political dissidents continue to be denied the right to travel abroad, including former political prisoners released under conditional freedom. In violation of International Labor Organization (ILO) statutes, Cubans working abroad, in the export processing zone at the Port of Mariel, or for foreign companies on the island are not paid directly, but rather through the Cuban state in Cuban, or nonconvertible, pesos.

A 2013 migration law rescinded the exit visa and letter of invitation that were previously required to travel abroad. Since then, the law has generally been respected, with record numbers of Cubans either traveling abroad temporarily or emigrating permanently. Driven in part by fears that the United States' Cuban Adjustment Act, which allows Cubans who reach U.S. territory to remain and gain legal residency, would be repealed as U.S.-Cuban relations thaw, the number of Cubans seeking entry to the United States spiked in late 2015 and continued to rise throughout 2016. U.S. Customs and Border Protection reported that fiscal year 2016 saw a historic exodus of 50,082 Cubans into the U.S., a 17.2 percent increase over fiscal year 2015.

The number of self-employment licenses rapidly expanded from 157,000 in October 2010 to more than 522,000 by November 2016. However, the extent of private employment opportunities remains limited, with almost no professional jobs included in the expanded list of legal self-employment occupations. In addition, many workers in Cuba's new non-agricultural cooperatives were forced into their positions as the only alternative to being laid off. Opening a cooperative even in today's more permissive environment is an arduous, multiyear bureaucratic task requiring municipal and ministerial approvals, with the final green light reserved for the Council of Ministers itself. Separately, in November 2016, Havana authorities said they would suspend the issuing of new restaurant licenses, and warned restaurant owners against violating regulations; with a recent influx of foreign tourists, analysts have suggested that authorities are seeking to curb the earnings of successful restaurants in order to prevent significant wealth disparities in the capital.

Private credit and wholesale access to merchandise for the nonstate sector remains largely nonexistent, which also limits the expansion of private activity. Only state enterprises can enter into economic agreements with foreigners as minority partners; ordinary citizens cannot participate. While new U.S. regulations that went into effect in 2015 now allow U.S. companies to sell inputs to and buy products directly from Cuban entrepreneurs, the Cuban government has yet to permit such activity from its side.

The Cuban constitution establishes full equality for women, and women hold nearly 49 percent of National Assembly seats. However, they make up only 24 percent of the PCC's politburo, 17 percent of the party secretariat, and 24 percent of the Council of Ministers. Only one woman has achieved the rank of vice president. Additionally, women make up only 38 percent of Cuba's work force, even as they are well represented in most professions and have equal access to higher education. Cuban women average less than half of what men earn, mostly because men have access to higher-paying jobs; the gender gap is exacerbated by uneven opportunities opened up by recent market-oriented reforms.

The U.S. State Department claims that the government of Cuba does not fully comply with minimum standards for the elimination of sex trafficking and does not recognize forced labor as a problem in the country. However, Cuba has recently made significant efforts to address trafficking, including the prosecution and conviction of 18 sex traffickers in 2014 and the provision of services to victims in those cases.

Cyprus

Political Rights Rating: 1
Civil Liberties Rating: 1
Freedom Rating: 1.0
Freedom Status: Free
Electoral Democracy: Yes

Population: 1,200,000
Capital: Nicosia

Note: The numerical ratings and status listed here do not reflect conditions in Northern Cyprus, which is examined in a separate report.

Ten-Year Ratings Timeline For Year Under Review (Political Rights, Civil Liberties, Status)

Year Under Review	2007	2008	2009	2010	2011	2012	2013	2014	2015	2016
Rating	1,1,F	1,1,F	1,1,F	1,1,F	1,1,F	1,1,F	1,1,F	1,1,F	1,1,F	1,1,F

Overview: The Republic of Cyprus is a parliamentary democracy that has de jure sovereignty over the entire island. In practice, however, the government controls only the southern, largely Greek-speaking part of the island, as the northern area is ruled by the self-declared Turkish Republic of Northern Cyprus, recognized only by Turkey. The two sections are separated by a UN buffer zone. Political rights and civil liberties are generally respected in the Republic of Cyprus. Ongoing concerns include societal discrimination against minority groups and flaws in the asylum system that lead to prolonged detention and premature deportations.

KEY DEVELOPMENTS IN 2016:

- In March, after years of austerity, Cyprus was able to exit a 2013 financial bailout agreement with the International Monetary Fund (IMF) and the European Union (EU) that had enabled it to survive a banking crisis.
- The center-right Democratic Rally (DISY) won the most seats in parliamentary elections in May, though it lost ground compared with 2011 as three new parties entered the parliament.
- The government continued UN-sponsored reunification talks with representatives of Northern Cyprus during the year, and a breakdown over territorial issues in November was followed by pledges to resume negotiations in early 2017.

EXECUTIVE SUMMARY

As the country's economy, banking system, and fiscal position continued to recover in 2016, Cyprus in March was able to formally exit the bailout agreement that it entered into with the IMF and the EU in 2013. In spite of this progress, the economy still faced many challenges, most notably a high level of nonperforming loans in the banking sector and a relatively large public debt.

The economic hardship that Cypriots have experienced in recent years continued to unsettle the political landscape. Parliamentary elections in May resulted in three new parties entering the parliament, including the far-right National Popular Front (ELAM), which secured 2 of the 56 seats at stake. The center-right DISY of President Nicos Anastasiades led the voting with 18 seats, down slightly from 2011, followed by the left-wing Progressive Party of the Working People (AKEL) with 16, also a decline. The Democratic Party (DIKO) received 9 seats, the Movement for Social Democracy (EDEK) took 3, and the Green Party secured 2. Aside from ELAM, the other two parties entering for the first time were the center-left Citizens' Alliance (SYPOL), which won 3 seats, and the right-wing Solidarity, an offshoot of DISY that also received 3 seats. Turnout was the second-lowest ever recorded at 66.7 percent, reflecting voter disillusionment.

Although only small numbers of irregular migrants and refugees have arrived in Cyprus in recent years, due in part to the difficulty of traveling on from Cyprus to more desirable locations in Northern Europe, the government continued to face criticism during 2016 for its slow processing of asylum applications, restrictive conditions for granting asylum, and long-term detention of asylum seekers in prison-like conditions.

Since the 2015 election of a new, pro-reunification president in Northern Cyprus, Mustafa Akıncı, talks between the two sides have raised hopes for a lasting solution to the island's partition, which resulted from a 1974 Turkish invasion of the north following a coup aimed at union with Greece. The talks broke down in November 2016 amid disagreement on the territorial divisions of a new federal state, among other issues, but representatives quickly agreed to resume the negotiations in January 2017.

POLITICAL RIGHTS: 38 / 40

A. Electoral Process: 11 / 12

B. Political Pluralism and Participation: 16 / 16

C. Functioning of Government: 11 / 12

CIVIL LIBERTIES: 56 / 60

D. Freedom of Expression and Belief: 15 / 16

E. Associational and Organizational Rights: 12 / 12

f. Rule of Law: 15 / 16

G. Personal Autonomy and Individual Rights: 14 / 16

This country report has been abridged for *Freedom in the World 2017*. For background information on political rights and civil liberties in Cyprus, see *Freedom in the World 2016*.

Czech Republic

Political Rights Rating: 1

Civil Liberties Rating: 1

Freedom Rating: 1.0

Freedom Status: Free

Electoral Democracy: Yes

Population: 10,600,000

Capital: Prague

Ten-Year Ratings Timeline For Year Under Review (Political Rights, Civil Liberties, Status)

Year Under Review	2007	2008	2009	2010	2011	2012	2013	2014	2015	2016
Rating	1,1,F	1,1,F	1,1,F	1,1,F	1,1,F	1,1,F	1,1,F	1,1,F	1,1,F	1,1,F

Overview: The Czech Republic is a parliamentary democracy in which political rights and civil liberties are generally respected. However, the country has experienced problems related to corruption and organized crime since its transition to democracy in 1990, and severe economic disparities between the majority community and the Romani minority are persistent. In recent years, illiberal rhetoric has become more common in the public sphere.

KEY DEVELOPMENTS IN 2016:

- The Movement of Dissatisfied Citizens (ANO) party, led by Deputy Prime Minister Andrej Babiš, won October's regional elections. Observers suggested that the victory may presage a strong showing for the ANO in parliamentary elections scheduled for 2017.
- In March, the European Anti-Fraud Office (OLAF) opened an investigation into alleged corruption at Agrofert, one of the firms Babiš controls.
- Issues related to the acceptance and integration of refugee and immigrant communities persisted throughout 2016. Several provocative demonstrations were held, including one at which a Koran was burned.

EXECUTIVE SUMMARY

Babiš's ANO won regional elections held in October. The victory, combined with robust polling numbers for the party, suggested that the ANO may see a strong showing in parliamentary elections scheduled for 2017. There was also speculation during the year that Babiš would eventually replace Bohuslav Sobotka—head of the Czech Social Democratic Party (ČSSD), which with the ANO and the Christian Democratic Party (KDU-ČSL) comprised the country's ruling coalition—as prime minister, even in spite of an ongoing investigation by OLAF into practices at Agrofert. Sobotka's ČSSD won elections to the Senate, held in two rounds in October, though its share of seats in the body decreased.

Corruption is a serious problem. A hint of the issue's scale was revealed during the Panama Papers scandal that emerged in April 2016, when a trove of documents was leaked from a Panama-based law firm and unveiled by media organizations. Of the 11 million documents released, over 250,000 had a connection to the Czech Republic, with nearly 300 Czech business figures appearing in the files. Many of the cases involved alleged tax evasion or money laundering.

Anti-immigrant, antirefugee, and anti-Islamic sentiment persists in the Czech Republic. Several provocative protests took place in 2016, some of which appeared to equate Islam with terrorism; at least one featured an organized Koran burning. The events contributed to a growing Islamophobia throughout the country and a chilling effect on the ability of Muslims to practice freely. At least one racially motivated attempted murder against a Muslim person was recorded in 2016.

Babiš and President Miloš Zeman both made public statements during the year that implied a connection between migration and terrorism. In August, Babiš, citing "what has happened in Europe," said he did not want "even a single refugee in the Czech Republic, not even temporarily." In an interview the previous month, Zeman exhorted people to "arm themselves" to guard against the threat of terrorism, and added that he might endorse the construction of a border fence if the country were to see an influx of migrants, which so far it has not. The remarks reflected growing illiberal discourse in the country.

Asylum seekers are routinely detained, and conditions in detention centers are generally poor. In February 2016, an arson attack was committed against a refugee center in Prague, leaving one person injured.

The Romany minority lacks meaningful political representation. None of the parties representing the estimated 250,000 Roma living in the country have reached the 5 percent parliamentary threshold, and Romany candidates lack adequate representation in the major parliamentary parties. Roma face discrimination in the job market and significantly poorer housing conditions, as well as occasional threats and violence from right-wing groups.

POLITICAL RIGHTS: 38 / 40

A. Electoral Process: 12 / 12

B. Political Pluralism and Participation: 15 / 16

C. Functioning of Government: 11 / 12

CIVIL LIBERTIES: 56 / 60 (− 1)

D. Freedom of Expression and Belief: 15 / 16 (− 1)

E. Associational and Organizational Rights: 12 / 12

F. Rule of Law: 14 / 16

G. Personal Autonomy and Individual Rights: 15 / 16

This country report has been abridged for *Freedom in the World 2017*. For background information on political rights and civil liberties in the Czech Republic, see *Freedom in the World 2016*.

Denmark

Political Rights Rating: 1
Civil Liberties Rating: 1
Freedom Rating: 1.0
Freedom Status: Free
Electoral Democracy: Yes

Population: 5,700,000
Capital: Copenhagen

Ten-Year Ratings Timeline For Year Under Review (Political Rights, Civil Liberties, Status)

Year Under Review Rating	2007	2008	2009	2010	2011	2012	2013	2014	2015	2016
	1,1,F	1,1,F	1,1,F	1,1,F	1,1,F	1,1,F	1,1,F	1,1,F	1,1,F	1, 1,F

Overview: Denmark is a robust democracy with regular free and fair elections. Its population enjoys full political rights, the government protects free expression and association, and the judiciary functions independently. However, with some of the strictest European laws for family reunification, long predating the 2015 migrant crisis, as well as more recent due process limitations for asylum seekers, Denmark has struggled to uphold all fundamental freedoms for its non-European populations.

KEY DEVELOPMENTS IN 2016:

- A November law allows foreigners to be detained or electronically tagged if they have been convicted of even minor crimes but cannot be deported due to conditions in their countries of origin.
- A January law allows border officials to seize refugees' personal property and also increased the mandatory waiting time for family reunification for people without permanent residence.
- In May, lawmakers announced that transsexuality will be removed from classification as a mental illness, effective January 1, 2017.

EXECUTIVE SUMMARY

Denmark regularly holds free and fair elections in an open political system. The government functions transparently and institutes strong safeguards against corruption. Most of the population enjoys a full range of unfettered civil liberties, and civil society is vibrant. A May law made Denmark the first country to no longer classify transsexuality as a mental disorder.

However, the Danish government has long imposed restrictions on its foreign-born population that make it stand out among its Nordic neighbors, and these have been further tightened in response to the massive increase in refugees to Europe in 2015. The year 2016 saw a string of legislative measures affecting immigrants, refugees, and asylum seekers. This began with a January law that extended the mandatory waiting time for family reunification (even for small children) for persons without permanent Danish residence from one to three years, and also authorized the confiscation of valuables carried by asylum seekers when they enter the country. In November, parliament passed a law allowing foreigners convicted of even minor crimes to be confined or electronically tagged without legal recourse if they cannot be deported due to conditions in their countries of origin. The Supreme Court in June ruled that Danish citizenship could be revoked from a man who also held a Moroccan passport after he was convicted of instigating terrorism.

POLITICAL RIGHTS: 40 / 40
A. Electoral Process: 12 / 12
B. Political Pluralism and Participation: 16 / 16
C. Functioning of Government: 12 / 12

CIVIL LIBERTIES: 57 / 60 (− 1)
D. Freedom of Expression and Belief: 16 / 16
E. Associational and Organizational Rights: 12 / 12
F. Rule of Law: 14 / 16 (− 1)
G. Personal Autonomy and Individual Rights: 15 / 16

This country report has been abridged for *Freedom in the World 2017*. For background information on political rights and civil liberties in Denmark, see *Freedom in the World 2016*.

Djibouti

Political Rights Rating: 6
Civil Liberties Rating: 5
Freedom Rating: 5.5
Freedom Status: Not Free
Electoral Democracy: No

Population: 900,000
Capital: Djibouti

Ten-Year Ratings Timeline For Year Under Review (Political Rights, Civil Liberties, Status)

Year Under Review	2007	2008	2009	2010	2011	2012	2013	2014	2015	2016
Rating	5,5,PF	5,5,PF	5,5,PF	6,5,NF	6,5,NF	6,5,NF	6,5,NF	6,5,NF	6,5,NF	6,5,NF

Overview: Djibouti is a republic ruled by a powerful president, Ismail Omar Guelleh, who has been in office since 1999 and is not subject to term limits. While Djibouti technically has a multiparty political system, the ruling Union for a Presidential Majority (UMP) has seized all state power. The opposition's ability to operate is severely constrained, and journalists and activists critical of Guelleh or the UMP are regularly harassed or arrested. Freedoms of assembly and association are restricted.

KEY DEVELOPMENTS IN 2016:
- President Ismail Omar Guelleh was reelected for a fourth term in April, in a poll that was boycotted by some opposition parties.
- Journalists and activists working on contentious issues, including the April presidential election and the killing of at least 19 people by police at a December 2015

religious demonstration, were subject to harassment and arbitrary arrest during the year.

EXECUTIVE SUMMARY

President Guelleh was reelected in April 2016 with 87 percent of the vote, in an election boycotted by the majority of the Djiboutian opposition. The run-up to the presidential election was marked by restrictions on free speech and the harassment and detention of opposition figures. Journalists from the independent internet radio station La Voix de Djibouti, run by exiles in Europe, and opposition-affiliated outlets were arrested in the months leading up to the election. Foreign journalists who covered election were also subject to government reprisals: a British Broadcasting Corp. (BBC) team was detained and deported from the country in April.

An agreement between the ruling UMP and the opposition Union for National Salvation (USN), reached in December 2014 after months of disputes and noncooperation following the 2013 parliamentary elections, was again neglected in 2016. While the opposition ended its boycott of parliament, it continued to claim that the government was neglecting key democratic reforms promised in the deal.

The government continued to harass and imprison human rights defenders in 2016. In January, Omar Ali Ewado—a leader of the Ligue Djiboutienne des Droits Humains (LDDH) who had been detained in December 2015 after publishing the names of people allegedly killed by police during a religious demonstration earlier that month—was convicted of inciting hatred and spreading false news. He was sentenced to three months in jail, but released in February after his sentence was overturned by the Appeals Court of Djibouti.

POLITICAL RIGHTS: 7 / 40 (− 2)

A. Electoral Process: 2 / 12 (− 1)

B. Political Pluralism and Participation: 3 / 16

C. Functioning of Government: 2 / 12 (− 1)

CIVIL LIBERTIES: 19 / 40

D. Freedom of Expression and Belief: 6 / 16

E. Associational and Organizational Rights: 3 / 12

F. Rule of Law: 4 / 16

G. Personal Autonomy and Individual Rights: 6 / 16

This country report has been abridged for *Freedom in the World 2017*. For background information on political rights and civil liberties in Djibouti, see *Freedom in the World 2016*.

Dominica

Political Rights Rating: 1
Civil Liberties Rating: 1
Freedom Rating: 1.0
Freedom Status: Free
Electoral Democracy: Yes

Population: 70,000
Capital: Roseau

Ten-Year Ratings Timeline For Year Under Review (Political Rights, Civil Liberties, Status)

Year Under Review	2007	2008	2009	2010	2011	2012	2013	2014	2015	2016
Rating	1,1,F	1,1,F	1,1,F	1,1,F	1,1,F	1,1,F	1,1,F	1,1,F	1,1,F	1,1,F

The country or territory displayed here received scores but no narrative report for this edition of *Freedom in the World.*

Dominican Republic

Political Rights Rating: 3
Civil Liberties Rating: 3
Freedom Rating: 3.0
Freedom Status: Partly Free
Electoral Democracy: Yes

Population: 10,600,000
Capital: Santo Domingo

Ten-Year Ratings Timeline For Year Under Review (Political Rights, Civil Liberties, Status)

Year Under Review	2007	2008	2009	2010	2011	2012	2013	2014	2015	2016
Rating	2,2,F	2,2,F	2,2,F	2,2,F	2,2,F	2,2,F	2,3,F	2,3,F	3,3,PF	3,3,PF

Overview: The Dominican Republic has a strong framework for the protection of political rights and civil liberties. However, pervasive corruption undermines state institutions, and discrimination against Dominicans of Haitian descent and Haitian migrants, as well as against LGBT (lesbian, gay, bisexual, and transgender) people, is a serious problem. Press freedom is restricted by criminal defamation laws and the harassment of journalists.

KEY DEVELOPMENTS IN 2016:
- Observers from the Organization of American States (OAS) deemed May's presidential, legislative, and municipal elections credible. However, they called for major reforms to guarantee equal access to party financing and media coverage, and expressed concern about serious complications involving new electronic voting and vote-counting infrastructure.
- In February, the Constitutional Court struck down sections of a press law criminalizing defamation of government bodies and public officials, but preserved some other criminal defamation provisions.
- In September, a lawyer working on issues related to discrimination against Dominicans of Haitian descent was attacked in connection with his work.

EXECUTIVE SUMMARY

The ruling Dominican Liberation Party (PLD) maintained its hold on power in simultaneous presidential, legislative, and municipal elections held in May 2016. An OAS observation mission called the polls credible, but cited a number of irregularities, including vote buying. It additionally called for significant structural reforms to promote fairness in the public financing of political parties and campaigns, and, citing a "high degree of unfairness in access to the media," called for mechanisms to guarantee better access to public and private media for smaller political parties.

Additionally, the introduction of a new electronic system for voter identification and registration, counting votes, and transmitting election results created significant complications during the election period. These included technical problems with voting equipment as well as inconsistencies in vote-counting procedures, as some parties, distrustful of the new system, insisted that votes at some locations be counted manually. Delays in tabulation resulted in the full final results not being made public until 13 days after the elections. Six people were killed in election-related violence the Central Election Board (JCE) head claimed had erupted out of frustration with delays created by demands for manual vote counting. Opposition parties blamed the JCE for problems with the polls, contributing to tensions surrounding November's elections by the PLD-controlled Senate of new JCE members.

Human rights violations against Dominicans of Haitian descent, as well as the reported mistreatment of Haitian immigrants, have continued in the wake of a 2013 Constitutional Court ruling that stripped thousands of Dominicans of Haitian descent of their nationality. In 2016, individuals who were able to apply for a restoration of nationality under legislation adopted after the 2013 ruling continued to report problems accessing citizenship documents and registering their children as Dominicans. Additionally, many people affected by the 2013 ruling were unable to exercise their right to vote in the 2016 elections. Lawyers and others working to defend the rights of Dominicans of Haitian descent have reported receiving threats. In September, a prominent lawyer working on the issue was attacked by unknown men in Santo Domingo, in what appeared to be retaliation for his work. The status of an investigation into the attack was unclear at year's end.

While the law guarantees freedom of speech and of the press, journalists face intimidation and violence when investigating sensitive issues, particularly drug trafficking and corruption. However, 2016 saw some advancement in press freedom after the Constitutional Court in February struck down a provision of the press law that criminalized defamation of government bodies and public officials. However, it maintained criminal penalties for defamation committed against private persons, the president, or foreign leaders. Separately, the Chamber of Deputies approved amendments to the Criminal Code that would decriminalize abortion when the mother's life is in danger, but maintained criminal penalties for abortion in all other cases, including for pregnancies resulting from rape and in which a fetus has malformations incompatible with life.

POLITICAL RIGHTS: 27 / 40 (− 2)

A. Electoral Process: 9 / 12 (− 1)

B. Political Pluralism and Participation: 10 / 16

C. Functioning of Government: 8 / 12 (− 1)

CIVIL LIBERTIES: 41 / 60

D. Freedom of Expression and Belief: 14 / 16

E. Associational and Organizational Rights: 10 / 12

F. Rule of Law: 8 / 16

G. Personal Autonomy and Individual Rights: 9 / 16

This country report has been abridged for *Freedom in the World 2017.* For background information on political rights and civil liberties in the Dominican Republic, see *Freedom in the World 2016.*

Ecuador

Political Rights Rating: 3
Civil Liberties Rating: 4
Freedom Rating: 3.5
Freedom Status: Partly Free
Electoral Democracy: Yes

Population: 16,500,000
Capital: Quito

Ratings Change: Ecuador's civil liberties rating declined from 3 to 4 due to the government's decision to order the closure of a major teachers' union as well as regulatory actions and legislation that threatened the sustainability of two graduate universities.

Ten-Year Ratings Timeline For Year Under Review (Political Rights, Civil Liberties, Status)

Year Under Review	2007	2008	2009	2010	2011	2012	2013	2014	2015	2016
Rating	3,3,PF	3,3,PF	3,3,PF	3,3,PF	3,3,PF	3,3,PF	3,3,PF	3,3,PF	3,3,PF	3,4,PF

Overview: Ecuador transitioned to democracy from a military regime in 1979, and since then has experienced the ouster of three presidents under popular or military pressure. Elections take place regularly amid a highly fragmented party system. A leftist government has ruled the country for the past decade, and has introduced a new constitution that guarantees the rights of women and minorities, among other improvements. However, the government has a poor record regarding respect for civil liberties, particularly freedom of expression.

KEY DEVELOPMENTS IN 2016:
- Journalistic coverage of the leaked documents dubbed the Panama Papers, which appeared in the international press beginning in April, triggered authorities to launch corruption investigations into Ecuadorian entities mentioned in the leak.
- In July, close to 150 Cuban nationals were detained and deported while trying to obtain authorization to seek asylum in the United States or Ecuador; human rights watchdogs decried due process violations during the deportation proceedings.
- In August, the government ordered the dissolution of the largest teachers' union in the country, claiming that the group had failed to fully disclose information about its leadership.
- In December, the National Assembly passed legislation eliminating public funding for research at universities that operate under international agreements; the legislation has the potential to undermine the sustainability of two graduate universities, Universidad Andina Simón Bolívar and FLACSO Ecuador.

EXECUTIVE SUMMARY

The administration of Rafael Correa, who has held presidential office since 2007, maintained pressures on the media environment and civil society in 2016. In August, the Ministry of Education declared the dissolution of the National Union of Teachers (UNE), the largest trade association for teachers in the country. The ministry claimed that UNE had failed to submit all information about its leadership as part of its state registration, and was in violation of regulations for the functioning of social organizations. Domestic and international rights groups, among them the International Labor Organization (ILO) and the Office of the UN High Commissioner for Human Rights (OHCHR), protested the decision, finding it a politically motivated violation of freedom of association. Academic freedom also faced threats in legislative amendments passed in December that cut research funding for universities operating under international agreements. The legislation, which affects two graduate universities in particular, followed vocal criticism of public funding for such institutions by Correa.

The government has increasingly cracked down on social media and other internet activity in recent years, leading some online outlets to disable public comment sections out of fear of reprisal. The local press watchdog Fundamedios reported that in 2016, officials continued monitoring speech on the social-media platform Twitter and filing complaints against accounts that are critical of the Correa administration.

In July, authorities detained and deported around 150 Cuban nationals who had established an encampment in a Quito park while attempting to gain asylum in the United States or Ecuador. Human rights watchdogs decried the move, claiming that the judicial proceedings involved in the deportations violated due process rights. Ecuador is the largest recipient of refugees in Latin America, and in 2016, the government continued to struggle to uphold refugees' rights.

Tensions between the presidency and the military surfaced in February, when Correa dismissed the military high command amid allegations that the Social Security Institute of the Armed Forces had overcharged the Ministry of the Environment in a land deal. Correa announced plans to withhold the overpaid sum, sparking popular protests over concerns about the impact on military pensions. The disagreement also led to the resignation of the minister of defense and prompted a cabinet reshuffle in March. Separately, international journalistic coverage of the Panama Papers, which made headlines beginning in April, triggered authorities to launch corruption investigations into Ecuadorian entities mentioned in the leaked documents.

POLITICAL RIGHTS: 24 / 40

A. Electoral Process: 7 / 12

The 2008 constitution provides for a directly elected president. The unicameral, 137-seat National Assembly is elected for four-year terms, with 116 members elected in 24 provinces (each province elects at least two representatives and then one additional representative for every 200,000 inhabitants), 15 elected through nationwide proportional representation, and 6 elected in multimember constituencies representing Ecuadorians living abroad. The president has the authority to dissolve the legislature once in his term, which triggers new elections for both the assembly and the presidency. The assembly can likewise dismiss the president, though under more stringent rules. The president can veto individual line items in legislation. The election law requires that women account for 50 percent of party lists in national legislative elections.

In the 2013 presidential election, Correa won a second term with more than 57 percent of the vote in the first round, followed by Guillermo Lasso Mendoza of the Creating Opportunities Movement (CREO) with 22 percent. In concurrent legislative elections, Correa's Alianza PAIS won an overwhelming 100 of the 137 seats. CREO took only 11 seats; the Social Christian Party won 6; Patriotic Society, Avanza, and the Pachakutik Plurinational Unity Movement won 5 each; and five smaller factions took 1 seat each. A 2008 constitutional mandate called for a significant female presence in public office; women won 53 of 137 assembly seats in the 2013 elections.

International observers reported that the elections were generally free and fair. According to the Organization of American States (OAS), the environment for political competition among candidates was more equal than in previous elections due to new regulations imposed during the campaign period. The OAS noted, however, that competition between candidates in the precampaign period remained unregulated, giving an advantage to the incumbent. Prior to the elections, the Correa administration promoted changes to the parliament's seat-allocation formula that favored larger parties, which critics warned would benefit PAIS.

In 2014, a majority in the National Assembly approved 15 constitutional amendments. Among other things, the changes lowered the minimum age of presidential candidates to 30 years, limited the subjects on which citizens and local governments could request a referendum, and eliminated term limits for elected officials. The removal of term limits included a provision restricting current officials who had already served two terms, including Correa, from running again in 2017, though these individuals would be eligible again beginning in 2021. The opposition and several civil society groups condemned the amendments.

In October 2016, the National Electoral Council opened the candidate registration process for the February 2017 general elections.

B. Political Pluralism and Participation: 11 / 16

For decades, Ecuador's political parties have been largely personality based, clientelist, and fragile. Correa's PAIS remains by far the largest party in the legislature. Other parties include CREO, the Social Christian Party, and the Patriotic Society Party.

The 2008 constitution mandated that political organizations register in order to be eligible for participation in the 2013 general elections, although the process drew controversy. In preparation for the 2014 local elections, the registry of local organizations expanded. At the end of 2016, there were more than 150 registered political organizations, most of them at the local level.

Ecuador's constitution promotes nondiscrimination and provides for the adoption of affirmative action measures to guarantee equality and representation of minorities. In practice, however, indigenous groups often lack a voice in key decisions pertaining to their land and resources. The Pachakutik movement is loosely affiliated with the Confederation of Indigenous Nationalities, the leading national organization representing indigenous groups.

C. Functioning of Government: 6 / 12

Ecuador has long been racked by corruption, and the weak judiciary and lack of investigative capacity in government oversight agencies contribute to an environment of impunity. Corruption investigations fall under the jurisdiction of the government's Office of Transparency and Social Control, created under the 2008 constitution. In 2013, the agency launched a national plan aimed at eradicating corruption by 2017. In April 2016, the National Assembly Justice Commission began investigating the involvement of Ecuadorian entities in potential financial wrongdoing suggested by the Panama Papers, a cache of documents leaked from a major offshore law firm. The initiative produced an August report on tax havens that included a recommendation for further investigations of institutions, officials, and private individuals. In May, former head of the state-owned oil company Petroecuador, Álex Bravo, was detained on charges of illicit enrichment. In June, Ecuadorian authorities dismantled a criminal network involved in money laundering and the illegal export of gold. Also in June, the National Assembly passed a law designed to help the detection, prevention, and prosecution of money laundering.

Ecuador was ranked 90 out of 176 countries and territories surveyed in Transparency International's 2016 Corruption Perceptions Index.

CIVIL LIBERTIES: 33 / 60 (− 2)

D. Freedom of Expression and Belief: 11 / 16 (− 1)

Ecuador remained a hostile environment for freedom of expression in 2016. The press watchdog Fundamedios recorded 535 cases of aggression against media workers during the year, of which 32 were instances of physical aggression. Correa continued to use national broadcasts to castigate opposition leaders and other critics. The government also made use of its unlimited access to public service airtime to interrupt news programming on privately owned stations for the purpose of discrediting journalists.

Criminal prosecution of defamation remains a problem. In September 2016, a judge sentenced Quito's CREO vice-mayor, Eduardo del Pozo, to 15 days in prison for defaming Correa. Del Pozo planned to appeal the sentence.

Ecuador's controversial Organic Law on Communications, approved by the National Assembly in 2013, has faced strong criticism from international press freedom groups and human rights commissions for overly broad restrictions on the media. Among other provisions, the legislation created powerful regulatory bodies with little independence from the executive, placed excessive controls on journalistic content, and imposed onerous obligations on journalists and media outlets, such as barring reporters from working unless they hold degrees from accredited institutions. The law also employs vague language that could be used to censor critical reporting, prohibiting "media lynching" and "character assassination." The former extends to investigative reporting, while the latter covers the dissemination of any information that could undermine the prestige of an individual or institution. The Constitutional Court upheld the law in 2014, rejecting a challenge by opposition politicians and civil society groups. According to Fundamedios, from October 2013 to June 2016, the law resulted in 398 sanctions, 98 percent of which were levied against privately owned media. In August 2016, the media regular sanctioned award-winning journalist Janet Hinostroza and the television network Teleamazonas, for which she hosts a program, for "media lynching" in their investigative reporting about a government purchase of medication. Before the sanction was announced, Correa personally denounced Hinostroza and Teleamazonas in his weekly television address.

The 2013 criminal code contains potential restrictions on freedom of expression, including provisions penalizing the propagation of information that could erode equality, the unauthorized dissemination of personal information, the publication of false news that could affect the economy, and the defense of someone sentenced for a crime. The code retained existing libel and terrorism clauses. A constitutional reform package approved in 2015 included a provision to make communications a "public service," which gives the government broad regulatory powers over the media.

Freedom of religion is constitutionally guaranteed and generally respected in practice.

In 2016, some government maneuvers around higher education funding threatened to compromise academic freedom. In December, the National Assembly approved changes to the Law on Higher Education that eliminate public funding for research at universities that operate in Ecuador under international agreements. Earlier in the year, Correa criticized the use of public funds by such institutions. Critics noted that the changes would severely undermine the viability of two graduate institutions, Universidad Andina Simón Bolívar and FLACSO Ecuador.

Critical content published online has been subject to increasing pressure from the government in recent years. Crackdowns on social media have led some online outlets to disable sections for public commentary for fear of reprisal, limiting the freedom of private discussion online. The government has employed private firm Ares Rights to force the removal of YouTube videos and Twitter posts that are critical of the government, mostly relying on copyright infringement as grounds. Fundamedios reported that more than 800 complaints against at least 292 Ecuadorian Twitter accounts were filed between mid-April and mid-July 2016. The complaints targeted accounts that had a significant following and that posted content criticizing the government.

E. Associational and Organizational Rights: 6 / 12 (− 1)

Numerous protests occur throughout the country without incident. However, national security legislation that predates the Correa administration provides a broad definition of sabotage and terrorism, extending to acts against persons and property by unarmed individuals. The use of such charges against protesters has increased under Correa. According to Human Rights Watch, delays in the appeals process of sabotage and terrorism cases are likely the result of political pressure.

Weeks of national protests in 2015 over indigenous rights left more than 100 injured, including civilians and police personnel. Watchdogs condemned police officers' use of excessive force and arbitrary detention in response to the events.

While the right to organize civic groups and unions is granted by law, domestic and international nongovernmental organizations (NGOs) have come under increasing government scrutiny and regulation. A 2013 presidential decree, codified in 2015, introduced onerous requirements for forming an NGO, granted officials broad authority to dissolve organizations, and obliged NGOs to register all members. Critics contended that the decree violated international standards, and activists challenged its constitutionality in Ecuadorian courts.

In December 2016, the government initiated the dissolution process of Acción Ecológica, an environmental NGO, arguing that the organization had diverged from its goals after it supported a Shuar community that clashed with police amid a conflict with a Chinese mining company. Authorities accused the organization of acting beyond its authority, participating in violence, and interfering in politics.

Private-sector labor unions have the right to strike, though the labor code limits public-sector strikes. The 2015 constitutional amendments limit public sector collective bargaining. There are more labor unions in the public than in the private sector. The ILO has recommended that Ecuador review a constitutional provision mandating that only one association represent public sectors workers. It is estimated that only a small portion of the general workforce is unionized, partly because many people work in the informal sector.

In August 2016, the Ministry of Education dissolved the UNE on the grounds that the union had failed to properly register its leadership and was noncompliant with regulations on social organizations. UNE sustained that its attempts to register its leadership encountered obstacles within the government. The dissolution was widely viewed as a political move and prompted criticism from the public and international organizations, including the ILO.

F. Rule of Law: 6 / 16

Ecuador's highest-ranking judicial bodies are the 21-member National Court of Justice and the nine-member Constitutional Court. Opposition members and foreign experts have expressed concern about the pronounced lack of transparency in the appointment process for the National Court of Justice, and the Constitutional Court has likewise faced criticism because members of its selection committee are closely aligned with the government. The system used by the Council of Popular Participation to vet candidates for the attorney general, appointed in 2011, was similarly criticized for its lack of transparency.

Judicial processes remain slow, with many inmates reaching the time limit for pretrial detention while their cases are still under investigation. Overcrowding plagues the prison system, and torture and ill-treatment of detainees and prisoners are widespread. The 2013 criminal code introduced more restrictive rules on pretrial detention, penalties for specific crimes such as hired killings, and tougher sentences for existing offenses. The government maintains strict visitation protocols for inmates' families.

There have been some tensions in the president's relationship with Ecuador's military. In February 2016, amid a dispute over a 2010 land deal between the military and the Ministry of the Environment, Correa dismissed the high command of the armed forces. The dismissals led to the resignation of the minister of defense and prompted Correa to initiate a cabinet reshuffle in March.

Indigenous people continue to suffer discrimination at many levels of society. In the Amazon region, indigenous groups have attempted to win a share of oil revenues and a voice in decisions on natural resources and development. The government, however, has steadfastly refused the claims of indigenous inhabitants, maintaining that development of protected land is a matter of national interest. Those who continue to campaign against the government often face harassment or violence. In reports submitted for Ecuador's 2017 United Nations Universal Periodic Review on Human Rights, several human rights organizations highlighted violations of the rights of prior consent and free association of indigenous peoples.

Ecuador is the largest recipient of refugees in Latin America. A 2015 report by the UN High Commissioner for Refugees (UNHCR) asserted that Ecuador needed to better uphold the right of asylum and to fight discrimination against refugees. In July 2016, authorities detained and deported around 150 Cuban nationals who were living in an encampment in Quito and protesting poor access to immigration and asylum mechanisms. Most of the individuals were attempting to obtain humanitarian visas from the Mexican government and continue to the United States; some had requested asylum in Ecuador. Human rights watchdogs condemned the move, arguing that the judges who presided over the deportation proceedings violated due process.

The government has shown some responsiveness in upholding the rights of LGBT (lesbian, gay, bisexual, and transgender) people. The constitution includes the right to decide one's sexual orientation, and discrimination based on sexual orientation is prohibited by law. Nevertheless, LGBT individuals continue to face discriminatory treatment.

G. Personal Autonomy and Individual Rights: 10 / 16

Freedom of movement outside and inside the country is largely unrestricted. Individuals can determine their place and type of employment. There has been some controversy over entrance to public institutions of higher education since the government introduced a nationwide examination and reorganized admission procedures.

Citizens have the right to own property and establish private businesses without undue influence by nonstate actors. While there may be delays due to red tape, Ecuador's business environment is close to the regional average in the World Bank's 2017 *Doing Business* report. The results of a 2011 referendum and a subsequent antimonopoly law prevent asset holders in private financial institutions or private companies in the communications sector from simultaneously holding stakes outside each of these sectors.

Employment discrimination is common. The government has taken steps to protect women's rights through public campaigns and legal measures. The 2013 criminal code included femicide as a crime, with penalties reaching 26 years in prison. Sexual harassment is punishable with up to two years in prison. From the 2013 enforcement of the code to April 2016, the attorney general's office investigated 84 cases of femicide, resulting in 24 guilty verdicts. The constitution does not provide for same-sex marriage, but civil unions are recognized.

Indigenous and Afro-Ecuadorian individuals, as well as migrants and refugees from Colombia, are most vulnerable to human trafficking in Ecuador.

Egypt

Political Rights Rating: 6
Civil Liberties Rating: 5
Freedom Rating: 5.5
Freedom Status: Not Free
Electoral Democracy: No

Population: 93,500,000
Capital: Cairo

Ten-Year Ratings Timeline For Year Under Review (Political Rights, Civil Liberties, Status)

Year Under Review	2007	2008	2009	2010	2011	2012	2013	2014	2015	2016
Rating	6,5,NF	6,5,NF	6,5,NF	6,5,NF	6,5,NF	5,5,PF	6,5,NF	6,5,NF	6,5,NF	6,5,NF

Overview: President Abdel Fattah al-Sisi, who first took power in a July 2013 coup, continues to govern Egypt in an authoritarian manner, though the election of a new parliament in late 2015 ended a period of rule by executive decree. Serious political opposition is virtually nonexistent, as both liberal and Islamist activists face criminal prosecution and imprisonment. Terrorism persists unabated in the Sinai Peninsula and has also struck the Egyptian mainland, despite the government's use of aggressive and often abusive tactics to combat it.

KEY DEVELOPMENTS IN 2016:

- In April, the government cracked down on demonstrators protesting a deal to transfer the sovereignty of Egyptian islands to Saudi Arabia. Dozens of people were beaten and arrested.
- In February, an Italian doctoral student, Giulio Regeni, was found dead in Cairo, and his body showed evidence of torture. Security forces were suspected of involvement in his abduction and murder.
- In November, the parliament passed a highly restrictive bill on nongovernmental organizations (NGOs) that effectively criminalized any civil society activity in the absence of approval from a new regulatory body dominated by security agencies. The measure had yet to be signed by the president at year's end.

- Sectarian attacks against Christians continued during the year, including a December church bombing by the Islamic State (IS) militant group that killed 25 worshipers.

EXECUTIVE SUMMARY

The overwhelmingly progovernment parliament elected in 2015 generally rubber-stamped legislation during 2016 and did not provide an effective check on the government of President Sisi.

The authorities harshly restricted freedoms of speech and assembly for activists from across the political spectrum, and the new NGO legislation passed in November threatened to further curtail the operations of independent civil society groups. The media were also targeted, with law enforcement agencies harassing and sometimes jailing journalists who reported on political opposition of any kind. Arbitrary travel bans increasingly affected academics and others seeking to visit or leave Egypt.

An armed insurgency by an IS affiliate based in the Sinai Peninsula continued to grow in 2016. The government maintained a state of emergency in large sections of northeastern Sinai, but it failed to halt terrorist attacks there and in other parts of the country.

Corruption, mismanagement, political unrest, and terrorist violence all contributed to the country's severe economic problems, which included inflation and food shortages. The International Monetary Fund approved a three-year, $12 billion loan in November, but the associated conditions, such as cuts to energy subsidies, were expected to impose further hardship on the population.

POLITICAL RIGHTS: 9 / 40

A. Electoral Process: 3 / 12

In July 2013, following massive protests calling for the resignation of elected president Mohamed Morsi of the Muslim Brotherhood's Freedom and Justice Party (FJP), the armed forces overthrew Morsi, suspended the constitution, and dissolved the upper house of parliament. The military—led by Sisi, then the armed forces commander and defense minister—installed a nominally civilian interim government but remained heavily involved in the political system. The courts had already dissolved the FJP-dominated lower house of parliament in 2012.

A new constitution was adopted by referendum under tightly controlled conditions in January 2014, and a presidential election was held in May 2014. Sisi resigned his post as head of the armed forces to stand as a candidate, and garnered more than 95 percent of the vote against a single opponent, leftist politician Hamdeen Sabbahi. However, no independent international monitors were able to verify the results. The vote was also marred by low turnout, the use of state resources to support Sisi's candidacy, voter intimidation, and arrests and assaults of poll monitors. With no legislature in place following his election, President Sisi ruled by decree.

Parliamentary elections took place in two stages from October to December 2015, and the unicameral House of Representatives was seated in January 2016. The elections featured low turnout, intimidation, and abuse of state resources. The progovernment coalition For the Love of Egypt, consisting of some 10 parties, won all 120 bloc-vote seats. Independents, a number of whom were aligned with the coalition, won 351 of the 448 constituency seats, and the coalition parties' candidates generally outpolled their rivals in the remaining districts. Just three parties outside For the Love of Egypt won more than 10 seats: Protectors of the Homeland (18), the Republican People's Party (13), and Al-Nour (11), a Salafist group that was the only major Islamist party to participate in the elections. In addition to the elected seats, 28 seats are reserved for presidential appointees. Many parties—including moderate Islamist parties and liberal and leftist factions—boycotted the elections and voiced serious reservations about their fairness, accusing security forces of harassment and intimidation. In January 2016, the parties associated with For the Love of Egypt formed a parliamentary bloc, In Support of Egypt, that controlled a majority of the chamber.

Egypt remained without elected local councils in 2016, as the parliament had yet to complete the necessary electoral legislation as required by the 2014 constitution. The last councils were elected in 2008 and dissolved in 2011 after the ouster of longtime authoritarian president Hosni Mubarak. As of the end of 2016, the elections were not expected to take place until the second half of 2017.

B. Political Pluralism and Participation: 4 / 16

The government systematically persecutes opposition parties and political movements, disrupting their operations and constraining their ability to organize. Large numbers of Muslim Brotherhood members and supporters, including nearly all of the organization's senior leadership and Morsi himself, were arrested following the coup, and arrests continued through 2016. Some Brotherhood members have been killed under unclear circumstances, with police reporting gun battles during attempted arrests and the group claiming summary executions. Civil society organizations estimate that as many as 40,000 people were being detained for political reasons as of 2016, most of them for real or suspected links to the Muslim Brotherhood. Authorities declared the Brotherhood a terrorist organization in December 2013, which allowed them to charge anyone participating in a pro-Morsi demonstration with terrorism and laid the foundation for the complete political isolation of the Islamist opposition.

The government has also persecuted non-Islamist critics and parties. For example, Alaa Abdel Fattah, perhaps Egypt's best-known secular activist, was sentenced to five years in prison in February 2015 for violating a highly restrictive law on public protests. The April 6 movement, one of the prodemocracy groups that catalyzed the January 2011 uprising against Mubarak, was banned in 2014. The group's general coordinator, Amr Ali, was sentenced to three years in prison on protest-related charges in February 2016; the sentence was reduced to two years on appeal in July.

Since the 2013 coup, the military has dominated the political system, with most power and patronage flowing from Sisi and his allies in the armed forces and security agencies. As of late 2016, more than two-thirds of Egypt's provincial governors were former military or police commanders.

The constitution bans parties based on religion, though a number of Islamist parties continue to operate in a precarious political and legal position. The Coptic Church leadership has allied itself with Sisi since the coup, apparently to ensure the security of its constituents. Coptic Christians, who account for some 10 percent of the population, are allocated 24 of the parliament's 120 party-list seats. Thirty-six Christians were elected in 2015, and an additional three were appointed by the president, for a total of 39 Christians in the parliament. The party-list quotas also set aside small numbers of seats for workers and farmers, people under 35, people with disabilities, and Egyptians living abroad.

C. Functioning of Government: 2 / 12

Egypt is governed by officials who were not freely elected, and the parliament does not provide an effective check on executive power. The 2014 constitution increased the military's independence from civilian oversight, including through the selection process for the post of defense minister, who must be a military officer. Sisi has ruled in a style that entrenches military privilege and shields the armed forces from accountability for their actions.

Corruption is pervasive at all levels of government. Official mechanisms for investigating and punishing corrupt behavior remain very weak, and the major prosecutions that began after Mubarak's ouster in 2011 have faltered since the 2013 coup. In May 2015, Mubarak was deemed to have completed a three-year sentence for embezzlement, though he remained confined to a military hospital and still faced an ongoing retrial in another case at the end of 2016. In October 2015, a court ordered the release of Mubarak's two sons with time served for their own corruption sentences, but separate charges against them for insider trading remained pending.

The head of Egypt's Central Auditing Authority, Hisham Geneina, was abruptly dismissed and placed under house arrest in March 2016. Sisi had granted himself power to dismiss the heads of state auditing bodies in a 2015 decree. The government accused Geneina of spreading "false news" after he estimated that losses from corruption in Egypt from 2012 to 2015 amounted to $76 billion. In July, he received a one-year suspended prison sentence and was ordered to pay a fine.

In August, a parliamentary committee tasked with investigating corruption in Egypt's system of food subsidies reported that government officials had embezzled more than $70 million by inflating wheat procurement figures. At least 13 officials were arrested in connection with the report's findings, and the cabinet minister responsible for food supplies was forced to resign. However, under a 2015 amendment to the penal code, defendants in financial corruption cases can avoid imprisonment by paying restitution, meaning those accused in the wheat scandal were unlikely to serve jail time.

The Sisi administration has offered very little transparency regarding government spending and operations. The International Budget Partnership gave Egypt a score of 16 out of 100 for budget transparency in its most recent assessment. In its 2017 budget proposal, the government allocated the equivalent of 1.6 percent of gross domestic product for health care and 3.1 percent for education, well short of the 3 percent and 4 percent mandated by the constitution, respectively. The military is notoriously opaque with respect to its own extensive business interests, including in major projects like the "New Suez Canal," and regarding multibillion-dollar arms deals with foreign powers.

CIVIL LIBERTIES: 17 / 60 (− 1)

D. Freedom of Expression and Belief: 5 / 16

Military authorities shut down virtually all Islamist and opposition media outlets following the 2013 coup and pressured others if they carried any critical coverage of the new government. As a result, state media and most surviving private outlets strongly support Sisi and the military.

Official censorship and self-censorship remained widespread in 2016. The Association for Freedom of Thought and Expression (AFTE), an Egyptian rights organization, documented 303 press freedom violations in the first half of the year, including censorship and physical abuse. Arrests of journalists on dubious charges continued, and it was increasingly difficult for media workers to access or report on the Sinai. The Committee to Protect Journalists found that 25 journalists remained behind bars as of December 2016, placing Egypt behind only Turkey and China for the number of reporters detained. The most serious violation occurred in May, when police took the unprecedented step of storming the headquarters of the Journalists' Syndicate to detain two wanted journalists who were seeking refuge in the building. The government then prosecuted the head of the syndicate and two of its board members for allegedly harboring the journalists. All three were sentenced to two years in prison in November, though they remained free at year's end pending an appeal.

Islam is the state religion, and most Egyptians are Sunni Muslims. Coptic Christians form a substantial minority, and there are very small numbers of Jews, Shiite Muslims, atheists, and Baha'is. The 2014 constitution made the right to freedom of religion "absolute" and was well received by religious minorities, though little has changed in practice since the document's adoption. Abuses against Copts continued in 2016, adding to numerous cases of forced displacement, physical assaults, bomb and arson attacks, and blocking of church construction in recent years. One of the worst incidents occurred in May, when a mob of Muslim men in Minya looted and burned the homes of several Christian families and stripped a Christian woman whose son they accused of having an affair with a Muslim woman. IS claimed responsibility for a December church bombing in Cairo that killed 25 people. Separately, in November, a Shiite man was allegedly abducted by security forces after he submitted a request to travel to Iraq for a religious pilgrimage.

Academic freedom has suffered since the 2013 coup. Despite a ban on political protests, universities have been a center of antigovernment demonstrations and the target of government crackdowns. A 2015 decree allows for the dismissal of university professors who engage in on-campus political activity, and in 2016 the government reportedly began imposing more systematic requirements for academics to obtain approval from security officials for travel abroad. In February, Italian doctoral student Giulio Regeni was found dead in Cairo with signs of severe torture, highlighting the dangers faced by foreign researchers, who are often under surveillance, informed on by citizens, and harassed by the government. Regeni's apparent torture and the fact that he was previously investigated and possibly detained at the time of his disappearance led many observers to conclude that security agencies were involved in his death.

Private discussion has become more guarded in the face of vigilantism and increased state monitoring of social media for critical content. Media personalities have called on the public to inform on anyone they suspect of undermining the state, and some arrests have reportedly stemmed from overheard conversations in public places. Social media users have faced arrest or prosecution for alleged offenses ranging from blasphemy to inciting protests or opposing the government online.

E. Associational and Organizational Rights: 4 / 12

Freedoms of assembly and association are tightly restricted. A November 2013 decree gave police great leeway to ban and forcibly disperse gatherings of 10 or more people. The law also prohibits all protests at places of worship and requires protest organizers to inform police at least three days in advance. In the period from the law's enactment to September 2016, some 37,000 legal or security measures were taken to implement it, including more than 19,000 arrests and 3,000 cases of detention and interrogation, according to local human rights activists.

Protests against the government were mounted throughout 2016, but they often ended in violent clashes with police and local residents, and police repeatedly used excessive force. In January, during the weeks leading up to planned demonstrations to commemorate the fifth anniversary of the 2011 revolution, police searched at least 5,000 homes in downtown Cairo. According to AFTE, at least 181 individuals were questioned or detained nationwide surrounding the anniversary. Activists protesting the government's transfer of sovereignty over two Egyptian islands to Saudi Arabia in April 2016 were also aggressively pursued, with at least 150 people arrested. Some of those detained were charged with a number of crimes and sentenced to jail. While a few remained behind bars at year's end, most were later released or given reduced sentences. The most prominent case was that of rights activist Malek Adly, who was detained in an undisclosed location for nearly four months before being released in August, though his trial was still pending.

In November 2016, the parliament passed even harsher legislation to replace the already strict Law on Associations, which governed the operations of NGOs. The new law, if signed by the president, would establish a new regulatory body dominated by security agencies. The measure also bans NGOs from engaging in what the government deems to be political work, and requires the regulator's approval for any field research or polling and any type of cooperation with foreign NGOs. NGO activities in border provinces require approval from the governor. Violators face prison terms of up to five years. Under a 2014 decree, members of NGOs who use foreign funding to commit acts that "harm the national interest" face life imprisonment and fines of 500,000 Egyptian pounds ($50,000). If an offender is a public servant or committed the violation for the purposes of terrorism, he or she could face the death penalty.

Egyptian NGOs faced harassment in the form of office raids, arrests of members, and restrictions on travel in 2016. In March, authorities revived a crackdown on organizations it accused of accepting foreign funding in defiance of Egyptian law, imposing travel bans and asset freezes on several prominent NGO leaders. They included Hossam Bahgat, former head of the Egyptian Initiative for Personal Rights, and Gamal Eid, head of the Arab Network for Human Rights Information. Such actions effectively shut down the operations of the targeted NGOs. Aya Hegazy, a dual American and Egyptian citizen who ran an NGO to help street children remained in pretrial detention for a second year. She had been arrested in 2014 on charges of exploiting street children for political protests and was demonized in the media, indicating that even NGOs focused on apolitical humanitarian issues faced persecution by the government.

Strikes played a significant role in the 2011 uprising, and workers formed two independent union federations in 2011 and 2013, ending the long-standing monopoly of a state-allied federation. Strikes continued amid the country's ongoing economic problems in 2016, with 493 labor protests reported in the first quarter of the year alone, a 25 percent increase over the same period in 2015. Authorities responded to the actions with raids, arrests, and intimidation.

F. Rule of Law: 2 / 16

The Supreme Judicial Council, a supervisory body of senior judges, nominates most members of the judiciary. However, the Justice Ministry plays a key role in assignments and transfers, giving it undue influence over the courts. Judges led the drafting of the 2014 constitution, which significantly enhanced the judiciary's autonomy, including by allowing each major judicial entity to receive its budget as a single line item and permitting the Supreme Constitutional Court to appoint its own chairman.

Although the constitution limits military trials of civilians to crimes directly involving the military, its personnel, or its property, an October 2014 presidential decree placed all "public and vital facilities" under military jurisdiction, resulting in the referral of thousands of civilian defendants to military courts. Charges brought in military courts are often vague or fabricated, defendants are denied due process, and basic evidentiary standards are routinely disregarded.

A number of cases in 2016 demonstrated a high degree of politicization in the court system, typically resulting in harsh punishments for perceived enemies of the government.

A military court sentenced eight civilians to death in May, allegedly relying on confessions obtained through torture. Their charges included belonging to the Muslim Brotherhood. Another 116 people were sentenced to life in prison in February for protest-related violence, but most were tried in absentia, including one who was just three years old; the authorities later admitted that the child's prosecution was a case of mistaken identity.

Police brutality and impunity for abuses by security forces were catalysts for the 2011 uprising, but no reforms have been enacted. Reports of alleged extrajudicial killings and forced disappearances continued throughout 2016, with estimates among various NGOs ranging from dozens to several hundred cases. Prison conditions are very poor; inmates are subject to torture, overcrowding, and a lack of sanitation and medical care. A highly controversial August 2015 antiterrorism law provided a vague definition for terrorism and granted law enforcement personnel sweeping powers and immunity while carrying out their duties.

Egypt was under a state of emergency from 1981 until May 2012, and for three months following the 2013 coup. The Emergency Law grants the government extensive powers of surveillance and detention. A state of emergency and nighttime curfew have been in place since October 2014 in Northern Sinai, with repeated three-month extensions. Nevertheless, fighting there continued throughout 2016, reportedly killing hundreds of civilians, security personnel, and militants.

LGBT (lesbian, gay, bisexual, and transgender) people face severe persecution, and conditions have grown worse under the Sisi regime. While same-sex sexual activity is not explicitly banned, LGBT people have been charged with prostitution or "debauchery." In April 2016, a court sentenced 11 men to between 3 and 12 years in prison on charges of debauchery. New raids and arrests were reported over the course of 2016.

G. Personal Autonomy and Individual Rights: 6 / 16 (− 1)

Freedom of movement and property rights have been severely affected by the government's counterinsurgency efforts in the Sinai. In addition to the curfew, checkpoints, and other travel restrictions, the military has summarily demolished buildings in the town of Rafah to create a buffer zone along the border with the Gaza Strip.

A growing list of rights activists, journalists, political party members, bloggers, and academics have been subjected to arbitrary travel bans in recent years, and the practice appeared to intensify during 2016. In addition to orders preventing Egyptians from traveling abroad, many foreign researchers or activists have been expelled or denied entry to the country.

The 2014 constitution clearly affirms the equality of the sexes, but this has not resulted in practical improvements for women. Thanks in large part to quotas, women won 75 seats in the 596-seat parliament in 2015, and another 14 were appointed by the president. Some laws and traditional practices discriminate against women, job discrimination is common, and Muslim women are disadvantaged by personal status laws. Domestic violence is widespread, and spousal rape is not illegal. Other problems include forced marriages and high rates of female genital mutilation or cutting. In August 2016, the parliament approved harsher penalties for female genital mutilation or cutting, but the ban on the practice has long been poorly enforced.

Violence against women has surfaced in new ways since 2011, particularly as women have participated in demonstrations and faced increased levels of sexual violence in public. A 2014 decree criminalized sexual harassment, with prison terms of up to five years, as part of a national strategy to combat violence against women. Critics argued that the law was inadequate and the strategy was failing, citing a lack of protection for witnesses, continued cases of group sexual harassment in public, and harassment by police officers, which deters women from reporting crimes.

Egyptian women and children, migrants from sub-Saharan Africa and Asia, and increasingly Syrian refugees are vulnerable to forced labor and sex trafficking in Egypt. The Egyptian authorities routinely punish individuals for offenses that stemmed directly from their circumstances as trafficking victims.

El Salvador

Political Rights Rating: 2
Civil Liberties Rating: 3
Freedom Rating: 2.5
Freedom Status: Free
Electoral Democracy: Yes

Population: 6,400,000
Capital: San Salvador

Ten-Year Ratings Timeline For Year Under Review (Political Rights, Civil Liberties, Status)

Year Under Review	2007	2008	2009	2010	2011	2012	2013	2014	2015	2016
Rating	2,3,F	2,3,F	2,3,F	2,3,F	2,3,F	2,3,F	2,3,F	2,3,F	2,3,F	2,3,F

Overview: Violence linked to criminal gangs remains a grave problem, and there is increasing concern about the influence such groups have in politics. The country has a lively press and civil society sector, though journalists risk harassment and violence in connection with work related to gang activity or corruption.

KEY DEVELOPMENTS IN 2016:

- The online news outlet *El Faro* publicized videos showing members of the country's two largest political parties making deals with gangs to buy votes ahead of the 2014 presidential election.
- In March, a radio journalist known for reporting on gang activity was murdered.
- In July, the Supreme Court repealed a 1993 amnesty law that had barred the prosecution of crimes and human rights violations committed during the 1980–92 civil war, saying the government had an obligation to investigate war crimes and to provide reparations.

EXECUTIVE SUMMARY

Due to rampant gang-related violence, El Salvador is considered one of the most dangerous countries in the world. While the homicide level fell in 2016 compared to the previous year, police still recorded 5,278 homicides, amounting to a rate of approximately 80 per 100,000 people. (In 2015, 6,656 homicides were recorded.) Authorities intensified their militarized response to the Mara Salvatrucha (MS-13) and Barrio 18 gangs during the year, and faced criticism from rights activists for the deadly confrontations between security forces and suspected gang members that frequently erupted. Some public officials have been implicated in gang activity.

Journalists whose work focuses on gangs and corruption continue to face harassment and violence. Nicolás García, a radio journalist who reported on gangs, was murdered in

March 2016, reportedly after experiencing harassment from MS-13 members who had insisted that he assist them by providing information on police activity.

Several electoral reforms were passed in 2016 in an effort to simplify the cross-party, or "voto cruzado," and proportional representation voting rules, which had created some confusion in the 2015 elections.

Separately, in July, the Constitutional Chamber of the Supreme Court ruled that a 1993 general amnesty law barring the prosecution of human rights violations committed during the civil war was unconstitutional. In its ruling, the court stated that the government had an obligation to investigate war crimes and to provide reparations.

POLITICAL RIGHTS: 34 / 40 (+ 1)

A. Electoral Process: 11 / 12 (+ 1)

El Salvador's president is elected for a five-year term. The 84-member, unicameral Legislative Assembly is elected for three years. Three candidates contended for the presidency in 2014: former guerilla Salvador Sánchez Cerén of the incumbent Farabundo Martí National Liberation Front (FMLN), Norman Quijano of Nationalist Republican Alliance (ARENA), and former president Antonio Saca of the Grand Alliance for National Unity (GANA). Cerén defeated Quijano in a very close runoff. Turnout was 60 percent. Quijano accused the Supreme Electoral Tribunal (TSE) of fraud, but domestic and international observers considered the elections free and fair.

Before the 2015 legislative and municipal elections, the Constitutional Chamber of the Supreme Court passed a number of rulings on the electoral system, including one allowing voters to cast ballots for candidates from more than one political party (cross-voting); previously, voters selected a party rather than individual candidates. The FMLN accused the Chamber of purposefully generating confusion before the election, while the Organization of American States (OAS) questioned whether the date of the decision allowed enough time for parties to adapt to the changes. Citing a lack of time, the legislature delegated to the TSE how it would count votes under the new rules in 2015.

In the 2015 elections, ARENA won 35 seats—32 on its own and 3 in coalition with the National Coalition Party (PCN). The FMLN won 31 seats, GANA won 11, and the rest went to smaller groupings. Turnout was 48 percent. Some vote buying was alleged in rural areas. The OAS observation mission declared the election broadly transparent and free. It did note that the TSE had difficulties in the counting and transmission of results. San Salvadoran candidates disputed their results, prompting the Constitutional Chamber to call for an unprecedented recount that did not affect the results, but delayed the seating of 24 deputies.

In 2015, residential voting was extended nationwide, and municipal elections were conducted under new proportional rules. In February and May of 2016, the legislature passed reforms that clarified the application of those rules and of the cross-party voting system. The reforms also prohibited changes to the electoral process one year before an election, and mandated that alternative candidates be listed on the ballot. However, in July 2016, the Chamber declared the 2015 election of alternate legislators unconstitutional, removing them from office and creating uncertainty for future elections.

The OAS, and other organizations, have repeatedly called for the TSE to update its list of registered voters.

B. Political Pluralism and Participation: 14 / 16

Since the end of the civil war in 1992, FMLN and ARENA have been the two largest political parties, though the newer GANA has significant support. Some Salvadorans continue to express concern that foreign governments and multinational corporations exert excessive influence over local and national government officials. Increasingly, there are concerns about the growing political influence of gangs. In March and May 2016, *El Faro* released videos that showed ARENA and the FMLN apparently making deals with gang leaders in exchange for votes ahead of the 2014 presidential election.

The current legislature includes no members who identify as representatives of ethnic minorities or indigenous groups, nor do these populations hold high-level government positions. A 2013 statute requires that 30 percent of legislative and municipal candidates be women; currently women hold 32 percent of seats in the Legislative Assembly.

C. Functioning of Government: 9 / 12

Corruption is a serious problem. There has been some progress in corruption investigations and prosecutions against officials from previous administrations, and the current one. However, a majority of crimes continue to go unpunished, and the FMLN has pushed back against investigations of its members. In January 2016, the United Nations announced the establishment of a U.S–funded program designed to assist El Salvador's attorney general with anticorruption investigations.

Nongovernmental organizations (NGOs) agree that while there are advances in the government's application of the Access to Public Information Law, passed in 2011, there is still room for improvement.

CIVIL LIBERTIES: 36 / 60

D. Freedom of Expression and Belief: 12 / 16

The constitution provides for freedom of the press, and while this right is generally respected, harassment and acts of violence following coverage of corruption and gang violence have led reporters to engage in self-censorship. Journalists continue to face intimidation and threats following their reporting on gangs, corruption, police impunity, and negotiations between the gangs and political parties. Nicolás García, a radio journalist who reported on gangs, was murdered in March 2016, reportedly after experiencing harassment from MS-13 members who had insisted that he assist them by providing information on police activity.

Salvadoran media are privately owned, but ownership is confined to a small group of businesspeople that manipulate reporting to protect their interests. ARENA-aligned Telecorporación Salvadoreña dominates the market, controlling three of the five private television networks. Online sites such as *El Faro* and *Contrapunto* provide alternative views and investigative reporting. Access to the internet is unrestricted. In May 2016, the legislature approved a package of amendments to the Telecommunications Act that were developed amid a robust debate that included civil society and private media outlets. Among other things, they included changes to how radio frequencies are allocated that gave greater representation to community media.

The government does not encroach upon religious freedom, and academic freedom is respected. Religious leaders working with former gang members or who have been critical of the government's security strategy have been harassed.

There have been no recent reports of extralegal surveillance or government interference in private discussions or communications. However, given the prevalence of gang activity throughout the country, Salvadorans take precautions when discussing matters of public security outside their homes in order to minimize the risk of retaliation.

E. Associational and Organizational Rights: 8 / 12

Freedoms of assembly and association are generally upheld, and public protests are permitted without obstruction. NGOs for the most part operate freely. Labor unions have long faced obstacles in a legal environment that has traditionally favored business interests, including light penalties for employers who interfere with strikes. The law prohibits strikes in sectors deemed essential, but is vague about the type of work falling within this designation. A number of strikes among both public- and private-sector workers took place in 2016; several involving health-care workers were ruled illegal.

F. Rule of Law: 8 / 16

El Salvador's judicial system remains weak and plagued by corruption and obstructionism. Judges are often affiliated with a particular party, and various parties have complained that some recent investigations and judicial decisions were politically motivated. Justice system officials have frequently been accused of brutality, corruption, and arbitrary arrest.

The government has enlisted the help of the military in its efforts to rein in gang activity. Authorities escalated a crackdown on gangs in 2016, and an increased rate of lethal armed confrontations between suspected gang members and security forces during the year drew concern from rights advocates and others about human rights violations perpetrated by police. In June, the director of the National Civil Police (PNC) announced that 346 suspected gang members had been killed since the start of the year in joint operations carried out by the police and the military, while the attorney general said in April that 50 police officers had been killed in by gang members so far in 2016.

In 2016, the government passed reforms that tightened its control of prisons, in large part to curtail the activities of gang leaders who continue to direct operations while incarcerated. Prisons remain extremely overcrowded, and conditions within can be lethal due to disease, lack of adequate medical care, and the risk of attack by other inmates. In June 2016, the Supreme Court's Constitutional Chamber ruled that prison conditions had deteriorated to the point of being unconstitutional. Prisoners held in pretrial detention account for more than 30 percent of inmates.

El Salvador is one of the most violent countries in the world. In 2016, police recorded 5,278 homicides—a rate of approximately 80 per 100,000 in 2016—compared to 6,656 in 2015. The country since 2011 has been on the U.S. list of "major" drug producing and transit countries.

In 2010, the legislature criminalized gang membership. In 2016, the legislature passed a series of antigang measures, among them one that criminalized negotiations with gangs. The 2006 Special Law against Acts of Terrorism allows street gangs and those who finance them to be treated as terrorists and expanded the use of wiretaps and the freezing of funds. However, despite a high number of such investigations, very few suspected gang members are convicted under the terrorism provisions.

In July 2016, the Supreme Court ruled that a 1993 general amnesty law barring the investigation and prosecution of human rights violations committed during the civil war was unconstitutional; in its ruling it stated that the government had an obligation to investigate war crimes and to provide reparations. The law's repeal will permit prosecutions related to the conflict, during which 75,000 people were tortured, unlawfully killed, or disappeared, according to Amnesty International.

Much of the indigenous population faces poverty, unemployment, and labor discrimination, and challenges with regard to land rights and access to credit. Article 63 of the Constitution, ratified in 2014, recognizes indigenous peoples and pledges to adopt policies that support indigenous cultural identity, values, and spirituality. In August 2016, the legislature approved a new Culture Law that includes a clause on the preservation of indigenous culture and language.

Discrimination based on sexual orientation is widespread, despite being illegal. According to local activists, the state's security apparatus and gangs are responsible for most violence against the LGBT community. Women continue to face questionable trials and high prison sentences for supposed abortions.

G. Personal Autonomy and Individual Rights: 8 / 16

Freedom of travel within El Salvador is complicated by the government's inability to control gang violence. The MS-13 and Barrio 18 gangs control certain neighborhoods, making it dangerous for citizens to travel, work, and live freely. The Global Report on Internal Displacement estimated that at the end of 2015, there were some 289,000 internally displaced persons in El Salvador, with most displacements due to gang violence and criminal activity, and tens of thousands of students have stopped attending school in 2015 due to violence. Businesses and private citizens are regularly subject to extortion, paying an estimated 3 percent of gross domestic product (GDP) to criminal groups.

Women are granted equal rights under the constitution, but are often subject to discrimination. Abortion is punishable by imprisonment even when the life of the mother is at risk or in cases of incest. Some women have been jailed despite credible claims that their pregnancies ended due to miscarriage. The Constitutional Chamber affirmed in 2013 that the "rights of the mother cannot be privileged over the fetus." In September 2016, one of the so-called Las 17—women who served jail time for pregnancy-related crimes—was released, though some of the women still remained in prison at year's end. Violence against women, including domestic violence, is a serious concern. In February 2016, the legislature created new tribunals to preside over cases that involve discrimination or violence against women.

Despite government efforts, El Salvador remains a source, transit, and destination country for the trafficking of women and children. Gangs often force children to sell drugs, and migrants traveling from or through El Salvador can fall victim to sex and labor trafficking rings. Corruption among public officials has stymied efforts to dismantle sex trafficking operations.

Equatorial Guinea

Political Rights Rating: 7
Civil Liberties Rating: 7
Freedom Rating: 7.0
Freedom Status: Not Free
Electoral Democracy: No

Population: 900,000
Capital: Malabo

Ten-Year Ratings Timeline For Year Under Review (Political Rights, Civil Liberties, Status)

Year Under Review	2007	2008	2009	2010	2011	2012	2013	2014	2015	2016
Rating	7,6,NF	7,7,NF	7,7,NF	7,7,NF	7,7,NF	7,7,NF	7,7,NF	7,7,NF	7,7,NF	7,7,NF

Overview: Equatorial Guinea holds regular elections, but the voting is neither free nor fair. The current president, who took power in a military coup that deposed his uncle, has led a highly repressive authoritarian regime since 1979. Oil wealth and political power are concentrated in the hands of the president's family. The government frequently detains the few opposition politicians in the country, and cracks down on any civil society groups that have the slightest appearance of being politically engaged. The government also censors and harasses the country's small number of journalists, including those who work for state media. The judiciary is under presidential control, and security forces engage in torture and other violence with impunity.

KEY DEVELOPMENTS IN 2016:

- President Teodoro Obiang Nguema Mbasogo was awarded a new seven-year term in a tightly controlled presidential election in April. The main opposition party boycotted the vote.
- In June, Obiang appointed one of his sons to serve as the sole vice president, a post that made him the legal successor to the 74-year-old incumbent.

EXECUTIVE SUMMARY

President Obiang was credited with 93.5 percent of the vote in the April 2016 presidential election. As with previous elections, the campaign took place in a highly restrictive environment. In March, the government suspended the activities of the Center for the Study and Initiatives for Development, a prominent civil society group. The main opposition party, Convergence for Social Democracy (CPDS), boycotted the election, and other factions faced police violence, detentions, and torture. One opposition figure who had been barred from running for president, Gabriel Nse Obiang Obono, was put under house arrest during the election, and police used live ammunition against supporters gathered at his home.

One of the president's sons, Teodoro "Teodorín" Nguema Obiang Mangue, was appointed in June to serve as the sole vice president, essentially confirming speculation that he was being groomed to succeed his father. There have been reports, however, that some political elites do not support Teodorín's succession. He had previously held the title of "second vice president," a position that did not exist in the constitution. Teodorín remained the focus of several international money-laundering investigations during the year.

POLITICAL RIGHTS: 1 / 40

A. Electoral Process: 0 / 12

B. Political Pluralism and Participation: 1 / 16

C. Functioning of Government: 0 / 12

CIVIL LIBERTIES: 7 / 60

D. Freedom of Expression and Belief: 4 / 16

E. Associational and Organizational Rights: 0 / 12

F. Rule of Law: 0 / 16

G. Personal Autonomy and Individual Rights: 3 / 16

This country report has been abridged for *Freedom in the World 2017*. For background information on political rights and civil liberties in Equatorial Guinea, see *Freedom in the World 2016*.

Eritrea

Political Rights Rating: 7
Civil Liberties Rating: 7
Freedom Rating: 7.0
Freedom Status: Not Free
Electoral Democracy: No

Population: 5,400,000
Capital: Asmara

Ten-Year Ratings Timeline For Year Under Review (Political Rights, Civil Liberties, Status

Year Under Review	2007	2008	2009	2010	2011	2012	2013	2014	2015	2016
Rating	7,6,NF	7,6,NF	7,7,NF	7,7,NF	7,7,NF	7,7,NF	7,7,NF	7,7,NF	7,7,NF	7,7,NF

Overview: Eritrea is an authoritarian, highly militarized state that has not held a national election since independence in 1993. The ruling People's Front for Democracy and Justice (PFDJ), headed by President Isaias Afwerki, is the sole political party. Rule of law is flouted, arbitrary detention is commonplace, and citizens are required to perform national service, often for their entire working lives. The government shut down all independent media in 2001, and freedoms of assembly and association are not recognized.

KEY DEVELOPMENTS IN 2016:

- In June, the UN Human Rights Council (UNHRC) recommended that the UN Security Council refer the situation in Eritrea to the prosecutor of the International Criminal Court (ICC). The council's commission of inquiry urged the ICC to investigate what it described as systematic and gross human rights violations that may amount to crimes against humanity.
- The Committee to Protect Journalists (CPJ) estimated that 17 journalists remained in prison in Eritrea at the end of the year, the highest number in sub-Saharan Africa.

EXECUTIVE SUMMARY

The June 2016 UNHRC commission of inquiry report on human rights conditions in Eritrea found that the government continued to enforce indefinite military service and was responsible for arbitrary detention, torture, rape, murder, persecution, imprisonment in violation of international law, and enforced disappearances. The report said the systematic nature of these actions suggested that crimes against humanity had been committed. Due to the refusal of the Eritrean government to cooperate with the commission, the report relied on first-hand testimony from 550 Eritreans who had fled the country. Eritrea's government rejected the findings, alleging that the commission had relied on biased testimony.

Despite these findings, the European Union (EU) signaled its readiness for more constructive relations with Eritrea. In January 2016, it signed a 200-million-euro ($222-million) development deal with Asmara. EU officials expressed hope that the deal would lead to improved conditions inside Eritrea and stem the flow of Eritreans fleeing for Europe. However, according to Human Rights Watch, there is little evidence that the Eritrean government had implemented promised reforms such as time limits and pay increases for conscripts. And Eritreans continued to flee to Europe in large numbers: according to the EU, there were more than 33,000 first-time asylum seekers in 2016.

Tensions remained high between Eritrea and Ethiopia, following armed confrontations by rival troops on their contested border in June. Eritrea accused it neighbor of instigating a series of artillery attacks.

POLITICAL RIGHTS: 1 / 40
A. Electoral Process: 0 / 12
B. Political Pluralism and Participation: 0 / 16
C. Functioning of Government: 1 / 12

CIVIL LIBERTIES: 2 / 60
D. Freedom of Expression and Belief: 0 / 16
E. Associational and Organizational Rights: 0 / 12
F. Rule of Law: 0 / 16
G. Personal Autonomy and Individual Rights: 2 / 16

This country report has been abridged for *Freedom in the World 2017*. For background information on political rights and civil liberties in Eritrea, see *Freedom in the World 2016*.

Estonia

Political Rights Rating: 1
Civil Liberties Rating: 1
Freedom Rating: 1.0
Freedom Status: Free
Electoral Democracy: Yes

Population: 1,300,000
Capital: Tallinn

Ten-Year Ratings Timeline For Year Under Review (Political Rights, Civil Liberties, Status)

Year Under Review	2007	2008	2009	2010	2011	2012	2013	2014	2015	2016
Rating	1,1,F	1,1,F	1,1,F	1,1,F	1,1,F	1,1,F	1,1,F	1,1,F	1,1,F	1,1,F

Overview: Robust democratic institutions have taken root in Estonia since it regained independence in 1991. Elections are regarded as free and fair, and political and civil rights are generally respected. However, about 6 percent of the country's population—mostly ethnic Russians—remain stateless and thus may not participate in national elections. Ethnic tensions remain an issue, as does economic inequality.

KEY DEVELOPMENTS IN 2016:

- In October, Kersti Kaljulaid became Estonia's first female president. A nonpartisan figure, the parliament elected her to the largely ceremonial post following five failed attempts to elect other candidates.
- Edgar Savisaar was removed as leader of the Center Party in a development seen as a means of distancing the party from the Russian government. The new Center Party leader, Jüri Ratas, became prime minister of a new coalition government after Prime Minister Taavi Rõivas of the Reform Party lost a confidence vote in November.

- The parliament struggled to adopt legislative changes required to fully implement a law allowing same-sex partnerships that confer most of the same rights as marriage.

EXECUTIVE SUMMARY

Due to infighting and the ideological diversity among its member parties, the broad coalition government headed by Reform Party leader Taavi Rõivas struggled to make timely decisions and approve public-sector reforms in 2016. The indirect presidential election held in 2016 also reflected Estonia's political fragmentation, as the parliament and later, the electoral college, were unable to approve a candidate in five attempts during August and September. A nonpartisan consensus candidate, Kersti Kaljulaid, was finally elected in October, with the support of 81 of 101 members of parliament.

In November, Rõivas lost a parliamentary confidence vote. The Reform Party's former coalition partners, the center-left Social Democratic Party (SDE) and the center-right Union of Pro Patria and Res Publica (IRL), agreed to form a new coalition with the Center Party, which draws much of its support from Estonia's Russian-speaking population. The coalition deal was sealed only after the Center Party replaced longtime party leader Edgar Savisaar—who in 2015 had been suspended from the duties of Tallinn city mayor due to corruption charges—with Jüri Ratas, who became the new prime minister. Ratas subsequently attempted to distance the party from a cooperation agreement with the Russian ruling party, United Russia, that was negotiated by Savisaar in 2004. However, Ratas declined to suspend it completely.

Meanwhile, the Russian occupation of Crimea and the ongoing crisis in Ukraine continued to contribute to widespread tensions in Estonia about the potential for Russian expansionism. In 2016, in reaction to heightened security concerns, Estonia started to build a 3-meter (10-foot) fence along parts of its border with Russia, and to install an accompanying surveillance system.

While residents of Estonia enjoy a high level of economic freedom, inequality is a concern, and about a quarter of the population remains at risk of poverty or social exclusion.

In 2014, Estonia's parliament narrowly approved legislation permitting same-sex partnerships, which confer most of the same rights as marriage. However, due to resistance from its socially conservative members, the parliament has struggled to adopt legislative changes required to fully implement the partnership law.

POLITICAL RIGHTS: 38 / 40

A. Electoral Process: 12 / 12

B. Political Pluralism and Participation: 15 / 16

C. Functioning of Government: 11 / 12

CIVIL LIBERTIES: 56 / 60

D. Freedom of Expression and Belief: 16 / 16

E. Associational and Organizational Rights: 12 / 12

F. Rule of Law: 14 / 16

G. Personal Autonomy and Individual Rights: 14 / 16

This country report has been abridged for *Freedom in the World 2017*. For background information on political rights and civil liberties in Estonia, see *Freedom in the World 2016*.

⬇ Ethiopia

Political Rights Rating: 7
Civil Liberties Rating: 6
Freedom Rating: 6.5
Freedom Status: Not Free
Electoral Democracy: No

Population: 101,700,000
Capital: Addis Ababa

Trend Arrow: Ethiopia received a downward trend arrow due to the security forces' dispro-portionate and often violent response to massive, primarily peaceful antigovernment pro-tests in the Oromia and Amhara regions, as well as an emergency declaration in October that gave the military sweeping powers to crack down on freedoms of expression and association.

Ten-Year Ratings Timeline For Year Under Review (Political Rights, Civil Liberties, Status)

Year Under Review	2007	2008	2009	2010	2011	2012	2013	2014	2015	2016
Rating	5,5,PF	5,5,PF	5,5,PF	6,6,NF	6,6,NF	6,6,NF	6,6,NF	6,6,NF	7,6,NF	7,6,NF

Overview: Ethiopia is an authoritarian state ruled by the Ethiopian People's Revolutionary Democratic Front (EPRDF), which has been in power since 1991 and currently holds every seat in parliament. Multiple flawed elections, including most recently in 2015, showcased the government's willingness to brutally repress the opposition and its supporters, journal-ists, and activists. Muslims and members of the Oromo ethnic group have been specifically singled out. Perceived political opponents are regularly harassed, detained, and prosecuted—often under the guise of Ethiopia's deeply flawed Anti-Terrorism Proclama-tion. The 2009 Charities and Societies Proclamation drastically impeded the activities of civil society groups.

KEY DEVELOPMENTS IN 2016:

- Hundreds of people were killed in a crackdown on antigovernment protests that took place primarily in the Oromia and Amhara regions throughout much of the year. The Ethiopian government admitted to at least 500 deaths since the protests began in November 2015, while some human rights organizations report that there were at least 800.
- Thousands of people have been detained in connection with the protests, and reports of mistreatment, including torture, while in custody are rife.
- In early October, Prime Minister Hailemariam Desalegn announced a six-month state of emergency that gives the government sweeping powers to deploy the mili-tary, further restrict speech and the media, impose curfews and movement restric-tions, and monitor communications.
- Throughout the year, the authorities disrupted internet and mobile phone networks, and temporarily blocked social-media platforms and certain news websites, in an effort to prevent people from organizing and communicating about the protests.

EXECUTIVE SUMMARY

Ethiopia was wracked by protests throughout much of 2016, a result of widespread and growing discontent with ethnic and political marginalization and repressive rule by the

EPRDF. The largely peaceful protests were frequently put down violently by the security forces. The demonstrations had begun over ethnic and land rights in November 2015 in the Oromia region, and intensified in 2016, with significant additional protests in Addis Ababa and the Amhara region.

In January, the government withdrew the contentious Addis Ababa Master Plan, which had been the rallying point for Oromo protesters who alleged that thousands of farmers would be displaced from their ancestral lands to make way for the capital's expansion. However, the announcement did little to staunch larger discontent with the EPRDF, and demonstrations took on broader antigovernment dimensions and appealed to Ethiopians across ethnic lines. The protests were regularly met with excessive force by the police and the military, including the use of live ammunition and tear gas against crowds. Tens of thousands of people were detained in police sweeps, and reports of mistreatment, including beatings and torture while in custody, were widespread. Among those arrested or charged were leaders of the opposition Oromo Federalist Congress, including party chairman Merera Gudina and deputy chairman Bekele Gerba. In October, the government admitted that more than 500 people had been killed in connection with the protests since November 2015, though some rights organizations reported that the true figure is at least 800.

In early October, the government announced a nationwide six-month state of emergency, enacting sweeping powers to deploy the military, restrict speech and the media, impose curfews and movement restrictions, and monitor communications. According to some estimates, nearly 24,000 Ethiopians were detained under the state of emergency, although about 10,000 were released in December. The demonstrations subsided in the wake of the emergency decree, but the government has taken little action to address the grievances of the protesters.

In September, the government pardoned some 700 prisoners in its annual gesture, including 135 Muslims who had been convicted on terrorism charges. However, key religious, ethnic, and political leaders, as well as at least 16 journalists, remained behind bars, and a number of new arrests occurred in 2016; countless other political dissidents are still facing terrorism charges in lengthy and ongoing trials.

Tensions between Ethiopia and Eritrea reached a boiling point in June, when the two militaries skirmished at the northern border town of Tsorona before returning to an uneasy peace.

POLITICAL RIGHTS: 4 / 40

A. Electoral Process: 1 / 12

Ethiopia's bicameral parliament is made up of a 153-seat upper house, the House of Federation, and a 547-seat lower house, the House of People's Representatives. The lower house is filled through popular elections, while the upper chamber is selected by state legislatures; members of both houses serve five-year terms. While the lower house's seats are equal to a fixed number of constituencies, the upper house's seats are adjusted in proportion with the population. The lower house selects the prime minister, who holds most executive power. The president, a largely ceremonial figure, serves up to two six-year terms and is indirectly elected by both houses. Hailemariam has served as prime minister since 2012, and Mulatu Teshome as president since 2013.

As in past contests, Ethiopia's 2015 parliamentary and regional elections were tightly controlled by the ruling coalition, the EPRDF, with reports of voter coercion, intimidation, and barriers to registration. Elections were held on time, and official results were released within a month. The opposition lost their sole seat in parliament, as the EPRDF and its allies took all 547 seats in the lower house. Both the opposition party coalition Medrek and the Semayawi Party, also known as the Blue Party, voiced serious concerns about the ruling party's behavior leading up to and on election day, and ultimately rejected the election's results.

The African Union (AU) was the only international organization to send election observers to Ethiopia's 2015 contest, and it declared elections "peaceful and credible," but noted irregularities including voter coercion and inconsistent poll hours. The European Union (EU) was not invited to observe, with EU officials noting that the EPRDF had rejected recommendations it issued following the 2010 elections.

Following massive nationwide demonstrations, the government announced in October 2016 that it would reform the country's electoral laws to allow for more inclusive governance; the details of the plan are not yet public.

B. Political Pluralism and Participation: 0 / 16

Opponents of the EPRDF find it nearly impossible to operate inside Ethiopia. In the lead-up to the 2015 elections, opposition party members were intimidated, detained, beaten, and arrested. Three opposition members were killed in the aftermath of the elections, though the Ethiopian government denies opposition claims that the killings were politically motivated.

Both the Unity for Democracy and Justice (UDJ) party, formerly represented by one seat in parliament, and the Semayawi Party alleged that the EPRDF used procedural technicalities to block their candidates' registration. Opposition parties also repeatedly questioned the independence of the National Electoral Board of Ethiopia.

Authorities frequently invoke antiterrorism legislation against dissenters. Bekele, the deputy chairman of the opposition Oromo Federalist Congress (OFC) and an advocate of nonviolent protest, was charged under the Anti-Terrorism Proclamation in April after being arrested in late 2015; like many other ethnic Oromos critical of EPRDF authorities, Bekele stands accused of belonging to the banned Oromo Liberation Front (OLF). In December, Merera, the OFC chairperson, was arrested for allegedly meeting with Berhanu Nega, a leader of Ginbot 7—considered a banned terror group by the Ethiopian government—while abroad. Closed court proceedings surrounding an investigation into the matter were ongoing at year's end. In May, Yonatan Tesfaye, the former Semayawi spokesperson who was arrested in 2015 after criticizing the EPRDF on Facebook, was charged with plotting terrorist acts on behalf of the OLF. In April, former Gambella regional governor Okello Akway Ochalla, a Norwegian citizen, was sentenced to nine years in prison under provisions of the Anti-Terrorism Proclamation after being illegally rendered from South Sudan in 2014; Okello had fled Ethiopia and sought asylum in Norway in the wake of the 2003 Gambella massacre, in which government forces had killed hundreds of ethnic Anuak people in Gambella town.

Political parties in Ethiopia are often ethnically based. The country's major ethnic parties are allied with the EPRDF, but have no room to effectively advocate for their constituents. The EPRDF coalition is comprised of four political parties and represents several ethnic groups. The government favors Tigrayan ethnic interests in economic and political matters, and the Tigrayan People's Liberation Front (TPLF) dominates the EPRDF. The 1995 constitution grants the right of secession to ethnically based states, but the government acquired powers in 2003 to intervene in states' affairs on issues of public security. Secessionist movements in Oromia and the Ogaden have largely failed after being put down by the military.

C. Functioning of Government: 3 / 12

Ethiopia's governance institutions are dominated by the EPRDF, which controlled the succession process following Prime Minister Meles Zenawi's death in 2012. The EPRDF continues its tight hold on Ethiopian politics under Hailemariam.

Despite legislative improvements, enforcement of corruption-related laws remains limited in practice, and corruption remains a significant problem. EPRDF officials reportedly receive preferential access to credit, land leases, and jobs. Petty corruption extends to lower-level officials, who, for example, solicit bribes in return for processing documents. In April 2016, Hailemariam put forward a bill authorizing the creation of a federal attorney general, who would handle corruption cases and report directly to the prime minister. It was approved in May, and Getachew Ambaye was appointed to the position soon after, relinquishing his post of justice minister. In December, about 130 people, including government officials, were arrested on corruption charges.

CIVIL LIBERTIES: 8 / 40 (− 3)

D. Freedom of Expression and Belief: 2 / 16 (− 1)

Ethiopia's media are dominated by state-owned broadcasters and government-oriented newspapers. Privately owned papers tend to steer clear of political issues and have low circulation, and journalists operating inside the country practice self-censorship. Defamation is a criminal offense, and a 2008 media law increased fines for defamation and allows prosecutors to pursue cases without complaints from aggrieved parties. The law also allows prosecutors to seize material before publication in the name of national security. A cybercrime law passed in June 2016 criminalized online speech deemed defamatory or pornographic, and outlined penalties for internet service providers that knowingly host such objectionable material. Activists expect that the law will be will be used against EPRDF opponents.

The Ethiopian government maintains the ability to censor critical or opposition websites and monitor dissidents' electronic communications. The state of emergency announced in October 2016 specifically banned people from listening to or watching broadcasts by Ethiopian Satellite Radio and Television (ESAT) and Oromo Media Network (OMN), both of which are based abroad. Localized internet and phone blackouts were regularly reported following mass demonstrations. Social media and messaging applications including WhatsApp and Twitter became largely inaccessible in parts of Oromia starting in March 2016, and sporadic cuts to those and other social media outlets were reported throughout wider areas on numerous occasions later in the year. Mobile internet was unavailable for more than a week immediately following the state of emergency declaration.

According to the Committee to Protect Journalists (CPJ), Ethiopia holds at least 16 journalists behind bars—the second-highest number of jailed journalists in sub-Saharan Africa. Restrictions are particularly tight on journalists perceived to be sympathetic to the ongoing Oromo and Amhara protests and, historically, protests by the Muslim community. In September 2016, Yusuf Getachew, editor of the now-defunct *Ye Muslimoch Guday* (Muslim Affairs) publication who was convicted on terrorism charges in 2015, was pardoned. In March, Yusuf's colleague, Solomon Kebede, received a sentence of several years' imprisonment in connection with coverage of 2012 protests by Ethiopia's Muslim community; however, he was freed in April. Two Bilal radio journalists who had also reported on Muslim protests—Khalid Mohammed and Darsema Sori—were convicted on terrorism charges in December, but had not been sentenced by year's end.

Negere Ethiopia editor in chief Getachew Shiferaw was arrested in late December 2015 and not charged under the Anti-Terrorism Proclamation until May, violating a provision that says authorities can only detain a suspect without charge for four months. His charges were later downgraded from terrorism to inciting violence. Oromo Radio and TV anchor Fikadu Mirkana was arrested in 2015 and charged under the Anti-Terrorism Proclamation, though he was released in April 2016. In May, *De Birhan* blogger Zelalem Workagenehu was sentenced to five years and four months in prison for purportedly plotting to overthrow the government. Two others that he was arrested with were acquitted, though they were immediately re-arrested and detained temporarily. In November, Zone 9 blogger Befeqadu Hailu was arrested; he was released with thousands of others in December after completing indoctrination sessions while incarcerated.

Foreign journalists also experienced harassment in 2016, particularly while reporting on contentious subjects including Ethiopia's drought and ongoing antigovernment demonstrations. Journalists with Bloomberg News and the American Public Broadcasting Service (PBS) and their Ethiopian assistants were detained while reporting outside of the capital in March and August, respectively.

Due to the risks of operating inside the country, many Ethiopian journalists work in exile. According to Human Rights Watch (HRW), since 2010 the Ethiopian government has developed a robust and sophisticated internet and mobile framework to monitor journalists and opposition groups, block access to unwanted websites or critical television and radio programs, and collect evidence for prosecutions in politically motivated trials.

Musicians perceived to be sympathetic to protesters—particularly Oromo musicians—have experienced targeted harassment and censorship. In late 2015, Oromo singer Hawi Tezera was temporarily detained, during which time she was reportedly tortured, following the release of a song considered antigovernment.

The constitution guarantees religious freedom, but the government has increasingly harassed the Muslim community, which comprises about 34 percent of the population. (About 44 percent of people in Ethiopia are Orthodox Christian, while about 19 percent are Protestant.) In 2015, 18 Muslim activists who were arrested following 2012 protests over alleged government involvement in the Muslim community's affairs were sentenced to prison terms of between 7 and 22 years on terrorism charges. The activists maintain their innocence. In September, 135 Muslims who had been convicted of crimes under the Anti-Terrorism Proclamation—including Yusuf of *Ye Muslimoch Guday* but excluding many of the protest leaders—were among those released in a mass pardon marking the Ethiopian New Year holiday. In December, 20 Ethiopian Muslims were found guilty of terrorism charges in connection with attempts to win the release of jailed members of the Ethiopian Muslim Arbitration Committee—a group of religious leaders who had attempted to negotiate with the government on behalf of the Muslim community.

Academic freedom is often restricted in Ethiopia. The government has accused universities of being pro-opposition and prohibits political activities on campuses. There are reports of students being pressured into joining the EPRDF in order to secure employment or places at universities; professors are similarly pressured in order to ensure favorable positions or promotions. The Ministry of Education closely monitors and regulates official curricula, and the research, speech, and assembly of both professors and students are frequently restricted.

Students have consistently been at the forefront of antigovernment protests and as a result make up a significant proportion of those who have been arrested, beaten, and killed in the unrest. Security officials have forcibly entered Ethiopian schools and universities to make arrests, sometimes intimidating or detaining minors who were involved or perceived to have been involved in the unrest; schools in the affected regions have been closed at times due to the ongoing crisis. In October 2016, outspoken blogger and Ambo University lecturer Seyoum Teshome was arrested on unclear charges, and held for two months before being released.

The presence of the EPRDF at all levels of society—directly and, increasingly, electronically—inhibits free private discussion. The EPRDF maintains a network of paid informants, and opposition politicians have accused the government of tapping their phones or monitoring their electronic communications. On October 4, Zone 9 blogger Natnael Feleke was arrested with two friends after criticizing the government in a public restaurant. They were released days later.

E. Associational and Organizational Rights: 0 / 12

Freedoms of assembly and association are guaranteed by the constitution but limited in practice. Organizers of large public meetings must request permission from the authorities 48 hours in advance. Applications by opposition groups are routinely denied and, in cases when approved, organizers are subject to government meddling to move dates or locations. The October 2016 state of emergency banned all "assembly or protest" without prior approval.

Demonstrations erupted in late 2015 after land was cleared for an investment project linked to the controversial Addis Ababa Master Plan, which envisioned the expansion of the capital into parts of Oromia State. Protests quickly spread throughout the region and continued throughout 2016, even as the government abandoned the Addis Ababa plan in January. Security forces responded to the demonstrations with overwhelming force, including by firing tear gas and live ammunition into crowds. By mid-year, demonstrations had spread to Amhara Region. During a particularly bloody weekend in August, at least 100 people were killed across Amhara and Oromia, including at least 30 people in the northern town of Bahir Dar. In October, a stampede reportedly started by security forces' firing of tear gas into a crowd at the Irreecha religious festival in Oromia killed at least 55 people. Throughout the year, some protesters were responsible for property damage and looting, including the targeting of at least 11 mostly foreign-owned factories and a tourist lodge in the wake of the Irreecha incident.

Tens of thousands have been arrested in connection with the protests, many of whom were held for months without charge. In October, 2,000 people were released from detention, and in December, another 9,800 were released, though the government has indicated that some 2,500 people will be tried for their role in the unrest.

In March, 20 Addis Ababa University students were arrested for an unauthorized protest in front of the American Embassy and 11 were later convicted under Ethiopia's criminal code, though they were released for time served.

The 2009 Charities and Societies Proclamation restricts the activities of foreign nongovernmental organizations (NGOs) by prohibiting work on political and human rights issues. Foreign NGOs are defined as groups receiving more than 10 percent of their funding from abroad. The law also limits the amount of money any NGO can spend on "administration," a controversial category that has included activities such as teacher or health-worker training. NGOs have struggled to maintain operations as a result of the law.

Trade unions rights are tightly restricted. Neither civil servants nor teachers have collective bargaining rights. All unions must be registered, and the government retains the authority to cancel registration. Two-thirds of union members belong to organizations affiliated with the Confederation of Ethiopian Trade Unions, which is under government influence.

Independent unions face harassment, and trade union leaders are regularly imprisoned. There has not been a legal strike since 1993.

F. Rule of Law: 2 / 16 (− 1)

The judiciary is officially independent, but its judgments rarely deviate from government policy. The 2009 antiterrorism law gives great discretion to security forces, allowing the detention of suspects for up to four months without charge. The October 2016 announcement of a six-month state of emergency further expands these powers, including by allowing lengthy detentions without charge and the nationwide deployment of the military.

Hundreds of people were killed in the crackdown on antigovernment protests that took place primarily in the Oromia and Amhara regions throughout much of the year. The Ethiopian government admitted to at least 500 deaths since the protests began in November 2015, while some human rights organizations reported that there were at least 800. A June 2016 report by the government-run Ethiopian Human Rights Commission found that security forces had used "proportional" force in responding to protests in Oromia, but had used "excessive" force against participants in a November 2015 protest in Amhara involving the Qimant people.

Conditions in Ethiopia's prisons are harsh, and detainees frequently report abuse, including regular reports of torture, especially in Ethiopia's notorious Maekelawi and Qilinto prisons. CPJ and Ethiopian sources reported that former *Feteh* editor Temesgen Desalegn, who was convicted on defamation charges in 2014 and sentenced to three years in prison, has been denied medical care and family visits. In January 2016 and again in July, Bekele and other Oromo political prisoners went on a hunger strike to protest their treatment in prison, including allegations that they were denied medical attention and access to legal counsel and their families. In September, a massive fire broke out at Qilinto prison, where a number of prominent political prisoners were being held. Witnesses reported gunfire after the fire broke out, and at least 23 inmates were killed in the incident. In November, a court charged 38 inmates with starting the fire.

The federal government generally has strong control and direction over the military, though forces such as the Liyu Police in Somali Region sometimes operate independently.

Repression of the Oromo and ethnic Somalis, and government attempts to co-opt their political parties into EPRDF allies, have fueled nationalism in the Oromia and Ogaden regions. Persistent claims that government troops in the Ogaden have committed war crimes are difficult to verify, as independent media are barred from the region.

Same-sex sexual activity is prohibited by law and punishable by up to 15 years' imprisonment.

G. Personal Autonomy and Individual Rights: 4 / 16 (− 1)

While Ethiopia's constitution establishes freedom of movement, it has been increasingly restricted through curfews and road closures in Oromia and Amhara Regions, where mass demonstrations have taken place. Protesters and political activists released from detention are often freed on the condition that they regularly check in with local police. Also under the state of emergency, refugees are forbidden to leave camps without "necessary authorization," and foreign diplomats were temporarily banned from traveling more than 40 kilometers (25 miles) outside of Addis Ababa. Free movement through the Somali Region remains limited. Under the state of emergency, businesses are prohibited from closing, as commerce strikes were initially used as a form of protest.

Private business opportunities are limited by rigid state control of economic life and the prevalence of state-owned enterprises. All land must be leased from the state. The government has evicted indigenous groups from various areas to make way for projects such as hydroelectric dams. It has also leased large tracts of land to foreign governments and investors for agricultural development in opaque deals that have displaced thousands of Ethiopians. Up to 70,000 people have been forced to move from the western Gambella region, although the government denies that the resettlement plans are connected to land investments. At least four people, including police officers, were killed in June 2016 during a clash between residents of a neighborhood of more than 30,000 houses in Addis Ababa, and police who entered the sector to demolish homes, which authorities said had been constructed illegally. Evictions have taken place in Lower Omo Valley, where government-run sugar plantations and hydroelectric dams have put thousands of pastoralists at risk by diverting their water supplies. Activists report that the December 2016 inauguration of the Gibe III dam on the Omo River will affect hundreds of thousands of farmers and fishers living downstream. Journalists and international organizations have persistently alleged that the government withholds development assistance from villages perceived as being unfriendly to the ruling party. Displacement resulting from the appropriation of land has driven much of the resentment behind recent antigovernment protests, and demonstrators have attacked foreign businesses perceived to be the recipients of unfair distribution of land by the Ethiopian government.

Women hold nearly 39 percent of seats in the lower house, 32 percent in the upper house, and three ministerial posts. Legislation protects women's rights, but these rights are routinely violated in practice. Enforcement of the law against rape and domestic abuse is patchy, and cases routinely stall in the courts. Female genital mutilation and forced child marriage are technically illegal, though there has been little effort to prosecute perpetrators. In 2015, Ethiopia enacted the Proclamation to Provide for the Prevention and Suppression of Trafficking in Persons and Smuggling of Migrants, which criminalizes human trafficking and enacts stricter penalties for child trafficking. Trafficking convictions have increased in recent years, though the U.S. government continues to urge its Ethiopian counterparts to more aggressively pursue trafficking cases. Many children continue to work in dangerous sectors and lack access to basic education and services.

Fiji

Political Rights Rating: 3
Civil Liberties Rating: 4 ↓
Freedom Rating: 3.5
Freedom Status: Partly Free
Electoral Democracy: Yes

Population: 900,000
Capital: Suva

Ratings Change: Fiji's civil liberties rating declined from 3 to 4 due to the increasing influence of the military in the country's police force, the prevalence of abuse by police and military personnel of prisoners and people accused of crimes, and the temporary detention of opposition members and others who took part in a public forum on the controversial 2013 constitution.

Ten-Year Ratings Timeline For Year Under Review (Political Rights, Civil Liberties, Status)

Year Under Review	2007	2008	2009	2010	2011	2012	2013	2014	2015	2016
Rating	6,4,PF	6,4,PF	6,4,PF	6,4,PF	6,4,PF	6,4,PF	6,4,PF	3,4,PF	3,3,PF	3,4,PF

Overview: The repressive climate that followed a 2006 coup has eased since democratic elections were held in 2014. However, the ruling party frequently interferes with opposition activities, the judiciary is subject to political influence, and military and police brutality is a significant problem.

KEY DEVELOPMENTS IN 2016:
- In September, police arrested several opposition leaders in connection with their participation in a public forum at which participants discussed the controversial 2013 constitution.
- Two opposition lawmakers were suspended from the parliament during the year, bringing the number of suspended opposition lawmakers to three.
- The appointment of former military figures to head the police force and prison system indicated a growing military influence in the criminal justice system.

EXECUTIVE SUMMARY

Fiji's democratic progress stalled in 2016, as the government interfered with the activities of the political opposition and the military gained influence in the criminal justice system.

In September, five opposition leaders were arrested in connection with their participation in a public discussion on the 2013 constitution; several organizers and other participants were also detained. While they were eventually released without charge, the events indicated the government's willingness to suppress public scrutiny of Fiji's controversial legal framework. The 2013 constitution was drawn up by the interim government of J. V. (Frank) Bainimarama (who is the current prime minister) after it had rejected a draft developed by an independent committee. The charter was adopted by decree, and cannot be amended without the support of both 75 percent of lawmakers, and a referendum backed by at least 75 percent of registered voters.

Bainimarama's Fiji First party won a parliamentary majority in 2014 elections, and since then has frequently pushed through bills and budgets with minimal input from the opposition. In June and September 2016, the parliament suspended two opposition lawmakers, the first for making derogatory comments aimed at the education minister, and the second for allegedly inciting racial antagonism towards the country's Muslim minority. The suspensions, which drew a rebuke from the Inter-Parliamentary Union, brought the total number of opposition legislators barred from the parliament to three. In May, the chair of the Public Accounts Committee, an opposition figure, was removed and replaced with a government ally.

Separately, municipal councils continue to be run by government-appointed administrators. The councils were dissolved in 2009, and subsequent pledges to hold municipal elections have yet to be realized.

Military and police brutality is a significant problem, with several serious incidents reported in 2016. In February, the High Court found five police officers and a soldier guilty of rape and sexual assault in a case involving a man who had died while in police custody in 2014. Military influence within the criminal justice system is growing. A former military officer was appointed the country's new police commissioner in May. In March, Francis Kean—a former Navy commander who was convicted of manslaughter in 2006, and who is also Prime Minister Bainimarama's brother-in-law—became the commissioner of the Fiji Corrections Service.

The government eased some restrictive policies in 2016. In October, bans on several foreign journalists were removed. A mission by the International Labor Organization (ILO) in January 2016 facilitated some compromises between the government and the country's unions, including the reinstatement of the automatic deduction of union dues from employee paychecks, and of employment tribunals to handle grievances.

POLITICAL RIGHTS: 25 / 40 (–2)

A. Electoral Process: 8 / 12 (− 1)

B. Political Pluralism and Participation: 10 / 16 (− 1)

C. Functioning of Government: 7 / 12

CIVIL LIBERTIES: 34 / 60 (− 1)

D. Freedom of Expression and Belief: 12 / 16 (+ 1)

E. Associational and Organizational Rights: 5 / 12

F. Rule of Law: 7 / 16 (− 2)

G. Personal Autonomy and Individual Rights: 10 / 16

This country report has been abridged for *Freedom in the World 2017.* For background information on political rights and civil liberties in Fiji, see *Freedom in the World 2016.*

Finland

Political Rights Rating: 1
Civil Liberties Rating: 1
Freedom Rating: 1.0
Freedom Status: Free
Electoral Democracy: Yes

Population: 5,500,000
Capital: Helsinki

Ten-Year Ratings Timeline For Year Under Review (Political Rights, Civil Liberties, Status)

Year Under Review	2007	2008	2009	2010	2011	2012	2013	2014	2 015	2016
Rating	1,1,F	1,1,F	1,1,F	1,1,F	1,1,F	1,1,F	1,1,F	1,1,F	1,1,F	1,1,F

Overview: Finland's parliamentary system features free and fair elections and robust multiparty competition. Corruption is not a significant problem, and freedoms of speech, religion, and association are respected. The judiciary is independent under the constitution and in practice. Women enjoy equal rights, as do citizens from ethnic minority groups, though harassment and hate speech aimed at minority groups do occur.

KEY DEVELOPMENTS IN 2016:

- In February, the parliament passed a law allowing same-sex marriage.
- In July, after a year of negotiations between trade unions, employer organizations, and government officials, the participants agreed to cut worker benefits and temporarily freeze wages in a bid to improve the country's economic competitiveness.

- A new law that took effect in September made the country's asylum policies more restrictive, for instance by reducing the time limit for appealing rejected applications.
- A regional politician with the right-wing Finns Party was removed from her leadership position in April and fined in December for writing anti-Muslim social media posts.

EXECUTIVE SUMMARY

Finland received only about 5,000 asylum applications in 2016, down from some 33,000 in 2015. As the number of new asylum seekers decreased, so did related hate crimes. Nevertheless, the government took some steps to tighten asylum laws during the year. Among other changes, the president signed legislation in August, to take effect in September, that reduced the time for appeals of rejected applications and limited the circumstances in which state-funded legal aid is provided.

In April, the first vice chair of the regional government in Pirkanmaa, Terhi Kiemunki of the Finns Party, was removed from her post over her anti-Muslim comments on Facebook. She requested a police investigation to clear her name, but in December she was found guilty of incitement against an ethnic group and ordered to pay a 450 ($500) fine. Amid other controversial posts by Finns Party lawmakers, party chairman Timo Soini in July urged members to think twice before making comments on social media. In November, the chair of the Finns Party Youth was charged with hate speech against Muslims; a trial was expected in early 2017.

The national broadcaster Yle participated in reporting in April on the so-called Panama Papers, a trove of leaked documents from a Panama-based law firm that revealed the widespread use of shell companies to avoid taxes and launder money. Several Finnish lawyers and businessmen were implicated. The Finnish tax authorities demanded that Yle hand over the leaked material, sparking a debate on press freedom and the confidentiality of journalistic sources. Yle refused to hand over the documents. Separately, in November, Prime Minister Juha Sipila faced criticism for a series of e-mail messages in which he appeared to pressure Yle reporters covering an alleged conflict of interest involving a company owned by his relatives.

POLITICAL RIGHTS: 40 / 40
A. Electoral Process: 12 / 12
B. Political Pluralism and Participation: 16 / 16
C. Functioning of Government: 12 / 12

CIVIL LIBERTIES: 60 / 60
D. Freedom of Expression and Belief: 16 / 16
E. Associational and Organizational Rights: 12 / 12
F. Rule of Law: 16 / 16
G. Personal Autonomy and Individual Rights: 16 / 16

This country report has been abridged for *Freedom in the World 2017*. For background information on political rights and civil liberties in Finland, see *Freedom in the World 2016*.

France

Political Rights Rating: 1
Civil Liberties Rating: 2 ↓
Freedom Rating: 1.5 ↓
Freedom Status: Free
Electoral Democracy: Yes

Population: 64,600,000
Capital: Paris

Ratings Change: France's civil liberties rating declined from 1 to 2 due to infringements on personal autonomy, particularly controls on dress and religious symbols, that disproportionately focus on women, following earlier deterioration related to terrorist attacks and aggressive counterterrorism measures.

Ten-Year Ratings Timeline For Year Under Review (Political Rights, Civil Liberties, Status)

Year Under Review	2007	2008	2009	2010	2011	2012	2013	2014	2015	2016
Rating	1,1,F	1,1,F	1,1,F	1,1,F	1,1,F	1,1,F	1,1,F	1,1,F	1,1,F	1,2,F

Overview: The French political system features vibrant democratic processes and generally strong protections for civil liberties and political rights. However, due to a number of deadly terrorist attacks in recent years, the government has been increasingly willing to curtail constitutional protections and empower law enforcement to act in ways that impinge on personal freedoms. Anti-Muslim and anti-immigrant sentiments have also become features of the political community.

KEY DEVELOPMENTS IN 2016:

- Multiple incidents of terrorist violence, including a July attack in Nice that killed 86 people, led to repeated extensions of a state of emergency, in place since November 2015.
- Beginning in late July, around 30 municipal governments issued short-term bans on the burkini, a full-body swimsuit, citing fears about the garment's links to Islamist extremism; the bans, as well as continuing concerns about terrorism, fueled public debate about French policies toward immigration and Islam.
- In November, the Republican Party conducted its first primary campaign ever, and voters selected former prime minister François Fillon to be the party's nominee for president in the 2017 election.

EXECUTIVE SUMMARY

Several terrorist attacks took place in France in 2016, and security concerns continued to influence political discussions and decisions. In June, a man claiming allegiance to the Islamic State (IS) killed a police commander and his wife in Magnanville. In July, a man drove a truck through a crowd that had gathered for a Bastille Day celebration in Nice, killing 86 people and injuring more than 300. Although IS claimed responsibility for the attack, police had not uncovered definitive evidence of operational links between the driver and the terrorist group at year's end. Also in July, two men claiming affiliation with IS stormed a Catholic church in Normandy during a mass, taking multiple hostages before brutally murdering the priest.

These and other attacks led the government to repeatedly extend France's state of emergency, first declared in November 2015 after a string of coordinated attacks in Paris. Local and international rights groups have criticized the extensions, voicing concerns with the French authorities' power to conduct raids, make arrests, block websites, and restrict free expression with little judicial oversight under the state of emergency. As part of its international campaign against terrorism, France continued its participation in a military coalition against IS, conducting air strikes and ground operations against targets in Iraq and Syria.

Political parties began laying the groundwork for the 2017 presidential election. Marine Le Pen, leader of the far-right National Front (FN) and a strong proponent of anti-immigration and Euroskeptic views, was widely expected to perform strongly in the vote. In December, incumbent president François Hollande announced he would not seek reelection, creating an open contest for the Socialist Party (PS) nomination. Against a backdrop of terrorist attacks, continuing migration flows from the Middle East and North Africa, and preparations for the election, public discussion was dominated by concerns about security, religion, and immigration during the year. In July and August, the mayors of more than two dozen towns issued short-term bans on the burkini based on security concerns, citing fears about the garment's links to Islamist extremism. In August, the Council of State, the highest administrative court in the country, ruled that the bans violate fundamental freedoms.

POLITICAL RIGHTS: 38 / 40

A. Electoral Process: 12 / 12

The French president and members of the lower house of Parliament, the 577-seat National Assembly, are elected to five-year terms. The upper house, the 348-seat Senate, is an indirectly elected body whose members serve six-year terms. The prime minister is appointed by the president, who is elected by direct, universal suffrage in a two-round system. In the 2012 presidential election, Hollande—a PS candidate—won the first round with 28.6 percent of the vote, beating incumbent Nicolas Sarkozy of the Union for a Popular Movement (UMP), who took 27.2 percent. Le Pen, leading the FN, placed third with 17.9 percent of the vote. Hollande won the election in the runoff, taking 51.6 percent of the vote to Sarkozy's 48.4 percent, and became France's first Socialist president since François Mitterrand left office in 1995.

In 2012, the center-left PS and its allies won an absolute majority of 314 seats in the National Assembly, while the UMP and its allies took 229 seats. In the 2014 Senate elections, the PS lost its majority to the UMP and the center-right Union of Democrats and Independents (UDI), while the FN won two seats—its first ever in the upper chamber.

In regional elections held in 2015, the FN led the first round of voting in 6 of the 13 regions at stake. The PS then withdrew from some races to encourage its supporters to vote for the Republicans—the successor of the UMP, which changed its name in May—in order to block the FN, which failed to win any regions in the second round.

B. Political Pluralism and Participation: 15 / 16

Parties organize and compete on a free and fair basis. The PS and the Republicans are the largest parties. Since taking over the FN in 2011, Le Pen has sought to normalize the party by toning down its more extreme rhetoric, but its politics remain anchored in anti-immigration, anti-Islam and anti–European Union (EU) sentiments.

In November 2016, the Republicans organized a primary to choose their candidate for the 2017 presidential election. Fillon beat Bordeaux mayor and former prime minister Alain

Juppé decisively in the second round, after Sarkozy was eliminated in the first round. The PS scheduled its primary for January 2017.

In August, Emanuel Macron announced his resignation from the position of economy minister in order to mount a bid for the presidential election. Macron ran under the banner of his newly established political party, En Marche! (Forward!).

The 2012 parliamentary elections yielded a record of eight new members from immigrant backgrounds. Nevertheless, they comprised less than 2 percent of the National Assembly, prompting renewed calls from minority rights groups for a law ensuring ethnic diversity in politics.

C. Functioning of Government: 11 / 12

A number of corruption cases linked to Sarkozy's presidency continued in 2016. In February, prosecutors brought charges against him for exceeding the legal spending limits on his 2012 reelection bid. The charges alleged that Sarkozy colluded with a public relations firm, Bygmalion, to falsify invoices that hid the extent of the company's spending on his campaign. Thirteen others, including Bygmalion executives and former Sarkozy aides, were also charged in connection to the case. In September, prosecutors recommended that the charges proceed to a full trial, though a final decision was not reached by year's end. Separately, in December, Christine Lagarde, a managing director at the International Monetary Fund and France's finance minister under Sarkozy, was convicted of negligence in the use of public funds. However, the court did not impose a sentence, leaving Lagarde without a penalty or a criminal record.

France was ranked 23 out of 176 countries and territories surveyed in Transparency International's 2016 Corruption Perceptions Index. In December 2016, Transparency France released a positive assessment of the country's anticorruption efforts under Hollande, including the establishment of new anticorruption bodies and a special prosecutor's office focusing on tax evasion. Many of these efforts were inaugurated following revelations in 2013 that France's budget minister, Jérôme Cahuzac, had engaged in tax fraud. He was convicted and sentenced to three years in prison in December 2016.

French law provides for public access to government information. France ranked 7 out of 102 countries assessed in the 2015 Open Budget Index, indicating very high levels of budgetary transparency and financial disclosure.

CIVIL LIBERTIES: 52 / 60 (− 1)

D. Freedom of Expression and Belief: 14 / 16

The media operate freely and represent a wide range of political opinions. Though a law from 1881 forbids "offending" various personages, including the president and foreign heads of state, the press is lively and critical in practice.

A 2014 counterterrorism law empowered authorities to block websites and bring criminal charges for incitement or glorification of terrorism, with penalties reaching seven years in prison. France's state-run privacy commission reported that between November 2015 and April 2016, French authorities used the law to take down more than 1,000 pieces of content from the internet, delist nearly 400 web addresses from search results, and block 68 websites. By the end of 2016, France had blocked more than 800 websites and delisted nearly 2,000 from search results, mostly over alleged support for terrorism.

The constitution protects freedom of religion. Strong antidefamation laws prohibit religiously motivated attacks, and Holocaust denial is illegal. France maintains the policy of *laïcité,* whereby religion and state affairs are strictly separated, though the government maintains relationships with organizations representing the country's three major religions (Christianity, Islam, and Judaism). France's relationship with its Muslim community has grown increasingly fraught in the wake of terrorist attacks in 2015 and 2016. Islamophobic rhetoric from prominent politicians on both the left and right is not uncommon. Domestic monitors recorded numerous offenses against Muslims in 2016. These included more than 400 cases of discrimination, nearly 40 physical assaults, 25 attacks on mosques and other religious buildings, and nearly 100 instances of verbal harassment. However, the Collective Against Islamophobia in France, a domestic organization, noted that the total number of recorded incidents was lower in 2016 than in previous years.

There are no restrictions on academic freedom in France. Private discussion is open and vibrant. However, in 2015, parliament approved a new law granting the government expanded powers to conduct domestic surveillance, including bulk collection of communications data as well as wider authority to use hidden cameras and microphones. The law authorizes the use of sophisticated intelligence technology to intercept all telephone conversations, text messages, and emails in targeted areas. The law only prescribes limited judicial oversight of these activities.

E. Associational and Organizational Rights: 11 / 12

Freedoms of assembly and association are normally respected, and nongovernmental organizations (NGOs) can generally operate freely. However, in September 2016, the FN mayor of the town of Hayange ordered the local branch of the major NGO Secours Populaire Français (French Popular Relief) to vacate its offices for allegedly engaging in pro-immigrant political activities. The group refused and continued to operate despite the eviction order, prompting the town to cut off utilities to the premises. The standoff had not been resolved at year's end.

Trade unions are strong despite declining membership and a lack of legal protections relative to more corporatist European countries. Beginning in March, thousands protested at recurrent demonstrations against changes to the country's labor code, which would have reduced protections for workers. Violent clashes with police led to a number of individuals receiving serious injuries, including a student who lost an eye in April and a man who was put into a coma in May. Only 48 cases of misconduct were opened against officers in subsequent months, a figure that watchdogs judged to be too low given the scale of the police response.

F. Rule of Law: 13 / 16

France has an independent judiciary, and the rule of law generally prevails in court proceedings. However, the state of emergency imposed after the November 2015 attacks in Paris has allowed authorities to take extraordinary measures, including conducting raids, detentions, and house arrests of suspects without warrants or judicial oversight. The order was extended multiple times in 2016. In December, parliament voted to keep it in place until the conclusion of the 2017 presidential election. According to Amnesty International, by the end of 2016, authorities had conducted more than 4,000 raids, upwards of 600 house arrests, and nearly 1,700 identity checks or car searches under the state of emergency. The report noted that these efforts have produced only 20 judicial investigations of terrorism-related crimes, leading many to criticize the maneuvers as too expansive.

In May 2016, the UN Committee against Torture criticized France over its use of excessive force during police operations conducted under the state of emergency. It also condemned the difficulty victims encountered in filing complaints, the failure to collect statistical data related to excessive force complaints, and inadequate consequences for officers who commit such actions.

Migrants and refugees in France continue to suffer both from societal discrimination and abuse by government officials. In October, authorities dismantled the makeshift migrant camp at Calais, which had grown notorious for its squalid conditions. The camp's residents—who by some estimates numbered as high as 9,000—were transported to alternative shelters. Surging immigration and refugee flows from Muslim-majority countries have exacerbated anti-Muslim sentiment, vandalism of mosques, verbal assaults, and xenophobic graffiti.

French law forbids the categorization of people according to ethnic origin, and no official statistics are collected on ethnicity. Discrimination based on sexual orientation is prohibited by law. New legislation, passed in October 2016, scrapped the requirement that transgender people undergo sterilization in order to legally change their gender.

G. Personal Autonomy and Individual Rights: 14 / 16 (− 1)

There are normally no restrictions on freedom of travel or choice of residence or employment in France, but a number of exceptions have been made in recent years. A 2014 counterterrorism law imposed a travel ban on anyone suspected of planning to become a jihadist; the passports of such individuals can be confiscated for a period of six months to two years. Separately, under the state of emergency still in force, authorities are empowered to place individuals under house arrest, require them to report to police stations, and confiscate their passports without prior judicial authorization. Hundreds of individuals have been confined to house arrest since the order was first implemented.

Private businesses are free to operate. In 2015, the government pushed through measures to liberalize multiple sectors of the economy; these measures aim to ease entry to certain professions, simplify the firing of employees, and allow businesses to open on Sundays in areas frequented by tourists. In August 2016, major reforms to the labor code were enacted, further shifting power over hiring, firing, and working conditions to businesses and away from labor.

Gender equality is protected in France, and constitutional reforms in 2008 institutionalized economic and social equality. After the 2012 elections, women held a record 27 percent of seats in the National Assembly. France legalized same-sex marriage in 2013.

A number of French laws on dress disproportionately affect women. A 2004 law bans "ostentatious" religious symbols in schools; Muslim girls' headscarves were widely seen as the main target of this law. In July 2016, more than 30 municipalities instituted short-term bans on burkinis, a type of full-body swimwear used by some Muslim women. In August, the country's highest administrative court struck down one town's ban on constitutional grounds. However, some mayors have refused to abide by the ruling, claiming that the decision does not apply to towns that were not parties in the suit.

Civil rights groups and scholars have reported evidence of labor market discrimination against women, French Muslims, immigrants of North African decent, and others outside the traditional elite. While France's government takes actions against human trafficking, the problem persists in the commercial sex trade; some victims are also forced into domestic labor.

Gabon

Political Rights Rating: 6
Civil Liberties Rating: 5
Freedom Rating: 5.5
Freedom Status: Not Free
Electoral Democracy: No

Population: 1,800,000
Capital: Libreville

Ten-Year Ratings Timeline For Year Under Review (Political Rights, Civil Liberties, Status)

Year Under Review	2007	2008	2009	2010	2011	2012	2013	2014	2015	2016
Rating	6,4,PF	6,4,PF	6,5,NF	6,5,NF	6,5,NF	6,5,NF	6,5,NF	6,5,NF	6,5,NF	6,5,NF

Overview: Although Gabon holds regular elections, President Ali Bongo Ondimba maintains political dominance through a pervasive patronage system and restrictions on dissent, having succeeded his father when he died after more than 40 years in power in 2009. The media carry some criticism of the government, but self-censorship is common, especially regarding the president. The executive branch effectively controls the judiciary, and prisoners suffer from harsh conditions and severe overcrowding. Other significant problems include discrimination against and exploitation of African immigrants and migrant workers, marginalization of indigenous peoples, and legal and de facto inequality for women.

KEY DEVELOPMENTS IN 2016:
- In August, election officials declared that Bongo had won a second seven-year term as president, defeating challenger Jean Ping, who was supported by a coalition of opposition parties and prominent figures who had left the ruling party.
- Violent protests erupted after the results were announced, the parliament building was set on fire, and security forces launched a crackdown to suppress dissent and deter assemblies.
- Amid the protests, the government blocked access to the internet and social media applications for several days, then maintained partial restrictions through late September.

EXECUTIVE SUMMARY

Gabon's August 2016 presidential election pitted incumbent president Bongo against Jean Ping of the opposition Union of Forces for Change. Ping, a diplomat who had long served as foreign minister under Bongo's late father, won the support of a number of opposition factions and benefited from major defections among the old guard of the ruling Gabonese Democratic Party (PDG), including Guy Nzouba-Ndama, who resigned as head of the National Assembly in March.

A few days after the voting, the national electoral commission declared Bongo the winner with 49.8 percent of the vote, compared with Ping's 48.2 percent. In the province of Haut-Ogooué, a Bongo family stronghold, turnout was reported at a dubious 99.9 percent, with 95 percent backing the incumbent, even though turnout in the rest of the country was just 54 percent. Both Ping and observers from the European Union called for a recount, and the results were sent to the Constitutional Court for review.

Meanwhile, violent protests erupted, the parliament building was set on fire, and security forces stormed Ping's headquarters. Estimates of the death toll from the unrest ranged from fewer than 10 to more than 50, and hundreds of others were arrested, though most were later released or freed pending trial. The government also shut down access to the internet on the night the results were announced, and it remained inaccessible for five days, after which it was restored for 12 hours a day and social media sites remained blocked. Full access was not restored until the end of September.

The Constitutional Court, which had rebuffed an observation mission from the African Union during its deliberations, confirmed and strengthened Bongo's victory, altering the result slightly to 50.66 percent for Bongo and 47.24 percent for Ping. The head of the court, Marie-Madeleine Mborantsuo, was reportedly the longtime mistress of Bongo's father. Bongo was later sworn in for his new term amid a heavy military presence in the capital.

POLITICAL RIGHTS: 8 / 40 (− 1)

A. Electoral Process: 2 / 12

B. Political Pluralism and Participation: 3 / 16 (− 1)

C. Functioning of Government: 3 / 12

CIVIL LIBERTIES: 24 / 60 (− 1)

D. Freedom of Expression and Belief: 9 / 16 (− 1)

E. Associational and Organizational Rights: 4 / 12

F. Rule of Law: 6 / 16

G. Personal Autonomy and Individual Rights: 5 / 16

This country report has been abridged for *Freedom in the World 2017*. For background information on political rights and civil liberties in Gabon, see *Freedom in the World 2016*.

The Gambia

Political Rights Rating: 6 ↑
Civil Liberties Rating: 6
Freedom Rating: 6.0
Freedom Status: Not Free
Electoral Democracy: No

Population: 2,100,000
Capital: Banjul

Ratings Change: The Gambia's political rights rating improved from 7 to 6 due to opposition candidate Adama Barrow's victory in the December 2016 presidential election, though the incumbent, Yahya Jammeh, was refusing to step down as of year's end.

Ten-Year Ratings Timeline For Year Under Review (Political Rights, Civil Liberties, Status)

Year Under Review	2007	2008	2009	2010	2011	2012	2013	2014	2015	2016
Rating	5,4,PF	5,4,PF	5,5,PF	5,5,PF	6,5,NF	6,6,NF	6,6,NF	6,6,NF	7,6,NF	6,6,NF

Overview: The Gambia was ruled for more than two decades by President Yahya Jammeh and his party, the Alliance for Patriotic Reorientation and Construction (APRC). Jammeh, who took power in a bloodless coup in 1994, oversaw a regime that showed little respect for political rights or civil liberties. Government opponents, independent journalists, and activists faced intimidation, arbitrary arrest, torture, and disappearance, while women and minorities lacked equal rights. The Gambia's elections have been marred by violence and rigging, but the December 2016 presidential vote resulted in a surprise victory for opposition candidate Adama Barrow. Jammeh initially accepted the results before rescinding his concession days later, and it was unclear at the end of the year how the impasse would be resolved.

KEY DEVELOPMENTS IN 2016:

- In April, the organizing secretary of the opposition United Democratic Party (UDP), Solo Sandeng, was reportedly tortured to death in state custody shortly after being detained during a peaceful demonstration for electoral reform.
- Days after Sandeng's arrest, UDP leader Ousainou Darboe was arrested during a peaceful protest to demand transparency about the fate of Sandeng and the release of political detainees. In July, Darboe and 29 other people were sentenced to three years in prison for their roles in the protests.
- In December, President Jammeh publicly conceded defeat to Barrow in that month's presidential election. Jammeh soon reneged on his statement, claimed that the election was not conducted fairly, called for a new vote, and filed a petition with the Supreme Court. However, the court lacked a quorum due to outstanding vacancies, and the dispute was unresolved at year's end.

EXECUTIVE SUMMARY

As the December 2016 presidential election approached, the government used violence and intimidation to suppress peaceful opposition protests calling for electoral reform. Many opposition figures were arrested and prosecuted, and at least two UDP figures—organizing secretary Solo Sandeng and local constituency official Ebrima Solo Krummah—died in government custody.

In a surprise result, the Independent Electoral Commission (IEC) announced that Barrow, a UDP leader supported by a coalition of opposition parties, had garnered a plurality in the election, defeating Jammeh and a third candidate to take the presidency. After initially accepting the outcome, Jammeh reversed himself and called for a new election, filing a challenge with the Supreme Court that remained pending at year's end.

Throughout the year, the Jammeh regime continued to curtail freedom of expression, in part by enforcing restrictive laws on sedition. Teranga FM radio director Alagie Abdoulie Ceesay, who had been detained on sedition charges in 2015, escaped from government custody in April 2016 and was later convicted in absentia.

The authorities similarly disregarded freedom of association and the rule of law during the year, arbitrarily detaining a number of activists in addition to those involved in the opposition protests. One such activist, trade union leader Sheriff Dibba, died in state custody in February. Jammeh also continued to denounce LGBT (lesbian, gay, bisexual, and transgender) people.

POLITICAL RIGHTS: 8 / 40 (+ 3)

A. Electoral Process: 3 / 12 (+ 2)

The president is elected by popular vote and is eligible for an unlimited number of five-year terms. Elections have typically been violent and rigged. The two-week official campaign period is the only time that state television and radio stations devote significant airtime to the opposition. Moreover, 2015 amendments to the election law increased the registration deposit for presidential candidates from 10,000 dalasi to 500,000 dalasi ($12,000), a considerable sum given the average annual income of $450. The amounts required from National Assembly and mayoral candidates were raised to 50,000 dalasi, and the sum for local council candidates was increased to 10,000 dalasi.

Ahead of the December 2016 presidential election, international observers were not allowed into The Gambia, and internet and international telephone services were cut on election day. Despite these and other obstacles to a free and fair election, the IEC was apparently able to conduct an impartial vote count, declaring that Barrow had won with 43.3 percent, followed by Jammeh with 39.6 percent and Mama Kandeh of the Gambia Democratic Congress (GDC) with 17.1 percent. Jammeh initially conceded defeat, but after a key member of the president-elect's coalition told Britain's *Guardian* newspaper that Jammeh would be prosecuted after stepping down, Jammeh reversed his position, called the election flawed, and said a new vote would be held. He submitted a petition to the Supreme Court, which had been crippled by vacancies since 2015 and appeared unable to hear the case.

In mid-December, the Economic Community of West African States (ECOWAS) authorized a standby force to intervene militarily if a peaceful transfer of power did not begin by the last day of Jammeh's mandate, January 18.

Of the 53 members of the unicameral National Assembly, 48 are elected by popular vote, with the remainder appointed by the president; members serve five-year terms. Six of seven opposition parties boycotted the most recent elections in 2012, after demands for electoral reform were rejected. The ruling APRC won 43 of the elected seats. African Union observers noted a "gross imbalance" between the resources of the APRC and those of other parties, and cited the presence of security personnel and traditional chiefs in polling stations. ECOWAS refused to send observers.

B. Political Pluralism and Participation: 5 / 16 (+ 1)

Jammeh and the APRC long dominated politics, and the politicized security forces suppressed the opposition during 2016. Sandeng, the UDP's organizing secretary, was arrested along with other opposition supporters in April for holding a protest calling for electoral reforms. He died in custody after reportedly being tortured. Two days after Sandeng's detention, the authorities arrested the leader of the UDP, Ousainou Darboe, and other important opposition officials for their role in another peaceful rally calling for the earlier detainees' release. Krummah, a UDP constituency official, died in custody in August, having been detained in another wave of arrests in May and allegedly tortured and denied medical treatment. By November, the government had arrested over 90 opposition supporters involved in election-related protests, according to Human Rights Watch. Thirty opposition figures, including Darboe, were prosecuted, convicted, and sentenced to three years in prison in July, though many were released on bail after Barrow's stunning election victory in December.

The 2015 election law amendments impose burdensome requirements on political parties. To register, parties must deposit over $12,000; gather the signatures of 10,000 registered voters, up from 500; ensure that all executive members live in The Gambia; have offices in each of the country's administrative regions; provide audited accounts to the IEC; and hold biannual congresses. In April 2016, the IEC said eight parties had met the requirements ahead of the presidential election, two had been deregistered, and one was dissolved.

Members of Jammeh's minority Jola ethnic group held important positions in the government in 2016, and the APRC's dominance limited the extent to which any group could freely participate in the political system.

C. Functioning of Government: 0 / 12

The president exercises most control over decision-making, and government operations are generally opaque. Official corruption remains a serious problem. In September 2016, Justice Minister Mama Fatima Singhateh said the government was set to validate a draft Anti-Corruption Bill backed by the UN Development Programme that would create a national Anti-Corruption Commission. Singhateh said the commission would investigate and facilitate prosecution of corruption cases, and would aid in asset recovery. However, in practice the Jammeh regime did not tolerate independent corruption monitoring by civil society groups or journalists, prosecutions of officials appeared limited and selective, and enforcement of asset-disclosure rules was weak. Asset declarations were required for all candidates in the 2016 presidential election, but Jammeh did not comply.

CIVIL LIBERTIES: 12 / 60 (− 1)

D. Freedom of Expression and Belief: 3 / 16

Laws on sedition give the government discretion in silencing dissent, and independent journalists are subject to harassment, arrest, and violence. There are harsh criminal penalties for use of the internet to criticize government officials and providing "false information" to a public servant. Alagie Abdoulie Ceesay, director of Taranga FM, was abducted by suspected government agents in July 2015, detained by the National Intelligence Agency (NIA) later that month, and charged with sedition for allegedly sharing an anti-Jammeh photograph via mobile phone. He was reportedly tortured in custody. In April 2016, Ceesay escaped from a hospital where he had been taken for treatment. In November, he was convicted in absentia on three counts of sedition and spreading of false news and sentenced to two years in prison and a fine of $4,670, according to media reports.

State-run outlets dominate the media landscape. There are no private television stations, but a small number of privately owned newspapers and radio stations operate. Many opposition and news websites are blocked. Self-censorship among journalists is common. In April 2016, the Gambian Press Union estimated that 20 percent of Gambian journalists were living in exile.

Religious freedom is enshrined in the constitution, but Jammeh declared the country to be an Islamic state in December 2015. He is supported by the Supreme Islamic Council, whose members have discriminated against Ahmadi Muslims. In June 2016, a police statement announced that music, dancing, and drumming would be banned during the month of Ramadan, and that violators would be subject to arrest. Religious instruction in schools is mandatory.

Academic freedom is severely limited at the University of The Gambia. Free and open private discussion is curtailed due to credible fears of government surveillance and retaliation. Despite the repressive environment, university student and faculty associations joined other civil society organizations in urging a peaceful handover of power from Jammeh to Barrow in December 2016.

E. Associational and Organizational Rights: 2 / 12 (− 1)

Freedoms of assembly and association are legally protected. However, Gambian criminal law calls for protest organizers to seek permits from the inspector general of police, and police do not reliably issue permits for such events. The crackdown on UDP-led protests in April 2016 was justified on the grounds that the organizers had not obtained permits.

Nongovernmental organizations (NGOs) in the country operate under constant threat of reprisals and detention of staff. Workers—except for civil servants, household workers, and security forces—can form unions, strike, and bargain for wages, but the labor minister has the discretion to exclude other categories of workers, and legal protections are poorly enforced. In January 2016, the government banned the GNTCA, which had demanded lower fuel prices, and several of its leaders were arrested. In February, GNTCA secretary general Sheriff Dibba died in government custody; international rights groups alleged that he had been denied proper medical attention after becoming ill during his detention, while the International Transport Workers' Federation cited reports that he had been tortured.

F. Rule of Law: 1 / 16

Although the constitution guarantees an independent judiciary, the president selects and dismisses judges. Jammeh's dismissal of judges from the Supreme Court in 2015 left it unable to hear cases after May of that year. In December 2016, when Jammeh filed a challenge to Barrow's election victory with the Supreme Court, Chief Justice Emmanuel Olusegun Fagbenle announced that the petition could not be heard before January 2017, as replacement judges had yet to be sworn in. Critics questioned the legitimacy of a process in which Jammeh would effectively be selecting the judges for his own case.

In October 2016, the government announced that The Gambia would withdraw from the International Criminal Court. However, following the presidential election, Barrow said he would reverse that decision.

The judicial system recognizes customary and Islamic law, primarily for personal status and family matters. Impunity for the security forces is a problem. The NIA is authorized to search, arrest, or seize any person or property without a warrant in the name of state security. Prisons are overcrowded and unsanitary, and torture is reportedly common.

Activists, journalists, and government opponents are often jailed without charge for longer than the 72 hours allowed by law. For instance, the former deputy minister of foreign affairs, Sarjo Jallow, was arrested in September 2016 and remained in state custody at year's end, reportedly held by the NIA without charge, even though the High Court in Banjul had granted him bail in October. Similarly, Haruna Gassama, president of the Rice Farmers' Cooperative Society, was detained by the NIA for 185 days in 2015, rearrested in April 2016, and still in incommunicado detention at year's end.

The Gambia's ethnic groups coexist in relative harmony, though Jammeh is accused of giving preferential treatment to the Jola, whose presence in the army reportedly increased after a 2014 coup attempt. In June 2016, Jammeh referred to Gambian members of the Mandinka ethnic group as foreigners and threatened them with death if they attempted to oppose him.

Consensual same-sex sexual relationships remain a criminal offense. Even an attempted sex act can draw seven years in prison, and defendants with repeat offenses or who are HIV positive face life imprisonment for "aggravated homosexuality." Jammeh continued to condemn homosexuality in inflammatory terms in 2016.

G. Personal Autonomy and Individual Rights: 6 / 16

State employees must obtain permission from the administration to travel abroad, and authorities often seize the documents of arrested individuals, preventing them from traveling after their release. Freedom of movement within the country is impaired by security checkpoints.

Property rights are not secure. Village chiefs allocate land for various uses, but poor record keeping and high rates of turnover in village hierarchies foster land disputes and confusion about ownership and leases. Problems with due process related to the illegal seizure of land also persist. Regulatory hurdles impede the establishment and operation of businesses.

Women enjoy less access to higher education, justice, and employment than men. Sharia (Islamic law) provisions on family law and inheritance discriminate against women. Rape and domestic violence are common, despite laws prohibiting them. In July 2016, the National Assembly passed a law criminalizing child marriage. Female genital mutilation is widespread, though it was criminalized in a 2015 law.

Although child labor and forced labor are illegal, women and children are subject to sex trafficking, domestic servitude, and forced begging. The government does little to prosecute offenders or to identify and protect victims of human trafficking.

Georgia

Political Rights Rating: 3
Civil Liberties Rating: 3
Freedom Rating: 3
Freedom Status: Partly Free
Electoral Democracy: Yes

Population: 4,000,000
Capital: Tbilisi

Note: The numerical rankings and subsequent report do not include South Ossetia or Abkhazia, which are considered in separate reports.

Ten-Year Ratings Timeline For Year Under Review (Political Rights, Civil Liberties, Status)

Year Under Review	2007	2008	2009	2010	2011	2012	2013	2014	2015	2016
Rating	4,4,PF	4,4,PF	4,4,PF	4,3,PF	4,3,PF	3,3,PF	3,3,PF	3,3,PF	3,3,PF	3,3,PF

Overview: Georgia holds regular and pluralistic elections, and its democratic trajectory has generally shown significant improvement in recent years. However, oligarchic actors hold outsized influence over policy and political choices, and judicial independence continues to be stymied by executive and legislative interests.

KEY DEVELOPMENTS IN 2016:

- Following competitive parliamentary elections in October, the new legislature—sworn in the following month—announced intentions to conduct fundamental constitutional reform, drawing immediate disapproval from opposition parties and a number of civil society groups.
- The Georgian Dream–Democratic Georgia party, the leader of the ruling Georgian Dream coalition, dominated the October elections and captured a supermajority.
- On a number of occasions during the year, the leader of the Constitutional Court complained about excessive pressure by government authorities; his comments earned the support of President Giorgi Margvelashvili but caused disagreement within the court itself.

EXECUTIVE SUMMARY

Georgia held national parliamentary elections in October. Georgian Dream ran as a single party without its coalition partners and emerged with the highest proportion of party votes, winning the bulk of majoritarian seats. The United National Movement (UNM), Georgian Dream's main rival, secured roughly a third of the proportional votes and none of the majoritarian seats. Observers found the elections to be competitive and largely fair.

Soon after the new legislators began their terms, the parliamentary leadership announced intentions to launch a far-reaching constitutional reform program in 2017, a controversial move that drew disagreement from opposition legislators, a number of civil society groups, and President Margvelashvili, who was elected as an independent candidate and remains unaffiliated with any political party. With its parliamentary dominance, the Georgian Dream party will likely dominate any constitutional commission charged with developing reforms.

The role of political interests in the judiciary remained a concern, and was apparent in several cases involving elected officials or government interests in general. On a number of occasions during the year, the president of the Constitutional Court complained of undue pressure and blackmail by government actors seeking particular outcomes in high-profile cases. His comments divided the Constitutional Court, with justices publicly agreeing with or opposing his claims. The court system's handling of the ownership dispute involving Rustavi 2, the country's main opposition channel, also suggested the continued involvement of political forces in the actions of the judiciary.

POLITICAL RIGHTS: 29 / 40

A. Electoral Process: 9 / 12

B. Political Pluralism and Participation: 11 / 16

C. Functioning of Government: 7 / 12

CIVIL LIBERTIES: 37 / 60

D. Freedom of Expression and Belief: 11 / 16

E. Associational and Organizational Rights: 8 / 12

F. Rule of Law: 8 / 16

G. Personal Autonomy and Individual Rights: 10 / 16

This country report has been abridged for *Freedom in the World 2017*. For background information on political rights and civil liberties in Georgia, see *Freedom in the World 2016*.

Germany

Political Rights: 1
Civil Liberties: 1
Freedom Rating: 1.0
Freedom Status: Free
Electoral Democracy: Yes

Population: 82,600,000
Capital: Berlin

Ten-Year Ratings Timeline For Year Under Review (Political Rights, Civil Liberties, Status)

Year Under Review	2007	2008	2009	2010	2011	2012	2013	2014	2015	2016
Rating	1,1,F	1,1,F	1,1,F	1,1,F	1,1,F	1,1,F	1,1,F	1,1,F	1,1,F	1,1,F

Overview: Germany, a member of the European Union (EU), is a representative democracy with a vibrant political culture and civil society. Political rights and civil liberties are largely assured both in law and practice. The political system is influenced by the country's totalitarian past, with constitutional safeguards designed to prevent authoritarian rule. Although generally stable since the mid-20th century, politics are experiencing tensions following an influx of asylum seekers into the country and the growing popularity of a right-wing party, among other issues.

KEY DEVELOPMENTS

- The right-wing, populist Alternative for Germany (AfD) party gained ground in several state-level elections, taking advantage of a wave of discontent with Chancellor Angela Merkel and Europe's immigration crisis.
- Attacks on refugee housing remained a major problem, and both refugees and religious minorities reported a significant number of threats as well as incidents of hate speech and violence.
- Several terrorist attacks took place during the year, the most serious one targeting a Berlin Christmas market in December and ending with 12 deaths and dozens of injuries.

EXECUTIVE SUMMARY

In 2016, Germany's public sphere continued to absorb the consequences of the record-breaking flow of asylum seekers into the country the previous year. Although the migration flow ebbed significantly, violence against refugees and their homes remained high. Religious minorities also reported high lebels of threats, hate speech, and even violence. Amid these tensions, support for the right-wing, populist, anti-immigration AfD grew in all five state-level elections that took place during the year.

A number of terrorist attacks shook Germany, including ones carried out in the name of or claimed by the Islamic State (IS) militant group. The most severe attack targeted a Christmas market in Berlin and left 12 people dead and dozens injured. Following two attacks in July, the Bundestag passed amendments to existing antiterrorism legislation to improve the German intelligence service's ability to cooperate and share information with foreign counterparts.

In March, German comedian Jan Böhmermann became the center of a freedom of expression controversy after performing a satirical poem about Turkish president Recep Tayyip Erdoğan. Using an obscure law that enables foreign heads of state to prosecute insult in German courts with authorization from the German government, Erdoğan took steps to launch a criminal case against Böhmermann. Merkel granted authorization for use of the law, and the case led to significant international outcry. Prosecutors dropped it in October, citing insufficient evidence, and authorities announced plans to review the legislation.

POLITICAL RIGHTS: 39 / 40

A. Electoral Process: 12 / 12

The German constitution provides for a lower house of parliament, the Bundestag (Federal Assembly), as well as an upper house, the Bundesrat (Federal Council), which represents the country's 16 federal states. The Bundestag is elected at least every four years through a mixture of proportional representation and single-member districts, which can lead the number of seats to vary from the minimum 598. Bundesrat members are appointed by state governments. Germany's head of state is a largely ceremonial president, chosen jointly by the Bundestag and a group of state representatives to serve up to two five-year terms. The chancellor—the head of government—is elected by the Bundestag and usually serves for the duration of a legislative session. The chancellor's term can be cut short only if the Bundestag chooses a replacement in a so-called constructive vote of no confidence. In Germany's federal system, state governments have considerable authority over matters such as education, policing, taxation, and spending.

Joachim Gauck was elected president in 2012. In the 2013 federal elections, a total of 631 representatives were elected to the Bundestag. Merkel's Christian Democratic Union (CDU) and its Bavarian sister party, the Christian Social Union (CSU), won 311 seats—the best showing for the Christian Democrats since 1990, when Germany reunified. The CDU's previous coalition partner, the pro–free market Free Democratic Party (FDP), failed to meet the 5 percent threshold to qualify for seats for the first time since 1949. The center-left Social Democratic Party (SPD) took 193 seats, and the Greens won 63. The far-left party the Left, which is widely viewed as a successor to the East German communists, took 64 seats. The AfD failed to qualify for seats. The CDU reached an agreement with the SPD to form a so-called grand coalition government, as they had done during Merkel's first term (2005–09).

In 2016, state-level elections took place in five German states. The AfD made considerable gains in these elections, winning 24 percent of the vote in Saxony-Anhalt and 21 percent in Mecklenburg-Western Pomerania.

B. Political Pluralism and Participation: 15 / 16

The dominant political parties have traditionally been the SPD and the CDU-CSU. Parties do not face undue restrictions on registration or operation, although under electoral laws that, for historical reasons, are intended to restrict the far left and far right, a party must receive either 5 percent of the national vote or win at least three directly elected seats to gain representation in the parliament.

The influence of Germany's extreme-right party, the National Democratic Party (NPD)—an anti-immigration, anti-EU party that has been accused of glorifying Adolf Hitler and the Third Reich—remains very limited. All 16 German states petitioned the Federal Constitutional Court in 2013 to ban the NPD, calling it a neo-Nazi antidemocratic group. Previous attempts to outlaw the party have failed. The movement against the NPD continued in 2016, but with no significant results.

Support for the AfD has grown in recent years. In addition to making gains in the 2016 state elections, the party won seven seats in the European Parliament elections in 2014. Several AfD members and deputies are linked to right-wing extremist groups. In 2016, Baden-Württemberg state legislator Wolfgang Gedeon left the party after publicly glorifying Holocaust deniers as dissidents.

The 2013 federal elections resulted in the first black members of the Bundestag, with one each from the CDU and the SPD. The CDU also saw its first Muslim deputy elected to the Bundestag. Overall, the number of Bundestag members from immigrant backgrounds rose from 21 to 34.

C. Functioning of Government: 12 / 12

Elected representatives decide and implement policy without undue interference.

Germany is free from pervasive corruption and was ranked 10 out of 176 countries and territories surveyed in Transparency International's 2016 Corruption Perceptions Index. However, watchdogs continue to express concerns about a controversial 2015 data retention law, which they view as a threat not just to general privacy but also to whistleblowers, who could be punished under a section detailing illegal data handling. Whistleblowers receive few legal protections in Germany.

The government is held accountable for its performance through open parliamentary debates, which are covered widely in the media. However, Transparency International and other nongovernmental organizations (NGOs) criticize Germany for having loose regulations on lobbying and lacking a centralized lobbying register, which stifle transparency in this area.

CIVIL LIBERTIES: 56 / 60

D. Freedom of Expression and Belief: 15 / 16

Freedom of expression is enshrined in the constitution, and the media are largely free and independent. Hate speech, such as racist agitation or anti-Semitism, is punishable by law. It is also illegal to advocate Nazism, deny the Holocaust, or glorify the ideology of Hitler. In March 2016, Böhmermann became the center of a freedom of expression scandal after reciting a satirical poem on television about Erdoğan. Following the broadcast, Erdoğan took steps toward prosecuting Böhmermann for insult, using a section of the German criminal code that allows a foreign head of state to undertake such proceedings if authorized to do so by the German government. Merkel faced widespread criticism by domestic and international media watchdogs as well as the public for granting authorization. Prosecutors ceased investigations in October, citing insufficient evidence, and a review of the relevant section of the criminal code was ongoing at year's end.

Internet access is generally unrestricted. In 2013, documents leaked by former U.S. National Security Agency (NSA) contractor Edward Snowden revealed that the NSA, in collaboration with Germany's Federal Intelligence Service (BND), had secretly collected extensive data on communications in Germany. In 2014, a parliamentary inquiry was launched into the nature of cooperation between the NSA and BND. The inquiry was ongoing in 2016. In October, the Bundestag passed a bill to reform the BND. Although the legislation strengthened government monitoring of and control over the BND, it also legalized some of the agency's controversial intelligence-gathering practices and expanded its power to monitor foreign entities. A number of minority parties and NGOs strongly opposed the bill and announced plans to challenge it.

Freedom of belief is legally protected. However, eight states have passed laws prohibiting female Muslim schoolteachers from wearing headscarves, while Berlin and the state of Hesse have adopted legislation banning headscarves for civil servants.

Violence against religious minorities remained a prominent issue throughout the year. According to the Interior Ministry, there were 91 attacks on mosques in 2016, the most prominent of them a bomb attack in Dresden in September. In April, a Sikh temple in Essen fell victim to a bomb attack. Police arrested a group of German-born youths with connections to Islamist extremists in subsequent investigations; the case had not concluded at year's end.

Academic freedom is respected, and private discussion is generally unrestricted. A debate surrounding censorship of online discussion continued in 2016, with several court cases leading to convictions for incitement of hatred on digital platforms.

E. Associational and Organizational Rights: 12 / 12

The right to peaceful assembly is respected in practice, except in the case of outlawed groups, such as those advocating Nazism or opposing democratic order. Civic groups and NGOs operate without hindrance.

Trade unions, farmers' groups, and business confederations are generally free to organize. In July, a federal court ruled that a 2012 strike by Frankfurt Airport air traffic controllers was unlawful, ordering their union to pay damages.

F. Rule of Law: 14 / 16

The judiciary is independent, and the rule of law prevails. Prison conditions are adequate, though the Council of Europe has criticized some of Germany's preventive detention practices.

The threat posed by terrorist groups to national and regional security remained a major concern in 2016 and contributed to social and political tensions. Two German terrorist attacks in July—a suicide bombing targeting visitors to a festival in Ansbach and an axe attack on a passenger train in Würzburg, were attributed to registered refugees associated with IS. In both cases, the perpetrators were killed and several bystanders injured. In December, Germany witnessed its worst terrorist incident in decades when a militant extremist drove a truck into a crowd at a Christmas market in Berlin, killing 12 and injuring dozens. The suspect, Tunisian citizen Anis Amri, was killed a few days later by police in Italy. The incident stirred up a renewed debate on Germany's security and migration policies. After the July attacks, legislators amended existing antiterrorism laws to improve the German domestic intelligence service's ability to cooperate and share information with foreign counterparts.

The constitution and other laws guarantee equality and prohibit discrimination on the basis of origin, gender, religion or belief, disability, age or sexual orientation. However, a number of obstacles stand in the way of equal treatment of all segments of the population. Following the record number of asylum seekers who entered Germany in 2015, significantly lower numbers were recorded in 2016—280,000, compared with 890,000 the previous year. Although the German government retains one of the most open policies toward asylum, the problem of violence against refugees persisted in 2016. There were 970 attacks on refugee housing during the year, most of them attributed to right-wing extremists. Separately, federal police recorded 11 attempted murders by right-wing extremists through October. In October, a police officer in Bavaria was killed in a shootout with a member of a so-called Reichsbürger group, a militant collective that refuses to accept the authority of the German state.

Rhetoric against refugees remained prominent in German public rhetoric. The anti-immigration, anti-Islam group known as the Patriotic Europeans Against the Islamization of the Occident (PEGIDA), which developed into a large protest movement in 2014, remained active in 2016 and continued to be one of the most vocal opponents of asylum and migration. In October, the group again made headlines when members disturbed celebrations of Germany's reunification day in Dresden, displaying signs and using language that mocked the country's political establishment, including Chancellor Merkel.

G. Personal Autonomy and Individual Rights: 15 / 16

Freedom of movement is legally protected and generally respected, although the refugee crisis and security concerns related to IS have led to some restrictions on travel. In 2015, the government introduced legislation allowing the confiscation of identity documents from German citizens suspected of terrorism as a way to prevent them from traveling abroad, particularly to Iraq and Syria. The rights to own property and engage in commercial activity are respected.

Women's rights are protected under antidiscrimination laws. However, a considerable gender wage gap persists, with women earning approximately 22 percent less in gross wages than men. A law requiring large German companies to reserve at least 30 percent of seats on their non-executive boards for women came into effect in 2016, but only affects a very limited number of companies. Following the 2013 federal elections, women gained 6 of the 16 federal cabinet positions and 36 percent of the seats in the Bundestag.

Limited same-sex partnership rights are respected. Adoption and tax legislation passed in 2014 gave equal rights to same-sex couples in these areas. However, the government does not grant same-sex couples the right to marry, instead providing the option of a civil partnership.

According to the U.S. State Department's 2016 Trafficking in Persons report, migrants from Eastern Europe, Africa, and Asia are targeted for sex trafficking and forced labor. Asylum seekers, especially unaccompanied minors, are also particularly vulnerable to exploitation.

Ghana

Political Rights Rating: 1
Civil Liberties Rating: 2
Freedom Rating: 1.5
Freedom Status: Free
Electoral Democracy: Yes

Population: 28,200,000
Capital: Accra

Ten-Year Ratings Timeline For Year Under Review (Political Rights, Civil Liberties, Status)

Year Under Review	2007	2008	2009	2010	2011	2012	2013	2014	2015	2016
Rating	1,2,F	1,2,F	1,2,F	1,2,F	1,2,F	1,2,F	1,2,F	1,2,F	1,2,F	1,2,F

Overview: Since 1992, Ghana has held competitive multiparty elections that have led to peaceful transfers of power between the two main political parties. Although Ghana has a relatively strong record of upholding civil liberties, discrimination against women and members of the LGBT (lesbian, gay, bisexual, and transgender) community continues. Some weaknesses in judicial independence and rule of law persist, and political corruption presents challenges to government performance.

KEY DEVELOPMENTS IN 2016:

- In a general election held in December, the New Patriotic Party (NPP) won a majority in Parliament, and its candidate, Nana Akufo-Addo, won the presidency.
- Despite several legal and logistical challenges leading up to the vote, observers concluded that the Electoral Commission (EC) conducted a relatively well-organized and transparent election, and that the vote was free, fair, and credible.
- In August, legislators passed the Petroleum and Oil Exploration Bill, which has the potential to enhance transparency and accountability in the oil and gas sector.
- The fallout of a judicial bribery scandal, which first emerged in 2015, continued during the year, with a number of judges dismissed from office.

EXECUTIVE SUMMARY

In December, Ghana set the stage for its third peaceful transfer of power since 1992 as voters elected Akufo-Addo of the NPP to presidential office and secured a parliamentary majority for the party. Despite a contentious campaign period that saw reports of inter-party violence, allegations of abuse of government resources, and complaints about incendiary campaign speech, domestic and international observers considered the vote to be largely free, fair, and credible. A preliminary report by a European Union (EU) observer mission commended the EC for its preparedness and transparency, but encouraged the institution to improve some aspects of its operations, including the quality of its framework for communicating with political parties.

Corruption continues to hinder government performance. During the year, fallout continued from a judicial bribery scandal that came to light in 2015, when a journalist publicized videos that seem to show numerous judges and other judicial officials accepting .bribes. In a positive step, legislators passed the Petroleum and Oil Exploration Bill in August. The legislation has the potential to enhance transparency and accountability in the oil and gas sector.

POLITICAL RIGHTS: 37 / 40

A. Electoral Process: 12 / 12

Ghana has experienced competitive multiparty elections since 1992. The president and vice president are directly elected on the same ticket for up to two four-year terms. Members of the unicameral, 275-seat Parliament are also elected for four-year terms.

In December 2016, Akufo-Addo was elected president with 53.9 percent of the vote, while incumbent John Mahama of the National Democratic Congress (NDC) took 44.4 percent. This represents the first time since the reintroduction of the multi-party system in 1992 that an incumbent president has stood for reelection and lost. In concurrent parliamentary elections, the NPP captured 169 seats while the NDC, which had held a majority going into elections, took the 106 remaining seats. International and domestic observers generally praised the elections, and all major political parties accepted the results.

Although the vote and its immediate aftermath were peaceful, the campaign period was contentious. There were several reports of clashes between NPP and NDC supporters, as well as attacks on EC officials. Moreover, representatives of civil society raised concerns about what they claimed were alarming levels of hate speech used by politicians, as well as the monetization of the electoral process and alleged abuse of state resources. In the week before voting began, the seven presidential candidates contesting the polls signed a commitment to the peaceful conduct of the elections.

The EC's preparations were shrouded in controversy. After the 2012 elections, the results of which the NPP had disputed, the Supreme Court recommended reform of the electoral process in a 2013 ruling. EC chair Charlotte Osei, appointed by Mahama in 2015, was expected to spearhead major changes. In May 2016, the Supreme Court ordered the EC to overhaul the voter register, after a case brought to the court alleged that the current voter register would undermine electoral integrity because it contained the names of foreigners and people under the legal voting age. The EC published an updated voter register in November.

In a controversial move, the EC disqualified 13 presidential candidates in October due to irregularities with their nomination papers or failure to pay the nomination fee. The Supreme Court rescinded the EC's decision in early November, giving the disqualified candidates an opportunity to rectify the problems. In the end, three of the originally disqualified candidates were allowed to stand for election. Political parties also criticized the EC for ineffective communication. Despite these challenges, domestic and international observers generally commended the EC for the conduct of the elections.

In July, a proposed constitutional amendment to move the date of the general election from December to November failed to gain the parliamentary supermajority required for passage. Opponents in Parliament indicated that the proposal had been raised too close to the electoral period, although they supported the change in principle.

B. Political Pluralism and Participation: 15 / 16

Ghana's multiparty system provides ample opportunity for opposition parties to meaningfully participate in the political process. The NPP and the NDC dominate the political system. The 2017 inauguration of Akufo-Addo will represent the country's third peaceful transfer of presidential power between the NPP and NDC. The legal framework provides for equal participation in political life for the country's various cultural, religious, and ethnic minorities. However, candidate nomination fees for the 2016 presidential and parliamentary elections were higher by 500 percent and 1,000 percent, respectively, than in the previous elections. This increase, along with the difficulties in the nomination procedures highlighted by the presidential candidate disqualifications, presented challenges to participation, especially for candidates from smaller parties. In September, the Progressive People's Party mounted a legal challenge against the nomination fees; the case was ultimately unsuccessful.

Despite the NPP's victories in the general election, political infighting plagued the party in 2016. The trial of the George Afoko, brother of former NPP chairman Paul Afoko, for the 2015 murder of Adams Mahama, NPP chairperson of the Upper East Region, was ongoing at year's end. A second alleged participant in the murder remained at large; a third man had been released on bail in 2015 after authorities determined there was not enough evidence to charge him in the crime. Paul Afoko was indefinitely suspended from the NPP after his brother's arrest, exacerbating internal divisions within the party; he challenged his suspension in court, but lost the case in August 2016.

The NPP is traditionally supported by the Akan people and the NDC by the Ewe and other northern groups. Although the lines have been blurred over the years, ethnicity continues to play a role in voting patterns and representation.

C. Functioning of Government: 10 / 12

Political corruption remains a problem, despite robust legal and institutional frameworks to combat it, active media coverage, and the government's willingness to investigate major scandals. The media, opposition parties, and nongovernmental organizations (NGOs) continue to criticize the government for ineffectiveness in preventing political corruption and prosecuting public officials suspected of malfeasance.

In June, critics accused President Mahama of accepting a car in 2012 from a Burkinabe construction firm bidding on a government contract. Mahama's administration denied that the car was a bribe and claimed that it had been added to the pool of government vehicles. An investigation by the Commission for Human Rights and Administrative Justice (CHRAJ)—Ghana's leading anticorruption body—concluded in September that the president's actions did not amount to corruption.

Civil society groups have expressed concern that Ghana's main anticorruption bodies, including the CHRAJ, are led by individuals operating in an acting capacity rather than as substantive chairs, which they said could undermine the agencies' rigor.

A court case involving legislator Abuga Pele, who was charged in 2014 for allegedly granting interest-free loans worth $100 million to private companies without parliamentary approval, continued in 2016.

Efforts to strengthen Ghana's institutional and legal anticorruption framework continued in 2016. Following the 2014 passage of the National Anti-Corruption Action Plan

(NACAP), which aims to improve the prevention, investigation, and prosecution of corruption by strengthening a number of state agencies, the government began a five-year partnership with the EU in 2016. Under its terms, the EU is set to provide 20 million to support Ghana's anticorruption efforts.

In August, Parliament approved the Petroleum Production and Exploration Bill, which supporters expect will increase accountability and transparency in Ghana's young oil and gas sector. Separately, despite over a decade of consideration by Parliament and renewed efforts by advocates in 2015 and 2016, the Right to Information Bill remained stalled.

CIVIL LiBERTIES: 46 / 60

D. Freedom of Expression and Belief: 14 / 16

Freedom of expression is constitutionally guaranteed and generally respected in practice. Ghana has a diverse and vibrant media landscape that includes state and privately owned television and radio stations, and several independent newspapers and magazines. While the internet has generally been unrestricted, Inspector General of Police John Kudalor indicated in May 2016 that he was considering blocking access to social media during the general election to prevent misinformation and maintain security. Amid heavy criticism from the political opposition, rights advocates, and a domestic anticensorship campaign, Mahama indicated in August that no such restrictions would be implemented. In June, the government withdrew the Interception of Postal Packets and Telecommunications Messages Bill, known as the "spy bill," from parliamentary consideration. Local and international rights groups had opposed certain provisions that had the potential to undermine the right to privacy in private communications.

Government agencies occasionally restrict press freedom through harassment and arrests of journalists, especially those reporting on politically sensitive issues. In September, the Bureau of National Investigations arrested writer and Mahama critic Fadi Dabboussi and held him for two days without access to legal counsel, reportedly because of allegations he had made about the president in a recently published book. Officials also reportedly raided his home and temporarily seized copies of the book.

Despite a statement from a Mahama aide that the president would look into the actions of presidential staffer Stan Dogbe, who allegedly attacked a journalist in 2015, there seemed to be no investigation in 2016. Dogbe continued to serve in his position during the year.

Although criminal libel and sedition laws were repealed in 2001, powerful figures attempt to use other aspects of the legal system to punish criticism. Paul Dery, one of 34 judges implicated in a high-profile bribery scandal in 2015, continued to pursue a legal battle in 2016 against Anas Aremeyaw Anas, the journalist responsible for publicizing videos that seemingly showed judicial officials accepting bribes.

Religious freedom is constitutionally and legally protected, and the government largely respects it in practice. However, Muslim families have complained that compulsory Christian prayer sessions and church services that are widespread in Ghana's public schools seek to promote Christianity and violate their children's religious freedom.

Academic freedom is legally guaranteed and upheld in practice, and private discussion is both free and vibrant.

E. Associational and Organizational Rights: 11 / 12

The rights to peaceful assembly and association are constitutionally guaranteed and generally respected. Permits are not required for meetings or demonstrations. Public discontent with the government's management of the economy and power sector prompted numerous public protests, demonstrations, and strikes in 2016.

NGOs are generally able to operate freely, and they play an important role in ensuring government accountability and transparency.

Under the constitution and 2003 labor laws, workers have the right to form and join trade unions. However, the government forbids or restricts labor action in a number of industries, including fuel distribution, public transportation, and the prison system.

F. Rule of Law: 11 / 16

Judicial independence in Ghana is constitutionally and legally enshrined. While the judiciary has demonstrated greater levels of impartiality in recent years, corruption remains a challenge. Following the 2015 scandal in which a series of videos published by Anas alleged that 34 judges and scores of other judicial officials had accepted bribes in exchange for favorable rulings, many members of the judiciary faced dismissal or administrative sanctions. Disciplinary action continued in 2016, and had affected more than 30 judges by year's end. Among those dismissed were high court judges.

Police in Ghana have a history of using excessive force, making arbitrary arrests, detaining suspects for extended periods, and taking bribes.

Ghana's prisons are overcrowded, and conditions are often life-threatening, though the prison service has attempted to reduce congestion and improve the treatment of inmates in recent years. Ghana continues to cooperate with the UN Refugee Agency to protect the rights of the thousands of refugees and asylum seekers in the country.

Communal and ethnic violence occasionally flare in Ghana. In July, reports emerged that at least nine people were killed in violence surrounding a chieftaincy dispute in the Bole Bamboi district in the Northern Region.

Ghanaian law prohibits "sexual intercourse with a person in an unnatural manner." LGBT people face societal discrimination. In May, a Muslim cleric, Mallam Abass Mahmud, was condemned by local and international activists for making incendiary comments about members of the LGBT community.

G. Personal Autonomy and Individual Rights: 10 / 16

Freedom of movement is guaranteed by the constitution and respected by the government, and Ghanaians are free to choose their place of residence. However, poorly developed road networks and banditry make travel outside the capital and touristic areas difficult. Police have been known to set up illegal checkpoints to demand bribes from travelers. Bribery is also rife in the education sector.

Weak rule of law, corruption, and an underregulated property rights system remain significant impediments to economic freedom and business confidence. Bribery is a common practice in starting a business and registering property.

Despite equal rights under the law, women suffer societal discrimination, especially in rural areas, where opportunities for education and employment are limited. However, women's enrollment in universities is increasing, and a number of women hold high-ranking positions in the government. Female legislators took 37 of the 275 parliamentary seats in the 2016 elections, the highest since the reintroduction of multiparty rule in 1992. Human rights groups sustain that more needs to be done to eliminate barriers for female participation in politics. In August, the cabinet approved the Affirmative Action Bill, which aims to increase women's political representation. The bill went on to be deliberated in Parliament, but had not passed at year's end.

Domestic violence and rape are serious problems, and the practice of female genital mutilation continues in the north. The government has worked to combat gender-based violence by expanding the police's domestic violence and victim support unit, creating gender-based violence courts, establishing domestic violence shelters, and training police and service providers likely to encounter domestic violence situations.

Ghana serves as a source, transit point, and destination for the trafficking of women and children for labor and sexual exploitation. Children in Ghana, especially in the region surrounding Lake Volta, are vulnerable to exploitation in the agricultural and fishing industries. While the government has taken some steps in recent years, it has not implemented appropriate legislation or adequately funded antitrafficking agencies. Ghana remained on the Tier 2 Watch List in the U.S. State Department's 2016 Trafficking in Persons Report.

Greece

Political Rights Rating: 2
Civil Liberties Rating: 2
Freedom Rating: 2.0
Freedom Status: Free
Electoral Democracy: Yes

Population: 10,800,000
Capital: Athens

Ten-Year Ratings Timeline For Year Under Review (Political Rights, Civil Liberties, Status)

Year Under Review	2007	2008	2009	2010	2011	2012	2013	2014	2015	2016
Rating	1,2,F	1,2,F	1,2,F	1,2,F	2,2,F	2,2,F	2,2,F	2,2,F	2,2,F	2,2,F

Overview: Greece's parliamentary democracy features vigorous competition between political parties and a strong if imperfect record of upholding civil liberties. Entrenched corruption has undermined the economy and state finances, and since the sovereign debt crisis of 2010, Greece's international creditors have imposed tight constraints on its fiscal policies. Other concerns include discrimination against immigrants and minorities as well as poor conditions for an influx of refugees and migrants in recent years.

KEY DEVELOPMENTS IN 2016:

- Although the flow of migrants and refugees eased during the year, more than 60,000 remained stranded in Greece at year's end, often living in squalid or dangerous conditions.
- In August, the parliament adopted measures that enabled the introduction of schooling for young migrants and refugees in the fall and the construction of a mosque in Athens to help serve the needs of Muslim residents, including refugees.
- In September, the government held an auction for television broadcast permits in an attempt to reorganize and regulate the sector, but the Council of State ruled the process unconstitutional in October.

EXECUTIVE SUMMARY

The economic impact of Greece's 2015 agreement with its international creditors was not as extreme as many feared, and the economy was expected to return to annual growth in 2017. The budget outlook also appeared more positive in 2016, with the year's primary surplus set to increase in 2017. Nonetheless, the economy remained fragile, and the government's ability to implement additional unpopular austerity measures was uncertain.

A March 2016 agreement between the European Union (EU) and Turkey limited the number of new refugees and migrants entering the country during the year, but Macedonia's decision the same month to close its southern border left a substantial number stranded in Greece. Irregular migration picked up again in the aftermath of the attempted coup in Turkey in July, and Greek officials, citing safety concerns, were reluctant to return the newly arrived refugees. By year's end, over 60,000 migrants and refugees were stranded in Greece as officials struggled to process asylum claims in a timely manner. Many camps and facilities suffered from squalid and dangerous living conditions, violence, harassment of women, and endangerment of children. EU emergency funds appeared insufficient, and Greek authorities had difficulty putting the money into action, though some funds were also channeled directly to nongovernmental organizations. On the positive side, the Greek government began incorporating refugee children into the school system in the fall, and the parliament voted in August to begin construction of an official mosque to serve Muslim residents of Athens, including many refugees. Muslims were previously forced to worship in improvised mosques and other informal gathering places.

Though acts of racist violence are an ongoing problem, the threat appears to have diminished somewhat since law enforcement agencies began investigating and prosecuting the illegal activities of the far-right Golden Dawn party. Dozens of party members and leaders remained on trial during 2016 in a case that got under way the previous year, with prosecutors arguing that Golden Dawn operated as a criminal enterprise. Separately, the parliament continued its efforts to hold members accountable for their actions, for example by voting in June to lift immunity for three lawmakers accused of various offenses: Pavlos Polakis and Christos Byialas of the ruling left-wing SYRIZA party and Nikos Mihos of Golden Dawn.

In late August and early September, the government attempted to reorganize the private television sector by holding an auction for broadcast permits under a law passed in 2015. Supplementary legislation adopted in February had authorized the government to administer the auction directly rather than through the National Council for Radio and Television, as the parliament had failed to reach agreement on the council's membership, leaving it unable to function. The new law also allowed the government to reduce the number of private nationwide broadcasters to four, from the current seven, leading critics to accuse SYRIZA of altering the media landscape in its favor. Station owners challenged the auction's legality, and the Council of State ruled in October that it was unconstitutional. A new auction was expected to be conducted by the media council in 2017.

POLITICAL RIGHTS: 35 / 40

A. Electoral Process: 12 / 12

B. Political Pluralism and Participation: 15 / 16

C. Functioning of Government: 8 / 12

CIVIL LIBERTIES: 49 / 60 (+ 1)

D. Freedom of Expression and Belief: 14 / 16

E. Associational and Organizational Rights: 11 / 12

F. Rule of Law: 11 / 16 (+ 1)

G. Personal Autonomy and Individual Rights: 13 / 16

This country report has been abridged for *Freedom in the World 2017*. For background information on political rights and civil liberties in Greece, see *Freedom in the World 2016*.

Grenada

Political Rights Rating: 1
Civil Liberties Rating: 2
Freedom Rating: 1.5
Freedom Status: Free
Electoral Democracy: Yes

Population: 100,000
Capital: St. George's

Ten-Year Ratings Timeline For Year Under Review (Political Rights, Civil Liberties, Status)

Year Under Review	2007	2008	2009	2010	2011	2012	2013	2014	2015	2016
Rating	1,2,F	1,2,F	1,2,F	1,2,F	1,2,F	1,2,F	1,2,F	1,2,F	1,2,F	1,2,F

The country or territory displayed here received scores but no narrative report for this edition of *Freedom in the World.*

Guatemala

Political Rights Rating: 4
Civil Liberties Rating: 4
Freedom Rating: 4.0
Freedom Status: Partly Free
Electoral Democracy: Yes

Population: 16,600,000
Capital: Guatemala City

Ten-Year Ratings Timeline For Year Under Review (Political Rights, Civil Liberties, Status)

Year Under Review	2007	2008	2009	2010	2011	2012	2013	2014	2015	2016
Rating	3,4,PF	3,4,PF	4,4,PF	4,4,PF	3,4,PF	3,4,PF	3,4,PF	3,4,PF	4,4,PF	4,4,PF

Overview: Organized crime and corruption severely impact the free functioning of government in Guatemala, which remains one of the most dangerous countries in Latin America. Indigenous peoples, women, and children continue to feel the brunt of this violence, with little recourse to justice. Journalists, activists, and public officials who confront crime, corruption, and other sensitive issues risk attack.

KEY DEVELOPMENTS IN 2016:

- In early September, President Jimmy Morales fired two high-ranking officers from the presidential security service after they came under investigation for unlawful surveillance of journalists, human right advocates, politicians, and business owners.
- The attorney general pursued high-level corruption cases, but faced severe intimidation for her efforts, including death threats.
- In February, in the Sepur Zarco trial, two officers were convicted of holding indigenous women in sexual slavery during the civil war.
- In April, the mandate of UN-backed International Commission against Impunity in Guatemala (CICIG) was extended to 2019.

EXECUTIVE SUMMARY

Guatemala's attorney general and the UN-backed CICIG continued to investigate and prosecute high-level cases of corruption and criminal behavior in 2016, with some investigations targeting members of Morales's administration and of his family. In September, Morales fired two high-ranking officers from the presidential security service after it emerged that they were being investigated for the unlawful surveillance of journalists, human right advocates, politicians, and business owners. Herbert Armando Melgar Padilla, a close advisor to the president, was also implicated. Around the time the spying allegations became public, Melgar Padilla had filled the seat of a congressman who suddenly stepped down, a development that allowed him to obtain parliamentary immunity.

The country's homicide rate continued to drop in 2016, for the seventh straight year. However, Guatemala is still plagued by violence, much of which is related to criminal groups, and in 2016 officials reported 4,550 homicides. Human rights defenders, members of the media, as well as labor, land, and indigenous rights activists face threats when their work is perceived to interfere with such groups' operations, or when it threatens to expose corruption.

Only a small number of perpetrators of human rights atrocities from the 1960–96 civil war have been prosecuted. In January 2016, 18 high-ranking officers were arrested in connection with massacres and disappearances in the 1980s. In February, there was a verdict in the Sepur Zarco trial against two officers. They were convicted for holding indigenous women in sexual slavery during the civil war.

POLITICAL RIGHTS: 23 / 40

A. Electoral Process: 8 / 12

The constitution stipulates a four-year presidential term and prohibits reelection. Members of the 158-seat, unicameral Congress are elected to four-year terms. In the September 2015 legislative election, the Renewed Democratic Liberty (LIDER) party won 45 seats and the National Unity for Hope (UNE) won 32. A new party, Todos, took 18 seats, as did the scandal-plagued Patriotic Party (PP); the PP had held 39 seats previously. Nine other parties took the remaining 45 seats. Morales won a plurality in the concomitant presidential vote and, with 67 percent, defeated former first lady Sandra Torres of the UNE in an October 2015 runoff. Turnout was 70 percent in September and 56 percent in October. The Supreme Electoral Tribunal (TSE) removed about 10 percent of voters from the register ahead of the elections because they were deceased or ineligible to participate.

The elections were generally judged as credible. As in the past, electoral observers reported irregularities, including intimidation, vote buying, and the burning of ballots and electoral boxes. Eleven municipal contests had to be repeated in October 2015. Throughout the electoral campaign, an estimated 20 election-related murders occurred, mostly involving mayoral candidates and their relatives.

Before the election, a CICIG report estimated that 50 percent of known campaign donations come from contractors doing business with the state, another 25 percent from organized crime groups. CICIG also said that nearly all parties spend more money than they report, and that they exceeded official spending limits.

In April 2016, the legislature approved reforms to the electoral law that among other things mandated stricter financial disclosure procedures that are overseen by the TSE. The legislature also adopted reforms that punish *transfuguismo*—the practice whereby deputies abandon the parties with which they are elected.

B. Political Pluralism and Participation: 10 / 16

Elections take place within a highly inchoate multiparty system. A total of 14 candidates vied for the presidency in 2015, and 13 political parties won congressional seats.

The government uses the military to maintain internal security, despite restrictions imposed by the 1996 peace accord that ended a 36-year civil war. The National Convergence Front (FCN), the party that backs Morales, was founded by a group of former military officials, and Morales's association with the party has raised questions about military influence in his administration. In June 2016, attempts to revive the annual military parade, after a nine-year hiatus, came under pressure from civil society actors who said holding the controversial event would be inappropriate due to a lack of progress in implementation of the peace accords. The president canceled the public parade, but organized a private one, as had taken place each year since the public one was banned.

Members of indigenous communities hold just 20 congressional seats, although they comprise 44 percent of the population. There are no indigenous members in the cabinet. In 2015, 113 out of 333 Guatemalan mayors were indigenous. In March 2016, the legislature rejected a proposed reform to electoral laws that would have mandated the equal inclusion of ethnic groups and women in party candidate lists.

C. Functioning of Government: 5 / 12

While ongoing efforts to combat corruption have lent some credibility to the justice system in recent years, corruption remains a serious problem. Few convictions have followed dozens of arrests connected to the various scandals that in 2015 brought down the administration of Otto Pérez Molina, though new arrests of ex-officials continued in 2016. Additionally, both Morales's son and his brother came under investigation in 2016 for possible involvement in the previous administration's network of corruption. The news outlet *La Hora*, after conducting an investigation, reported that Pérez and former Vice President Roxana Baldetti remain involved in criminal activity even after being jailed in connection with their roles in a wide-ranging corruption scheme; they were formally charged with money laundering and the illegal financing of political parties in June 2016. In September, a lax, 30-month suspended sentence was handed down to Édgar Barquín, a former central bank head who was convicted of laundering some $30 million.

In January 2016, CICIG and the attorney general announced a plan to investigate corruption at the municipal level.

Despite 2015 reforms in that make the processes for issuing government contracts more transparent, abuses remain. Reports also reveal that construction firms under government contracts often face extortion demands.

In October 2016, the Human Rights Ombudsman reported that there are challenges in the implementation of the Law on Access to Information. The Ombudsman found that some municipalities lack the necessary infrastructure to accept and process information requests and that public information offices frequently fail to publish data about public expenditures as required.

CIVIL LIBERTIES: 31 / 60

D. Freedom of Expression and Belief: 11 / 16 (− 1)

While the constitution protects freedom of speech, journalists often face threats and practice self-censorship when covering sensitive topics such as drug trafficking, corruption, organized crime, and human rights violations. Threats come from public officials, drug traffickers, individuals aligned with companies operating in indigenous communities, and local security forces. Nine journalists were murdered in 2016, according to the Guatemalan press freedom group CERIGUA.

Mexican businessman Remigio Ángel González owns a monopoly of broadcast television networks and has significant holdings in radio. Newspaper ownership is also concentrated. Most papers have centrist or conservative editorial views. While the government is making an effort to improve the country's telecommunications infrastructure, internet access remains limited.

The constitution guarantees religious freedom. However, indigenous communities have faced discrimination for openly practicing the Mayan religion.

Although the government does not interfere with academic freedom, scholars have received death threats for questioning past human rights abuses or continuing injustices.

In early September 2016, Morales fired two high-ranking officers from the presidential security service after they came under investigation for unlawful surveillance of journalists, human right advocates, politicians, and business owners. Melgar Padilla, a close advisor to the president, was also implicated. Herbert Armando Melgar Padilla, a close advisor to the president, was also implicated. Around the time the spying allegations became public, Melgar Padilla had filled the seat of a congressman who suddenly stepped down, a development that allowed him to obtain parliamentary immunity.

E. Associational and Organizational Rights: 6 / 12

The constitution guarantees freedom of assembly, but this right is not always guaranteed in practice. Police frequently threaten force and have at times used violence against protesters. In September 2016, authorities issued an emergency decree that allowed them to break up demonstrations and meetings that "contributed to or incited" disturbances to public order, but quickly repealed it after an outcry from civil society groups and some public officials.

The constitution guarantees freedom of association, and a variety of nongovernmental organizations (NGOs) operate in Guatemala, though they face significant obstacles. The Guatemalan rights group the Unit for the Protection of Human Rights Defenders (UDEFEGUA) reported in December 2016 that human rights advocates had experienced 223 attacks during the first 11 months of the year, and that 14 rights activists had been murdered.

Guatemala is home to a vigorous labor movement, but workers are frequently denied the right to organize and face mass firings and blacklisting, especially in export-processing zones. Trade-union members are also subject to intimidation, violence, and murder, particularly in rural areas. According to the International Trade Union Confederation, Guatemala is one of the most dangerous countries for unionists, and a number of labor figures were killed in 2016. Among them was the deputy coordinator for the Legal Advice Commission, one of the larger unions, who was shot to death in June.

F. Rule of Law: 6 / 16 (+ 1)

The judiciary is hobbled by corruption, inefficiency, capacity shortages, and the intimidation of judges and prosecutors. Witnesses and judicial-sector workers continue to be threatened and, in some cases, murdered. In April 2016, the three branches of government inaugurated a national dialogue process to propose judicial reforms. In June, the legislature approved a measure, based on recommendations issued in 2015, that created a new mechanism for evaluating and sanctioning judges.

The increasing independence of the attorney general's office and its work with CICIG to root out corruption reflect a strengthening of the justice system in Guatemala. However, the attorney general has faced serious intimidation, including death threats, in connection with her work investigating the systemic syphoning of state funds by public and private actors. In August 2016, she reported that unknown parties had spied on her home using a drone. In April 2016, the government extended CICIG's mandate until 2019.

Police are accused of torture, extortion, kidnapping, extrajudicial killings, and drug-related crimes. Prison facilities are grossly overcrowded and rife with gang and drug-related violence and corruption. Prison riots are common, and are frequently deadly. In July 2016, an ex-army captain who ran a powerful criminal operation, and twelve others, were killed during a prison riot. People in pretrial detention comprise a large percentage of those in detention facilities. In 2016, the prisons operated without permanent directors.

The country's homicide rate continued to drop in 2016, for the seventh straight year. However, violent crime is a serious problem. In 2016, officials reported 4,550 homicides, compared to 4,778 in 2015. Violence related to the transport of drugs between South America and the United States has spilled over the border from Mexico, with rival Mexican and Guatemalan gangs battling for territory. These groups operate with impunity in the northern jungles. For most of 2016, Morales did not have a cohesive plan to address the country's violence. In August 2016, he met with other presidents in the region to discuss an antigang strategy.

The extrajudicial lynching of suspected criminals by private citizens occurs frequently.

A small number of perpetrators of human rights atrocities from the 1960–96 civil war have been being prosecuted, and cases continued in 2016. In January, 18 high-ranking officers joined those arrested in connection with massacres and disappearances in the 1980s. In February, in the Sepur Zarco trial, two officers were convicted for holding indigenous women in sexual slavery during the civil war. A close adviser to the president is facing charges of massacres during the conflict. The trial of Ríos Montt—whose 2013 conviction for genocide was overturned by the Constitutional Court 10 days after it was issued—was scheduled to begin in January 2016, but has been repeatedly postponed. He has been declared medically unfit to stand trial and will not face criminal penalties if convicted.

Indigenous communities suffer from high rates of poverty, illiteracy, and infant mortality. Indigenous women are particularly marginalized. Discrimination against the Mayan community is a major concern.

Members of the LGBT (lesbian, gay, bisexual, and transgender) community are not covered under antidiscrimination laws. They face discrimination, violence, and police abuse. The country's human rights ombudsman has stated that people suffering from HIV/AIDS also face discrimination. In January 2016, the first, openly gay person was sworn into the legislature.

G. Personal Autonomy and Individual Rights: 8 / 16

Nonstate actors, including gangs and organized criminal groups, threaten freedom of travel, residence, and employment, often through threats or acts of violence, with women being particularly vulnerable. Between January and September 2016, 112 people had been killed while using the public transport system. The Internal Displacement Monitoring Center estimates that in 2015, there were 251,000 internal displacements, largely due to violence. Property rights and economic freedom rarely extend beyond Guatemalans with wealth and political connections. Private businesses continue to experience high rates of contraband smuggling and extortion by criminal groups.

In recent years, the government approved the eviction of indigenous groups to make way for mining, hydroelectric, and other development projects. In a victory to such groups, in December 2016, a mining company was forced to stop a hydroelectric project due to local protests. In a 2016 lawsuit, a Mayan woman claimed that workers with a Canadian mining company had sexually assaulted her before setting her home on fire; she filed the case in Canada, instead of Guatemala, due to the low rate of successful prosecutions in domestic cases involving claims by indigenous people against foreign corporations.

The constitution prohibits discrimination based on gender, though inequalities between men and women persist. Sexual harassment in the workplace is not penalized. Young women who migrate to the capital for work are vulnerable to harassment and inhumane labor conditions. Physical and sexual violence against women and children remains widespread, with perpetrators rarely prosecuted.

According to the National Institute of Forensic Science (INACIF), 739 women were victims of a violent death in 2016. Women are underrepresented in government posts. Currently, 9 of 338 elected mayors are women, and only 13 percent of elected legislators are women.

Guatemala has one of the highest rates of child labor in the Americas. Criminal gangs often force children and young men to join their organizations or perform work for them, and government officials are complicit in trafficking.

Guinea

Political Rights Rating: 5
Civil Liberties Rating: 5
Freedom Rating: 5.0
Freedom Status: Partly Free
Electoral Democracy: No

Population: 11,200,000
Capital: Conakry

Ten-Year Ratings Timeline For Year Under Review (Political Rights, Civil Liberties, Status)

Year Under Review	2007	2008	2009	2010	2011	2012	2013	2014	2015	2016
Rating	6,5,NF	7,5,NF	7,6,NF	5,5,PF	5,5,PF	5,5,PF	5,5,PF	5,5,PF	5,5,PF	5,5,PF

Overview: Since Guinea returned to civilian rule in 2010 following a 2008 military coup and decades of authoritarian governance, elections have been plagued by violence, delays, and other flaws. The government uses restrictive criminal laws to discourage dissent, and political disputes are often exacerbated by ethnic divisions and pervasive corruption. Regular abuse of civilians by military and police forces reflects a deep-seated culture of impunity.

KEY DEVELOPMENTS IN 2016:

- A new criminal code adopted in July outlawed torture but appeared to exclude a range of abusive practices from the definition. It also retained criminal penalties for defamation, among other problematic provisions.
- In August, a senior member of the political opposition, Ousmane Gaoual Diallo, received a suspended two-year prison sentence for making statements that were deemed offensive to the president.
- Overdue local elections were tentatively scheduled for early 2017 under a political accord reached in October.
- A number of journalists were reportedly detained and beaten by security forces, and one was killed, while attempting to cover politically sensitive events during the year.

EXECUTIVE SUMMARY

In June 2016, the World Health Organization declared an end to transmission of the Ebola virus in Guinea, where a deadly regional outbreak had begun in 2013. A similar declaration in late December 2015 had been followed by new cases. The outbreak as a whole killed over 2,500 people in Guinea, devastated the fragile economy, and increased mistrust of the government.

Disputes over long-delayed local elections continued to fuel tensions between the governing and opposition parties in 2016. Local balloting originally due in 2010 had been repeatedly postponed, and the country had not held such elections since 2005. In October, the opposition announced a political agreement to schedule the vote for February 2017, but it remained unclear at year's end whether the plan would proceed. Contributing to the tensions, the government repeatedly failed to respect the freedoms of peaceful assembly and expression during the year. Journalists and opposition protesters faced violence and harassment from security forces, as well as prosecution for offenses such as insulting the president.

Corruption remained pervasive, and the courts suffered from a long-standing lack of resources and capacity. Impunity for Guinea's security forces also persisted, with little accountability for the hundreds of deaths and injuries they had inflicted on protesters and other civilians over the past decade.

POLITICAL RIGHTS: 17 / 40

A. Electoral Process: 6 / 12

Guinea's president is elected by popular vote for up to two five-year terms. In the 2015 election, incumbent president Alpha Condé of the Rally of the Guinean People (RPG) defeated former prime minister Cellou Dalein Diallo of the Union of Democratic Forces of Guinea (UFDG), taking 57.8 percent of the vote to secure a second and final term. The months preceding the election were characterized by ethnic tensions, violence between RPG and UFDG supporters, and deadly clashes between opposition supporters and security forces. Election day itself was peaceful, but opposition candidates filed unsuccessful legal challenges of the results, claiming fraud and vote rigging. Despite a number of logistical problems, international observers deemed the vote valid.

Of the unicameral National Assembly's 114 seats, 38 are awarded through single-member constituency races and 76 are filled through nationwide proportional representation, all for five-year terms. The 2013 parliamentary elections were also marred by deadly violence, ethnic tensions, and disputes over the rules governing the polls. The RPG won 53 seats, the UFDG won 37 seats, and a dozen smaller parties divided the remainder.

Local elections were last held in 2005. The next balloting was due in 2010, but was postponed during the transition to civilian rule after the 2008 military coup. The local elections were then scheduled for early 2014, between the parliamentary and presidential elections, only to be repeatedly delayed, with the government at times citing the Ebola crisis. Negotiations between the major parties during 2016 resulted in a tentative plan, announced in October, to hold the elections in February 2017. The agreement also called for reform of the electoral commission.

B. Political Pluralism and Participation: 8 / 16

The main political parties are the RPG and the UFDG. More than 130 parties are registered, most of which have clear ethnic or regional bases. Relations between the RPG and opposition parties are strained, and violent election-related clashes between RPG supporters, who are predominantly drawn from the Malinké ethnic group, and UFDG supporters, who are largely from the Peul ethnic group, have inflamed tensions.

During 2016, political disputes including the overdue local elections led to further confrontations between the government and opposition. Authorities blocked a women's opposition protest march in April, and in August a senior UFDG lawmaker, Ousmane Gaoual Diallo, received a two-year suspended prison sentence for statements that were deemed insulting to President Condé. Also in August, opposition parties held demonstrations in Conakry that brought an estimated half a million supporters into the streets. Though the protests were largely peaceful, a policeman shot and killed a bystander, resulting in the officer's reported arrest. Tensions between the UFDG and RPG eased somewhat after the conclusion of the political accord in October.

Separately, rifts within the UFDG erupted into violence in February, when ousted party vice president Amadou Oury Bah was barred from a meeting at the UFDG headquarters. Amid clashes between his supporters and those of party president Cellou Dalein Diallo, journalist El-Hadj Mohamed Diallo was fatally shot. Of the 20 UFDG supporters arrested over the incident, one subsequently died in pretrial detention, and 17 others were freed in August.

C. Functioning of Government: 3 / 12

The legitimacy of executive and legislative officials is undermined by the flawed electoral process, and their ability to determine and implement laws and policies without undue interference is impeded by factors including impunity among security forces and rampant corruption.

The National Anti-Corruption Agency (ANLC) reports directly to the presidency, and is considered to be underfunded and understaffed. A government audit whose findings were released in October 2016 uncovered thousands of civil service positions held by absent or deceased workers.

While Guinea was declared in full compliance with the Extractive Industry Transparency Initiative in 2014, allegations of high-level corruption in the mining sector have continued. In May 2016, the international anticorruption watchdog Global Witness alleged that Sable Mining supported President Condé's 2010 election campaign, using his son as an intermediary, in return for the iron-mining license that it later received. The president denied any wrongdoing and said the government would work with Global Witness to collect evidence for an investigation. Separately, U.S. authorities in August arrested Samuel Mebiame, the son of a former prime minister of Gabon, for allegedly paying bribes to Guinean officials to secure mining concessions. In November, mining giant Rio Tinto admitted to paying over $10 million to a presidential adviser to secure a mining concession.

Guinean authorities took some steps to punish corruption outside the mining sector. In July, two officials were convicted for embezzlement of funds earmarked for Ebola relief. Also that month, three officials were convicted for selling diplomatic passports.

An access to information law adopted in 2010 has never been effectively implemented.

CIVIL LIBERTIES: 24 / 40 (+ 1)

D. Freedom of Expression and Belief: 10 / 16 (+ 1)

The 2010 constitution guarantees media freedom, but Guinea has struggled to uphold freedom of expression in practice. A new criminal code adopted in July 2016 retained penalties of up to five years in prison for defamation or insult of public figures. A cybersecurity law passed the previous month criminalized similar offenses online, as well as the dissemination of information that is false, protected on national security grounds, or "likely to disturb law and order or public security or jeopardize human dignity."

Among other physical attacks and criminal charges against journalists during the year, in February gendarmes reportedly beat a journalist while he was filming a protest and destroyed his camera. In June, a radio host was fined 1 million Guinean francs ($115) after a listener called in and made remarks deemed insulting to the president. The caller, also a journalist, received a one-year prison sentence in absentia and a fine of 1.5 million francs. Separately that month, presidential guards reportedly detained and beat a journalist and destroyed his equipment after he photographed Condé in front of RPG headquarters. In August, police allegedly detained and beat a journalist while he was attempting to cover the trial of opposition politician Ousmane Gaoual Diallo.

Several dozen newspapers publish regularly in Guinea, though most have small circulations. More than 30 private radio stations and a few private television stations compete with the public broadcaster, Radio Télévision Guinéenne (RTG). Due to the high illiteracy rate, most of the population accesses information through radio; internet access remains limited to urban areas.

Religious rights are generally respected in practice. Some non-Muslim government workers have reported occasional discrimination. People who convert from Islam to Christianity sometimes encounter pressure from members of their community.

Academic freedom has historically faced political restrictions under authoritarian regimes. The problem has eased in recent years, particularly since the return to civilian rule in 2010, though self-censorship still tends to reduce the vibrancy of academic debate.

There are few limits on free and open private discussion.

E. Associational and Organizational Rights: 5 / 12

Freedom of assembly is enshrined in the constitution, but this right is often restricted. In practice, assemblies held without notification, a requirement under Guinean law, are considered unauthorized and are often violently dispersed, leading to deaths, injuries, and arrests. Several such incidents occurred during 2016. In August, local human rights groups denounced the arrest of a dozen young protesters who had gathered to demonstrate against the poor living conditions that have compelled many Guineans to undertake the dangerous journey across the Mediterranean to Europe.

Freedom of association is generally respected. However, Guinean civil society remains weak, ethnically divided, and subject to periodic harassment and intimidation. Although workers are allowed to form trade unions, strike, and bargain collectively, they must provide 10 days' notice before striking, and strikes are banned in broadly defined essential services. Public-and private-sector unions mounted a four-day general strike in February 2016 over low wages and high fuel prices before reaching an agreement with the government. Sixteen trade union members who had been arrested during the strike were released. In March, five members of a union for retired military personnel were sentenced to six months in jail and fines of 1 million francs for insulting the president.

F. Rule of Law: 4 / 16

The judicial system has demonstrated some degree of independence since 2010, though the courts remain understaffed and underfunded, and have been slow to adjudicate high-profile criminal cases—most prominently, the massacre of more than 150 opposition protesters by the forces of the military junta at Conakry stadium in 2009. Judges investigating the massacre have made some progress, and a number of current and former officials have been charged, but the case remains at the investigation stage.

The new criminal code adopted by the National Assembly in July 2016 abolished the death penalty and explicitly outlawed torture for the first time. However, the military code of justice retained the death penalty for certain offenses, and human rights watchdogs noted that the new criminal code categorized a number of acts that fall within the international definition of torture as merely "inhuman and cruel," a category that does not carry any explicit penalties in the code.

Security forces continue to engage in arbitrary arrests and torture of detainees with impunity. However, unlike in previous years, at least some personnel were arrested or investigated for abuses during 2016. For example, 11 soldiers were charged over an incident in June in which the beating of a truck driver sparked violent confrontations between civilians and security forces.

Prison conditions remain harsh and are sometimes life threatening. Most prisoners are in prolonged pretrial detention, which contributes to severe overcrowding. In 2015 the government adopted a plan of priority actions for justice reform, and it has begun to build and staff new courthouses and construct a new prison, though progress has reportedly stalled.

Antidiscrimination laws do not protect LGBT (lesbian, gay, bisexual, and transgender) people. Same-sex sexual activity is a criminal offense that can be punished with up to three years in prison, and although this law is rarely enforced, LGBT people have been arrested on lesser charges.

G. Personal Autonomy and Individual Rights: 5 / 16

Freedom of movement has long been hindered by rampant crime and ubiquitous security checkpoints, but restrictions related to the Ebola epidemic have largely been removed.

Private business activity is hampered by corruption and political instability, among other factors. A centralized Agency for the Promotion of Private Investments aims to ease the business registration process. Following recent reforms, property registration processes have become faster and less expensive.

Societal discrimination against women is pervasive, and Guinea ranked 122 out of 144 countries on the World Economic Forum's 2016 Gender Gap Index. Under the electoral law, at least 30 percent of the candidates on the proportional representation lists for the National Assembly must be women. Women hold nearly 22 percent of the seats in the assembly. Rape and sexual harassment are common but underreported due to fears of stigmatization. While women have legal access to land, credit, and business, they are disadvantaged by inheritance laws and the traditional justice system. Guinean law allows husbands to forbid their wives from working. Female genital mutilation is illegal but nearly ubiquitous, affecting up to 97 percent of all girls and women in the country, the second-highest rate in the world. In August 2016, the government launched a campaign to discourage the practice. The new criminal code adopted in July set the legal age for marriage at 18, but early and forced marriages remained extremely common.

Guinean women and children are subject to sex trafficking and forced labor in various industries. Guinean boys have been forced to work in mines in Guinea and in neighboring countries, and women and children have been trafficked for sexual exploitation to other parts of West Africa as well as Europe and the Middle East. The 2016 criminal code specifically criminalized trafficking in persons and debt bondage, but reduced the minimum penalties for such crimes, and enforcement has been weak.

Guinea-Bissau

Political Rights Rating: 5
Civil Liberties Rating: 5
Freedom Rating: 5.0
Freedom Status: Partly Free
Electoral Democracy: No

Population: 1,900,000
Capital: Bissau

Ten-Year Ratings Timeline For Year Under Review (Political Rights, Civil Liberties, Status)

Year Under Review	2007	2008	2009	2010	2011	2012	2013	2014	2015	2016
Rating	4,4,PF	4,4,PF	4,4,PF	4,4,PF	4,4,PF	6,5,PF	6,5,NF	5,5,PF	5,5,PF	5,5,PF

Overview: Guinea-Bissau's 2014 elections, held two years after a military coup, marked a significant improvement in democratic governance. However, the country remains politically fragile, with the months since the elections marked by divisions in the ruling party and the rise and fall of numerous prime ministers. Corruption remains a major problem, bolstered by the country's prominent role in international drug trafficking and by the government's limited resources to combat it. Violence and homicides remain serious issues.

KEY DEVELOPMENTS IN 2016:

- President José Mário Vaz's rule has been marked by frequent political shifts. Under his administration, by November 2016 the country had seen five prime ministers in the course of nine months.
- A number of protests took place during the year, during which participants expressed their dismay with ongoing political instability. One such demonstration in May, held outside the presidential palace, ended in violence when police employed force against protesters who were burning tires and throwing rocks.
- In June, authorities temporarily suspended the political debate radio program "Cartas na Mesa," in a signal of the government's willingness to suppress public scrutiny of officials.

EXECUTIVE SUMMARY

Tensions between President Vaz and members of his own African Party for the Independence of Guinea and Cabo Verde (PAIGC) remained high in 2016. Vaz dissolved the government and removed Prime Minister Carlos Correia in May, replacing him with Baciro Djá; he then replaced Djá with Umaro Sissoco Embaló in November, making Embaló the fifth prime minister to come to power in just nine months. The frequent changes in the government have led to protests and threatened flows of international aid and trade. However, the military has refrained from intervening—a positive sign, given Guinea-Bissau's history of coups. The head of the armed forces, Biaguê Nan Tan, reaffirmed in November 2016 that the military would stay out of political affairs.

International donors, encouraged by successful elections in 2014, have acted to support economic and political stability in Guinea-Bissau, and the economy has been growing. However, the government remains highly dependent on foreign aid, and donors pull back funding when the situation becomes unstable. Corruption remains a major problem, bolstered by Guinea-Bissau's prominent role in international drug trafficking and by the government's limited resources to combat it.

In June 2016, the national radio broadcaster Rádio Difusão Nacional (RDN) temporarily suspended the political debate program "Cartas na Mesa" in a signal of the government's willingness to suppress public scrutiny of officials. Separately, protests in May against the dismissal of Correia and appointment of Djá as the new prime minister were dispersed by police using tear gas and physical force after protestors began throwing stones and setting tires on fire.

The judiciary and criminal justice system remain weak, and violence and homicides are serious problems. However, conditions with regard to arbitrary arrest and detention appear to have durably improved since the country's return to electoral politics in 2014.

POLITICAL RIGHTS: 16 / 40

A. Electoral Process: 7 / 12

B. Political Pluralism and Participation: 8 / 16

C. Functioning of Government: 1 / 12

CIVIL LIBERTIES: 24 / 60 (+ 1)

D. Freedom of Expression and Belief: 10 / 16

E. Associational and Organizational Rights: 5 / 12

F. Rule of Law: 4 / 16 (+ 1)

G. Personal Autonomy and Individual Rights: 5 / 16

This country report has been abridged for *Freedom in the World 2017*. For background information on political rights and civil liberties in Guinea-Bissau, see *Freedom in the World 2016*.

Guyana

Political Rights Rating: 2
Civil Liberties Rating: 3
Freedom Rating: 2.5
Freedom Status: Free
Electoral Democracy: Yes

Population: 800,000
Capital: Georgetown

Ten-Year Ratings Timeline For Year Under Review (Political Rights, Civil Liberties, Status)

Year Under Review	2007	2008	2009	2010	2011	2012	2013	2014	2015	2016
Rating	2,3,F	2,3,F	2,3,F	2,3,F	2,3,F	2,3,F	2,3,F	2,3,F	2,3,F	2,3,F

The country or territory displayed here received scores but no narrative report for this edition of *Freedom in the World*.

Haiti

Political Rights: 5
Civil Liberties: 5
Freedom Rating: 5.0
Freedom Status: Partly Free
Electoral Democracy: No

Population: 11,100,000
Capital: Port-au-Prince

Ten-Year Ratings Timeline For Year Under Review (Political Rights, Civil Liberties, Status)

Year Under Review Rating	2007	2008	2009	2010	2011	2012	2013	2014	2015	2016
	4,5,PF	4,5,PF	4,5,PF	4,5,PF	4,5,PF	4,5,PF	4,5,PF	5,5,PF	5,5,PF	5,5,PF

Overview: Weak institutions and corruption hinder the capacities of the Haitian government, and international actors wield significant influence in the country. Haiti continues to recover from devastating hurricanes that damaged crops and infrastructure, displaced thousands, and inflicted widespread hardship.

KEY DEVELOPMENTS IN 2016:

- Jovenel Moïse, the preferred candidate of former president Michel Martelly, won a November rerun of the previous year's flawed presidential election. But because an electoral tribunal had not formally verified the vote by year's end, interim president Jocelerme Privert remained in office.
- In January, most members of the legislature were sworn in, despite serious questions about the legitimacy of the 2015 legislative polls.
- Hurricane Matthew struck the country in October, killing some 500 people, displacing thousands, and inflicting widespread hardship.

EXECUTIVE SUMMARY

President Michel Martelly's term ended in February 2016, but due to the postponement of the second round of the 2015 presidential election, there was no successor to assume office. The National Assembly (a joint session of parliament) subsequently elected the National Assembly president, Senator Jocelerme Privert, to serve as interim president, and he was sworn in with a mandate to restore confidence in the electoral process within 120 days. When Privert's mandate expired in June, opposition parliamentarians refused to meet the quorum necessary to extend it or propose a replacement, leaving Privert in office. A rerun of the 2015 presidential election took place in November, with Moïse, Martelly's handpicked successor, winning 55.6 percent of the vote, according to provisional results. The election, which saw voter turnout of only 21 percent, was considered an improvement compared to the 2015 polls but was nonetheless contested. Privert remained in office at year's end, because an electoral tribunal tasked with assessing claims of fraud in the November poll had not yet issued a ruling.

Though the 2015 legislative elections were widely considered fraudulent, the majority of parliament took office in January 2016. Despite a constitutional guarantee of 30 percent female representation in public offices, only 3 women sit in the 118-seat Chamber of Deputies.

Hurricane Matthew caused significant damage in October, killing more than 500 people, displacing some 175,000, and inflicting widespread hardship. Matthew destroyed crops across the region, resulting in a sharp increase in food prices and pushing some 800,000 people into severe food insecurity, according to the United Nations Office for the Coordination of Humanitarian Affairs.

POLITICAL RIGHTS: 15 / 40 (− 2)

A. Electoral Process: 3 / 12 (− 1)

Haiti's constitution provides for a president elected for a five-year term, a parliament composed of a Senate, whose 30 members serve six-year terms, and a Chamber of Deputies whose 118 members serve four-year terms. The prime minister is appointed by the president and approved by the parliament. According to the constitution, a National Assembly, or joint session of parliament, may be called under certain circumstances.

A number of electoral councils appointed by President Martelly did not meet constitutional requirements and did not receive parliamentary approval; that, combined with pushback from the opposition, delayed 2011 and 2013 midterm elections. By January 2015, the terms of two-thirds of the Senate, all members of the Chamber of Deputies, and all mayors had expired. The vacancies allowed the executive branch to govern with little legislative supervision.

The United States, United Nations, and Organization of American States (OAS) all provided significant support for long-awaited presidential, legislative, and local elections held in 2015. The elections were rife with disorder, fraud, and violence, and were marked by very low voter turnout. A network of Haitian observers labeled the vote "an affront to democratic standards," and considered the irregularities serious enough to jeopardize the legitimacy of the legislature. No party won a parliamentary majority. The Haitian Tet Kale Party (PHTK), which supports Martelly, took 26 seats in the Chamber of Deputies and was aided by an additional 15 won by three of its allies. The Vérité (Truth) party won 13 seats, and smaller parties divided the remainder. Of the contested seats in the Senate, PHTK ally Konvansyon Inite Demokratik (KID) and Vérité won 3 seats each, PHTK won 2 seats, and 4 smaller parties captured 1 seat each. Despite concerns about the election's credibility, 92 parliamentarians took office in January 2016.

The presidential runoff election was postponed until January 2016, but amid growing calls for an investigation into possible fraud in the first round of presidential voting, it was then postponed indefinitely. At the end of Martelly's term in February, Privert was elected interim president by the National Assembly and sworn in with a mandate to restore confidence in the electoral process within 120 days.

Meanwhile, based on the recommendations of two official commissions that investigated claims of fraud, a new electoral council agreed to rerun the presidential election in October. In response, the European Union (EU) withdrew its electoral observation mission and the United States withdrew its electoral funding. Haiti pledged to fund the elections itself. The election was postponed after Hurricane Matthew struck in early October. When it was held in November, Moïse, a businessman who belonged to the PHTK, came in first in the provisional results with 55.6 percent of the vote, followed by Jude Célestin of the Alternative League for the Progress and Emancipation of Haiti (LAPEH) with 19.5 percent. Turnout for the poll was again very low, at 21 percent, and various allegations of fraud followed. Logistical hurdles, inconsistent electoral lists, and inaccessibility of voting centers, especially in flooded, hurricane-affected areas, prevented some people from voting. Nevertheless, the election was generally considered an improvement over the previous year's.

At year's end, verification of final election results by a tribunal was still pending, and Privert remained in office.

B. Political Pluralism and Participation: 8 / 16

Political parties generally do not face legal or administrative barriers to registering or running in elections. Notwithstanding improvements in recent years, the electoral system appears to favor the preferences of incumbent powers. The number of members required to form a political party was decreased from 500 to 20 in 2014, leading to a proliferation of new groups, many of which were suspected to be formed in order to aid Martelly and his allies. The electoral council and Haitian police failed to punish perpetrators of the 2015 electoral fraud and violence. A Haitian observer mission concluded that the PHTK had been the most aggressive in committing fraud and acts of election-related violence.

Haitians' political choices are free from domination by domestic military powers and religious hierarchies. However, weak state capacity and corruption hinder the state from effectively asserting a central role in development, and international actors wield significant influence. The Haitian army was disbanded in 1995, but the UN Stabilization Mission in Haiti (MINUSTAH) has been in the country since 2004. Bringing thousands of foreign military and police personnel to Haiti, MINUSTAH is perceived as an occupying force by many Haitians. MINUSTAH's mission was extended for six months in October 2016.

C. Functioning of Government: 4 / 12 (− 1)

An interim president, election chaos, and corruption allegations impaired governance in 2016. When Privert's 120-day mandate expired in June, opposition parliamentarians refused to meet the quorum necessary to extend his mandate or propose a replacement, leaving Privert in office. He remained in office at year's end, after the year's presidential election, because Moïse's victory had yet to be formally verified.

Corruption is a serious problem. In 2016, the corruption investigation against Nonie Mathieu, a former president of the Superior Court of Auditors and Administrative Disputes (CSC/CA), Haiti's government watchdog of public funds, for allegedly misappropriating hundreds of thousands of dollars, advanced. In August, a Senate anticorruption commission headed by Senator Youri Latortue, who is himself suspected of corruption, recommended she be prosecuted.

The Haitian government and civil society organizations reduced the number of possible fatalities from Hurricane Matthew through prior warnings and evacuations, but the efforts, according to observers, were inadequate and not systemic. In the aftermath of the hurricane, there were reports that efforts of local government authorities had not been coordinated, and that local mayors had hoarded emergency aid supplies to distribute to their followers.

CIVIL LIBERTIES: 24 / 60

D. Freedom of Expression and Belief: 10 / 16

The constitution guarantees freedom of expression, but press freedom is constrained by the feeble judiciary and the inability of police to adequately protect journalists from threats and violence. Media and other observers have expressed concern about government interference with freedom of the press. Martelly, a former pop music star, released a sexually suggestive song for Haiti's annual carnival in February 2016 that belittled Liliane Pierre-Paul, a radio reporter and human rights activist, using crude language. Separately, in June, the television station Télé Pluriel was attacked by assailants armed with automatic weapons, in an incident thought to be election related. With a literacy rate of 60 percent and little print or online news material in Haitian Creole, radio remains the main source of information.

The government generally respects religious and academic freedoms. Haitians are generally free to engage in private political discussions while in public. The government is not known to block websites or illegally monitor private online communications.

E. Associational and Organizational Rights: 4 / 12

The 1987 constitution guarantees freedoms of assembly and association, though these freedoms are often violated in practice. Antigovernment demonstrations in response to electoral fraud became violent in January and November 2016, with reports of violence committed by police.

Activists with nongovernmental organizations (NGOs) that confront sensitive topics risk threats and violence. Activist Davidtchen Siméon, of the leftist Movement of Liberty, Equality of the Haitians for Fraternity (MOLEGHAF), which opposes MINUSTAH, was shot to death in August 2016 by a group of armed men that witnesses said included police officers. MOLEGHAF leader David Oxygène later reported being threatened by one of the officers accused of involvement in Siméon's killing. Pierre Espérance, director of the human rights organization the National Network for the Defense of Human Rights (RNDDH), received an envelope containing a bullet and a note threatening him and his family in December.

The ability to unionize is protected under the law, though the union movement in Haiti is weak and lacks collective bargaining power. Workers frequently face harassment and other repercussions for organizing. A five-month strike at the state's general hospital in Port-au-Prince to contest the working conditions of medical staff and the lack of medical supplies ended in September 2016.

F. Rule of Law: 4 / 16

The judicial system is under resourced and inefficient, and is burdened by a large backlog of cases, underpaid staff, outdated legal codes, and poor facilities. Bribery common at all levels of the judicial system. Official court business is conducted primarily in French, rendering proceedings only marginally comprehensible to many of those involved.

Police are regularly accused of abusing suspects and detainees. Haitian law guarantees a hearing within 48 hours after arrest, yet much of the prison population is in prolonged pretrial detention, including most minors and women held in the system. In September 2016, interim president Privert created a nine-member commission to analyze the problem of extended pretrial detention. The prison system is severely overcrowded. In October, more than 170 prisoners escaped the Arcahaie prison in northern Haiti; only 10 were reportedly recaptured.

Considerable discrimination exists against people with disabilities. Three deaf women were murdered in March 2016 in what appeared to be a hate crime. Three people had been arrested for the crime by mid-year.

Discrimination against women and LGBT (lesbian, gay, bisexual, and transgender) individuals is pervasive within the legal system and in broader society. In September 2016, organizers of an LGBT art event received death threats. The event was canceled by the Port-au-Prince authorities and publicly condemned by Senator Jean Renel Senatus, who stated that the festival promoted values that were contrary to Haiti's social and cultural morals. Spousal rape, sexual harassment, and discrimination on the basis of sexual orientation are not criminalized.

G. Personal Autonomy and Individual Rights: 6 / 16

The neighboring Dominican Republic has begun to enforce laws that prevent people of Haitian descent from exercising their political and civil rights. In response, tens of thousands of people of Haitian origin, including many unaccompanied minors, have been repatriated from Dominican Republic, or have entered Haiti for fear of staying. Additionally, in

September 2016, the United States announced that it would begin deporting Haitians who had been in the country since a devastating 2010 earthquake; the deportations were temporarily put on hold after Hurricane Matthew struck but commenced in November. Haitian officials offer few services and resources to returnees, who often struggle to survive, given the country's 60 percent unemployment rate and broader lack of government services. At the end of 2016, 46,691 persons displaced by the 2010 earthquake still lived in makeshift camps around Port-au-Prince. In addition, in November, some 14,000 people displaced by Hurricane Matthew were living in shelters.

Difficulty registering property, enforcing contracts, and getting credit led to Haiti being ranked 181 out of 190 by the World Bank's *Ease of Doing Business Report.* Spotty record keeping and corruption result in severe inconsistencies in property-rights enforcement; those with political and economic connections frequently rely on extrajudicial means of enforcement.

The government generally respects freedom of movement and the rights of individuals to choose their own employment, education, and residence. Although the government does not restrict these activities, freedom to engage in them highly depends on economic means. Economic insecurity is a main contributor to Haitians' inability to enforce their individual rights. Sixty percent of Haitians earn the equivalent of one dollar a day or less. Almost half of Haiti's children do not attend school.

According to the U.S. State Department's 2016 *Trafficking in Persons Report,* Haiti is a source, transit, and destination country for the trafficking of men, women, and children for the purposes of forced labor and sexual exploitation.

Honduras

Political Rights Rating: 4
Civil Liberties Rating: 4
Freedom Rating: 4.0
Freedom Status: Partly Free
Electoral Democracy: No

Population: 8,200,000
Capital: Tegucigalpa

Ten-Year Ratings Timeline For Year Under Review (Political Rights, Civil Liberties, Status)

Year Under Review	2007	2008	2009	2010	2011	2012	2013	2014	2015	2016
Rating	3,3,PF	3,3,PF	4,4,PF	4,4,PF	4,4,PF	4,4,PF	4,4,PF	4,4,PF	4,4,PF	4,4,PF

Overview: Honduras is a multiparty democracy, but institutional weakness, corruption, violence, and impunity undermine its stability. Journalists, human rights defenders, and political activists face significant threats, including harassment, surveillance, detention, and murder. Though it has fallen in recent years, Honduras's murder rate remains among the highest per capita in the world.

KEY DEVELOPMENTS IN 2016

- In March, internationally recognized rights activist Berta Cáceres was murdered in her home after campaigning against the construction of a dam on indigenous lands.
- In April, leaked documents revealed that high-ranking police officials had been involved in the 2009 killing of Honduras's top antidrug official, and in the murder

of his deputy two years later. Major reforms to the national police force followed the revelations.

* The Mission to Support the Fight against Corruption and Impunity in Honduras (MACCIH), a body established in a 2015 agreement between the Honduran government and the Organization of American States (OAS), began work in April.
* In August, Congress rejected an opposition-backed initiative to hold a plebiscite on a controversial 2015 Supreme Court decision to allow presidential reelection. In November, President Juan Orlando Hernández announced he would seek a second term.

EXECUTIVE SUMMARY

The March 2016 murder of Cáceres, a high-profile rights activist, and the revelation in April that top police officials had been involved in the past murders of two top antidrug officials, drew renewed international attention to pervasive violence, corruption, and impunity in Honduras. The country is among the most dangerous in the world for rights activists to operate, and its per capita murder rate is among the world's highest. Attacks generally go unpunished, leaving a pervasive climate of impunity.

In response to the revelations of high-level police officials' involvement in the murders of the antidrug officials, a Special Commission for the Purging and Reform of the National Police was formed in April 2016. During the year it conducted investigations and instituted various organizational changes to the police force, including the discharge of more than 1,000 police officials.

In response to national and international pressure over a scandal involving the misappropriation of social security funds, the Hernández government in 2015 signed an agreement with the OAS to create MACCIH, which began operating in April 2016. During the year, the body investigated the social security scandal, and helped to develop a party financing law and a new court system for corruption cases.

In August, Congress rejected an opposition-backed initiative to hold a plebiscite on a controversial 2015 Supreme Court decision to allow presidential reelection. Opponents of the ruling say the Supreme Court lacked the authority to overturn the article of the constitution that banned presidents from running for a second term. In November, amid the controversy, President Hernández announced that he would run for a second term in 2017.

POLITICAL RIGHTS: 19 / 40

A. Electoral Process: 7 / 12

The president is elected by popular vote for a four-year term. The leading candidate is only required to win a plurality; there is no runoff system. In a controversial 2015 decision, the Honduran Supreme Court voided Article 239 of the constitution, which had limited presidents to one term; the development exacerbated existing political polarization and the opposition attempted unsuccessfully to reverse the move in 2016. In November, the president announced plans to run for a second term.

Members of the 128-seat, unicameral National Congress are elected for four-year terms using proportional representation by department.

Election observers noted a number of irregularities in the 2013 general elections, including the harassment of international observers by immigration officials, vote buying, problems with voter rolls, and potential fraud in the transmission of tally sheets to the country's electoral body, the Supreme Electoral Tribunal (TSE). More than a dozen opposition activists and candidates were murdered during the campaigning period. The TSE conducted a partial recount, but ultimately certified Hernández's victory.

OAS monitors found that the TSE did not have clear rules for processing candidate registration applications and along with European Union monitors also noted inconsistencies in the development of voter lists. The OAS also found that campaign finance laws in Honduras were not stringent enough to ensure fair and transparent elections.

B. Political Pluralism and Participation: 8 / 16 (− 1)

Political parties are largely free to operate, though power has mostly been concentrated in the hands of the Liberal Party (PL) and the National Party (PN) since the early 1980s. In 2013, Liberation and Refoundation Party (LIBRE), the Anti-Corruption Party (PAC), and the Patriotic Alliance Party (ALIANZA) all participated in elections for the first time, winning a significant share of the vote and disrupting the dominance of the PL and the PN.

The military, after decades of ruling Honduras, remains politically powerful. President Hernández's appointments of military officials to civilian posts, many related to security, have underscored that influence.

In August 2016, Congress rejected an opposition-backed initiative to hold a plebiscite on the Supreme Court's 2015 decision to allow presidential reelection, with opponents of the ruling saying that the Supreme Court did not have the authority to overturn the relevant article of the constitution. This rejection has exacerbated a constitutional crisis that began with the 2009 coup against Mario Zelaya, who was ousted when he had attempted to eliminate term limits through constitutional reforms. President Hernández is running for a second term in 2017; police broke up some demonstrations against the constitutional changes and his reelection campaign in 2016.

Minorities are underrepresented in Honduras's political system. Following the 2013 elections, 33 of 128 seats in Congress were held by women; only 22 of 298 mayoralties were held by women. No representatives of the Afro-Honduran (Garifuna) population were elected to Congress in 2013; one English-speaking Afro-Honduran and one Miskito person won seats. No election materials were printed in indigenous languages. In 2014, the Ministry for Indigenous Peoples and Afro-Hondurans was folded into the Ministry of Development and Social Inclusion, a move criticized by indigenous rights activists.

C. Functioning of Government: 4 / 12 (+ 1)

In 2014, the Hernández administration eliminated five cabinet-level ministries and created seven umbrella ministries in an effort to cut costs. Critics have argued that the restructuring concentrated power in too few hands.

Corruption remains a serious problem. In 2016, nine mayors were arrested for a variety of crimes, including homicide, drug trafficking, and money laundering, although two were later exonerated. As of October 2016, over 30 mayors, congressmen, judges, military officials, and police officers were under investigation for links to organized crime.

A scandal involving top officials with the Honduran Institute of Social Security (IHSS) in the misappropriation of more than $300 million in public funds broke in 2015. Later that year, Hernández admitted that his 2013 election campaign had accepted funds linked to companies implicated in the scandal, though he denied knowledge of any wrongdoing. In October 2015, the Hernández government signed an agreement with the OAS to create the MACCIH, which began operating in April 2016 and has since begun investigating the social security scandal. It also helped develop a party financing law that was approved in October, and assisted in the establishment of a new court system for corruption cases. However, local human rights and anti-impunity groups have expressed disappointment with MACCIH's mandate, saying its powers are limited.

The Law on Classification of Public Documents Related to Security and National Defense, a 2014 statute allowing the government to withhold information on those topics for up to 25 years, continued to undermine transparency. The law covers information regarding the military police budget, which is funded by a security tax.

CIVIL LIBERTIES: 27 / 60 (+ 1)

D. Freedom of Expression and Belief: 9 / 16

Authorities systematically violate the constitution's press freedom guarantees. Reporters and outlets covering sensitive topics or who are perceived as critical of authorities risk assaults, threats, blocked transmissions, and harassment.

In August 2016, television reporter Ariel Armando D'Vicente was convicted of criminal defamation and sentenced to three years in prison, and banned from practicing journalism for three years; the charges were filed in connection with his reporting on police involvement with criminal groups. In May, Honduran journalist Félix Molina was shot in a taxi in Tegucigalpa, the country's capital; the attack, from which he recovered, took place not long after he had published an article on the murder of indigenous rights leader Berta Cáceres.

A 2015 law to protect journalists, human rights defenders, and administrators of justice took effect in 2016 following a lengthy process to establish its internal regulations. Feedback on the performance of the mechanism created by the law to protect these at-risk populations has been mixed, and it continues to face budgetary and staffing challenges. Most attacks against journalists go unprosecuted, creating a climate of impunity that encourages self-censorship.

Freedom of religion is broadly respected. Academic freedom is threatened as educators are subject to extortion by gang members, who control all or parts of schools in some areas. In 2016, members of a student movement demanding participation in university governance and protesting privatization of public education claimed that authorities were improperly suppressing their demonstrations.

Access to the internet use is generally unrestricted. However, under the Special Law on Interception of Private Communications, passed in 2011, the government can intercept online and telephone messages. Violence, threats, and intimidation by state and nonstate actors curtails open and free private discussion among the general population.

E. Associational and Organizational Rights: 5 / 12

Constitutional guarantees of freedoms of assembly and association are not consistently upheld. Human rights defenders and political activists continued to face significant threats in 2016, including harassment, surveillance, detention, and murder.

In March 2016, prominent indigenous rights leader Berta Cáceres was shot to death in her home, after receiving more than 30 death threats connected to her opposition of a dam project on indigenous lands. Months later, a former Honduran soldier told Britain's *Guardian* newspaper that Cáceres's name had been included on a Honduran military hit list. Six people were arrested in connection with her murder, including people associated with the construction company behind the dam, Desarollos Energéticos S.A. (DESA), as well as two active military members and one retired military officer. Case files for Cáceres's murder were stolen from the car of a judge involved in the case in September 2016, casting suspicion on the investigation. Assaults, threats, and intimidation against environmental activists, particularly members of Cáceres's organization, increased after her murder. In October, Amnesty International named Honduras a "no-go zone" for human rights defenders.

International bodies have noted that the registration process for nongovernmental organizations (NGOs) has become overly complicated; some NGOs have suggested that the moves are intended to silence criticism.

Labor unions are well organized and can strike, though labor actions often result in clashes with security forces. Threats, surveillance and attacks against union leaders and blacklisting of employees who sought to form unions remained problems in 2016.

F. Rule of Law: 5 / 16 (+ 1)

Political and business elites exert excessive influence over the Honduran judiciary, including the Supreme Court. Judicial appointments are made with little transparency. Judges have been removed from their posts for political reasons, and a number of legal professionals have been killed in recent years. Prosecutors and whistleblowers handling corruption cases are often subject to threats of violence.

In a controversial move in 2012, Congress voted to remove four of the five justices in the Supreme Court's constitutional chamber after they ruled a police reform law unconstitutional. In 2013, the legislature granted itself the power to remove from office the president, Supreme Court justices, legislators, and other officials. It also curtailed the power of the Supreme Court's constitutional chamber and revoked the right of citizens to challenge the constitutionality of laws.

The government continued to rely on the armed forces to fight crime in 2016, and critics contend that too much power is concentrated in the hands of the military. Army officers have been found guilty of involvement in drug trafficking and other crimes. An increase in reported abuses, including murder, illegal detention, and torture has accompanied the militarization of domestic policing. Private security guards have also committed abuses.

The police force is highly corrupt, and officers engage in criminal activities including drug trafficking and extortion. In September 2016, an internal police investigation revealed that 81 police officers, among them high-ranking officials, had been working for a gang and that some were involved in mass killings of civilians. In April, the media publicized leaked documents showing that high-level officials within the National Police had been involved in the 2009 murder of Honduras's top antidrug official, Julián Arístides González, and in the 2011 murder of González's top adviser. Internal police investigations into both crimes had concluded that the officials were involved in both murders, but the results were only made public after being leaked. Soon after, a Special Commission for the Purging and Reform of the National Police was formed. As of November 2016, hundreds of officials had been dismissed. Other proposed changes to the police system include modifying training procedures, eliminating redundant positions, and implementing a new organizational structure to increase transparency and create specific and functional roles within the police force.

While the murder rate in Honduras has declined in recent years, it continues to be one of the highest in the world at approximately 58.83 murders per 100,000 inhabitants in 2016, according to police.

Impunity is a serious problem in Honduras. Many crimes committed in Honduras are never reported, and police investigate only a small percentage percent of those that are. A new maximum security prison opened in 2016, marking an initial step toward a planned redesign of the country's correctional system, but prison conditions are generally harsh, with overcrowding of up to 200 percent, lengthy pretrial detention, and rampant inmate violence that generally goes unpunished. Prosecutors say protection for witnesses in criminal cases is insufficient.

Although there is an official human rights ombudsman, critics claim that the work of the office is politicized. Discrimination against the indigenous and Garifuna populations is widespread. Both groups experience high rates of poverty and socioeconomic exclusion.

The LGBT (lesbian, gay, bisexual, and transgender) community faces discrimination, harassment, and physical threats. A 2005 constitutional amendment prohibits same-sex marriage and same-sex adoption. Rights groups have reported the violent deaths of over 200 LGBT activists and individuals between 2009 and 2016.

G. Personal Autonomy and Individual Rights: 8 / 16

Honduras's ongoing violence and impunity have reduced personal autonomy for people in Honduras. Hondurans living in particularly violent neighborhoods have been forced to abandon their homes and businesses. Children have been fleeing the country to avoid forced recruitment into gangs. Corruption remains a serious problem in the private sector.

The conflict between indigenous groups, authorities, and private actors persisted in 2016, with clashes among peasants, landowners' private security forces, and state forces. Indigenous and Garifuna residents have faced various abuses at the hands of property developers and their allies, including corrupt titling processes, acts of violence, forcible eviction and unfair compensation for expropriated land. The clearing of land for clandestine airstrips used in the drug trade has increased pressure on indigenous groups in remote areas of the country.

Violence against women is a serious problem, and femicide has risen dramatically in recent years. Many of these murders, like most homicides in Honduras, go unpunished, even as femicide was added as a crime to the penal code in 2013. Women remain vulnerable to exploitation by employers, particularly in the low-wage *maquiladora* (assembly plant) export sector.

Child labor is a problem in rural areas and in the informal economy. Honduras is primarily a source country for human trafficking, and women and children are particularly vulnerable to being trafficked for the sex trade and forced labor. Domestically, gangs have forced Hondurans to traffic drugs, perform sex work, and carry out violent acts. Police and government officials have been implicated in protecting sex trafficking rings and paying for sex acts.

Hungary

Political Rights Rating: 3 ↓
Civil Liberties Rating: 2
Freedom Rating: 2.5 ↓
Freedom Status: Free
Electoral Democracy: Yes

Population: 9,800,000
Capital: Budapest

Ratings Change: Hungary's political rights rating declined from 2 to 3 due to government practices that curtailed the ability of the opposition to freely and meaningfully participate in the formal political system, as well as continuing impunity for high-level corruption.

Ten-Year Ratings Timeline For Year Under Review (Political Rights, Civil Liberties, Status)

Year Under Review	2007	2008	2009	2010	2011	2012	2013	2014	2015	2016
Rating	1,1,F	1,1,F	1,1,F	1,1,F	1,2,F	1,2,F	1,2,F	2,2,F	2,2,F	3,2,F

Overview: Since taking power in 2010, Prime Minister Viktor Orbán's Alliance of Young Democrats–Hungarian Civic Union (Fidesz) has pushed through constitutional and legal changes that have allowed it to consolidate control over the country's independent institutions. Following a dip in its popularity in 2014 and 2015, support for the party has recently increased, likely in response to its hard-line policies on migration.

KEY DEVELOPMENTS IN 2016:

- In February, a group of men physically prevented an opposition lawmaker from filing a referendum initiative on an unpopular government-backed law. The perpetrators were not held accountable.
- In October, a government-initiated referendum was held on a European Union (EU) asylum quota plan that would require Hungary to take in about 1,300 refugees housed in other EU countries. Despite heavy government spending on frequently xenophobic campaign materials, the referendum, which participating voters overwhelmingly approved, was ultimately invalid due to low voter turnout.
- In April, the release of information about several foundations created and endowed by central bank revealed a number of questionable transactions, including ones that benefit the bank's director and his allies.
- In October, Hungary's leading political daily, *Népszabadság*, was shuttered. Its closure came after it had uncovered a string of scandals involving the ruling party.

EXECUTIVE SUMMARY

Support for Prime Minister Viktor Orbán's Alliance of Young Democrats–Hungarian Civic Union (Fidesz) increased in 2016, likely reflecting support for the government's tough stance on migration. During the year, the government refused to take in some 1,300 asylum seekers and examine their applications under the EU's quota system, and challenged the underlying regulation before the European Court of Justice, in addition to holding a referendum on the issue.

Orbán announced the referendum on the EU asylum quota in February 2016, one day after a widely criticized incident at the National Election Office in which an opposition lawmaker was physically prevented by roughly a dozen men from submitting a separate referendum initiative against an unpopular, Fidesz-backed law requiring most stores to close on Sundays. The Supreme Court weeks later confirmed the opposition's referendum initiative, declaring that the use of physical force to block its filing had been illegal. The government then repealed the Sunday closure law before a referendum on the issue could take place.

The government-initiated asylum referendum was held in October, amid serious concerns over the constitutionality of the question. Following an expensive government campaign marked by xenophobic rhetoric, participating voters overwhelmingly agreed that Hungary should reject the European quota. However, turnout was only 41.3 percent, short of the 50 percent threshold needed for the referendum to be considered valid.

In March, the Constitutional Court ruled that the Hungarian Central Bank could not withhold data about public funds it had disbursed to six foundations the bank had established, which amounted to about $1 billion. The following month, information released regarding the foundations' operations revealed a number of questionable transactions, including ones that benefit the bank's director and his allies.

Hungary's media situation came under international scrutiny after the country's leading political daily, *Népszabadság*, was abruptly closed after it ran a series of articles scrutinizing actions of ruling-party members. Shortly after the suspension, the newspaper's publisher was sold to a company linked to a close ally of Prime Minister Orbán.

POLITICAL RIGHTS: 29 / 40 (− 3)

A. Electoral Process: 9 / 12

Voters elect representatives every four years to a 199-seat, unicameral National Assembly under a mixed system of proportional and direct representation (106 from districts and 93 from compensatory party lists). The National Assembly elects both the president and the prime minister. The president's duties are mainly ceremonial, but he can influence appointments and return legislation for further consideration before signing it into law.

The coalition of Fidesz and its junior coalition partner, the Christian Democratic People's Party (KDNP), won 2014 parliamentary elections with 45 percent of the vote, capturing exactly two-thirds (133) of the seats. Unity—a new coalition of five leftist parties—won 38 seats. The far-right-wing Jobbik took 23 seats, while the green-liberal Politics Can Be Different party (LMP) won 5 seats.

Throughout the rancorous campaign, opposition parties criticized recent changes to electoral legislation, including rules that facilitated the creation of instant parties, splitting the antigovernment vote; alleged gerrymandering in the ruling coalition's favor; and the government's heavy influence over state television and radio. Most of these grievances were echoed in critical assessments from international transparency watchdogs and an Organization for Security and Co-operation in Europe (OSCE) election-monitoring delegation, which also pointed to strong government influence over media and advertising outlets and grossly unequal financial resources. Election monitors also suggested that the dual system for foreign voters, under which ethnic Hungarians who have been awarded citizenship but have never lived in the country can register and vote more easily than native Hungarian citizens living abroad, "undermine[s] the principle of equal suffrage."

In 2015, Zoltán Kész, an independent candidate who drew support from left-wing parties, won with 43 percent of the vote in a parliamentary by-election in Veszprém, a traditional Fidesz stronghold. The Fidesz-KDNP coalition consequently lost the two-thirds parliamentary supermajority it had held since 2010.

B. Political Pluralism and Participation: 13 / 16 (− 2)

Political parties are able to organize without interference. After Fidesz's electoral victories in 2014, public support for the party declined significantly due to corruption allegations, political infighting, and an attempt to tax internet traffic, among other factors. However, the 2015 refugee crisis and the referendum on the EU asylum quota proposal offered opportunities for Fidesz to reassert itself among anti-immigrant and Euroskeptic voters. The ruling party's popularity, which was at a two-year low in the first half of 2015, grew in 2015 and in the second half of 2016. Parties must take at least 5 percent of the national vote to win parliament seats by proportional representation.

Fidesz and its allies have increasingly harnessed their political and economic power to prevent the opposition from influencing policy. In recent years, the government has made efforts to block referendum proposals at odds with its policies. In February 2016, an opposition politician, István Nyakó of the Socialist Party, was physically prevented by roughly a dozen men from submitting to the National Election Commission a referendum initiative against an unpopular, Fidesz-backed law requiring most stores to close on Sundays. However, the Supreme Court weeks later confirmed the referendum initiative, declaring that the use of physical force to block Nyakó had been illegal. The government subsequently moved to repeal the Sunday closure law before the referendum—which if approved was likely to damage the ruling coalition's popularity—could take place. Although it is a crime under

Hungarian law to obstruct referendum initiatives by force or threat of force, the men who blocked Nyakó were never charged.

Both the National Election Commission and the Supreme Court allowed the government's referendum initiative challenging EU asylum quotas, despite legal objections maintaining that the question could not be put to a national referendum because it challenged the country's obligations under an international treaty. The referendum campaign was unequal and costly. The government spent heavily on billboards, television campaigns, and mailings, and public media outlets echoed the government's negative view of refugees ahead of the vote. The opposition parties were divided over strategy, with Jobbik officially supporting the government's initiative, and most left-wing parties calling on voters to stay home. The satirical Two-Tailed Dog Party (MKKP) relied on donations to launch the most visible antigovernment campaign, which called on voters to spoil their ballots. The overwhelming majority of the valid votes (98.4 percent) agreed with the government's position rejecting the European quota, but turnout was only 41.3 percent, short of the 50 percent threshold needed for the vote to be considered valid. Nevertheless, the prime minister subsequently announced that there was a "new unity" and that the ruling parties would seek to amend the constitution, inserting clauses that confirm the protection of the "constitutional identity" of the country and ban the settlement of "aliens" in Hungary. The amendment failed to clear a parliamentary vote in November, with Fidesz lacking a two-thirds majority and opposition parties abstaining.

Hungary's constitution guarantees the right of ethnic minorities to form self-governing bodies, and all 13 recognized minorities have done so. Minorities can also register to vote for special minority lists—with a preferential vote threshold—in parliamentary elections, but they are then excluded from general party-list voting. None of the 13 minority lists won enough votes to secure a seat in 2014, meaning each is represented only by a nonvoting spokesperson. The Roma population in particular has long been underrepresented in political office.

C. Functioning of Government: 7 / 12 (− 1)

Corruption remains a problem in Hungary, and instances of high-level government corruption have not been properly investigated. The lack of an appropriate public-spending database presents an obstacle to the transparency of government finances. Transparency International's Hungary chapter has reported that that a number of companies with close ties to the government are supported primarily by public funds. Fidesz-allied businessmen who have fallen out of favor, like Lajos Simicska and Zoltán Spéder, have experienced financial and legal pressure. In 2015, Hungary's public procurement board banned Simicska's construction firm Közgép—which had won billions of forints in state contracts before the emergence of a rift between Simicska and Orbán—from participating in public tenders for three years. Spéder, a businessman with holdings in media and the financial sector, came under police investigation as did several of his companies in 2016, after an apparent falling out with the ruling party.

In March 2016, the governing majority adopted a controversial amendment to the law on postal services that limited the scope of public information that could be disclosed about the postal services' dealings with private companies. The same month, the parliament adopted an amendment to the law on the Hungarian National Bank that restricted public access to data on the functioning of six foundations the bank had created and endowed. European Central Bank head Mario Draghi, assessing the Hungarian National Bank's activities in a July 2016 letter, found that these foundations "could be perceived as potentially being in conflict with the monetary financing prohibition" applicable to central banks. The two legislative measures together shielded access to information on public funds amounting to more than $1 billion.

President János Áder declined to sign the national bank amendment, and instead referred it to the Constitutional Court, which struck it down. Much of the information revealed in April, following the court decision, showed irregular spending by the foundations, including decisions that benefit central bank head György Matolcsy, a close ally of Orbán and a former minister of economy, and Matolcsy's allies.

CIVIL LIBERTIES: 47 / 60

D. Freedom of Expression and Belief: 13 / 16

Hungary's constitution protects freedoms of speech and the press, but complex and extensive media legislation enacted under the Fidesz government has undermined these guarantees. Since 2011, media outlets must register with the National Media and Infocommunications Authority (NMHH), which can revoke licenses for infractions. A Media Council under the NMHH can close outlets or impose fines of up to $950,000 for failure to register or for airing content that incites hatred. Fidesz, with its parliamentary supermajority, controlled the initial appointments to the Media Council, whose members serve nine-year terms; it now requires some outside support for the approval of its nominees. The government has withdrawn most advertising from independent media since Fidesz took power in 2010.

Editorial bias and political pressure are problems at both public and private media outlets. The largest political daily, the liberal *Népszabadság*, abruptly ceased its operations in October 2016. While its Austrian investor owner cited economic reasons for the closure, the move came after the paper published stories of alleged misspending of public funds by senior government officials. Shortly after it ceased publication, *Népszabadság*'s parent company was sold to a firm linked to Orbán ally Lorinc Mészáros. In December, *Népszabadság*'s new owner announced that it did not plan to reopen the paper. There is a growing number of progovernment media outlets, including private companies, operating with heavy support from the state and state-affiliated entities. The government does not restrict or monitor the internet.

The constitution guarantees religious freedom and provides for the separation of church and state, although these guarantees were weakened in the 2011 constitution, whose preamble makes direct references to Christianity, including the recognition of "the role of Christianity in preserving nationhood." Adherents of all religions are generally free to worship. However, a two-thirds parliamentary majority must approve the right of any religious community or church to receive tax and other benefits reserved for "accepted churches." Both the Constitutional Court and the European Court of Human Rights have found the law in violation of the Hungarian constitution and the European Convention on Human Rights, respectively. A 2015 government proposal sought to remedy this while maintaining limitations, but it did not get a two-thirds majority in the parliament.

The state generally does not restrict academic freedom. However, a gradual overhaul of the public education system has raised concerns about excessive government influence on school curriculums, and legislation adopted in 2014 allows for government-appointed chancellors empowered to make financial decisions at public universities. Selective support by the government of certain academic institutions also threatens academic autonomy. There are no significant constraints on freedom of private discussion in Hungary.

E. Associational and Organizational Rights: 11 / 12

The constitution provides for freedoms of assembly and association, and the government generally respects these rights in practice. However, in July 2016, the Constitutional

Court dismissed a challenge to a ban on demonstrations at the Supreme Court and the home of the prime minister. Separately, people opposed to a government project to create a museum district in a public park in Budapest set up an encampment to prevent the cutting of a large number of trees, but were forcibly removed by security personnel in June and July.

A broad array of nongovernmental organizations (NGOs) operate in Hungary, but groups pursuing activities counter to government priorities have come under pressure in recent years. Since taking power, the Fidesz government has instituted burdensome registration and reporting requirements for NGOs, and some groups have seen their offices illegally raided by police. As part of the campaign for the referendum on the EU asylum quota proposal, Fidesz lawmaker Szilárd Németh called for a security screening of NGOs that opposed the referendum initiative. A 2016 report by the UN Special Rapporteur on the situation of human rights defenders noted a "general stigmatization" of NGOs and "shrinking civil society space," and called on the government to "refrain from criminalizing defenders' peaceful and legitimate activities." Recent years have seen the creation of a number of GONGOs, or government-organized NGOs, many of which were active during the migration crisis. State funding to NGOs and other civil society groups is distributed through the National Cooperation Fund (NEA), whose nine-member council is dominated by government and parliamentary appointees.

The government recognizes workers' rights to form associations and petition public authorities. Trade unions represent less than 30 percent of the workforce.

F. Rule of Law: 10 / 16

Judicial independence is a matter of concern. All of the 11 judges put on the Constitutional Court between 2010 and 2014 were appointed by the Fidesz government, and rulings in recent years have favored government interests. It was only well after the government lost its two-thirds majority that one opposition party—the green-liberal LMP—was included in the discussions over the election of four new judges, in November 2016.

In March 2016, the government declared a nationwide "state of national crisis," expanding the designation from a handful of counties where it was first declared the previous year; the declaration was made in response to "mass immigration," despite the fact that the number of people arriving in the country remained under the legal threshold for declaring this type of special legal order. A new government-initiated Sixth Amendment to the Fundamental Law—a draft of which was kept secret until it was leaked by a Jobbik politician—created a new type of special order granting extraordinary powers to the government in the case of a "terrorist threat." It was approved in June.

Prisons are generally approaching European standards, though overcrowding, inadequate medical care, and poor sanitation remain problems.

According to the UN High Commissioner for Refugees (UNHCR), Hungary fails to observe its obligations under international and European law protecting asylum seekers, and the European Commission started an infringement procedure against Hungary concerning its asylum law in December 2015. The erection of a fence along its border in 2015, to be extended and strengthened according to government plans; the recognition of Serbia and Turkey as "safe third countries"; the criminalization of irregular entry; and the creation of "transit zones" outside of the fence have been criticized as deterring applicants from access to asylum. Only around 15 people are allowed into a transit zone each day, and the government holds asylum seekers in dire conditions. The asylum system serving those who are eventually let in the country has been scaled back, relegating even recognized refugees to live without work or shelter. Legislation adopted in 2015 allowed Hungary's army to enforce border controls, restrict civil liberties, and employ "coercive weapons." A 2016 law allows police forces to "escort" out of the country migrants found within 8 kilometers (5 miles) inside Hungary's borders. The government continues to recruit "border hunter action units" that receive expedited training. During the year, Human Rights Watch reported cases of police violence against asylum seekers at the border. The government also impedes humanitarian efforts by NGOs and activists seeking to assist migrants and asylum seekers.

The government disseminated xenophobic propaganda in the period leading up to the October 2016 quota referendum with heavy spending on billboards, television campaigns, and mailings, connecting asylum seekers and immigrants to acts of crime and terrorism. In July 2016, Prime Minister Orbán called immigration a "poison."

G. Personal Autonomy and Individual Rights: 13 / 16

Hungarians enjoy freedom of travel and choice of residence, employment, and institution of higher education. Citizens have the right to own property and establish private businesses. Critics of recent sectoral taxes see them as efforts by the state to drive out or take over foreign businesses. Recent difficulties of business owners who have fallen out of favor with the government illustrate the extent to which business success depends on government connections.

Women possess the same legal rights as men, but they face employment discrimination and tend to be underrepresented in high-level business positions and political life. Women hold no cabinet posts and only 20 of 199 seats in the National Assembly, or 10 percent—the lowest percentage in the EU, with even lower representation (7 percent) among members of the ruling parties. The UN working group on discrimination against women found especially problematic "the pervasive and flagrant stereotyping of women, with repeated statements by some public figures that women are unsuited to political power and insistence on woman's role as primarily wife and mother." The right to life from conception is protected under the 2011 Fundamental Law, but access to abortions remained largely unrestricted in 2016. Discrimination on the basis of sexual orientation is banned under the Act on Equal Opportunity. However, in 2016, the government inserted into a budget bill an amendment seeking to make it easier to deny benefits to same-sex couples. The proposal was ultimately withdrawn after extensive media coverage and public criticism. The constitution enshrines the concept of marriage as a union between a man and a woman.

Hungary is a transit point, source, and destination for trafficked persons, including women trafficked for prostitution, and the country's efforts to support and reintegrate victims are insufficient. Roma women, men, and children; those who have been raised in state-run children's homes; and unaccompanied asylum seekers are particularly vulnerable.

Hungary has taken a number of steps to improve monitoring of Roma rights and equal treatment, but Roma, who form Hungary's largest ethnic minority, still face widespread discrimination, societal exclusion, and poverty. Roma students continue to be segregated and improperly placed in schools for children with mental disabilities. The European Commission in May 2016 sent a formal notice to the Hungarian government that it was beginning an infringement procedure on the discrimination of Roma children in education.

Iceland

Political Rights Rating: 1
Civil Liberties Rating: 1
Freedom Rating: 1.0
Freedom Status: Free
Electoral Democracy: Yes

Population: 300,000
Capital: Reykjavík

Ten-Year Ratings Timeline For Year Under Review (Political Rights, Civil Liberties, Status)

Year Under Review	2007	2008	2009	2010	2011	2012	2013	2014	2015	2016
Rating	1,1,F	1,1,F	1,1,F	1,1,F	1,1,F	1,1,F	1,1,F	1,1,F	1,1,F	1,1,F

The country or territory displayed here received scores but no narrative report for this edition of *Freedom in the World.*

India

Political Rights Rating: 2
Civil Liberties Rating: 3
Freedom Rating: 2.5
Freedom Status: Free
Electoral Democracy: Yes

Population: 1,328,900,000
Capital: New Delhi

Note: The numerical ratings and status listed above do not reflect conditions in Indian-controlled Kashmir, which is examined in a separate report.

Ten-Year Ratings Timeline For Year Under Review (Political Rights, Civil Liberties, Status)

Year Under Review	2007	2008	2009	2010	2011	2012	2013	2014	2015	2016
Rating	2,3,F	2,3,F	2,3,F	2,3,F	2,3,F	2,3,F	2,3,F	2,3,F	2,3,F	2,3,F

Overview: India maintains a robust electoral democracy with a competitive multiparty system at federal and state levels. However, politics (and business) are beset by corruption. The constitution guarantees freedom of expression and the news media are vibrant, even as speech and reportage deemed seditious or harmful to religious sentiment is routinely censored and punished. India's minority groups—notably Muslims, scheduled castes (Dalits), and scheduled tribes (Adivasis)—enjoy legal equality and sometimes benefit from affirmative action programs. However, they remain economically and socially marginalized and have been the victims of violent attacks.

KEY DEVELOPMENTS IN 2016:

- Vigilante cow-protection groups associated with nationalist Hindu organizations engaged in a number of assaults on Dalits and Muslims. Prime Minister Narendra Modi has been criticized for failing to promptly condemn the attacks.

- In February, the arrest of student protesters in Delhi on sedition charges raised concerns about freedom of expression on university campuses.
- The government passed two major economic reforms in 2016—the Goods and Services Tax bill and a demonetization policy—aimed at reducing corruption.
- Tens of millions of public sector workers went on strike for 24 hours in September to demand the establishment of a monthly minimum wage.

EXECUTIVE SUMMARY

State elections in early 2016 brought mixed news for Prime Minister Modi's incumbent Bharatiya Janata Party (BJP), which secured a legislative majority in the northeastern state of Assam for the first time, but failed to make significant inroads among voters in the south. In two of the most consequential economic reforms since economic liberalization in 1991, the government passed a major overhaul of its taxation regime and withdrew the two most common currency bills from circulation; the reforms were aimed at combatting corruption.

In February, sedition cases were initiated against student activists in connection with a protest marking the state execution of a Kashmiri separatist who was hanged in 2013 following a terrorism conviction. Separately, a professor at the University of Mysore was arrested in June in connection with a speech the previous year in which he allegedly insulted a Hindu deity. The events had a chilling effect among Indian intellectuals.

Meanwhile, threats to freedom of expression—including intimidation of and attacks against journalists and users of online social media—continued. There is increasing concern about the harassment of bloggers and social-media users by Hindu nationalists.

POLITICAL RIGHTS: 35 / 40

A. Electoral Process: 12 / 12

Elections in India are generally free and fair. Members of the lower house of parliament, the 545-seat Lok Sabha (House of the People), are directly elected in single-member constituencies for five-year terms, except for two appointed members representing Indians of European descent. The Lok Sabha determines the leadership and composition of the government. Most members of the less powerful 250-seat upper house, the Rajya Sabha (Council of States), are elected by state legislatures using a proportional-representation system to serve staggered six-year terms; up to 12 members are appointed. Executive power is vested in a prime minister and cabinet. The president, who plays a largely symbolic role, is chosen for a five-year term by state and national lawmakers. Current president Pranab Mukherjee, a former cabinet minister and veteran Congress Party leader, was elected in 2012.

In the 2014 Lok Sabha elections, the BJP won 282 seats and its National Democratic Alliance (NDA) coalition won 336 seats, ensuring a stable majority for the new government; turnout was 66 percent. The incumbent Congress Party and its United Progressive Alliance (UPA), headed by Rahul Gandhi, won just 44 and 60 seats, respectively. Modi, a three-term chief minister from the western state of Gujarat, was sworn in as prime minister. The elections, conducted with electronic voting machines, were broadly free and fair.

The Congress Party and its allies still controlled the Rajya Sabha in 2016; the BJP-led alliance held only 72 (out of 250) seats. The BJP controls the governments of 8 of India's 29 states and is a governing coalition partner in an additional 5 states.

Elections were held for five state governments in 2016. In West Bengal, postelection violence carried out by activists from several parties marred the contest. Notably, the BJP became the governing party in the northeastern state of Assam for the first time, but failed to make significant inroads with voters in the south. Across all states, the 2016 polls were generally regarded as free and fair.

B. Political Pluralism and Participation: 14 / 16

India hosts a dynamic multiparty system. Recent elections have tended to result in ruling coalitions involving large numbers of parties. In 2014, the two main national parties won only about 50 percent of the vote combined. Nonetheless, the disproportionate translation of votes to seats put the BJP in the clear majority in the lower house, marking the first time a single party won a majority of seats in the Lok Sabha since 1984. It also relegated the Congress Party to its weakest position to date. Support for Congress appeared to weaken further in 2016, prompting many to question its future electoral prospects.

Political participation is affected to a certain degree by insurgent violence in some areas, and ongoing practical disadvantages for marginalized segments of the population. Nevertheless, women, religious and ethnic minorities, and the poor vote in large numbers. There is some political representation for historically marginalized groups. Twenty-two Muslims were elected to the Lok Sabha in 2014. Quotas for the chamber ensure that 84 and 47 seats are reserved for the so-called scheduled castes (Dalits) and scheduled tribes (Adivasis), respectively. There are similar quotas for these historically disadvantaged groups in state assemblies. The current BJP government includes just 2 Muslim ministers out of 75, the lowest number since independence. Two states—Haryana and Rajasthan—have instituted educational requirements for candidates in local elections. It is widely thought that this stipulation disproportionately prevents members of lower castes, and particularly women, from standing for elective office.

Modi is a controversial figure given his role as chief minister during the 2002 Gujarat riots, an outbreak of communal violence in which more than 1,000 Muslims were killed, and in which he has been accused of complicity. There was evidence of a BJP strategy of communal polarization in the states of Uttar Pradesh and Assam in 2013 and 2014 during the parliamentary election campaign. There are reports that the BJP has been employing a similar strategy of communal polarization to rouse support in the lead-up to 2017 state elections in Uttar Pradesh. Notably, BJP politicians, including the national party president, have insinuated that Hindus were forced to flee the town of Kairana in the western part of the state due to intimidation by Muslim gangs. Whether such an exodus actually occurred is disputed.

C. Functioning of Government: 9 / 12

Elected leaders have the authority to govern in practice, and civilian control of the military is codified in the constitution. However, political corruption has a negative effect on government efficiency and economic performance. Though politicians and civil servants at all levels are regularly caught accepting bribes or engaging in other corrupt behavior, a great deal of corruption goes unnoticed and unpunished. This is particularly the case in the energy and construction sectors, and in state infrastructure projects more broadly. However, the passage of the Goods and Services Tax bill in August 2016 constituted a major legislative accomplishment, and is expected to limit tax evasion and reduce opportunities for graft in interstate commerce. In November, the government announced the demonetization of 500- and 1,000-rupee notes in a bid to reduce the incidence of "black money," or untaxed money earned on the black market.

The Lokpal and Lokayuktas Act, which the president signed in 2014, creates independent government bodies tasked with receiving complaints of corruption against public servants or politicians, investigating claims, and pursuing convictions through the courts. Modi and members of his government have signaled support for the law, but two years on, there is little evidence that it is being effectively implemented.

The 2005 Right to Information (RTI) Act is widely used to improve transparency and expose corrupt activities, though there are questions about its enforcement. Since the enactment of the RTI Act, at least 56 right-to-information users and activists have been murdered, and more than 311 have been assaulted or harassed. In 2015, the Lok Sabha adopted amendments to the 2014 Whistleblowers Protection Act. Opposition members criticized the changes for diluting the effectiveness of the act, which was already regarded as limited in scope. Debate on the amendments in the Rajya Sabha is still pending.

CIVIL LIBERTIES: 42 / 60

D. Freedom of Expression and Belief: 13 / 16

The private media are vigorous and diverse, and investigations and scrutiny of politicians are common. Nevertheless, revelations of close relationships between politicians, business executives, and lobbyists and some leading media personalities and owners of media outlets have dented public confidence in the press. In October, a prominent television station declined to air an interview with a major opposition-party politician and former finance minister, apparently because he had been critical of the Modi government's "surgical strikes" on Pakistani targets across the Line of Control (LOC) demarcating the Indian- and Pakistani-held parts of Kashmir. Separately, in July, three Chinese journalists were denied visa renewals by the Indian government and expelled from the country; a Chinese state-owned newspaper suggested that this was punishment for China's objection to India joining the Nuclear Suppliers Group.

Journalists risk harassment and sometimes, physical violence. In 2016, at least two journalists were killed in connection with their work, and three others were killed under circumstances where the motive remained unclear, according to the Committee to Protect Journalists. There is increasing concern about harassment of bloggers and social-media users by Hindu nationalists.

Internet access is largely unrestricted, though officials periodically implement overly broad blocks on supposedly offensive content to prevent communal or political unrest. The 2000 Information Technology Act criminalizes the sending of offensive messages by computer, and this has been interpreted to allow for censorship of critical commentary on political parties and specific politicians. The authorities have also used security laws, criminal defamation legislation, hate-speech laws, and contempt-of-court charges to curb critical voices on both social media and traditional media platforms.

Hindus make up about 80 percent of the population. The Indian state is formally secular. Freedom of religion is constitutionally guaranteed and generally respected in practice. However, legislation in several Hindu-majority states criminalizes religious conversions that take place as a result of "force" or "allurement," which can be broadly interpreted to prosecute proselytizers. Some states require government permission for conversion.

An array of Hindu nationalist organizations and some local media outlets promote antiminority views, a practice that critics charge is tolerated or even encouraged by the Hindu nationalist government of Prime Minister Modi. Like the year before it, 2016 saw a series of attacks on minorities tied to the alleged slaughter or mishandling of cows (animals held to be sacred by Hindus). Ruling-party politicians have called for the release of those charged with the lynching of a Muslim man in 2015, demanding instead that the victim's family be prosecuted for cow slaughter. Self-styled *gau rakshaks* (cow protectors) have engaged in vigilante violence against Dalit communities in Gujarat and Karnataka. Modi has been criticized for failing to promptly condemn the perpetrators of such attacks.

Academic freedom is generally robust, though intimidation of professors, students, and institutions over political and religious issues has been increasing. In February 2016, Kanhaiya Kumar, a student leader at Jawaharlal Nehru University in New Delhi, was remanded in custody on charges of sedition for having led protests on the anniversary of the 2013 execution of Mohammad Afzal Guru, who had been convicted of involvement in a 2001 terrorist attack on the parliament. The arrest sparked a wave of protests, intensified by a video apparently showing Kumar being beaten en route to court. At least two more students were later accused of sedition over involvement with the protest, but were released on bail after turning themselves in. Separately, a professor at the University of Mysore was arrested in June 2016 for a speech the previous year that allegedly insulted a Hindu deity. The events have had a chilling effect among Indian intellectuals.

Private discussion in India is generally open and free. However, a nationwide Central Monitoring System launched in 2013 is meant to enable authorities to intercept any digital communication in real time without judicial oversight; India does not have a privacy law to protect citizens in case of abuse.

E. Associational and Organizational Rights: 10 / 12

There are some restrictions on freedoms of assembly and association. Section 144 of the criminal procedure code empowers the authorities to restrict free assembly and impose curfews whenever "immediate prevention or speedy remedy" is required. State laws based on this standard are often abused to limit the holding of meetings and assemblies. Nevertheless, protest events take place regularly.

Human rights organizations operate freely, but they continue to face threats, legal harassment, excessive police force, and occasionally lethal violence. While India is home to a strong civil society sector and academic community, foreign monitors and journalists are at times denied visas to conduct research in the country on human rights and other topics. Under certain circumstances, the Foreign Contributions Regulation Act (FCRA) permits the federal government to deny nongovernmental organizations (NGOs) access to foreign funding. The government has been accused of abusing this power to target political opponents. In April 2015, the authorities canceled the FCRA licenses of some 9,000 charities for failing to declare details about foreign donations. In June 2016, the Home Affairs ministry withdrew FCRA registration from the Sabrang Trust, an NGO that has advocated for the victims of the 2002 riots in Gujarat. The Trust had received funding from the Ford Foundation, which, as a result of this relationship, had been placed on a government watchlist for a number of months; the designation required the foundation to seek specific clearance from the Home Ministry before funding individuals or organizations.

Although workers in the formal economy regularly exercise their rights to bargain collectively and strike, the Essential Services Maintenance Act has enabled the government to ban certain strikes. Tens of millions of public sector workers went on strike countrywide for 24 hours on September 2016 to demand a monthly minimum wage.

F. Rule of Law: 9 / 16

The judiciary is independent of the executive branch. Judges have displayed considerable activism in response to public-interest litigation matters. However, the lower levels of the judiciary in particular have been rife with corruption, and most citizens have great difficulty securing justice through the courts. The system is severely backlogged and understaffed, leading to lengthy pretrial detention for a large number of suspects, many of whom remain in jail longer than the duration of any sentence they might receive if convicted.

Police torture, abuse, and corruption are entrenched in the law enforcement system. Citizens frequently face substantial obstacles, including demands for bribes, and in getting the police to file a First Information Report, which is necessary to trigger an investigation of an alleged crime. Custodial rape of female detainees continues to be a problem, as does routine abuse of ordinary prisoners, particularly minorities and members of the lower castes. In the country's largest state of Uttar Pradesh, 428 deaths occurred in police or judicial custody between October 2015 and September 2016, according to the National Human Rights Commission (NHRC).

The NHRC is headed by a retired Supreme Court judge and handles roughly 8,000 complaints each year. While it monitors abuses, initiates investigations, makes independent assessments, and conducts training sessions for the police and others, its recommendations are often not implemented and it has few enforcement powers. The commission also lacks jurisdiction over the armed forces, one of the principal agents of abuse in several parts of the country. The NHRC nevertheless makes a contribution to accountability by submitting reports to international bodies such as the UN Human Rights Council, often contradicting the government's account of its own performance.

Security forces operating in the context of regional insurgencies continue to be implicated in extrajudicial killings, rape, torture, arbitrary detention, kidnappings, and destruction of homes. The criminal procedure code requires that the government approve the prosecution of security force members; approval is rarely granted, leading to impunity. The Armed Forces Special Powers Act grants security forces broad authority to arrest, detain, and use force against suspects in restive areas; civil society organizations and multiple UN human rights bodies have called for the act to be repealed. A number of other security laws allow detention without charge or based on vaguely worded offenses.

The Maoist insurgency in the east-central hills region of India is of serious concern, although the annual number of casualties has decreased since its peak in 2010. Among other abuses, the rebels have allegedly imposed illegal taxes, seized food and shelter, and engaged in abduction and forced recruitment of children and adults. Local civilians and journalists who are perceived to be pro-government have been targeted. Tens of thousands of civilians have been displaced by the violence and live in government-run camps.

Separately, in India's seven northeastern states, more than 40 insurgent factions—seeking either greater autonomy or complete independence for their ethnic or tribal groups—continue to attack security forces and engage in intertribal violence. Such fighters have been implicated in numerous bombings, killings, abductions, and rapes of civilians, and they operate extensive extortion networks. The number of deaths related to the northeastern insurgencies decreased from 273 in 2015 to 165 in 2016, according to the South Asia Terrorism Portal, which monitors such violence.

The criminal justice system fails to provide equal protection to marginalized groups. Muslims, who make up about 14 percent of the population, are underrepresented in the security forces as well as in the foreign and intelligence services. In parts of the country, particularly in rural areas, informal community councils issue edicts concerning social customs. Their decisions sometimes result in violence or persecution aimed at those perceived to have transgressed social norms, especially women and members of the lower castes.

The constitution bars discrimination based on caste, and laws set aside quotas in education and government jobs for historically underprivileged scheduled tribes, Dalits, and groups categorized by the government as "other backward classes." However, members of the lower castes and minorities continue to face routine discrimination and violence. Many Dalits are denied access to land and other public amenities, are abused by landlords and police, and work in miserable conditions.

The penal code forbids "intercourse against the order of nature." Discrimination against LGBT (lesbian, gay, bisexual, and transgender) people continues, including violence and harassment in some cases, though the Supreme Court recognized transgender people as a third gender in 2014. In June 2016, the Indian government opted to abstain on a vote at the UN Human Rights Council in which a resolution was being passed to establish a special office for addressing LGBT discrimination worldwide.

G. Personal Autonomy and Individual Rights: 10 / 16

Freedom of movement is hampered in some parts of the country by insurgent violence or communal tensions, though violence from insurgencies has decreased in recent years. Property rights are somewhat tenuous for tribal groups and other marginalized communities, and members of these groups are often denied adequate resettlement opportunities and compensation when their lands are seized for development projects. While many states have laws to prevent transfers of tribal land to nontribal groups, the practice is reportedly widespread, particularly with respect to the mining and timber industries.

There is some degree of female representation in government. Modi's cabinet includes seven female ministers. For the bulk of the year, chief ministers in the states of Tamil Nadu, Jammu and Kashmir, Rajasthan, and West Bengal were women. Female quotas are in place for elected positions in India's three-tier local government system.

Rape, harassment, and other transgressions against women are serious problems, and lower-caste and tribal women are particularly vulnerable. Mass demonstrations after the fatal gang rape of a woman on a Delhi bus in 2012 prompted the government to enact significant legal reforms. However, egregious new cases emerged in 2016, including the July gang rape of a mother and 14-year-old daughter in Uttar Pradesh, leading to calls for further action. Despite criminalization and hundreds of convictions each year, dowry demands persist. A 2006 law banned dowry-related harassment, widened the definition of domestic violence to include emotional or verbal abuse, and criminalized spousal rape. However, reports indicate that enforcement is poor. Statistics suggest that murders and suicides associated with dowry disputes are on the rise in parts of the country.

Muslim personal laws and traditional Hindu practices discriminate against women in terms of inheritance, adoption, and property rights. The Muslim divorce custom of "triple talaq," by which a Muslim man can unilaterally divorce his wife by saying "talaq" three times, faced a constitutional challenge in 2016. The Modi government has come out against the practice, but others maintain that it is a religious freedom that should remain constitutionally guarded. The malign neglect of female children after birth remains a concern, as does the banned but growing use of prenatal sex-determination tests to selectively abort female fetuses.

Article 23 of the constitution bans human trafficking, and bonded labor is illegal, but the practice is fairly common. Estimates of the number of affected workers range from 20 to 50 million. The government passed a controversial law in July 2016 allowing children below the age of 14 to engage in "home-based work," as well as other occupations between the ages of 14 and 18. Children are banned from working in potentially hazardous industries, though in practice the law is routinely flouted.

Indonesia

Political Rights Rating: 2
Civil Liberties Rating: 4
Freedom Rating: 3.0
Freedom Status: Partly Free
Electoral Democracy: Yes

Population: 259,400,000
Capital: Jakarta

Ten-Year Ratings Timeline For Year Under Review (Political Rights, Civil Liberties, Status)

Year Under Review	2007	2008	2009	2010	2011	2012	2013	2014	2015	2016
Rating	2,3,F	2,3,F	2,3,F	2,3,F	2,3,F	2,3,F	2,4,PF	2,4,PF	2,4,PF	2,4,PF

Overview: Indonesia has made impressive democratic gains since the fall of an authoritarian regime led by President Suharto in 1998, establishing significant pluralism in politics and the media and undergoing multiple, peaceful transfers of power between parties. However, the country continues to struggle with challenges including systemic corruption, discrimination and violence against some minority groups, separatist tensions in the Papua region, and the politicized use of defamation and blasphemy laws.

KEY DEVELOPMENTS IN 2016:

- In January, after local residents in Kalimantan attacked settlements established by the banned religious group Gafatar, hundreds of members were forcibly transferred to their home districts and subjected to "reeducation" sessions.
- More than 2,000 people were reportedly arrested during the year for participating in nonviolent rallies supporting independence for the provinces of Papua and West Papua.
- Setya Novanto—who had stepped down as parliament speaker in 2015 after being accused of attempted extortion—won the chairmanship of the second-largest political party, Golkar, in May and resumed his position as speaker in December following a favorable court ruling.
- In September, Jakarta governor Basuki Tjahaja Purnama ("Ahok"), an ethnic Chinese Christian who was preparing to run in the February 2017 gubernatorial election, made remarks that critics claimed were blasphemous toward Islam, leading to criminal charges and a series of protests in the city.

EXECUTIVE SUMMARY

President Joko Widodo (Jokowi) continued to work with entrenched elites to advance his economic development agenda in 2016, at times at the expense of democratic reforms. He made multiple appointments during the year that appeared to clash with his stated goals of advancing anticorruption efforts and addressing past human rights abuses. While he took office in 2014 with only a minority ruling coalition in the parliament, other parties have gradually joined the bloc, including Golkar and the United Development Party (PPP), which both underwent progovernment leadership changes in 2016.

Religious and other minorities faced ongoing harassment and intimidation, often with the tacit approval of local governments and security forces. Suspected members of the banned religious organization Gafatar were increasingly targeted in 2016 as part of a growing trend of using defamation and blasphemy laws to limit the public expression of minority faiths and political opinions. Followers of Ahmadiyya and Shia Islam also suffered discrimination and violent attacks. In addition, women and LGBT (lesbian, gay, bisexual, and transgender) people remained subject to discriminatory local bylaws regulating dress and behavior.

While Jokowi has claimed that easing separatist tensions in the provinces of Papua and West Papua is a priority, various government agencies and security forces have often openly or subtly contradicted his stated intentions. The presence of international media and nongovernmental organizations (NGOs) in the region remained restricted in 2016, despite government assurances to the contrary.

POLITICAL RIGHTS: 31 / 40

A. Electoral Process: 11 / 12

The president is directly elected and serves as both head of state and head of government. The House of Representatives (DPR), with 560 seats, is the main parliamentary chamber. The 132-member House of Regional Representatives (DPD) is responsible for monitoring laws related to regional autonomy, and may also propose bills on the topic. All legislators serve five-year terms with no term limit. Presidents and vice presidents can serve up to two five-year terms.

Jokowi, the candidate of the Indonesian Democratic Party of Struggle (PDI-P), won the 2014 presidential election with 53 percent of the vote, defeating former general Prabowo Subianto. The PDI-P, the party of former president Megawati Sukarnoputri, led that year's DPR elections with 19 percent of the vote and 109 seats. Golkar, the party of former president Suharto, won 91 seats, followed by Prabowo's Great Indonesia Movement Party (Gerindra) with 73 seats. The Democratic Party (PD) of outgoing president Susilo Bambang Yudhoyono received 61 seats. Three Islamic parties—the National Mandate Party (PAN), the National Awakening Party (PKB), and the PPP—increased their total vote share, taking 49, 47, and 39 seats, respectively. A fourth, the Prosperous Justice Party (PKS), fell to 40 seats. NasDem and the People's Conscience Party (Hanura) won the remainder, with 35 and 16 seats, respectively. Irregularities were reported in some regions, including political violence during the preelection period in Aceh and voter-list inflation, ballot stuffing, and community bloc voting in Papua.

In June 2016 the parliament revised the law governing local elections. Among other changes, the new law requires that the Election Oversight Agency (Bawaslu) and the General Elections Commission (KPU) consult with the parliament and the government before issuing any new regulations or decisions, and states that the consultation results are binding. Activists expressed concern that the rules would reduce electoral authorities' independence.

Under a 2012 law, the hereditary sultan of Yogyakarta is that region's unelected governor. The position is nonpartisan, and the sultan is subject to a verification process with minimum requirements—such as education—every five years beginning in 2016. The prince of Paku Alaman serves as deputy governor of the region.

B. Political Pluralism and Participation: 14 / 16

The right to organize political parties is respected, though in recent years the election laws have been amended to favor large parties by imposing eligibility requirements for parliamentary and presidential candidacy. Only 12 parties passed verification processes for the 2014 national elections, down from 48 in 1999. One new national party, NasDem, competed in the 2014 elections. Gerindra and Hanura competed for the first time in 2009.

Since Jokowi took office with a minority coalition in the parliament in 2014, opposition parties have been encouraged to join the government bloc through cabinet appointments and executive interference in internal party matters, perpetuating a trend seen under previous administrations. Executive actions—tacit or otherwise—exacerbated the internal disputes of the PPP and Golkar, contributing to leadership changes for both in 2016. The PPP aimed to end a nearly two-year schism by choosing a new, progovernment chairman in April, confirming the party's place in the ruling coalition. Golkar chose a new chairman in May and moved from the opposition to the government bloc.

Some local governments have discriminated against minorities by restricting access to national identification cards, birth certificates, marriage licenses, and other bureaucratic necessities, limiting their political rights and electoral opportunities. However, despite growing religious intolerance and historical hostility toward certain ethnic groups, a number of minority politicians have achieved important posts. Ahok, an ethnic Chinese Christian, rose from deputy governor to governor of Jakarta when Jokowi, then the incumbent governor, became president in 2014. Ahok was seeking election as governor in his own right in early 2017, with the backing of major parties including PDI-P and Golkar, though his political rivals joined with Islamist hard-liners in calling for him to be jailed for allegedly blasphemous comments he made in September 2016. He had accused opponents of distorting a Quranic verse to claim that Muslims could not vote for a non-Muslim. The incident touched off a series of large protests, and a trial was pending at year's end.

C. Functioning of Government: 6 / 12

Elected officials determine the policies of the government, though national authorities have faced difficulties in implementing decisions due to resistance at the local and regional level. Separately, observers have warned that the military is regaining influence over political and economic affairs.

Corruption remains endemic, including in the parliament and the police. In 2016, the Corruption Eradication Commission (KPK) began focusing on corruption in the judiciary after previous campaigns against high-profile corruption in business and the government. Defendants who received prison sentences during the year included former cabinet ministers, a member of parliament, an army general, and a well-known criminal defense attorney convicted of bribing judges.

However, Setya Novanto, who resigned as DPR speaker in 2015 amid allegations that he had demanded a 20 percent stake in mining company Freeport Indonesia in exchange for an expedited contract renewal, rejuvenated his political career by winning the chairmanship of Golkar in May. In September he won a Constitutional Court ruling that incriminating recordings of him could not be used as evidence in the extortion case, as they had not been made by law enforcement officials. The DPR's ethics board subsequently cleared Setya of wrongdoing, and he reclaimed his position as speaker in December.

Acrimony between rival agencies has hindered anticorruption efforts. In particular, the KPK and the national police have engaged in a series of disputes since 2009, reflecting deeper disagreement over governance reform among political elites. In September 2016, Jokowi appointed Budi Gunawan to serve as chief of national intelligence; Budi's 2015 nomination as national police chief, despite corruption allegations against him, had set off a public outcry and a major clash with the KPK.

Civil society groups are able to comment on and influence pending policies or legislation. However, government transparency is limited by broad exemptions in the freedom of information law and obstacles such as a 2011 law that criminalizes the leaking of vaguely defined state secrets to the public.

CIVIL LIBERTIES: 34 / 60

D. Freedom of Expression and Belief: 12 / 16

Indonesia hosts a vibrant and diverse media environment, though press freedom is hampered by a number of legal and regulatory restrictions. Licensing rules are stringent but unevenly enforced, meaning that thousands of television and radio stations operate illegally. Before 2015, foreign journalists were not authorized to travel to the provinces of Papua and West Papua without special permission; Jokowi announced an end to the rule that year, but journalists seeking to visit the region have continued to report bureaucratic obstacles.

Reporters sometimes face violence and intimidation, which frequently goes unpunished. Journalists often practice self-censorship to avoid running afoul of civil and criminal defamation laws. The 2008 Law on Electronic Information and Transactions (ITE Law) extended libel and other restrictions to online media, criminalizing the distribution or accessibility of information or documents that are "contrary to the moral norms of Indonesia" or related to gambling, blackmail, or defamation. An amendment to the law passed in October 2016 allows individuals to obtain court orders to delete online information deemed "no longer relevant," potentially permitting powerful figures to retroactively censor critical reporting. A report by the organization SAFEnet noted a steady increase in the use of the ITE Law since 2008, with cases often brought against anticorruption activists, whistleblowers, and journalists.

Censorship and self-censorship of books and films for allegedly obscene or blasphemous content are fairly common. Official and unofficial censorship has long been in place regarding a period in 1965–66 ("Gestapu") when alleged members of the Indonesia Communist Party (PKI) were massacred. In recent years, as public dialogue has increased amid the publication of new books and documentaries about the era, censorship has also increased.

Indonesia officially recognizes Islam, Protestantism, Roman Catholicism, Hinduism, Buddhism, and Confucianism, though local customary practices (*adat*) also exist. Individuals have the option of leaving the religion section of their identity cards blank, but those who do—including adherents of faiths outside the six recognized religions—often face discrimination; in December 2016 the government asked the Constitutional Court to rule on allowing other faiths to appear on identity cards. Atheism is not accepted, and the criminal code contains provisions against blasphemy, penalizing those who "distort" or "misrepresent" recognized faiths.

National and local governments have repeatedly failed to protect religious minorities from violence and discrimination, and exhibited bias in investigations and prosecutions. To obtain a permit to build a new house of worship, a religious group must gather the signatures of 90 congregation members and 60 local residents of different faiths; the rule has been used to block or target minority religious sites. Mobs periodically attack houses of worship belonging to groups that form a minority in their area.

Violence and intimidation against Ahmadiyya, an Islamic sect with approximately 400,000 Indonesian followers, persisted in 2016, and the central government continued to tolerate persecution of the group by local governments. The Shiite Muslim minority has also suffered violence and intimidation, including forced conversion.

In 2016, attacks escalated against Gafatar, a heterodox Muslim group that was accused of combining the teachings of Islam, Christianity, and Judaism. It was formed in 2011, but was formally disbanded in 2015 after the government refused to grant it a registration permit. In January and February, Gafatar communities in Kalimantan were threatened or attacked by mobs as security forces stood by, and as many as 7,900 people were forcibly relocated to their hometowns in Java and elsewhere, with many also subjected to "reeducation" sessions. In March, following a February fatwa against the group by the Indonesian Ulema Council (MUI), the Home and Religious Affairs Ministries issued a joint decree banning any proselytizing activities by the group's former members and requiring them to uphold peace and order. Several Gafatar leaders have been arrested or sentenced to prison on blasphemy and other charges.

In recent years, hard-line Islamist groups such as the Islamic Defenders Front (FPI) have engaged in raids and extrajudicial enforcement of Sharia bylaws, and pressured local governments to close churches and non-Sunni mosques. Their violent activities are not supported by the country's main Islamic organizations, but they often have the support of high-ranking government officials, and security forces have been criticized for tacitly aiding them by ignoring their abuses.

Academic freedom in Indonesia is generally respected, though there are sporadic reports of pressure from groups such as FPI to cancel lectures that feature minority faiths or related issues. There are no major obstacles to open and free private discussion.

E. Associational and Organizational Rights: 8 / 12

Freedom of assembly is usually upheld, and peaceful protests are common in the capital. However, assemblies in support of minority groups or to address sensitive political topics—such as Gestapu and Indonesia's leftist past, women's rights, or regional separatism—are regularly dispersed, with participants facing intimidation or violence from a combination of hard-line vigilantes and police. Among other incidents during 2016, FPI forcibly broke up a public event organized by a mainstream Islamic student group in Riau Province in April. In December, nearly a dozen individuals linked to the anti-Ahok protests were arrested and investigated for allegedly conspiring to overthrow the government, among other possible offenses. A 2010 regulation allows national police to use live ammunition to quell situations of "anarchic violence."

Flag-raising ceremonies and independence rallies in Maluku and Papua are routinely dispersed, often violently, and participants have been tried for treason. The Jakarta Legal Aid Institute (LBH Jakarta) reported in October 2016 that between April and September the authorities had arrested more than 2,280 Papuans for nonviolent demonstrations. In December, a series of demonstrations backing Papuan independence in multiple cities across the country resulted in some 500 arrests and multiple charges of treason.

Indonesia hosts a strong and active array of civil society organizations, but some human rights groups are subject to government monitoring and interference, and activists working on a variety of sensitive issues remain targets for human rights abuses. A 2013 law on mass organizations requires all civic and religious NGOs to register with the government and submit to regular reviews of their activities. It limits the types of activities NGOs can undertake, requires formal government approval to operate, and bars them from committing blasphemy or espousing ideas that conflict with the official Pancasila ideology, such as atheism and communism. The government is empowered to dissolve noncompliant organizations.

Workers can join independent unions, bargain collectively, and with the exception of civil servants, stage strikes. Legal strikes can be unduly delayed by obligatory arbitration processes, and laws against antiunion discrimination are not well enforced. Some unions have resorted to violence in their negotiations with employers, and labor-related demonstrations are common.

F. Rule of Law: 5 / 16

The judiciary, particularly the Constitutional Court, has demonstrated its independence in some cases, but the court system remains plagued by corruption and other weaknesses. A 2015 report by Amnesty International found that many defendants are denied proper access to legal counsel, including in death penalty cases. Jokowi's administration has revived the application of the death penalty for drug-trafficking crimes. Four convicts were executed for such offenses in 2016, and at least 46 new death sentences were issued, in addition to 14 death sentences for murder. In May 2016, Jokowi issued a decree—later approved by the parliament—that authorizes harsher punishments for child sex offenders, including the death penalty and chemical castration.

The security forces are also rife with corruption and other abuses, and personnel regularly go unpunished or receive lenient sentences for human rights violations. In December 2016, the national police issued a regulation that prohibits law enforcement agencies from investigating a police officer without the preapproval of the national police chief. Military service members accused of crimes against civilians are tried in military courts, which lack impartiality and often impose light punishments. Torture by law enforcement officers is not specifically criminalized. KontraS (Commission for the Disappeared and Victims of Violence) identified 260 victims of torture between mid-2015 and mid-2016, with most cases perpetrated by police, followed by the military and prison officers. Poor prison governance is compounded by endemic overcrowding and corruption. Prison riots and protests over lack of services have led to numerous jailbreaks.

Jokowi has pledged to address the human rights abuses of previous decades, and the government organized a symposium on the 1965–66 massacres in April 2016, but plans for a nonjudicial reconciliation mechanism have made little progress and drawn criticism for a lack of transparency. Moreover, in 2016 Jokowi appointed a security minister who had been accused of crimes against humanity dating to 1999.

Security forces have been fairly successful in suppressing the country's terrorist networks. Nevertheless, hundreds of Indonesians have reportedly traveled to Syria and Iraq to join jihadist groups, raising the threat of domestic attacks. Among other events in 2016, a group of four attackers targeted police and civilians with firearms and suicide bombings in Jakarta in January, killing four people before being killed themselves. The Islamic State (IS) militant group claimed responsibility. In July, a suicide bomber attacked a police station in Central Java, though only the bomber was killed. Later than month, security forces killed IS-linked militant leader Abu Wardah Santoso in a gun battle in Central Sulawesi.

Since the 1950s, separatists have waged a low-grade insurgency in the provinces of Papua and West Papua, where the central government's exploitation of natural resources and a heavy police and military presence have stirred resentment. Deadly confrontations between security forces and protesters are common, as are extrajudicial killings, tribal conflict, and violence related to labor disputes at foreign-operated mines and other resource-extraction enterprises. Jokowi has stated that achieving peace and development in Papua and West Papua is a priority of his presidency, but government ministries and agencies have at times openly contradicted his stated goals, and little progress was made in 2016.

A number of districts have issued local ordinances based on Sharia that in many cases are unconstitutional, contradict Indonesia's international human rights commitments, or are difficult to enforce due to lack of clarity. Many are never reported to the Home Affairs Ministry for review. In 2015, Aceh implemented a new Sharia-based criminal code that applies even to non-Muslims and includes corporal punishment in the form of caning. At least 100 people were caned in 2016, including a Christian woman convicted of selling alcohol.

LGBT (lesbian, gay, bisexual, and transgender) people face widespread discrimination, harassment by local officials, and attacks by hard-line Islamist groups that sometimes enjoy support from local authorities. In addition to the many local bylaws—in Aceh and elsewhere—that effectively criminalize LGBT people, a 2008 antipornography law labels same-sex sexual acts as "deviant." Transgender people are routinely arrested and sent for counseling. Among other incidents in 2016, the authorities closed an Islamic boarding school for transgender students and moved to block social media applications serving the LGBT community.

Ethnic Chinese, who make up as little as 1 percent of the population but are resented by some for reputedly holding much of the country's wealth, continue to face harassment. In addition, ethnic Chinese in Yogyakarta face restrictions on the right to own private property under a 1975 decree that contradicts national laws.

Indonesia grants temporary protection to refugees and migrants, including those stranded at sea, but the country is not a party to the 1951 Refugee Convention and does not accept refugees for asylum and resettlement.

G. Personal Autonomy and Individual Rights: 9 / 16

Freedom of travel and choice of residence, employment, and higher education are generally respected. However, the ability to obtain public employment or operate businesses is often limited by the need for bribes or other inducements.

Property rights are threatened by mining and logging activity on communal land and state appropriation of land claimed by indigenous groups. In 2013, the Constitutional Court ruled that indigenous people have the right to manage "customary forest" lands they inhabit. A 2015 ministerial regulation called for mining and plantation companies to allocate at least 20 percent of their land concessions for management and use by local people, though many companies reportedly failed to comply.

Discrimination against women persists, including in the workplace. Working men receive tax benefits that are unavailable to their wives, as husbands are deemed the heads of households. A 2008 law states that 30 percent of a political party's candidates and board members must be women. In 2014, 94 women (approximately 17 percent) were elected to the 560-seat DPR. Abortion is illegal except to save a woman's life or in instances of rape. Adults over 15 years of age must have corroboration and witnesses to bring rape charges.

Sharia-based ordinances in a number of districts infringe on women's constitutional rights, and the ordinances' restrictions on dress, public conduct, and sexual activity are disproportionately enforced against women and LGBT people. Women applying to work for the police and military must undergo "virginity tests" in some areas.

Marriages must be conducted under the supervision of a recognized religion, which can sometimes obstruct interfaith marriages; civil marriage is not possible. Divorce is legal, but civil servants seeking divorce must first undergo a mediation and approval process through a government personnel agency.

Many Indonesian workers are trafficked abroad for forced labor, including women in domestic service and men in the fishing industry. Traffickers are often able to avoid punishment due to corruption among law enforcement officials.

Iran

Political Rights Rating: 6
Civil Liberties Rating: 6
Freedom Rating: 6.0
Freedom Status: Not Free
Electoral Democracy: No

Population: 79,500,000
Capital: Tehran

Ten-Year Ratings Timeline For Year Under Review (Political Rights, Civil Liberties, Status)

Year Under Review	2007	2008	2009	2010	2011	2012	2013	2014	2015	2016
Rating	6,6,NF	6,6,NF	6,6,NF	6,6,NF	6,6,NF	6,6,NF	6,6,NF	6,6,NF	6,6,NF	6,6,NF

Overview: The Islamic Republic of Iran holds elections regularly, but they fall short of democratic standards due to the role of the hard-line Guardian Council, which disqualifies all candidates deemed insufficiently loyal to the clerical establishment. Ultimate power rests in the hands of the country's supreme leader, Ayatollah Ali Khamenei, and the unelected institutions under his control.

KEY DEVELOPMENTS IN 2016:

- In February, Iran held elections for the parliament and the Assembly of Experts, the body tasked with appointing and monitoring the supreme leader. Most reformist candidates were disqualified by the Guardian Council.
- In May, prominent human rights defender Narges Mohammadi was sentenced to 16 years in prison on national security charges stemming from her activism, including membership in a group that aims to reduce the high number of executions in Iran. The sentence was upheld on appeal in September.
- In August, Iranian authorities hanged 25 Sunni Muslim prisoners who had been convicted on terrorism-related charges; human rights organizations and lawyers representing some of the men cited a pattern of due process violations in the cases. Iran also continued to impose the death penalty on juvenile offenders, including a prisoner who had been convicted of raping a teenage boy when he was 17.
- In October, a court in Iran sentenced an Iranian-American businessman and his 80-year-old father to 10 years in prison for collaborating with the U.S. government. Their friends and family dismissed the charges, calling the men "hostages" of the Iranian regime.

EXECUTIVE SUMMARY

Human rights abuses continued unabated in 2016, with the authorities carrying out Iran's largest mass execution in years and launching a renewed crackdown on women's rights activists. The regime maintained restrictions on freedom of expression, both offline and online, and made further arrests of journalists, bloggers, labor union activists, and dual nationals visiting the country, with some facing heavy prison sentences.

Hard-liners in control of powerful institutions, including the judiciary and the Islamic Revolutionary Guard Corps (IRGC), were behind many of the year's abuses. There were no indications that President Hassan Rouhani, a self-proclaimed moderate seeking reelection in 2017, was willing or able to push back against repressive forces and deliver the greater social freedoms he had promised.

Opposition leaders Mir Hossein Mousavi, his wife Zahra Rahnavard, and reformist cleric Mehdi Karroubi remained under house arrest for a sixth year without being formally charged or put on trial. As in 2015, the media were barred from quoting or reporting on former president Mohammad Khatami, another important reformist figure.

POLITICAL RIGHTS: 7 / 40

A. Electoral Process: 3 / 12

The supreme leader, who has no fixed term, is the highest authority in the country. He is the commander in chief of the armed forces and appoints the head of the judiciary, the heads of state broadcast media, and the Expediency Council—a body tasked with mediating disputes between the Guardian Council and the parliament. He also appoints six of the members of the Guardian Council; the other six are jurists nominated by the head of the judiciary and confirmed by the parliament, all for six-year terms. The supreme leader is appointed by the Assembly of Experts, which also monitors his work. However, in practice his decisions appear to go unchallenged by the assembly, whose proceedings are kept confidential. The current supreme leader, Ali Khamenei, succeeded Islamic Republic founder Ruhollah Khomeini in 1989.

Elections in Iran are not free and fair, according to international standards. The Guardian Council, controlled by hard-line conservatives, vets all candidates for the parliament, presidency, and the Assembly of Experts—a body of 86 clerics who are elected to eight-year terms by popular vote. The council has in the past rejected candidates who are not considered insiders or deemed fully loyal to the clerical establishment, as well as women seeking to run in the presidential election. As a result, Iranian voters are given a limited choice of candidates.

The president, the second-highest-ranking official in the Islamic Republic, is elected by popular vote for four years and can serve two consecutive terms. Ahead of the 2013 election, the Guardian Council disqualified more than 600 candidates, including former president Akbar Hashemi Rafsanjani and Rahim Mashaei, an aide to incumbent president Mahmoud Ahmadinejad, apparently due to political infighting. Nearly all of the eight approved candidates, including Rouhani, were deemed close to Khamenei. Only one reformist candidate, who was widely seen as lacking both charisma and significant popular support, was allowed to run. In the run-up to the election, censorship increased, the government intensified its press crackdown, and authorities restricted the already slow speed of the internet. However, Rouhani's victory—with nearly 51 percent of the vote amid 72 percent turnout—appeared to reflect the choice of the voters.

In February 2016, elections were held for the both the parliament and the Assembly of Experts. Only 51 percent of candidates who had applied to run for parliament were approved by the Guardian Council, the lowest figure to date. Only 20 percent of candidates were approved to run for the assembly, also a record low. Human Rights Watch reported that a significant number of candidates were disqualified due to their political beliefs and their prior convictions for supposed national security crimes that stemmed from legitimate political activities. Reformist politician Hossein Marashi said that only 30 reformist candidates were approved to run, out of more than 3,000 who had applied.

After the first round of parliamentary elections was held in February, a runoff took place in April for all constituencies where no candidate garnered at least 25 percent of the vote. At the end of the process, relatively moderate Rouhani supporters held more than 40 percent of seats in the parliament, while independents—who included a number of reformists—and hard-liners each took about a third. The result was perceived as a victory

Country Reports 247

for moderates and reformists, though the exact orientations and allegiances of individual lawmakers are often unclear. Moderates and reformists similarly made symbolic gains in the Assembly of Experts, but because so many had been disqualified, the supposedly moderate lists included conservative candidates. A majority of the new assembly ultimately chose hard-line cleric Ahmad Jannati, head of the Guardian Council, as the body's chairman.

B. Political Pluralism and Participation: 2 / 16

Only political parties and factions loyal to the establishment and to the state ideology are permitted to operate. Reformist parties and politicians have come under increased state repression, especially since 2009.

In 2015, two new reformist parties—Nedaye Iranian (Voice of Iranians) and Ettehad Mellat Iran (Iranian National Unity)—were established ahead of the 2016 parliamentary elections. However, most candidates from these and other reformist groups were disqualified by the Guardian Council ahead of the voting.

Iran's leading opposition figures—Mir Hossein Mousavi; his wife, university professor Zahra Rahnavard; and reformist cleric Mehdi Karroubi—have been under house arrest since February 2011 with no access to the outside world. Mousavi and Karroubi were presidential candidates in the disputed 2009 election, and the three are seen as the leaders of the reformist Green Movement, whose mass protests were brutally suppressed following that vote.

The parliament grants five seats to recognized non-Muslim minorities: Jews, Armenian Christians, Assyrian and Chaldean Christians, and Zoroastrians. However, ethnic and especially religious minorities are rarely awarded senior government posts, and their political representation remains weak.

C. Functioning of Government: 2 / 12

The elected president's powers are limited by the supreme leader and other unelected authorities. The powers of the elected parliament are similarly restricted by the supreme leader and the unelected Guardian Council, which must approve all bills before they can become law. The council often rejects bills it deems un-Islamic. Nevertheless, the parliament has been a platform for heated political debate and criticism of the government, and legislators have frequently challenged presidents and their policies.

Corruption remains endemic at all levels of the bureaucracy, despite regular calls by authorities to tackle the problem. Powerful actors involved in the economy, including the IRGC and bonyads (endowed foundations), are above scrutiny, and restrictions on the media and civil society activists prevent them from serving as independent watchdogs to ensure transparency and accountability.

CIVIL LIBERTIES: 10 / 60

D. Freedom of Expression and Belief: 2 / 16

Freedom of expression and access to information remain severely limited both online and offline. The state broadcasting company is tightly controlled by hard-liners and influenced by the security apparatus. News and analysis are heavily censored, while critics and opposition members are rarely, if ever, given a platform on state-controlled television, which remains a major source of information for many Iranians. State television has a record of airing confessions extracted from political prisoners under duress, and it routinely carries reports aimed at discrediting dissidents and opposition activists.

Satellite dishes are banned, and Persian-language broadcasts from outside the country are regularly jammed. Authorities periodically raid private homes and confiscate satellite dishes.

Newspapers and magazines face censorship and warnings from authorities about which topics to cover and how. At least two publications were temporarily suspended during 2016 for critical coverage that was deemed insulting to the authorities, as were several news websites. Journalists state that they are often forced to practice self-censorship when working on sensitive issues.

According to the Committee to Protect Journalists, eight journalists were behind bars in Iran at year's end, down from 19 in 2015, marking the first time in eight years that Iran was not among the world's top five jailers of journalists. *Washington Post* reporter Jason Rezaian, who had been in custody since mid-2014, was released from prison along with three other Iranian-Americans in a January 2016 prisoner exchange with the United States.

Journalists continued to faced arrest, prosecution, and imprisonment throughout the year. In April, a court in Tehran sentenced three journalists—Ehsan Mazandarani, Saman Safarzaee, and Afarin Chitsaz—to between five and 10 years in prison on numerous political and security charges; the terms were later reduced to two years on appeal. In August, a revolutionary court sentenced journalist Issa Saharkhiz to three years in prison for allegedly insulting the supreme leader and disseminating antistate propaganda. His sentence was reduced to 21 months in September.

Also in September, reformist journalist Sadra Mohaghegh was detained at his home in Tehran. Though the reason for his arrest was not clear, the semiofficial Mehr News Agency accused him of working against state interests. Yashar Soltani, editor of the website Memari News, was detained the same month following a complaint by Tehran's mayor and the chair of its municipal council. Soltani had reported that the municipal government was illegally transferring favorable land and housing to state officials.

Tens of thousands of foreign-based websites remain filtered, including news sites and social media, which have otherwise become a relatively free platform of expression for many Iranians. The government has said it is pursuing "smart filtering" for social-networking sites such as Instagram, allowing it to block certain content without obstructing the entire service.

Authorities continue to persecute online activists and scrutinize users' internet activity. Well-known internet activist and founder of the popular Weblogina portal Arash Zad, detained since 2015 on unknown charges, remained behind bars. In May 2016, authorities announced an operation targeting "un-Islamic" online modeling agencies. Several people were arrested for posting pictures of women without the obligatory hijab on websites such as Instagram. In August, the IRGC said its cybersecurity arm had spoken to or interrogated about 450 administrators of social media groups over allegedly "immoral" content and warned them against future transgressions.

Various forms of art face restrictions in Iran. All books must be approved by the Ministry of Culture in order to receive a publishing license. Scores of books have been banned, while their authors have been accused of subversion. Filmmakers also face censorship and official pressure. In June 2016, filmmaker Hossein Rajabian, his brother, musician Mehdi Rajabian, and an associated musician, Yousef Emadi, began serving three-year prison sentences after being arrested in 2015 for allegedly distributing underground music. In October, the writer and activist Golrokh Ebrahimi Iraee was taken to jail to begin serving a six-year sentence for her authorship of an unpublished story about the practice of execution by stoning in Iran.

Iran is home to a majority Shiite Muslim population and Sunni, Baha'i, Christian, and Zoroastrian minorities. The constitution recognizes only Zoroastrians, Jews, and certain Christian communities as religious minorities, and they are relatively free to worship. The regime cracks down on Muslims who are deemed to be at variance with the state ideology and interpretation of Islam. Spiritual leader Mohammad Ali Taheri has been in jail since 2011 for founding a group centered on mysticism whose beliefs and practices are allegedly un-Islamic. Sunni Muslims complain that they have been prevented from building mosques in major cities and face difficulty obtaining government jobs. In recent years, there has been increased pressure on the Sufi Muslim order Nematollahi Gonabadi, including destruction of their places of worship and the jailing of some of their members.

The government also subjects some non-Muslim minorities to repressive policies and discrimination. Baha'is are systematically persecuted, sentenced to prison, and banned from access to higher education. In October 2016, 14 Baha'is were arrested in the city of Shiraz, though the charges against them were not clear. The Baha'i International Community has also reported the destruction of cemeteries and the closure of Baha'i-owned businesses in recent years. There is an ongoing crackdown on Christian converts. In the past several years, a number of informal house churches have been raided and their pastors detained.

Academic freedom remains limited in Iran, despite attempts by Rouhani's government to ease the harsh repression universities have experienced since 2009. Khamenei has warned that universities should not be turned into centers for political activities. Amnesty International estimates that hundreds of students have been prevented from continuing their studies for political reasons or because they belong to the Baha'i community. In March 2016, Iranian-Canadian academic Homa Hoodfar was detained while traveling in Iran, and authorities confiscated her passport and prevented her from returning to Canada. She was questioned by police for months before being arrested and imprisoned in June. In October, she was released after spending four months in prison, where she had been subjected to harsh interrogations.

Iran's vaguely defined restrictions on speech, harsh criminal penalties, and state monitoring of online communications are among several factors that deter citizens from engaging in open and free private discussion.

E. Associational and Organizational Rights: 1 / 12

The constitution states that public demonstrations may be held if they are not "detrimental to the fundamental principles of Islam." In practice, only state-sanctioned demonstrations are typically permitted, while other gatherings have in recent years been forcibly dispersed by security personnel, who detain participants. In October 2016, for example, police made hundreds of arrests after thousands of people gathered in Fars Province for an unusually large annual celebration of Cyrus the Great, a pre-Islamic Persian king known for religious tolerance. By December more than 70 detainees had been sentenced to jail terms of up to eight years, though appeals were pending at year's end.

Nongovernmental organizations that work on nonpolitical issues such as poverty and the environment are allowed to operate relatively freely. Other groups, especially those that have highlighted human rights violations, have been suppressed. They include the Center for Human Rights Defenders, which remains closed with several of its members in jail, and the Mourning Mothers of Iran (Mothers of Laleh Park), which had been gathering in a Tehran park to bring attention to human rights abuses.

Iran does not permit the creation of labor unions; only state-sponsored labor councils are allowed. Labor rights groups have come under pressure in recent years, and more than a dozen activists have been sentenced to prison. Three prominent teachers' union activists were temporarily released in 2016 after undergoing hunger strikes in prison, but they were later ordered to complete their sentences.

F. Rule of Law: 3 / 16

The judicial system is used as a tool to silence critics and opposition members. The head of the judiciary is appointed by the supreme leader for a five-year term. Under the current head, Ayatollah Sadegh Larijani, human rights advocates and political activists have been subjected to unfair trials, and the security apparatus's influence over judges has reportedly grown.

Iran, after China, carries out the largest number of executions in the world each year, and the annual total has increased under Larijani. Convicts can be executed for offenses other than murder, such as drug trafficking, and for crimes they committed when they were less than 18 years old. According to the UN special rapporteur on the human rights situation in Iran, at least 200 individuals were reportedly executed in the first half of 2016. Though this represented a decrease in the rate of executions compared with the previous year, the rapporteur noted that such patterns are common around elections. In August, Iran hanged 25 Sunnis in a single day for their alleged involvement in terrorist violence. As in previous years, Iran refused to allow a visit to the country by the UN special rapporteur.

Lawyers taking up sensitive political cases have been jailed and banned from practicing, including prominent human rights lawyer Abdolfatah Soltani. A number of lawyers have been forced to leave the country to escape prosecution.

Activists are routinely arrested without warrants, held indefinitely without formal charges, and denied access to legal counsel or any contact with the outside world. Many are later convicted on vague security charges in trials that sometimes last only a few minutes. Activists say they have been beaten during interrogation, forced into false confessions, and subjected to psychological pressure, including threats that their relatives will be arrested. In the past few years, the IRGC's intelligence unit appears to have increased its involvement in political repression. The unit reportedly controls a section of Tehran's Evin prison.

Amnesty International reported that authorities engaged in a campaign of harassment against women's rights activists early in 2016, subjecting more than a dozen to harsh interrogations and threatening them with arrest and imprisonment. In September 2016, an appeals court upheld a 16-year prison sentence imposed in May against prominent human rights defender Narges Mohammadi for a variety of security charges stemming from her activism, including membership in a group that aims to reduce the high number of executions in Iran. In October, a court sentenced an Iranian-American businessman, Siamak Namazi, and his 80-year-old father, Bagher Namazi, to 10 years in prison for allegedly colluding with the United States.

Security forces are seldom held responsible for human rights violations.

Ethnic minorities complain of various forms of discrimination, including restrictions on the use of their languages. Some provinces with large minority populations remain underdeveloped. Activists campaigning for more ethnic rights and greater autonomy have come under pressure from authorities, and some have been jailed.

The penal code criminalizes all sexual relations outside of traditional marriage, and Iran is among the few countries where individuals can be put to death for consensual same-sex conduct. Members of the LGBT (lesbian, gay, bisexual, and transgender) community face harassment and discrimination, though the problem is underreported due to the criminalized and hidden nature of these groups in Iran.

G. Personal Autonomy and Individual Rights: 4 / 16

Freedom of movement is restricted, particularly for women and perceived opponents of the regime. Women are banned from certain public places, such as sports stadiums, and can obtain a passport to travel abroad only with the permission of their fathers or husbands. Many journalists and activists have been prevented from leaving the country.

Iranians have the legal right to own property and establish private businesses. However, powerful institutions like the IRGC play a dominant role in the economy, and bribery is said to be widespread in the business environment, including for registration and obtaining business licenses.

The government interferes in most aspects of citizens' private lives. Home parties are often raided and citizens detained or fined for drinking alcohol or mingling with members of the opposite sex. In May 2016, some 30 students were each given 99 lashes for attending a mixed-sex graduation party in Qazvin. Women are regularly harassed and detained by the police for not fully observing the obligatory Islamic dress code. An increasing number of women defy the state by wearing tight clothes and short coats.

Women remain significantly underrepresented in politics and government, though Rouhani has appointed three women among his vice presidents, and four women have been appointed as governors. During the 2016 parliamentary elections, 17 women were elected to serve as representatives, the highest number in the Islamic Republic's history. Women are denied equal rights in divorce, child custody, and inheritance. A woman's testimony in court is given only half the weight of a man's, and the monetary compensation awarded to a female victim's family upon her death is half that owed to the family of a male victim.

The government provides no protection to women and children forced into sex trafficking, and both Iranians and migrant workers from countries like Afghanistan and Pakistan are subject to forced labor and debt bondage.

Iraq

Political Rights Rating: 5
Civil Liberties Rating: 6
Freedom Rating: 5.5
Freedom Status: Not Free
Electoral Democracy: No

Population: 38,100,000
Capital: Baghdad

Ten-Year Ratings Timeline For Year Under Review (Political Rights, Civil Liberties, Status)

Year Under Review	2007	2008	2009	2010	2011	2012	2013	2014	2015	2016
Rating	6,6,NF	6,6,NF	5,6,NF	5,6,NF	5,6,NF	6,6,NF	5,6,NF	6,6,NF	5,6,NF	5,6,NF

Overview: Iraq holds regular, competitive elections, and the country's various partisan, religious, and ethnic groups enjoy some representation in the political system. However, democratic governance is seriously impeded in practice by problems including corruption, severe insecurity, and the influence of foreign powers. Iraqis living in areas controlled by the Islamic State (IS) militant group exercise virtually no political or personal freedoms.

KEY DEVELOPMENTS IN 2016:

- The Iraqi government regained significant territory from IS in both Anbar and Nineveh Provinces, though a number of areas—including large parts of Mosul—remained under IS control at year's end.
- Many Sunni Arabs were displaced by the battles against IS, and some also faced abuse by their liberators, particularly the Shiite militias fighting alongside Iraqi government forces.
- The prime minister's attempt in February to form a technocratic cabinet—which threatened the allocation of positions based on ethno-sectarian and partisan considerations—touched off months of protests and political infighting, with some factions holding an illegal rump parliamentary session in April in a bid to replace the speaker and other key officials.
- Opposition lawmakers led by former prime minister Nouri al-Maliki succeeded in removing the ministers of defense and finance in August and September, citing corruption allegations, and the vital posts remained vacant at year's end.

EXECUTIVE SUMMARY

In 2016, Iraqi government forces and their allies—including a U.S.-led coalition, *peshmerga* units reporting to the Kurdistan Regional Government (KRG), Shiite militia groups organized as the Popular Mobilization Forces (PMF), and various other ethnic and tribal militias—retook significant territory held by IS since at least 2014. Ramadi, the capital of Anbar Province, was fully recaptured early in the year, and the Anbar city of Fallujah was taken in June. By October government forces had begun an offensive on Mosul, a major city and capital of Nineveh Province in the north. However, at year's end IS still controlled portions of Mosul, Hawija, Al-Qaim, and Tal Afar, as well as some surrounding areas.

The battles themselves raised new challenges to Baghdad's sovereignty, with Iran actively supporting key Shiite militias, the Kurds expanding the de facto territory of their autonomous region, and the Turkish military staking out an unapproved presence in the Mosul area to support allied militias and oppose Kurdish fighters associated with the Kurdistan Workers' Party (PKK), an armed Kurdish separatist group that has carried out terrorist attacks in Turkey.

The fighting also continued to exacerbate the deep rifts that made Iraq vulnerable to IS infiltration in the first place. The PMF and to a lesser extent government forces sometimes mistreated Sunni civilians in areas retaken from IS, and the government remained unable to care adequately for displaced Sunnis. Nor was the state able to protect Shiite civilians from IS terrorist attacks meant to drive a wedge between the Sunni and Shiite populations.

Meanwhile, Iraq's political establishment descended into near-chaos during the year. The Shiite coalition that had dominated the parliament shattered over whether to end the long-standing, unwritten ethno-sectarian allocation of government positions in favor of a more technocratic cabinet. Former prime minister al-Maliki, a supporter of the status quo, squared off against followers of rival Shiite political leader Moqtada al-Sadr, who insisted on reform; both sides threatened to bring down Prime Minister Haidar al-Abadi's government if their demands were not met, and other groups splintered or maneuvered as the crisis unfolded. Abadi's attempt to reshuffle the cabinet, initiated in February, remained unresolved at year's end, with a number of key ministerial posts left vacant.

Kurdish politics also proved dysfunctional in 2016. The Kurdistan Parliament effectively remained suspended amid a political stalemate that began when Masoud Barzani's already extended term as KRG president expired in 2015. Barzani's party defended his right to stay in office until conditions permitted new elections, while other parties called for reforms that would shift power to the legislature.

POLITICAL RIGHTS: 12 / 40

A. Electoral Process: 8 / 12

Iraq's parliament, the Council of Representatives (CoR), is elected every four years. The CoR currently has 328 members elected through multimember open lists for each province. Seats are allocated by population, but because Iraq has not conducted a nation-wide census since 1987, their distribution is certainly flawed. Once seated after elections, the CoR elects a president. The largest bloc in the parliament then nominates one of its members to be prime minister, and the president formally appoints him to office. The prime minister forms a government that assumes most executive power.

The constitution calls for a second legislative chamber to represent provincial interests, the Federal Council, but this body has never been formed. Provincial councils are elected every four years. Until recently, the borders of the provinces were generally accepted. However, in 2015 the KRG designated Halabja as a new province, splitting it off from Suley-maniyah in a move that has not been universally recognized. In 2016 the Kurds proposed dividing Nineveh into three new provinces, at least one of which would presumably join the KRG.

Iraqi elections are generally considered to be competitive and relatively well adminis-tered given the challenge of chronic political violence. Voting is monitored by the Indepen-dent High Electoral Commission (IHEC), political parties, foreign and domestic media outlets, Iraqi nongovernmental organizations (NGOs), and international observers. Provin-cial elections were scheduled for 2017, and the IHEC began updating voter rolls and regis-tering new voters in 2016, but it was unclear whether the country's security situation would permit the elections to proceed as planned. The next parliamentary elections were scheduled for 2018.

In the 2014 parliamentary elections, al-Maliki's Shiite-led State of Law coalition won 95 seats, making it the largest grouping. A Shiite bloc associated with Moqtada al-Sadr placed second with 34 seats, followed by a third Shiite coalition, Al-Muwatin, with 31 seats. A Sunni-led bloc, Muttahidoon, took 28 seats; a secular nationalist coalition led by Ayad Allawi, Al-Wataniya, received 21; and two Kurdish parties, the Kurdistan Democratic Party (KDP) and the Patriotic Union of Kurdistan (PUK), took 25 and 21 seats, respectively. The remainder was divided among several smaller parties. After tense and protracted negotia-tions, the new parliament eventually approved a government headed by al-Abadi.

The KRG, comprising the northern provinces of Erbil, Dohuk, Suleymaniyah, and Halabja, has its own flag, military (the *peshmerga*), official language, and other institutions. The region elects a 111-seat Kurdistan Parliament through closed party-list proportional representation in a single district. The 2013 elections resulted in the new Gorran (Change) movement (24 seats) displacing the PUK (18) as the second-largest party after the KDP (38). Smaller factions and minority representatives made up the remainder. Kurdish voters also elect provincial councils and vote in national elections. The KRG president, who con-trols many key institutions without legislative oversight, is normally elected directly every four years. However, after holding the office for eight years, Barzani of the KDP had his term extended by two years in a 2013 political agreement with the PUK, and in 2015 he extended his term by another two years unilaterally, citing a legal opinion from a KRG advisory council. That move was endorsed by the KDP but strongly rejected by Gorran and the PUK, which called for an overhaul of KRG political institutions. The dispute remained unresolved in 2016, and a de facto suspension of the Kurdish legislature continued through-out the year.

B. Political Pluralism and Participation: 5 / 16

The constitution guarantees the freedom to form and join political parties, apart from the Baath Party. In July 2016, the parliament passed legislation that strengthened the consti-tutional ban on the Baath Party, criminalizing Baathist protests and the promotion of Baa-thist ideas. The measure applies to any group that supports racism, terrorism, sectarianism, sectarian cleansing, and other ideas contrary to democracy or the peaceful transfer of power. Individual Iraqis' freedom to run for office is limited by a "good conduct" requirement in the electoral law and by the Accountability and Justice Commission, which disqualifies candidates and officials with ties to the former Baath Party. Many Sunnis view the commis-sion as discriminatory. Despite these barriers, Iraqis run for office, form parties, and take part in politics in large numbers.

As in past years, political activity was impaired in 2016 by violence, both threatened and actual. The problem was especially acute in territories still under IS control, but intimi-dation of those active in public life occurs throughout Iraq. The political system is also distorted by interference from foreign powers and the allocation of key offices according to informal ethno-sectarian criteria, which reduces the likelihood that politicians will act in the interests of the whole country and the viability of non-ethno-sectarian parties and movements.

A system of reserved seats ensures representation in the CoR for many of Iraq's smaller religious and ethnic minorities. There are five seats for Christians and one each for Yazidis, Sabean Mandaeans, and Shabaks. The Kurdish legislature reserves five seats for Turkomans, five for Chaldean and Assyrian Christians, and one for Armenians. Sunni Arabs, Iraq's largest minority, argue that Shiite dominance of the political system keeps them out of positions of influence.

C. Functioning of Government: 2 / 12

Governance in Iraq is hampered by factors including IS control over territory in the northwest, rampant corruption, and ethno-sectarian divisions. The political disorder of 2016 featured a splintering of alliances, both within and across ethno-sectarian blocs, and repeated attempts to influence parliamentary outcomes through illegal and even violent means.

Al-Sadr's supporters organized aggressive protests to advance his demands for radical anticorruption measures and a technocratic cabinet, ultimately occupying the government district of Baghdad and violently storming the parliament building in April, forcing elected representatives to flee temporarily. Also that month, a disparate group of Sunni, Sadrist, and other Shiite lawmakers occupied the CoR and held a rogue session that attempted to change the leadership, though it lacked a quorum. Al-Maliki later organized some elements of that group into an opposition Reform Front that sought to weaken al-Abadi's government by initiating corruption investigations against ministers and bringing votes to remove them. The initiative succeeded in ousting Defense Minister Khalid al-Obeidi in August and Finance Minister Hoshyar Zebari in September. Although al-Abadi managed to install some technocratic ministers, those two crucial posts remained vacant at year's end, as did that of interior minister; the incumbent interior minister had resigned in July following a massive suicide bombing in central Baghdad.

Many parties' resistance to a technocratic cabinet reflected the extent to which they benefit financially from control over ministries. In August, the head of the country's Integrity Commission demanded that political parties abolish affiliated committees that broker deals between the ministries and private businesses. The home of at least one technocratic minister was attacked by gunmen in September, and members of the Integrity Commission are reportedly exposed to chronic threats and deadly violence.

Separately, the political standoff in the KRG also contributed to governmental dysfunction, with the legislature unable to convene and the president remaining in office without an electoral mandate. The crisis has opened up debate on the entire Kurdish institutional structure. Gorran, the PUK, and their allies have demanded a reformed system in which a largely symbolic president is elected by the parliament. Barzani, with the backing of the KDP, insists on maintaining the current system and refuses to leave office. His wealthy family remains a powerful political and economic force in the region, with his son serving as the KRG's intelligence chief and his nephew as prime minister.

DISCRETIONARY POLITICAL RIGHTS QUESTION B: $-3 / 0$

IS continued its efforts to change the religious demography in areas it controlled or could attack in 2016. In occupied regions, Shiites, Christians, Yazidis, Shabaks, Sabeans, and Kaka'i faced executions, forced conversion, discriminatory "taxation," and enslavement that entailed sexual violence. IS also destroyed or repurposed churches and shrines. IS terrorist attacks outside its territory often struck Shiite targets. In areas where the *peshmerga* captured territory from IS, displaced Arab residents were frequently barred from returning, a form of population transfer that Kurdish forces justified as a security measure.

CIVIL LIBERTIES: 15 / 60

D. Freedom of Expression and Belief: 5 / 16

The constitution guarantees freedom of expression and media freedom so long as "public order" and "morality" are maintained. Iraq's media scene appears diverse, but many outlets are controlled by political parties. The few independent newspapers have suffered from economic pressures in recent years, forcing some to close. Journalists face the threat of lawsuits or retaliation in an environment characterized by corruption and violence. Bloggers and others who disseminate information online are also at risk. At least six journalists were killed in connection with their work in 2016, according to the Committee to Protect Journalists (CPJ). In one case for which CPJ had not confirmed the motive, journalist Wedad Hussein Ali of the PKK-affiliated website Roj News was murdered in the Kurdish region in August.

The constitution guarantees freedom of belief, but in practice many Iraqis were targeted for their religious identity during 2016. IS continued to kill Shiites, whom it considers to be apostates, either in terrorist bombings or after capture. Abducted Yazidi women have been forced to serve IS members as sex slaves. Some Christians survived in IS areas by paying a special tax, but they lived under the constant threat of violence and abuse. Sunnis who resisted the militants' interpretation of Islamic law were also killed in large numbers. Sunnis suspected of supporting IS faced execution or property loss at the hands of progovernment forces, particularly Shiite militias.

None of the several universities that closed as a result of IS's 2014 invasion was able to resume normal functioning in 2016. According to the UN Children's Fund (UNICEF), approximately 3.5 million Iraqi children's education was interrupted during the year by IS and the military campaign against it. Schools throughout Iraq are overcrowded, due in part to corrupt mismanagement and population movements. In IS-held areas where university or secondary school classes have resumed, the militants permit no teaching of music, history, literature, or art, often focusing instead on paramilitary training.

Free and open private discussion is limited by the fear of informants in IS-affected areas. Speech in other parts of Iraq is more free, though the threat of political or sectarian violence remains a deterrent.

E. Associational and Organizational Rights: 6 / 12

The constitution guarantees freedom of assembly, and this right is increasingly respected in practice, though deadly violence still occurs. In 2016, multiple large and confrontational demonstrations by Sadrists and others were able to proceed in southern Iraq and central Baghdad, though clashes with security forces ensued when protesters stormed government buildings and attacked officials, and at least four demonstrators were reportedly killed.

NGOs enjoy societal support and a relatively hospitable regulatory environment, though they must register with the government and obtain approval from the Accountability and Justice Commission. In the KRG, NGOs must renew their registration annually. The main obstacles to NGO operations are a lack of security and impunity for past attacks.

A new Iraqi labor law that generally meets international standards was adopted in 2015 and took effect in February 2016, though the KRG was considering drafting its own labor laws, adding to doubts about the national legislation's implementation and enforcement. The law allows collective bargaining even by workers without a union, improves the rights of subcontractors and migrant workers, and permits workers to strike, among other features. However, it does not apply to civil servants or security forces. Some state officials and private employers reportedly discouraged union activity with threats, dismissals, and other deterrents during 2016.

F. Rule of Law: 0 / 16

The judiciary is influenced by corruption, political pressure, tribal forces, and religious interests. Due to distrust of or lack of access to the courts, many Iraqis have turned to tribal bodies to settle disputes, even those involving major crimes. In 2016, the country's highest court played a role in the political dispute over al-Abadi's cabinet reshuffle, ruling in June that an April parliament session to approve several of the prime minister's appointees had used unconstitutional procedures, but also that the rump parliament formed earlier that month by rogue lawmakers was invalid.

Large numbers of detainees are held in government prisons without charge. Many were arrested under a vaguely worded antiterrorism law passed in 2005. Iraqi prisons are overcrowded and dangerous. Amnesty International documented extremely poor conditions in counterterrorism detention facilities in Anbar Province in 2016. The use of torture to elicit confessions is widespread.

The number of death sentences and executions increased dramatically in 2016 despite enduring flaws in the integrity of the criminal justice system. By July there were over 3,000 people on death row, and at least 88 inmates were executed during the year, according to Amnesty International. In August, after a brief trial based on confessions that were allegedly obtained through torture, the state executed 36 men convicted in the IS massacre of hundreds of Iraqi military recruits in 2014.

IS intensified its terrorist bombing campaign in government-held areas in 2016, with one attack in Baghdad in July killing some 300 people in the predominantly Shiite area of Karrada. Additional threats to civilian safety arose from IS atrocities in areas under its control as well as fighting between the militants and progovernment forces. IS reportedly forced large groups of people into Mosul to serve as human shields against bombardment. Meanwhile, many Sunnis in liberated areas were illegally detained, beaten, robbed, tortured, and murdered, most often by the PMF. The authorities launched investigations into these crimes, but it remained unclear whether perpetrators were ultimately punished.

According to the UN Assistance Mission for Iraq, at least 6,878 civilians were killed and 12,388 were injured in 2016 as a result of armed conflict and related violence, though the mission cautioned that its figures were incomplete.

Same-sex sexual relations are not illegal in Iraq, but LGBT (lesbian, gay, bisexual, and transgender) people risk violence—including execution in IS-held areas—if they are open about their identity. Other disadvantaged groups in the country include Iraqis of African descent, who suffer from high rates of extreme poverty and discrimination.

G. Personal Autonomy and Individual Rights: 4 / 16

Freedom of movement, choice of residence, and property rights have all suffered from the conflict with IS. Roughly three million people remained internally displaced during 2016, and the number was expected to rise as fighting in Mosul intensified. In the KRG, displaced persons have reported being forced to enter camps against their will.

Iraqi women face problems including domestic violence, early marriage, and discrimination on issues governed by personal status law such as marriage, divorce and inheritance. Women living in IS-held areas risked beatings or execution if they left home without full veils, gloves, and a male guardian. They also faced rape and forced marriages, while captive Yazidi women and girls in particular were subjected to sex slavery and other egregious abuses. The government continues to prevent NGOs from legally providing shelter to women fleeing gender-based violence. At least one-fourth of the seats in the Iraqi parliament and 30 percent of the seats in the Kurdish parliament must go to women, though such representation has had little obvious effect on state protections for women in practice.

Refugees and internally displaced persons are especially vulnerable to human trafficking and sexual exploitation. Other victims of human trafficking in Iraq include foreign migrant workers, children engaged in forced begging, and child soldiers recruited primarily by IS, though the PMF and some Kurdish and tribal militias also reportedly recruit child soldiers.

Ireland

Political Rights Rating: 1
Civil Liberties Rating: 1
Freedom Rating: 1.0
Freedom Status: Free
Electoral Democracy: Yes

Population: 4,700,000
Capital: Dublin

Ten-Year Ratings Timeline For Year Under Review (Political Rights, Civil Liberties, Status)

Year Under Review	2007	2008	2009	2010	2011	2012	2013	2014	2015	2016
Rating	1,1,F	1,1,F	1,1,F	1,1,F	1,1,F	1,1,F	1,1,F	1,1,F	1,1,F	1,1,F

Overview: Ireland is a stable democracy that holds regular free and fair elections. Political rights and civil liberties are robust, although the government suffers from some incidence of corruption. While the Catholic Church maintains a strong influence and abortion rights remain restricted, members of all religious groups may practice freely and same-sex marriage is legal. There is some limited societal discrimination, especially against the traditionally nomadic Irish Travellers.

KEY DEVELOPMENTS IN 2016:

- General elections took place on February 26. Fine Gael remained the largest party, but with far fewer seats than in the 2011 general election, while Fianna Fáil more than doubled its share of the vote. Sinn Féin came in third.
- After protracted postelection negotiations lasting 63 days, Fine Gael joined Fianna Fáil in a minority-led government.
- In September, a large prochoice demonstration took place in Dublin calling for repeal of the eighth amendment of the constitution that gives equal rights to the life of the mother and the unborn; the law remained unchanged at year's end.

EXECUTIVE SUMMARY

Ireland is a stable and robust democracy. As in the past, 2016 national elections saw no major irregularities or unequal campaigning opportunities. Free expression and association as well as the functioning of the judiciary are unhampered. Among its European peers, Ireland is most distinguished by its strict abortion laws protected by the constitution. However, the population is more socially liberal, as evidenced by a 2015 referendum that approved the extension of marriage rights to same-sex couples and resulted in a constitutional amendment. Ireland also has relatively high levels of governmental corruption compared to its neighbors, marked by cronyism, political patronage, and illegal donations.

Societal discrimination against the small Irish Traveller population remains, particularly in housing and employment. Only in 2015 did the parliament pass legislation to curtail an exemption that allowed health and educational institutions run by religious entities to practice employment discrimination on religious grounds, for example on the basis of sexual orientation. Unusually severe prison conditions were highlighted by a 2015 Council of Europe report that criticized the continued lack of toilet access in some cells; the government has taken steps to address this.

POLITICAL RIGHTS: 39 / 40

A. Electoral Process: 12 / 12

B. Political Pluralism and Participation: 16 / 16

C. Functioning of Government: 11 / 12

CIVIL LIBERTIES: 57 / 60

D. Freedom of Expression and Belief: 16 / 16

E. Associational and Organizational Rights: 12 / 12

F. Rule of Law: 14 / 16

G. Personal Autonomy and Individual Rights: 15 / 16

This country report has been abridged for *Freedom in the World 2017*. For background information on political rights and civil liberties in Ireland, see *Freedom in the World 2016*.

Israel

Political Rights Rating: 1   **Population:** 8,200,000
[Note: There are an estimated 386,000 Israeli settlers in the West Bank, about 21,000 in the Golan Heights, and 201,000 in East Jerusalem.]
Civil Liberties Rating: 2   **Capital:** Jerusalem
Freedom Rating: 1.5
Freedom Status: Free
Electoral Democracy: Yes

Note: The numerical ratings and status listed above do not reflect conditions in the West Bank and the Gaza Strip, which are examined in separate reports.

Ten-Year Ratings Timeline For Year Under Review (Political Rights, Civil Liberties, Status)

Year Under Review	2007	2008	2009	2010	2011	2012	2013	2014	2015	2016
Rating	1,2,F	1,2,F	1,2,F	1,2,F	1,2,F	1,2,F	1,2,F	1,2,F	1,2,F	1,2,F

Overview: Israel is a multiparty democracy with strong and independent institutions that guarantee political rights and civil liberties for most of the population. Although the judiciary is active in protecting minority rights, the ruling elite has traditionally discriminated against the Arab and, to a lesser degree, the ultra-Orthodox and Ethiopian minorities.

KEY DEVELOPMENTS IN 2016:

- In July, the Knesset (parliament) approved a law that allows it to expel any members found to have incited racism or supported armed struggle against the state of Israel. Critics of the measure described it as a means of silencing Arab representatives.
- In July 2016, Israelis of Ethiopian origin took to the streets of Tel Aviv to protest against police brutality and discrimination, with police arresting participants who tried to block a highway.
- A reported 414 Palestinian children (aged 12–17) from the occupied territories were being held in Israeli military detention as of April 2016, more than double the figure from a year earlier.

EXECUTIVE SUMMARY

The environment for civil society groups and minorities in Israel did not improve in 2016, as restrictions on nongovernmental organizations (NGOs) and Knesset members reinforced a recent trend of intolerance for dissent. A wave of stabbing and other attacks against Jewish Israeli citizens that began in late 2015 continued to influence politics and society, despite a relative easing of tensions during the year. In July, the Knesset approved separate bills that increase penalties for flag desecration, require certain NGOs to routinely publicize their reliance on foreign funding, and allow the parliament to remove members who incite racism or support armed struggle against the state of Israel. Opponents said the latter two measures targeted left-leaning human rights groups and Arab Knesset members, respectively. Also in July, the government outlawed Al-Hirak al-Shababi (Youth Movement), a Palestinian group, and in August it reported plans to ban the radical Islamist group Hizb ut-Tahrir.

Meanwhile, hundreds of Palestinians were in administrative detention in 2016, hundreds of Palestinian children remained in military prisons, and Arab citizens of Israel—who often identify as Palestinian—continued to face disadvantages in areas such as education, social services, and housing. However, Arabs were not the only minority suffering from discrimination, as Israelis of Ethiopian origin have experienced a pattern of racism, including at the hands of police. In July Ethiopian Israelis took to the streets of Tel Aviv in a major demonstration, with police arresting protesters after some attempted to block a highway.

POLITICAL RIGHTS: 36 / 40

A. Electoral Process: 12 / 12

A largely ceremonial president is elected by the 120-seat parliament, the Knesset, for one seven-year term. In 2014, Reuven Rivlin of the right-leaning Likud party was elected to replace outgoing president Shimon Peres, receiving 63 votes in a runoff against Meir Sheetrit of the centrist Hatnuah party.

The prime minister is usually the leader of the largest faction in the Knesset, members of which are elected by party-list proportional representation for four-year terms. A low electoral threshold to win representation has led to unstable coalitions, though the threshold was raised in 2014 from 2 to 3.25 percent. Among other changes adopted in the same legislation, the no-confidence procedure was altered so that opponents hoping to oust a sitting government must simultaneously vote in a new one.

Israeli elections are free and fair. In the March 2015 Knesset elections, Likud, led by incumbent prime minister Benjamin Netanyahu, secured 30 seats, followed by the center-left Zionist Union with 24. The Joint List—a coalition of parties representing Arab citizens of Israel—earned 13 seats; the centrist Yesh Atid (There Is a Future), 11; Kulanu, also centrist, 10; Habayit Hayehudi (Jewish Home), 8; the ultra-Orthodox parties Shas and United Torah Judaism, 7 and 6, respectively; the right-wing Yisrael Beiteinu, 6; and the left-wing Meretz party, 5. In May 2015, after lengthy negotiations, Netanyahu formed a new coalition government made up of Likud, Kulanu, Jewish Home, Shas, and United Torah Judaism. In May 2016 the coalition was expanded to include Yisrael Beiteinu, whose leader, Avigdor Lieberman, became defense minister.

B. Political Pluralism and Participation: 14 / 16

Israel hosts a diverse and competitive multiparty system. However, parties or candidates that deny Israel's Jewish character, oppose democracy, or incite racism are prohibited. In July 2016 the Knesset approved a law that allows it to remove any members who incite racism or support armed struggle against the state of Israel. Critics of the law alleged that it was aimed at silencing Arab representatives. Three-quarters of the Knesset would have to vote to oust a member, who could then appeal to the Supreme Court.

Arab or Palestinian citizens of Israel enjoy equal rights in principle, as enshrined in Israel's Basic Law, but face some discrimination in practice, both legally and informally. The Joint List's representation in the Knesset falls short of Arabs' roughly one-fifth share of Israel's population, though some vote or run as candidates for other parties. No Arab party has ever been formally included in a governing coalition, and Arabs generally do not serve in senior positions in government. Although Israeli identity cards issued since 2005 have not classified residents by ethnicity, Jewish Israelis can often be identified by the inclusion of their Hebrew birth date.

After Israel's annexation of East Jerusalem in 1967, which has not been recognized internationally, Arab residents were issued Israeli identity cards and given the option of obtaining Israeli citizenship, though most declined for political reasons. These noncitizens can vote in municipal as well as Palestinian Authority elections, and remain eligible to apply for Israeli citizenship. However, Israeli law strips noncitizens of their Jerusalem residency if they are away for more than three months.

A 2003 law, renewed in 2013, denies citizenship and residency status to Palestinian residents of the West Bank or Gaza Strip who are married to Israeli citizens. While the measure was criticized as blatantly discriminatory, supporters cited evidence that a significant share of past suicide bombers had acquired Israeli identity cards via family reunification. A 2011 law allows the courts to revoke the citizenship of any Israeli convicted of spying, treason, or aiding the enemy.

Under the 1948 Law of Return, Jewish immigrants and their immediate families are granted Israeli citizenship and residence rights; other immigrants must apply for these rights.

C. Functioning of Government: 10 / 12

The government and parliament are free to set and implement policies and laws without undue interference from unelected entities.

A strong societal intolerance for graft has been reinforced by frequent high-level corruption investigations. Scandals and criminal cases in recent years have implicated several senior officials. The most prominent example is that of Ehud Olmert, who resigned as prime minister in 2008 amid graft allegations. After the Supreme Court in December 2015 reduced his original 2014 sentence of six years, in February 2016 Olmert went to jail to serve a 19-month sentence for bribery. In September, Olmert was convicted of fraud and breach of trust in a separate case involving cash he accepted from an American businessman, Morris Talansky, and was sentenced to an additional eight months in prison.

Prime Minister Netanyahu has been the subject of a number of corruption probes by the media and state authorities, though none had resulted in formal charges as of 2016.

CIVIL LIBERTIES: 44 / 60

D. Freedom of Expression and Belief: 12 / 16

The Israeli media are vibrant and free to criticize government policy. However, the diversity and editorial independence of both print and broadcast media have been threatened in recent years by financial difficulties in the industry. All Israeli newspapers are privately owned, though ownership is concentrated among a small number of companies, some of which display a clear partisan bias. Internet access is widespread and unrestricted. The Israel Broadcasting Authority operates public radio and television services, and commercial broadcasts are widely available. Most Israelis subscribe to cable or satellite television. While the scope of permissible reporting is generally broad, print articles on security matters are subject to a military censor, and the censor has sought to expand its supervision to bloggers and social media. The Government Press Office has occasionally withheld press cards from journalists, especially Palestinians, to restrict them from entering Israel, citing security considerations.

Investigative journalists came under increased pressure from politicians during 2016, with Netanyahu in particular issuing unusually harsh denunciations of senior reporters with the commercial television stations Channel 2 and Channel 10. Netanyahu's dual role as communications minister has raised questions about political bias and conflicts of interest in the ministry's regulation of the media and telecommunications.

There are some restrictions on political expression, including constraints on any local authorities or state-funded groups that commemorate the 1948 displacement of Palestinians, support armed resistance or racism against Israel, or desecrate national symbols. The 2011 Boycott Law exposes Israeli individuals and groups to civil lawsuits if they advocate an economic, cultural, or academic boycott of the state of Israel or West Bank settlements. A law adopted in July 2016 sharply increased penalties for desecrating the Israeli flag, calling for up to three years in prison and over $15,000 in fines.

While Israel defines itself as a Jewish state, freedom of religion is largely respected. Christian, Muslim, and Baha'i communities have jurisdiction over their own members in matters of marriage, divorce, and burial. The Orthodox establishment governs personal status matters among Jews, drawing objections from many non-Orthodox and secular Israelis. In a milestone case in 2011, an Israeli Jew won the right to an identity card that excluded his Hebrew birth date. Nevertheless, in 2013 the Supreme Court ruled against an appeal that would have allowed individuals to declare their ethnic "nationality" in Israel's population registry to be "Israeli" rather than "Jewish."

Ultra-Orthodox Jews, or Haredim, were exempt from compulsory military service under the 2002 Tal Law, which expired in 2012 after the High Court of Justice ruled it unconstitutional. In 2014, the Knesset enacted a law to formally end the exemption, but legislation adopted in November 2015 effectively postponed enforcement of the 2014 measure until 2023.

Although the law protects the religious sites of non-Jewish minorities, they face discrimination in the allocation of state resources, and a number of Christian and Muslim sites were attacked or vandalized in 2015 and to a much lesser extent in 2016. In September 2015, the government agreed to increase funding for private Christian schools in Israel for the 2015–16 school year and reexamine their legal status and future funding after the schools, representing 33,000 students, carried out a month-long strike over their unequal treatment by the state. However, there were considerable delays in the distribution of the new funds in 2016.

Citing security concerns, Israeli authorities have set limits on Muslim worshippers' access to the Temple Mount/Haram al-Sharif in Jerusalem with increasing frequency in recent years. Clashes between Palestinians and Israeli police in the area in 2015 and 2016 were driven partly by rumors that Israel was planning to change the existing rules and allow Jews to pray in the Muslim compound, which the government strongly denied.

Primary and secondary education is universal, though divided into multiple public school systems (state, state-religious, Haredi, and Arab, the last of which uses the common curriculum but provides instruction in Arabic). School quality and resources are generally lower in mostly non-Jewish communities. Israel's universities have long been centers for dissent and are open to all students based on merit, though security-related restrictions on movement limit access for West Bank and Gaza residents in practice.

While private discussion in Israel is generally open and free, it has been affected by security conditions in recent years. Palestinians in the country faced increased societal and other pressure in response to their remarks during a 2014 Israeli military campaign against Hamas militants in Gaza. Dozens were reportedly fired or disciplined by employers for views expressed on social media and elsewhere, and tensions persisted to some extent in 2016.

E. Associational and Organizational Rights: 10 / 12

Israel has an active civil society, and demonstrations are widely permitted and typically peaceful, though groups committed to the destruction of Israel are banned from demonstrating. In July 2016 Israelis of Ethiopian origin organized a protest against police brutality and discrimination in Tel Aviv. Several participants were arrested for disruption of public order after attempting to block a highway.

A law that took effect in 2012 requires NGOs to submit financial reports four times a year on support received from foreign government sources. In July 2016, the Knesset approved a law requiring NGOs that receive more than half of their funding from foreign governments to disclose this fact publicly and in any written or oral communications with elected officials. An especially controversial provision of the bill, requiring representatives of such NGOs to wear a special badge in the Knesset building, was dropped from the final version.

Also in July, the government outlawed the Palestinian youth group Al-Hirak al-Shababi due to its alleged violent activities and links with Iran and the Lebanese militant group Hezbollah. In August, Internal Security Minister Gilad Erdan announced plans to ban Hizb ut-Tahrir, a radical Islamist organization whose ideology he likened to that of the militant group Islamic State (IS), but no actual ban was subsequently reported. In December the Defense Ministry outlawed a Turkish group, the Kanadil Institute for Humanitarian Aid and Development, because it allegedly channeled funds to the Palestinian militant group Hamas and the Muslim Brotherhood.

Workers may join unions and have the right to strike and bargain collectively. Most of the workforce either belongs to Histadrut, the national labor federation, or is covered by its social programs and bargaining agreements.

F. Rule of Law: 11 / 16

The judiciary is independent and regularly rules against the government. Over the years, the Supreme Court has played an increasingly central role in protecting minorities and overturning decisions by the government and the parliament when they threaten human rights. The Supreme Court hears direct petitions from both citizens and Palestinian residents of the West Bank and Gaza Strip, and the state generally adheres to court rulings.

The Emergency Powers (Detention) Law of 1979 provides for administrative detention without trial for renewable six-month terms. According to the human rights group B'Tselem, there were 644 Palestinians in administrative detention in Israel Prison Service facilities at the end of August 2016, up from 584 at the end of 2015. Such detention rarely lasts for more than two years. Under criminal law, individuals suspected of security offenses can be held for up to 96 hours without judicial review under certain circumstances, compared with a maximum of 48 hours in other cases, and be denied access to an attorney for up to 21 days.

Israel's High Court of Justice banned torture in a 1999 ruling, but said physical coercion might be permissible during interrogations in cases involving an imminent threat. Human rights organizations accuse the authorities of continuing to use some forms of physical abuse and other measures such as isolation, sleep deprivation, psychological threats and pressure, painful binding, and humiliation.

Hunger strikes by Palestinian detainees have become increasingly common. Among several other such actions during the year, 65 detainees aligned with the left-wing Popular Front for the Liberation of Palestine (PFLP) went on a hunger strike in June 2016 to support

Bilal Kayed, a PFLP member who was administratively detained after completing a 14-year sentence. Kayed ended his hunger strike in August after he reached a deal with the Israeli authorities, who agreed to release him in December. Also in August, more than 200 Hamas members detained in Israel went on a hunger strike to protest body searches and improve prison conditions. The protest ended days later, after an agreement was reached.

According to Defense for Children International (DCI) Palestine, 414 Palestinian children (aged 12–17) from the occupied territories were being held in Israeli military detention as of April 2016, up from 164 at the same time in 2015. Although Israeli law prohibits the detention of children younger than 12, some are occasionally held. Most Palestinian child detainees are serving sentences of several weeks or months—handed down by a special military court for minors created in 2009—for throwing stones or other projectiles at Israeli troops in the West Bank; acquittals on such charges are very rare. East Jerusalem Palestinian minors are tried in Israeli civilian juvenile courts.

The authorities took a number of steps to crack down on violent protests in 2015. The Knesset passed legislation imposing harsher sentences for stone-throwing offenses under Israeli criminal law, with penalties of up to 20 years in prison for adults who throw objects at a vehicle with intent to harm the occupants. Moreover, the government authorized police to fire small-caliber bullets at stone throwers if a third party's life is threatened, not just when the officer's own life is in danger. Finally, the Knesset approved three-year minimum prison sentences for stone-throwing offenses in Israel, as well as the suspension of social benefits for the parents of juvenile offenders. Meanwhile, human rights groups in late 2015 accused police of using deadly force against some perpetrators of stabbing and vehicular attacks when they did not pose a lethal threat.

In addition to attacks by Palestinians on the ground during the year, Israeli civilians—particularly those living near border areas—faced occasional rocket and artillery fire from war-torn Syria and the Gaza Strip. However, the rate of fire was far lower than during the major Israel-Hamas conflicts of 2008–9, 2012, and 2014.

About 93 percent of the land in Israel is publicly owned, including some 12.5 percent owned by the Jewish National Fund (JNF-KKL). In 2005, the Supreme Court and attorney general ruled against the JNF-KKL's marketing property only to Jews, while the Knesset made several unsuccessful attempts to override those rulings. In practice, the JNF-KKL continues its Jewish-only land-leasing policy, partly as a result of a land-swap arrangement with the Israel Land Authority. In 2014 the Supreme Court upheld 2011 legislation that allows Jewish communities of up to 400 residents in the Negev and Galilee to exclude prospective residents based on "social suitability," meaning they could effectively bar non-Jews and other marginalized groups. In September 2016 a group of NGOs petitioned the Supreme Court, challenging the JNF-KKL's role in marketing Israeli land and focusing particularly on its discrimination against non-Jews.

Arab or Palestinian citizens of Israel face de facto discrimination in education, social services, and access to housing and related permits. Aside from the Druze minority, they are exempted from military conscription, though they may volunteer. Those who do not serve are ineligible for the associated benefits, including scholarships and housing loans. Many of Israel's roughly 230,000 Bedouin citizens live in towns and villages not recognized by the state. Those in unrecognized villages cannot claim social services, are in some cases off the electricity grid, and have no official land rights, and the government routinely demolishes their unlicensed structures. A lack of bomb shelters puts them at additional risk from Gaza-based rocket fire.

Israelis of Ethiopian origin, numbering around 130,000, suffer from some discrimination and lag behind the general population economically despite government integration efforts. Although Ethiopian Israelis mounted protests against police brutality and discrimination in 2015 and 2016, in August Israel's police commissioner defended the practice of racially profiling them, along with Arabs and other "immigrant" groups, claiming that statistics showed they were more likely to be involved in crime. In July, a regional labor court ordered the state to provide compensation to Ethiopian Israeli religious leaders who had long faced wage and other discrimination relative to their non-Ethiopian colleagues.

Israel has sought to block asylum seekers and migrants from Africa by erecting a fence along its border with Egypt. Individuals who enter the country irregularly, including asylum seekers, can be detained for up to a year without charges. Asylum applications, when fully processed, are nearly always rejected. Of some 60,000 African asylum seekers who have entered since 2005, mostly from Sudan and Eritrea, more than 10,000 have left under pressure, agreeing to be repatriated or deported to a third country such as Uganda or Rwanda.

G. Personal Autonomy and Individual Rights: 11 / 16

Security measures can sometimes present obstacles to freedom of movement, though military checkpoints are restricted to the West Bank. By law, all citizens must carry identification cards. Informal local rules that prevent driving on the Sabbath and Jewish holidays can also hamper free movement.

Property rights within Israel are effectively protected, and business activity is generally free of undue interference. Businesses face a low risk of expropriation or criminal activity, and corruption is only a minor nuisance for private investors.

Women have achieved substantial parity at almost all levels of Israeli society. However, Palestinian women and religious Jewish women face some discrimination. Many ultra-Orthodox Jewish communities enforce gender separation. In 2012, the Supreme Court ruled against gender-segregated buses. Nevertheless, many women still sit at the rear of buses on certain lines, and there are occasionally violent Haredi attacks on buses where the practice is not observed, along with attacks against women and girls deemed to be dressed immodestly. Since religious courts oversee marriage rules, marriages between Jews and non-Jews are not recognized by the state unless conducted abroad, nor are marriages involving a Muslim woman and a non-Muslim man. A law passed in 2010 permits nonreligious civil unions, but they are restricted to cases where the individuals have no religion, and they are seldom used.

Israel has recognized same-sex marriages conducted abroad since 2006, and a Tel Aviv family court granted the first same-sex divorce in 2012. Nonbiological parents in same-sex partnerships are eligible for guardianship rights, and openly gay Israelis are permitted to serve in the military. The Israel Prison Service permits same-sex conjugal visits.

Israel remains a destination for human-trafficking victims, and African migrants and asylum seekers residing in the country are especially vulnerable to forced labor and sex trafficking. The government works actively to combat trafficking and protect victims, though the U.S. State Department's *Trafficking in Persons Report* describes many of the penalties imposed by courts as inadequate.

Israel's roughly 80,000 legal foreign workers are formally protected from exploitation by employers, but these guarantees are poorly enforced. About 17,000 foreigners work in the country illegally, according to official data. Histadrut has opened membership to foreign workers and called on employers to grant them equal rights.

Italy

Political Rights Rating: 1
Civil Liberties Rating: 1
Freedom Rating: 1.0
Freedom Status: Free
Electoral Democracy: Yes

Population: 60,600,000
Capital: Rome

Ten-Year Ratings Timeline For Year Under Review (Political Rights, Civil Liberties, Status)

Year Under Review	2007	2008	2009	2010	2011	2012	2013	2014	2015	2016
Rating	1,1,F	1,2,F	1,2,F	1,2,F	1,1,F	2,1,F	1,1,F	1,1,F	1,1,F	1,1,F

Overview: Italy's parliamentary system features competitive multiparty elections. The Vatican has traditionally held significant influence over the country's politics, and ties between organized crime and public officials persist. Civil liberties are generally respected, though the judicial system is undermined by long trial delays and the influence of organized crime.

KEY DEVELOPMENTS IN 2016:

- In May, the parliament approved a law recognizing same-sex civil unions, providing same-sex couples with the opportunity to claim nearly all of the rights conferred by marriage.
- Authorities struggled to provide adequate housing for asylum seekers and refugees and to process asylum applications in a timely manner, as the country continued to experience large-scale migration by sea from the Middle East and North Africa.

EXECUTIVE SUMMARY

In 2016, the parliament approved same-sex civil unions, after a lively debate that lasted for nearly two years. The law provides same-sex couples who enter a civil union with almost all rights conferred by marriage. The possibility of stepchild adoption was removed from the legislation, however.

Italy continued to face large-scale migration by sea from the Middle East and North Africa during 2016, with over 180,000 registered arrivals during the year. Immediate emergency services for arriving migrants, many of whom were asylum seekers, were routine and included medical treatment, food, water, and temporary shelter. However, the authorities still struggled to provide adequate longer-term housing and ensure the timely processing of asylum applications. Reports of excessive use of force by police against migrants have persisted.

A controversial new electoral law approved in 2015 entered into force in July 2016. The measure, designed to encourage majorities and avoid postelection deadlock, mandates that a party that wins more than 40 percent of the popular vote in a legislative election be granted at least 54 percent of seats in the lower house; if no party wins more than 40 percent, a special election round is held in which the winning party receives at least 54 percent of lower-house seats. The Constitutional Court is expected to rule on the reform's legality in 2017.

Separately, constitutional reforms designed to streamline Italy's time-consuming legislative processes by reducing the size and powers of the Senate were approved by parliament in April 2016, but rejected by voters in a December referendum amid concerns that the changes could give outsized powers to the prime minister. Prime Minister Matteo Renzi subsequently resigned and was replaced by foreign affairs minister Paolo Gentiloni.

POLITICAL RIGHTS: 36 / 40
A. Electoral Process: 12 / 12
B. Political Pluralism and Participation: 14 / 16
C. Functioning of Government: 10 / 12

CIVIL LIBERTIES: 53 / 60
D. Freedom of Expression and Belief: 15 / 16
E. Associational and Organizational Rights: 12 / 12
F. Rule of Law: 12 / 16
G. Personal Autonomy and Individual Rights: 14 / 16

This country report has been abridged for *Freedom in the World 2017*. For background information on political rights and civil liberties in Italy, see *Freedom in the World 2016*.

Jamaica

Political Rights: 2
Civil Liberties: 3
Freedom Ratings: 2.5
Freedom Status: Free
Electoral Democracy: Yes

Population: 2,700,000
Capital: Kingston

Ten-Year Ratings Timeline For Year Under Review (Political Rights, Civil Liberties, Status)

Year Under Review	2007	2008	2009	2010	2011	2012	2013	2014	2015	2016
Rating	2,3,F	2,3,F	2,3,F	2,3,F	2,3,F	2,3,F	2,3,F	2,3,F	2,3,F	2,3,F

Overview: Jamaica's political institutions are democratic, with competitive elections and orderly rotations of power. However, corruption remains a serious problem, and long-standing relationships between officials and organized crime figures are thought to persist. Gang and vigilante violence remains a concern, as does harassment and violence against LGBT (lesbian, gay, bisexual, and transgender) people.

KEY DEVELOPMENTS IN 2016:
- The Jamaica Labour Party (JLP) won a narrow victory in February's legislative elections, pushing the incumbent People's National Party (PNP) into opposition. Monitors deemed the elections competitive and credible, but noted some instances of election-related violence.
- In July, the PNP's treasurer levied allegations that senior party officials had misappropriated millions of dollars' worth of campaign donations ahead of the 2016 polls.

- A commission tasked with investigating severe violence that accompanied a 2010 police operation in Kingston found that security forces had acted disproportionately, and recommended that the government apologize for the events and provide victims with compensation and counseling services.

EXECUTIVE SUMMARY

Monitors from the Organization for American States (OAS) deemed the February 2016 general elections competitive and credible, but recorded instances of election-related violence ahead of the polls. The opposition JLP won 32 seats in the legislature in a narrow victory over the PNP, which took 31; no other parties won representation. JLP leader Andrew Holness was sworn in as the new prime minister in March.

Separately, in a July report, the PNP's treasurer accused unnamed senior party leaders of siphoning off millions of dollars' worth of funds donated to the party in order to bolster their personal campaigns for February's elections. Jamaica's Office of the Contractor General (OCG) was investigating the matter at year's end.

In December, an investigative commission tasked with providing an objective review of the state of emergency declared in 2010 in response to violence in the Tivoli Gardens neighborhood of Kingston issued its findings; during the state of emergency, more than 70 civilians were killed in an operation aimed at arresting an alleged drug trafficker. The report found that while the state of emergency had been justified, "its execution by some members of the security forces was disproportionate, unjustified and unjustifiable," and recommended that the government issue an apology for the events and provide counseling services and compensation to victims.

POLITICAL RIGHTS: 34 / 40

A. Electoral Process: 12 / 12

B. Political Pluralism and Participation: 13 / 16

C. Functioning of Government: 9 / 12

CIVIL LIBERTIES: 41 / 60

D. Freedom of Expression and Belief: 15 / 16

E. Associational and Organizational Rights: 9 / 12

F. Rule of Law: 7 / 16

G. Personal Autonomy and Individual Rights: 10 / 16

This country report has been abridged for *Freedom in the World 2017*. For background information on political rights and civil liberties in Jamaica, see *Freedom in the World 2016*.

Japan

Political Rights Rating: 1
Civil Liberties Rating: 1
Freedom Rating: 1.0
Freedom Status: Free
Electoral Democracy: Yes

Population: 125,300,000
Capital: Tokyo

Ten-Year Ratings Timeline For Year Under Review (Political Rights, Civil Liberties, Status)

Year Under Review	2007	2008	2009	2010	2011	2012	2013	2014	2015	2016
Rating	1,2,F	1,2,F	1,2,F	1,2,F	1,2,F	1,2,F	1,1,F	1,1,F	1,1,F	1,1,F

Overview: Japan is a parliamentary democracy with a multiparty system. The ruling Liberal Democratic Party (LDP) has governed for most of the period since 1955, though it has served two stints in opposition since the 1990s. Political rights and civil liberties are generally well respected. Outstanding challenges include ethnic and gender-based discrimination, claims of unduly close relations between government and the business sector, and politically fraught disagreements over the legacy of the pre-1945 regime and the future of Japan's military, or Self-Defense Forces.

KEY DEVELOPMENTS IN 2016:

- The LDP and its junior coalition partner gained ground in July elections for the upper house of parliament, giving them enough seats to pass possible constitutional revisions.
- Also in July, former defense minister Yuriko Koike was elected as Tokyo's first female governor, having run as an independent after the LDP endorsed a rival candidate.
- Press freedom watchdogs reported media self-censorship in response to government complaints about coverage, with three television presenters losing their positions in March due to perceived government pressure.

EXECUTIVE SUMMARY

In July 2016 elections for the House of Councillors, the upper house of Japan's National Diet, the ruling coalition of the LDP and Kōmeitō won a decisive victory. The opposition Democratic Party of Japan (DPJ) had merged in March with the Japan Innovation Party to contest the elections as the new Democratic Party (DP). It also agreed not to compete with three smaller parties in an unsuccessful bid to deny the LDP the two-thirds majority it would need to adopt constitutional amendments.

The government of Prime Minister Shinzō Abe has called for amendments that would loosen constraints on military action by Japan's Self-Defense Forces, among other revisions. It took no major steps toward such a change during the year, though as part of a cabinet shuffle in August, Abe appointed a hawkish supporter of constitutional revision, Tomomi Inada, to the post of defense minister.

POLITICAL RIGHTS: 40 / 40

A. Electoral Process: 12 / 12

Japan is a parliamentary democracy, with representative assemblies at the municipal, prefectural, and national levels. The national assembly, or Diet, has two chambers. The more powerful lower house, the House of Representatives, is made up of 475 members elected to four-year terms. The upper house, the House of Councillors, has 242 members serving six-year terms, with half up for election every three years. The House of Representatives has a mixture of single-seat constituencies and proportional representation, while the House of Councillors uses a mixture of single- and multimember districts and nationwide proportional representation.

The House of Representatives elects the prime minister. The prime minister and his cabinet can dissolve the lower house, but not the upper house. The lower house can also pass a no-confidence resolution that forces the cabinet to either resign or dissolve the House of Representatives. Japan's emperor serves in a ceremonial capacity.

Elections in Japan are free and fair. In snap elections for the House of Representatives in December 2014, the LDP won 291 seats, and its coalition partner, Kōmeitō, won 35, meaning they would retain a two-thirds majority. The DJP won 73 seats, the newly formed Japan Innovation Party took 41 seats, the Japanese Communist Party secured 21, and the remaining seats were divided among smaller parties.

As a result of the July 2016 upper house elections, the LDP had 122 seats and Kōmeitō had 25. The opposition DP had 50 seats, and the Japanese Communist Party had 14. Five smaller groups and independents made up the remainder, and some supported the LDP's constitutional revision plan, giving it the two-thirds majority needed for passage. Any amendments would need to pass with supermajorities in both houses and win approval in a referendum to take effect.

There is a notable degree of malapportionment in both chambers of parliament, to the benefit of the rural districts from which the LDP draws significant support. A handful of Supreme Court rulings in recent years seemed to encourage the Diet to address the issue, but reforms so far have been minor. Due to limited redistricting, the highest vote-value disparity in the 2016 elections, about 3.08 to 1, was lower than in the previous upper house elections in 2013, when the figure was estimated at 4.77 to 1. Several court rulings during the year still found the districts to be "in a state of unconstitutionality," but declined to invalidate the elections.

The June 2016 resignation of Tokyo governor Yoichi Masuzoe over his misuse of public funds triggered a gubernatorial election in July. Former defense minister Yuriko Koike, an LDP member who ran as an independent, easily defeated opponents endorsed by the LDP and the DP, taking about 44 percent of the vote.

B. Political Pluralism and Participation: 16 / 16

The LDP is an ideologically broad party whose members' political beliefs range from the center to the far right, though they share a commitment to economic growth and free enterprise. The party has been a dominant force in Japanese politics since its creation in 1955, though it was voted out of office twice—for a brief period in 1993–94, after a significant group of LDP Diet members formed a reformist opposition faction, and from 2009 to 2012, when a series of three DPJ prime ministers held power.

Japan's other parliamentary parties represent a variety of views. They include the liberal or center-left DP; the conservative Kōmeitō, which began as the political extension of a lay Buddhist movement; the Japanese Communist Party, which retains a substantial following; and the Social Democratic Party. Koike's victory in the 2016 Tokyo governor's race fueled speculation on whether she would lead a new opposition group or seek national office through the LDP.

People's political choices are free from domination by powerful interests. There are no legal barriers preventing ethnic and religious minorities from freely participating in the political process. In September 2016, the DP elected Renhō Murata, whose father was Taiwanese, as its new leader.

C. Functioning of Government: 12 / 12

Elected officials are free to govern without interference, though Japanese bureaucrats have a strong degree of control over policy. While corruption in government is generally low, and petty bribery is very rare, observers have expressed concerns about unduly close relationships between some government officials and business leaders. Retiring bureaucrats often quickly secure high-paying positions with companies that receive significant government contracts. The practice has increasingly drawn criticism from across the political spectrum.

An October 2015 report by the free expression advocacy group Article 19 found that the country's access to information legislation, which came into force in 2001, has not always been implemented effectively, with requesters encountering high fees and lengthy waits. All 47 of Japan's prefectures have also enacted laws ensuring citizens' access to information.

The 2013 Act on the Protection of Specially Designated Secrets allows for unclassified information to be automatically shared with the public, but it also empowers state agencies to protect information on a range of security or diplomatic matters, with criminal penalties for those who reveal designated secrets, including journalists.

CIVIL LIBERTIES: 56 / 60
D. Freedom of Expression and Belief: 15 / 16

Japan has a free and highly competitive media landscape. Under the traditional *kisha kurabu* (press club) system, institutions such as government ministries and corporate organizations have restricted the release of news to those journalists and media outlets with membership in their clubs, essentially exchanging access for moderate coverage and discouraging critical articles. In recent years, online media and weekly newsmagazines have begun challenging the daily papers' dominance of political news with more aggressive reporting. The government does not restrict internet access.

There were reports in 2016 of government pressure on media outlets to refrain from critical coverage. In March, three prominent television news presenters were removed from their positions by their respective networks following indirect warnings from the government in February that broadcasters could theoretically be shut down for political bias. After a country visit in April, the UN special rapporteur on freedom of expression noted apparently high levels of self-censorship in print and broadcast media.

Freedom of religion is mandated in the constitution, and there are no substantial barriers to religious expression. Aside from the traditional religions of Buddhism and Shintoism, Japan is home to small Christian and Muslim populations. There have been reports of significant state surveillance of the Muslim community; officials have tacitly acknowledged some such programs, and defended them as within legal limits.

There are no restrictions on academic freedom, but education has long been a focus of public and political debate. While there is not a national curriculum or single official history text, the Ministry of Education's screening process has approved textbooks that downplay Japan's history of imperialism and war atrocities. Conservatives in the LDP and the Ministry of Education often clash with the more left-leaning teachers' union. At the university level, there is a wide diversity of views among faculty and active academic debate on a broad range of issues. The government does not restrict private discussion.

E. Associational and Organizational Rights: 12 / 12

Freedom of assembly is protected under the constitution. Protests, large and small, take place frequently. Demonstrations against the U.S. military presence on Okinawa continued in 2016, with tens of thousands of participants gathering in June after an American base worker was arrested in May for the murder of a local woman.

Nongovernmental organizations (NGOs) are legally recognized and protected under the 1999 Law to Promote Specified Nonprofit Activities, and they remained diverse and active in 2016. Labor unions are also active, but because most private-sector unions are small and company specific, the labor movement has never achieved its potential nationwide influence. While labor laws are generally adhered to, there are some restrictions on the ability to strike and bargain for those employed in certain essential sectors, including health care and transportation.

F. Rule of Law: 15 / 16

Japan's judiciary is independent. There are several levels of courts, and suspects generally receive fair public trials by an impartial tribunal within three months of being detained. For serious criminal cases, a judicial panel composed of professional judges and *saiban-in* (lay judges), selected from the general public, rule on defendants. Police may detain suspects for up to 23 days without charge in order to extract confessions. Foreign analysts have questioned the high rate at which they say warrants are issued, and have claimed that people are often detained on flimsy evidence, arrested multiple times for the same alleged crime, or subjected to lengthy or coercive interrogations. Observers have also argued that trials often favor the prosecution.

There are frequent reports of substandard medical care in Japanese prisons. Prisoners facing death sentences or accused of crimes that could carry the death penalty are held in solitary confinement, sometimes for years at a time.

Organized crime is fairly prominent, particularly in the construction and nightlife industries. Police worked during 2016 to suppress a conflict between Japan's largest criminal organization, the Yamaguchi-gumi, and a splinter group that broke away in 2015, arresting hundreds of members of both groups by September.

The constitution prohibits discrimination based on race, creed, sex, or social status. Entrenched societal discrimination prevents Japan's estimated three million *burakumin*—descendants of feudal-era outcasts—and the indigenous Ainu minority from gaining equal access to housing and employment, though such forms of discrimination are slowly waning as traditional social distinctions weaken. Japan-born descendants of colonial subjects (particularly ethnic Koreans and Chinese) continue to suffer similar disadvantages.

Antidiscrimination laws do not cover sexual orientation or gender identity, and laws on rape and prostitution do not address same-sex activity. LGBT (lesbian, gay, bisexual, and transgender) people reportedly face social stigma and in some cases harassment.

G. Personal Autonomy and Individual Rights: 14 / 16

Citizens enjoy broad personal autonomy in their choices of residence, profession, and education. Property rights are generally respected. People are free to establish private businesses, but can face financial and other obstacles in Japan's heavily regulated economy.

Although women enjoy legal equality, discrimination in employment and sexual harassment on the job are common. Violence against women often goes unreported due to concerns about family reputation and other social mores. A 2015 Supreme Court ruling upheld a law requiring married couples to use the same surname, and a Tokyo court ruled in

October 2016 that a married female plaintiff did not have the right to use her birth name at work. Women remain underrepresented in government, with some 9 percent of seats in the Diet's lower house and about 21 percent in the upper house, though by the end of 2016 women held the important positions of Tokyo governor, leader of the opposition, defense minister, and internal affairs minister.

Traffickers frequently bring foreign women into the country for forced sex work in brothels and clubs by arranging fraudulent marriages with Japanese men. Some Japanese women and girls are also at risk of sex trafficking. Foreign workers enrolled in state-backed technical "internships" sometimes face exploitative conditions and forced labor; in November 2016 the Diet passed legislation designed to strengthen oversight of the program and punish violations.

Jordan

Political Rights: 5 ↑
Civil Liberties: 5
Freedom Rating: 5.0
Freedom Status: Partly Free
Electoral Democracy: No

Population: 8,200,000
Capital: Amman

Status Change, Ratings Change: Jordan's status improved from Not Free to Partly Free, and its political rights rating improved from 6 to 5, due to electoral law changes that led to somewhat fairer parliamentary elections.

Ten-Year Ratings Timeline For Year Under Review (Political Rights, Civil Liberties, Status)

Year Under Review	2007	2008	2009	2010	2011	2012	2013	2014	2015	2016
Rating	5,4,PF	5,5,PF	6,5,PF	6,5,NF	6,5,NF	6,5,NF	6,5,NF	6,5,NF	6,5,NF	5,5,PF

Overview: Jordan is a hereditary monarchy in which the king holds ultimate power over policymaking. The lower house is elected, and while electoral laws have limited the development of opposition parties in the past, reforms contributed to somewhat fairer elections in 2016. Press freedom is curtailed by strict media laws and the intimidation of journalists, and the judicial system is neither independent nor does it fully adhere to international standards.

KEY DEVELOPMENTS IN 2016:

- September's parliamentary elections took place under a new electoral law mandating a proportional representation system in place of the previous single nontransferable vote system, which had been criticized for favoring progovernment tribal elites. The main opposition Islamic Action Front (IAF), the political wing of the Muslim Brotherhood in Jordan, consequently returned to formal politics after boycotting past elections, but won just 16 seats out of the 130 contested.
- In April, with little public debate, Jordan's parliament amended the constitution to reinforce the king's control over succession, the judiciary, the Senate, and the police.

- In September, well-known writer Nahed Hattar was assassinated outside a court-room where he was facing blasphemy charges.

EXECUTIVE SUMMARY

In September, Jordan elected its lower house under a new electoral law, adopted in March, which mandated a proportional representation system and included new districts boosting representation for urban areas where support for the opposition is strong. Jordan's main opposition party, the IAF, consequently participated fully in elections for the first time in years; the party had boycotted the 2010 and 2013 polls in protest of Jordan's use of a single nontransferable voting system, which it and other parties had criticized for favoring progovernment tribal elites. The IAF-led coalition won just 16 seats of the 130 contested; most of those elected were independent candidates considered loyal to the monarchy. Turnout was low, at 31 percent, with analysts attributing the apparent lack of enthusiasm to popular frustration with the overall weakness of the parliament, which rarely initiates legislation, and instead approves, rejects, or amends bills proposed by the cabinet. The official count of participating voters was also depressed because the new reforms made registration for elections mandatory, thus increasing the number of eligible voters on the rolls by over one million people compared to the 2013 elections. Domestic and international monitors praised the elections as well-administered, and more inclusive than past polls.

Separately, in April, the government approved a set of constitutional amendments that gave King Abdullah II absolute power to appoint constitutional court and Senate members, as well as the chief of the parliamentary police; in the past the king formally consulted the prime minister and cabinet on such key appointments. The amendments also permitted Abdullah to unilaterally name a crown prince and deputy king. The opposition and others criticized the changes as a weakening of the separation of powers between the executive, legislature, and judiciary. The changes were approved two weeks after being introduced to the parliament, leaving little opportunity for public debate.

The presence of over 600,000 refugees from neighboring Syria continues to strain Jordan's public services. In 2016, Jordan sought to curb the influx of refugees by sealing two key checkpoints on the Syrian border in the wake of an June attack there by the Islamic State (IS) militant group, which killed seven border guards. The move left approximately 85,000 people stranded in a desolate strip of land between the Jordanian and Syrian borders, with limited access to food and basic services.

The kingdom continued to restrict civil liberties in 2016 in response to the security threat posed by regional and local militants. Those who made public statements perceived as supportive of the militants were detained on several occasions. In its efforts to set strict parameters for religious discourse, the state also charged Nahed Hattar, a well-known Christian writer and commentator, with blasphemy and inciting sectarian strife over a cartoon that depicted God as in the service of an IS militant. In September, Hattar was shot to death outside the court where he was facing charges.

POLITICAL RIGHTS: 12 / 40 (+ 1)

A. Electoral Process: 3 / 12 (+ 1)

B. Political Pluralism and Participation: 6 / 16

C. Functioning of Government: 3 / 12

CIVIL LIBERTIES: 25 / 60

D. Freedom of Expression and Belief: 7 / 16

E. Associational and Organizational Rights: 4 / 12

F. Rule of Law: 6 / 16

G. Personal Autonomy and Individual Rights: 8 / 16

This country report has been abridged for *Freedom in the World 2017.* For background information on political rights and civil liberties in Jordan, see *Freedom in the World 2016.*

Kazakhstan

Political Rights Rating: 7 ↓
Civil Liberties Rating: 5
Freedom Rating: 6.0
Freedom Status: Not Free
Electoral Democracy: No

Population: 17,800,000
Capital: Astana

Ratings Change: Kazakhstan's political rights rating declined from 6 to 7 due to voters' lack of access to any genuine political choice and the continuation of efforts by the government to stifle opportunities for opposition groups.

Ten-Year Ratings Timeline For Year Under Review (Political Rights, Civil Liberties, Status)

Year Under Review Rating	2007	2008	2009	2010	2011	2012	2013	2014	2015	2016
	6,5,NF	6,5,NF	6,5,NF	6,5,NF	6,5,NF	6,5,NF	6,5,NF	6,5,NF	6,5,NF	7,5,NF

Overview: Kazakhstan has been ruled by President Nursultan Nazarbayev, the former first secretary of its branch of the Soviet-era Communist Party, since independence in 1991. While there are regular parliamentary and presidential elections, none to date have been considered free or fair by reputable international observers, and all major parties exhibit political loyalty to the president. The authorities have consistently marginalized or imprisoned genuine opposition figures. The media are either in state hands or owned by government-friendly businessmen. Freedoms of speech and assembly remain restricted, criticism of Nazarbayev is not permitted, and corruption is endemic.

KEY DEVELOPMENTS IN 2016:

- In March, early elections were held for the lower house of Parliament. Nazarbayev's Nur Otan party secured an overwhelming majority of seats in a process that did not meet international democratic standards.
- In April and May, thousands of people across Kazakhstan protested against a proposed reform of the land code that would allow long-term leases for foreigners. While there was no major violence against demonstrators, the authorities sought to curb the protests by blocking roads and detaining activists and organizers.
- Opposition leader Vladimir Kozlov was released early from prison in August, having been sentenced to seven and a half years in 2012 for his alleged involvement in inciting social unrest in Zhanaozen in 2011.

EXECUTIVE SUMMARY

In March 2016, President Nazarbayev's Nur Otan party won a lopsided victory in early parliamentary elections, capturing 84 of the lower house's 98 directly elected seats—one more than in 2012. Two other parties that are generally loyal to the president, Ak Zhol and the Communist People's Party, each secured 7 seats. The elections took place against a backdrop of low prices for the country's oil and gas exports, which have slowed economic growth and forced devaluations of the national currency.

Protests took place in several cities across the country in April and May in response to proposed reforms of the land code that would allow foreign entities to lease agricultural land for up to 25 years, rather than the current maximum of 10 years. The authorities generally did not use direct violence to suppress the demonstrations, but hundreds of organizers and participants were arrested, in many cases preemptively, and some 50 journalists were also detained as they attempted to report on the events. While most were quickly released, two leading activists were eventually sentenced to five years in prison in November on charges including incitement of social discord, and others faced lesser penalties. Police also physically blocked access to planned protest areas, used social media monitoring to identify and intimidate organizers, and apparently disrupted access to some social media applications at crucial times. In light of the opposition to the proposed reform, Nazarbayev postponed the plan by five years and set up a commission to review the matter.

In June, a group of up to 26 suspected Islamist militants attacked weapons shops and security installations in the city of Aktobe. At least 25 people were killed, including 18 attackers. A gunman later struck a police station in Almaty in July, killing eight police officers and two civilians. The government has sought to prevent Islamist violence in part by exerting tight control over religious groups and materials that it deems "extremist" or "nontraditional," though such restrictions extend to nonviolent Muslim and Christian groups as well.

Nazarbayev undertook a major government shuffle in September. Long-serving prime minister Karim Masimov was transferred to lead the National Security Committee (KNB) and replaced in the premiership by Deputy Prime Minister Bakytzhan Sagintayev. Nazarbayev's daughter, Dariga Nazarbayeva, was removed from her position as deputy prime minister and appointed to a seat in the Senate.

Also during the year, the authorities continued to arrest and prosecute journalists and social media users on a range of criminal charges. In one high-profile example, Seytkazy Matayev, the head of the Kazakh Union of Journalists and chair of the National Press Club, and his son Aset Matayev, director of the independent news agency KazTag, were detained in February on fraud and embezzlement charges. Observers speculated on possible political or corrupt motivations behind the prosecution; both defendants had complained of recent government harassment and said the case was an effort to suppress their work. Matayev and his son were found guilty in October and sentenced to six and five years in prison, respectively.

The government remained sensitive to the perceived threat of Russian nationalism. In January, authorities arrested Shymkent-based businessman Tokhtar Tuleshov, who was known for his close Russian ties. He was sentenced in November to 21 years in prison for alleged extremism, possession of illegal weapons, and plotting to overthrow the government. He also faced a separate trial on charges that he had financed that year's land code protests.

POLITICAL RIGHTS: 5 / 40 (− 1)

A. Electoral Process: 1 / 12 (− 1)

B. Political Pluralism and Participation: 3 / 16

C. Functioning of Government: 1 / 12

CIVIL LIBERTIES: 17 / 60 (− 1)

D. Freedom of Expression and Belief: 4 / 16

E. Associational and Organizational Rights: 1 / 12 (− 1)

F. Rule of Law: 4 / 16

G. Personal Autonomy and Individual Rights: 8 / 16

This country report has been abridged for *Freedom in the World 2017*. For background information on political rights and civil liberties in Kazakhstan, see *Freedom in the World 2016*.

Kenya

Political Rights Rating: 4
Civil Liberties Rating: 4
Freedom Rating: 4.0
Freedom Status: Partly Free
Electoral Democracy: Yes

Population: 45,400,000
Capital: Nairobi

Ten-Year Ratings Timeline For Year Under Review (Political Rights, Civil Liberties, Status)

Year Under Review	2007	2008	2009	2010	2011	2012	2013	2014	2015	2016
Rating	4,3,PF	4,3,PF	4,4,PF	4,3,PF	4,3,PF	4,4,PF	4,4,PF	4,4,PF	4,4,PF	4,4,PF

Overview: Kenya is a multiparty democracy that holds regular elections, but its political rights and civil liberties are seriously undermined by pervasive corruption and cronyism, police brutality, and ethnic rivalries that are exploited by political leaders. The country has also struggled to cope with the threat of terrorism emanating from neighboring Somalia; counterterrorism efforts often feature abusive and discriminatory tactics targeting the Muslim and ethnic Somali communities.

KEY DEVELOPMENTS IN 2016:

- After Islamist militants killed at least 141 Kenyan soldiers in Somalia in January, Kenyan authorities arrested a journalist and a blogger for sharing information related to the attack on social media, adding to a pattern of restrictions on freedom of expression. In April, a judge struck down the legal provision under which the two were arrested.
- In June, police officers allegedly tortured and murdered the accuser in a police brutality case, along with his lawyer and a driver. The incident highlighted the broader problem of criminality and excessive force among law enforcement agencies.
- Members of the electoral commission resigned in October as part of a political agreement to reform the body ahead of general elections in 2017. The deal came after a failed constitutional referendum bid and a series of major protests by the opposition, which argued that the existing electoral system was deeply flawed.

EXECUTIVE SUMMARY

A decline in domestic terrorist attacks in 2016 was overshadowed by an apparent rise in the use of lethal force by Kenyan police. An October study found that in the first eight months of the year, police officers killed a total of 122 civilians, a 7 percent increase over the same period in 2015. Police brutality was on display in May and June, when the opposition organized demonstrations aimed at overhauling the electoral commission. At least five demonstrators were killed amid police beatings, tear gas, and gunfire ammunition.

In the year's most prominent incident of police violence, human rights lawyer Willie Kimani, his client Josephat Mwenda, and their driver, Joseph Muiruri, were killed in June. Kimani was representing Mwenda in a court case in which the latter accused police officers of misuse of lethal force. The three were allegedly tortured and then dumped in a river. Five police officers were charged with the murders. Government statistics released in May provided another indication of alarming criminality among police, showing that police officers were implicated in over a third of the crimes reported in 2015.

The year also featured attempts by the government to limit freedom of expression. Journalists, bloggers, and activists were arrested or prosecuted on a variety of charges, and officials allegedly pressured media outlets to curb unfavorable coverage. In January, the *Daily Nation* fired an editor over an opinion piece that was critical of the administration, and in March the same paper severed ties with a cartoonist known for his biting critiques of powerful figures. Despite these pressures, many media houses continued to produce aggressive reporting on the government, and a number of activists used the country's moderately independent judicial system to fight back against threats to freedom of expression.

POLITICAL RIGHTS: 22 / 40

A. Electoral Process: 7 / 12

Under a constitution approved by voters in 2010, the president and deputy president, who can serve up to two five-year terms, are directly elected by majority vote; they are also required to win 25 percent of the votes in at least half of Kenya's newly created 47 counties.

The legislature consists of the National Assembly (349 members) and the Senate (67 senators). In the National Assembly, 290 members are directly elected from single-member constituencies. A further 47 special women representatives are elected from the counties, and political parties nominate 12 additional members according to the share of seats won. The Senate has 47 elected members representing the counties, 16 special women representatives nominated by political parties based on the share of seats won, and four nominated members representing youth and people with disabilities. Both houses have speakers who are ex-officio members.

In the 2013 general elections, the ruling Jubilee Coalition took 167 National Assembly seats and 30 Senate seats. The opposition Coalition for Reforms and Democracy (CORD) won 141 and 28 seats in the assembly and Senate, respectively. In the presidential race, Uhuru Kenyatta of Jubilee won with 50.07 percent of the vote, followed by Raila Odinga of CORD with 43.7 percent. Amid serious questions surrounding the tabulation of results, CORD alleged widespread vote rigging in a petition to the Supreme Court, but the court declined to annul the results.

The 47 counties have elected governors, deputy governors, and assemblies. Following the 2013 general elections, the Jubilee Coalition held governorships in 18 counties, while CORD won in 23. Governors serve for a term of five years, renewable once.

With the next elections expected in August 2017, CORD pushed during 2016 for a reform of the Independent Electoral and Boundaries Commission (IEBC) and other aspects of the electoral system. It first sought to initiate a process for the adoption of constitutional amendments to that end, which required gathering at least a million signatures. The effort failed after the IEBC ruled in March that only about 890,000 of the 1.6 million signatures submitted were valid. CORD then mobilized its supporters in May and June for weekly street demonstrations that paralyzed Kenya's urban centers. This forced the government to the negotiating table, and in August the two sides reached an agreement under which the IEBC would be restructured to include direct party representation. The incumbent commissioners submitted their resignations in October, and an appointment process for new commissioners was under way at year's end.

B. Political Pluralism and Participation: 10 / 16

Citizens are free to organize into political parties that represent a range of ideological, regional, and ethnic interests, but Kenyan parties are notoriously weak, often amalgamated into coalitions designed only to contest elections. Under the Political Parties Act, parties that receive at least 5 percent of the votes cast in a national election are eligible for public funds.

During the 2013 elections, powerful economic interests posed impediments to political choice. Unverified sums of money were used during the campaign in the absence of an adequate campaign finance law, and there was evidence of direct vote buying by candidates from both coalitions.

The 2010 constitution was intended to reduce the role of ethnicity in elections. Fiscal and political devolution, implemented in 2013, has served to generate more intraethnic competition at the county level. Nevertheless, the ongoing politicization of ethnicity at the national level hinders effective representation of different segments of Kenya's diverse population, limits voter choice, and impedes meaningful policy debates. Although the Political Parties Act requires each party to have at least 1,000 members in 24 of the 47 counties to ensure diversity, the major coalitions continue to reflect distinctive—though rarely exclusive—ethnic alliances.

The stipulation that all voters must possess a National Identity Card impedes historically marginalized groups from obtaining greater access to the political process, particularly the nearly seven million pastoralists from the upper Rift Valley and North Eastern regions.

C. Functioning of Government: 5 / 12

The ability of elected officials to set and implement policy is seriously undermined by corruption and other forms of dysfunction. The devolution process has exposed capacity deficits at the county level, with most county governments struggling to absorb funds and failing to meet spending targets for development projects. At the national level, an auditor general's report on government financial statements for the 2014–15 fiscal year gave a clean (unqualified) audit opinion for only about 25 percent of the statements assessed.

Major corruption scandals continued to be reported in the media during 2016. They included opposition claims that a portion of the revenue from a sale of $2.8 billion in Eurobonds had been misappropriated by the government; revelations that some $17.4 million, more than double the initial estimate, had been lost in a 2015 embezzlement scandal centered on the National Youth Service; and the improper awarding of Health Ministry contracts reserved for marginalized groups, in some cases to companies owned by the president's relatives.

State institutions tasked with combating corruption have been ineffective. In August 2016, the head of the Ethics and Anti-Corruption Commission (EACC) resigned under pressure over allegations that a company run by his wife had benefited from National Youth

Service contracts. Some reform projects, like the Integrated Financial Management Information System (IFMIS), launched in 2014 as an online clearinghouse for state procurements, appear to have made the problem worse. Misuse of IFMIS was alleged in both the National Youth Service and Health Ministry scandals. The EACC's weakness is compounded by shortcomings at the Office of the Director of Public Prosecutions (ODPP) and in the judiciary. It was reported in October 2016 that out of 5,551 cases investigated by the EACC in the 2014–15 fiscal year, only 117 (2 percent) were forwarded to the ODPP, and of these the ODPP managed to secure a single conviction.

The president signed the Access to Information Act in August 2016, enabling citizen information requests and requiring disclosures on government contracts. Officials who improperly withhold information can face fines or prison terms. Transparency advocates welcomed the law, but noted a broadly defined exemption for national security matters and called for careful consultation on implementing regulations.

CIVIL LIBERTIES: 29 / 60

D. Freedom of Expression and Belief: 10 / 16 (− 1)

The 2010 constitution strengthened protections for freedoms of speech and of the press, and there is a large, independent, and active media sector in Kenya. The media notably reported on corruption scandals reaching the highest levels of government during 2016. However, several laws restrict press freedom, and the government and security forces harass journalists, leading to self-censorship in some cases. Many journalists and activists have turned to online outlets and social media platforms to bypass political and business influences at established media groups.

In January 2016, the interior minister issued a directive against the dissemination of images showing the victims of a devastating Islamist militant attack in Somalia that killed at least 141 Kenyan soldiers. Later that month, a journalist and a blogger who had reported on the attack were arrested and charged under Section 29 of the Information and Communications Act, which banned the "improper use of a licensed communications system." The vaguely defined offense has allowed authorities to arrest and charge numerous online journalists and bloggers who convey critical information on government officials. In April 2016, the High Court declared Section 29 unconstitutional, and related cases were subsequently dropped.

The government and some business groups have used other forms of influence to shape news coverage, including defamation suits and manipulation of advertising purchases, sometimes leading major media groups to avoid sensitive content. In January 2016, the *Daily Nation* fired editor Denis Galava after he wrote an editorial that was critical of the government. In March, the newspaper fired Godfrey Mwampembwa (Gado), a cartoonist known for skewering powerful figures. Mwampembwa was later hired by a competing newspaper, the *Standard*. Also during the year, the courts ordered media outlets including the *Standard* and the *Daily Nation* to pay substantial monetary damages in defamation cases, several of which were filed by judges.

The government generally respects the constitutional guarantee of freedom of religion. However, counterterrorism operations against the Somalia-based Shabaab militant group have left Muslims exposed to state violence and intimidation. In July 2016, Human Rights Watch reported that it had documented at least 34 enforced disappearances and 11 extrajudicial killings between 2013 and 2015, all involving people taken into custody during counterterrorism operations.

Academic freedom in Kenya, though traditionally robust, is increasingly threatened by ethnic politics and political violence. Student union elections have led to allegations of fraud and violent protests. Police reportedly used beatings and other abuse to quell protests over a student election at the University of Nairobi in April 2016. In addition, there is growing evidence that ethnic considerations have influenced university hiring, leaving the staff of some institutions with significant ethnic imbalances.

The relatively unfettered freedom of private discussion in Kenya has suffered somewhat from state counterterrorism operations and intimidation by security forces and ethnically affiliated gangs.

E. Associational and Organizational Rights: 7 / 12 (+ 1)

The constitution guarantees the freedoms of assembly and association. The law requires organizers of public meetings to notify local police in advance, and in practice police have regularly prohibited gatherings on security or other grounds, or violently dispersed assemblies that they had not explicitly banned. Among other episodes in 2016, police used beatings, tear gas, and live ammunition to break up CORD protests calling for electoral reform in May and June. At least five demonstrators were killed.

Kenya has an active nongovernmental organization (NGO) sector, but civil society groups have faced growing obstacles in recent years, including repeated government attempts to deregister hundreds of NGOs for alleged financial violations. The moves were seen in part as an effort to silence criticism of the government's human rights record. In 2016, the government again failed to put into effect the 2013 Public Benefit Organizations Act, which was expected to provide a more transparent and supportive legal framework for NGO registration and activity. While delaying implementation, officials have sought to introduce restrictive amendments to the law. In June 2016 the government announced that it would strictly enforce laws placing limits on work permits and salaries for foreign workers, specifically threatening the status of those employed by NGOs.

The 2010 constitution affirmed the rights of trade unions to establish their own agendas, bargain collectively, and strike. Unions are active in Kenya, with approximately 40 unions representing nearly two million workers. Most unions are affiliated with the Central Organization of Trade Unions (COTU). In June 2016, the government agreed to a new pay deal with teachers' unions, which had mounted a strike over the issue in 2015. A full collective-bargaining agreement was completed in October. In December, Kenyan doctors went on strike over pay and working conditions that had apparently grown worse after the devolution of health services to the county level.

F. Rule of Law: 5 / 16

The 2010 constitution enhanced the independence of the judiciary, but Kenya has struggled to entrench the rule of law in practice. The country's respected chief justice, Willy Mutunga, retired from office in June 2016, raising concerns as to whether the judiciary would continue on a reformist path. The constitution sets a mandatory retirement age of 70, and Mutunga stepped down a year earlier than necessary. Two other Supreme Court justices, Philip Tunoi and deputy chief justice Kalpana Rawal, were forced to retire the same month after controversial but unsuccessful attempts to stay on beyond the age limit. Tunoi was facing bribery allegations at the time. David Maraga was nominated as the new chief justice in September, and in October he and the replacements for the other two retired justices were sworn into office. The independent Judicial Services Commission handles the vetting and appointment of judges, including the chief justice. In May, the High Court struck down a legal amendment that would have directed the commission to submit three names for chief justice to the president rather than one, effectively giving the president discretion over the appointment.

The police service is thoroughly undermined by corruption and criminality. Government statistics released in May 2016 showed that police officers were implicated in over a third of the crimes reported in 2015. In October, the *Daily Nation* reported that in the first eight months of 2016, at least 122 civilians had been shot dead by police, a 7 percent increase over the same period in 2015.

The year's most brazen crime occurred in June, when police officers allegedly abducted, tortured, and murdered human rights lawyer Willie Kimani; his client, Josephat Mwenda, who had filed a complaint against an officer for illegally shooting him; and their driver, Joseph Muiruri. The three men's bodies were found in a river about a week after they went missing. Five police officers were facing trial for the murders at year's end. A number of other high-profile crimes remained unsolved during the year, including the May murder of a prominent businessman and opposition supporter, Jacob Juma. Opposition leader Raila Odinga claimed that a police hit squad was responsible.

Despite aggressive government counterterrorism efforts, the Shabaab continued to mount deadly attacks on Kenyan soil, particularly near the border with Somalia. While the number of attacks appeared to decline compared with the previous year, notable incidents in 2016 included a July shooting attack on two buses that killed at least six people in Mandera County in the northeast, and an October raid on a guesthouse in the same county that killed 12 people.

Ethnic Somalis—both Kenyan citizens and refugees from neighboring Somalia—have borne the brunt of arbitrary arrests and a range of other abuses linked to the counterterrorism campaign. As of 2016 there were more than 500,000 refugees in Kenya, including some 330,000 Somalis. In recent years there has been increased social and political pressure to expel Somali refugees, and tens of thousands have been repatriated under UN supervision. The government in May announced plans to close the massive Dadaab refugee camp in November, but later extended the deadline by six months.

Consensual same-sex sexual activity is criminalized under the penal code, with a maximum penalty of 14 years in prison. Members of the LGBT (lesbian, gay, bisexual, and transgender) community continue to face discrimination, abuse, and violent attacks. In June 2016, a High Court judge in Mombasa upheld the use of forced anal examinations and testing for HIV and hepatitis B as a means of gathering supposed evidence of same-sex sexual activity. The UN special rapporteur on torture and other experts have condemned such practices.

G. Personal Autonomy and Individual Rights: 7 / 16

While the constitution provides protections for freedom of movement and related rights, they are impeded in practice by security concerns and ethnic tensions that lead many residents to avoid certain parts of the country.

Organized crime continues to threaten legitimate business activity in Kenya. Political corruption and ethnic favoritism also affect the business sector and exacerbate existing imbalances in wealth and access to economic opportunities, including public-sector jobs.

The 2015 Protection against Domestic Violence Act criminalized a range of abuses including forced marriage, spousal rape, and female genital mutilation. However, rape and domestic violence reportedly remain common and are rarely prosecuted. Customary law often trumps statutory law, leaving women with few remedies for discriminatory customary practices. Underage marriage is illegal but still occurs. Women face disparities in education and are underrepresented in politics and government. The constitution calls for all elected and appointed state institutions to have no more than two-thirds of their members from the same gender, but institutions that continued to fall short of that standard in 2016 included the cabinet and both houses of Parliament.

Refugees and asylum seekers from neighboring countries, particularly children, have been vulnerable to sex trafficking and forced labor in Kenya, though Kenyan children are also subject to such abuses. Kenyan workers are recruited for employment abroad in sometimes exploitative conditions, particularly in the Middle East.

Kiribati

Political Rights Rating: 1
Civil Liberties Rating: 1
Freedom Rating: 1.0
Freedom Status: Free
Electoral Democracy: Yes

Population: 100,000
Capital: Tarawa

Ten-Year Ratings Timeline For Year Under Review (Political Rights, Civil Liberties, Status)

Year Under Review	2007	2008	2009	2010	2011	2012	2013	2014	2015	2016
Rating	1,1,F	1,1,F	1,1,F	1,1,F	1,1,F	1,1,F	1,1,F	1,1,F	1,1,F	1,1,F

The country or territory displayed here received scores but no narrative report for this edition of *Freedom in the World*.

Kosovo

Political Rights Rating: 3
Civil Liberties Rating: 4
Freedom Rating: 3.5
Freedom Status: Partly Free
Electoral Democracy: Yes

Population: 1,800,000
Capital: Priština

Ten-Year Ratings Timeline For Year Under Review (Political Rights, Civil Liberties, Status)

Year Under Review	2007	2008	2009	2010	2011	2012	2013	2014	2015	2016
Rating	6,5,NF	6,5,NF	5,4,PF	5,4,PF	5,4,PF	5,4,PF	5,4,PF	4,4,PF	3,4,PF	3,4,PF

Overview: Kosovo's institutions remain weak, and rampant corruption has given rise to deep public distrust in the government. Journalists face serious pressure, and risk being attacked in connection with their reporting. While Kosovo holds credible and relatively well-administered elections, politics in recent years have been dominated by a polarized dispute over the Association/Community of Serb-majority Municipalities, which is meant to allow greater autonomy for Kosovo's ethnic Serb minority population. Its implementation is key to Kosovo's eventual accession to the European Union (EU), but it is vehemently opposed by parties that believe it threatens Kosovo's sovereignty.

KEY DEVELOPMENTS IN 2016:

- Political opposition, which on a number of instances became violent, hampered the implementation of an EU-brokered agreement to boost autonomy for the ethnic Serb minority, as well as parliamentary approval of a border demarcation agreement with Montenegro that was also backed by the EU.
- In August, a rocket-propelled grenade was fired at the parliament building. Six people, all reportedly members of an opposition party, were arrested in connection with the attack.
- In January, a new war crimes tribunal was established in The Hague, the Netherlands, to handle cases concerning alleged war crimes carried out by the Kosovo Liberation Army (KLA) during the 1999 conflict.
- The first Serbian Orthodox Synod held in Kosovo since the 1999 conflict took place in May.

EXECUTIVE SUMMARY

Opposition protests, some of which turned violent, hampered policymaking in 2016. Three opposition parties—the Movement for Self-Determination (Vetëvendosje), the Alliance for the Future of Kosovo (AAK), and the Initiative for Kosovo (Nisma)—led a campaign against an EU-brokered deal to establish the Association/Community of Serb-majority Municipalities, which is meant to allow greater autonomy for Kosovo's ethnic Serb population; the opposition coalition also opposed another EU-backed deal on border demarcation with Montenegro, which they argued deprived Kosovo of land. Opposition protests took place both on the streets, where firebombs were occasionally deployed by participants of mass demonstrations, and inside the parliament, where tear gas was released on a number of occasions. In February, such disruptions accompanied the election by parliament of Hashim Thaçi, a leading politician with the Democratic Party of Kosovo (PDK), as president. In August, a rocket-propelled grenade was fired at the parliament building. Six people were arrested in connection with the attack, all of them reportedly members of Vetëvendosje.

Meanwhile, in July 2016 the government established a working group, which included Serb representatives, to draft a statute for the Association/Community of Serb-majority Municipalities.

Journalists report frequent harassment and intimidation, and occasional physical attacks. There were at least two instances in 2016 in which media workers with the public broadcaster were targeted by explosive devices, though no one was injured. One attack took place in a reporter's backyard, and the other at the outlet's offices.

The constitution guarantees religious freedom. In an encouraging development, the first Serbian Orthodox Synod held in Kosovo since the 1999 conflict took place in May. Two minor security incidents were recorded, but the event otherwise took place peacefully. However, as in previous years, Serbian Orthodox structures were vandalized in 2016.

In January, a new war crimes tribunal was established in The Hague to prosecute former KLA fighters. The opposition had opposed the court's establishment, arguing that it violated Kosovo's sovereignty, but its legal appeal was struck down in 2015.

POLITICAL RIGHTS: 24 / 40

A. Electoral Process: 9 / 12

B. Political Pluralism and Participation: 10 / 16

C. Functioning of Government: 5 / 12

CIVIL LIBERTIES: 28 / 60

D. Freedom of Expression and Belief: 9 / 16

E. Associational and Organizational Rights: 6 / 12

F. Rule of Law: 6 / 16

G. Personal Autonomy and Individual Rights: 7 / 16

This country report has been abridged for *Freedom in the World 2017.* For background information on political rights and civil liberties in the Kosovo, see *Freedom in the World 2016.*

Kuwait

Political Rights Rating: 5
Civil Liberties Rating: 5
Freedom Ratings: 5.0
Freedom Status: Partly Free
Electoral Democracy: No

Population: 4,000,000
Capital: Kuwait City

Ten-Year Ratings Timeline For Year Under Review (Political Rights, Civil Liberties, Status)

Year Under Review	2007	2008	2009	2010	2011	2012	2013	2014	2015	2016
Rating	4,4,PF	4,4,PF	4,4,PF	4,5,PF	4,5,PF	5,5,PF	5,5,PF	5,5,PF	5,5 PF	5,5,PF

Overview: Kuwait is a constitutional emirate ruled by the Sabah family. While the monarchy holds executive power and dominates the judiciary, the elected parliament plays an influential role, often challenging the government. Partly due to friction between lawmakers and the executive, government turnover and snap parliamentary elections have been frequent since 2011. In recent years, with a surge in demands for greater political rights, state authorities have narrowed freedoms of speech and assembly.

KEY DEVELOPMENTS IN 2016:

- A 2015 cybercrimes law that took effect in January criminalized online criticism of state officials, members of the royal family, religious figures, and foreign leaders, prescribing prison terms of up to 10 years.
- In April, some 20,000 oil workers went on strike to protest austerity measures linked to low global oil prices. The walkout, which nearly halved Kuwait's oil production, ended after three days to allow for negotiations.
- Amid criticism in the parliament about the government's management of the economic crisis and moves to raise fuel prices, the emir dissolved the legislature in October, prompting elections in November.

EXECUTIVE SUMMARY

Persistently low oil prices strained Kuwait's economy in 2016 and put pressure on its extensive social benefits. In July, the government said it had posted a rare budget deficit of some $15 billion in the fiscal year that ended in March. Authorities responded to the crisis by adopting austerity measures, including public-sector job cuts and reduced subsidies for water, electricity, and fuel. Some members of parliament challenged the government on its policies and alleged profligacy by senior officials and members of the ruling family.

In an apparent effort to ward off further criticism, the emir dissolved the parliament and called new elections for November. Opposition factions—including Islamist, nationalist, and liberal groupings that had boycotted the last elections in 2013—won 24 of the 50 seats, though the system is formally nonpartisan. Only 20 of the incumbent members were reelected; voter turnout was high at about 70 percent. One woman was among those who won seats.

Also during the year, the authorities arrested and punished a number of government critics for their speech online, aided by a new cybercrimes law that took effect in January. A separate law adopted that month required all online media to obtain a government license, and legislation passed in June barred electoral participation by those convicted of blasphemy or insulting the emir. Among other individual cases during the year, in March authorities arrested Salam Abdullah Ashtil Dossari, an expatriate who had been living in Britain, for insulting Gulf Cooperation Council leaders online. In April, former lawmaker Mubarak al-Dowaila, who had been acquitted in 2015 of insulting the United Arab Emirates on television in 2014, was sentenced to two years in prison by an appellate court. In May, three members of the ruling family were sentenced to five years in prison for insulting the judiciary on social media. In September, human rights activist Sara al-Drees was arrested for insulting the emir on social media; she was released on bail pending trial, but faced up to five years in prison.

Shiite Muslims, who comprise about a third of the population, enjoy equal political rights but have experienced increased harassment in recent years. In January, a court sentenced two Shiite men, one of them an Iranian citizen, to death as part of a larger trial of suspected members of the Iranian-backed militant group Hezbollah. Some of the defendants accused the authorities of torturing them to extract confessions.

POLITICAL RIGHTS: 13 / 40

A. Electoral Process: 2 / 12

B. Political Pluralism and Participation: 7 / 16

C. Functioning of Government: 4 / 12

CIVIL LIBERTIES: 23 / 60

D. Freedom of Expression and Belief: 6 / 16

E. Associational and Organizational Rights: 4 / 12

F. Rule of Law: 7 / 16

G. Personal Autonomy and Individual Rights: 6 / 16

This country report has been abridged for *Freedom in the World 2017*. For background information on political rights and civil liberties in Kuwait, see *Freedom in the World 2016*.

Kyrgyzstan

Political Rights Rating: 5
Civil Liberties Rating: 5
Freedom Rating: 5.0
Freedom Status: Partly Free
Electoral Democracy: No

Population: 6,100,000
Capital: Bishkek

Ten-Year Ratings Timeline For Year Under Review (Political Rights, Civil Liberties, Status)

Year Under Review	2007	2008	2009	2010	2011	2012	2013	2014	2015	2016
Rating	5,4,PF	5,4,PF	6,5,NF	5,5,PF	5,5,PF	5,5,PF	5,5,PF	5,5,PF	5,5,PF	5,5,PF

Overview: After two revolutions that ousted authoritarian presidents in 2005 and 2010, Kyrgyzstan adopted a parliamentary form of government, and multiparty coalitions have since been the norm. However, power remains in the hands of an entrenched political elite, and corruption is pervasive. Authorities have harshly suppressed dissent from human rights activists, particularly those linked to the Uzbek minority, which bore the brunt of ethnic violence in 2010. In recent years, President Almazbek Atambayev and his party have sought to consolidate executive power, threatening political pluralism.

KEY DEVELOPMENTS IN 2016:

- The coalition government, led by the Social Democratic Party of Kyrgyzstan (SDPK), collapsed in October amid disagreement over a proposed referendum to amend the constitution. The SDPK organized a new coalition in November.
- The referendum passed in December despite low turnout, and the resulting constitutional changes were expected to strengthen the positions of president and prime minister ahead of a presidential election in 2017.

EXECUTIVE SUMMARY

In July 2016, after years of pressure from the international community, Kyrgyzstan's Supreme Court set aside the life sentence of jailed ethnic Uzbek activist Azimjon Askarov, but ordered him to be retried on allegations that he fomented interethnic violence in 2010. The court decision followed an April ruling by the UN Human Rights Committee (UNHRC), which found that Askarov had not received a fair trial and had been tortured and otherwise mistreated. The committee called for him to be immediately freed.

In September, the parliament began to consider a proposed referendum on constitutional amendments despite a previous consensus that the 2010 document should not be fundamentally altered for 10 years. Two junior partners in the ruling coalition refused to back the proposal, prompting President Atambayev's SDPK to withdraw from the coalition and bring down the government. The amendments would apparently strengthen the executive, weaken judicial independence, and allow the government to rebuff rulings by international human rights bodies—a direct response to the UNHRC decision. Critics said the changes were likely to reinforce the position of the SDPK as Kyrgyzstan's dominant party, though the full implications of some of the 26 amendments were unclear even to legal experts.

The proposal nevertheless won passage in the parliament in early November, and the SDPK formed a new governing coalition. The final referendum language was not released to the public until mid-November, roughly a month before the scheduled vote. Multiple reports indicated that the government used administrative resources to mobilize support for the referendum, and the proposal ultimately passed amid low turnout. The amendments were due to be signed into law in early 2017.

POLITICAL RIGHTS: 13 / 40 (− 1)

A. Electoral Process: 5 / 12 (− 1)

Constitutional changes adopted in 2010 expanded the unicameral parliament from 90 to 120 deputies, with no party allowed to hold more than 65 seats. Parliamentary elections are to be held every five years. The directly elected president, who shares executive power with the prime minister, serves a single six-year term with no possibility of reelection and has the power to veto legislation.

Observers from the Organization for Security and Co-operation in Europe (OSCE) judged the 2011 presidential election to have been free and competitive, though marred by widespread problems with voter lists and numerous faults in the tabulation process. Atambayev, then the incumbent prime minister, defeated 15 other candidates and took 63 percent of the vote.

OSCE observers found that the October 2015 parliamentary elections were competitive and that the 14 registered parties offered voters a wide range of options. However, the monitoring group noted significant procedural problems, flaws in the rollout of a new biometric registration system, inadequate media coverage, and widespread allegations of vote buying. Civil society groups and media reports raised concerns that the SDPK had used state resources and pressure on public employees to enhance its position. Six parties cleared the 7 percent national threshold to secure representation. SDPK led the voting with 38 seats, followed by Respublika–Ata Jurt (28), the Kyrgyzstan party (18), Onuguu-Progress (13), Bir Bol (12), and Ata Meken (11).

In October 2016, the SDPK-led coalition government collapsed after Ata Meken and Onuguu-Progress refused to back plans to amend the constitution. In November, a new government was formed by SDPK, Kyrgyzstan, and Bir Bol, and the parliament passed the final language for a raft of 26 constitutional amendments that would be submitted to voters in a simple yes-or-no referendum scheduled for December, leaving the public only a month to understand and debate the changes. The initiative passed with an overwhelming 80 percent of the referendum vote, but only 42 percent of eligible voters participated; this was enough to overcome the 30 percent threshold required for the vote to be valid. Multiple reports indicated that state employees, especially university and college teachers, were ordered to campaign for the initiative and for SDPK candidates in local elections held the same day, contributing to illegal use of administrative resources by the government.

B. Political Pluralism and Participation: 6 / 16

Citizens have the freedom to organize political parties and groupings, especially at the local level. However, in addition to the 7 percent national threshold, parties must win at least 0.7 percent of the vote in each of the country's nine regional divisions to secure seats in the parliament, which discourages locally organized groups from participating in national politics. Political parties are primarily vehicles for a handful of strong personalities, rather than mass organizations with clear ideologies and policy platforms. Although the 2015 elections featured several new parties, almost all were the result of splits or mergers among the factions in the previous parliament, meaning the actual roster of deputies changed very little.

The 2010 constitutional reforms aimed to ensure political pluralism and prevent the reemergence of an authoritarian, superpresidential system. Since 2012, however, observers have noted signs that President Atambayev was consolidating power and using executive agencies to target political enemies. Opposition members and outside observers have accused the SDPK of attempting to improperly influence electoral and judicial outcomes. The constitutional amendments approved in 2016 included measures that made it more difficult to bring down a sitting government or withdraw from a coalition, effectively solidifying the position of the SDPK.

Although a variety of opposition groups held peaceful rallies during 2016, protesters have frequently complained of interference and pressure from local and national authorities as well as from counterprotesters. In May, a small political opposition group calling itself the People's Parliament planned a rally and called on Atambayev to resign. Five members were arrested on charges of plotting to violently overthrow the government.

Ethnic minority groups face additional forms of political marginalization. After several years of relative quiet, in 2016 ethnic Uzbeks were again used as scapegoats on various issues by politicians from the Kyrgyz majority. In August, a suicide bomber attacked the Chinese embassy in Bishkek, killing only himself; the government publicly named a number of ethnic Uzbeks as suspected accomplices, several of whom publicly professed their innocence. In September, Atambayev asked prosecutors to investigate some of his former colleagues in the 2010 interim government who had recently expressed opposition to the SDPK-backed constitutional reforms, suggesting that they had colluded with alleged Uzbek separatists to foment ethnic violence in 2010. Also that month, the government indicated that it would downgrade the status of the OSCE office in Bishkek after ethnic Uzbek political exile Kadyrzhan Batyrov addressed an OSCE conference in Warsaw.

C. Functioning of Government: 4 / 12

The 2010 constitution's division of power between the president, prime minister, and parliament left some issues unresolved. In the years since, a series of prime ministers have clashed with Atambayev over their respective roles, contributing to the instability of coalition governments.

Corruption is pervasive in Kyrgyzstani society, and transparency in government operations remains inadequate. Despite multiple rounds of constitutional and statutory changes, the country has long been trapped in a cycle in which predatory political elites use government resources to reward clients—including organized crime figures—and punish opponents. In April 2016, Prime Minister Temir Sariyev and his cabinet were forced to resign over allegations that a road-construction tender had been rigged in favor of a Chinese company. The transport minister accused Sariyev of benefiting personally from the tender. Several other corruption scandals involving lower-level officials were reported during the year.

A new anticorruption office within the State Committee of National Security (GKNB) was formed in 2012. The office has primarily been used to target the administration's political enemies in the parliament and city governments.

DISCRETIONARY POLITICAL RIGHTS QUESTION B: −2 / 0

Southern Kyrgyzstan has yet to fully recover from the ethnic upheaval of June 2010, which included numerous documented instances of government involvement or connivance in violence against ethnic Uzbeks in the region, with the aim of tipping the political and economic balance in favor of the Kyrgyz elite. Though some initial steps have been taken to restore Uzbek-language media, the political economy of the south remains deeply altered.

CIVIL LIBERTIES: 24 / 60

D. Freedom of Expression and Belief: 9 / 16

The media landscape remained divided along ethnic lines in 2016, with improved conditions for Kyrgyz-language media since 2010 and continuing challenges for both Uzbek-language outlets and critical Russian-language media. Independent Uzbek-language media virtually ceased to exist in southern Kyrgyzstan after the 2010 ethnic violence, as major Uzbek television and radio outlets were closed down. Although some outlets have opened since then, Uzbek media representation is extremely limited, and staff at remaining outlets continue to be persecuted. Prosecutions for inciting hatred have focused exclusively on minority writers despite the prevalence of openly racist and anti-Semitic articles in Kyrgyz-language media. A 2014 law criminalized the publication of "false information relating to a crime or offense" in the media, which international monitors saw as a contradiction of the country's 2011 decriminalization of defamation. The law assigns penalties of up to three years in prison, or five years if the claim serves the interests of organized crime or is linked to the fabrication of evidence. News websites, blogs, and online forums are increasingly important alternative sources of information for those with access.

In June 2016, the parliament passed the first reading of a measure limiting foreign ownership of media companies operating in Kyrgyzstan. The proposal remained in draft form at the end of the year, with activists raising concerns that it was primarily an attempt to limit Radio Free Europe/Radio Liberty's Kyrgyz service in the country.

All religious organizations must register with the authorities, a process that is often cumbersome and arbitrary. The 2009 Law on Religion deems all unregistered groups illegal and bans proselytizing, private religious education, and the wearing of headscarves in schools. Religious groups outside the traditional Muslim and Orthodox Christian mainstream reportedly have difficulty obtaining registration. The government monitors and restricts Islamist groups that it regards as a threat to national security, particularly Hizb ut-Tahrir.

While private discussion is generally free in the country, state and local authorities regularly raid private homes where they believe Hizb ut-Tahrir members or certain religious minorities, such as Jehovah's Witnesses, are meeting to discuss their beliefs.

The government does not formally restrict academic freedom, though teachers and students reportedly face pressure to participate in political campaigns and voting, as with the 2016 constitutional referendum and local elections.

E. Associational and Organizational Rights: 4 / 12

A 2012 law allows peaceful assembly, and small protests and civil disobedience actions, such as blocking roads, take place regularly. Nevertheless, domestic and international watchdogs remain concerned about police violations of the right to demonstrate, including arrests and other forms of interference, as with the preemptive arrests of People's Parliament leaders who were planning a rally in May 2016. Intimidation by counterprotesters has also emerged as a problem in recent years.

Nongovernmental organizations (NGOs) participate actively in civic and political life, and public advisory councils were established in the parliament and most ministries in 2011, permitting improved monitoring and advocacy by NGOs. However, rising nationalism continues to affect both ethnic Kyrgyz and ethnic Uzbek NGO activists. Human rights workers who support Uzbek abuse victims face threats, harassment, and physical attacks. Ultranationalists have stepped up harassment of U.S. and European NGOs as well as domestic counterparts that are perceived to be favored by Western actors. In 2016, human rights activists Tolekan Ismailova and Aziza Abdirasulova repeatedly faced public smears or threats, in some cases from President Atambayev and other politicians and officials; one series of incidents followed the two activists' participation in the OSCE conference in Warsaw in September. In a positive development, a bill emulating a Russian law that requires NGOs to register as "foreign agents" if they receive foreign funding was rejected by the parliament in May 2016 on its final reading, even after revisions that would have reduced its impact.

Kyrgyzstani law provides for the formation of trade unions, which are generally able to operate without obstruction. However, strikes are prohibited in many sectors. Legal enforcement of union rights is weak, and employers do not always respect collective-bargaining agreements.

F. Rule of Law: 4 / 16

The judiciary is not independent and remains dominated by the executive branch. Corruption among judges is widespread. Defendants' rights, including the presumption of innocence, are not always respected, and there are credible reports of torture during arrest and interrogation. Most such reports do not lead to investigations and convictions, and evidence allegedly obtained through torture is regularly accepted in courts.

The widespread and extensively documented violence against the Uzbek community in southern Kyrgyzstan in 2010 cast a harsh light on the plight of ethnic minorities, and few perpetrators have been brought to justice. Uzbeks, who make up nearly half of the population in Osh, have long demanded more political and cultural rights, including greater representation in government, more Uzbek-language schools, and official status for the Uzbek language. Ethnic minorities continue to face discrimination on economic, security, and other matters.

Same-sex sexual activity is not illegal, but discrimination against and abuse of LGBT (lesbian, gay, bisexual, and transgender) people at the hands of police are pervasive. A bill similar to Russia's ban on "propaganda of nontraditional sexual relations" remained stalled in the parliament during 2016, but the December constitutional amendments included a clause that formalized a de facto ban on same-sex marriage.

G. Personal Autonomy and Individual Rights: 7 / 16

The government generally respects the right of unrestricted travel to and from Kyrgyzstan. However, barriers to internal migration include a requirement that citizens obtain permits to work and settle in particular areas of the country.

Personal connections, corruption, organized crime, and widespread poverty limit business competition and equality of opportunity. Companies that had belonged to the family of ousted president Kurmanbek Bakiyev were nationalized in 2010 pending a new process of privatization. That year's ethnic violence affected property rights in the south, as many businesses, mainly owned by ethnic Uzbeks, were destroyed or seized.

Despite achieving notable leadership positions, women remain underrepresented at higher levels of government and business. Cultural traditions and apathy among law enforcement officials discourage victims of domestic violence and rape from contacting the authorities. The practice of bride abduction persists despite the strengthening of legal penalties in 2013, and few perpetrators are prosecuted. In November 2016, the parliament passed a law introducing criminal penalties for anyone carrying out or enabling underage marriages.

The trafficking of women and girls into forced prostitution abroad is a serious problem. Police have been accused of complicity in the trafficking and exploitation of victims. Kyrgyzstani men are especially vulnerable to trafficking for forced labor abroad.

Laos

Political Rights Rating: 7
Civil Liberties Rating: 6
Freedom Rating: 6.5
Freedom Status: Not Free
Electoral Democracy: No

Population: 7,100,000
Capital: Vientiane

Ten-Year Ratings Timeline For Year Under Review (Political Rights, Civil Liberties, Status)

Year Under Review Rating	2007	2008	2009	2010	2011	2012	2013	2014	2015	2016
	7,6,NF	7,6,NF	7,6,NF	7,6,NF	7,6,NF	7,6,NF	7,6,NF	7,6,NF	7,6,NF	7,6,NF

Overview: Laos is a one-party state in which the ruling Lao People's Revolutionary Party (LPRP) dominates all aspects of politics and government and harshly restricts civil liberties. There is no organized opposition and no truly independent civil society. News coverage of the country is limited by the remoteness of some areas, repression of domestic media, and the opaque nature of the regime. Economic development has led to a rising tide of disputes over land and environmental issues, as well as corruption and the growth of an illegal economy. Such disputes frequently lead to violence, including by the security forces.

KEY DEVELOPMENTS IN 2016:

- Tightly controlled legislative elections in March resulted in a new National Assembly, which chose incumbent vice president Bounnhang Vorachith as the new president in April. He had been named LPRP general secretary at a party congress in January.
- In February and March, security forces arrested three Laotian citizens who had used social media to criticize the state while working in Thailand. They were detained upon returning to Laos to renew their passports and reportedly remained in custody at year's end.
- Laos hosted the Association of Southeast Asian Nations (ASEAN) summit in September, but it refused to host a related civil society gathering, which was held in Timor-Leste instead.
- Violence increased in central and northern Laos during the year, particularly in areas with a history of conflict between security forces and ethnic Hmong militants.

EXECUTIVE SUMMARY

The LPRP selected new leaders through an opaque process at a party congress in January. Vice President Bounnhang Vorachith, who became general secretary of the party, was then elected as state president by the National Assembly in April following legislative elections in March. Thongloun Sisoulith, previously the deputy prime minister and foreign minister, was promoted to prime minister. The LPRP won 144 of 149 seats in the legislative elections, with the remainder going to carefully vetted independents.

The Laotian government continued to tighten its control over domestic dissent in 2016, partly by monitoring citizens' activity on social media. In at least three cases, individuals were apparently arrested for comments they posted while working abroad. The authorities also suppressed independent civil society activity. Although Laos hosted the annual ASEAN summit in September, it would not host the parallel ASEAN People's Forum, a gathering of regional civil society groups. The forum was held in Timor-Leste instead, and participants reported that the Laotian delegation was hand-picked and pressured by the Laotian government to minimize criticism of its record.

Political and ethnic violence surged during the year. There were a series of attacks on buses and trucks in areas of central and northern Laos that have been plagued by banditry and violent Hmong opposition groups. There were also numerous attacks on Chinese nationals in Vientiane, Xaisomboun, and other parts of the country. The government remained largely silent about the violence, including the possible identities and motives of the perpetrators. Some observers suggested that local anger at the environmental destruction caused by foreign-owned mining, logging, and farming concessions contributed to the attacks on Chinese nationals.

POLITICAL RIGHTS: 1 / 40

A. Electoral Process: 0 / 12

B. Political Pluralism and Participation: 0 / 16

C. Functioning of Government: 1 / 12

CIVIL LIBERTIES: 11 / 40

D. Freedom of Expression and Belief: 4 / 16

E. Associational and Organizational Rights: 0 / 12

F. Rule of Law: 2 / 16

G. Personal Autonomy and Individual Rights: 5 / 16

This country report has been abridged for *Freedom in the World 2017*. For background information on political rights and civil liberties in Laos, see *Freedom in the World 2016*.

Latvia

Political Rights Rating: 1 ↑
Civil Liberties Rating: 2
Freedom Rating: 1.5
Freedom Status: Free
Electoral Democracy: Yes

Population: 2,000,000
Capital: Riga

Ratings Change: Latvia's political rights rating improved from 2 to 1 due to a gradual decrease in the influence of oligarchic business interests on political affairs.

Ten-Year Ratings Timeline For Year Under Review (Political Rights, Civil Liberties, Status)

Year Under Review	2007	2008	2009	2010	2011	2012	2013	2014	2015	2016
Rating	2,1,F	2,1,F	2,1,F	2,2,F	2,2,F	2,2,F	2,2,F	2,2,F	2,2,F	1,2,F

Overview: Latvia has successfully developed into a democracy since regaining independence in 1991. Elections are regarded as free and fair, and political and civil rights are generally respected in practice. Nevertheless, ethnic tensions between the country's Latvians and its Russians, many of whom are regarded as noncitizens, are acute. Latvia is also troubled by corruption and relatively high income inequality.

KEY DEVELOPMENTS IN 2016:

- In February, a new government headed by Māris Kučinskis of the Union of Greens and Farmers (ZZS) was installed, though the party composition of the ruling coalition remained the same.
- In July, Latvia became a member of the Organization for Economic Co-operation and Development (OECD). Against this background, the country has increased efforts to fight corruption and international money laundering.
- In November, the parliament approved an amendment that would allow teachers to be fired if they were found to be "disloyal" to the Latvian state. The measure appeared set to take effect in 2017.
- In July, it was revealed that the National Electronic Mass Media Council (NEPLP) had asked police to find a journalist's source, after she published an investigative story revealing likely appointees to its board.

EXECUTIVE SUMMARY

In February 2016, Kučinskis of the ZZS was appointed prime minister of Latvia. He replaced Laimdota Straujuma of the Unity party, who had resigned in December 2015 following internal strife within both Unity and the ruling coalition, though the party composition of the ruling coalition remained intact. In addition to the ZZS and Unity, it also includes the nationalist National Alliance. It took nearly another three months to prepare a government program, which upon its release prioritized strengthening the economy and national security, and reforming the education and health care sectors.

In July 2016, Latvia became a member of the OECD, boosting its international credibility and providing an additional impetus to increase transparency and tackle the rather neglected issue of international money laundering, though concrete results of any initiative addressing the latter were yet to be seen at year's end. Meanwhile, state institutions have taken active steps to combat corruption and tax evasion, but the effectiveness of any reforms has been hampered by the institutions' inability to consolidate power within their own fields of competence. In May, the head of the State Revenues Service resigned, saying she was struggling to implement planned reforms—among them measures aimed at increasing transparency—due to internal tensions and resistance from allied institutions. Meanwhile, despite legislative changes aimed at consolidating the Corruption Prevention and Combating Bureau of Latvia (KNAB) and making it more autonomous, throughout the year its work was marred by public controversies and infighting. During the year, the selection of the new KNAB chief, as well as of the Revenue Service, was delayed and contributed to tensions within the ruling coalition.

Recent years have seen a gradual decrease in the influence of oligarchs in Latvia—attributable mainly to reforms in party financing mechanisms and anticorruption operations—leaving government and political institutions more responsive and accountable to citizens.

Press freedom is generally respected in Latvia, though libel remains a criminal offense. In July 2016, a scandal erupted around the NEPLP, after it was revealed that in March it had requested that police uncover the source of the journalist who had discovered and publicized likely appointees to its board, ahead of the body's formal announcement.

Geopolitical tensions continued to exacerbate the existing social and political divide between the country's ethnic Latvians and its sizable ethnic Russian minority. About 250,000 Latvian residents, mostly ethnic Russians, still do not have citizenship status and altogether any voting rights, and unemployment is higher among Russians than Latvians. In November, the parliament approved an amendment that would allow teachers to be fired if they were found to be "disloyal" to Latvia. The legislation was set to take effect in 2017, and had been introduced after a teacher sparked controversy by suggesting in a radio interview that he was not loyal to the Latvian state.

POLITICAL RIGHTS: 36 / 40 (+ 1)

A. Electoral Process: 12 / 12

B. Political Pluralism and Participation: 15 / 16 (+ 1)

C. Functioning of Government: 9 / 12

CIVIL LIBERTIES: 51 / 60

D. Freedom of Expression and Belief: 15 / 16

E. Associational and Organizational Rights: 12 / 12

F. Rule of Law: 12 / 16

G. Personal Autonomy and Individual Rights: 12 / 16

This country report has been abridged for *Freedom in the World 2017*. For background information on political rights and civil liberties in Latvia, see *Freedom in the World 2016*.

Lebanon

Political Rights Rating: 5
Civil Liberties Rating: 4
Freedom Rating: 4.5
Freedom Status: Partly Free
Electoral Democracy: No

Population: 6,200,000
Capital: Beirut

Ten-Year Ratings Timeline For Year Under Review (Political Rights, Civil Liberties, Status)

Year Under Review	2007	2008	2009	2 010	2011	2012	2013	2014	2015	2016
Rating	5,4,PF	5,4,PF	5,3,PF	5,3,PF	5,4, PF	5,4,PF	5,4,PF	5,4,PF	5,4,PF	5,4,PF

Overview: Lebanon's troubled political system ensures representation for its many sectarian communities, but suppresses competition within each community and impedes the rise of cross-sectarian or secularist parties. Parliamentary elections have been repeatedly postponed amid partisan gridlock and security threats linked to the war in neighboring Syria. Residents enjoy some civil liberties and media pluralism, but the rule of law is undermined by political interference and partisan militias, and the country has struggled to cope with an influx of Syrian and other refugees who make up more than a quarter of its population.

KEY DEVELOPMENTS IN 2016:

- In October, the National Assembly elected Michel Aoun as president, ending a two-year vacancy.

- Aoun asked former prime minister Saad Hariri to lead a new unity cabinet, which was approved by the National Assembly in late December.
- Municipal elections were held in May for the first time in six years, though long-overdue parliamentary elections were not expected until 2017 at the earliest.

EXECUTIVE SUMMARY

Lebanon made some progress toward ending its political dysfunction in 2016. Local elections in more than a thousand municipalities were held in May, in some cases featuring vigorous competition. The new, civil society–based list Beirut Madinati (Beirut My City) won 40 percent of the vote in the capital, campaigning on a platform of practical urban governance and transparency rather than traditional factional loyalties.

In October, the National Assembly's main parties and movements reached a deal to elect Michel Aoun, a longtime political and military leader from the Maronite Christian community, as president, ending a two-year vacancy. Aoun then named Saad Hariri, a Sunni Muslim political leader, to serve as prime minister, and his 30-member cabinet was approved by the National Assembly in late December. The cabinet included all major factions except the Kataeb Party, a Christian group also known as the Phalangist party, which rejected the position it was offered. The cabinet also featured new posts responsible for women's affairs, refugee affairs, and combating corruption, reflecting key challenges facing the country. However, the appointment of a man to the women's affairs post was met with public derision.

Despite the successful municipal voting and the progress in the executive branch, it remained unclear whether parliamentary elections would be held as planned by mid-2017, when the current legislature's mandate—already extended repeatedly since its elected term ended in 2013—was due to expire.

Meanwhile, among other ongoing governance problems, a garbage crisis stemming from the closure of Beirut's main landfill in 2015 continued without a sustainable solution, and the rule of law was threatened by terrorist violence and arbitrary restrictions—including arrests and curfews—on Syrian refugees.

POLITICAL RIGHTS: 14 / 40 (+ 1)

A. Electoral Process: 3 / 12 (+ 1)

The president is selected every six years by the 128-member National Assembly, which in turn is elected for four-year terms. The president and parliament nominate the prime minister, who, along with the president, chooses the cabinet, subject to parliamentary approval. The unwritten National Pact of 1943 stipulates that the president must be a Maronite Christian, the prime minister a Sunni Muslim, and the speaker of the National Assembly a Shiite Muslim. Parliamentary seats are divided among major sects under a constitutional formula that does not reflect their current demographic weight. No official census has been conducted since the 1930s. The sectarian political balance has been periodically reaffirmed and occasionally modified by foreign-brokered agreements.

The last parliamentary elections were held in June 2009. The March 14 coalition, headed by Sunni Muslim parties, won 71 seats, while the rival March 8 coalition, backed by the Shiite militant group Hezbollah, took 57 seats. Although the elections were conducted peacefully and judged to be free and fair in some respects, vote buying was reported to be rampant, and the electoral framework retained a number of fundamental structural flaws linked to the country's sectarian political system. New elections were due in June 2013, but disagreement over electoral reforms led the parliament to extend its own term until late

2014. Citing security concerns associated with the Syrian conflict, lawmakers that year extended their mandate again, this time until June 2017.

The presidency, vacant since the term of Michel Suleiman expired in 2014, was filled through the October 2016 election of Michel Aoun, who nominated Saad Hariri of the March 14 coalition as prime minister in November. Nabih Berri, affiliated with the Amal movement and backed by Hezbollah, retained his post as parliament speaker, a position he has held since 1992. Hariri's unity cabinet, which included representatives of most major factions, was approved by the assembly in late December.

Relatively successful and peaceful municipal council elections were held in May across the country, marking the first subnational elections since 2010. More than 30,000 candidates participated in contests in 1,015 municipalities, though turnout was generally low.

B. Political Pluralism and Participation: 9 / 16

Two major factions, each comprising more than a dozen political parties, have dominated Lebanese politics since 2005: the March 8 coalition, of which Hezbollah is the most powerful member and which is seen as aligned with the Syrian regime, Iran, and Russia; and the March 14 bloc, headed by Sunni Muslims and associated with Saudi Arabia, Europe, and the United States. Christian factions are divided between the two blocs, and a predominantly Druze party has adopted positions that straddle the political divide. These long-standing incumbent parties faced strong challenges or setbacks in a number of the 2016 municipal council elections. Beirut Madinati, a new electoral list characterized by political independents and a technocratic policy agenda, garnered 40 percent of the vote in the capital, but a bloc of establishment parties still captured all of the council seats.

Although the political system features a variety of competing parties, their activities are inhibited by periodic violence, intimidation, and entrenched patronage networks—in some cases linked to foreign funding—that make it difficult for new groups to emerge or existing groups to modify their positions or policies. Lebanese voters' political choices are also restricted by the sectarian electoral system and a related requirement that citizens vote in their ancestral hometowns, which discourages the rise of multiconfessional or secularist parties. The established sectarian parties are often headed by prominent families, with key positions effectively handed down from one generation to the next.

The rigid formula for allocation of elected positions ensures that nearly all recognized confessional groups are represented, but it does not reflect their actual shares of the population. Refugees, including large, decades-old Palestinian communities, are not eligible for citizenship and have no political rights.

C. Functioning of Government: 2 / 12

Sectarian and partisan divisions, exacerbated by foreign interference and more recently the Syrian civil war, have frequently prevented Lebanese governments from forming and operating effectively and independently after elections. The extended presidential vacancy and the National Assembly's ongoing lack of an electoral mandate have further undermined the government's legitimacy. The authority of the government is also limited in practice by the power of autonomous militant groups, such as Hezbollah.

Political and bureaucratic corruption is widespread, businesses routinely pay bribes and cultivate ties with politicians to win contracts, and anticorruption laws are loosely enforced. In an indication of institutional dysfunction, the national government has not passed an annual budget since 2005, meaning state expenditures are irregular, lacking in oversight, and prone to corrupt manipulation. The garbage crisis that began in 2015, when authorities closed the capital's main landfill without preparing a replacement site, remained unresolved in 2016 amid corruption and other concerns. Temporary dumps were used during the year, including one near Beirut's international airport and another near a commercial and residential neighborhood, Bourj Hammoud, provoking renewed protests and resulting in periodic pile-ups of garbage.

Corruption has extended to contracts for aid to refugees. Some nongovernmental organizations (NGOs) have allegedly siphoned off funds from international agencies, with cooperation from corrupt Lebanese officials, or wasted resources on excessive salaries and benefits for senior employees. Donor concerns about corruption were believed to be one factor behind chronic shortfalls in aid for Syrian refugees.

CIVIL LIBERTIES: 30 / 60

D. Freedom of Expression and Belief: 11 / 16

Freedom of expression and freedom of the press are guaranteed by law. The country's media are among the most open and diverse in the region, but nearly all outlets have ties to sectarian leaders or groups, and consequently practice self-censorship and maintain a specific, often partisan, editorial line. Censorship of books, movies, plays, and other artistic work is common, especially when the work involves politics, religion, sex, or Israel.

It is a criminal offense to criticize or defame the president or Lebanese security forces, and an audiovisual media law bans broadcasts that seek to harm the state or its foreign relations or incite sectarian violence, among other broadly worded provisions. These and similar laws have been used to intimate and prosecute journalists who disseminate criticism of the government or powerful nonstate actors. On at least two occasions in 2016, authorities summoned journalists for questioning about their work.

The Netherlands-based Special Tribunal for Lebanon (STL) continued to adjudicate contempt of court cases related to media exposure of confidential witnesses in its investigation of the 2005 assassination of former prime minister Rafik Hariri. In March 2016, an STL appellate panel overturned the 2015 conviction of Al-Jadeed TV's Karma Khayat, but in July the tribunal convicted and fined *Al-Akhbar* newspaper and its editor in chief for the public identification of 32 confidential witnesses.

Journalists and media outlets occasionally face intimidation or violence in response to their reporting. In April 2016, the Beirut offices of the London-based newspaper *Asharq al-Awsat* were attacked by protesters over a cartoon deemed offensive to Lebanon.

Freedom of religion is guaranteed in the constitution and protected in practice. Every confessional group manages its own family and personal-status laws, and has its own religious courts to adjudicate such matters. Proselytizing, while not punishable by law, is strongly discouraged by religious leaders and communities, sometimes with the threat of violence. Blasphemy is a criminal offense that carries up to one year in prison. Political strife between religious groups has persisted to some extent since the 1975–90 civil war, and such differences—particularly between Sunnis and Shiites—have been exacerbated in recent years by the civil war in Syria.

Academic freedom is generally unimpaired, though defamation and blasphemy laws could deter open debate. Private discussion is similarly uninhibited. However, the government reportedly monitors social media, and users occasionally face arrests, short detentions, or fines for their remarks. In two cases during 2016, a human rights lawyer and a journalism student were temporarily detained and faced defamation charges for social media posts that criticized the state.

E. Associational and Organizational Rights: 7 / 12

The constitution guarantees the freedoms of assembly and association, and the government generally respects these rights, though police have cracked down in the past on demonstrations against the government or the Syrian regime. Garbage-related protests in 2015 featured clashes between police and demonstrators, but those in 2016 were generally peaceful. More than a dozen demonstrators faced charges in military courts for the 2015 violence, though none were in detention during 2016.

Civil society organizations have long operated openly in Lebanon, with some constraints. All NGOs must be registered with the Interior Ministry. The ministry may force an NGO to undergo an approval process and investigate its founders, and representatives of the ministry must be invited to observe voting on bylaws and boards of directors.

Trade unions are often tightly linked to political organizations, and in recent years they have been subordinate to their political partners. The Labor Ministry has broad authority over the formation of unions, union elections, and the administrative dissolution of unions. Collective bargaining and especially strikes are subject to onerous restrictions. Public employees, agricultural workers, and household workers are not protected by the labor code and have no legal right to organize, though they have formed unrecognized representative organizations in practice.

F. Rule of Law: 5 / 16

Political forces hold sway over the formally independent judiciary. The Supreme Judicial Council is composed of 10 judges, eight of whom are nominated by the president and the cabinet. Other judges are nominated by the council, approved by the Justice Ministry, and vetted by opposition and government parties.

While the regular judiciary generally follows international standards of criminal procedure, these standards are not followed in the military courts, which have been tasked with cases against Islamist militants, human rights activists, and alleged Israeli spies, among others. Security forces reportedly use torture and other abuse to obtain confessions. Prison conditions remain poor, with severe overcrowding, and pretrial detention often lasts years. Inmates at Roumieh prison launched a protest against harsh conditions and ill-treatment following the death of a prisoner in May 2016.

Security threats and militant activity related to the Syrian civil war persisted in 2016. Among other violent incidents during the year, a wave of suicide bombings struck a Lebanese Christian village near the Syrian border in June, killing five people and wounding many others. There was no official claim of responsibility for the attack. In response, Lebanese security forces imposed curfews on Syrian refugees in the area and conducted hundreds of arbitrary arrests, although the interior minister said the attack originated inside Syria.

There were roughly 1.5 million Syrian refugees in Lebanon as of 2016, of whom about one-third were not registered with the UN refugee agency; the government had instructed the agency to suspend registrations in 2015. Syrian refugees reportedly faced arbitrary arrests and other forms of harassment from both security forces and Lebanese civilians. Most refugee households included at least some members who lacked a residency permit owing to stricter government regulations, exposing them to arrest, and a large majority lived in poverty, partly due to limitations on refugees' employment options.

About 450,000 Palestinian refugees were registered in Lebanon, though fewer than 300,000 were believed to reside in the country in 2016. They also face certain restrictions on economic activity, contributing to widespread poverty.

LGBT (lesbian, gay, bisexual, and transgender) people face both official and societal discrimination and harassment. The penal code prescribes up to one year in prison for "sexual intercourse against nature," though this is rarely enforced. NGOs work to uphold the human rights of LGBT people, and social acceptance is more common in urban and cosmopolitan areas, particularly in Beirut.

G. Personal Autonomy and Individual Rights: 7 / 16

Impediments to freedom of movement include de facto sectarian boundaries in some areas and curfews on Syrian refugees in many municipalities. Even longtime Palestinian refugee residents face restrictions on employment and property ownership. A 2010 law allowed them access to social security benefits, end-of-service compensation, and the right to bring complaints before labor courts, but closed off access to skilled professions. At least 250,000 Syrian children were without access to education in 2016. Business activity in Lebanon is impaired by bureaucratic obstacles and corrupt patronage networks.

Women are granted equal rights in the constitution, but they are disadvantaged under the sectarian personal-status laws on issues such as divorce, inheritance, and child custody. Under a 1925 law, women cannot pass their nationality to non-Lebanese husbands or children. A 2014 law that criminalized domestic violence failed to criminalize spousal rape.

Both Lebanese and foreign nationals are subjected to forced labor and sex trafficking in Lebanon. Refugees and foreign household workers are especially vulnerable to exploitation. Authorities often arrest victims of trafficking for crimes committed as a result of their being trafficked.

Lesotho

Political Rights Rating: 3
Civil Liberties Rating: 3
Freedom Rating: 3.0
Freedom Status: Partly Free
Electoral Democracy: Yes

Population: 2,200,000
Capital: Maseru

Ten-Year Ratings Timeline For Year Under Review (Political Rights, Civil Liberties, Status)

Year Under Review	2007	2008	2009	2010	2011	2012	2013	2014	2015	2016
Rating	2,3,F	2,3,F	3,3,PF	3,3,PF	3,3,PF	2,3,F	2,3,F	2,3,F	3,3,PF	3,3,PF

Overview: In recent years, political instability and accompanying violence have severely hampered the country's development, as has an ongoing drought. Corruption is rife in all sectors of government and public services. Customary practice and law restricts women's rights in areas such as property, inheritance, and marriage and divorce.

KEY DEVELOPMENTS IN 2016:

* The year was marked by politically motivated assassinations and attempted assassinations against journalists, academics, and political figures.
* In November, Lesotho Defense Force (LDF) head Tlali Kamoli, who many see as a primary instigator of the country's security challenges, was forced into early retirement.

EXECUTIVE SUMMARY

Lesotho remained in crisis in 2016, with politics entangled in disputes among factions of the LDF. Politically motivated assassinations and assassination attempts continued with impunity. In June, the daughter of a lawmaker with the All Basotho Convention (ABC) was shot dead. In October, the editor in chief of the *Lesotho Times* was shot four times, but survived. In May, the home of Mafa Sejanamane, an academic and prominent government critic, was shot at, though he was not injured in the attack. The ongoing violence has cast a chill over political discourse in the country.

As of October 2016, the police had yet to take statements from the family of Maaparankoe Mahao, the former leader of the LDF who was killed in 2015 amid murky circumstances; the defense minister claims that Mahao was killed in an operation to arrest him on charges of mutiny, but the opposition and civil society groups have labeled his death an assassination. Notably, police had yet to contact Mahao's two nephews, who were in the car with him at the time he was shot.

In November, LDF head Tlali Kamoli, who many see as a primary instigator of the country's security challenges and who some suspect of ordering Mahao's killing, was forced into early retirement.

A devastating drought has gripped the country for the last several years, resulting in a heavy reliance on imported foodstuffs that has strained public finances. Lesotho is one of the world's largest per capita recipients of overseas development aid, with some 11 percent of national income derived from such assistance. The ongoing political instability in the country threatens the aid's continuance.

POLITICAL RIGHTS: 27 / 40 (− 1)

A. Electoral Process: 10 / 12

B. Political Pluralism and Participation: 11 / 16 (− 1)

C. Functioning of Government: 6 / 12

CIVIL LIBERTIES: 37 / 60 (− 2)

D. Freedom of Expression and Belief: 12 / 16 (− 2)

E. Associational and Organizational Rights: 7 / 12

F. Rule of Law: 9 / 16

G. Personal Autonomy and Individual Rights: 9 / 16

This country report has been abridged for *Freedom in the World 2017*. For background information on political rights and civil liberties in Lesotho, see *Freedom in the World 2016*.

Liberia

Political Rights Rating: 3
Civil Liberties Rating: 4
Freedom Rating: 3.5
Freedom Status: Partly Free
Electoral Democracy: Yes

Population: 4,600,000
Capital: Monrovia

Ten-Year Ratings Timeline For Year Under Review (Political Rights, Civil Liberties, Status)

Year Under Review	2007	2008	2009	2010	2011	2012	2013	2014	2015	2016
Rating	3,4,PF	3,4,PF	3,4,PF	3,4,PF	3,4,PF	3,4,PF	3,4,PF	3,4,PF	3,4,PF	3,4,PF

Overview: Liberia has enjoyed more than a decade of peace and stability since a 14-year period of intermittent civil war ended in 2003. During this time, the country has made considerable progress toward rebuilding government capacity, reestablishing the rule of law, and ensuring the political rights and civil liberties of citizens. However, Liberia still faces serious issues with corruption and unequal justice.

KEY DEVELOPMENTS IN 2016:

- With presidential and legislative elections scheduled for October 2017, Liberia's political landscape saw jockeying among parties and politicians, amid a peaceful environment. By year's end, a number of credible contenders for the presidency had emerged.
- In September, in an effort to address underrepresentation of women in government, Liberia's legislature passed the Equal Representation and Participation Act, creating five seats for female politicians in the House of Representatives, along with one for young people and one for people with disabilities.
- The UN Security Council voted in December to extend the mandate of the UN Mission in Liberia (UNMIL) until March 2018.

EXECUTIVE SUMMARY

Liberia's political landscape in 2016 was dominated by preparations for the 2017 presidential and legislative elections. Because incumbent president Ellen Johnson Sirleaf is constitutionally barred from serving a third term, the election will bring about the first transition of power since the end of the civil wars in 2003. Several candidates have emerged as top contenders for the presidency, including Vice President Joseph Boakai of the ruling Unity Party (UP); George Weah, a senator and standard-bearer for the Congress for Democratic Change (CDC); and Benoni Urey, a businessman affiliated with the All Liberian Party (ALP). Despite fears among some observers that the election could destabilize the country, in 2016 all stakeholders appeared to be committed to a peaceful electoral process.

The government has continued to pursue its anticorruption agenda, though progress has been slow and corruption remains pervasive. In May 2016, the government launched an investigation into a corruption scandal involving mining contracts, which led to bribery charges against the speaker of the House of Representatives, as well as a senator.

In recent years, rulings by the nation's highest court have reflected judicial independence and the court's continued willingness to intervene to protect people's rights. However, petty corruption and a lack of capacity within lower-level courts and security sectors remained major impediments to the rule of law.

POLITICAL RIGHTS: 28 / 40

A. Electoral Process: 9 / 12

Liberia has a bicameral legislature composed of a 30-member Senate and a 73-member House of Representatives; senators are elected to nine-year terms, and representatives to six-year terms. Staggered senatorial elections were introduced in 2011. The president can serve up to two six-year terms.

Since the end of the civil wars in 2003, Liberia has held two presidential elections. The most recent was in 2011, when incumbent president Sirleaf of the UP secured 44 percent of the vote in the first round, while Winston Tubman, of the opposition CDC, took 32 percent. Sirleaf was reelected after winning 91 percent of the vote in a runoff. Although opposition members alleged fraud and corruption, international and local observers found that the elections had been comparatively free, fair, and peaceful, though there were isolated incidents of violence before and after the voting, and the government briefly shut down radio and television stations with perceived pro-CDC biases before the vote.

Elections to 15 of Liberia's 30 Senate seats were held in December 2014 after several months of delay due to the Ebola crisis, and turnout was depressed by fears of Ebola. The election resulted in major losses for incumbent politicians in general and the UP in particular, attributed to widespread discontent with the government's handling of the Ebola crisis. The UP held just eight seats in the body after the polls. The CDC and National Patriotic Party (NPP) were left with four Senate seats each after votes were tabulated, with the remainder of seats held by smaller parties or independents, except for a single seat that was left vacant. Although beset with restrictions under a state of emergency, the 2014 Senate elections were deemed "free, fair, credible, and transparent" by an observer mission from the Economic Community of West African States (ECOWAS).

Liberia's next national election is scheduled for October 2017. Sirleaf will not be in the running, as presidents are constitutionally barred from running for more than two terms. Sirleaf is supporting incumbent vice president Boakai of the UP, who has emerged as a major contender. Other contenders include Weah, a senator and standard-bearer for the CDC, and Urey, a prominent businessman in the telecommunications sector, who is affiliated with the ALP.

In 2016, all parties appeared committed to ensuring elections are peaceful, and support for a democratic process among citizens is strong. Although campaigning is not expected to begin in earnest until summer of 2017, candidates appear set to campaign in a free and fair environment.

B. Political Pluralism and Participation: 12 / 16

Political parties do not face undue legal or practical obstacles that prevent them from operating. Allegations of undue influence or pressure on voters by powerful groups are rare. Opposition parties hold significant support among the population and, in the 2014 Senate elections, demonstrated the ability to convert this support into political power.

Though Liberians elected Africa's first female head of state, women are underrepresented in government, and hold only 12 percent of legislative seats and 6 percent of positions in local government, despite a 2014 electoral law mandating that neither men nor women can comprise more than 70 percent of the candidates listed by any political party. Recognizing the need for further reform, in September 2016 the legislature passed the Equal Representation and Participation Act, which created five seats reserved for female politicians in the House of Representatives, as well as one for youth, and one for people with disabilities. It is set to take effect in time for the 2017 elections.

Ethnic and religious minority groups generally enjoy full political rights and electoral opportunities, though some minorities—especially the Mandingo and Fulani peoples—continue to be stigmatized as outsiders. Candidates occasionally exploit these biases to rally their constituents. Additionally, members of Lebanese and Asian minority groups whose families have lived in Liberia for several generations are denied citizenship, and therefore may not vote or participate in the political process.

C. Functioning of Government: 7 / 12

Once elected, new government officials are duly installed in office, and elected legislators generally operate without interference from nonstate actors, foreign governments, or unelected officials.

Liberia boasts a number of institutions devoted to fighting corruption—including the Liberia Anti-Corruption Commission (LACC), the General Auditing Commission, and the Public Procurement and Concessions Commission—but they lack the resources and capacity to function effectively, and corruption remains pervasive. Widespread government distrust is thought to have contributed to the spread of Ebola in 2014, as there was low support for government-backed control policies and preventative measures. A May 2016 report by Global Witness, an international anticorruption group, reported that a series of questionable payments had been made by the British company Sable Mining to House Speaker Alex Tyler and other high-ranking government officials. The payments, believed to total more than $1 million, were allegedly made in 2010 during the firm's attempt to gain an iron ore concession in the north of the country. Later in the month, Tyler and a senator were indicted on charges including bribery; Tyler resigned as House Speaker in September, and proceedings against them were underway at year's end.

President Sirleaf has been repeatedly accused of nepotism when filling lucrative bureaucratic posts within her administration. Charles Sirleaf, one of her sons, was appointed the interim head of the central bank in February 2016, while Fumba Sirleaf, another son, heads the National Security Agency.

Liberia's Freedom of Information Act is rarely used, and government responsiveness to requests tends to be slow. Liberia was the first African state to comply with Extractive Industries Transparency Initiative (EITI) rules governing natural-resource extraction, and in 2016 it remained EITI compliant. In November, the legislature passed the Petroleum Law, which compels all oil companies to disclose their ownership and mandates that all petroleum contracts be awarded through competitive bidding.

CIVIL LIBERTIES: 34 / 60 (+ 1)

D. Freedom of Expression and Belief: 11 / 16 (+ 1)

A variety of newspapers operate in Liberia, though most are published in the capital. Numerous radio stations operate across the country. The government does not restrict internet access, but poor infrastructure and high costs limit usage to a small fraction of the population.

Despite becoming to a signatory in 2012 to the Declaration of Table Mountain, a pan-African initiative that calls for the abolition of criminal defamation laws, Liberia has long been criticized for its onerous criminal and civil libel laws, which are used to harass and intimidate journalists and activists. In 2016 the government continued to use libel and sedition laws to clamp down on dissent. Following the mysterious death of Harry Greaves, a prominent businessman and government critic whose body was found on a beach in Monrovia in January, human rights activist Vandalark Patricks was arrested and charged with sedition and criminal libel after calling for mass protests against what he alleged to be a government plot to assassinate political opponents. While an independent investigation found no evidence of criminal wrongdoing in the death of Greaves, the government's willingness to quickly detain critics on allegations of sedition and criminal libel is alarming. In addition, in September an activist was charged with criminal coercion for his investigation into a government-backed loan program for businesses in the city of Buchanan. In July, the opposition radio station Voice FM was temporarily shut down for lacking an operating permit. And in October, the publisher of the *Hot Pepper* newspaper, Philipbert Browne, was arrested for libel and detained for several days after publishing an article in which a teenage girl claimed that a legislator had raped her. Physical attacks against media workers are occasionally reported. In May 2016, journalist Wremongar Joe was physically attacked for refusing to delete footage he had taken of a brawl that involved a legislator.

Religious freedom is protected in the constitution, and there is no official religion. Liberia is, however, a de facto Christian state, and the Muslim minority frequently reports discrimination. In 2015, a proposal to amend the constitution in order to establish Christianity as the official state religion was decried by Muslim leaders, and contributed to interreligious tensions. Though the proposal appeared to have the support of numerous lawmakers, the house speaker indicated his opposition in April 2016 and President Sirleaf has maintained opposition to the bill. Separately, the Palm oil company Golden Veroleum (GVL) reportedly bulldozed religious shrines in October as part of its expansion plans.

The government does not restrict academic freedom, though educational quality and infrastructure remain grossly inadequate. People are generally free to engage in private discussion while in public spaces. The government is not known to illegally monitor online communications.

E. Associational and Organizational Rights: 8 / 12

Freedom of association is constitutionally guaranteed and largely respected in Liberia. Numerous civil society groups, including human rights organizations, operate in the country.

The rights of workers to strike, organize, and bargain collectively are recognized, but labor laws remain in need of reform. Labor disputes can turn violent, particularly at the country's various mines and rubber plantations.

F. Rule of Law: 7 / 16

Constitutional provisions guarantee an independent judiciary. Although petty corruption and backlogs remain major impediments to justice, recent rulings by the nation's highest court point to increased judicial independence and increased willingness to intervene to protect people's rights. However, lower-level courts continue to struggle to provide justice to ordinary citizens. Corruption remains rampant, judges are subject to interference, and courts are hamstrung by case backlogs.

Lack of discipline, absenteeism, and corruption continue to plague the police and armed forces, hampering their ability to enforce laws and bring justice to those who have been the victims of crimes. As a result, many in Liberia turn to extrajudicial means of justice, including attacks and property damage. People accused of witchcraft can face the practice of "trial by ordeal," in which they are subjected to abuses amounting to torture. Prisons are notorious for inadequate medical care, food, and sanitation; lax security; and prolonged pretrial detentions.

LGBT (lesbian, gay, bisexual, and transgender) people face social stigma and the threat of violence and harassment. Under the penal code, "voluntary sodomy" is a misdemeanor offense that can carry up to a year in prison. A local LGBT rights group reported in October 2016 that several people were arrested on allegations of sodomy, including one person who was arrested after reporting a robbery to police.

G. Personal Autonomy and Individual Rights: 8 / 16

Personal autonomy and individual rights are constitutionally protected in Liberia, and the government does not restrict freedom of travel, or choice of residence, employment, or institutions of higher education. However, equality of opportunity is limited in part by the low quality of public education. The government has tried to address low numeracy and literacy skills among young people by expanding vocational training, and more controversially, by partnering in April 2016 with a private company that provides primary education at a low cost.

Conflicts over land access and ownership remain pervasive. Many of these conflicts originated in the civil wars and subsequent internal migration, displacement, and resettlement. Others are the result of opaque concession agreements granting foreign corporations access to lands for production of tropical timber, palm oil, and other products. A large fraction of the country's land mass is thought to be owned by private logging and other companies. A 2015 report by Global Witness criticized the government for helping the palm oil company Golden Veroleum pressure local communities to enter into concession agreements with little understanding of their terms and conditions. In addition, mechanisms for compensating local communities in concession areas remain inadequate and have led to violent protests. In 2016, there were reports that Golden Veroleum had turned land traditionally held by communities into its own palm oil plantations, and had stationed armed guards around them.

While men and women enjoy equal legal rights under civil law, customary law remains dominant in many parts of the country, especially in rural areas, creating gender discrepancies in access to land, custody of children, and impartial adjudication of disputes. Violence against women and children, particularly rape, is a pervasive problem. In April 2016, the government proposed legislation against female genital mutilation, a process many Liberian women have experienced.

Human trafficking for the purpose of forced labor and prostitution remains a problem in Liberia, with most victims trafficked from Liberia's rural areas to its cities. Many trafficking victims are children, who can be found working in diamond mines, agricultural operations, or as domestic laborers, or engaged in forced begging or prostitution.

Libya

Political Rights Rating: 7 ↓
Civil Liberties Rating: 6
Freedom Rating: 6.5
Freedom Status: Not Free
Electoral Democracy: No

Population: 6,300,000
Capital: Tripoli

Ratings Change: Libya's political rights rating declined from 6 to 7 due to wide-ranging problems associated with the ongoing political and security crisis, including overdue elections and the lack of a fully functional government with nationwide recognition and authority.

Ten-Year Ratings Timeline for Year Under Review (Political Rights, Civil Liberties, Status)

Year Under Review	2007	2008	2009	2010	20 11	2012	2013	2014	2015	201
Rating	7,7,NF	7,7,NF	7,7,NF	7,7,NF	7,6,NF	4,5,PF	4,5,PF	6,6,NF	6,6,NF	7,6,NF

Overview: While a popular armed uprising in 2011 deposed longtime dictator Mu'ammar al-Qadhafi, Libya is now wracked by political, security, and economic crises, and a UN-brokered deal designed to bring rival administrations together in a unity government has failed to come to fruition. Awash in weapons and hundreds of armed groups, criminal networks have flourished, and a faction of the Islamic State (IS) extremist group has emerged.

Fighting has displaced hundreds of thousands of people and disrupted basic services. Human rights conditions have deteriorated, and impunity reigns.

KEY DEVELOPMENTS IN 2016:

- The UN-backed Libyan Political Agreement (LPA), signed in December 2015, failed to unify the country's rival political and military authorities under a single administration. The country had three competing governments at year's end. In October, there was a failed coup attempt by one administration against UN-backed authorities in Tripoli.
- General Khalifa Haftar, commander of the Libyan National Army in the east of the country, refused to endorse the UN-backed deal, and strengthened his foothold in eastern Libya. A number of elected civilian mayors in areas under his control were replaced by military governors, including in Benghazi, where new authorities implemented a measure requiring military approval for demonstrations.
- Local armed forces, primarily from the city of Misrata and nominally affiliated with the UN-backed government, fought the Islamic State (IS) extremist group in the coastal city of Sirte. Beginning in August, U.S. airstrikes supported the operations and by year's end most IS fighters had been pushed out of the city. However, IS maintained a presence elsewhere in Libya.
- The human rights situation continued to deteriorate amid ongoing armed conflicts between the hundreds of militant groups operating in Libya, and an economic crisis that left many without basic services. The UN Office for Humanitarian Affairs estimated that 1.3 million people in Libya will require humanitarian assistance in 2017.

EXECUTIVE SUMMARY

Five years after the downfall of longtime dictator Mu'ammar al-Qadhafi, Libya remains deeply divided between political and military actors, and internationally backed efforts to reach political consensus and establish a single government with authority over the whole country have failed. The human rights situation continues to deteriorate amid ongoing armed conflicts between the hundreds of militant groups and an economic crisis that has left many without basic services, including electricity.

In late 2015, following 18 months of UN-led negotiations, representatives from two competing governments—the Tubruk-based House of Representatives (HoR), which enjoyed widespread international recognition, and the Tripoli-based General National Congress (GNC)—signed the LPA. The agreement was intended to end the political gridlock and armed fighting that started in 2014 between the rival HoR and GNC, each of which had its own allied military coalitions, and reconcile them within a single administration. The appointment of a nine-member Presidency Council (PC) under the leadership of Prime Minister Fayez al-Serraj followed. The PC assumed office in Tripoli in March 2016; it was tasked with forming a unity government, the Government of National Accord (GNA), to serve as an executive branch. Under the LPA, the HoR would act as a primary legislature, while GNC members would form the State Council, a secondary consultative body. The agreement was designed to be in effect until the adoption of a new constitution and the subsequent holding of parliamentary elections.

However, at the end of 2016, the HoR had yet to pass a measure approving the LPA's provisions—including one formally establishing the HoR as the country's legislature. In August, the HoR voted overwhelmingly to reject a GNA cabinet proposed by the PC.

At year's end Libya thus had three competing governments: the United Nations–backed PC, in Tripoli, which the international community continued to back; the National Salvation Government (NSG), the successor to the GNC, also based in Tripoli; and the interim government associated with the HoR in eastern Al-Bayda and Tubruk, respectively. The LPA's primary effect was to reconfigure much of the internal strife in Libya as between supporters and opponents of the PC and the internationally-backed agreement itself.

Meanwhile, Libya's Constitutional Drafting Assembly (CDA), a body that was previously neutral and uncontested, in 2016 became mired in political infighting.

Amid the security vacuum and a breakdown in law and order, IS established a presence in the coastal city of Sirte, though local armed groups, assisted by U.S. airstrikes, mostly dislodged IS fighters from the city by year's end. However, the group maintained a presence in other parts of Libya, including around Benghazi and Derna.

Oil production, the main source of revenue in Libya, has declined massively in recent years and the financial situation continues to deteriorate. The human rights situation has also worsened, as armed groups on all sides commit human rights violations.

POLITICAL RIGHTS: 3 / 40 (− 3)

A. Electoral Process: 1 / 12 (− 3)

An August 2011 constitutional declaration, issued by an unelected National Transitional Council, serves as the governing document for the ongoing transitional period between the revolution and the adoption of a permanent constitution. Amid the political crisis that unfolded in 2014 and 2015 between rival governments and military coalitions in the east and west of the country, the United Nations launched a political dialogue process that ended with the signing of the LPA in December 2015 in Skhirat, Morocco, and the establishment of a nine-member Presidency Council tasked with forming a unity government, the GNA.

While the United Nations and many world powers voiced support for the LPA and PC in 2016, their legitimacy is contested domestically. In October 2016, power struggles in Tripoli underscored the weak position of UN-backed prime minister–designate Serraj and the PC. That month, Khalifa al-Ghwell, the Tripoli-based prime minister of the NSG, and former members of the defunct legislative GNC seized several state buildings, and declared the GNA "void," though they could not garner much support and ultimately failed to displace UN-backed authorities from Tripoli. Meanwhile, the HoR in 2016 declined to approve a constitutional amendment, as envisioned by the LPA, that would formally approve the LPA's provisions and establish the HoR as Libya's legislative authority; this was largely because HoR head Aquila Saleh and General Haftar, who commands the HoR-aligned Libyan National Army, objected to an LPA provision that subordinated the military to the PC. Furthermore, as General Haftar consolidated his control over eastern Libya during the year, both he and his chief of staff fired a number of elected municipal mayors and installed military figures in their place, including in Benghazi, Libya's second-largest city.

Additionally, the Constitutional Drafting Assembly (CDA), which had been uncontested and maintained neutrality throughout the 2014–15 conflict, in 2016 became embroiled in political infighting. The LPA's time line rests on the CDA's completion of a new constitution and the HoR and State Council's approval of the new charter. The CDA released a second draft constitution in February 2016 after consultative sessions that took place in Oman, which included roughly half of its members.

While an electoral law was published in the aftermath of the 2011 revolution and an electoral commission was appointed, in practice Libya lacks a functioning electoral framework.

B. Political Pluralism and Participation: 2 / 16

More than 100 parties or lists spanning the political spectrum, from socialists to Islamists, organized to participate in the 2012 GNC elections, marking a clear departure from the Qadhafi era, during which political parties were illegal and all independent political activity was banned. However, the legitimacy and integrity of the new parties steadily eroded, and all candidates in the 2014 elections were required to run as independents. Civilian politics and public participation were further marginalized by and subordinated to armed groups, as two opposing military coalitions in the east and west fought for control of the country and against extremist forces, including IS.

Throughout 2016, political life in Libya was mired in obstructionist, zero-sum politics. The UN-backed PC, currently located off a naval base in Tripoli, had yet to secure control and reconcile rival political and military actors. Major world powers reiterated support for the UN-brokered LPA and PC during the year, and in April, the European Union (EU) sanctioned three political personalities who opposed the unity government: Nouri Abusahmain, former head of the GNC; Ghwell, of the NSG; and Saleh, speaker of the HoR in the east.

C. Functioning of Government: 0 / 12

None of the country's rival political and military camps constituted an effective national government in 2016. While the GNA enjoys strong backing from the international community, its domestic security is based on a fragile arrangement with various armed groups. Even before the rift between the HoR and GNC opened in 2014, the authority of elected officials was limited due to underdeveloped state institutions and the presence of autonomous regional armed groups, which by some counts number more than 1,700.

Corruption has long been pervasive in both the private sector and the government. The fall of the Qadhafi regime initially raised hopes that the level of graft would decline, but oil interests, foreign governments, smuggling syndicates, and armed groups still wield undue influence, especially in the south, and opportunities for corruption and criminal activity abound in the absence of effective fiscal, judicial, and commercial institutions.

CIVIL LIBERTIES: 10 / 60 (−4)

D. Freedom of Expression: 4 / 16 (−2)

The fall of the Qadhafi regime lifted restrictions on the long-repressed media sector. Citizen journalism became more common, and media outlets ranging from satellite television and radio stations to print publications multiplied in number. However, media freedom is increasingly limited by political and criminal violence that has made objective reporting dangerous. Many journalists and media outlets have censored themselves or ceased operations to avoid retribution by armed groups. Threats and violent reprisals for reporting have prompted a growing number of journalists to flee the country. Post-Qadhafi authorities have sometimes sought to curb free expression through the approval of restrictive laws codifying insult crimes. The GNC has in the past directed a state internet service provider to turn over certain data, and to ban access to websites that hosted content dealing with Christianity or atheism, or which were deemed pornographic.

Nearly all Libyans are Sunni Muslims, but Christians form a small minority, with most hailing from neighboring countries. Some Salafi Muslim groups, whose beliefs reject the veneration of saints, have destroyed or vandalized Sufi Muslim shrines. Egyptian Coptic Christian communities have been targeted by armed groups, including IS.

Close state supervision of education ended along with Qadhafi's regime. However, laws guaranteeing academic freedom have not been passed, and by mid-2016 hundreds of schools across the country were closed due to a breakdown in the rule of law, or damage to facilities inflicted during fighting between various armed groups.

Although open and free private discussion improved dramatically after 2011, the ongoing hostilities have taken their toll, with many Libyans increasingly withdrawing from political life or avoiding criticism of powerful actors, particularly in the eastern regions dominated by General Haftar's forces.

E. Associational and Organizational Rights: 2 / 12 (− 1)

A 2012 law on freedom of assembly is generally compatible with international human rights principles. However, fighting and related disorder seriously deter peaceful assemblies in many areas. After General Haftar replaced the elected mayor of Benghazi with a military leader, the new authorities banned demonstrations without prior approval from the military.

A multitude of domestic nongovernmental organizations (NGOs) formed after the 2011 revolution. However, the number of active NGOs continued to decline in 2016, due to armed conflict and the departure of international donors. Armed groups with varying political, tribal, and geographic affiliations have targeted civil society activists with impunity. Many NGO workers have fled abroad or ceased their activism in the wake of grave threats to themselves or their families.

Some trade unions, previously outlawed, formed after 2011, but they remain in their organizational infancy.

F. Rule of Law: 0 / 16 (− 1)

The role of the judiciary remains unclear without a permanent constitution, and judges, prosecutors, and police officers in postrevolutionary Libya face frequent threats and attacks. By the end of 2016 the country's judicial system had essentially collapsed, with courts across the country nonfunctional and impunity widespread. In some cases, nonstate dispute mechanisms have filled the void.

Investigations into a large number of cases involving torture and extrajudicial executions before and during the 2011 revolution, including the killing of Qadhafi, have made little progress. Thousands of individuals remain in the custody of militia or government groups despite the absence of any formal trial or sentencing.

Libya's warring militias operate with little regard for civilian lives. Various armed groups have carried out indiscriminate shelling of civilian areas, abductions, torture, executions, and the destruction of property. The war's main battleground has been Benghazi, though fighting has taken place across the country. In 2016, eastern Libya saw a spate of kidnappings and other attacks targeting government officials, activists, and journalists. Fighting in Benghazi in 2016 resulted in many casualties, including of civilians, and widespread hardship. In the south, tribal clashes also resulted in casualties during the year.

The U.S. State Department has estimated that hundreds of people were killed in 2016 due to violent acts committed by extremist groups including IS, Ansar al-Sharia, and al-Qaida in the Islamic Maghreb (AQIM). In 2016, local armed forces, primarily from the city of Misrata and nominally affiliated with the UN-backed government, fought IS in the coastal city of Sirte, with some assistance from U.S. air strikes beginning in August, and had mostly dislodged IS fighters from the city by the year's end. However, IS maintained a presence in other parts of Libya, including around Benghazi and Derna.

Separately, General Haftar, who is seen as an anti-Islamist figure and enjoys backing from the United Arab Emirates and Egypt, strengthened his foothold over Libya's eastern region, particularly after the successful takeover of the Gulf of Sidra oil crescent in September 2016.

Libyans from certain tribes and communities—often those perceived as pro-Qadhafi—have faced discrimination, violence, and displacement since 2011. Migrant workers from sub-Saharan Africa have also been subject to discrimination and mistreatment, particularly at the hands of armed groups. The Tebu and Tuareg minorities in the south face discrimination.

Under Libya's penal code, sexual activity between members of the same sex is punishable by up to five years in prison. LGBT (lesbian, gay, bisexual, and transgender) people face severe discrimination and harassment, and have been targeted by militant groups.

G. Personal Autonomy and Individual Rights: 4 / 16

The 2011 constitutional declaration guarantees freedom of movement, but violence has disrupted normal activity in major cities. Airports in Benghazi, Tripoli, Sabha, and Misrata have been attacked and destroyed, severely limiting access to air travel. The UN Office for Humanitarian Affairs has estimated that 1.3 million people in Libya will need humanitarian assistance in 2017, including more than 313,000 who are internally displaced. Many others have reportedly sought safety in neighboring Tunisia and Egypt. Government and militia checkpoints also restrict movement within Libya, while poor security conditions more generally affect movement as well as access to healthcare, education, and work.

While Libyans have the right to own property and can start businesses, regulations and protections are not upheld in practice. Businesses and homes have been confiscated by militants, particularly in Libya's eastern regions and in Benghazi, and ongoing unrest has severely disrupted ordinary commerce.

Threats and harassment against women, especially female activists, are common. Forced labor, sexual exploitation, abuse in detention facilities, and starvation are widespread among migrants and refugees from sub-Saharan Africa and elsewhere, many of who are beholden to human traffickers. Libya lacks comprehensive laws criminalizing human trafficking, and the authorities have been either incapable of enforcing existing bans or complicit in trafficking activity. Traffickers have taken advantage of civil unrest to establish enterprises in which refugees and migrants are loaded into overcrowded boats that are abandoned in the Mediterranean Sea, where passengers hope to be rescued and taken to Europe. The voyages are often deadly.

Liechtenstein

Political Rights Rating: 2
Civil Liberties Rating: 1
Freedom Rating: 1.5
Freedom Status: Free
Electoral Democracy: Yes

Population: 40,000
Capital: Vaduz

Ten-Year Ratings Timeline For Year Under Review (Political Rights, Civil Liberties, Status)

Year Under Review	2007	2008	2009	2010	2011	2012	2013	2014	2015	2016
Rating	1,1,F	1,1,F	1,1,F	1,1,F	1,1,F	1,1,F	1,1,F	1,1,F	1,1,F	2,1,F

The country or territory displayed here received scores but no narrative report for this edition of *Freedom in the World*.

Lithuania

Political Rights Rating: 1
Civil Liberties Rating: 1
Freedom Rating: 1.0
Freedom Status: Free
Electoral Democracy: Yes

Population: 2,900,000
Capital: Vilnius

Ten-Year Ratings Timeline For Year Under Review (Political Rights, Civil Liberties, Status)

Year Under Review	2007	2008	2009	2010	2011	2012	2013	2014	2015	2016
Rating	1,1,F	1,1,F	1,1,F	1,1,F	1,1,F	1,1,F	1,1,F	1,1,F	1,1,F	1,1,F

Overview: Lithuania is an electoral democracy in which political rights and civil liberties are generally respected. However, corruption and income inequality are serious issues that often arouse public dissatisfaction with the government.

KEY DEVELOPMENTS IN 2016:

- Top officials from three major parties were implicated in separate bribery scandals.
- A perception of widespread corruption among the mainstream political parties contributed to a surge in support for the centrist Lithuanian Peasant and Green Union (LPGU), which won 56 seats in the 141-seat parliament in October's elections—the largest plurality achieved by a single party in two decades. It had held one seat in the legislature previously.

EXECUTIVE SUMMARY

High-profile corruption claims that emerged in 2016 raised questions about the trustworthiness of Lithuania's mainstream parties. Serious accusations of bribery were levied against Liberal Movement (LRLS) leader Eligijus Masiulis, who had been a potential candidate for prime minister but resigned from the party and the parliament in May; Vytautas Gapšys, one of the leaders of the Labor Party (DP), who was accused of taking a bribe from MG Baltics, the same firm implicated in the bribery claims against Masiulis; and Rolandas Paksas, the leader of the Order and Justice (TT) party, who was accused of taking a bribe from the owner of the prominent Lithuanian newspaper *Lietuvos Rytas*. The Lithuanian Special Investigation Service (STT) was investigating the cases at year's end.

The allegations proved beneficial to the opposition LPGU, which in 2016 elections saw its share of seats in the 141-member parliament rise to 56 from a single seat previously; its performance in the polls gave it the largest plurality seen in Lithuania in two decades. Voter turnout was low, at barely 50 percent in the first round and about 38 percent in the second, both of which were held in October. The LPGU in November formed a coalition government with the Social Democratic Party of Lithuania (LSDP).

The elections were considered free and fair, though the election commission faced criticism for delays in announcing the official results, which were linked to issues with new electronic infrastructure for the polls. While relatively few irregularities were reported, there was one notable case of vote buying, to benefit TT. In late October, the election commission stripped lawmaker Kestas Komskis of TT of his parliamentary mandate in connection with the events.

While residents of Lithuania enjoy a high level of economic freedom, inequality is a concern, and about 30 percent of the population remains at risk of poverty or social exclusion.

POLITICAL RIGHTS: 38 / 40

A. Electoral Process: 12 / 12

B. Political Pluralism and Participation: 16 / 16

C. Functioning of Government: 10 / 12

CIVIL LIBERTIES: 53 / 60

D. Freedom of Expression and Belief: 16 / 16

E. Associational and Organizational Rights: 11 / 12

F. Rule of Law: 13 / 16

G. Personal Autonomy and Individual Rights: 13 / 16

This country report has been abridged for *Freedom in the World 2017*. For background information on political rights and civil liberties in Lithuania, see *Freedom in the World 2016*.

Luxembourg

Political Rights Rating: 1
Civil Liberties Rating: 1
Freedom Rating: 1.0
Freedom Status: Free
Electoral Democracy: Yes

Population: 600,000
Capital: Luxembourg

Ten-Year Ratings Timeline For Year Under Review (Political Rights, Civil Liberties, Status)

Year Under Review	2007	2008	2009	2010	2011	2012	2013	2014	2015	2016
Rating	1,1,F	1,1,F	1,1,F	1,1,F	1,1,F	1,1,F	1,1,F	1,1,F	1,1,F	1,1,F

The country or territory displayed here received scores but no narrative report for this edition of *Freedom in the World*.

Macedonia

Political Rights Rating: 4
Civil Liberties Rating: 3
Freedom Rating: 3.5
Freedom Status: Partly Free
Electoral Democracy: No

Population: 2,100,000
Capital: Skopje

Ten-Year Ratings Timeline For Year Under Review (Political Rights, Civil Liberties, Status)

Year Under Review	2007	2008	2009	2010	2011	2012	2013	2014	2015	2016
Rating	3,3,PF	3,3,PF	3,3,PF	3,3,PF	3,3,PF	3,3,PF	3,3,PF	4,3,PF	4,3,PF	4,3,PF

Overview: Credible allegations of a massive, government-sponsored wiretapping and surveillance program that emerged in 2015 prompted a crisis that has paralyzed normal political activity and given way to regular antigovernment demonstrations. An internationally backed special prosecutor tasked with investigating the wiretapping scandal has made some progress, but faces interference.

KEY DEVELOPMENTS IN 2016:

- Prime Minister Nikola Gruevski resigned in January as part of an internationally brokered political deal that envisioned snap elections later in the year.
- Gruevski's Internal Macedonian Revolutionary Organization–Democratic Party for Macedonian National Unity (VMRO-DPMNE) narrowly won snap elections that were held in December after a series of delays. While an Organization for Security and Co-operation in Europe (OSCE) monitoring mission deemed the polls "competitive," they were marked by an atmosphere of mistrust, and serious irregularities were reported.
- Though it faced obstruction by police, domestic prosecutors, and the president, a special prosecutor appointed by local and international authorities to investigate the revelations of the wiretapping program made some progress.
- In December, the Public Revenue Office said it would increase financial inspections of nongovernmental organizations (NGOs), in what was seen as an attempt to place pressure on groups critical of the VMRO-DPMNE.

EXECUTIVE SUMMARY

Following the 2015 revelation of a massive wiretapping and surveillance program—allegedly directed by Gruevski's administration and operated by the secret service—Macedonia saw months of protests against the VMRO-DPMNE–led government and the wholesale interruption of normal parliamentary activity. The intervention of U.S. and European mediators somewhat stabilized the situation, and eventually led to the resignation of Gruevski in a January 2016 deal that envisioned snap elections being held by mid-April. The elections were twice delayed after the opposition indicated it would not participate, citing excessive government influence on the media and problems with voter rolls. Following a June 2016 deal designed to address opposition concerns, the elections were finally held in December, and resulted in a narrow VMRO-DPMNE victory. However, domestic monitors raised serious issues with the voter rolls. An OSCE monitoring mission voiced similar concerns, noted instances of voter intimidation, and concluded that the polls were marked by "a lack of public trust in institutions and the political establishment." No new government had been formed at year's end.

Meanwhile, police and domestic prosecutors obstructed the work of a special prosecutor appointed to investigate the wiretapping scandal. In April 2016, the president pardoned dozens of people being investigated. The move prompted mass protests, and the pardons were later rescinded.

The country's crisis of governance continued to spur civil society activity in 2016, with a wave of civil disobedience by opposition supporters being dubbed the "Colorful Revolution," after the protesters' propensity to pelt government buildings and riot police with paint-filled balloons.

Separately, there has been little headway in illuminating the events of April and May 2015, when clashes between government security forces and purported ethnic Albanian militants at a border crossing and the town of Kumanovo left at least 20 gunmen and police dead. Allegations that the VMRO-DMPNE somehow orchestrated the events in order to draw attention away from the wiretapping scandal continue to hang over the incidents, which served as a worrying reminder of cleavages that exist between the country's ethnic Albanian minority and ethnic Macedonia majority. However, antigovernment demonstrations have been multiethnic, and notably, in December, two ethnic Albanians were elected to the legislature as members of a party traditionally dominated by ethnic Macedonians.

POLITICAL RIGHTS: 21 / 40 (− 1)

A. Electoral Process: 6 / 12

Members of the unicameral, 120-seat Assembly are elected to four-year terms by proportional representation. The Assembly elects the prime minister, who holds most executive power. The president is elected to a five-year term through a direct popular vote. Most postindependence elections have met international standards, although following the outbreak of the wiretapping scandal in 2015, Macedonia authorities struggled to organize the snap polls mandated by an internationally brokered political deal. They were finally held in December 2016, following another internationally backed political deal designed to address opposition concerns about voter rolls and media coverage of the campaign.

Days ahead of the polls, domestic election monitors noted that the names of so-called phantom voters remained on electoral rolls, casting doubt on the legitimacy of the entire exercise, and the subsequent results. While the elections took place on December 11, the opposition demanded a recount, and final results were not released until late in the month. The VMRO-DPMNE–led bloc won 51 seats in the assembly (down from 61 previously), while the opposition coalition led by the Social Democratic Union of Macedonia (SDSM) secured 49. The remaining 20 seats were split among four ethnic Albanian parties, with the VMRO-DPMNE–aligned Democratic Union for Integration (DUI) winning 10 seats, the upstart Besa Movement winning five, the newly formed Alliance for Albanians (AS) winning three, and the Democratic Party of Albanians (DPA) winning two. A new government had not yet formed by year's end. An OSCE monitoring mission deemed the polls "competitive," but said issues with the media and voter rolls had "yet to be addressed in a sustainable manner," noted instances of voter intimidation, and concluded that the polls were marked by "a lack of public trust in institutions and the political establishment."

Some of the wiretapped conversations released by the opposition in 2015 appeared to indicate that senior VMRO-DPMNE figures had engaged in election fraud during both the 2013 local and 2014 parliamentary elections, and these concerns likewise clouded the 2016 results. The parliament adopted a number of changes to the electoral code in November 2015 as part of an EU-backed political agreement, addressing key opposition concerns.

B. Political Pluralism and Participation: 10 / 16

The constitution protects the right to establish and join political parties. The center-right VMRO-DPMNE has won every parliamentary election since 2006, ruling in coalition with a number of parties representing ethnic minorities. The left-leaning SDSM held power through much of the 1990s and early 2000s, and is currently the leading opposition party. It has boycotted the parliament on several occasions in recent years over claims of electoral fraud and issues related to the wiretap scandal.

Ethnic Albanians make up about 25 percent of the population. A political party representing Albanians has sat in each ruling coalition, and certain types of legislation must pass with a majority of legislators from both major ethnic groups in the Assembly. Notably, two incoming lawmakers with the traditionally Macedonian-dominated SDSM are Albanian, a new development in a party system that has been dominated by ethnic-based or nationalist options. Macedonians living abroad can elect up to three Assembly members.

Politically fraught violence between ethnic Macedonians and ethnic Albanians erupts occasionally, though there were no such incidents reported in 2016. Recent antigovernment protests have generally been multiethnic in character.

C. Functioning of Government: 5 / 12 (− 1)

The continuing political crisis has given rise to severe gridlock in democratic processes and the operations of elected officials. While mediation efforts by the United States and EU have eased tensions in the country, Macedonia is still fundamentally in crisis.

Corruption is a serious problem. While anticorruption legislation is in place, and measures to clarify party funding and prevent conflicts of interest have been strengthened, implementation is weak. Graft and misconduct are widespread in public procurement. The Public Prosecutor's Office for Organized Crime and Corruption suffers from low administrative capacity.

CIVIL LIBERTIES: 36 / 60 (+ 1)

D. Freedom of Expression and Belief: 10 / 16

The constitution provides for freedom of the press. However, Macedonian media are subject to political pressure and harassment, resulting in self-censorship. The arrest in April 2016 and continued detention of Zoran Božinovski, a reporter critical of the government, has drawn condemnation from local and international observers. Wiretap recordings released by the opposition in 2015 appeared to reveal conversations between high-level government functionaries and the staff of several major television stations—including the public broadcaster and Sitel, a private, progovernment television station with national reach—indicating that the government was directly influencing editorial policies. Internet access is unrestricted.

The constitution guarantees freedom of religion. A long-standing dispute between the breakaway Macedonian Orthodox Church and the canonically recognized Serbian Orthodox Church remains unresolved. Islamophobia is present in the rhetoric of politicians and in public discourse.

Although academic freedom is generally unrestricted, the education system is weak by European standards. Textbooks barely cover the postindependence period, primarily because ethnic Macedonians and ethnic Albanians interpret the 2001 civil conflict differently. Increasingly, schools are becoming ethnically segregated.

Space for free private discussion contracted in the wake of the opposition's credible allegations of widespread government wiretapping and monitoring of private citizens, journalists, politicians, and religious leaders.

E. Associational and Organizational Rights: 8 / 12

Constitutional guarantees of freedoms of assembly and association are generally respected. Mass antigovernment protests, led by student and opposition figures, continued throughout 2016. The protests have sometimes given way to property damage, and are typically monitored by riot police.

NGOs have generally operated freely but the VMRO-DPMNE has increasingly characterized groups that challenge it as enemies of the state. In December 2016, Macedonia's public revenue office announced that it would increase financial inspections of NGOs, in what was widely seen as an attempt to place pressure on critical groups.

Workers may organize and bargain collectively, though trade unions lack stable financing and skilled managers, and journalists have reportedly been fired for their union activities. The informal and grey economy is large, leaving many workers vulnerable to abuses by employers.

F. Rule of Law: 8 / 16 (+ 1)

While Macedonia has carried out comprehensive reforms of the judiciary over the past decade, fundamental problems remain, including concerns over the weak independence of the Constitutional Court. While the special prosecutor appointed to investigate the wiretap allegations has begun formally charging public officials with wrongdoing, movement remains slow and uneven, in part due to efforts to obstruct the office's operations. In April 2016, President Gjorge Ivanov ordered that the office cease operations and pardoned dozens of people it was investigating—most of whom were affiliated with the VMRO-DPMNE—prompting widespread protests. The pardons were later revoked. However, the Special Prosecutor's Office continued to face obstruction, including difficulties collecting evidence from police and in taking over cases from the Macedonian prosecutor's office.

While trials for the suspected militants behind the 2015 violence in Kumanovo have begun, many residents and civil society observers of the proceedings continued to express doubts as to the veracity of government claims, and the fairness of the trials themselves. No such violence was repeated in 2016.

Roma, ethnic Albanians, and other vulnerable groups face discrimination. Minority groups have criticized the ongoing Skopje 2014 urban development plan, arguing that its themes ignore their heritage and present a monoethnic image of the country. Rights groups and others have condemned Macedonian police for numerous instances of violence against refugees passing through Macedonia on their way to locations to the country's north.

A 2010 antidiscrimination law does not prohibit discrimination on the basis of sexual orientation or gender identity, and anti-LGBT (lesbian, gay, bisexual, and transgender) sentiment is widespread.

G. Personal Autonomy and Individual Rights: 10 / 16

Travel and movement are generally unrestricted. Membership in a party within the ruling coalition is often an informal precondition for employment in the public sector. While the government has streamlined procedures to launch a business, licensing fees can be prohibitively expensive. Unemployment has been estimated at about 27 percent, but the actual figure may be smaller given Macedonia's sizable shadow economy.

In 2014, the VMRO-DPMNE proposed a constitutional amendment that would narrow the definition of marriage, making it applicable only to a relationship between a man and a woman. The parliament voted to approve the amendment in January 2015, and took further steps to complicate the possibility of future civil-union legislation being enacted. LGBT issues and people, however, have gained increased visibility during the course of the ongoing antigovernment demonstrations.

While women in Macedonia enjoy the same legal rights as men, societal attitudes limit their participation in non-traditional roles, and women rarely participate in local politics. In Albanian Muslim areas, many women are subject to proxy voting by male relatives. In the December 2016 election, 38 women were elected to the legislature. Despite the ongoing implementation of a strategy against domestic violence, it remains a serious problem, as does the trafficking of women for forced labor and sex work.

Madagascar

Political Rights Rating: 3
Civil Liberties Rating: 4
Freedom Rating: 3.5
Freedom Status: Partly Free
Electoral Democracy: Yes

Population: 23,700,000
Capital: Antananarivo

Ten-Year Ratings Timeline For Year Under Review (Political Rights, Civil Liberties, Status)

Year Under Review	2007	2008	2009	2010	2011	2012	2013	2014	2015	2016
Rating	4,3,PF	4,3,PF	6,4,PF	6,4,PF	6,4,PF	6,4,PF	5,4,PF	4,4,PF	3,4,PF	3,4,PF

Overview: An unelected administration governed Madagascar for five years following a 2009 coup, but the country has since returned to electoral politics through presidential, parliamentary, and municipal elections. However, few governing bodies are truly independent from the president. Corruption and a lack of government accountability remain problematic. Independent journalists face pressure from authorities, and demonstrations are frequently banned or dispersed. The government has struggled to manage lawlessness in the southeast.

KEY DEVELOPMENTS IN 2016:

- The country adopted a new Communication Code that increased penalties for defamation.
- In October, the United Nations reported that nearly 850,000 people were in need of immediate humanitarian assistance due to a severe drought.
- Three people were killed and scores were injured in a grenade attack at the main Independence Day celebration in the capital.

EXECUTIVE SUMMARY

While Madagascar has returned to electoral politics since a 2009 coup, the country's political framework is constituted by a fragile arrangement of personal networks through which the administration of President Hery Rajaonarimampianina develops and implements policy. In April 2016, President Rajaonarimampianina appointed his third prime minister in three years in a chaotic process in which the previous prime minister learned of his dismissal only after the announcement of the new one was made. Meanwhile, opposition political movements continued to demand the president's resignation, while in May a sitting senator was arrested amid rumors of another coup attempt.

During the year, lawmakers approved, and Rajaonarimampianina promulgated, a new Communication Code that included several provisions that could be used to restrict media freedom. Though initially expected to lift older provisions that allowed jail terms for defamation of public officials, the new code increased the possible fines for defamation, and contained penalties for offenses including using media to discourage participation in national celebrations, and disseminating information harmful to the country's currency. It also allowed for the confiscation of equipment or the outright closure of press outfits deemed repeat violators of the new code.

Popular discontent increased in 2016, amid a stagnant economy and an unresponsive political system. Demonstrations against the presence of foreign mining companies and land expropriation, and against the new Communication Code, took place during the year. Many demonstrations were banned or dispersed by authorities, particularly those against the new press restrictions. Police sometimes used excessive force when breaking up anti-government gatherings.

Separately, at the Independence Day celebration in the capital in June, a grenade explosion killed three people and wounded over 90 in what authorities characterized as an act of political terrorism.

In October, the United Nations reported that nearly 850,000 people were in need of immediate humanitarian assistance due to a severe drought.

POLITICAL RIGHTS: 24 / 40

A. Electoral Process: 9 / 12

B. Political Pluralism and Participation: 10 / 16

C. Functioning of Government: 5 / 12

CIVIL LIBERTIES: 32 / 60

D. Freedom of Expression and Belief: 10 / 16

E. Associational and Organizational Rights: 8 / 12

F. Rule of Law: 6 / 16

G. Personal Autonomy and Individual Rights: 8 / 16

This country report has been abridged for *Freedom in the World 2017*. For background information on political rights and civil liberties in Madagascar, see *Freedom in the World 2016*.

Malawi

Political Rights Rating: 3
Civil Liberties Rating: 3
Freedom Rating: 3.0
Freedom Status: Partly Free
Electoral Democracy: Yes

Population: 17,200,000
Capital: Lilongwe

Ten-Year Ratings Timeline For Year Under Review (Political Rights, Civil Liberties, Status)

Year Under Review	2007	2008	2009	2010	2011	2012	2013	2014	2015	2016
Rating	4,4,PF	4,4,PF	3,4,PF	3,4,PF	3,4,PF	3,4,PF	3,4,PF	3,4,PF	3,3,PF	3,3,PF

Overview: Malawi holds regular elections and has undergone multiple transfers of power between political parties, though the changes were frequently a result of rifts among ruling elites rather than competition between distinct parties. Political rights and civil liberties are for the most part respected by the state. However, corruption is endemic, police brutality and arbitrary arrests are common, and discrimination and violence toward women, minority groups, and people with albinism remain problems.

KEY DEVELOPMENTS IN 2016:

- President Peter Mutharika remained abroad for a month with little explanation after attending the UN General Assembly in September, sparking speculation that he was ill or even dead. Upon his return, he criticized the media and opposition parties for spreading rumors.
- Three opposition lawmakers were charged with treason in February for their communications on social media. They remained free on bail.
- In November, the national ombudsman implicated senior officials in a corrupt scheme involving tractors intended for small-scale farmers.

EXECUTIVE SUMMARY

The opposition Malawi Congress Party (MCP) won three out of five parliament seats at stake in November 2016 by-elections, with the ruling Democratic Progressive Party (DPP) securing the other two. The Malawi Electoral Commission (MEC) had attempted to improve its performance ahead of the voting, relieving several officials of their duties in August in response to an audit that found alleged malfeasance, and implementing procedural reforms in October. Nevertheless, opposition candidates accused the DPP of disrupting their rallies, offering food gifts to voters, and using state funds for campaigning. An assistant to the vice president was accused of impersonating an MEC official during one of the by-elections.

Authorities took several actions that infringed on freedom of expression during the year. In December, the Malawi Communications Regulatory Authority (MCRA) fined a private radio station for what it deemed to be unbalanced media coverage, following an August interview the station conducted with an opposition legislator who was critical of the government. A man was arrested in February for throwing stones at a picture of Mutharika, and a student was arrested in March for insulting the president while travelling on public transportation. Three opposition lawmakers were arrested on treason charges in February for statements they made in a discussion group on the social media platform WhatsApp; they remained free on bail at year's end.

In a positive step, however, the parliament in December passed an access to information bill that received praise from media freedom advocates. The president was expected to sign the measure in early 2017.

The prosecution of the main suspects in the 2013 "Cashgate" corruption scandal continued to drag on in 2016. Meanwhile, in November, the national ombudsman published a report exposing another corruption scandal, known as "Tractorgate," in which the government sold off tractors that were meant to be distributed to farmers. High-level officials were identified as beneficiaries, including the parliament speaker, the foreign minister, and the president's chief of staff. The ombudsman reportedly received death threats during the investigation. In late December, the attorney general obtained a court order that effectively blocked implementation of the ombudsman's recommendations, temporarily shielding the officials implicated in the scandal.

Security forces repeatedly arrested protesters during the year. In March, more than a dozen youths were detained for an antigovernment demonstration in which they draped a coffin in the colors of the DPP. More than 30 students were arrested during student protests against tuition fee hikes in July and August; the protests eventually compelled the government to scale down the fee increases. In October, three activists were arrested for staging a protest over electricity blackouts. Separately, strikes remained common among public-sector workers, who often experience delays in their already low pay.

The killing and mutilation of people with albinism and a ritual cleansing practice that involves men being paid to have sex with young girls—both longtime problems rooted in cultural beliefs—came to the fore in 2016. President Mutharika called for additional efforts to address both issues. A law passed in July increased the penalties for albinism-related crimes. Child marriage also remained a problem despite a 2015 law setting the minimum age at 18, with experts noting that the legislation appeared to conflict with the constitution and customary law. About half of Malawian girls marry before the age of 18.

POLITICAL RIGHTS: 26 / 40 (− 1)

A. Electoral Process: 8 / 12

B. Political Pluralism and Participation: 12 / 16

C. Functioning of Government: 6 / 12 (-1)

CIVIL LIBERTIES: 37 / 60

D. Freedom of Expression and Belief: 13 / 16

E. Associational and Organizational Rights: 8 / 12

F. Rule of Law: 9 / 16

G. Personal Autonomy and Individual Rights: 7 / 16

This country report has been abridged for *Freedom in the World 2017*. For background information on political rights and civil liberties in Malawi, see *Freedom in the World 2016*.

Malaysia

Political Rights Rating: 4
Civil Liberties Rating: 4
Freedom Rating: 4.0
Freedom Status: Partly Free
Electoral Democracy: No

Population: 30,800,000
Capital: Kuala Lumpur

Ten-Year Ratings Timeline For Year Under Review (Political Rights, Civil Liberties, Status)

Year Under Review	2007	2008	2009	2010	2011	2012	2013	2014	2015	2016
Rating	4,4,PF	4,4,PF	4,4,PF	4,4,PF	4,4,PF	4,4,PF	4,4,PF	4,4,PF	4,4,PF	4,4,PF

Overview: Although Malaysia holds regular elections, it has been ruled by the same political coalition since independence in 1957. The coalition has maintained power by manipulating electoral districts, appealing to ethnic nationalism, and suppressing criticism through restrictive speech laws and politicized prosecutions of opposition leaders.

KEY DEVELOPMENTS IN 2016

- The coalition of civil society organizations and opposition parties known as Bersih (Clean) continued their campaign for electoral and other reforms with rallies in November across the country and abroad, including tens of thousands of people in the capital.
- The government's arrest of several key activists and organizers the day before the rally is the latest in a series of heavy-handed attempts to quell and silence civil society activism.
- Press freedom violations continue, including the shut down of independent news site the *Malaysian Insider* in March after the government ordered one of its reports to be blocked.
- In November, a court found opposition politician Rafizi Ramli guilty of disclosing state secrets after he made public the Auditor General's report on the 1MDB scandal.

EXECUTIVE SUMMARY

Malaysia holds regular elections, but it falls short of international standards. The political playing field is tilted toward the ruling party through measures such as gerrymandering of electoral districts, unequal candidate access to the media, and restrictions on campaigning, in addition to election day fraud. In noncampaign periods, opposition figures continue to face charges for sedition and other criminal offenses for criticizing the government or organizing demonstrations, and the government influences the judiciary for political ends. In November 2016, a court ruled against opposition politician Rafizi Ramli for making public a report on the ongoing 1MDB scandal. Prime Minister Najib Razak's mismanagement of and possible embezzlement from state development fund 1MDB has continued to be highly controversial domestically and internationally.

Tens of thousands of people congregated for the Bersih 5 rally in November in Kuala Lumpur, which built on four previous rallies over the past decade in favor of anticorruption reforms and other democratic improvements. This year, the government intensified its crackdown on the movement, raiding the offices of the organizers and arresting leaders and participants.

Religious minorities including Shiites face discriminatory treatment that is often ignored by the government, though some ruling party members articulate the need for a tolerant and inclusive form of Islam in Malaysia. Muslims are subject to Sharia (Islamic law), leading to unequal treatment particularly of women and LGBT persons. Free expression faces a range of restrictions, many of which have recently spread to the internet. The government can suspend or revoke publishing licenses and censorship is common. The government engages in legal harassment of critical voices using a range of laws at its disposal.

POLITICAL RIGHTS: 18 / 40

A. Electoral Process: 6 / 12

The paramount ruler, the monarch and titular head of state, is elected for five-year terms by fellow hereditary rulers from nine of Malaysia's 13 states. A new king, Sultan Muhammad V, was sworn in on December 13, 2016. The role of the king is largely ceremonial.

Executive power is vested in the prime minister and cabinet. The leader of the coalition that wins a plurality of seats in legislative elections becomes the prime minister. The upper house of the bicameral Parliament, the Senate, consists of 44 members appointed by the king and 26 members elected by the 13 state legislatures, serving three-year terms. The House of Representatives, or Dewan Rakyat, has 222 seats; its members are elected by popular vote at least every five years.

The ruling National Front (BN) coalition won the 2013 parliamentary elections, capturing 133 seats in the lower house despite receiving only 47 percent of the overall popular vote. The opposition and observers accused the BN of electoral fraud, citing irregularities such as phantom voting and power outages in vote-tallying centers in a number of constituencies that opposition parties hoped to win. The Election Commission is frequently accused of manipulating electoral rolls and gerrymandering districts to aid the ruling coalition, and the Registrar of Societies arbitrarily decides which parties can participate in politics. Although a government committee issued recommendations for electoral reforms in 2012, there is continuing skepticism over their implementation.

B. Political Pluralism and Participation: 7 / 16

The BN and its pre-1973 predecessor organization have governed Malaysia since independence in 1957. Most of its constituent parties have an ethnic or regional base, including the dominant United Malays National Organization (UMNO) and the United Traditional Bumiputera Party, whose stronghold is in Sarawak. The delineation of electoral districts gives uneven voting power to ethnic Malays and other indigenous groups, especially those in rural areas, at the expense of groups considered more likely to vote for the opposition, such as city dwellers and ethnic minorities.

In addition to the skewed electoral system, opposition parties face obstacles such as unequal access to the media, restrictions on campaigning and freedom of assembly, and politicized prosecutions. In recent years, politicians and political activists have increasingly been charged with sedition and other criminal offenses for criticizing the government or organizing demonstrations. In November 2016, a court found opposition politician Rafizi Ramli guilty of disclosing state secrets after he made public the Auditor General's report on the 1MDB scandal, a ruling condemned by human rights groups. People's Justice Party (PKR) leader Anwar Ibrahim has been dogged by claims that he "sodomized" a male aide in 2008, a charge seen as politically motivated. He was acquitted in 2012, but the Court of Appeal reversed that verdict and sentenced him to five years in prison in 2014. The Federal Court, Malaysia's highest court, confirmed the sentence in 2015, and in December 2016 a five-judge panel denied his appeal for a review.

C. Functioning of Government: 5 / 12

Elected officials determine and implement government policy, but the unfair electoral framework weakens their legitimacy, and corruption provides a strong incentive to serve partisan patronage networks rather than the public interest.

Government favoritism and blurred distinctions between public and private enterprises create conditions conducive to corruption. Officials regularly move back and forth between the private and public sectors, fostering opportunities for collusion and graft. Political parties are allowed to own or have financial holdings in corporate enterprises. Several government-affiliated organizations have been involved in scandals.

The corruption scandal involving the state-owned 1MDB development fund is ongoing. The U.S. Department of Justice announced in July 2016 that it would seize U.S. assets amounting to more than $1 billion from people connected to Prime Minister Razak in a move intended to stem illicit finance and money laundering.

Meanwhile, Najib worked to suppress scrutiny within the government and his own party. In 2015, he replaced the attorney general and fired cabinet ministers, including Deputy Prime Minister Muhyiddin Yassin, who had been critical of Najib's handling of the scandal. Najib then promoted four members of a parliamentary committee investigating 1MDB to his cabinet, temporarily halting the committee's work.

CIVIL LIBERTIES: 26 / 60 (− 1)

D. Freedom of Expression and Belief: 7 / 16

Freedom of expression is constitutionally guaranteed but restricted in practice. A 2012 amendment to the Printing Presses and Publications Act retains the home minister's authority to suspend or revoke publishing licenses but allows judicial review of such decisions. Most private publications are controlled by parties or businesses allied with the BN, as are most private television stations, which generally censor programming according to government guidelines. State outlets reflect government views. Books and films are directly censored or banned for profanity, violence, and political and religious content.

The internet is an outlet for some free discussion and the exposure of political corruption, but the Malaysian Communication and Multimedia Commission (MCMC) monitors websites and can order the removal of material considered provocative or subversive. A 2012 amendment to the 1950 Evidence Act holds owners and editors of websites, providers of web-hosting services, and owners of computers or mobile devices accountable for information published through their services or property. The government engages in legal harassment of critical voices, charging them under defamation laws, the Official Secrets Act, and the Sedition Act—all of which include imprisonment as a possible penalty. In March 2016, an independent Malaysian news site, the *Malaysian Insider*, shut down. Though officially for administrative reason, the closure came just after the MCMC ordered the site blocked in response to a report it published claiming that the local antigraft agency had sufficient evidence to bring criminal charges against Razak.

Political satire is also heavily regulated by the Communications and Multimedia Act (CMA), and transgressors may face imprisonment and/or large fines for communication that is "obscene, indecent, false, menacing or offensive in character with intent to annoy, abuse, threaten or harass another person." In June 2016, Malaysian artist Fahmi Reza was charged under the CMA and investigated for sedition after he posted a caricature of Razak online. The editors and cofounders of the news website Malaysiakini were charged in November under the CMA, with a pending sentence of up to one year in jail.

While some members of the BN government continue to articulate the need for a tolerant and inclusive form of Islam in Malaysia, religious freedom is restricted. Ethnic Malays are defined under the constitution as Muslims. Practicing a version of Islam other than Sunni Islam is prohibited, and Shiites face discrimination. Muslim children and civil servants are required to receive religious education using government-approved curriculums and instructors. Proselytizing among Muslims by other religious groups is prohibited, and a 2007 ruling by the Federal Court effectively made it impossible for Muslims to have their conversions to other faiths recognized by the state. Non-Muslims are not able to build houses of worship as easily as Muslims, and the state retains the right to demolish unregistered religious statues and houses of worship.

Teachers and students espousing antigovernment views or engaging in political activity are subject to disciplinary action under the Universities and University Colleges Act (UUCA) of 1971.

Open and free private discussion has been undermined in recent years by increasing use of sedition and other charges to suppress critical speech, the ban on non-Muslims' use of the word "Allah," and growing state enforcement of conservative social norms.

E. Associational and Organizational Rights: 5 / 12 (− 1)

Freedoms of assembly and association are limited on the grounds of maintaining security and public order. Street protests are prohibited, with high fines for noncompliance. The law delineates 21 public places where assemblies cannot be held—including within 50 meters of houses of worship, schools, and hospitals—and prohibits persons under the age of 15 from attending any public assembly.

Leading up to the Bersih 5.0 rally in November in Kuala Lumpur and other cities that pushed for electoral and anticorruption reforms, the government intensified its previous crackdown on Bersih activists, raiding the offices of the organizers and arresting the chairperson and secretariat manager. The police also seized computers, mobile phones, and other documents. Other activists were arrested under Penal Code provisions criminalizing rioting. The government banned Bersih in 2015 after it organized similar mass demonstrations.

The Societies Act of 1996 defines a society as any association of seven or more people, excluding schools, businesses, and trade unions. Societies must be approved and registered by the government, which has refused or revoked registrations for political reasons. Numerous nongovernmental organizations (NGOs) operate in Malaysia, but some international human rights organizations are forbidden from forming local branches. The government is investigating many NGOs, including Bersih 2.0, for accepting foreign funds on the grounds that foreign intervention might destabilize democracy.

Most Malaysian workers can join trade unions, but the law contravenes international guidelines by restricting unions to representing workers in a single or similar trade. The director general of trade unions can refuse or withdraw registration arbitrarily. Collective bargaining is limited, as is the right to strike.

F. Rule of Law: 5 / 16

Judicial independence is compromised by extensive executive influence. Arbitrary or politically motivated verdicts are common, as seen in the convictions of Anwar Ibrahim in 1999, 2000, and 2014 on charges of corruption and sodomy. Malaysia's secular legal system is based on English common law. However, Muslims are subject to Sharia (Islamic law), the interpretation of which varies regionally, and the constitution's Article 121 stipulates that all matters related to Islam should be heard in Sharia courts. This results in vastly different treatment of Muslims and non-Muslims regarding "moral" and family law issues.

Allegations of torture and abuse, including deaths, in police custody continue to be reported, and a number of criminal offenses can be punished with caning. The 2012 Security Offences (Special Measures) Act allows police to detain anyone for up to 28 days without judicial review for broadly defined "security offenses," and suspects may be held for 48 hours before being granted access to a lawyer. The government used the act to briefly detain the leader of Bersih 2.0 in November 2016. A 2013 amendment to the Prevention of Crime Act (PCA), a law ostensibly aimed at combating organized crime, allows a five-member board to order the detention of individuals listed by the Home Ministry for renewable two-year terms without trial or legal representation. The 2015 Prevention of Terrorism Act (POTA) together with the National Security Council (NSC) Act from the same year gives the NSC—led by the prime minister—wide powers of arrest, search, and seizure without a warrant in areas deemed as security risks and within the pretext of countering terrorism. The NSC Act entered into force in August 2016. Government critics and opposition members argue that these laws widen government's power to reintroduce indefinite detention without trial and could be misused to undermine human rights and democracy.

Although the constitution provides for equal treatment of all citizens, it grants a "special position" to ethnic Malays and other indigenous people, known collectively as *bumiputera.*

The government maintains programs intended to boost the economic status of bumiputera, who receive preferential treatment in areas including property ownership, higher education, civil service jobs, business affairs, and government contracts.

LGBT (lesbian, gay, bisexual, and transgender) Malaysians face widespread discrimination and harassment. Same-sex sexual relations are punishable by up to 20 years in prison under the penal code, and some states apply their own penalties to Muslims under Sharia statutes. The Ministries of Health and Education conduct campaigns to "prevent, overcome, and correct" symptoms of homosexuality in children, while the Ministry of Information has banned television and radio shows depicting gay characters. The Malaysian Islamic Development Department operates camps to "rehabilitate" transgender Muslims. In July 2016, the Kuala Lumpur High Court ordered the National Registration Department (NRD) to update a transgender man's identity card to reflect his gender identity and chosen name. The decision has been lauded by LGBT activists as it "gives new hope" for the trans community in the country.

G. Personal Autonomy and Individual Rights: 9 / 16

Citizens are generally free to travel within and outside of Malaysia, as well as to change residence and employment. Malaysia is recognized as having a vibrant private business sector. However, professional and business opportunities and access to higher education are affected by regulations and practices favoring ethnic Malays and those with connections to political elites. Bribery is common in the private sector, and Malaysia ranks second on the *Economist*'s list of countries with the most crony capitalism.

Women are underrepresented in politics, the civil service, and professional fields such as law, medicine, banking, and business. Violence against women remains a serious problem. Muslim women are legally disadvantaged because their family grievances are heard in Sharia courts, where men are favored in matters including inheritance and divorce, and women's testimony is not given equal weight.

Foreign household workers are often subject to exploitation and abuse by employers. An estimated two million foreigners work illegally in various industries and are vulnerable to forced labor and sexual abuse. If arrested and found guilty of immigration offenses, they can be caned and detained indefinitely pending deportation. Legislation passed in 2015 granted greater rights and protections to human trafficking victims, but implementation remains problematic.

Maldives

Political Rights Rating: 5 ↓
Civil Liberties Rating: 5
Freedom Rating: 5.0
Freedom Status: Partly Free
Electoral Democracy: No

Population: 400,000
Capital: Malé

Ratings Change: The Maldives' political rights rating declined from 4 to 5 due to the systematic repression of the opposition and the emergence of a massive corruption case involving the improper lease and sale of islands and lagoons, in which senior officials have been implicated.

Ten-Year Ratings Timeline For Year Under Review (Political Rights, Civil Liberties, Status)

Year Under Review	2007	2008	2009	2010	2011	2012	2013	2014	2015	2016
Rating	6,5,NF	4,4,PF	3,4,PF	3,4,PF	3,4,PF	5,4,PF	4,4,PF	4,4,PF	4,5,NF	5,5,PF

Overview: Following several decades of rule by former President Maumoon Abdul Gayoom, the Maldives held its first multiparty presidential election in 2008. However, democratic gains have been reversed in recent years amid a severe crackdown on the opposition and the introduction of laws restricting speech and assembly. Widespread financial and judicial corruption has further eroded public confidence in the government.

KEY DEVELOPMENTS

- In August, the parliament recriminalized defamation and imposed new restrictions on the right to assemble freely.
- Former president Mohamed Nasheed was granted asylum in the United Kingdom, and in June announced the establishment of a new opposition body. The group was promptly declared illegal and its activities in Maldives were suppressed.
- Several opposition figures were charged with or convicted of security-related offenses, including terrorism.
- Senior officials were implicated in the embezzlement of more than 1.2 billion rufiyaa (US$79 million) from the state-run tourism office.

EXECUTIVE SUMMARY

The administration of President Abdulla Yameen continued to suppress the political opposition through the enactment and enforcement of harsh restrictions on free speech and assembly, and through the manipulation of political processes including election timelines and the registration of opposition party members.

In May 2016, former president Nasheed—whose 2015 arrest, flawed trial, and conviction on terrorism-related charges sent shockwaves through the political landscape—was granted asylum by the United Kingdom, where he had been permitted to travel to receive medical treatment. In June, Nasheed announced the establishment of a new opposition body, the Maldives United Opposition (MUO), which took the form of a shadow cabinet and whose stated aim was to remove Yameen through lawful mechanisms and restore democratic rule. Nasheed took an advisory role in the body.

Maldivian authorities promptly declared the MUO illegal and its rallies in the Maldives were dispersed by police, some of whom reportedly removed their nametags as they moved against the demonstrators. MUO spokesperson Ahmed Mahloof, who is also a member of parliament, was arrested in July while promoting a MUO rally; he remained in jail at year's end after being convicted of police obstruction and handed two sentences totaling nearly 11 months. Additionally, in October MUO deputy leader Ali Waheed, who is also chairperson of the opposition Maldivian Democratic Party (MDP) and who lived in exile in the United Kingdom, was charged with terrorism, reportedly in connection with his participation in a 2015 mass protest during which participants called for the release of detained opposition figures, and had seen clashes between participants and police. Separately, the leader of the Islamist Adhaalath Party, Imran Abdulla, in February was convicted of terrorism-related charges involving his participation in the same protest, and he received a sentence of 12 years.

The courts and Election Commission (EC) also announced decisions that benefitted the ruling Progressive Party of Maldives (PPM) during the year. In November, the EC deregistered almost half of all MDP members, citing their failure to adhere to a law requiring them to submit their fingerprints to it. In December, a civil court ruled that the EC must postpone local council elections set for January 2017 because the ruling party, embroiled in a leadership dispute, was not sufficiently prepared for them.

Meanwhile, the biggest corruption scandal in the country's history came to light in 2016, when senior officials were implicated in the embezzlement of more than 1.2 billion rufiyaa (US$79 million) from the state-owned Maldives Marketing and Public Relations Corporation (MMPRC); the scandal involved the improper lease and sale of islands and lagoons. Former vice president Ahmed Adeeb and two others were convicted on corruption charges in relation to the scandal and issued jail sentences ranging between two and eight years. Whistleblower Gasim Abdul Kareem, who helped expose the corruption and was consequently convicted in a closed trial of data theft and illegal disclosure of information, was in released in November, with authorities ruling that he had served his eight-month sentence while in pretrial detention.

In August, the parliament approved and Yameen ratified new legislation criminalizing and raising fines for defamation to up to 2 million rufiyaa (US$130,000). Those who fail to pay the fines can be jailed for up to six months. Several media outlets were forced to close during the year following decisions by the courts or by regulators, prompting alarm among press freedom advocates. Also in August, the parliament approved and Yameen ratified a new law mandating that organizers of protests, marches, and other gatherings either obtain prior written permission from the police for the event, or be held only in special areas designated by the Ministry of Home Affairs.

In October, the Maldives quit the Commonwealth after facing scrutiny from the body over its failure to implement judicial and other reforms, reflecting a worrying disengagement from the international community.

POLITICAL RIGHTS: 17 / 40 (− 2)

A. Electoral Process: 7 / 12

B. Political Pluralism and Participation: 5 / 16 (− 1)

C. Functioning of Government: 5 / 12 (− 1)

CIVIL LIBERTIES: 23 / 60 (− 1)

D. Freedom of Expression and Belief: 5 / 16 (− 1)

E. Associational and Organizational Rights: 5 / 12

F. Rule of Law: 6 / 16

G. Personal Autonomy and Individual Rights: 7 / 16

This country report has been abridged for *Freedom in the World 2017*. For background information on political rights and civil liberties in the Maldives, see *Freedom in the World 2016*.

Mali

Political Rights Rating: 5
Civil Liberties Rating: 4
Freedom Rating: 4.5
Freedom Status: Partly Free
Electoral Democracy: No

Population: 17,300,000
Capital: Bamako

Ten-Year Ratings Timeline For Year Under Review (Political Rights, Civil Liberties, Status)

Year Under Review	2007	2008	2009	2010	2011	2012	2013	2014	2015	2016
Rating	2,3,F	2,3,F	2,3,F	2,3,F	2,3,F	7,5,NF	5,4,PF	5,4,PF	5,4,PF	5,4,PF

Overview: Mali experienced a political transition away from authoritarian rule beginning in the early 1990s, and gradually built up its democratic institutions for about 20 years. However, the country displayed characteristics of state fragility along the way that eventually contributed to a 2012 military coup, and a rebellion in northern Mali that erupted the same year. Though constitutional rule was restored and a peace agreement signed in the north, the events have left an enduring situation of insecurity.

KEY DEVELOPMENTS IN 2016:

- Fighting among militant groups persisted in northern and central Mali, hindering the delivery of basic services, interfering with political activities including the year's local elections, and undermining the rule of law in the affected areas.
- Protests in Kidal in April and Gao in July culminated in deadly confrontations between demonstrators and UN peacekeeping forces and Malian security forces, respectively.
- In September, the parliament passed a bill to amend the electoral code, despite criticism from opposition parties that the provisions favored established parties and were thus undemocratic.
- Local elections were held in most of the country's communes in November, despite objections and boycotts by opposition parties and other groups.

EXECUTIVE SUMMARY

In 2016, Mali continued to struggle with recovery from the rebellion in the north, which erupted in 2012 and was led by Tuareg rebels but complicated by the involvement of Islamist militants. A 2015 peace agreement, negotiated under the auspices of the United Nations and Algeria, called for the creation of regional elected bodies but stopped short of establishing federalism for northern Mali, which was the rebels' main demand. In 2016, its implementation continued to be delayed, and violence among various armed groups, including multiple Islamist militant factions that were not involved in the peace process, continued in northern and, increasingly, in central Mali. The violence hindered the delivery of basic services, interfered with political activities including the year's local elections, and undermined the rule of law in the affected areas.

The government held local elections in most of the country's 703 communes in November 2016, though voting was canceled in 58 northern and central communes for security reasons, and some opposition parties and militant groups that had signed the 2015 peace agreement called for the polls to be delayed, citing inadequate preparations, instability, or the risk of electoral fraud. Nevertheless, the vote was generally considered credible in regions where it was held, despite some reports of violence and intimidation.

In September 2016, parliament passed a bill to amend the electoral code, despite complaints by opposition parties that the provisions favored candidates from major parties. The amendments require every candidate for president to collect the signatures of at least 10 deputies or 5 municipal councilors from each region, as well as from Bamako. They also fixed the deposit amount required of presidential candidates at 25 million CFA francs ($42,000) rather than 10 million ($17,000), as provided by the old electoral law.

Corruption remains a major problem. In August, the Malian government announced that it had identified 13,000 nonexistant or irregular government employees; Information Minister Mountaga Tall said their removal from the government payrolls would save approximately $50 million.

The constitution guarantees freedom of assembly, but the risk of violence during public gatherings persists, especially in northern and central Mali. In April 2016, a protest in Kidal that followed French forces' detention of people suspected of having links to regional militants culminated in a confrontation with UN peacekeeping forces, and two demonstrators were killed. In July, Malian forces in the northern city of Gao fired into a demonstration against the installation of interim local authorities, killing three people and wounding at least 31 others.

Separately, in late November, the trial of Amadou Sanogo—the former army captain who staged a military coup in Mali in 2012—and 16 codefendants began on charges related to the abduction and killing of killing 21 soldiers. The trial was soon adjourned until 2017.

Conditions in northern Mali have left many refugees unable or unwilling to return. According to the United Nations, there were more than 138,000 Malian refugees outside the country as of December 2016, and more than 36,000 people displaced inside the country as of October 2016.

POLITICAL RIGHTS: 17 / 40

A. Electoral Process: 6 / 12

B. Political Pluralism and Participation: 7 / 16

C. Functioning of Government: 4 / 12

CIVIL LIBERTIES: 28 / 60

D. Freedom of Expression and Belief: 12 / 16

E. Associational and Organizational Rights: 6 / 12

F. Rule of Law: 6 / 16

G. Personal Autonomy and Individual Rights: 4 / 16

Explanatory Note: This country report has been abridged for *Freedom in the World 2017.* For background information on political rights and civil liberties in Mali, see *Freedom in the World 2016.*

Malta

Political Rights Rating: 1
Civil Liberties Rating: 1
Freedom Rating: 1.0
Freedom Status: Free
Electoral Democracy: Yes

Population: 400,000
Capital: Valletta

Ten-Year Ratings Timeline For Year Under Review (Political Rights, Civil Liberties, Status)

Year Under Review	2007	2008	2009	2010	2011	2012	2013	2014	2 015	2016
Rating	1,1,F	1,1,F	1,1,F	1,1,F	1,1,F	1,1,F	1,1,F	1,1,F	1,1,F	1,1,F

The country or territory displayed here received scores but no narrative report for this edition of *Freedom in the World*.

Marshall Islands

Political Rights Rating: 1
Civil Liberties Rating: 1
Freedom Rating: 1.0
Freedom Status: Free
Electoral Democracy: Yes

Population: 60,000
Capital: Majuro

Ten-Year Ratings Timeline For Year Under Review (Political Rights, Civil Liberties, Status)

Year Under Review	2007	2008	2009	2010	2011	2012	2013	2014	2015	2016
Rating	1,1,F	1,1,F	1,1,F	1,1,F	1,1,F	1,1,F	1,1,F	1,1,F	1,1,F	1,1,F

The country or territory displayed here received scores but no narrative report for this edition of *Freedom in the World*.

Mauritania

Political Rights Rating: 6
Civil Liberties Rating: 5
Freedom Rating: 5.5
Freedom Status: Not Free
Electoral Democracy: No

Population: 4,200,000
Capital: Nouakchott

Ten-Year Ratings Timeline For Year Under Review (Political Rights, Civil Liberties, Status)

Year Under Review	2007	2008	2009	2010	2011	2012	2013	2014	2015	2016
Rating	4,4,PF	6,5,NF	6,5,NF	6,5,NF	6,5,NF	6,5,NF	6,5,NF	6,5,NF	6,5,NF	6,5,NF

Overview: The current leadership in Mauritania came to power in 2008 through a military coup. It has since confirmed its position in flawed elections that were boycotted by the main opposition parties. The government has adopted a number of laws ostensibly meant to address the problem of institutionalized slavery and discrimination, but it continues to arrest antislavery activists and threaten bloggers who criticize the system with punishments including the death penalty. Corruption linked to extractive industries also remains a concern.

KEY DEVELOPMENTS IN 2016:

- In April, an appellate court upheld a 2014 death sentence against Mohamed Cheikh Ould Mohamed M'Kheitir, a blogger who was convicted of apostasy for posting an article in which he criticized the use of Islam to justify social discrimination in the country. An appeal to the Supreme Court was pending at year's end.
- In May, Biram Dah Abeid and Bilal Ramdhane, two leaders of the antislavery Initiative for the Resurgence of the Abolitionist Movement in Mauritania (IRA Mauritania), were released from prison after serving 20 months of a two-year sentence.
- Thirteen other antislavery activists were arrested after a protest and sentenced to prison terms of up to 15 years in June and July. The sentences, for offenses such as rebellion and membership in an unregistered organization, were significantly reduced on appeal in November, and all but three were released by the end of the year. Protests demanding the release of the activists had been violently dispersed by police.

EXECUTIVE SUMMARY

In September and October 2016, the government organized a dialogue with political parties and civil society groups to discuss major institutional reforms as well as social and political grievances. Mainstream opposition parties refused to participate in the event, adhering to a boycott strategy that had led them to sit out parliamentary and presidential elections in 2013 and 2014. The opposition considered President Mohamed Ould Abdel Aziz's regime to be illegitimate due to its origins in the 2008 coup and its disrespect for civil liberties and the rule of law. Nevertheless, the dialogue produced plans for constitutional amendments that would eliminate the indirectly elected Senate and create elected regional councils, among other changes.

While many Mauritanians welcomed the proposed reforms, others voiced concern that the real motive behind the constitutional initiative was to lift presidential term limits and allow Abdel Aziz to seek a third term.

Restrictions on civil liberties persisted throughout 2016, as the authorities continued to jail antislavery activists and harass journalists and bloggers who reported on politically sensitive topics.

POLITICAL RIGHTS: 9 / 40

A. Electoral Process: 3 / 12

B. Political Pluralism and Participation: 2 / 16

C. Functioning of Government: 4 / 12

CIVIL LIBERTIES: 21 / 60

D. Freedom of Expression and Belief: 9 / 16

E. Associational and Organizational Rights: 4 / 12

F. Rule of Law: 4 / 16

G. Personal Autonomy and Individual Rights: 4 / 16

This country report has been abridged for *Freedom in the World 2017*. For background information on political rights and civil liberties in Mauritania, see *Freedom in the World 2016*.

Mauritius

Political Rights Rating: 1
Civil Liberties Rating: 2
Freedom Rating: 1.5
Freedom Status: Free
Electoral Democracy: Yes

Population: 1,300,000
Capital: Port Louis

Ten-Year Ratings Timeline For Year Under Review (Political Rights, Civil Liberties, Status)

Year Under Review	2007	2008	2009	2010	2011	2012	2013	2014	2015	2016
Rating	1,2,F	1,2,F	1,2,F	1,2,F	1,2,F	1,2,F	1,2,F	1,2,F	1,2,F	1,2,F

The country or territory displayed here received scores but no narrative report for this edition of *Freedom in the World*.

Mexico

Political Rights Rating: 3
Civil Liberties Rating: 3
Freedom Rating: 3.0
Freedom Status: Partly Free
Electoral Democracy: Yes

Population: 128,600,000
Capital: Mexico City

Ten-Year Ratings Timeline For Year Under Review (Political Rights, Civil Liberties, Status)

Year Under Review	2007	2008	2009	2010	2011	2012	2013	2014	2 015	2016
Rating	2,3,F	2,3,F	2,3,F	3,3,PF	3,3,PF	3,3,PF	3,3,PF	3,3,PF	3,3,PF	3,3,PF

Overview: Mexico has been an electoral democracy since 2000, and alternation in power between the leading parties is routine at both the federal and state levels. However, the country suffers from severe rule-of-law deficits that limit full citizen enjoyment of political rights and civil liberties. Violence perpetrated by organized criminals, corruption among government officials, human rights abuses by both state and nonstate actors, and a climate of impunity are among the most visible of Mexico's many governance challenges.

KEY DEVELOPMENTS IN 2016

- Corruption accusations against government officials, particularly at the state level, contributed to multiple losses for the ruling Institutional Revolutionary Party (PRI) in gubernatorial elections in June.

- Little progress was made in the investigation of the 2014 disappearance of 43 students, an event that continues to generate outrage and protests. In April, international investigators released a report questioning key elements of the government's narrative.
- Criminal violence rose sharply during the year, and by October, homicide cases had reached their highest levels since the current government took office in late 2012.

EXECUTIVE SUMMARY

The administration of President Enrique Peña Nieto, head of the Institutional Revolutionary Party (PRI), began its term in December 2012 with a promising set of reforms accompanied by slowing homicide rates, generating optimism about Mexico's economic and social direction. However, starting in 2014 the government's narrative of progress has been undermined by corruption scandals and rights abuses. The problems continued in 2016, with an increase in homicide rates, corruption scandals implicating high-level PRI officials, and tension with international rights observers over the government's investigation of the 2014 disappearance of 43 college students in Iguala, Guerrero.

The results of gubernatorial elections in 12 states in June illustrated the effects of mounting corruption scandals involving government officials. PRI candidates lost races in several states in which incumbents had been accused of graft, including the populous states of Veracruz and Chihuahua; notably, the elections also marked the first time in the PRI's history it lost the governorship of Veracruz, as well as those of Quintana Roo and Tamaulipas. In the fall, arrest warrants were issued for outgoing Veracruz governor Javier Duarte de Ochoa of the PRI and outgoing Sonora governor Guillermo Padrés Elías of the National Action Party (PAN); Padrés turned himself in to authorities in November, while Duarte remained at large at the year's end.

Weak accountability for human rights violations also generated political discontent throughout the year. Judicial processes surrounding the Iguala disappearances continued against scores of local police, drug gang members, and the mayor of the city and his wife, but as of year's end no convictions had been achieved. In June, government cooperation with a group of international experts backed by the Inter-American Commission on Human Rights (IACHR), ended when the government opted not to renew the agreement governing the group's mission. In April, the experts had released the latest of a series of reports assailing investigative and procedural lapses in the government's investigation; the report cast renewed doubt on the government's conclusion that the students' remains had been burned in a municipal dump, and alleged that the testimony the government's description of the crime rested on had been extracted by torturing suspects. The state agreed in July to an accord that authorized a reduced presence by the investigative group.

Other manifestations of accountability shortcomings included the May dismissal of charges against soldiers accused of murder following a 2014 confrontation between criminals and an army unit in the State of Mexico that left 22 people dead. In August, the National Human Rights Commission (CNDH) accused the federal police of covering up extrajudicial executions following a 2015 raid that resulted in the deaths of 42 alleged gang members and a police officer. Rights watchers also decried the slow pace of investigations into the June deaths of eight protesters at the hands of the federal police during violent teachers' protests in Oaxaca. The steadily rising violence throughout the year undermined the message of security improvements that the government had broadcast during the initial years of the Peña Nieto administration.

POLITICAL RIGHTS: 28 / 40

A. Electoral Process: 9 / 12

The president is elected to a six-year term and cannot be reelected. The bicameral Congress consists of the 128-member Senate and the 500-member Chamber of Deputies. Senators are elected for six-year terms through a mix of direct voting and proportional representation, with at least two parties represented in each state's delegation. In the Chamber of Deputies, 300 members are elected through direct representation and 200 through proportional representation, each for three-year terms. Under 2013 electoral reforms, current members of Congress are no longer barred from reelection and candidates are permitted to run as independents. As of 2018, elected senators will be eligible to serve up to two six-year terms; deputies will be permitted to serve up to four three-year terms. In Mexico's federal system, the elected governor and legislature in each of the 31 states have significant governing responsibility, including oversight of most of the country's beleaguered police forces.

Peña Nieto won the 2012 presidential election with 38 percent of the vote, followed by veteran Party of the Democratic Revolution (PRD) leader Andrés Manuel López Obrador with 31 percent. Although López Obrador initially refused to accept the results, alleging infractions such as widespread vote buying, overspending, and media bias, the Federal Electoral Tribunal found insufficient evidence to invalidate the election. In 2015 midterm elections, the PRI and allied parties overcame poor government approval ratings to garner a 260-seat majority in the lower chamber. The right-wing PAN won 108 seats, while left-wing parties (the PRD, the López Obrador-led National Regeneration Movement [MORENA], and the Citizens' Movement) won 120. No coalition commands a majority in the Senate, where the PRI–Green Party alliance won 61 seats in 2012, the PAN took 38, and the PRD won 22.

Mexico's National Electoral Institute (INE) supervises elections and enforces political party laws, including strict regulations on campaign financing and the content of political advertising—although control is weaker in practice. Both the 2012 and 2015 elections were generally considered free and fair, but complaints persisted. The primary accusations in 2012—which concerned alleged instances of vote buying and collusion between the PRI and dominant broadcaster Televisa—were instrumental in sparking a significant anti-PRI student movement. At the state level, allegations of misuse of public resources to favor specific gubernatorial candidates are frequent. The 2013 political reform broadened the INE's power to oversee state elections, and the agency was generally considered to have competently managed balloting in the 2015 midterms and 2016 state races. However, political analysts fault the INE's unwillingness to adequately punish campaign violations. Numerous irregularities were reported in the 2016 elections, including carousel voting and destruction of ballots, with the most reports coming from Veracruz State.

B. Political Pluralism and Participation: 12 / 16

Mexico's multiparty system features few official restrictions on political organization and activity. Power has changed hands twice at the national level since 2000, and opposition parties are also competitive in many states. However, in states with lower levels of multiparty contestation, locally dominant political actors often govern in a highly opaque manner that limits political activity and citizen participation, and opens the door to corruption and organized crime.

The PRI returned to national government in 2012 after losing two consecutive presidential races to the right-leaning PAN. The PRI ruled Mexico without interruption from 1929 to 2000, and many Mexicans still question its commitment to full democracy. Its ally the Green Party is viewed as a particularly feckless seeker of control over public funds. The left, which had previously been dominated by the PRD, fragmented prior to the 2015 midterms, with López Obrador forming his own party, MORENA, which in 2016 won 22 of the 60 elected seats on the constituent assembly tasked with drafting a constitution in Mexico City; the remaining 40 deputies are appointed by the PRI-dominated legislative branch and Peña Nieto.

Politicians and municipal governments have been subject to significant pressure from criminal groups in recent years. Six mayors were assassinated in 2016, adding to a tally of over 80 mayors and ex-mayors killed since 2006.

Indigenous Mexicans are not blocked from participating in the political process, and federal and state laws prescribe procedures for the integration of traditional community customs. However, indigenous groups remain underrepresented in formal political institutions.

C. Functioning of Government: 7 / 12

Organized crime and related violence have limited the effective governing authority of elected officials in some areas of the country. Members of organized crime groups have persisted in their attempts to infiltrate local governments to ensure their own impunity. The mass student disappearance in Iguala in 2014 has been linked to a deeply corrupt local government working in conjunction with a drug gang. In the most violent regions, the provision of public services has become more difficult, as public-sector employees such as teachers face extortion.

Official corruption remains a serious problem. Billions of dollars in illegal drug money—as well as large quantities of powerful firearms—enter the country each year from the United States, and such funds affect politics, particularly at the state and local levels. Attempts to prosecute officials for alleged involvement in corrupt or criminal activity have often failed due to the weakness of the cases brought by the state. Punitive measures have generally focused on low- and mid-level officials, with lower pressure on high-ranking elected officials. The extent of state-level corruption uncovered in Veracruz—where the governor and his cronies are accused of pilfering hundreds of millions of dollars in 2015 alone by robbing the pension fund and channeling government contracts through shadow companies—led to a sharp outcry and the October 2016 resignation of Veracruz governor Duarte, who was charged with corruption and subsequently fled from authorities.

Pressure for reform has intensified since 2014, when it was revealed that the president's wife and the finance minister had purchased multimillion-dollar houses from an active government contractor. In 2015, all were cleared of wrongdoing following a widely derided investigation; however, the civil society outcry about lack of progress in combatting corruption contributed to the 2015 passage of constitutional amendments creating a new National Anticorruption System that grants more autonomy to auditors and prosecutors. These were followed in June 2016 by a set of bills to implement the reforms, which notably featured intensive cooperation with civil society groups. However, a provision giving the sitting prosecutor general a nine-year term once the autonomy provisions take effect yielded controversy when PRI senator and government ally Raúl Cervantes Andrade was appointed prosecutor general in October 2016.

Despite some limitations, a 2002 freedom of information law has successfully strengthened transparency at the federal level, though implementation has slowed and enforcement is uneven across states. A new and more extensive transparency law passed in 2015 was mostly praised by good governance advocates, although controversies over denial of access to files pertaining to abuses by state security forces persisted.

CIVIL LIBERTIES: 37 / 60

D. Freedom of Expression and Belief: 13 / 16

Legal and constitutional guarantees of free speech have been improving gradually, but the security environment for journalists remains highly problematic. While some major media outlets have reduced or eliminated their dependence on the government for advertising and subsidies, the distribution of government advertising still affects coverage, particularly at the local level. Broadcast media are dominated by a corporate duopoly composed of Televisa and TV Azteca, which together control approximately 95 percent of the free-to-air market. Televisa has faced accusations of supporting specific politicians over the years, usually from the PRI. A 2013 telecommunications law established a new telecommunications regulator, strengthened the Federal Economic Competition Commission, and resulted in the creation of two new free-to-air channels, the first of which arrived on the airwaves in October 2016. However, civil society groups have criticized the limited scope of the reforms, and the winners of the auctioned airwaves—one of which subsequently was stripped of its frequency for nonpayment—were not considered likely to offer significant new competition.

Reporters probing police issues, drug trafficking, and official corruption face an increasingly high risk of physical harm. According to the Committee to Protect Journalists (CPJ), nine journalists were murdered in 2016, and the organization confirmed that two of the journalists were killed for reasons connected to their jobs. Self-censorship has increased, with many newspapers in violent areas avoiding publication of stories concerning organized crime. Press watchdog groups hailed the 2012 federalization of crimes against journalists as well as a 2015 law in Mexico City aimed at protecting journalists and human rights defenders, but they have decried the slow pace of the federal government's special prosecutor for crimes against freedom of expression since the office gained authority in 2013. Despite improvements in legal status, community radio stations continue to face occasional harassment from criminals and state authorities.

Mexico has been at the forefront of citizen-led efforts to ensure internet access. The government amended Article 6 of the constitution in 2013 to make access to the internet a civil right. However, gangs have targeted bloggers and online journalists who report on organized crime, issuing threats and periodically murdering online writers.

Religious freedom is protected by the constitution and is generally respected in practice. The government does not restrict academic freedom, though university students are sometimes threatened for their political activism. While there are no formal impediments to free and open discussion, fear of criminal monitoring restricts citizens' willingness to converse publicly about crime in some areas of the country.

E. Associational and Organizational Rights: 8 / 12

Constitutional guarantees regarding free assembly and association are largely upheld, but political and civic expression is restricted in some regions. The most extensive and controversial protests in 2016 were carried out by teachers' unions; the events paralyzed economic activity in several southern states for months. In June, a federal police–led effort to clear a highway in Oaxaca being blocked by teachers' union members and local residents led to the deaths of eight protesters, with scores more injured, under circumstances that remained murky months later.

Although highly active, nongovernmental organizations sometimes face violent resistance, including threats and murders. Activists representing indigenous groups contesting large-scale infrastructure projects have been particularly vulnerable. In 2012, civil society pressure prompted the government to create a Protection Mechanism for Human Rights Defenders and Journalists. As of mid-2016 it had offered protection to 333 people since its inception, but has also been critiqued by rights groups as slow and suffering from insufficient governmental commitment. On multiple occasions in early 2016, government officials or their allies verbally attacked prominent human rights advocates, baselessly describing them as members of a "mafia" group reaping financial gains from criticism of the government.

Trade unions, long a pillar of the PRI, have diminished significantly, but independent unions still face interference from the government. Informal, nontransparent negotiations between employers and politically connected union leaders often result in "protection contracts" that govern employee rights but are never seen by workers. Several large unions are considered opaque and antagonistic to necessary policy reforms. Longtime teachers' union leader Elba Esther Gordillo—widely perceived as extremely corrupt—was arrested in 2013 and charged with embezzling more than $150 million; she remained in detention throughout 2016, though since January she has been held at a Mexico City hospital due to health concerns.

F. Rule of Law: 6 / 16

Mexico's justice system is plagued by delays, unpredictability, and corruption, leading to pervasive impunity. A 2008 constitutional reform replaced the civil-inquisitorial trial system with an oral-adversarial one. Although it was expected to strengthen due process while increasing efficiency and impartiality, human rights groups raised concerns about the weak protections it affords to those suspected of involvement in organized crime. Implementation of the new system was technically completed in June 2016, but analysts noted that absent more thorough training at all levels, from police to judges, the credibility of the new system would be at risk.

Abuses during criminal investigations are rife; in 2015, a UN special rapporteur released a report characterizing torture as "generalized" within Mexican police forces, generating a diplomatic spat. The government has also faced domestic and international pressure to confront the problem of forced disappearance, which affects an unknown portion of the more than 28,000 Mexicans listed as disappeared in a national registry. The weakness of forensic investigations was notably highlighted when experts from the Interdisciplinary Group of Independent Experts (GIEI)—a body established in an agreement between the IACHR, the Mexican government, and organizations representing the Iguala victims' family members—produced evidence that the head of the federal criminal investigation unit had made an unregistered appearance at the San Juan River shortly before the only identifiable remains of the murdered Iguala students were found there. The official, Tomás Zerón de Lucio, resigned from his position in September 2016 following months of criticism, though shortly afterward he was appointed technical secretary of the National Security Council. The GIEI report, released in April, also cast doubt on the government's claims that the students' remains were incinerated at a Cocula dump, and alleged that the testimony the government's description of the crime rested on had been extracted through torture. The government declined to renew the GIEI's mission weeks after the report was released, but later agreed to allow it to continue working in a reduced capacity.

Coordination among Mexico's many federal, state, and local law enforcement entities has long been problematic, and the Peña Nieto administration has pursued streamlined chains of command. In zones plagued by crime, federal troops have temporarily replaced local police forces. Critics contend that federal intervention decreases incentives for governors to undertake systemic reforms, and in practice implementation of such reforms at the local level has been largely unsuccessful. Despite a 2009 law ordering all members of the police to be vetted, thousands of police who failed to meet requirements have remained on the job.

Lower courts—and law enforcement in general—are undermined by widespread bribery and suffer from limited capacity. According to a government survey released in September 2016, over 93 percent of crimes committed in 2015 went unreported because the underpaid police are viewed as either inept or in league with criminals. Even when investigations are conducted, only a handful of crimes end in convictions. Prisons are violent and overcrowded, and it is not uncommon for prisoners to continue criminal activity while incarcerated. In February 2016, 49 prisoners died in a riot in a state prison in Monterrey. The 2015 escape of drug lord Joaquín "El Chapo" Guzmán from a high-security federal prison illustrated the depth of corruption in the criminal justice system; Guzmán was recaptured in January 2016. The CNDH, long maligned due to its perceived passivity in the face of rampant rights abuses, began to regain some credibility following the appointment of a new director in 2014, and in August 2016 it issued a report accusing the federal police of covering up extrajudicial executions following a 2015 raid outside the city of Guadalajara that resulted in the deaths of 42 alleged gangsters and a police officer.

Presidential authority over the armed forces is extensive, but the military has historically operated beyond public scrutiny. Human rights advocates for years have expressed concern about a lack of accountability for rights abuses including torture, forced disappearances, and extrajudicial executions. Military personnel are generally tried in military courts, but a bill passed in 2014 shifted the venue of trials for violations of civilians' rights to civilian courts. While a handful of soldiers have been convicted of crimes including torture and murder, the status of many processes remains unclear. Rights watchers viewed the May 2016 dismissal of charges against three soldiers indicted for the 2014 State of Mexico massacre as a grave setback in an emblematic case. In November 2016, several bills to allow the military to perform police-like tasks in order to "safeguard internal security" were introduced in Congress; they remained pending at year's end.

The number of deaths attributed to organized crime rose sharply each year between 2007 and 2011, declined from 2012 to 2014, and subsequently began trending upward. Violence in 2016 spiked in Colima, Zacatecas, Tijuana, and Mexico City, while remaining acute in Guerrero. Gang murders continue to feature extreme brutality designed to maximize the psychological impact on civilians, authorities, and rival groups.

In recent years, the government has taken a number of steps to curb violence and ease popular frustration with the problem. These include engaging in consultations with civic leaders, the continued deployment of troops, the reformation of the federal police and development of the National Gendarmerie, and the decriminalization of possession of small quantities of drugs. The Peña Nieto administration has been less vocal on matters of public safety than its predecessor, but it has maintained many of the former administration's strategies, including use of the military. However, after three straight years of declines, the murder rate increased by more than 8 percent in 2015, and an additional 22 percent in 2016, generating renewed pressure for strategic changes in state efforts to contain the carnage.

Mexican law bans discrimination based on ethnic origin, gender, age, religion, and sexual orientation. Nevertheless, the large indigenous population has been subject to social and economic discrimination, and 70 percent of the indigenous population lives in poverty. Southern states with high concentrations of indigenous residents suffer from particularly deficient services. Indigenous groups have been harmed by criminal violence; in recent years, a series of communities in Guerrero and Michoacán have formed self-defense groups, some of which were subsequently legalized. In addition, disputes over land issues within indigenous groups have occasionally become violent, particularly in the states of Chiapas and Oaxaca.

G. Personal Autonomy and Individual Rights: 10 / 16

Criminals have impeded freedom of movement by blocking major roads in several states in recent years, and ordinary citizens avoid roads in many rural areas after dark. Rights groups frequently detail the persecution and criminal predation faced by migrants from Central America, many of whom move through Mexico to reach the United States. Despite government initiatives to improve protections, pressure from the United States to crack down on migration pathways generated ongoing accusations of abuses against migrants in 2016. Separately, in late 2014 the Internal Displacement Monitoring Center estimated that there were more than 280,000 internally displaced people (IDPs) in Mexico, many of whom had fled cartel-related violence.

Property rights in Mexico are protected by a modern legal framework, but the weakness of the judicial system, frequent solicitation of bribes by bureaucrats and officials, and the high incidence of criminal extortion harm security of property for many individuals and businesses. Large-scale development projects have been accompanied by controversy in recent years, and in September 2016 the UN Working Group on Business and Human Rights urged greater consultation with indigenous groups to minimize the damaging effects of such projects.

Women play a prominent role in social and political life, and female representatives increased their share of seats in the Chamber of Deputies to 42 percent in the 2015 elections. However, sexual abuse and domestic violence against women are common, and perpetrators are rarely punished. Implementation of a 2007 law designed to protect women from such crimes remains halting, particularly at the state level, and impunity is the norm for the killers of hundreds of women each year. As of the end of 2016, authorities in the states of Mexico, Michoacán, Morelos, Chiapas, Nuevo León, Veracruz, and Jalisco had issued "gender alerts," thereby triggering greater scrutiny and an influx of resources to combat an epidemic of violence against women. Abortion has been a contentious issue in recent years, with many states reacting to Mexico City's 2007 liberalization of abortion laws by strengthening their own criminal bans on the procedure.

Mexico has taken significant steps toward LGBT equality, courtesy of Supreme Court rulings in 2015 that struck down state laws defining the purpose of marriage as procreation. However, implementing the jurisprudence in all Mexican states will take time, as the court's rulings do not apply in blanket form. In May 2016, Peña Nieto proposed a constitutional amendment legalizing same-sex marriage, but the project encountered opposition from the Catholic Church and was shelved in November.

Mexico is a major source, transit, and destination country for trafficking in persons, including women and children, many of whom are subject to forced labor and sexual exploitation. Organized criminal gangs are heavily involved in human trafficking in Mexico and into the United States. Government corruption is a significant concern as many officials are bribed by or aide traffickers.

Micronesia

Political Rights Rating: 1
Civil Liberties Rating: 1
Freedom Rating: 1.0
Freedom Status: Free
Electoral Democracy: Yes

Population: 100,000
Capital: Palikir

Ten-Year Ratings Timeline For Year Under Review (Political Rights, Civil Liberties, Status)

Year Under Review	2007	2008	2009	2010	2011	2012	2013	2014	2015	2016
Rating	1,1,F	1,1,F	1,1,F	1,1,F	1,1,F	1,1,F	1,1,F	1,1,F	1,1,F	1,1,F

The country or territory displayed here received scores but no narrative report for this edition of *Freedom in the World.*

Moldova

Political Rights Rating: 3
Civil Liberties Rating: 3
Freedom Rating: 3.0
Freedom Status: Partly Free
Electoral Democracy: Yes

Population: 3,600,000
Capital: Chişinău

Note: The numerical ratings and status listed above do not reflect conditions in Transnistria, which is examined in a separate report.

Ten-Year Ratings Timeline For Year Under Review (Political Rights, Civil Liberties, Status)

Year Under Review	2007	2008	2009	2010	2011	2012	2013	2014	2015	2016
Rating	3,4,PF	4,4,PF	3,4,PF	3,3,PF	3,3,PF	3,3,PF	3,3,PF	3,3,PF	3,3,PF	3,3,PF

Overview: Moldova is a multiparty democracy that holds regular, credible elections, but struggles with serious corruption among public officials and within the judicial system. The country continues to reel from a 2014 banking scandal, which led to a bailout that devastated its national budget and fostered deep mistrust in the political establishment.

KEY DEVELOPMENTS IN 2016:

- In June, former prime minister Vlad Filat, who during his 2009–13 tenure had worked to bring Moldova closer to the European Union (EU), was convicted on corruption charges related to a banking scandal that had rocked Moldovan politics. He was sentenced to nine years in prison.
- In March, the Constitutional Court struck down constitutional amendments mandating parliamentary selection of the president, paving the way for the first direct presidential election since 1996.

- Socialist Party leader Igor Dodon won the presidency in two rounds of an election held in October and November. In his campaign, Dodon promised to bring about prosperity through closer ties with Russia, and his victory highlighted voters' rejection of pro-European parties that had been embroiled in numerous scandals.
- Several controversies involving members of the judicial system drew attention to continuing issues with corruption in the courts.

EXECUTIVE SUMMARY

Moldovan politics in 2016 largely revolved around political and economic fallout from the corruption scandal that emerged in late 2014, in which the central bank had eventually taken control of three troubled financial institutions, and an independent assessment concluded that $1 billion had disappeared from the banks in a fraudulent borrowing scheme. In June 2016, former prime minister Vlad Filat was convicted on corruption charges related to the scandal and sentenced to nine years in prison; Filat, a member of the center-right Liberal Democratic Party of Moldova (PLDM), had worked to bring Moldova closer to the EU, but had become embroiled in multiple corruption cases and in 2015 was stripped of parliamentary immunity.

In the wake of the banking scandal, many people turned against the European-leaning yet oligarchic parties that dominated previous governments, including the one headed by Filat. Popular support for Russian-oriented parties has since been building. Newly created political movements seeking to capture pro-European and anti-oligarchic ground have also seen increasing popularity. Meanwhile, some corruption investigations are progressing, and the political situation stabilized somewhat in 2016 compared to the previous year.

In March, Moldova's Constitutional Court struck down constitutional amendments mandating that the president be elected by the parliament, paving the way for a popular vote for president later in the year. The court's decision prompted criticism from some political parties and from civil society, who said it had acted outside its jurisdiction. Nevertheless, Moldova subsequently held its first direct presidential election since 1996, in two rounds held in October and November 2016. Socialist Party leader and prominent Russophile Igor Dodon won in the second round; he had campaigned on boosting the economy by establishing closer ties with Russia. Monitors deemed the vote credible, but noted issues with media bias and misuse of administrative resources, while some overseas voting posts in Western Europe reportedly ran out of ballots. The vote for Dodon brought into sharp relief voters' ambivalence toward the EU and their rejection of previous pro-European parliamentary coalitions that were bedeviled by corruption crises. (Earlier, in January, a pro-European coalition government was voted in, amid calls by protesters and pro-Russian lawmakers for snap legislative elections.)

Several incidents in 2016 prompted concern about politicization, corruption, and a lack of professionalism within the judicial system. In March, a judge was appointed to the Supreme Court of Justice despite failing to meet requirements for financial disclosures, and amid questions about whether she had adequately managed past caseloads. As Moldova lost cases at the European Court of Human Rights and was required to pay damages to plaintiffs, Minister of Justice Vladimir Cebotari called for those Moldovan judges and officials who lost the cases to bear the costs of those payments, saying their personal property could be confiscated, if necessary. In May, a court suspended the popular mayor of Taraclia, Sergei Filipov, ostensibly for the improper removal of trees from public property. Filipov called the move political retaliation for his refusal to support the Democratic Party of Moldova (PDM) presidential candidate in a past election. He was reinstated after a court battle, and while the issue was ultimately adjudicated in Moldovan courts, the head of the EU's delegation to Moldova highlighted the case as emblematic of Moldova's problems with a politicized judiciary.

POLITICAL RIGHTS: 27 / 40 (+ 2)

A. Electoral Process: 10 / 12

B. Political Pluralism and Participation: 12 / 16 (+ 1)

C. Functioning of Government: 5 / 12 (+ 1) .

CIVIL LIBERTIES: 35 / 60

D. Freedom of Expression and Belief: 12 / 16 (+ 1)

E. Associational and Organizational Rights: 8 / 12

F. Rule of Law: 6 / 16 (− 1)

G. Personal Autonomy and Individual Rights: 9 / 16

This country report has been abridged for *Freedom in the World 2017*. For background information on political rights and civil liberties in Moldova, see *Freedom in the World 2016*.

Monaco

Political Rights Rating: 3
Civil Liberties Rating: 1
Freedom Rating: 2
Freedom Status: Free
Electoral Democracy: Yes

Population: 40,100
Capital: Monaco

Ten-Year Ratings Timeline For Year Under Review (Political Rights, Civil Liberties, Status)

Year Under Review	2007	2008	2009	2010	2011	2012	2013	2014	2015	2016
Rating	2,1,F	2,1,F	2,1,F	2,1,F	2,1,F	2,1,F	2,1,F	2,1,F	2,1,F	3,1,F

The country or territory displayed here received scores but no narrative report for this edition of *Freedom in the World*.

Mongolia

Political Rights Rating: 1
Civil Liberties Rating: 2
Freedom Rating: 1.5
Freedom Status: Free
Electoral Democracy: Yes

Population: 3,100,000
Capital: Ulaanbaatar

Ten-Year Ratings Timeline For Year Under Review (Political Rights, Civil Liberties, Status)

Year Under Review Rating	2007	2008	2009	2010	2011	2012	2013	2014	2015	2016
	2,2,F	2,2,F	2,2,F	2,2,F	2,2,F	1,2,F	1,2,F	1,2,F	1,2,F	1,2,F

Overview: Following a peaceful revolution in 1990, Mongolia began holding multiparty elections and has since established itself as an electoral democracy. While parties, and in particular the two dominant parties, remain rooted in patronage relations, and widespread corruption hinders development, political freedoms and civil liberties are firmly institutionalized.

KEY DEVELOPMENTS IN 2016:
- In the spring, the country shifted from a mixed electoral system to a majoritarian system, in an opaque process that drew criticism from an Organization for Security and Co-operation in Europe (OSCE) election monitoring mission.
- The opposition Mongolian People's Party (MPP) won June's polls with 45 percent of the popular vote, a result that gave it 65 of the 76 seats in the legislature. The incumbent Democratic Party (DP) won 33 percent of the vote, giving it nine seats.
- A slew of election-related defamation complaints were lodged in the weeks leading up to the polls, contributing to a perceived chilling of political discourse.

EXECUTIVE SUMMARY

In April 2016, the Mongolian High Court invalidated a part of the electoral law that had permitted a mixed electoral system, ruling that it failed to comply with a section of the constitution calling for direct elections. The parliament then approved legislation mandating a majoritarian, or first-past-the-post, system with 76 single-mandate constituencies. The OSCE criticized the reform process as rushed and opaque, and noted that the new districts were drawn inequitably.

In June parliamentary elections under the new system, the opposition MPP won 45 percent of the popular vote, a result that gave it 65 of the 76 seats in the legislature. The incumbent DP won 33 percent of the vote, giving it nine seats. The Mongolian People's Revolutionary Party (MPRP), won a single seat, as did an independent candidate. The Civil Will Green Party was eliminated from parliament. The OSCE mission said polling took place in an orderly manner.

Some journalists and activists reported a sense of unease about the potential for targeted enforcement of election laws officials say are intended to ensure fair media coverage of elections, but which critics argue threaten press freedom. Journalists reportedly asked authorities for clarification of some such laws, but did not receive any. Police reported receiving 209 allegations of defamation committed against candidates between June 10 and June 29, the day of the polls, though not all complaints were investigated and it was unclear if prosecutions arose from any of those that were. A sense of unease was echoed by some members of the general public who perceived a chilling of political discourse, and in particular of criticism of political parties, that was not observed in previous elections.

POLITICAL RIGHTS: 36 / 40
A. Electoral Process: 11 / 12
B. Political Pluralism and Participation: 16 / 16
C. Functioning of Government: 9 / 12

CIVIL LIBERTIES: 49 / 60 (− 1)
D. Freedom of Expression and Belief: 14 / 16 (− 1)
E. Associational and Organizational Rights: 11 / 12
F. Rule of Law: 12 / 16
G. Personal Autonomy and Individual Rights: 12 / 16

This country report has been abridged for *Freedom in the World 2017*. For background information on political rights and civil liberties in Mongolia, see *Freedom in the World 2016*.

Montenegro

Political Rights Rating: 3
Civil Liberties Rating: 3
Freedom Rating: 3.0
Freedom Status: Partly Free
Electoral Democracy: Yes

Population: 600,000
Capital: Podgorica

Ten-Year Ratings Timeline For Year Under Review (Political Rights, Civil Liberties, Status)

Year Under Review	2007	2008	2009	2010	2011	2012	2013	2014	2015	2016
Rating	3,3,PF	3,3,PF	3,2,F	3,2,F	3,2,F	3,2,F	3,2,F	3,2,F	3,3,PF	3,3,PF

Overview: While numerous political parties compete for power in Montenegro, the opposition is fragmented, and the governing Democratic Party of Socialists (DPS) has been in power since 1991. Corruption is a serious issue. Investigative journalists and journalists critical of the government face pressure.

KEY DEVELOPMENTS in 2016:

- A number of irregularities were reported during October's parliamentary polls, including alleged vote-buying by the governing DPS and an election-day shutdown of mobile messaging services. The opposition called the polls fraudulent and subsequently boycotted the parliament.
- The DPS won the most seats in the elections, and formed a government with the support of smaller parties. Duško Marković became prime minister, replacing long-time leader Milo Đukanović.

- On election day, authorities announced that 20 people had been arrested for allegedly plotting a coup, which reportedly involved a planned assassination attempt on Đukanović. Đukanović accused the opposition Democratic Front (DF) of involvement with the suspected coup planners, while the DF claimed that Đukanović manufactured the controversy to create an advantage for the DPS in the elections.
- Jovo Martinović, an investigative reporter detained in late 2015 on charges of drug trafficking, remained in custody at year's end.

EXECUTIVE SUMMARY

Prime Minister Milo Đukanović has served as either prime minister or president for most of the last two decades, and wields great influence in Montenegro. He framed the October 2016 parliamentary election as a choice between his administration, which had pursued membership to the European Union (EU) and North Atlantic Treaty Organization (NATO), and opposition parties he decried as seeking to turn the country into a "Russian colony," even as some opposition parties also supported NATO membership. His DPS posted the strongest performance in the polls, taking 36 seats in the 81-seat parliament—5 seats short of a governing majority. The DF, the main opposition party, took 18 seats. After several weeks of coalition talks, the DPS formed a government with several smaller parties that won representation, and the parliament then confirmed Duško Marković as the new prime minister in November. Marković was considered an ally of Đukanović, who as DPS chairman was expected to retain influence in the government.

Alleging electoral fraud, the opposition rejected the polls' results, and boycotted the parliament throughout the rest of the year. While election monitors from the Organization for Security and Co-operation in Europe (OSCE) ultimately assessed the polls as credible, numerous violations were reported, and the EU days after the election issued a statement of concern in which it called for fraud claims to be investigated. The Montenegro-based NGO MANS accused the Montenegrin government of trading tax or debt relief for votes, estimating that the DPS could have effectively bought as many as six legislative seats through such efforts. The government also suspended mobile messaging applications including Viber and WhatsApp on election day, citing "illegal marketing" taking place on the platforms.

Additionally, on the day of the election, the Montenegrin government arrested 20 Serbian and Montenegrin citizens on charges of plotting a coup; the group's plans allegedly included breaking into the parliament, attacking police, and assassinating Đukanović. A few suspects were subsequently released but others remained in detention at year's end, including figures described as Russian nationalists who had fought alongside pro-Russian forces in eastern Ukraine. Đukanović publicly accused the DF of plotting the alleged coup, but offered no evidence for his claims; the DF in turn accused Đukanović of manufacturing the events as a means of securing support for the DPS in the elections. Later in the year, Montenegrin authorities issued arrest warrants for two Russian and three Serbian citizens on charges of leading the alleged coup.

Journalist Jovo Martinović, known for his coverage of organized crime, was detained in late 2015, and in April 2016 was charged with involvement in a drug smuggling operation he had been investigating. He remained in detention at year's end, and argues that his contact with members of the smuggling operation fell within his work as a journalist.

POLITICAL RIGHTS: 26 / 40 (− 1)

A. Electoral Process: 8 / 12 (− 1)

B. Political Pluralism and Participation: 11 / 16

C. Functioning of Government: 7 / 12

CIVIL LIBERTIES: 43 / 60

D. Freedom of Expression and Belief: 12 / 16

E. Associational and Organizational Rights: 9 / 12

F. Rule of Law: 10 / 16

G. Personal Autonomy and Individual Rights: 12 / 16

This country report has been abridged for *Freedom in the World 2017*. For background information on political rights and civil liberties in Montenegro, see *Freedom in the World 2016*.

Morocco

Political Rights Rating: 5
Civil Liberties Rating: 4
Freedom Rating: 4.5
Freedom Status: Partly Free
Electoral Democracy: No

Population: 34,700,000
Capital: Rabat

Note: The numerical ratings and status listed above do not reflect conditions in Western Sahara, which is examined in a separate report.

Ten-Year Ratings Timeline For Year Under Review (Political Rights, Civil Liberties, Status)

Year Under Review	2007	2008	2009	2010	2011	2012	2013	2014	2015	2016
Rating	5,4,PF	5,4,PF	5,4,PF	5,4,PF	5,4,PF	5,4,PF	5,4,PF	5,4,PF	5,4,PF	5,4,PF

Overview: Morocco holds regular multiparty elections for parliament, and reforms in 2011 formally shifted some power over government from the monarchy to the elected legislature. Nevertheless, King Mohammed VI maintains dominance through a combination of substantial formal powers and informal lines of influence in the state and society, including his control over security forces, religious authority, and strong appeals to nationalism.

KEY DEVELOPMENTS IN 2016:

- Prime Minister Abdelilah Benkirane's Party of Justice and Development (PJD), a moderate Islamist group, retained its plurality in October parliamentary elections, outpolling its main rival, the royalist Party of Authenticity and Modernity (PAM). The PJD was expected to lead a new coalition government, which had yet to be formed at year's end.
- Nationwide protests against abuse of power erupted in late October after a fish vendor was crushed to death in a garbage truck during a confrontation with police; images of the incident were disseminated on social media.
- A new press code adopted in July removed imprisonment as a punishment for press offenses, but journalists could still be jailed for similar violations under the penal code.

EXECUTIVE SUMMARY

The ruling PJD maintained its position in October 2016 parliamentary elections, which were the second to be held since 2011 constitutional reforms began requiring that the prime minister be selected from the party with a plurality of seats. Days after the elections, the king asked Prime Minister Benkirane to form a new government, but coalition talks were ongoing at year's end, slowed in part by disagreement over the inclusion of the nationalist party Istiqlal.

In the run-up to the elections in September, the government announced that it had broken up a terrorist cell linked to the Islamic State (IS) militant group, which was allegedly planning to mount attacks in the north. In October, the government reported that it had arrested 10 women suspected of being IS suicide bombers who intended to strike during the voting.

The government continued to restrict personal freedoms and journalistic coverage of sensitive subjects in 2016, with reporters and activists sometimes facing fines and jail sentences. A large number of protests on various topics proceeded peacefully during the year, though the authorities used violence to disperse demonstrations in some cases.

POLITICAL RIGHTS: 15 / 40

A. Electoral Process: 5 / 12

King Mohammed VI and his close advisers and associates hold political, social, and economic power in Morocco. Constitutional reforms in 2011 required the king to appoint the prime minister from the party that wins the most seats in parliamentary elections, and to consult the prime minister before dissolving Parliament, though they preserved most of the king's existing powers. The monarch can disband the legislature, rule by decree, and dismiss or appoint cabinet members. He sets national and foreign policy, commands the armed forces and intelligence services, and presides over the judicial system. One of the king's constitutional titles is "commander of the faithful," giving his authority a claim to religious legitimacy.

The lower house of parliament, the Chamber of Representatives, has 395 directly elected members who serve for five-year terms. Of these, 305 seats are elected from 92 multimember constituencies. The remaining 90 seats are elected from a single nationwide constituency, with 60 seats reserved for women and 30 for people under the age of 40. Members of the 120-seat upper house, the Chamber of Counselors, are chosen by an electoral college to serve six-year terms.

In 2015, Morocco held its first regional and municipal elections since the adoption of the new constitution, garnering 53 percent voter turnout. The PJD came in first at the regional level, winning 26 percent of all available seats; the PAM won 19 percent, while Istiqlal took 18 percent. Due to the geographic distribution of the seats won, the PAM won five out of the country's 12 regional councils, while the PJD won just two. At the municipal level, PAM came in first with 21 percent of all available seats, while the PJD and Istiqlal each took 16 percent. Importantly, the PJD won majorities on the councils of most large cities. Under a rule that took effect in 2009, women are guaranteed 12 percent of the seats in local elections.

In the October 2016 parliamentary elections, the PJD placed first with 125 seats in the Chamber of Representatives, followed by the PAM with 102. Both increased their share of seats compared with 2011. Istiqlal fell by 14 seats to 46; the National Rally of Independents (RNI) declined 15 seats to 37; the Popular Movement (MP) declined 5 seats to 27; and the Socialist Union of Popular Forces (USFP) declined 19 seats to 20. Official turnout was 43 percent of registered voters, lower than the 45 percent in 2011 and representing only 23 percent of eligible voters.

In September, Justice Minister Mustapha Ramid of the PJD accused Interior Minister Mohamed Hassad, a technocrat appointed by the king, of manipulating the upcoming elections, saying he was making decisions on electoral administration unilaterally. The government approved 4,000 election observers out of 5,000 applicants, including 92 foreign observers connected to five international organizations. A notable exception was the Carter Center, which was excluded. Human Rights Watch criticized the decision as part of a trend of reduced access to the country for international nongovernmental organizations (NGOs). After the elections, the National Council of Human Rights released a report noting isolated irregularities, including cases of vote buying.

B. Political Pluralism and Participation: 7 / 16

Morocco has a multiparty system, but the parties are fragmented and generally unable to assert themselves relative to the power of the palace. Prior to 2011, the PJD was a vocal opposition party, though it remained respectful of the monarchy. Another Islamist group, the Justice and Charity movement, is illegal and does not participate in the electoral process, though its other activities are largely tolerated by the authorities. Of the two main parties, the PJD polls strongly in urban areas, while the PAM dominates rural areas. Smaller parties tend to be unstable, sometimes built around the personalities of their leaders.

For decades, the indigenous peoples grouped under the term Berber or Amazigh have had an uneasy relationship with the palace. Prominent Amazigh elites enjoy access to the monarchy and also have their interests represented in Parliament, but the bulk of the ethnically indigenous population is marginalized. The official recognition of Tamazight languages alongside Arabic in the 2011 constitutional reform was seen as a step toward greater equality in politics and government.

C. Functioning of Government: 3 / 12

While elected officials are duly installed in government, their power to shape policy is sharply constrained by the role of the king and his advisers, who control most of the levers of power.

Corruption is rife in state institutions and the economy. Despite the government's rhetoric on combating corruption, it has a mixed record on enforcement. After considerable political maneuvering, the powers of the main anticorruption body, the Central Authority for the Prevention of Corruption (ICPC), were strengthened in 2015. At the party level, the PJD benefits from a perception that it is relatively free of corruption.

For the past several years, the government has published the annual budget and other financial information online and has proactively discussed such matters with the press. However, overall transparency is limited, as the monarchy plays an outsized role in the economy and is the majority stakeholder in a vast array of private and public-sector firms.

CIVIL LIBERTIES: 26 / 60

D. Freedom of Expression and Belief: 7 / 16 (− 1)

The state dominates the broadcast media, but more affluent segments of society have access to foreign satellite television channels. Although the independent press enjoys a significant degree of freedom when reporting on economic and social policies, the authorities use an array of financial and legal mechanisms to punish critical journalists, particularly those who focus on the king, his family, the status of Western Sahara, or Islam. The monarchy allegedly instructs businesses not to buy advertisements in publications that have criticized the government, or punishes those that do. The authorities also occasionally disrupt websites and internet platforms; bloggers and other internet users are harassed for posting content that offends the monarchy.

A new press code approved by parliament in July 2016 eliminated imprisonment as a penalty for press offenses, such as insulting the king or malicious publication of false news, prescribing suspensions or fines instead. However, journalists could still face prison terms for similar offenses under the penal code.

Journalists remained subject to legal harassment in 2016. Hicham Mansouri, a project manager with the Moroccan Association of Investigative Journalism (AMJI) who in 2015 was arrested and charged with committing adultery, was released from prison in January 2016 after serving a 10-month sentence. He told a press conference that he had been physically abused and questioned extensively about his possible involvement with Islamist movements rather than the adultery charges. Mansouri and six others also faced a pending trial on separate charges for running a training program for citizen journalists. Amnesty International denounced the proceedings as an unwarranted restriction of freedom of expression. Journalist and activist Ali Anouzla was charged in January for an interview with foreign media in which he allegedly questioned the status of Western Sahara; after Anouzla insisted that he had been misquoted, the charges were dropped in May.

Nearly all Moroccans are Muslims. While the small Jewish community is permitted to practice its faith without government interference, Moroccan authorities are increasingly intolerant of social and religious diversity. The government exercises strict control over Muslim religious institutions in the name of countering extremism. All imams preaching in mosques are required to obtain state certification, and mosques and sermons are regularly monitored by the authorities. The government operates a large and well-financed training program for imams and female religious counselors tasked with promoting a state-sanctioned version of Islam, which some critics charge is also intended to promote political quiescence.

While university campuses generally provide a space for open discussion, professors practice self-censorship when dealing with sensitive topics like Western Sahara, the monarchy, and Islam.

There is some freedom of private discussion, but state surveillance of online activity and personal communications has been a growing concern in recent years.

E. Associational and Organizational Rights: 6 / 12 (+ 1)

Freedom of assembly is not always respected. The authorities sometimes use excessive force and violence to disperse even peaceful protests, and harass activists involved in organizing demonstrations that criticize the government. While such practices continued in 2016, the year also featured a number of large protests that proceeded without incident, including a series of demonstrations across the country triggered by the widely publicized death of a fish vendor in a confrontation with police.

Civil society organizations are quite active, but they are subject to legal harassment, travel restrictions, and other impediments to their work. The authorities routinely deny registration to NGOs with links to Justice and Charity or that assert the rights of marginalized communities. Officials also raise obstacles to events held by local human rights groups and increasingly expel or bar entry to representatives of international human rights organizations.

Workers are permitted to form and join independent trade unions, and the 2004 labor law prevents employers from punishing workers who do so, but there are undue legal and employer restrictions on collective bargaining and strikes. The authorities sometimes forcibly break up labor actions that clash with the government's policies or interests. Police attacked labor-related protests by student teachers in Inezgane in January 2016, as well as sit-ins by unionized steelworkers in Casablanca in May. Union-led protests against government-backed pension reforms during the year were largely peaceful, though they failed to prevent the changes from being adopted.

F. Rule of Law: 6 / 16

The judiciary is not independent of the monarchy, and the courts are regularly used to punish government opponents. Arbitrary arrests and torture still occur. Right advocates report that torture remains widespread among Moroccan security forces and detention centers, especially against advocates for the independence of Western Sahara, leftists, Islamists, and other government critics.

Public frustration with abusive police practices fueled the protests over the October 2016 death of fish vendor Mouhcine Fikri. His 1,000 pounds of swordfish had been confiscated by authorities because it was caught out of season. When he climbed into a garbage truck to retrieve the fish, the trash compactor was turned on—allegedly on orders from a police officer—and he was killed. Eleven people were arrested for Fikri's death in November, including two police officers. The largely peaceful demonstrations subsided somewhat over the subsequent weeks.

The Moroccan LGBT (lesbian, gay, bisexual, and transgender) community faces harsh discrimination and occasional violence. Same-sex sexual relations can be punished with up to three years in prison, though the presence of LGBT foreigners is generally tolerated in tourist areas.

Amazigh and other communities that do not identify with the dominant Arab culture tend to face educational and economic disadvantages. The government has made some efforts to rectify past Arabization policies; since the 2011 constitutional reforms granted official status to Tamazight languages, they and Amazigh culture have been promoted in schools. However, independent groups that promote local Amazigh rights and identities have faced government interference.

The government granted temporary residency permits to hundreds of recognized refugees and thousands of African migrants who met certain conditions in 2016, as part of an ongoing effort to regularize their status. However, authorities continued to face accusations of excessive force in their efforts to block irregular migrants seeking entry to the Spanish enclaves of Ceuta and Melilla.

G. Personal Autonomy and Individual Rights: 7 / 16

Freedoms of movement, employment, and education are guaranteed by law in Morocco, but poor economic conditions and corruption limit these rights in practice. Widespread bribery, nepotism, and misconduct within the educational sector constrain merit-based advancement.

Morocco ranked 68 out of 190 countries in the World Bank's 2017 *Doing Business* report, released in October 2016, and 85 out of 178 countries on the Heritage Foundation's 2016 *Index of Economic Freedom*, indicating a mixed legal environment for the smooth operation of private businesses. Although starting a business is a relatively quick and simple process, regulatory and market hurdles create difficulties.

Nearly 50 percent of Morocco's land is held collectively by tribes, which allocate its use based on the needs of the community, while smallholders and a few larger agricultural groups control almost one-third. Most agricultural land is administered according to religious and customary law, which generally respects the ownership and usage rights of its residents and laborers.

By regional standards, Moroccan laws are relatively progressive on women's rights issues. Gender equality is recognized in the 2011 constitution, and the 2004 family code has been lauded for granting women increased rights in the areas of marriage, divorce, and child custody. Various other laws aim to protect women's interests. Nevertheless, inheritance rules remain discriminatory, spousal rape is not a crime, and domestic violence against women is rarely reported or punished due to social stigma. Women continue to face significant discrimination at the societal level. All extramarital sexual activity is illegal.

Child laborers, especially girls working as domestic helpers, are denied basic rights. In July 2016, parliament passed a new labor law for domestic workers that requires written contracts, sets a minimum age of 18 (with a five-year phase-in period during which those aged 16 and 17 are allowed to work), stipulates weekly rest periods, and provides minimum wage guidelines. The quality of enforcement of the law, which was set to take effect in 2017, remained to be seen. Separately, parliament in May adopted a law to criminalize human trafficking; existing measures had defined and banned only some forms of trafficking and left many victims unprotected.

↓ Mozambique

Political Rights Rating: 4
Civil Liberties Rating: 4
Freedom Rating: 4.0
Freedom Status: Partly Free
Electoral Democracy: No

Population: 27,200,000
Capital: Maputo

Trend Arrow: Mozambique received a downward trend arrow due to an increase in political tensions and violence, including the abuse of civilian populations by security forces, which caused thousands of people to flee to Malawi.

Ten-Year Ratings Timeline For Year Under Review (Political Rights, Civil Liberties, Status)

Year Under Review	2007	2008	2009	2010	2011	2012	2013	2014	2015	2016
Rating	3,3,PF	3,3,PF	4,3,PF	4,3,PF	4,3,PF	4,3,PF	4,3,PF	4,3,PF	4,4,PF	4,4,F

Overview: Mozambique has been governed by the same political party since its 1975 independence, and the ruling party's unbroken incumbency has allowed it to establish significant control over state institutions. The opposition has disputed the results of recent elections, and its armed wing has fought a low-level conflict against government forces for the last several years. Mozambique also struggles with corruption, and journalists who report on it and other sensitive issues risk violent attacks.

KEY DEVELOPMENTS IN 2016:

- Armed conflict continued between government security forces and the opposition Mozambique National Resistance (RENAMO). Government forces were implicated in human rights abuses against civilians, and the ongoing violence has driven thousands of refugees into Malawi and Zimbabwe.
- While no deal was achieved in several rounds of internationally mediated peace negotiations, President Filipe Nyusi of the ruling Front for the Liberation of Mozambique (FRELIMO) and RENAMO leader Alfonso Dhlakama agreed to a seven-day ceasefire in late December.
- In October, Jeremias Pondeca, a senior RENAMO negotiator, was assassinated while jogging in Maputo.
- In April, the government was revealed to have taken out nearly $2 billion in secret loans in 2013 and 2014. In December, a parliamentary committee ruled that the government had broken the law by failing to seek parliament's approval for the loans. In the scandal's wake, major donors, including the World Bank and International Monetary Fund (IMF), suspended budget assistance to the country.

EXECUTIVE SUMMARY

Ongoing, low-level fighting between government security forces and RENAMO in the country's central and northwestern regions resulted in the deaths of dozens of people and forced thousands of refugees into neighboring Malawi and Zimbabwe in 2016. Acts of violence against civilians, including summary executions and acts of sexual violence, were reported; most documented attacks were found to have been committed by government security forces, with many abuses apparently based on perceived or actual political affiliation. In addition, officials from both FRELIMO and RENAMO have been targeted in violent attacks, with at least 10 apparent political assassinations having occurred since 2015. In October 2016, Jeremias Pondeca, a senior RENAMO negotiator, was assassinated while jogging in Maputo.

Internationally mediated peace talks that opened in 2015 took place throughout the year, with participants attempting to negotiate agreements on RENAMO's calls for decentralization and for its fighters to be integrated into the national security forces, among other issues. In late December, President Nyusi and Dhlakama, RENAMO's leader, agreed to a 7-day ceasefire.

There were numerous instances of attacks against and intimidation of journalists in 2016. In May, political analyst José Jaime Macuane, a regular commentator on the independent television station STV and a critic of government policies and organized crime, was kidnapped and shot in the legs by unknown attackers. In December, in the conflict-affected Manica province, men claiming to be police officers raided the home of John Chekwa, a community radio journalist and @*Verdade* correspondent known for his reporting on the ongoing conflict and citizens' grievances. The assailants confiscated items of value and abducted and threatened to kill Chekwa's son, who later escaped. Several journalists also faced dubious defamation cases during the year.

In April 2016, it emerged that the Mozambican government had taken out almost $2 billion in secret loans in 2013 and 2014. The revelation outraged the Mozambican public, exacerbated an existing economic crisis, prompted the World Bank and IMF to suspend budget assistance to the country, and generally called into question the ruling party's commitment to transparency and its ability to manage the economy. In December, a parliamentary commission of inquiry concluded that the government had acted illegally by failing to acquire permission from the legislature before taking on the loans, which contributed to a national debt amounting to more than 80 percent of gross domestic product as of September. President Nyusi, who served as defense minister at the time the loans were agreed, claimed that his staff had known nothing about the issue.

POLITICAL RIGHTS: 20 / 40 (-2)

A. Electoral Process: 6 / 12

B. Political Pluralism and Participation: 9 / 16 (− 1)

C. Functioning of Government: 5 / 12 (− 1)

CIVIL LIBERTIES: 33 / 60 (− 1)

D. Freedom of Expression and Belief: 11 / 16

E. Associational and Organizational Rights: 7 / 12

F. Rule of Law: 7 / 16

G. Personal Autonomy and Individual Rights: 8 / 16 (− 1)

This country report has been abridged for *Freedom in the World 2017*. For background information on political rights and civil liberties in Mozambique, see *Freedom in the World 2016*.

Myanmar

Political Rights Rating: 5 ↑
Civil Liberties Rating: 5
Freedom Rating: 5.0
Freedom Status: Partly Free
Electoral Democracy: No

Population: 52,400,000
Capital: Nay Pyi Taw

Status Change, Ratings Change: Myanmar's status improved from Not Free to Partly Free, and its political rights rating improved from 6 to 5, after lawmakers conducted the country's first relatively free presidential election through an indirect vote by the parliament, and as the new government began work on a series of policy reforms aimed at improving civil liberties.

Ten-Year Ratings Timeline For Year Under Review (Political Rights, Civil Liberties, Status)

Year Under Review	2007	2008	2009	2010	2011	2012	2013	2014	2015	2016
Rating	7,7,NF	7,7,NF	7,7,NF	7,7,NF	7,6,NF	6,5,NF	6,5,NF	6,6,NF	6,5,NF	5,5,PF

Overview: Myanmar's transition from military dictatorship toward democracy is ongoing, with relatively free parliamentary elections in 2015 ushering in a peaceful transfer of power to the National League for Democracy (NLD). However, ethnic peace remains elusive as military offensives and other violent conflicts offset a government push for more comprehensive negotiations with ethnic armed groups. Persecution of the country's mostly Muslim Rohingya minority has created sustained refugee outflows.

KEY DEVELOPMENTS IN 2016:

- Following the NLD's overwhelming victory in 2015 parliamentary elections, the ruling Union and Solidarity Development Party (USDP) and military representatives accepted the results, setting the stage for a peaceful transfer of political power. The NLD-led parliament held its opening session in February and elected the country's new president in March.
- Over the military's objections, in April the parliament installed NLD leader Aung San Suu Kyi—who was constitutionally barred from the presidency—in the newly created post of state counselor, granting her authority to direct policies not under military jurisdiction.
- The government took several steps that signaled an opening of associational and organizational space, including scrapping the restrictive Emergency Provisions Act, releasing dozens of students who had been arrested the previous year on unlawful assembly charges, and engaging with nongovernmental organizations (NGOs).
- The NLD government's push for the creation of a more comprehensive peace mechanism was hampered by military offensives against various ethnic rebel groups, attacks by such groups against security forces, and continued divisions among signatories and nonsignatories to a 2015 national cease-fire agreement.

EXECUTIVE SUMMARY

The USDP and military representatives accepted the results of parliamentary elections held in 2015, permitting a historic transfer of political power to an NLD-dominated parliament, which opened its first session in February 2016. In March, Htin Kyaw, the NLD's primary presidential candidate, won the presidency with 360 of the 652 parliamentary votes cast in the country's first relatively free presidential election. Days later, NLD lawmakers approved a bill that elevated party leader Aung San Suu Kyi, who was constitutionally barred from running for the presidency because members of her immediate family hold foreign citizenship, to the newly created and powerful position of state counselor. The USDP condemned the move as an improper consolidation of power.

The NLD government in 2016 took a series of actions that indicated an opening of associational and organizational space following decades of military dictatorship. Government representatives made efforts to engage with civil society groups, in particular by holding consultations regarding the implementation of laws on NGO registration. In April, a court ordered the release of 69 students who had been arrested the previous year on unlawful assembly charges, and in October, the government repealed the Emergency Provisions Act, which the military government had frequently employed to jail political activists. However, concerns about freedom of expression persisted amid a spike in prosecutions for online defamation under the 2013 Telecommunications Law.

Separately, while corruption remained rampant at both the national and local levels, the new NLD government took modest steps to address the problem. In April, Aung San Suu Kyi issued an official regulation banning civil servants from accepting gifts worth more than 25,000 kyat ($21).

The NLD government struggled to negotiate a more comprehensive peace agreement with the many ethnic armed groups in Myanmar. Aung San Suu Kyi convened a high-profile peace conference in August, though officials later downplayed it as a trust-building exercise for the hundreds of delegates who attended. Military offensives against various ethnic rebel groups, and attacks by such groups against security forces, continued. In October, armed men attacked police posts in Rakhine State, killing nine officers; officials blamed the Rohingya Solidarity Organisation (RSO), a militant group that was active in the 1980s and 1990s. Security forces subsequently launched violent reprisals against the local Rohingya Muslim population, which reportedly included torture and rape, worsening the community's already dire humanitarian situation and causing a new outflow of refugees to Bangladesh. Separately, activists continued to report abuses by the military against civilians in Northern Shan and Kachin States, where fighting between armed groups and state forces has increased in recent years.

POLITICAL RIGHTS: 14 / 40 (+ 3)

A. Electoral Process: 5 / 12 (+ 2)

Under the 2008 constitution, whose drafting was controlled by the military, the bicameral Assembly of the Union consists of the 440-seat House of Representatives, or lower house, and the 224-seat House of Nationalities, or upper house. Representatives serve five-year terms. A quarter of the seats in both houses are reserved for the military and filled through appointment by the commander in chief, an officer with broad powers who is selected by the military-dominated National Defense and Security Council (NDSC).

The legislature elects the president. Military members have the right to nominate one of the three presidential candidates, and the elected members of each chamber nominate the other two. The candidate with the largest number of votes in a combined parliamentary vote wins the presidency; the other two candidates become vice presidents. The NLD selected Htin Kyaw as its primary presidential candidate, and he won the presidency with 360 of the 652 parliamentary votes cast in the March 2016 election. The first vice president was Myint Swe, the military-nominated candidate, and the second vice president was Henry Van Thio, also of the NLD.

Unlike with the 2010 parliamentary elections, international electoral observers concluded that the 2015 polls were generally credible and that the outcome reflected the will of the people, despite a campaign period marked by anti-Muslim rhetoric, the exclusion of Muslim candidates, and the disenfranchisement of hundreds of thousands of Rohingya, most of whom are Muslim. The NLD won 135 of the 168 elected seats in the upper house, 255 of 330 elected seats in the lower house, and 496 of 659 seats across 14 state and regional legislatures. The military-backed USDP placed second with 12 seats in the upper house, 30 in the lower house, and 76 in the states and regions. (Myanmar's first-past-the-post system allowed the NLD to translate its popular vote margin into a much larger majority in terms of seats; it took 57 percent of the popular vote, compared with the USDP's 28 percent.) The remaining seats were captured by ethnic minority and other parties as well as independents. While ethnic parties fared poorly overall, the Shan Nationalities League for Democracy (SNLD) and the Arakan National Party (ANP) performed well in their respective states.

After the elections, commander in chief Min Aung Hlaing, former military ruler Than Shwe, and outgoing president Thein Sein each met with Aung San Suu Kyi and agreed to support a smooth transition. However, constitutional provisions barred the NLD leader from becoming president due to the foreign nationality of her immediate family members. Changes to the constitution require a three-quarters parliamentary supermajority, meaning military support would be required in practice. To circumvent these restrictions, the NLD used its parliamentary majority to create the new post of state counselor, a powerful role akin to that of a prime minister, which Aung San Suu Kyi assumed in April 2016 amid military objections.

B. Political Pluralism and Participation: 8 / 16

New political parties were generally allowed to register and compete in the 2015 elections, which featured fewer restrictions on party organization and voter mobilization than the 2010 vote. Only sporadic interference from government officials was reported. Ninety-one parties competed in the elections, and many of them, including the NLD, convened meetings and large rallies throughout the country.

The government has allowed members of the parliament to speak about democratic rights since 2011. While the legislators' time to speak has often been severely limited, many of their speeches receive coverage in the domestic media. Since winning a seat in 2012 by-elections, Aung San Suu Kyi has gained political influence, as demonstrated by the NLD's dramatic 2015 electoral victory. However, critics argue that she has failed to strongly challenge incumbent interests or alter state policy. She and her aides have notably downplayed the plight of the Rohingya minority.

The military retains considerable power over political affairs, though the 2015 results and subsequent transition talks suggested a waning ability or determination to influence electoral outcomes. The 2008 constitution allows the military to dissolve the civilian government and parliament and rule directly if the president declares a state of emergency. The military has the right to administer its own affairs, and members of the former military government received blanket immunity for all official acts.

Minority groups face restrictions on their political rights and electoral opportunities. A 2014 amendment to the Political Parties Registration Law prohibited residents without full citizenship from forming political parties or contesting elections. The measure effectively curbed political participation by Rohingya, who were rendered stateless by a 1982 law and lack full citizenship documents. A sitting Rohingya lawmaker from the USDP was barred from running in 2015. That year, under pressure from Buddhist nationalists, the president issued a decree revoking the temporary identification cards, or "white cards," that had allowed Rohingya to vote in previous elections. A Constitutional Tribunal ruling later in 2015 then found that voting by white-card holders was unconstitutional. Nearly all Rohingya were consequently left off the voter rolls for the 2015 elections. Other Muslims with citizenship documents were able to vote, but of more than 6,000 candidates on the final list, only about 28 were Muslim. A total of 75 candidates were disqualified by election officials, including a number of Rohingyas and other Muslims.

C. Functioning of Government: 4 / 12 (+ 1)

Though the NLD has begun to lay out plans for policy changes among its various ministry portfolios, the military remains a dominant force in policymaking, particularly through its constitutional control over the Defense, Home Affairs, and Border Affairs Ministries. The military effectively controls at least six seats on the powerful 11-member NDSC. Over one-fifth of the total budget is devoted to the military. Although the military budget remains opaque and the 2011 Special Funds Law allows the military to circumvent parliamentary oversight to access additional funds, details on part of the budget were shared publicly for the first time in 2015 and faced limited parliamentary scrutiny.

Corruption is rampant at both the national and local levels. In a first step to address the problem, Aung San Suu Kyi in April 2016 issued an official regulation banning civil servants from accepting gifts worth more than 25,000 kyat ($21). An Anti-Corruption Commission established in 2014 has only penalized a handful of people in connection with its investigations. Privatization of state-owned companies and other economic reforms in recent years have allegedly benefited family members and associates of senior officials. The government has ignored tax evasion by the country's wealthiest companies and individuals.

Discretionary Political Rights Question B: − 3 / 0

The government has long used violence, displacement, and other tactics to alter the demographics of states with ethnic unrest or insurgencies. The Rohingya in Rakhine State have faced particularly harsh restrictions for decades, including limits on family size and the ability and right to marry. Hundreds of Rohingya remain imprisoned for dubious offenses such as marrying an unapproved spouse. Children born to unrecognized couples or beyond a two-child limit imposed on Rohingya in some areas are often denied legal status and services. The 2015 revocation and confiscation of temporary identification cards led to the disenfranchisement and loss of citizenship rights for hundreds of thousands of Rohingya. Human rights experts have continued to label the abuses against the Rohingya as crimes against humanity, while some analysts have argued that they constitute either genocide or a precursor to genocide.

In August 2016, the NLD government created a joint advisory panel led by former UN secretary general Kofi Annan to help develop conflict-resolution mechanisms to address tensions between Buddhists and Muslims (mainly Rohingya) in Rakhine State, and to ensure the delivery of humanitarian aid there, among other tasks. However, the group failed to include a single Rohingya representative, nor was it mandated to investigate human rights abuses.

In October, armed men attacked police posts in Rakhine State, killing nine officers; officials blamed the Rohingya Solidarity Organisation (RSO), a militant group that was active in the 1980s and 1990s. Security forces launched a severe crackdown on Rohingya communities in the northern part of the state, which reportedly included torture and rape, worsening already dire humanitarian conditions and causing a new outflow of refugees to Bangladesh.

CIVIL LIBERTIES: 18 / 60 (+ 1)

D. Freedom of Expression and Belief: 7 / 16

Media freedoms have improved substantially since the official end of government censorship and prepublication approval in 2012. However, other restrictions limit journalists' freedom. Existing media laws allow authorities to deny licenses to outlets whose reporting is considered to have insulted religion or endangered national security, and the threat of prosecution under criminal defamation laws has encouraged a climate of pervasive self-censorship.

In 2016, there was a notable increase in the number of defamation cases brought against journalists and social media users, some of which were initiated in response to criticism of government or military authorities. Those involving online commentary were generally filed under the broadly worded 2013 Telecommunications Law, which allows penalties of up to three years in prison. The editor in chief of the independent *Daily Eleven* and the chief executive of its parent company were imprisoned on defamation charges in November, in connection with an article implicating the chief minister of Yangon in illegal business dealings with a drug trafficker. Separately, a journalist fired from the English-language *Myanmar Times* claimed that the government had pressured the paper to dismiss her following the October publication of an article on allegations that the security forces had raped more than two dozen women in Rakhine State.

Reporters covering sensitive topics risk harassment and physical violence. In December, journalist Soe Moe Tun was found beaten to death after reporting on the illegal logging industry. The Myanmar Journalists' Association reported that another journalist had relocated to a different town after being threatened by individuals in the logging industry.

Previous constraints on internet access have largely unraveled, and the proliferation of smartphones has rapidly increased usage, but internet activity is still subject to criminal punishment under broadly worded legal provisions. The Electronic Transactions Law, which has been used to criminalize political activism on the internet, mandates fines or prison terms of three to seven years for "any act detrimental to" state security, law and order, community peace and tranquility, national solidarity, the national economy, or national culture, including "receiving or sending" related information. Journalists and others have faced cyberattacks and attempts to infiltrate their e-mail accounts by both state and nonstate actors.

The 2008 constitution provides for freedom of religion. It distinguishes Buddhism as the majority religion, but also recognizes Christianity, Islam, Hinduism, and animism. The government occasionally interferes with religious assemblies and attempts to control the Buddhist clergy. Authorities have also discriminated against minority religious groups, refusing to grant them permission to hold gatherings and restricting educational activities, proselytizing, and construction of houses of worship. Influential Buddhist monks in Karen State have built pagodas in church and mosque compounds, increasing tensions within diverse communities.

Anti-Muslim hate speech and discrimination continued to spread during 2016. In April, the newly appointed religious affairs minister suggested in a radio interview that members of the country's Muslim and Hindu minorities were not full citizens, sparking both criticism and strident statements of support. Social media and some state institutions and mainstream news websites have amplified such communal tensions. Ma Ba Tha, or the Committee for the Protection of Nationality and Religion, agitates for the protection of Buddhist privileges, urges boycotts against Muslim-run businesses, and disseminates anti-Muslim propaganda. In September, three Muslim men were arrested and imprisoned for illegally importing cows for the Eid al-Adha celebration.

In 2015, the parliament approved a revised version of a controversial education law, initially passed in 2014, that failed to meet student demands concerning decentralization, access to instruction in local languages, curriculum reform, and a clear role for student unions in setting education policy, among other issues. Opponents of the new law said it perpetuated the country's authoritarian approach to academic freedom, and student leaders pledged to continue pressing their demands.

The ability to engage in open and free private discussion without criminal repercussions has increased markedly since political reforms began under the previous administration. However, general surveillance by local security officials, under the purview of the military-controlled Home Affairs Ministry, remains a common practice. In September 2016, a parliamentary committee submitted draft legislation that would offer better protections from state surveillance.

E. Associational and Organizational Rights: 5 / 12 (+ 1)

Under the Peaceful Assembly and Peaceful Procession Law, as revised in 2014, holding a demonstration without government "consent" is punishable with up to six months in prison; a variety of other vaguely worded violations can draw lesser penalties. Authorities arrested a number of demonstrators under the law during the 2015 election campaign. However, in April 2016, the president pardoned 69 students arrested the previous year. A new

Peaceful Assembly and Procession Bill proposed in the legislature still includes criminal penalties for vaguely worded offenses.

The 2014 Association Registration Law features simple, voluntary registration procedures for local and international NGOs and no restrictions or criminal punishments for noncompliance. Although the law was seen a positive development, in 2015 the Home Affairs Ministry issued implementing regulations that required NGOs to obtain government approval prior to registration, drawing sharp criticism from civil society leaders. However, consultations between civil society and the relevant committee in the new NLD government were held in 2016 to draw attention to the law and provide clarity on implementation rules.

Independent trade unions were banned until 2011, and union organizers continue to face retaliation for their work. In recent years, factory workers have held strikes in Yangon with fewer repercussions than in the past, though arrests for striking and other labor activism persisted in 2016. A 2013 law allowed for a minimum wage, and in 2015, after two years of heated negotiations, the figure was set at $2.80 per day.

F. Rule of Law: 1 / 16

The judiciary is not independent. Judges are appointed or approved by the government and adjudicate cases according to its decrees. Administrative detention laws allow individuals to be held without charge, trial, or access to legal counsel for up to five years if deemed a threat to state security or sovereignty. According to a report by the Assistance Association for Political Prisoners (Burma), at the end of November 2016 there were 195 political prisoners in the country, of whom 87 were currently serving sentences, 24 were in pretrial detention, and 84 were awaiting trial outside of prison. In October the parliament repealed the 1950 Emergency Provisions Act, which the previous military government had invoked frequently to silence and imprison dissidents.

Some of the country's worst human rights abuses, commonly committed by government troops, are against ethnic minorities, especially the Kachin, Shan, Chin, Karen, and Rohingya. Riots and mob violence against Rohingya and other Muslims have killed hundreds of people, displaced thousands of residents, and destroyed hundreds of properties, including religious sites, since 2012. The government's failure to protect victims, conduct investigations, and punish perpetrators is well documented. The anti-Muslim Ma Ba Tha and the similar 969 movement have been accused of stoking outbreaks of violence with inflammatory sermons, leaflets, and other materials, and local government officials have actively sought out administrative loopholes to destroy Muslim schools and houses of worship.

The government continued to negotiate with armed ethnic minority groups in 2016, but a comprehensive agreement regarding federalism and adherence to the 2008 constitution remained elusive. Discussions were hampered by persistent fighting in some regions, including military offensives in Kachin State and in Shan State.

A number of laws create a hostile environment for LGBT (lesbian, gay, bisexual, and transgender) people. Same-sex sexual conduct is criminalized under the penal code, and police subject LGBT people to harassment, extortion, and physical and sexual abuse.

G. Personal Autonomy and Individual Rights: 5 / 16

Freedom of internal travel is generally respected outside of conflict zones. Numerous exiled activists who returned to the country have experienced substantial delays and evasion from government authorities when attempting to renew visas and residency permits, despite the call for exiles to return to work for the country's development. Illegal toll collection by state and nonstate actors has been a problem in some areas. The parliament voted in September 2016 to repeal a long-standing rule requiring overnight houseguests to be registered with local authorities, which particularly affected low-income people and activists and created opportunities for harassment, extortion, and invasions of privacy. Guests staying for more than a month must still be registered.

Contentious disputes over land grabbing and business projects that violate human rights continued in 2016. Instances of forced eviction and displacement, lack of sufficient compensation, and direct violence by state security officials abound. As of June 2015, the parliament's Farmland Investigation Commission reported that it had heard about 20,000 of the 30,000 cases submitted since 2013, and decided in favor of compensation for claimants in only 4 percent of the cases heard—a number that activists generally view as much too low. The NLD government's newly formed Central Committee on Confiscated Farmlands and Other Lands has been accused of including members who were themselves involved in land grabs.

Women of some classes have traditionally enjoyed high social and economic status, but women remain underrepresented in the government and civil service. Notwithstanding the prominence of Aung San Suu Kyi, whose father led Myanmar's independence struggle, few women have achieved recognition in politics, and she remains the only woman of ministerial rank in the current NLD cabinet. Sixty-four women were elected to the new parliament in 2015, up from 28 in the outgoing body.

Laws protecting women from violence and exploitation are inadequate, and violence against women is a persistent problem. The army has a record of using rape as a weapon of war against ethnic minority women, and security personnel typically enjoy impunity for sexual violence. Human trafficking is also a concern; the country was designated in June 2016 as one of the worst performers in the U.S. State Department's annual *Trafficking in Persons Report* due to the prevalence of child soldiers and forced labor.

Child labor is endemic in Myanmar. The International Labour Organization estimated in 2015 that nearly 1.1 million children, almost 10 percent of all children in the country, engaged in child labor. To address international concerns and improve childhood development, the government in 2014 had announced plans for a policy to end child labor. Various commercial and other interests continue to use forced labor despite a formal ban on the practice since 2000.

Namibia

Political Rights Rating: 2
Civil Liberties Rating: 2
Freedom Rating: 2.0
Freedom Status: Free
Electoral Democracy: Yes

Population: 2,500,000
Capital: Windhoek

Ten-Year Ratings Timeline For Year Under Review (Political Rights, Civil Liberties, Status)

Year Under Review	2007	2008	2009	2010	2011	2012	2013	2014	2015	2016
Rating	2,2,F	2,2,F	2,2,F	2,2,F	2,2,F	2,2,F	2,2,F	2,2,F	2,2,F	2,2,F

Overview: Namibia is a stable multiparty democracy, though the ruling party, SWAPO, has overwhelmingly won every election since independence. Protections for civil liberties are generally robust. Minority ethnic groups claim that the government favors the majority

Ovambo—which dominates SWAPO—in allocating funding and services, and the nomadic San people suffer from poverty and marginalization. Other human rights concerns include the criminalization of same-sex sexual relations under colonial-era laws and discrimination against women under customary law and other traditional societal practices.

KEY DEVELOPMENTS IN 2016:

- A corruption case dating to 2009 faced further obstacles as the defendants sought to have the trial judge removed.
- Both the state and defendants in a collection of treason cases linked to secessionism in the Caprivi region pursued appeals of their 2015 verdicts during the year.
- In April, authorities temporarily detained two Japanese journalists shortly after they interviewed a cabinet minister about Namibia's use of North Korean workers on military construction projects. The journalists were released, and their seized equipment was eventually returned.

EXECUTIVE SUMMARY

A long-running corruption trial continued to face delays during 2016, as the Supreme Court heard arguments in June on the defendants' petition to have the trial judge, Maphios Cheda, removed from the case. Prosecutors accused three business partners—former public service commissioner Teckla Lameck, Jerobeam Mokaxwa, and Chinese national Yang Fan, whose employer had close ties to the Chinese Communist Party—of defrauding the state in 2009 through inflated contract prices, among other offenses. The Supreme Court was still considering Cheda's removal at year's end.

Although the High Court issued verdicts in 2015 for the last of more than 100 alleged secessionists who were accused of treason and other crimes related to fighting in Namibia's Caprivi region between 1998 and 1999, a series of related court proceedings began in 2016. These included defendants' appeals of their convictions, civil suits against the state by those found not guilty, and state appeals of the acquittals. Hearings were expected to continue in 2017.

The issue of land reform remained a contentious one in 2016. A small white minority owns just under half of Namibia's arable land, and redistribution has been slow and fraught with disagreement. In August, the radical Affirmative Repositioning (AR) movement threatened to take the government to court for failing to make affordable, rent-controlled land available as previously agreed. Disputes over land policy have divided SWAPO in recent years; four SWAPO youth wing officials were reinstated in the party after a court ruled in April that their 2015 expulsions—largely for involvement with or support of AR—had violated the party's own rules.

POLITICAL RIGHTS: 30 / 40

A. Electoral Process: 10 / 12

B. Political Pluralism and Participation: 11 / 16

C. Functioning of Government: 9 / 12

CIVIL LIBERTIES: 47 / 60

D. Freedom of Expression and Belief: 14 / 16

E. Associational and Organizational Rights: 12 / 12

F. Rule of Law: 11 / 16

G. Personal Autonomy and Individual Rights: 10 / 16

This country report has been abridged for *Freedom in the World 2017*. For background information on political rights and civil liberties in Namibia, see *Freedom in the World 2016*.

Nauru

Political Rights Rating: 2
Civil Liberties Rating: 2
Freedom Rating: 2.0
Freedom Status: Free
Electoral Democracy: Yes

Population: 10,000
Capital: Yaren

Ten-Year Ratings Timeline For Year Under Review (Political Rights, Civil Liberties, Status)

Year Under Review	2007	2008	2009	2010	2011	2012	2013	2014	2015	2016
Rating	1,1,F	1,1,F	1,1,F	1,1,F	1,1,F	1,1,F	1,1,F	1,2,F	2,2,F	2,2,F

Overview: Citizens of Nauru generally enjoy political rights and civil liberties, though the government has taken steps to sideline its political opponents, and intense political rivalries and the use of parliamentary no-confidence votes have been a source of instability. Corruption is a serious problem. The government is heavily reliant on funding it receives from Australia for housing a processing center for asylum seekers. Authorities restrict foreign journalists' and activists' access to the facility, which has attracted international criticism for abuses committed against the asylum seekers who were forcibly transferred there.

KEY DEVELOPMENTS IN 2016:

- In August, Amnesty International reported that conditions in the Australian-run processing center for asylum seekers remained dire, citing among other issues grossly inadequate housing and frequent self-harm and suicide attempts by residents.
- The government headed by President Baron Waqa was returned to office in July elections with an increased majority.
- Foreign journalists reported being denied visas ahead of the elections. After the polls, the justice minister berated foreign outlets over critical coverage of the processing center for asylum seekers.
- Days after the election, the government approved a bill creating the new post of assistant minister, and subsequently installed seven assistant ministers. The move was seen as an attempt by Waqa to consolidate power.

EXECUTIVE SUMMARY

Elections in July 2016 to Nauru's 19-member unicameral parliament saw the Waqa-led government return with an increased majority. After his reelection by the parliament, Waqa moved to consolidate power by appointing seven people to the post of assistant minister, a new position created with the approval of the 2016 Assistant Ministers Bill a few days after the elections.

Corruption is a serious problem. Allegations of improper payments to senior government officials, including Waqa, by an Australian phosphate company continued to emerge in 2016, with the Australian Broadcasting Company (ABC) in September reporting on the existence of bank records supporting claims that the company had given money to the family of Justice Minister David Adeang. In April, a major Australian bank announced it would cancel all operations involving the Nauru government and public bodies, with media reports suggesting that the decision came in response to concerns about financial mismanagement.

Media in Nauru is government owned, with the exception of opposition newsletters. Foreign news sources are available. The social networking website Facebook remained inaccessible in Nauru in 2016.

The government appears determined to silence international criticism of extremely poor conditions faced by asylum seekers at the Australian-run facility by restricting or interfering with the activities of foreign media and nongovernmental organization (NGO) workers. In what was widely characterized as a means of deterring reporting on the asylum facility, the visa application fee for foreign journalists was raised to $8,000 in 2014, up from $400. There were reports of foreign journalists being denied visas to cover the 2016 elections. In a statement shortly after the polls, Adeang said the reelection of Waqa's government "humiliated" journalists from Australia and New Zealand, suggesting that they had sought to discredit the administration through critical reporting on the asylum center; he added that they should "show more respect" to the country. Additionally, government officials including Adeang have pressured members of the judiciary who issued rulings or voiced opinions contrary to government policies, including on refugees and antigovernment protests.

An August report by Amnesty International documented "appalling abuse" of the asylum seekers who had been forcibly transferred to the Nauru processing center. The report noted among other things grossly inadequate housing; the denial of health care for life-threatening conditions; and a high rate of self-harm and suicide attempts among residents who suffer "overwhelming despair" as they wait, at times for years, for their asylum applications to be processed. Australia pays Nauru about $35 million per year to house the facility, which is operated by private contractors paid for by Australia.

POLITICAL RIGHTS: 35 / 40

A. Electoral Process: 12 / 12

B. Political Pluralism and Participation: 15 / 16

C. Functioning of Government: 8 / 12

CIVIL LIBERTIES: 46 / 60 (− 3)

D. Freedom of Expression and Belief: 13 / 16

E. Associational and Organizational Rights: 9 / 12 (− 1)

F. Rule of Law: 10 / 16 (− 2)

G. Personal Autonomy and Individual Rights: 14 / 16

This country report has been abridged for *Freedom in the World 2017*. For background information on political rights and civil liberties in Nauru, see *Freedom in the World 2016*.

Nepal

Political Rights Rating: 3
Civil Liberties Rating: 4
Freedom Rating: 3.5
Freedom Status: Partly Free
Electoral Democracy: Yes

Population: 28,400,000
Capital: Kathmandu

Ten-Year Ratings Timeline For Year Under Review (Political Rights, Civil Liberties, Status)

Year Under Review	2007	2008	2009	2010	2011	2012	2013	2014	2015	2016
Rating	5,4,PF	4,4,PF	4,4,PF	4,4,PF	4,4,PF	4,4,PF	4,4,PF	3,4,PF	3,4,PF	3,4,PF

Overview: After ending a decade-long civil war in 2006, Nepal held competitive national elections in 2008 and 2013, and adopted a permanent constitution in 2015. However, successive coalition governments have proven unstable as rival factions pursue their interests in establishing the details of a new constitutional order, and political protests often lead to violence. Corruption is endemic in politics, government, and the judicial system. The police service has been accused of criminality and excessive force or torture, and prison conditions are poor. Journalists often face violence or harassment in the course of their work. Other problems include discrimination against low-caste Hindus, ethnic minorities, and Christians; gender-based violence and underage marriage; sex trafficking of women and girls; and bonded or child labor.

KEY DEVELOPMENTS IN 2016:

- Ethnic Madhesi protesters ended a months-long blockade along the Indian border in February, though they continued to object to elements of the new constitution.
- Prime Minister Khadga Prasad Sharma Oli resigned in July after the Maoist party withdrew support from his coalition government, and Maoist leader Pushpa Kamal Dahal was elected prime minister by a new coalition in August.
- The government failed to push through crucial constitutional amendments by year's end, raising concerns that local, provincial, and federal elections could not be held by January 2018 as scheduled.

EXECUTIVE SUMMARY

Nepal experienced continued political turmoil during 2016 as the government and parliament sought to implement the 2015 constitution, which had drawn opposition from various groups over its provisions on citizenship, federalism, and political representation. However, violence and obstacles to freedom of movement declined over the course of the year. In February, opposition parties representing ethnic Madhesis in southern Nepal finally ended a border blockade that had effectively cut off supplies from India for 135 days and prompted deadly clashes with security forces. The groups maintained that the constitution's reorganization of the country into seven provinces, among other provisions, would weaken their influence.

In January 2016, as part of an effort to address the Madhesi concerns, parliament approved a constitutional amendment that prioritized population over geography in the delineation of electoral constituencies. However, the Madhesi parties criticized it as inadequate, and a number of other constitutional concerns—including the role of districts as administrative units and quota formulas for various minorities and disadvantaged groups—remained unresolved. Critics of the constitution also objected to its citizenship provisions, which allow the children of Nepali mothers and non-Nepali fathers to acquire only naturalized citizenship; naturalized citizens are ineligible for the highest executive, legislative, and judicial offices.

In May, Prime Minister Oli of the Communist Party of Nepal–Unified Marxist-Leninist (CPN-UML) struck a nine-point deal with the Maoists—who changed their name later that month to the Communist Party of Nepal (Maoist Centre)—to maintain his coalition government. The agreement included a pledge to withdraw or offer clemency on any court cases related to human rights abuses during the 1996–2006 civil war, despite previous Supreme Court rulings curbing the government's ability to grant amnesty for such crimes.

Oli ultimately failed to implement the deal and resigned in late July to avoid a no-confidence vote in parliament. Maoist party chairman Pushpa Kamal Dahal, also known as Prachanda, was elected to replace him in early August, forming a coalition with the Nepali Congress party and leaving the CPN-UML in opposition. His government was Nepal's ninth since 2008. It drafted a constitutional amendment bill to address some of the outstanding grievances with the 2015 charter, but because amendments require a two-thirds majority to pass, the CPN-UML was able to block it, and it had yet to be adopted at year's end.

A number of incidents during the year raised concerns about freedom of expression and freedom of assembly. For example, in May, a Canadian man was arrested and deported for pro-Madhesi posts on social media, and a photojournalist was arrested and temporarily detained for reporting on a symbolic protest outside a government complex. Other journalists faced short detentions or physical assaults. In June, the government issued a directive requiring online media to register and giving itself broad authority to block online content.

POLITICAL RIGHTS: 24 / 40 (− 1)

A. Electoral Process: 9 / 12

B. Political Pluralism and Participation: 10 / 16 (− 1)

C. Functioning of Government: 5 / 12

CIVIL LIBERTIES: 28 / 60 (+ 2)

D. Freedom of Expression and Belief: 9 / 16

E. Associational and Organizational Rights: 5 / 12

F. Rule of Law: 6 / 16 (+ 1)

G. Personal Autonomy and Individual Rights: 8 / 16 (+ 1)

This country report has been abridged for *Freedom in the World 2017*. For background information on political rights and civil liberties in Nepal, see *Freedom in the World 2016*.

Netherlands

Political Rights Rating: 1
Civil Liberties Rating: 1
Freedom Rating: 1.0
Freedom Status: Free
Electoral Democracy: Yes

Population: 17,000,000
Capital: Amsterdam

Ten-Year Ratings Time-line For Year Under Review (Political Rights, Civil Liberties, Status)

Year Under Review	2007	2008	2009	2010	2011	2012	2013	2014	2015	2016
Rating	1,1,F	1,1,F	1,1,F	1,1,F	1,1,F	1,1,F	1,1,F	1,1,F	1,1,F	1,1,F

Overview: The Netherlands is a parliamentary democracy with a strong record of safeguarding political rights and civil liberties. Nevertheless, the political debate and policymaking in recent years have reflected a growing wariness of immigration and Muslim minorities.

KEY DEVELOPMENTS IN 2016:

- Dutch voters rejected a European Union (EU) association agreement with Ukraine in April, though the referendum was nonbinding.
- In September, a majority in the parliament expressed support for a repeal of the country's lèse majesté laws.
- In November, the lower house of parliament passed a ban on face-covering garments in some public settings, but it had yet to be considered by the Senate.
- Geert Wilders, leader of the xenophobic right-wing Party for Freedom (PVV), was found guilty in December of insulting and inciting racial discrimination against people of Moroccan origin in a 2014 speech. However, he was acquitted of inciting hatred and received no penalty for his conviction.

EXECUTIVE SUMMARY

The approach of general elections scheduled for March 2017 influenced the political debate in the Netherlands throughout 2016, with the government and various parties taking up contentious topics related to immigration, integration, and Dutch sovereignty.

In April, voters rejected an EU association agreement with Ukraine after anti-EU activists organized an online petition to bring the matter to a nonbinding referendum. Although more than 61 percent of participants vote against the deal, turnout was only about 32 percent. The agreement, which the government had already signed, was expected to proceed despite the vote.

The government continued to tighten its asylum policies during the year, adding to its list of "safe countries of origin" in February and again in October. Applicants from the listed countries are entitled to a single hearing and must leave the country immediately if their claim is denied, even if they plan to appeal.

In May, Minister of Social Affairs and Employment Lodewijk Asscher sent a letter to municipalities and local mosques to remind them of a rarely enforced 2009 law that requires foreign imams, priests, and other religious functionaries to have a work permit before they can preach in the Netherlands. Also that month, the lower house of parliament approved legislation that would allow the government to strip dual citizens of Dutch nationality if it finds that they joined a terrorist group abroad and pose a threat to national security. In

November, the lower house passed a ban on clothing that covers the face in certain public settings, including schools, hospitals, public transportation, and government buildings. The Senate was considering both bills at year's end.

Separately, in September, Prime Minister Mark Rutte's center-right People's Party for Freedom and Democracy (VVD) said it would support a proposal by the liberal party Democrats 66 (D66) to repeal the country's antiquated lèse-majesté laws, giving the plan a majority, though the parliament had yet to act on the matter at year's end. The laws have occasionally been enforced in recent years. In July, a man was sentenced to 30 days in jail after calling the king a murderer, rapist, and thief on social media.

POLITICAL RIGHTS: 40 / 40
A. Electoral Process: 12 / 12
B. Political Pluralism and Participation: 16 / 16
C. Functioning of Government: 12 / 12

CIVIL LIBERTIES: 59 / 60
D. Freedom of Expression and Belief: 16 / 16
E. Associational and Organizational Rights: 12 / 12
F. Rule of Law: 15 / 16
G. Personal Autonomy and Individual Rights: 16 / 16

This country report has been abridged for *Freedom in the World 2017*. For background information on political rights and civil liberties in the Netherlands, see *Freedom in the World 2016*.

New Zealand

Political Rights Rating: 1
Civil Liberties Rating: 1
Freedom Rating: 1.0
Freedom Status: Free
Electoral Democracy: Yes

Population: 4,700,000
Capital: Wellington

Ten-Year Ratings Timeline For Year Under Review (Political Rights, Civil Liberties, Status)

Year Under Review	2007	2008	2009	2010	2011	2012	2013	2014	2 015	2016
Rating	1,1,F	1,1,F	1,1,F	1,1,F	1,1,F	1,1,F	1,1,F	1,1,F	1,1,F	1,1,F

Overview: New Zealand has a strong record of providing for and protecting fundamental freedoms. Free and fair elections take place regularly, people can exercise their political rights, and free expression and other civil liberties are protected. Among the greatest concerns is *de facto* discrimination against New Zealand's Maori people and some immigrant communities, although the government has made significant efforts in recent years to improve representation of their interests.

KEY DEVELOPMENTS IN 2016:

- The government introduced a bill in August to tighten rules regarding foreign trusts after the Panama Papers scandal highlighted New Zealand as a possible haven for so-called gray money—wealthy individuals using anonymous offshore entities to hide their assets.
- Also in August, the government introduced an intelligence and security bill that would enhance interagency cooperation while allowing for more interception of private communications and collection of citizens' personal information.
- In December, Bill English was sworn in as prime minister following the unexpected resignation, for personal reasons, of long-serving prime minister John Key.

EXECUTIVE SUMMARY

New Zealand has a robust and well-established democracy. Free and fair elections take place regularly and the population is able to organize in a range of political parties and participate in the political process. Although New Zealand is one of the least corrupt countries in the world, the government continues to fight corruption in government and business. For example, in response to the Panama Papers leak in 2016, which referenced New Zealand as a possible haven for offshore investors, the government drafted a bill to tighten registration and transparency regulations for foreign trusts.

In August, the government introduced a sweeping new intelligence and security bill to enable more cooperation among New Zealand's intelligence and law enforcement agencies. As an example of New Zealand's open public discourse, the bill faced robust parliamentary debate and public comment. The bill was pending at year's end.

While individuals enjoy a wide range of civil liberties largely unrestricted, New Zealand continues to struggle to fully uphold the rights of its indigenous and Pacific islander populations, who lag behind the European-descended majority in social and economic status. The Maori population has become more assertive in its claims for land, resources, and compensation from the government in recent years, and the Maori Party is part of the ruling government coalition.

POLITICAL RIGHTS: 40 / 40

A. Electoral Process: 12 / 12

B. Political Pluralism and Participation: 16 / 16

C. Functioning of Government: 12 / 12

CIVIL LIBERTIES: 58 / 60

D. Freedom of Expression and Belief: 16 / 16

E. Associational and Organizational Rights: 12 / 12

F. Rule of Law: 15 / 16

G. Personal Autonomy and Individual Rights: 15 / 16

This country report has been abridged for *Freedom in the World 2017*. For background information on political rights and civil liberties in New Zealand, see *Freedom in the World 2016*.

⬇ Nicaragua

Political Rights Rating: 5 ↓
Civil Liberties Rating: 4 ↓
Freedom Rating: 4.5
Freedom Status: Partly Free
Electoral Democracy: No

Population: 6,300,000
Capital: Managua

Ratings Change, Trend Arrow: Nicaragua's political rights rating declined from 4 to 5, its civil liberties rating declined from 3 to 4, and it received a downward trend arrow due to a court's ouster of the leader of the main opposition party and the National Assembly's expulsion of 16 opposition lawmakers in the run-up to November elections, combined with government efforts to silence journalists and academics with opposing views.

Ten-Year Ratings Timeline For Year Under Review (Political Rights, Civil Liberties, Status)

Year Under Review	2007	2008	2009	2010	2011	2012	2013	2014	2015	2016
Rating	3,3,PF	4,3,PF	4,4,PF	4,4,PF	5,4,PF	5,4,PF	4,3,PF	4,3,PF	4,3,PF	5,4,PF

Overview: The election of Sandinista leader Daniel Ortega in 2006 began a period of democratic deterioration in Nicaragua that continues today. President Ortega has consolidated all branches of government under his party's control, limited fundamental freedoms, and allowed unchecked corruption to pervade the government. In 2014, the National Assembly approved constitutional amendments that paved the way for Ortega to win a third consecutive term in November 2016.

KEY DEVELOPMENTS IN 2016

- In November, President Ortega was reelected for a third term, with his wife chosen as vice president. Ortega received more than 72 percent of the vote, with the next closest competitor receiving just 15 percent. The Sandinista party also expanded its already significant majority in the National Assembly.
- In June, the Supreme Court removed the leader of the opposition Independent Liberation Party (PLI), severely limiting the competitiveness of the November election. In July, the Supreme Electoral Council (CSE) pushed 16 opposition members of the National Assembly from their seats for failure to recognize the actions of the Supreme Court.
- Freedom of expression and association continued to decline as environmental activists and investigators of the interoceanic canal project were detained and sometimes expelled.

EXECUTIVE SUMMARY

In 2016, the ruling Sandinista National Liberation Front (FSLN) tightened its grip on power. The Nicaraguan Supreme Court stripped the main opposition candidate for president of his party's leadership in June, and the following month the CSE removed 16 opposition members from the National Assembly for their failure to recognize the new party leader. This resulted in certain defeat for the opposition in the November elections. Despite regular protests against deteriorating democratic conditions, Ortega enjoyed high approval ratings, largely as a result of his handling of the economy and popular social programs.

The Ortega administration engages in systematic efforts to obstruct and discredit critics, and the environment for the media has been in steady decline in recent years. Corruption has been a major issue, with Ortega's sons and daughters appointed to prominent positions such as ambassador and presidential adviser, and his wife elected as vice president. Significant concerns have also been raised over the lack of transparency and consultation in the project to dig the interoceanic canal across Nicaragua, which was approved quickly and with little public debate. Protests against the plans continued in 2016. Foreign researchers and journalists investigating the project have been detained and removed from the country. In July, six foreign activists holding environmental workshops were expelled.

POLITICAL RIGHTS: 14 / 40 (− 5)

A. Electoral Process: 3 / 12 (− 3)

The constitution provides for a directly elected president and a 92-member unicameral National Assembly. Two seats in the legislature are reserved for the previous president and the runner-up in the most recent presidential election. Presidential and legislative elections are both held every five years. Since constitutional reforms that went into effect in 2014, presidents are elected with a simple plurality of the vote. The reforms also eliminated term limits and mandated that half of all candidates for elected office be women.

President Ortega was reelected in November 2016 with over 72 percent of the vote. The previous June, the Supreme Court expelled the main opposition candidate, Eduardo Montealegre, from his Independent Liberation Party (PLI), replacing him with a pro-Ortega leader. The following month, the Supreme Electoral Council (CSE) removed 16 members of the National Assembly for their refusal to accept the court's decision. In November, Maximino Rodríguez of the Constitutionalist Liberal Party (PLC) received 15 percent of the vote, with no other candidate reaching 5 percent, including the replacement PLI candidate. Ortega's wife, Rosario Murillo, ran as the vice presidential candidate despite opposition voices decrying this as further evidence of the Ortega administration's consolidation of power. In the legislative elections, Ortega's FSLN increased its majority to 70 seats in the National Assembly, followed by the PLC with 13 seats. The PLI won just 2 seats, in contrast to the 26 seats it won in the 2011 election. Ortega refused to allow international election observers into the country.

Numerous changes to the municipal electoral law approved in 2012 include a provision allowing mayors to run for reelection and a requirement that half of each party's candidates for mayoralties and council seats be women.

Nicaragua's North Atlantic Autonomous Region (RAAN) and South Atlantic Autonomous Region (RAAS) have regional councils, for which elections were last held in 2014. The FSLN won 52 percent of the votes in the RAAN, followed by the majority-indigenous YATAMA party with 21 percent; the PLI and the PLC won the remainder. In the RAAS, the FSLN garnered 48 percent of the vote; the PLC, the PLI, YATAMA, and the Multi-Ethnic Indigenous Party each won small portions. YATAMA supporters organized minor protests following the vote.

The selection of Judith Silva, who had been nominated by President Ortega, to fill the vacant position for CSE magistrate in 2015 renewed concerns about the institution's independence.

B. Political Pluralism and Participation: 6 / 16 (− 1)

The formerly dominant PLC has experienced a sharp decline in its voter base since 1999, while the FSLN's backing has increased. Public opinion polls consistently reveal high levels of popularity for Ortega and the FSLN.

The FSLN's majority in the National Assembly enables it to pass laws without requiring support from opposition parties. As a result of the 2014 constitutional reforms, legislators who do not vote with their party may lose their seats. In 2014, the PLI and PLC signed a pact in hopes of launching a unified opposition for the 2016 elections. Their efforts were undermined by the Nicaraguan Supreme Court, which in June 2016 disqualified the leader of the PLI from his party. In July, the CSE removed 16 legislators who refused to recognize the new leadership from the National Assembly.

Minority groups, especially the indigenous inhabitants of Nicaragua's eastern and Caribbean regions, frequently complain that they are politically underrepresented and that the government and the FSLN largely ignore their grievances.

C. Functioning of Government: 5 / 12 (− 1)

The FSLN dominates most public institutions, working closely with labor and private business in a tripartite alliance (COSEP) that is recognized in Article 98 of the constitution. The manipulation of the 2016 election and the expulsion of 16 opposition politicians from the legislature have prevented freely elected representatives from determining government policies. Constitutional reforms passed in 2014 include the ability of the president to issue binding decrees, to appoint active military personnel to executive-level positions previously designated for civilians, and to direct changes in tax policy without legislative approval.

Corruption charges against high-ranking government officials are rare except in the most egregious cases, and corruption cases against opposition figures are often criticized for being politically motivated. Ortega's sons and daughters have been appointed to prominent positions such as ambassador and presidential adviser. The Communications and Citizenry Council, which oversees the government's press relations, is directed by First Lady Rosario Murillo and has been accused of limiting access to information. Murillo became vice president following the 2016 presidential election.

The 2007 Law on Access to Public Information requires public entities and private companies doing business with the state to disclose certain information. However, it preserves the government's right to protect information related to state security.

A wide range of civil society groups have raised concerns over the lack of transparency and consultation in the project to dig the interoceanic canal across Nicaragua, which was approved quickly and with little public debate. Results of environmental studies detailing the human and environmental toll have been kept from the public.

CIVIL LIBERTIES: 33 / 60 (− 2)

D. Freedom of Expression and Belief: 11 / 16 (− 1)

The constitution calls for a free press. Radio remains the main source of information in Nicaragua. Six television networks, including a state-owned network, are based in the capital; many favor particular political factions. Three national newspapers cover a variety of political viewpoints, though coverage is polarized. Access to the internet is unrestricted.

The press has faced increased political and judicial harassment since 2007, and the Ortega administration engages in systematic efforts to obstruct and discredit media critics. Journalists, including several reporters with the newspaper *El Nuevo Diario*, have received death threats. In 2015, reporters faced harassment from police and some were detained while they were covering protests related to the opposition's push for electoral reforms, as well as demonstrations against the canal project. In June 2016, police briefly detained a photojournalist investigating the canal. Members of the ruling elite have acquired stakes in media outlets and have used their influence as owners to sideline independent journalists.

In October 2016, the director of *Confidencial*, a notable opposition magazine, accused the Nicaraguan army of spying on the publication. President Ortega has not held an open-access press conference since 2007.

Religious and academic freedoms are generally respected, although some university-level academics refrain from open criticism of the government.

Private discussion is generally free, though there are increasing reports of self-censorship. Both private citizens and government employees have complained of retaliation for opposing the interoceanic canal project.

E. Associational and Organizational Rights: 5 / 12 (− 1)

Nicaraguan law recognizes freedoms of assembly and association, but in practice respect for these rights has been problematic. While public demonstrations are generally permitted, members of the opposition have accused the police of failing to protect demonstrators and of engaging in partisan behavior. Gangs with tacit government support have reportedly attacked antigovernment protesters. In 2015, police clashed with protesters in a labor dispute at El Limón mine, resulting in injuries to both sides and the death of one police officer.

Although nongovernmental organizations (NGOs) are active, they have faced harassment and occasional violence in recent years. NGOs have also been weakened by the system of Citizens' Power Councils, which operate from the neighborhood to the federal level. Critics say they blur the line between state and party institutions, and that they are highly politicized. In June 2016, a professor researching the interoceanic canal was deported. Organizations representing the interests of indigenous groups in the scope of the canal project have been marginalized.

The FSLN controls many of the country's labor unions, and the legal rights of non-FSLN unions are not fully guaranteed. Although the law recognizes the right to strike, unions must clear a number of hurdles, and approval from the Ministry of Labor is almost never granted. Employers sometimes form their own unions to avoid recognizing legitimate organizations. Employees have reportedly been dismissed for union activities, and citizens have no effective recourse when those in power violate labor laws.

F. Rule of Law: 7 / 16

The judiciary remains dominated by FSLN and PLC appointees, and the Supreme Court is a largely politicized body controlled by Sandinista judges. The court system also suffers from corruption, long delays, a large backlog of cases, and a severe shortage of public defenders. Access to justice is especially deficient in rural areas and on the Caribbean coast.

Despite long-term improvements, the security forces remain understaffed and poorly funded, and human rights abuses still occur. Forced confessions and arbitrary arrests continue. Nicaragua has generally been spared the high rates of crime and gang violence that plague its neighbors to the north, and the police have been active in combating drug trafficking and organized crime. Generally considered to be the most professionalized in the region, the police have come under increasing criticism for skirmishes with civilians. In 2015, Nicaraguan police killed three members of one family, including two children, during a botched antidrug operation. Nine police officers were sentenced to 11 years in prison after being convicted on various charges related to the incident. Also in 2015, police and military allegedly used tear gas and rubber bullets to turn back a group of Cuban migrants seeking to reach the United States by traveling through Nicaragua from Costa Rica. Prison conditions are poor and overcrowding is a problem.

Changes to the military code in 2014 gave the army a role in internal security at the discretion of the president, further concentrating power under the executive. Critics suggested that it opened the military to executive manipulation. A 2014 law that restructured the National Police allows the president to appoint and extend the terms of the body's director, increases service eligibility, and permits members of the National Police to engage in political campaigning and political party activity. The Sovereign Security Law, passed in 2015, has been criticized for blurring the line between public safety and national security by potentially militarizing civilian agencies, and because the threats it combats are defined too broadly. Those concerns were heightened by the failure of the Ortega administration to issue a regulatory decree by the February 2016 deadline, thus requiring the National Assembly to draft it. Without that guidance, application of the law could be very broad.

The constitution and laws nominally recognize the rights of indigenous communities, but those rights have not been respected in practice. Approximately 5 percent of the population is indigenous and lives mostly in the RAAN and the RAAS.

Same-sex marriage and civil unions remain barred in Nicaragua, and the country's LGBT (lesbian, gay, bisexual, and transgender) population is subject to intermittent threats and discriminatory treatment. LGBT activists blasted the family code, which went into effect in 2015, for defining marriage as a union between a man and a woman and, as such, depriving same-sex couples the right to adopt children or the ability to receive fertility treatment. A resolution approved in 2014 prohibits discrimination in health service provision based on sexual identity, though few steps have been taken toward implementation.

G. Personal Autonomy and Individual Rights: 10 / 16

Governmental and nonstate actors generally respect travel, residence, and employment choices. Property rights are protected on paper but can be tenuous in practice. Titles are often contested, and individuals with connections to the FSLN sometimes enjoy an advantage during property disputes.

Property owners in the construction zone for the new canal have complained that they have felt intimidated, sometimes with violence, by surveyors with the backing of the army and police. Indigenous groups and farmers have raised concerns that they will be negatively impacted by the digging of the canal. Protests against the project continued into 2016.

In 2015, land conflicts in the RAAN resulted in forced displacements and clashes between indigenous groups, settlers, and police, as disputes over indigenous lands turned violent. Dozens were injured and at least nine were killed in September alone, with YATAMA leader Mario Lemans among the deceased. Hundreds of members of the Miskito community sought refuge in Honduras from the violence. Residents and human rights groups claimed that the Nicaraguan government, regional government, and the police had done little to stop the violence or to protect the property rights of indigenous communities. In August 2016, two Miskito men were kidnapped during a clash with settlers and found dead 11 days later.

In 2016, Nicaragua was ranked 10 out of 144 countries surveyed in the World Economic Forum's *Global Gender Gap Report,* indicating that its gender-based disparities are among the smallest in the world. However, violence against women and children, including sexual and domestic abuse, remains widespread and underreported; few cases are ever prosecuted. The 2012 Comprehensive Law Against Violence toward Women addresses both physical and structural forms of violence, and recognizes violence against women as a matter of public health and safety. The legislation codified femicide and establishes sentencing guidelines for physical and psychological abuses against women. A 2013 reform to the law allows mediation between the victim and accuser, despite concerns from rights groups. The family code includes protections for pregnant minors, the elderly, and ethnic minorities; establishes equal duties of mothers and fathers; and prohibits physical punishment of children.

Abortion is illegal and punishable by imprisonment, even when performed to save the mother's life or in cases of rape or incest. Scores of deaths stemming from the ban have been reported in recent years.

Human trafficking is a significant issue in Nicaragua, which serves as a source country for women and children forced into prostitution. A 2010 law classifies human trafficking as a form of organized crime. Adults and children are also vulnerable to forced labor in some sectors. In 2016, the U.S. State Department's *Trafficking in Persons Report* noted inadequate protections for victims and the vulnerability of women on the Atlantic Coast, where institutions are weaker and crime is more prevalent. The National Assembly's passage of a law in 2015 meant to address human trafficking is a sign of some progress. The law establishes prison terms of up to 20 years, creates a databank to track cases, and enables the confiscation of property gained through human trafficking.

Niger

Political Rights Rating: 4
Civil Liberties Rating: 4 ↓
Freedom Rating: 4.0
Freedom Status: Partly Free
Electoral Democracy: No

Population: 19,700,000
Capital: Niamey

Rating Change: Niger's political rights rating declined from 3 to 4 due to the repressive conditions surrounding the 2016 presidential and legislative elections, including harassment of the opposition, as well as alleged irregularities in the balloting itself.

Ten-Year Ratings Timeline For Year Under Review (Political Rights, Civil Liberties, Status)

Year Under Review	2007	2008	2009	2010	2011	2012	2013	2014	2015	2016
Rating	3,4,PF	3,4,PF	5,4,PF	5,4,PF	3,4,PF	3,4,PF	3,4,PF	3,4,PF	3,4,PF	4,4,PF

Overview: The current regime in Niger was democratically elected in 2011, and reelected in 2016 in a polling process reportedly plagued by serious irregularities. The struggle to meet the security challenges that surround Niger has served as an alibi for the government to restrict freedoms and civil liberties. Security, transparency, economic prosperity, and gender equality are limited.

KEY DEVELOPMENTS IN 2016:

- In February and March, Niger held legislative and presidential elections in an environment in which the primary opponent of the incumbent president was held in jail. Widespread electoral irregularities were reported.
- Authorities in October announced the formation of a unity government, after one of the major opposition parties joined the ruling coalition.
- In June, the government banned an international correspondent from the country in connection with her coverage of Boko Haram violence. A few days later, a local

civil society activist was sentenced to six months in jail for criticizing the government in a Facebook comment.

- In December, more than 30 Boko Haram fighters turned themselves in to the government, in what appeared to be the first abandonment of the jihadist insurgent movement by Nigerien recruits.

EXECUTIVE SUMMARY

President Mahamadou Issoufou was reelected for a second five-year term in March. The elections happened in a context of political tension, as opposition leader Hama Amadou, Issoufou's most significant challenger for the presidency, was jailed during the entire electoral process, accused of involvement in a baby-trafficking scandal. The opposition boycotted the second round of the presidential poll, which Issoufou won with 92 percent of the vote. In legislative polls held in February, Issoufou's Party for Democracy and Socialism (PNDS) won 75 seats in the 171-seat legislature, while Amadou's Nigerien Democratic Movement for an African Federation (MODEN/FA) won 25 seats, and former prime minister Seini Oumarou's National Movement for a Developing Society (MNSD) took 20 seats. Thirteen smaller parties divided the remaining seats. The elections were reportedly plagued with irregularities such as vote buying, underage voting, and rigging of election results, and combined with pressure by the government on the opposition, effectively resulted in the installation of a government that was not freely and fairly elected. The local elections, initially scheduled to take place in July 2016, were postponed. Amadou was bailed in March, after the presidential election was completed.

Although no major outbreaks of violence occurred during the electoral process, tension between government and opposition supporters was high, and often took on an ethno-regionalist character. In October 2016, authorities announced the formation of a government of national unity after the opposition MNSD joined the ruling majority. A new cabinet with 42 ministers was subsequently announced, prompting criticism for being excessively large at a time when the country was experiencing an economic downturn, and the government was struggling to provide basic services.

These political tensions mounted against a backdrop of a deteriorating security situation, as Islamic insurgent groups active in neighboring countries threatened to encroach on Niger. Although Niger has so far managed to maintain a precarious stability, it has undermined civil liberties in the process. The fight against the militant group Boko Haram has led the government to declare states of emergency in the Diffa region near the border with Nigeria, allowing the army to engage in mass arrests and detain those suspected of links with terrorist organizations. Journalists, demonstrators, and civil society activists have faced harassment and obstruction by officials who cite security grounds to justify their actions.

In December 2016, more than 30 Boko Haram fighters surrendered their weapons and turned themselves in to the government, in what appeared to be the first abandonment of the jihadist insurgent movement by Nigerien recruits. They will reportedly receive amnesty and participate in deradicalization and reintegration programs.

POLITICAL RIGHTS: 21 / 40 (− 3)

A. Electoral Process: 6 / 12 (− 2)

B. Political Pluralism and Participation: 9 / 16

C. Functioning of Government: 6 / 12 (− 1)

CIVIL LIBERTIES: 28 / 60

D. Freedom of Expression and Belief: 11 / 16

E. Associational and Organizational Rights: 6 / 12

F. Rule of Law: 5 / 16

G. Personal Autonomy and Individual Rights: 6 / 16

This country report has been abridged for *Freedom in the World 2017*. For background information on political rights and civil liberties in Niger, see *Freedom in the World 2016*.

Nigeria

Political Rights Rating: 3
Civil Liberties Rating: 5
Freedom Rating: 4.0
Freedom Status: Partly Free
Electoral Democracy: Yes

Population: 186,500,000
Capital: Abuja

Ratings change: Nigeria's political rights rating improved from 4 to 3 due to increased transparency under the administration of President Muhammadu Buhari, and military gains against the militant group Boko Haram that led to a significant reduction in the group's ability to alter the religious and ethnic composition of the northeast.

Ten-Year Ratings Timeline For Year Under Review (Political Rights, Civil Liberties, Status)

Year Under Review	2007	2008	2009	2010	2011	2012	2013	2014	2015	2016
Rating	4,4,PF	4,4,PF	5,4,PF	4,4,PF	4,4,PF	4,4,PF	4,4,PF	4,5,PF	4,5,PF	3,5,PF

Overview: Nigeria has made significant improvements in the competiveness and quality of national elections in recent years, though political corruption remains endemic. Militant and extremist groups and security officials consistently violate the human rights of Nigerians, while religious and ethnic bias as well as discrimination against women and the LGBT (lesbian, gay, bisexual, and transgender) community are pervasive.

KEY DEVELOPMENTS IN 2016:

- Counterinsurgency efforts weakened Boko Haram's capacity to launch attacks in the northeastern regions. However, humanitarian conditions there became increasingly dire, with some 1.8 million people displaced, and many more facing malnutrition.
- Security conditions worsened elsewhere, with the resurgence of militants in the Niger Delta, and increased ethnic and communal clashes in and around the middle belt.
- The administration of President Muhammadu Buhari continued its drive to reduce graft and improve transparency, and announced in June that authorities had recovered $9 billion in stolen assets since Buhari took office in 2015.
- Rights groups accused Nigerian security forces of committing gross human rights violations with impunity, including extrajudicial killings, arbitrary mass arrests, illegal detentions, and torture of civilians.

EXECUTIVE SUMMARY

The security situation in Nigeria remained challenging in 2016 due to the ongoing insurgency in the northeast by the militant Islamist group Boko Haram; renewed militancy in the Niger Delta; and intersectarian and communal clashes in and around the middle belt. The counterinsurgency offensive of the Multinational Joint Task Force (MNJTF), which included soldiers from Nigeria, Niger, Cameroon, Chad, and Benin, diminished the capacity of Boko Haram to coordinate large-scale attacks. However, humanitarian conditions in the northeast remained grave. At year's end some 1.8 million people had been internally displaced by the conflict, and many more faced food insecurity. In Borno State, some 50,000 people faced starvation conditions.

Militants in the restive Niger Delta, including a new group called the Niger Delta Avengers, launched a series of attacks on oil installations during the year. In August, amnesty payments to militants, which Buhari had halted previously, were resumed in hopes of curbing the attacks. Furthermore, up to September, about 870 people had died in sectarian and communal clashes, including many involving Fulani herdsmen in and around the country's middle belt, according to the Council on Foreign Relations.

Reports from domestic and international advocacy groups indicated that government forces, including the military and police, continued to commit gross human rights violations with impunity, including extrajudicial killings, arbitrary mass arrests, illegal detentions, and torture of civilians.

Buhari's administration continued its fight against corruption by expanding reforms to the oil and security sectors. Several high-ranking military and government officials were arrested on corruption-related charges in 2016, while Buhari's government announced in June that authorities had recovered $9 billion in stolen assets since Buhari took office in 2015.

POLITICAL RIGHTS: 25 / 40 (+ 2)

A. Electoral Process: 9 / 12

The president is elected by popular vote for no more than two four-year terms. Members of the bicameral National Assembly, consisting of the 109-seat Senate and the 360-seat House of Representatives, are elected for four-year terms. While elections that followed Nigeria's return to a multiparty system in 1999 were marred by gross irregularities, the 2011 polls marked the beginning of a departure from this trend.

The 2015 presidential and legislative elections were regarded as competitive and generally well conducted by local and international observer organizations. They represented a milestone in the country's democratic development, marking the first time that the opposition gained power at the national level through elections. Although the voting had been postponed by approximately six weeks, with officials citing insecurity in the northeast, the delay did not adversely affect the integrity of the process. Instead it appeared to have given the Independent National Electoral Commission (INEC) more time to improve the distribution of permanent voter cards, pilot a new electronic voter-identification system, and fine-tune its election machinery. However, hundreds of thousands of Nigerians were still prevented from voting, either because they were internally displaced by the Boko Haram insurgency, or because they failed to receive their permanent voter cards in time. There were far fewer election-related deaths in 2015 than there were during the 2011 election cycle.

Buhari, the candidate of the All Progressives Congress (APC), won the presidential contest, defeating incumbent president Goodluck Jonathan of the Peoples Democratic Party (PDP), 54 percent to 45 percent. Jonathan quickly conceded defeat, helping to ensure a peaceful and orderly rotation of power. APC candidates also won a majority in the legislative elections. In the House of Representatives, the APC took 212 of 360 seats, while the PDP won 140, and smaller parties captured the remaining eight. In the Senate, the APC won 60 of 109 seats, while the PDP secured 49. At the state level, the APC captured a majority of the contested governorships.

There were some difficulties surrounding 2016 regional elections. A gubernatorial election in Edo state, originally scheduled for September 10, was postponed for over two weeks due to security concerns. Separately, there were over 250 conflict-related deaths during the lead-up to and aftermath of a March rerun of legislative elections in Rivers State.

In December, Buhari swore in six new commissioners to the INEC; he had previously held off on swearing them in to ensure that the 12 commissioners' terms were staggered. Some critics had suggested that vacancies on the INEC had contributed to some regional electoral difficulties.

B. Political Pluralism and Participation: 10 / 16

Nigeria's multiparty system provides an opportunity for opposition parties to gain power through elections, as demonstrated by the APC's sweeping victory in 2015. Buhari's defeat of Jonathan represented the first time that a sitting Nigerian president was democratically replaced. The vote appeared to reflect the ethnic and religious divisions in the country, with Buhari, a northern Muslim, winning primarily in the northern states, and Jonathan, a Christian from the southern Niger Delta region, gaining an overwhelming majority in the south. However, Buhari's ability to gain support from many non-northern and non-Muslim voters was a significant factor in his success.

Despite the improved elections and peaceful rotation of power, citizens' political choices remain impaired or undermined to some degree by vote buying and intimidation, the influence of powerful domestic and international economic interests on policymaking, and the local domination of either the Nigerian military or Boko Haram militants in regions affected by the insurgency.

Although in 2014, the 36 state legislatures approved proposed amendments to the 1999 constitution, neither Jonathan nor Buhari assented to these changes. In 2016, the National Assembly reopened debate on a series of proposed amendments, including one that would remove the need for presidential assent for constitutional amendments to be adopted.

C. Functioning of Government: 6 / 12 (+ 1)

Corruption remains pervasive, particularly in the oil and security sectors. However, the Buhari administration has undertaken a series of reforms aimed at reducing graft and improving transparency. Among them were a restructuring of the state-owned Nigerian National Petroleum Corporation (NNPC); the establishment of a committee to investigate procurement fraud in the military; and the May 2016 removal of the fuel subsidy, the administration of which had opened avenues for corruption. The government's efforts led to several officials being charged with corruption and, according to an announcement in June, the recovery of approximately $9 billion in stolen assets between May 2015 and May 2016. The Economic and Financial Crimes Commission (EFCC) and the Independent Corrupt Practices Commission (ICPC) opened investigations into several high-level current and former officials during the year. The opposition PDP has accused the federal government of political bias in its anticorruption efforts by disproportionately targeting its members.

Buhari signed the 2016 federal budget into law in May—almost five months after it was proposed—due to several scandals, including the disappearance of hard copies of the budget from the Senate in January, as well as large discrepancies in budgetary allocations.

Despite the passage of the 2011 Freedom of Information Act, which guarantees the right to access public records, nongovernmental organizations (NGOs) have criticized government agencies for routinely refusing to release information sought through the law. Nevertheless, Nigeria saw improvements in transparency initiatives in 2016, with the NNPC earning praise in August from the Extractive Industries and Transparency Initiative (EITI) for its implementation of the initiative's standards. In July, Buhari appointed Maikanti Kacalla Baru to be the new head of NNPC, in a move that observers saw as a continuation of the corporation's reform efforts under Buhari. In April, after soliciting public input, the government released a development plan it and several international organizations had developed for conflict-damaged northeastern Nigeria.

DISCRETIONARY POLITICAL RIGHTS QUESTION B: 0 / 0 (+ 1)

In recent years, Boko Haram has been accused of attempting to alter the religious and ethnic composition of the northeast by targeting Christians and moderate Muslims through mass killings, kidnappings, and other human rights abuses. However, in 2016, the Nigerian and allied regional military forces reclaimed most, if not all, of the territory once controlled by the group and limited the group's capacity to launch large-scale offensives. Furthermore, the number of casualties related to the conflict fell by 73 percent compared to 2015, according to figures from the Institute for Security Studies. The developments have significantly diminished Boko Haram's capacity to continue altering the religious composition of the northeast.

CIVIL LIBERTIES: 25 / 40

D. Freedom of Expression and Belief: 9 / 16

Freedom of speech, expression, and the press are constitutionally guaranteed. However, these rights are limited by laws on sedition, criminal defamation, and publication of false news. Sharia statutes in 12 northern states impose severe penalties for alleged press offenses. Government officials also restrict press freedom by publicly criticizing, harassing, and arresting journalists, especially when they cover corruption scandals, human rights violations, or separatist and communal violence. In August 2016, the military announced that freelance journalist Ahmad Salkida, who had been reporting on the Boko Haram insurgency since 2006, was wanted for questioning and could be charged under a terrorism law if he did not provide information. On his return to Nigeria from his home in the United Arab Emirates, Salkida was detained and questioned without a lawyer before being released the following day. Journalists and media entities have also been attacked and intimidated by nonstate actors, including Boko Haram. There were no reports that the government restricted access to the internet.

Religious freedom is constitutionally and legally protected and is generally respected by the government in practice. Nevertheless, in some instances state and local governments have placed limits on religious activities and endorsed a dominant faith, and recent polling has indicated some level of mistrust between various religious communities. In October 2016, police in Kaduna banned the Islamic Movement in Nigeria (IMN), the country's largest Shiite organization. At least 11 people died that month during the annual Ashura processions, an important Shiite rite that some areas in the north had attempted to ban, after clashes erupted between Nigerian police, Sunni mobs, and Shiite participants. Separately, in a victory for religious freedom, high courts in two southwest states, Osun and Lagos, ruled in June and July, respectively, that bans on female Muslim students wearing hijabs in schools were unconstitutional.

Nonstate actors have also attempted to limit religious freedom. Boko Haram has explicitly targeted Christians and moderate Muslims, and their respective houses of worship. Periodic communal clashes between Muslims and Christians have broken out for decades in and around the states of Kaduna and Plateau, often killing hundreds of people and displacing thousands at a time.

The federal government generally respects academic freedom. However, some state governments mandate religious instruction in elementary and secondary curriculums, and student admission and faculty hiring policies are subject to political interference. Boko Haram's assault on secular education included the closure or destruction of primary, secondary, and tertiary institutions. In October, negotiations between government, military, and civil society representatives and Boko Haram led to the release of 21 girls whom Boko Haram had abducted from a school in the town of Chibok in 2014. However, almost 200 of the girls abducted from the Chibok school remained unaccounted for at year's end, and are suspected to be in the custody of Boko Haram.

There was no evidence of government authorities monitoring electronic communications between private citizens.

E. Associational and Organizational Rights: 7 / 12

The rights to peaceful assembly and association are constitutionally guaranteed. However, federal and state governments frequently ban public events perceived as threatening national security, including those that could incite political, ethnic, or religious tension. Rights groups have criticized federal and state government for banning protests and frustrating protestors associated with various movements throughout the country. These include a September 2016 protest by the IMN in Abuja and various pro-Biafran independence protests in southeastern states. According to a November report issued by Amnesty International, peaceful Biafran independence protesters have frequently faced arrest and violence, including the use of deadly force, at the hands of security forces.

Nigeria has a broad and vibrant civil society. Members of some organizations faced intimidation and physical harm for speaking out against Boko Haram, or encountered obstacles when investigating alleged human rights abuses committed by the military against Boko Haram suspects. Groups operating in the restive Niger Delta region face similar impediments.

Under the constitution, workers have the right to form and join trade unions, engage in collective bargaining, and conduct strikes. Nevertheless, the government forbids strike action in a number of essential services, including public transportation and security.

F. Rule of Law: 4 / 16

Judicial independence is constitutionally and legally enshrined. The judiciary has achieved some degree of independence and professionalism in practice, but political interference, corruption, and a lack of funding, equipment, and training remain important problems. A number of prominent judges were arrested on corruption-related charges in 2016, while several others were sanctioned by the Nigerian Judicial Council for malpractice. Certain departments, particularly the Court of Appeals, have frequently rejected election challenges or allegations of corruption against powerful elites, raising doubts about their impartiality.

Despite pressure from international human rights groups, torture has yet to be criminalized. In June 2016, the Senate passed its first reading of an antitorture bill that had already been approved in the House of Representatives. However, the bill had not been passed by year's end. There were numerous allegations of torture, extortion, and bribe taking within the police force in 2016. Amnesty International released a report in September claiming that some members of the Special Anti-Robbery Squad (SARS) carried out a torture, bribery, and extortion racket, in which they tortured suspected criminals and demanded bribes from suspects and their families to secure the suspects' freedom. The Nigerian Police immediately denied the allegations and condemned the report, but the inspector general of police also issued a warning to SARS against committing torture or other violations of due process of the law.

The military has also been widely criticized for pervasive corruption and human rights abuses. In January, the Kaduna State government launched a judicial commission of inquiry into the alleged massacre the previous month of hundreds of Shiite Muslim members of the IMN in Kaduna by the Nigerian military. In July, the commission's nonbinding report was made public; it found the army responsible for the unlawful killing of civilians. The commission called for the prosecution of soldiers who were involved, and for Nigeria's security agencies to improve their monitoring and surveillance of groups like IMN. Meanwhile, international and domestic rights groups continue to condemn the military for extrajudicial killings and other abuses, including acts of torture carried out during counterinsurgency efforts in the northeast. An Amnesty International report released in November accused the security forces of carrying out 150 extrajudicial killings against peaceful pro-Biafra activists between August 2015 and August 2016. In April, the International Criminal Court (ICC) began an investigation of alleged human rights abuses committed by the Nigerian military and Boko Haram. In February, the military announced that it was establishing an office of human rights where Nigerians could lodge complaints about human rights abuses, though its impact remains to be seen.

The multinational offensive against Boko Haram continued during 2016, further diminishing the group's capacity to occupy territory and launch large-scale attacks against military and civilian targets in Nigeria and neighboring countries. However, the insurgency continues to engage in asymmetric warfare, including the use of women and children in suicide attacks against civilian towns in the northeast. Since the start of the year, the conflict has claimed the lives of approximately 2,900 people. This, however, represents a sharp reduction in conflict-related causalities compared to the corresponding period in 2015. According to the International Crisis Group (ICG), about 1.8 million people remained internally displaced in northeast Nigeria in December and 9.2 million residents of the region required humanitarian assistance as of May. Separately, militants in the Niger Delta attacked oil installations in 2016, and sectarian and communal clashes continued to occur in the country's middle belt.

Violent crime in certain areas of Nigeria is a serious problem, as is the trafficking of drugs and small arms. Abductions are common in the Niger Delta and the southeastern states of Abia, Imo, and Anambra. Political figures, the wealthy, and foreigners are most frequently targeted. In September, Margaret Emefiele, the wife of Godwin Emefiele, the governor of the Central Bank of Nigeria, was kidnapped by an armed gang and rescued the following day by security agencies. Nine suspects, including two army members, were arrested in connection with her kidnapping.

Despite constitutional safeguards against ethnic discrimination, many ethnic minorities experience bias by state governments and other societal groups in areas including employment, education, and housing. The government and society continue to discriminate against LGBT (lesbian, gay, bisexual, and transgender) people. An October 2016 report by Human Rights Watch found no evidence that the 2014 Same Sex Marriage (Prohibition) Act had resulted in any prosecutions, but said that because of the law, LGBT people face increased violence and discrimination from the public and police. In northern states, same-sex relationships can be punished by death under Sharia statutes.

G. Personal Autonomy and Individual Rights: 5 / 16

Freedom of internal movement and foreign travel are legally guaranteed. However, security officials frequently impose dusk-to-dawn curfews in areas affected by communal violence or the Islamist insurgency.

Nigeria's largely unregulated property rights system hinders citizens and private business from engaging in the efficient and legal purchase or sale of land and other types of property. According to the World Bank's Doing Business Report for 2017, Nigeria ranked 169 out of 190 countries; the country showed improvements in credit accessibility and the ease of starting a business, but continued to rank near the bottom of the index with respect to property registration and the ease of paying taxes.

Women's representation in government worsened following the 2015 elections. Women maintained eight of 109 Senate seats, but in the House of Representatives women currently hold 18 of 360 seats, compared with 24 following the 2011 elections. Of the 37 ministers named to Buhari's cabinet, only six were women. This amounted to 16 percent female representation in the cabinet, compared with 31 percent in the previous administration.

Many families choose to send sons to school while daughters become street vendors or domestic workers. Women experience discrimination in employment. Gender discrimination is significant in the states governed by Sharia statutes. Women belonging to certain ethnic groups are often denied equal rights to inherit property due to customary laws and practices. Despite the existence of strict laws against rape, domestic violence, female genital mutilation, and child marriage, these offenses remain widespread, with low rates of reporting and prosecution.

Nigerian organized crime groups are heavily involved in human trafficking. Boko Haram has subjected children to forced labor and sex slavery. Both Boko Haram and a civilian vigilante group that opposes the militants have forcibly recruited child soldiers, according to the U.S. State Department. Meanwhile, as of year's end, several of Nigeria's states had not implemented the 2003 Child Rights Act, which protects children from discrimination based on sex, ethnicity, and other factors. In September 2016, the acting director general of the National Agency for the Prohibition of Trafficking in Persons (NAPTIP), said that some two million Nigerian women and children are victims of trafficking each year. He said that since his agency's inception in 2003, 269 people had been convicted of trafficking, including seven so far in 2016.

North Korea

Political Rights Rating: 7
Civil Liberties Rating: 7
Freedom Rating: 7.0
Freedom Status: Not Free
Electoral Democracy: No

Population: 25,100,000
Capital: Pyongyang

Ten-Year Ratings Timeline For Year Under Review (Political Rights, Civil Liberties, Status)

Year Under Review	2007	2008	2009	2010	2011	2012	2013	2014	2015	2016
Rating	7,7,NF	7,7,NF	7,7,NF	7,7,NF	7,7,NF	7,7,NF	7,7,NF	7,7,NF	7,7,NF	7,7,NF

Overview: North Korea is a single-party state led by a dynastic totalitarian dictatorship. Surveillance is pervasive, arbitrary arrests and detention are common, and punishments for political offenses are severe. The state maintains a system of camps for political prisoners where torture, forced labor, starvation, and other atrocities take place. A UN commission of inquiry into the human rights situation in North Korea in 2014 found violations to be widespread, grave, and systematic, rising to the level of crimes against humanity.

KEY DEVELOPMENTS IN 2016:

- In 2016, North Korea conducted two nuclear weapons tests, a satellite launch, and more than 20 ballistic missile tests, drawing condemnation and harsher sanctions from the international community.
- In May, the ruling Korean Workers' Party (KWP) held its first congress in 36 years, which reinforced the state's ideological roots, announced a new Five-Year Plan, and created the post of KWP chairman for incumbent leader Kim Jong-un.
- At the June session of the Supreme People's Assembly, North Korea's rubber-stamp parliament, the State Affairs Commission was established as the government's new top power organ, with Kim Jong-un serving as chairman.

EXECUTIVE SUMMARY

North Korea began 2016 by conducting a nuclear weapons test in January and a satellite launch in February, both prohibited under existing UN resolutions. In response, the UN Security Council adopted Resolution 2270, which imposed tougher sanctions on the country, including restrictions on mineral exports. Nevertheless, the regime subsequently proceeded with more than 20 ballistic missile tests, as well as its fifth nuclear test in September. The Security Council followed up with additional sanctions in November.

In May, the ruling KWP held its first party congress since 1980 and its seventh overall. The party introduced a new Five-Year Plan at the gathering, and adopted revisions to its charter, including the institutionalization of the so-called *byungjin* policy of dual nuclear and economic development and the creation of the post of party chairman for Kim Jong-un. In June, the Supreme People's Assembly adopted constitutional changes that established the State Affairs Commission, replacing the National Defense Commission as the highest ruling organ.

In August, flooding caused by Typhoon Lionrock devastated parts of North Hamgyong Province, killing hundreds of people, destroying tens of thousands of homes, and leaving at least 140,000 people in urgent need of assistance. The scale of the disaster led North Korea to move domestic resources to this area and seek international humanitarian assistance. However, international responses were limited due to the regime's provocative behavior throughout the year.

POLITICAL RIGHTS: 0 / 40

A. Electoral Process: 0 / 12

Kim Jong-un became the country's supreme leader after the death of his father, Kim Jong-il, in December 2011. The elder Kim had led North Korea since the 1994 death of his own father, Kim Il-sung, to whom the office of president was permanently dedicated in a 1998 constitutional revision. In June 2016, the Supreme People's Assembly established the State Affairs Commission as the country's top ruling organ and elected Kim Jong-un as chairman. Kim already held a variety of other titles, including first chairman of the National

Defense Commission—previously the highest state body—and supreme commander of the Korean People's Army.

The 687-seat Supreme People's Assembly is elected to five-year terms. All candidates for office, who run unopposed, are preselected by and from the KWP and a handful of subordinate parties and organizations. Kim Jong-un was among those who won seats in the most recent national elections, held in March 2014. The official voter turnout was 99.97 percent.

Elections were held in July 2015 for 28,452 provincial, city, and county people's assembly members. Voter turnout was again reported to be 99.97 percent, with all candidates preselected by the KWP and running unopposed.

B. Political Pluralism and Participation: 0 / 16

North Korea is effectively a one-party state. Although a small number of minor parties and organizations exist legally, all are members of the Democratic Front for the Reunification of the Fatherland, a KWP-led umbrella group that selects all candidates for elected office. The ruling party has been dominated by the Kim family since its founding. The late Kim Jong-il was dubbed the "eternal general secretary" of the party after his death.

In May 2016, the KWP held its seventh party congress, the first since 1980. In a tightly controlled process, delegates reiterated the ideological underpinnings of the party, reviewed its performance, and introduced a new Five-Year Plan, also the first since 1980. Key changes to the KWP charter that were adopted at the gathering institutionalized the *byungjin* policy of dual nuclear and economic development and established the new leadership positions of chairman and vice chairman. Kim Jong-un, previously the party's "first secretary," was elected chairman, and other elections for key committees were held, including the Central Committee.

Any political dissent or opposition is harshly punished, and even the KWP is subject to regular purges aimed at reinforcing the leader's personal authority. Executions of dismissed cabinet officials continued to be reported in 2016.

North Korea is ethnically homogeneous, with only small Chinese populations and few foreign residents. Foreigners are not allowed to join the KWP or serve in the military or government.

C. Functioning of Government: 0 / 12

North Korea's dictatorial government is neither transparent in its operations nor accountable to the public. Information about the functioning of state institutions is tightly controlled for both domestic and external audiences. Most observers must glean evidence from state media, defector testimony, or secret informants inside the country, and the accuracy and reliability of these sources varies considerably. Corruption is believed to be endemic at every level of the state and economy, and bribery is pervasive.

CIVIL LIBERTIES: 3 / 60

D. Freedom of Expression and Belief: 0 / 16

All domestic media outlets are run by the state. Televisions and radios are permanently fixed to state channels, and all publications are subject to strict supervision and censorship. In recent years, several foreign news agencies have established bureau offices in Pyongyang: the U.S.-based Associated Press, Russia's Sputnik International (formerly RIA Novosti), Japan's Kyodo, and China's Xinhua. In September 2016, Agence France-Presse officially opened its Pyongyang bureau, though it will largely be limited to filing photos and video. A British Broadcasting Corporation crew was detained and expelled in May for coverage that the authorities found objectionable.

Access to the global internet is restricted to a small number of people in the government and academia, and others have access to a national intranet on which foreign websites are blocked. Alternative information sources, including mobile telephones, pirated recordings of South Korean dramas, and radios capable of receiving foreign programs are increasingly available. Mobile-phone service was launched in 2008, and there were more than three million subscriptions as of 2015, though phone calls and text messages are generally recorded and transcribed for monitoring purposes. Foreigners, who operate on a separate network, have been allowed to bring mobile phones into the country and have access to 3G service, enabling live social-media feeds out of North Korea.

Although freedom of religion is guaranteed by the constitution, it does not exist in practice. State-sanctioned churches maintain a token presence in Pyongyang, and some North Koreans who live near the Chinese border are known to practice their faiths furtively. However, intense state indoctrination and repression preclude free exercise of religion.

There is no academic freedom. The state must approve all curriculums, including those of educational programs led by foreigners. Although some North Koreans are permitted to study abroad, at both universities and short-term educational training programs, those granted such opportunities are subject to monitoring and reprisals for perceived disloyalty.

Nearly all forms of private communication are monitored by a huge network of informants.

E. Associational and Organizational Rights: 0 / 12

Freedom of assembly is not recognized, and there are no known associations or organizations other than those created by the state. Strikes, collective bargaining, and other organized labor activities are illegal.

F. Rule of Law: 0 / 16

North Korea does not have an independent judiciary. The UN General Assembly has recognized and condemned the country's severe human rights violations, including torture, public executions, extrajudicial and arbitrary detention, and forced labor by detainees; the absence of due process and the rule of law; and death sentences for political offenses. A UN commission of inquiry into the human rights situation in North Korea in 2014 found these violations to be widespread, grave, and systematic, rising to the level of crimes against humanity. Since then, there have been ongoing efforts to convince the UN Security Council to refer the case to the International Criminal Court.

It is estimated that 80,000 to 120,000 political prisoners are held in detention camps in the country. Inmates face brutal conditions, and collective or familial punishment for suspected dissent by an individual is common practice.

Ignoring international objections, the Chinese government continues to return refugees and defectors to North Korea, where they are subject to torture, harsh imprisonment, or execution. North Korean authorities regularly detain foreign citizens on various charges, obtaining coerced confessions, sometimes imposing harsh prison terms, and typically using the detainees as diplomatic leverage before eventually granting their release.

The most prevalent form of discrimination is based on perceived political and ideological nonconformity rather than ethnicity. All citizens are classified according to their family's level of loyalty and proximity to the leadership under a semihereditary caste-like system known as *songbun*.

Laws do not prohibit same-sex sexual activity, but the government maintains that the practice does not exist in North Korea.

G. Personal Autonomy and Individual Rights: 3 / 16

Citizens have no freedom of movement, and forced internal resettlement is routine. Emigration is illegal, but many North Koreans have escaped via China. Access to Pyongyang, where the availability of food, housing, and health care is somewhat better than in the rest of the country, is tightly restricted. Recently, this disparity has increased, with the capital featuring more luxuries for a growing middle class. A person's *songbun* classification affects his or her place of residence as well as employment and educational opportunities, access to medical facilities, and even access to stores. Foreign residents tend to have somewhat more freedom of movement, being able to travel abroad and participate in trade.

The formal economy remains both centrally planned and grossly mismanaged. Business activity is also hobbled by a lack of infrastructure, a scarcity of energy and raw materials, an inability to borrow on world markets or from multilateral banks because of sanctions, lingering foreign debt, and ideological isolationism. However, expanding informal and government-approved private markets and service industries have provided many North Koreans with a growing field of activity that is comparatively free from government control, if not from bribery and extortion; some have managed to engage in cross-border trade with China. In addition, a greater emphasis on building special economic zones has led to conditions more conducive to foreign investment. Local officials have had some authority in the management of these zones and over small-scale experiments with economic policies.

Women have formal equality, but they face rigid discrimination in practice and are poorly represented at high levels of government and in public employment. Although they have fewer opportunities in the formal sector, women are economically active outside the socialist system, exposing them to arbitrary state restrictions.

UN bodies have noted the use of forced abortions and infanticide against pregnant women who are forcibly repatriated from China. There have been widespread reports of trafficked women and girls among the tens of thousands of North Koreans who have recently crossed into China. Prostitution is rampant in ordinary residential areas.

Forced labor is common in prison camps, mass mobilization programs, and state-run contracting arrangements in which North Korean workers are sent abroad.

Norway

Political Rights Rating: 1
Civil Liberties Rating: 1
Freedom Rating: 1.0
Freedom Status: Free
Electoral Democracy: Yes

Population: 5,200,000
Capital: Oslo

Ten-Year Ratings Timeline For Year Under Review (Political Rights, Civil Liberties, Status)

Year Under Review	2007	2008	2009	2010	2011	2012	2013	2014	2015	2016
Rating	1,1,F	1,1,F	1,1,F	1,1,F	1,1,F	1,1,F	1,1,F	1,1,F	1,1,F	1,1,F

Overview: Norway has one of the most robust democracies in the world. The government regularly rotates through free and fair elections. Candidates have largely equal campaign opportunities and represent the interests of broad segments of the population. Civil liberties are upheld, and journalists and other civil society actors call attention to weaknesses and hold the government to account in addressing them.

KEY DEVELOPMENT IN 2016:

- The government further tightened asylum laws in June, though legislation was less restrictive than draft bills tabled in the spring.
- In April, a Norwegian court ruled that prison authorities had violated the human rights of convicted mass murderer and right-wing terrorist Anders Behring Breivik by keeping him in solitary confinement, despite what could be argued are luxury conditions by global prison standards.
- In June, the legislature passed a new health law that will allow transgender people to self-declare their legal gender, rather than first undergoing evaluations and surgery as in the past.

EXECUTIVE SUMMARY

Norway is a well-established democracy with regular free and fair elections. Political power generally alternates between the Labor Party and Conservative-led coalitions. The indigenous Sami population, in addition to participating in the national political process, has its own legislature. Freedom of expression is strongly defended, with several court cases involving violent extremists testing the boundaries of this freedom.

Rule of law is upheld. Despite Norway having some of the best prison conditions in the world, a controversial district court ruling in April 2016 determined that authorities had violated the human rights of convicted mass murderer and right-wing terrorist Anders Behring Breivik for keeping him in solitary confinement; the case is under appeal.

The continued influx of refugees and other migrants has dominated the political debate in Norway in 2015 and 2016. The government further restricted access to asylum through 2016 legislation that builds on a stringent law from the previous December, though the tightening was scaled back from bills tabled in April. Amnesty International and other watchdogs have criticized the laws. In January, after Russia temporarily stopped patrolling certain border checkpoints, Norway returned a swell of refugees and migrants to that country without individually reviewing their cases, thus violating the principle of non-refoulement.

POLITICAL RIGHTS: 40 / 40

A. Electoral Process: 12 / 12

B. Political Pluralism and Participation: 16 / 16

C. Functioning of Government: 12 / 12

CIVIL LIBERTIES: 60 / 60

D. Freedom of Expression and Belief: 16 / 16

E. Associational and Organizational Rights: 12 / 12

F. Rule of Law: 16 / 16

G. Personal Autonomy and Individual Rights: 16 / 16

This country report has been abridged for *Freedom in the World 2017.* For background information on political rights and civil liberties in Norway, see *Freedom in the World 2016.*

Oman

Political Rights Rating: 6
Civil Liberties Rating: 5
Freedom Rating: 5.5
Freedom Status: Not Free
Electoral Democracy: No

Population: 4,400,000
Capital: Muscat

Ten-Year Ratings Timeline For Year Under Review (Political Rights, Civil Liberties, Status)

Year Under Review	2007	2008	2009	2010	2011	2012	2013	2014	2015	2006
Rating	6,5,NF	6,5,NF	6,5,NF	6,5,NF	6,5,NF	6,5,NF	6,5,NF	6,5,NF	6,5,NF	6,5,NF

Overview: Oman is a hereditary monarchy, and power is concentrated in the hands of Sultan Qaboos bin Said al-Said, who has ruled since 1970. The regime imposes limits on virtually all political rights and civil liberties, and responds particularly harshly to criticism and dissent.

KEY DEVELOPMENTS IN 2016:

- Authorities arrested and imprisoned several human rights activists, intellectuals, and ordinary citizens for expressing views that criticized or were deemed threatening to the regime.
- In July and August, authorities arrested two editors and a journalist from the *Al-Zaman* newspaper in connection to articles about state interference in the judiciary; all three received prison sentences and fines in a trial in September, with the presiding judge also ordering the closure of the paper.
- In December, an appeals court reversed the closure of *Al-Zaman* and acquitted one of the defendants.

EXECUTIVE SUMMARY

Oman's lagging economy and budget deficit contributed to heightened political tensions in 2016, particularly as the government took steps to reduce or eliminate longstanding social and economic programs. Activists and critics of the regime were vocal during the year about corruption and mismanagement of state resources, and used both the traditional press and online platforms to express their views. In this tense environment, state authorities stepped up efforts to silence voices that criticized or were otherwise deemed a threat to the regime.

The most notable case of the year involved the *Al-Zaman* newspaper, which in July published two reports alleging that under state pressure, the head of Oman's Supreme Court had directly influenced the outcome of a high-profile inheritance dispute. In July and August, authorities arrested two editors and a journalist working for the paper, charging them with vaguely defined offenses that included undermining state prestige, disrupting public order, and misusing the internet. The Ministry of Information also ordered that *Al-Zaman* cease operations. A court in September confirmed the closure and convicted all three individuals, although an appeals court in December acquitted the journalist, reduced the prison sentences of the two editors, and reversed the paper's closure.

In a number of separate cases, authorities prosecuted activists, intellectuals, and ordinary citizens for exercising freedom of expression in the press or on social media platforms. In November, an appeals court upheld a fine and a one-year prison sentence against Said Jaddad, an activist, for inciting discord and threatening national unity in a blog post about a 2011 uprising. In April, authorities arrested Abdullah Habib, a prominent intellectual, and held him incommunicado for several weeks. Watchdogs noted that the arrest was likely connected to Habib's Facebook posts about the 2011 and other uprisings in Oman.

POLITICAL RIGHTS: 8 / 40

A. Electoral Process: 2 / 12

B. Political Pluralism and Participation: 2 / 16

C. Functioning of Government: 2 / 12

Discretionary Political Rights Question A: 2 / 4

CIVIL LIBERTIES: 17 / 60

D. Freedom of Expression and Belief: 5 / 16

E. Associational and Organizational Rights: 3 / 12

F. Rule of Law: 4 / 16

G. Personal Autonomy and Individual Rights: 5 / 16

This country report has been abridged for *Freedom in the World 2017*. For background information on political rights and civil liberties in Oman, see *Freedom in the World 2016.*

Pakistan

Political Rights Rating: 4
Civil Liberties Rating: 5
Freedom Rating: 4.5
Freedom Status: Partly Free
Electoral Democracy: Yes

Population: 203,400,000
Capital: Islamabad

Note: The numerical ratings and status listed above do not reflect conditions in Pakistani-controlled Kashmir, which is examined in a separate report.

Ten-Year Ratings Time-line For Year Under Review (Political Rights, Civil Liberties, Status)

Year Under Review	2007	2008	2009	2010	2011	2012	2013	2014	2015	2016
Rating	6,5,NF	4,5,PF	4,5,PF	4,5,PF	4,5,PF	4,5,PF	4,5,PF	4,5,PF	4,5,PF	4,5,PF

Overview: Pakistan has a thriving and competitive multiparty system. However, the military exerts enormous influence over security and other issues. Islamist extremist violence targets religious minorities and those deemed impediments to Islamization. The military and intelligence services enjoy impunity for indiscriminate use of force. Authorities routinely curtail freedom of expression and association.

KEY DEVELOPMENTS IN 2016:

- Terrorist violence declined sharply, in large part due to a deescalation of an insurgency in the Federally Administered Tribal Areas (FATA).
- Documents released in the Panama Papers leak raised questions about undisclosed assets held by Prime Minister Nawaz Sharif's family. In November, following a series of antigovernment protests, the Supreme Court began hearings into the matter.
- In August, the National Assembly passed the Prevention of Electronic Crimes Bill, which failed to include safeguards proposed by civil society and digital activists.
- In November, Sharif appointed a new chief of army staff in line with the constitution, indicating a consolidation of the civilian leadership's role in national policymaking.

EXECUTIVE SUMMARY

Pakistan remained relatively stable in 2016. Terrorist violence continued to decline, with the South Asia Terrorism Portal counting 1,803 terrorism-related fatalities during the year, about half the number it had documented in 2015. The cumulative effect of the army's clearance of terrorist sanctuaries in Waziristan, and intelligence-led operations elsewhere in the country, was that radical Islamist violence no longer directly threatened democratic order.

In October, a series of antigovernment protests took place at which demonstrators expressed anger over documents released in the Panama Papers leak that raised questions about undisclosed assets held by Prime Minister Sharif's family. Hundreds of demonstrators were detained following violent clashes with police, who employed tear gas and rubber bullets against the crowd. The Supreme Court opened hearings into corruption allegations against Sharif in November. Meanwhile, the army leadership was changed in line with the constitutional process and normal timeline, reflecting some consolidation of the civilian leadership's role in national policymaking.

There was little progress on expanding civil liberties in 2016. Instead, a restrictive law governing the use of the internet was passed, and civil society organizations faced a continuing clampdown. An orchestrated campaign of harassment against Afghan refugees in Pakistan, launched during the summer, precipitated a mass exodus to Afghanistan despite continuing insecurity there.

POLITICAL RIGHTS: 21 / 40 (+ 1)

A. Electoral Process: 7 / 12

Pakistan consists of four provinces (Baluchistan, Punjab, Sindhi, and Khyber Pakhtunkhwa, or KPK) and two federal territories (the FATA and the Islamabad Capital Territory). The parliament (Majlis-i-Shoora) is bicameral, with a 342-member National Assembly (NA) and a 104-member Senate. The constitution provides for a parliamentary system of government headed by a prime minister. An electoral college of the Senate, the NA, and the provincial assemblies elects the president for up to two five-year terms.

The Senate provides equal representation to all units of the federation. Each provincial assembly chooses 23 members, NA members representing the FATA elect eight, and four are chosen by the NA to represent the capital territory. Senators serve six-year terms, with half of the seats up for election every three years.

Members of the NA are elected for five years. Of the 342 seats, 272 are filled through direct elections in single-member districts, 60 are reserved for women, and 10 are reserved for non-Muslim minorities. The reserved seats are filled through a proportional representation system with closed party lists. The seats for women are allocated in proportion to the number of general seats a party gains in each of the provinces. The provincial assemblies employ a similar electoral system.

International and domestic election observers judged the 2013 elections favorably, citing active competition and campaigning. Voter turnout was 55 percent. The Pakistan Muslim League–Nawaz (PML-N) overtook the incumbent Pakistan People's Party (PPP) at the federal level, winning 126 of the directly elected seats in the NA. The PPP won 31 seats and Pakistan Tehreek-e-Insaf (PTI) took 28. Various smaller parties won less than 20 directly elected seats each. The PML-N formed a governing majority with the help of allied independents, and Sharif became prime minister.

The 18th constitutional amendment, adopted in 2010, significantly decentralized power from the federal level to the provinces. Under this arrangement, the provincial assemblies and governments have legislative and executive responsibilities, including in health, education, and local government. The 2013 provincial elections left a different party in government in each of the four provinces: PML-N in Punjab, PPP in Sindhi, a PTI-led coalition in KPK, and a National Party/PML-N coalition in Baluchistan.

Effort continued in 2016 to clear electoral business left over from the 2013 national and provincial elections, as election tribunals settled petitions relating to winning candidates accused of serious violations of electoral law, and several by-elections were held.

B. Political Pluralism and Participation: 8 / 16

Pakistan has a thriving and competitive multiparty system. Opposition parties are generally free to operate both inside and outside the assemblies. The PPP, which had been defeated by the PML-N in 2013 federal elections, attempted to rebuild its national base in 2016, with former Pakistani president and party co-chairman Asif Ali Zardari returning to Pakistan in December after spending a year and a half abroad. Meanwhile, his son, Bilawal Bhutto Zardari, the PPP's other co-chairman, staged a series of rallies during the year. In contrast, the strongest party in Karachi, the Muttahida Qaumi Movement (MQM), faced a crackdown by authorities, who closed the party's offices and arrested influential members after exiled party leader Altaf Hussain gave an August address that was highly critical of the army. Demonstrators allegedly affiliated with the party had subsequently launched a violent attack on two television stations. The MQM nevertheless continued operating during the year, participating in by-elections and the Sindh assembly.

There is a history of use of accountability mechanisms against national politicians, some of which has been selective and discriminatory. However, in 2016 the main focus on accountability for national politicians revolved around whether Prime Minister Sharif would be held to account on claims of concealing assets. In November, the Supreme Court appointed a one-judge commission to investigate the issue. Proceedings were still underway at the year end.

Terrorist violence fell further in 2016. There were no assassinations of prominent political figures and the army saw success in pushing radical Islamist groups out of the remainder of their main sanctuaries. Therefore, despite the periodic mass-casualty terrorist attacks that occur in all provinces, terrorist violence did not represent a direct threat to the democratic order.

Since 2002, a joint electorate system has allowed members of minorities to participate in the general vote while also being represented by reserved seats in the national and provincial assemblies through the party-list system. However, the participation of non-Muslims in the political system continues to be marginal. Political parties nominate members to legislative seats reserved for non-Muslim minorities, leaving non-Muslim voters with little say in selecting the parliamentarians who supposedly represent them. Ahmadis, members of a heterodox Muslim sect, face political discrimination and are registered on a separate voter roll.

C. Functioning of Government: 6 / 12 (+ 1)

The shifting terms of civil-military relations remained one of the most important underlying themes in national politics. The most concrete development in 2016 was the November appointment by the prime minister, in line with the constitution, of Qamar Javed Bajwa as the new chief of army staff. The high-profile incumbent, Raheel Sharif, retired in November without seeking an extension, thus breaking with the precedent set by previous army chief Ashfaq Parvez Kayani, who had maneuvered to stay on for a second term. In December, the intelligence chief was also replaced. Both moves indicated a consolidation of the civilian leadership's role in national policymaking. However, the military continued to exert enormous influence in the conduct of relations with India and on internal security issues, such as the prioritization of areas for counterterrorism operations.

The National Accountability Bureau (NAB) is Pakistan's premier anticorruption body. In 2016 it continued to pursue dozens of "mega cases" involving investigation or prosecution of public representatives and commercial figures accused of serious corruption. Popular perception was that corruption remained endemic in public bodies.

Accessing official information remains difficult, and existing provisions for obtaining public records are ineffective. At the end of 2016, lawmakers had yet to approve a draft freedom of information bill, which would replace a 2002 ordinance on the topic and had drawn praise from local and international transparency advocates. Think tanks, civil society organizations, and universities all contribute to lively debate on many aspects of public policy. However, debate on certain aspects of national security policy, particularly the military's alleged support for militant groups targeting Afghanistan and Indian Kashmir, have in effect remained taboo.

CIVIL LIBERTIES: 22 / 60 (+ 1)

D. Freedom of Expression and Belief: 6 / 16 (+ 1)

Pakistan has a vibrant media sector that presents a range of news and opinions and hosts lively debates on current affairs. However, there is a history of violence and intimidation selectively directed against media figures by both intelligence agencies and violent extremist groups, and the Committee to Protect Journalists (CPJ) documented two journalists' murders in 2016. The perpetrators of such violence enjoy impunity.

The military retained a prominent place in the media landscape, in part relying on the well-resourced Inter-Services Public Relations (ISPR) to maintain its profile and project its perspectives. The Pakistan Electronic Media Regulatory Authority (PEMRA) awards radio and television licenses, maintains a code of conduct which was toughened in 2015, and exercises the power to suspend operators. In October 2016, PEMRA banned the transmission of radio and television broadcasts from India, days after the Indian government had banned Pakistani actors and actresses from working in Indian films; the developments came amid increasing tensions along the Line of Control (LoC) demarcating the Indian- and Pakistani-held parts of Kashmir. The Pakistani Broadcasters Association indicated that they would legally challenge the order, which appeared to be in place at year's end.

More than 200,000 websites are banned in the country because of their allegedly anti-Islamic, pornographic, or blasphemous content. The Pakistan Telecommunications Authority (PTA) in January 2016 lifted a three-year ban on the video-hosting website YouTube, with the launch of a new country-specific version of the service and a protocol for the authorities to approach Google, YouTube's parent company, to suppress objectionable material.

In August, after a year of controversy, the NA passed the Prevention of Electronic Crimes Bill (PECB). While civil society was heavily involved in debate surrounding the bill, activists complained that the act as passed gives the executive-controlled PTA unchecked powers to censor material on the internet. The act also increases punishments for some offenses already in the penal code and relaxes safeguards against surveillance and breach of privacy.

Constitutional guarantees of freedom of religion and protection of minorities have not provided effective checks to discriminatory legislation, social prejudice, and sectarian violence. Members of the Hindu community have complained of vulnerability to kidnapping and forced conversions, and some continue to migrate to India, where they are housed in refugee camps. High-profile blasphemy cases and mob violence have affected the Christian community and others. The most specific discriminatory legislation has been directed at the Ahmadi community, who are prohibited from asserting themselves as Muslims. In December 2016, in Chakwal District, a mob attacked Ahmadis in their place of worship, ultimately setting fire to the building and wounding several people. The mob action occurred soon after a rare example of public recognition of members of the Ahmadi community; days before, Prime Minister Sharif announced that he was renaming the physics department of Quaid-i-Azam University in Islamabad after Nobel Prize winner Abdus Salam, a theoretical physicist who belonged to the Ahmadi community.

Pakistan has a long history of using education to portray Hindus and other non-Muslims negatively and to rationalize enmity between Pakistan and India. Attempts to modernize education and introduce tolerance into school textbooks have proven slow and controversial. In recent years, some space has opened for scholars to discuss sensitive issues involving the military. However, the threat of accusations of blasphemy or reprisals from the military still obliges ordinary Pakistanis to self-censor on topics of religion and security.

E. Associational and Organizational Rights: 6 / 12

The constitution guarantees the rights to associate, demonstrate, and organize, but the government sporadically imposes arbitrary restrictions to temporarily ban gatherings or any activity designated a threat to public order, often invoking Section 144 of the Penal Code. Authorities violently dispersed antigovernment protests that took place in Islamabad and Rawalpindi in October 2016, and arrested hundreds of people under Section 144.

The government, acting at both the federal and provincial level, in recent years has significantly limited the ability of civil society organizations to function by enforcing rigid regulatory and reporting rules. Among them are requirements that international and domestic organizations seek official "no-objection certificates" (NOCs) before launching various projects. Foreign NGOs were required to undergo a cumbersome reregistration process under a 2015 initiative, and many had yet to secure official status by the end of 2016.

The rights of workers to organize and form trade unions are recognized in law, and the constitution grants unions the rights to collective bargaining and to strike. However, many categories of workers are excluded from these protections. The procedures that need to be followed for a strike to be legal are onerous. Nevertheless, strikes are organized regularly.

Roughly 70 percent of the workforce is employed in the informal sector, where there is limited unionization.

F. Rule of Law: 4 / 16

Over the last decade, executive interference in the higher judiciary has decreased, and the judiciary in some cases holds the executive to account. However, the broader justice system is marred by endemic problems including corruption, intimidation, a large backlog of cases, insecurity, and low conviction rates for serious crimes. A separate Federal Sharia Court is empowered to determine whether a provision of law goes against Islamic injunctions. Some communities resort to informal forms of justice, leading to decisions outside formal safeguards.

The National Commission for Human Rights, now in its second year of operation, has made little progress in strengthening human rights protections in the country.

Military courts with powers to try civilians accused of terrorist-related offenses were established in 2015 in the wake of a deadly terrorist attack on a military school, and continued to operate throughout 2016. These courts have convicted scores of people, at least 140 of whom received death sentences; of those, 12 people had been executed by the end of 2016. The courts have drawn significant criticism for their lack of transparency and absence of safeguards to ensure fair trials. Strikingly, the army claimed in November 2016 that over 90 percent of those convicted in the courts had given a confession. The courts' mandate will end in early 2017. In addition to the military courts, the government continued to seek implementation of death sentences awarded by the judiciary, and more than 400 Pakistanis have been executed since the lifting of the death penalty moratorium in December 2014. Separately, the Protection of Pakistan Act, which gave authorities broad license to carry out arrests and detentions, expired in July 2016 and was not extended.

The FATA are governed by the president. They are subject to the Frontier Crimes Regulation (FCR) and lie outside the jurisdiction of the Pakistan Supreme Court. The FCR authorizes the government's political agents and tribal leaders to apply customary law, and provides for collective punishment. In 2016, a government committee recommended that the FATA integrate with KPK, though there is no clear timetable for implementation.

The military and the intelligence services enjoy impunity for indiscriminate use of force. Extrajudicial killings, enforced disappearances, torture, and other abuses are common. Terrorism suspects, Balochi and Sindhi nationalists, journalists, researchers, and social workers have all been victims of alleged disappearance.

Insurgencies and military efforts to counter them continued to disrupt residents' lives in 2016, though a deescalation of the insurgency in the FATA was a primary contributor to the national-level reduction in terrorist violence; terrorism-related fatalities fell approximately 50 percent in 2016 compared to the previous year, to 1,803. The army continued security operations in Karachi, which significantly brought down levels of violence there. A major insurgency continued in Baluchistan, and the army also notably deployed in Rajanpur, reportedly to root out a local criminal group. The Tehreek-i-Taliban Pakistan (TTP) and its offshoots, along with the regional branch of Islamic State militant group and its ally Lashkar-e-Jhangvi, claimed responsibility for high-casualty attacks against civilians and security forces during the year.

Pakistan has long hosted some 1.5 million registered Afghan refugees, with approximately one million more unregistered. These include a generation of refugees born and raised in Pakistan, with little or no experience of Afghanistan. The UN Refugee Agency and Pakistani authorities periodically negotiate extensions to refugees' authorized stays. During the summer of 2016, authorities in Khyber Pakhtunkhwa, Punjab, and Baluchistan launched what amounted to a campaign of harassment of Afghan communities. Measures taken included mass arrests and deportations, restriction on the ability to rent property, evictions, exclusion from schools, adverse commentary amounting to hate speech, and tighter control of border crossings. Hundreds of thousands of refugees returned to Afghanistan, where security and economic conditions were likely to leave the uprooted refugees vulnerable.

Members of the transgender and intersex community are authorized to register for official documents under a "third gender" classification recognized by the Supreme Court in 2009. In a ruling in 2011, the court granted them the right to vote, enabling them to participate in the 2013 elections. Nonetheless, the LGBT (lesbian, gay, bisexual, and transgender) community are subject to societal and legal discrimination. The penal code prescribes prison terms for consensual sex "against the order of nature." Although prosecutions are rare, such laws deter LGBT people from acknowledging their orientation or reporting abuses. Transgender and intersex people face de facto discrimination in housing and employment. They are also refused inheritance rights. Many are forced into prostitution or to beg in order to survive.

G. Personal Autonomy and Individual Rights: 6 / 16

There are few legal limitations on citizens' travel or their choice of residence, employment, or institution of higher learning. The main tool for restricting foreign travel is the Exit Control List, which blocks named individuals from using official exit points from the country. The list is meant to include those who pose a security threat and those facing court proceedings, but on occasion it has been used against civil society activists who have worked on issues embarrassing to officials. Some 5,000 names were removed from the list after the Interior Ministry ordered a review of it in 2015. In October 2016, a senior reporter was added to the list after publishing an article discussing counterterrorism strategy, but was soon removed following an outcry from media freedom advocates. The Supreme Court in December ordered the removal of former president Pervez Musharraf from the list, allowing him to leave Pakistan for medical treatment; Musharraf faced treason charges at the time. Separately, restrictions on movement in the FATA were imposed as the army carried out counterinsurgency operations and resettlement programs.

Pakistan's rampant corruption, weak regulatory environment, and ineffective legal system undermine property rights and economic freedom.

A number of reforms have been enacted in recent years to improve conditions for women. However, the implementation of protective laws has been weak, and violence against women continues unabated. In addition to acid attacks, domestic violence, rape, and so-called honor crimes, women face restrictions on voting and education, especially in KPK, the FATA, and Baluchistan. Political parties maintain women's wings that are active during elections. However, currently no women hold posts in the federal cabinet or at the helm of mainstream political parties.

Exploitative forms of labor remain common, in particular in the brick kiln industry, where owners have significant political influence that protects them from prosecution. Though bonded and child labor are outlawed, they are widespread in practice.

Palau

Political Rights Rating: 1
Civil Liberties Rating: 1
Freedom Rating: 1.0
Freedom Status: Free
Electoral Democracy: Yes

Population: 20,000
Capital: Melekeok

Ten-Year Ratings Timeline For Year Under Review (Political Rights, Civil Liberties, Status)

Year Under Review	2007	2008	2009	2010	2011	2012	2013	2014	2015	2016
Rating	1,1,F	1,1,F	1,1,F	1,1,F	1,1,F	1,1,F	1,1,F	1,1,F	1,1,F	1,1,F

The country or territory displayed here received scores but no narrative report for this edition of *Freedom in the World.*

Panama

Political Rights Rating: 2
Civil Liberties Rating: 2
Freedom Rating: 2.0
Freedom Status: Free
Electoral Democracy: Yes

Population: 4,000,000
Capital: Panama City

Ten-Year Ratings Timeline For Year Under ReviewRights, Civil Liberties, Status)

Year Under Review	2007	2008	2009	2010	2011	2012	2013	2014	2015	2016
Rating	1,2,F	1,2,F	1,2,F	1,2,F	1,2,F	1,2,F	2,2,F	2,2,F	2,2,F	2,2,F

Overview: Panama's political institutions are democratic, with competitive elections and orderly rotations of power. Freedoms of expression and association are generally respected. However, corruption and impunity are serious challenges, affecting the police, the judiciary, and the highest levels of government. Discrimination against darker-skinned Panamanians is common, and indigenous groups have struggled to uphold their substantial legal rights with respect to land and development projects.

KEY DEVELOPMENTS IN 2016:

- Two prominent members of a committee established to examine malfeasance in Panama's financial system resigned in August, citing government obstruction.
- In September, the government requested the extradition of former president Ricardo Martinelli from the United States amid multiple ongoing investigations into corruption linked to his administration.
- A Dutch journalist was detained for over a month on a 2012 defamation conviction before being released by presidential decree in December.

EXECUTIVE SUMMARY

Panama's authorities continued to grapple with corruption in government and the private sector in 2016. More than 200 investigations were under way into wrongdoing linked to the administration of former president Martinelli, who had fled to the United States in 2015. The Supreme Court ordered his detention late that year, and in September 2016 Panama requested his extradition.

The Panama Papers, a trove of documents leaked from a Panama-based law firm and unveiled by media organizations in April 2016, provided further evidence of the country's role in a global network of money laundering and other hidden financial dealings. That month, President Juan Carlos Varela created an independent committee to evaluate the financial system, but two prominent members resigned in August, accusing the government of restricting the scope of their work and failing to guarantee that their findings would be made public.

Independent or critical journalists reportedly faced editorial pressure from the government during the year. Both public officials and private businessmen regularly bring defamation cases against the media. In November, Dutch journalist Okke Ornstein was detained over a 2012 defamation conviction in a case filed by a Canadian businessman. He had been sentenced to 20 months in prison, though authorities had made no attempt to arrest him before. Following objections from press freedom groups and Dutch diplomats, President Varela signed a decree that enabled Ornstein's release in late December.

The number of recorded homicides declined to 374 in 2016, from 434 in 2015. However, the prison population was at 121 percent of intended capacity, with pretrial detainees accounting for a majority of the total. The overall incarceration rate remains one of the highest in the world at more than 420 per 100,000 inhabitants.

A dispute between the government and indigenous communities over a hydroelectric dam project continued in 2016, prompting a series of demonstrations and the arrest of some protest leaders. A negotiated agreement was rejected by an indigenous congress in September, but a pair of Supreme Court rulings in December favored the project, and flooding of land above the dam was under way at year's end.

POLITICAL RIGHTS: 35 / 40

A. Electoral Process: 12 / 12

B. Political Pluralism and Participation: 15 / 16

C. Functioning of Government: 8 / 12

CIVIL LIBERTIES: 48 / 60

D. Freedom of Expression and Belief: 15 / 16

E. Associational and Organizational Rights: 11 / 12

F. Rule of Law: 10 / 16

G. Personal Autonomy and Individual Rights: 12 / 16

This country report has been abridged for *Freedom in the World 2017*. For background information on political rights and civil liberties in Panama, see *Freedom in the World 2016*.

Papua New Guinea

Political Rights Rating: 3 ↑
Civil Liberties Rating: 3
Freedom Rating: 3.0
Freedom Status: Partly Free
Electoral Democracy: Yes

Population: 8,200,000
Capital: Port Moresby

Ratings Change: Papua New Guinea's political rights ratings improved from 4 to 3 because there is robust competition among political parties, which may form freely and have repeatedly risen to power by winning credible elections.

Ten-Year Ratings Timeline For Year Under Review (Political Rights, Civil Liberties, Status)

Year Under Review	2007	2008	2009	2010	2011	2012	2013	2014	2015	2016
Rating	3,3,PF	4,3,PF	4,3,PF	4,3,PF	4,3,PF	4,3,PF	3,3,PF	4,3,PF	4,3,PF	3,3,PF

Overview: Papua New Guinea has a reasonably open democratic system, though corruption among public officials and a lack of will to address it remain serious problems. The country is home to a relatively free media. Controversy persists over the presence of an Australian-run center for asylum seekers, which has faced criticism for poor conditions. A 2005 agreement ended a civil war in Bougainville and provided for an independence referendum now expected in 2019, though the current authorities have indicated that they oppose Bougainville's secession.

KEY DEVELOPMENTS IN 2016:

- In June, police fired on student protesters in Port Moresby as the students prepared to march to the parliament to call for Prime Minister Peter O'Neill's resignation. Police said 23 people were injured.
- In July, O'Neill easily survived a parliamentary no-confidence vote.
- In August, O'Neill announced a significant hike in the nomination fee for candidates contesting the 2017 legislative elections. Critics said the increased fee, ostensibly meant to support the operations of the Electoral Commission, would exclude candidates who could not afford to pay it.
- In April, the Supreme Court ruled an Australian-run facility for asylum seekers unconstitutional, saying its residents were held there against their will, thus violating their personal liberty. The facility, which is located on Manus Island and has faced criticism for poor conditions within, remained open at year's end.

EXECUTIVE SUMMARY

In 2016, Prime Minister O'Neill fended off widespread criticism over longstanding corruption allegations that involved millions of dollars' worth of public funds allegedly paid out to a private law firm. He easily survived a parliamentary no-confidence vote in July, with 21 lawmakers voting for his removal and 85 voting in his favor. The vote came after a June incident at a campus of the University of Papua New Guinea in Port Moresby, in which police had opened fire on students as they prepared to march to the parliament to call for O'Neill's resignation; police said 23 people were injured. Transport workers also took strike actions during the year to protest O'Neill's continued leadership.

In August, O'Neill announced a hike in the nomination fee for candidates contesting the 2017 legislative elections to 10,000 kina ($3,150), a substantial increase from the previous rate of 2,000 kina ($630). The fee increase was purportedly aimed at filling a gap in funding for the Electoral Commission, but critics said it would effectively reduce the number of candidates by excluding ones that could not afford to pay it.

Pervasive corruption is the biggest hindrance to development, and the country's anticorruption bureaucracies have been subject to political interference. Plans to establish a new Independent Commission against Corruption had not been realized at the end of 2016. A previous anticorruption body known as Taskforce Sweep was eventually defunded after bringing corruption claims against O'Neill.

Controversy persists over the country's agreement with Australia regarding asylum seekers, in which migrants from third-party countries that reach Australia are sent to an Australian-run detention center on Manus Island while their asylum applications are processed. The Supreme Court ruled the Manus Island center unconstitutional in April 2016, saying its residents were held there against their will, thus violating their personal liberty. It issued an order that Papua New Guinea and Australia work to relocate the asylum seekers held there, but the center remained operational at year's end. In December, asylum seekers temporarily seized control of sections of the facility following the death of a 27-year-old Sudanese detainee they said had been denied adequate medical care.

O'Neill has indicated that he opposes the secession of Bougainville from Papua New Guinea, and that he views the planned 2019 independence referendum as nonbinding, with any vote for independence subject to approval by the country's parliament.

POLITICAL RIGHTS: 26 / 40 (+ 3)

A. Electoral Process: 9 / 12

B. Political Pluralism and Participation: 13 / 16 (+ 3)

C. Functioning of Government: 4 / 12

CIVIL LIBERTIES: 38 / 60 (+ 2)

D. Freedom of Expression and Belief: 13 / 16 (+ 1)

E. Associational and Organizational Rights: 9 / 12

F. Rule of Law: 7 / 16

G. Personal Autonomy and Individual Rights: 9 / 16 (+ 1)

This country report has been abridged for *Freedom in the World 2017*. For background information on political rights and civil liberties in Papua New Guinea, see *Freedom in the World 2016*.

Paraguay

Political Rights Rating: 3
Civil Liberties Rating: 3
Freedom Rating: 3.0
Freedom Status: Partly Free
Electoral Democracy: Yes

Population: 7,000,000
Capital: Asunción

Ten-Year Ratings Timeline For Year Under Review (Political Rights, Civil Liberties, Status)

Year Under Review	2007	2008	2009	2010	2011	2012	2013	2014	2015	2016
Rating	3,3,PF	3,3,PF	3,3,PF	3,3,PF	3,3,PF	3,3,PF	3,3,PF	3,3,PF	3,3,PF	3,3,PF

Overview: Paraguay maintains a democratic political system, but it is dominated by the conservative Colorado Party, which resumed its many decades in government shortly after the four-year tenure of a liberal president ended in a controversial impeachment in 2012. Rampant corruption and organized crime are key impediments to good governance and security. Indigenous populations, which suffer disproportionately from poverty, have struggled to assert their land rights.

KEY DEVELOPMENTS IN 2016:

- Government forces continued to combat the Paraguayan People's Army (EPP), a Marxist guerrilla group that operates primarily in the north. The government accused the EPP of killing eight soldiers and abducting three civilians during the year.
- A law enacted in September was designed to protect children against abuse, including in the context of child labor, which remains a pervasive problem in the country.
- In December, the president signed a law meant to address violence against women, in part by providing for shelters and establishing femicide—the murder of a woman based largely on her gender—as a crime punishable with 10 to 30 years in prison.

EXECUTIVE SUMMARY

President Horacio Cartes was praised in 2016 for increasing economic opportunity and curbing crime in the country since he took office in 2013. However, Cartes's market-oriented policies and widespread government corruption stoked protests by campesinos (small-scale farmers or farmworkers), indigenous people, and an emboldened student movement that has demanded comprehensive university reforms.

Cartes and conservative lawmakers resisted international pressure to ease the country's strict ban on abortion and adopt laws to prevent discrimination against LGBT (lesbian, gay, bisexual, and transgender) people. Paraguay has more Roman Catholics per capita than any other country in the region, and the government enjoys the support of a significant portion of the population on these issues.

While no journalists were killed during 2016, direct pressure by criminal groups and corrupt authorities often leads reporters to censor themselves, especially in remote border areas. Private media owners also exert influence over journalists, and a media group linked to President Cartes has expanded its holdings in recent years.

POLITICAL RIGHTS: 27 / 40

A. Electoral Process: 10 / 12

B. Political Pluralism and Participation: 12 / 16

C. Functioning of Government: 5 / 12

CIVIL LIBERTIES: 37 / 60

D. Freedom of Expression and Belief: 12 / 16

E. Associational and Organizational Rights: 8 / 12

F. Rule of Law: 7 / 16

G. Personal Autonomy and Individual Rights: 10 / 16

This country report has been abridged for *Freedom in the World 2017*. For background information on political rights and civil liberties in Paraguay, see *Freedom in the World 2016*.

Peru

Political Rights Rating: 2
Civil Liberties Rating: 3
Freedom Rating: 2.5
Freedom Status: Free
Electoral Democracy: Yes

Population: 31,500,000
Capital: Lima

Ten-Year Ratings Timeline For Year Under Review (Political Rights, Civil Liberties, Status)

Year Under Review	2007	2008	2009	2010	2011	2012	2013	2014	2015	2016
Rating	2,3,F	2,3,F	2,3,F	2,3,F	2,3,F	2,3,F	2,3,F	2,3,F	2,3,F	2,3,F

Overview: Despite a history of authoritarian rule, Peru has established democratic political institutions and undergone multiple peaceful transfers of power in recent years. Corruption continues to be a serious concern. Indigenous groups suffer from inadequate political representation and exclusion from decisions on land use and other issues, though the government has taken some steps to address those problems in recent years. Protests and activism related to land use have often led to violence and the use of lethal force by police. While the media are active and largely privately owned, their independence is hampered by the threat of physical attacks and defamation charges, as well as ownership concentration.

KEY DEVELOPMENTS IN 2016:
- Pedro Pablo Kuczynski, a center-right former prime minister, narrowly won the presidency in a June runoff against Keiko Fujimori, the daughter of former authoritarian president Alberto Fujimori.
- Fujimori's Popular Force party won an absolute majority in the April congressional elections, taking 73 out of 130 seats.
- A series of corruption scandals led to the resignations of Popular Force secretary general Joaquín Ramírez in May and three advisers to Kuczynski in October.

EXECUTIVE SUMMARY

Peru's 2016 general elections were considered free and fair. The presidential race was hotly contested, with Keiko Fujimori leading a field of 10 candidates in the first round in April, then losing to Kuczynski in the June runoff by just 0.2 percentage points. However, Fujimori's Popular Force party took 73 out of 130 seats in the April congressional elections, followed by the left-leaning Broad Front with 20, Kuczynski's Peruvians for Change party with 18, and three smaller parties with the remainder. President Kuczynski assumed office in July.

International election observers expressed concerns about insufficient controls on campaign finances, including a lack of limits on spending by political parties. While the National Board of Elections (JNE) was applauded for its efforts to improve transparency, inadequate enforcement mechanisms led to the perception that abuse of campaign finance laws was widespread. Observers criticized the enactment of a 2015 reform to the Political Parties Law after elections had already been called, which caused confusion about which laws were in effect. However, the reform proved to be a useful tool for protecting electoral integrity, as the JNE effectively applied it in disqualifying two candidates, one of them for vote buying.

The conviction of journalists on charges of defamation reinforced concerns about outdated legal restrictions on freedom of expression in Peru. Among other cases during the year, Fernando Valenica was charged with libeling the former president, Alan García, and Rafael León was charged with defamation for publishing a piece in 2014 that was critical of a fellow journalist. They received fines and suspended jail sentences in April and May, respectively, though both sentences were later overturned on appeal. Separately, newspaper editor Ronald Daniel Ormeño was temporarily jailed in September for failing to pay damages in a libel case dating to 2013. Physical attacks and threats against journalists remained common; at least one journalist, radio host Hernán Choquepata Ordoñez, was murdered during the year, though the motive for the November killing was unclear.

Local disputes and protests—often related to extractive industries, land rights, and resource allocation among marginalized populations—regularly result in deaths and injuries. In September 2016, more than 50 indigenous residents of the Amazon province of Bagua were finally acquitted of murder and other charges stemming from deadly clashes between police and land-rights protesters in 2009. No state officials were prosecuted for their role in the incident.

NOTE: BELOW THIS LINE UNEDITED

POLITICAL RIGHTS: 30 / 40

A. Electoral Process: 10 / 12

The president and the 130-member unicameral Congress are elected for five-year terms. Congressional balloting employs an open-list, region-based system of proportional representation, with a 5-percent vote hurdle for a party to enter the legislature.

The 2016 general elections were closely contested, with Pedro Pablo Kuczynski ultimately winning by a historically small margin. After a competitive first round with 10 candidates, in which Keiko Fujimori won 39.9 percent of the vote, well ahead of any other candidate, Pedro Pablo Kuczynski and Fujimori entered a runoff in June, which Kuczynski won, 50.1 percent to 49.9 percent. In the concurrent legislative elections, Fujimori's Popular Force party captured 73 of the 130 seats, followed by Kuczynski's Peruvians for Change with 18 seats and Broad Front with 20 seats.[1]

While international observers deemed the elections and fair, they raised concerns regarding campaign financing. Though there are limits on individual donations, there are

---

1. http://perureports.com/2016-elections-peru/

no constraints on spending by political parties. Political parties are required to disclose funding sources in regular reporting, but due to the lack of enforcement mechanisms to ensure compliance, observers believe the reports provided were incomplete.[2] The enactment of a 2015 reform to the Political Party Law was largely viewed as complicating an already-opaque process. However, the electoral authority (JNE) effectively applied the reform to disqualify candidates Cesar Acuña for vote-buying and Julio Guzman for failing to complete required paperwork.[3] Campaign ethics were a serious issue, as the Secretary General of the Popular Force party, Joaquin Ramirez, resigned under allegations of corruption and possible money laundering.[4] Key advisers to the Kuczynski campaign resigned after incriminating audiotapes surfaced in October.[5]

Local and regional elections in October 2014 followed the pattern of previous cycles, with most elected officials representing regional movements rather than fragmented national parties. In Lima, the election returned former mayor Luis Castañeda to office despite past controversies. Accusations of collusion between local candidates and criminals are common; in the aftermath of the elections, 227 contributors to political parties were linked by the electoral authorities to various illicit activities.

B. Political Pluralism and Participation: 13 / 16

Peruvian parties, while competitive, are both highly fragmented and extremely personalized. In the December 2015 National Corruption Survey, 64 percent of Peruvians described the performance of political parties as bad or very bad. Moves toward decentralization over the last decade have strengthened the role and influence of regional presidents, though they have often been accused of corruption.

The concerns of ethnic and cultural minorities, especially in remote mountain or Amazonian areas, remain inadequately addressed among parties with national scope, which contributes to regular episodes of acute social conflict in the provinces. The 2011 Law of Prior Consultation has fostered increased recognition and encouragement of indigenous participation and consultation rights, but analysts agree that there is still ample room to improve the Peruvian state's integration of indigenous political agendas into mainstream national debate.

C. Functioning of Government: 7 / 12

Corruption remains a critical problem in Peru. According to the 2015 National Corruption Survey, nearly 80 percent of Peruvians think corruption increased under the Humala government, and 85 percent view the central government as "little" or "not at all" effective in fighting corruption. Checks on political parties' campaign financing are weak, especially at the subnational level, where drug trafficking activity flourishes. Peru was ranked 88 out of 168 countries and territories surveyed in Transparency International's 2015 Corruption Perceptions Index.

Corruption scandals persisted in 2016. In March, Brazilian officials announced they were investigating now-former President Ollanta Humala for allegedly accepting bribes of up to three million dollars from a Brazilian engineering firm.[6] After corruption had featured prominently in the presidential campaign, three advisers to President Kuczynski—Carlos Moreno, José Labán, and Jorge Villacorta—stepped down in October amid allegations that

2. https://eeas.europa.eu/election-observation-missions/eom-peru-2016/305/preliminary-statement-a-democratic-and-broadly-accepted-although-atypical-electoral-process_en

3. https://redaccion.lamula.pe/2016/02/23/elecciones-2016-estas-son-las-reglas-vigentes-para-los-partidos-politicos/jorgepaucar/

4. http://larepublica.pe/politica/768690-joaquin-ramirez-renuncia-la-secretaria-general-de-fuerza-popular

5. http://larepublica.pe/politica/812197-renuncian-asesores-de-ppk-jose-laban-y-jorge-villacorta

6. http://www.worldpoliticsreview.com/trend-lines/18165/impunity-allows-corruption-to-flourish-in-peru

they had engaged in corruption during the campaign.[7] In response to the allegations, Kuczynski announced a series of measures to combat corruption, including a law that would ban those who have been charged with corruption from returning to public office.[8]

Some government agencies have made progress on transparency, but much information related to defense and security policies remains classified under a 2012 law.

CIVIL LIBERTIES: 41 / 60

D. Freedom of Expression and Belief: 15 / 16

Peru's dynamic press is mostly privately owned. The 2013 purchase of the EPENSA newspaper group by the *El Comercio* conglomerate—which now controls nearly 80 percent of the market—ignited an intense debate over the concentration of media ownership. The Constitutional Tribunal (TC) still has yet to rule on an injunction filed in 2013 claiming that the merger infringed on a constitutional article barring the "cornering" of the media market.[9]

Attacks against journalists in response to negative media coverage are common, especially at the subnational level. Reporters often receive threats when reporting on corruption, while many physical attacks occur in the context of protests over resource extraction issues. Low pay leaves reporters susceptible to bribery, and media outlets remain dependent on advertising by large retailers and the state. Defamation is criminalized, and journalists are regularly convicted under such charges, though their sentences are usually suspended. In 2016, Fernando Valencia was charged with libeling former president Alan García,[10] and Rafael Leon was charged with defamation for publishing a critical piece in 2014 of then-mayor of Lima, Susana Villaran.[11] Valencia was sentenced to over a year in prison, though the sentence was suspended, and both were forced to pay fines.

The Peruvian constitution guarantees freedom of religion and belief, rights that are generally respected. The Roman Catholic Church nevertheless receives preferential treatment from the state, and an influential bloc of Catholic congressional representatives helps limit potential changes on social issues such as same-sex marriage and abortion.

The government restricts neither academic freedom nor access to the internet, which had a penetration rate of 58 percent in 2016.[12]

E. Associational and Organizational Rights: 8 / 12

The authorities generally recognize and respect the constitutionally guaranteed right to peaceful assembly. However, the government has also frequently resorted to declarations of states of emergency and done little to prevent excessive use of force by security personnel confronting protests. At least 51 Peruvians were killed in protests between the start of Humala's term and October 2015. Very few members of the police or military have faced charges for protest-related incidents in recent years. Several decrees and laws since 2010 have limited police and military responsibility in the event of injury or death during demonstrations. In 2015, the TC ruled unconstitutional a provision broadening military jurisdiction

---

7. http://larepublica.pe/politica/812197-renuncian-asesores-de-ppk-jose-laban-y-jorge-villacorta
8. http://aristeguinoticias.com/1810/mundo/aprobaran-muerte-civil-para-politicos-corruptos-en-peru
-video/
9. http://larepublica.pe/impresa/politica/812965-sip-invoca-al-poder-judicial-que-resuelva-demanda
-por-concentracion-de-medios
10. http://en.sipiapa.org/notas/1210208-peru-journalist-found-guilty-of-defamation
11. http://larepublica.pe/politica/764630-rafo-leon-hoy-dictan-sentencia-periodista-por-presunta
-difamacion
12. http://www.internetworldstats.com/sa/pe.htm

in cases when the security forces are involved in civilian deaths, but upheld the executive's capacity to deploy the armed forces in a variety of social conflict situations.

Despite substantial efforts by the state ombudsman and the recently created National Office of Dialogue, the governmental approach to local grievances typically eschews mediation and early intervention in favor of reactive repression. On September 22, 12 Amazon indigenous leaders were finally acquitted of chargers of murder, inciting rebellion, and causing serious injury, in the wake of the Bagua protests and subsequent police massacre in June 2009.[13]

Freedom of association is generally respected. In recent years, however, anti-mining activists have been subject to arbitrary arrest or questionable legal charges, while several nongovernmental organizations have experienced various forms of intimidation.

Peruvian law recognizes the right of workers to organize and bargain collectively. Strikes are legal with advance notification to the Ministry of Labor, but few strikers abide by this regulation. Less than 10 percent of the formal-sector workforce is unionized.

F. Rule of Law: 8 / 16

The judiciary is perceived as the most corrupt institution in the country. A controversial set of appointments in 2013—later rescinded in the wake of public protests—greatly undermined the credibility of the relatively independent TC. Attention by civil society organizations has increasingly focused on the National Judiciary Council, which appoints judges and prosecutors and monitors alleged cases of judicial corruption.

The situation in Peruvian jails is extremely poor. The average population is 75,000 inmates—230 percent of capacity—more than half of whom are in pretrial detention. Since 2006, an adversarial justice system designed to improve the speed and fairness of judicial proceedings has slowly been implemented. Many indigenous Peruvians pass through the justice system without sufficient Spanish to adequately understand their cases or fully exercise their rights, and the state fails to provide sufficient translation services.

According to the 2014 Latin American Public Opinion Project (LAPOP) survey, Peru had the highest crime victimization rate of 28 countries in the Americas, and local polls often confirm crime as Peruvians' principal concern.

Since the 2003 publication of Peru's Truth and Reconciliation Commission Report on the internal conflict against Shining Path guerrillas—which took 69,000 lives in the 1980s and 1990s—justice has been served in some significant cases. Most notable is the conviction of former president Alberto Fujimori for overseeing death-squad killings and two kidnappings. The García government made almost no efforts to prioritize justice for cases of human rights abuse by state actors during the 1980s and 1990s, and the Humala administration was similarly passive. The military continues to obstruct those investigating past violations. However, in November 2015 the government declared the reparation of victims of forced sterilizations during Fujimori's government a matter of "national interest" and created a victims' registry to better target their legal assistance and health and psychological needs.

Remnants of the Shining Path involved in the drug trade continue to clash with security forces in the Apurimac-Ene River Valley (VRAE) and Upper Huallaga zones. Coca eradication efforts and economic development programs in other regions have failed to reverse a trend toward increased coca production.

Native Quechua speakers and Afro-Peruvians are subject to discrimination. Peru is a particularly hostile country toward the LGBT (lesbian, gay, bisexual, and transgender) population. Many cases of discrimination and violence are reported each year; in a survey

---

13. http://amazonwatch.org/news/2016/0922-peru-amazon-leaders-acquitted-of-killing-police-during-clash

conducted in 2014, nearly 90 percent of Lima's LGBT residents reported being the victim of physical violence due to their sexual preference. The Humala administration removed any mention of targeted LGBT policies from the National Plan of Human Rights (2014–16).

G. Personal Autonomy and Individual Rights: 10 / 16

Peru does not place formal restrictions on movement, but the frequency of protests can disrupt travel in certain areas, occasionally for prolonged periods. Discrimination against indigenous populations remains pervasive with regard to land use and property rights. Afro-Peruvians remain especially vulnerable and invisible to public policy. Humala's government nonetheless instituted some programs and initiatives to better ensure the exercise of indigenous rights. The Prior Consultation Law is a notable example: despite some criticism by activists, the law is widely accepted, even by the extractive sector, and has resulted in positive outcomes for communities that have taken part in consultation processes.

Domestic violence is widespread in Peru, with more than half of Peruvian women reporting instances of physical or emotional abuse. In recent years, women have advanced into leadership roles in various companies and government agencies, but there are still no specific gender policies to ensure equal rights between men and women. A proposal to recognize civil unions for same-sex partners, rejected by Congress in 2015, was reintroduced in 2016.

Peruvian women and girls—especially from the indigenous community—fall victim to sex trafficking within the country, including near mining facilities. Men, women, and children are subject to forced labor in the mines, in related industries, and in the informal economy. According to the U.S. State Department's 2015 *Trafficking in Persons Report*, government enforcement of an anti-trafficking law has been "uneven."

Philippines

Political Rights Rating: 3
Civil Liberties Rating: 3
Freedom Rating: 3.0
Freedom Status: Partly Free
Electoral Democracy: Yes

Population: 102,600,000
Capital: Manila

Ten-Year Ratings Timeline For Year Under Review (Political Rights, Civil Liberties, Status)

Year Under Review	2007	2008	2009	2010	2011	2012	2013	2014	2015	2016
Rating	4,3,PF	4,3,PF	4,3,PF	3,3,PF	3,3,PF	3,3,PF	3,3,PF	3,3,PF	3,3,PF	3,3,PF

Overview: Governing infrastructure is well developed in the Philippines, but the rule of law and application of justice are haphazard and heavily favor ruling dynastic elites. Long-term violent insurgencies have continued for decades. Impunity remains the norm for crimes against activists and journalists, and newly elected president Rodrigo Duterte's war on drugs has led to a surge in extrajudicial killings and vigilante justice.

KEY DEVELOPMENTS IN 2016:

- Newly elected president Rodrigo Duterte's war on drugs saw the extrajudicial killing of more than 6,000 people in both police operations and at the hands of vigilantes.

- Duterte's threats against journalists and civil society activists exacerbated their already dangerous operating atmosphere.
- In February, the Philippine Congress quashed the Bangsamoro Basic Law (BBL), under which a new self-governing region, Bangsamoro, would replace and add territory to the current Autonomous Region in Muslim Mindanao (ARMM). The BBL was the next critical step outlined in a landmark 2014 peace treaty between the previous administration of President Benigno Aquino and the Moro Islamic Liberation Front (MILF), the country's largest rebel group.
- In July, Duterte issued an order establishing the country's first freedom of information directive, though it only applied to the executive branch.

EXECUTIVE SUMMARY

Rodrigo Duterte was elected president in May 2016 after running on a law and order campaign. His ensuing war on drugs saw the extrajudicial killing of more than 6,000 people in both police operations and vigilante justice, which Duterte appeared to encourage. During the year Duterte also publicly threatened journalists and civil society activists, exacerbating an already dangerous environment. Three journalists were killed in 2016, according to the Committee to Protect Journalists (CPJ), though the motives for their murders was unclear. An environmental activist and two labor leaders were also killed during the year.

In December, Vice President Leni Robredo resigned as chairperson of the Housing and Urban Development Coordinating Council, a cabinet position, citing "major differences in principles and values" with Duterte. Robredo, who had voiced opposition to the drug war and other policy initiatives, stayed on as vice president.

In February, the Philippine Congress quashed the Bangsamoro Basic Law, under which a new self-governing region, Bangsamoro, would replace and add territory to the current Autonomous Region in Muslim Mindanao. The BBL was the next critical step outlined in a landmark 2014 peace treaty between the previous Aquino administration and the Moro Islamic Liberation Front (MILF), the country's largest rebel group. The lack of an agreement, which could have ended more than 40 years of separatist violence among Moros, as the region's Muslim population is known, means that peace remained elusive even as the newly elected president's peace team talked of creating a more inclusive replacement agreement in 2017.

In July 2016, the president issued an order establishing the country's first freedom of information directive, though it applied solely to the executive branch. Separately, in an effort to address longstanding concerns about media freedom and the safety of journalists, in October Duterte issued an order creating the Presidential Task Force on Violations of the Right to Life, Liberty, and Security of the Members of the Media. However, it had yet to open a major investigation by year's end.

POLITICAL RIGHTS: 27 / 40

A. Electoral Process: 9 / 12

The Philippines' directly elected president is limited to a single six-year term. The vice president is directly elected on a separate ticket and may serve up to two successive six-year terms. Rodrigo Duterte won the May 2016 presidential election with 39 percent of the vote, followed by Manuel Roxas II with 23 percent. Maria Leonor "Leni" Robredo won the closely contested vice presidency with 35 percent of the vote, followed by Ferdinand Marcos Jr. with 35 percent. Several other candidates also competed for both offices.

In the bicameral Congress, the 24 members of the Senate are elected on a nationwide ballot and serve six-year terms, with half of the seats up for election every three years. The

297 members of the House of Representatives serve three-year terms, with 238 elected in single-member constituencies and the remainder elected through party-list voting. In the 2016 congressional elections, no single party won an outright majority in either house, but President Duterte's PDP-Laban Party secured unprecedented majority alliances in both chambers.

While open and competitive, elections in the Philippines are typically marred by fraud, intimidation, and political violence. The 2016 national elections were credible, and while they were marked by dozens of incidents of election-related violence, including a number of killings, there were fewer such incidents compared to previous election years. Other persistent problems included media bias, which tends to favor wealthier candidates, and vote buying, offers for which affected nearly 20 percent of voters in 2016, according to one survey.

The president appoints the Commission on Elections (Comelec). Although discredited in past scandals, Comelec's performance was generally praised in 2016. Approximately 1.3 million overseas voters were registered for the 2016 elections compared to 700,000 for the 2013 midterm elections; registration requirements for overseas voters had been eased in 2013. Appointments or promotions in government offices are banned in the period surrounding elections.

B. Political Pluralism and Participation: 11 / 16

The Philippines has a strong record of open competition among multiple parties, though candidates and political parties typically have weak ideological identities. Legislative coalitions are exceptionally fluid, and members of Congress often change party affiliation.

Distribution of power is heavily affected by kinship networks. Political dynasties are particularly prevalent at the provincial and municipal levels, and those that vie for national office often draw on a regional base of support. The nature of election-related funding contributes to the concentration of power: there are no limits on individuals' or companies' contributions to candidates, and a significant portion of political donations come from a relatively small number of donors. There have been several unsuccessful attempts to pass an anti-dynasty law limiting the number of members of a single family that may run for or hold political office at the same time. The Roman Catholic Church has historically played a significant role in politics.

The activities of armed rebel groups continue to affect political activity in the country. In areas dominated by the leftist New People's Army (NPA), for example, candidates face demands for money in exchange for a rebel "permit" to campaign.

In 2013, the Supreme Court ruled that the party-list portion of the electoral framework for the House of Representatives, traditionally meant to represent marginalized or underrepresented demographic groups, could also be open to other groups, including national political parties, provided that they do not stand in the single-member constituency contests. Critics of the decision warned that it would allow the wealthy and powerful to gain more congressional seats at the expense of marginalized groups. A number of party-list groups gained seats in 2016 not by representing national sectors or interests as intended, but through substantial support from kinship networks in single geographic regions.

C. Functioning of Government: 7 / 12

Elected government officials and legislative representatives determine state policies, but corruption and cronyism are rife, including in business. A few dozen families continue to hold a disproportionate share of land, corporate wealth, and political authority. Local "bosses" often control their respective areas, limiting accountability and committing abuses of power.

Investigations and trials over lawmakers' misuse of local development funds were ongoing at the end of 2016; the program in question, which allowed discretionary allocations by members of Congress, was discontinued in 2013 after an audit found widespread abuses.

A culture of impunity, stemming in part from backlogs in the judicial system, hampers the fight against corruption. The country's official anticorruption agencies, the Office of the Ombudsman and the Presidential Anti-Graft Commission (PAGC), have mixed records. The PAGC lacks enforcement capabilities. The current ombudsman has focused on major cases against senior government officials and those involving large sums of money, but some cases have languished for years in the special anticorruption court (Sandiganbayan). At the end of 2016, the court had a backlog of 4,214 cases compared to 3,206 cases at the end of 2015.

The country lacks a nationwide freedom of information law. In July 2016, Duterte issued an order establishing the country's first freedom of information directive, though it mandating public disclosure only by the executive branch, and did not apply to the legislature or judiciary, and in August the government proposed a long list of types of requests that would be exempt from the order. Local governments have been required to post procurement and budget data on their websites, and in 2012 the national government began participatory budgeting at various levels.

CIVIL LIBERTIES: 36 / 60 (− 2)

D. Freedom of Expression and Belief: 14 / 16

The constitution provides for freedoms of expression and the press. The private media are vibrant and outspoken, although content often consists more of innuendo and sensationalism than substantive investigative reporting. The country's many state-owned television and radio stations cover controversial topics and criticize the government, but they too lack strict journalistic ethics. While the censorship board has broad powers to edit or ban content, government censorship is generally not a serious problem in practice.

However, the Philippines remains one of the most dangerous places in the world for journalists, and hostile rhetoric toward members of the media by Duterte further exacerbated an already perilous situation in 2016; Duterte, for example, weeks after his election asserted that "corrupt" reporters "are not exempted from assassination." According to CPJ, three reporters were murdered in 2016. Though none of the killings could be definitively linked to the victims' work, each had reported on sensitive issues, including official corruption and organized crime. Two people were convicted of murdering journalists in 2016, though impunity remains the norm for attacks against media workers. In October 2016, President Duterte announced the creation of the Presidential Task Force on Violations of the Right to Life, Liberty, and Security of the Members of the Media, but no major investigations had been opened by year's end.

Other obstacles to press freedom include Executive Order 608, which established a National Security Clearance System to protect classified information, and the Human Security Act, which allows journalists to be wiretapped based on suspicion of involvement in terrorism. Libel is a criminal offense, and libel cases have been used frequently to quiet criticism of public officials.

The internet is widely available. However, rights groups have expressed concern about censorship of anonymous online criticism and the criminalization of libelous posts.

Freedom of religion is guaranteed under the constitution and generally respected in practice. Academic freedom is also generally respected, and there are no significant impediments to free and open private discussion.

E. Associational and Organizational Rights: 8 / 12 (− 1)

Citizen activism and public discussion are robust, and demonstrations are common. However, permits are required for rallies, and police sometimes use violence to disperse antigovernment protests.

Assassination of civil society activists is a serious problem in the Philippines, and President Duterte's public threats against activists who oppose his policies, including his administration's violent war on drugs have exacerbated an already dangerous atmosphere. Gloria Capitan, an environmental activist, was murdered inside of her family's business in Bataan in July, and labor activists Orlando Abangan and Edilberto Miralles were both gunned down in the span of a week in September. The cases remain unsolved. Labor rights and farmers' organizations dedicated to ending extrajudicial killings and helping families of the disappeared face serious threats, and their offices have occasionally been raided by authorities. Despite the danger, the Philippines hosts many active human rights and social welfare groups, and the civil society sector as a whole has grown more robust in recent years.

Trade unions are independent, but in order to register, a union must represent at least 20 percent of a given bargaining unit. Large firms are increasingly using contract workers, who are prohibited from joining unions. Less than 10 percent of the labor force is unionized. Among unionized workers collective bargaining is common, and strikes may be called, though unions must provide notice and obtain majority approval from their members. Violence against labor leaders has been part of the broader trend of extrajudicial killings over the past decade.

F. Rule of Law: 4 / 16 (− 1)

Judicial independence has traditionally been strong, particularly in the Supreme Court. The efforts of the judiciary are stymied, however, by inefficiency, low pay, intimidation, corruption, and high vacancy rates, all of which have contributed to excessive delays and significant case backlogs. Judges and lawyers often depend on local power holders for basic resources and salaries, which can lead to compromised verdicts.

The trial for alleged perpetrators of the 2009 Maguindanao massacre, in which 58 civilians—including 32 journalists—were killed to stop the registration of a local political candidate, continued in 2016. The process has featured flawed forensic investigations and intimidation of and attacks against witnesses; at least eight witnesses and witnesses' relatives have been killed since 2009. The media have complained of limited access to court proceedings.

Arbitrary detention, disappearances, kidnappings, and abuse of suspects continue. President Duterte's war on drugs led to the extrajudicial killing of more than 6,000 people in 2016, including a number of innocent civilians, from the time he entered office on June 30. Between July 1 and December 14, police killed 2,102 "suspected drug personalities" according to the Philippine National Police; police statistics attributed an additional 3,993 deaths between July 1 and December 12 to "unidentified gunmen." Convictions for extrajudicial killings and other such crimes are extremely rare, and Duterte has appeared to encourage such actions, revealing in December 2016 that he had killed suspected drug dealers and users himself during his time as mayor of Davao.

The police and military have also been implicated in corruption, extortion, torture of detainees, extrajudicial killings, and involvement in local rackets. Lack of effective witness protection has been a key obstacle to investigations against members of the security forces. With drug users fearfully turning themselves in to police en masse, dangerously crowded prison conditions and extended wait times for access to justice for even minor infractions have become the norm.

Kidnappings for ransom remain common in the south, perpetrated in large part by the Islamist militant group Abu Sayyaf; victims whose ransoms are not paid have been beheaded, including Canadian tourists John Ridsdel and Robert Hall in April and June 2016, respectively. Abu Sayyaf also regularly carries out bombings and other attacks. In September 2016, a bomb attack in Davao claimed by Abu Sayyaf killed at least 14 people and wounded dozens more. Since the current administration came to power, military operations have led to a serious weakening of the group. As of October 2016, 14 hostages had been released or escaped since Duterte took office; in mid-December a military official reported that the group continued to hold 23 hostages.

In August, the Duterte government engaged in a second official round of peace negotiations with the Communist Party of the Philippines–New People's Army–National Democratic Front of the Philippines (CPP-NPA-NDFP), restoring hope that the nearly 50-year violent insurgency could see a peaceful end for the first time since negotiations broke down in under the previous administration. Deadly clashes between the leftist group's militarized wing, the NPA, and the Philippine army continue to occur regularly, though the violence has declined over recent years.

Perceptions of relative socioeconomic deprivation and political disenfranchisement, along with resentment toward Christian settlements in traditionally Muslim areas, have played a central role in the Philippines' Muslim separatist movements. The related conflict has caused severe hardship on Mindanao and nearby islands, and has resulted in more than 120,000 deaths and the displacement of tens of thousands of people since it erupted in 1972. Both government and rebel forces have committed summary killings and other human rights abuses. Several peace deals have fallen through as a result of the failure to effectively disarm, demobilize, and reintegrate former rebels, but a landmark comprehensive agreement was reached in 2014 with the Moro Islamic Liberation Front (MILF), the country's largest rebel group, paving the way for a new legal and governing framework, namely the Bangsamoro Basic Law, for the region.

However, after a botched antiterrorism raid in January 2015 that left dead 44 elite police officers, 18 members of the MILF, five members of the Bangsamoro Islamic Freedom Fighters (BIFF, a splinter faction that opposes the peace process), and several civilians, Congress postponed deliberations on the BBL. Despite President Duterte's public support for the BBL and a comprehensive peace settlement, in addition to new trust-building joint antidrug campaigns between the Philippine Armed Forces and the MILF, a formal agreement remained elusive through 2016.

Indigenous rights are generally upheld, but land disputes and local development projects regularly cause friction and sometimes lead to violence. Indigenous people often live in conflict areas and are targeted by combatants for their perceived loyalties.

LGBT people face bias in employment, education, and other services, as well as societal discrimination. In September, Congresswoman Geraldine Roman, the Philippines' first transgender person elected to national office, advocated for a House bill prohibiting at a national level discrimination based on sexual orientation or gender identity. The Senate proposed companion legislation, though the measure had yet to pass at year's end.

G. Personal Autonomy and Individual Rights: 10 / 16

Outside of conflict zones, citizens enjoy freedom of travel and choice of residence. Private business activity is often dependent on the support of local power brokers in the complex patronage system that extends through the country's social, political, and economic spheres.

Although more women than men now enter high schools and universities, women face some discrimination in private-sector employment, and those in Mindanao enjoy considerably fewer rights in practice. Divorce is illegal in the Philippines, though annulments are allowed under specified circumstances; Muslims may divorce via Sharia (Islamic law) courts. Violence against women continues to be a significant problem, and while spousal rape is a crime, very few cases are prosecuted.

In 2014, the Supreme Court upheld the constitutionality of the landmark Reproductive Health Law, which provides state funding for contraceptives in public clinics, reproductive health care, and sex education in schools. However, the Philippine Congress denied funding for the program in January 2016 in a bid backed by elements of the country's powerful Catholic Church. Health workers may deny services in non-life-threatening circumstances if they have moral or religious misgivings.

The Philippines is a source country for human trafficking, with some Filipinos abroad forced to work in the fishing, shipping, construction or other industries, or forced to engage in sex work. The country's various insurgent groups have been accused of using child soldiers. NGOs have reported increases in the number of child sex tourists traveling to the country.

⬇ Poland

Political Rights Rating: 1
Civil Liberties Rating: 2 ↓
Freedom Rating: 1.5
Freedom Status: Free
Electoral Democracy: Yes

Population: 38,400,000
Capital: Warsaw

Ratings Change, Trend Arrow: Poland's civil liberties rating declined from 1 to 2, and it received a downward trend arrow, due to sustained attempts by the ruling Law and Justice (PiS) party, through hastily drafted legislation and other measures, to increase government influence over the country's media, judiciary, civil service, and education system.

Ten-Year Ratings Timeline for Year under Review (Political Rights, Civil Liberties, Status)

Year Under Review	2007	2008	2009	2010	2011	2012	2013	2014	2015	2016
Rating	1,1,F	1,1,F	1,1,F	1,1,F	1,1,F	1,1,F	1,1,F	1,1,F	1,1,F	1,2,F

Overview: Poland's democratic institutions took root at the start of its postcommunist transition in 1989. Rapid economic growth and other societal changes have benefited some segments of the population more than others, contributing to a deep divide between liberal, pro-European parties and those purporting to defend national interests and "traditional" Polish Catholic values. Since taking power in late 2015, the conservative PiS party has enacted measures that increase political influence over state institutions, raising serious concerns about Poland's democratic trajectory.

KEY DEVELOPMENTS IN 2016:

- In January, the European Commission (EC) initiated its first-ever probe into a European Union (EU) member state's commitment to the rule of law, focusing on the PiS government's moves to curb the powers of the Constitutional Tribunal (TK) and alter its composition.

- Several key pieces of legislation, including one that increased government influence over public broadcasters, were enacted through fast-tracked procedures that did not allow for significant consultation or debate.
- In December, attempts to limit media access to the parliament triggered protests by opposition lawmakers on the lower chamber's floor, as well as mass demonstrations outside the building. PiS deputies then passed the 2017 budget in a separate room with only a few opposition deputies present; journalists were barred from entering.
- Throughout the year, the government attempted to silence or discredit academics, journalists, and others whose work challenged PiS's preferred historical narrative.

EXECUTIVE SUMMARY

During its first full year in power, PiS worked to increase its influence over state institutions and discredit the previous coalition government and its perceived allies in the media and the courts. Throughout 2016, controversial PiS initiatives prompted mass demonstrations and denunciations from domestic and international human rights groups.

In response to PiS's attempts to alter TK procedures and interfere with the appointment of its judges, the EC in January initiated an official review of Poland's commitment to EU standards for adherence to the rule of law. A standoff between PiS and the TK continued over the course of the year and appeared to draw to a close with the December expiration of the term of TK president Andrzej Rzepliński, who was appointed in 2007 by the previous government and had resisted PiS's legislative attempts to curb the TK's authority. The PiS government subsequently approved a measure granting the state president greater influence over the appointment of a new TK president. Julia Przylebska, a PiS ally, was tapped for the job, clearing the way for PiS-appointed judges to form a majority on the tribunal. A day after Przylebska's appointment, EC vice president Frans Timmermans declared that there were "persistent problems with the rule of law" in Poland, and gave the government two months to address EC criticism, but declined to specify consequences for failure to do so.

In October, tens of thousands of women and many men took to the streets to protest a citizen-backed initiative that would have eliminated most of the exceptions to Poland's ban on abortion. Lawmakers, under public pressure, ultimately voted down the initiative. A major opposition-led protest in December followed the government's decision to limit journalists' access to the parliament. The protest movement continued in the wake of PiS's contentious approval of the 2017 budget, which was conducted by a show of hands in a side chamber that media representatives were barred from entering. Many critics called the procedure illegal.

Citing a need to "depoliticize the airwaves," PiS moved rapidly after taking power in late 2015 to pass a controversial amendment to Poland's media law, which took effect in January. The measure ended the mandates of the heads of Poland's public television and radio broadcasters and empowered the treasury minister to appoint their successors. A series of dismissals at public media channels followed, while a number of managers who expected to be sacked chose to resign.

A new civil service law that lowered the standards for recruitment to senior posts and allowed for arbitrary dismissal also took effect in January, raising concerns about politicization.

Separately, PiS worked throughout the year to suppress the dissemination of information detailing the involvement of Polish people in World War II–era atrocities, both by putting pressure on Holocaust historians and by creating avenues for greater government involvement at national institutions that focus on Polish history. The efforts prompted sharp criticism from the academic community.

POLITICAL RIGHTS: 37 / 40 (− 1)

A. Electoral Process: 12 / 12

The president of Poland is directly elected for up to two five-year terms, and members of the bicameral National Assembly are elected for four-year terms. The president's appointment of a prime minister must be confirmed by the 460-seat Sejm, the National Assembly's lower house, which is elected by proportional representation. The 100 members of the Senate, the upper house, can delay and amend legislation, but have few other powers. While the prime minister is responsible for most government policy, the president also has influence, particularly over defense and foreign policy matters.

Andrzej Duda of PiS won the second round of Poland's May 2015 presidential election with 52 percent of the vote, defeating popular incumbent Bronislaw Komorowski. Duda's victory was interpreted by many observers as a protest vote against the ruling center-right Civic Platform (PO), which had led Poland's government since 2007, and with which Komorowski was associated.

PiS won a landslide victory of 37.5 percent in the October 2015 parliamentary elections, increasing its representation in the Sejm to a total of 235 seats. It was the first party in postcommunist Poland to win an outright parliamentary majority, allowing it to rule without coalition partners. Beata Szydlo was elected prime minister, though her role was soon eclipsed in practice by that of PiS's chairman, former prime minister Jaroslaw Kaczyński. PO came in second with slightly more than 24 percent of the vote and 138 seats. Third and fourth place both went to new parties: Kukiz'15, a right-wing, antiestablishment party led by former rock musician Pawel Kukiz, which took 42 seats; and the probusiness party Modern, led by economist Ryszard Petru, which won 28. The agrarian Polish People's Party (PSL) won 5 percent of the vote and 16 seats. A representative of the ethnic German minority received the remaining seat. In the Senate, PiS took 61 seats, PO 34, and PSL 1.

B. Political Pluralism and Participation: 16 / 16

Poland's political parties organize and operate freely. PO and PiS have dominated the political scene since 2005, with relations between the two parties becoming increasingly polarized.

PiS won a narrow parliamentary majority in 2015, so it requires the support of other parties to obtain the two-thirds supermajority needed for any constitutional changes. Following the United Left (ZL) alliance's failure to cross the 5 percent electoral threshold for representation in 2015, there are now no left-leaning parties in the parliament. Voter turnout for the 2015 parliamentary elections was low, at 51.6 percent.

Ethnic, religious, and other minority groups enjoy full political rights and electoral opportunities. Their political parties are not subject to the minimum vote threshold for parliamentary representation.

C. Functioning of Government: 9 / 12 (− 1)

Freely elected officials can determine and implement laws and policies without interference in Poland, but anticorruption laws are not always effectively enforced. Several notable corruption probes that emerged in 2016 pointed to ongoing problems in state institutions. In October, a Defense Ministry official, Bartlomiej Misiewicz, came under investigation after *Newsweek Polska* accused him of attempting to bribe opposition politicians to switch allegiances by offering them jobs at state-run companies. The case was assigned to district attorney Magdalena Witko, the wife of a former PiS deputy, prompting opposition claims of a conflict of interest. The inquiry followed revelations that Defense Minister Antoni Macierewicz had appointed Misiewicz, his former assistant, to a position on the board of a state-owned defense company for which he had few qualifications. Opposition parties argued that Misiewicz was just one of many unfit appointments to state companies based on cronyism and party loyalty. In September, Szydlo announced plans to make personnel and systemic changes to address the problem, saying "we did make some mistakes." It was unclear at year's end if changes to recruitment standards had been adopted.

In November, prosecutors charged the head of the Supreme Audit Office (NIK), Krzysztof Kwiatkowski, a former PO senator and justice minister, with influencing the office's recruitment process. Separately, Józef Pinior, a leader of Poland's Solidarity trade union movement who represented PO in the Senate from 2011 to 2015, was arrested the same month along with 10 others in connection with bribery allegations.

PiS has employed opaque practices to pass laws, including fast-tracking procedures that leave little time for public comment on proposed legislation. Fast-tracked amendments to the Civil Service Act that took effect in January 2016 lowered the standards of recruitment for higher civil service posts, and allowed for arbitrary dismissal. Similarly fast-tracked media legislation, which gave the government greater control over the public broadcasters, took effect the same month.

CIVIL LIBERTIES: 52 / 60 (− 3)

D. Freedom of Expression and Belief: 14 / 16 (− 2)

The constitution guarantees freedom of expression and forbids censorship. Libel remains a criminal offense, though a 2009 amendment to the criminal code eased penalties. A person may be found guilty of blasphemy, punishable by a fine of 5,000 zloty ($1,250) or up to two years in prison, even if the offense was unintentional. Poland's media are pluralistic and mostly privately owned. The government does not restrict internet access.

PiS has drawn sharp criticism from the EU and press freedom advocacy groups for its move to increase the government's authority over public broadcasters. On the last day of 2015, PiS deputies in the Sejm passed an amendment to Poland's media law that ended the mandates of the heads of the public television and radio broadcasters and empowered the treasury minister, rather than an independent body, to appoint their successors. PiS defended the move as an attempt to depoliticize the airwaves. The leadership of the public broadcasters was quickly replaced with PiS appointees; several managers at the influential public television station, TVP, resigned in protest before they could be fired. The new TVP president was the deputy minister of culture and former parliamentarian Jacek Kurski, who once described himself as the PiS founders' "bull terrier." He was officially appointed to a four-year term in October, though TVP toed the government line throughout 2016. Meanwhile, large state-owned companies have redirected their advertising spending to progovernment media, effectively penalizing private outlets that were seen as sympathetic to the opposition.

While journalists are not allowed in the main parliament chamber, they have traditionally waited in the halls, where they were able to interview lawmakers. In December 2016, PiS deputies decided to limit this access, starting in January 2017, to preapproved journalists. In protest, opposition lawmakers occupied the speaker's podium to block a vote on the 2017 national budget. The ruling party responded by passing the budget with a show of hands in a side chamber that media representatives were barred from entering. Many critics called the procedure illegal.

Separately, in April 2016, conservative weekly *Do Rzeczy* publicized an audio recording of what it described as a 2014 conversation between an aide to former PO prime minister Donald Tusk and the late Jan Kulczyk, then Poland's wealthiest businessman, about coverage critical of Tusk's family by the popular tabloid *Fakt*. Kulczyk agreed to discuss the matter with *Fakt*'s owner; according to *Do Rzeczy*, the conversation took place weeks before *Fakt*'s editor was removed.

The state respects freedom of religion. The PiS government is aligned with the Roman Catholic Church, which has significant influence in the country. Religious groups are not required to register with the authorities but receive tax benefits if they do. There is a formal ban on state funding for church construction, but a church can obtain Culture Ministry funding in practice if it includes a museum—as does the Temple of Divine Providence in Warsaw. In September 2016, the government, which contributed about $10 million to the Catholic temple's construction from 2007 to 2014, agreed to continue financing the institution as a comanager.

The ruling party has sought to discredit academics who challenge its preferred historical narrative, which largely omits the involvement of Poles in World War II–era atrocities. In April 2016, prosecutors questioned Holocaust historian and Princeton University professor Jan Gross for five hours over allegations that he had publicly insulted the nation. The claims stemmed from a 2015 article in which he had stated that during World War II, Poles killed more Jews than they had Nazis. Duda's office had also considered stripping Gross of the Order of Merit he was awarded in 1996. His questioning and the president's proposal drew sharp criticism from intellectuals in Poland and abroad. In December 2016, the director of the Polish Culture Institute in Berlin was fired after Poland's ambassador to Germany called for her departure in connection with "too much Jewish-themed programming."

Separately, new legislation governing the state's Institute of National Remembrance (IPN), a body formed in 1998 to investigate crimes committed under both the Nazi occupation and communist rule, entered into force in June 2016. Among other changes, the law, drafted by PiS, cut short the mandate of the IPN's governing council, which was replaced with a nine-member panel selected by the Sejm, the Senate, and the president. In July, the panel recommended Jaroslaw Szarek, a historian who has expressed views in line with the government's preferred narrative, to serve as the institute's new head. The planned opening of a new World War II museum in Gdańsk was delayed in 2016 as the government sought to replace the collection's global perspective with a narrower focus on Polish suffering and sacrifice, prompting criticism from historians.

In December 2016, the Sejm approved a PiS-authored overhaul of the education system, which eliminated middle schools in favor of eight years of primary school, followed by high school or trade school. Critics have expressed concern that the shift could usher in new curriculum and staff changes aimed at indoctrinating students with the ruling party's brand of patriotism. Among other laws passed during the same parliamentary session, held without opposition deputies present, was one that allows the government to appoint directors and deputy directors of state research institutes without a competitive hiring process. The new legislation, condemned by the Polish Academy of Sciences and the academic community at large, also eliminated the requirement that directors speak a second language.

People are free to engage in private discussions on political and other matters without fear of harassment or detention by the authorities.

E. Associational and Organizational Rights: 12 / 12

Freedom of association is generally respected in law and in practice. Poles hold public demonstrations with some regularity, though local authorities can limit demonstrations in their districts on grounds of maintaining public order.

In a late-night parliamentary vote in December 2016, the Sejm passed legislation that gives priority to repeated rallies organized in the same place on predictable dates, and requires separate gatherings to keep a distance of at least 100 meters. PiS, which sponsored the bill, said its intention was to prevent conflicts between demonstrators, but critics called the measure a restriction on freedoms of assembly and speech. Duda referred the legislation to the TK, and it had not been signed at year's end.

Nongovernmental organizations (NGOs) generally operate without government interference. However, in November 2016, Szydlo announced plans for a new, centralized civil society department that some observers said could allow the government to pressure NGOs. Human rights advocates have charged that progovernment media frame NGOs—particularly those receiving foreign funding—as working against the country's interests. Several news stories broadcast on TVP during the year appeared intended to discredit NGOs and protest movements that were critical of the government.

Poland has a robust labor movement, though certain groups—including the self-employed, private contractors, and those in essential services—cannot join unions. Complicated legal procedures hinder workers' ability to strike.

F. Rule of Law: 12 / 16 (−1)

Since taking office, the PiS government has faced criticism from the United States, the EU, and rights groups for working to curb the powers of the TK and to alter its composition in ways that hamper its ability to serve as a check on the political branches. The EC in January 2016 initiated an official review of Poland's commitment to EU standards for adherence to the rule of law in connection with the matter.

The year was marked by legal wrangling between the PiS-led legislature, which passed a series of laws that created inefficiencies in the TK and otherwise interfered with its functioning, and the court itself, which ruled most of the changes unconstitutional. However, the government refused to publish some of those rulings, meaning they technically never became binding. As a result of a dispute over the appointment of TK judges, which began during the 2015 parliamentary election campaign, the TK had only 12 out of 15 seats filled for most of 2016.

The term of TK president Rzepliński, who was appointed in 2007 by the previous government and resisted PiS's legislative attempts to curb the court's authority, ended in December. That day, Duda signed into law additional changes to TK procedures that gave him increased influence over court appointments. Przylebska, whom many consider unqualified, was named TK president, prompting further membership changes that left PiS-appointed judges with a majority on the tribunal. (In accordance with existing TK law, the court had convened a general assembly earlier in the month to choose Rzepliński's successor, but PiS-backed judges called in sick to prevent a quorum.) A day after Przylebska's appointment, EC vice president Timmermans declared that there were "persistent problems with the rule of law" in Poland, and gave the government two months to address EC criticism, but declined to specify consequences for failure to do so.

Separately, in March 2016, the government merged the office of the justice minister with that of the public prosecutor general, a move that gave the government greater influence over prosecutions. Justice Minister Zbigniew Ziobro, who thus became public prosecutor general, was known for pursuing corruption and cronyism cases against political opponents when he had held both posts between 2005 and 2007.

In June 2016, Duda signed new antiterrorism legislation that gave authorities more leeway to monitor the movements of foreign citizens without prior court approval, and permitted suspects to be held without judicial review for up to two weeks. The legislation was submitted to the TK by the national ombudsman, who said ambiguous provisions on collecting individuals' data, arresting civilians, prohibiting demonstrations, and blocking internet access violated the constitution as well as the European Convention on Human Rights.

Pretrial detention periods can be lengthy, and prison conditions are poor by European standards.

Ethnic minorities generally enjoy generous legal rights and protections. Some groups, particularly the Roma, experience employment and housing discrimination, racially motivated insults, and occasional physical attacks. Members of the LGBT (lesbian, gay, bisexual, transgender) community continue to face discrimination. Data released in November 2016 by the National Prosecutor's Office showed a 13 percent increase in hate crimes during the first half of 2016. Approximately half of all reported incidents related to hate speech on the internet, but the category of "physical violence or threats" (14 percent of the total) increased by over 40 percent compared with the same period in 2015. The most frequent targets of such attacks were Muslims, or people believed to be Muslim by their attackers. In April, the government abolished the Council for the Prevention of Racial Discrimination, Xenophobia, and Related Intolerance.

G. Personal Autonomy and Individual Rights: 14 / 16

Citizens enjoy freedom of travel and choice of residence, employment, and institution of higher education. Citizens have the right to own property and establish private businesses.

Women hold senior positions in government and the private sector, including about 27 percent of the seats in the Sejm. Both PO and PiS fielded female candidates for the position of prime minister in the 2015 elections.

Under Polish law, abortion is permissible through the 12th week of pregnancy only if a woman's health or life are jeopardized, if the pregnancy is a result of a criminal act such as rape, or if the fetus is severely damaged. Legislation proposed in September 2016 would have removed most of these exceptions to the ban and made illegal abortions punishable by five years in prison. Following mass protests, PiS leaders distanced themselves from the legislation, which failed to pass. In November, the Sejm adopted legislation that provided financial incentives for women to carry fetuses with severe disabilities or terminal illnesses to term.

Domestic violence against women remains a serious concern, as does trafficking in women and girls for the purpose of prostitution. In May 2016, the government withdrew funding from the Women's Rights Center (CPK), which has provided support to victims of domestic violence for over 20 years. The state's justification was that the CPK offers help only to women, rather than to all victims of abuse.

The U.S. State Department's 2016 *Trafficking in Persons Report* noted an uptick in labor trafficking throughout Poland, with Romany children in particular being subjected to forced begging.

Portugal

Political Rights Rating: 1
Civil Liberties Rating: 1
Freedom Rating: 1.0
Freedom Status: Free
Electoral Democracy: Yes

Population: 10,300,000
Capital: Lisbon

Ten-Year Ratings Timeline For Year Under Review (Political Rights, Civil Liberties, Status)

Year Under Review	2007	2008	2009	2010	2011	2012	2013	2014	2015	2016
Rating	1,1,F	1,1,F	1,1,F	1,1,F	1,1,F	1,1,F	1,1,F	1,1,F	1,1,F	1,1,F

Overview: Portugal is a stable parliamentary democracy with a multiparty political system and regular transfers of power between the two largest parties. Civil liberties are generally well protected. Ongoing concerns include corruption, certain legal constraints on journalism, and poor or abusive conditions for prisoners. However, prosecutors have pursued corruption cases against top officials, and the courts often rule in favor of journalists' rights.

KEY DEVELOPMENTS IN 2016:

- Marcelo Rebelo de Sousa, a center-right candidate supported by the opposition Social Democratic Party (PSD) and its allies, won the presidential election in January.
- Among other high-profile corruption cases, prosecutors continued their long-running investigation of former prime minister José Sócrates, who had been arrested in 2014 for suspected tax fraud and money laundering.
- Journalists ran afoul of judicial secrecy laws in their coverage of ongoing corruption cases. Prosecutors requested a trial against 13 journalists in connection with the Sócrates probe in June, and filed charges in September against 11 journalists who reported on a separate case involving abuses in a residency program for foreign investors.

EXECUTIVE SUMMARY

In the January 2016 presidential election, former PSD politician Marcelo Rebelo de Sousa won with 52 percent of the vote, easily defeating a leftist candidate backed by the ruling Socialist Party (PS), António Sampaio da Nóvoa, who took less than 23 percent. Prime Minister António Costa of the PS holds most executive power in Portugal's parliamentary system, but the president can force reviews of legislation and call early elections.

Several new cases of corruption arose during 2016, and some investigations from previous years—including one targeting former prime minister José Sócrates—were ongoing. In February, prosecutor Orlando Figueira was arrested for allegedly taking bribes to drop a probe into malfeasance by the current vice president of Angola. In May, a judge ruled that 17 people implicated in the so-called golden visa scandal, including a former interior minister, would have to stand trial. The case involved corruption related to a program allowing foreign investors to obtain visas and eventually apply for residency and citizenship.

Prosecutors targeted journalists in two separate cases during the year, accusing them of violating judicial secrecy by reporting on ongoing corruption investigations. In June, the Lisbon public prosecutor requested a trial against 13 journalists from three media outlets for their coverage of the Sócrates investigation. The evidence was being reviewed by a magistrate at year's end. Similarly in September, prosecutors in the capital charged 11 journalists for their coverage of the golden visa case, arguing that they had published privileged information.

Journalists also risk civil and criminal defamation charges. In one high-profile case, former police inspector Gonçalo Amaral was ordered in 2015 to pay over €500,000 ($560,000) in damages to the parents of Madeleine McCann, who went missing from a Portuguese resort town in 2007, due to claims in his book that McCann's parents were involved in her disappearance. However, the decision was overturned on appeal in April 2016. Separately in November, a former intelligence chief, Jorge Silva Carvalho, received a suspended prison sentence and was ordered to pay compensation for illegally accessing the telephone records of journalist Nuno Simas in 2011 in an attempt to identify a source.

POLITICAL RIGHTS: 39 / 40

A. Electoral Process: 12 / 12

B. Political Pluralism and Participation: 16 / 16

C. Functioning of Government: 11 / 12

CIVIL LIBERTIES: 58 / 60

D. Freedom of Expression and Belief: 16 / 16

E. Associational and Organizational Rights: 12 / 12

F. Rule of Law: 15 / 16

G. Personal Autonomy and Individual Rights: 15 / 16

This country report has been abridged for *Freedom in the World 2017*. For background information on political rights and civil liberties in Portugal, see *Freedom in the World 2016*.

Qatar

Political Rights Rating: 6
Civil Liberties Rating: 5
Freedom Rating: 5.5
Freedom Status: Not Free
Electoral Democracy: No

Population: 2,500,000
Capital: Doha

Ten-Year Ratings Timeline For Year Under Review (Political Rights, Civil Liberties, Status)

Year Under Review	2007	2008	2009	2010	2011	2012	2013	2014	2015	2016
Rating	6,5,NF	6,5,NF	6,5,NF	6,5,NF	6,5,NF	6,5,NF	6,5,NF	6,5,NF	6,5,NF	6,5,NF

Overview: Qatar's hereditary emir holds all executive and legislative authority, and ultimately controls the judiciary as well. Political parties are not permitted, and the only elections are for an advisory municipal council. While Qatari citizens are among the wealthiest in the world, more than four-fifths of the population are expatriates with no political rights, few civil liberties, and limited access to economic opportunity.

KEY DEVELOPMENTS IN 2016:

- In June, the emir issued a decree that extended the term of the fully appointed Advisory Council by another three years, postponing the first elections for the council until at least 2019.
- In November, authorities blocked access to Doha News, a popular online outlet that had provided critical reporting on sensitive topics.
- Qatar continued to face international scrutiny over the alleged mistreatment of migrant workers, particularly those involved in construction projects related to soccer's World Cup, which the emirate was scheduled to host in 2022.

EXECUTIVE SUMMARY

The government of Sheikh Tamim bin Hamad al-Thani, Qatar's emir since 2013, continued to grapple with the effects of low oil and gas prices and a related slowdown in public spending in 2016. A cabinet shuffle in January, part of a gradual process by which the emir was replacing officials appointed by his father, also featured the consolidation of several ministries to reduce costs. The country remained involved in Saudi-led military operations in Yemen and made efforts to repair relations with fellow Gulf Cooperation Council (GCC) states after a serious rift in 2014 over Qatar's support for the Muslim Brotherhood.

Qatari citizens have been spared from the brunt of austerity measures, whose impact has fallen hardest on the expatriate population. Spending continued in 2016 on preparations for the 2022 World Cup, which have drawn international attention to labor exploitation in Qatar. Large numbers of migrant workers reportedly faced abusive conditions that sometimes amounted to forced labor.

POLITICAL RIGHTS: 9 / 40

A. Electoral Process: 2 / 12

The head of state is the emir, whose family holds a monopoly on political power. The emir appoints the prime minister and cabinet, and also selects an heir-apparent after consulting with the ruling family and other notables. In 2013, Sheikh Hamad bin Khalifa al-Thani abdicated after serving as emir since 1995. His successor, Sheikh Tamim, was his fourth-born son. Sheikh Abdullah bin Nasser bin Khalifa al-Thani, the former head of state security and a member of the ruling family, became prime minister as well as interior minister.

The constitution, approved in a 2003 referendum, stipulates that 30 of the 45 seats of the Advisory Council (Majlis al-Shura) should be filled through elections every four years; the emir would appoint the other 15 members. However, elections have yet to take place, so all members are currently appointed. Elections scheduled for 2013 were postponed by three years, ostensibly due to the transfer of power to Tamim. In June 2016, the emir issued a decree extending the term of the existing council by another three years.

The country held its first nonpartisan elections in 1999 for the 29-member Central Municipal Council, a body designed to advise the minister for municipal affairs. Its members serve four-year terms. In the most recent council elections, held in 2015, five of the 130 candidates were women, and two of them won seats, up from one in the previous council. Although turnout rose substantially to 70 percent of registered voters, from 43 percent in 2011, the actual number registered fell by 40 percent to a record low of 21,735, out of roughly 150,000 eligible voters.

All Qatari citizens over the age of 18 are eligible to vote, with the exception of those in the military and those working for the Interior Ministry. However, more than 80 percent of the country's population is composed of foreign nationals, who are not eligible to vote.

B. Political Pluralism and Participation: 2 / 16

The government does not permit the existence of political parties. All candidates for municipal elections run as independents, and tribal and family ties continue to play an influential role in political affairs. The system as a whole is dominated by the ruling family. While some members of the noncitizen majority work as senior government employees and judges, they have no formal political rights.

C. Functioning of Government: 3 / 12

Decision-making authority is concentrated in the hands of the emir and his family. Critics continue to complain of a lack of transparency in state procurement, which allegedly depends on personal connections. Qatar has been accused of corrupt practices in its bid to host the 2022 World Cup. Official information in general is very tightly controlled. Nevertheless, the authorities regularly punish lower-level public officials for bribery and embezzlement. More than a dozen such cases were reported during 2016, and in October the emir signed a law empowering the State Audit Bureau to make some aspects of its findings public, though the security ministries remained exempt from its oversight.

DISCRETIONARY POLITICAL RIGHTS QUESTION A: 2 / 4

Citizens can petition elected local government representatives who have limited powers over municipal services; these representatives report to the Ministry of Municipality and Environment. However, the record low rate of registration for the 2015 municipal council elections suggested waning public confidence in the ability of existing institutions to communicate citizens' concerns, particularly in light of the continued failure to hold Advisory Council elections.

CIVIL LIBERTIES: 17 / 60 (− 1)

D. Freedom of Expression and Belief: 7 / 16 (− 1)

Although the constitution guarantees freedom of expression, both print and broadcast media are influenced by leading families and subject to state censorship. The main daily newspapers are privately owned, but their owners and boards include members of the ruling family. In 1996, the emir permitted the creation of Al-Jazeera, a television network that has achieved a global reach. Although it is privately held, the government has reportedly paid for the network's operating costs since its inception. Al-Jazeera generally does not cover Qatari politics. All journalists in Qatar practice a high degree of self-censorship and face possible jail sentences for defamation and other press offenses. Social media users can also face criminal penalties for posting politically sensitive content. In March 2016, the emir pardoned a poet who had been sentenced in 2013 to 15 years in prison for poems posted online that were critical of Qatari and other Arab leaders.

Foreign journalists continued to encounter official interference during 2016. Three journalists working for the Danish Broadcasting Corporation were detained in May after filming a soccer tournament for migrant workers outside Doha. Before they were released, the crew were made to sign confessions that they had trespassed and filmed without permission.

A 2014 law on cybercrimes prescribes up to three years in prison for a range of vaguely worded offenses, including online dissemination of "false news" or content that undermines "general order." Publishing personal or family information can draw prison time and fines even if the content is accurate. In October 2016, Doha News, a local English-language website that has reported on sensitive topics, published an editorial arguing that the cybercrimes law was being "exploited by criminals and individuals with personal agendas to silence others," noting that one of its own reporters had been detained for questioning in July over an article that identified a convicted child molester by name. In November, Doha News reported that access to its site had been blocked indefinitely by Qatar's two internet service providers, allegedly due to problems with its license.

Islam is the official religion, though the constitution explicitly provides for freedom of worship. The Ministry of Islamic Affairs regulates clerical matters and the construction of mosques. Several churches have been built for Qatar's growing Christian community. The constitution guarantees freedom of opinion and academic research, but scholars often self-censor on politically sensitive topics. Several foreign universities have established branches in Qatar under a program to strengthen the country's educational institutions.

While residents enjoy some freedom of private discussion, security forces reportedly monitor personal communications, and noncitizens often self-censor to avoid jeopardizing their work and residency status.

E. Associational and Organizational Rights: 2 / 12

While the constitution grants freedoms of assembly and association, these rights are limited by law and in practice. Protests are rare, with the government restricting the public's ability to organize demonstrations. All nongovernmental organizations need state permission to operate, and the government closely monitors their activities. There are no independent human rights organizations, though a government-appointed National Human Rights Committee, which includes members of civil society and government ministries, investigates alleged abuses.

A 2005 labor law expanded some worker protections, but the rights to form unions and to strike remain restricted. The only trade union allowed to operate is the General Union of Workers of Qatar, and the law prohibits membership for noncitizens, government employees, and household workers. Onerous administrative and financial requirements deter the formation of professional associations.

F. Rule of Law: 4 / 16

Despite constitutional guarantees, the judiciary is not independent in practice. The majority of Qatar's judges are foreign nationals who are appointed and removed by the emir. The judicial system consists of Sharia (Islamic law) courts, which have jurisdiction over a narrow range of issues including family law, and civil law courts, which have jurisdiction over criminal, commercial, and civil cases.

Although the constitution protects individuals from arbitrary arrest and detention and bans torture, a 2002 law allows the suspension of these guarantees for the "protection of society." The law empowers the interior minister to detain a defendant for crimes related to national security on the recommendation of the director general of public security.

The integrity of Qatar's judicial system became the focus of attention in 2015, when the Court of Appeal overturned convictions of involuntary manslaughter for several people, including a member of the ruling family, in connection with the 2012 Villaggio Mall fire, which killed 19 people. The decision was criticized for alleged bias in favor of the defendants. In February 2016, the Court of Cassation ordered a retrial before the Court of Appeal, but the latter ruled in April that the defendants would pay compensation to the victims' families rather than facing jail time. An appeal of that verdict was pending at year's end.

LGBT (lesbian, gay, bisexual, and transgender) people face legal and societal discrimination, and same-sex relationships must be hidden in practice. Vague wording in the penal code can be interpreted to criminalize same-sex sexual activity, and both criminal law and Sharia prohibit any sexual acts outside of heterosexual marriage. In June 2016, a non-Muslim Dutch woman received a one-year suspended sentence for extramarital sex and was deported after reporting that she had been drugged and raped. A Syrian Muslim man accused in the case received corporal punishment for extramarital sex and consumption of alcohol.

G. Personal Autonomy and Individual Rights: 4 / 16

Qataris face no apparent restrictions on freedom of movement within Qatar or on type or place of employment. Such freedoms, however, are not extended to noncitizens and foreign workers. Unlike citizens, noncitizens must pay for services including education and utilities, and face discrimination in housing and other areas. Qataris are permitted to own property and start private businesses, although the process of obtaining necessary commercial permits can be cumbersome. Noncitizens are generally barred from owning property.

While the constitution treats women as full and equal persons, and gender-based discrimination is banned, women face de facto discrimination in the workforce. A 2006 family law regulates issues such as inheritance, child custody, marriage, and divorce. While the law expanded protections for women, they continue to face disadvantages, including societal discrimination, and have few effective legal mechanisms to contest incidents of bias.

Domestic violence is not specifically criminalized, though the 2011–16 National Development Strategy included plans for laws against domestic violence, increased legal protections for victims, and robust social support services. A small state-sponsored shelter serves abused women and children and, in cooperation with the public prosecutor's office, facilitates the legal response to cases of abuse.

Many foreign nationals, who make up over 90 percent of the workforce, face economic abuses including the withholding of salaries, contract manipulation, poor living conditions, and excessive working hours. However, fear of job loss and deportation often prevents them from asserting their limited rights. Female household workers are particularly vulnerable to abuse and exploitation. Migrants building the infrastructure for the 2022 World Cup continued to work in harsh conditions in 2016. There have been reports of workers not receiving wages for more than a year and being stranded in Qatar after the collapse of the contracting companies that employed them.

A modest 2015 reform law that took effect in December 2016 ostensibly eased foreign workers' ability to change employers at the end of a contract and leave the country without an employer's permission, but analysts noted that workers still could not change jobs during a contract period, and that employers could now hold workers' passports legally and remained empowered to block exit visas.

Romania

Political Rights Rating: 2
Civil Liberties Rating: 2
Freedom Rating: 2.0
Freedom Status: Free
Electoral Democracy: Yes

Population: 19,800,000
Capital: Bucharest

Ten-Year Ratings Timeline For Year Under Review (Political Rights, Civil Liberties, Status)

Year Under Review	2007	2008	2009	2010	2011	2012	2013	2014	2015	2016
Rating	2,2,F	2,2,F	2,2,F	2,2,F	2,2,F	2,2,F	2,2,F	2,2,F	2,2,F	2,2,F

Overview: Romania's multiparty system has ensured regular rotations of power, and executive authority is often divided between a president and prime minister from different parties. Civil liberties are generally respected, though ongoing concerns include police brutality, discrimination against Roma and other vulnerable groups, and corruption and political influence in the judiciary. Key media outlets are controlled by businessmen with political interests. While political corruption remains an entrenched problem, prosecutors have made major progress in holding senior politicians accountable in recent years, raising tensions between investigators and elected officials.

KEY DEVELOPMENTS IN 2016:

- The caretaker government installed in late 2015 took a number of steps to strengthen transparency and access to information during the year.
- In March, the government enacted new regulations on prison and detention conditions that were expected to improve food and medical care, counseling, and communication with law enforcement authorities and families, and would allow electronic monitoring of convicts outside prisons.
- Parliamentary elections were held in December, and a new government headed by the Social Democratic Party (PSD) was set to take office in early 2017.

EXECUTIVE SUMMARY

Parliamentary elections were held in December 2016 under a new electoral law adopted the previous year. It lowered the number of members needed to create a new political party from 25,000 to three, leading to the registration of many new parties. The law also allowed mail-in voting for citizens living abroad, though participation was limited; fewer than 9,000 people registered to vote by mail, and some 4,000 ballots were cast by mail. New technological measures were introduced to help prevent fraud, including video cameras to record the ballot count.

The size of each chamber of parliament was reduced in keeping with the electoral law, and all members were elected under a party-list proportional representation system. The PSD won a plurality, taking 154 of 329 seats in the Chamber of Deputies and 67 of 136 seats in the Senate. The National Liberal Party (PNL) placed second with 69 and 30. The Save Romania Union (USR)—a new, broad-based centrist party formed after the June local elections—came in third, taking 30 lower house seats and 13 in the Senate. The Democratic Alliance of Hungarians in Romania (UDMR) captured 21 and nine, the Alliance of Democrats and Liberals (ALDE) took 20 and nine, and the Popular Movement Party (PMP), led by former president Traian Băsescu, received 18 and 8. The remaining 17 members of the Chamber of Deputies represented ethnic minorities. A new cabinet led by the PSD's Sorin Grindeanu in coalition with the ALDE, a PNL splinter party, was expected to be confirmed in early January 2017.

Despite the acknowledged improvements, the elections revealed some gaps in the new electoral code, such as flawed procedures for vetting candidate eligibility, registering as an observer, and conducting ballot recounts. Analysts also noted a scarcity of regulations on party financing.

For the year before the elections, Romania was governed by a technocratic caretaker cabinet, with Dacian Cioloş as prime minister. It sought to work with parliament, but continued the practice of using emergency ordinances to pass legislation. The government also implemented a variety of administrative reforms aimed at improving transparency and access to information; for example, the new Ministry for Public Consultation and Civic Dialogue—created at the end of 2015—launched an online platform offering fiscal and budgetary information on thousands of public institutions and approved the creation of a registry for lobbyists.

The work of the National Anticorruption Directorate (DNA) continued to meet with resistance from much of the political class and their media allies, and related disputes were adjudicated by the Constitutional Court. In February, the court barred the DNA from using intelligence agency wiretaps, meaning prosecutors would have to build their own surveillance capacity. In June, the court ruled against decriminalizing abuse of power, but limited its application to actual breaches of the law rather than cases in which officials inflicted harm by doing their jobs improperly. In October, the court blocked a bill passed by parliament in June that would have exempted many lawmakers from conflict-of-interest charges related to the hiring of relatives.

The DNA's head, Laura Codruța Kövesi, was also the target of illegal surveillance and harassment during the year. A former Romanian intelligence officer was detained for such abuses in September, and members of a private Israeli intelligence firm admitted their involvement in October. Separately, Kövesi was cleared of academic plagiarism accusations in December, and her accuser, a businessman and former lawmaker facing corruption charges, fled the country.

Meanwhile, the DNA continued to pursue numerous cases against current and former high-ranking officials, and the caretaker government forced some of its own ministers to step down in response to scandals or poor performance.

POLITICAL RIGHTS: 35 / 40 (+ 1)

A. Electoral Process: 11 / 12

B. Political Pluralism and Participation: 14 / 16

C. Functioning of Government: 10 / 12 (+ 1)

CIVIL LIBERTIES: 49 / 60

D. Freedom of Expression and Belief: 14 / 16

E. Associational and Organizational Rights: 11 / 12

F. Rule of Law: 12 / 16

G. Personal Autonomy and Individual Rights: 12 / 16

This country report has been abridged for *Freedom in the World 2017*. For background information on political rights and civil liberties in Romania, see *Freedom in the World 2016*.

Russia

Political Rights Rating: 7 ↓
Civil Liberties Rating: 6
Freedom Rating: 6.5
Freedom Status: Not Free
Electoral Democracy: No

Population: 144,300,000
Capital: Moscow

Ratings Change: Russia's political rights rating declined from 6 to 7 due to the heavily flawed 2016 legislative elections, which further excluded opposition forces from the political process.

Ten-Year Ratings Timeline For Year Under Review (Political Rights, Civil Liberties, Status)

Year Under Review	2007	2008	2009	2010	2011	2012	2013	2014	2015	2016
Rating	6,5,NF	6,5,NF	6,5,NF	6,5,NF	6,5,NF	6,5,NF	6,5,NF	6,6,NF	6,6,NF	7,6,NF

Overview: In Russia's authoritarian government, power is concentrated in the hands of President Vladimir Putin. With loyalist security forces, a subservient judiciary, and a legislature dominated by his United Russia party, Putin is able to manipulate elections and inhibit formal opposition. The government also has strong control of the media environment, and has been able to retain domestic support despite an ongoing economic slump and strong international criticism. The country's rampant corruption is one notable threat to state power, as it facilitates shifting links among bureaucrats and organized crime groups.

KEY DEVELOPMENTS IN 2016:

- Amid historically low turnout, elections in September produced a supermajority for the ruling United Russia party in the State Duma, the lower legislative house.
- In July, Putin created the National Guard of Russia, a force devoted to maintaining public order; critics noted that the body is likely to be used to prevent unwanted public protests.
- Space for independent voices in the media continued to diminish, particularly after a series of politically motivated personnel changes at the RBC media group.
- The Levada Center, among many other organizations, was added to the list of "foreign agents" by the Justice Ministry during the year; the authorities continued requiring groups that receive foreign funding and engage in loosely defined political activities to adopt the label.

EXECUTIVE SUMMARY

Russia's economic downturn continued in 2016, and the Kremlin worked to preempt potential domestic discontent through several means, including focusing public attention on foreign interventions. Authorities continued incorporating Crimea into the administration of the Russian Federation, maintained support for separatist militants in eastern Ukraine, and expanded military support for Bashar al-Assad's regime in Syria.

Historically low turnout marked the Duma elections in September, in which United Russia captured 343 of 450 seats, solidifying its grip on the legislative branch of government. Voters also cast ballots in a number of regional races, which United Russia dominated. The restrictive political atmosphere—characterized by the state's grip on the flow of information, limitations on activism, and hostility to opposition—undercut competition and freedom of choice. In October, the Levada Center, a local independent research organization, published the results of its post-election polling, noting that approximately a third of respondents believed the elections to have been unfair. Nevertheless, half of those polled expressed satisfaction with the electoral results. Following the elections, legislators approved the nomination of Vyacheslav Volodin, a close Putin ally and his former first deputy chief of staff, to the position of Duma speaker. The move, part of a broader reshuffle of the political elite, was perceived to bolster executive control over the legislature in preparation for presidential elections in 2018.

In September, the Federal Antimonopoly Service reported that the state controls 70 percent of the economy either directly or through state-owned enterprises. Throughout the year, the Kremlin utilized its vast resources to pressure opposition entities and critical voices. Authorities continued to restrict the activities of civil society groups, increasing pressure on independent groups—including the Levada Center—by declaring them "foreign agents." The regime also intensified its grip on the country's media environment, saturating the landscape with nationalist propaganda while suppressing remaining sources of independent information. The editorial leadership of RBC came under fire in May in connection to reporting on the president's family and friends. Three editors at outlets owned by the media group were pushed out amid rumors of pressure from the Kremlin, and replaced in July by recruits from the state-owned TASS news agency; many RBC reporters resigned in protest.

POLITICAL RIGHTS: 5 / 40 (-2)

A. Electoral Process: 0 / 12 (-1)

The 1993 constitution established a strong presidency with the power to dismiss and appoint, pending parliamentary confirmation, the prime minister. Putin served two four-year presidential terms from 2000 to 2008, and remained the de facto paramount leader while working as prime minister until 2012, violating the spirit if not the letter of the constitution's two-term limit. In the 2012 presidential election, Putin benefited from advantages including preferential media treatment, numerous abuses of incumbency, and procedural irregularities during the vote count. He won an official 63.6 percent of the vote against a field of weak, hand-chosen opponents. Communist Party leader Gennadiy Zyuganov took second place with 17.2 percent. Under a 2008 constitutional amendment, Putin is now serving a six-year term, and will be eligible for another in 2018.

The Federal Assembly consists of the 450-seat State Duma and an upper chamber, the 170-seat Federation Council. Half the members of the upper chamber are appointed by governors and half by regional legislatures, usually with strong federal input. Since 2011, only locally elected politicians have been eligible to serve in the Federation Council; the change was designed to benefit United Russia, as most local officeholders are party members.

The 2008 constitutional amendment extended Duma terms from four to five years. Following the 2011 State Duma elections, when the ruling United Russia party scored just less than 50 percent of the vote in flawed elections that sparked street protests, the Kremlin rewrote the electoral law, restoring the mixed system abandoned after the 2003 elections, under which half of Duma members are elected by proportional representation and half in single-member districts. The reform also moved elections from December to September.

The changes had the desired effect in September 2016, when United Russia won 343 seats in the 450-seat State Duma, gaining a supermajority that allows it to change the constitution without the support of other parties. Kremlin-approved parties won the bulk of all remaining seats. The Central Electoral Commission (CEC) reported a turnout of 48 percent, the lowest in Russia's post-Soviet history.

The Organization for Security and Co-operation in Europe's Office for Democratic Institutions and Human Rights noted that "democratic commitments continue to be challenged and the electoral environment was negatively affected by restrictions to fundamental freedoms and political rights, firmly controlled media and a tightening grip on civil society." The election monitoring group Golos deemed the elections "far from being truly free and fair." The group also noted that there were half as many independent election observers in 2016 as in 2011. Reported violations included ballot stuffing, pressure on voters, and illegal campaigning. A number of opposition candidates were simply not permitted to register, so the outcome of many races was clear even before election day. Statistical analysis of the results conducted by Sergei Shpilkin—a physicist and independent election monitor—suggested irregularities in the voting consistent with systematic cheating, with high turnout areas backing United Russia.

A 2012 law restored gubernatorial elections, ending a system of presidential appointments that dated to 2004. The new rules allowed federal and regional officials to screen the candidates for governor, and United Russia candidates have dominated almost every subsequent election. The party swept gubernatorial and regional legislative races in 2016. Ramzan Kadyrov won a reported 98 percent of the vote in Chechnya.

B. Political Pluralism and Participation: 3 / 16

Legislation enacted in 2012 liberalized party registration rules, allowing the creation of hundreds of new parties. However, none posed a significant threat to the authorities, and many seemed designed to encourage division and confusion among the opposition.

Opposition politicians and activists are frequently targeted with fabricated criminal cases and other forms of administrative harassment. Opposition leader Aleksey Navalny's brother was sentenced to three and a half years in prison on trumped-up fraud charges in 2014, and he remained behind bars in 2016 in an apparent attempt to limit Navalny's activities. In December, Navalny announced plans to challenge Putin in the 2018 presidential election, although a protracted embezzlement case—ongoing at the end of 2016—could bar him from competing if it results in a conviction.

Five individuals went on trial in October for the February 2015 assassination of opposition leader Boris Nemtsov. The trial was ongoing at year's end, and it remained unclear who had ordered the killing.

The formation of parties based on ethnicity or religion is not permitted by law. In practice, many ethnic minority regions are carefully monitored and controlled by federal authorities. Most republics in the restive North Caucasus area and some autonomous districts in energy-rich western Siberia have opted out of direct gubernatorial elections; instead, their legislatures choose a governor from candidates proposed by the president.

C. Functioning of Government: 2 / 12 (− 1)

There is little transparency and accountability in the day-to-day workings of the government. Decisions are adopted behind closed doors by a small group of individuals—led by Putin—whose identities are often unclear, and announced to the population after the fact. Numerous structural and personnel changes within the government occurred in 2016 as Putin sought to preserve his power in an atmosphere of declining resources, as well as to plan ahead for the 2018 presidential race. The president broke with past practices and dismissed a number of loyal subordinates; among those affected was his chief of staff Sergei Ivanov, whom Putin replaced with Ivanov's own deputy, Anton Vaino.

Corruption in the government and business world is pervasive, and a growing lack of accountability enables bureaucrats to act with impunity. Many analysts have argued that the political system is essentially a kleptocracy, in which ruling elites plunder public wealth to enrich themselves. In September, Navalny's Anti-Corruption Foundation published an exposé of an extravagant country home tied to—but not directly owned by—Prime Minister Dmitry Medvedev, detailing a number of suspicious transactions involved in the compound's acquisition, expansion, and renovation.

In a shocking case in September 2016, authorities arrested Dmitry Zakharchenko, a senior anticorruption official in the Ministry of the Interior, after discovering that he possessed some $120 million in cash and 300 million in foreign bank accounts; investigators reported that he had hidden the cash at the home of his sister and used accounts registered in his father's name. Many political analysts suggested that the arrest was a reflection of infighting within the Russian elite, and a breach in the complex networks that support corrupt activities. Separately, in November, the arrest of Economy Minister Aleksey Ulyukayev on bribery charges signaled that even sitting ministers could now be prosecuted on corruption charges, breaking with a tradition of immunity. These events did little to change the extent of overall corruption in the system, however.

CIVIL LIBERTIES: 15 / 60

D. Freedom of Expression and Belief: 3 / 16

Although the constitution provides for freedom of speech, vague laws on extremism grant the authorities great discretion to crack down on any speech, organization, or activity that lacks official support. The government controls, directly or through state-owned companies and friendly business magnates, all of the national television networks and many radio and print outlets, as well as most of the media advertising market. These media effectively serve as vehicles for Kremlin propaganda, which vociferously backs Putin's actions in Ukraine and Syria and denounces foreign and domestic opponents.

Only a small and shrinking number of radio stations and print outlets with limited reach offer a diverse range of viewpoints. The government regularly pressures media houses and workers for investigating or reporting on corruption. In one such case, three top editors at RBC outlets—Roman Badanin, Yelizaveta Osetinskaya, and Maksim Solyus—were dismissed in May 2016 amid rumors of government pressure. Watchdogs and the independent media community noted that the dismissals were tied to articles about Putin's immediate family as well as a close friend of the president's whose offshore accounts appeared in the Panama Papers. Editors from TASS, the state news agency, were recruited as replacements.

Separately, in a case brought by Rosneft head Igor Sechin against *Novaya Gazeta,* a Moscow court ruled in favor of Sechin, who had filed the suit over an article linking his wife to a luxury yacht. The court ruled that the paper had improperly implied wrongdoing and ordered the offending article to be redacted, although *Novaya Gazeta* announced plans to appeal. Sechin also successfully sued the parent company of *Vedomosti* as well as a journalist working for the daily over a July article connecting Sechin to a luxury development outside of a Moscow. The court ordered the destruction of all remaining copies of *Vedomosti* containing the story.

In September, authorities detained Roman Sushchenko, a Paris-based correspondent for Ukraine's state news agency, and claimed that he was an intelligence officer collecting information on the Russian military—a claim that his employer denied. Sushchenko remained in custody at year's end. Also in September, award-winning journalist Denis Korotkov was arrested while investigating voter fraud during the parliamentary elections. A St. Petersburg court ultimately dismissed the case against him.

Violations of media freedom, including violence against journalists, generally go unpunished. Although five men were sentenced in 2014 for the 2006 killing of journalist Anna Politkovskaya, the identity of those responsible for arranging her murder remained unclear in 2016.

Freedom of religion is respected unevenly. A 1997 law on religion gives the state extensive control and makes it difficult for new or independent groups to operate. The Russian Orthodox Church has a privileged position, working closely with the government on foreign and domestic policy priorities. In 2009, the president authorized religious instruction in public schools. Regional authorities continue to harass nontraditional groups, such as Jehovah's Witnesses and Mormons. The so-called Yarovaya Law, ostensibly targeting terrorism, includes new powers that the authorities can use to repress religious groups in Russia on the grounds of fighting extremism.

The education system is marred by bureaucratic interference, international isolation, and increasing pressure to toe the Kremlin line on politically sensitive topics, though some academics continue to express dissenting views. The appointment of Olga Vasilyeva to the post of minister of education and science in August raised worries from critics, particularly regarding her strong support for the Russian Orthodox Church and her claim that estimates of the number of people who suffered under Stalinism have been exaggerated.

Pervasive, hyperpatriotic propaganda and political repression over the past two years have had a cumulative impact on open and free private discussion, and the chilling effect is exacerbated by growing state efforts to control expression on the internet. More than 70 percent of Russians have internet access, and penetration continues to increase. Discussion on the internet had been largely unrestricted until 2012, but following large antigovernment demonstrations in 2011 and 2012, the Kremlin adopted a series of laws that gave it more power to shut down critical websites. The independent research group Roskomsvoboda reported that by year's end, more than a million websites had been blocked through unlawful means. The Kremlin also employs numerous "trolls" to disrupt online discussions and intimidate users.

Individuals continued to face legal repercussions for exercising freedom of expression online, particularly under anti-extremism legislation. In December 2016, a court in Tyumen sentenced Aleksei Kungurov to two years in a penal colony for "justifying terrorism" in a blog post in which Kungurov criticized Russia's actions in Syria. In a separate case, Sochi resident Oksana Sevastidi received a seven-year sentence in March for texting about the location of Russian military equipment in the lead-up to the 2008 Russo-Georgian war. Sevastidi was only arrested in 2015 and tried in a secret court in the southern Krasnodar region without adequate counsel, raising serious questions about the nature of the charges as well as due process.

E. Associational and Organizational Rights: 3 / 12

The government has consistently reduced the space for freedoms of assembly and association. Overwhelming police responses, the use of force, routine arrests, and harsh fines and prison sentences have discouraged unsanctioned protests, though pro-Kremlin groups are able to demonstrate freely. In July, Putin signed the Yarovaya Law, two pieces of counterterrorism legislation that strengthen punishments for terrorism and extremism, increase Russia surveillance capabilities, criminalize withholding information about certain crimes from the authorities, and ease state monitoring of phone and internet communications. Critics claimed that the law would make it easier for the authorities to stifle dissent.

The government continued its relentless campaign against nongovernmental organizations (NGOs) in 2016. By the end of 2016, the Justice Ministry had included 154 Russian organizations on its list of "foreign agents." On the eve of the State Duma elections, the authorities added the Levada Center, Russia's most prominent independent pollster, to the roster. Among other prominent additions in 2016 were Memorial International and the Environmental Watch on North Caucasus, both of which conduct independent research about Russian policies. Among others, the Justice Ministry also gave the label to volunteer firefighters in Krasnodar. The designation and related requirements—such as marking all published works with the "foreign agent" label—make it extremely difficult for groups to pursue their objectives.

While trade union rights are legally protected, they are limited in practice. Strikes and worker protests have occurred in prominent industries, such as automobile manufacturing, but antiunion discrimination and reprisals for strikes are not uncommon, and employers often ignore collective-bargaining rights. The largest labor federation works in close cooperation with the Kremlin, though independent unions are active in some industrial sectors and regions.

F. Rule of Law: 2 / 16

The judiciary lacks independence from the executive branch, and career advancement is effectively tied to compliance with Kremlin preferences. A 2014 law merged the Supreme Arbitration Court, which headed the system of courts handling commercial disputes, into the Supreme Court, which oversees courts of general jurisdiction and will now also supervise the arbitration courts. The Supreme Arbitration Court had been widely respected as one of the most independent of Russia's courts. In April 2016, a Russian court ruling on a dispute over prisoners' voting rights was the first to use a 2015 law that allows the Russian judiciary to reject international court decisions; in this case, the international ruling had come from the European Court for Human Rights. In November, Putin withdrew Russia from the International Criminal Court after the body issued a report of preliminary findings calling the fighting in Crimea and eastern Ukraine an "international armed conflict" between Ukraine and Russia.

Ildar Dadin, an activist sentenced in 2015 to two and a half years in prison for participating in multiple unsanctioned protests within a period of 180 days, claimed that he was being tortured and beaten while in custody. A letter detailing Dadin's experiences, smuggled out of the penal colony housing him, caused national and international uproar when it was picked up by the media in November 2016, and focused attention on numerous other cases of severe mistreatment in Russian prisons.

In April, Putin ordered the creation of a new force devoted to maintaining public order, the National Guard. After its establishment under the formal control of the presidency in July, Putin appointed his former chief bodyguard, Viktor Zolotov, as head of the new force, which is set to have a membership of 350,000–400,000 individuals, many of them former security personnel. Although the National Guard is ostensibly devoted to combatting terrorism and extremism, critics fear that it could be used to block popular protest and serve as a tool for disciplining the Russian elite.

Parts of the country, especially the North Caucasus area, suffer from high levels of violence. Hundreds of officials, insurgents, and civilians die each year in bombings, gun battles, and assassinations. In Chechnya, Kadyrov imposes tight control over his republic with the support of a militia and a flow of generous subsidies from Moscow. The result is superficial peace and prosperity that mask personalized and arbitrary rule, fierce repression and intimidation, economic inequality, and impunity for abuses.

Immigrants and ethnic minorities—particularly those who appear to be from the Caucasus or Central Asia—face governmental and societal discrimination and harassment. LGBT (lesbian, gay, bisexual, and transgender) people are subject to considerable discrimination as well. A 2013 law banned dissemination of information promoting "nontraditional sexual relationships," putting legal pressure on LGBT activists and encouraging harassment.

G. Personal Autonomy and Individual Rights: 7 / 16

The government places some restrictions on freedoms of movement and residence. Adults must carry internal passports while traveling and to obtain many government services. Some regional authorities impose registration rules that limit the right of citizens to choose their place of residence, typically targeting ethnic minorities and migrants from the Caucasus and Central Asia. More than four million employees tied to the military and security services were banned from traveling abroad under rules issued during 2014.

State takeovers of key industries and large tax penalties imposed on select companies have illustrated the precarious nature of property rights in the country, especially when political interests are involved.

Women are underrepresented in politics and government. They hold less than a fifth of seats in the State Duma and the Federation Council. Only three of 32 cabinet members are women. Domestic violence against women continues to be a serious problem, and police are often reluctant to intervene in what they regard as internal family matters.

Migrant workers are often exposed to exploitative labor conditions. Both Russians facing economic hardship and migrants to Russia from neighboring countries are subject to sex and labor trafficking.

Rwanda

Political Rights Rating: 6
Civil Liberties Rating: 6
Freedom Rating: 6.0
Freedom Status: Not Free
Electoral Democracy: No

Population: 11,900,000
Capital: Kigali

Ten-Year Ratings Timeline For Year Under Review (Political Rights, Civil Liberties, Status)

Year Under Review 1Rating	2007	2008	2009	2010	2011	2012	2013	2014	2015	2016
	6,5,NF	6,5,NF	6,5,NF	6,5,NF	6,5,NF	6,6,NF	6,5,NF	6,6,NF	6,6,NF	6,6,NF

Overview: The Rwandan Patriotic Front (RPF), led by President Paul Kagame, has ruled the country since 1994, when it ousted forces responsible for that year's genocide and ended a civil war. While the regime has maintained peace and economic growth, it has also suppressed political dissent though pervasive surveillance, intimidation, and suspected assassinations. Recent constitutional changes could allow Kagame to serve another three terms as president.

KEY DEVELOPMENTS IN 2016:

- Kagame confirmed in January that he would seek a new term in the presidential election scheduled for 2017.
- In February, the government withdrew the right of individuals and organizations to file appeals before the African Court on Human and People's Rights (ACHPR), cutting off access for those who are denied justice by domestic courts.
- Journalists and members of banned opposition groups reportedly faced arbitrary arrests, beatings, politicized prosecutions, and enforced disappearances during the year.

EXECUTIVE SUMMARY

With the next presidential election approaching in 2017, President Kagame announced in January that he would run for another seven-year term. Under constitutional amendments adopted in 2015, he would also be eligible for two five-year terms beginning in 2024. Although the ruling RPF and most other legal political parties supported Kagame, the small opposition Democratic Green Party of Rwanda (DGPR)—which has no parliamentary representation—nominated Frank Habineza as its candidate in December.

Kagame's would-be challenger in the 2010 election, Victoire Ingabire, remained behind bars on politically motivated charges in 2016, as did many other dissidents. In late February, shortly before the Tanzania-based ACHPR was to hear Ingabire's appeal of her 15-year prison sentence, the Rwandan government withdrew from a protocol allowing individuals and nongovernmental organizations (NGOs) to bring cases before the court. However, the ACHPR ruled in September that the withdrawal would not affect pending cases.

Rwandan authorities continued to suppress dissent through violence and intimidation. A number of journalists and opposition members, including individuals affiliated with Ingabire's banned United Democratic Forces–Inkingi (FDU-Inkingi) party, were allegedly subjected to enforced disappearance, trumped-up criminal charges, arbitrary arrests, and physical abuse in custody during the year.

POLITICAL RIGHTS: 8 / 40

A. Electoral Process: 2 / 12

Rwanda's 2003 constitution grants broad powers to the president, who has the authority to appoint the prime minister and dissolve the bicameral parliament. Amendments passed in 2015 retained a two-term limit for the presidency and shortened the terms from seven to five years. The changes also explicitly stated, however, that the current president—Paul Kagame—was eligible for one additional seven-year term, after which he may run for two of the new five-year terms, which would extend Kagame's rule until 2034. Kagame announced in January 2016 that he would indeed seek reelection in 2017.

The 26-seat Senate, the upper house, consists of 12 members elected by regional councils, eight appointed by the president, four chosen by a forum of political parties, and two elected representatives of universities, all serving eight-year terms. The 80-seat Chamber of Deputies, the lower house, includes 53 directly elected members, 24 women chosen by local councils, two members from the National Youth Council, and one member from the Federation of Associations of the Disabled, all serving five-year terms. The 2003 constitution requires women to occupy at least 30 percent of the seats in each chamber of Parliament.

Kagame had no serious challengers in the 2010 presidential election, as key candidates and parties were arrested or denied registration. He won reelection with an official 93 percent of the vote. The RPF similarly dominated the most recent elections for the Chamber of Deputies in 2013, capturing 41 of the elected seats. Two allied parties, the Social Democratic Party and the Liberal Party, won seven and five seats, respectively. The RPF faced only limited competition from other parties in local elections held in early 2016.

The 2015 constitutional amendments were adopted through a flawed petition and referendum process. Rights groups and news organizations cited reports that some signatures on the petition were not given voluntarily, and the referendum passed in December 2015 with 98 percent of voters endorsing the amendments, according to the National Electoral Commission. The government limited the political activities of groups opposed to the amendments, and the referendum was not monitored by any independent international observer groups.

B. Political Pluralism and Participation: 1 / 16

The constitution permits political parties to exist but under strict controls, and its emphasis on "national unity" effectively limits political pluralism. Parties closely identified with the 1994 genocide are banned, as are parties based on ethnicity or religion. Although the RPF is still dominated by Tutsis, these restrictions have been used to ban other political parties that might challenge the RPF, regardless of ethnicity. Most recognized opposition parties are tied to the RPF in practice. The DGPR is perhaps the only legal party that offers genuine opposition, though it has no seats in parliament. It filed unsuccessful legal appeals against the 2015 referendum process, and as of December 2016 it was the only party to have nominated a candidate to challenge Kagame for the presidency in 2017, naming Frank Habineza as its standard-bearer that month.

In the run-up to the 2010 presidential poll, the government had prevented new political parties from registering and arrested the leaders of several existing parties, effectively preventing them from fielding candidates. Victoire Ingabire, the leader of FDU-Inkingi and one of Kagame's strongest opponents, was arrested twice in 2010, including before the election, and convicted in 2012 of engaging in terrorist activities. The case was widely seen as politically motivated. After an appeal of her initial eight-year prison sentence, the Supreme Court increased the prison term to 15 years in 2013. In 2014, the ACHPR agreed to hear Ingabire's case, and she remained in prison during 2016—with inconsistent access to her lawyer and other visitors—as that process moved forward.

A number of people connected to Ingabire or the FDU-Inkingi were allegedly subject to arbitrary arrest, forced disappearance, and physical abuse in 2016. They included activist Illuminée Iragena, who went missing in March and was thought to have died in prison as a result of torture. Separately, after visiting Ingabire in prison in March, FDU-Inkingi member Léonille Gasengayire was arrested and detained for three days, during which she was beaten. She was released without charges but then arrested again in August and charged with inciting insurrection. Another FDU-Inkingi member, Théophile Ntirutwa, was arrested in September, beaten, and questioned about his party membership before being released after two days.

Opposition figures residing outside of Rwanda have also been threatened, attacked, forcibly disappeared, or killed. Former members of the Rwandan security forces living in exile have gone missing, while others have been targeted for assassination.

Although the constitution calls on the president to ensure "representation of historically marginalized communities" in the Senate through his appointees, asserting one's ethnic identity in politics is banned, meaning the level of representation is unclear.

C. Functioning of Government: 5 / 12

Government policy is largely set and implemented by the executive, with the security and intelligence services playing a powerful role. Parliament generally lacks independence, merely endorsing presidential initiatives.

Government countermeasures, including regular prosecutions of low-level officials, have helped limit corruption, but graft remains a problem. Few independent organizations and media outlets are able to investigate or report on corruption issues due to fear of government reprisals. In 2013, Gustave Makonene, an anticorruption campaigner working for Transparency International Rwanda, was found murdered in northwestern Rwanda. Two police corporals were convicted in 2015 and sentenced to 20 years in prison for killing Makonene because he had information on their smuggling operation.

A 2013 law provides comprehensive access to information, but implementation has been weak. In 2015, Rwandan NGOs working with the Office of the Ombudsman launched a web portal called Sobanukirwa to make the process of requesting access to government documents easier. Data for 2016 suggested that only a small fraction of requests result in positive and timely responses.

CIVIL LIBERTIES: 16 / 40

D. Freedom of Expression and Belief: 4 / 16

The government imposes legal restrictions and informal controls on freedoms of the press and expression. A 2013 media law, initially lauded for expanding the rights of journalists and recognizing freedom for online communications, threatened to limit press freedom, including through the creation of a government body with the power to set conditions for both local and foreign media outlets to operate. More often, restrictions on journalists take the form of criminal charges and intimidation. In January 2016, writer and editor John Williams Ntwali, whose reporting had been critical of the government, was arrested, accused of rape (later reduced to indecent exposure), and illegally detained for 13 days. In February, the offices of the *East African* newspaper were raided by police, who seized materials and arrested a journalist, Yvan Mushiga. In August, radio journalist John

Ndabarasa—a relative of a former bodyguard of President Kagame who had been sentenced to life imprisonment for treason in 2014—went missing.

Many Rwandan journalists have fled the country and work in exile. Due in part to this phenomenon, the government has increasingly blocked access to news websites based abroad. The British Broadcasting Corporation's Kinyarwanda-language service has been suspended in the country since 2014.

Religious freedom is generally respected. Relations between religious leaders and the government are sometimes tense, in part because of the involvement of clergy in the 1994 genocide. Fear among teachers and students of being labeled "divisionist" constrains academic freedom at all levels of education.

The space for free private discussion remained limited in 2016 amid indications that the government monitors e-mail and other personal communications. The Law Relating to the Interception of Communications, enacted in 2013, authorizes high-ranking security officials to monitor e-mail and telephone conversations of individuals considered potential threats to public security. Social media are widely believed to be monitored, and the law allows for government hacking of telecommunications networks.

E. Associational and Organizational Rights: 2 / 12

Although the constitution guarantees freedoms of assembly and association, these rights are limited in practice. Fear of arrest often leads individuals and organizations to refrain from exercising their right to peaceful assembly. Registration and reporting requirements for both domestic and foreign NGOs are onerous, and activities that the government defines as divisive are prohibited. Delays in the registration renewal of the Human Rights League in the Great Lakes Region (LDGL) left it unable to operate between February and November 2016, and LDGL official Epimack Kwokwo, a Congolese national, was ordered to leave the country in May. Several organizations have been banned in recent years, leading others to self-censor, though civil society organizations that do not focus on democracy or human rights are able to function without direct government interference. The government has been accused of employing infiltration tactics against human rights organizations similar to those used against opposition political parties.The constitution provides for the rights to form trade unions, engage in collective bargaining, and strike, but free collective bargaining and strikes are limited by binding arbitration rules and rare in practice. Public workers and employees in broadly defined "essential services" are generally not allowed to strike.

F. Rule of Law: 3 / 16

The Rwandan judiciary lacks independence from the executive. The DGPR alleged that government pressure led several lawyers to withdraw from representing it in the party's legal challenge to the 2015 constitutional amendments. In February 2016, the government withdrew the right of individuals and NGOs to bring cases before the ACHPR, which they had been permitted to do since 2013. The court ruled in September that the change would not affect cases that were already pending and would not take effect for one year. In October, the cabinet passed a resolution for consideration by Parliament that called for the creation of a Court of Appeals, to serve as an additional judicial tier beneath the Supreme Court and help address a backlog of cases under review.

Police officers sometimes use excessive force, and local officials periodically ignore due process. The construction of new prisons during the past decade has improved prison conditions, and the inmate population has declined somewhat in recent years, but conditions remain poor in some facilities. Alleged dissidents have increasingly been subject to unlawful imprisonment, torture, and ill-treatment in custody. While political disappearances were apparently less common in 2016 than in some previous years, several people held by the authorities were either out of contact for lengthy periods of time or otherwise unaccounted for. A 2015 Human Rights Watch (HRW) report accused the Rwandan government of illegally detaining people from the streets of Kigali—including sex workers, street children, homeless people, and suspected petty criminals—at the Gikondo Transit Center in the Kigali suburbs, where the report said numerous human rights abuses occurred. HRW reported in July 2016 that conditions remained poor at the Gikondo center, which held hundreds of people at any one time, and noted similar abuses at other transit centers.

Equal treatment for all citizens under the law is guaranteed, and there are legal protections against discrimination. However, the Tutsi minority group is often accused of receiving preferential treatment for high-ranking jobs and university scholarships under the pretext of an affirmative action program for "genocide survivors." Additional preferences are afforded to those who returned from exile communities after 1994, particularly in Uganda. The indigenous Twa minority continues to suffer from de facto disadvantages in education, employment, and health care.

Same-sex sexual activity is not criminalized in Rwanda, though social stigma still exists for LGBT (lesbian, gay, bisexual, and transgender) people. No laws specifically provide protection against discrimination based on sexual orientation or gender identity.

G. Personal Autonomy and Individual Rights: 7 / 16

An easily attainable national identity card is required to move within the country. All government officials must receive approval from the president or prime minister's office before traveling for personal or professional reasons. For most citizens there are no formal restrictions on property rights, freedom of travel, or choice of employment, residence, or institution of higher education, although Hutus often face unofficial discrimination when seeking public employment or government scholarships.

Rwanda was ranked 56 out of 190 countries in the World Bank's 2017 *Doing Business* report, which was released in October 2016, placing second in sub-Saharan Africa. The country ranked third in sub-Saharan Africa, and 52 out of 138 economies, in the World Economic Forum's *Global Competitiveness Report 2016–2017*, indicating relatively well-functioning institutions and a low level of direct government control over the economy.

Women currently hold 10 of the 26 Senate seats and 49 of the 80 seats in the Chamber of Deputies. De facto discrimination against women persists. Domestic violence is illegal but remains widespread.

Human trafficking within Rwanda is limited in scale, and mostly consists of children forced into domestic service. Burundian refugees are also vulnerable to exploitation, however, including coercive recruitment into armed groups. Government officials have sometimes been complicit in trafficking crimes.

Saint Kitts and Nevis

Political Rights Rating: 1
Civil Liberties Rating: 1
Freedom Rating: 1.0
Freedom Status: Free
Electoral Democracy: Yes

Population: 50,000
Capital: Basseterre

Ratings Change: Saint Kitts and Nevis's political rights rating declined from 1 to 2 due to problems with the 2015 elections, including unequal access to the media and financial resources, final determination of a number of constituency boundaries only a few days before the polling, and refusal of the supervisor of elections to publish the results on schedule.

Ten-Year Ratings Timeline For Year Under Review (Political Rights, Civil Liberties, Status)

Year Under Review	2007	2008	2009	2010	2011	2012	2013	2014	2015	2016
Rating	1,1,F	1,1,F	1,1,F	1,1,F	1,1,F	1,1,F	1,1,F	1,1,F	2,1,F	1,1,F

The country or territory displayed here received scores but no narrative report for this edition of *Freedom in the World.*

Saint Lucia

Political Rights Rating: 1
Civil Liberties Rating: 1
Freedom Rating: 1.0
Freedom Status: Free
Electoral Democracy: Yes

Population: 200,000
Capital: Castries

Ten-Year Ratings Timeline For Year Under Review (Political Rights, Civil Liberties, Status)

Year Under Review	2007	2008	2009	2010	2011	2012	2013	2014	2 015	2016
Rating	1,1,F	1,1,F	1,1,F	1,1,F	1,1,F	1,1,F	1,1,F	1,1,F	1,1,F	1,1,F

The country or territory displayed here received scores but no narrative report for this edition of *Freedom in the World.*

Saint Vincent and the Grenadines

Political Rights Rating: 1
Civil Liberties Rating: 1
Freedom Rating: 1.0
Freedom Status: Free
Electoral Democracy: Yes

Population: 100,000
Capital: Kingstown

Ten-Year Ratings Timeline For Year Under Review (Political Rights, Civil Liberties, Status)

Year Under Review	2007	2008	2009	2010	2011	2012	2013	2014	2015	2016
Rating	2,1,F	2,1,F	2,1,F	1,1,F	1,1,F	1,1,F	1,1,F	1,1,F	1,1,F	1,1,F

The country or territory displayed here received scores but no narrative report for this edition of *Freedom in the World.*

Samoa

Political Rights Rating: 2
Civil Liberties Rating: 2
Freedom Rating: 2.0
Freedom Status: Free
Electoral Democracy: Yes

Population: 200,000
Capital: Apia

Ten-Year Ratings Timeline For Year Under Review (Political Rights, Civil Liberties, Status)

Year Under Review	2007	2008	2009	2010	2011	2012	2013	2014	2015	2016
Rating	2,2,F	2,2,F	2,2,F	2,2,F	2,2,F	2,2,F	2,2,F	2,2,F	2,2,F	2,2,F

The country or territory displayed here received scores but no narrative report for this edition of *Freedom in the World*.

San Marino

Political Rights Rating: 1
Civil Liberties Rating: 1
Freedom Rating: 1.0
Freedom Status: Free
Electoral Democracy: Yes

Population: 30,000
Capital: San Marino

Ten-Year Ratings Timeline For Year Under Review (Political Rights, Civil Liberties, Status)

Year Under Review	2007	2008	2009	2010	2011	2012	2013	2014	2015	2016
Rating	1,1,F	1,1,F	1,1,F	1,1,F	1,1,F	1,1,F	1,1,F	1,1,F	1,1,F	1,1,F

The country or territory displayed here received scores but no narrative report for this edition of *Freedom in the World*.

São Tomé and Príncipe

Political Rights Rating: 2
Civil Liberties Rating: 2
Freedom Rating: 2.0
Freedom Status: Free
Electoral Democracy: Yes

Population: 200,000
Capital: São Tomé

Ten-Year Ratings Timeline For Year Under Review (Political Rights, Civil Liberties, Status)

Year Under Review	2007	2008	2009	2010	2011	2012	2013	2014	2015	2016
Rating	2,2,F	2,2,F	2,2,F	2,2,F	2,2,F	2,2,F	2,2,F	2,2,F	2,2,F	2,2,F

The country or territory displayed here received scores but no narrative report for this edition of *Freedom in the World.*

Saudi Arabia

Political Rights Rating: 7
Civil Liberties Rating: 7
Freedom Rating: 7.0
Freedom Status: Not Free
Electoral Democracy: No

Population: 31,700,000
Capital: Riyadh

Ten-Year Ratings Timeline For Year Under Review (Political Rights, Civil Liberties, Status)

Year Under Review	2007	2008	2009	2010	2011	2012	2013	2014	2015	2016
Rating	7,6,NF	7,6,NF	7,6,NF	7,6,NF	7,7,NF	7,7,NF	7,7,NF	7,7,NF	7,7NF	7,7,NF

Overview: Ruled by the Saud family since its founding in 1932, the Kingdom of Saudi Arabia restricts almost all political rights and civil liberties through a combination of oppressive laws and the use of force. No officials at the national level are elected. The regime extends some authority to clerics who follow the austere Wahhabi interpretation of Sunni Islam in exchange for affirmation of the monarchy's religious legitimacy. Ruling elites rely on extensive surveillance, the criminalization of dissent, appeals to sectarianism, and public spending supported by oil revenues to maintain power.

KEY DEVELOPMENTS IN 2016:

- In January, the regime executed one of the kingdom's most prominent Shiite Muslim clerics as part of its ongoing crackdown against the religious minority.
- More than 150 people were executed during 2016, the second consecutive year in which the total passed that threshold. Defendants are generally denied due process, and many are executed for crimes other than murder.
- In April, against a backdrop of low oil prices and a struggling economy, the deputy crown prince announced an economic reform package called Saudi Vision 2030, without promising any significant political reforms.
- As the Saudi military continued its controversial bombing campaign against rebel forces in neighboring Yemen, cross-border attacks by the rebels occasionally caused deaths and injuries in the kingdom.

EXECUTIVE SUMMARY

Beleaguered by a second full year of low oil prices, Saudi Arabia's leaders struggled to manage a weak economy in 2016. In January, Deputy Crown Prince Mohammed bin Salman al-Saud, son of King Salman bin Abdulaziz al-Saud, announced that the state was planning to privatize a minority stake in the national oil company; subsequent statements indicated that the sale would be held by 2018. In April, the prince mapped out an ambitious economic strategy called Saudi Vision 2030 that aimed to overhaul the country's economy, including by "Saudiizing" the labor force to reduce unemployment among citizens, diversifying away from oil, privatizing more of the state-controlled economy, and cutting state spending and subsidies. The plan did not address political reform or offer to expand heavily restricted political rights and civil liberties. Meanwhile, Saudi officials in November agreed to an oil production cut by the Organization of the Petroleum Exporting Countries (OPEC), the first in eight years, as part of a bid to shore up prices.

With significant logistical and political support from the United States and Britain, Saudi Arabia continued its destructive military campaign in neighboring Yemen, where groups loyal to Saudi-backed president Abd Rabbuh Mansur Hadi were locked in a civil war against Houthi rebels and allied forces linked to former president Ali Abdullah Saleh. Saudi leaders maintained that the Houthis, who sometimes launched raids or missile attacks across Saudi Arabia's southern border, were proxies for Shiite-ruled Iran, the kingdom's regional rival.

Saudi internal security forces continued their oppression of the Shiite religious minority. In January, the authorities executed a prominent Shiite cleric and outspoken critic of the regime, Nimr al-Nimr. Ali Mohammed al-Nimr, the cleric's nephew, remained on death row for his participation as a teenager in 2011 protests that led to clashes with security forces. In June, a Saudi court sentenced 14 Shiites to death for alleged attacks on security personnel during the same wave of protests, which the regime characterized as terrorism.

As in previous years, Saudi human rights and political activists were systematically persecuted and imprisoned in 2016. Despite its poor record, Saudi Arabia was reelected to its seat on the UN Human Rights Council in October. In a modest reform in April, the government announced that the religious police no longer had the authority to pursue or detain civilians, and that they could operate only during business hours, reporting violations to the civil police. The religious police had faced public criticism for abusive behavior in recent years.

POLITICAL RIGHTS: 3 / 40

A. Electoral Process: 0 / 12

The 1992 Basic Law declares that the Koran and the Sunna (the guidance set by the deeds and sayings of the prophet Muhammad) are the country's constitution. The cabinet, which is appointed by the king, passes legislation that becomes law once ratified by royal decree. The king also appoints the 150 members of the Majlis al-Shura (Consultative Council), who serve in an advisory capacity, for four-year terms. Limited elections for advisory councils at the municipal level were introduced in 2005, though these bodies exercise little real power. In municipal elections held in 2015, women were able to vote and stand as candidates for the first time—a right granted by a 2011 royal decree. Two-thirds of the seats on the 284 councils were open to voting, while the minister of municipal and rural affairs held responsibility for filling the remainder through appointment. Women won approximately 1 percent of contested seats.

In May 2016, King Salman announced significant changes to the cabinet. Most importantly, a series of moves resulted in the dismissal of longtime oil minister Ali al-Naimi. He was replaced by Khalid al-Faleh, chairman of the state oil company Aramco, who assumed control over a renamed Ministry of Energy, Industry, and Mineral Resources. The cabinet reshuffle signaled the king's support for the new economic strategy overseen by his son, Deputy Crown Prince Mohammed bin Salman, who is also the defense minister. The move also raised questions about whether the prince's rapid rise and influence would unsettle the line of succession. Interior Minister Mohammed bin Nayef, the current crown prince, is widely seen as a rival to Mohammed bin Salman, his younger cousin.

B. Political Pluralism and Participation: 0 / 16

Political parties are forbidden, and organized political opposition exists only outside the country. Political dissent is criminalized. Activists who challenge the kingdom's record on political inclusion or call for constitutional changes are treated harshly. Raef Badawi, a human rights activist and founder of the website Liberal Saudi Network, remained behind bars in 2016 after being sentenced in 2014 to 10 years in prison and 1,000 lashes for "insulting Islam." Badawi was subjected to a first round of flogging in early 2015, and a report that surfaced in October claimed that a second round was imminent. The kingdom's crackdown on one of the country's most prominent political rights organizations, the Saudi Civil and Political Rights Association (ACPRA), continued in 2016. In April ACPRA founding member Issa al-Hamid was sentenced to nine years in prison, extended later in 2016 to 11 years. In June his colleague and fellow ACPRA member Abdulaziz al-Shubaili was sentenced to eight years in prison. Several other ACPRA members remained imprisoned in 2016. In January Samar Badawi, wife of the imprisoned activist Waleed Abu al-Khair and sister of Raef Badawi, was briefly detained by police in Jeddah.

The Muslim Brotherhood, a Sunni Islamist political organization, and Hezbollah, the Lebanon-based and Iranian-backed Shiite militia group, have been designated as terrorist organizations in Saudi Arabia since 2014, reflecting official concerns about the domestic popularity of both entities, which are considered threats to the regime.

C. Functioning of Government: 1 / 12

The kingdom's few elected officials have little or no influence over national laws and policies. Corruption remains a significant problem, despite some earlier moves to hold certain officials accountable, and the functioning of government is largely opaque. Following a deadly stampede during the hajj in 2015, which drew international criticism of the infrastructure and safety measures provided by Saudi authorities, the government refused to amend its official death toll of 769, despite estimates by international news organizations that exceeded 2,400.

The Saudi state also remains notably opaque in its financial practices. Although the government generates massive revenue from the sale of oil, which it redistributes through social welfare programs and as patronage, little is known about its accounting or the various direct ways in which the state's wealth becomes a source of private privilege for the royal family and its clients. Anticipating ongoing economic pressure from low global oil prices, Deputy Crown Prince Mohammed bin Salman announced his reform plan, Saudi Vision 2030, in April 2016. The strategy is intended to reduce the kingdom's dependence on oil and, in the short term, begin dismantling long-standing elements of the welfare state as part of a push for greater austerity. Saudi Vision 2030, which also sought extensive privatization of government-owned sectors of the economy, to reduce youth unemployment, and to develop new industries, was considered largely aspirational by some analysts. Previous leaders had attempted to introduce similar measures, only to face political blowback and stubborn patterns of corruption. Meanwhile, Saudi Arabia agreed to a first round of oil production cuts among global oil producers in late November 2016, with the goal of bolstering prices and generating more revenue.

DISCRETIONARY POLITICAL RIGHTS QUESTION A: 2 / 4

In addition to drawing advice from the Consultative Council, the monarchy has a tradition of consulting with select members of Saudi society. However, the process is not equally open to all citizens. From the king to local governors, royal family officials periodically host meetings for citizens to air grievances and seek access to money or power. These meetings are irregular, and while they afford some citizens rare opportunities to meet with the powerful, the outcomes reinforce the personalized nature of authority.

CIVIL LIBERTIES: 7 / 60

D. Freedom of Expression and Belief: 3 / 16

The government tightly controls domestic media content and dominates regional print and satellite-television coverage, with members of the royal family owning major stakes in news outlets in multiple countries. Government officials have banned journalists and editors who publish articles deemed offensive to the religious establishment or the ruling authorities. A 2011 royal decree amended the press law to criminalize, among other things, any criticism of the country's grand mufti, the Council of Senior Religious Scholars, or government officials; violations can result in fines and forced closure of media outlets.

The regime has taken steps to limit the influence of online media, blocking access to large numbers of websites that are considered immoral or politically sensitive. A 2011 law requires all blogs and websites, or anyone posting news or commentary online, to have a license from the Ministry of Information or face fines and possible closure of the website.

Authorities continue to target writers and activists who use the internet to express their views. In December 2016, Issa al-Nukhaifi, an activist critical of corruption and the government's conduct of the war in Yemen, was arrested for his posts on Twitter.

Islam is the official religion, and all Saudis are required by law to be Muslims. A 2014 royal decree punishes atheism with up to 20 years in prison. The government prohibits the public practice of any religion other than Islam and restricts the religious practices of the Shiite and Sufi Muslim minority sects. The construction of Shiite mosques is constrained through licensing rules and prohibited outside of Eastern Province, where most Shiites live. Although the government recognizes the right of non-Muslims to worship in private, it does not always respect this right in practice.

Online commentary that touches on religion can be harshly punished. In February 2016, a Saudi court sentenced a man to 10 years in prison and 2,000 lashes for embracing atheism in postings on social media. In March, journalist Alaa Brinji was sentenced to five years in prison for insulting the regime and criticizing the country's crackdown on Shiites in Eastern Province.

Academic freedom is restricted, and informers monitor classrooms for compliance with curriculum rules, including a ban on teaching secular philosophy and religions other than Islam. Despite changes to textbooks in recent years, intolerance in the classroom remains a significant problem, as some educators continue to espouse discriminatory and hateful views of non-Muslims and Muslim minority sects.

Saudis are able to engage in some degree of private discussion on political and other topics, including criticism of certain aspects of government performance, both online and offline. However, severe criminal penalties deter more direct criticism of the regime and free discussion on topics like religion or the royal family.

E. Associational and Organizational Rights: 0 / 12

Freedoms of assembly and association are not upheld. The government frequently detains political activists who stage demonstrations or engage in other civic advocacy. While no massive protests have taken place in the kingdom, smaller demonstrations have become more common. The largest of these occur in Eastern Province. In 2016, protests broke out in the province after prominent Shiite cleric and political dissident Sheikh Nimr al-Nimr, who was arrested in 2012 for leading antigovernment demonstrations and calling for an end to sectarian discrimination, was executed in January. His nephew Ali Mohammed al-Nimr, arrested at age 17 in 2012 for participating in protests, also faced execution in 2016, but his sentence had yet to be carried out at year's end.

Saudi Arabia has no associations law and has historically approved licenses only for charitable organizations. No laws protect the rights to form independent labor unions, bargain collectively, or engage in strikes. Workers who engage in union activity are subject to dismissal or imprisonment.

F. Rule of Law: 2 / 16

The judiciary, which must coordinate its decisions with the executive branch, is not independent. A special commission of judicial experts writes law that serves as the foundation for verdicts in the court system, which is grounded in Sharia (Islamic law). While Saudi courts have historically relied on the Hanbali school of Islamic jurisprudence, the commission incorporates all four Sunni Muslim legal schools in drafting new guidelines.

Defendants' rights are poorly protected by law and not respected in practice. Detainees are often denied access to legal counsel during interrogation, and lengthy pretrial detention and detention without charge are common. Capital punishment, usually carried out by beheading, is applied to a wide range of crimes; juvenile offenders are not exempt from the penalty. According to international media reports, Saudi authorities carried out more than 150 executions in 2016.

The penal code bans torture, but allegations of torture by police and prison officials are common, and access to prisoners by independent human rights and legal organizations is strictly limited. A sweeping new antiterrorism law, which includes lengthy prison sentences for criticizing the monarchy or the government, went into effect in 2014. Among other provisions, it expanded the power of police to conduct raids against suspected antigovernment activity without judicial approval.

Local affiliates of the Islamic State (IS) militant group carried out several terrorist bombings and bombing attempts in 2016. Attacks on a Shiite mosque in Al-Ahsa in the Eastern Province that killed four people in January were attributed to IS. In July, a suicide bombing in Medina also killed four people. Two other attacks were attempted the same day in the Shiite community of Qatif and near the U.S. consulate in Jeddah. In May, security forces reportedly broke up an IS cell in a suburb of Mecca. Separately, Yemeni rebel forces continued to fire missiles and other ordnance into Saudi territory in 2016, killing small numbers of Saudi civilians.

Substantial prejudice against ethnic, religious, and national minorities prevails. Shiites, who make up 10 to 15 percent of the population, are underrepresented in senior government positions, and Shiite activism has faced repression by security forces. Shiites have also been subject to physical assaults by both state and nonstate actors.

G. Personal Autonomy and Individual Rights: 2 / 16

Freedom of movement is restricted in some cases. The government punishes activists and critics by limiting their ability to travel outside the country, and reform advocates are routinely stripped of their passports.

While a great deal of business activity is connected to members of the government, the ruling family, or other elite families, officials have given assurances that special industrial and commercial zones are free from interference by the royal family.

Women are not treated as equal members of society, and many laws discriminate against them. They are not permitted to drive cars, despite the advocacy efforts of a civic movement aimed at lifting the ban, and must obtain permission from a male guardian in order to travel within or outside of the country. According to prevailing interpretations of Sharia in Saudi Arabia, daughters generally receive half the inheritance awarded to their brothers, and the testimony of one man is equal to that of two women. Moreover, Saudi women seeking access to the courts must be represented by a male.

The religious police enforce a strict policy of gender segregation and often harass women, using physical punishment to ensure compliance with conservative standards of dress in public. However, an April 2016 government decree revoked the religious police's authority to pursue or arrest suspects or ask for their identification—meaning they must report alleged violations to regular police instead—and requires them to work only during specified office hours. In December, a Twitter user in Riyadh, Malak al-Shehri, posted a photo of herself on the street without the obligatory hijab or abaya. She was subsequently arrested for "violations of general morals."

Same-sex marriage is not legal. All sexual activity outside of marriage, including same-sex activity, is criminalized, and the death penalty can be applied in certain circumstances. A 2013 law defines and criminalizes domestic abuse, prescribing fines and up to a year in prison for perpetrators. However, according to analysis by Human Rights Watch, the law lacks clarity on enforcement mechanisms.

Education and economic rights for Saudi women have improved somewhat in recent years. More than half of the country's university students are now female, although they do not enjoy equal access to classes and facilities. Women gained the right to hold commercial licenses in 2004. In 2008, the Saudi Human Rights Commission established a women's branch to investigate cases of human rights violations against women and children, but it has not consistently carried out serious investigations or brought cases against violators.

A 2005 labor law that extended various protections and benefits to previously unregulated categories of workers also banned child labor and established a 75 percent quota for Saudi citizens in each company's workforce, though a series of government policies have since set more modest interim "Saudiization" goals due to the difficulty of reaching such a high target. Foreign workers—of whom there are more than seven million in the country, making up more than half of the active labor force—have historically enjoyed virtually no legal protections and remain vulnerable to trafficking and forced labor, primarily through the exploitation of the visa-sponsorship system. In 2014, the Ministry of Labor ruled that expatriate workers who are not paid their salaries for more than three consecutive months are free to switch their work sponsors without approval. A number of amendments to the labor law that went into effect in 2015 contained broader rights and protections for workers in the private sector. The labor law does not apply to household workers, who remain particularly vulnerable to exploitation.

Senegal

Political Rights Rating: 2
Civil Liberties Rating: 2
Freedom Rating: 2.0
Freedom Status: Free
Electoral Democracy: Yes

Population: 14,800,000
Capital: Dakar

Ten-Year Ratings Timeline For Year Under Review (Political Rights, Civil Liberties, Status)

Year Under Review	2007	2008	2009	2010	2011	2012	2013	2014	2015	2016
Rating	2,3,PF	3,3,PF	3,3,PF	3,3,PF	3,3,PF	2,3,F	2,2,F	2,2 F	2,2,F	2,2,F

Overview: Senegal is one of Africa's most stable democracies and has undergone two peaceful transfers of power between rival parties since 2000. The government's respect for civil liberties has improved over time, and the country is known for its independent media and public engagement in free expression and debate. Ongoing challenges include corruption in government, weaknesses in the rule of law, and inadequate protections for the rights of women and LGBT (lesbian, gay, bisexual, and transgender) people.

KEY DEVELOPMENTS IN 2016:

- In March, referendum voters approved constitutional amendments that reduced the presidential term from seven years to five, effective after President Macky Sall's current term.
- In May, former Chadian dictator Hissène Habré was convicted and sentenced to life in prison for crimes against humanity, torture, and sex crimes at the Extraordinary African Chambers in Dakar. The special tribunal was created to try Habré, who had lived in Senegal since he was overthrown in 1990.
- In June, President Sall commuted the prison term of Karim Wade, the son of former president Abdoulaye Wade, who had been sentenced to six years in prison for illicit enrichment in 2015. Though he was released early, Wade was still required to pay a fine of $229 million.

EXECUTIVE SUMMARY

Senegalese citizens voted "yes" on a March 2016 constitutional referendum that, among other amendments, reduced presidential terms from seven to five years, not counting President Sall's current term.

Corruption in government remained the subject of lively public debate. Karim Wade, the son of former president Abdoulaye Wade, had been sentenced in 2015 to six years in prison for illicit enrichment after a controversial trial at the Court of Repression of Illicit Enrichment (CREI); human rights groups had criticized the court for due process violations including prolonged pretrial detention. In June 2016, President Sall commuted the remainder of Wade's sentence but left him responsible for paying a $229 million fine.

Meanwhile, Sall's administration faced allegations of nepotism and opacity. In May, the National Anti-Corruption Commission (OFNAC) published its first annual report, which included critiques of officials close to Sall. The commission's head, Nafi Ngom Keïta, was fired in July. The government said she had leaked confidential state data and attempted to manipulate public opinion, but her supporters claimed that her firing was retaliatory. In August, Sall fired the country's chief inspector of taxes and customs, Ousmane Sonko, after Sonko voiced concerns about corruption in the government. Sonko, who was also the head of a political party, was accused of violating rules of professional discretion, a charge he denied. In October, the president's brother, Aliou Sall, resigned from the Senegalese branch of an international corporation that held stakes in oil and gas fields in the country, following criticism about the impropriety of his position.

While freedoms of expression and assembly remained relatively robust, they faced ongoing pressure. In February and March, authorities attempted to punish unfavorable coverage of the constitutional referendum by the media outlet Walfadjri, temporarily detaining a journalist, demanding recordings of a particular television segment, and trying unsuccessfully to cut the outlet's broadcast signal. The state has considerable discretion to prohibit or control public assemblies, and officials banned or rerouted a number of demonstrations in 2016. In February, the authorities prohibited a proposed rally against the constitutional referendum.

The rule of law was generally respected during the year, though the judiciary is exposed to executive and other influences, and marginalized groups are subject to discrimination. Same-sex sexual activity is a crime punishable by up to five years in prison. In March, on a university campus in Dakar, a male student accused of making sexual advances to another male student was chased and threatened by a violent mob. Violence against women, trafficking in persons, and forced begging by Quranic school students are long-standing problems; the government announced a new crackdown on child begging in 2016. Conditions for women have gradually improved in some respects. For example, rates of female genital mutilation are thought to have declined over time due in part to campaigns to discourage the practice.

POLITICAL RIGHTS: 32 / 40 (− 1)
A. Electoral Process: 11 / 12
B. Political Pluralism and Participation: 13 / 16
C. Functioning of Government: 8 / 12 (− 1)

CIVIL LIBERTIES: 46 / 60 (+ 1)
D. Freedom of Expression and Belief: 15 / 16
E. Associational and Organizational Rights: 10 / 12
F. Rule of Law: 10 / 16
G. Personal Autonomy and Individual Rights: 11 / 16 (+ 1)

This country report has been abridged for *Freedom in the World 2017*. For background information on political rights and civil liberties in Senegal, see *Freedom in the World 2016*.

Serbia

Political Rights Rating: 3 ↓
Civil Liberties Rating: 2
Freedom Rating: 2.5
Freedom Status: Free
Electoral Democracy: Yes

Population: 7,100,000
Capital: Belgrade

Ratings Change: Serbia's political rights rating declined from 2 to 3 due to serious irregularities in the 2016 parliamentary elections.

Ten-Year Ratings Timeline For Year Under Review (Political Rights, Civil Liberties, Status)

Year Under Review	2007	2008	2009	2010	2011	2012	2013	2014	2015	2016
Rating	3,2,F	3,2,F	2,2,F	2,2,F	2,2,F	2,2,F	2,2,F	2,2,F	2,2,F	3,2,F

Overview: Serbia is a parliamentary republic in which political parties may form freely and compete in generally credible elections. However, political rights and civil liberties have eroded in recent years under Prime Minister Aleksandar Vučić and his Serbian Progressive Party (SNS), which took power in 2012. The government has drawn repeated criticism for imposing various forms of political pressure on independent media and civil society organizations. Nevertheless, the country has moved forward in its bid to join the European Union (EU).

KEY DEVELOPMENTS IN 2016:

- The governing SNS won snap parliamentary elections in April, but took 27 fewer seats than in the last elections in 2014, and the allied Socialist Party of Serbia (SPS) lost 15 seats. Left- and right-wing parties not seated in the previous parliament made gains.
- Voting was rerun at 15 polling stations due to reports of electoral irregularities and claims by the opposition that the SNS had stuffed ballot boxes, while international monitors raised a number of other concerns.
- Following the SNS's strong performance in elections for the legislature of the autonomous province of Vojvodina, a number of journalists were dismissed from the provincial public broadcaster in what many described as a politically motivated purge.
- In December a former police spokesman was acquitted of endangering members of a nongovernmental organization (NGO) that called attention to Serbian involvement in the Yugoslav wars of the 1990s. He had suggested in a social media post that members of the group should be attacked.

EXECUTIVE SUMMARY

In January, Prime Minister Vučić called snap parliamentary elections, which were held in April—the country's third such polls in four years. The SNS won the most seats, and the allied SPS, led by Foreign Minister Ivica Dačić, finished a distant second. However, the parties together lost 42 seats in the parliament, with the far-right Serbian Radical Party (SRS), the conservative and Euroskeptic Dveri–Democratic Party of Serbia, and the progressive Enough Is Enough grouping making up much of the difference. Vučić did not present a cabinet until August, leaving normal government activity at a near-standstill for the first half of the year.

Both domestic observers and international monitors expressed concern about the conduct of the elections. Voting was rerun at 15 polling stations amid reports of electoral irregularities and claims by the opposition that the SNS had stuffed ballot boxes. Opposition parties questioned the independence of the Republic Electoral Commission (RIK), and international monitors criticized its procedures for filing election-related complaints. The international monitors also expressed concern about voting pressure on public-sector workers by the SNS.

Vučić's government continued its campaign against critical and independent media in 2016, notably by hosting an exhibition at a Belgrade art gallery in which media outlets that had criticized the government were depicted as liars. Separately, following the SNS's strong performance in elections to the Vojvodina provincial assembly, a number of journalists, including top editors, were dismissed from the public broadcaster Radio Television Vojvodina (RTV), in what many called a politically motivated purge.

NGOs that have taken critical stances toward the government or addressed sensitive or controversial topics faced pressure during the year. In January, a brick was thrown through the window of a building where several NGO offices are located. In March, the director of the Center for Euro-Atlantic Studies was placed under police protection in response to repeated threats.

POLITICAL RIGHTS: 29 / 40 (− 1)

A. Electoral Process: 9 / 12 (− 1)

The Serbian National Assembly is a unicameral, 250-seat legislature, with deputies elected to four-year terms according to closed party lists in a proportional representation vote. The assembly elects the prime minister. The president, a largely ceremonial post, is popularly elected for up to two five-year terms. In 2012, Tomislav Nikolić, a former SNS leader, defeated incumbent president and Democratic Party (DS) leader Boris Tadić in a presidential runoff, taking 51 percent of the vote. The next presidential election was scheduled for 2017.

In January 2016, Prime Minister Vučić called snap parliamentary elections. While he cited a need for a new government with a full four-year term in order to implement reforms that would prepare the country for EU accession, critics characterized the move as an effort by the SNS, which had posted a landslide victory in 2014 polls, to further consolidate political power. The snap elections were eventually set to take place in April, alongside local and regional elections that were being held according to schedule, prompting speculation that Vučić sought to use his national campaign effort to bolster the SNS in local races.

While the SNS and its coalition partners won the largest portion of the vote in the 2016 polls—enabling Vučić to remain prime minister—they lost 27 seats in the parliament, falling from 158 to 131. Foreign Minister Dačić's SPS and its allies took 29 seats, 15 fewer than they had held before the polls. Flagging support for the SNS and SPS allowed for gains by right-wing and progressive parties that had not held seats in the previous parliament. The far-right Serbian Radical Party (SRS), led by Vojislav Šešelj—who was acquitted of war crimes by a UN tribunal just weeks before the elections—placed third with 22 seats, returning to the parliament after a four-year absence. The conservative and Euroskeptic Dveri–Democratic Party of Serbia, which supports stronger ties between Serbia and Russia, won 13 seats. The progressive Enough Is Enough movement, founded by former economy minister Saša Radulović in 2014, took 16 seats.

A coalition led by the DS won 16 seats, down from 19 in the previous parliament. The pro-EU Alliance for a Better Serbia bloc, led by former president Tadić, won 13 seats, down from 18. The remaining seats went to smaller parties representing ethnic minorities. The SNS performed well in local elections, particularly in Vojvodina, where the DS had previously enjoyed broad support. Turnout was 56 percent, roughly the same as for the 2012 and 2014 parliamentary polls. After months of negotiations, Vučić presented his cabinet in August, which the parliament subsequently approved.

Both domestic observers and international monitors expressed concern about the conduct of the elections. In their aftermath, leaders of several opposition parties with widely varying political platforms banded together to accuse the SNS of rigging the polls, including by orchestrating the submission of ballots for dead or nonexistent people and otherwise tampering with ballot boxes. They also called into question the independence of the RIK, which is responsible for administering elections, noting that its president was an SNS member. Election observers from the Organization for Security and Co-operation in Europe (OSCE) noted pressure on public-sector workers to vote for the ruling party; an outsized presence at official events during the campaign by the SNS and SPS, which blurred the line between state and party activities; and self-censorship among media outlets, which was attributed to government pressure and effectively narrowed the coverage available to voters.

The RIK received dozens of appeals for reruns at various polling stations due to electoral irregularities. It ultimately upheld 15 of them. (The reruns resulted in the Dveri–Democratic Party of Serbia crossing the 5 percent threshold for representation in the parliament.) OSCE monitors criticized the RIK in a postelection report, which found that the 24-hour time period to file complaints about electoral violations was too short. It added that monitors had also received reports of citizens who wanted to file complaints, but either feared retribution or had no confidence that the relevant investigatory and judicial bodies would act on them. Courts had limited the RIK's authority in ways that created inefficiencies in addressing such complaints, the report noted.

Political parties must submit candidate lists to the commission at least 15 days ahead of a scheduled election, and the body has the right to return lists if they are not in compliance with electoral rules.

B. Political Pluralism and Participation: 13 / 16

Political parties may be established freely and can typically operate without encountering formal restrictions. Serbian voters are generally able to vote for the party they prefer without facing intimidation or coercion, though the ruling SNS was criticized for pressuring public-sector workers ahead of the 2016 polls. In addition, a group of DS supporters were attacked in March while participating in a voter outreach campaign in Belgrade. One person was injured, and several suspects were later arrested.

Since the ouster of authoritarian leader Slobodan Milošević in 2000, Serbian politics have featured orderly transfers of power between competing parties. In 2014, the landslide victory of the SNS bloc gave the party control of the executive and legislative branches of government—a rare occurrence in the usually contested political sphere. While the SNS retained control in 2016, it lost ground to smaller parties in the parliament.

The country's 5 percent electoral threshold for parliamentary representation does not apply to parties representing ethnic minorities. Groups centered on the ethnic Albanian, Bosniak, Slovak, and Hungarian communities won a total of 10 seats in the 2016 elections. Nevertheless, ethnic minorities have a relatively muted voice in Serbian politics in practice. No party representing the interests of the Romany minority ran in the 2016 elections.

Political parties adhered to laws requiring mixed-gender party lists ahead of the 2016 polls. Vučić's government included for the first time a member of Serbia's LGBT (lesbian, gay, bisexual, and transgender) community, Ana Brnabić, who became minister of public administration and local self-government.

C. Functioning of Government: 7 / 12

While freely elected officials are generally able to determine and implement laws and policies without interference, corruption remains a problem in many areas, including the security, education, housing, and labor sectors, as well as in privatization processes and the judiciary. The Anti-Corruption Council, made up of six members, was established in 2001 to handle corruption complaints. Other entities that combat corruption include the Anti-Corruption Agency and the ombudsman, known as the Protector of Citizens of Serbia. However, these institutions lack a track record of successful investigations and prosecutions. The ombudsman has faced attacks in progovernment media in connection with charges he brought against members of the military police in 2015.

Vučić's government has received sustained criticism for a lack of transparency surrounding the Belgrade Waterfront Project, an ambitious bid to develop property along the Sava River. Among other complaints, critics note that authorities unilaterally tapped a United Arab Emirates–based developer as the project's primary funder, and that plans for financing the project are generally unclear. Serbia's commissioner for information and personal data protection received threats after calling for an investigation of the demolition of homes in the capital's Savamala district, where the Belgrade Waterfront Project is to be constructed. The April demolitions were carried out at night by masked men who allegedly mistreated onlookers.

CIVIL LIBERTIES: 47 / 60 (− 1)

D. Freedom of Expression and Belief: 14 / 16

The government has shown growing hostility toward independent and critical media in recent years. Investigative journalists or those critical of the government frequently encounter aggressive rhetoric from senior officials, and are frequently smeared in progovernment media as criminals or members of foreign intelligence agencies. In July 2016, the government hosted an exhibition at a Belgrade art gallery in which media outlets that had criticized Vučić and his allies were depicted as liars.

While there is no official censorship in Serbia, many media outlets are thought to be aligned with specific political parties, and the public broadcaster Radio Television of Serbia (RTS) remains subject to heavy government influence. Following the SNS's strong performance in elections for the provincial assembly in Vojvodina in 2016, a number of journalists, including top editors, were dismissed from RTV, the provincial public broadcaster, in what many described as a politically motivated purge.

Changes to the criminal code in 2012 removed defamation as a criminal offense, though the code retains provisions criminalizing insult. Funds for media advertising are controlled by a small number of economic and political actors. Media ownership is not fully transparent, and ownership of large, influential print media outlets in Serbia is often unclear.

In January 2016, it was reported that SNS lawmakers had introduced legislation that would have prevented photographers from obtaining copyright protection for their work. The bill was abandoned after photojournalists protested.

The constitution guarantees freedom of religion, which is generally respected in practice. However, given the legacy of socialism, many citizens remain secular. Academic freedom is generally upheld, though accusations that politicians had plagiarized academic papers have raised questions about the quality and integrity of the Serbian education system.

The U.S. State Department has expressed concern about "credible reports" that Serbian authorities monitor private online communications without first obtaining the necessary legal permission to do so, which could affect citizens' right to open and free private discussion.

E. Associational and Organizational Rights: 10 / 12 (− 1)

Serbians enjoy freedoms of assembly and association. In 2016, for the third consecutive year, the government permitted a parade in support of LGBT rights. It proceeded without incident in September, with riot police providing security and some government officials participating. At least half a dozen large demonstrations against the Belgrade Waterfront Project also took place during the year.

Foreign and domestic NGOs generally operate freely, though those that have taken openly critical stances toward the government or address sensitive or controversial topics have faced pressure. Members of Women in Black, an NGO that is critical of the legacy of Serbian involvement in the Yugoslav wars of the 1990s, are frequently harassed by both civilians and police. In December 2016, former antiterrorist police spokesman Radomir Počuča was acquitted of endangering the group's members; he had been charged in connection with a 2014 post on Facebook in which he suggested that they should be attacked. Separately, in January, a brick was thrown through the window of Belgrade's Human Rights House, where several NGO offices are located. And in March, the director of the Center for

Euro-Atlantic Studies was placed under police protection as a result of repeated threats against her. Many NGOs receive international funding.

Workers may join unions, engage in collective bargaining, and strike, but the International Confederation of Trade Unions has reported that organizing efforts and strikes are substantially restricted in practice. There are numerous professional associations in the country, such as the Journalists' Association of Serbia (UNS) and the Judges' Association of Serbia (JAS).

F. Rule of Law: 10 / 16

The judiciary operates independently, but endemic problems continue to plague the court system, including corruption, lengthy trials, and obstacles to equal treatment, such as high fees and a lack of uniform access to legal aid. In a 2016 report, the Anti-Corruption Council noted some small improvements, citing more complete staffing of courts and progress in some old cases, but concluded that there was little transparency in the judicial system and that the government "continues to violate the presumption of innocence."

Chief war crimes prosecutor Vladimir Vukčević resigned his position in January 2016, and the post remained vacant at year's end. While eight people were indicted for war crimes in 2016, no prosecutions can move forward until the position is filled.

Prisons generally meet international standards, though overcrowding is an issue, and health care facilities are often inadequate. Radical right-wing organizations and violent sports fans who target ethnic minorities and others remain a serious concern.

In 2015, Serbia became a key transit country for refugees and migrants trying to reach northern Europe. In general, the authorities were praised for their handling of a difficult situation, but the burden on the country increased after Hungary closed its border with Serbia that fall. Thousands of refugees aiming to seek asylum in the EU states to the north remained stuck in squalid camps in Serbia in 2016.

The treatment of LGBT people is problematic, with threats and attacks often going unsolved despite a law banning discrimination based on sexual orientation and gender identity. While public attitudes are changing as more LGBT people decide to live openly, Serbian society is still somewhat resistant to the trend. Increasingly tolerant actions by the government appear to be influencing those holding more conservative views.

G. Personal Autonomy and Individual Rights: 13 / 16

Serbian citizens are free to choose their employment and education, and have the right to travel. Many of these choices are constrained by socioeconomic factors, such as slow economic growth and high unemployment rates. Serbian citizens have been able to enter the Schengen area of the EU without a visa since 2010.

In general, property rights are respected, but adjudication of disputes is slow. In 2016, a number of homes were demolished under highly questionable circumstances to make way for the Belgrade Waterfront Project. Serbian citizens can start their own businesses, although bureaucratic obstacles make the process difficult. There are instances of nepotism in higher education and employment.

Women enjoy legal equality with men as indicated in the Serbian constitution. There are several antidiscrimination and gender equality laws in place. According to electoral regulations, women must account for at least 33 percent of a party's candidate list, and women currently hold 38 percent of seats in the parliament. However, women face undue challenges on the job market, and those of childbearing age are often illegally asked if they plan to start a family. Domestic violence remains a problem.

Migrants and refugees passing through the country are particularly susceptible to sexual or labor exploitation, as are Romany children. Efforts to address human trafficking have tapered off in recent years, in part because government attention has been redirected toward management of the refugee crisis. In 2016, officials established a new office within the national police force intended to streamline antitrafficking efforts, but it has not been sufficiently staffed.

Seychelles

Political Rights Rating: 3
Civil Liberties Rating: 3
Freedom Rating: 3.0
Freedom Status: Partly Free
Electoral Democracy: Yes

Population: 93,000
Capital: Victoria

Ten-Year Ratings Timeline For Year Under Review (Political Rights, Civil Liberties, Status

Year Under Review	2007	2008	2009	2010	2011	2012	2013	2014	2015	2016
Rating	3,3,PF	3,3,PF	3,3,PF	3,3,PF	3,3,PF	3,3,PF	3,3,PF	3,3,PF	3,3,PF	3,3,PF

The country or territory displayed here received scores but no narrative report for this edition of *Freedom in the World*.

Sierra Leone

Political Rights Rating: 3
Civil Liberties Rating: 3
Freedom Rating: 3.0
Freedom Status: Partly Free
Electoral Democracy: Yes

Population: 6,600,000
Capital: Freetown

Ten-Year Ratings Timeline For Year Under Review (Political Rights, Civil Liberties, Status)

Year Under Review	2007	2008	2009	2010	2011	2012	2013	2014	2015	2016
Rating	3,3,PF	3,3,PF	3,3,PF	3,3,PF	3,3,PF	2,3,F	3,3,PF	3,3,PF	3,3,PF	3,3,PF

Overview: Sierra Leone has held three rounds of national elections since the end of its civil war in 2002, including one that resulted in an orderly transfer of power to the opposition in 2007. However, opposition parties have faced police violence and restrictions on assembly. Government corruption is pervasive, and the work of journalists is hampered by the threat of defamation charges. Other long-standing concerns include gender-based violence, child marriage, and female genital mutilation (FGM).

KEY DEVELOPMENTS IN 2016:

- Sierra Leone was finally declared free of the Ebola virus in March 2016, after a series of new cases prompted the withdrawal of a similar declaration in November 2015.

- Freedom of movement improved during the year due to the lifting of restrictions meant to curb the spread of Ebola.
- Police fired tear gas and live bullets to break up some protests, including an independence day event organized by the main opposition party in April.

EXECUTIVE SUMMARY

The World Health Organization declared Sierra Leone to be free of the Ebola virus in March 2016, marking the end of a devastating outbreak that took hold in 2014. Already one of the world's poorest countries before the epidemic, Sierra Leone faced the difficult task of rebuilding its economy amid the social and political challenges associated with rapid population growth and high youth unemployment.

The country continued to struggle with rampant corruption in government. In recent years, the Sierra Leone Anti-Corruption Commission (ACC) has made some progress toward uncovering corruption among high-level officials, but it has a poor prosecutorial record, especially in trials involving President Ernest Bai Koroma's friends, family, and political allies.

The opposition faced some restrictions on its activities in 2016, raising concerns about the campaign environment ahead of national elections in early 2018. In April, the opposition Sierra Leone People's Party (SLPP) was denied a permit to march in Freetown on independence day, leading to clashes in which the police fired live rounds and tear gas at demonstrators. About 30 people were arrested, and several received jail sentences of six months; one received a nine-month term. Also that month, the SLPP cast doubt on the credibility of newly released provisional results of the 2015 census, which showed major population increases in strongholds of the ruling All People's Congress (APC) party, though UN agencies reportedly endorsed the results.

Journalists and social media users risked short-term arrest and other reprisals for critical coverage or commentary. For example, in July, a radio station manager was temporarily forced into hiding after receiving threatening telephone calls over the station's reporting on floods associated with illegal mining in the Kono district. Separately, at least two people were killed in August when police opened fire on protesters opposed to the relocation of a local youth center. While a police complaints board investigated the incident, no charges were reported.

Weak protection of women's rights remained a prominent problem during the year. In March, President Koroma rejected a bill passed unanimously by parliament that would have legalized abortion at up to 12 weeks of pregnancy under any circumstances and up to 24 weeks under special circumstances. In August, the death of a teenage girl during an FGM procedure led to the arrest of four people involved in the incident and renewed calls to ban the practice, which had been temporarily suspended in connection with the Ebola crisis.

POLITICAL RIGHTS: 28 / 40

A. Electoral Process: 10 / 12

B. Political Pluralism and Participation: 11 / 16

C. Functioning of Government: 7 / 12

CIVIL LIBERTIES: 38 / 60 (+ 1)

D. Freedom of Expression and Belief: 12 / 16

E. Associational and Organizational Rights: 7 / 12

F. Rule of Law: 9 / 16
G. Personal Autonomy and Individual Rights: 10 / 16 (+ 1)

This country report has been abridged for *Freedom in the World 2017*. For background information on political rights and civil liberties in Sierra Leone, see *Freedom in the World 2016*.

Singapore

Political Rights Rating: 4
Civil Liberties Rating: 4
Freedom Rating: 4.0
Freedom Status: Partly Free
Electoral Democracy: No

Population: 5,600,000
Capital: Singapore

Ten-Year Ratings Timeline For Year Under Review (Political Rights, Civil Liberties, Status)

Year Under Review	2007	2008	2009	2010	2011	2012	2013	2014	2015	2016
Rating	5,4,PF	5,4,PF	5,4,PF	5,4,PF	4,4,PF	4,4,PF	4,4,PF	4,4,PF	4,4,PF	4,4,PF

Overview: Singapore's parliamentary political system has been dominated by the ruling People's Action Party (PAP) and the family of current prime minister Lee Hsien Loong since 1959. The electoral and legal framework that the PAP has constructed allows for some political pluralism and considerable economic prosperity, but it effectively limits opportunities for the growth of credible opposition parties and constrains freedoms of expression, assembly, and association.

KEY DEVELOPMENTS IN 2016:
- In November, Parliament approved constitutional changes that set new candidacy requirements for presidential elections. Critics said the revisions would block the candidacy of a government critic who had narrowly lost the last presidential race in 2011.
- The courts continued hand down jail terms for critical online speech, with defendants in at least two prominent cases pleading guilty during the year.

EXECUTIVE SUMMARY
Government-backed constitutional amendments adopted by parliament in November 2016 tightened the eligibility rules for presidential candidates ahead of the next election for head of state, expected in 2017. One change established that none of Singapore's three main ethnic groupings—Malays, Chinese, and Indians or others—may be excluded from the presidency for more than five consecutive terms. Since the office has been held by ethnic Indian or Chinese presidents for the past five terms, the next president would apparently have to be a Malay. Critics of the measure noted that this would exclude Tan Cheng Bock, a government critic who had narrowly lost the 2011 race.

Another revision included in the package will require that presidential candidates from the private sector—as opposed to senior officials with at least three years of service—have experience leading a company with at least S$500 million ($370 million) in shareholder equity, up from S$100 million in paid-up capital. The amendments would also grant greater oversight powers to the Council of Presidential Advisers, particularly with respect to the country's financial reserves.

The prime minister in January had proposed additional constitutional changes that would increase the minimum number of opposition representatives in Parliament from 9 to 12, strengthen the voting powers of the opposition representatives who are appointed to meet that minimum figure, and raise the number of single-member constituencies at the expense of group constituencies. However, these proposals had yet to be adopted at year's end.

Although Singapore is often praised for a perceived lack of corruption, transparency and accountability remained concerns. Ministers in the government can serve in several capacities simultaneously, and legislators often serve on the boards of private companies, including as chairpersons, which creates conflicts of interest. Singapore was the fourth-worst-ranked country in the *Economist*'s 2016 "crony-capitalism index," which aims to measure the degree to which accumulation of private wealth depends on political connections.

Bloggers increasingly risk civil suits or criminal charges in connection with their work. The founders of a news portal that had been closed down in 2015, Ai Takagi and Yang Kaiheng, were sentenced to 10 months and 8 months in prison in March and June, respectively, after pleading guilty to sedition charges. In September, 17-year-old blogger Amos Yee Pang Sang was sentenced to six weeks in prison after pleading guilty to wounding religious feelings; he had received a similar penalty in 2015. Yee sought political asylum in the United States in December.

POLITICAL RIGHTS: 19 / 40

A. Electoral Process: 4 / 12

B. Political Pluralism and Participation: 8 / 16

C. Functioning of Government: 7 / 12

CIVIL LIBERTIES: 32 / 60

D. Freedom of Expression and Belief: 9 / 16

E. Associational and Organizational Rights: 4 / 12

F. Rule of Law: 7 / 16

G. Personal Autonomy and Individual Rights: 12 / 16

This country report has been abridged for *Freedom in the World 2017*. For background information on political rights and civil liberties in Singapore, see *Freedom in the World 2016*.

Slovakia

Political Rights Rating: 1
Civil Liberties Rating: 1
Freedom Rating: 1.0
Freedom Status: Free
Electoral Democracy: Yes

Population: 5,400,000
Capital: Bratislava

Ten-Year Ratings Timeline For Year Under Review (Political Rights, Civil Liberties, Status)

Year Under Review	2007	2008	2009	2010	2011	2012	2013	2014	2015	2016
Rating	1,1,F	1,1,F	1,1,F	1,1,F	1,1,F	1,1,F	1,1,F	1,1,F	1,1,F	1,1,F

Overview: Slovakia's parliamentary system ensures regular multiparty elections and peaceful transfers of power between rival parties. While civil liberties are generally protected, democratic institutions are hampered by cronyism and political corruption, entrenched discrimination against the Romany minority, and growing political hostility toward potential migrants and refugees who could augment Slovakia's tiny Muslim population. Such concerns have fueled the rise of right-wing nationalist parties in recent years.

KEY DEVELOPMENTS IN 2016:

- The ruling party, Direction–Social Democracy (Smer-SD), lost its outright majority in March parliamentary elections and formed a coalition with two other parties, including the nationalist Slovak People's Party (SNS). A party led by the neo-Nazi Marián Kotleba entered the parliament with 8 percent of the vote.
- New corruption allegations against Interior Minister Robert Kaliňák, involving links to a businessman facing tax fraud charges, sparked months of protests and a failed no-confidence motion against Kaliňák and Prime Minister Robert Fico in September. In a positive step in October, the parliament adopted a law to block shell companies from involvement in the public procurement process.
- Throughout the year, Fico and other government officials characterized Muslim migrants as a threat to European security. The parliament voted in November to increase the membership threshold, from 20,000 to 50,000, for religious groups seeking official recognition or state benefits, in what was seen as an effort to prevent future registration of Muslim groups. The president vetoed the measure in December, returning it to the parliament for reconsideration.

EXECUTIVE SUMMARY

Slovakia held elections for the 150-seat unicameral parliament in March 2016. The ruling Smer-SD secured 49 seats, losing its parliamentary majority, while the liberal center-right Freedom and Solidarity (SaS) placed second with 21 seats, and the conservative Ordinary People and Independent Personalities (OLANO–NOVA) took 19. Most-Híd (Bridge), which advocates better cooperation between the country's ethnic Hungarian minority and ethnic Slovak majority, took 11 seats.

Two far-right parties fared well, apparently benefiting from the government's warnings that Slovakia risked being overrun by Muslim refugees. The nationalist SNS won 15 seats, while the People's Party–Our Slovakia (LSNS), led by neo-Nazi regional governor Marián Kotleba, took 14 seats. The new parties We Are Family, led by wealthy businessman Boris

Kollár, and Siet (Network), headed by prominent conservative lawyer Radoslav Procházka, ran on anticorruption platforms and captured 11 and 10 seats, respectively.

Negotiations on a new government eventually yielded a four-party coalition composed of Smer-SD, SNS, Siet, and Most-Híd. Siet subsequently split and began to lose members, dropping out of the coalition in August.

Although Slovakia assumed the presidency of the European Union (EU) for the first time in July, Prime Minister Fico continued to push back strongly against the EU's mandatory refugee resettlement quotas, finding common ground with the leaders of neighboring Poland and Hungary. In November, Slovakia presented the European Council with an alternative plan for resettling migrants. Throughout the year, the government used anti-Muslim and anti-immigrant rhetoric to underscore its stance against perceived threats to Slovakia's sovereignty, security, and "values."

In October, the parliament voted to impose new rules on the conduct of deputies during parliamentary sessions, including time limits on speeches and a ban on leaflets and audiovisual presentations. The speaker will be allowed to launch disciplinary proceedings against unruly deputies. President Andrej Kiska initially vetoed the legislation on the grounds that it was aimed at restricting the effective operation of the opposition, but the parliament overrode the veto.

Relations between the government and critical media outlets remained tense. Fico made headlines in November by calling some reporters "dirty, anti-Slovak prostitutes" following reports on possible corruption in state procurements. Journalists in the country continued to face the threat of criminal penalties for defamation and Holocaust denial.

Other corruption allegations dogged current and former public officials in 2016. Marek Gajdoš, head of the long-running "Gorilla file" investigation, stepped down in October, citing "intolerable" pressure by his superiors. He asserted that most of the allegations in the file—a leaked document on state surveillance of allegedly corrupt relationships between politicians and prominent businessmen—have turned out to be accurate, despite authorities' reluctance to validate the material's authenticity.

A stalemate between the president and parliament over the appointment of Constitutional Court judges persisted, leaving the 13-member court with three vacant seats.

POLITICAL RIGHTS: 36 / 40

A. Electoral Process: 12 / 12

B. Political Pluralism and Participation: 15 / 16

C. Functioning of Government: 9 / 12

CIVIL LIBERTIES: 53 / 60

D. Freedom of Expression and Belief: 15 / 16

E. Associational and Organizational Rights: 12 / 12

F. Rule of Law: 12 / 16

G. Personal Autonomy and Individual Rights: 14 / 16

This country report has been abridged for *Freedom in the World 2017*. For background information on political rights and civil liberties in Slovakia, see *Freedom in the World 2016*.

Slovenia

Political Rights Rating: 1
Civil Liberties Rating: 1
Freedom Rating: 1.0
Freedom Status: Free
Electoral Democracy: Yes

Population: 2,100,000
Capital: Ljubljana

Ten-Year Ratings Timeline For Year Under Review (Political Rights, Civil Liberties, Status)

Year Under Review	2007	2008	2009	2010	2011	2012	2013	2014	2015	2016
Rating	1,1,F	1,1,F	1,1,F	1,1,F	1,1,F	1,1,F	1,1,F	1,1,F	1,1,F	1,1,F

Overview: Slovenia is a parliamentary republic with a freely elected government, and political rights and civil liberties are generally respected. A handful of harsh media laws, including one criminalizing defamation, occasionally limit press freedom.

KEY DEVELOPMENTS IN 2016:

- In April, the National Assembly passed a law allowing same-sex couples to enter partnerships that grant them most of the same rights as married couples.
- Also in April, the government announced plans to construct a new prison facility by 2020, in order to ease persistent overcrowding.
- Noting its satisfaction with the process, the Council of Europe in May ended its supervision of damage payments the European Court of Human Rights (ECHR) had ordered Slovenia to pay to a group of people known as "the erased." They had been removed from official records after failing to apply for citizenship or permanent residency following Slovenian independence, losing some rights as a result.

EXECUTIVE SUMMARY

Slovenia's National Assembly in April approved a new law that granted people entering same-sex partnerships most of the same rights conferred by marriage. However, the law did not grant same-sex couples the right to adopt children or undergo in-vitro fertilization procedures, and marriage is still legally defined as a union between a man and a woman.

While prison conditions meet international standards, overcrowding has been a problem. To address it, the government announced in April that it is building a new prison facility, to be completed by 2020.

In May, the Committee of Ministers of the Council of Europe officially closed the examination of Kurić v. Slovenia, known as "the erased" case, saying it was satisfied that Slovenia fulfilled its obligation to pay compensation to the victims as demanded by the ECHR. The examination's closure represented a major milestone in Slovenia's attempts to address of decades-long violations of the rights of so-called erased people, who were removed from official registers after failing to apply for citizenship or residency after Slovenian independence was declared. Legislation adopted in 2010 reinstated the legal status of the "erased," but implementation has been problematic, and court proceedings in some individual cases continued in 2016.

Slovenia housed over 350 refugees, asylum seekers, and migrants in its asylum centers in 2016. In September, refugees demonstrated at an asylum center in Vič over bureaucratic delays related to the status of their asylum claims, which prevented them from attending school and gaining lawful employment while residing in Slovenia.

POLITICAL RIGHTS: 39 / 40
A. Electoral Process: 12 / 12
B. Political Pluralism and Participation: 16 / 16
C. Functioning of Government: 11 / 12

CIVIL LIBERTIES: 53 / 60
D. Freedom of Expression and Belief: 14 / 16
E. Associational and Organizational Rights: 12 / 12
F. Rule of Law: 14 / 16
G. Personal Autonomy and Individual Rights: 13 / 16

This country report has been abridged for *Freedom in the World 2017.* For background information on political rights and civil liberties in Slovenia, see *Freedom in the World 2016.*

Solomon Islands

Political Rights Rating: 3
Civil Liberties Rating: 2 ↑
Freedom Rating: 2.5
Freedom Status: Free
Electoral Democracy: Yes

Population: 700,000
Capital: Honiara

Status Change, Ratings Change: The Solomon Islands' status improved from Partly Free to Free, and its civil liberties rating improved from 3 to 2, due to a recent record of free competition among opposing political groupings and a pattern of increased judicial independence.

Ten-Year Ratings Timeline For Year Under Review (Political Rights, Civil Liberties, Status)

Year Under Review	2007	2008	2009	2010	2011	2012	2013	2014	2015	2016
Rating	4,3,PF	4,3,PF	4,3,PF	4,3,PF	4,3,PF	4,3,PF	4,3,PF	3,3,PF	3,3,PF	3,2,F

Overview: Political rights and civil liberties are generally respected in the Solomon Islands, though corruption remains a serious issue, and the government does not operate with openness and transparency. Violence against women is a significant problem.

KEY DEVELOPMENTS IN 2016:
- Investigations by a new anticorruption body known as Taskforce Janus led to the arrest of several high-profile government officials.
- A law criminalizing domestic violence and enabling victims to apply for protection orders came into force.

- In October, the Solomon Islands Court of Appeal upheld a government decision to make legislators' salaries tax-free.

EXECUTIVE SUMMARY

The most recent parliamentary elections, held in 2014, brought the government of Prime Minister Manasseh Sogavare to power and were considered a significant improvement over previous polls. The improvements were largely attributed to the introduction of a biometric voter registration system, as well as a single ballot box system, both of which reduced incidents of electoral corruption and fraud. There are several political parties, but alliances are driven more by personal ties and local allegiances than formal policy platforms or ideology. Independent candidates dominated the 2014 polls, taking 32 of the 50 seats in the legislature.

The so-called second election, in which a parliamentary majority elects the prime minister, is the focus of many of the country's political difficulties. Lawmakers either without party affiliation, or affiliated but prepared to switch sides in search of ministerial portfolios, frequently form factional alliances seemingly in contrast with the platforms they ran on. Additionally, there have been reports of businesses offering incentives for lawmakers to vote a particular way. Splits within the cabinet are frequent, and ministers often conduct their affairs unilaterally.

Sogavare pledged to usher in new anticorruption laws in 2016, but has had difficulty acquiring parliamentary support. However, in December, investigations by a new anticorruption body known as Taskforce Janus led to the arrest of Edmond Sikua, the permanent secretary of the Ministry of Police, National Security, and Correctional Services, for allegedly manipulating his ministry's tendering process to favor a family-owned firm. The financial controller in Sikua's ministry and an inland revenue officer were also arrested during the year as a result of Taskforce Janus investigations.

In 2015, a parliamentary commission granted lifetime pension payments to all lawmakers, as well as tax-free status on their salaries. The benefits' introduction drew strong public criticism given the size of the national debt, high unemployment, and other public spending needs. Later in 2015, the High Court ruled that granting payments tax-free to lawmakers was unconstitutional, but the ruling was overturned in October 2016, with the Solomon Islands Court of Appeal saying that while the move was unpopular, it was not unconstitutional. Generally, the courts have demonstrated greater independence in recent years.

Discrimination limits economic and political opportunities for women. Rape and other forms of violence against women and girls are serious problems. The 2014 Family Protection Act, which formally criminalized domestic violence and enabled victims to apply for protection orders, came into force in 2016.

POLITICAL RIGHTS: 27 / 40 (+ 2)

A. Electoral Process: 9 / 12

B. Political Pluralism and Participation: 13 / 16 (+ 3)

C. Functioning of Government: 5 / 12 (− 1)

CIVIL LIBERTIES: 44 / 60 (+ 1)

D. Freedom of Expression and Belief: 14 / 16

E. Associational and Organizational Rights: 9 / 12

F. Rule of Law: 9 / 16 (+ 1)

G. Personal Autonomy and Individual Rights: 12 / 16

This country report has been abridged for *Freedom in the World 2017*. For background information on political rights and civil liberties in the Solomon Islands, see *Freedom in the World 2016*.

Somalia

Political Rights Rating: 7
Civil Liberties Rating: 7
Freedom Rating: 7.0
Freedom Status: Not Free
Electoral Democracy: No

Population: 11,100,000
Capital: Mogadishu

Note: The numerical ratings and status listed above do not reflect conditions in Somaliland, which is examined in a separate report.

Ten-Year Ratings Timeline For Year Under Review (Political Rights, Civil Liberties, Status)

Year Under Review	2007	2008	2009	2010	2011	2012	2013	2014	2015	2016
Rating	7,7,NF	7,7,NF	7,7,NF	7,7,NF	7,7,NF	7,7,NF	7,7,NF	7,7,NF	7,7,NF	7,7,NF

Overview: Somalia has struggled to reestablish a functioning state since the collapse of an authoritarian regime in 1991. No direct national elections have been held to date, and the country's territory is divided among an internationally supported national government, the Shabaab militant group, a semiautonomous government in the Puntland region, and a separatist government in the Somaliland region. Political affairs are dominated by clan divisions, and ongoing insecurity has restrained the development of the economy and robust media and civil society sectors. In the absence of an effective court system, impunity for human rights abuses by both state and nonstate actors is the norm.

KEY DEVELOPMENTS IN 2016:

- Indirect elections for the bicameral parliament began in October and continued through the end of the year, by which time most seats had been filled. Clan elders chose members of a limited electoral college, who in turn cast the votes for lawmakers. The resulting parliament was expected to vote on a new president in early 2017.
- The Shabaab militant group continued to carry out regular attacks on military, government, and civilian targets, employing suicide bombings, assassinations, mortar fire, and guerrilla-style assaults. The militants committed numerous human rights violations in areas under their control, though clan militias and progovernment forces were also criticized for violence and abuses against civilians.
- There were more than 1.1 million internally displaced people in 2016, including some 400,000 in Mogadishu.

EXECUTIVE SUMMARY

Somalia's internationally recognized government proceeded with a plan for indirect parliamentary elections in 2016, as the security situation and other factors precluded direct national elections based on universal suffrage. Members of the 54-seat upper house were elected by state assemblies, while the lower house was elected under a system in which 135 clan elders chose 275 electoral colleges, each of which comprised 51 people and elected one lawmaker.

The voting began behind schedule in October, and after a series of further delays, some seats had yet to be filled at year's end. Once the parliamentary elections could be completed in early 2017, the new members would elect a president for a four-year term. Corruption and vote buying reportedly played a major role in the elections. Direct national voting was not expected until 2020 at the earliest.

Although the elections were largely based on clan divisions, legislation signed by President Hassan Sheikh Mohamud in September would allow formal registration of political parties—for the first time since 1969—after the completion of the election process. Some political associations had previously operated as de facto parties. Members of the new parliament were obliged to join a party by October 2018.

Somalian civil society has made modest gains in recent years as the government and international troops have reclaimed territory from the Shabaab, an extremist group that once controlled most of southern Somalia. There are functioning universities in Mogadishu and some other cities, and local nongovernmental organizations have been able to conduct a range of activities with international support, depending on security conditions. A relatively dynamic media sector, particularly radio stations and online outlets, has also developed in what remains an extremely inhospitable environment, with raids and arrests at media offices and at least three journalists killed in connection with their work during 2016, according to the Committee to Protect Journalists. A new media law signed by the president in January raised concerns about arbitrary or restrictive regulations.

Meanwhile, the Shabaab are still an active presence in the country despite the combined efforts of the Somalian military and the African Union Mission in Somalia (AMISOM). The militant group continued to attack both civilian and military targets throughout 2016. Additional abuses—including arbitrary arrests, extrajudicial killings, and indiscriminate attacks that resulted in civilian casualties—were reportedly committed by government forces as well as clan militias and AMISOM troops. In this volatile environment, violence against women has continued to escalate, and minors are allegedly recruited by all armed groups. The weak judicial system means that customary or Islamic courts are often the prevailing source of adjudication, particularly in more remote areas of the country.

POLITICAL RIGHTS: 0 / 40

A. Electoral Process: 0 / 12

B. Political Pluralism and Participation: 0 / 16

C. Functioning of Government: 0 / 12

CIVIL LIBERTIES: 5 / 60 (+ 3)

D. Freedom of Expression and Belief: 3 / 16 (+ 2)

E. Associational and Organizational Rights: 1 / 12 (+ 1)

F. Rule of Law: 0 / 16

G. Personal Autonomy and Individual Rights: 1 / 16

This country report has been abridged for *Freedom in the World 2017*. For background information on political rights and civil liberties in Somalia, see *Freedom in the World 2016*.

South Africa

Political Rights Rating: 2
Civil Liberties Rating: 2
Freedom Rating: 2.0
Freedom Status: Free
Electoral Democracy: Yes

Population: 55,700,000
Capital: Tshwane/Pretoria

Ten-Year Ratings Timeline For Year Under Review (Political Rights, Civil Liberties, Status)

Year Under Review	2007	2008	2009	2010	2011	2012	2013	2014	2015	2016
Rating	2,2,F	2,2,F	2,2,F	2,2,F	2,2,F	2,2,F	2,2,F	2,2,F	2,2,F	2,2,F

Overview: South Africa is a constitutional democracy. Since the end of apartheid in 1994, it has been regarded globally as a proponent of human rights and a leader on the African continent. However, in recent years, the ruling African National Congress (ANC) has been accused of undermining state institutions in order to protect corrupt officials and preserve its power as its support base begins to wane.

KEY DEVELOPMENTS IN 2016:

- The long-ruling African National Congress (ANC) suffered a major setback in local elections in August, losing control of three of the country's main municipalities.
- President Jacob Zuma faced mounting pressure amid corruption scandals, including a report from the public protector detailing the extent of influence over the government held by a wealthy family, the Guptas.
- In July, South Africa's public broadcaster, the South African Broadcasting Corporation (SABC), fired eight journalists for criticizing a new editorial policy that banned the broadcast of violent protests; the courts later reinstated the journalists and the Independent Communications Authority of South Africa (ICASA) ordered the reversal of the ban.
- In October, the executive unilaterally initiated South Africa's withdrawal from the International Criminal Court (ICC) without consulting parliament.

EXECUTIVE SUMMARY

President Jacob Zuma faced mounting corruption scandals in 2016, further undermining the reputation of the ANC and likely contributing to setbacks for the party in August local elections. The Constitutional Court, South Africa's highest court, ruled in March that Zuma should pay back some of the money spent on upgrades to his private home in Nkandla, KwaZulu-Natal. In April, the North Guateng High Court ruled that Zuma should face 783 corruption and fraud charges that had been dropped by the National Prosecuting Authority (NPA) in 2009. And in November, the former public protector released a report about the wide scale of "state capture" by the Guptas, a wealthy Indian immigrant family that had close ties to Zuma.

In the August elections, the ANC garnered its lowest share of the vote nationally since taking power after the end of apartheid in 1994. The preelection environment was marred by violence and suspected political killings.

Unrest that began in 2015 continued at universities throughout the country in 2016, as students protested tuition fee increases and a lack of racial transformation on campuses. Although the student protests did not always remain peaceful, the response of police and private security to the protests was at times disproportionate and included the use of rubber bullets, tear gas, and stun grenades against students.

POLITICAL RIGHTS: 33 / 40

A. Electoral Process: 12 / 12

Elections for the 400-seat National Assembly, the lower house of the bicameral parliament, are determined by party-list proportional representation. The 90 members of the upper chamber, the National Council of Provinces, are selected by provincial legislatures. The National Assembly elects the president to serve concurrently with its five-year term, and can vote to replace him or her at any time. Presidents can serve a maximum of two terms.

The most recent national elections, held in 2014, were declared free and fair by domestic and international observers. The ANC won, though with a smaller majority than in previous elections—a trend that has persisted for three consecutive elections. The ANC took 62.2 percent of the national vote, 249 of 400 seats in the National Assembly, and clear majorities in eight of nine provinces. The Democratic Alliance (DA) remained the largest opposition party, winning 89 seats with 22.2 percent of the vote, up from 16.7 percent in the previous election, and maintained control over the Western Cape. The newly formed leftist Economic Freedom Fighters (EFF) won 25 seats, the Inkhatha Freedom Party (IFP) took 10 seats, and nine smaller parties shared the remainder. The National Assembly elected Zuma for a second term as president.

In August 2016, South Africa held municipal elections, which regional observers assessed as free and fair. The ANC's national share of the vote dropped to 53.9 percent, marking the first time it had garnered less than 60 percent of the national vote in any election it had contested. The DA formed postelection coalitions or agreements with smaller parties in order to gain control over three key metropolitan municipalities previously governed by the ANC: Johannesburg, the economic capital; Tshwane, the metropolitan area that includes Pretoria, the national capital; and Nelson Mandela Bay, which includes a major seaport, Port Elizabeth.

The Independent Electoral Commission (IEC) is largely considered independent and the electoral framework fair. However, the IEC's independence has come under greater scrutiny in recent years, and the 2016 local elections were seen as an important test of the body's autonomy, given that the ANC lost significant ground. In September 2016, a media report emerged that IEC deputy chairperson Terry Tselane had written a letter to his colleagues on the commission complaining about an incident in which, following the declaration of the results of the municipal elections, senior ANC officials had angrily criticized him in the presence of Zuma, referring to him as "an enemy." The ANC denied that an attempt to intimidate Tselane had occurred.

B. Political Pluralism and Participation: 14 / 16 (+ 1)

The ANC, which is part of a tripartite governing alliance with the Congress of South African Trade Unions (COSATU) and the South African Communist Party (SACP), has won every election since 1994. Nevertheless, opposition parties are able to compete in elections, and there are frequent upsets, most recently in the 2016 municipal elections.

Factional conflicts within the ANC are increasingly aired in public. Several senior current and former ANC members have called on Zuma to resign, including the chief ANC whip in Parliament. In November, at least three cabinet ministers reportedly supported an unsuccessful motion for Zuma to resign at a meeting of the ANC's national executive committee.

Since the 2014 legislative elections, parliamentary sessions have taken on a more adversarial tone. In April 2016, Zuma survived an attempted impeachment initiated by the DA after the Constitutional Court ruled that the president had violated the constitution in the matter of the upgrades to his home in Nkandla. In May 2016, the EFF's parliamentarians were forcibly removed from Parliament after they said they planned to disrupt Zuma's attempts to speak. In the ensuing scuffle, according to a parliamentary statement, security personnel were assaulted and property damaged by EFF supporters protesting the removal of the parliamentarians.

South Africa has long been plagued by low-intensity political violence—including assassinations—with much of the violence concentrated in KwaZulu-Natal province. Both factionalism within the ANC and inter-party disputes have led to violence. In the run-up to the 2016 local elections, there were over a dozen suspected political killings in KwaZulu-Natal. Days of rioting in Tshwane in June—sparked by ANC supporters' dissatisfaction with the party's mayoral candidate—left at least five people dead, shops looted, and vehicles set on fire. The DA and the EFF complained that intimidation by ANC supporters hindered their campaigning in the run-up to the local elections, and the EFF accused ANC members of violence against its supporters. In April and May, respectively, two EFF supporters died after being attacked while campaigning in Gauteng province.

The political process is free from domination by the military, which is professional and largely stays out of politics. The constitution prohibits discrimination and provides full political rights for all adult citizens.

C. Functioning of Government: 7 / 12 (− 1)

Pervasive corruption and apparent interference by non-elected actors hampers the proper functioning of government. Despite comprehensive anticorruption laws and several agencies tasked with combating corruption, enforcement remains inadequate.

In November, a report by former public protector Thuli Madonsela, whose term had ended the previous month, was made public. The report concerned allegations of "state capture," or the exercise of inappropriate authority over state matters by private entities, by the Gupta family. The report, which calls for the creation of a judicial inquiry commission to investigate the issue, implicates the Guptas in Zuma's ill-fated and short-lived appointment of Des van Rooyen as finance minister—which led to a crash in the value of the rand in 2015—and includes allegations of a failed attempt to bribe another potential finance minister. The report also contains allegations that the Guptas may have used their influence over the state-owned energy provider, Eskom, to acquire a coal supplier to the company on more advantageous terms. The Guptas denied the allegations contained in the report.

One of South Africa's highest-profile corruption cases reached a climax in March when the Constitutional Court ordered Zuma to pay back a portion of the 246 million rand ($23 million) spent on upgrades to his home in Nkandla. A 2014 report compiled by Madonsela had found that Zuma derived undue personal benefit from the renovations, which were ostensibly initiated for security reasons, and said that Zuma should repay a portion of the funds. The court found that Zuma had violated the constitution by failing to comply with the report. In September, seven years after the upgrades began, Zuma paid back 7.8 million rand using a loan.

In April 2016, the North Guateng High Court found that the NPA's 2009 decision to drop 783 fraud, racketeering, and corruption charges against Zuma was "irrational" and should be set aside. Zuma and the head of the NPA tried unsuccessfully to appeal the April decision.

CIVIL LIBERTIES: 45 / 60 (− 1)

D. Freedom of Expression and Belief: 15 / 16

Freedoms of expression and the press are protected in the constitution and generally respected in practice. South Africa features a vibrant and often adversarial media landscape, including independent civic groups that help counter government efforts to encroach on freedom of expression. Nonetheless, concerns about press freedom have grown in recent years amid increasing government pressure on both state-run and independent outlets.

A number of recent incidents have compromised the credibility and independence of the SABC, the outlet with the largest reach in the country. The most high-profile incident came in May, when the SABC banned the broadcast of violent protests taking place across the country. The broadcaster's controversial chief operating officer, Hlaudi Motsoeneng—a political ally of Zuma—said it was the role of the SABC to "educate the citizens," and that coverage of the unrest could encourage further violence. Critics of the ban alleged that the broadcaster had enacted it in order to avoid unflattering coverage for the ANC in the run-up to the August local elections. Amid protests against the ban from journalists, civil society, and the opposition, the Independent Communications Authority of South Africa (ICASA) ordered its reversal in July.

Seven SABC journalists and one contracted freelance journalist were fired by the SABC in July after criticizing the protest ban policy. The journalists were reinstated later in the month following a ruling by the Labour Court in Johannesburg.

In May, the DA filed a complaint with ICASA after the SABC refused to air its election advertisements. In early June, the SABC agreed to air the ads. In June, Motsoeneng reportedly directed SABC staff not to engage in tough questioning of Zuma or to cover him negatively.

In September, Motsoeneng was removed from his position at the SABC after a court found that his appointment had been improper, but he was immediately rehired in another position by the broadcaster's board; in December, a court ordered that he be removed from his new post as well.

Offsetting the turmoil at the SABC, private newspapers and magazines are often critical of powerful figures and institutions and remain a crucial check on the government. Internet access is unrestricted and growing rapidly, reaching around 52 percent penetration in 2015. However, many South Africans cannot afford connectivity.

Freedom of religion and academic freedom are constitutionally guaranteed and actively protected by the government. Religious leaders and academics are largely free to engage in discussions of a political nature without fear of adverse consequences. However, after coming under heavy criticism from the South African Council of Churches, Zuma in December told religious leaders to stay out of political affairs. He later clarified that he meant they should "avoid becoming embroiled in divisive party political squabbles." Violence between student protesters and police and private security on university campuses amid demonstrations related to tuition fees have disrupted academic life.

. South Africans are generally free to engage in private conversations of a political nature without harassment. However, a March report from the UN Human Rights Committee expressed concern about the government's use of surveillance and the law governing it, the 2002 Regulation of Interception of Communications and Provision of Communication-Related Information Act.

E. Associational and Organizational Rights: 11 / 12 (− 1)

The constitution guarantees freedoms of association and peaceful assembly. Freedom of assembly is generally respected, and South Africa has a vibrant protest culture. Demonstrators must notify police ahead of time but are rarely prohibited from gathering. Protests over the government's shortcomings in the provision of public services are common in South Africa, and sometimes turn violent. Police have faced accusations of provoking some protest violence.

Student protests over tuition fees, which began the previous year, continued in 2016 at universities throughout the country, and sometimes turned violent. On several occasions, police used tear gas, stun grenades, and rubber bullets at students. In September, one student reported that she had been raped by a police officer in Pietermaritzburg, and in October police allegedly abducted a student leader in Johannesburg and dumped him in a neighboring province, Limpopo.

South Africa hosts a vibrant civil society. Nongovernmental organizations (NGOs) can register and operate freely, and lawmakers regularly accept input from NGOs on pending legislation. However, in April David Mahlobo, the minister of state security, accused some NGOs of working with foreign powers against South African interests.

South African workers are generally free to form, join, and participate in independent trade unions, and the country's labor laws offer unionized workers a litany of protections. Contract workers and those in the informal sector enjoy fewer safeguards. Strike activity is very common, and unionized workers often secure above-inflation wage increases. COSATU dominates the labor landscape but faces growing challenges from factionalism as well as independent unions. Union rivalries, especially in mining, sometimes result in the use of violent tactics to recruit and retain members and to attack opponents; violent and illegal strikes have also increased in recent years.

F. Rule of Law: 9 / 16

The constitution guarantees judicial independence, and courts operate with substantial autonomy. The Judicial Services Commission appoints Constitutional Court judges based on both merit and efforts to racially diversify the judiciary. A number of recent court judgments held the executive and legislative branches to account in such a manner as to suggest that the judiciary commands significant independence. Most notably, in the Nkandla matter, the Constitutional Court found that Zuma had failed to uphold the constitution and that a resolution of parliament saying he did not have to comply with Madonsela's 2014 report was "inconsistent with" the constitution and "invalid."

In October 2016, South Africa became the first country to file a notice of intent to withdraw from the ICC. The DA immediately challenged the legality of the move, saying the executive had acted unilaterally and was required to consult parliament before taking such an action. The decision was announced weeks before the Constitutional Court was due to hear a government appeal against a March 2016 Supreme Court of Appeal ruling that South Africa had violated the Rome Statute of the ICC and domestic law by not arresting Sudanese president Omar al-Bashir, who had been indicted by the ICC, during a June 2015 visit by Bashir to South Africa. The government in October 2016 said it was withdrawing its appeal against the earlier ruling.

Prosecutorial independence has been undermined in recent years. The NPA has experienced a string of politically motivated appointments and ousters. Along with the Police

Services Directorate for Priority Crime Investigation, known as the Hawks—which is responsible for combatting corruption and other serious crimes—the NPA appeared to be engaged in a political battle against Finance Minister Pravin Gordhan, with whom Zuma has frequently clashed. In October 2016, the NPA brought fraud charges against Gordhan; the charges were suddenly withdrawn later that month amid mounting pressure from opposition parties, NGOs, and senior ANC figures. Before the charges were withdrawn, evidence emerged that critics said indicated that the NPA and the Hawks had not considered all the evidence at the time the charges were announced and had subsequently sought to gather evidence to support the prosecution, including by the use of coercive tactics.

Shortages of judicial staff and financial resources undermine defendants' procedural rights, including the rights to a timely trial and state-funded legal counsel. According to a Judicial Inspectorate for Correctional Services (JICS) 2015–16 annual report, there is severe overcrowding in some prisons. During this period, 62 unnatural deaths were reported in prisons and there were 811 complaints of assault by prison officials on inmates. According to the 2015–16 Department of Correctional Services report, detainees wait an average of nearly six months before trial, and some are held beyond the legal maximum of two years.

Customary law plays a significant role in areas that under apartheid had been designated as land reserves for the country's black population. Traditional councils in these areas have authority over some aspects of local administration and can enforce customary law as long as it does not contravene the constitution. While this policy reduces the burden on state courts, customary law is replete with discriminatory provisions affecting women and certain minorities.

Despite constitutional prohibitions, there are many reports of police torture and excessive force during arrest, interrogation, and detention. The Independent Police Investigative Directorate (IPID) is required by law to investigate allegations of police offenses or misconduct. In its annual report for the 2015–16 fiscal year, the IPID recorded 582 reported deaths either in police custody or by police action, 112 reported rapes by police officers, 145 reports of torture, and 3,509 reports of assault. Overall, there was a 6 percent decrease in total reported incidents from the previous period.

South Africa has one of the highest rates of violent crime in the world. After a decline, murder, attempted murder, and armed robbery increased for the fourth consecutive fiscal year in 2015–16. Vigilantism remains a problem.

The constitution prohibits discrimination based on a range of categories, including race, sexual orientation, and culture. State bodies such as the South African Human Rights Commission and the Office of the Public Protector are empowered to investigate and prosecute discrimination cases. Affirmative-action legislation has benefited previously disadvantaged racial groups in public and private employment as well as in education but racial imbalances in the workforce persist. White people, constituting a small minority, still own a majority of the country's business assets. The indigenous, nomadic Khoikhoi and Khomani San peoples suffer from social and legal discrimination.

Xenophobic violence against immigrants from other African countries has broken out sporadically in recent years. In April 2016, foreign-owned shops were looted in Cape Town. A government-commissioned report on the causes and consequences of a spring 2015 spree of xenophobic violence in KwaZulu-Natal, released in April 2016, found that the attacks were immediately caused by a purposeful attempt by local businesspeople to push out competition from establishments owned by foreigners. The investigation found that the spread of sensationalism and misinformation by media organizations and on social media also contributed to the violence.

South Africa has one of the world's most liberal legal environments for LGBT (lesbian, gay, bisexual, and transgender) people. Discrimination on the basis of sexual orientation is prohibited in the constitution, same-sex couples have the same adoption rights as heterosexual married couples, and same-sex marriage is legal. However, there are frequent reports of physical attacks against LGBT people, including instances of so-called corrective rape, in which lesbians are raped by men who claim that the action can change the victim's sexual orientation.

G. Personal Autonomy and Individual Rights: 10 / 16

While there are no official restrictions on housing, employment, or freedom of movement for most South Africans, travel and some other personal freedoms are inhibited by the country's high crime rate. For many foreigners, the threat of xenophobic violence impedes freedom of movement as well. The legacy of apartheid continues to segregate the population and restrict nonwhite opportunity for employment and education.

The state generally protects citizens from arbitrary deprivation of property. However, the vast majority of farmland remains in the hands of white South Africans, who make up some 9 percent of the population. Illegal squatting on white-owned farms is common, as are attacks on white farm owners. The government has lagged far behind its own targets for land reform to address the legacy of apartheid.

In May 2016, parliament passed a new land Expropriation Bill, which had not been signed into law by the end of the year. The bill called for an end to the current "willing buyer, willing seller" policy and would allow for the compulsory purchase by the government of land in the "public interest."

The constitution guarantees equal rights for women, which are actively promoted by the Commission on Gender Equality. Nevertheless, women suffer de facto discrimination with regard to marriage, divorce, inheritance, and property rights, particularly in rural areas. Sexual harassment is common, and reports of forced marriages persist. Women are also subject to wage discrimination in the workplace and are not well represented in top management positions. Women are better represented in government, holding 42 percent of the seats in the National Assembly. Female premiers lead two of the nine provinces. Despite a robust legal framework criminalizing domestic violence and rape, both are grave problems. Only a small percentage of rapes are reported.

South Africans, predominantly from rural regions, as well as foreign migrants are vulnerable to sex trafficking and forced labor. Organized criminal syndicates are responsible for the bulk of trafficking.

Inequality levels in South Africa are among the highest in the world. Only a small percentage of the population benefits from large state industries and the economy is controlled by a relatively small number of people belonging to the political and business elite.

South Korea

Political Rights Rating: 2
Civil Liberties Rating: 2
Freedom Rating: 2.0
Freedom Status: Free
Electoral Democracy: Yes

Population: 50,800,000
Capital: Seoul

Ten-Year Ratings Timeline For Year Under Review (Political Rights, Civil Liberties, Status)

Year Under Review	2007	2008	2009	2010	2011	2012	2013	2014	2015	2016
Rating	1,2,F	1,2,F	1,2,F	1,2,F	1,2,F	1,2,F	2,2,F	2,2,F	2,2,F	2,2,F

Overview: South Korea's democratic system features regular rotations of power and robust political pluralism, with the two largest parties representing conservative and liberal views. Personal freedoms are generally respected, though the country continues to struggle with minority rights and social integration, especially for North Korean defectors, LGBT (lesbian, gay, bisexual, and transgender) people, and immigrants. The population is also subject to legal bans on pro–North Korean activity, which have sometimes been invoked to curb legitimate political expression.

KEY DEVELOPMENTS IN 2016:

- In April legislative elections, the liberal opposition Minjoo Party won an upset victory, narrowly edging out the ruling conservative Saenuri Party.
- A scandal that broke in October revealed corruption and extensive interference in state affairs by Choi Soon-sil, a longtime friend of President Park Geun-hye.
- In response, protests calling for Park's resignation ensued across the country, and the National Assembly voted in December to impeach her. The Constitutional Court was considering the matter at year's end.

EXECUTIVE SUMMARY

The Minjoo Party's narrow defeat of the Saenuri Party in April 2016 legislative elections was seen as a rebuke of Park Geun-hye's performance as president, with voters acting on frustration over a sluggish economy, a growing number of corruption scandals, allegations of abuse of power, mounting tensions with North Korea, and the imposition of a new antiterrorism law that could be used to limit political dissent.

In October, the media exposed a scandal surrounding the relationship between Park and her close friend Choi Soon-sil. The president had allegedly allowed Choi to access confidential information and exploit her friendship to influence government affairs and extort money and favors from third parties. Choi was arrested, and multiple investigations were under way at year's end.

Park initially issued two public apologies for her misconduct, replaced officials who had come under suspicion, and nominated a new prime minister, though the National Assembly quickly rejected her choice, leaving incumbent Hwang Kyo-ahn in office.

Protests calling for Park's resignation or impeachment steadily grew in size, and the National Assembly ultimately voted to impeach her in early December. Executive authority was transferred to the prime minister pending a Constitutional Court review of the charges against Park. A decision was due within 180 days, after which either a presidential election would be held or Park's powers would be restored.

POLITICAL RIGHTS: 32 / 40 (− 2)

A. Electoral Process: 11 / 12

The 1988 constitution vests executive power in a directly elected president, who is limited to a single five-year term. In the 2012 presidential election, Park of the Saenuri Party defeated Democratic United Party (DUP) candidate Moon Jae-in, 52 percent to 48 percent, to become the first female president of the Republic of Korea.

The unicameral National Assembly is composed of 300 members serving four-year terms. In the April 2016 legislative elections, the Minjoo Party (formerly the New Politics Alliance for Democracy, or NPAD) won 123 seats, while Saenuri won only 122. The centrist People's Party won 38 seats, and minor parties and independents secured the remaining 17 seats. Although liberal and centrist opposition parties won a total of 167 seats, they failed to gain the 180-seat supermajority needed to pass major reform legislation.

In December 2016, the National Assembly voted—234 to 56—to impeach Park based on 13 allegations of misconduct stemming from the Choi scandal, handing the case over to the Constitutional Court for review. Presidential authority was transferred to the prime minister pending the court's decision.

B. Political Pluralism and Participation: 13 / 16

Political pluralism is robust, with multiple parties competing for power and succeeding one another in government. The two dominant parties as of 2016 were the ruling conservative Saenuri Party and the liberal Minjoo Party, though party structures and coalitions are relatively fluid. In December 2016, after Park's impeachment, the New Reform Conservative Party was established as the result of a split in Saenuri.

Only once, in December 2014, has a political party—the United Progressive Party—been dissolved by the Constitutional Court on the grounds that it violated the National Security Law, which bans pro–North Korean activities. Separately, the National Intelligence Service (NIS) has been implicated in a series of scandals in recent years, including allegations that it interfered in political affairs and sought to influence the 2012 election in Park's favor.

Although ethnic minority citizens enjoy full political rights under the law, they rarely win political representation. Philippine-born Jasmine Lee of Saenuri lost her National Assembly seat in the 2016 elections, leaving no lawmakers of non-Korean ethnicity in the chamber.

C. Functioning of Government: 8 / 12 (− 2)

Elected officials generally determine and implement state policy without undue interference from unelected entities and interests. However, despite government anticorruption efforts, bribery, influence peddling, and extortion persist in politics, business, and everyday life.

The controversial Kim Young-ran Act, which took effect in September 2016, establishes stiff punishments for those convicted of accepting bribes, and eliminates the need to prove a direct link between a gift and a favor to secure a conviction. The law targets government officials, but it is also applicable to spouses, journalists, and educators—roughly 4 million people. It sets strict limits on acceptable costs of meals and gifts if a conflict of interest is possible.

In October, a major corruption scandal revealed extensive collusion between President Park and her close friend Choi Soon-sil, who held no government office. Media and law enforcement investigations uncovered evidence that Park's administration had shared confidential and even classified information with Choi, and that Choi used her relationship with Park to manipulate government affairs and extort money and favors from others, including major corporations. Choi was arrested, and a special prosecutor was assigned to the case. Park herself was immune from prosecution until formally removed from office by the Constitutional Court.

CIVIL LIBERTIES: 50 / 60 (+ 1)

D. Freedom of Expression and Belief: 13 / 16 (+ 1)

The news media are generally free and competitive. Newspapers are privately owned and report aggressively on government policies and allegations of official and corporate wrongdoing. Some forms of official censorship are legal, however. Under the National Security Law, listening to North Korean radio is illegal, as is posting pro-North messages online; authorities have deleted tens of thousands of posts deemed to be pro-North, drawing accusations that the law's broadly written provisions are being used to circumscribe political expression. Journalists at major news outlets have faced political interference from managers or the government. Under the Park administration, there was more liberal use of defamation charges against government critics, with possible punishments of up to seven years in prison. Nevertheless, the media reported extensively on the Choi scandal during 2016.

The constitution provides for freedom of religion, and it is respected in practice.

Academic freedom is mostly unrestricted, though the National Security Law limits statements supporting the North Korean regime or communism. In addition, the new anticorruption law subjects public and private school teachers and administrators to the same oversight as public officials, potentially exposing educators to increased government influence or intimidation. In late 2015, the Park administration announced its decision to require middle and high schools to use history textbooks produced by an official institute, rather than choosing from a variety of options. However, the Ministry of Education reversed the requirement after Park's impeachment in 2016.

Private discussion is typically free and open, and the government generally respects citizens' right to privacy. A wiretap law sets the conditions under which the government may monitor telephone calls, mail, and e-mail. In March 2016, a new antiterrorism law was adopted after an eight-day filibuster attempt by the opposition. The legislation grants the NIS expanded authority to conduct wiretaps, and its vague definition of "terrorism" raised concerns that it would enable the agency to monitor government critics, particularly online.

E. Associational and Organizational Rights: 11 / 12

The government generally respects freedoms of assembly and association, which are protected under the constitution. However, several legal provisions conflict with these principles, creating tension between the police and protesters over the application of the law. For instance, the Law on Assembly and Demonstration prohibits activities that might cause social unrest, and police must be notified of all demonstrations. Local nongovernmental organizations (NGOs) have alleged that police who mistreat demonstrators have not been penalized equally with protesters under this law. In the wake of sometimes violent antigovernment protests in 2015, a June 2016 report from the UN special rapporteur on freedoms of assembly and association criticized South Korean police tactics that increased the risk of clashes and injuries at protests, including excessive use of water cannons and bus barricades.

Police and protesters largely avoided serious confrontations during a series of major political protests that began in July 2016—when the government announced plans to deploy a controversial U.S. missile-defense system on South Korean soil—and peaked ahead of Park's impeachment in December.

Human rights groups, social welfare organizations, and other NGOs are active and generally operate freely. The country's independent labor unions advocate workers' interests, organizing high-profile strikes and demonstrations that sometimes lead to arrests. However, labor unions in general have diminished in strength and popularity, especially as the employment of temporary workers increases. Several unionists remained in detention during 2016 after facing charges for the labor-related political protests in 2015, and the president of the Korean Confederation of Trade Unions was sentenced to five years in prison in July 2016—reduced to three years on appeal in December—for offenses linked to the protest violence. In late September, Korean Public Service and Transport Workers' Union affiliates began a strike against new labor guidelines that allowed for workers to be fired more easily, among other provisions. An October strike of more than 7,000 owner-operators in the trucking industry against plans to deregulate the transport sector was declared illegal by the government, leading to dozens of arrests.

F. Rule of Law: 13 / 16

The judiciary is generally considered to be independent. Judges render verdicts in all cases. While there is no trial by jury, an advisory jury system has been in place since 2008, and judges largely respect juries' decisions. Reports of beatings or intimidation by guards in South Korea's prisons are infrequent.

The country's few ethnic minorities encounter legal and societal discrimination. Residents who are not ethnic Koreans face extreme difficulties obtaining citizenship, which is based on parentage rather than place of birth. Lack of citizenship bars them from the civil service and limits job opportunities at some major corporations. A 2016 report by the National Human Rights Commission of Korea found that children of foreign-born residents in South Korea suffer from racial discrimination and systemic exclusion from the education and medical systems. It is estimated that there are some 20,000 stateless children residing in South Korea.

There were roughly 30,000 North Korean defectors in South Korea at the end of 2016. Defectors are eligible for South Korean citizenship, but they can face months of detention and interrogations upon arrival, and some have reported abuse in custody and societal discrimination. In March 2016, the National Assembly passed the North Korean Human Rights Act, which created transparent guidelines to safeguard the human rights of current and former North Korean citizens. It establishes a Human Rights Advisory Committee within the Ministry of Unification to develop a long-term plan addressing human rights dialogue and humanitarian assistance, and a Human Rights Foundation to conduct policy research on these topics and provide support to NGOs working on North Korean human rights issues.

Same-sex sexual relations are generally legal, and the law bars discrimination based on sexual orientation, but transgender people are not specifically protected, and societal discrimination against LGBT people persists. In July 2016, the Constitutional Court upheld a provision of the Military Criminal Act that bans sexual acts between male soldiers.

G. Personal Autonomy and Individual Rights: 13 / 16

Travel both within South Korea and abroad is unrestricted, though travel to North Korea requires government approval. South Korea fully recognizes property rights and has a well-developed body of laws governing the establishment of commercial enterprises, though the economy remains dominated by large family-owned conglomerates that have been accused of collusion with political figures, as evidenced in the Choi scandal.

South Korean women have legal equality, and a 2005 Supreme Court ruling granted married women equal rights with respect to inheritance. Women face social and employment discrimination in practice, and continue to be underrepresented in government. According to the World Economic Forum's 2016 Global Gender Gap Index, South Korea ranks 116 out of 144 countries in terms of gender parity. In January 2016, as part of an effort to combat domestic violence, the government proposed stronger penalties for stalking, including up to two years in prison rather than the small fine prescribed under current law.

In May 2016, the first lawsuit seeking recognition of same-sex marriage was rejected by a district court, which upheld the definition of marriage under the Act on Family Registration as a union between different sexes.

Foreign migrant workers are vulnerable to debt bondage and forced labor, including forced prostitution. Korean women and foreign women recruited by international marriage brokers can also become sex-trafficking victims. Although the government actively prosecutes human trafficking cases, those convicted often receive light punishments.

⬇ South Sudan

Political Rights Rating: 7
Civil Liberties Rating: 7 ↓
Freedom Rating: 7.0
Freedom Status: Not Free
Electoral Democracy: No

Population: 12,700,000
Capital: Juba

Ratings Change, Trend Arrow: South Sudan's civil liberties rating declined from 6 to 7, and it received a downward trend arrow, due to the collapse of a peace deal, the resumption of civil war, and egregious human rights abuses carried out against civilians, in many cases by government forces.

Ten-Year Ratings Timeline For Year Under Review (Political Rights, Civil Liberties, Status)

Year Under Review	2007	2008	2009	2010	2011	2012	2013	2014	2015	2016
Rating	—	—	—	—	6,5,NF	6,5,NF	6,6,NF	7,6,NF	7,6,NF	7,7,NF

Overview: South Sudan, which gained independence from Sudan in 2011, has been ravaged by civil war since late 2013, when a rift between President Salva Kiir and his recently dismissed vice president, Riek Machar, triggered fighting among their supporters and divided the country along ethnic lines. Overdue national elections have yet to be held, and the incumbent leadership has presided over rampant corruption, economic collapse, and atrocities against civilians, journalists, and aid workers.

KEY DEVELOPMENTS IN 2016:

- A cease-fire between armed factions loyal to President Kiir and First Vice President Machar unraveled in July. Heavy fighting broke out in the capital, signaling the resumption of the civil war.

- Machar himself fled the country, traveling to the Democratic Republic of Congo and Sudan before resurfacing in South Africa. He urged followers to continue the war. Machar was replaced as vice president by Taban Deng Gai.
- After existing UN peacekeepers failed to protect civilians from atrocities by the combatants, the UN Security Council in August authorized a new Regional Protection Force that would have a stronger mandate to secure Juba. It had yet to deploy at year's end.

EXECUTIVE SUMMARY

An August 2015 agreement to end South Sudan's civil war, already threatened by cease-fire violations and signs that the two sides were rearming themselves for further clashes, broke down completely in July 2016, apparently due to bad faith by the signatories and their inability to control armed supporters. Fighting erupted in Juba between forces loyal to President Kiir and First Vice President Machar, amid conflicting accounts of what triggered the violence. Within days, several hundred people had been killed, and pro-Machar forces had been routed. Machar, who accused Kiir of trying to kill him, fled Juba and later emerged in Sudan and South Africa, where he called on supporters to continue the fight.

As the violence escalated in Juba, peacekeepers with the UN Mission in South Sudan (UNMISS) failed in their mandate to protect civilians. Soldiers from the Sudan People's Liberation Army (SPLA)—South Sudan's military—and other forces aligned with Kiir murdered and raped people on the basis of their ethnic origin and attacked foreign aid workers and diplomats. In August, the UN Security Council authorized a new Regional Protection Force of 4,000 troops to supplement 13,000 UNMISS peacekeepers; the new force would be able to take more aggressive measures to secure Juba and the surrounding area. Kiir's government initially resisted the move, but formally accepted it in November under the threat of a UN arms embargo. The first troops had not yet deployed as of December.

The fighting in 2016 was not confined to the capital. Widespread violence affected the greater Upper Nile region, Western Bahr el-Ghazal State, and parts of the country that were previously spared the worst of the conflict, including greater Equatoria. Civilians were deliberately targeted for attack by combatants on all sides, who committed repeated acts of murder, rape, torture, and looting, according to multiple reports by the United Nations, the African Union (AU), and other observers. In one of the worst incidents, civilians taking shelter at an UNMISS base in Malakal were attacked by SPLA troops and allied militias in February. At least 30 people were killed.

By late 2016, nearly 1.9 million citizens were internally displaced, including 200,000 people who were taking shelter at UNMISS bases. More than 300,000 refugees had fled to Uganda alone since the resumption of large-scale violence in July, contributing to a total of almost 1.5 million South Sudanese refugees in neighboring countries. In December, the World Food Programme (WFP) estimated that 3.6 million people were in immediate need of food assistance, partly as a result of the conflict.

POLITICAL RIGHTS: −2 / 40 (−4)

A. Electoral Process: 1 / 12 (−2)

Kiir was elected president of the semiautonomous region of Southern Sudan in 2010, and inherited the presidency of South Sudan when it gained independence in 2011. A revised version of Southern Sudan's 2005 interim constitution, adopted at independence, gives sweeping powers to the executive. The president cannot be impeached and has the authority to fire state governors and dissolve the parliament and state assemblies. A permanent constitution was due to be passed by 2015, but the National Constitutional Review Commission had yet to produce a draft in 2016.

In principle, significant powers are devolved to the state assemblies, but they have exercised little autonomy in practice. At the end of 2015, Kiir pushed ahead with controversial plans to reorganize state boundaries, increasing the number of states from 10 to 28 and potentially stoking further ethnic conflict. Kiir handpicked the new states' governors, who took office in December 2015. The opposition strongly rejected the move.

Kiir has yet to face an electoral test since 2010 because national polls, scheduled for 2015, were postponed due to the civil war. The August 2015 peace deal established a national unity government for 30 months, with elections meant to take place at least 60 days before the end of its mandate. The Transitional Government of National Unity (TGNU) was formed in April 2016 after months of delay. Machar, whose dismissal as vice president in 2013 helped precipitate the civil war, was restored to power as first vice president. However, after fighting resumed in July, Kiir replaced Machar with Taban Deng Gai, effectively ending the power-sharing arrangement.

South Sudan's bicameral National Legislature is dominated by the SPLM. The upper chamber, the Council of States, includes 20 former members of Sudan's Council of States, plus 30 members appointed by Kiir. The lower house, the 332-seat National Legislative Assembly (NLA), comprised members of the preindependence Southern legislature who were elected in 2010, plus 96 former members of Sudan's National Assembly and 66 additional members appointed by the president. Under the peace agreement of August 2015, another 68 seats were added to this body by appointment, forming the Transitional National Legislative Assembly (TNLA).

The new allocation of legislative and executive posts under the peace deal ultimately failed to resolve the dispute behind the civil war, and as of 2016, both branches of government lacked a legitimate electoral mandate.

B. Political Pluralism and Participation: 1 / 16

The SPLM dominates the political landscape and uses its power and resources to sideline opposition parties, which are largely irrelevant. Although a handful of non-SPLM parties are represented in the 400-seat TNLA, they lack the resources to operate effectively and the experience to formulate policy and set party platforms.

Most political competition takes place within the SPLM. Kiir's faction is deeply intolerant of internal dissent, and his dismissal of opponents in 2013 raised political tensions during the run-up to the civil war. Following the 2015 peace deal, the TGNU was formed to include the SPLM faction headed by Machar, the SPLM in Opposition (SPLM-IO). However, Kiir reverted to previous practices when the civil war resumed in mid-2016. In July and August, he replaced several opposition-oriented members of the TGNU with loyalists.

A September report produced by a panel of experts for the UN Security Council found that the appointment of Taban Deng Gai as first vice president and Stephen Dhieu Dau as finance minister were particularly likely to anger ethnic groups linked to Machar's forces. The panel observed that the war had become a contest between elements of Kiir's Dinka ethnic group and other ethnicities. It noted that a Dinka group calling itself the Jieng Council of Elders had met regularly with the president and mobilized opposition to the peace deal.

South Sudan's military, the SPLA, exercises an overbearing influence over political affairs and public life, and the activities of various other armed groups tied to political and ethnic factions have made political participation by ordinary civilians all but impossible.

C. Functioning of Government: 0 / 12 (− 1)

South Sudan's government and legislature, which lack electoral legitimacy, are unable to exercise control over the national territory, and corruption is pervasive among the political elite. No one has been held accountable for the squandering of the country's considerable oil wealth, and the war economy has provided additional opportunities for illicit gain. According to a January 2016 UN report, the former minister of petroleum and mining used funds from the national oil company to supply the military and arm ethnic militias. In September, the Enough Project, a U.S. advocacy organization, accused senior officials such as Kiir, Machar, and SPLA chief of staff Paul Malong Awan of using their positions to pursue commercial ventures and make procurement deals that enabled them to amass great wealth, much of which was laundered overseas. State institutions tasked with promoting transparency and accountability are weak and underfunded.

DISCRETIONARY POLITICAL RIGHTS QUESTION B: − 4 / 0 (− 1)

Combatants on both sides of the civil war have killed, murdered, raped, tortured, and destroyed the homes and livestock of civilians because of their ethnicity. While some of these atrocities were the result of poorly disciplined fighters acting on their own initiative, others appear to have been officially planned and coordinated, according to international observers. An AU investigation into human rights abuses in the opening days of the civil war in 2013 suggested that mass killings of up to 20,000 members of the Nuer ethnic group were carried out by members of the state security forces and the Presidential Guard. The September 2016 expert report for the UN Security Council concluded that widespread attacks on civilians based on ethnicity during the fighting in Juba in July were likely coordinated at "the highest levels of the SPLA command structure." In December, the UN Commission on Human Rights in South Sudan found that ethnic cleansing was under way in parts of the country, and raised the possibility of a Rwanda-like genocide in the near future. The overall death toll remained unknown in 2016, though the most conservative estimates were in the tens of thousands.

CIVIL LIBERTIES: 6 / 60 (− 6)

D. Freedom of Expression and Belief: 4 / 16

The operating environment for journalists worsened after independence and has further deteriorated since the outbreak of the civil war. The government has detained or harassed reporters who tried to interview rebel leaders or provide balanced coverage of the conflict. As a result, many reporters exercise self-censorship, while others have left the country altogether. Several journalists have been killed since the war began, though in some cases the violence was not necessarily related to their work. In July 2016, for instance, Internews journalist John Gatluak was killed when SPLA soldiers stormed the Terrain hotel compound in Juba. Witnesses said he was shot dead because he was Nuer.

Members of the National Security Service (NSS) have ordered the closure of newspapers in response to their coverage. In September 2016, the independent *Nation Mirror*, a previous target of the authorities, was ordered closed without a specific explanation. In July, the editor in chief of the *Juba Monitor* newspaper, Alfred Taban, was arrested after the paper published editorials calling on Kiir and Machar to step down. He was charged with publishing false information before being released on bail later that month. Also in July, the editor in chief of *Al-Watan*, an Arabic-language daily, was detained for publishing what was described as an inaccurate report. In December, Justin Lynch of the Associated Press, the last foreign journalist based in South Sudan, was arrested and deported by the NSS without an official explanation. He had reported on human rights abuses in the country.

The interim constitution guarantees religious freedom, but houses of worship—used as places of refuge for civilians—have been attacked by gunmen seeking members of rival ethnic groups. There are no government restrictions on academic freedom, though basic access to education is limited outside state capitals. The education system has been seriously disrupted by the civil war, with many schools closed or commandeered for military use.

Private discussion of political issues in public places is impeded by fear of harassment or retribution at the hands of authorities. The NSS tracks and intimidates perceived critics of the government and is believed to use telephone surveillance to monitor opponents. The government also reportedly intimidates those who post critical comments online.

E. Associational and Organizational Rights: 2 / 12 (− 1)

Freedoms of assembly and association are enshrined in the interim constitution but have been seriously eroded in practice. While protests do occur, they have been met with excessive force by the authorities.

Two bills that became law in February 2016 placed severe restrictions on the operations of nongovernmental organizations (NGOs). The Non-Governmental Organizations Act and the Relief and Rehabilitation Commission Act, which require all NGOs to register with the authorities, have been used to justify the intimidation of civil society activists and the seizure of their assets. At least four groups were told that their registration was under threat due to their "political" activities. International organizations also faced operational restrictions. In December, the country director of the Norwegian Refugee Council was expelled without explanation, along with another senior manager.

South Sudan is a dangerous place for humanitarian workers, who have been systematically targeted by combatants. At least 67 national and international aid workers have been killed since the start of the civil war, according to a UN Security Council report in November 2016. Both sides in the civil war have looted humanitarian supplies and prevented the delivery of aid. In July, a South Sudan Red Cross warehouse in Juba was bombed and looted, while later that month, soldiers used trucks and cranes to steal 4,500 tons of food from a WFP depot. The authorities have attacked and intimidated UNMISS personnel, fired at UNMISS compounds, and obstructed peacekeeping operations. A UN panel recorded more than 640 instances in which UN operations were targeted or obstructed in the first nine months of 2016. In the July attack on the Terrain hotel compound, which housed local and foreign staff of international organizations in Juba, SPLA troops beat foreign nationals and raped at least five international aid workers. Also in July, the top representative of the UN Educational, Scientific and Cultural Organization (UNESCO) in South Sudan was shot and seriously wounded when progovernment gunmen fired on his vehicle.

South Sudan has yet to pass a comprehensive labor law; a Sudanese law that predates independence remains in force. While it allows workers to form independent unions, it does not provide protections for strikes and collective bargaining. A 2013 law regulates union operations, and the government holds extensive authority to intervene in union affairs. A Workers' Trade Union Federation, formed in 2010, has about 65,000 members, most of whom are public employees.

F. Rule of Law: 0 / 16 (− 1)

Although its interim constitution guarantees an independent judiciary, South Sudan's legal system is characterized by a culture of impunity. The judiciary and law enforcement agencies lack the capacity and apparently the will to hold perpetrators accountable for the many human rights violations committed since the start of the civil war. Judges are few in number, the mechanism for appointments is unclear, and the court system is under huge strain. According to the U.S. State Department, pretrial detainees account for between one-third and two-thirds of the prison population. Inefficiencies in the justice system have led to indefinite detention. Prison facilities feature crowded, unsanitary conditions and insufficient food for inmates. Children and the mentally ill are routinely detained with the general prison population.

The NSS, which reports directly to the president, has been responsible for arbitrary arrests and other abuses. Under the National Security Service Law, which came into force in 2015, the NSS has almost unlimited powers to detain and interrogate suspects. UN reports recorded multiple examples of politically motivated arrests in 2016.

Members of the SPLA, the South Sudan National Police Service (SSNPS), and the NSS have played a central role in the violence that has engulfed South Sudan since 2013. UNMISS, the AU, and human rights organizations have accused members of the security services of involvement in extrajudicial killings, attacks on civilians, enforced disappearances, destruction of property, and sexual violence. Civilians have also faced egregious atrocities at the hands of rebel forces and various other militias that operate in the country's security vacuum.

As part of the 2015 peace deal, the warring parties agreed to establish a hybrid tribunal under AU authority to prosecute genocide and other serious crimes. They also agreed that the TGNU would set up a truth and reconciliation commission within six months to document human rights abuses. After many delays, the process to establish a commission got under way in December 2016. In August, South Sudan said it had court-martialed 60 soldiers for offenses related to the violence in Juba the previous month. A military spokesman said the offenses included murder, shooting, and looting, but gave no details about how many had been convicted and what sentences they received.

Same-sex sexual conduct is not explicitly illegal in South Sudan, but "carnal intercourse against the order of nature" is punishable by up to 10 years in prison. LGBT (lesbian, gay, bisexual, and transgender) individuals face widespread discrimination and stigma.

G. Personal Autonomy and Individual Rights: 0 / 16 (−4)

South Sudan's interim constitution enshrines the rights of free movement and residence, as well as the right to an education. In reality, the civil war, multiple local conflicts, and poor to nonexistent service delivery have made it impossible for many people to exercise these basic rights.

Land use and ownership are frequent causes of conflict in South Sudan, and returning refugees from earlier wars have exacerbated the problem. Property rights are weak and not respected in practice. There have been multiple allegations of land grabbing and forced evictions in recent years.

The interim constitution guarantees the rights of women to equal pay and property ownership. However, women are routinely exposed to discriminatory practices and domestic abuse. The prevalence of child marriage contributes to low levels of educational attainment among girls. Official figures suggest that almost half of girls aged 15 to 19 are married. Combatants have committed systematic and widespread sexual and gender-based violence against women during the civil war. In 2016, the United Nations recorded 217 cases of sexual violence, mostly against Nuer women, between July 8 and July 25 in Juba alone.

Sex and labor trafficking is widespread, with rural woman and girls, the internally displaced, and migrants from neighboring countries among the most vulnerable to exploitation. The two main armed factions have committed to end the use of child soldiers, but there were multiple reports that armed groups continued to recruit children in 2016.

The population has also suffered from the consequences of an economic collapse brought on by government mismanagement, corruption, and the pursuit of war. The rate of inflation was reported at more than 660 percent in August 2016, and in December the WFP reported that more than 3.6 million people were severely food insecure, with malnutrition beyond emergency levels in seven of South Sudan's 10 original states.

Spain

Political Rights Rating: 1
Civil Liberties Rating: 1
Freedom Rating: 1.0
Freedom Status: Free
Electoral Democracy: Yes

Population: 43,300,000
Capital: Madrid

Ten-Year Ratings Timeline For Year Under Review (Political Rights, Civil Liberties, Status)

Year Under Review	2007	2008	2009	2010	2011	2012	2013	2014	2015	2016
Rating	1,1,F	1,1,F	1,1,F	1,1,F	1,1,F	1,1,F	1,1,F	1,1,F	1,1,F	1,1,F

Overview: Spain's parliamentary system features competitive multiparty elections and peaceful transfers of power between rival parties. The rule of law prevails, and civil liberties are generally respected. Although political corruption remains a concern, high-ranking politicians and other powerful figures have been successfully prosecuted. Restrictive legislation adopted in recent years poses a threat to otherwise robust freedoms of expression and assembly, and peaceful separatist movements in some regions represent an ongoing challenge to the country's constitutional system and territorial integrity.

KEY DEVELOPMENTS IN 2016:

- Mariano Rajoy of the conservative Popular Party (PP) was sworn in as prime minister in October, ending a lengthy impasse that began when the divided parliament was unable to agree on a new government following December 2015 elections, necessitating new elections in June 2016. Rajoy's new government still lacked a legislative majority.
- Carles Puigdemont of the Catalan separatist party Junts pel Sí (Together for Yes) became president of the Catalonia region in January 2016 following regional elections in late 2015. In October, the Catalan parliament voted to hold a referendum on independence in September 2017, despite warnings issued by the Constitutional Court and the Catalonian High Court.
- In September regional elections, the PP won an absolute majority in Galicia, while in the Basque region, the incumbent center-right Basque Nationalist Party secured the presidency with support from the Basque Socialist Party, having outpolled the left-wing separatist party EH Bildu.

EXECUTIVE SUMMARY

Spain lacked a government for most of 2016 after two rounds of parliamentary elections left no single party with a majority. Either the PP or the Spanish Socialist Workers' Party (PSOE) have typically held a majority in recent decades, but the success of two new parties—the left-wing Podemos and center-right Ciudadanos—in the December 2015 elections triggered months of fruitless coalition talks, followed by fresh elections in June 2016. The PP emerged with 137 seats in the 350-seat Chamber of Deputies, followed by PSOE with 85, Podemos with 45, Ciudadanos with 32, and several smaller parties with the remainder.

The deadlock was finally broken in October, when members of PSOE, concerned about the ramifications of continued disarray, decided to abstain from the vote for prime minister, allowing incumbent Mariano Rajoy of PP—who had been serving in a caretaker capacity since the 2015 vote—to take office. A new cabinet was appointed in November. PSOE leader Pedro Sánchez, who opposed the abstentions, resigned his position as general secretary of the party. PSOE was set to choose a new leadership in 2017.

Meanwhile, the separatist government in Catalonia continued to push for a referendum on independence, and elections were held in Galicia and the Basque region in September. Also during 2016, the authorities actively enforced controversial public security legislation that took effect in mid-2015, issuing numerous fines for disrespect of police officers and other offenses. At least one journalist was fined for publishing unauthorized photographs of a police operation. Separately, two puppeteers were charged and briefly detained for allegedly glorifying terrorism and inciting hatred in one of their satirical performances; the case was pending at year's end. A rap musician and a poet have faced prosecutions on similar charges.

The year featured several ongoing corruption cases, with defendants including politicians, wealthy businessmen, and members of the royal family. The PP was facing a sprawling investigation into an illicit bribes-for-contracts network that involved key political and business figures. The central trial in the case began in October 2016, but the overall probe had nearly 200 official suspects.

POLITICAL RIGHTS: 38 / 40 (− 1)

A. Electoral Process: 12 / 12

B. Political Pluralism and Participation: 16 / 16

C. Functioning of Government: 10 / 12 (− 1)

CIVIL LIBERTIES: 56 / 60

D. Freedom of Expression and Belief: 15 / 16

E. Associational and Organizational Rights: 11 / 12

F. Rule of Law: 15 / 16

G. Personal Autonomy and Individual Rights: 15 / 16

This country report has been abridged for *Freedom in the World 2017.* For background information on political rights and civil liberties in Spain, see *Freedom in the World 2016.*

Sri Lanka

Political Rights Rating: 3 ↑
Civil Liberties Rating: 4
Freedom Rating: 3.5
Freedom Status: Partly Free
Electoral Democracy: Yes

Population: 20,900,000
Capital: Colombo

Ratings Change: Sri Lanka's political rights rating improved from 4 to 3 due to ongoing reforms to the constitution and electoral processes, and because the government has taken steps to combat corruption.

Ten-Year Ratings Timeline For Year Under Review (Political Rights, Civil Liberties, Status)

Year Under Review	2007	2008	2009	2010	2011	2012	2013	2014	2 015	2016
Rating	4,4,PF	4,4,PF	4,4,PF	5,4,PF	5,4,PF	5,4,PF	5,4,PF	5,5,PF	4,4,PF	3,4,PF

Overview: Mahinda Rajapaksa oversaw the abolition of term limits after he was reelected president in 2010, and suppressed criticism from dissenters while consolidating power. Rajapaksa suffered a surprise defeat in the 2015 elections, and since then Sri Lanka has experienced improvements in political and civil liberties under the new administration of President Maithripala Sirisena.

KEY DEVELOPMENTS IN 2016

- In June, parliament passed a long-awaited Right to Information Act.
- In August, parliament approved a bill that established an Office of Missing Persons, marking a step forward in the transitional justice and reconciliation process.

EXECUTIVE SUMMARY

President Maithripala Sirisena's administration continued working on electoral, constitutional, and other reforms, and sought out public input on these processes. The Right to Information Act, which had been introduced in 2015, was approved by the parliament in June, and the Information Ministry worked on preparations for its full implementation in 2017. In August, parliament approved legislation that established an Office of Missing Persons, which is tasked with setting up a database of missing persons, advocating for the missing persons and their families, and recommending redress. Separately, a draft constitution with new checks on executive power is expected to be released in 2017.

An opposition political grouping known as the Joint Opposition experienced some pressure during the year, with Sirisena at one point threatening to reveal "secrets" about its members. Separately, Sirisena accused an independent anticorruption commission of politicization, in remarks that drew widespread criticism as a departure from his government's anticorruption efforts, which have included a number of high profile investigations.

Religious extremist groups continued to harass minorities and advocates of religious tolerance, albeit with less frequency than in previous years.

POLITICAL RIGHTS: 24 / 40 (+ 1)

A. Electoral Process: 8 / 12

The 1978 constitution vested strong executive powers in the president, but the approval in 2015 of the 19th Amendment curtailed those powers somewhat by reintroducing term limits—limiting the president to two five-year terms—and requiring the president to consult the prime minister on ministerial appointments. The prime minister heads the leading party in parliament, but has limited authority. The 225-member unicameral parliament is elected for six-year terms through a mixed proportional representation system.

In the January 2015 presidential election, President Mahinda Rajapaksa suffered a surprise defeat, with his opponent, Sirisena, winning 51 percent of the vote; turnout was a record 82 percent.

In the August 2015 parliamentary elections, the United National Party (UNP) led a coalition, the National Front for Good Governance, to a modest victory, winning 106 seats, a 46-seat increase from the 2010 polls. The United People's Freedom Alliance (UPFA) took 95 seats, a decline of 49, while the Tamil National Alliance (TNA), the largest party representing the ethnic minority, won 16 seats, an increase of two. The UNP formed a government with the backing of smaller parties on a platform of undertaking a wide range of electoral and governance-related reforms. Ranil Wickremesinghe, long-time leader of the UNP, became prime minister, and a new cabinet was drawn from a range of coalition partners, including the Sri Lanka Freedom Party (SLFP), one of the parties that comprised the UPFA.

In the run-up to the presidential election, groups such as the Center for Monitoring Election Violence (CMEV) accused the government of acts of violence and of inappropriate use of state resources—particularly transportation, infrastructure, police services, and the media. While dozens of violent incidents were reported prior to the parliamentary elections later in 2015—including several murders—the polling itself was considered credible.

Local elections, originally set for 2015, had still not been held by the end of 2016, with the government citing issues involving the delimitation of voting districts.

Lawmakers continued debating electoral reforms in 2016, but progress was slow, due in part to differing opinions over whether constitutional reforms should come before or after electoral ones. A draft constitution with new checks on executive power is expected to be released in 2017.

B. Political Pluralism and Participation: 10 / 16

A range of political parties, some of which explicitly represent the interests of ethnic and religious minority groups, are able to operate freely and contest elections. In addition to Prime Wickremesinghe's UNP and the UPFA, other major parties include the Marxist Janatha Vimukthi Peramuna (JVP); the TNA and several smaller Tamil parties; the Buddhist nationalist Jathika Hela Urumaya (JHU); and the Sri Lankan Muslim Congress, the country's largest Muslim party.

Following a 2015 coalition agreement between the UNP and SLFP, disgruntled SLFP members including Rajapaksa, along with other lawmakers, vowed to sit in the opposition, and this political bloc experienced pressure in 2016. The parliament speaker drew criticism in February after refusing to recognize the group, known as the Joint Opposition, as an independent parliamentary grouping, while President Sirisena in August threatened that he would reveal "secrets" about his rivals within the group if they formally established a new party.

Harassment of opposition politicians also took place in the lead-up to the January 2015 election, but declined markedly for the August 2015 parliamentary polls. Tamil political parties and civilians faced less harassment and fewer hindrances in voting during 2015 presidential and parliamentary elections, compared to the 2010 elections.

C. Functioning of Government: 7 / 12 (+ 1)

Government accountability has improved under Sirisena, as the Rajapaksa family's power over various ministries waned and parliament has taken a greater role in setting policy. The passage of the 19th Amendment in 2015 and the strengthening of independent commissions—including the National Human Rights Commission and the National Police Commission—represented important steps toward improving accountability mechanisms and reversing Rajapaksa's consolidation of executive power.

The Sirisena administration continued its efforts to fight corruption in 2016, though some critics note that a flurry of corruption investigations and related arrests have led to few major prosecutions. Several investigations focused on members of Rajapaksa's family. In June, Namal Rajapaksa, his oldest son, was arrested on charges related to an allegedly illicit real estate deal.

Separately, President Sirisena in October 2016 accused an independent antigraft commission of political bias; his statement was widely characterized as a departure from his administration's ongoing anticorruption efforts, and as serving to undermine the commission. The commission's head resigned in the wake of Sirisena's remarks.

In June 2016, parliament passed a right to information act the cabinet had approved in late 2015. The Information Ministry began training staff and setting up specialized departments in preparation for the act's implementation in 2017.

DISCRETIONARY POLITICAL RIGHTS QUESTION B: (− 1 / 0)

Following the end of the Sri Lankan Civil War in 2009, the traditionally Tamil areas of the north and east have seen a heightened military presence. The Rajapaksa government encouraged settlement by ethnic Sinhalese civilians by providing land certificates, housing, and other infrastructure with the aim of diluting Tamil dominance in these areas. While such policies have ended under the new government, and some land has been released, displacement of Tamil civilians remains a concern.

CIVIL LIBERTIES: 32 / 60

D. Freedom of Expression and Belief: 9 / 16

Freedom of expression is guaranteed in the constitution, and respect for this right has dramatically improved since 2015. Since then, laws restricting media freedom have been invoked less frequently, verbal and physical attacks on journalists have decreased, and several investigations into journalists' killings have been reopened.

However, media space is not entirely free. Senior officials have expressed hostility toward the media in public remarks, including the country's prime minister, who in July 2016 publicly claimed that some journalists were "conspiring against the government," and threatened to name the purported offenders. Earlier in the year, a cabinet official warned journalists not to cover activities of the Joint Opposition. The government in March also renewed calls for news websites to register with the Media Ministry or risk being deemed unlawful; in the past, failure to register had been cited as a pretext to shut down websites that were critical of the government. In September, a 26-year-old man was arrested for video recording on his mobile phone the president landing in a helicopter; he was later released on bail.

The constitution gives special status to Buddhism. Religious minorities face discrimination and occasional violence. Tensions between the Buddhist majority and the Christian and Muslim minorities—particularly evangelical Christian groups, which are accused of forced conversions—sporadically flare into attacks by Buddhist extremists. In recent years, the minority Ahmadiyya Muslim sect has faced increased threats and attacks from Sunni Muslims, who accuse Ahmadis of apostasy. In August 2016, Buddhist extremists disrupted a peaceful vigil meant to promote religious tolerance. Separately, in 2016, Tamil groups in the north drew attention to the construction of Buddhist structures in close proximity to Hindu places of worship, and in areas where they said there were no Buddhists.

Academic freedom is generally respected, but there are occasional reports of politicization in universities and a lack of tolerance for dissenting views by both professors and students, particularly for academics who study Tamil issues, according to the Federation of University Teachers' Associations.

The current government is not known to monitor or restrict access to the internet, and private discussion remains fairly free.

E. Associational and Organizational Rights: 8 / 12

Although demonstrations occur regularly, authorities sometimes restrict freedom of assembly. Police occasionally use tear gas and water cannons to disperse protesters, and were slow to respond to the disruption of the August 2016 vigil for religious tolerance. The army has imposed some restrictions on assembly in the north and east, particularly for planned memorial events concerning the end of the long-running civil war between the government and ethnic Tamil rebels.

Conditions for nongovernmental organizations (NGOs) have improved dramatically since the new government took office in 2015, with a lessening of official harassment and interference. However, some NGOs have faced difficulty operating in the northern and eastern areas of the country, although the United Nations and humanitarian organizations are generally given adequate access to former conflict zones. In 2016, the government notably engaged with civil society groups on several initiatives, including the Right to Information Act.

Most of Sri Lanka's trade unions are independent and legally allowed to engage in collective bargaining, but this right is poorly respected. Except for civil servants, most workers can hold strikes, though the 1989 Essential Services Act allows the president to declare any strike illegal. While more than 70 percent of the mainly Tamil workers on tea plantations are unionized, employers routinely violate their rights. Harassment of labor activists and official intolerance of union activities, particularly in export processing zones, are regularly reported.

F. Rule of Law: 7 / 16

Corruption and politicization remains common in the lower courts, but the level of threats and political interference that occurred under Rajapaksa has abated somewhat under the new government. However, in 2016 there was evidence of the executive attempting to influence the judiciary; for instance, Prime Minister Wickremesinghe in July asked the parliament speaker to overrule a Supreme Court judgment.

Police and security forces occasionally engage in abusive practices, including arbitrary arrest, extrajudicial execution, forced disappearance, custodial rape, torture, and prolonged detention without trial, all of which disproportionately affect Tamils. Due to huge backlogs and a lack of resources, independent commissions have been slow to investigate allegations of police and military misconduct.

Under the Prevention of Terrorism Act (PTA), suspects can be detained for up to 18 months without trial. The law has been used to detain perceived enemies of the government, and many detained under the PTA's provisions have been held for longer than the law mandates is legal; civil society groups have been clamoring for its repeal. A draft of a new

Counter Terrorism Act (CTA) intended to replace the PTA was released in October 2016, but prompted concern among civil society groups and other observers for its broad scope and lack of oversight provisions.

Some 65,000 disappearances have been reported since the government began accepting such reports in 1994; the disappearances occurred during two conflicts: an uprising in the late 1980s, and the 26-year civil war that ended in 2009. In August 2016, parliament approved legislation that established an Office of Missing Persons, which is tasked with setting up a database of missing persons, advocating for the missing persons and their families, and recommending redress. While the development won praise from domestic and international observers, rights advocates also said the government failed to consult adequately with the families of missing persons as the bill was being developed. Separately, the Internal Displacement Monitoring Center estimated that around 73,700 internally displaced persons remained in Sri Lanka as of July 2015.

Tamils report systematic discrimination in areas including government employment, university education, and access to justice. The status of Sinhala as the official language puts Tamils and other non-Sinhala speakers at a disadvantage. Ethnic tensions occasionally lead to violence.

LGBT (lesbian, gay, bisexual, and transgender) people face societal discrimination, occasional instances of violence and some official harassment, though government officials have stated that LGBT people are constitutionally protected from discrimination. Sex "against the order of nature" is a criminal offense, but cases are rarely prosecuted. An August 2016 report by Human Rights Watch found that transgender people in particular face discrimination, including the inability to update their identity documentation with their preferred gender and police harassment at checkpoints.

G. Personal Autonomy and Individual Rights: 8 / 16

Freedom of movement is restricted by security checkpoints, particularly in the north, but recent years have seen greater freedom of travel. Government appropriation of land in the north and east as part of economic development projects or "high security zones" following the end of the civil war had prevented local people from returning to their property. However, the Sirisena administration has released some military-held land for resettlement by displaced civilians. There have been few official attempts to help Muslims forcibly ejected from the north by the Liberation Tigers of Tamil Eelam (LTTE or Tamil Tigers) rebel group in the early 1990s to return to their homes. Access to education is affected by corruption from the primary through the tertiary levels.

Women are underrepresented in politics, on independent commissions, and in the civil service. Female employees in the private sector face sexual harassment as well as discrimination in salary and promotion opportunities. Rape of women and children and domestic violence remain serious problems. Although women have equal rights under civil and criminal law, matters related to the family—including marriage, divorce, child custody, and inheritance—are adjudicated under the customary law of each ethnic or religious group, and the application of these laws sometimes results in discrimination against women. Women make up just 35 percent of the labor force, and they are also often barred from access to information and communications technology, particularly in rural areas, and are more susceptible to poverty.

Although the government has increased penalties for employing minors, thousands of children continue to work as household servants, and many face abuse. Throughout the country, the military's role and expanded size under former president Rajapaksa and its presence in a variety of economic sectors—including tourism and infrastructure projects—remain causes for concern.

Sudan

Political Rights Rating: 7
Civil Liberties Rating: 7
Freedom Rating: 7.0
Freedom Status: Not Free
Electoral Democracy: No

Population: 42,100,000
Capital: Khartoum

Ten-Year Ratings Timeline For Year Under Review (Political Rights, Civil Liberties, Status)

Year Under Review	2007	2008	2009	2010	2011	2012	2013	2014	2015	2016
Rating	7,7,NF	7,7,NF	7,7,NF	7,7,NF	7,7,NF	7,7,NF	7,7,NF	7,7,NF	7,7,NF	7,7,NF

Overview: Sudan's political system is dominated by an authoritarian president, Omar al-Bashir, and his National Congress Party (NCP), which rely on a combination of repression and inducements to remain in power. The regime violently represses—including through attacks on civilians—groups representing regions, religions, and ethnicities that do not share its narrow nationalist vision. Civil society encounters severe restrictions, religious rights are not respected, and the media is closely monitored.

KEY DEVELOPMENTS IN 2016:

- In October, President Omar al-Bashir announced the conclusion of a National Dialogue with some opposition parties and the formation of a government of national unity within 90 days; however, most opposition and civil society groups boycotted this process.
- In March, the government unilaterally signed a so-called Roadmap Agreement, mediated by the African Union (AU), to end conflicts in Sudan's Darfur region and the states of South Kordofan and Blue Nile. Some—but not all—of Sudan's political and armed opposition groups followed suit in August. However, negotiations with the armed groups soon stalled over the terms of a cease-fire, and did not produce a final agreement by year's end.
- In June, the UN/African Union Hybrid Operation in Darfur (UNAMID) to renewed its mandate for one year.

EXECUTIVE SUMMARY

Despite publicly pursuing negotiations with opposition and rebel groups, Sudan's government continued to attack civilians in conflict areas and repress all forms of dissent throughout 2016. On the political front, there were tentative signs of progress in October, when President al-Bashir declared the end of a year-long National Dialogue with a small number of opposition parties and the transition to a government of national unity within 90 days. The United States "noted" the development but urged Sudan to consider it as only an initial step toward a more inclusive political agreement. A larger coalition of opposition entities—including political parties, armed groups, and civil society representatives—

rejected the process and demanded a genuinely inclusive dialogue with the government, to be staged abroad and mediated by the AU.

In Darfur, fighting raged for much of the year, particularly in the Jebel Marra region. A referendum in April 2016 confirmed Darfur's current administrative arrangements and was presented by the government as a landmark step toward ending the conflict. However, the vote was boycotted by the opposition and criticized by the international community. In August, two of Darfur's three main rebel groups joined political opposition parties in signing the so-called Roadmap Agreement mediated by the AU. The agreement—which also covered South Kordofan and Blue Nile—was meant to initiate negotiations on a comprehensive political settlement but quickly stalled, in part over accusations that the government had used chemical weapons against civilians. Of the estimated 2.6 million people displaced by the conflict, more than 80,000 fled Darfur between January and August 2016.

Civilians continued to bear the heaviest burden of the five-year-long conflict in South Kordofan and Blue Nile. Government forces persisted with indiscriminate aerial bombings, killing six children during one attack in May. The government and the main rebel group, the Sudan People's Liberation Movement-North (SPLM-North), signed the Roadmap Agreement but could not reach a deal to provide humanitarian access to the region.

Economic hardship intensified for many Sudanese when the government accelerated its austerity measures by removing fuel subsidies in November. Demonstrators took to the streets of Khartoum and other cities to protest the price rises that followed, leading to the arrests of scores of political activists from some of Sudan's main opposition parties. In December, authorities carried out mass arrests on the eve of a planned civil disobedience campaign related to the price increases.

Sudan's powerful National Intelligence and Security Service (NISS) continued to routinely confiscate printed editions of newspapers considered to be in violation of the Press and Publication Act in 2016, leading to crippling financial losses for media houses. In May, five separate editions of the independent daily newspaper *Al-Jareeda* were seized by NISS officers without explanation. Another spate of confiscations occurred during the anti-austerity protests in November and December. The print runs of seven newspapers were seized, including four progovernment publications.

POLITICAL RIGHTS: 2 / 40

A. Electoral Process: 2 / 12

B. Political Pluralism and Participation: 3 / 16

C. Functioning of Government: 1 / 12

Discretionary Political Rights Question B: −4 / 0

CIVIL LIBERTIES: 4 / 60

D. Freedom of Expression and Belief: 2 / 16

E. Associational and Organizational Rights: 1 / 12

F. Rule of Law: 0 / 16

G. Personal Autonomy and Individual Rights: 1 / 16

This country report has been abridged for *Freedom in the World 2017*. For background information on political rights and civil liberties in Sudan, see *Freedom in the World 2016*.

Suriname

Political Rights Rating: 2
Civil Liberties Rating: 3 ↓
Freedom Rating: 2.5
Freedom Status: Free
Electoral Democracy: Yes

Population: 500,000
Capital: Paramaribo

Ratings Change: Suriname's civil liberties rating declined from 2 to 3 due to the judiciary's lack of financial independence from the executive and the ruling party's deliberate failure to proceed with the long-delayed formation of a Constitutional Court.

Ten-Year Ratings Timeline For Year Under Review (Political Rights, Civil Liberties, Status)

Year Under Review	2007	2008	2009	2010	2011	2012	2013	2014	2015	2016
Rating	2,2,F	2,2,F	2,2,F	2,2,F	2,2,F	2,2,F	2,2,F	2,2,F	2,3,F	2,3,F

The country or territory displayed here received scores but no narrative report for this edition of *Freedom in the World.*

Swaziland

Political Rights Rating: 7
Civil Liberties Rating: 5
Freedom Rating: 6.0
Freedom Status: Not Free
Electoral Democracy: No

Population: 1,300,000
Capital: Mbabane (administrative), Lobamba (legislative, royal)

Ten-Year Ratings Timeline For Year Under Review (Political Rights, Civil Liberties, Status)

Year Under Review	2007	2008	2009	2010	2011	2012	2013	2014	2 015	2016
Rating	7,5,NF	7,5,NF	7,5,NF	7,5,NF	7,5,NF	7,5,NF	7,5,NF	7,5,NF	7,5,NF	7,5,NF

Overview: Swaziland, currently ruled by King Mswati III, is often described as the last absolute monarchy in Africa. The king appoints the prime minister and a large portion of the bicameral parliament, dominates the judicial appointment process, and effectively controls local governance through traditional chiefs. The king and his government determine policy and legislation; members of parliament cannot initiate legislation or oversee the king's budget. Political parties are unable to register or participate in elections, meaning candidates must run as individuals. Political dissent and civic or labor activism are subject to harsh punishment under laws on sedition and other offenses. Those who criticize the monarchy can also face exclusion from traditional patronage systems. Additional human rights problems include discrimination against women, ethnic minorities, people with albinism, and LGBT (lesbian, gay, bisexual, and transgender) people, as well as lack of enforcement of laws against child labor and exploitation.

KEY DEVELOPMENTS IN 2016:

- In February, as police attempted to disperse students who were protesting funding problems at the University of Swaziland, an armored vehicle was driven into the crowd, severely injuring one student. There were no reports of any punishment for the incident by year's end.
- In September, the High Court found that provisions of two security laws violated constitutional rights. The Supreme Court was expected to hear an appeal of the ruling.

EXECUTIVE SUMMARY

Despite Swaziland's poor record on democracy and human rights, King Mswati III commenced his one-year chairmanship of the Southern African Development Community (SADC) in August 2016, receiving a tacit vote of support from the region's governments. On the eve of the SADC summit that month, the king used a traditional people's assembly to castigate trade union leaders who had criticized Swaziland's labor rights violations in international forums. Police continued to harass trade unions during the year, blocking demonstrations, raiding offices, and assaulting striking workers.

A report released in October by the International Trade Union Confederation detailed labor exploitation and land confiscation in Swaziland's vital sugar industry, which is dominated by a royally controlled investment fund. The *Times of Swaziland*, the country's only ostensibly independent newspaper, allegedly engaged in self-censorship in its coverage of the report to avoid any criticism of the king.

In September, the High Court found that sections of the Suppression of Terrorism Act and the Sedition and Subversive Activities Act were in violation of the constitution's protections for freedom of expression and freedom of association. The government filed an appeal with the Supreme Court, though there were concerns about that court's impartiality. In May, the king had appointed seven lawyers to serve as acting Supreme Court judges without adhering to constitutional procedures; the Law Society of Swaziland, which called for permanent judges to be constitutionally appointed, boycotted the court's November session.

POLITICAL RIGHTS: 1 / 40

A. Electoral Process: 0 / 12

B. Political Pluralism and Participation: 1 / 16

C. Functioning of Government: 0 / 12

CIVIL IIBERTIES: 17 / 60

D. Freedom of Expression and Belief: 7 / 16

E. Associational and Organizational Rights: 2 / 12

F. Rule of Law: 4 / 16

G. Personal Autonomy and Individual Rights: 4 / 16

This country report has been abridged for *Freedom in the World 2017*. For background information on political rights and civil liberties in Swaziland, see *Freedom in the World 2016*.

Sweden

Political Rights Rating: 1
Civil Liberties Rating: 1
Freedom Rating: 1.0
Freedom Status: Free
Electoral Democracy: Yes

Population 9,900,000
Capital: Stockholm

Ten-Year Ratings Timeline For Year Under Review (Political Rights, Civil Liberties, Status)

Year Under Review	2007	2008	2009	2010	2011	2012	2013	2014	2015	2016
Rating	1,1,F	1,1,F	1,1,F	1,1,F	1,1,F	1,1,F	1,1,F	1,1,F	1,1,F	1,1,F

Overview: Sweden is a parliamentary monarchy with free and fair elections and a strong multiparty system. Civil liberties and political rights are legally guaranteed and respected in practice, and the rule of law prevails.

KEY DEVELOPMENT IN 2016:

- Reports published during the year indicated an uptick in violence by nonstate actors, including car fires and assaults against security personnel, and analysts pointed to social segregation and greater inequality as contributing factors.
- The government continued dealing with the consequences of an unprecedented influx of asylum seekers, and aligned national asylum regulations with the minimum standards set by the European Union (EU).
- In June, a court found the Swedish state guilty of discrimination in a case involving a register of Roma individuals maintained by police in Skåne, the country's southernmost county.

EXECUTIVE SUMMARY

An unprecedented influx of asylum seekers in 2015 led to political tensions as well as a strain on government resources, both of which persisted through 2016. Although Sweden's asylum and immigration policies had been among the most liberal in the EU, this influx led to a number of reversals in both policies and attitudes, and in 2016, officials aligned asylum regulations with the minimum standards set by the EU.

Sweden remains a country where civil and political freedoms are strongly protected by law and in practice, but a number of civil liberties issues unfolded in 2016. In June, a 2013 scandal—in which the Skåne police department was found to maintain a registry of individuals of Roma heritage—made headlines again. That month, in a case brought by 11 individuals who had appeared on the list, the Stockholm district court found that the Swedish state was guilt of ethnic discrimination. The state appealed, and the case was ongoing at year's end. In its most recent periodic review of Sweden, concluded in 2015, the United Nations largely applauded the government but noted the need to better address discrimination against Roma people, and also criticized the use of lengthy detention periods and the lack of robust mechanisms against human trafficking.

Acts of violence by nonstate actors, particularly car fires and attacks against public safety officers, remained a concern in 2016. In July and August alone, there were more than 70 car fires in the city of Malmö. Experts pointed to social segregation and greater inequality as contributing factors to these issues.

POLITICAL RIGHTS: 40 / 40
A. Electoral Process: 12 / 12
B. Political Pluralism and Participation: 16 / 16
C. Functioning of Government: 12 / 12

CIVIL LIBERTIES: 60 / 60
D. Freedom of Expression and Belief: 16 / 16
E. Associational and Organizational Rights: 12 / 12
F. Rule of Law: 16 / 16
G. Personal Autonomy and Individual Rights: 16 / 16

This country report has been abridged for *Freedom in the World 2017*. For background information on political rights and civil liberties in Sweden, see *Freedom in the World 2016*.

Switzerland

Political Rights Rating: 1
Civil Liberties Rating: 1
Freedom Rating: 1.0
Freedom Status: Free
Electoral Democracy: Yes

Population: 8,400,000
Capital: Bern

Ten-Year Ratings Timeline For Year Under Review (Political Rights, Civil Liberties, Status)

Year Under Review	2007	2008	2009	2010	2011	2012	2013	2014	2015	2016
Rating	1,1,F	1,1,F	1,1,F	1,1,F	1,1,F	1,1,F	1,1,F	1,1,F	1,1,F	1,1,F

Overview: The political system of Switzerland is characterized by decentralization and direct democracy. The multilingual state is typically governed by a broad coalition that includes members from the four largest political parties represented in the parliament. The 26 cantons that make up the Swiss Confederation have considerable decision-making power, and the public is often asked to weigh in on policy matters through referendums. Civil liberties are generally respected in the country, though laws and policies adopted in recent years have reflected a growing wariness of immigration and minority groups of foreign origin, which sometimes face societal discrimination.

KEY DEVELOPMENTS IN 2016:
- In February, Swiss referendum voters rejected a proposed law that would have forced the government to expel foreigners for even minor crimes.
- In September, the lower house of parliament approved a bill that would impose a national ban on face-covering veils. The measure was under consideration by the upper house at year's end.
- Also in September, referendum voters endorsed a law that considerably expanded the surveillance powers of the Swiss security services.

EXECUTIVE SUMMARY

Swiss policymakers continued to grapple with overlapping concerns about immigration, integration, and security during 2016. In a February referendum, citizens rejected an initiative by the right-wing Swiss People's Party (SVP) that called for authorities to automatically expel foreigners convicted of at least two minor crimes within a span of 10 years. Separately in June, voters approved a measure to reduce processing times for asylum applications and provide asylum seekers with legal assistance and more financial aid.

However, efforts to ban certain practices associated with fundamentalist forms of Islam appeared to move forward during the year. A law that came into force in the Italian-speaking canton of Ticino in July banned face-covering veils, following a 2013 referendum and several legal battles. The law prescribes fines of up to 10,000 francs ($10,000). In September, the National Council narrowly voted for a nationwide ban on such veils; at year's end the legislation was before the Council of States, the upper house of the Swiss parliament, though it was considered unlikely to pass. A discussion broke out in the canton of Basel over two male Muslim students' refusal to shake a female teacher's hand on religious grounds. The canton authorities concluded in May that the students had no right to deny the traditional handshake to their teacher, and that their parents could be fined if they persisted.

In April, local authorities in Bern banned a demonstration by the Islamic Central Council of Switzerland (IZRS), citing security concerns. IZRS claims to represent Muslims in Switzerland, but it has often been criticized for making radical statements and maintaining links to Salafi movements.

Swiss citizens who seek to travel abroad to fight on behalf of terrorist groups are subject to prosecution, and a suspect was sentenced to prison for the offense for the first time in August. Amid growing concerns about terrorism, Swiss voters in September approved a law that significantly expanded the surveillance powers of the Swiss security services. Though their activities would be subject to judicial oversight, Swiss agencies would be able to use a range of surveillance technologies and cooperate with foreign counterparts.

POLITICAL RIGHTS: 39 / 40

A. Electoral Process: 12 / 12

B. Political Pluralism and Participation: 15 / 16

C. Functioning of Government: 12 / 12

CIVIL LIBERTIES: 57 / 60

D. Freedom of Expression and Belief: 15 / 16

E. Associational and Organizational Rights: 12 / 12

F. Rule of Law: 15 / 16

G. Personal Autonomy and Individual Rights: 15 / 16

This country report has been abridged for *Freedom in the World 2017*. For background information on political rights and civil liberties in Switzerland, see *Freedom in the World 2016*.

Syria

Political Rights Rating: 7
Civil Liberties Rating: 7
Freedom Rating: 7.0
Freedom Status: Not Free
Electoral Democracy: No

Population: 17,200,000
Capital: Damascus

Ten-Year Ratings Timeline For Year Under Review (Political Rights, Civil Liberties, Status)

Year Under Review	2007	2008	2009	2010	2011	2012	2013	2014	2015	2016
Rating	7,6,NF	7,6,NF	7,6,NF	7,6,NF	7,7,NF	7,7,NF	7,7,NF	7,7,NF	7,7,NF	7,7,NF

Overview: Syria's civil war has bred an atmosphere of extreme violence, impunity, and intolerance by state and nonstate actors alike. In much of the country, people cannot meaningfully participate in political or civic life. Those that do risk harassment, detention, or death.

KEY DEVELOPMENTS IN 2016:

- The ruling Baath Party and allied factions took 200 of the 250 contested seats in parliamentary elections held in government-controlled areas.
- The government transferred thousands of civilians from besieged areas taken from rebels to other parts of the country.
- At least 14 journalists were killed in connection with their work in 2016, according to the Committee to Protect Journalists.
- Over a million people were thought to be living under siege conditions.

EXECUTIVE SUMMARY

Syria's civil war continued unabated in 2016, with the country effectively divided into four main zones, controlled, respectively, by the repressive government of President Bashar al-Assad; multiple militias comprising opposition forces; the Islamic State (IS) militant group; and Kurdish authorities. By the end of 2016, the conflict had internally displaced some 6.3 million people and created 4.8 million Syrian refugees. By September 2016, roughly 430,000 people had been killed during the conflict since it started in 2011, according to the independent Syrian Observatory for Human Rights. Institutions and rule of law continued to weaken during the year, and corruption was rampant in regime and opposition-held areas.

In April 2016, parliamentary elections took place in government-controlled areas amid an opposition boycott, heavy repression, and open warfare in parts of the country. However, political power remains monopolized by President Assad, his family, and their security and business allies, though foreign actors also express influence.

The regime besieged major opposition-held population centers in a "surrender or starve" strategy by which it limited aid deliveries, and displaced thousands of civilians from captured rebel areas. There were consistent reports of torture and mistreatment of detainees held in government custody. Insurgents also committed serious human rights violations, including detention, torture, and execution of perceived political dissidents and rivals, though conduct varied between different rebel groups. Receding state control in some areas, on the other hand, has allowed for freer expression. The opposition in exile is comprised of delegates from various opposition groups and has been recognized as the legitimate representative of the Syrian people by the Arab League, the United States, and many European countries. However, it does not effectively represent the demands and interests of the population in rebel-held areas.

POLITICAL RIGHTS: −3 / 40

A. Electoral Process: 0 / 12

Bashar al-Assad assumed power after the death of his father, longtime president Hafez al-Assad, in 2000. Constitutional revisions adopted in 2012 introduced presidential elections, replacing a referendum system in which the ruling Baath Party candidate nominated a single candidate. However, among other restrictions, candidates needed support from at least 35 members of parliament to qualify for consideration.

Assad was reelected for a third term in 2014 with what the government claimed was 88.7 percent of the vote amid 73.4 percent turnout. The voting was conducted only in government-controlled areas in a climate of severe repression. Observers were invited from friendly authoritarian countries including North Korea, while major democratic states denounced the voting as illegitimate.

Members of the 250-seat, unicameral People's Council serve four-year terms but hold little independent legislative power. Almost all power rests in the executive branch. The most recent legislative elections were held in April 2016, in government-controlled territory. Several opposition groups traditionally tolerated by the authorities boycotted the polls, and state workers reportedly faced pressure to vote. Members of the military were permitted for participate in the election for the first time. The ruling Baath Party and allied factions took 200 of the 250 contested seats.

Opposition-held Syria—as distinguished from IS and Kurdish territory—continued to lack an effective or unified governing structure in 2016. The National Coalition for Syrian Revolutionary and Opposition Forces, or Etilaf, was formed in 2012 to act as the opposition's international representative body. Comprising delegates from opposition groups in exile, it has been recognized as the legitimate representative of the Syrian people by the Arab League, the United States, and many European countries. Etilaf has undergone several changes of leadership through internal elections; in March 2016, it elected Anas al-Abdah as president. These elections are competitive to an extent, but heavily influenced by the coalition's foreign backers. Moreover, Etilaf's links to local leaders and fighters inside Syria remain tenuous, casting serious doubt on the degree to which it is genuinely representative of civilians or fighters in the country.

Provisional local councils in certain rebel-held areas have organized rudimentary elections, and some appear to have been fairly competitive and even impartially monitored. Separately, Syria's Kurdish north, known locally as Rojava, declared autonomy from Damascus in 2014 and adopted a provisional constitution. It has decentralized political and administrative structures and decision-making, allowing elections at the neighborhood and municipal levels. However, in Rojava and elsewhere, experiments in civilian self-government are vulnerable to derailment by hostile militant groups, bombardment and siege by regime forces, and chronic resource shortages. IS does not allow elections of any kind in areas under its control.

B. Political Pluralism and Participation: 0 / 16

Formally, the state forbids parties based on religious, tribal, or regional affiliation. Until a 2011 decree allowed the formation of new parties, the only legal factions were the Baath

Party and its several small coalition partners. Independent candidates are heavily vetted and closely allied with the regime. The 2012 constitutional reforms relaxed rules regarding the participation of non-Baathist parties, but in practice, the government maintains a powerful intelligence and security apparatus to monitor and punish opposition movements that could emerge as serious challengers to Assad's rule.

Within the domestic progovernment camp, politics, security, and decision making are dominated by Assad, his extended family, and a close circle of business and security allies. Although the government is often described as an Alawite regime and a protector of religious minorities, it is not an authentic vehicle for these groups' political interests. Political access is a function not primarily of sect, but of proximity and loyalty to Assad and his associates. The political elite is not exclusively Alawite and includes members of the majority Sunni sect, which also makes up most of the rebel movement; meanwhile, Alawites, Christians, and Druze outside Assad's inner circle are just as politically disenfranchised as the broader Sunni population. Foreign actors including Iran, Hezbollah, and Russia also exert heavy influence over the regime due to their critical contribution to the war effort.

Political activity in rebel-held areas is more vigorous than in regime areas, but it is still seriously constrained, and in some places nonexistent. Civilians' political aspirations are often subordinated to local armed groups. Opposition territory is divided among moderate, Islamist, and radical jihadist rebels, with varying implications for local political life. Local councils are often sponsored or appointed by prominent families and armed groups, and overwhelmed by addressing humanitarian needs and delivering basic services.

In the Kurdish region, in theory the decentralized governance structure allows for wide political participation, including by ethnic and religious minorities. However, the Democratic Union Party (PYD), the most powerful Syrian Kurdish group, dominates politics and the Kurdish-led armed forces in practice. It has been accused of arbitrarily detaining perceived opponents.

No political activity is permitted in IS-controlled territory. Those who oppose IS rule must either refrain from expressing their views openly or flee to other areas, as dissent is severely punished.

C. Functioning of Government: 0 / 12

Government institutions lacked public accountability and were plagued by corruption even before the armed conflict. Authority lies with the president and his political, security, and business allies rather than formal institutions, and corruption is rampant.

Those who question state policies or use of public funds face harassment, imprisonment, or death. Members and allies of the ruling family are said to own or control much of the Syrian economy. The civil war has created new opportunities for corruption between the government, loyalist armed forces, and the private sector. The regime has regularly distributed patronage in the form of public resources, and implemented policies to benefit favored industries and companies, to secure its support base. Government contracts and trade deals have also been awarded to allies like Iran, possibly as compensation for political and military aid. Even basic state services are extended or withheld based on a community's demonstrated political loyalty to the Assad regime, providing additional leverage for bribe-seeking officials. In September 2016, dozens of aid groups suspended their participation in joint relief efforts with the United Nations, saying that Assad was manipulating the aid distribution process in ways that deprived certain areas of assistance.

The government's lack of public accountability has worsened during the civil war amid the rise of militias that are nominally loyal to the regime but largely autonomous and free to exploit the population in regime-held areas. They have reportedly engaged in looting, extortion, and the erection of arbitrary checkpoints.

Corruption is also widespread in rebel-held areas. Some rebel commanders, including from brigades nominally aligned with democratic powers and their allies, have been accused of looting, extortion, and theft. In addition, local administrators and activists complain that little of the international aid reportedly given to opposition representatives abroad seems to reach them, raising suspicions of graft.

Islamist factions appear somewhat more disciplined and eager to enforce their decrees, though the more extreme militant groups such as IS are not accountable to the public. IS runs an extensive extortion network and smuggling operations that extends into Iraq and Turkey.

DISCRETIONARY POLITICAL RIGHTS QUESTION B: − 3 / 0

The armed conflict is largely sectarian, with Sunni Arab civilians bearing the brunt of government and progovernment militia attacks, some Islamist factions persecuting minorities and others they deem insufficiently pious, and civilians of all confessions seeking safety among their respective groups. The result is significant, ongoing change in the country's demographics, including as deliberate military strategy. The Assad regime in 2016 forcibly transferred thousands of people from rebel-held areas to other parts of the country; rebels were effectively forced to assent to the evacuations as a result of the "surrender or starve" strategy by which the government had blocked aid deliveries to rebel-held areas. Separately, in 2015 Amnesty International accused Kurdish militias of destroying Arab and Turkmen settlements and displacing their inhabitants for suspected sympathies with IS or other rebels.

CIVIL LIBERTIES: 2 / 60

D. Freedom of Expression and Belief: 2 / 16

The constitution nominally guarantees freedom of speech and the press, but this is not implemented in practice. Freedom of expression is heavily restricted in government-held areas, and journalists or ordinary citizens who criticize the state face censorship, detention, torture, and death. The regime controls most domestic news outlets, substantially hindering access to information. All media must obtain permission to operate from the Interior Ministry. Private media in government areas are generally owned by figures associated with the regime. The state has stopped trying to block Facebook but instead uses it to monitor opponents and dissidents. Meanwhile, the progovernment Syrian Electronic Army has mounted several cyberattacks on opposition supporters, activists, and major foreign media.

Media freedom varies in rebel territory, but local outlets are generally under heavy pressure to support the dominant militant faction in the area. Journalists face physical danger throughout Syria. At least 14 journalists were killed in connection with their work in 2016, according to the Committee to Protect Journalists, bringing that total to 108 since early 2011. Several were executed by the Islamic State. Others were killed by unclaimed terrorist bombings or regime shelling or air strikes. Many journalists remained missing, were kidnapped, or imprisoned but eventually released.

While the constitution mandates that the president be a Muslim, there is no state religion, and the regime has generally allowed freedom of worship as long as religious activities are not politically subversive. The government monitors mosques and controls the appointment of Muslim religious leaders. In opposition-held areas, freedom of worship also generally prevails, except under extremist Islamist groups. IS has destroyed numerous religious and cultural sites and artifacts in its region, and harshly restricts any religious activity that does not conform to its version of Sunni Islam. Christians in IS-held areas are reportedly forced to pay special taxes and remove all outward symbols of their faith from their homes and persons. The war has increased sectarian hostility and polarization in both government and rebel-held areas. The regime has massacred Sunni civilians, while Sunni extremists have done the same to non-Sunni civilians.

Academic freedom is heavily restricted. University professors in government-held areas have been dismissed or imprisoned for expressing dissent, and some have been killed for supporting regime opponents. The civil war has greatly disrupted education in general. Combatants on all sides have regularly attacked or commandeered schools. IS has reconstituted an educational system of sorts in some of its territory, though it is based on religious and political indoctrination. Schooling in regime areas continues to emphasize political indoctrination as well. The PYD began to introduce Kurdish-language education in 2015, with critics alleging that its curriculum too served to advance the party's political agenda.

Private discussion is subject to heavy surveillance in areas controlled by the government and IS, but the environment is somewhat more open than before the uprising in some areas where government control has receded, though this depends which particular militias control them. The PYD and Jaish al-Islam, an opposition group with a presence in eastern Ghouta, allegedly suppress freedom of speech in their territory. The Assad government monitors online communications, including e-mail and social media, and persecutes internet users engaging in speech it objects to.

E. Associational and Organizational Rights: 0 / 12

Freedom of assembly is severely restricted across Syria. Opposition protests in government-held areas are usually met with gunfire, mass arrests, and torture of those detained. The regime generally denies registration to nongovernmental organizations with reformist or human rights missions, and regularly conducts raids and searches to detain civic and political activists. IS, the PYD, and some rebel factions have also used force to suppress civilian dissent and demonstrations.

A variety of new grassroots civil society networks emerged in many parts of Syria following the 2011 uprising, monitoring human rights abuses by all sides and attempting to provide humanitarian and other services in opposition areas. However, such activists face violence, intimidation, and detention by armed groups, and must operate secretly in some cases.

Professional syndicates in state-held areas are controlled by the Baath Party, and all labor unions must belong to the General Federation of Trade Unions, a nominally independent grouping that the government uses to control union activity. The war's economic and political pressures have made functioning labor relations virtually impossible across the country.

F. Rule of Law: 0 / 16

The constitution forbids government interference in the civil judiciary, but all judges and prosecutors must belong to the Baath Party and are in practice beholden to the political leadership. Military officers can try civilians in both conventional military courts and field courts. While civilians may appeal military court decisions with the military chamber of the Court of Cassation, military judges are neither independent nor impartial, as they are subordinate to the military command.

Government forces have arrested and tortured tens of thousands of people since the uprising began in 2011. In 2014, a military police forensic photographer defected and revealed some 55,000 images documenting the large-scale torture, starvation, and death of prisoners. In 2015, Human Rights Watch concluded the photos showed at least 6,786 different detainees who had died in government custody and showed signs of torture and other abuse. The Syrian Network for Human Rights documented more than 10,000 arbitrary arrests in 2016.

IS and some other Islamist militant groups have set up crude religious courts in their areas, imposing harsh punishments for perceived offenses by civilians. IS routinely carries out public executions, and insurgent factions including Jabhat al-Nusra have also been accused of summary killings of civilians and torture of detainees. More generally, the breakdown of state authority and the proliferation of both loyalist and rebel militias has led to warlordism, crime, and arbitrary abuse by all sides.

The Kurdish minority has historically faced official discrimination and severe restrictions on work, travel, property ownership, and cultural and linguistic expression, though their situation improved significantly after 2011 due to receding state authority. Syrian law also discriminates against LGBT (lesbian, gay, bisexual, and transgender) people; according to the 1949 penal code, "unnatural sexual intercourse" is punishable with up to three years in prison. Separately, there were multiple reports in 2015 of IS executing men for their alleged homosexuality.

G. Personal Autonomy and Individual Rights: 0 / 16

The proliferation of checkpoints manned by various armed groups, heavy combat, and general insecurity have severely restricted the free movement of people and vital supplies since 2011. The regime has systematically blockaded regions controlled by rebels, and rebel and IS forces have done the same to regime-held territories. As of May 2016, more than 1,000,000 Syrians were living under siege conditions, according to the Syria Institute, a U.S.-based think tank.

Rampant corruption predated the Syrian uprising, affecting the daily lives of Syrians. Citizens are frequently required to bribe officials to complete bureaucratic procedures, and business investors and owners must often pay bribes to operate. Since the war broke out, Syrians who fear persecution have been wary of approaching official institutions to request critical documentation, and must resort to the black market. Rebel groups, IS, regime, and Kurdish forces also extort businesses and confiscate private property to varying degrees.

Women are underrepresented in Syrian politics and government, and face serious legal discrimination. They hold just 13 percent of seats in the legislature, though some have been appointed to senior positions, including speaker of parliament and one of the two vice presidential posts. Husbands may prevent their wives from leaving the country with their children, and women cannot pass citizenship on to their children. Male perpetrators of killings classified as "honor crimes" can receive reduced sentences under the penal code. Personal status law for Muslims is governed by Sharia (Islamic law) and is discriminatory in marriage, divorce, and inheritance matters. Church law governs personal status issues for Christians, in some cases barring divorce.

In addition to increased sexual violence associated with the armed conflict, domestic abuse is endemic. Rates of early marriage are reportedly high, with displaced and refugee families in particular marrying off young daughters as a perceived safeguard against rape, a means of covering up such crimes, or a response to economic pressure. Forced prostitution and human trafficking are also serious problems among these populations.

Conditions for women are uneven in areas outside government control, ranging from extreme discrimination, sexual slavery, and onerous codes of dress and behavior in IS territory, to formal equality under the PYD in Kurdish areas. All government positions in Rojava are reportedly shared between a man and a woman, and women are well represented in political life and military service.

Forced labor is widespread in Syria, as many armed groups are engaged in forced conscription or the use of child soldiers.

Taiwan

Political Rights Rating: 1
Civil Liberties Rating: 1 ↑
Freedom Rating: 1.0
Freedom Status: Free
Electoral Democracy: Yes

Population: 23,500,000
Capital: Taipei

Ratings Change: Taiwan's civil liberties rating improved from 2 to 1 due to demonstrations of media independence and academic freedom in recent years, including in media coverage of the 2016 elections.

Ten-Year Ratings Timeline For Year Under Review (Political Rights, Civil Liberties, Status)

Year Under Review	2007	2008	2009	2010	2011	2012	2013	2014	2015	2016
Rating	2,1,F	2,1,F	1,2,F	1,2,F	1,2,F	1,2,F	1,2,F	1,2,F	1,2,F	1,1,F

Overview: Taiwan's vibrant and competitive democratic system has allowed three peaceful transfers of power between rival parties since 2000, and protections for civil liberties are generally robust. Ongoing concerns include Chinese efforts to influence policymaking and some sectors of the economy, foreign migrant workers' vulnerability to exploitation, and disputes over the land and housing rights of both ordinary citizens and Taiwan's indigenous people.

KEY DEVELOPMENTS IN 2016:

- The opposition Democratic Progressive Party (DPP) won a sweeping victory in January general elections, capturing both the presidency and a majority in the Legislative Yuan.
- A scandal over weak oversight of the state-controlled Mega Financial Holdings Company forced the head of Taiwan's top financial regulator to step down in October.
- Also in October, the DPP introduced draft legislation that would formally recognize same-sex marriage.

EXECUTIVE SUMMARY

Amid widespread dissatisfaction with a slowing economy and the incumbent Kuomintang (KMT) government's policy of closer ties with China, voters handed the opposition DPP a resounding victory in January general elections. Tsai Ing-wen, the DPP's chairperson, became the country's first female president, and the party won a substantial legislative majority.

The new government subsequently made commitments to better protect the rights of marginalized and vulnerable populations, including indigenous communities, foreign migrant workers, and LGBT (lesbian, gay, bisexual, and transgender) people. The administration also faced concern over a perceived lack of oversight of state-controlled financial institutions and the need for a reform of housing laws to secure residency rights in the context of development projects.

POLITICAl RIGHTS: 37 / 40

A. Electoral Process: 12 / 12

The president, who is directly elected for up to two four-year terms, appoints the premier with the consent of the national legislature (Legislative Yuan), which consists of 113 members serving four-year terms. The Executive Yuan, or cabinet, is made up of ministers appointed by the president on the recommendation of the premier. The three other branches of government are the judiciary (Judicial Yuan), a watchdog body (Control Yuan), and a branch responsible for civil-service examinations (Examination Yuan). Direct elections for both the president, held since 1996, and for the legislature, held since 1991, have been considered generally free.

In the January 2016 general elections, Tsai of the DPP won 56 percent of the presidential vote, followed by the KMT's Eric Chu Li-lun with 31 percent and James Soong Chu-yu of the People First Party (PFP) with 12.8 percent. Tsai's margin of victory was the largest since presidential elections were first held in 1996. The DPP also won 68 out of 113 seats in the Legislative Yuan, leaving the KMT with 35, the New Power Party with five, PFP with three, and the Non-Partisan Solidarity Union and an independent with one seat each.

Elections in Taiwan are administered by the Central Election Commission. The law mandates that no political party may hold more than one-third of the seats on the commission. Since 2007, instances of vote buying and other electoral irregularities have gradually waned thanks to tighter enforcement of anticorruption laws.

B. Political Pluralism and Participation: 15 / 16

Taiwan's multiparty system features vigorous competition between the two major parties, the KMT and the DPP. Opposition parties are able to function without interference.

The KMT, which governed Taiwan as an authoritarian, one-party state for decades until democratic reforms took hold in the 1980s and 1990s, retained a considerable financial advantage over its rivals in recent years, benefitting from the fact that the business sector generally favored the party's China-friendly policies. In contrast, the DPP has traditionally favored greater independence from China. The DPP's victory in the 2016 presidential and legislative elections was seen as a public rejection of the KMT's economic management and approach to relations with China. The results also led to Taiwan's third peaceful transfer of power between parties, after previous handovers in 2000 and 2008.

Taiwan's constitution grants all citizens the right to vote, including members of 16 indigenous tribes, who make up roughly 2 percent of the population. Six seats in the Legislative Yuan are reserved for indigenous candidates elected by indigenous voters. An additional two indigenous candidates won seats in 2016 through normal party-list voting.

C. Functioning of Government: 10 / 12

Though consideration of China necessarily plays a significant role in Taiwanese politics, elected officials in Taiwan are free to set and implement policy without undue interference from foreign or other unelected actors.

Corruption is significantly less pervasive than in the past, but it remains a problem. Politics and big business are closely intertwined, leading to malfeasance in government procurement. In August 2016, the state-controlled financial institution Mega Financial Holding Company was heavily fined for breaching U.S. laws against money laundering, prompting concerns over the Taiwan government's capacity to independently oversee the firm's financial compliance. The chairman of the Financial Supervisory Commission, Taiwan's top financial regulator, resigned in October as a result of the scandal. Also in August, seven Taiwan Railways Administration officials were convicted and sentenced for accepting sex-related services in exchange for business contracts over six years.

CIVIL LIBERTIES: 54 / 60 (+ 2)

D. Freedom of Expression and Belief: 16 / 16 (+ 2)

Taiwan's media reflect a diversity of views and report aggressively on government policies and corruption allegations, though many outlets display strong party affiliation in their coverage. Beijing has sought to exert influence on Taiwanese media. A number of media owners have significant business interests in China or rely on advertising by Chinese companies, leaving them vulnerable to pressure and prone to self-censorship on topics considered sensitive by the Chinese government. In recent years, Taiwanese regulators have successfully resisted proposed mergers that would have placed important media outlets in the hands of businessmen with significant ties to China, and the Taiwanese press was able to report freely on the 2016 elections. The government does not restrict internet access.

Taiwanese of all faiths can worship freely. Religious organizations that choose to register with the government receive tax-exempt status. Educators in Taiwan can generally write and lecture without interference, and past practices—including prosecutions—aimed at restricting academics' political activism have been rare in recent years. Private discussion is open and free, and there were no reports of the government illegally monitoring online communication.

E. Associational and Organizational Rights: 11 / 12

Taiwan's Assembly and Parade Act, passed in 1988, enables authorities to prosecute protesters who fail to obtain a permit or follow orders to disperse, but freedom of assembly is largely respected in practice. In recent years, there has been an increase in youth-led demonstrations. More than 30 people were arrested during a July 2015 protest over proposed changes to the high school curriculum that were seen by some as pro-Beijing, but only five of the student protesters were eventually convicted in September 2016 on obstruction of justice and coercion charges linked to a break-in at the Ministry of Education, and none faced jail time. Separately, in May 2016, the new government dropped legal complaints against 126 student protesters who had occupied a government building as part of the so-called Sunflower Movement in 2014, which was prompted by concerns about a KMT-backed trade agreement with China.

All civic organizations must register with the government, though registration is freely granted. Nongovernmental organizations typically operate without harassment.

Trade unions are independent, and most workers enjoy freedom of association, though the government strictly regulates the right to strike. Among other barriers, teachers, workers in the defense industry, and government employees are prohibited from striking.

F. Rule of Law: 14 / 16

Taiwan's judiciary is independent, and trials are generally fair. Police largely respect the ban on arbitrary detention, and attorneys are allowed to monitor interrogations to prevent torture. After a four-year moratorium on the use of the death penalty, the government reinstated the practice in 2010. Condemned inmates, after being sedated, are shot from behind at close range. Family members of inmates facing the death penalty are typically not informed about scheduled dates of executions. Authorities executed one inmate in 2016, down from six in 2015.

The constitution provides for the equality of all citizens, though the island's indigenous people continue to face social and economic discrimination, leading to high unemployment levels, lower wages, and barriers to education and social services. In August 2016, President Tsai offered the government's first formal apology to indigenous people for "the suffering and injustice you endured over the past 400 years." She also announced the launch of a justice commission to investigate their historical mistreatment. Nonetheless, disputes over indigenous lands continue amid stalled efforts to pass legislation on indigenous autonomy.

Taiwanese law prohibits discrimination in employment based on sexual orientation, and violence against LGBT people is adequately addressed by police.

Taiwanese law does not allow for asylum or refugee status. However, in July 2016 a long-awaited draft bill to address the problem passed its first review by the Internal Administration Committee of the Legislative Yuan.

G. Personal Autonomy and Individual Rights: 13 / 16

Taiwan's residents enjoy freedom of movement, and Taiwanese authorities have gradually eased restrictions on travel between Taiwan and China in recent years. A program launched in 2011 allows Chinese tourists to travel to Taiwan without supervision, with a cap on the daily number raised to 5,000 in 2015. However, Chinese authorities reportedly moved to reduce cross-strait tourism after the DPP government took office in 2016.

Urban renewal projects and conversions of agricultural land for industrial or residential use have been criticized for unfairly displacing residents. In August 2016, demonstrations were held to protest a lack of transparency and public consultation concerning planned demolitions of homes and local markets to make way for three major development projects in the city of Kaohsiung. Evictions and demolitions continued through October, even as protests persisted. Housing advocates have called for legal amendments to clarify residency rights, including protections against forced eviction, and establish an appeals system to review alleged violations.

The constitution guarantees women equal rights, though Taiwanese women continue to face discrimination in employment and compensation. The 2016 elections increased women's overall political representation, with female candidates winning the presidency and a record 38 percent of seats in the Legislative Yuan. In October, the DPP introduced a draft bill in the Legislative Yuan that would formally recognize same-sex marriage. Amendments to the Nationality Act adopted in December eased regulations that limit access to citizenship for the foreign spouses of Taiwanese nationals.

Over 600,000 foreign migrants work in Taiwan, with a substantial number working as domestic helpers and fishermen; most come from Indonesia, Vietnam, Thailand, and the Philippines. Foreign domestic workers and fishermen are not covered by Taiwan's Labour Standards Act, meaning they are excluded from minimum wage, overtime, and paid leave protections. As a result, foreign workers in these and other fields are at substantial risk of exploitation, with widespread accounts of unpaid wages, poor working conditions, and physical and sexual abuse, as well as extortion and fraud at the hands of recruitment and brokerage agencies. In July 2016, President Tsai publicly committed to improving protections for foreign workers, and the government promulgated new legislation that established stricter rules and stronger punishments to combat worker exploitation by Taiwanese fishing companies.

Tajikistan

Political Rights Ratings: 7
Civil Liberties Ratings: 6
Freedom Rating: 6.5
Freedom Status: Not Free
Electoral Democracy: No

Population: 8,600,000
Capital: Dushanbe

Ten-Year Ratings Timeline For Year Under Review (Political Rights, Civil Liberties, Status)

Year Under Review	2007	2008	2009	2010	2011	2012	2013	2014	2015	2006
Rating	6,5,NF	6,5,NF	6,5,NF	6,5,NF	6,5,NF	6,6,NF	6,6,NF	6,6,NF	7,6,NF	7,6,NF

Overview: Political rights and civil liberties in Tajikistan are severely curtailed by the government of President Emomali Rahmon, which sustains a campaign of repression against political opposition, dissent, and criticism.

KEY DEVELOPMENTS IN 2016:

- In May, voters approved a package of 41 constitutional amendments that, among other things, significantly strengthened executive power, including by removing presidential term limits.
- Taking the repression of opposition voices to another level, authorities prosecuted lawyers who had represented members of the banned Islamic Renaissance Party of Tajikistan (IRPT) in court.
- In November, the independent media outlets *Nigoh* and TojNews announced that they were ceasing operations.

EXECUTIVE SUMMARY

The government continued to arbitrarily limit free speech, access to information, and the right to civic organization in 2016. In May, authorities held a referendum on a controversial package of constitutional amendments, which voters approved. Among other things, the amendments formally removed presidential term limits, introduced a prohibition on faith-based political groups, and lowered the minimum age for presidential candidates from 35 to 30. The changes effectively allow Rahmon to rule indefinitely, and also render his 29-year-old son eligible for candidacy in the 2020 presidential polls.

The government continued a legal and media campaign against former members of the country's largest opposition group, the IRPT, which was banned and declared a terrorist organization in 2015. After arresting many of its leaders and sentencing them to long prison terms in 2015, the regime expanded efforts to suppress the IRPT, and initiated prosecution against lawyers who represented IRPT members. In October, the Supreme Court convicted two such legal professionals of extremism and related charges. After exiled former members of the IRPT and another opposition entity, Group 24, spoke at a conference organized by the Organization for Security and Co-operation in Europe (OSCE) in Warsaw, authorities in Tajikistan harassed, threatened, and arrested members of their families.

Independent voices within the media continued to face dire conditions. In November, two prominent independent outlets—the *Nigoh* newspaper and TojNews website—announced their closures, noting that conditions in the country no longer allowed for them to continue operations.

POLITICAL RIGHTS: 1 / 40 (− 1)

A. Electoral Process: 0 / 12 (− 1)

B. Political Pluralism and Participation: 0 / 16

C. Functioning of Government: 1 / 12

CIVIL LIBERTIES: 10 / 60 (− 4)

D. Freedom of Expression and Belief: 2 / 16 (− 2)

E. Associational and Organizational Rights: 2 / 12 (− 1)

F. Rule of Law: 2 / 16 (− 1)

G. Personal Autonomy and Individual Rights: 4 / 16

This country report has been abridged for *Freedom in the World 2017.* For background information on political rights and civil liberties in Tajikistan, see *Freedom in the World 2016.*

Tanzania

Political Rights: 3
Civil Liberties: 4
Freedom Rating 3.5
Freedom Status: Partly Free
Electoral Democracy: Yes

Population: 54,200,000
Capital: Dodoma

Ten-Year Ratings Timeline For Year Under Review (Political Rights, Civil Liberties, Status)

Year Under Review	2007	2008	2009	2010	2011	2012	2013	2014	2015	2016
Rating	4,3,PF	4,3,PF	4,3,PF	3,3,PF	3,3,PF	3,3,PF	3,3,PF	3,3,PF	3,4,PF	3,4,PF

Overview: Although Tanzania has held five consecutive multiparty elections since its transition from a one-party state in the early 1990s, the presence of formal opposition remains limited within the government, and the ruling party, Chama Cha Mapinduzi (CCM), has retained power for over half a century. Civil liberties concerns include government limitations on freedom of expression as well as recent legislation and official rhetoric that have had a chilling effect on civil society.

KEY DEVELOPMENTS IN 2016:

- A number of moves by the authorities threatened the exercise of civil liberties, including an indefinite ban on public assemblies, implemented in June, and the halting of public broadcasts of parliamentary sessions, implemented in April.
- Zanzibar held elections in March, following an annulment of its 2015 polls; the opposition boycotted the vote, allowing the CCM to win the presidency and every legislative seat.
- Authorities used the controversial 2015 Cybercrimes Act to prosecute critics of the ruling party.

- The president signed another piece of restrictive legislation, the Media Services Bill, in November, raising concerns from watchdogs about expanded government powers to curb freedom of expression.

EXECUTIVE SUMMARY

The aftermath of Tanzania's 2015 national elections, which were the country's most competitive to date but also featured controversy, drove political developments in early 2016. The elections in the semi-autonomous archipelago of Zanzibar had been annulled before the official announcement of the results, and a second vote was held in March 2016. The opposition formally boycotted the elections, as the Civic United Front (CUF) claimed that the 2015 elections had been voided because it appeared to be winning. The lead-up to the vote was tense, with episodes of violence against opposition members and journalists as well as a heightened military presence. The CCM easily won every seat in the legislature and took the presidency, resulting in the dissolution of a power-sharing government that had been formed in 2010 and allocated executive positions to both major parties. Although Tanzania's opposition had successfully organized a coalition for the 2015 elections, it showed weakness and fragmentation in 2016. Following signs of infighting, the chairman of the CUF was expelled in September.

There was a significant crackdown on civil liberties during the year. The Cybercrimes Act, rushed through the legislature in 2015, was used against critics of the regime on a number of occasions. The law gives the government significant leeway to arrest anyone for publishing information deemed false, deceptive, misleading, or inaccurate and to levy heavy penalties against individuals involved in a host of criminalized cyberactivities. Under this law, one man was convicted in June of calling President Magufuli an "imbecile" on Facebook. The Media Services Bill, signed into law in November, raised alarm in the media community, with critics noting that it could constrain the types of stories published by journalists. In April, the Information Ministry announced that broadcasts of parliamentary sessions would cease, a move that significantly undermined the public's ability to access official information. Separately, in June, the government imposed a ban on all public demonstrations and rallies, curtailing individuals' right to exercise freedom of assembly.

POLITICAL RIGHTS: 25 / 40 (− 2)

A. Electoral Process: 7 / 12 (− 1)

The president of Tanzania is elected by direct popular vote for up to two five-year terms. Legislative authority lies with a unicameral, 393-seat National Assembly (the Bunge) whose members serve five-year terms. Of these, 264 are directly elected in single-member constituencies, 113 are reserved for women elected by political parties, 10 are filled by presidential appointment, 5 are for members of the Zanzibar legislature, and 1 is held by the attorney general. Zanzibar elects its own president and 85-seat House of Representatives, whose members serve five-year terms and are seated through a mix of direct elections and appointments. Zanzibar maintains largely independent jurisdiction over its internal affairs.

The 2015 national elections saw a voter turnout of 65 percent, compared with 43 percent in 2010. In the presidential race, the CCM's John Magufuli won with 58 percent of the vote, while Edward Lowassa of Chama Cha Demokrasia na Maendeleo (CHADEMA) took 40 percent. In the National Assembly, the CCM won 189 of the directly elected seats. Opposition parties, many of which had coordinated candidates through a unified coalition, gained their largest representation yet. CHADEMA won 70 of the directly elected seats, the CUF took 42, and the Alliance for Change and Transparency (ACT) and the National Convention for Construction and Reform (NCCR)–Mageuzi each won one.

Domestic and international observers generally deemed the 2015 elections to be credible, but noted a number of areas of concern. An observer mission from the European Union (EU) described "highly competitive, generally well organized elections, but with insufficient efforts at transparency from the election administrations." The EU mission noted that the CCM had drawn on state resources, such as public stadiums, to support its campaign.

In addition, the simultaneous elections in Zanzibar featured irregularities. Prior to the announcement of official results, Zanzibar Electoral Commission (ZEC) Chair Jecha Salim Jecha declared the elections for the president and legislature null and void, claiming the process had not been conducted in accordance with the law. In a joint statement, observer missions from the Commonwealth, the Southern African Development Community, the African Union, and the EU expressed "great concern" at the ZEC's move and noted that they had assessed the voting to be conducted according to the law. The CUF claimed that authorities annulled the vote because the CCM appeared to be losing. The annulment of Zanzibar's presidential election and simultaneous acceptance of the Zanzibari vote for the mainland presidential election undermined the fairness of the electoral framework. The framework is facilitated by the National Election Commission (NEC) and the ZEC, both of which are appointed by the Tanzanian president and whose independence has been questioned. The president maintains the ability to appoint regional and district commissioners, who are influential during elections.

A second Zanzibari election, held in March 2016, was boycotted by the opposition, and the CCM won the presidency and the entire legislature. Ahead of the elections, the military increased its presence on Zanzibar, and there were reports of political party offices being torched and journalists and opposition members harassed and even, in some cases, abducted. Without an opposition, CCM legislators voted in September to change Zanzibar's constitution, eliminating a 2010 amendment establishing the Government of National Unity, a CCM-CUF power-sharing arrangement that had been considered a milestone for stability.

Tanzania's constitution was passed in 1977, when the country was under single-party rule. In 2014, the presidentially appointed Constitutional Review Commission submitted its second draft of a new constitution to the Constituent Assembly (CA), a body of 640 Tanzanian and Zanzibari legislators and presidential appointees, for approval. The draft proposed a three-tiered federal state, fewer cabinet members, independent candidature, limits on executive appointment, and an explicit bill of rights. Shortly afterward, Tanzania's three primary opposition parties quit the CA, claiming that their input was being ignored. Nevertheless, the CA passed a controversial draft that year. Opposition parties sought a judicial block to the document, suggesting it was passed without a quorum, and initiated a nationwide campaign to garner public support for their position. Though the government scheduled a nationwide referendum on the proposed constitution in 2015, the NEC announced an indefinite delay, citing an inability to implement a new biometric voter registration system in time for voting. No referendum on the matter was held in 2016.

B. Political Pluralism and Participation: 11 / 16 (− 1)

Tanzanians have the right to organize into political parties, and there is growing support for the opposition. The constitution permits political parties to form "shadow governments" while in opposition. Four opposition parties—the CUF, CHADEMA, NCCR-Mageuzi, and the National League for Democracy (NLD)—supported a single presidential candidate and coordinated parliamentary candidates for the 2015 elections. Past attempts to form opposition alliances had failed. This coalition, known as the Coalition for a People's Constitution,

Ukawa, formed during the CA process and posed the most significant threat to CCM's rule in the country's history.

In June 2016, authorities announced an indefinite ban on all demonstrations and rallies, curtailing the ability of political parties to hold assemblies in public. The government clarified the following month that the opposition could hold small constituency meetings, but the effects of the ban were nevertheless overwhelmingly negative. CHADEMA canceled plans for a nationwide rally in September following warnings from the police.

Opposition parties report regular harassment and intimidation by the ruling party and various state institutions, including the police. In December, police interrogated Tundu Lissu, the chief legal adviser of CHADEMA, for six hours about his claim regarding the government's alleged use of torture chambers, among other things. In November, CHADEMA parliamentarian Godbless Lema was arrested and charged with inciting mutiny and insulting the president. He remained in detention at the end of 2016.

Both CHADEMA and the CUF have struggled with internal crises over the last two years. In 2015, CHADEMA leader Wilbroad Slaa resigned after Ukawa selected Edward Lowassa as its presidential candidate, citing Lowassa's involvement in a corruption scandal. A power struggle within the CUF led to the expulsion of its former leader, Ibrahim Lipumba, in September 2016.

People's choices are influenced by threats from military forces and the use of material incentives by the ruling party.

Cultural, ethnic, religious, and other minority groups have full political rights, but parties formed on explicitly ethnic or religious bases are prohibited.

C. Functioning of Government: 7 / 12

Magufuli, a technocrat, has taken a number of cost-cutting measures, including replacing an annual independence day celebration with a national street cleaning day, shrinking the cabinet from 30 to 19 members, and reducing the salaries of senior officials, the latter of which he announced in March 2016.

Despite the presence of the Prevention and Combating Corruption Bureau (PCCB), corruption is pervasive in all aspects of political and commercial life in Tanzania. The PCCB has been accused of focusing on low-level corruption and doing little to address graft committed by senior government officials. In 2015, Magufuli dismissed the director general of the PCCB for negligence. In January 2016, Dickson Maimu, head of the National Identification Authority (NIDA), was suspended to allow authorities to investigate his possible involvement in a corrupt identification card project. Maimu and five other NIDA officials were charged with abuse of power, among other offenses, in August.

The government remains sporadically responsive to citizen input between elections, and people generally have access to public information. However, in April 2016, live broadcasts of parliamentary sessions were suspended. Justified as a cost-cutting measure by the government, the move was widely criticized by local and domestic rights groups. The parliament inconsistently publishes legislation, committee reports, budgets, and other documents.

CIVIL LIBERTIES: 33 / 40
D. Freedom of Expression and Belief: 9 / 16

Although the constitution provides for freedom of speech, it does not specifically guarantee freedom of the press. Current laws give authorities broad discretion to restrict media on the basis of national security or public interest, and difficult registration processes hinder print and electronic media. The government increased its crackdown on the media in 2016.

The 2015 Cybercrimes Act gives the government significant leeway to arrest anyone perceived of publishing information deemed false, deceptive, misleading, or inaccurate and to levy heavy penalties against individuals involved in a host of criminalized cyberactivities. In December 2016, the High Court struck down a section of the law that allowed suspects who voluntarily confess to receive penalties before trial. The rest of the law was deemed constitutional. In June, a court sentenced a private citizen to three years in jail and a 7 million shilling ($3,100) fine for insulting Magufuli on Facebook. His sentence was subsequently reduced to only the fine. In September, five individuals were charged under the Electronic and Postal Communications Act No. 3 of 2010 over commentary about Magufuli on WhatsApp. In December, police raided the office of the popular online discussion website, JamiiForums, and interrogated employees. The raid came a day after police arrested the site's cofounder, Maxence Melo. He was detained for seven days and charged with obstructing a police investigation and using an unregistered domain. Melo later claimed that police had asked for the identities of whistleblowers who used the site. In December, the chief legal adviser of CHADEMA claimed that 142 people were arrested under the Cybercrimes Act from May to November 2016.

In November, Magufuli signed the Media Service Bill into law. The act seemingly aims to professionalize the journalism sector, and requires employers to provide insurance and social security. However, media stakeholders have objected to the constraints it places on journalists and news outlets, including the ambiguous prohibition of stories that would cause "grievance" to citizens. The act also includes a provision to create a government-controlled accreditation board empowered to suspend journalists. Reporters operating without a press card could be subject to three or more years in prison and at least a five million shilling ($2,200) fine under the law. In addition, the law empowers the information minister to set licensing requirements for newspapers.

In July, the television program "Take One" was forced to publicly apologize for LGBT advocacy, and in October, the telecommunications regulator suspended the program due to sexual content.

In July, a court convicted a police officer of manslaughter in the 2012 death of journalist Daudi Mwangosi, and sentenced him to 15 years in prison.

Press freedom in Zanzibar is more constrained than on the mainland. The Zanzibari government owns the only daily newspaper, and private media other than radio are nearly nonexistent. Journalist Salma Said was abducted and held for two days by unidentified men during the March 2016 electoral period.

Freedom of religion is generally respected. Relations between the various faiths are largely peaceful, though there have been periodic instances of violence. Politicians have used the specter of Islamic radicalism in Zanzibar to advance political goals.

Historically, there have been few government restrictions on academic freedom. The 2015 Statistics Act—which requires data released publicly to be first approved by the National Bureau of Statistics—has not yet, as feared by the law's critics, disproportionately affected researchers and academics.

People actively engage in private discussions, but the CCM uses a system of party-affiliated cells in urban and rural areas for public monitoring.

E. Associational and Organizational Rights: 6 / 12

The constitution guarantees freedom of assembly, but the government can limit this right. All assemblies require police approval, and critical political demonstrations are at times actively discouraged. In July 2016, authorities banned all public gatherings until further notice. CHADEMA's proposed "Day of Defiance" rally, scheduled for September and subsequently canceled, faced threats from the regional commissioner of Dar es Salaam, who instructed police to assault demonstrators.

There is generally freedom for nongovernmental organizations (NGOs), and more than 4,000 are registered. While current laws give the government the right to deregister NGOs, there has been little interference in NGO activity. Many groups, such as Research and Education for Democracy in Tanzania and the Legal and Human Rights Centrer, publish reports that are critical of the government. However, in September, two civil society leaders in Zanzibar criticized the government for politicizing civil society and failing to address issues raised by NGO stakeholders.

Trade unions are ostensibly independent of the government and are coordinated by the Trade Union Congress of Tanzania and the Zanzibar Trade Union Congress. The Tanzania Federation of Cooperatives represents most of Tanzania's agricultural sector. Essential public service workers are barred from striking, and other workers are restricted by complex notification and mediation requirements. Strikes are infrequent on both the mainland and Zanzibar.

F. Rule of Law: 9 / 16

Tanzania's judiciary suffers from underfunding and corruption. Judges are political appointees, and the judiciary does not have an independent budget, which makes it vulnerable to political pressure. Rule of law does not always prevail in civil and criminal matters.

Despite recent improvements, policies and rules regarding arrest and pretrial detention are often ignored. Prisoners suffer from harsh conditions, including overcrowding and poor medical care. Security forces reportedly abuse, threaten, and mistreat civilians routinely and with limited accountability. Vigilante justice and mob violence are common, and security forces are often unable or unwilling to enforce the rule of law.

Tanzania's albino population has faced increasing violence over recent years. Albino body parts are believed to bring good luck, leading to the trafficking, death, and dismemberment of many albinos. In September 2016, unknown attackers attempted to chop off the legs and hands of the leader of an albino society. The Tanzania Albinism Society, an umbrella organization, aims to protect albinos, and the government has established sanctuaries for those who flee their communities.

Same-sex sexual relations are illegal and punishable by lengthy prison terms, and members of the LGBT (lesbian, gay, bisexual, and transgender) community face discrimination and police abuse. Most hide their sexual orientation. In September, the deputy health minister threatened to ban NGOs that support LGBT causes and blamed LGBT people for spreading HIV. In July, the regional commissioner of Dar es Salaam claimed that he would monitor social media posts to find and arrest gay people.

More than 250,000 refugees from conflicts in neighboring countries reside in Tanzania.

As of April, Tanzania was home to over 130,000 Burundian refugees, many of whom entered the country in 2015 following an outbreak of civil unrest. Refugee camps are overburdened.

Human rights advocates have criticized the 2002 Prevention of Terrorism Act for giving police and immigration officials sweeping powers to arrest suspected illegal immigrants.

G. Personal Autonomy and Individual Rights: 9 / 16

Citizens generally enjoy basic freedoms in travel, residence, employment, and education. However, the prevalence of petty corruption can inhibit these freedoms.

Tanzanians have the right to establish private businesses but are often required to pay bribes to set up and operate them. The state remains the owner of all land and leases to individuals and private entities, leading to clashes between citizens and private companies. A 2016 report by a special commission appointed by the Mines Ministry estimated that over the last decade, police were responsible for 65 deaths and 270 injuries during clashes with villagers at a Canadian-owned mine in northern Tanzania. Land-use conflicts exist in ancestral lands and near nature reserves and national parks, where the government has restricted grazing.

Women's rights are constitutionally guaranteed but not uniformly protected. Rape, female genital mutilation, and domestic violence are reportedly common but rarely prosecuted. Around 37 percent of underage girls are married. To help combat this problem, the Constitutional Court established in July 2016 that the minimum marriage age is 18. Women have high descriptive representation due to gender quotas in Tanzania's legislatures. In 2015, Samia Suluhu Hassan became the country's first woman vice president. Four female ministers and five female deputy ministers serve in the cabinet.

In September 2016, the government announced that it would bolster its border security to target human trafficking.

Equality of economic opportunity is limited, and there is continued economic exploitation. Poverty, especially in rural areas, affects approximately 33 percent of the population.

Thailand

Political Rights Rating: 6
Civil Liberties Rating: 5
Freedom Rating: 5.5
Freedom Status: Not Free
Electoral Democracy: No

Population: 65,300,000
Capital: Bangkok

Ten-Year Ratings Timeline For Year Under Review (Political Rights, Civil Liberties, Status)

Year Under Review	2007	2008	2009	2010	2011	2012	2013	2014	2015	2016
Rating	6,4,PF	5,4,PF	5,4,PF	5,4,PF	4,4,PF	4,4,PF	4,4,PF	6,5,NF	6,5,NF	6,5,NF

Overview: Thailand is ruled by a military junta that launched a coup in 2014, claiming that it would put an end to a political crisis that had gripped the country for almost a decade. As the military government goes about remaking the political system, it has exercised unchecked powers granted through an article of the interim constitution to impose extensive restrictions on civil and political rights, and to suppress dissent.

KEY DEVELOPMENTS IN 2016:

- In August, voters approved a referendum on a draft constitution that would weaken political parties, strengthen unelected bodies, and entrench the military's presence in politics.
- Authorities placed severe restrictions on free expression ahead of the vote, including through the 2016 Referendum Act, which criminalized the expression of opinions "inconsistent with the truth." Over 100 people were arrested for offenses related to the referendum.
- In September, the government issued an order that halted the practice of trying civilians accused of national security, lèse-majesté, and certain other crimes in

military courts. However, the order is not retroactive and does not cover cases that had already entered the military court system.

- Following the death of King Bhumibol Adulyadej in October, the military government intensified restrictions on speech deemed offensive to the monarchy as it worked to manage the period of transition.

EXECUTIVE SUMMARY

The National Council for Peace and Order (NCPO), the military junta that seized power in a 2014 coup, continued to impose extensive restrictions on political rights and civil liberties in 2016, including through the use of an article of the interim constitution that gives the head of the NCPO unchecked powers. Activists who express opposition to the government are monitored, summoned, arrested, and detained on accusations of breaking a raft of laws that limit freedom of expression and assembly.

While the NCPO's road map for a return to civilian rule has shifted several times since 2014, a draft constitution was released in March 2016, and 61 percent of voters approved the draft in a national referendum held in August. The new charter aims to weaken political parties and elected representatives, strengthen unelected councils and bureaucrats, and entrench the military's presence in politics. The draft was developed without meaningful citizen input, and public discussions and debates to promote awareness and understanding of its content were not permitted. The 2016 Referendum Act banned campaigning on the charter or expressing opinions that were "inconsistent with the truth;" violations carried penalties of up to 10 years in jail. When students and other civil society activists tried to distribute flyers about the charter or advocate for voting against it, they were arrested; when academics tried to hold seminars to analyze its contents, security officials forced them to cancel the events.

The death of King Bhumibol Adulyadej in October ended a 70-year reign. His son, Crown Prince Maha Vajiralongkorn, in December accepted the invitation of the National Legislative Assembly (NLA) to succeed his late father. The junta intensified restrictions on speech deemed offensive to the monarchy as it worked to manage the period of transition.

In September, the government issued an order that halted the practice of trying civilians accused of national security and lèse-majesté crimes, and of violating NCPO orders, in military courts. However, the order is not retroactive and does not cover cases that already entered the military court system.

POLITICAL RIGHTS: 7 / 40

A. Electoral Process: 1 / 12

Under the 2007 constitution that was drafted after the 2006 military coup, Thailand was governed through a bicameral parliamentary system. In late 2013, amid mass antigovernment protests, elections were called in an attempt to end a persistent deadlock between Prime Minister Yingluck Shinawatra's Pheua Thai Party (PTP) and the opposition Democrat Party (DP) and People's Democratic Reform Committee (PDRC). Elections were held in early 2014, but protests disrupted the voting process in some constituencies, eventually prompting the Constitutional Court to call new national elections. Before the polls could take place, the Constitutional Court found Yingluck and nine cabinet members guilty of abuse of power for 2011 personnel changes that granted the post of national police chief to a relative of Yingluck's; she subsequently complied with the court's order to step down as caretaker prime minister. A military coup in May 2014 forestalled further electoral plans.

General Prayuth Chan-ocha, the army chief at the time of the coup, became both head of the NCPO and prime minister. An interim constitution promulgated by the NCPO in July 2014 created a 220-seat National Legislative Assembly (NLA)—which formally installed the prime minister and cabinet—and the 250-member National Reform Council (NRC). The NRC was designed to provide the leadership with recommendations for reform of all aspects of governance and the political process. Both the NRC and the NLA were comprised of members appointed by the NCPO, and were dominated by current and former military officers and individuals who had opposed the Yingluck government. However, the NRC was dissolved following its rejection of a draft constitution in September 2015. A National Reform Steering Assembly (NRSA) was then convened to replace it. The new body consisted of 200 members appointed by the head of the NCPO, and included academics, representatives of political parties, former members of the NRC, and a significant number of military and police members.

The effort to draft a new permanent constitution was a major component of the military's road map back to electoral democracy. Following the NRC's rejection of the first draft constitution, the military government in late 2015 appointed a new Constitutional Drafting Committee (CDC) tasked with producing another draft. The draft was developed without public comment and unveiled in March 2016, and then voted on in an August referendum.

While voting day proceeded peacefully, the period leading up to the referendum was marked by the suppression of dissent. The NLA passed the Referendum Act, which prohibited the expression of opinions and distribution of information about the charter that was "inconsistent with the truth," and which carried a penalty of up to 10 years in prison. Authorities banned public seminars and debates on the contents of the draft constitution, and arrested those who campaigned against the charter or disseminated leaflets and booklets on the draft. Using a combination of the Referendum Act, limits on political gatherings, a 2015 law on public assemblies, and restrictions on media, authorities made over 100 arrests related to the referendum. While one regional Asian monitoring network was allowed to perform random polling station checks on election day, local civil society organizations were prohibited from conducting monitoring of the referendum process.

The turnout for the referendum was low, at roughly 55 percent of eligible voters; about 61 percent of them voted to approve the charter, paving the way, according to the junta's timeline, for elections to be held in late 2017 after the development of various organic laws.

The charter contained features that critics across the spectrum of Thailand's political factions claimed would weaken political parties and elected officials while strengthening unelected institutions. In the mixed-member apportionment system introduced in the charter, there will be 350 constituency seats and 150 party-list seats in the House of Representatives, the lower house of parliament, with lawmakers serving four-year terms. Citizens will cast only one vote, rather than two distinct votes, which counts for a candidate as well as for that candidate's party for the party list seats. Experts anticipate that without separate votes for each type of seat, parties will have difficulty gaining a majority, which could lead to unstable coalition governments.

All 250 seats in the Senate, or upper house, will be appointed for the first five-year term by the junta and include six seats reserved for senior military officials. Subsequent Senates will be appointed by a selection committee whose members will be drawn from various professional groups. Unelected bodies, such as the Constitutional Court, will be strengthened to check elected governments.

The government also inserted a second question into the referendum ballot related to whether the Senate could join the lower house in appointing a prime minister; the question was approved by 58 percent of voters.

B. Political Pluralism and Participation: 3 / 16

Since Thaksin Shinawatra, Yingluck's brother, and his Thai Rak Thai (TRT) party came to power in 2001, there have been two main political factions in Thailand's system: the DP, which is today associated with traditional elites, and the TRT and its successors (the People's Power Party and the PTP). The latter have won every election since 2001. While the actions of the NCPO have favored the interests of the DP's core supporters, leaders of both the DP and the PTP have been kept on the sidelines of the political process since the 2014 coup.

Following the coup, political parties continued to be regulated under a 2007 law. However, the NCPO enacted measures banning the formation of new political parties and prohibiting existing parties from meeting or conducting political activities, including any party-wide deliberations on the constitutional drafting process. State funding for political parties was also suspended. Following the completion of the final draft of the constitution, the CDC and Election Commission have been tasked with drafting organic laws, including one governing political parties, which are scheduled to be completed in 2017.

The sweeping scope of the military government's powers, facilitated by Article 44 of the interim constitution, continued to undermine citizens' ability to participate in the political process. Orders issued under Article 44 not only imposed restrictions on expression and assembly, but also granted the head of the NCPO absolute power beyond legislative or judicial oversight. In 2016, the NCPO used this article to remove government officials from office and fast-track various policies without public input.

The constitution approved in 2016 will institutionalize the military's influence in political processes, both through its presence in the upper house of parliament as well as through its connections with allies placed in ostensibly independent agencies tasked with checking the powers of elected government.

Members of Thailand's ethnic and religious minority groups are poorly represented in national politics.

C. Functioning of Government: 3 / 12

The NLA, which serves in place of an elected parliament, continued in 2016 to consider draft legislation and pass laws that were criticized for infringing on citizens' rights and for lacking public input. Additional military officials were appointed to the NLA in October, reportedly amid public concern about the new members' lack of legislative qualifications.

Corruption is widespread at all levels of Thai society. The National Anti-Corruption Commission (NACC) receives a high number of complaints each year. The NLA passed bills to establish a special court, which opened in October, to handle corruption cases in response to the backlog confronted by the NACC and the Public Anti-Corruption Commission.

A criminal negligence case that was lodged in 2015 against former prime minister Yingluck in connection with a rice-subsidy scheme was still ongoing at year's end. However, the government issued an administrative order in October imposing on her a $1 billion fine for her role in the scheme, even before the case has been concluded.

In 2016, the NCPO had to address allegations of nepotism and cronyism against one of its members, General Preecha Chan-ocha, who is the brother of the head of the NCPO and had served as permanent secretary of the ministry of defense. Media reports in September revealed that a company owned by general's son was awarded military construction contracts by the army division where his father once held a post. General Preecha and other military officials denied that any improprieties had taken place, and the issue faded from public attention.

CIVIL LIBERTIES: 25 / 60

D. Freedom of Expression and Belief: 6 / 16

Since taking power in 2014, the NCPO has systematically used censorship, intimidation, and legal action to suppress freedom of speech. Journalists and media outlets risk penalties for violating an NCPO ban on material that "maliciously" criticizes the government or is deemed divisive. Outlets face suspension and revocation of their operating licenses. In July 2016, the government invoked Article 44 to give legal immunity to the National Broadcasting and Telecommunications Commission (NBTC) when it imposes regulatory actions on television and radio outlets deemed to have violated national security. A proposed media regulation bill also provoked concern among Thai media associations, and six such groups in December 2016 submitted an open letter to the media reform committee saying the bill would permit interference by politicians in media outlets' operations.

Defamation is a criminal offense, and charges are often used by politicians and companies to silence opponents, critics, and activists. Frequently paired with accusations of defamation and other offenses are charges under the 2007 Computer Crimes Act (CCA), which assigns significant prison terms for the online publication of false information deemed to endanger the public or national security, and allows the government to review the data of individual web users for a select number of preceding days. The CCA has been invoked against whistle-blowers and government critics. In a high-profile case, a British human rights activist was found guilty in September 2016 of defamation and of violating the CCA in connection with 2013 allegations that a Thai fruit wholesale company had committed labor rights violations. Additionally, three human rights advocates were accused by the Internal Security Operations Command (ISOC) in June of defamation and CCA violations for their report chronicling allegations that ISOC counterinsurgency agents had tortured people during operations in the southern part of the country in 2014 and 2015.

In December, the NLA passed amendments to the CCA that will intensify existing constraints on internet freedom. Ambiguous language related to the type of information that could be deemed "false" or "distorted" grants authorities considerable discretion in judging whether an individual violates the law, making it vulnerable to abuse. Another component that provoked concern is the establishment of a computer data screening committee empowered to request court orders to delete content that is not illegal, but which it determines is contrary to public morals. Internet service providers will also continue to face punishment for objectionable content if they do not take action to follow government requests to remove offending information. The authorities continue to block sites that are critical of the government or deemed insulting to the monarchy.

The number of lèse-majesté cases, covered under Article 112 of the criminal code, has sharply increased under the NCPO. Cases have been used to target activists, scholars, students, journalists, and politicians, and accusations have also been lodged by citizens against one another. In addition to authorities' monitoring of social media sites for such violations, this type of social surveillance has also been undertaken by citizens who, either with the backing of the government or on their own initiative, scan online postings and report them to authorities. In a 2016 case demonstrating the scope of what can be considered a lèse-majesté case, a student activist's mother was accused in May of committing such an offense by acknowledging a private Facebook message that contained an alleged lèse-majesté violation. Authorities maintained that by replying with a single word, which Human Rights Watch characterized as a "non-committal, colloquial 'yes' in the Thai language," she had failed to reject the comment.

During the sensitive period after King Bhumibol's death in October 2016, the NCPO signaled that it would intensify restrictions on speech it deemed offensive to the monarchy.

Within the first week after his death was announced, 12 cases of violations of Article 112 had already been reported to authorities. The NBTC asked internet service providers to monitor social media activity and block "inappropriate" content related to the monarchy. The companies' failure to do so would be considered a crime. The internet service providers were also requested to issue instructions to their users on how to report violations found on messaging applications and platforms such as Facebook and YouTube. During the mourning period, there were a number of reports of citizens verbally and physically attacking individuals accused of insulting the monarchy before police extracted the targets from the assaults and charged them with lèse-majesté violations. While the NCPO said it does not condone such attacks and encouraged the public to use legal reporting processes, the minister of justice was quoted as saying that this type of "social sanction" was useful in addressing lèse-majesté offenses. In December, a student activist became the first person to be charged under the reign of the new king for posting on Facebook a link to a controversial profile of the new monarch and an excerpt of the article.

While the 2007 constitution explicitly prohibited discrimination based on religious belief, the current interim constitution only states in general terms that rights and freedoms will be protected in line with "existing international obligations." While there is no official state religion, speech considered insulting to Buddhism is prohibited by law. A long-running civil conflict in the south, which pits ethnic Malay Muslims against ethnic Thai Buddhists, continues to undermine citizens' ability to practice their religions. Nevertheless, religious freedom in the majority of the country is generally respected, religious organizations operate freely, and there is no systemic or institutional discrimination based on religion. When concerns emerged over potential bias toward Buddhism in an article in the newly approved constitution, which stated that the government would promote and protect Theravada Buddhism, the head of the NCPO attempted to allay concerns by using his powers under Article 44 to issue an order clarifying that the state would protect all religions.

Academic freedom is constrained under the NCPO. University discussions and seminars on topics regarded as politically sensitive are subject to monitoring or outright cancellation by government authorities, who also require organizers to request permission to hold such events. Academics working on sensitive topics are subjected to oppressive tactics including summonses for questioning, home visits by security officials, and surveillance of their activities.

E. Associational and Organizational Rights: 4 / 12

Prohibitions on political gatherings of five or more people continued to be enforced in 2016, and those who engaged in symbolic actions advocating for democracy and human rights and protests against military rule faced a spectrum of consequences, including being warned, fined, arrested, or charged with violating NCPO orders.

A public assembly law approved in 2015 requires protest organizers to notify the police 24 hours in advance of the event, and sets limits on where demonstrations can take place. Authorities cited the law throughout 2016 to disperse labor union rallies and various gatherings by activists.

Thailand has a vibrant civil society, but groups focused on defending human rights or freedom of expression faced restrictions. The NCPO often insisted that such activities break laws concerning political gatherings, or create "public disturbances." When activities were allowed to move forward, authorities cautioned organizers against opposing NCPO policies ahead of time and heavily monitored the events. In 2016, restrictions contained within the Referendum Act and NCPO orders on political gatherings were invoked as reasons for canceling a number of seminars and public discussions on the draft constitution organized by universities and other civil society groups. In one notable case, authorities not only arrested the organizers of a public discussion on the charter, but also three people who identified themselves as only observers of the activity; two of them were human rights documentation officers from the legal assistance group Thai Lawyers for Human Rights.

Thai trade unions are independent and have the right to collectively bargain. However, civil servants and Thailand's numerous temporary workers do not have the right to form unions, and less than 2 percent of the total workforce is unionized. Antiunion discrimination in the private sector is common, and legal protections for union members are weak and poorly enforced.

F. Rule of Law: 5 / 16

Although the interim constitution grants independence to the judiciary, the military courts' jurisdiction over certain types of civilian cases, including those related to lèse-majesté and national security offenses, effectively compromises judicial independence. Military court cases initiated during the martial-law period starting in May 2014 feature no right to appeal, but convictions in cases tried after the revocation of martial law in April 2015 can be appealed. NCPO orders issued in 2015 under Article 44 of the interim constitution allow the detention of individuals without charge for up to seven days. The orders also expanded the authority of military officers in the area of law enforcement, permitting them to arrest, detain, and investigate crimes related to the monarchy and national security.

In September 2016, the government issued an order that halted the practice of trying civilians accused of national security and lèse-majesté crimes and of violating NCPO orders in military courts. However, the NCPO order is not retroactive and does not cover over 1,000 cases that have already entered the military court system. Furthermore, human rights activists contend that this move should not obscure the fact that laws criminalizing dissent, allowing arbitrary arrests, and broadening policing powers of the military remain in place.

A combination of martial law and emergency rule has been in effect for over a decade in the four southernmost provinces, where Malay Muslims form a majority and a separatist insurgency has been ongoing since the 1940s. Civilians are regularly targeted in shootings, bombings, and arson attacks, and insurgents have focused on schools and teachers as symbols of the Thai state. Counterinsurgency operations have involved the indiscriminate detention of thousands of suspected militants and sympathizers, and there are long-standing and credible reports of torture and other human rights violations, including extrajudicial killings, by both government forces and insurgents. The police and military often operate with impunity. Peace negotiations between the government and the dominant southern militant group, the National Revolutionary Front (BRN), were suspended in 2013. Although the NCPO had engaged in several rounds of informal talks in 2015 with the Mara Patani Consultative Council, a coalition of six armed groups, the official dialogue process stalled in 2016.

Other regions of the country have generally been free from terrorism or insurgencies. However, in August 2016, a series of bombings occurred across multiple provinces in the southern part of the country. The coordinated attacks differed from other attacks in that they took place in tourist cities considered to be outside the theater of conflict. No group immediately claimed responsibility for the attacks, but security analysts noted that they shared characteristics with those conducted by southern insurgent groups. Authorities have been reluctant to confirm a connection to the insurgency.

In Thailand's north, so-called hill tribes are not fully integrated into society. Many lack formal citizenship, which renders them ineligible to vote, own land, attend state schools, or receive protection under labor laws.

Thailand is known for its tolerance of the LGBT (lesbian, gay, bisexual, and transgender) community, though societal acceptance is higher for tourists and expatriates than for nationals, and unequal treatment and stigmatization remain challenges.

Thailand has not ratified the UN convention on refugees, who risk detention as unauthorized migrants and often lack access to asylum procedures.

G. Personal Autonomy and Individual Rights: 10 / 16

Except in areas affected by civil conflict, citizens have freedom of travel and choice of residence. Citizens also have freedom of employment and higher education. The rights to property and to establish businesses are protected by law, though in practice business activity is affected by some bureaucratic delays, and at times by the influence of security forces and organized crime.

While women have the same legal rights as men, they remain subject to economic discrimination in practice, and are vulnerable to domestic abuse, rape, and sex trafficking. Sex tourism has been a key part of the economy in some urban and resort areas.

Exploitation and trafficking of migrant workers from Myanmar, Cambodia, and Laos are serious and ongoing problems, as are child and sweatshop labor. Porous borders and government indifference, if not outright collusion, have helped to fuel migrant smuggling networks.

Timor-Leste

Political Rights Rating: 3
Civil Liberties Rating: 3
Freedom Rating: 3.0
Freedom Status: Partly Free
Electoral Democracy: Yes

Population: 1,300,000
Capital: Dili

Ten-Year Ratings Timeline For Year Under Review (Political Rights, Civil Liberties, Status)

Year Under Review	2007	2008	2009	2010	2011	2012	2013	2014	2015	2016
Rating	3,4,PF	3,4,PF	3,4,PF	3,4,PF	3,4,PF	3,4,PF	3,4,PF	3,3,PF	3,3,PF	3,3,PF

Overview: Timor-Leste has held competitive elections and undergone peaceful transfers of power, but its democratic institutions remain fragile, and disputes among the major personalities from the independence struggle tend to dominate political affairs. Judicial independence and due process are undermined by serious capacity deficits as well as political influence. Wealth and power are concentrated among a small elite, raising concerns about corruption, but media coverage of such topics is sometimes affected by self-censorship and the threat of legal reprisals.

KEY DEVELOPMENTS IN 2016:

- In February, President Taur Matan Ruak harshly criticized powerful figures in the government and parliament, arguing that a 2015 political pact between the two main parties had benefited the ruling elite at the expense of good governance.
- In January, Prime Minister Rui Maria de Araújo launched a criminal defamation case against a journalist and his editor for a 2015 report on alleged bid-rigging for

contracts at the Ministry of Finance during Araújo's tenure as a ministry adviser. A trial was under way at year's end.

- Parliament adopted a new law on local elections in May, and elections for district and village representatives were held in October and November.
- In a high-profile corruption case dating to 2012, former finance minister Emilia Pires was found guilty in December of awarding contracts to a company owned by her husband. Sentencing was expected in early 2017.

EXECUTIVE SUMMARY

A unity government formed in 2015 between Timor-Leste's two largest parties, which left little meaningful opposition in parliament, grew increasingly intolerant of criticism in 2016. In February, amid a dispute between parliament and President Ruak over the appointment of the chief and deputy chief of the armed forces, Ruak harshly criticized the unity pact for enabling powerful figures like former prime ministers Kay Rala Xanana Gusmão of the National Congress for Timorese Reconstruction (CNRT) and Mari Alkatiri of the Revolutionary Front for an Independent Timor-Leste (Fretilin) to amass personal wealth and privileges without the scrutiny of an opposition party. Members of parliament threatened Ruak with impeachment, and Fretilin leaders warned that the country could return to instability if the president persisted in his attacks.

With presidential and parliamentary elections scheduled for 2017, parliament in June amended the Law on Electoral Administration to change the composition of the National Election Commission. The panel's size was reduced from 15 to 7 members, civil society representatives were no longer included, and the government and parliament together selected a majority of the new commissioners. The law was enacted over the objections of President Ruak, who noted that it enabled the replacement of incumbent commissioners before their terms had expired.

Also in June, the president signed a new law passed by parliament in May that governed local elections. Suco (district) councils would comprise the suco chief, aldeia (village) representatives, aldeia chiefs, traditional authorities, and male and female youth representatives. The new law provides for the direct election of aldeia representatives—one woman and one man from each aldeia. Each suco chief election must have at least one female candidate. The elections proceeded in October and November, and 21 women were elected as suco chiefs, an increase from 11 in 2009 but still a small fraction among the country's 442 sucos.

Economic growth continued to be the government's primary concern in 2016. The government depends on large drawdowns from its Petroleum Fund to finance infrastructure development projects and programs that ensure peace and stability, including payments to veterans of the independence struggle and army deserters who catalyzed a security crisis in 2006. The withdrawals have exceeded sustainable levels for several years, and income from the fund has dropped as a result of the reduction in global oil prices.

POLITICAL RIGHTS: 29 / 40

A. Electoral Process: 11 / 12

B. Political Pluralism and Participation: 12 / 16

C. Functioning of Government: 6 / 12

CIVIL LIBERTIES: 36 / 60

D. Freedom of Expression and Belief: 12 / 16

E. Associational and Organizational Rights: 8 / 12

F. Rule of Law: 7 / 16

G. Personal Autonomy and Individual Rights: 9 / 16

This country report has been abridged for *Freedom in the World 2017*. For background information on political rights and civil liberties in Timor-Leste, see *Freedom in the World 2016.*

Togo

Political Rights Rating: 4
Civil Liberties Rating: 4
Freedom Rating: 4.0
Freedom Status: Partly Free
Electoral Democracy: No

Population: 7,500,000
Capital: Lomé

Ten-Year Ratings Timeline For Year Under Review (Political Rights, Civil Liberties, Status)

Year Under Review	2007	2008	2009	2010	2011	2012	2013	2014	2015	2016
Rating	5,5,PF	5,5,PF	5,4,PF	5,4,PF	5,4,PF	5,4,PF	4,4,PF	4,4,PF	4,4,PF	4,4,PF

Overview: Togo has held regular multiparty elections since the current constitution was adopted in 1992. However, the country's politics have been dominated since 1963 by Gnassingbé Eyadéma and his son, the current president, Faure Gnassingbé. Advantages including a security service dominated by the president's ethnic group, disproportionately drawn election districts, and a fractured opposition have helped President Gnassingbé and his party hold on to power. However, recently the legislature has passed laws to promote good governance and human rights in response to domestic and international pressure. While political violence scarred Togo between 1958 and 2005, it has been rare in recent years.

KEY DEVELOPMENTS In 2016:
- In UN-backed meetings held in December, the government met with opposition representatives to discuss plans to hold local elections, though no date was set. The country has not held local elections since 1986.
- In March, the National Assembly approved a freedom of information law.
- Also in March, the National Assembly adopted a law establishing a mechanism within the National Human Rights Commission to prevent torture, but the new body's independence was questioned.

EXECUTIVE SUMMARY

In 2016, opposition parties and international donors continued to call for the restoration of presidential term limits, which were eliminated in 2002, and the organization of local elections, which have not been held since 1986, in violation of the 1992 constitution; local officials are instead appointed by the president. In March, the government agreed to began public consultations in preparation for local elections, and in December, government and opposition representatives participated in UN-backed meetings in preparation for local polls. The opposition called for the polls to be held in 2017, but the government has stated a preference that they be conducted the following year to make time for adequate preparations.

The National Assembly continued to pass laws to promote good governance and human rights in response to domestic and international demands, but the enforcement bodies often lack independence. For example, the National Assembly adopted a law to establish a mechanism within the National Human Rights Commission to prevent torture, but the measure allows the president to appoint the new body's members without parliamentary approval.

Separately, a freedom of information law was approved in March, though it contains exemptions for some kinds of information, including that deemed relevant to national security.

Opposition leaders boycotted the country's official independence celebration in April, in protest of the omission of opposition figures from the independent electoral commission, the ongoing failure to hold local elections, and the failure of Togo's Truth, Justice, and Reconciliation Commission (TJRC) to adequately address past violence committed by members of Gnassingbé's Union for the Republic (UNIR) and its supporters.

POLITICAL RIGHTS: 18 / 40

A. Electoral Process: 6 / 12

The president is elected to a five-year term and appoints the prime minister. The 1992 constitution included a two-term limit for the president, but this was removed by the legislature in 2002 to enable the current president's father, Eyadéma Gnassingbé, to run for a third term, and Togo remains without term limits despite numerous attempts by the opposition to reinstate them. In 2015, the younger Gnassingbé won reelection with 59 percent of the vote, a slightly smaller percentage than he received in the 2010 polls. At 61 percent, voter turnout was lower than at any time since he was first elected.

The African Union (AU) observer mission deemed the election largely free and fair. However, opposition critiques of the new electronic vote-tabulation system and delays in appointing the electoral commission's vice president—a post that by law must be held by a member of the opposition—until the eve of the vote itself reinforced a lack of public faith in the electoral process. The vote was also postponed by 10 days to accommodate voter list revisions called for by the Economic Community of West African States (ECOWAS). While all presidential candidates were given equal airtime on public media during the election period, the main opposition candidate, Jean-Pierre Fabre, was reportedly prohibited from broadcasting a message viewed as critical of the government.

Fabre and his followers protested the election's result. However, opposition leaders declined to dispute it at the Constitutional Court, saying the court was tilted in favor of Gnassingbé.

The 91 members of the unicameral National Assembly are elected to five-year terms. Legislative elections were held in 2013 after much delay. International observers considered them to be credible and transparent, though the opposition disputed the results. Gnassingbé's UNIR won 62 seats and 23 of the country's 28 electoral zones, including some opposition strongholds. This result was bolstered by district gerrymandering that heavily favors UNIR. The opposition Save Togo Collective (CST) won 19 seats, the Rainbow Coalition won six seats, the Union of Forces for Change (UFC) won three, and an independent candidate won one seat.

The 1992 Constitution states that local territories administer themselves by elected councils, but local elections have not been held since 1986. In response to criticism by opposition parties and international donors, the government agreed in March 2016 to begin public consultations in preparation for local elections. In December, the government described local elections as a priority at UN-backed meetings with the opposition. The opposition called for the polls to be held in 2017, but the government has stated a preference they be conducted the following year to make time for adequate preparations.

B. Political Pluralism and Participation: 7 / 16

Although opposition parties are free to operate, the structure of the electoral system, including district allocations dramatically favoring the UNIR and the single election round, have helped Gnassingbé and his party remain in power. The opposition is weakened by internal divisions. The results of the 2015 presidential election added another five years to the Gnassingbé family's decades long hold on power.

The opposition, led by Fabre, continued to voice their grievances against the government in 2016. Opposition figures including Fabre boycotted the country's official independence celebration in April 2016 in protest of the omission of opposition leaders from the independent electoral commission, the ongoing failure to hold local elections, and the failure of the TJRC to adequately address past violence committed by UNIR members and supporters. Fabre delivered a similar message at an opposition colloquium in October. (Implementing recommendations of the TJRC are at the president's discretion; one of these recommendations, to restore the two-term limit, was ignored when the president was elected for a third term in 2015.) Fabre's party, the National Alliance for Change (ANC), participated in the December meeting to discuss local elections.

Separately, Antoine Randolph, head of the National Rally for Democracy and Pan-Africanism (RNDP), a mostly dormant opposition party, was arrested by the Togolese intelligence services in February 2016 under mysterious circumstances, and released nearly one month later.

The government is dominated by Gnassingbé's Kabyé ethnic group, who also make up the vast majority of the security services. The Éwé, Togo's largest ethnic group, are persistently excluded from influential government positions, but are prominent within the opposition.

C. Functioning of Government: 5 / 12

The National Assembly was freely elected in 2013 and has influence over policy, but in the absence of local elections, local officials are appointed by the president. Perhaps as a result of the lack of local elected officials, a 2014 Afrobarometer survey indicated that the vast majority of Togolese citizens have little to no interaction with their political representatives, and instead tend to reach out to religious figures and traditional leaders. However, the government began discussions of local elections in in December 2016 meetings on decentralization that were attended by opposition representatives, and supported by the UN Development Program (UNDP).

Corruption remains a serious problem. Reforms in 2015 empowered the National Assembly to appoint members of the Anticorruption Commission (CAC), but the body has been slow to make progress, in part due to a weak legal mandate, and appears to be aligned with the president and UNIR. In July 2015, the National Assembly passed a law to create a new body under the auspices of the CAC to prevent and combat corruption. Four out of the seven members are to be appointed by the president, raising concerns about its independence. A year later, there appears to have been little activity by the new body.

Also in 2015, a group of 40 nongovernmental organizations (NGOs) created a civil society anticorruption network, intended to serve as an independent body to support the capacity of existing anticorruption actors, expand judicial reform, and inform the public about the negative consequences of corruption. The NGO network held at least one meeting in 2016, but its impact remains unclear.

In March 2016, the National Assembly approved a new freedom of information law guaranteeing the right to access government information, though some information was exempted from the law on security or privacy grounds. A National Statistics Institute makes monthly national accounts and other information available on the internet.

CIVIL LIBERTIES: 30 / 60

D. Freedom of Expression and Belief: 9 / 16

Freedom of the press is guaranteed by law but can be disregarded in practice. The availability of diverse and critical voices in the media has increased in recent years. While the government can hand down punishments to critical journalists by invoking punitive laws, there appear to have been no such prosecutions in 2016, though some journalists faced charges the previous year. The National Assembly passed a new Criminal Code in 2015 that punishes the publication of false information with between six months and two years in prison and a hefty fine. Journalists' associations and media outlets in Togo have spoken out against the new law, while the government defends it as a necessary step to fight cyber-crime and terrorism. The High Authority of Broadcasting and Communications (HAAC), Togo's main state regulatory body, can impose severe penalties—including the suspension of publications or broadcasts and the confiscation of press cards—if journalists are found to have made "serious errors" or are "endangering national security."

Access to the internet is generally unrestricted. Although penetration is low, Togolese activity online is increasing, and internet access is now free at public universities.

Religious freedom is constitutionally protected and generally respected. Islam and Christianity are recognized as official religions; other religious groups must register as associations.

Academic freedom is somewhat limited. Government security forces are believed to maintain a presence on university campuses and have cracked down on student protests in past years. However, university figures are able to engage in political discussions, and have participated in recent debates surrounding the issue of constitutional reform.

Citizens are increasingly able to speak openly in private discussion, though political discussion is prohibited on religious radio and television stations.

E. Associational and Organizational Rights: 7 / 12

Freedom of assembly is sometimes restricted, particularly in election years. A 2011 law requires that demonstrations receive prior authorization and only be held during certain times of the day. The amended penal code adopted in 2015 further limits the right to peaceful assembly, by outlawing both participation in and organization of assemblies that have not been granted administrative approval. Those prosecuted under the law can face prison sentences up to five years if violence occurred at an unauthorized demonstration. A leader of a human rights group was arrested in March 2016 for organizing a sit-in that had been refused by local authorities. However, in May, supporters of opposition parties protested for local elections and other reforms, apparently without incident.

Police in recent years have refrained from employing violence against opposition protests. However, police did open fire on a student protest in March 2015. Separately, following the government's attempts to revitalize an inhabited nature reserve in the north of the country, protests by local residents in November 2015 turned violent after security forces opened fire on peaceful protesters; seven protesters and one local police officer were killed.

As of March 2016, five men remain in prison in connection with that protest, including four organizers who claim they did not initiate or encourage the violence.

Freedom of association is largely respected, and NGOs generally operate without government interference.

Togo's constitution guarantees the right to form and join labor unions, though workers' rights in the lucrative export-processing zone are regularly violated.

F. Rule of Law: 7 / 16

The judicial system lacks resources and is heavily influenced by the presidency. The Constitutional Court in particular is believed to be partial to UNIR; Fabre chose not to appeal the 2015 election results with the court for this reason. In 2015, the government announced plans to improve the judiciary; these included providing greater access to the courts and modernizing judicial facilities. That year, the High Court of Magistrates also cracked down on judicial corruption by suspending and firing two judges for "unethical behavior."

In March 2016, the National Assembly adopted a law to establish a mechanism within the National Human Rights Commission to prevent torture, but the law allows the president to appoint its members without parliamentary approval, raising concerns about the new body's independence.

Lengthy pretrial detention is a serious problem, particularly for Gnassingbé's political opponents. One former minister accused of fraud in 2012 was released from jail in February 2016, but the charges against him have not been dropped.

Prisons suffer from overcrowding and inadequate food and medical care, sometimes resulting in deaths among inmates from preventable or curable diseases. The government periodically releases prisoners to address overcrowding, but the process by which individuals are chosen for release is not sufficiently transparent.

The 2015 penal code criminalizes torture. However, its definition of torture does not conform to the definition in the UN Convention against Torture.

Many of these gradual moves on the part of the government directed at the judiciary and prisons came in response to recommendations from the 2012 TJRC, which investigated political violence and human rights violations that occurred in Togo between 1958 and 2005. Despite these apparent efforts, impunity persists for many Gnassingbé supporters, perpetuating a climate of fear for those critical of the government.

The north and south of the country have historically been divided along political and ethnic lines. Discrimination among the country's 40 ethnic groups occurs. Same-sex sexual activity continues to be punishable by fines and up to three years in prison under the revised penal code passed in 2015. The relevant laws are rarely enforced, though LGBT (lesbian, gay, bisexual, and transgender) people face societal discrimination.

G. Personal Autonomy and Individual Rights: 7 / 16

Travel within Togo can involve arbitrary traffic stops as a means for police to coerce drivers into paying bribes.

Some 60 percent of the population is employed in agriculture. The country is increasingly seen as a Western-friendly investment environment and has moved to privatize a number of industries and implement reforms to reduce the time and financial means necessary to start a business.

A 2013 amendment to the Electoral Code requires that women have equal representation on party lists. The Law on Political Party and Electoral Campaign Funding, passed after the 2013 legislative elections, requires that a portion of a party's public financing be determined in proportion to the number of women from that party elected in the most recent national and local elections. Of the 91 seats in the National Assembly, 16 are held by women. A 2014 provision to the Family Code assigned women equal status in the household as well improved inheritance rights. Even so, women's opportunities for education and employment are limited. Spousal abuse is widespread, though the new penal code provides for five to 10 years in prison for rape and no longer excludes spousal rape.

The government has been making increasing efforts to reduce trafficking, which is most common in (though not limited to) the sex industry and for forced labor inside Togo.

Tonga

Political Rights Rating: 2
Civil Liberties Rating: 2
Freedom Rating: 2.0
Freedom Status: Free
Electoral Democracy: Yes

Population: 103,300
Capital: Nuku'alofa

Ten-Year Ratings Timeline For Year Under Review (Political Rights, Civil Liberties, Status)

Year Under Review	2007	2008	2009	2010	2011	2012	2013	2014	2015	2016
Rating	5,3,PF	5,3,PF	5,3,PF	3,3,PF	3,3,PF	3,2,F	2,2,F	2,2,F	2,2,F	2,2,F

The country or territory displayed here received scores but no narrative report for this edition of *Freedom in the World*.

Trinidad and Tobago

Political Rights Ratings: 2
Civil Liberties Rating: 2
Freedom Rating: 2.0
Freedom Status: Free
Electoral Democracy: Yes

Population: 1,400,000
Capital: Port of Spain

Ten-Year Ratings Timeline For Year Under Review (Political Rights, Civil Liberties, Status)

Year Under Review	2007	2008	2009	2010	2011	2012	2013	2014	2015	2016
Rating	2,2,F	2,2,F	2,2,F	2,2,F	2,2,F	2,2,F	2,2,F	2,2,F	2,2,F	2,2,F

Overview: Since independence, Trinidad and Tobago has maintained a robust parliamentary democracy with a vibrant media and civil society. However, organized crime contributes to a difficult security environment, and corruption remains a challenge.

KEY DEVELOPMENTS IN 2016:

- The country continued to grapple with violent crime, linked mainly to drug trafficking.

- In October, a court invalidated the 2015 Bail (Amendment) Act, which stipulated that people accused of certain gang-related crimes were ineligible for bail for 120 days after being charged.

EXECUTIVE SUMMARY

Trinidad and Tobago continues to maintain a fairly robust democracy, despite problems with corruption and organized crime. The media is vibrant and freedoms of assembly and association are generally respected.

In September 2016, a disagreement between President Anthony Carmona and Prime Minister Keith Rowley was made public by media reports. The dispute centered on a meeting between Carmona and National Security Minister Edmund Dillon regarding the security environment in the country. Rowley said the meeting had improperly taken place without his knowledge; Carmona claimed that he had notified the prime minister of the meeting, and affirmed his respect for the separation of powers. The dispute raised some concerns about the general transparency of government operations. Separately, in June, Government Senator Hafeez Ali of the governing People's National Movement (PNM) resigned after sexually explicit videos of him spread across social media websites. Ali said the video was released as part of an extortion plot against him.

Meanwhile, the country continued to grapple with violent crime linked mainly to drug trafficking. Some observers expressed concern that the crisis in nearby Venezuela could contribute to an increase in the number of illegal firearms entering the country.

The 2015 Bail (Amendment) Act, which mandated that people accused of certain gang-related crimes were ineligible for bail for 120 days after being charged, was deemed unconstitutional in October. The ruling paved the way for people who were held on remand under the law to sue the government.

POLITICAl RIGHTS: 33 / 40

A. Electoral Process: 11 / 12

B. Political Pluralism and Participation: 13 / 16

C. Functioning of Government: 9 / 12

CIVIL LIBERTIES: 48 / 60

D. Freedom of Expression and Belief: 15 / 16

E. Associational and Organizational Rights: 11 / 12

F. Rule of Law: 9 / 16

G. Personal Autonomy and Individual Rights: 13 / 16

This country report has been abridged for *Freedom in the World 2017*. For background information on political rights and civil liberties in Trinidad and Tobago, see *Freedom in the World 2016*.

Tunisia

Political Rights Rating: 1
Civil Liberties Rating: 3
Freedom Rating: 2.0
Freedom Status: Free
Electoral Democracy: Yes

Population: 11,300,000
Capital: Tunis

Ten-Year Ratings Timeline For Year Under Review (Political Rights, Civil Liberties, Status)

Year Under Review	2007	2008	2009	2010	2011	2012	2013	2014	2015	2016
Rating	7,5,NF	7,5,NF	7,5,NF	7,5,NF	3,4,PF	3,4,PF	3,3,PF	1,3,F	1,3,F	1,3,F

Overview: Since ousting a longtime autocrat from power in 2011, Tunisia has transitioned to a functioning, if precarious, democracy in which citizens enjoy unprecedented political rights and civil liberties. Corruption, economic challenges, and security threats remain obstacles to full democratic consolidation.

KEY DEVELOPMENTS IN 2016:

- In March, dozens of gunmen with links to the Islamic State (IS) militant group attacked the town of Ben Guerdane, near the Libyan border. The ensuing battle left 36 militants, seven civilians, and 12 members of the Tunisian security forces dead.
- In June, the parliament adopted a robust gender parity law for candidates in local elections, though officials indicated that the next elections, set for March 2017, would be postponed.
- Amid increasing concerns about security threats and a weak economy, Prime Minister Habib Essid lost a July confidence vote in the parliament, and his government stepped down. A new national unity government took office in late August.
- In November, the Truth and Dignity Commission held two public hearings on national television and radio, offering victims of human rights abuses under the former regime a chance to share their testimony.

EXECUTIVE SUMMARY

Tunisia took important, if modest, steps in 2016 toward preserving the democratic gains of the previous five years and improving civil liberties, even as ongoing economic stagnation and security challenges threatened the system's stability. New legislation established the Supreme Judicial Council, a body charged with ensuring the independence of the judiciary and appointing Constitutional Court judges, and council members were elected in October. In September, the parliament approved a long-awaited investment code that was expected to help attract foreign direct investment and reduce state interference in economic activity. And in June, the parliament adopted a gender parity law to ensure greater representation of women in local elections, though the elections planned for March 2017 were postponed.

In a sign of ongoing frustration with the lack of economic progress, protests broke out across the country in January. Police met the demonstrations with greater restraint than in recent years, when security forces had sometimes responded to protests with excessive or even deadly force. A major attack on the town of Ben Guerdane in March by militants affiliated with IS highlighted ongoing security threats that have triggered successive states of emergency.

At the start of the year, a number of parliament members with the leading political party, the secularist Nidaa Tounes, broke away after two years of growing internal disagreements. The development left Nidaa Tounes with 64 seats and handed a plurality to the moderate Islamist party Ennahda, which held 69. In July, the government of Habib Essid, an independent who had initially enjoyed the backing of both Nidaa Tounes and Ennahda but had struggled to address security threats and the faltering economy, was forced to step down after failing to win a vote of confidence. A national unity government assumed office in August, with Youssef Chahed of Nidaa Tounes as prime minister.

A controversial bill that would grant amnesty to individuals implicated in economic crimes under the former regime in exchange for their return of stolen assets to the state continued to meet resistance in civil society during the year, with activists claiming that it would undermine existing reconciliation programs. However, leading factions in the parliament indicated their intention to approve the measure.

POLITICAL RIGHTS: 37 / 40 (− 1)

A. Electoral Process: 11 / 12 (− 1)

Tunisia's 2014 constitution established a unicameral legislative body, the Assembly of the Representatives of the People (ARP), and a semipresidential system in which the majority party in the parliament selects a head of government, while a popularly elected president serves as head of state and exercises circumscribed powers. The ARP consists of 217 representatives serving five-year terms, with members elected on party lists in 33 multimember constituencies.

Parliamentary elections held in October 2014 featured high turnout, with 67 percent of registered voters participating. Nidaa Tounes, established two years earlier with the goal of blunting the momentum of Ennahda, won a plurality of the vote and 86 seats. Ennahda placed second with 69 seats, 20 fewer than in 2011. Three other parties won enough seats to play significant roles in government formation: the populist-centrist Free Patriotic Union (UPL) won 16 seats, the leftist Popular Front garnered 15, and the center-right Afek Tounes won eight. Eleven other parties each obtained between one and four seats, and two seats went to independents.

A presidential election was held in November 2014, with 64 percent of registered voters casting ballots in the first round. Beji Caid Essebsi, the leader of Nidaa Tounes, won 40 percent of the vote, followed by incumbent Mohamed Moncef Marzouki of Congress for the Republic, with 33 percent. Essebsi then defeated Marzouki in the runoff, 55 percent to 44 percent. International and local observers concluded that the 2014 elections were free and fair.

Essebsi tasked Essid, an independent technocrat, with forming a government. The ARP's approval of Essid's cabinet in February 2015 completed the transition to a fully democratic system at the legislative and executive levels under the new constitution. Essid's government, comprising members of Nidaa Tounes, Ennahda, UPL, and Afek Tounes, remained in office through the first half of 2016.

In January 2016, 22 representatives from Nidaa Tounes resigned from the party to form a new bloc, Al-Horra, reducing Nidaa Tounes to 64 seats and leaving Ennahda as the largest party. That development, combined with growing concern over the government's handling of security threats and widespread frustration with a lack of economic progress, prompted Essebsi to call for a new national unity government in June. The following month, Essid lost a vote of confidence in the parliament, and his government stepped down. Essebsi tapped Chahed, an agricultural economist and Nidaa Tounes member, to serve as prime minister. His government, comprising members of Nidaa Tounes, Ennahda, and five smaller parties, plus two figures close to the Tunisian General Labor Union (UGTT), took office in August.

The Independent High Authority for Elections (ISIE), a neutral nine-member commission, is tasked with supervising parliamentary and presidential elections. The constitution also calls for a system of local governance based on municipal, district-level, and regional elections. Those votes have been repeatedly postponed, due in part to a lack of resources and disagreements as to whether members of the security forces should participate. The government has pledged that the polls will be held in 2017, though a plan to hold them in March of that year was abandoned in 2016.

Observers praised the 2014 electoral law for providing a credible framework that would reflect the will of the voters. However, the law's gender parity provisions, which required men and women to alternate within each party list but stopped short of requiring that men and women alternate at the head of lists across regions, attracted criticism. In June 2016, the ARP adopted an amendment to legislation governing municipal and regional elections that mandated horizontal and vertical parity, meaning parties must have equal numbers of men and women at the head of their lists, in addition to alternating between men and women within each list.

B. Political Pluralism and Participation: 16 / 16

Seventy parties participated in the 2014 elections. The two dominant parties were Nidaa Tounes, a secularist coalition of leftists, trade unionists, businesspeople, and members of the former government of Zine el-Abidine Ben Ali (who was ousted as president in a popular revolution in 2011), and Ennahda, a moderate Islamist party that had been banned under Ben Ali's regime. Throughout 2015, a power struggle played out within Nidaa Tounes between the leftist faction, led by the party's secretary general, Mohsen Marzouk, and ancien régime elements led by Hafedh Caid Essebsi, the current president's son. In March 2016, Marzouk announced the formation of a new party, the Tounes Movement Project, which was expected to contest the next elections. Al-Horra, the parliamentary bloc that departed Nidaa Tounes in January, supported Marzouk.

The Tunisian military, historically marginalized by the political leadership, remained politically neutral in 2016. The military's budget has significantly expanded in the past several years, and it has established its own intelligence and security services. While generally viewed as positive developments aimed at correcting long-standing internal dysfunction, these changes have led some experts to caution against an unwarranted increase in the military's powers. Concerns over the military's potential politicization emerged in September 2016, following a controversial proposal to amend the electoral law to extend voting rights to members of the armed forces and police. The proposal had not been approved by year's end, but unions representing the security forces campaigned vigorously in favor of the amendment.

The government and both domestic and international nongovernmental organizations (NGOs) have worked to increase the political participation of marginalized groups, including disabled Tunisians, and ensure their inclusion in elections.

C. Functioning of Government: 9 / 12

Freely elected officials determine and implement laws and policies without interference in Tunisia, and the 2011 removal of Ben Ali and his close relatives and associates, who had used their positions to create private monopolies in several sectors, represented an important step in combating corruption and eliminating conflicts of interest. The 2014 constitution called for the eventual creation of a Good Governance and Anti-Corruption Commission, but few prosecutions have occurred to date, with the exception of in absentia trials for members of the Ben Ali and Trabelsi clans—the families of the ousted president and his wife. Petty corruption continues to plague the country, with tax evasion, falsification of documents, and bribery rampant in the civil service.

A proposed "reconciliation law" approved by Essid's cabinet in 2015 would suspend all legal proceedings and investigations into public corruption committed under the Ben Ali regime in exchange for implicated individuals' agreement to return stolen assets to the state. In 2016, the bill continued to face resistance from civil society and some factions in the parliament, with representatives claiming that its enactment would undermine existing reconciliation programs. The leading political parties indicated that they would support the measure, though the bill had not come up for a vote by year's end.

Since the revolution, Tunisia has improved its record on government transparency. A 2011 decree requires internal documents of public institutions to be made available to the public. The 2014 constitution established the right of access to information, along with an independent commission to monitor compliance. In March 2016, the ARP adopted a freedom of information law, though it was criticized by watchdog groups for its security-related exemptions.

CIVIL LIBERTIES: 42 / 60

D. Freedom of Expression and Belief: 13 / 16

The constitution guarantees freedom of opinion, thought, expression, information, and publication, subject to some restrictions. However, journalists continued to face obstacles in 2016. In February, political cartoonist Lotfi Ben Sassi alleged that he had received threats of administrative sanctions and pressure from the editor in chief of the state-run newspaper *La Presse* over cartoons mocking Tunisia's reliance on foreign assistance, particularly from the United States. In September, officials at the private television station Attessia said government officials had pressured them not to air a prerecorded interview with former president Marzouki, though it broadcast the interview anyway.

Article 91 of the military justice code criminalizes "insulting the flag or the army," and a number of bloggers and journalists have been prosecuted under the provision. In October 2016, a military court issued a warrant for the arrest of Mohamed Haj Mansour following his online newspaper's publication of an article alleging that Israel was behind the army's recent purchase of defective military equipment. Independent journalist Jamel Arfaoui and Rached Khiari, editor of the newspaper *Al-Sadaa*, were charged under the military justice code in September and November for separate articles; at year's end both were free pending trial.

Authorities do not restrict access to the internet or illegally monitor users' online activity.

The constitution calls for freedom of belief and conscience for all religions, as well as for the nonreligious, and bans campaigns against apostasy and incitement to hatred and violence on religious grounds. While the constitution identifies Islam as the state religion and requires the president to be a Muslim, no constitutional provision identifies Sharia (Islamic law) as a source of legislation. The state retains influence over the internal affairs of religious institutions, particularly at mosques, where it continues to appoint local imams and bans unauthorized activity.

Article 33 of the constitution explicitly protects academic freedom, which continues to improve in practice. Private discussion is largely open and free.

E. Associational and Organizational Rights: 9 / 12

The constitution guarantees the rights to assembly and peaceful demonstration. Public demonstrations on political, social, and economic issues regularly take place, although a controversial counterterrorism law adopted in 2015, and successive states of emergency issued in response to terrorist attacks, have imposed constraints on public demonstrations. In January 2016, protests over soaring unemployment erupted in Kasserine Governorate and spread to cities around the country after a jobless man was electrocuted while standing on top of a power pole to protest his removal from consideration for public-sector jobs. The protests subsided by late February, and observers credited the police with demonstrating greater restraint than in previous years.

The constitution protects the freedom to establish political parties, unions, and associations. Tens of thousands of new civil society organizations began operating after the revolution, and NGO conferences were held throughout the country during 2016.

The constitution guarantees the right to form labor unions and to strike. The Tunisian economy has been rocked by continuous strikes across all sectors since the revolution, with participants demanding labor reform, better wages, and improved workplace conditions. In August 2016, Chahed announced that his government would penalize labor actions aimed at disrupting production, but offered assurances that the constitutional right to strike would be upheld. In November, the country's largest trade union, the UGTT, called for a strike of public-sector workers following a wage dispute with the government. However, the planned action was canceled in December after the government agreed to increase civil service salaries.

F. Rule of Law: 9 / 16

The constitution calls for a robust and independent judiciary. Judicial reform since the revolution has proceeded slowly, with numerous Ben Ali–era judges remaining on the bench and successive governments regularly attempting to manipulate the courts. Legislation adopted in March 2016 established the Supreme Judicial Council, a body charged with ensuring the independence of the judiciary and appointing Constitutional Court judges. Council members were elected in October by thousands of legal professionals.

In June 2014, Tunisia established a Truth and Dignity Commission (TDC) to examine political, economic, and social crimes committed since 1956. The TDC's director, Sihem Ben Sedrine, reported in February 2016 that she still had not been granted access to Interior Ministry archives, though she did obtain access to the presidential archives after initially being blocked the previous year. In November, the TDC broadcast its first two public hearings on national television and radio. By December, the commission had registered over 62,000 complaints and heard 11,000 testimonies documenting cases of economic corruption and human rights violations such as torture and sexual abuse against men, women, and children.

Security issues, particularly threats from violent groups within the Salafi Muslim community, are a major concern for the government. A 2015 antiterrorism law gives police expanded surveillance and detention powers, allows terrorism suspects to be tried in closed-door hearings, and permits witnesses in such trials to remain anonymous. In March 2016, dozens of militants with links to IS attacked the town of Ben Guerdane near the Libyan border, targeting police and army outposts before being repelled by security forces. The initial attack left 36 militants, seven civilians, and 12 members of the armed forces dead, and security forces killed 14 more militants in operations over the next several days to secure the town.

The constitution refers to state protections for persons with special needs, prohibiting all forms of discrimination and providing aid for their integration into society. It also calls for the state to create a culture of diversity. However, LGBT (lesbian, gay, bisexual, and transgender) people continue to face discrimination in law and society, and the penal code calls for a three-year prison sentence for "sodomy." In January 2016, a court in Tunis ordered the LGBT rights group Shams to suspend activities for 30 days. The decision was reversed on appeal in February, although Shams activists continued to face harassment by the police. In March, a judge acquitted eight youths charged with same-sex sexual acts, the first such acquittal in Tunisian history, though they remained in jail on separate drug charges.

Tunisia has no asylum law, leaving the United Nations as the sole entity processing claims of refugee status in the country. Irregular migrants and asylum seekers are often housed in informal detention centers, where they suffer from substandard living conditions. Delays in the issuance of residency permits make it impossible for many to work legally, forcing them to take informal jobs with no labor protections. A draft law that would normalize the status of asylum seekers and increase their rights and protections had yet to be passed at the end of 2016.

G. Personal Autonomy and Individual Rights: 11 / 16

Freedom of movement has improved substantially since 2011. The constitution guarantees freedom of movement within the country, as well as the freedom to travel abroad. Unlike in some other countries in the region, women do not require the permission of a male relative to travel. In 2016 the border with Libya was closed on numerous occasions in response to terrorist attacks, and a nationwide curfew was imposed following the demonstrations that broke out in January. The curfew was lifted in February, though a state of emergency has been repeatedly renewed since late 2015 and remained in place throughout the year.

The protection of property rights continued to be an area of concern, closely linked to high levels of corruption as well as a large backlog of property disputes. The 2014 constitution introduced new protections for property, including intellectual property, but their implementation has yet to be seen. In September 2016, the parliament approved a long-awaited investment code that was expected to help attract foreign direct investment and reduce state interference in economic activity.

Tunisia has long been praised for relatively progressive social policies, especially in the areas of family law and women's rights. The constitution guarantees equality before the law for men and women, and the 1956 personal status code, which also grants women equality with men, has remained in force. The code provides women with equal rights in divorce, and children born to Tunisian mothers and foreign fathers are automatically granted citizenship. Medical abortion is legal. Currently, 68 women serve in the parliament, and 8 of the 40 ministers and secretaries of state in Chahed's government are women.

Areas of ongoing concern for women's rights include social discrimination, domestic abuse, and unequal inheritance laws. A proposed law introduced in the parliament in May 2016 would allow families to manage their estates as they wished, in an effort to establish equity for women and men in matters of inheritance. The bill elicited opposition from various factions in the parliament, as well as from the Mufti of the Republic, the country's leading religious authority. It had not passed by year's end.

Tunisian women and children are subject to sex trafficking and forced domestic work in both Tunisia and abroad. Refugees and other migrants are also susceptible to exploitation by traffickers.

⬇ Turkey

Political Rights Rating: 4 ↓
Civil Liberties Rating: 5 ↓
Freedom Rating: 4.5
Freedom Status: Partly Free
Electoral Democracy: No

Population: 79,500,000
Capital: Ankara

Ratings Change, Trend Arrow: Turkey's political rights rating declined from 3 to 4, its civil liberties rating declined from 4 to 5, and it received a downward trend arrow due to the security and political repercussions of an attempted coup in July, which led the government to declare a state of emergency and carry out mass arrests and firings of civil servants, academics, journalists, opposition figures, and other perceived enemies.

Ten-Year Ratings Timeline For Year Under Review (Political Rights, Civil Liberties, Status)

Year Under Review	2007	2008	2009	2010	2011	2012	2013	2014	2015	2016
Rating	3,3,PF	3,3,PF	3,3,PF	3,3,PF	3,3,PF	3,4,PF	3,4,PF	3,4,PF	3,4,PF	4,5,PF

Overview: The Republic of Turkey regularly holds multiparty elections. Although the prime minister traditionally held most executive power, Recep Tayyip Erdoğan has dominated the government since moving from the premiership to the presidency in 2014. The Justice and Development Party (AKP) has been the ruling party since 2002. After initially passing some liberalizing reforms, the government has shown decreasing respect for political rights and civil liberties, especially in the past five years. Problem areas include minority rights, free expression, associational rights, corruption, and the rule of law.

KEY DEVELOPMENTS IN 2016:

- The government survived an attempted military coup in July, in which more than 260 people were killed.
- In the wake of the coup, the government declared a state of emergency that was later extended through the end of the year. Over 150,000 people—including soldiers, police, judicial officials, civil servants, academics, and schoolteachers—were detained, arrested, or dismissed from their positions in a massive purge of suspected coup plotters and other perceived enemies of the state.
- In May, Binali Yıldırım, a close ally of President Erdoğan, replaced Ahmet Davutoğlu as prime minister.
- There were several terrorist attacks linked to the Islamic State (IS) militant group or Kurdish insurgents, including a June attack on Istanbul's Atatürk Airport, an August suicide bombing in Gaziantep, and December bombings outside a soccer stadium in Istanbul.

EXECUTIVE SUMMARY

On July 15, antigovernment forces in the Turkish military moved to overthrow the elected government. Thanks in part to massive civilian demonstrations, the government survived the coup attempt. Over 260 people were killed and roughly 2,000 were wounded in related violence. President Erdoğan claimed that Fethullah Gülen, an Islamic preacher living in self-imposed exile in the U.S. state of Pennsylvania, was the mastermind behind the attack on the government. Gülen's organization, which the government had previously described as a terrorist group, had been officially designated as such a few weeks before the coup attempt.

The government declared a three-month state of emergency, allowing the president to rule by decree and derogate constitutional protections. Over 150,000 soldiers, judges, police, civil servants, academics, and teachers were detained by authorities or dismissed from their jobs for alleged loyalties to Gülen, Kurdish militants, or other antigovernment forces. Gülen-affiliated schools and universities were closed. Scores of media outlets and hundreds of civic organizations—some of which were Kurdish oriented or simply critical of the government—were also closed. The state of emergency was extended through year's end in October, raising serious concerns about accountability, civil liberties, and the rule of law.

Even prior to the coup, freedom for media and free expression had declined. In March, the government took over *Zaman*, a leading daily newspaper that was supportive of Gülen. Social media users and others continued to be charged with insulting state leaders. Academics who signed a petition calling for peace talks with Kurdish militants in January were accused by Erdoğan of being "treasonous," and dozens of the signatories faced criminal investigations and dismissal from their positions over the course of the year.

In May, Binali Yıldırım, a close ally of President Erdoğan, replaced Ahmet Davutoğlu as prime minister and leader of the ruling AKP. Critics suggested that Erdoğan, whose position as president is supposed to be nonpartisan, was the force behind this change. Yıldırım had expressed strong support for Erdoğan's proposal to amend the constitution and strengthen presidential powers, while Davutoğlu had faced months of criticism in pro-AKP media outlets for insufficient loyalty to Erdoğan.

Turkey suffered terrorist attacks by both IS and Kurdish militants during the year. The government used antiterrorism laws to ban Kurdish organizations and remove mayors who were members of the Kurdish-oriented Peoples' Democratic Party (HDP). A constitutional amendment signed in June facilitated the removal of lawmakers' parliamentary immunity, exposing numerous deputies from the HDP and the secularist opposition Republican Peoples' Party (CHP) to prosecution. In November, 12 HDP deputies, including the party's two coleaders, were arrested for refusing to give testimony in an investigation of alleged "terrorist propaganda."

POLITICAL RIGHTS: 18 / 40 (− 6)

A. Electoral Process: 8 / 12 (− 1)

Turkey has a semipresidential system of government. The prime minister is the head of government and under the constitution holds most executive authority. The president is the head of state and has a legislative veto as well as power to appoint judges and prosecutors. In 2014, Erdoğan became the country's first popularly elected president, winning a once-renewable five-year term with 51.8 percent of the vote; presidents were previously chosen by the parliament. Some domestic and international observers, such as the Organization for

Security and Co-operation in Europe (OSCE), pointed to irregularities in the election campaign, including media bias and self-censorship, misuse of state resources to support Erdoğan, lack of transparency in campaign finances, and cases of voter fraud.

The unicameral parliament, the 550-seat Grand National Assembly, is elected by proportional representation for a four-year term. The most recent elections were in November 2015. They were called by President Erdoğan after no party won a majority in June 2015 elections and a coalition government could not be formed. In the November vote, the AKP won 49 percent of the ballots and 317 seats, giving it a clear parliamentary majority. The CHP won 134 seats with 25 percent of the vote, whereas the HDP and the Nationalist Action Party (MHP) won 59 and 40 seats, respectively. Many reports cited irregularities in the electoral process. Erdoğan campaigned for the AKP in the June elections, in violation of the president's nonpartisan status under both precedent and law. Opponents of the government also alleged media bias and censorship, noting that the state-owned TRT television station provided extensive coverage of the AKP's campaign while giving far less time to opposition parties and rejecting some of their advertisements. The HDP suffered from terrorist attacks, arrests, and mob violence. The OSCE, while acknowledging that Turkish voters had a choice among parties and that the vote count was transparent, concluded that media restrictions and violence severely hindered the campaign.

After the November 2015 elections, Davutoğlu of the AKP remained prime minister, but he resigned in May 2016 and was replaced by Yıldırım, a longtime ally of Erdoğan. Some reports indicated that Erdoğan orchestrated this change, believing Davutoğlu was insufficiently supportive of his efforts to amend the constitution to strengthen presidential powers.

Judges on the Supreme Electoral Council (YSK) oversee voting procedures. In June 2016, the parliament passed a judicial reform bill that allowed AKP-dominated judicial bodies to replace most YSK judges in September. In addition, three YSK judges were arrested in July for their alleged involvement in the coup.

B. Political Pluralism and Participation: 7 / 16 (− 2)

Turkey has a competitive multiparty system, with four parties represented in parliament. However, the rise of new parties is inhibited by the 10 percent vote threshold for parliamentary representation, and parties can be disbanded for endorsing policies that are not in agreement with constitutional parameters. This rule has been applied in the past to Islamist and Kurdish-oriented parties. After a cease-fire with the militant Kurdistan Workers' Party (PKK) collapsed in 2015, the government accused the HDP of being a proxy for the PKK. Erdoğan has called for HDP deputies linked to the PKK to be prosecuted.

In May 2016, the parliament approved a constitutional amendment to facilitate the removal of deputies' immunity from prosecution. Over 150 lawmakers, mostly from the HDP and CHP, subsequently had their immunity lifted for supposed links to terrorism or corruption. In June, files on 57 deputies were sent to the Ministry of Justice for possible prosecution, and in August two HDP deputies, including the party's cochair, were indicted for engaging in "terrorist propaganda." HDP officials in Istanbul were detained after state raids on the party's offices in August. In September, the government removed 28 HDP mayors from their posts, citing links to either the PKK or Gülen's organization. In November, 12 HDP deputies, including the party's coleaders, were arrested for refusing to cooperate in other cases involving alleged terrorist activities. Between October and December, 45 more mayors were dismissed, and by the end of the year 2,700 local HDP politicians had been jailed.

The military has historically been a dominant force in politics. Under the AKP, various reforms and controversial, politically motivated prosecutions have increased civilian control over the military. The attempted coup in July therefore came as a surprise to many. After the government reestablished its authority, it purged over 10,000 military personnel, including nearly half of all generals and admirals; many were also subsequently arrested.

C. Functioning of Government: 3 / 12 (− 3)

The May 2016 ouster of Davutoğlu illustrated the declining power of the Grand National Assembly compared with the presidency. The state of emergency, announced in July after the coup attempt and renewed for another three months in October, placed additional powers in the hands of the president. Furthermore, local self-government has been compromised, as the Interior Ministry took over dozens of municipalities in the southeastern part of the country after their elected HDP mayors were dismissed.

Corruption—including money laundering, bribery, and collusion in the allocation of government contracts—remains a major problem. In April 2016, Transparency International released a report highlighting the poor implementation of measures to combat corruption, and ineffective checks on power holders. Rather than investigating widely publicized corruption allegations, the government tends to attribute them to rogue elements in the police and judiciary that are allegedly part of an antigovernment "parallel state" linked to Gülen's network.

Anti-Gülen operations accelerated after the July coup attempt. Under the state of emergency, roughly 120,000 police, civil servants, military personnel, teachers, and academics were dismissed or suspended; by November, 37,000 others had been formally arrested for political reasons. The state of emergency also raised serious questions about accountability and transparency, as it removed important checks on state power. It effectively derogated the constitution and the European Convention on Human Rights, allowing the president to suspend civil liberties and rule by decree, without oversight from the Constitutional Court. The Council of Europe has criticized the state of emergency for bestowing "almost unlimited discretionary powers" on the government.

CIVIL LIBERTIES: 20 / 60 (− 9)

D. Freedom of Expression and Belief: 6 / 16 (− 2)

Freedom of expression is constitutionally guaranteed. However, in recent years dozens of intellectuals and journalists have been jailed, particularly on terrorism charges or for insulting state leaders, with more than 3,000 cases opened on the latter charge during Erdoğan's presidency. High-profile events in 2016 included the government's March seizure of *Zaman*, a leading daily newspaper that had been supportive of Gülen and critical of the government. Its offices were raided by police, and a demonstration in support of the paper was broken up with tear gas. After the editors were replaced, the paper began adopting progovernment positions. In April, Dutch-Turkish journalist Ebru Umar was arrested for insulting Erdoğan, and in May a former Miss Turkey was found guilty of the same offense. Also in May, a Turkish court sentenced *Cumhuriyet* editor Can Dündar to nearly six years in prison for revealing state secrets; hours earlier, a man had tried to shoot him during a break in the trial. In June, a Turkish representative of Reporters Without Borders and the president of the Human Rights Foundation of Turkey were arrested for publishing material that allegedly included "terrorist propaganda" during their stints as temporary editors of the pro-Kurdish newspaper *Özgür Gündem*.

The authorities carried out a severe crackdown on the media after the July coup attempt. Decree Order 668 allows the state to shutter outlets and seize their assets on national security grounds. Within two weeks of the coup, 131 media outlets were closed, including dozens of national and regional newspapers, three wire services, 16 television stations, and 23 radio stations, and arrest warrants were issued for 89 journalists. In August, the government closed *Özgür Gündem* and detained over 20 of its journalists. In September, more than 20 Kurdish-language and leftist television and radio stations were shut down. In October, the editor and at least a dozen staff from *Cumhuriyet* were detained for publishing material that was allegedly supportive of the coup attempt. By the end of October, over 170 outlets had been closed and more than 700 journalists had their credentials revoked. The Committee to Protect Journalists reported in December that 81 journalists were behind bars in Turkey, the most in any country in the world. In addition, ownership of many remaining media outlets has been transferred to AKP supporters, with the result that access to independent, critical media is extremely limited.

Infringements on internet freedom have mounted. A law that took effect in June 2016 permits the government to suspend or block internet access in case of war or national emergency. Social media were blocked after the June attack on the Istanbul airport and during the coup attempt in July. During the first half of 2016, Twitter reported nearly 2,500 requests from the Turkish government, police, or courts to remove content, affecting nearly 15,000 accounts, by far the most for any country in the world. After the coup, pro-Gülen websites and others critical of the government were blocked or taken down.

The constitution protects freedom of religion, and religious expression has become more prominent in the public sphere under the AKP. Critics charge that the AKP has a religious agenda favoring Sunni Muslims, evidenced by the expansion of the Directorate of Religious Affairs and the alleged use of this institution for political patronage and to deliver government-friendly sermons in mosques. The Alevi minority, a non-Sunni Muslim group, has historically faced violence and discrimination. In April 2016, the European Court of Human Rights ruled that Alevis were subject to discrimination because the state refused to recognize their faith and provide support for their houses of worship, as it does for Sunni mosques. Three non-Muslim religious groups—Jews, Orthodox Christians, and Armenian Christians—are officially recognized. However, disputes over property and prohibitions on training of clergy remain problems for these communities. In April 2016, the government seized several Christian churches in Diyarbakır, claiming that the move was part of a historical restoration.

Academic freedom has become a major concern. In January 2016, over 1,400 Turkish academics signed a petition calling for an end to the military campaign against Kurdish population centers. Erdoğan called this action treasonous, and Turkish signatories were placed under investigation. More than two dozen were detained by police, and several were dismissed from their jobs. After the July coup, all university deans were forced to resign, while universities were required to submit a report naming faculty with suspected links to Gülen. Close to 4,000 academics were suspended, and 15 universities were closed. The government also ordered the closure of over 1,000 private schools allegedly affiliated with Gülen and dismissed more than 11,000 teachers suspected of pro-PKK activities.

Self-censorship on controversial issues is commonplace, and even private discussion has become more constrained amid the postcoup crackdown.

E. Associational and Organizational Rights: 3 / 12 (−3)

Freedoms of association and assembly are protected in the constitution, and Turkey has an active civil society. Since the 2013 Gezi Park protests, however, the authorities have broken up numerous demonstrations and passed laws to expand police powers to use force against protesters. In May 2016, police in Istanbul used tear gas to disperse May Day gatherings and detained over 200 demonstrators. In June, police forcibly broke up a demonstration against an earlier mob attack on music fans who were consuming alcohol. After the July coup attempt, there were numerous large progovernment demonstrations throughout the country; some of these included leaders from the CHP and MHP. But the state of emergency gave authorities the power to impose curfews and declare certain public and private areas off limits, and to ban or restrict meetings, gatherings, and rallies. In September, in southeastern Turkey, protests against the postcoup purges were dispersed with water cannons and tear gas, and dozens of people were arrested.

Turkey has a large number of active nongovernmental organizations (NGOs). However, authorities have monitored and harassed many NGOs in recent years, in particular those affiliated with Gülen's Hizmet movement. In the aftermath of the coup, 1,229 foundations and associations and 19 trade unions were shut down without judicial proceedings. In November, 375 more associations and NGOs were closed for alleged links to terrorists, and their assets were seized by the government. These included several charities, medical and lawyers' associations, and groups advocating for women's and children's rights.

There are four national trade union confederations. Trade unions have traditionally been active in organizing antigovernment protests. Nevertheless, union activity, including the right to strike, remains limited by law and in practice, and antiunion activities by employers are common. Because of various threshold requirements, only half of union members in Turkey enjoy collective-bargaining rights, and fewer than 10 percent of workers are unionized. In June 2016, the leader of the Confederation of Progressive Trade Unions of Turkey was arrested for allegedly insulting Erdoğan. In September, union protests in Bursa were forcibly broken up by police acting under the state of emergency.

F. Rule of Law: 4 / 16 (− 2)

The constitution provides for an independent judiciary, but the government has been able to influence judges through appointments, promotions, and financing. Antiterrorism laws have been widely employed to investigate and prosecute critics of the government. Reassignments of thousands of police officers, judges, and prosecutors, which began in 2014, continued into 2016. The government also passed laws to gain more control over the courts. In June, the government issued a decree to reassign 3,750 judges and prosecutors, promoting those who had issued rulings favorable to the government. In the aftermath of the July coup attempt, over 2,700 more judges and prosecutors were dismissed or arrested, including two Constitutional Court judges, who were jailed for alleged connections to Gülen. A law adopted at the end of June overhauled higher judicial organs, including the Supreme Court of Appeals and the Council of State, leading to a mass dismissal of judges.

Under the state of emergency, tens of thousands of people have been detained, and the maximum permissible pretrial detention period has been extended from four to 30 days. Family members of suspects have also been detained and arrested. Human rights watchdogs have decried the conditions under which those accused of organizing or supporting the coup have been held, citing little or no access to lawyers as well as evidence of beatings, torture, and forced confessions. The Constitutional Court lacks the power to review or overturn executive decrees during the state of emergency.

A cease-fire with the PKK ended in July 2015, leading to guerrilla attacks and intense urban fighting in the southeast. The International Crisis Group reports that more than 2,400 people—PKK fighters, Turkish security forces, and civilians—had died by December 2016, double the casualty rate during the last period of intense fighting from 2011 to 2012.

According to Amnesty International, by the end of 2016 over 500,000 people had been displaced due to fighting in Kurdish-majority regions. Several terrorist attacks have been attributed to Kurdish groups. In February and March of 2016, the Kurdistan Freedom Falcons (TAK), an offshoot of the PKK, claimed responsibility for suicide bombings in Ankara directed against military personnel that claimed 28 and 37 lives, respectively. In October, a car bomb in Hakkâri Province killed 10 soldiers and eight civilians. In December, TAK claimed responsibility for a suicide bombing outside a soccer stadium in Istanbul that killed 39 people. Turkish security forces have been accused of committing numerous atrocities, including the killing of more than 160 Kurdish civilians in February in the town of Cizre, which was under curfew.

Turkey has suffered from several terrorist attacks attributed to IS. These include a suicide bombing that killed at least 10 people in Istanbul's Sultanahmet district in January, a June attack on Istanbul's Atatürk Airport that killed 44, and an August bombing of a wedding in Gaziantep that killed 57. Security forces conducted anti-IS raids throughout 2016, and in August Turkish ground forces entered Syria to free territory held by the group.

Turkey harbors over 2.8 million refugees from Syria. Refugees have access to education and health care, and in January 2016 Turkey passed a new law allowing them to work legally, although few refugees are in a position to take advantage of these legal protections. In March, Turkey signed an agreement with the European Union (EU) under which migrants and refugees are to be returned to Turkey if they cross irregularly into EU territory. Critics of the deal argued that Turkey is unable to provide adequate services for refugees, even with promised EU aid.

Same-sex sexual activity is legally permitted, but LGBT (lesbian, gay, bisexual, and transgender) people are subject to widespread discrimination, police harassment, and occasional violence. There is no legislation to protect people from discrimination based on sexual orientation or gender identity. In June 2016, the government refused to grant permission for an Istanbul gay pride parade on security grounds.

G. Personal Autonomy and Individual Rights: 7 / 16 (− 2)

Freedom of travel and choice of residence and employment are generally respected, though movement in parts of the southeast was seriously hampered throughout 2016 by curfews, checkpoints, and fighting between security forces and PKK militants. As part of the state of emergency after the July coup, academics were temporarily prohibited from leaving the country. Tens of thousands of people who have been dismissed from jobs in the postcoup purges have also had their passports revoked.

There is a right to private property, but since 2013 many critics of the government have been subjected to intrusive tax and regulatory inspections. After the July coup attempt, the government raided numerous companies linked to Gülen, including Akfa Holding, Kaynak Holding, and Boydak Holding. Their assets have been seized and management turned over to state-appointed trustees. By the end of 2016, hundreds of companies and thousands of properties worth nearly $10 billion had been confiscated. Assets of closed NGOs have also been turned over to the state.

The constitution grants women full equality before the law, but only about 32 percent of working-age women participate in the labor force. One cabinet minister is female. Turkey ranked 130 out of 144 countries in the World Economic Forum's 2016 Global Gender Gap report. In March 2016, Erdoğan, who has claimed that gender equality is "against nature," proposed reforms that would embrace "Turkish-style" women's rights. In May, he condemned use of birth control and declared that women who work are "deficient" and "half-people." Some issues, in particular the problem of violence against women, have gained more visibility in recent years. However, critics argue that the government is often more concerned with family integrity than women's rights. For example, a parliamentary commission on protecting the integrity of the family issued a May 2016 report that proposed lowering the legal age of marriage to 15, favored mediation over shelter for abused women, and urged more involvement by the Religious Affairs Directorate in family counseling. In November, the government proposed a bill that would lift some convictions for child sexual assault if the perpetrators marry their victims; the measure was withdrawn amid domestic and international protest.

Syrian refugees and other migrants have been subjected to sex trafficking and forced labor. In February 2016, the government moved to increase criminal penalties for trafficking in persons. A U.S. State Department report issued in July noted some progress but suggested that more attention needed to be devoted to the issue, including more vigorous efforts to identify and support victims.

Turkmenistan

Political Rights Rating: 7
Civil Liberties Rating: 7
Freedom Rating: 7.0
Freedom Status: Not Free
Electoral Democracy: No

Population: 5,400,000
Capital: Ashgabat

Ten-Year Ratings Timeline For Year Under Review (Political Rights, Civil Liberties, Status)

Year Under Review	2007	2008	2009	2010	2011	2012	2013	2014	2015	2016
Rating	7,7,NF	7,7,NF	7,7,NF	7,7,NF	7,7,NF	7,7,NF	7,7,NF	7,7,NF	7,7,NF	7,7,NF

Overview: Turkmenistan is a highly repressive authoritarian state where citizens' political rights and civil liberties are almost completely denied in practice. Saparmurat Niyazov, the president of Turkmenistan from independence until his death in 2006, created a pervasive personality cult, and his successor, Gurbanguly Berdimuhamedov, has sought to replace it with his own. Elections in Turkmenistan are controlled by the state, ensuring nearly unanimous victories for the president and his party. Corruption is systemic, religious groups and minorities are persecuted, and political dissent is not tolerated. Numerous political prisoners remain behind bars or unaccounted for, and reports of torture and other human rights abuses are common.

KEY DEVELOPMENTS IN 2016:

- In September, the legislature adopted constitutional revisions that removed the age limit of 70 for presidential candidates and increased presidential terms from five years to seven.
- Changes to the law on religion enacted in March raised new obstacles for religious groups seeking registration. Activities by unregistered groups are considered illegal.
- Journalists and others who disseminated information about the economic situation faced harassment and violence, as authorities attempted to suppress evidence of hardship associated with low global energy prices.

EXECUTIVE SUMMARY

President Berdimuhamedov took a number of steps to reinforce his control over the state during 2016, apparently motivated by the worsening economic situation. With persistently low oil and gas prices driving down export revenues, there were reports of unpaid wages and food shortages across the country.

In September, the parliament enacted constitutional changes that removed the age ceiling of 70 for presidential candidates and extended presidential terms from five years to seven. The revisions meant that Berdimuhamedov, still just 59, could continue to seek reelection indefinitely and would not have to renew his mandate as often. The next presidential election was due in 2017. Meanwhile, the president also moved to bolster the position of his son, Serdar Berdimuhamedov. He was appointed as deputy minister of foreign affairs in July and won a parliament seat in a November by-election that received virtually no media coverage.

Also during the year, the president arbitrarily dismissed cabinet ministers and many local officials, and eliminated both the Ministry of Oil and Gas and the State Agency for Managing Hydrocarbon Resources in July, citing corruption and poor performance. The moves were seen as part of an effort to cut expenses, maintain presidential dominance, and shift blame for the economic crisis.

State authorities continued to limit the availability of independent information, harass and imprison critics and their relatives, and persecute ethnic minorities and religious groups. In March the president signed legislation that tightened restrictions on religious freedom, in part by raising the membership threshold for registration of a religious group from 5 to 50. Only registered religious groups are able to operate legally.

Local journalists working with U.S.-funded Radio Free Europe/Radio Liberty's Turkmen-language service faced persistent harassment during the year. For example, Soltan Achilova was questioned by police, then assaulted by unknown attackers who seized her camera, after taking photographs of a supermarket queue in October. She was threatened and assaulted again later in the year. Another contributor to the news service who had reported on the economic situation, Khudayberdy Allashov, was arrested along with his mother in December when police raided his home and beat him. They were charged with possessing illegal chewing tobacco and remained in detention at year's end.

Among other hostile acts against family members of government critics, the brother of exiled dissident journalist Chary Annamuradov was kidnapped and beaten to death in September.

POLITICAL RIGHTS: 0 / 40

A. Electoral Process: 0 / 12

B. Political Pluralism and Participation: 0 / 16

C. Functioning of Government: 0 / 12

CIVIL LIBERTIES: 4 / 60

D. Freedom of Expression and Belief: 1 / 16

E. Associational and Organizational Rights: 0 / 12

F. Rule of Law: 0 / 16

G. Personal Autonomy and Individual Rights: 3 / 16

This country report has been abridged for *Freedom in the World 2017*. For background information on political rights and civil liberties in Turkmenistan, see *Freedom in the World 2016*.

Tuvalu

Political Rights Rating: 1
Civil Liberties Rating: 1
Freedom Rating: 1.0
Freedom Status: Free
Electoral Democracy: Yes

Population: 10,000
Capital: Funafuti

Ten-Year Ratings Timeline For Year Under Review (Political Rights, Civil Liberties, Status)

Year Under Review	2007	2008	2009	2010	2011	2012	2013	2014	2015	2016
Rating	1,1,F	1,1,F	1,1,F	1,1,F	1,1,F	1,1,F	1,1,F	1,1,F	1,1,F	1,1,F

the country or territory displayed here received scores but no narrative report for this edition of *Freedom in the World.*

Uganda

Political Rights Rating: 6
Civil Liberties Rating: 5
Freedom Rating: 5.5
Freedom Status: Not Free
Electoral Democracy: No

Population: 36,600,000
Capital: Kampala

Ten-Year Ratings Timeline For Year Under Review (Political Rights, Civil Liberties, Status)

Year Under Review	2007	2008	2009	2010	2011	2012	2013	2014	2015	2016
Rating	5,4,PF	5,4,PF	5,4,PF	5,4,PF	5,4,PF	5,4,PF	6,4,PF	6,5,NF	6,5,NF	6,5,NF

Overview: While Uganda holds regular elections, their credibility has deteriorated over time, and the country has been ruled by the same party and president since 1986. The ruling party, the National Resistance Movement (NRM), retains power through the manipulation of state resources, intimidation by security forces, and politicized prosecutions of opposition leaders. Uganda's civil society and media sectors remain vibrant, despite suffering sporadic legal and extralegal harassment and state violence. The LGBT (lesbian, gay, bisexual, and transgender) community remains under threat.

KEY DEVELOPMENTS IN 2016:

- In February, Uganda held deeply flawed general elections that featured harassment and violence against the opposition, among other abuses. President Yoweri Museveni of the ruling NRM was officially awarded another five-year term in office.
- In May, Kizza Besigye, the leading opposition presidential candidate, was charged with treason following months of arrests, detentions, and periods of house arrest.
- Legislation enacted in January contained ill-defined regulatory provisions for nongovernmental organizations (NGOs) that could allow government interference, and extralegal intimidation remained a serious challenge to civil society advocacy.

EXECUTIVE SUMMARY

In 2016, Uganda held its third general elections since the transition to a multiparty system in 2005. While incumbent president Museveni was reelected, the polls were marred by severe intimidation of voters and the opposition, the repeated arrest of presidential challenger Kizza Besigye, the use of state resources for the ruling party's campaign, and significant delays in voting.

The president signed the Non-Governmental Organisations (NGO) Act in January, despite criticism that its ambiguous language could be used to ban groups that challenge the government. The authorities also interfered with the free flow of information, shutting down access to social media in the periods around the February elections and the presidential inauguration in May. Police brutality and harassment intensified during the year, targeting opposition candidates, their supporters, and civil society activists. Separately, although the controversial Anti-Homosexuality Act (AHA) was struck down on a technicality in 2014, a 2016 report showed that the LGBT community continued to experience human rights abuses.

POLITICAL RIGHTS: 11 / 40

A. Electoral Process: 3 / 12

Uganda's single-chamber Parliament and president are elected for five-year terms. In the February 2016 presidential contest, Museveni extended his 30-year rule with another five-year term by securing 60.6 percent of the vote, according to official results. Besigye of the opposition Forum for Democratic Change (FDC) placed second with 35.6 percent. Due to the introduction of new constituencies, a total of 426 members of parliament (MPs) were chosen in the 2016 legislative elections, including 289 elected in single-member districts, 112 elected to reserved seats for women, and 25 chosen to represent special interest groups (the military, youth, people with disabilities, and trade unions). The ruling party, the NRM, won an absolute majority with 293 seats, while independents won 66 seats, the FDC won 36, and smaller parties took the remainder. Additional ex-officio seats are held by cabinet ministers, who are appointed by the president and do not have voting rights.

According to international and regional observers, the 2016 elections were undermined by problems including the misuse of state resources and flawed administration by the Electoral Commission (EC). On election day, the EC experienced significant technical and logistical challenges, causing some citizens to wait for hours to cast their votes. The EC extended the voting time for polling stations that opened late, with voting in some areas continuing for an extra day even as counting was well under way. This fueled existing mistrust of the EC and raised suspicions of malfeasance. Besigye and the FDC leadership contended that fraud and intimidation of the opposition had marred the entire electoral process.

Former prime minister Amama Mbabazi, who placed a distant third in the presidential race, petitioned the Supreme Court in March to nullify the elections. Although the court acknowledged a number of irregularities—including violations by the EC, interference by public officials, the arrest of opposition candidates, the delayed delivery of voting materials to polling places, and unfair public media coverage—it ultimately ruled that these problems did not affect the results to an extent that would justify an annulment.

The president appoints the members of the EC with the approval of parliament. The incumbent commission's term was due to end in 2016. In August, an NRM MP proposed a constitutional amendment that would provide EC commissioners with open-ended terms, but the measure was met with resistance by activists and opposition MPs who saw it as a way for the ruling party to permanently secure its position. In November, the president nominated a new chair, vice chair, and commissioners for the EC, and parliament approved them in December.

B. Political Pluralism and Participation: 5 / 16

While opposition groups have suffered from infighting and funding shortages, their ability to compete in elections is largely hindered by restrictive party registration requirements and candidate eligibility rules, the use of government resources to support NRM candidates, a lack of access to state media coverage, state violence and harassment, and paramilitary groups that intimidate voters and government opponents.

Throughout the 2016 electoral period, violence, intimidation, and harassment toward opposition parties—especially the FDC and its supporters—were particularly acute. Days before the elections, Besigye was arrested on his way to a campaign rally on the grounds that he was disrupting traffic and business in Kampala. He was arrested again on election day after trying to inform police of electoral violations. The following day, police stormed FDC headquarters and arrested Besigye yet again along with other FDC leaders. For weeks afterward, Besigye was held under house arrest or moved between police stations and his home without formal charges ever being filed. Police argued that they were using their powers of "preventative arrest" to disrupt activities or statements that could incite violence or defiance of the law. The day after the elections, police also surrounded the home of Mbabazi, who was barred from leaving but not arrested.

In May, Besigye was charged with treason for a video in which he held a mock presidential inauguration for himself, and due to allegations that he had incited people to overthrow the government. After two months in detention, Besigye was released on bail in July. The case remained pending at year's end.

The military is closely aligned with Museveni and holds 10 seats in parliament. During the 2016 election period, the military and police services worked to dissuade any protests against the results, mounting a visible armed security presence with heavy deployments in and around the capital. They repeatedly used excessive force to disperse opposition gatherings.

The dominant position and coercive tactics of the NRM impede free political participation and advocacy of interests by Uganda's various ethnic groups, including those affiliated with traditional kingdoms as well as smaller indigenous groups.

C. Functioning of Government: 3 / 12

Power is concentrated in the hands of the NRM leadership, the security forces, and especially the president, who retains office through a deeply flawed electoral process. Ordinary MPs and civic groups have little practical ability to influence legislation or government policies.

Despite high-profile scandals, investigations, increased media attention, and laws and institutions designed to combat corruption, malfeasance continues and top government officials are rarely prosecuted for such offenses. The World Bank has estimated that corruption costs Uganda 500 billion shillings ($145 million) a year, and in August 2016 the bank decided to withhold new lending to the country due to reports of persistent corruption and political kickbacks.

CIVIL LIBERTIES: 24 / 60 (− 1)

D. Freedom of Expression and Belief: 9 / 16

Constitutional protections for freedoms of expression and the press are often undermined by provisions in the penal code, including laws on criminal libel and treason, as well as by extralegal government actions.

Uganda has nearly 200 private radio stations and dozens of television stations and print outlets. Independent journalists and media outlets are often critical of the government, but in recent years they have faced escalating government restrictions and intimidation. More than a dozen journalists were arrested and beaten by state officials in 2016, in some cases during live broadcasts. In May, the government banned journalists from reporting on opposition activities, threatening arrest or cancelation of their licenses if they failed to comply.

Ahead of the February elections, the Uganda Communications Commission (UCC) temporarily blocked access to the social media platforms Twitter, WhatsApp, and Facebook, citing security concerns. Many Ugandans were able to circumvent the restriction by using virtual private networks (VPNs). The UCC shut down access to social media platforms again on the day of Museveni's inauguration in May.

There is no state religion, and freedom of worship is both constitutionally protected and generally respected in practice. However, the government has barred religious leaders from engaging in political debates and restricted religious groups whose members allegedly pose security risks. A series of Muslim clerics have been murdered in recent years, and in December 2016 police raided mosques and carried out arrests in search of those responsible for the killings and other criminal activity, drawing complaints that the officers acted arbitrarily and unlawfully.

Academic freedom has been undermined by alleged surveillance of university lectures by security officials, and by the need for professors to obtain permission to hold public meetings at universities. In November 2016, after weeks of student protests and a strike by faculty who said the government had defaulted on payment of their allowances, Museveni shut down Makerere University, Uganda's largest. Lecturers agreed to suspend the strike in December, and students were to resume classes at the beginning of 2017.

In addition to the threat of state surveillance, free and open private discussion is limited by a climate of intimidation pertaining to sexual orientation and gender identity. For example, LGBT individuals and others face the fear of being "outed" by tabloid newspapers that publicly identify real or perceived gay men and lesbians, along with personal details and photos.

E. Associational and Organizational Rights: 4 / 12

Freedom of assembly is restricted by law and in practice. Among other repressive provisions, the 2013 Public Order Management Act (POMA) requires groups to register with local police in writing three days before any gathering, public or private, to discuss political issues. The police have broad authority to deny approval for such meetings if they are not deemed to be in the "public interest," and to use force to disperse assemblies judged unlawful. The POMA was used numerous times as the justification for arresting opposition candidates and supporters during the 2016 campaign period.

Freedom of association is guaranteed in the constitution but often restricted. Civil society in Uganda is active, and several NGOs address politically sensitive issues. However, their existence and activities are vulnerable to legal restrictions and the manipulation of burdensome registration requirements. More than two dozen NGO offices have suffered suspicious break-ins since 2012, with intruders sometimes focusing on documents rather than valuable equipment. A security guard was reportedly drugged in one April 2016 incident, and another guard was killed in May. Police have failed to actively investigate the crimes.

Museveni signed the new NGO Act into law in January. Opponents of the measure noted that it contained a number of provisions that could allow the government to shutter organizations and jail their members for vaguely worded offenses, such as engagement in acts that are "prejudicial to the security and laws of Uganda" or to "the interests of Uganda and the dignity of the people of Uganda."

Workers' rights to organize, bargain collectively, and strike are recognized by law, except for workers providing essential government services. However, legal protections often go unenforced. Many private firms refuse to recognize unions, and strikers are sometimes arrested.

F. Rule of Law: 4 / 16 (− 1)

Executive and military influence undermines judicial independence, as does systemic corruption. Prolonged pretrial detention, inadequate resources, and poor judicial administration also impede access to justice. The prison system is operating at more than twice its intended capacity, with pretrial detainees constituting more than half of the prison population. Rape, extrajudicial violence, and torture and abuse of suspects and detainees by security forces are persistent problems.

The justice system's handling of politically charged cases surrounding the 2016 elections underscored its lack of impartiality. In response to Besigye's arrest on treason charges, the president of the Uganda Law Society questioned the independence of the judiciary in dealing with political cases and cautioned that the courts should not be used to settle political disputes.

Security forces violently dispersed opposition supporters who gathered to welcome Besigye after his release on bail in July. Opposition MPs called for an investigation into the police beatings, which were captured on video. Victims sued police commanders for alleged torture and violations of their constitutional rights, but in August a court halted the proceedings.

Separately in June, FDC MP Michael Kabaziguruka and more than two dozen others, including military personnel, were charged with treason for allegedly plotting to overthrow the government. A trial before a military court was pending at year's end.

In November, Ugandan security forces stormed the royal enclosures and palaces of the traditional Rwenzururu Kingdom in the Rwenzori region, after palace guards allegedly attacked police stations. The fighting left more than 100 people dead, and human rights groups cited evidence of indiscriminate violence and summary executions on the part of security forces. The Rwenzururu king and many of his guards were arrested and charged with offenses including murder, treason, and terrorism. Analysts noted possible political motives behind the violence, as voters in the Rwenzori region heavily favored the opposition in the recent elections.

The AHA, which criminalized homosexuality, was struck down in 2014, but the LGBT community continues to face overt hostility from the government and much of society. According to an April 2016 report by Sexual Minorities Uganda, LGBT people suffered 264 verified cases of human rights abuses between May 2014 and the end of 2015; 84 involved loss of property or employment and other forms of intimidation, while 48 involved violence, including "torture by the state." In August, police raided an event during Ugandan LGBT Pride celebrations and beat participants, arresting 16 people and holding them temporarily under abusive conditions.

G. Personal Autonomy and Individual Rights: 7 / 16

Freedom of movement in Uganda is largely unrestricted. Bribery is common in many facets of life, such as interacting with traffic police, gaining admittance to some institutions of higher education, and obtaining government jobs. Licenses are required to start a business, obtain construction permits, and register property, and the multistage processes involve numerous opportunities for officials to seek bribes. Customary land tenure is widespread in the north, and land disputes—some of them violent—are common, particularly when private development projects are at stake.

Although the constitution prohibits discrimination on the basis of gender and acknowledges the equal rights of women, gender discrimination remains pronounced, particularly in rural areas. Women hold about a third of the seats in parliament, and a third of local council seats are reserved for women. The law gives women the right to inherit land, but discriminatory customs often trump legal provisions in practice. Rape and domestic violence are widespread and underreported, and offenders are rarely prosecuted. Cultural practices such as female genital mutilation persist, despite the 2010 Prohibition of Female Genital Mutilation Act.

Poor enforcement of labor laws contributes to unsafe or exploitative conditions for many workers. Child labor in agriculture, domestic service, and a variety of other industries is a significant problem, as is sexual exploitation of minors. Ritual sacrifice of abducted children has reportedly increased in recent years, with six killings reported ahead of the 2016 elections.

Ukraine

Political Rights Rating: 3
Civil Liberties Rating: 3
Freedom Rating: 3.0
Freedom Status: Partly Free
Electoral Democracy: Yes

Population: 42,700,000
Capital: Kyiv

Note: The numerical ratings and status listed above do not reflect conditions in Crimea, which is examined in a separate report. *Freedom in the World* country reports assess the level of political rights and civil liberties in a given geographical area, regardless of whether they are affected by the state, nonstate actors, or foreign powers. Disputed territories are sometimes assessed separately if they meet certain criteria, including boundaries that are sufficiently stable to allow year-on-year comparisons. For more information, see the report methodology and FAQ.

Ten-Year Ratings Timeline For Year Under Review (Political Rights, Civil Liberties, Status)

Year Under Review	2007	2008	2009	2010	2011	2012	2013	2014	2015	2016
Rating	3,2,F	3,2,F	3,2,F	3,3,PF	4,3,PF	4,3,PF	4,3,PF	3,3,PF	3,3,PF	3,3,PF

Overview: Ukraine continues to recover from the disorder that surrounded the ouster of Viktor Yanukovych from the presidency in 2014, as well as the related crisis sparked by Russia's occupation of Crimea and military support for separatists in the Donbas area of eastern Ukraine. The authorities' failure to prosecute extensive high-level corruption has undermined the popularity of the government and affected reform efforts in a wide range of sectors. In the sphere of civil liberties, political pressure and attacks on journalists have threatened freedom of the press.

KEY DEVELOPMENTS IN 2016:

- Amid extended political deadlock over reform and anticorruption efforts, Prime Minister Arseniy Yatsenyuk resigned in April at the request of President Petro Poroshenko. Volodymyr Groysman, a close Poroshenko ally, replaced Yatsenyuk.
- The front lines in the Donbas regions of Donetsk and Luhansk remained largely unchanged during the year, with only minor outbreaks of combat between government forces and Russian-backed separatists, and significantly fewer casualties than in 2014 or 2015.
- In July, a car bomb killed prominent journalist Pavel Sheremet in Kyiv, heightening concerns about the safety and freedom of journalists. Several other media professionals and organizations—in both government-controlled and separatist-held areas—faced violence, threats, and harassment during the year.
- Strong protection from security forces ensured that a Kyiv LGBT (lesbian, gay, bisexual, and transgender) pride parade could proceed without violence in June, though some other LGBT events outside the capital were threatened or attacked.

EXECUTIVE SUMMARY

Political infighting consumed much of the early months of 2016. President Poroshenko requested the resignation of Prime Minister Yatsenyuk in February, but failed to gather the necessary support in the parliament, where Yatsenyuk's People's Front is the second-largest party. Yatsenyuk resigned in April, along with many ministers who were outspoken advocates of reform, and was replaced by Groysman. The Yatsenyuk government had achieved notable reforms in the gas and banking sectors, and Groysman moved ahead with changes in the electricity sector, eliminating some opportunities for corruption. In June, the parliament passed long-promised legislation aimed at increasing independence and reducing malfeasance in the judiciary. Nevertheless, other anticorruption efforts moved slowly throughout the year.

The Minsk II agreement, a cease-fire deal brokered by France and Germany in early 2015, remained formally in effect in 2016, but low-intensity combat continued along the line of contact in eastern Ukraine. In a December 2016 report, the Office of the UN High Commissioner for Human Rights (OHCHR) noted that at least 9,733 people had been killed and more than 22,000 wounded in Ukraine from the outbreak of the conflict in April 2014 to November 2016. In April, the Ministry of Social Policy reported that it had registered approximately 1.7 million internally displaced persons (IDPs) from Crimea and the Donbas. IDPs continued to experience difficulties in accessing public services in 2016.

The situation in the Donbas separatist entities, the self-styled Luhansk People's Republic (LNR) and Donetsk People's Republic (DNR), remained unstable, with several killings and arrests among the rebel leadership. Following an alleged coup attempt against Luhansk leader Igor Plotnitsky in August, the separatist leaders purged dozens of political and military personnel. In October, a bomb killed Arsen Pavlov, a Russian national and one of the most prominent separatist military leaders in Donetsk. Local elections and administration in these two regions remained contentious issues. In October, despite some preparation by separatist authorities in both Donetsk and Luhansk, the regions' leaders announced the cancelation of voting, which had been scheduled for November. Details about the framework and conduct of future elections in separatist-held areas were still unclear at year's end.

The Ukrainian government made little progress in meeting domestic and international demands to investigate and prosecute crimes committed during the last months of the Yanukovych administration in late 2013 and early 2014, which included the shooting of protesters.

POLITICAL RIGHTS: 25 / 40

A. Electoral Process: 9 / 12

The president is elected to a maximum of two five-year terms. After Yanukovych fled the country in February 2014, a snap presidential election was held that May. Poroshenko won 54.7 percent of the overall vote and majorities in regions across the country. The process was largely considered free and fair by international observers, although voting could not take place in Crimea and some districts in the east.

Citizens elect delegates to the Verkhovna Rada (Supreme Council), the 450-seat unicameral parliament, for five-year terms, according to a system in which half of the members are chosen by closed-list proportional representation and half in single-member districts. The early parliamentary elections held in October 2014 produced a legislature with a reformist majority. Petro Poroshenko's Bloc won 133 seats, former prime minister Arseniy Yatsenyuk's People's Front took 81, Self-Reliance 33, the Opposition Bloc 29, the Radical Party 22, and Fatherland 19. Several smaller parties and 96 independents divided the remainder. While the elections were generally deemed free and fair, voting was again impossible in Crimea and separatist-held parts of Donetsk and Luhansk, where many citizens would likely have voted against the winning reformist parties. As a result of the occupation, the elections filled only 423 of the parliament's 450 seats.

In October 2015, Ukraine held elections for more than 10,000 mayors and 155,970 local, district, and regional council members, with 132 political parties participating. Turnout was 46.6 percent. Petro Poroshenko's Bloc and its allies won more than 16,500 seats, while former prime minister Yuliya Tymoshenko's Fatherland party placed second with over 8,000 seats. The Opposition Bloc, a successor to Yanukovych's Party of Regions, did well in some of the eastern and southern regions, taking over 4,000 seats.

B. Political Pluralism and Participation: 10 / 16

Since the fall of Yanukovych, Ukraine's political party system has experienced extreme volatility. The Communist Party was banned in 2015, and other older parties have all but disappeared, while a variety of new groups have formed and won important offices. A key problem has been that the parties often rely on the country's politically connected business magnates, or oligarchs, for their funding. A new law that came into force in July 2016 subjects party funding and expenditures to public reporting and oversight requirements and provides parliamentary parties with state funding beginning in 2017. The latter provision effectively favors established parties over newcomers. The party landscape continued to evolve in 2016, with the small Democratic Alliance party growing thanks to defections by high-profile reformists. A fledgling far-right party, the National Corps, was created in October by the Azov Battalion—a nationalist volunteer paramilitary unit that has been incorporated into Ukraine's National Guard.

Russia maintained a powerful influence over the course of Ukrainian political life through its occupation of Crimea, involvement in the fighting in the east, imposition of economic sanctions on the rest of the country, and manipulation of the price Ukraine pays for natural gas. Concerns about national security and Russian influence have contributed to a shrinking space for criticism of the Ukrainian authorities and military, and for discussions on resolving the conflict in the east through political means. Journalist Ruslan Kotsaba, arrested in early 2015 and charged with treason for his calls to resist military conscription, was convicted in May 2016 of "obstructing the activities of Ukraine's armed forces" and sentenced to three and a half years in prison, though he was then acquitted on appeal and released in July. Lawmaker and military veteran Nadiya Savchenko faced widespread criticism for meeting with separatist leaders in Minsk and advocating a political dialogue to end the fighting.

Ethnic minorities are able to participate freely in political affairs in Ukraine. However, their voting and representation has been hindered by factors including the conflict in the Donbas, illiteracy and lack of identity documents for many Roma, and rules against running as an independent for many local, district, and regional offices.

C. Functioning of Government: 6 / 12

Poroshenko's removal of Yatsenyuk has considerably strengthened the power of the president. Yanukovych in 2010 had overseen the restoration of the 1996 constitution, which featured a dominant presidency, but a 386–0 vote by the parliament in 2014 reversed that move, reviving the 2004 charter. The latter, the product of a compromise during the Orange Revolution, had shifted power to the prime minister and cabinet and made them responsible to the parliament, though the president retained control over the foreign and defense ministers and the head of the security service. This division of power had led to infighting between the president and prime minister between 2004 and 2010, and similar rifts began to emerge in 2015. However, in April 2016, Poroshenko secured a dominant position by placing a close ally in the prime minister's office.

Aside from the conflict in the east, the main obstacle to effective governance in Ukraine is corruption, and the vast majority of citizens have been deeply disappointed with the government's slow progress in combating it since Yanukovych's departure in 2014. No major figures have been arrested, and the government has recovered almost none of the billions of dollars in assets that were allegedly looted under previous administrations.

Oligarchs continue to exert considerable influence over Ukrainian life through their control of some 70 percent of the economy, much of the media, and the financing of political parties. Poroshenko, a wealthy businessman who is counted among them, remains at the center of controversy. Former member of parliament Oleksandr Onishchenko, after fleeing abroad, accused him of offering bribes to lawmakers and extorting money from state companies. Odesa governor Mikheil Saakashvili resigned from his post in November 2016, claiming that the president and other high-level officials were taking advantage of the system for personal gain. Poroshenko has not honored campaign promises to sell most of his extensive assets, and his son Oleksiy Poroshenko is now a member of parliament and an increasingly powerful businessman, drawing comparisons to Yanukovych, whose sons also became power brokers.

Another key problem is pervasive corruption among Ukraine's prosecutors and judges. Under intense pressure from his critics and civil society, Poroshenko in February initiated the removal of Prosecutor General Viktor Shokin, who was seen as blocking anticorruption reforms, and replaced him in May with loyalist Yuriy Lutsenko, who lacks legal training. Before his removal by the parliament in March, Shokin sacked his deputy, corruption fighter Davit Sakvarelidze; another reformist deputy prosecutor general, Vitaliy Kasko, had resigned earlier. Although the parliament adopted a lustration law in 2014, it has not been used against prosecutors and judges.

The National Anti-Corruption Bureau of Ukraine (NABU), set up to investigate corrupt officials, began operating in 2015, but critics warned that it would be ineffective without reforms in the prosecutor's office and judiciary. It lacks sufficient personnel and powers, according to NABU head Artem Sytnyk, and faces institutional resistance to its work. In August 2016, for example, NABU officials conducting a criminal investigation into a department of the Prosecutor General's Office were detained and allegedly beaten by members of the targeted unit. Poroshenko's administration is seen as supporting the prosecutors over NABU.

Nongovernmental organizations (NGOs) focused on combating corruption complained in June that they were not properly included in the process of choosing the new leaders of the National Agency for the Prevention of Corruption (NAZK), as required by law. Also during the year, one prominent anticorruption NGO was targeted by prosecutors with an intrusive criminal investigation in apparent retribution for its work.

Ukraine has made some progress in advancing transparency, requiring that banks publish the identity of their owners. Under pressure from the European Union (EU), the parliament in March 2016 passed a law obliging politicians and bureaucrats to file electronic declarations of their assets by October 31. The measure exposed large amounts of property and cash held by Ukrainian officials who had no obvious means of earning such wealth. While the disclosures received significant media attention and bolstered civil society anticorruption efforts, critics warned that the NAZK lacked the capacity to properly investigate the declarations, and few criminal cases had been reported by year's end.

CIVIL LIBERTIES: 36 / 60

D. Freedom of Expression and Belief: 11 / 16

The constitution guarantees freedoms of speech and expression, and libel is not a criminal offense. The media landscape features considerable pluralism and open criticism of the government. However, business magnates with varying political interests own and influence many outlets. Poroshenko owns the television network Fifth Channel and has rebuffed press freedom groups' calls to honor his earlier promise to sell it. Among other key media owners are Ihor Kolomoysky (1 + 1), Dmytro Firtash (Inter), Rinat Akhmetov (Ukraine), Viktor Pinchuk (Novy Kanal, STB, ICTV), and Andriy Podshchypkov, whose cable and satellite broadcaster 112 Ukraine is often critical of Poroshenko. In 2014, the Interior Ministry banned the broadcast of over a dozen Russian channels, arguing that the country's information space had to be protected from Russia's "propaganda of war and violence."

Despite the pluralism of the Ukrainian media, many problems persist. In September 2016, VoxUkraine published a two-year analysis showing that the top four weekly television news programs only made negative references to President Poroshenko in 1 to 2 percent of their reports. At a June news conference, Poroshenko asked journalists not to write negative stories about Ukraine. He has also sought to block coverage of Onishchenko's corruption accusations by threatening lawsuits.

Journalists continue to face the threat of violence and intimidation. In July, a car bomb killed prominent journalist Pavel Sheremet, who wrote for the independent online newspaper *Ukrayinska Pravda*. In September, intruders set fire to the offices of Inter, which many Ukrainians view as having a pro-Russian bias. In May, Myrotvorets (Peacemaker), a website whose stated goal is to identify Ukraine's enemies, listed the names, employers, and contact information of more than 4,000 Ukrainian and foreign journalists who had received press credentials from separatist forces to report on fighting in the east. The website claimed that the journalists were supporting the separatists by seeking and receiving such accreditation, though many journalists stressed their need to receive accreditation in order to operate safely in separatist-controlled areas. Interior Minister Arsen Avakov defended the website's action. Other journalists who are critical of the government have been threatened and beaten. Deputy Information Policy Minister Tetyana Popova resigned in August, protesting the authorities' failure to prosecute attacks against journalists and defend free speech.

The constitution and a 1991 law define religious rights in Ukraine, and these are generally respected. However, the conflict has increased friction between rival branches of the Orthodox Church, and smaller religious groups continue to report some discrimination. In the DNR and LNR, separatist forces have reportedly persecuted Protestant and other non–Russian Orthodox denominations, forcing them to flee or operate underground churches.

A June 2014 law dramatically reduced the government's control over education and allowed universities much greater freedom in designing their own programs. Universities also gained an expanded ability to manage their own finances, and faculty members were permitted to devote more of their time to research activities.

Ukrainians generally enjoy open and free private discussion, although the polarizing effects of the conflict have weighed on political expression, and intimidation prevails in the separatist-held areas.

E. Associational and Organizational Rights: 9 / 12

The constitution guarantees the right to peaceful assembly but requires organizers to give the authorities advance notice of any demonstrations. While officials generally create an open environment for public gatherings in practice, Ukraine lacks a law governing the conduct of demonstrations and specifically providing for freedom of assembly. Moreover, threats and violence by nonstate actors sometimes prevent certain groups from holding events, particularly those advocating equal rights for LGBT people.

Civil society has flourished since 2014, as civic groups with a variety of social, political, cultural, and economic agendas have emerged or become reinvigorated. Trade unions function in the country, but strikes and worker protests are infrequent, as the largest trade union, stemming from the Soviet-era labor federation, lacks independence from the government and employers in practice. Factory owners are still able to pressure their workers to vote according to the owners' preferences.

F. Rule of Law: 6 / 16

Ukraine has long suffered from politicized courts, and judges were subject to intense political pressure under Yanukovych. An April 2014 judicial reform law sought to weaken the top-down power of court chairmen, who assign cases to specific judges and often make decisions about judges' salaries and other work conditions. Despite these reforms, Poroshenko has been unwilling to give up his control of the judicial branch. The senior prosecutors and law enforcement officials he has appointed are frequently criticized for failing to arrest high-level suspects on corruption charges.

In June 2016, the parliament approved constitutional amendments that changed Ukraine's system for appointing judges. They will be chosen by a judicial council rather than the parliament, which should help shield them from political influence. The amendments also call for specialized anticorruption courts that will be independent of the existing system. However, before the courts are created, a new law must be enacted to clarify their operations and the selection process for their judges. Full implementation could therefore be delayed until 2019.

In 2015, Ukraine introduced new patrol police in several cities. Though the police were initially popular, they came under attack from the unreformed prosecutor's office. First Deputy Interior Minister Eka Zguladze, who was in charge of the new police force, resigned after the downfall of Yatsenyuk government and warned that the patrol police could not survive as an "island" amid corrupt institutions.

Due to the ongoing fighting in eastern Ukraine, substantial parts of the population face extensive violence—including inaccurate or indiscriminate shelling by both sides. The separatist rulers of the DNR and LNR have "undermined the human rights of the estimated 2.7 million people residing under their control," according to the OHCHR. Meanwhile, there has been insufficient progress in bringing to justice the individuals responsible for political violence in Kyiv and Odesa in 2014 that killed some 150 people.

A July 2016 report by Amnesty International and Human Rights Watch alleged that the Security Service of Ukraine (SBU) was illegally holding and torturing suspected separatist fighters in unlawful detention facilities. The groups detailed alleged abuses in the cases of nine individuals held by the SBU, mainly in 2015 and the first half of 2016, as well as nine individuals held by the Russian-backed separatists. The SBU reacted to the document by releasing 13 prisoners; no similar response by the separatists, whose violations were reportedly much greater in number, was reported.

Although the national government has generally protected the legal rights of minority groups, the Romany population continues to suffer from discrimination. In one high-profile incident in 2016, dozens of Roma fled the village of Loshchynivka in southern Ukraine in August, when villagers blamed them for the rape and killing of a nine-year-old girl. Roma often live in substandard housing in marginal areas.

The LGBT community also faces bias and hostility in Ukraine. A June 2016 pride parade in Kyiv proceeded without violence thanks to strong protection from the security forces, though the heavy police presence made the march almost inaccessible. Public events on LGBT issues were disrupted in Zaporizhya, Odesa, and Lviv, through either violence or pressure by right-wing groups. Incidents of homophobic and transphobic violence are rarely investigated or prosecuted by the authorities, and there is no effective hate-crime legislation in place.

G. Personal Autonomy and Individual Rights: 10 / 16

The ongoing conflict with Russian-backed separatists in the east has displaced many residents from their homes and hampered freedom of movement within the country.

The separatist-controlled territories are largely lawless, with armed groups controlling public buildings and looting local businesses for supplies. Numerous reports indicate that separatist commanders force local residents to perform menial tasks. In the rest of Ukraine, private businesses continue to suffer at the hands of corrupt bureaucrats, tax collectors, and corporate raiders.

Gender discrimination is prohibited under the constitution, but government officials demonstrate little interest in or understanding of the problem. Human rights groups have reported that employers openly discriminate on the basis of gender, physical appearance, and age. Women currently make up about 12 percent of the parliament. A new local elections law, adopted in 2015, includes a 30 percent quota for women on the party lists, but there are no sanctions for parties that do not comply. The new law on party financing provides financial incentives for parties to achieve gender equality.

The trafficking of women domestically and abroad for the purpose of prostitution remains a major problem. The IDP population is especially vulnerable to exploitation for sex trafficking and forced labor. Separatist forces have reportedly recruited children as soldiers and informants.

United Arab Emirates

Political Rights Rating: 6
Civil Liberties Rating: 6
Freedom Rating: 6.0
Freedom Status: Not Free
Electoral Democracy: No

Population: 9,300,000
Capital: Abu Dhabi

Ten-Year Ratings Timeline For Year Under Review (Political Rights, Civil Liberties, Status)

Year Under Review	2007	2008	2009	2010	2011	2012	2013	2014	2015	2016
Rating	6,5,NF	6,5,NF	6,5,NF	6,5,NF	6,6,NF	6,6,NF	6,6,NF	6,6,NF	6,6,NF	6,6,NF

Overview: The United Arab Emirates (UAE) is a federation of seven emirates led in practice by Abu Dhabi, the largest by area and richest in natural resources. Limited elections are held for a federal advisory body, but political parties are banned, and all executive, legislative, and judicial authority ultimately rests with the seven hereditary rulers. The civil liberties of both citizens and noncitizens, who make up an overwhelming majority of the population, are subject to significant restrictions.

KEY DEVELOPMENTS IN 2016:

- In July, the government issued a law that increased penalties for using a virtual private network (VPN) to commit a crime, potentially deterring those who employ such tools to circumvent online censorship.
- In November, an Emirati dissident who had initially been arrested in Indonesia was sentenced to 10 years in prison as part of a broader crackdown on individuals accused of links to the Muslim Brotherhood.
- Another Emirati citizen, academic and activist Nasser bin Ghaith, was on trial during the year for critical online comments about the authorities and his own claims of torture, as well as alleged collaboration with Islamist political groups. He had been detained incommunicado or in solitary confinement since his August 2015 arrest.

EXECUTIVE SUMMARY

The government of the UAE continued to suppress dissent in 2016, restricting the use of social media and utilizing an expansive antiterrorism law that criminalizes criticism of the regime. The authorities remained especially focused on activists with real or suspected ties to Islamist political groups, which—like all political parties—are banned even if they do not espouse violence.

Sheikh Mohammed bin Zayed al-Nahyan, the crown prince of Abu Dhabi, the most powerful of the seven emirates, has reportedly taken on most policymaking authority since his older brother, UAE president and Abu Dhabi emir Khalifa bin Zayed al-Nahyan, suffered a stroke in 2014. Under Sheikh Mohammed's leadership, the country has pursued an active foreign policy, deploying financial, diplomatic, and even military resources to combat perceived Islamist or pro-Iranian threats across the region. It has provided support for the anti-Islamist Egyptian government, participated in a Saudi-led coalition against Shiite-affiliated antigovernment forces in Yemen, and backed an anti-Islamist factional leader in Libya.

Economic disparities persist among UAE citizens across the seven emirates, and between citizens and many noncitizen residents, who constitute nearly 90 percent of the total population. Noncitizens have borne the brunt of government austerity measures associated with lower oil and gas revenues in recent years.

POLITICAL RIGHTS: 7 / 40

A. Electoral Process: 1 / 12

All decisions about political leadership rest with the dynastic rulers of the seven emirates, who form the Federal Supreme Council, the country's highest executive and legislative body. These leaders select a president and vice president, and the president appoints a prime minister and cabinet. The emirate of Abu Dhabi, the major oil producer in the UAE, has controlled the federation's presidency since its inception in 1971. In 2006, Sheikh Mohammed bin Rashid al-Maktoum succeeded his late brother as ruler of the emirate of Dubai and prime minister of the UAE.

The 40-seat Federal National Council (FNC) serves as an advisory body, reviewing proposed laws and questioning federal government ministers. Under reforms implemented in 2006, half of its members are elected by an electoral college chosen by the seven rulers, while the government directly appoints the other half. After previous rounds in 2006 and 2011, the third elections to the FNC took place in 2015, and while the size of the electoral college was expanded to more than 224,000 members—some 34 times larger than in 2006—voter turnout remained low, at 35 percent. Overseas voting was permitted for the first time.

B. Political Pluralism and Participation: 2 / 16

Political parties are banned in the UAE. The allocation of positions in the government is determined largely by tribal loyalties and economic power.

Since 2011, the authorities have aggressively cracked down on suspected members of the Association for Reform and Guidance, or Al-Islah—a group formed in 1974 to peacefully advocate for democratic reform—accusing them of being foreign agents of the Muslim Brotherhood intent on overthrowing the government. The government officially declared the Muslim Brotherhood a terrorist organization in 2014. Dozens of activists, civil society leaders, academics, and students remained behind bars as part of the crackdown in 2016. In December 2015, one defendant, Abdulrahman bin Sobeih, who had been convicted in absentia, was forcibly returned from Indonesia to the UAE. He was put on trial in March 2016, found guilty of being a member of Al-Islah, and sentenced in November to a 10-year prison term.

Citizens are believed to constitute only about 11 percent of the population. Noncitizens —including many expatriate minority groups and some stateless residents—have few opportunities for participation and representation in politics.

C. Functioning of Government: 2 / 12

Although unelected officials determine and implement all laws and policies with little independent oversight, the UAE is considered one of the least corrupt countries in the Middle East, and the government has taken steps in recent years to increase efficiency and streamline bureaucracy. In 2015, the leadership launched a 2 billion dirham ($550 million) innovation fund to help reform public services and advance the country's commercial interests; the fund is managed by the Ministry of Finance. These and other initiatives are part of the government's broader "UAE Vision 2021" plan, aimed at making improvements in key governmental, social, economic, and technological areas.

Transparency surrounding such projects—and in government in general—is low, and despite legal provisions, accessing public information remains difficult. Public officials are not required to disclose information about their income or assets.

DISCRETIONARY POLITICAL RIGHTS QUESTION A: 2 / 4

Citizens have some limited opportunities to express their interests through traditional consultative sessions, including during an open *majlis*, or council. The participation of women in consultative processes is limited, however, and the severe difficulty of acquiring citizenship leaves the noncitizen majority without meaningful prospects for political engagement.

CIVIL LIBERTIES: 13 / 60

D. Freedom of Expression and Belief: 4 / 16

Although the constitution provides for some freedom of expression, the government restricts this right in practice. The 1980 Publications and Publishing Law, considered one of the most restrictive press laws in the Arab world, regulates all aspects of the media. It prohibits criticism of the government, its allies, and religion and also bans pornography. Journalists commonly practice self-censorship, and outlets frequently publish government statements without criticism or comment. Media operate with relatively more freedom in four "free media zones"—areas in which foreign outlets produce material for foreign audiences—but the zones remain subject to UAE media laws and have additional regulatory codes and authorities.

A number of other laws, such as a 2014 antiterrorism law and a 2015 measure against hate speech and discrimination, feature broadly worded offenses that can be used to restrict free expression. A 2012 cybercrimes law allows fines and imprisonment for anyone who publishes online content that insults the state, organizes antigovernment protests, or is deemed a threat to national security. Amendments to the law issued in July 2016 increased the penalties for using a VPN to commit a crime, permitting fines of up to 2 million dirhams ($540,000) in addition to possible jail time. Separately, academic and human rights activist Nasser bin Ghaith was put on trial in 2016 after being arrested in August 2015 for online postings that criticized UAE and Egyptian authorities and for alleged collaboration with banned Islamist groups such as Al-Islah. He was held incommunicado until a court appearance in April, and claimed to have been tortured in custody. The trial made little progress during the year, and bin Ghaith remained in solitary confinement at year's end.

The constitution provides for freedom of religion. Islam is the official religion, and the majority of citizens are Sunni Muslims. The minority Shiite Muslim sect and non-Muslims are free to worship without interference. The government controls content in nearly all Sunni mosques.

The Ministry of Education censors textbooks and curriculums in both public and private schools. Several foreign universities have opened satellite campuses in the UAE, although faculties are careful to avoid criticizing the government for fear of losing funding. In 2015, UAE officials barred entry to a professor from New York University (NYU) who was an outspoken critic of the country's treatment of migrant workers and had planned to travel to Abu Dhabi—where NYU maintains a campus—to conduct research on that topic.

Social media platforms are heavily monitored by the government. The openness of private discussion is limited by sensitivities surrounding a range of topics, including government policy and officials, the ruling family, and Islam.

E. Associational and Organizational Rights: 2 / 12

The government places tight constraints on freedoms of assembly and association. Public meetings require government permits. Nongovernmental organizations must register with the Ministry of Social Affairs and can receive subsidies from the government, though they are subject to many burdensome restrictions.

Workers—most of whom are foreign—do not have the right to organize, bargain collectively, or strike. Workers occasionally protest against unpaid wages and poor working and living conditions, but such demonstrations are typically dispersed by security personnel.

F. Rule of Law: 3 / 16

The judiciary is not independent, with court rulings subject to review by the political leadership. The legal system is divided into Sharia (Islamic law) courts, which address family and criminal matters, and secular courts, which cover civil law. Sharia courts sometimes impose flogging sentences for drug use, prostitution, and adultery.

While the federal Interior Ministry oversees police forces, each emirate's force enjoys considerable autonomy. Arbitrary arrests and detention have been reported, particularly of foreign residents. Detainees are often denied adequate access to legal counsel during interrogations, and lengthy detention without charge is not uncommon. Authorities have been criticized by international human rights organizations for failure to investigate allegations of torture and mistreatment in custody. Prisons in the larger emirates are overcrowded.

The 2014 antiterrorism law allows the cabinet to determine whether groups are terrorist organizations and assigns fines of up to $27 million, custodial sentences of up to life in prison, and death sentences for terrorist offenses. The law is broad and ambiguous, describing violations such as "antagonizing the state" and "undermining social peace."

In the first half of 2016, the State Security Chamber at the Abu Dhabi Supreme Court acquitted several Libyan nationals, including U.S. and Canadian dual citizens, who had been held in secret detention since 2014 in some cases, charged with terrorism offenses and supporting militants in Libya. In February 2016, the UN special rapporteur on torture said there was credible evidence that they had been tortured in custody.

Discrimination against noncitizens and foreign workers is common. While the Interior Ministry has established methods for stateless persons, known as *bidoon*, to apply for citizenship, the government uses unclear criteria in approving or rejecting such requests. Same-sex relations are illegal, and LGBT (lesbian, gay, bisexual, and transgender) people are subject to widespread social stigma and discrimination.

G. Personal Autonomy and Individual Rights: 4 / 16

Emiratis face no apparent restrictions on freedom of movement within the UAE or on their type or place of employment, although migrant workers' visas and legal status are tied to an employer's sponsorship, meaning they can be punished or deported for leaving employment without meeting certain criteria.

The UAE has made reforms in recent years to ease procedures for establishing and operating businesses. However, the government and ruling families exercise outsized influence over the economy and are involved in many of the country's major economic and commercial initiatives.

The constitution does not address gender equality. Muslim women are forbidden to marry non-Muslims and receive smaller inheritances than men. No laws protect against spousal rape, and men are permitted to physically discipline their wives. Women are politically underrepresented, though they have in recent years received appointments to various levels of government, including the cabinet. Although only one woman was elected to the FNC in 2015, another eight were appointed by the government, and one of them was named as speaker and president of the body, marking the first time that the position has been held by a woman.

Despite a 2006 antitrafficking law and the opening of new shelters for female victims, the government has failed to adequately address human trafficking. Migrants in particular are at high risk of being trafficked for the purposes of forced labor and sexual exploitation. Foreign workers are often subjected to harsh working conditions, physical abuse, and withholding of passports with little to no access to legal recourse.

A series of ministerial decrees issued in 2015 aimed to give migrant workers more flexibility to terminate employment under certain conditions—including through indemnification or in the case of extended nonpayment of wages—and to combat abusive practices like contract substitution, in which a worker is recruited with one contract abroad but forced to sign a less favorable agreement upon arrival in the UAE. Foreign household workers are not covered by those decrees or by labor laws in general, leaving them especially vulnerable. In December 2016, the cabinet transferred oversight responsibility for such workers from immigration officials to the labor ministry, raising the possibility of improved protections.

United Kingdom

Political Rights: 1
Civil Liberties: 1
Freedom Rating: 1.0
Status: Free
Electoral Democracy: Yes

Population: 65,600,000
Capital: London

Ten-Year Ratings Timeline For Year Under Review (Political Rights, Civil Liberties, Status)

Year Under Review	2007	2008	2009	2010	2011	2012	2013	2014	2015	2016
Rating	1,1,F	1,1,F	1,1,F	1,1,F	1,1,F	1,1,F	1,1,F	1,1,F	1,1,F	1,1,F

Overview: The United Kingdom (UK)—comprised of England, Scotland, Northern Ireland, and Wales—is a stable democracy that regularly holds free elections and is home to a vibrant free press. While the government enforces robust protections for political rights and civil liberties, recent years have seen concerns about increased government surveillance of residents, as well as rising Islamophobia and anti-immigrant sentiment. In a 2016 referendum, UK voters narrowly voted to leave the European Union (EU), in a development that will have political and economic reverberations both domestically and across Europe in the coming years.

KEY DEVELOPMENTS IN 2016

- In a June referendum that sent shockwaves across the continent, voters chose to leave the EU by a margin of 51.9 percent, in what became known as "Brexit," a word coined to capture Britain's exit from the union. A desire to reduce immigration was a critical concern among "Leave" voters.

- Prime Minister David Cameron, who led the "Remain" campaign, resigned following the Brexit vote and was replaced by Theresa May, who was appointed following a Conservative Party leadership contest.
- Street crime and harassment against immigrants and Muslims increased in the wake of the 2015 terrorist attacks in Paris and continued throughout the contentious campaign surrounding the EU referendum, during which elements of the Leave side blamed immigrants for economic woes and stress on social services.
- Jo Cox, a Labour MP who supported the Remain campaign, was murdered by a far-right extremist a week before the referendum. The attacker was convicted and sentenced to life in prison in November.

EXECUTIVE SUMMARY

The referendum in June 2016 to decide whether the UK should leave or remain in the EU resulted in a 51.9 percent vote to leave, upending UK politics. The Leave campaign centered in large part on the issue of immigration, with proponents arguing that the sizable number of EU nationals living and working in the UK had done harm to the economy and overburdened its network of social services. The Remain campaign had emphasized economic benefits of immigration and EU membership, and the UK's commitment to the liberal democratic values the EU embodied. However, the Remain campaign was widely described as listless and hampered by divisions between Cameron and Labour Party leader Jeremy Corbyn.

Cameron, whose Conservative Party had won general elections held in 2015, announced his intention to resign the day after the vote, triggering a Conservative Party leadership election that resulted in the appointment of Prime Minister Theresa May in July. Prime Minister May quickly vowed to curb immigration.

The Brexit campaign and the vote's results, as well as the political aftermath of the 2015 terrorist attacks in Paris, brought about widespread concerns of rising anti-immigrant and anti-Muslim sentiment in the country, with the Council of Europe expressing concerns about hate speech among politicians and in popular tabloid newspapers. Police in December also recorded an 18.2 percent increase in racist and religious hate crimes over the previous year. Additionally, days before the Brexit vote, Labour MP Jo Cox—who had campaigned for the Remain side—was killed by a far-right-wing extremist. The assailant was convicted of murder in November, with the presiding judge imposing a life sentence for what he described as a crime committed to advance Nazi ideology.

Mass surveillance by the security services, including the Government Communications Headquarters (GCHQ), remained a concern during the year. In December, the European Court of Justice (ECJ) ruled, in a case concerning the 2014 Data Retention and Investigatory Powers Act (DRIPA), that "general and indiscriminate" retention of e-mails and electronic communications by the government was illegal unless it was targeted in order to fight cases of serious crimes, including terrorism. However, DRIPA was replaced in November 2016 by the new Investigatory Powers Act, which permitted even greater surveillance. At year's end, UK courts were set to decide how to implement December's ECJ ruling under domestic laws. The ruling could prompt legal cases against the new legislation—though if the UK leaves the EU, it will no longer be bound by ECJ decisions.

POLITICAL RIGHTS: 40 / 40

A. Electoral Process: 12 / 12

Each of the members of the House of Commons, the dominant, lower chamber of the bicameral parliament, is elected in a single-member district. Executive power rests with the prime minister and cabinet, who must have the support of the Commons. The House of Lords, Parliament's upper chamber, can delay legislation initiated in the Commons. The Commons must reconsider any measure defeated by the Lords, but it can ultimately overrule the upper chamber. The Lords' approximately 800 members consist mostly of "life peers" nominated by successive governments. There are also 90 hereditary peers (nobles) and 26 bishops and archbishops of the Church of England. The monarch, Queen Elizabeth II, plays a largely ceremonial role as head of state. Elections in Britain are consistently free and fair.

The Conservative Party, which had been ruling in coalition with a smaller party, the Liberal Democrats, won an unexpected victory in the 2015 general elections, taking 36.9 percent of the popular vote and increasing its share of Commons seats by 24 for a total of 330, an outright majority. The second-ranked Labour Party took 30.4 percent of the vote and 232 seats, a loss of 26. The Scottish National Party (SNP) won 4.7 percent of the vote and 56 seats, an increase of 50. The Liberal Democrats won 7.9 percent of the vote and lost 49 seats, leaving them with just eight. The Euroskeptic, populist United Kingdom Independence Party (UKIP), campaigning on an anti-immigration platform, secured only one seat, despite having won the country's 2014 European Parliament elections and taken two Commons seats in 2014 by-elections. Turnout for the 2015 voting was 66.1 percent. Local elections in England took place on the same day, with the Conservatives winning control of 163 of 279 councils; Labour placed second with control of 74 councils.

In February 2016, Prime Minister Cameron scheduled a June referendum on membership in the EU, fulfilling a years-old pledge to hold a vote on the issue. He led the Remain campaign. The referendum resulted in a 51.9 percent vote to leave the EU, against 48.1 percent who voted to remain. The results revealed deep divisions within the UK: England and Wales voted to leave by 53.4 percent and 52.5 percent, respectively; while voters in Scotland chose to remain by 62 percent, as did voters Northern Ireland, by 55.8 percent. Cameron resigned the day after the vote, triggering a Conservative Party leadership election that resulted in the appointment of May as Prime Minister in July. She proclaimed that "Brexit means Brexit" and assembled a team to prepare for the negotiations to leave the EU. Meanwhile, the main opposition Labour Party embarked on a protracted leadership battle that resulted in the incumbent Jeremy Corbyn being reelected in September. Nigel Farage, head of the UKIP—which claimed much of the credit for the Brexit vote's results— resigned in July, saying he had fulfilled his political ambitions. Paul Nuttall was elected the UKIP's new leader in November.

In the wake of the referendum result both Scotland and Northern Ireland began exploring political solutions to maintain their membership in the EU. SNP leader Nicola Sturgeon suggested that Scotland might seek a new referendum on independence if the UK pursued "hard Brexit" policies that could reintroduce strict border controls and lead the UK to leave the EU's common market. In Northern Ireland, the referendum's result gave rise to politically sensitive questions about how to resolve the Brexit vote with provisions of the 1998 Good Friday peace agreement.

In May 2016, regional elections to the Northern Ireland and Welsh Assemblies, as well the Scottish Parliament, took place. The Democratic Unionist Party (DUP) remained the largest party after elections to the Northern Ireland Assembly. Sinn Féin and the Social Democratic and Labour Party (SDLP) lost votes, coming in second and fourth, respectively. The Ulster Unionist Party (UUP) was the third biggest party. In the Welsh Assembly, Labour remained the largest party, while UKIP won seats in the Assembly for the first time. In Scotland, the governing SNP remained the largest party, with the Conservatives surpassing Labour to become the second-largest party.

In December 2016, the government announced that it would soon begin requiring voters to produce identification in order to vote, drawing criticism that such a requirement would discourage participation among poorer voters. Officials also said they would prevent political activists from distributing absentee ballots.

B. Political Pluralism and Participation: 16 / 16

The Conservative Party and Labour Party have dominated British politics for decades, though several other parties regularly win seats in Parliament. The SNP supplanted the Liberal Democrats as the third-largest party in the 2015 elections. Smaller parties, such as UKIP and the Greens, fare better in races for the European Parliament, which feature proportional-representation voting.

Under Britain's system of "devolution," the UK Parliament has granted certain powers to subnational legislatures, augmenting the political representation of regional populations as well as parties like the SNP. In Wales, Plaid Cymru champions Welsh nationalism. A 2011 referendum increased the Welsh Assembly's autonomy, giving it authority to make laws in 20 subject areas without consulting Parliament.

The 2016 Scotland Act, approved in March, transferred further powers to the Scottish parliament in areas such as taxation, welfare, and abortion law, in line with a pledge made by the main British parties ahead of the 2014 referendum on Scottish independence, which had been defeated.

In Northern Ireland, the main Catholic and republican parties are Sinn Féin and the SDLP, while the leading Protestant and unionist parties are the UUP and the DUP. The armed struggle between unionists and Irish nationalists over governance in Northern Ireland largely ended with the 1998 Good Friday peace agreement, which established the Northern Ireland Assembly.

C. Functioning of Government: 12 / 12

Britain's freely elected officials make and implement national policy, and corruption is not pervasive, though high-profile scandals have damaged political reputations under both Labour and Conservative governments. The Bribery Act, which is considered one of the most sweeping pieces of antibribery legislation in the world, came into force in 2011. In 2015, then first minister of Northern Ireland Peter Robinson was accused of accepting millions of dollars in kickbacks to sell assets managed by the Republic of Ireland's National Asset Management Agency (NAMA) to the U.S. investment firm Cerberus. An investigation of the sale was ongoing at year's end.

Parties in the United Kingdom are financed through membership fees, donations, and state funding (if they are in opposition), and there have been scandals over donations to political parties. A lobbying register established in 2015 was criticized for its narrow scope and lack of enforcement mechanisms.

A 2013 World Bank study concluded that Britain's freedom of information laws are "reasonably successful." Civil liberties groups and the press have criticized government-proposed reforms to limit freedom of information requests.

CIVIL LIBERTIES: 55 / 60

D. Freedom of Expression and Belief: 14 / 16 (+ 1)

Press freedom is legally protected, and the media are lively and competitive. Daily newspapers span the political spectrum, though economic pressures and rising internet use have driven some smaller papers out of business. On rare occasions, the courts have imposed so-called superinjunctions that forbid the media from reporting on certain information or even the existence of the injunction itself.

The state-owned British Broadcasting Corporation (BBC) is editorially independent and competitive with its counterparts in the commercial market. A series of scandals have plagued the broadcaster in recent years, including the convictions of several employees and former employees for sexual and verbal abuse in 2013, and a controversy involving senior managers who were given inordinately high severance payouts and executive pay.

In the wake of a 2011 scandal in which reporters at the *News of the World* were accused of hacking the voicemails of hundreds of public figures and crime victims, a 2013 royal charter created a special panel that would certify an independent regulatory body for the press. Press freedom advocates have questioned the independence of the Press Recognition Panel established by the charter, suggesting that it is too closely linked to the government. In October 2016, a regulator known as Impress received recognition under the royal charter and was later endorsed by the National Union of Journalists (NUJ). With the establishment of a royal charter–approved regulator, officials may invoke Section 40 of the Crime and Courts Act, through which tough financial penalties can be imposed on publications that fail to register with it.

The 2013 Defamation Act overhauled the country's plaintiff-friendly libel laws, introducing a "public interest" defense, setting more stringent requirements for claimants, and making it more difficult for foreigners to file complaints in cases with little connection to Britain. The number of problematic defamation cases has decreased in recent years.

The government does not restrict internet access. New online criminal offenses were introduced in 2015 under the Criminal Justice and Courts Act, including the dissemination of images of a naked person without the subject's consent, also known as "revenge porn."

Although the Church of England and the Church of Scotland have official status, freedom of religion is protected in law and practice. A 2006 law bans incitement to religious hatred, with a maximum penalty of seven years in prison. Nevertheless, minority groups, particularly Muslims, report discrimination, harassment, and occasional assaults. The Muslim community has come under threat and Muslims have faced occasional violence from far-right groups like the English Defence League. In the weeks following the 2015 terrorist attacks in Paris, the Metropolitan Police reported that Islamophobic hate crimes in London tripled; in 2016, the police recorded an 18.2 percent increase in racist and religious hate crimes over the previous year.

Academic freedom is generally respected. However, the Counter-Terrorism and Security Act of 2015 requires schools and universities to prevent students from being drawn into terrorism and to vet the remarks of visiting speakers as part of that effort. The new legal obligation raised concerns that open debate and academic inquiry could be stifled. A Private Member's Bill was presented to parliament in June 2016 to repeal provisions in the Counter-Terrorism and Security Act that require teachers and those caring for children to report evidence of extremism among children in preschool or primary school settings. Its second reading will take place in early 2017.

The effects of mass surveillance on free and open private discussion are also a growing concern. In 2015, a government-commissioned report on surveillance by British security agencies held that although the power to collect bulk communications data on British citizens may be justified, privacy concerns must be considered early in the collection process. It also stated that judges, rather than ministers, should authorize warrants for the collection of data related to criminal matters, and that there should be judicial review of warrants related to national security that are authorized by ministers.

DRIPA, the 2014 law governing intelligence agencies' authority to monitor communications data, was replaced in November 2016 by the Investigatory Powers Act, known by critics as the "snooper's charter." DRIPA had been ruled unlawful by the High Court in 2015, in part because it allowed the agencies to conduct surveillance without judicial oversight. It was also struck down in December 2016 by the ECJ, which held that the government could use "bulk data" or "mass surveillance" collection only to deal with serious crime and that there should be restrictions on access to data to protect against violations of citizens' privacy.

The new Investigatory Powers Act requires communications companies to store metadata on customers' activity for 12 months and, in some cases allows this information to be accessed by police and other security officials without a warrant. However, judicial commissioners must review ministerial authorization of warrants for the actual interception of communications, including their content. The new law could be subject to legal challenges as a result of the ECJ ruling, although if the United Kingdom withdraws from the EU, it will not be bound by rulings of the ECJ.

E. Associational and Organizational Rights: 12 / 12

Freedoms of assembly and association are respected, though police have been criticized for certain crowd-control tactics in recent years. A number of demonstrations and assemblies were organized during 2016, including rallies across the country against a British exit from the EU, following the June referendum result.

Civic and nongovernmental organizations (NGOs) operate freely. Groups identified as terrorist organizations can be banned, and there are concerns that the legal definition is broad enough that it could be interpreted to encompass legitimate associations and activism. Surveillance of NGOs has also drawn criticism. In 2015, the Investigatory Powers Tribunal (IPT) disclosed that Amnesty International was among the groups whose data GCHQ had accessed and illegally retained. The U.S.-based NGO Human Rights Watch (HRW) filed a complaint in 2015 with the tribunal alleging that its communications had also been the target of such surveillance, which had entailed cooperation with the U.S. National Security Agency. In May 2016 the IPT ruled in the HRW case that data collected on persons "situated outside" the United Kingdom cannot give rise to a claim of infringement of the right to privacy under UK law and the European Convention on Human Rights. In November, HRW filed a challenge with the European Court on Human Rights to force the IPT to state whether or not the group had been subject to GCHQ surveillance, and if so, whether such surveillance was illegal.

A lobbying law adopted in 2014 was heavily criticized for limiting the amount of money organizations can spend during election years; opponents assert that the law's ambiguous language could lead to self-censorship and hinder the work of smaller groups.

Workers have the right to organize trade unions, which have traditionally played a central role in the Labour Party. The rights to bargain collectively and strike are also respected.

F. Rule of Law: 14 / 16 (− 1)

A new Supreme Court began functioning in 2009, transferring final judicial authority from the House of Lords. In 2015, the Criminal Justice and Courts Act, a sweeping legal reform law, came into effect. Among other things, it increased maximum prison sentences for terrorists and pedophiles, made certain kinds of extreme pornography illegal, and introduced measures to reduce recidivism.

The police maintain high professional standards. While prisons generally adhere to international guidelines, an increase in violence and suicides in jails was reported after recent austerity cuts resulted in reduced prison staffing, and the Prison Governors Association in October 2016 called for a public inquiry into the problem. Inmates are banned from voting. Although the European Court of Human Rights has ruled on several occasions that this is a violation of prisoners' rights, an EU court ruled in 2015 that voting bans can be legal for prisoners convicted of serious crimes.

Britain's strict antiterrorism laws allow authorities to control the movement of terrorism suspects when the evidence against them is insufficient for prosecution or deportation. The 2015 Counter-Terrorism and Security Act has been criticized for giving excessive powers to police, including the authority to seize travel documents of individuals attempting to leave the country if they are suspected of planning to engage in terrorist-related activities abroad, and to forcibly relocate terrorism suspects within the country up to 200 miles away from their homes.

Anti-immigrant rhetoric surrounding the EU referendum campaign appeared to fuel a spike in harassment of and physical attacks against foreigners in the UK, many of which targeted immigrants from Poland. In an attack that shook the country's politics days before the referendum, Labour MP Jo Cox, an advocate for the Remain campaign, was murdered by a far-right extremist who had shouted "Britain first" as he shot and stabbed her. The assailant was convicted of murder in November, with the presiding judge imposing a life sentence for what he described as a crime committed to advance Nazi ideology. There have also been concerns about rising Islamophobia in the wake of the 2015 Paris terrorist attacks.

Immigrants and their descendants receive equal treatment under the law, but generally face living standards below the national average. The Immigration Act 2016, which took effect in July, requires landlords to check the immigration status of their tenants, obliges banks to perform background checks before opening an account, and makes it a criminal offense for migrants to obtain jobs without appropriate paperwork. It also allows police to seize vehicles belonging to illegal migrants and allows authorities to electronically track those released on bail while awaiting deportation.

In 2015, the High Court found that the government's fast-track procedure for asylum seekers—under which failed applicants were detained while their appeals were processed in an expedited manner—unlawfully prioritized speed over fairness. The Court of Appeal confirmed the ruling later that year and the system was suspended, although it is not yet clear what kind of system has replaced it. Meanwhile, in January 2016, former prisons and probation ombudsman Stephen Shaw submitted to parliament a series of recommendations to improve the welfare of vulnerable asylum-seekers in detention. The "Shaw Report," commissioned by the government in 2015, said too many asylum-seekers were being detained, and among other things recommended a ban on the detention of pregnant asylum-seekers and limits on the amount of time other asylum-seekers may be detained.

The authorities actively enforce a 2010 law barring discrimination on the basis of factors including sexual orientation and gender reassignment.

G. Personal Autonomy and Individual Rights: 15 / 16

Citizens generally enjoy freedom of travel and choice of residence, employment, and institution of higher education. Economic activity is not excessively influenced by the government.

A government-commissioned report by Dame Louise Casey on social integration in the United Kingdom released in December 2016 expressed concern about the social and economic isolation of many members of ethnic and religious minorities and of the poor. The report also criticized "regressive religious and cultural practices" in segments of some communities.

While women receive equal treatment under the law, they remain underrepresented in top positions in politics and business. The number of women in the House of Commons rose to 192, or 30 percent, as a result of the 2015 elections, from about 23 percent before the elections. Gender discrimination persists in the workplace in practice. Abortion is legal in Great Britain, though heavily restricted in Northern Ireland, where it is allowed only to protect the life or the long-term health of the mother.

Same-sex marriage became legal in 2013. Religious organizations are permitted to refuse to conduct same-sex marriages.

The Modern Slavery Act, which increases punishments for human traffickers and offers greater protections for victims, became law in 2015. Children and migrant workers are among those most vulnerable to forced labor and sex trafficking.

United States of America

Political Rights Rating: 1
Civil Liberties Rating: 1
Freedom Rating: 1.0
Freedom Status: Free
Electoral Democracy: Yes

Population: 323,900,000
Capital: Washington, D.C.

Ten-Year Ratings Timeline For Year Under Review (Political Rights, Civil Liberties, Status)

Year Under Review	2007	2008	2009	2010	2011	2012	2013	2014	2015	2016
Rating	1,1,F	1,1,F	1,1,F	1,1,F	1,1,F	1,1,F	1,1,F	1,1,F	1,1,F	1,1,F

Overview: The United States is arguably the world's oldest democracy. Its people benefit from a vibrant electoral system, a strong rule-of-law tradition, robust freedoms of expression and religious belief, and a wide array of other civil liberties. The United States remains a major destination point for immigrants and has largely been successful in integrating newcomers from all backgrounds. However, in recent years the country's democratic institutions have suffered some erosion, as reflected in legislative gridlock, dysfunction in the criminal justice system, and growing disparities in wealth and economic opportunity.

KEY DEVELOPMENTS IN 2016:

- Wealthy businessman Donald Trump, the Republican Party nominee, defeated Hillary Clinton of the Democratic Party in the November presidential election. Although Clinton received the most votes at the national level, Trump won the presidency by securing a decisive majority in the state-based Electoral College.
- Beginning in October, U.S. intelligence agencies officially accused Russia of interfering in the election process, in part by hacking into the computer systems of the Democratic Party and leaking its internal communications.
- Supreme Court justice Antonin Scalia died in February, but Republican leaders in the Senate refused to hold confirmation hearings for outgoing president Barack Obama's nominee to replace him, arguing that the next president should make the appointment. The vacancy remained open at year's end.

EXECUTIVE SUMMARY

Celebrity real-estate developer Donald Trump, an outsider candidate with no previous political experience, won the November presidential election after a year-and-a-half campaign. He secured the Republican Party's nomination in July after defeating a large field of opponents, including several seasoned politicians, in the primary elections. He then scored a major upset in the general election against Democratic Party nominee Hillary Clinton, a former first lady, senator, and secretary of state. Republicans also maintained their majorities in the Senate and the House of Representatives, meaning one party would control both the presidency and Congress for the first time since 2010.

The hard-fought electoral campaign reflected a country that is deeply polarized, not only along party lines, but also along lines of race, gender, geography, and education. Trump ultimately prevailed by winning over white working-class voters in key states, defeating a Clinton coalition that relied more on college-educated white voters and racial and ethnic minorities.

The campaign was also notable for Trump's use of a personal social media account, live rallies, and other means of communicating directly with voters instead of costly television advertising, the typical centerpiece of campaign messaging in recent elections. The news media challenged the veracity of many of Trump's campaign statements, most notably his assertion that the election system was rigged in Clinton's favor.

The election was marred by alleged Russian interference, with U.S. intelligence officials citing strong evidence that hackers tied to the Kremlin had stolen documents from the Democratic Party and leaked them over the course of the campaign period. Clinton's bid was separately hampered by a federal investigation into her improper use of a private e-mail server during her tenure as secretary of state, though investigators eventually decided against filing charges.

Throughout 2016, President Barack Obama's legislative agenda continued to be stymied by Republican opposition in Congress. As a result, Obama used executive authority to advance his priorities in areas including the environment, foreign policy, and health and labor standards. Senate Republicans refused to hold confirmation hearings for Obama's nominee to replace Supreme Court justice Antonin Scalia, who died in February, leaving the court with eight members.

POLITICAL RIGHTS: 36 / 40

A. Electoral Process: 11 / 12

The United States is a presidential republic, with the president serving as both head of state and head of government. Cabinet secretaries and other key officials are nominated by the president and confirmed by the Senate, the upper house of the bicameral Congress. Presidential elections are decided by an Electoral College, making it possible for a candidate to win the presidency while losing the national popular vote. Electoral College votes are apportioned to each state based on the size of its congressional representation. In most cases, all of the electors in a particular state cast their ballots for the candidate who won the statewide popular vote, regardless of the margin. Two states, Maine and Nebraska, have chosen to divide their electoral votes between the candidates based on their popular-vote performance in each congressional district. In 2016, Trump won the Electoral College vote, 304 to 227, while finishing nearly three million votes behind Clinton in the popular ballot. The 2016 election marked the second time since 2000 that the candidate with the most popular votes lost in the Electoral College.

The Senate consists of 100 members—two from each of the 50 states regardless of population—serving six-year terms, with one-third coming up for election every two years. The lower chamber, the House of Representatives, consists of 435 members serving two-year terms. All national legislators are elected directly by voters in the districts or states that they represent. In a practice known as gerrymandering, the boundaries of House districts, and those for state legislatures, are often drawn to maximize the advantage of the party in power in a given state. The capital district, Puerto Rico, and four overseas U.S. territories are each represented by an elected delegate in the House who can perform most legislative functions but cannot participate in floor votes.

In the 2016 congressional elections, Republicans retained control of the Senate with 52 seats. Democrats hold 46 seats, and there are two independent senators who generally vote with the Democrats. Republicans also retained their majority in the House, taking 241 seats, versus 194 for the Democrats. Republicans currently control the majority of state governorships and legislatures. Turnout for the 2016 general elections was approximately 55 percent of voting-age citizens, roughly in line with past elections.

In some states, citizens have a wide-ranging ability to influence legislation through referendums. Such direct-democracy mechanisms, often initiated by signature campaigns, have been hailed by some as a reflection of the openness of the U.S. system. However, they have also been criticized on the grounds that they can lead to incoherent governance, undermine representative democracy, and weaken the party system. In 2016, referendums in various states resulted in the legalization of recreational use of marijuana, curbs on plastic shopping bags, and increases in the state minimum wage, among many other topics.

B. Political Pluralism and Participation: 14 / 16 (− 1)

The intensely competitive U.S. political environment is dominated by two major parties, the right-leaning Republicans and the left-leaning Democrats. The country's "first past the post" or majoritarian electoral system discourages the emergence of additional parties, as do a number of specific legal and other hurdles. However, the two parties' primary elections allow for an array of views and candidates to enter the political system. Trump, himself an unorthodox Republican, defeated not only mainstream politicians but also opponents whose positions ranged from libertarian to Christian conservative. Clinton won her party's nomination after a powerful challenge by Senator Bernie Sanders, a democratic socialist who subsequently secured changes to the party platform.

On occasion, independent or third-party candidates have significantly influenced politics at the presidential and state levels, and a number of newer parties, such as the Green Party or groups aligned with organized labor, have modestly affected politics in certain municipalities in recent years. In the 2016 presidential election, Libertarian Party candidate Gary Johnson received 3.3 percent of the popular vote, while Jill Stein of the Green Party received 1 percent.

Election campaigns in the United States are long and expensive. The two main parties and the constituency and interest groups that support them have used an array of methods to circumvent legal restrictions on campaign spending, and the Supreme Court on several occasions has struck down such restrictions, finding that they violated free-speech rights. In the 2016 campaign, Clinton and her supporters spent more than $1 billion, about twice the amount spent by Trump and his allies, according to some estimates. In previous campaigns, candidates relied heavily on television advertising, especially in states where competition was expected to be close. Trump relied less on such expensive purchases, instead conveying his message by attracting television news coverage and issuing regular, provocative statements through social media, especially his personal Twitter account.

The theft and disclosure of Democratic Party communications, which U.S. intelligence agencies attributed to hackers linked to the Russian government, attracted ample media attention and was believed to have damaged the campaigns of Clinton and other Democratic candidates, though there was no firm evidence that it actually shifted voter allegiances. Trump, who advocated a more cooperative policy toward Russia, repeatedly expressed doubt that Moscow was to blame for the hacking.

A number of important laws are designed to ensure the political rights of racial and ethnic minorities. However, in 2013 the Supreme Court invalidated portions of the Voting Rights Act of 1965, a measure adopted to deal with entrenched racial bias in the political process. Subsequently, many states enacted laws that required voters to present certain forms of identification, rolled back innovations like early voting that contributed to high rates of minority participation, or altered polling locations in ways that could disproportionately harm minority voters. Some of these state laws were struck down by federal courts, but 14 states had new restrictive voting laws in place for the 2016 elections—the first presidential vote since the 2013 ruling. There were 868 fewer polling stations in states formerly subject to special scrutiny under the Voting Rights Act, with one county in Arizona providing a single polling place for every 21,000 voters. Sponsors of such legislation say the intent is to cut expenses or combat voter fraud, though studies by experts and the bipartisan testimony of election officials indicate that election fraud is a negligible problem in the United States.

Religious groups and racial or ethnic minorities have been able to gain a political voice through participation in the two main parties. Leaders of both parties have traditionally made an effort to appeal to all segments of the population and address issues of concern to each, or at a minimum to avoid alienating any major demographic group. The 2016 elections stood out for the unusually divisive rhetoric of the Republican presidential nominee. Trump made statements that were widely seen as offensive to Latinos, Muslims, people with disabilities, and women, among others. His ability to do so without suffering significant political repercussions raised fears that these groups' interests would not be represented in the new administration.

C. Functioning of Government: 11 / 12 (+ 1)

Federal policymaking and government have been hampered in recent years by partisan gridlock in Congress, and between Congress and the executive branch. Impasses over taxation, federal debt, and spending bills have repeatedly threatened to halt government operations or trigger a default on public debt. During six of his eight years as president, Obama faced a dominant Republican opposition in Congress that rejected the overwhelming majority of his legislative proposals. In response, he sought to push through his agenda through various executive and regulatory actions, bypassing Congress. Obama issued significant changes in environmental standards, health and safety regulations, and the treatment of undocumented immigrants. Some of these actions were invalidated by federal courts.

American society has a tradition of intolerance toward government corruption, and the media are aggressive in reporting on such malfeasance. Cases of corruption at the federal level have been relatively rare or small in scale in recent years. The most serious abuses have instead been uncovered among state and local officials.

The United States was the first country to adopt a Freedom of Information Act (FOIA). A substantial number of auditing and investigative agencies function independently of political influence. Such bodies are often spurred to action by the investigative work of journalists. Federal agencies regularly place information relevant to their mandates on websites to broaden public access.

Early in his administration, Obama instructed federal agencies to adopt a cooperative attitude toward public information requests. During much of his tenure, however, he encountered criticism for engendering an environment of excessive secrecy. The Justice Department initiated nine prosecutions of leakers or whistle-blowers, more than in all previous administrations combined. Prosecutors have at times sought to compel journalists to reveal the sources of leaked national security information, and the administration was accused of implementing an aggressive policy to discourage government officials from having contact with the media.

In a change over the last two years, the administration has refrained from efforts to compel testimony from journalists in leak cases and issued guidelines to limit such actions. While federal agencies' responses to FOIA requests remained problematic, according to data for the 2015 fiscal year, Obama signed the FOIA Improvement Act in June 2016, codifying a presumption of disclosure and reducing procedural barriers for requesters, among other reforms.

CIVIL LIBERTIES: 53 / 60 (− 1)

D. Freedom of Expression and Belief: 16 / 16 (+ 1)

The United States has a free, diverse, and constitutionally protected press. While newspapers have been in economic decline for a number of years, the media environment retains a high degree of pluralism. Internet access is widespread and unrestricted, and news websites now constitute a major source of political news, along with cable television networks and talk-radio programs. News coverage has also grown more polarized, with particular outlets and their star commentators providing a consistently right-or left-leaning perspective. Several journalists were arrested while covering demonstrations during 2016, including four who faced serious charges after filming incidents linked to protests against an oil pipeline in North Dakota; those charges were later dropped. In October, the Committee to Protect Journalists declared Trump a threat to media freedom, citing his verbal attacks on individual reporters, his campaign's denial of credentials to critical outlets, and his call to expand the scope of U.S. libel laws. Other freedom of expression groups issued similar statements of concern about the incoming administration. After the election, Trump stepped back from his proposal on libel laws.

The United States has a long tradition of religious freedom. The constitution protects the free exercise of religion while barring any official endorsement of a religious faith, and there are no direct government subsidies to houses of worship. The debate over the role of religion in public life is ongoing, however, and religious groups often mobilize to influence political discussions on the diverse issues in which they take an interest. The Supreme Court regularly adjudicates difficult cases involving the relationship between church and state.

The academic sphere features a substantial level of intellectual freedom. In one potential threat to freedom of expression on campus, university officials have been criticized for giving in to pressure from student activist groups that object to speakers who have been invited to campus events. Speakers have regularly been disinvited or decided to withdraw from appearances after protests were launched. Students have also mounted protests over issues related to gender, race, ethnicity, and other identity categories, sometimes demanding changes to teaching and hiring practices.

Americans generally enjoy open and free private discussion, including on the internet. Civil libertarians, many lawmakers, and other observers have pointed to the real and potential effects of National Security Agency (NSA) data collection and other forms of government monitoring on the rights of U.S. citizens. However, the USA Freedom Act of 2015 banned the bulk collection of citizens' telephone and internet records, and in 2016 the FBI abandoned a controversial attempt to force the technology firm Apple to break through its own security features—designed to protect user communications—as part of a terrorism investigation. A broader debate about possible restrictions on encryption technology remains unresolved. Concerns about state surveillance were displaced during 2016 by new attention on foreign hacking as well as user intimidation on social media.

E. Associational and Organizational Rights: 10 / 12 (− 1)

In general, officials respect the right to public assembly. Demonstrations against government policies are frequently held in Washington, New York, and other major cities. In response to acts of violence committed in the course of some past demonstrations, local authorities often place restrictions on the location or duration of large protests directed at meetings of international institutions, political party conventions, or targets in the financial sector. During 2016, a number of protesters attending Trump campaign rallies were intimidated or physically attacked by Trump supporters, at times with the encouragement of the candidate. The year's major demonstrations—focused on improper police use of force against black civilians, a controversial oil pipeline near indigenous land in North Dakota, and Trump's election victory—were largely peaceful but featured episodic clashes with police or security guards, leading to scores of injuries and arrests.

The United States gives wide freedom to trade associations, nongovernmental organizations, minority rights advocates, and issue-oriented pressure groups to organize and pursue their civic or policy agendas.

Federal law guarantees trade unions the right to organize and engage in collective bargaining. The right to strike is also guaranteed. Over the years, however, the strength of organized labor has declined, and just 6.4 percent of the private-sector workforce is currently represented by unions. While public-sector unions have higher rates of membership, with 34.4 percent in 2016, they have come under pressure from officials concerned about the cost of compensation and pensions to states and municipalities. The overall unionization rate in the United States is 10.7 percent. The country's labor code and decisions by the National Labor Relations Board (NLRB) during Republican presidencies have been regarded as impediments to organizing efforts, although the board was sympathetic to unionization during the Obama presidency. Union organizing is also hampered by strong resistance from private employers. In 2016, West Virginia became the 26th state to adopt "right to work" legislation, which weakens unions by allowing workers who benefit from union bargaining efforts to opt out of paying union dues or fees.

F. Rule of Law: 12 / 16 (− 1)

Judicial independence is respected. Although the courts have occasionally been accused of intervening in areas that are best left to the political branches, most observers regard the judiciary as one of the country's strongest democratic institutions. Concern has been raised about a trend toward the politicization of judicial elections in some states. Much attention has also been paid to the ideological composition of the Supreme Court, which has issued a series of major decisions by a one-vote margin and is currently seen as having a conservative majority. In 2016, the Republican majority in the Senate refused to hold hearings or schedule a confirmation vote on Merrick Garland, a federal judge named by President Obama to fill the Supreme Court vacancy created by the death of Justice Antonin Scalia in February. The Republicans asserted that Obama's successor should fill the vacancy, with some arguing that Scalia, a staunch conservative, should be replaced with another conservative. The delay left the court with eight justices, meaning it was unable to reach majority decisions on a number of issues during the year.

While the United States has a strong rule-of-law tradition, the criminal justice system's treatment of minority groups has long been a problem. Black and Latino inmates account for a disproportionately large percentage of the prison population. Civil liberties organizations and other groups have also argued more broadly that there are too many Americans in prison, that prison sentences are often excessive, that too many prisoners are relegated to solitary confinement or other maximum-security arrangements, and that too many people are incarcerated for minor drug offenses. A broad left-right political coalition calling for reform on the last issue has emerged despite increased partisan rancor on other matters. Although the U.S. incarceration rate has declined somewhat in recent years, it remains easily one of the highest in the world. Additional calls for prison reform have focused on the incidence of violence and rape behind bars.

Many critics of the incarceration problem point to abuses and deficiencies at other stages of the legal process. Media reports and analyses in recent years have drawn new attention to the extensive use of plea bargaining in criminal cases, with prosecutors employing the threat of harsh sentences to avoid trial and effectively reducing the role of the judiciary; the practice of imposing court fees or fines for minor offenses as a means of raising budget revenues, which can lead to jail terms for those who fail to pay; deficiencies in the parole system; and long-standing funding shortages for public defenders, who represent low-income criminal defendants.

The increased focus on the criminal justice system has coincided with a series of widely publicized incidents in which police actions led to the deaths of black civilians. A number of the confrontations were captured on video, and some recordings appeared to show unjustified use of force by the officers in question. Even as more cases emerged in 2016, individual black gunmen shot and killed police officers in Dallas and Baton Rouge in July, in what were seen as revenge attacks. The Justice Department has launched investigations into police practices and imposed reforms in a number of municipalities. Because officers often avoid indictments for controversial shootings, critics have called for sweeping changes to the grand jury system and the appointment of special prosecutors for such cases. Some jurisdictions have enacted policies requiring police to wear body cameras and record interactions with civilians.

Use of the death penalty has declined significantly in recent years. There were 20 executions, in five states, in 2016—the lowest number in a quarter century. The death penalty has been formally abolished by 19 states; in another 16 states where it remains on the books, executions have not been carried out for the past five years or more. The most recent federal execution was in 2003. Of particular importance in this trend has been the exoneration of some death-row inmates based on new DNA testing, as well as legal challenges to the constitutionality of the prevailing methods of lethal injection. The Supreme Court has effectively ruled out the death penalty for crimes other than murder and in cases where the perpetrator is a juvenile or mentally disabled, among other restrictions. In 2012, the court further decided that juvenile offenders could not be subjected to mandatory sentences of life imprisonment without the possibility of parole.

Among Obama's principal goals on assuming office in 2009 was the closure of the offshore U.S. detention facility at Guantanamo Bay, Cuba, which has been used to hold terrorism suspects captured abroad in the early 2000s, in many cases without formal charge or trial. While Obama succeeded in repatriating or resettling 179 people, reducing the population of detainees to 59 by the end of 2016, he was unable to shut down the facility, largely because Congress expressly forbade the transfer of detainees to the U.S. mainland.

Islamist terrorist attacks and other mass shootings remained a concern during 2016, as did rising murder rates in certain cities, especially Chicago. However, the overall homicide rate, 4.9 per 100,000 inhabitants as of 2015, remains relatively low by regional and historical standards. The country's most deadly attack in 2016 occurred in June, when a gunman who declared allegiance to the Syria-based Islamic State militant group killed 49 people at a nightclub in Orlando, Florida.

The United States is one of the world's most racially and ethnically diverse societies. In recent years, residents and citizens of Latin American ancestry have replaced black Americans as the largest minority group, and the majority held by the non-Latino white population has declined. An array of policies and programs are designed to protect the rights of minorities, including laws to prevent workplace discrimination. However, the black population and some other groups continue to suffer from disparities in overall economic standing, educational attainment, and other social indicators. In 2016, the Supreme Court again confirmed the constitutionality of considering race or ethnicity as one of many factors in university admissions to ensure student diversity, but several states have banned the practice outright through referendums.

Federal antidiscrimination legislation does not include LGBT (lesbian, gay, bisexual, and transgender) people as a protected class, though many states have enacted such protections. The government bans discrimination based on sexual orientation or gender identity in federal employment and among federal contractors. The rights of transgender people became a subject of court battles and national debate in 2016 after North Carolina passed a law requiring individuals in public buildings to use restrooms that correspond with the gender on their birth certificate. The Obama administration issued legal guidelines in May that instructed school districts to allow transgender students to use bathrooms that correspond with their gender identity, but enforcement was blocked as federal courts considered challenges to the rule.

The United States has generally maintained liberal immigration policies in recent decades. Most observers believe that the country has struck a balance that both encourages assimilation and permits new immigrants to maintain their religious and cultural customs. Many Americans remain troubled by the large number of immigrants in the country illegally, however, and the government has responded by strengthening border security and stepping up deportation efforts. The Obama administration focused its enforcement policies on criminals and other high-priority categories of migrants while explicitly sparing groups like those who entered the country illegally as children. During the 2016 presidential campaign, Trump pledged to build a "wall" along the southern border and accelerate deportations. Responding to concerns about terrorism and the Obama administration's efforts to take in greater numbers of Syrian refugees, Trump also publicly considered a variety of measures to limit or monitor the presence of refugees, Muslim immigrants, or Muslims in general.

G. Personal Autonomy and Individual Rights: 15 / 16

Citizens of the United States enjoy freedom of movement and a high level of personal autonomy. The right to own property is protected by law, and business entrepreneurship is encouraged as a matter of government policy.

Women have made important strides toward equality over the past several decades. They now constitute almost half of the American workforce and are well represented in professions like law, medicine, and journalism. In 2015, the Defense Department announced that all combat roles in the military were open to women. Although women with recent university degrees have effectively attained parity with men, the average compensation for female workers is roughly 80 percent of that for male workers. In the past several years, a number of new state laws have been designed to restrict women's access to abortion without breaching prior court decisions, and some have survived initial judicial scrutiny, adding to state-by-state variation in access.

In 2015, the Supreme Court found that all states must allow same-sex marriage. The practice had already become legal in most states through court decisions, legislative action, or referendums, but the new ruling invalidated laws in a minority of states that still barred same-sex couples from marrying.

The "American dream"—the notion of a fair society in which hard work will bring economic and social advancement, regardless of the circumstances of one's birth—is a core part of the country's identity, and voters tend to favor government policies that enhance equality of opportunity. Recently, however, studies have shown a widening inequality in wealth and a narrowing of access to upward mobility. One key driver of inequality is the widening gap between Americans with university degrees and those with a high school degree or less. A number of states and municipalities have enacted substantial hikes in the minimum wage, but wages overall have remained stagnant for many years, and the number of well-compensated jobs for the less-educated have fallen steeply.

Uruguay

Political Rights Rating: 1
Civil Liberties Rating: 1
Freedom Rating: 1.0
Electoral Status: Free
Electoral Democracy: Yes

Population: 3,500,000
Capital: Montevideo

Ten-Year Ratings Timeline For Year Under Review (Political Rights, Civil Liberties, Status)

Year Under Review	2007	2008	2009	2010	2011	2012	2013	2014	2015	2016
Rating	1,1,F	1,1,F	1,1,F	1,1,F	1,1,F	1,1,F	1,1,F	1,1,F	1,1,F	1,1,F

Overview: Uruguay has a historically strong democratic governance structure and a positive record of upholding political rights and civil liberties while also working toward social inclusion. Although all citizens enjoy legal equality, there are still disparities in treatment and political representation for women, Uruguayans of African descent, and the indigenous population.

KEY DEVELOPMENTS IN 2016:

- Six former detainees who had been released to Uruguay from the U.S. military facility in Guantánamo Bay, Cuba, in 2014 continued to protest their presence in the country, demanding to be sent elsewhere and reunite with their families. One man engaged in a lengthy hunger strike during 2016 and twice made unsuccessful attempts to leave Uruguay.
- In March, a Jewish community leader was stabbed to death in what appeared to be an anti-Semitic attack. The alleged perpetrator was arrested, charged, and eventually committed to a psychiatric hospital.

EXECUTIVE SUMMARY

Violent crime remained a problem in Uruguay during 2016, though the rates were still fairly low for the region, and statistics for the year showed a decrease in key categories compared with 2015. Homicides, for example, fell to 265 from 293, for a rate of 7.6 per 100,000 inhabitants. Much of the rise in criminal activity over the past several years has been linked to the transnational drug trade.

In April, the government introduced legislation designed to define and combat gender-based violence, including femicide. A bill proposed in September would create a special prosecutors' office focused on crimes against humanity dating to the military regime that ended in 1985. The measures were still under consideration by lawmakers at year's end.

POLITICAL RIGHTS: 40 / 40

A. Electoral Process: 12 / 12

B. Political Pluralism and Participation: 16 / 16

C. Functioning of Government: 12 / 12

CIVIL LIBERTIES: 58 / 60

D. Freedom of Expression and Belief: 16 / 16

E. Associational and Organizational Rights: 12 / 12

F. Rule of Law: 15 / 16

G. Personal Autonomy and Individual Rights: 15 / 16

This country report has been abridged for *Freedom in the World 2017*. For background information on political rights and civil liberties in Uruguay, see *Freedom in the World 2016*.

Uzbekistan

Political Rights Rating: 7
Civil Liberties Rating: 7
Freedom Rating: 7.0
Freedom Status: Not Free
Electoral Democracy: No

Population: 31,900,000
Capital: Tashkent

Ten-Year Ratings Timeline For Year Under Review (Political Rights, Civil Liberties, Status)

Year Under Review	2007	2008	2009	2010	2011	2012	2013	2014	2015	2016
Ratings	7,7,NF	7,7,NF	7,7,NF	7,7,NF	7,7,NF	7,7,NF	7,7,NF	7,7,NF	7,7,NF	7,7,NF

Overview: Uzbekistan is ruled by a highly repressive authoritarian regime. No genuine opposition parties operate legally, and domestic supporters or family members of exiled opposition figures are persecuted. The legislature and judiciary effectively serve as instruments of the executive branch. The media are tightly controlled by the state, and journalists who work with foreign outlets are subject to detention and other abuses. There is little account-ability for endemic corruption or torture of detainees; the government holds numerous pris-oners on political or religious grounds. Dissent is suppressed in part through surveillance and intimidation by a network of neighborhood councils.

KEY DEVELOPMENTS IN 2016:

- Islam Karimov, Uzbekistan's president since independence in 1991, was reported dead in September and replaced by the incumbent prime minister, despite constitu-tional provisions designating the head of the Senate as acting president in such circumstances.
- The annual cotton harvest again relied on forced labor by state employees, and activists and journalists who attempted to document the practice faced detention and physical abuse.

EXECUTIVE SUMMARY

In late August, amid rumors about President Karimov's health, the government admit-ted that he had suffered a stroke and was hospitalized. Officials confirmed Karimov's death on September 2, but gave no information about who had assumed his duties. The constitu-tion called for the Senate chairman to become acting president, but on September 8 the parliament appointed Prime Minister Shavkat Mirziyoyev to hold the post, apparently bypassing constitutional order. Mirziyoyev won a special presidential election in December, taking a reported 88.6 percent of the vote and defeating nominal challengers whose parties in some cases openly campaigned for the incumbent. Election monitors from the Organiza-tion for Security and Co-operation in Europe concluded that the process was "devoid of genuine competition."

In his first four months in power, Mirziyoyev issued decrees that reinstated some former officials who had fallen out of favor with Karimov, announced the partial privatization of key state-owned enterprises, took steps to ease international travel and commerce, and promised to make the government serve the people, instead of the other way around. In addition, former lawmaker and Karimov opponent Samandar Kukanov was amnestied in November after nearly 24 years in prison, and a number of blocked foreign news sites reportedly became accessible to internet users in late December. In response to such moves, many prominent opposition figures—including some who had been imprisoned on political charges under Karimov—spoke out in support of Mirziyoyev and expressed hope for seri-ous reforms. However, Mirziyoyev had yet to propose major structural changes that would expand the political rights and civil liberties of Uzbekistani citizens.

The government continued to prosecute religion-based offenses in 2016, and increas-ingly focused on returning migrant workers accused of supporting banned groups. The trials in such cases are closed, making it impossible to evaluate the evidence on which convictions are based. Authorities also repeatedly raided the homes of people whose relatives living abroad were suspected of extremism. In April the president signed criminal code amend-ments that prescribed up to eight years in prison for promoting religious extremism in the media or online.

The country's few remaining human rights activists faced ongoing harassment, prose-cutions, travel restrictions, and violence during the year, particularly when attempting to document conditions for workers during the annual cotton harvest. As in previous years, the harvest featured state-organized forced labor by public employees and some reports of labor by students under age 18. In October, police temporarily detained Elena Urlaeva, head of the Human Rights Alliance (HRA), along with photographer Timur Karpov and two

French researchers as they monitored the cotton harvest. Urlaeva was separated from the others and subjected to invasive searches, threats, and beatings; she suffered similar treatment in another incident later that month. Earlier in the year she had been forcibly detained in a psychiatric facility for several weeks.

POLITICAL RIGHTS: 0 / 40
A. Electoral Process: 0 / 12
B. Political Pluralism and Participation: 0 / 16
C. Functioning of Government: 0 / 12

CIVIL LIBERTIES: 3 / 60
D. Freedom of Expression and Belief: 0 / 16
E. Associational and Organizational Rights: 0 / 12
F. Rule of Law: 0 / 16
G. Personal Autonomy and Individual Rights: 3 / 16

This country report has been abridged for *Freedom in the World 2017*. For background information on political rights and civil liberties in Uzbekistan, see *Freedom in the World 2016*.

Vanuatu

Political Rights Ratings: 2
Civil Liberties Ratings: 2
Freedom Rating: 2.0
Freedom Status: Free
Electoral Democracy: Yes

Population: 300,000
Capital: Port Vila

Ten-Year Ratings Timeline For Year Under Review (Political Rights, Civil Liberties, Status)

Year Under Review	2007	2008	2009	2010	2011	2012	2013	2014	2015	2016
Rating	2,2,F	2,2,F	2,2,F	2,2,F	2,2,F	2,2,F	2,2,F	2,2,F	2,2,F	2,2,F

The country or territory displayed here received scores but no narrative report for this edition of *Freedom in the World*.

Venezuela

Political Rights Rating: 6 ↓
Civil Liberties Rating: 5
Freedom Rating: 5.5
Freedom Status: Not Free
Electoral Democracy: No

Population: 31,000,000
Capital: Caracas

Status Change, Ratings Change: Venezuela's status declined from Partly Free to Not Free, and its political rights rating declined from 5 to 6, due to efforts by the executive branch and the politicized judiciary to curtail the power of the opposition-controlled legislature, including a series of court rulings that invalidated new laws, usurped legislative authority to review the national budget, and blocked legislative efforts to address the country's economic and humanitarian crisis.

Ten-Year Ratings Timeline For Year Under Review (Political Rights, Civil Liberties, Status)

Year Under Review	2007	2008	2009	2010	2011	2012	2013	2014	2015	2016
Rating	4,4,PF	4,4,PF	5,4,PF	5,5,PF	5,5,PF	5,5,PF	5,5,PF	5,5,PF	5,5,PF	6,5,NF

Overview: The ruling political movement formed by late president Hugo Chávez has presided over a deterioration in democratic institutions since 1999, but conditions have grown sharply worse in recent years due to a concentration of power in the executive and harsher crackdowns on the opposition. The opposition-controlled legislature's powers have been curtailed by a politicized judiciary that serves the executive's interests. Government corruption is pervasive, and law enforcement has proven unable to halt violent crime. The authorities have restricted civil liberties and prosecuted perceived opponents without regard for due process.

KEY DEVELOPMENTS IN 2016:

- Following the opposition's victory in December 2015 parliamentary elections, the Supreme Tribunal of Justice (TSJ) barred three opposition lawmakers from taking their seats in January due to alleged electoral irregularities, denying the opposition a supermajority that would have given it greater powers. The court later nullified most legislation that had been passed by the opposition-controlled National Assembly, and stripped the chamber of certain functions.
- In October, the National Electoral Council (CNE) blocked a proposed referendum to recall President Nicolás Maduro, citing dubious allegations of fraud in the opposition's signature drive for the vote, and separately postponed December gubernatorial and local elections until mid-2017.
- The intelligence service detained opposition politicians on trumped-up charges during the year, often violating due process.
- Despite a growing humanitarian crisis linked to the collapsing economy, the government and the TSJ obstructed the National Assembly's attempts to pass economic reforms and enable Venezuela to receive foreign medical aid.

EXECUTIVE SUMMARY

Following the victory of the opposition Democratic Unity Roundtable (MUD) in December 2015 elections for the National Assembly, the governing United Socialist Party of Venezuela (PSUV) moved quickly to diminish the effects of the election result. A decision by the TSJ prevented four lawmakers, including three from the opposition, from taking their seats in January, thereby stripping the opposition of its supermajority, which is needed to make appointments to the CNE and other key institutions. Throughout the year, the TSJ—stacked with PSUV appointees—repeatedly ruled that legislation passed by the National Assembly was unconstitutional, including a bill that would have enabled foreign humanitarian aid to Venezuela and an amnesty law intended to free political prisoners. The tribunal also stripped the assembly of certain constitutional functions, such as the ability to approve the federal budget.

As part of its bid to retain power, the PSUV government resorted to imprisoning more opposition politicians, detaining journalists, and intimidating state employees. Some 55 people were added to the ranks of political prisoners during 2016, according to the nongovernmental organization Foro Penal, with a total of 103 behind bars or under house arrest at year's end. In some cases, Venezuelan intelligence officials arrested and held opposition activists in violation of due process, and many detainees reported physical abuse in custody.

Food and medication shortages worsened and runaway inflation intensified during the year, but the Maduro administration remained unwilling to acknowledge or address the crisis. Growing frustration with the government's performance brought citizens to the streets, with nearly one million residents marching in Caracas in early September, according to opposition estimates.

Meanwhile, the opposition leadership focused on organizing a presidential recall referendum, as allowed by the constitution. Despite onerous hurdles established by the CNE, the opposition peacefully complied with all of the requirements. However, in October the council suspended the referendum process until at least 2017, virtually ensuring that Maduro would remain in power through the end of his term. The widely condemned decision, which prompted another round of large protests, was based on unproven allegations of fraud in the initial stages of the opposition's signature drive for the referendum, long after the CNE itself had checked for irregularities.

The suspension of the referendum process, together with a separate decision that month to postpone elections for governors and mayors until 2017, signaled the authorities' new willingness to disrupt important electoral processes in order to prevent further opposition victories.

POLITICAL RIGHTS: 11 / 40 (− 4)

A. Electoral Process: 5 / 12

The president serves six-year terms, and since 2009 neither the president nor other elected officials have been subject to term limits. The most recent presidential election was held in April 2013, after longtime incumbent Hugo Chávez died of cancer. Maduro, Chávez's vice president and handpicked successor, narrowly defeated opposition leader Henrique Capriles, 50.6 percent to 49.1 percent. Turnout was nearly 80 percent. Maduro was officially declared the winner by the Chavista-dominated CNE. The opposition accused the government of multiple violations, including election-day abuses and the rampant misuse of state resources during the campaign, and for the first time since 2005 it refused to accept the outcome's legitimacy without a more complete audit. Protests in the election's immediate aftermath left nine people dead and hundreds injured. A limited audit conducted by the CNE revealed few discrepancies, while the TSJ rejected the opposition petitions in August 2013, thereby concluding the electoral process.

The unicameral, 167-seat National Assembly is popularly elected for five-year terms, using a mix of majoritarian and proportional-representation voting. Three seats are reserved for indigenous representatives. The 2015 elections were marred by a delayed initial announcement, a campaign environment clearly tilted in favor of the ruling PSUV, disqualifications of prominent opposition candidates, government abuse of public resources to boost voter support, uneven access to the state-dominated media, a near extinction of independent traditional media, a lack of international observers, some violence, and reported intimidation and monitoring by superiors of state employees with the aim of ensuring that they voted for the government, followed by threats and firings after the results were announced.

Nonetheless, the MUD coalition won 109 seats, and MUD-aligned candidates won the three indigenous seats, leaving the PSUV with just 55. Under a 2009 electoral reform, the system gives a notable seat advantage to the party with the most votes, allowing the MUD to achieve its strong victory with only about 56 percent of the national vote; the PSUV received some 41 percent of the vote. In late 2015, government challenges against opposition victories—and specifically the TSJ's decision to invalidate the votes for four representatives, three of whom were members of the opposition—deprived the MUD of a two-thirds majority in the assembly that would have allowed it to adopt legislation and make appointments without support from PSUV legislators.

In October 2016, the CNE announced that gubernatorial and local elections, originally scheduled for December, would be postponed until mid-2017, without offering further details.

B. Political Pluralism and Participation: 6 / 16 (−2)

The MUD's 2015 campaign and eventual victory in the legislative elections demonstrated that it had improved its ability to compete electorally. However, the aftermath of the election underscored the fact that for the opposition, victory at the polls does not necessarily translate into governing power or influence over policymaking. Opposition leadership in some states and localities has been blunted in recent years by laws allowing the national government to cut budgets and strip important functions from subnational administrations.

Opposition leader Leopoldo López remained imprisoned throughout 2016, having been held in a military prison since February 2014 for supposedly instigating violence during that year's protests. In September 2015 he was sentenced to 13 years and nine months in prison following a closed-door trial in which the judge blocked most of the evidence and witnesses proposed by the defense. Daniel Ceballos, the former mayor of San Cristóbal who was jailed in 2014 and then kept under house arrest for allegedly inciting or failing to halt violent demonstrations, was detained again in August 2016 after reportedly being told he was being taken to a medical exam.

Among other cases, Yon Goicoechea, a prominent leader of the opposition party Popular Will, disappeared in late August 2016 and was subsequently reported to have been arrested by the Bolivarian National Intelligence Service (SEBIN), which accused him of possessing explosives. Delson Guarate, mayor of Mario Briceño Iragorry in the state of Aragua, was arrested by SEBIN in September for alleged possession of firearms, among other charges. Alejandro Puglia, a journalist and employee of the National Assembly, was also arrested by SEBIN in September for possessing a drone. Caracas mayor Antonio Ledezma, who was detained in February 2015, remained under house arrest in 2016 for supposedly plotting a coup against the government. Francisco Márquez and Gabriel San Miguel of Popular Will were arrested while collecting signatures for the recall petition; they were both released by October and subsequently left the country. At least 55 people were added to the ranks of political prisoners in 2016, according to the Venezuelan watchdog Foro Penal, for a total of 103 behind bars or under house arrest at year's end.

As support grew for the recall referendum during the year, PSUV officials, including Maduro, threatened those who might consider supporting it. State employees were told they would lose their jobs if they endorsed the referendum.

After initially postponing the referendum until 2017 and imposing a higher threshold for signatures, in October 2016 the CNE suspended the process indefinitely. The constitution states that if the president is recalled during the last two years of his term, the vice president serves out the remainder of the term, in lieu of an early election. Thus the CNE's decision staved off the possibility of an opposition candidate taking the presidency. The

CNE in September had mandated that the signatures gathered must meet a threshold of 20 percent of all voters in each state, rather than 20 percent nationwide. In addition, citizens were required to provide their fingerprint alongside their signature, potentially deterring those who feared government reprisals.

While Venezuela's constitution provides specific protection for minorities, historically marginalized groups have been particularly affected by the economic and health crisis. Food and medication shortages, the spread of infectious diseases, and rampant crime have undermined the ability of Venezuela's poorest and most vulnerable citizens to participate politically.

C. Functioning of Government: 0 / 12 (− 2)

Venezuela did not function as a representative democracy in 2016. The opposition-controlled legislature had virtually no ability to carry out its constitutional mandate, as the TSJ repeatedly struck down its bills and curtailed its authority. The tribunal impeded the National Assembly from taking actions to address the economic crisis, including by invalidating a law to allow Venezuela to receive foreign humanitarian aid. It deemed an opposition-backed bill to free political prisoners unconstitutional. It blocked the assembly from conducting a review of the federal budget, thus allowing the executive branch to unilaterally develop and implement a new budget. It disallowed the assembly from filling two vacancies on the CNE. And the TSJ's nullification of the votes for four elected assembly members—three of whom were affiliated with the MUD coalition—effectively revoked the opposition's veto-proof supermajority. Opposition leaders claimed that the decision was politically motivated and undermined the people's will.

The government's economic policies—particularly its currency and price controls—have greatly increased opportunities for corruption, black-market activity, and collusion between public officials and organized crime networks. The government loses billions of dollars in revenue per year to gasoline smuggling. Continued restrictions on foreign currency and imports have greatly affected poor and middle-class Venezuelans and exacerbated the effects of the economic crisis, while elite groups and favored entities such as the military benefit from valuable exemptions and privileges. The government's decision in December 2016 to take the 100-bolivar note out of circulation prompted major protests and looting, as citizens waited in long lines to deposit their expiring currency and replacement notes remained unavailable. Ultimately, the government decided to extend use of the bill until January 2017.

There is little transparency regarding government spending, which has often outpaced the budgeted amount. The government failed to publish vital economic data, including monthly inflation statistics, for most of the year. Venezuela has received over $65 billion in loans from China since 2007, adding to concerns about the opaque allocation of resources.

CIVIL LIBERTIES: 19 / 60 (− 1)

D. Freedom of Expression and Belief: 8 / 16

The Chávez and Maduro governments, claiming that the private media were controlled by the right, have sought to build a state communications infrastructure with the aim of propagating their political and ideological program. This state media apparatus includes not only the television station VTV, which has modernized and expanded its signal to cover the entire national territory, but also Vive TV, Ávila TV, and Telesur, as well as a large number of state-owned newspapers.

Laws such as the 2004 Law on Social Responsibility of Radio and Television give the government the authority to control media content, and because the judiciary and regulatory agencies lack political independence, the legal framework is effectively used to control or punish any media owner or journalist whom the leadership perceives as an adversary. Critical media also face harassment in the form of tax penalties, equipment confiscation, and withdrawal of government advertising. A series of private news outlets have changed ownership under financial pressure in recent years, and their coverage subsequently grew more favorable to the authorities.

Intimidation, physical attacks, confiscations of equipment, and detentions and arrests of journalists continued in 2016, particularly for those seeking to bring economic struggles, the health crisis, and other significant concerns to light. The Institute for Press and Society, a local media watchdog, recorded 546 violations of press freedom during the first seven months of 2016, compared with 287 in the same period in 2015. Digital media outlets are increasingly targeted, and many journalists have had their social media accounts hacked in recent years.

During a visit to Nueva Esparta in early September 2016, President Maduro was chased down the street by protesters in an area that had previously been considered progovernment. Law enforcement officials and government personnel reportedly searched homes and confiscated mobile phones in an attempt to suppress video evidence of the incident. The following day, journalist Braulio Jatar of the news website Reporte Confidencial was detained for alleged money laundering, though many observers suggested that the arrest was linked to his coverage of the presidential visit. He remained in custody at year's end, allegedly under harsh conditions.

Constitutional guarantees of religious freedom are generally respected, though tensions between the government and the Roman Catholic Church remain high. Government relations with the small Jewish community have also been strained at times.

Academic freedom came under mounting pressure during Chávez's tenure, and a school curriculum developed by his government emphasizes socialist concepts. A 2008 Organic Education Law included ambiguities that could lead to restrictions on private education and increased control by the government and communal councils. In universities, elections for student associations and administration positions have become more politicized, and rival groups of students have clashed over both academic and political matters. In 2016, budget cuts and broader funding issues remained serious challenges that undermined universities' autonomy.

In recent years the government has repeatedly aired illegally intercepted conversations of opposition members, and ordinary Venezuelans have become more reticent about calling attention to their political views in situations where they might be overheard.

E. Associational and Organizational Rights: 3 / 12

Although freedom of peaceful assembly is guaranteed in the constitution, the right to protest has become a sensitive topic in recent years, and human rights groups have criticized legal amendments that make it easier to charge protesters with serious crimes. Widespread antigovernment protests during 2014 featured violence on the part of both police and demonstrators. More than 40 people were reportedly killed, and at least 3,100 were arrested, in many cases through targeted raids on their homes.

Citizens returned to the streets in 2016 to express frustration with the country's economic problems and their discontent with President Maduro. A protest on September 1 reportedly drew a million participants, though government officials disputed such estimates.

Some opposition leaders were arrested before and after the protests, including Yon Goicoechea and Alejandro Puglia. From January to September, Foro Penal registered over 2,000 arbitrary detentions in the context of public demonstrations. Protests on October 26 drew hundreds of thousands of people, resulting in at least 120 injuries and over 200 arrests.

The government has sought to undermine the legitimacy of human rights and other civil society groups by questioning their international ties. The 2010 Law on Political Sovereignty and National Self-Determination threatens sanctions against any "political organization" that receives foreign funding or hosts foreign visitors who criticize the government. Dozens of civil society activists have been physically attacked in recent years, and other forms of harassment are common, including bureaucratic hurdles to registration. The Inter-American Commission on Human Rights has repeatedly expressed alarm over government intimidation against activists.

Workers are legally entitled to form unions, bargain collectively, and strike, with some restrictions on public-sector workers' ability to strike. Control of unions has shifted from traditional opposition-allied labor leaders to new workers' organizations that are often aligned with the government. The competition has contributed to a substantial increase in labor violence as well as confusion and delays during industry-wide collective bargaining.

F. Rule of Law: 1 / 16

Politicization of the judicial branch increased dramatically under Chávez, and has progressed even further under Maduro. High courts generally do not rule against the government. Conviction rates for violent crimes remain low, the public defender system is underfunded, and most judges and prosecutors lack tenure, undermining their autonomy.

The National Assembly has the authority to remove and appoint judges to the TSJ, which controls the rest of the judiciary and is viewed as friendly to the government. In October 2015, a group of TSJ judges requested early retirement, allowing the outgoing legislature to appoint 13 new judges to serve 12-year terms on the 32-member tribunal in December. The move was seen as an attempt to ensure PSUV control over the judiciary despite the opposition's election victory.

The police and military have been prone to corruption, widespread arbitrary detention and torture of suspects, and extrajudicial killings, with few convictions. Military officials, many of them in active service, occupy a number of top positions in government ministries and state-level administrations, and the armed forces perform routine government duties, blurring the lines between civilian and military functions. In 2016, SEBIN increasingly carried out policing functions and arrested opposition politicians and journalists without informing the Public Ministry or presenting official charges. Foreign governments allege that the military has adopted a permissive attitude toward drug trafficking. Prison conditions in Venezuela remain among the worst in the Americas, featuring gang violence, rioting, overcrowding, and lack of proper sanitation. The Venezuelan Prison Observatory reported 173 deaths within prison walls in 2016.

Venezuela's violent crime rate ranks among the highest in the world and is a major source of popular discontent. According to the attorney general's office, homicides increased by nearly 50 percent from January to March 2016 compared with the first three months of 2014. According to Insight Crime, a foundation that studies organized crime in Latin America, 4,156 people were killed in police and military clashes with criminal groups from January to September 2016.

The formal and constitutional rights of indigenous people, who make up about 2 percent of the population, improved under the 1999 constitution, though such rights are seldom enforced by local authorities. Indigenous communities trying to defend their land rights are subject to abuses, particularly along the Colombian border. Afro-Venezuelans also remain marginalized and underrepresented among the country's political and economic elite, despite some state efforts to ameliorate conditions.

Although discrimination based on sexual orientation is barred, LGBT (lesbian, gay, bisexual, and transgender) Venezuelans face widespread de facto discrimination and are occasionally subjected to violence. In the December 2015 elections, transgender lawyer and political activist Tamara Adrián won a position in the National Assembly as an alternate deputy (*diputado suplente*), though she was forced to register under the name she received at birth. Another alternate, Rosmit Mantilla, a gay activist, was one of three assembly candidates to win their elections while behind bars, having been arrested in 2014 after joining that year's protests.

G. Personal Autonomy and Individual Rights: 7 / 16 (− 1)

The country's currency controls and other economic policies, combined with a decline in the number of flights to and from Venezuela, have made it extremely difficult for Venezuelans to travel abroad. In April 2015, the government announced a reduction in the amount of foreign currency to be made available for the purpose of travel. After closing the border with Colombia in 2015, ostensibly to stop smuggling activities that officials blamed for food shortages, the government partially reopened the border in mid-2016. However, the border was briefly closed again in December in relation to the removal of the 100-bolivar note from circulation.

Property rights have also been affected by years of price controls, nationalizations, overregulation, and corruption. While the pace of expropriation has declined in recent years—due in part to the state's dominant position in many strategic industries—the government has continued to threaten to nationalize businesses deemed to lack commitment to revolutionary goals. Accusations of mismanagement, underinvestment, graft, and politicized hiring practices within state-owned enterprises are common.

Women are guaranteed progressive rights in the 1999 constitution, and a 2007 law was designed to combat violence against women. However, domestic violence and rape remain common and are rarely punished in practice. Women are poorly represented in government, with just 14 percent of the seats in the National Assembly, but they hold a number of important offices in the executive branch.

Trafficking of women remains inadequately addressed by the authorities. Venezuelan women and children are subjected to sex trafficking both within Venezuela and in neighboring countries. Migrants to Venezuela are also subjected to forced labor and sex trafficking.

With job opportunities growing scarce and wages not keeping up with hyperinflation, more citizens have turned to jobs in the informal economy, including illegal mining and other dangerous, unregulated activities. Many Venezuelans, particularly young people, have emigrated due to a lack of employment opportunities and severe shortages of basic goods.

Vietnam

Political Rights Ratings: 7
Civil Liberties Ratings: 5
Freedom Rating: 6.0
Freedom Status: Not Free
Electoral Democracy: No

Population: 92,700,000
Capital: Hanoi

Ten-Year Ratings Timeline for Year Under Review (Political Rights, Civil Liberties, Status)

Year Under Review	2007	2008	2009	2010	2011	2012	2013	2014	2015	2016
Rating	7,5,NF	7,5,NF	7,5,NF	7,5,NF	7,5,NF	7,5,NF	7,5,NF	7,5,NF	7,5,NF	7,5,NF

Overview: Vietnam is a one-party state, dominated for decades by the ruling Communist Party of Vietnam (CPV). Although some independent candidates are technically allowed to run in legislative elections, most are banned in practice. Freedom of expression, religious freedom, and civil society activism are highly restricted. The authorities have increasingly cracked down on citizens' use of social media and the internet in general to spread uncensored information and galvanize dissent.

KEY DEVELOPMENTS In 2016:

- In January, the ruling CPV held its 12th Party Congress and chose new leaders in a highly opaque manner.
- Legislative elections were held in May. Most independent candidates were prevented from running, though a handful managed to win seats.
- In April and May, large protests erupted over alleged pollution of Vietnamese waters by a Taiwanese-owned steel mill. The government eventually forced the company to pay a fine, but protests continued, and hundreds of demonstrators were detained.
- In July, an international tribunal ruled against China on its territorial claims in the South China Sea. The Vietnamese government attempted to quell celebratory anti-China demonstrations in response to the ruling.

EXECUTIVE SUMMARY

Nguyễn Phú Trọng was reelected as general secretary of the CPV at the 12th Party Congress in January 2016, while Trần Đại Quang was nominated to become state president and Nguyễn Xuân Phúc to become prime minister. The latter two were confirmed in office by the National Assembly in April. None of the three officials have expressed public support for a shift toward political reforms.

Vietnam held mostly pro forma legislative elections in May. Although the CPV dominated the new legislature, a handful of independent candidates were allowed to participate.

Also in May, U.S. president Barack Obama visited Vietnam in a sign of closer strategic ties between the two countries. Obama met with several civil society activists in Hanoi, but a number of prominent figures were barred from attending. Throughout 2016, the authorities continued to arrest and imprison well-known dissident bloggers, ordinary internet users who posted critical content, and members of religious groups that operate outside of CPV control.

POLITICAL RIGHTS: 3 / 40

A. Electoral Process: 0 / 12

The CPV is the country's only state-recognized political party, and its Politburo and Central Committee are effectively the country's top decision-making bodies. The unicameral National Assembly, whose maximum of 500 members are elected to five-year terms, generally follows CPV dictates. The president is elected by the National Assembly for a five-year term, and is responsible for appointing the prime minister, who is confirmed by the legislature.

Nominees for president and prime minister were chosen at the CPV's 12th Party Congress in January 2016, which also featured the reelection of Nguyễn Phú Trọng as the party's general secretary. He apparently defeated a bid for the position by former prime minister Nguyễn Tấn Dũng, though the process was largely opaque. In April, the National Assembly formally confirmed Trần Đại Quang as president and Nguyễn Xuân Phúc as prime minister.

In the tightly controlled May 2016 elections for the National Assembly, the CPV took 473 seats, candidates vetted by the CPV but technically independent took 19 seats, and the remaining 2 winners were self-nominated. More than 100 independent candidates, including many young civil society activists, were barred from running in the elections.

B. Political Pluralism and Participation: 1 / 16

The CPV enjoys a monopoly on political power, and no other parties are allowed to operate legally. Leaders and members of illegal opposition parties are subject to arrest and imprisonment. The Vietnam Fatherland Front (VFF), responsible for vetting all candidates for the National Assembly, is ostensibly an alliance of organizations representing the people, but in practice it acts as an arm of the CPV.

Splits between factions within the party exist, but they are not openly aired. In January 2016, infighting over who would be chosen as general secretary was revealed to the public in part through a series of leaks and counterleaks to various Vietnamese media.

Although ethnic minorities are represented within the CPV, they are rarely allowed to rise to senior leadership positions. A law that took effect in 2015 requires 18 percent of the final candidates for National Assembly elections to be ethnic minorities. Ethnic minorities held about 17 percent of seats in the National Assembly after the 2016 elections, and occupied one position in the cabinet.

C. Functioning of Government: 2 / 12

The CPV leadership determines and implements government policy, but it is not freely elected or accountable to the public, and it operates with considerable opacity. Membership in the CPV is widely viewed as a means of enhancing one's personal wealth and connections, and corruption and nepotism are ongoing problems within the party.

CPV and government leaders have acknowledged growing public discontent with corruption, and the authorities periodically prosecute high-profile officials and businessmen for malfeasance. However, observers argue that enforcement is selective and often linked to political rivalries, and those who attempt to independently expose corruption continue to face censorship and arrest.

The National Assembly passed an access to information law in April 2016, but it barred disclosure of information on "politics, defense, national security, foreign relations, economics, technology, or any other areas regulated by the law." Information would also be withheld if it could harm "the interests of the state, national defense and security, social security, and the health of the community." Human rights groups criticized the sweeping restrictions, as well as a ban on citizens using or disseminating information that could damage the state, public order, or social morality, or that would amount to defamation. Implementation was not expected until 2018.

CIVIL LIBERTIES: 17 / 60

D. Freedom of Expression and Belief: 4 / 16

The state controls all print and broadcast media, and authorities actively silence critical journalists and bloggers through arrest, prosecution, and other means of harassment. A 2006 decree prescribes fines for any publication that denies revolutionary achievements, spreads "harmful" information, or exhibits "reactionary ideology." Decree 72, issued in 2013, gave the state sweeping new powers to restrict speech on blogs and social media. In April 2016, the National Assembly passed an ambiguous media law—to take effect in 2017—that banned prepublication censorship of print and broadcast media and criminalized threats or other actions that interfere with journalistic activities, among other provisions, but also introduced several vaguely worded new offenses that could be used to punish journalists.

New arrests, criminal convictions, and physical assaults against journalists and bloggers continued to be reported during 2016. Among a number of other cases, two prominent bloggers who had been in detention since 2014, Nguyễn Hữu Vinh and Nguyễn Thị Minh Thúy, were sentenced in March to five and three years in prison, respectively, for infringing upon the interests of the state. In a separate case that month, freelance journalist and blogger Nguyễn Đình Ngọc (also known as Nguyễn Ngọc Già), who had also been detained since 2014, was sentenced to four years in prison—later reduced to three years on appeal—and three years of probation for propagandizing against the state.

Three Vietnamese reporters were beaten by security forces in July while investigating an alleged spill of toxic chemicals in the northern Phú Ninh district. In August, two members of an online dissident group, Nguyễn Hữu Quốc Duy and Nguy?n Hữu Thiên An, were sentenced to three and two years in prison, respectively, for allegedly disseminating antigovernment propaganda, including on Facebook. In October, dissident blogger Nguy?n Ngọc Nhu Quỳnh, also known as Mẹ Nâm (Mother Mushroom), was arrested for allegedly "propagandizing against the state," and she remained in incommunicado detention at year's end. Blogger Ho Van Hai was arrested on similar charges in November. There were at least eight journalists behind bars in Vietnam as of December, according to the Committee to Protect Journalists.

Foreign media representatives must notify authorities if they travel outside Hanoi, and the government has at times refused visas for foreign journalists who report on sensitive topics. Satellite television is officially restricted to senior officials, international hotels, and foreign businesses, though many private homes and businesses have satellite dishes.

A 2003 law bans the receipt and distribution of antigovernment e-mail. Websites considered reactionary are blocked, and owners of domestic websites must submit plans for their content for official approval. Internet cafés are required to register the personal information of users and record the sites they visit. Internet service providers face fines and closure for violating censorship rules.

Despite government restrictions on internet activity, many Vietnamese use the web and social media to participate in political debate, often employing technical circumvention methods to avoid censorship and maintain anonymity. The authorities have deployed progovernment social media users to manipulate public opinion online.

Religious freedoms remain restricted. All religious groups and most individual clergy members are required to join a party-controlled supervisory body and obtain permission for most activities. A law on belief and religion passed by the National Assembly in November 2016 reinforced registration requirements, allowed extensive state interference in religious groups' internal affairs, and gave the authorities broad discretion to penalize religious activity.

The Roman Catholic Church selects its own bishops and priests, but they must be approved by the government. Christians continue to be persecuted, particularly outside of major cities and among ethnic minority groups. In one incident in April 2016, the wife of an imprisoned Vietnamese Mennonite pastor was reportedly beaten by security forces after meeting a delegation of U.S. diplomats investigating religious freedom issues. Members of unregistered Christian, Hoa Hao, Cao Dai, and other groups also face regular arrests and harassment from local and provincial authorities, and dozens of prisoners are believed to be behind bars in connection with their religious beliefs.

Academic freedom is limited. University professors must refrain from criticizing government policies and adhere to party views when teaching or writing on political topics. Although citizens enjoy more freedom in private discussions than in the past, authorities continue to punish those who openly criticize the state.

E. Associational and Organizational Rights: 1 / 12

Freedoms of association and assembly are tightly restricted. Organizations must apply for official permission to assemble, and security forces routinely use excessive force to disperse unauthorized demonstrations. Among other incidents during 2016, police broke up national protests against land seizures in February, and detained hundreds of people beginning in April while attempting to suppress a series of large protests sparked by pollution from a Taiwanese-owned steel mill that had allegedly caused fish kills in coastal waters. Those protests were accompanied by multiple reports of police beating demonstrators and activists, including when they were in custody. In July, the authorities intervened to block anti-China demonstrations following a ruling by the Netherlands-based Permanent Court of Arbitration in favor of the Philippines in a case on China's territorial claims in the South China Sea. Activists gathering to hold such demonstrations were quickly arrested.

Private organizations outside the umbrella of the VFF are discouraged. A small but active community of nongovernmental groups promotes environmental conservation, land rights, women's development, and public health, but human rights organizations and other private groups with rights-oriented agendas are generally banned. Land tenure has become one of the most contentious issues in the country. In March 2016, two land rights activists were sentenced to three years in prison, and a third received a four-year sentence, for holding an antigovernment protest in Ho Chi Minh City in 2014. In May, the government allowed some civil society activists to meet with the visiting U.S. president, but used security forces to prevent other activists from leaving their homes to attend. Both police and thugs in civilian clothes frequently assault civil society activists and other perceived opponents of the government with impunity.

The Vietnam General Conference of Labor (VGCL) is Vietnam's only legal labor federation and is controlled by the CPV. Vietnam agreed in principle to allow the formation of independent unions as part of the Trans-Pacific Partnership trade agreement, but those commitments were in doubt at the end of 2016, as the United States appeared likely to withdraw from and thus scuttle the pact. In recent years the Vietnamese government has permitted hundreds of independent "labor associations" without formal union status to represent workers at individual firms and in some service industries. Strikes by these associations are relatively common, despite being technically illegal. Farmer and worker protests against local government abuses, such as land confiscations and unfair or harsh working conditions, have also become more common. The central leadership often responds by pressuring local governments and businesses to comply with tax laws, environmental regulations, and wage agreements.

F. Rule of Law: 4 / 16

Vietnam's judiciary is subservient to the CPV, which controls the courts at all levels. Defendants have a constitutional right to counsel, but lawyers are scarce, and many are reluctant to take on human rights and other sensitive cases for fear of state harassment and retribution, including arrest. Defense lawyers do not have the right to call witnesses and often report insufficient time to meet with their clients. In national security cases, police can detain suspects for up to 20 months without access to counsel.

The police are known to abuse suspects and prisoners, sometimes resulting in death or serious injury, and prison conditions are poor. New police regulations that took effect in 2014 codified rules for police investigations and prohibited police coercion during interrogations. Some human rights groups praised the measure as a step forward, but critics raised concerns about enforcement and argued that the reforms failed to protect due process rights.

Ethnic minorities, who often adhere to minority religions, face discrimination in mainstream society, and some local officials restrict their access to schooling and jobs. Minorities generally have little input on development projects that affect their livelihoods and communities.

The law does not prohibit discrimination based on sexual orientation or gender identity, and societal discrimination remains a problem. However, there is no ban on same-sex sexual activity, and the government has been relatively open to calls for equal rights for LGBT (lesbian, gay, bisexual, and transgender) people in recent years. Annual LGBT pride events were held across the country for a fifth year in August 2016.

G. Personal Autonomy and Individual Rights: 8 / 16

Although freedom of movement is protected by law, residency rules limit access to services for those who migrate within the country without permission, and authorities have restricted the movement of political dissidents and ethnic minorities on other grounds. Vietnamese citizens who are repatriated after attempting to seek asylum abroad can face harassment or imprisonment under the penal code. In April and May 2016, eight people were sentenced to between two and four years in prison after being intercepted at sea by Australian forces and returned to Vietnam in 2015.

All land is owned by the state, which grants land-use rights and leases to farmers, developers, and others. The seizure of land for economic development projects is often accompanied by violence, accusations of corruption, and prosecutions of those who protest the confiscations.

Women generally have equal access to education, and men and women receive similar treatment in the legal system. Women secured 132 seats in the National Assembly in the 2016 elections. Although economic opportunities have grown for women, they continue to face discrimination in wages and promotion. Domestic violence against women reportedly remains common, and the law calls for the state to initiate criminal as opposed to civil procedures only when the victim is seriously injured.

In 2015, Vietnam repealed a legal ban on same-sex marriages, but the government still does not officially recognize such unions. A revised civil code passed that year recognized transgender people's right to legally change their gender identity, but only after undergoing sex reassignment surgery.

Enforcement of labor laws covering child labor, workplace safety, and other issues remains poor. Vietnamese women seeking work abroad are subject to sex trafficking in nearby Asian countries, and internationally brokered marriages sometimes lead to domestic servitude and forced prostitution. Male migrant workers are also vulnerable to forced labor abroad in a variety of industries.

Yemen

Political Rights Rating: 7
Civil Liberties Rating: 6
Freedom Rating: 6.5
Freedom Status: Not Free
Electoral Democracy: No

Population: 27,500,000
Capital: Sanaa

Ten-Year Ratings Timeline For Year Under Review (Political Rights, Civil Liberties, Status)

Year Under Review	2007	2008	2009	2010	2011	2012	2013	2014	2015	2016
Rating	5,5,PF	5,5,PF	6,5,NF	6,5,NF	6,6,NF	6,6,NF	6,6,NF	6,6,NF	7,6,NF	7,6,NF

Overview: Yemen has been devastated by a civil war that began in 2015, when incumbent president Abd Rabbu Mansur Hadi fled the capital and foreign powers led by Saudi Arabia intervened to support his government against the Houthi rebel movement—rooted in the Zaidi Shiite community, which forms a large minority in Yemen—and allied forces linked to former president Ali Abdullah Saleh. The civilian population has suffered from direct violence by both sides, as well as hunger and disease caused by the belligerents' interruption of trade and aid. Elections are long overdue, normal political activity has halted, and key state institutions have ceased to function across the country. Terrorist networks have taken advantage of the disorder, seizing territory in some areas and encouraging sectarian hostility.

KEY DEVELOPMENTS IN 2016:

- Several rounds of peace talks and abortive cease-fires during the year failed to halt the civil war, and the United States and some European allies continued to support the Saudi-led coalition, including by providing weapons, logistical aid, and intelligence for military targeting.
- The United Nations estimated in August that at least 10,000 people had been killed during the war to date. A cholera outbreak in October presented a new threat, sickening more than 12,700 people and killing nearly 100 by year's end.
- Civilian activists, aid workers, and journalists were targeted by combatants. At least six journalists were killed in connection with their work during the year, and several others were abducted.

EXECUTIVE SUMMARY

In July 2016, as Yemen's civil war continued with no end in sight, the Houthi rebel movement and former president Saleh's political party announced plans to form a new government. In August they appointed a 10-person Supreme Political Council, which in turn declared the formation of the new government in November. The unconstitutional process was not recognized by the international community.

Although the rebel forces controlled the capital and much of the country's north and west, the Hadi government and its allies—headed by Saudi Arabia—attempted to press in on this territory from all directions, particularly from their base in the southern port of Aden. A Saudi-led air campaign supported by the United States and some European governments struck civilian infrastructure and population centers throughout the year, repeatedly hitting medical facilities. In an especially deadly attack in October, an air strike on a funeral in Sanaa killed at least 140 people. The Saudi-led coalition reportedly used internationally banned munitions, such as cluster bombs, that tend to increase civilian casualties. Several rounds of peace talks during the summer and late fall, including a series of short ceasefires, failed to make significant progress.

The war, combined with a blockade that prevented food, medicine, and other vital supplies from reaching rebel-held areas, intensified hardships for civilians during the year. The United Nations estimated that more than half of the population lacked adequate access to food and that two to three million people were internally displaced. The majority of Yemen's health facilities were shuttered or not fully functioning by the end of 2016, crippling the country's ability to stem a cholera outbreak that began in October.

Two major extremist groups, Al-Qaeda in the Arabian Peninsula (AQAP) and the Islamic State (IS), retained pockets of territory in the southeast and carried out terrorist attacks throughout the year. The pro-Hadi coalition was at times accused of tacitly cooperating with Sunni extremist fighters against the Shiite-led Houthis, who in turn were alleged to draw material support from Iran. The United States, in addition to aiding the coalition, periodically carried out direct attacks on suspected AQAP targets inside Yemen.

POLITICAL RIGHTS: 2 / 40 (− 2)

A. Electoral Process: 0 / 12 (− 2)

Under the existing constitution, the president is elected for seven-year terms and appoints the 111 members of the largely advisory upper house of parliament, the Majlis al-Shura (Consultative Council). The 301 members of the lower house, the House of Representatives, are elected to serve six-year terms. Provincial councils and governors are also elected.

Parliamentary elections have been repeatedly postponed. The original six-year mandate of the last parliament expired in 2009, and elections were put off again in 2011 amid a popular uprising against longtime president Saleh. In November of that year, under sustained pressure from the United States, the United Nations, and the Gulf Cooperation Council, Saleh signed a Saudi-brokered agreement that transferred his powers to then vice president Hadi in exchange for immunity from prosecution for his role in a violent crackdown on the antigovernment protests. In February 2012, Yemeni voters confirmed Hadi, who ran unopposed, as interim president with a two-year term. In January 2014, the multiparty National Dialogue Conference (NDC), a months-long initiative in which more than 500 delegates aimed to reach agreement on Yemen's political future, concluded with a plan to transform the country into a federated state of six regions. The NDC also extended Hadi's term for one year so that the proposed reforms could be finalized in a new constitution.

However, the constitutional drafting process and election schedule were thrown into disarray by the Houthis, an armed rebel movement rooted in the Zaidi Shiite population of northwestern Yemen. Houthi forces took over large swaths of the country, eventually occupying Sanaa in September 2014. The Houthis subsequently refused to evacuate the capital as part of a tentative power-sharing agreement, leading Hadi and his cabinet to resign and then flee into exile in early 2015. Meanwhile, the Houthis disbanded the parliament and assumed control of state institutions. Hadi retained international recognition as president but had no clear mandate and little control over the country.

In July 2016 the Houthis and Saleh-affiliated elements of the former ruling party, the General People's Congress (GPC), reached an agreement that cleared the way for a new government, excluding pro-Hadi forces. In August they appointed a 10-person Supreme Political Council, which in turn announced the formation of the new government in November. The unconstitutional move was seen a blow to UN-led peace efforts, which aimed to negotiate a power-sharing government that included both sides in the civil war.

B. Political Pluralism and Participation: 1 / 16

The Houthis and their allies have harshly suppressed political dissent in areas under their control since 2015. In May 2016, Amnesty International reported on a sample of 60 cases in which Houthi forces had arbitrarily detained journalists, professionals, and politicians between December 2014 and March 2016. Many were affiliated with the opposition party Islah, which had expressed support for the Saudi-led coalition in 2015.

Ordinary political activity is also impeded by the presence of multiple armed groups in other parts of the country, including Sunni extremist groups, southern separatists, foreign troops from the Saudi-led coalition, Hadi government troops, and local or partisan militias.

C. Functioning of Government: 1 / 12

Yemen has no functioning central government, and any state institutions that continue to operate are controlled by unelected officials and armed groups. The Hadi government is largely dependent on its foreign patrons, particularly Saudi Arabia. Government transparency and accountability were minimal even before the outbreak of war in 2015, as a network of corruption and patronage established under Saleh remained entrenched in public institutions, and formal anticorruption mechanisms were largely ineffective.

The central bank, which had continued to function despite the war, was bifurcated in September 2016, when Hadi changed its leadership and ordered it to relocate to Aden. A rebel-backed version survived in Sanaa, with the Houthis launching a campaign to solicit public "donations" to support it, but salary payments to public employees and other fundamental tasks broke down across the country. The disruption to legal commerce increased reliance on the black market and created further opportunities for fraud and bribery.

CIVIL LIBERTIES: 12 / 60 (− 1)

D. Freedom of Expression and Belief: 5 / 16

Legislation such as the Press and Publications Law long restricted reporting, and the state has historically controlled most terrestrial television and radio, though there were several privately owned radio stations. Since the outbreak of conflict, the belligerents have either taken over or enforced self-censorship at any surviving media outlets in the country. In 2016, Houthi-backed authorities reportedly blocked certain news websites, online messaging and social media platforms, and satellite broadcasts. Internet service was also apparently threatened by damage to infrastructure and reduced access to electricity.

Journalists were subject to arbitrary detention, abduction, and murder during the year. At least six journalists were killed in connection with their work, according to the Committee to Protect Journalists, and more than a dozen were being detained by the Houthis or AQAP at year's end.

Islam is the official religion, and the constitution declares Sharia (Islamic law) to be the source of all legislation. Yemen has few non-Muslim religious minorities; their rights have traditionally been respected in practice, though conversion from Islam and proselytizing to Muslims is prohibited. The outbreak of war has inflamed sectarian tensions between the Shiite Houthis and Sunni militant groups. Some terrorist attacks since 2015 have targeted Shiite mosques, and militants killed 16 people in an attack on a Christian-run nursing home in March 2016. Houthi authorities arrested dozens of members of the Baha'i community in August, though most were later released.

Strong politicization of campus life, including tensions between supporters of the GPC and the Islah party, historically infringed on academic freedom at universities. Since 2015, Houthi forces have detained scholars as part of their crackdown on dissent. The war has also led to damage to school facilities across the country, suspensions of classes and other activities at schools and universities, and deaths of children caught in either errant or deliberate military attacks on schools. Millions of students no longer attend school as a result of the war.

Freedom of private discussion is severely limited as a result of intimidation by armed groups and unchecked surveillance by the Houthi authorities.

E. Associational and Organizational Rights: 3 / 12

Yemenis have historically enjoyed some freedom of assembly, with periodic restrictions and sometimes deadly interventions by the government. There were frequent demonstrations against both the Houthi authorities and the pro-Hadi coalition's air strikes in 2016. Houthi forces have reportedly used violence and live ammunition to suppress critical protests in areas under their control.

Freedom of association is constitutionally guaranteed. A large number of nongovernmental organizations (NGOs) work in the country, though their ability to function is restricted in practice. Houthi forces continued to raid the offices of NGOs, including human rights organizations and international aid groups, during 2016.

The law acknowledges the right of workers to form and join trade unions, but in practice these organizations have had little freedom to operate. Virtually all unions belong to a single labor federation, and the government is empowered to veto collective bargaining agreements. Normal union activity has been disrupted by the civil war and the related breakdown of the economy.

F. Rule of Law: 2 / 16

The judiciary, though nominally independent, is susceptible to interference from various political factions. Authorities have a poor record of enforcing judicial rulings, particularly those issued against prominent tribal or political leaders. Lacking an effective court system, citizens often resort to tribal forms of justice and customary law, practices that have increased as the influence of the state has continued to deteriorate. The war has periodically halted the operations of some municipal and judicial offices, although the Ministry of Justice in Sanaa continued to operate under Houthi influence in 2016.

Arbitrary detention is common, with hundreds of cases documented in the past two years. Many amount to enforced disappearances, with no available information about the victims' status or location. Detainees are often held at unofficial detention sites. As with other state institutions, security and intelligence agencies like the Political Security Organization (PSO) have been split into parallel Houthi- and Hadi-controlled structures, which each operating in territory controlled by its side in the civil war. Houthi-backed authorities controlled most of Yemen's prison facilities during 2016, and instances of torture and other abuse were reported.

The civil war has resulted in widespread violence across the country. Coalition air strikes have failed to distinguish between military and civilian targets, and artillery fire from Houthi forces has been similarly indiscriminate. A number of other armed factions, including foreign military units and extremist groups like AQAP, operate in the country with impunity for any abuses. The United States carried out roughly 30 drone strikes on suspected AQAP targets over the course of 2016, including an attack in March that reportedly killed dozens of fighters. The United Nations estimated in August that at least 10,000 people had been killed since the start of the war.

Despite the growing sectarian rift between the Sunni Muslim majority and the large Zaidi Shiite minority, Yemen is relatively homogeneous in terms of language and ethnicity. However, a caste-like minority group with East African origins, known as the Akhdam or Muhamasheen, make up as much as 10 percent of the population, according to some estimates. They face severe social discrimination and poverty.

Migrants and refugees fleeing war and poverty in the Horn of Africa continued to arrive in Yemen during 2016, with nearly 106,000 people having made the crossing as of November, an increase over the previous year. Some 268,000 refugees were already in the country as of April 2016, according to UN data. Many of those entering were seeking work in the Gulf states but faced harsh conditions, violence, and barriers to further travel once in Yemen.

Same-sex sexual activity is illegal, with possible penalties including lashes, imprisonment, and death. Due to the severe threats they face, few LGBT (lesbian, gay, bisexual, and transgender) Yemenis reveal their sexual identity.

G. Personal Autonomy and Individual Rights: 2 / 16 (− 1)

Freedom of movement, property rights, and business activity have been badly disrupted by the civil war and unchecked corruption. Estimates of internally displaced people at the end of 2016 ranged from two to three million, and movement within the country was impaired by combat, damage to infrastructure, and checkpoints at which a variety of armed groups engaged in harassment and extortion.

Women continue to face discrimination in many aspects of life. A woman must obtain permission from her husband or father to receive a passport and travel abroad, cannot confer citizenship on a foreign-born spouse, and can transfer Yemeni citizenship to her children only in special circumstances. Women are vastly underrepresented in public office; there was just one woman in the lower house of parliament before it was dissolved. School enrollment and educational attainment rates for girls fall far behind those for boys. Yemen's penal code allows lenient sentences for those convicted of "honor crimes"—assaults or killings of women by family members for alleged immoral behavior. Although the law prohibits female genital mutilation, it is still prevalent in some areas. Extremist groups have attempted to impose crude versions of Sharia in territory under their control. In January 2016, AQAP forces reportedly stoned a married woman to death for alleged adultery in southern Yemen.

The war has increased the risk of human trafficking, and after 2015 the government was no longer able to pursue antitrafficking efforts it had previously begun. Migrants, refugees, and the internally displaced are especially vulnerable to exploitation.

The conflict has also resulted in severe economic hardship for the civilian population in general. Border controls and naval blockades imposed by the Saudi-led coalition contributed to shortages of food, medicine, fuel, and other essential imports in 2016, leaving the public more exposed to famine and disease as well as coercion and deprivation by armed groups and black-market traders. About 14 million people were considered food insecure during the year, and half of them were severely food insecure.

↓ Zambia

Political Rights Rating: 4
Civil Liberties Rating: 4
Freedom Rating: 4.0
Freedom Status: Partly Free
Electoral Democracy: No

Population: 15,900,000
Capital: Lusaka

Ratings Change, Trend Arrow: Zambia's political rights rating declined from 3 to 4, and it received a downward trend arrow, due to the restrictive environment for the opposition in the run-up to general elections, including unequal media access for opposition candidates and the use of the Public Order Act to ban opposition rallies.

Ten-Year Ratings Timeline For Year Under Review (Political Rights, Civil Liberties, Status)

Year Under Review	2007	2008	2009	2010	2011	2012	2013	2014	2015	2016
Rating	3,4,PF	3,3,PF	3,4,PF	3,4,PF	3,4,PF	3,4,PF	3,4,PF	3,4,PF	3,4,PF	4,4,PF

Overview: Zambia is a multiparty democracy that holds regular elections. However, opposition parties face onerous legal and practical obstacles in their operations. The government regularly invokes the law to restrict freedom of expression, and peaceful demonstrations—particularly those organized by the opposition—are frequently restricted or banned.

KEY DEVELOPMENTS IN 2016

- President Edgar Lungu of the Patriotic Front (PF) won a narrow victory in a presidential election held in August.
- The opposition disputed the election's result, but the Constitutional Court dismissed their petition on dubious procedural grounds.
- Police frequently invoked the Public Order Act and other laws to limit opposition activities.
- The government shut down the *Post*, a critical newspaper, and suspended the broadcast licenses of a number of private media outlets, particularly those that covered the opposition.

EXECUTIVE SUMMARY

In August, President Edgar Lungu of the PF was narrowly reelected, with 50.35 percent of the vote. The opposition United Party for National Development (UPND) disputed the result on grounds that the PF and Electoral Commission of Zambia (ECZ) had worked together to manipulate the vote, and filed a complaint with the Constitutional Court. The court in early September dismissed the petition on procedural grounds, without holding a hearing on its merits. Lungu and his running mate, Inonge Wina, were sworn in for a full five-year term later that month. In concurrent parliamentary elections, the PF won 80 seats, followed by the UPND, which took 58.

Violence between supporters of the PF and the UPND had escalated weeks before the poll, leading to a localized 10-day ban on campaigning in July. Private media outlets that hosted opposition members were harassed, restricted, or shut down, while opposition political rallies were cancelled after authorities invoked the Public Order Act.

Just ahead of elections, newly appointed judges on the Constitutional Court ruled that 64 of Lungu's ministers had unconstitutionally remained in office during the campaign period, allowing them improper access to government resources.

POLITICAL RIGHTS: 23 / 40 (− 3)

A. Electoral Process: 6 / 12 (− 2)

The president and the unicameral National Assembly are elected to serve concurrent five-year terms. The National Assembly is comprised of 156 elected members, and eight members appointed by the president. In the August 2016 presidential election, Edgar Lungu of the PF was narrowly reelected with 50.35 percent of the vote, defeating Hakainde Hichilema of the UPND, who took 47.67 percent; presidential candidates were required to take over 50 percent of the vote for an outright win. In concurrent parliamentary elections, the PF won 80 seats, followed by the UPND, which took 58. A voter registration drive resulted in turnout of 56 percent, up from a historic low of 32 percent in the 2015 presidential by-election. Despite the high turnout, a concurrent referendum that would have made changes to the Bill of Rights failed to achieve the voting threshold of 50 percent needed in order to be considered binding. International election observers noted a number of serious issues, but deemed the polls generally credible.

Government repression of the opposition as well as violence during the campaign period contributed to the restrictive environment that surrounded the 2016 elections. In the weeks leading up to the poll, a number of private media outlets that had offered positive coverage of the opposition were harassed, restricted, or shut down by authorities. Opposition activities received little coverage in state media, and police improperly invoked the Public Order Act to curtail opposition events, notably those of the UPND. Political violence between supporters of the PF and the UPND escalated, leading in July to a 10-day ban by the ECZ on campaign activities in Lusaka, and in the southern district of Namwala.

In August 2016, the Constitutional Court ruled that Lungu's 64 government ministers had remained in office unconstitutionally after Parliament was adjourned in May. Among them were a number of deputy ministers whose posts had been abolished when Lungu signed an amended constitution into law in January. By remaining in office during the campaign period, the ministers had improperly retained access to government resources.

The opposition disputed the result of the presidential election, but the Constitutional Court dismissed the petition on dubious procedural grounds. On August 15, four days after the election, Lungu was declared victorious. On August 19, the UPND filed a petition at the Constitutional Court disputing the results, saying that the PF and the ECZ had worked together to manipulate the poll. After some procedural confusion, the Constitutional Court in early September, in a three to two vote, suddenly dismissed the UPND's petition without holding a hearing on its merits, saying the time period it had to decide on the matter had expired. But while the constitution mandates that the Constitutional Court must hear such electoral complaints within 14 days of their formal submission, it does not stipulate a period in which a decision must be rendered. The court was criticized by the opposition and the U.S.-based nongovernmental organization (NGO) the Carter Center, among others, as failing to meet its obligations to guarantee due process.

In January 2016, Lungu signed a package of constitutional amendments, which among other changes introduced a clause requiring presidential candidates to select a running mate who would take over the presidency in the event of the head of state's death, and a threshold of over 50 percent for an outright win in the presidential election.

Separately, some elements of a new electoral law passed in June were not fully applied during the 2016 polls, in part because stakeholders did not have enough time to thoroughly review the law's provisions, and due to discrepancies between its contents and elements of the constitution.

B. Political Pluralism and Participation: 11 / 16

Political parties are registered under the Societies Act and do not regularly face onerous registration requirements. The major political parties are the PF and the UPND. The Movement for Multiparty Democracy (MMD)—which was in office from 1991 to 2011—splintered due to infighting and PF efforts to coopt its members.

In the 2016 legislative elections, the PF won 80 seats, down from the 87 it held previously; the UPND took 58 seats, up from 31 previously; and the MMD won three seats, down from the 36 previously. The Forum for Democracy and Development (FDD) continued to hold just one seat, while independent candidates took 14 seats. During campaigning, authorities restricted numerous opposition events by invoking the Public Order Act, and made efforts to limit opposition figures' access to media coverage, both through legal harassment of outlets covering their activities and by denying them coverage on state-owned media.

The constitution prohibits the formation of political parties aimed exclusively at representing the interests of a particular ethnic group. However, a number of political parties claim tribal areas as political strongholds. The government in practice does not limit the political rights of people belonging to ethnic minorities.

C. Functioning of Government: 6 / 12 (−)

Political violence and restrictions on opposition activities ahead of the 2016 elections created an environment in which voters were less able to freely elect representatives to determine government policies.

Corruption is widespread, though the PF has taken some steps to fight graft. In 2012, the National Assembly reinserted the key "abuse of office" clause of the Anti-Corruption Act, which had been removed by the MMD-dominated legislature in 2010. The clause allows for the prosecution of public officials for abuse of authority or misuse of public funds. However, many prosecutions and court decisions in Zambia are thought to reflect political motivations.

There were some improvements in government openness and transparency in 2016. Throughout the year, ministers issued unprompted statements in parliament, while Lungu held one press conference in May—his second in two years and the PF's second in five years. Access to information legislation was drafted in 2002, but was never approved.

CIVIL LIBERTIES: 33 / 60 (−1)

D. Freedom of Expression and Belief: 10 / 16 (−1)

Freedoms of expression and of the press are constitutionally guaranteed, but the government frequently restricted these rights in practice in 2016. The public media—consisting of the Zambia National Broadcasting Corporation (ZNBC) and the widely circulated *Zambia Daily Mail* and *Times of Zambia*—continue to report along progovernment lines, and generally failed to cover the activities of the opposition during 2016 election campaigns. The ZNBC dominates the broadcast media, though several private stations, a few of which are sharply critical of the government, have the capacity to reach large portions of the population.

Journalists at community and privately owned outlets continued to face harassment by police, government officials, and PF supporters throughout 2016, especially in retaliation for hosting opposition figures, and a high rate of such harassment further encouraged self-censorship. A longstanding harassment campaign against Fred M'Membe and his *Post* newspaper continued during the year, with authorities in June closing down the publication over claims it owed 68 billion kwacha ($6.3 million) in taxes—a charge M'Membe disputed. Police confiscated copies of the newspaper and arrested M'membe, as well as his wife, Mutinta Mazoka M'Membe, and deputy managing editor Joseph Mwenda. They were later released after being charged with forgery and trespassing. Separately, the *Zambian Watchdog*, an independent news outlet, was blocked and its Facebook page was taken down in September amid unexplained circumstances. There were numerous incidents in which police interfered with the operations of radio stations that hosted opposition figures, often by suspending their licenses on dubious grounds.

Constitutionally protected religious freedom is respected in practice. The government does not restrict academic freedom. Private discussion is generally free in Zambia, though the government appears to monitor and periodically restrict access to opposition websites.

E. Associational and Organizational Rights: 7 / 12

Freedom of assembly is guaranteed under the constitution but is not consistently respected by the government. Under the Public Order Act, police must receive a week's notice before all demonstrations. The police can choose where and when rallies are held, as well as who can address them. While the law does not require people to obtain a permit for a demonstration, the police in 2016 continued to deny and cancel permits for opposition demonstrations. In July, police cancelled two UPND rallies in Lusaka's Chawama and Kanyama townships, and a UPND supporter was shot dead by police as they dispersed supporters protesting after the cancellations. In October, police in Luanshya arrested the UPND's Hichilema and his deputy, Geoffrey Bwalya Mwamba, for obstructing traffic, sedition, and holding a meeting in Mpongwe without a permit; their trial was expected to take place in early 2017.

Freedom of association is guaranteed by law but is not always respected in practice. NGOs are required to register and reregister every five years under the 2009 NGO Act, which had been signed into law but not implemented. In 2013, the PF attempted to implement the law, initially requiring every group to register or face a ban. A group of NGOs resisted it as a violation of the right to free association, and mounted a legal challenge. In 2014, the government and some NGOs agreed to resolve the dispute out of court, leading to a suspension of the forced registration provision and negotiations on a self-regulatory framework. No amendments had been made to the law by the end of 2016.

The law provides for the right to join unions, strike, and bargain collectively. Historically, Zambia's trade unions were among Africa's strongest, but the leading bodies, including the Zambia Congress of Trade Unions (ZCTU), have faced marginalization under PF rule.

F. Rule of Law: 8 / 16

While judicial independence is guaranteed by law, the government often does not respect it in practice. Zambia's courts lack qualified personnel and resources, and significant trial delays are common. In September, the Constitutional Court suddenly dismissed the UPND's challenge of the presidential election's result on dubious procedural grounds.

Pretrial detainees are sometimes held for years under harsh conditions, and many of the accused lack access to legal aid, owing to limited resources. In rural areas, customary courts of variable quality and consistency—whose decisions often conflict with the constitution and national law—decide many civil matters.

Allegations of police brutality are widespread, and security forces have generally operated with impunity. In October, state police in Lusaka assaulted Komboni Radio's director, Lesa Kasoma, after the suspension of her station by the Independent Broadcasting Authority (IBA) had ended. In October, police in Luanshya assaulted UPND supporters at a police station after Hichilema and Mwamba were arrested. There are reports of forced labor, abuse of inmates by authorities, and deplorable health conditions in the country's prisons.

Presidents since independence, including Lungu, have failed to honor the 1964 Barotse-land Agreement, which promised the Western Province limited local self-governance and future discussions of greater autonomy. Several people accused of leading a separatist movement there have faced trial for treason in recent years.

Consensual sexual activity between members of the same sex is illegal under a law criminalizing "acts against the order of nature," an offense punishable by prison sentences of between 15 years and life.

G. Personal Autonomy and Individual Rights: 8 / 16

The government generally respects the constitutionally protected rights of free internal movement and foreign travel. However, movement is often hindered by petty corruption, such as police demands for bribes at roadblocks, for which perpetrators are rarely prosecuted. During the 2016 campaigning period, purported security concerns periodically resulted in restricted movements, including use of airspace, by opposition candidates and their supporters.

Most agricultural land is administered according to customary law. However, the president retains ultimate authority over all land in the country and can intercede to block or compel its sale or transfer. Zambia ranks low on indexes of economic freedom; processes for starting and operating businesses can be opaque and time-consuming.

Societal discrimination, low literacy levels, and violence remain serious obstacles to women's rights. Discrimination against women is especially prevalent in customary courts, where they are considered subordinate with respect to property, inheritance, and marriage. Zambia's child marriage rate is one of the highest in the world. Domestic abuse is common, and traditional norms inhibit many women from reporting assaults. Rape is widespread and punishable by up to life in prison with hard labor; however, the law is not adequately enforced. Spousal rape is not considered a crime.

Child labor in dangerous industries, including mining, is a problem in Zambia. According to the U.S. State Department's 2016 Trafficking in Persons report, the government does not fully comply with the minimum standards for the elimination of trafficking, but is making efforts to do so.

Zimbabwe

Political Rights Rating: 5
Civil Liberties Rating: 5
Freedom Rating: 5.0
Freedom Status: Partly Free
Electoral Democracy: No

Population: 16,000,000
Capital: Harare

Ten-Year Ratings Timeline For Year Under Review (Political Rights, Civil Liberties, Status)

Year Under Review	2007	2008	2009	2010	2011	2012	2013	2014	2015	2016
Rating	7,6,NF	7,6,NF	6,6,NF	6,6,NF	6,6,NF	6,6,NF	5,6,NF	5,6,NF	5,5,PF	5,5,PF

Overview: President Robert Mugabe and his Zimbabwe African National Union–Patriotic Front (ZANU-PF) have dominated Zimbabwean politics since independence in 1980, in part by carrying out severe and often violent crackdowns against the political opposition, critical media, and other dissenters. A fragile power-sharing arrangement helped the country recover somewhat in the years after a 2008 political and economic crisis. However, in recent years the ZANU-PF has been fragmenting as politicians jockey for position to succeed the aging Mugabe. Meanwhile, the country has seen burgeoning protests over issues including rampant corruption and the deteriorating economy.

KEY DEVELOPMENTS IN 2016:

- Protest actions initiated by hashtag campaigns, such as #ThisFlag and #Tajamuka, began in June, including a July 6 strike that paralyzed much of the country. Police violently dispersed many demonstrations, and hundreds of protesters remained in detention at year's end.
- Factional fighting within the ZANU-PF over who will succeed 92-year-old president Mugabe intensified during the year, and in July, the Zimbabwe National Liberation War Veterans Association (ZNLWVA), previously a key ally of Mugabe, publicly withdrew its support.
- A cash crisis had dire effects on the economy, as public-sector workers saw their salaries repeatedly delayed, and banks imposed limits on withdrawals.
- In November, the introduction of deeply unpopular bond notes raised concerns about a return to the hyperinflation experienced about a decade earlier.

EXECUTIVE SUMMARY

In 2016, factional wars within the ruling ZANU-PF party intensified, contributing to a further crisis of governance within Zimbabwe. Politicians—including President Mugabe's wife Grace Mugabe and Vice President Emmerson Mnangagwa—jockeyed for position amid widespread speculation about the state of Mugabe's health. In a surprising turn, leaders of the ZNLWVA—who had backed Mugabe since the struggle for independence—withdrew their support in July, calling Mugabe "dictatorial" and blaming him for strife across the country. Although the opposition remains weak and divided, at year's end it came together to demand electoral reforms ahead of the 2018 elections. In December, ZANU-PF elected Mugabe as its presidential candidate for 2018.

Meanwhile, a cash crisis paralyzed the Zimbabwean economy. The crisis left the government unable to pay civil servants—who make up a significant portion of the country's workforce—for long periods of time, and forced banks to place strict limits on cash withdrawals.

The effects of the economic crisis and other grievances prompted a wave of protests led by social movements including This Flag and Tajamuka. In response to the protests, authorities violently disbursed gatherings and arrested hundreds of people, many of whom remained in detention at year's end. Zimbabwean activists reported that state security forces carried out threats, abductions, and torture of social-movement leaders.

In an attempt to fix the economy, the government introduced so-called bond notes in November. The unpopular move was widely regarded as a means of reintroducing the Zimbabwean dollar, which was abandoned in 2009 after the inflation rate had reached 13 billion percent the previous year. In the meantime, rampant corruption—including an unaccounted-for $15 billion in diamond revenue—as well as repercussions of land-reform policies and an unclear indigenization policy, continued to hamper economic recovery.

POLITICAL RIGHTS: 12 / 40

A. Electoral Process: 3 / 12

Zimbabwe has a bicameral legislature. In the lower chamber, the 270-seat National Assembly, 210 members are elected through a first-past-the-post system with one member per constituency, and 60 female members are elected by proportional representation. The 80-seat Senate includes six members from each of Zimbabwe's 10 provinces who are elected through proportional representation, and 20 appointed members, including 18 traditional leaders and two members representing people with disabilities. Members in both houses serve five-year terms.

The 2013 constitution limited the president to two five-year terms, removed the presidential power to veto legislation and dismiss Parliament, and devolved some powers to the provinces. The new constitution also empowered the president's political party, not parliament, to select a presidential successor in the case of the president's retirement or death while in office. In 2014, amendments were made to the ruling ZANU-PF party's constitution that changed the procedures under which members of the party's executive, including its president, were to be appointed. The amendments, which were reportedly approved through methods falling outside proper procedures, left the country without a clear succession path should the president die or retire. Despite being 92 years old and in visibly fragile health, ZANU-PF in December 2016 endorsed Mugabe as its candidate for the 2018 presidential election.

Although far less violent than the 2008 elections, the 2013 presidential and parliamentary elections were marred by serious irregularities. Mugabe won the presidency with 61 percent of the vote; his opponent, Morgan Tsvangirai, head of the main opposition Movement for Democratic Change-Tsvangirai (MDC-T), took 34 percent. ZANU-PF also captured 197 seats in the National Assembly, compared with 70 for the MDC-T. The Zimbabwe Electoral Coalition (ZEC) reported widespread electoral violations, but monitors from the African Union (AU) and the Southern African Development Community (SADC) deemed the irregularities not severe enough to have affected the result.

In September 2016, by-elections were held in the constituency of Norton. Former ZANU-PF member Temba Mliswa, who ran as an independent, defeated ZANU-PF's candidate. Allegations of violence and intimidation by ZANU-PF members against Mliswa's supporters were reported; election monitors also reported that ZANU-PF had attempted to buy votes by giving away food and land.

The 2012 Electoral Amendment Act reconstituted the ZEC with new commissioners nominated by all political parties. However, its independence from ZANU-PF has been questioned, and opposition figures object that its chairwoman also serves as head of the Judicial Service Commission. The 2012 act also mandated, among other provisions, that the voter rolls be kept in both printed and electronic form by the ZEC and be provided to the public upon request. Legal loopholes that permit the printing of extra ballots, unfair media coverage, and interference of police officers in voter choice remain unrevised.

In 2016, the MDC-T continued to boycott by-elections until electoral reforms were put in place. In August, 18 political parties that had united in 2015 to form the National Election Reform Agenda (NERA) held a massive demonstration, demanding electoral reforms before the 2018 elections. Many have expressed doubt that reforms will be achieved, and in September 2016, Jonathan Moyo, minister of higher and tertiary education, stated that implementing them would constitute "reforming ourselves out of power."

In August 2016, the ZEC confirmed that, due to lack of funds, it was registering voters only in constituencies where by-elections were being held, despite the 2004 Electoral Act mandating that voter registration be an ongoing process. Opposition leaders dismissed the excuse, and allege that disfranchising voters is one of the ways that ZANU-PF is already rigging the 2018 elections.

B. Political Pluralism and Participation: 6 / 16

ZANU-PF has dominated politics since Zimbabwe's independence in 1980; however, intense infighting over who will succeed Mugabe has led to the formation of splinter groups within and outside the party. Joice Mujuru, who was replaced as vice president in 2014 and expelled from ZANU-PF, emerged as the leader of a breakaway faction, People First, during 2015; many of her supporters have been purged from political posts since her expulsion. Current vice president Mnangagwa heads another faction that draws significant support from the military. A relatively new third faction, known as G40, is comprised of younger party members who oppose liberal reforms. President Mugabe's wife, Grace Mugabe, has also emerged as a political leader and draws support from G40.

The main opposition party, the MDC, has also split into multiple factions but the MDC-T remains the largest opposition group. In August 2016, Tsvangirai and Mujuru held a well-attended joint rally that prompted talk of a formal alliance. In December, numerous opposition parties held talks to discuss forming a united coalition against the ZANU-PF.

The ruling party uses state institutions as well as violence and intimidation to punish opposition politicians, their supporters, and critical political activists. In October 2016, MDC-T lawmakers reportedly received threatening text messages warning them not to disrupt Mugabe's annual speech to parliament. In 2016, the opposition People's Democratic Party (PDP) repeatedly accused ZANU-PF of coercing traditional chiefs into intimidating opposition supporters on its behalf. In September, the Zimbabwe Human Rights Commission released a report alleging that the government uses food aid politically, giving it to supporters and denying it to areas where support for opposition parties is strong.

Zimbabwe's ethnic Shona majority dominates ZANU-PF and the MDC-T, and in the past, members of the Ndebele minority have complained of political marginalization.

C. Functioning of Government: 3 / 12

The civilian leadership has only partial electoral legitimacy, and the commanders of the highly partisan military, police, and intelligence agencies continue to play a central role in government decision making. The Central Intelligence Office (CIO) remains closely tied to the presidency and free from any substantial regulation by the legislature or civilian bureaucracy.

Due to the succession crisis and the state of the economy, much everyday government activity has been brought to a standstill. At the beginning of 2016, civil servants had not yet been given their November 2015 bonuses; the payments, as well as regular salaries, were repeatedly delayed throughout 2016. Claims of pay discrimination surfaced, with the government allegedly paying members of the military first and teachers last. The economic crisis has also resulted in reduced public services, with the situation exacerbated by the worst drought in 35 years.

Government effectiveness has been undermined by the use of appointments for political patronage and nepotism. In October 2016, there was public outcry over the appointment of Mugabe's son-in-law as the chief operating officer of Air Zimbabwe, the ailing national airline. The president regularly reshuffles the cabinet, and in 2015 increased the number of ministers to more than 72, each of whom receives large salaries and allowances, vehicles, housing, and special staff.

Corruption is endemic. In September 2016, a local firm released an audit of the Zimbabwe Revenue Authority revealing that over US$20 million had been lost through corrupt activities within the agency. In February 2016, Mugabe admitted that $US15 billion worth of diamond revenue was unaccounted for.

The Zimbabwe Anti-Corruption Commission (ZACC) has little independent investigative or enforcement capacity. In July 2016, the ZACC, originally housed under the Ministry of Home Affairs, was moved to the Office of the President and Cabinet. The ZACC has reportedly fallen prey to the ongoing factionalism within ZANU-PF, with different groups attempting to persuade it to prosecute members of rival factions. The body's efforts to arrest Moyo on charges of illegal diversion of government funds were reportedly halted by Mugabe in October 2016, though he was eventually arrested the following month, with a case against him ongoing at year's end.

CIVIL LIBERTIES: 20 / 60

D. Freedom of Expression and Belief: 8 / 16

Although the constitution protects freedoms of the media and expression, the country's repressive legal framework—including the Access to Information and Protection of Privacy Act, the Official Secrets Act, the Public Order and Security Act (POSA), and the Criminal Law (Codification and Reform) Act (CLCRA)—has yet to be reformed.

In February 2016, the Constitutional Court declared that Section 96 of the CLCRA, which allowed authorities to impose prison sentences of up to two years for defamation, was unconstitutional. However, throughout 2016 police continued to arrest and charge individuals who criticized Mugabe under CLCRA provisions prohibiting insult or so-called nuisance crimes. In July, the ZNLWVA information secretary was charged under the insult law for disseminating a statement that was sharply critical of the president, but charges against him and several other ZNLWVA members involved in the case were effectively dismissed in November. In April, a man was charged with criminal nuisance for sharing an audio message on WhatsApp that alluded to Mugabe's poor health and waning government duties.

The state-controlled Zimbabwe Broadcasting Corporation (ZBC) continues to dominate broadcast media. The government also controls the two main daily newspapers, though there are a number of independent print outlets. In July 2016, the Constitutional Court ruled that all Zimbabweans with a device capable of receiving radio or television signals must pay license fees to the ZBC. Commercial radio licenses issued to date have generally gone to state-controlled companies or individuals with close links to the ruling party.

Internet access and usage have expanded rapidly in recent years despite frequent power outages. In April, Mugabe warned citizens that the government would begin regulating access to different websites, adding that China's government had taken similar actions in the name of national security.

While internet access is rarely blocked or filtered, in July 2016 communications networks were disrupted amid escalating protests. Also in July, the Postal and Telecommunications Regulatory Authority of Zimbabwe warned citizens against "the gross irresponsible use of social media and telecommunication services," threatening to disconnect and prosecute anyone sharing material considered subversive. In August, the country's army commander characterized the use of social media to organize protests against the government as "cyber warfare," and threatened a response. That month, a draft Computer Crime and Cyber Crime Bill containing provisions that allowed police to intercept private communications and seize electronic devices began circulating, though it had not been passed by year's end.

Freedom of religion is generally respected in Zimbabwe.

Political pressure on teachers and academics has eased in recent years, though the state still responds with force to student protests. Prominent academics rank among the government's most vociferous critics, and some are allowed to operate with little interference. Mugabe serves as the chancellor of all eight state-run universities, and the Ministry of Higher Education supervises education policy at universities. Nevertheless, there is respect for academic freedom in many government institutions.

Zimbabweans enjoy some freedom and openness in private discussion, but official monitoring of public gatherings, prosecution of offenses like insulting the president, and the threat of political violence serve as deterrents to unfettered speech.

E. Associational and Organizational Rights: 4 / 12

Freedom of assembly and association are guaranteed in the constitution but are subject to restrictions. In 2016, citizens increasingly engaged in public protests at which they decried economic difficulties and poor governance, and demanded electoral reforms. Prominent protest movements included This Flag and Tajamuka, both of which heavily employed social media to spread their messages and organize protest actions, including a July strike that shut down normal activities across large parts of the country. In response, the police and army violently dispersed numerous protests, drawing sharp rebukes from various governments and civil society organizations. Hundreds of demonstrators were arrested and charged with criminal offenses under the CLCRA, and at the end of 2016, over 100 people who had protested against the government were awaiting trial on trumped-up charges, according to Zimbabwe Lawyers for Human Rights. Three activists were reportedly abducted and tortured by state security agents in the fall.

The POSA is routinely used by the police to deny protest permits. In October 2016, the Harare High Court upheld a 30-day ban on protests. While many opposition and grassroots protests were dispersed, large ZANU-PF rallies were permitted to take place.

Nongovernmental organizations (NGOs) are active and generally professional. They remain subject to legal restrictions under the POSA, the CLCRA, and the Private Voluntary Organisations Act, despite the rights laid out in the constitution. In September 2016, two employees of the Crisis in Zimbabwe Coalition, an alliance of civil society organizations, received anonymous telephone threats for arranging mass protests, with some observers alleging that the threats originated with the CIO.

The Labour Act allows the government to veto collective-bargaining agreements that it deems harmful to the economy. Strikes are allowed except in "essential" industries. The

Zimbabwe Congress of Trade Union in June, following a strike that began in March by unpaid National Railways of Zimbabwe employees, submitted a complaint to the International Labor Organization requesting it mediate between the government and the workers.

F. Rule of Law: 3 / 16

The executive branch has exerted considerable pressure on the courts or sought to circumvent their authority over the years, but a recent series of rulings appears to reflect increasing judicial independence. In August 2016, the High Court ruled that a major opposition rally could go forward after police in Harare had tried to suppress it. (Police violently dispersed the protest anyway, in violation of the order.) In July, a judge dismissed criminal charges against Pastor Evan Mawarire, leader of the This Flag movement, who according to his lawyer had been accused of trying to overthrow the government. In another decision celebrated by rights activists, a High Court judge in September suspended a two-week ban on demonstrations. Days ahead of the decision, Mugabe had claimed that judges who ruled to permit demonstrations over police objections endangered the public peace, and the remarks were widely interpreted as an attempt to intimidate members of the judiciary.

Toward the year's end, a court battle emerged concerning the procedure by which the chief justice is appointed. Observers said the battle, which involved a proposed constitutional amendment that would allow the president to appoint the chief justice alone rather than selecting from candidates screened by the Judicial Service Committee, reflected factional wrangling within ZANU-PF. Separately, in July, Attorney General Johannes Tomana was suspended on abuse-of-office allegations. While the charges may be founded, they are also widely viewed as part of ZANU-PF's factional quarrels.

The constitution gives arrested suspects the right to contact relatives, advisers, and visitors; to be informed of their rights; and to be released after 48 hours unless a court orders them to remain detained. However, these rights are often violated in practice. Security forces abuse citizens, frequently ignoring basic rights regarding detention, searches, and seizures. During the fall, reports emerged that security forces had abducted and tortured protesters.

Lengthy pretrial detention remains a problem, and despite some improvements in recent years, prison conditions are harsh and sometimes life-threatening. Overcrowding, poor sanitation, and food shortages have contributed to the spread of HIV/AIDS, tuberculosis, and other illnesses among inmates.

Discrimination on the basis of a broad range of characteristics is prohibited under the 2013 constitution. However, discrimination on the basis of sexual orientation or gender identity is not expressly prohibited. Sex between men is a criminal offense and can be punished with a fine and up to one year in prison. Mugabe has been vocal in his opposition to same-sex sexual relations, and LGBT (lesbian, gay, bisexual, and transgender) groups have been subject to regular harassment by security forces.

G. Personal Autonomy and Individual Rights: 5 / 16

Passport offices, which in the past were characterized by long queues and instances of bribery, have since become more efficient. However, high passport fees continue to inhibit legal travel abroad. Badly underfunded immigration and border authorities lack the capacity to efficiently enforce travel restrictions, and border posts have been described as overcrowded and staffed by corrupt officials.

Property rights are not respected. In January 2016, the government demolished the homes of over 100 families who resided on land intended for the expansion of Harare International Airport. In response to the residents' subsequent lawsuit, the High Court ruled the following month that the demolitions, which took place without notice and without a court order, were illegal.

In rural areas, the nationalization of land has left both commercial farmers and small-holders with limited security of tenure. Farmers without a title to their land have little collateral to use for bank loans. In September 2016, the ZANU-PF youth secretary called for the seizure of land from the few remaining white farmers. In February, around 90 black farmers who had benefited from previous land reform programs received 90-day eviction notices from the government. While the orders did not provide any explanation, some observers suggested that their land may be used to reward youths and war veterans who had assisted in ousting former party executives. In August, the ZNLWVA secretary general's farm was occupied by apparent ZANU-PF supporters, following his participation in a statement critical of Mugabe; a court later ordered them to leave. Also in August, it was reported that the government might charge rent to farmers who had settled on land that was confiscated during the nationalization process. Failure to pay could result in repossession.

The 2007 Indigenization and Economic Empowerment Act stipulates that 51 percent of the shares in all large companies operating in Zimbabwe must be owned by black Zimbabweans, and the government has indicated that it will close firms that do not comply. The law has discouraged foreign investment.

In November 2016, the Reserve Bank of Zimbabwe introduced "bond notes," a new currency pegged to the U.S. dollar, into circulation. The issuance occurred before a case could be heard in the High Court on the legality to do so. The unpopular move was widely regarded as a means of reintroducing the Zimbabwean dollar, which was abandoned in 2009 after the inflation rate had reached 13 billion percent the previous year.

In March 2016, the government banned import of certain products in an attempt to reduce the country's import bill and protect local businesses. The move provoked protests by informal cross-border traders, whose livelihoods would be affected.

Women enjoy extensive legal protections, and serve as ministers and deputies in the national and local governments. However, societal discrimination and domestic violence persist, and sexual abuse is widespread. In 2016, there were reports of female lawmakers being assaulted while carrying out government business. In October 2016, MDC-T legislator Jessie Majome was attacked by suspected ZANU-PF youths while attending a public hearing on electoral reforms. Also that month, police officers allegedly sexually molested two female MDC-T legislators on the floor of the National Assembly while the police attempted to remove another MDC-T legislator. A ZANU-PF legislator, Munyaradzi Kereke, was convicted of rape in July in a private lawsuit; though the crime occurred six years earlier, the attorney general's office had declined to prosecute him.

In January 2016, the Constitutional Court banned child marriage and set the minimum age of marriage for both men and women at 18. This nullified part of the Marriage Act, which had set the minimum age of marriage for women at 16, compared to 18 for men.

Zimbabwean women and girls are subjected to sex trafficking and forced labor, particularly in border areas. In 2016, 150 Zimbabwean women that had been trafficked to the Middle East were brought home, with the assistance of civil society and the Zimbabwe government. However, around 60 women still remain.

Abkhazia

Political Rights Rating: 4
Civil Liberties Rating: 5
Freedom Rating: 4.5
Freedom Status: Partly Free

Population: 243,000

Ten-Year Ratings Timeline For Year Under Review (Political Rights, Civil Liberties, Status)

Year Under Review	2007	2008	2009	2010	2011	2012	2013	2014	2015	2016
Rating	5,5,PF	5,5,PF	5,5,PF	5,5,PF	5,5,PF	4,5,PF	4,5,PF	4,5,PF	4,5,PF	4,5,PF

Overview: Abkhazia, a breakaway region of Georgia, has enjoyed de facto independence since the end of a civil conflict in 1993, and the last pocket of government-controlled territory was captured by separatist forces during a war that drew in Russian troops in 2008. The Abkhaz government is financially dependent on Russia, which maintains a military presence in the territory and is one of a handful of states that recognizes Abkhazia's independence. Nevertheless, the political system features significant opposition and civil society activity, and most residents reportedly oppose formal annexation by Russia. While local broadcast media are largely controlled by the government, there are some independent print and online outlets. Freedom of assembly is usually respected. Ongoing problems include a deeply flawed criminal justice system and discrimination against ethnic Georgians.

KEY DEVELOPMENTS IN 2016:

- In July, a referendum on whether to hold a snap presidential election failed to gain the required voter turnout after it was boycotted by both the opposition and government supporters.
- In December, amid opposition demands for his resignation, President Raul Khajimba agreed to appoint opposition nominees to a number of government posts.
- Local elections were held in April, and polling places were opened in September to allow residents to participate in Russia's parliamentary elections.
- In February, Khajimba signed legislation that criminalized all abortions in an apparent attempt to increase the birth rate.

EXECUTIVE SUMMARY

In April 2016, Amtsakhara and other opposition parties petitioned the Central Election Commission (CEC) to hold a referendum on an early presidential election, having collected some 19,000 signatures, almost double the required 10,000. Their grievances against incumbent president Raul Khajimba included his alleged failure to implement democratic reforms, work cooperatively with other parties and the parliament, and improve the economy and state management of Russian aid.

Khajimba allowed the referendum to proceed in July, but gave the opposition little time to prepare and refused to postpone it. Amid growing acrimony, both the president and the opposition ultimately urged supporters to boycott the vote, and it garnered turnout of just 1.23 percent, rendering it invalid. The opposition then continued to demand Khajimba's resignation.

In December, he reached a compromise with some elements of the opposition, agreeing to appoint its nominees as vice premier, prosecutor general, and various deputy ministers and agency heads. The opposition would also be able to fill positions at the CEC and the Constitutional Court. Furthermore, the president expressed support for proposed constitutional amendments that would bar him from dismissing the premier without the parliament's consent, among other changes. Amtsakhara did not join the agreement.

The year featured several incidents of political violence. In April, the car of an opposition lawmaker was blown up in Sukhumi, though it was not occupied at the time; he had strongly objected to a proposal that month—which was ultimately defeated—to lift a ban on selling land to foreigners. In July, opposition protesters repeatedly attempted to storm the Interior Ministry building. And in October, a suicide bomber killed himself outside the headquarters of the state broadcaster.

Local elections held across Abkhazia in April drew a relatively low turnout, and the voting was postponed in the Gali district because so many of its ethnic Georgian residents lacked documents from Abkhaz authorities. In September, nine polling stations were opened across Abkhazia so that residents, most of whom hold Russian passports, could participate in Russia's parliamentary elections. Georgia strongly condemned the move.

In November, in keeping with a treaty originally signed in 2014, Russia ratified a plan to form a joint military force with Abkhazia that would be under Russian command. Some elements of the treaty had generated considerable resistance in Abkhazia during 2015 on the grounds that they infringed on sovereignty, but implementation continued to move forward in 2016.

Political Rights: 18 / 40 (− 1)
A. Electoral Process: 6 / 12
B. Political Pluralism and Participation: 8 / 16
C. Functioning of Government: 4 / 12 (− 1)

CIVIL LIBERTIES: 23 / 60
D. Freedom of Expression and Belief: 8 / 16
E. Associational and Organizational Rights: 6 / 12
F. Rule of Law: 4 / 16
G. Personal Autonomy and Individual Rights: 5 / 16

This territory report has been abridged for *Freedom in the World 2017*. For background information on political rights and civil liberties in Abkhazia, see *Freedom in the World 2016*.

Crimea

Political Rights Rating: 7
Civil Liberties Rating: 6
Freedom Rating: 6.5
Freedom Status: Not Free

Population: 2,300,000

Ten-Year Ratings Timeline For Year Under Review (Political Rights, Civil Liberties, Status)

Year Under Review Rating	2007	2008	2009	2010	2011	2012	2013	2014	2015	2016
	—	—	—	—	—	—	—	7,6,NF	7,6,NF	7,6,NF

Overview: In early 2014, Russian forces invaded the autonomous Ukrainian region of Crimea, which was then quickly incorporated into the Russian Federation through a referendum that was widely condemned as having been conducted in violation of international law. The occupation government severely limits political and civil rights, has silenced independent media, and employs antiterrorism and other laws against political dissidents. Some members of the peninsula's indigenous Tatar minority continue to vocally oppose the annexation, despite the risk of imprisonment.

KEY DEVELOPMENTS IN 2016:

- In November, the International Criminal Court stated in preliminary findings that the annexation of Crimea constituted a violation of Ukraine's territorial integrity and was "equivalent to an international armed conflict between Ukraine and the Russian Federation."
- In September, elections for the Russian State Duma were held in Crimea. Local rights activists reported that some residents were threatened with dismissal from their jobs if they failed to vote, or were pressured to attend a preelection rally for Russian president Vladimir Putin's United Russia party.
- Crimean Tatar activist Ervin Ibragimov was abducted in May, and his whereabouts were unknown at year's end.

EXECUTIVE SUMMARY

Russian occupation authorities enforced their control over Crimea for a third year in 2016, notably repressing Crimean Tatar activists, further limiting the media available to Crimean residents, and pressuring local voters to participate in Russia's State Duma elections in September. In August, President Putin claimed that Russia had thwarted an incursion into the territory by Ukrainian saboteurs planning terrorist acts, though he provided little evidence to support the allegations, which Ukrainian authorities said were fabricated. The following day, Putin accused Ukraine of attempting to provoke violence in Crimea, and Russian officials announced naval exercises in the Black Sea. Separately, Russian authorities banned the Mejlis, the official but nongovernmental representative body of the Crimean Tatar people, purportedly because its members engaged in "extremist activity." Both episodes reflected Russian authorities' strategy of pointing to the alleged presence of extremists as justification for tightening their grip on the territory.

In addition to the Mejlis closure, occupation authorities—whose leadership was largely imposed by Moscow and included individuals with ties to organized crime—continued to harass members of the Crimean Tatar minority, with the most outspoken activists facing political persecution. Since the 2014 invasion, Tatar media outlets have been shuttered and many Tatar-owned businesses arbitrarily closed.

While some Crimeans hoped that the Russian occupation would improve their standard of living, prices for many goods have soared, wages and pensions have not kept pace, and the important tourism and agriculture industries are under heavy strain.

The international community continues to oppose the Russian occupation of Crimea. In late 2016, the United States imposed new sanctions against Russian firms and individuals doing business in Crimea—particularly those involved in the construction of a bridge connecting the peninsula to the Russian mainland—and against a number of officials in the occupation government.

POLITICAL RIGHTS: − 1 / 40

A. Electoral Process: 0 / 12

Under the administrative system established by Russia, the Crimean Peninsula is divided into the Republic of Crimea and the federal city of Sevastopol, a port of roughly 380,000 residents that had also been governed separately under Ukrainian control. Sevastopol's political institutions largely mirror those of Crimea proper.

The head of the Republic of Crimea is elected by its legislature, the State Council of Crimea, for up to two consecutive five-year terms. Lawmakers choose the leader based on a list of nominees prepared by the Russian president. In October 2014, they unanimously elected Sergey Aksyonov as the head of the republic, and he simultaneously served as prime minister. Aksyonov had been the acting leader of Crimea since February 2014, when a group of armed men forced legislators to elect him prime minister at gunpoint. He had reputedly been involved in organized crime during the 1990s.

The State Council consists of 75 members elected for a term of five years. Two-thirds of the members are elected by party list and one-third in single-member districts. Legislative elections under the Russian-organized Crimean constitution took place in September 2014, on the same day as Russia's regional elections. All of the parties allowed to participate supported the annexation, pro-Ukraine parties were excluded, and the Tatar minority boycotted the voting. The ruling party in Russia, United Russia, took 70 seats, while the ultranationalist LDPR (formerly known as the Liberal Democratic Party of Russia) secured the remaining 5 seats. No other parties crossed the 5 percent vote threshold to enter the legislature. The elections received little international recognition.

In September 2016 the occupation authorities conducted elections for the Russian State Duma in Crimea. Local rights activists reported that public- and private-sector workers were threatened with dismissal from their jobs if they failed to vote, and some municipal officials were pressured to attend a preelection rally for United Russia.

B. Political Pluralism and Participation: 0 / 16

The occupation authorities use intimidation and harassment to eliminate any public opposition to Russia's annexation of Crimea and to the current government. Russia's Federal Security Service (FSB), the local police, and "self-defense" units made up of pro-Russian residents enforce this political order. Ukrainian political parties are not able to operate, and the Crimean Tatars—the only group that has continued to openly oppose the Russian occupation—have faced considerable political persecution. The headquarters of the 33-member Mejlis, the Tatars' representative body, was seized and closed by the authorities in 2014. The incumbent chairman of the body, Refat Chubarov, and Tatar leader Mustafa Dzhemilev have been banned from the territory since then. In April 2016, the Russian Justice Ministry suspended the Mejlis for "extremist activity." A week later, Crimea's Supreme Court formally banned the Mejlis, and the Russian Supreme Court confirmed the decision in September.

Political dissidents are subject to harassment, arrest, and persecution. Tatar activist Ervin Ibragimov was abducted in May 2016, and his whereabouts were unknown at year's end. Ilmi Umerov, a former Mejlis deputy chairman who has vocally rejected the annexation, was forced into a psychiatric hospital in August. He was released three weeks later, but faced charges under a section of the Russian criminal code allowing authorities to prosecute public opposition to the annexation. Several Tatar activists were arrested in October and charged with belonging to the Islamist group Hizb ut-Tahrir, which is banned in Russia.

C. Functioning of Government: 0 / 12

All major policy decisions are made in Moscow and executed by Putin's representatives in Crimea or the local authorities, who were not freely elected and are beholden to Moscow. The collapse of the territory's key tourism and agricultural sectors following the occupation has left Crimea heavily reliant on Russian subsidies. International sanctions and the lack of a land connection to Russia put the region under severe logistical stress.

Bureaucratic infighting, corruption scandals, and tensions between federal and local authorities interfered with governance in 2016, particularly as various Russian companies sought access to Crimea's assets. The FSB has arrested a number of Crimean officials as part of an ostensible campaign against the territory's widespread corruption. Many of the arrests were related to allegations that local authorities embezzled Russian funds meant to support the occupation.

DISCRETIONARY POLITICAL RIGHTS QUESTION B: − 1 / 0

Russian and local pro-Russian officials' policies and actions in Crimea have led to an influx of 30,000 to 35,000 Russian troops and additional civilian personnel, an outflow of many ethnic Ukrainians, and the persecution of ethnic Tatars. The Russian occupation also represents a major setback to Tatars' long-term campaign to reestablish property and other rights that were lost in a Soviet-era mass deportation of the group.

CIVIL LIBERTIES: 9 / 60

D. Freedom of Expression and Belief: 3 / 16

Free speech is severely limited in Crimea. In addition to other restrictive Russian laws, an amendment to the Russian criminal code that took effect in 2014 banned public calls for action aimed at violating Russia's territorial integrity, meaning statements against the annexation, including in the media, can be punished with up to five years in prison.

The Russian telecommunications agency Roskomnadzor required all media outlets to seek registration under Russian regulations by April 2015. Before the annexation, there were approximately 3,000 outlets in Crimea. After the 2015 deadline, Roskomnadzor reported that 232 outlets were registered and authorized to operate. The occupation authorities have essentially cut the territory off from access to Ukrainian television, with armed men seizing the transmission centers in 2014 and imposing Russian broadcasts. Independent and pro-Ukraine media no longer function in Crimea, nor do outlets serving the Tatar community.

Crimea's internet service providers must operate under Russia's draconian media laws. In April 2016, journalist Mykola Semena of the news website Krym.Realii, the Crimean service of Radio Free Europe/Radio Liberty (RFE/RL), was taken into custody in connection with an article in which he expressed support for a civic blockade of the peninsula imposed by Ukrainian activists. He faced a possible five-year prison sentence for extremism. Also during the year, the authorities took steps to block online news outlets including Krym.Realii, Sobytiya Kryma, ATR, and Chernomorskaya TRC.

The occupation authorities have forced religious organizations to reregister. At the time of annexation, there were approximately 1,400 registered religious groups in Crimea and 674 additional communities operating without registration. As of August 2015, there were only 53 locally registered religious organizations, in addition to a few groups registered through an alternative procedure in Moscow. Mosques associated with Crimean Tatars have been denied permission to register. Followers of the Ukrainian Orthodox Church, which has not been banned, face pressure from occupation authorities. In October 2016, a Ukrainian

Orthodox official was briefly detained upon returning to Crimea after attending a session of the Parliamentary Assembly of the Council of Europe (PACE), at which he condemned the repression of Ukrainian Orthodox Christians and of the Ukrainian language in Crimea.

Schools must use the Russian state curriculum. Instruction in the Ukrainian language has been almost completely eliminated, and authorities have also drastically reduced the availability of education in the Tatar language.

The FSB reportedly encourages residents to inform on individuals who express opposition to the annexation, and a climate of fear and intimidation seriously inhibits private discussion of political matters.

E. Associational and Organizational Rights: 1 / 12

Freedoms of assembly and association are restricted. The de facto authorities, including the FSB, repress all independent political and civic organizations. Nongovernmental organizations (NGOs) are subject to harsh Russian laws that enable state interference and obstruct foreign funding.

Trade union rights are formally protected under Russian law, but limited in practice. As in both Ukraine and Russia, employers are often able to engage in antiunion discrimination and violate collective-bargaining rights. Pro-Russian authorities have threatened to nationalize property owned by labor unions in Crimea.

F. Rule of Law: 0 / 16

Under Moscow's rule, Crimea is subject to the Russian judicial system, which lacks independence and is effectively dominated by the executive branch. Russian laws bar dual citizenship for public officials, and Crimean judges were required to receive Russian citizenship in order to return to their positions after the annexation.

Crimes attributed to "self-defense" units and other pro-Russian forces since 2014—including the alleged murder of some activists, abductions and disappearances, and arbitrary expropriations—have gone unpunished. Russia continues to imprison prominent dissidents such as Ukrainian film director Oleh Sentsov, who actively opposed Russia's annexation of Crimea, and his codefendant, activist Oleksandr Kolchenko, both of whom received lengthy prison sentences in 2015. Sentsov has reported abuse in custody, and many international leaders and human rights organizations designated the two as political prisoners.

After the annexation, Crimea became subject to Russia's 2013 law banning dissemination of information that promotes "nontraditional sexual relationships," which tightly restricts the activities of LGBT (lesbian, gay, bisexual, and transgender) people and organizations.

G. Personal Autonomy and Individual Rights: 6 / 16

The occupation authorities have sought to compel Crimea's residents to accept Russian citizenship and surrender their Ukrainian passports. Those who fail to do so face the threat of dismissal from employment, loss of property rights, inability to travel to mainland Ukraine and elsewhere, and eventual deportation as foreigners.

Property rights are poorly protected, and the Russian invasion has resulted in a redistribution of assets in favor of Russian and pro-Russian entities. The occupation authorities have seized Ukrainian state property, and a law passed by the Crimean legislature in 2014 allows the government to condemn and purchase "strategic" assets.

Same-sex marriage is not legal under Russian law. Government officials demonstrate little interest in or understanding of gender-equality issues. Domestic violence against women remains a serious problem in Crimea, and Russian laws do not offer strong protections. Discrimination on the basis of gender, physical appearance, and age is not uncommon. Women hold 14 of the 75 seats in the State Council of Crimea.

As in both Ukraine and Russia, migrant workers, women, and children are vulnerable to trafficking for the purposes of forced labor or sexual exploitation.

Gaza Strip

Political Rights Rating: 7
Civil Liberties Rating: 6
Freedom Rating: 6.5
Freedom Status: Not Free

Population: 1,753,000

Note: The numerical ratings and status listed above do not reflect conditions in Israel or the West Bank, which are examined in separate reports. Prior to its 2011 edition, *Freedom in the World* featured one report for Israeli-occupied portions of the West Bank and Gaza Strip and another for Palestinian-administered portions.

Ten-Year Ratings Timeline For Year Under Review (Political Rights, Civil Liberties, Status)

Year Under Review	2007	2008	2009	2010	2011	2012	2013	2014	2015	2016
Rating	—	—	—	6,6,NF	6,6,NF	6,6,NF	7,6,NF	7,6,NF	7,6,NF	7,6,NF

Overview: The political rights and civil liberties of Gaza residents are severely constrained by multiple layers of interference. Israel's de facto blockade of the territory, along with its periodic military incursions and rule of law violations, has imposed serious hardship on the civilian population, as has Egypt's tight control over the Rafah border crossing in the south. Meanwhile, the Hamas militant group governs Gaza without democratic legitimacy, and its unresolved schism with the Palestinian Authority (PA) in the West Bank has contributed to legal confusion and repeated postponement of overdue elections.

KEY DEVELOPMENTS IN 2016:

- Hamas and the West Bank–based PA agreed to hold joint local elections in the West Bank and Gaza Strip in October, but the PA government chose to postpone them all by at least four months after the PA High Court of Justice suspended the Gaza voting due to legal irregularities.
- Nongovernmental organizations (NGOs) came under scrutiny and pressure from both Israeli and Hamas authorities, with Hamas attempting to impose its own regulations and Israel accusing some aid workers of links to Hamas.
- Reconstruction efforts in the wake of a 2014 conflict between Israel and Hamas faltered during the year due to Israeli-imposed restrictions on the entry of building supplies into Gaza.

EXECUTIVE SUMMARY

The Gaza Strip remained without an elected government in 2016, as PA presidential and legislative elections were last held in 2005 and 2006, respectively. Hamas retained de facto governing authority in Gaza due to a 2007 schism with the rival Fatah faction, which controls the PA structure in the West Bank.

In June, the Ramallah-based PA cabinet announced that municipal elections would be held in October, and Hamas stated in July that it would participate in the voting, meaning elections could be held in both the West Bank and Gaza. However, after the PA High Court of Justice found that elections could not proceed in Gaza or East Jerusalem, the PA cabinet decided to postpone all voting by at least four months, drawing objections from Hamas.

Also during the year, Hamas carried out its first executions since 2014, in contravention of PA law, and continued attempts to impose its own regulations on foreign journalists and NGOs. Separately, Israeli authorities accused certain aid workers of colluding with Hamas, which Israel considers a terrorist organization, and maintained tight restrictions on the movement of people and goods to and from Gaza, impeding civilian life and reconstruction efforts dating to Israel's 2014 conflict with Hamas. The unemployment rate exceeded 40 percent, and some 80 percent of the population remained dependent on international aid.

POLITICAL RIGHTS: 3 / 40

A. Electoral Process: 0 / 12

Most residents of the Gaza Strip are refugees or descendants of refugees from the 1948 Arab-Israeli war. They and the original inhabitants of Gaza hold PA identity documents. The Hamas-controlled government in the territory has claimed to be the legitimate leadership of the PA. However, the PA—an interim self-governing body created by the 1993 Oslo Accords—is effectively fractured, and Hamas officials implement PA law selectively.

Under the laws in place for the most recent PA elections, the PA president is elected to four-year terms. The prime minister is nominated by the president and requires the support of the unicameral, 132-seat Palestinian Legislative Council (PLC), which also serves four-year terms.

International observers judged the 2005 presidential election to be generally free and fair. However, PA president Mahmoud Abbas lost control over Gaza after the 2007 Fatah-Hamas schism, and Prime Minister Ismail Haniya of Hamas continued to lead the government in Gaza despite being formally dismissed by Abbas. Other Hamas ministers remained in their posts in Gaza after almost all Fatah-affiliated leaders were expelled or fled to the West Bank. When Abbas's elected term expired in 2009, Hamas argued that the PA Basic Law empowered the head of the PLC—Aziz Dweik of Hamas—to serve as acting president.

Voting in Gaza during the 2006 PLC elections was deemed largely fair by international observers. Hamas won 74 seats overall, while Fatah took 45. The subsequent Hamas-Fatah rift, combined with Israel's detention of many (especially Hamas-affiliated) lawmakers, prevented the PLC from operating, and its term expired in 2010. No elections have been held since 2006; Gaza did not participate in 2012 local elections in the West Bank.

After the PA government in Ramallah called municipal elections for October 2016, Hamas agreed to participate, and election officials began preparations for balloting across the West Bank and Gaza Strip. In September, however, the PA High Court of Justice suspended the elections, citing ongoing disputes about the exclusion of Israeli-controlled East Jerusalem and the legality of preelection court judgements in Gaza that affected the candidate lists. In early October, the High Court ruled that the elections could proceed in the West Bank only, leading the PA government to postpone all municipal elections by at least four months.

Abbas and the Hamas leadership met in Doha, Qatar, at the end of October, affirming the territorial unity of the West Bank and Gaza as part of the Palestinian state, but no concrete commitments on elections emerged.

B. Political Pluralism and Participation: 2 / 16

Since the 2007 schism, Gaza has effectively functioned as a one-party state under Hamas rule. Fatah is largely suppressed, with smaller factions tolerated to varying degrees. In the run-up to the planned 2016 municipal elections, Hamas-administered courts disqualified several electoral lists, leading to criticism that it was trying to prevent Fatah victories. Hamas then criticized the High Court of Justice rulings and the PA decision to suspend all municipal voting, accusing Abbas and Fatah of attempting to avoid an electoral defeat.

In general there is little display of opposition party activity, and party organizing is negligible. The militant Islamic Jihad faction was allowed to demonstrate in 2016, but human rights groups have documented multiple incidents in which Hamas used excessive force or arbitrary detention against its political opponents and critics.

Israel's ongoing blockade of Gaza, in place since 2007, continued to hamper the development of normal civilian political competition, partly by providing a pretext for most political factions to maintain armed wings, seek patronage from foreign powers with their own political agendas, and neglect basic governance concerns.

C. Functioning of Government: 1 / 12

The expiration of the presidential and parliamentary terms in 2009 and 2010 has left Gaza's authorities with no electoral mandate. The ability of Gazan officials to make and implement policy is limited by Israeli and Egyptian border controls, Israeli military actions, and the ongoing schism with the internationally recognized PA structure in the West Bank.

Humanitarian organizations and donor countries allege that Hamas exerts significant control over the distribution of funds and goods in Gaza, and allocates resources according to political criteria with little or no transparency, creating ample opportunity for corruption. The flow of aid is crucial to daily life, as the UN Relief and Works Agency (UNRWA) has reported that about 80 percent of the population is dependent on international assistance.

Meanwhile, partly as a result of the continued political rupture with the West Bank, tens of thousands of public workers in Gaza remained without regular pay during 2016, threatening basic government functions. Hamas has suffered in recent years from a decline in funding from foreign patrons as well as a crackdown on economically important smuggling routes from Egypt, while the Ramallah-based PA has been reluctant to recognize and pay civil servants hired by the Hamas government since 2007.

CIVIL LIBERTIES: 9 / 60

D. Freedom of Expression and Belief: 4 / 16

The media are not free in Gaza. Following the 2007 schism, Hamas security forces closed down pro-Fatah media outlets and began exerting pressure on media critics, including through the use of arbitrary arrest, detention, beatings, and other tactics of intimidation. These abuses came despite the Haniya-led government's Order 128/2007, which instructed security forces to respect "political and media freedoms." The Palestinian Basic Law also guarantees freedom of expression and media freedom. In 2012, Hamas's media office banned Palestinian journalists from giving interviews to or working with Israeli media. In 2016, foreign journalists reported various arbitrarily enforced restrictions on their work, including detentions and interrogations, excessive registration fees for vehicles, and unreasonable conditions attached to permits.

Some restrictions imposed in 2007 have been eased. In 2014, Hamas lifted a ban on the distribution of three West Bank newspapers—*Al-Ayyam*, *Al-Quds*, and *Al-Hayat al-Jadida*—that are generally associated with Fatah; it has also allowed the transmission of

PA-controlled Palestine TV. Blogging and other online media activities are generally allowed, but critical journalists, bloggers, and users of social media have at times faced harassment and arrests by Hamas authorities. The Palestinian Center for Development and Media Freedoms (MADA) reported 48 media freedom violations by Palestinian forces in Gaza in 2016, down from 76 in 2015 but still higher than in many previous years. Among other cases during the year, Palestinian journalist Ayman Alul was detained for several days in January, allegedly tortured, and released by Hamas authorities after pledging not to cover political affairs in Gaza. In September, journalist Mohammed Othman was similarly arrested and allegedly abused in retaliation for his work.

The Israeli blockade and Egyptian controls on the Rafah crossing restrict the movement of journalists. Israeli authorities repeatedly prevented Gaza-based journalists from traveling to the West Bank. For example, some 28 journalists were reportedly barred from making the trip in November to cover a Fatah party conference, despite having applied for permits.

Freedom of religion is restricted in Gaza. The PA Basic Law declares Islam to be the official religion of Palestine and states that "respect and sanctity of all other heavenly religions (Judaism and Christianity) shall be maintained." Hamas authorities have enforced traditional Sunni Islamic practices and conservative dress, and have attempted to exert political control over mosques.

Hamas has taken over the education system, aside from schools run by the United Nations. A teachers' strike in 2009 led to the replacement of many strikers with new, Hamas-allied teachers. Thousands of teachers are subject to irregular pay as part of the broader financial problems affecting civil servants. Hamas security officials have reportedly confiscated "immoral" books from (mostly university) bookstores in recent years. Israeli and Egyptian restrictions on trade and travel have limited access to educational materials, and university students have difficulty leaving the territory to study abroad. Gazans are now mostly absent from West Bank universities.

Intimidation by Hamas militants and other armed groups have some effect on open and free private discussion in Gaza, and the authorities reportedly monitor social media for critical content.

E. Associational and Organizational Rights: 3 / 12

Hamas significantly restricts freedoms of assembly and association, with security forces violently dispersing unapproved public gatherings of Fatah and other groups. Israeli forces regularly fire on demonstrations near the border fence.

There is a broad range of Palestinian NGOs and civic groups, and Hamas operates a large social-services network. However, Hamas has restricted the activities of aid organizations that do not submit to its regulations, and many civic associations have been shut down for political reasons since the 2007 PA split. Aid and reconstruction efforts after the 2014 conflict, led by UN agencies, have been held up in part by disagreements over international and PA access to the territory and control over border crossings.

Israeli authorities denied travel permits for many NGO personnel during 2016, citing security concerns. In one high-profile case in August, Israel charged the director of World Vision in Gaza with diverting $50 million over a seven-year period from the aid group to Hamas. He was arrested at the Erez Crossing and arraigned in a closed hearing. Similar charges of assisting Hamas were levied that month against a Gazan employee of a UN agency, and Save the Children said it was investigating possible Hamas ties to one of its workers. The cases helped to cast suspicion on aid activities in Gaza and led some donors to withdraw or review their funding.

Independent labor unions in Gaza continue to function, and PA workers have staged strikes against Hamas-led management. The Fatah-aligned Palestinian General Federation of Trade Unions, the largest union body in the territories, has seen its operations curtailed. It still negotiates with employers to resolve labor disputes, but workers have little leverage due to the territory's dire economic situation, extremely high unemployment, and the dysfunctional court system, which impedes enforcement of labor protections.

F. Rule of Law: 0 / 16

Laws governing Palestinians in the Gaza Strip derive from Ottoman, British Mandate, Jordanian, Egyptian, PA, and Islamic law, as well as Israeli military orders. The judicial system is not independent, and Palestinian judges lack proper training and experience. Hamas security forces and militants continued to carry out arbitrary arrests and detentions in 2016, and torture of detainees and criminal suspects was reported. The Palestinian human rights ombudsman agency, the Independent Commission for Human Rights, receives complaints from Gaza residents but has limited access to Hamas detention centers and Gaza's central prison.

According to the Palestinian Center for Human Rights, Hamas-led military courts issued at least a dozen death sentences in 2016. A smaller number of death sentences handed down by civilian courts included one against a 26-year-old woman who was convicted in a secret trial in October of killing her allegedly abusive husband. The Hamas authorities carried out their first executions since 2014 in May, putting three convicted murderers to death without the legally required approval of President Abbas.

There were 336 Palestinian security detainees and prisoners from Gaza in Israeli prisons as of August 2016, according to the Israeli human rights organization B'Tselem. The group also reported that Israeli forces killed at least eight Gaza residents in 2016, including civilian protesters and farmers working close to the border. Some deaths also resulted from Israeli air strikes and exchanges of fire with Gaza-based militants, who launched rockets into Israel sporadically during the year.

Vulnerable groups including LGBT (lesbian, gay, bisexual, and transgender) people reportedly face societal discrimination and official harassment in Gaza. Laws dating to the British Mandate authorize up to 10 years in prison for sexual acts between men.

G. Personal Autonomy and Individual Rights: 2 / 16

Freedom of movement in Gaza is severely restricted, and conditions worsened in 2014 as civilians were displaced within the territory by fighting between Israel and Hamas. Roughly 20,000 homes were destroyed or rendered uninhabitable, and nearly 500,000 people were displaced. Only a fraction of the damaged or destroyed homes had been reconstructed by the end of 2016. The effort was further hampered in April, when Israeli officials suspended cement shipments for the private sector for nearly two months; subsequent shipments remained far below demand. Unexploded ordnance also presented a lingering obstacle to internal movement.

Both Israel and Egypt exercised tight control over border areas, and Hamas imposed its own restrictions, for example by requiring exit permits for outgoing travelers. The Rafah border crossing with Egypt was opened only sporadically during 2016, continuing a sharp drop in the number of Gazans entering and exiting the Gaza Strip since the current Egyptian regime came to power in 2013. Only a limited number of people were allowed to cross into Israel for humanitarian or business reasons.

Under Hamas, personal status law is derived almost entirely from Sharia (Islamic law), which puts women at a stark disadvantage in matters of marriage, divorce, and inheritance, and domestic abuse. Rape and domestic violence remain underreported and frequently go unpunished, as authorities are allegedly reluctant to pursue such cases. So-called honor killings reportedly continue to occur, though information on the situation in Gaza is limited. The Hamas authorities have enforced restrictions on women's attire and behavior that is deemed immoral.

The blockade of Gaza's land borders and coastline has greatly reduced economic opportunity in the territory. A dense network of tunnels beneath Gaza's border with Egypt has facilitated much economic activity and is also used to transport weapons. However, the tunnels are sometimes bombed by Israel, and since 2013, Egyptian authorities have made an aggressive effort to shut them down. In 2015 Egypt began flooding the tunnels with seawater, which also threatens drinking water and farmland.

Israeli's intermittent restrictions on the entry of construction materials into Gaza have hampered the economy. Israeli forces also prevented farming near the border fence and limited Gazan fishermen's access to coastal waters beyond six nautical miles from shore during most of 2016. Hamas has imposed price controls and other rules that may further dampen economic activity. The unemployment rate, at about 42 percent, remained among the highest in the world in 2016, according to the World Bank. The youth unemployment rate was nearly 60 percent.

➡ Hong Kong

Political Rights Rating: 5
Civil Liberties Rating: 2
Freedom Rating: 3.5
Freedom Status: Partly Free

Population: 7,400,000

Trend Arrow: Hong Kong received a downward trend arrow due to Beijing's encroachment on freedoms in the territory, reflected in the detention by mainland authorities of five Hong Kong booksellers, shrinking journalistic and academic independence, and the central government's unilateral reinterpretation of the Basic Law in an apparent bid to exclude pro-independence and prodemocracy lawmakers from the Legislative Council.

Ten-Year Ratings Timeline For Year Under Review (Political Rights, Civil Liberties, Status)

Year Under Review	2007	2008	2009	2010	2011	2012	2013	2014	2015	2016
Rating	5,2,PF	5,2,PF	5,2,PF	5,2,PF	5,2,PF	5,2,PF	5,2,PF	5,2,PF	5,2,PF	5,2,PF

Overview: The people of Hong Kong, a special administrative region of China, have traditionally enjoyed substantial civil liberties and the rule of law under their local constitution, the Basic Law. However, the chief executive and half of the Legislative Council are chosen through indirect electoral systems that favor pro-Beijing figures, and the territory's freedoms and autonomy have come under threat in recent years due to growing political and economic pressure from the mainland.

KEY DEVELOPMENTS IN 2016:

- Ahead of Legislative Council elections in September, Hong Kong authorities refused to register a new pro-independence political party and invalidated the nominations of six "localist" candidates in connection with their views on self-determination for the territory.

- In November, the National People's Congress in Beijing issued an unsolicited interpretation of Hong Kong's Basic Law that requires oaths of office to be given "sincerely and solemnly," effectively barring two newly elected localists from taking their seats in the Legislative Council and prompting legal challenges against the status of four other lawmakers.
- Five Hong Kong booksellers, known for their publication and distribution of books that were critical of the Chinese leadership, resurfaced in early 2016 after their disappearance in late 2015, confirming that they had been in the custody of mainland police and issuing statements that raised suspicions of coercion.

EXECUTIVE SUMMARY

Hong Kong voters turned out in large numbers for the September 2016 Legislative Council (Legco) elections, which featured the emergence of a localist movement alongside existing pro-Beijing and prodemocracy camps. The new movement, which grew out of the 2014 Umbrella Movement protests, emphasizes greater autonomy or independence from mainland control, as opposed to the prodemocracy camp's push for direct elections as promised in Hong Kong's Basic Law under the current "one country, two systems" framework for Chinese rule. The localists faced major obstacles from Hong Kong authorities, including refusal to register a newly formed localist party and the invalidation of the nominations of some localist candidates due to their political views. Nonetheless, other localist candidates won 6 of the 70 Legco seats. Pro-Beijing parties won 40 seats, prodemocracy parties won 23, and the remaining seat went to an independent.

After some winning localist and prodemocracy candidates altered their oaths of office as a form of protest, the National People's Congress in Beijing issued an unusual interpretation of the Basic Law in November, declaring that such oaths must be given "sincerely and solemnly" to be valid. Unlike previous interpretations, it was issued while local courts were still considering the case at hand, and without a request from the Hong Kong government. Two localists were consequently barred from taking their seats, and Hong Kong authorities challenged the validity of the oaths of four other lawmakers who had already been seated. While the former case was awaiting a final appeal at year's end, the courts had yet to rule on the latter.

Separately, five Hong Kong booksellers who disappeared in late 2015 resurfaced in early 2016, officially confirming that they were in the custody of mainland authorities. Their company had been known for publishing and distributing books that were critical of China's leaders. Each made public statements through state and Hong Kong media in which they "confessed" to wrongdoing, though observers cast doubt on the authenticity of the statements given China's record of obtaining forced confessions. One of the detainees, after returning to Hong Kong in June, spoke out against the circumstances of his detention and said his confession had been forced and scripted. The case raised concerns about civil liberties and the rule of law in Hong Kong, as it suggested that residents were vulnerable to punishment in the mainland's politically controlled justice system for actions taken at home.

Hong Kong press freedom advocates continued to criticize the creeping growth of pro-Beijing pressure on journalistic expression, accusing media owners of encouraging self-censorship to favor the central government's interests. Meanwhile, students and scholars staged demonstrations against increasing pro-Beijing influence on academic administration.

POLITICAL RIGHTS: 16 / 40

A. Electoral Process: 3 / 12

Hong Kong's 1997 Basic Law calls for the election of a chief executive and a unicameral Legislative Council. Under 2010 electoral reforms, the chief executive, who serves a five-year term, is chosen by a 1,200-member election committee. Some 200,000 "functional constituency" voters—representatives of elite business and social sectors, many with close Beijing ties—elect 900 of the committee's members, and the remaining 300 consist of Legco members, Hong Kong delegates to China's National People's Congress (NPC), religious representatives, and Hong Kong members of the Chinese People's Political Consultative Conference (CPPCC), an advisory body to the Chinese government.

In 2012, the election committee chose CPPCC member Leung Chun-ying as the chief executive. He won 689 of the 1,050 valid votes cast following an unusually competitive race against two other candidates—Henry Tang, a high-ranking Hong Kong civil servant who took 285 votes, and Democratic Party leader Albert Ho, who secured 76. China's Liaison Office in Hong Kong reportedly lobbied election committee members to vote for Leung and pressured media outlets to remove critical coverage of him ahead of the balloting.

Of the 70 Legco seats, 30 are elected by functional constituency voters, 35 are chosen through direct elections in five geographical constituencies, and the remaining five are directly elected after nominations by Hong Kong's 18 district councils from among their own members. All Legco members serve four-year terms.

In the months before the September 2016 Legco elections, the Electoral Affairs Commission (EAC) announced a measure requiring all candidates to sign a form confirming their belief that Hong Kong is unquestionably a part of China, based on certain Basic Law provisions. The move was seen as an attempt to exclude localist candidates. The EAC ultimately invalidated the nominations of six localist candidates, either for refusal to sign the form or, in the case of some who ultimately did sign, because the EAC was nonetheless unconvinced that they were sincere in changing their previous views on independence. A number of other candidates were approved despite failing to sign the declaration. In October, one of the six disqualified candidates filed a lawsuit challenging the constitutionality of the EAC's actions. A hearing was expected in 2017.

Despite the initial obstacles, localist candidates won six seats in the September elections, which featured turnout of 58 percent. Moreover, localist candidates collectively garnered 19 percent of the votes cast in the five geographical constituencies.The results confirmed their status as a small but growing political force, complicating the traditional division between pro-Beijing parties, which won 40 seats, and prodemocracy parties, which won 23 seats. An independent took the remaining seat.

In October, after a number of newly elected localist and prodemocracy Legco members used their swearing-in ceremonies to make political statements, in some cases altering the wording of their oaths, the oaths of two localists—Sixtus Baggio Leung Chung-hang and Yau Wai-ching—were rejected. Amid calls for their disqualification, the Legco was eventually adjourned, blocking the two from retaking their oaths. In November, the NPC Standing Committee issued an official interpretation of Basic Law provisions concerning oaths of office, stating that all oaths must be taken "sincerely and solemnly." Subsequently, a court of first instance disqualified Leung and Yau, and the ruling was upheld by the High Court. In December, the two petitioned the Court of Final Appeal. Meanwhile, based on the NPC interpretation, Hong Kong authorities filed cases aimed at disqualifying four prodemocracy Legco members who had already been sworn in and seated.

B. Political Pluralism and Participation: 7 / 16

Hong Kong residents' political choices are limited by the semidemocratic electoral system, which ensures the dominance of pro-Beijing interests. While the Basic Law states that universal suffrage is the "ultimate aim," only incremental changes have been permitted to date.

Some 18 political parties are currently represented in the Legco. The largest pro-Beijing party is the Democratic Alliance for the Betterment and Progress of Hong Kong. The main parties in the prodemocracy camp are the Civic Party and the Democratic Party, and key localist groupings include Youngspiration and Civic Passion. The Chinese Communist Party (CCP) is not formally registered in Hong Kong but exercises considerable influence. In March 2016, the Hong Kong Companies Registry refused to register the new Hong Kong National Party on grounds that its proindependence platform constituted illegal activity.

While there are no legal restrictions on ethnic minorities participating in politics or running for office, the Legco had no ethnic minority members as of 2016.

C. Functioning of Government: 6 / 12

Directly elected officials have little ability to set and implement government policies under the territory's political system, and mainland authorities are highly influential. The Basic Law restricts the Legco's lawmaking powers, prohibiting legislators from introducing bills that would affect Hong Kong's public spending, governmental operations, or political structure. Most policymaking authority rests with officials who are appointed or indirectly elected in ways that protect Beijing's interests.

Hong Kong is generally regarded as having low corruption rates, and high-ranking officials have been successfully prosecuted for graft-related offenses.

CIVIL LIBERTIES: 45 / 60 (− 2)

D. Freedom of Expression and Belief: 12 / 16

The Basic Law upholds freedoms of speech, press, and publication. Residents have access to a variety of print and broadcast news sources. Foreign media generally operate without interference. The mainland's internet censorship regime does not apply in Hong Kong, and residents enjoy unrestricted access to a wide range of sites. However, in recent years the Hong Kong and Chinese governments, as well as businesses with close ties to Beijing, have increased political and economic pressure on media independence.

In December 2015, the mainland e-commerce giant Alibaba acquired the *South China Morning Post*, Hong Kong's leading English-language newspaper, adding to fears that its editorial independence was eroding. The new ownership took effect in April 2016.

In another sign of China's influence, a number of local news outlets appeared to participate in well-established Chinese government tactics of publicly airing dubious "confessions" of guilt without trial. In July and August, for example, the *South China Morning Post* and *Oriental Daily* newspapers respectively published "confessions" by legal assistant Zhao Wei and rights defense lawyer Wang Yu, both of whom had been detained in a massive 2015 crackdown against mainland lawyers and activists. Observers questioned the authenticity of the "confessions," and neither newspaper explained how the interviews were arranged, prompting criticism that they had compromised their independence by serving as Chinese government mouthpieces.

The disappearance of the five Hong Kong booksellers in late 2015, and their reemergence in Chinese custody in early 2016, had a chilling effect on expression in the territory, with several vendors declining to distribute books that were critical of Chinese authorities, even though such activity is legal in Hong Kong.

Religious freedom is generally respected in Hong Kong. Adherents of the Falun Gong spiritual movement, which is persecuted in mainland China, are free to practice in public.

However, in recent years they have been confronted and harassed by members of the Hong Kong Youth Care Association (HKYCA), which has ties to the CCP.

University professors can generally write and lecture freely, and political debate on campuses is lively. However, a series of incidents in recent years have stoked concerns that Beijing is putting greater pressure on Hong Kong's academic sphere. In January 2016, student demonstrations and boycotts erupted at the University of Hong Kong to protest the chief executive's appointment of a pro-Beijing official to head the university's governing council. The students' concerns were echoed during the year by a number of public figures and former officials who warned of growing interference by the Hong Kong government and mainland authorities with Hong Kong's colleges and universities.

Private discussion is open and free in Hong Kong, though mainland security agencies are suspected of monitoring the communications of prodemocracy activists.

E. Associational and Organizational Rights: 8 / 12

The Basic Law guarantees freedoms of assembly and association. The Public Order Ordinance requires organizers to give police seven days' notice before protests and to obtain official assent, which is rarely denied. However, prosecutions against leading participants in the Umbrella Movement have raised concerns about shrinking space for public assembly and association in Hong Kong. Drawing more than 100,000 people at its peak, the 2014 movement featured long-term encampments that paralyzed key commercial and government districts. Police made only sporadic and partial attempts to break up the camps. Nevertheless, their increased use of baton charges, pepper spray, and arrests to clear the last groups of protesters that year drew fresh criticism. The encampments also faced assaults by counterdemonstrators, many of whom were later found to have links with criminal gangs.

Most of the hundreds of people arrested during the Umbrella Movement were quickly released, although about 160 were later charged. In July 2016, student leaders Joshua Wong and Alex Chow were found guilty of participating in an "unlawful assembly," while colleague Nathan Law was found guilty of "inciting others to take part in an unlawful assembly" under the Public Order Ordinance. However, their sentences were light, ranging from community service to a suspended jail term of three weeks.

Prior to and during a May 2016 visit by Zhang Dejiang, chairman of the NPC Standing Committee, authorities took steps to make it difficult for demonstrators to confront the official. Protesters could congregate only in specified areas a long distance away from meeting venues, and prodemocracy protesters were arrested for trying to hang banners demanding universal suffrage.

Also in 2016, annual mass demonstrations on June 4 and July 1, marking the 1989 Tiananmen Square crackdown and the 1997 handover of Hong Kong from Britain to China, drew tens of thousands of people without major incident.

Hong Kong hosts a vibrant and largely unfettered nongovernmental organization (NGO) sector, including a number of groups that focus on human rights in mainland China. Trade unions are independent, but collective-bargaining rights are not recognized, and protections against antiunion discrimination are weak.

F. Rule of Law: 12 / 16 (− 2)

The judiciary is largely independent, and the trial process is generally fair. However, the NPC reserves the right to make final interpretations of the Basic Law, effectively limiting the power of Hong Kong's Court of Final Appeal. The NPC's November 2016 interpretation regarding oaths of office was unusual in a number of respects, particularly the fact that it was issued without a request from the Hong Kong government and before the local courts had ruled on the matter in question. It was therefore seen as a blow to the independence of the territory's legal system. Critics also noted that the interpretation introduced subjective concepts like "sincerity" and "solemnity" that could lead to politicized enforcement.

Police are forbidden by law to employ torture, disappearance, arbitrary arrest and detention, and other forms of abuse. They generally respect this ban in practice, and complaints of abuse are investigated. However, the case of the five booksellers cast doubt on Hong Kong's capacity to protect its residents from similar abuses by mainland authorities.

Before their disappearances in late 2015, one of the five men was last seen in Thailand, three were last seen in mainland China, and the fifth was apparently abducted directly from Hong Kong by Chinese agents. In January 2016, letters purportedly from one of the men stated that he was willingly cooperating with authorities in China, and that there was no need for concern. Chinese authorities confirmed his detention later that month. Also in January, a second bookseller was paraded on China's state television, where he "confessed" to his involvement in an unrelated fatal car accident years earlier. In February, the remaining three men appeared on Hong Kong's Phoenix TV, admitting to distributing unlicensed books on the mainland and confirming that they too were detained by Chinese authorities.

Eventually, four of the five booksellers were allowed to return to Hong Kong, but three stayed only briefly, and one—Gui Minhai, a Swedish citizen—remained detained on the mainland under suspicion of unnamed "criminal activities." Gui's family and the Swedish government were not told of his whereabouts or any charges against him, rendering him forcibly disappeared under international law. One of the returnees, Lam Wing-kee, held a news conference in June to describe his detention by Chinese authorities on the mainland. He said they interrogated him about his company's activities, including information about both authors and consumers of certain politically sensitive books, and forced him to read a scripted public "confession." He refused to return to mainland China despite orders to do so from Chinese police.

Hong Kong authorities insisted that they were not informed by mainland authorities about the circumstances of the disappearances, prompting concern about the system of reciprocal notification of cross-border detentions that is supposed to be in place between Hong Kong and the mainland. Officials emphasized that it is not legally possible to hand a Hong Kong resident over to Chinese authorities without an extradition agreement. However, police dropped an investigation into the abduction of Lee Bo, the bookseller who was allegedly seized in Hong Kong and smuggled across the border to the mainland, at the request of Lee and his family.

Citizens are generally treated equally under the law, though South Asian minorities face language barriers and de facto discrimination in education and employment. Antidiscrimination laws do not specifically protect LGBT (lesbian, gay, bisexual, and transgender) people.

More than 11,000 refugees were thought to be in Hong Kong as of June 2016, with most coming from South or Southeast Asia. While the government does not accept refugees for settlement, it does offer protection from refoulement, and those deemed eligible can be referred to UN officials for third-country resettlement. However, only 52 of more than 8,000 claims have been approved by authorities since 2009, raising serious doubts about the fairness of the process.

G. Personal Autonomy and Individual Rights: 13 / 16

Hong Kong residents generally enjoy freedom of movement, though authorities periodically deny entry to visiting political activists and Falun Gong practitioners, raising suspicions of a Beijing-imposed blacklist. While property rights are largely respected, collusion among powerful businessmen with political connections is perceived as an impediment to fair economic competition.

Women in Hong Kong are protected by law from discrimination and abuse. However, they continue to face de facto inequality in employment opportunities, salary, inheritance, and welfare. Only 11 of the 70 Legco members are women, and there are no women on the Court of Final Appeal.

Hong Kong remains a destination and transit point for human trafficking linked to sexual exploitation and forced labor. The territory's roughly 330,000 foreign household workers are vulnerable to abuse. They are often required by recruitment agencies to pay exorbitant fees, and since they may face deportation if dismissed, many are reluctant to bring complaints against employers. There have been reports of abuses against sex workers by law enforcement officers, including entrapment and other misuses of police powers. There are also reports of discrimination by police and correctional officers against sex workers who identify as transgender, and an overall unwillingness of sex workers to report assaults out of fear of prosecution for solicitation.

Indian Kashmir

Political Rights Rating: 4
Civil Liberties Rating: 4
Freedom Rating: 4.0
Freedom Status: Partly Free

Population: 12,500,000

Ten-Year Ratings Timeline For Year Under Review (Political Rights, Civil Liberties, Status)

Year Under Review	2007	2008	2009	2010	2011	2012	2013	2014	2015	2016
Rating	5,4,PF	5,4,PF	4,4,PF	4,5,PF	4,4,PF	4,4,PF	4,4,PF	4,4,PF	4,4,PF	4,4,PF

Overview: Control of Kashmir has been divided between India and Pakistan since 1948. In Indian-administered Kashmir, both separatist and jihadist militants have waged a protracted insurgency against the government. The state enjoys substantial autonomy under Article 370 of India's constitution. Competitive elections are held, but they have often been marred by the threat of violence and other flaws. Indian security forces are frequently accused of human rights violations and effectively enjoy broad impunity under the law. Curfews, newspaper bans, and internet and mobile phone blackouts are routinely imposed during times of unrest.

KEY DEVELOPMENTS IN 2016:
- Chief Minister Mufti Mohammad Sayeed died in January. He was succeeded in April by his daughter Mehbooba Mufti, president of the ruling People's Democratic Party, making her the state's first female chief minister.
- There was a dramatic increase in violence after security forces killed a popular separatist militant leader in July. Protests and strikes over the subsequent months resulted in the imposition of prolonged curfews, media censorship, and internet and mobile phone outages.
- A militant attack on an Indian army base in September led Indian forces to launch "surgical strikes" on Pakistani targets across the Line of Control (LoC).

EXECUTIVE SUMMARY

After several years of relative stability, the situation in Indian-administered Kashmir deteriorated sharply in the second half of 2016. In July, security forces killed Burhan Muzaffar Wani, a 22-year-old separatist militant leader who was active on social media and enjoyed broad popular support. Months of protests and clashes with police ensued, during which about 90 civilians reportedly died. The use of birdshot—lead pellets fired from shotguns—by security forces was also blamed for thousands of injuries, many of them resulting in blindness. Curfews were imposed in parts of the state, limiting freedom of movement and other civil liberties.

At the same time, internet services and mobile phone connectivity were suspended, printing of newspapers was briefly disallowed, and public transportation came to a standstill. Schools remained shut for extended periods. In October, the state government drew heavy criticism for prohibiting the publication of a local English-language newspaper, the *Kashmir Reader*, on the grounds that it carried incendiary content. The ban was lifted in December.

With the sharp drop-off in tourism, the region's economy suffered. In addition, panchayat (local council) elections scheduled for 2016 were postponed until 2017. In September, Khurram Parvez, an activist who was set to deliver a report on abuses in Kashmir to the UN Human Rights Council, was prevented from leaving India without explanation. He was then detained without charge under the Public Safety Act until a court ordered his release in November.

In September, four militants crossed the LoC and launched an attack on Indian army brigade headquarters in the town of Uri; 18 Indian soldiers were killed. Suspecting Pakistani involvement, India retaliated in a series of "surgical strikes" across the LoC. A total of 267 civilians, security personnel, and militants were killed in militant-related violence in 2016, compared with 174 deaths in 2015.

The annual Amarnath Yatra—a major Hindu procession—was repeatedly suspended in July for security reasons. In September, Hindu-Muslim clashes erupted in Rajouri district and a curfew was put in place after a man was beaten based on false suspicions that he had slaughtered a cow.

POLITICAL RIGHTS: 22 / 40

A. Electoral Process: 9 / 12

B. Political Pluralism and Participation: 9 / 16

C. Functioning of Government: 4 / 12

CIVIL LIBERTIES: 28 / 60 (− 1)

D. Freedom of Expression and Belief: 9 / 16

E. Associational and Organizational Rights: 5 / 12 (− 1)

F. Rule of Law: 6 / 16

G. Personal Autonomy and Individual Rights: 8 / 16

This territory report has been abridged for *Freedom in the World 2017*. For background information on political rights and civil liberties in Indian Kashmir, see *Freedom in the World 2016*.

Nagorno-Karabakh

Political Rights Rating: 5
Civil Liberties Rating: 5
Freedom Rating: 5.0
Freedom Status: Partly Free

Population: 146,600

Ten-Year Ratings Timeline For Year Under Review (Political Rights, Civil Liberties, Status)

Year Under Review	2007	2008	2009	2010	2011	2012	2013	2014	2015	2016
Rating	5,5,PF	5,5,PF	5,5,PF	6,5,NF	6,5,NF	5,5,PF	5,5,PF	5,5,PF	5,5,PF	5,5,PF

Overview: Nagorno-Karabakh is a breakaway territory that has enjoyed de facto independence from Azerbaijan since 1994, when it reached a ceasefire with Azerbaijani forces following a war for independence. The territory's population is majority Armenian, and Nagorno-Karabakh retains close political, economic, and military ties with Armenia. The security situation, exacerbated by regular violations of the ceasefire and the threat of renewed war, have a deeply negative impact on political rights and civil liberties.

KEY DEVELOPMENTS IN 2016:

- Heavy clashes erupted in April along the line of contact with Azerbaijan; although estimates of casualties varied wildly, most international sources agreed that the incident represented the worst violence since the 1994 ceasefire.
- In June, a group of men in military uniforms attacked and kidnapped a National Revival Party legislator; after his release, he claimed that the attack was politically motivated intimidation.
- In November, a constitutional commission—formed earlier in the year by request of the territory's president—published a new draft constitution that, among other things, would shift Nagorno-Karabakh's government from a semipresidential to a fully presidential system.
- The presidents of Armenia and Azerbaijan met to discuss the conflict on a few occasions during the year; negotiations led by the Organization for Security and Co-operation in Europe (OSCE), launched in 1992, also continued.

EXECUTIVE SUMMARY

In April, four days of heavy violence broke out along the line of contact between Azerbaijani forces and Karabakh troops, who are backed by the Armenian military. The fighting, which came to be known as the "Four Day War" among the local population, represented the worst episode of violence since the two sides reached a ceasefire in 1994. Although casualty estimates by the two sides varied wildly, the U.S. State Department noted that approximately 350 people died in the fighting, including civilians on both sides of the frontline. Azerbaijani forces gained small areas of land along the line of contact. The clashes heightened overall security concerns and led to significant social and political tensions in the territory.

In March, a special commission formed at the initiative of President Bako Sahakyan began to review Nagorno-Karabakh's constitution. The commission noted the need to thoroughly reform the territory's basic law, and unveiled a draft constitution to the public in

November. Among other things, the draft envisions a fully presidential system of government, as opposed to the current semipresidential system in which power is shared by the executive and legislative branches. Analysts noted that the territory's heightened security concerns figured prominently into the proposed legislation, which will likely be put to a referendum in 2017.

Relations between the country's main parties and the small opposition were tense in 2016. Given the territory's delicate geopolitical status, internal dissent and opposition have often been regarded as signs of disloyalty and even a security risk. In June, a group of men attacked and kidnapped Hayk Khanumyan, a legislator and member of the National Revival Party, one of the two opposition groups represented in the parliament. After his release, Khanumyan claimed that he recognized the perpetrators and that the attack—which took place in broad daylight in the territory's capital—was likely meant to intimidate him to leave Nagorno-Karabakh.

POLITICAL RIGHTS: 15 / 40
A. Electoral Process: 6 / 12
B. Political Pluralism and Participation: 6 / 16
C. Functioning of Government: 3 / 12

CIVIL LIBERTIES: 18 / 60
D. Freedom of Expression and Belief: 6 / 16
E. Associational and Organizational Rights: 3 / 12
F. Rule of Law: 4 / 12
G. Personal Autonomy and Individual Rights: 5 / 16

This territory report has been abridged for *Freedom in the World 2017*. For background information on political rights and civil liberties in Nagorno-Karabakh, see *Freedom in the World 2016*.

Northern Cyprus

Political Rights Rating: 2
Civil Liberties Rating: 2
Freedom Rating: 2.0
Freedom Status: Free

Population: 300,000

Ten-Year Ratings Timeline For Year Under Review (Political Rights, Civil Liberties, Status)

Year Under Review	2007	2008	2009	2010	2011	2011	2013	2014	2015	2016
Rating	2,2,F	2,2,F	2,2,F	2,2,F	2,2,F	2,2,F	2,2,F	2,2,F	2,2,F	2,2,F

Overview: The Turkish Republic of Northern Cyprus (TRNC) is a self-declared state recognized only by Turkey. It has a democratic political system in which multiple parties compete for power. Civil liberties, including freedom of assembly and the rights of nongovernmental organizations, are generally upheld. Turkey exercises considerable political and economic influence over the TRNC, in part through its military presence, control over security forces, and migration from the mainland. Other concerns include corruption, discrimination against minority communities, violations of due process, and poor prison conditions.

KEY DEVELOPMENTS IN 2016:

- The TRNC and Turkey concluded a controversial water agreement in March and an economic aid protocol in May, prompting accusations of growing Turkish influence aimed at thwarting reunification efforts with the rest of Cyprus.
- In April, a coalition government between the center-left Republican Turkish Party (CTP) and the right-wing National Unity Party (UBP) collapsed. The UBP, which was seen as closer to Ankara, then formed a new government with the center-right Democratic Party (DP).

EXECUTIVE SUMMARY

Political disagreements over the TRNC's relationship with Turkey contributed to a collapse of the governing coalition in April.

The friction began in January, when an economic protocol between Turkey and the TRNC formally expired, and Turkey suspended its financial support for the republic, generating a budgetary crisis. In March, Turkey and the TRNC concluded a controversial agreement whereby Turkey will supply the TRNC with fresh water, but the TRNC commits to buying the water at whatever prices are set by a private Turkish company, which will obtain control over the water distribution system. The UBP then left the governing coalition in early April and formed a new coalition with the DP, leaving the CTP—which seeks reconciliation with the Greek Cypriots and EU membership—in opposition. Hüseyin Özgürgün of the UBP became prime minister.

In May, the government concluded a new economic protocol with Ankara, whereby Turkey will provide $1.2 billion in aid over three years. As part of the deal, the TRNC committed to budget cuts and privatization of ports, telecommunications, and electricity infrastructure—which will likely result in Turkish ownership of those assets—as well as the creation of a "coordination office" for youth and sports that gives Turkish ministries authority over scholarships, camps, and facilities. Critics of the deal argued that the provisions would undermine Cypriot reunification talks and move the republic closer to annexation by Turkey.

Although TRNC president Mustafa Akıncı, who has pledged to reunify the island as a bicommunal federal state, continued to support the negotiations with the Republic of Cyprus, the UBP-DP government took a number of other actions that complicated the talks. For example, in May the authorities restricted most Orthodox churches to one service per year, citing limited resources to provide security. After the July coup attempt in Turkey, the TRNC declared the organization of U.S.-based Islamic preacher Fethullah Gülen to be a "terrorist organization" and reportedly cooperated with Turkey's efforts to identify Gülen supporters on the island. In June, the TRNC passed a law that made it more difficult for Turkish migrants to receive TRNC citizenship, offering them permanent residence permits instead. In August, however, an opposition leader in the TRNC claimed that the government, under pressure from Turkey, was issuing citizenship to 500 settlers a month.

Meanwhile, the TRNC's Immovable Property Commission—tasked with resolving claims by Greek Cypriots who owned property in the north before the island's 1974 division—continued to operate, though its work has been hampered by a lack of funding from Turkey. As of December 2016, the commission had settled a total of 805 claims out of 6,308 applications and awarded over $300 million in compensation.

Freedoms of assembly and association are generally upheld in Northern Cyprus, and the year featured a series of protests linked to political developments. Trade unions protested both the March water agreement and the May economic protocol with Turkey, and in August they demonstrated in favor of President Akıncı's reunification efforts and against the new right-wing government. In August, over 80 groups participated in a protest against Turkish influence in the TRNC. In December, unions staged a general strike to protest the government's decision to follow Turkey in not implementing daylight-savings time.

Although prostitution is nominally illegal, human trafficking and forced prostitution are serious problems. According to the U.S. State Department, the TRNC lacks an antitrafficking law and does not fund antitrafficking efforts. The government reaps tax revenue from an industry of nightclubs where forced prostitution by foreign women is tacitly permitted; foreign trafficking victims are routinely deported.

POLITICAL RIGHTS: 32 / 40

A. Electoral Process: 11 / 12

B. Political Pluralism and Participation: 12 / 16

C. Functioning of Government: 9 / 12

CIVIL LIBERTIES: 48 / 60 (+ 1)

D. Freedom of Expression and Belief: 14 / 16

E. Associational and Organizational Rights: 11 / 12 (+2)

F. Rule of Law: 12 / 16

G. Personal Autonomy and Individual Rights: 11 / 16 (− 1)

This territory report has been abridged for *Freedom in the World 2017*. For background information on political rights and civil liberties in Northern Cyprus, see *Freedom in the World 2016*.

Pakistani Kashmir

Political Rights Rating: 6   **Population:** 5,800,000
Civil Liberties Rating: 5
Freedom Rating: 5.5
Freedom Status: Not Free

Ten-Year Ratings Timeline For Year Under Review (Political Rights, Civil Liberties, Status)

Year Under Review	2007	2008	2009	2010	2011	2012	2013	2014	2015	2016
Rating	7,5,NF	6,5,NF	6,5,NF	6,5,NF	6,5,NF	6,5,NF	6,5,NF	6,5,NF	6,5,NF	6,5,NF

Overview: Pakistani Kashmir comprises those parts of the pre-1947 princely state that are now controlled by Pakistan. It is currently administered as two territories: Azad Jammu and Kashmir (AJK) and Gilgit-Baltistan (GB). Each has an elected assembly and government with limited autonomy, but they lack the parliamentary representation and other rights of Pakistani provinces, and Pakistani federal institutions have predominant influence over security, the courts, and most important policy matters. Politics within the two territories are carefully managed to promote the idea of Kashmir's eventual accession to Pakistan. Freedoms of expression and assembly, and any political activity deemed contrary to Pakistan's policy on Kashmir, are restricted.

KEY DEVELOPMENTS IN 2016:

- In June, an appellate court confirmed a sentence of life in prison for a left-wing activist in GB, preventing him from running in a legislative by-election.
- Pakistan's ruling party won AJK's legislative elections in July, installing its choices for prime minister and president of the territory.
- Heavy firing across the Line of Control (LoC) resumed in the second half of the year, reportedly causing civilian casualties.

EXECUTIVE SUMMARY

Elections for the AJK Legislative Assembly were held in July 2016. The Pakistan Muslim League–Nawaz (PML-N), Pakistan's ruling party, took 31 out of 41 seats. The local branch of the Pakistan People's Party (PPP) won three seats, as did the Muslim Conference, and the Pakistan Tehreek-e-Insaf secured two. The remaining two seats were won by the Jammu Kashmir Peoples Party and an independent. The new assembly elected the local PML-N leader, Raja Farooq Haider, as prime minister. In August, it elected Masood Khan, formerly a senior Pakistani diplomat, as president.

The election process was largely peaceful, though both the PPP and the local PTI leader complained of preelection manipulation, including the use of federal development funds to boost support for the PML-N.

In April, the GB Legislative Assembly (GBLA) elected its six representatives to the 15-member GB Council, four of whom were nominated by the PML-N. The council, which retains control over strategically important policy matters in GB, is chaired by the Pakistani prime minister and vice-chaired by a federally appointed governor, and also includes the chief minister of GB. The remaining six members are appointed by the Pakistani prime minister from among federal ministers and Parliament members.

In June, GB's Supreme Appellate Court upheld the 2014 life sentence of activist Baba Jan, a leader of the left-wing Awami Workers Party, for his alleged role in a violent 2011 protest by landslide victims. Critics viewed the case as a politically motivated. Baba Jan, while behind bars, had placed second in a GBLA race in 2015, and after the winner was appointed as GB governor later that year, he prepared to seek the seat again in the ensuring by-election. However, the by-election was repeatedly postponed until after the court confirmed his sentence and prevented him from standing. A PML-N candidate ultimately won the seat in September.

Political debate and demonstrations continued during the year over whether GB should be declared a province of Pakistan. Supporters argued that such a formalized constitutional status would give residents greater rights and representation in Islamabad, and resolve legal concerns about Chinese investment in the China-Pakistan Economic Corridor (CPEC), a massive transport and energy infrastructure project that would run through GB. Opponents, particularly in AJK, warned that the change would erode the larger region's disputed status and solidify India's claims on its portion of Kashmir, while others favored greater autonomy or independence for GB. Some protests related to these issues and the CPEC resulted in arrests and criminal charges.

Exchanges of shelling and gunfire with Indian forces across the LoC began to increase in July as Indian authorities struggled with protests over the killing of a popular Kashmiri militant leader. In September, India blamed infiltrators from AJK for a militant attack on an army camp in Uri, and heavier firing ensued, further disrupting civilian life in areas along the LoC. Pakistani officials reported dozens of civilian deaths during the year.

POLITICAL RIGHTS: 9 / 40
A. Electoral Process: 4 / 12
B. Political Pluralism and Participation: 4 / 16
C. Functioning of Government: 3 / 12

DISCRETIONARY POLITICAL RIGHTS QUESTION B: − 2 / 0

CIVIL LIBERTIES: 19 / 60
D. Freedom of Expression and Belief: 6 / 16
E. Associational and Organizational Rights: 4 / 12
F. Rule of Law: 3 / 16
G. Personal Autonomy and Individual Rights: 6 / 16

This territory report has been abridged for *Freedom in the World 2017.* For background information on political rights and civil liberties in Pakistani Kashmir, see *Freedom in the World 2016.*

Somaliland

Political Rights Rating: 5
Civil Liberties Rating: 5
Freedom Rating: 5.0
Freedom Status: Partly Free

Population: 3,500,000

Ten-Year Ratings Timeline For Year Under Review (Political Rights, Civil Liberties, Status)

Year Under Review	2007	2008	2009	2010	2011	2012	2013	2014	2015	2016
Rating	5,4,PF	5,4,PF	5,5,PF	4,5,PF	4,5,PF	4,5,PF	4,5,PF	4,5,PF	5,5,PF	5,5,PF

Overview: While past elections in Somaliland have been generally free and fair, scheduled polls are frequently postponed, and clan politics dominate the political landscape. Journalists face pressure from authorities, and police occasionally employ excessive force or detain suspects for longer than permitted under the law. Violence against women remains a problem.

KEY DEVELOPMENTS IN 2016:
- Parliamentary and presidential elections were delayed once again, undermining Somaliland's credibility as an advancing democracy. The last presidential election was held in 2010, and the last parliamentary polls in 2005.
- Registration for fresh voter rolls began in January and was completed in September.
- The Somaliland-based Human Rights Centre (HRC) documented an increase in the number of journalists detained.

EXECUTIVE SUMMARY

Despite ongoing preparations for long-delayed elections, in September 2016 President Ahmed Mohamed Mohamoud Silanyo's administration announced that both presidential and parliamentary polls would be postponed once again, with the parliamentary polls to be held in October 2017 and the presidential election the following month. Officials cited among other reasons an imbalance in regional allocation of parliamentary seats, and the absence of promised international aid. Under a previous agreement, the elections had been set to take place in March 2017, and would be preceded by voter registration for a new voter roll.

The voter registration process began in January 2016, and the process was completed in September, though the registry had yet to be finalized at year's end. A 2016 amendment to the voter registration law allowed the final voter register to be produced "within" six months of the election rather than six months prior, as had been mandated previously. The amendment drew some criticism for leaving a vague deadline.

Meanwhile, the government continued to suppress critical media coverage. According to the Somaliland-based Human Rights Centre (HRC), 28 journalists were detained between December 2015 and December 2016, up from 19 in the previous year's reporting period. Among the detentions reported by HRC was that of Abdirahman Ahmed Elser, who was detained in January at the request of the Ministry of Environment over a story on the environmental impact of charcoal production. Several other journalists faced charges or were detained in connection with stories critical of authorities. Separately, no progress has been made on a promised broadcast law that could introduce independent radio to Somaliland.

The judiciary is underfunded and lacks independence, and the Supreme Court in the past has been largely ineffective. However, a new chief justice appointed in 2015, Adan H. Ali Ahmed, enjoys strong support from civil society, and in 2016 he made some progress on a mandate to harmonize and modernize judicial structures.

POLITICAL RIGHTS: 15 / 40

A. Electoral Process: 2 / 12

B. Political Pluralism and Participation: 9 / 16

C. Functioning of Government: 4 / 12

CIVIL LIBERTIES: 25 / 60

D. Freedom of Expression and Belief: 7 / 16

E. Associational and Organizational Rights: 5 / 12

F. Rule of Law: 7 / 16

G. Personal Autonomy and Individual Rights: 6 / 16

This country report has been abridged for *Freedom in the World 2017*. For background information on political rights and civil liberties in Somaliland, see *Freedom in the World 2016*.

South Ossetia

Political Rights Rating: 7   **Population:** 54,000
Civil Liberties Rating: 6
Freedom Rating: 6.5
Freedom Status: Not Free

Ten-Year Ratings Timeline For Year Under Review (Political Rights, Civil Liberties, Status)

Year Under Review Rating	2007	2008	2009	2010	2011	2012	2013	2014	2015	2016
	—	7,6,NF	7,6,NF	7,6,NF	7,6,NF	7,6,NF	7,6,NF	7,6,NF	7,6,NF	7,6,NF

Overview: Large parts of South Ossetia, a breakaway territory of Georgia, enjoyed de facto independence after a civil conflict ended in 1992. A 2008 war that drew in Russian forces resulted in the expulsion of the remaining Georgian government presence and of many ethnic Georgian civilians. Only Russia and a handful of other states have since recognized South Ossetia's independence. The territory remains almost entirely dependent on Russia, and Moscow exerts a decisive influence over politics and governance. Local media are largely controlled by the authorities, who also restrict or closely monitor civil society activity. The judiciary is subject to political influence and manipulation. Physical abuse and poor conditions are reportedly common in prisons and detention centers.

KEY DEVELOPMENTS IN 2016:

- The president announced in May that a referendum on joining the Russian Federation would not be held until after the next presidential election in 2017.
- Ten polling stations were opened across the territory to allow the many residents with Russian citizenship to vote in Russia's parliamentary elections in September, drawing objections from the Georgian government.
- In October, leaked e-mails suggested that Russian officials carefully managed the legislative process in South Ossetia, adding to perceptions of extensive control by Moscow.

EXECUTIVE SUMMARY

With a presidential election scheduled for April 2017, South Ossetia's political leaders clashed during 2016 over how to approach the goal of union with Russia. In May, President Leonid Tibilov, an independent, postponed a planned referendum on the issue until after the upcoming election. He favored a plebiscite on whether to amend the constitution to empower the president to request incorporation into the Russian Federation, effectively giving the leadership—and by implication Moscow—greater discretion on when to formally seek annexation. His political rival, parliament speaker Anatoliy Bibilov of the United Ossetia party, advocated an outright poll on whether to unite with Russia.

A third possible contender, former president Eduard Kokoity, announced plans to seek reelection to his old post in November. However, according to electoral laws, candidates must have permanently resided in South Ossetia for 10 years. Kokoity had lived in Russia since leaving office in 2011, meaning he could be disqualified.

The territory's government remained heavily dependent on Russian aid, which made up more than 90 percent of its budget for 2016. A leak of e-mails apparently tied to senior Kremlin adviser Vladislav Surkov in October shed further light on the extent of Russian involvement. According to the documents, Moscow carefully managed the drafting and adoption of legislation by the South Ossetian parliament.

The local authorities continued to impose restrictions on critical journalists and media outlets during the year. In October, the chief prosecutor's office banned two websites for slandering government officials and brought criminal charges against two journalists and an internet user on similar grounds.

In February, South Ossetian security officials began requiring civilians to apply for permission before visiting villages along the boundary with Georgian-controlled territory. The tighter restrictions met with opposition from local residents, who organized a small protest in July.

POLITICAL RIGHTS: 2 / 40

A. Electoral Process: 2 / 12

B. Political Pluralism and Participation: 2 / 16

C. Functioning of Government: 0 / 12

DISCRETIONARY POLITICAL RIGHTS QUESTION B: − 2 / 0

CIVIL LIBERTIES: 9 / 60

D. Freedom of Expression and Belief: 4 / 16

E. Associational and Organizational Rights: 1 / 12

F. Rule of Law: 1 / 16

G. Personal Autonomy and Individual Rights: 3 / 16

This territory report has been abridged for *Freedom in the World 2017*. For background information on political rights and civil liberties in South Ossetia, see *Freedom in the World 2016*.

Tibet

Population: 3,200,000

[Note: This figure covers only the Tibet Autonomous Region. Areas of eastern Tibet that were incorporated into neighboring Chinese provinces are also assessed in the report below.]

Political Rights Rating: 7
Civil Liberties Rating: 7
Freedom Rating: 7.0
Freedom Status: Not Free

Ten-Year Ratings Timeline For Year Under Review(Political Rights, Civil Liberties, Status)

Year Under Review	2007	2008	2009	2010	2011	2012	2013	2014	2015	2016	
Rating	7,7,NF	7,7,NF	7,7,NF	7,7,NF	7,7,NF	7,7,NF	7,7,NF	7,7,NF	7,7,NF	7,7,NF	

Overview: Tibet is ruled by the Chinese Communist Party (CCP) government based in Beijing, with local decision-making power concentrated in the hands of Chinese party officials. Residents of both Chinese and Tibetan ethnicity are denied fundamental rights, but the authorities are especially rigorous in suppressing any signs of dissent among Tibetans, including manifestations of religious belief and cultural identity. State policies encourage migration from other parts of China, reducing the ethnic Tibetan share of the population.

KEY DEVELOPMENTS IN 2016:

- A Tibetan blogger who had been detained in 2015 was sentenced in February to three years in prison on separatism charges, one of many laypeople and monastics who faced detention for peaceful expression of their beliefs or criticism of the Chinese government.
- At an April party conference, Chinese president Xi Jinping and other CCP leaders called for the "Sinicization" of all religions, adding to concerns that the government sought to extinguish Tibetan religious and cultural identity.
- In June, authorities ordered a sharp reduction in the number of nuns and monks residing at Larung Gar, one of the world's largest centers for Tibetan Buddhist learning, in the Garzê Tibetan Autonomous Prefecture in Sichuan Province. Demolitions and evictions ensued the following month.

EXECUTIVE SUMMARY

The Chinese government continued to implement draconian public surveillance and enforcement measures in 2016 as part of a significant expansion of its "stability maintenance" policies in Tibet since an outbreak of protests and interethnic violence in 2008, and particularly since a change in national leadership in 2013. Observers documented wide-ranging violations of fundamental rights, including an alarming rate of detentions, prosecutions, and convictions of Tibetans for the peaceful exercise of their freedoms of expression, assembly, and religious belief.

Officials also ratcheted up Chinese nationalist rhetoric, including calls for the "Sinicization" of all religions, while moving forward with vast development and urbanization projects despite protests from the affected Tibetan communities.

POLITICAL RIGHTS: −2 / 40

A. Electoral Process: 0 / 12

The Chinese government rules Tibet through administration of the Tibet Autonomous Region (TAR) and 12 Tibetan autonomous prefectures or counties in the nearby provinces of Sichuan, Qinghai, Gansu, and Yunnan. Under the Chinese constitution, autonomous areas have the right to formulate their own regulations and implement national legislation in accordance with local conditions. In practice, however, decision-making authority is concentrated in the hands of ethnic (Han) Chinese officials of the CCP, which has a monopoly on political power. In August 2016, Wu Yingjie replaced Chen Quanguo as TAR party secretary. The few ethnic Tibetans who occupy senior positions serve mostly as figureheads and echo official doctrine. Losang Gyaltsen, an ethnic Tibetan, has been chairman of the TAR government since 2013. As in other jurisdictions of China, there are no direct elections above the lowest administrative levels, and aggressive state interference ensures that competitive races with independent candidates are exceedingly rare.

B. Political Pluralism and Participation: 0 / 16

All organized political activity outside the CCP is illegal and harshly punished, as is any evidence of loyalty to or communication with the Tibetan government in exile, based in Dharamsala, India. The exile government includes an elected parliament serving five-year terms, a Supreme Justice Commission that adjudicates civil disputes, and a directly elected prime minister, also serving five-year terms. Votes are collected from the Tibetan diaspora around the world. The unelected Dalai Lama, the Tibetan spiritual leader who also traditionally served as head of state, renounced his political role in 2011. Lobsang Sangay was elected prime minister in the same year, replacing a two-term incumbent and becoming the exile government's top political official; he was reelected in April 2016.

Political opportunities for ethnic Tibetans within Tibet remain limited by the dominance of ethnic Chinese officials at all levels of the CCP. The ethnic Tibetan population's concerns about and objections to party policies are actively suppressed.

C. Functioning of Government: 1 / 12

Unelected CCP officials determine and implement government policies in Tibet. As in the rest of China, corruption is believed to be extensive. Little information is available on the scale of the problem, but there have been moves in recent years to curb graft among the region's officials as part of Chinese president Xi's nationwide anticorruption campaign. For instance, following investigations that began in 2015, Chinese prosecutors filed corruption charges in September 2016 against Le Dake, a former TAR legislator. He was found guilty of taking bribes and sentenced to a 13-year prison term in December. Despite this anticorruption climate, prosecutions are believed to be politically selective, and whistle-blowers and activists who challenge their superiors or take their complaints public still face substantial risks. In October, a Tibetan township official who had raised questions about corruption was released after serving a 15-month prison term for "illegal activities," in what was apparently a retaliatory prosecution.

Discretionary Political Rights Question B: − 3 / 0

The Chinese government's economic development programs in Tibet have strongly encouraged ethnic Chinese migration to the region, disproportionately benefited ethnic Chinese residents, and exacerbated the marginalization of ethnic Tibetans, who have also been displaced by mass resettlement campaigns. Ethnic Tibetans account for some 90 percent of the permanently registered population of the TAR, but many ethnic Chinese migrants have moved to the region without changing permanent residency. In recent years, officials have announced major new urbanization projects that risk further diluting the region's Tibetan population; one such plan aims to increase the "permanent urban population" of Tibet by approximately 30 percent by 2020, with many new settlers likely to be ethnic Chinese.

CIVIL LIBERTIES: 3 / 60

D. Freedom of Expression and Belief: 0 / 16

Chinese authorities tightly restrict all news media in Tibet. Individuals who use the internet, social media, or other means to disseminate dissenting views or share politically sensitive content face arrest and harsh penalties. Tibetan cultural expression, which the authorities associate with separatism, is subject to especially harsh restrictions; those incarcerated in recent years have included scores of Tibetan writers, intellectuals, and musicians. Among other prominent cases in 2016, blogger Drukar Gyal (Druklo) was sentenced to three years in prison in February on charges of inciting separatism and endangering social stability; before his detention in early 2015, he had written about the increased armed security presence in Tibet and the political repression of Tibetans by Chinese authorities. Writer and monk Jo Lobsang Jamyang (Lomik), who had also been detained in 2015 after publishing articles that were critical of government policies, was sentenced to a prison term of seven and a half years in May.

Deliberate internet blackouts are common in Tibet, including in areas where public demonstrations have occurred. International broadcasts are jammed, and personal communications devices are periodically confiscated and searched. The online censorship and monitoring systems in place across China are applied even more stringently in the TAR.

Access to the TAR is highly restricted for foreign journalists, who are also regularly prevented from entering Tibetan areas of Sichuan and other provinces, though no permission is technically required to travel there. The Foreign Correspondents' Club of China reported in April 2016 that foreign journalists are limited to government-approved trips and face restrictions on their movement once in Tibetan areas. Tibetans who communicate with foreign media without permission risk arrest and prosecution. Businessman Tashi Wangchuck was detained in January and accused of inciting separatism after being interviewed by the *New York Times* in 2015 on Tibetan-language education; a court in Qinghai Province was considering a possible trial at year's end.

Freedom of religion is harshly restricted in Tibet, in large part because the authorities interpret reverence for the Dalai Lama and adherence to the region's unique form of Buddhism as a threat to CCP rule. At an April 2016 party conference, President Xi repeated calls for the "Sinicization" of all religions, warning against "overseas infiltrations via religious means" and "ideological infringement by extremists." A number of Tibetan Buddhist monks were arrested during the year for publicly protesting state repression, opposing land grabs, or displaying images of the Dalai Lama. Possession of Dalai Lama–related materials—especially in the TAR—can lead to official harassment, arrest, and punishment, including restrictions on commercial activity and loss of welfare benefits. In January and March, authorities in Tibetan areas of Sichuan and Qinghai Provinces, respectively, issued bans on displaying images of the Dalai Lama in shops and religious settings.

Religious Affairs Bureaus control who can study in monasteries and nunneries. Officials enforce a minimum age requirement of 18 for those who wish to become monks or nuns, although some institutions continue to accept younger children without registration. Monks and nuns are required to sign a declaration rejecting Tibetan independence, expressing loyalty to the government, and denouncing the Dalai Lama. Since 2012, the CCP has set up committees of government officials within monasteries to manage their daily operations and enforce party indoctrination campaigns. Police posts are increasingly common even in smaller monasteries.

Ideological education campaigns reach most monasteries and nunneries in the region. Such campaigns typically force participants to recognize the CCP claim that China "liberated" Tibet and to denounce the Dalai Lama. The effort has also been extended to the lay population in recent years, with students, civil servants, and farmers required to participate in discussions, singing sessions, and propaganda film screenings.

In June 2016, authorities ordered a sharp reduction in the size of Larung Gar—a major center for Tibetan Buddhist learning located in the Garzê Tibetan Autonomous Prefecture in Sichuan Province—to a maximum of 5,000 occupants, down from an estimated 10,000 to 30,000 occupants. Demolitions at the site began in July, and many of the evicted monks and nuns were reportedly forced to undergo political "reeducation" before being sent to their home districts.

University professors cannot lecture on certain topics, and many must attend political indoctrination sessions. The government restricts course materials to prevent circulation of unofficial versions of Tibetan history, and has reduced use of Tibetan as the language of instruction in schools in recent years.

Freedom of private discussion is severely limited by factors including the authorities' monitoring of electronic communications, the heavy security presence, and regular ideological campaigns in Tibetan areas.

E. Associational and Organizational Rights: 0 / 12

Chinese authorities severely restrict freedoms of assembly and association, particularly as the government has intensified its "stability maintenance" policy throughout Tibet. A Human Rights Watch report released in May 2016 documented a significant increase in control and surveillance of public gatherings and associations in rural areas in recent years, expanding the tightest restrictions beyond major towns. Independent trade unions and human rights groups are illegal, and even nonviolent protesters are often violently dispersed and harshly punished. Nongovernmental organizations (NGOs), including those focused only on apolitical issues like development and public health, operate under highly restrictive agreements. Nevertheless, Tibetans continue to seek avenues for expressing dissatisfaction with government policies. In May 2016, over 100 Tibetan demonstrators staged a peaceful protest in Sichuan's Garzê Tibetan Autonomous Prefecture against Chinese mining operations that threatened the environment. Similarly, in June, at least seven Tibetan demonstrators were detained after hundreds participated in a nine-day protest against a gold-mining project at a sacred site in Gansu Province. As in the rest of China, authorities have occasionally responded to environmental protests with minor concessions, such as temporary suspension of mining operations.

F. Rule of Law: 0 / 16

The CCP controls the judicial system in Tibet, and courts consequently lack independence. Critics of Chinese rule continue to face arrests, disappearances, and torture in custody. According to a partial database compiled by the U.S. Congressional-Executive Commission on China, there were 650 Tibetan political prisoners behind bars as of August 1, 2016. Defendants lack access to meaningful legal representation. Trials are closed if state security is invoked, and sometimes even when no political crime is listed. Chinese lawyers who offer to defend Tibetan suspects have been harassed or disbarred. Security forces routinely engage in arbitrary detention, and detainees' families are often left uninformed as to their whereabouts or well-being. There have been reports that Tibetan prisoners of conscience have died in custody under circumstances indicating torture. In February 2016, for instance, a Tibetan man died after suspected torture while serving a 13-year prison term for refusing to fly a Chinese flag.

At least three Tibetans reportedly self-immolated to protest Chinese rule during 2016, but instances of self-immolation have steadily declined in recent years, apparently due in part to state-imposed deterrents. Officials have responded to immolation incidents with information blackouts, a heightened security presence, and increased surveillance. Official guidelines state that engaging in self-immolations and organizing, assisting, or gathering crowds related to such acts should be considered criminal offenses, including intentional homicide in some cases. The government has also employed collective-punishment tactics to discourage self-immolations and other protests, imposing financial penalties on families, canceling public benefits for the households of self-immolators or other activists, and ending state-funded projects in their villages.

LGBT (lesbian, gay, bisexual, and transgender) people suffer from discrimination, though same-sex activities are not criminalized. No LGBT-focused groups operate in the TAR, and social pressures discourage discussion of LGBT issues.

G. Personal Autonomy and Individual Rights: 3 / 16

Obstacles including troop deployments, checkpoints, roadblocks, required bureaucratic approvals, and passport restrictions impede freedom of movement within and beyond Tibetan areas, particularly for travel to and from the TAR. Increased security efforts and Nepalese government cooperation have made it difficult for Tibetans to cross the border into Nepal. Fewer than a hundred Tibetans have reportedly made the crossing each year since 2014, down from more than 2,000 in 2007. Obtaining a passport for foreign travel is extremely difficult for Tibetans.

Authorities continue to restrict access to the TAR for human rights researchers, as well as for some tourists. Foreigners are often denied entry surrounding politically sensitive dates, such as the anniversary of the 2008 protests. During other periods, tourists must travel in groups and obtain official permission to visit the TAR, and even then, last-minute travel bans are periodically imposed.

Tibetans receive preferential treatment in university admission examinations, but this is often not enough to secure entrance. The dominant role of the Chinese language in education and employment limits opportunities for many Tibetans. Private employers favor ethnic Chinese for many jobs, and Tibetans reportedly find it more difficult to obtain permits and loans to open businesses.

Since 2003, the authorities have intensified efforts to resettle rural and nomadic Tibetans—forcibly or with incentives—into permanent-housing areas with little economic infrastructure. According to Human Rights Watch, more than two million TAR residents have been resettled since 2006. Many have reportedly tried to return to their previous lands, risking conflict with officials.

China's restrictive family-planning policies are more leniently enforced for Tibetans and other ethnic minorities. Officials limit urban Tibetans to two children and encourage rural Tibetans to stop at three. As a result, the TAR is one of the few areas of China without a skewed sex ratio. Women are well represented in many public-sector jobs and CCP posts within the TAR, though most high-level officials are men. Women reportedly suffer specific religious and political persecution related to Chinese suppression of Tibetan identity. Tibetan women continue to be targets of human trafficking, with many taken to China for domestic service or forced marriages.

Transnistria

Political Rights Rating: 6
Civil Liberties Rating: 6
Freedom Rating: 6.0
Freedom Status: Not Free

Population: 476,000

Ten-Year Ratings Timeline For Year Under Review (Political Rights, Civil Liberties, Status)

Year Under Review	2007	2008	2009	2010	2011	2012	2013	2014	2015	2016
Rating	6,6,NF	6,6,NF	6,6,NF	6,6,NF	6 6,NF	6,6,NF	6,6,NF	6,6,NF	6,6,NF	6,6,NF

Overview: Transnistria, a breakaway region of Moldova in which ethnic Russians and Ukrainians together outnumber ethnic Moldovans, has enjoyed de facto independence since a brief civil conflict in 1992, though it is internationally recognized as a part of Moldova. Its government and economy are heavily dependent on subsidies from Russia, which maintains a military presence in the territory. Political competition is limited, and the dominant party is aligned with Sheriff Enterprises, a monopolistic business conglomerate that is Transnistria's largest employer and taxpayer. Nearly all media outlets are controlled by the state or Sheriff Enterprises, and all civil society activities must be coordinated with local authorities. The justice system features arbitrary or politically motivated arrests, harsh prison conditions, and reports of torture. The ethnic Moldovan (Romanian-speaking) minority faces discrimination, and same-sex sexual activity is illegal.

KEY DEVELOPMENTS IN 2016:

- Vadim Krasnoselsky of the Obnovleniye (Renewal) party, which is associated with Sheriff Enterprises, defeated incumbent Yevgeniy Shevchuk in the December presidential election.
- Russian and Transnistrian troops held join military exercises in August, underscoring the close relationship between Moscow and Tiraspol.

EXECUTIVE SUMMARY

The December 2016 presidential election was held in the context of worsening economic conditions. Exports declined during the year, the Transnistrian ruble lost value, and in July Ukraine began restricting the flow of goods directly into the territory by rail, forcing such traffic to flow through Moldova proper. Obnovleniye, which controlled the legislature, accused President Shevchuk of embezzling Russian subsidies, while Shevchuk's government backed a bill calling on Sheriff Enterprises to repay $250 million of the state benefits it had received between 2007 and 2011 in order to help cover public expenses.

Krasnoselsky, the speaker of parliament, won the election in the first round with 62 percent of the vote. Shevchuk, who had been a leading figure in Obnovleniye before he split with the party in 2011, took 27 percent, and the remainder was divided among four other candidates. Voter turnout was 59 percent.

During the campaign, the main contenders competed to demonstrate their pro-Russian credentials. Transnistrian forces held joint military exercises with Russian troops in August, and in September Shevchuk issued a decree mandating that Transnistria adjust its legislation to comport with Russian laws in order to realize the result of a 2006 referendum in which the territory's voters affirmed the independence of Transnistria and their desire for it to join the Russian Federation.

Also in September, the parliament passed legislation giving itself greater authority over state media outlets, including the power to appoint editorial staff, and restricting the ability of any branch of government to establish media outlets without cooperation from the other branches. Moreover, the legislation enabled officials to limit media access to their activities and bar the use of recording devices. Other laws passed that month imposed restrictions or penalties related to unauthorized distribution of religious literature, preaching in public spaces, and organized religious activities in residential buildings.

POLITICAL RIGHTS: 10 / 40

A. Electoral Process: 3 / 12

B. Political Pluralism and Participation: 5 / 16

C. Functioning of Government: 2 / 12

CIVIL LIBERTIES: 14 / 60

D. Freedom of Expression and Belief: 5 / 16

E. Associational and Organizational Rights: 2 / 12

F. Rule of Law: 2 / 16
G. Personal Autonomy and Individual Rights: 5 / 16

This territory report has been abridged for *Freedom in the World 2017*. For background information on political rights and civil liberties in Transnistria, see *Freedom in the World 2016*.

West Bank

Population: 2,698,000

[Note: This figure represents the Palestinian population only.]
Political Rights Rating: 7 ↓
Civil Liberties Rating: 5
Freedom Rating: 6.0
Freedom Status: Not Free

Ratings Change: The West Bank's political rights rating declined from 6 to 7 due to the controversial postponement of municipal elections, which adversely affected the ability of opposition forces to meaningfully compete in the political arena.

Note: The numerical ratings and status listed above do not reflect conditions in Israel or the Gaza Strip, which are examined in separate reports. Prior to its 2011 edition, *Freedom in the World* featured one report for Israeli-occupied portions of the West Bank and Gaza Strip and another for Palestinian-administered portions.

Ten-Year Ratings Timeline For Year Under Review (Political Rights, Civil Liberties, Status)

Year Under Review	2007	2008	2009	2010	2011	2012	2013	2014	2015	2016
Rating	—	—	—	6,5,NF	6,5,NF	6,5,NF	6,5,NF	6,5,NF	6,5,NF	7,5,NF

Overview: The West Bank is under Israeli military occupation and is subject to the partial jurisdiction of the Palestinian Authority (PA), which is operating under an expired presidential mandate and has no functioning legislature. The Israeli occupation entails substantial physical barriers and constraints on movement, demolitions of homes and businesses, severe restrictions on political and civil liberties, and expanding Jewish settlements. The PA itself has grown more authoritarian, engaging in crackdowns on the media and human rights activists who criticize its rule.

KEY DEVELOPMENTS IN 2016:
- The PA postponed all local elections planned for October after its highest court ruled that voting could not proceed in East Jerusalem or Gaza, though critics of the move argued that it was politically motivated.
- The number of Israeli demolitions and seizures of Palestinian-owned structures nearly doubled compared with 2015, whereas Israel approved $20 million in additional funding for Jewish settlements in June.
- The PA reportedly revoked the licenses of dozens of nongovernmental organizations (NGOs) during the year, citing legal irregularities.

- Israeli forces temporarily cut off all access to several villages following terrorist attacks on nearby Jewish settlements, disrupting entire communities' livelihoods for days or weeks at a time.

EXECUTIVE SUMMARY

Mahmoud Abbas marked his 11th year as president of the PA in 2016, as well as his seventh year without an electoral mandate, having remained in office beyond his original four-year term. The PA also remained without a legislature, as the council elected in 2006 was unable to function after a 2007 schism between Abbas's Fatah faction and the Islamist group Hamas, which seized control of the Gaza Strip. That legislature's term expired in 2010.

Local elections planned for October were postponed following a ruling by the PA's High Court of Justice that voting could not proceed in Gaza or East Jerusalem. The postponement, which affected the entire territory, drew harsh criticism from Hamas and independents, as many perceived the decision as a politicized effort to ward off challenges to Abbas's rule. Separately in August, PA security officers beat a shooting suspect to death in custody, drawing criticism from multiple political factions and outside observers amid concerns about a deteriorating political and human rights environment.

Israel maintained restrictions on movement for the Palestinian population while promoting the growth of Jewish settlements, despite new censure at the UN Security Council, which adopted a resolution stating that the settlements lacked "legal validity" and calling for a halt to all settlement activity.

POLITICAL RIGHTS: 5 / 40 (− 1)

A. Electoral Process: 2 / 12

Palestinian residents of the West Bank fall under the overlapping control of Israel and the PA, an interim self-governing body created by the 1993 Oslo Accords with partial jurisdiction in the West Bank and Gaza Strip. Jewish settlers in the West Bank are Israeli citizens. Israel claims full sovereignty over East Jerusalem, though its annexation of the area is not internationally recognized, and most Palestinian residents do not hold Israeli citizenship.

Under the laws in place for the most recent PA elections, the PA president is elected to four-year terms. The prime minister is nominated by the president and requires the support of the unicameral, 132-seat Palestinian Legislative Council (PLC), which also serves four-year terms.

Voting in the West Bank during the 2005 presidential and 2006 PLC elections was deemed largely free and fair by international observers. Abbas won the presidency with 62 percent of the vote, but Hamas led the PLC balloting with 74 seats, leaving Fatah with 45. The two factions formed a unity government headed by Prime Minister Ismail Haniya of Hamas.

After the 2007 schism between the two groups left Hamas in de facto control of the Gaza Strip, Abbas appointed a new prime minister and cabinet in the West Bank without the PLC's approval. In 2008, PA security forces arrested hundreds of Hamas members and supporters. The rift, combined with Israel's detention of many Palestinian lawmakers, prevented the PLC from functioning, and its term expired in 2010. Meanwhile, the Fatah-led Palestine Liberation Organization (PLO) indefinitely extended Abbas's presidential term after his electoral mandate expired in 2009.

Also in 2009, Abbas issued a law permitting the Fatah-affiliated minister of local government to dissolve municipal councils elected in 2005 after their four-year mandates expired, leading to the replacement of nearly all Hamas-affiliated municipal officials in the West Bank with Fatah loyalists. In 2012, elections were held for more than 90 of the West Bank's 353 municipalities amid some accusations of unfairness, with Hamas and Islamic Jihad boycotting. Only half of eligible Palestinians registered to participate, and only 54 percent of those registered actually voted. Fatah won 40 percent of the seats at stake; others were taken by independents, including many former Fatah members.

The PA cabinet scheduled local elections for October 2016 across the Palestinian territories, following an agreement with Hamas to allow it to administer elections in Gaza. In September, however, the PA High Court of Justice suspended the elections, citing ongoing disputes about the exclusion of East Jerusalem and the legality of preelection court judgments in Gaza. In early October, the High Court ruled that the elections could proceed in the West Bank only, leading the PA government to postpone all municipal elections by at least four months.

Renewed discussions on forming a national unity government and ending the Fatah-led PA's schism with Hamas were under way at the end of 2016, though repeated attempts at such a reconciliation had failed to gain traction in previous years.

B. Political Pluralism and Participation: 4 / 16 (− 1)

The PA and Israeli forces in the West Bank have largely sought to suppress Hamas since its 2006 election victory, intermittently engaging in mass arrests and closures of affiliated organizations. Abbas and his government have also taken administrative and bureaucratic actions to marginalize potential political rivals within Fatah; he was reelected as Fatah's leader by handpicked delegates at a November 2016 party conference. A number of smaller Palestinian parties continue to operate, including through membership in the PLO.

Israeli authorities arrested the Hamas representative on the Palestinian Central Elections Commission (CEC) in August 2016 in advance of the planned municipal voting. The CEC certified approximately 860 political party and independent candidate lists for 416 districts in the West Bank and Gaza Strip. The PA's postponement of the elections was widely perceived as an effort to block anticipated Hamas and independent gains at the council level.

Palestinian residents of East Jerusalem who do not hold Israeli citizenship can participate in Israeli municipal elections, but are precluded from voting in Knesset (parliament) elections. They are formally entitled to vote in PA presidential and legislative elections, according to the 1993 Oslo Accords. In the 2006 PLC elections, Israel did not allow Hamas to campaign in the city. Hundreds of checkpoints, roadblocks, permit restrictions, and the security barrier that Israel has constructed along the West Bank side of the pre-1967 border also present obstacles to political participation, both in East Jerusalem and across the West Bank. The PA's inability to organize municipal elections in East Jerusalem due to Israeli control was cited as part of the rationale for postponing the broader municipal voting in 2016.

C. Functioning of Government: 2 / 12

The PA lacks an elected executive and legislature, as the PLC ceased functioning after the 2007 schism and both its and Abbas's electoral mandates have long since expired. Moreover, the PA's ability to implement policy decisions is limited in practice by direct Israeli control over much of the West Bank, including the movement and travel of PA officials, staff, and related personnel and contractors. Israel sometimes withholds the transfer of tax revenues to the PA. Israeli authorities have also routinely imprisoned PLC members, particularly Hamas deputies, as Israel regards Hamas as an illegal terrorist organization. As of October 2016, six PLC members were imprisoned.

In 2015, the PA Anti-Corruption Commission put forward an anticorruption strategy for 2015–18. The Coalition for Accountability and Integrity (AMAN) reported in April 2016 that there was increased public awareness of anticorruption mechanisms, but noted continuing government corruption in a number of areas, including favoritism in the allocation of public-sector jobs and contracts and a lack of transparency in budgetary matters.

The cabinet has discussed the adoption of an access to information law with civil society groups, but passage of a draft law stalled in 2015. In March 2016, a coalition of NGOs, including AMAN, formed a crisis management cell to monitor the PA's executive decision-making, citing opaque procedures for the formation of policies and legislation.

DISCRETIONARY POLITICAL RIGHTS QUESTION B: $-3 / 0$

Jewish settlements, related seizures of Palestinian land, and home demolitions in the West Bank spiked in 2016. According to the UN Office for the Coordination of Human Affairs (UNOCHA), 1,093 Palestinian-owned structures in the West Bank, including East Jerusalem, were demolished or seized during the year, nearly double the number for 2015, with a comparative monthly average of 91 versus 46. More than 1,600 Palestinians were displaced as result of these demolitions or seizures. A fraction of such demolitions are conducted to punish families of Palestinians accused of perpetrating violence against Israelis or in the course of military operations. Israel cited a lack of Israeli-issued building permits for the majority of demolitions and seizures, which occurred in East Jerusalem and in Area C, the portion of the West Bank under its direct administrative and security control.

In June 2016, Israel reportedly approved $20 million in additional financing for Jewish settlements in the West Bank and continued throughout the year to retroactively formalize certain ad hoc settlement outposts. As of the summer, Israel was moving ahead with plans to build more than 1,735 housing units in the West Bank, including 1,000 in East Jerusalem. In December, the UN Security Council adopted Resolution 2334, declaring that the settlements lacked "legal validity" and calling for all settlement activity to cease. Approximately 600,000 Jewish settlers were living in the West Bank, including East Jerusalem, as of 2016.

CIVIL LIBERTIES: 23 / 60 (-1)

D. Freedom of Expression and Belief: 8 / 16 (-1)

The media are not free in the West Bank. Under a 1995 PA press law, journalists may be fined and jailed, and newspapers closed, for publishing "secret information" on PA security forces or news that might harm national unity or incite violence. Media outlets are routinely pressured to provide favorable coverage of the PA and Fatah. Journalists and bloggers who criticize the PA or Fatah have faced arbitrary arrests, threats, and physical abuse. Reporters are also subject to administrative detention and assault by Israeli forces. Since 2007, both the PA and Israeli forces have regularly suppressed Hamas-affiliated media outlets in the West Bank.

The Palestinian Center for Development and Media Freedoms (MADA) reported 86 press freedom violations—including physical assaults—by Palestinian forces in the West Bank in 2016, down from 116 the previous year. According to the same report, Israeli authorities were responsible for 249 violations in the Palestinian territories, down from 407 in 2015. Although the figures reflected a general reduction in unrest and violence compared with 2014 and 2015, they still represented an increase from pre-2014 statistics.

The PA Basic Law declares Islam to be the official religion of Palestine and states that "respect and sanctity of all other heavenly religions (Judaism and Christianity) shall be maintained." Blasphemy against Islam is a criminal offense. Some Palestinian Christians have experienced intimidation and harassment by radical Islamist groups and PA officials.

Restrictions on movement and access serve as a general barrier to freedom of religion for Palestinians in the West Bank. Israel permits limited Palestinian access to Al-Aqsa Mosque in East Jerusalem during Muslim holidays. In 2016, male access to the site for Friday prayers was restricted to boys under age 12 and men over age 45. New rules also precluded access for Palestinians resident in select East Jerusalem neighborhoods. Attacks on religious sites by radical Jewish settlers, including vandalism of churches and mosques, have increased in recent years.

The PA has administrative authority over Palestinian education. Israeli movement restrictions limit access to academic institutions. Schools have sometimes been damaged during military actions, and student travel between the West Bank and the Gaza Strip has been limited.

Israeli academic institutions in the West Bank increasingly face international and domestic boycotts. Primary and secondary education in West Bank settlements is administered by Israel, though religious schools have significant discretion over curriculums. According to the Association for Civil Rights in Israel, East Jerusalem's schools are badly underfunded compared with schools in West Jerusalem.

Private discussion is relatively open and free, though both Israeli and PA security forces are known to monitor online activity and arrest individuals for alleged incitement or criticism of the Palestinian authorities.

E. Associational and Organizational Rights: 5 / 12

The PA requires permits for demonstrations, and those held to protest against PA policies are generally dispersed. Israel's Military Order 101 requires a permit for all "political" demonstrations of more than 10 people; demonstrations in Israeli-controlled areas are routinely broken up with force, occasionally resulting in fatalities. Such clashes increased in 2015, as Israeli forces sought to restrict and disperse frequent and sometimes violent demonstrations, declaring some protest areas to be closed military zones. Similar confrontations occurred during 2016.

A broad range of NGOs are able to operate in the West Bank, though in 2016 the PA cracked down on some civil society groups, reportedly closing 50 NGOs and charities in May and 16 in July due to alleged legal irregularities. Israeli restrictions on movement within the West Bank and between the West Bank and Gaza Strip further undermine Palestinian civil society, and human rights NGOs reportedly face harassment and threats from settlers and right-wing Israeli groups. Many Hamas-affiliated groups were shut down following the 2007 schism, and others have been periodically targeted in subsequent years. Activists who criticize the PA leadership can face harassment and abuse by security services.

Workers may establish unions without government authorization, but labor protections in general are poorly enforced. Palestinian workers seeking to strike must submit to arbitration by the PA Labor Ministry, and various other rules make it difficult to mount a legal strike. Palestinian workers in Jerusalem are subject to Israeli labor law.

F. Rule of Law: 5 / 16

The nascent PA judicial system is partly independent. West Bank law derives from Ottoman, British Mandate, and Jordanian law; Israeli law and military orders; and the Palestinian Basic Law and PA legislation. The PA High Judicial Council holds a mandate to appoint judges upon approval of the PA president. The court system allows for the right of appeal. Enforcement of judicial decisions is impeded by PA noncompliance as well as lack of Palestinian jurisdiction in Area C, which covers 60 percent of West Bank territory. Palestinians can appeal Israeli military orders and actions before the Israeli Supreme Court. While the court is often deferential to Israeli authorities, there have been a number of decisions in favor of Palestinian petitioners in recent years.

The PA has a military court system that lacks almost all due process, including the right to appeal sentences, and can impose the death penalty. No executions have been carried out since 2005, however. The PA military courts handle cases on a range of security offenses, on collaborating with Israel, and on drug trafficking. Human rights groups regularly document allegations of arbitrary detention and torture, and PA security officers are rarely punished for such abuses. In August 2016, following the killing of two Palestinian security officers in Nablus, PA forces killed two suspects who they said were armed. Days later, they arrested a third man said to be involved—Ahmad Izz Halaweh, a high-ranking member of a radical armed offshoot of Fatah—who was beaten to death in custody. The incident touched off riots and a further crackdown by the security services.

Palestinians are subject to Israel's military court system for a variety of offenses, from terrorism to illegally entering Israel and traffic violations. Jewish settlers are tried in Israeli civilian courts. Palestinians are regularly detained without charges for extended periods. Petitions challenging administrative detentions and prison sentences are reviewed in secrecy. According to the Israeli human rights group B'Tselem, there were 5,859 Palestinian security detainees and prisoners from the West Bank held in Israeli prisons or military facilities as of August 2016, including 646 administrative detainees and 335 minors.

Most convictions in Israeli military courts are based on confessions, sometimes obtained through coercion. Israel's Supreme Court banned torture in a 1999 ruling, but physical coercion is considered permissible when the prisoner is believed to have vital information about impending attacks. Human rights groups criticize Israeli interrogation methods, which allegedly include some forms of physical abuse, isolation, sleep deprivation, psychological pressure, and threats of violence against detainees and their relatives.

Most Palestinian child detainees are serving sentences of less than a year for throwing stones or other projectiles at Israeli forces in the West Bank, handed down by a special court for minors; acquittals on such charges are very rare. Defense for Children International (DCI) Palestine reports that most of these children are taken from their homes in the middle of the night, interrogated without a parent or lawyer, and subjected to threats as well as physical and verbal abuse. East Jerusalem Palestinian minors are tried in Israeli civilian juvenile courts.

Militant Jewish settlers continued to attack Palestinian individuals and property in 2016, often with the aim of driving Palestinians off their agricultural land. Most perpetrators of such activity enjoy impunity. Israeli soldiers accused of excessive force or abuse of Palestinian civilians are subject to Israeli military law, though convictions, which are rare, typically result in light sentences. In March 2016, soldier Elor Azaria was caught on video killing a wounded and disarmed Palestinian attacker in Hebron. He was tried for manslaughter and was awaiting a verdict at year's end.

Although LGBT (lesbian, gay, bisexual, and transgender) people in the West Bank do not face prosecution for same-sex activity, they are reportedly subject to harassment and abuse by PA authorities and members of society.

G. Personal Autonomy and Individual Rights: 5 / 16

Israeli checkpoints, roadblocks, travel permits, and other restrictions continue to seriously constrain freedom of movement, stunt trade, and limit Palestinian access to jobs, hospitals, and schools. The number of physical barriers decreased in early 2016; however, Israel appeared to step up a practice of cutting off entire communities from key transportation routes following Palestinian attacks on Israeli settlers. In July, one village had its access points sealed after a teenage resident stabbed and killed an Israeli girl in a nearby settlement. The village was cut off for 34 days, and 2,771 permits to work in Israel were canceled. The village was shut down again in September following the killing of two youths accused of attacking Israelis. Israel also continued its practice of revoking work permits for family members of alleged attackers.

The Israeli security barrier, most of which runs through West Bank territory and which was declared illegal in 2004 by the International Court of Justice, continues to separate families and communities and cause general hardship and disruption of services. Israel has not provided compensation to Palestinians who lost access to livelihoods and property due to the barrier.

Palestinian women are underrepresented in most professions and encounter discrimination in employment, though they have equal access to universities. Palestinian laws and societal norms, derived in part from Sharia (Islamic law), disadvantage women in marriage, divorce, and inheritance. For Christians, personal status issues are governed by ecclesiastical courts. Rape and domestic abuse remain underreported and frequently go unpunished, as authorities are allegedly reluctant to pursue such cases. So-called honor killings continue to be reported.

The PA has no law focused on combating trafficking in persons. Some Palestinians—both children and adults—reportedly work in exploitative conditions in Israeli settlements, where the PA has no jurisdiction. Israeli labor laws are rarely applied to protect such workers.

Western Sahara

Political Rights Rating: 7
Civil Liberties Rating: 7
Freedom Rating: 7.0
Freedom Status: Not Free
Electoral Democracy: No

Population: 600,000
Capital: Laâyoune

Ten-Year Ratings Timeline For Year Under Review (Political Rights, Civil Liberties, Status)

Year Under Review	2007	2008	2009	2010	2011	2012	2013	2014	2015	2016
Rating	7,6,NF	7,6,NF	7,6,NF	7,6,NF	7,7,NF	7,7,NF	7,7,NF	7,7,NF	7,7,NF	7,7,NF

Overview: The sovereignty of Western Sahara is the subject of longstanding dispute. Morocco claims authority over the territory, but the Polisario Front—a nationalist liberation movement comprised of members of the Sahrawi ethnic group—leads an independence movement. There are no free elections in Western Sahara. Morocco harshly represses Sahrawi activism. Corruption is rampant at all levels; freedoms of expression and assembly are severely restricted, as is the right to unimpeded movement; and most residents live in harsh conditions.

KEY DEVELOPMENTS IN 2016:

- In a reflection of ongoing tensions, both Moroccan authorities and the Polisario Front deployed new security forces in the Guerguerat region.
- In March, Moroccan authorities expelled dozens of civilian UN staff members, after UN Secretary General Ban Ki Moon referred to Moroccan "occupation" of Western Sahara.
- In October, Moroccan authorities expelled a Spanish human rights expert who had been invited to appear at an event hosted by a newly recognized Saharawi rights group.

EXECUTIVE SUMMARY

Longstanding tensions between Moroccan authorities and the Polisario Front continued in 2016. Meanwhile, the United Nations Mission for the Referendum in Western Sahara (MINURSO), established in 1991 to implement a national referendum on independence for the territory, had yet to fulfill its mandate at year's end. The UN Security Council renewed MINURSO's mission for another year in April.

A few weeks prior to the Security Council vote, Ban sparked a diplomatic dispute when, while visiting a Sahrawi refugee camp in Tindouf, Algeria, he referred to Morocco's "occupation" of Western Sahara. Morocco expelled dozens of civilian UN staff members at MINURSO's office in Laâyoune in retaliation, though some returned later in the year. Tensions flared again in August, when Moroccan authorities sent security forces into the Guerguerat region, on the southern border with Mauritania, saying they were necessary to combat smuggling and drug trafficking. The Polisario Front protested the police action, and set up its own outpost near the Moroccan one.

In 2015, Moroccan officials permitted the Sahrawi Association of Victims of Human Rights Abuses Committed by the Moroccan State to legally register its status as a nongovernmental organization (NGO), winning praise from the human rights community. However, in 2016 Moroccan authorities interfered with its activities, including by expelling in October a Spanish human rights expert the group had invited to Western Sahara for an event.

POLITICAL RIGHTS: − 3 / 40 (− 1)

A. Electoral Process: 0 / 12

B. Political Pluralism and Participation: 0 / 16

C. Functioning of Government: 0 / 12

DISCRETIONARY POLITICAL RIGHTS QUESTION B: − 3 / 0 (− 1)

CIVIL LIBERTIES: 7 / 60

D. Freedom of Expression and Belief: 3 / 16

E. Associational and Organizational Rights: 0 / 12

F. Rule of Law: 0 / 16

G. Personal Autonomy and Individual Rights: 4 / 16

This country report has been abridged for *Freedom in the World 2017*. For background information on political rights and civil liberties in Western Sahara, see *Freedom in the World 2016*.

Survey Methodology

INTRODUCTION

Freedom in the World is an annual global report on political rights and civil liberties, composed of numerical ratings and descriptive texts for each country and a select group of related and disputed territories. The 2017 edition covers developments in 195 countries and 14 territories from January 1, 2016, through December 31, 2016.

The report's methodology is derived in large measure from the Universal Declaration of Human Rights, adopted by the UN General Assembly in 1948. *Freedom in the World* is based on the premise that these standards apply to all countries and territories, irrespective of geographical location, ethnic or religious composition, or level of economic development. *Freedom in the World* operates from the assumption that freedom for all peoples is best achieved in liberal democratic societies.

Freedom in the World assesses the real-world rights and freedoms enjoyed by individuals, rather than governments or government performance per se. Political rights and civil liberties can be affected by both state and nonstate actors, including insurgents and other armed groups.

Freedom House does not equate legal guarantees of rights with the on-the-ground fulfillment of those rights. While both laws and actual practices are factored into the ratings decisions, greater emphasis is placed on implementation.

Countries and territories with small populations are not penalized for lacking pluralism in the political system or civil society if these limitations are determined to be a function of size and not overt restrictions by the government or other powerful actors.

Territories are selected for inclusion in *Freedom in the World* based on their political significance and size. Freedom House divides territories into two categories: related territories and disputed territories. Related territories are in some relation of dependency to a sovereign state, and the relationship is not currently in serious legal or political dispute. Disputed territories are areas within internationally recognized sovereign states whose status is in serious political or violent dispute, and whose conditions differ substantially from those of the relevant sovereign states. They are often outside of central government control and characterized by intense, longtime, and widespread insurgency or independence movements that enjoy popular support. Freedom House typically takes no position on territorial or separatist disputes as such, focusing instead on the level of political rights and civil liberties in a given geographical area.

HISTORY OF *FREEDOM IN THE WORLD*

Freedom House's first year-end reviews of freedom began in the 1950s as the *Balance Sheet of Freedom*. This modest report provided assessments of political trends and their implications for individual freedom. In 1972, Freedom House launched a new, more comprehensive annual study called *The Comparative Study of Freedom*. Raymond Gastil, a Harvard-trained specialist in regional studies from the University of Washington in Seattle, developed the methodology, which assigned political rights and civil liberties ratings to 151 countries and 45 territories and categorized them as Free, Partly Free, or Not Free. The findings appeared each year in Freedom House's *Freedom at Issue* bimonthly journal (later titled *Freedom Review*). *Freedom in the World* first appeared in book form in 1978 and included short narratives for each country and territory rated in the study, as well as a series of essays by leading scholars on related issues. *Freedom in the World* continued to be produced by Gastil until 1989, when a larger team of in-house analysts was established. In the mid-1990s, the expansion of the country and territory narratives demanded the hiring of outside analysts—a group of regional experts from the academic, media, and human rights communities—and the project has continued to grow in size and scope in the years since.

The methodology is reviewed periodically, and a number of modest changes have been made over the years to adapt to evolving ideas about political rights and civil liberties. However, the time-series data are not revised retroactively, and any changes to the methodology are introduced incrementally in order to ensure the comparability of the ratings from year to year.

RESEARCH AND RATINGS REVIEW PROCESS

Freedom in the World is produced each year by a team of in-house and external analysts and expert advisers from the academic, think tank, and human rights communities. The 2017 edition involved more than 100 analysts and nearly 30 advisers. The analysts, who prepare the draft reports and scores, use a broad range of sources, including news articles, academic analyses, reports from nongovernmental organizations, and individual professional contacts. The analysts score countries based on the conditions and events within their borders during the coverage period. The analysts' proposed scores are discussed and defended at annual review meetings, organized by region and attended by Freedom House staff and a panel of the expert advisers. The final scores represent the consensus of the analysts, advisers, and staff, and are intended to be comparable from year to year and across countries and regions. The advisers also provide a detailed review of and commentary on a number of key country and territory reports. Although an element of subjectivity is unavoidable in such an enterprise, the ratings process emphasizes methodological consistency, intellectual rigor, and balanced and unbiased judgments.

RATINGS PROCESS

Freedom in the World uses a three-tiered rating system, consisting of **scores**, **ratings**, and **status**. The complete list of the questions used in the scoring process, and the tables for converting scores to ratings and ratings to status, appear at the end of this essay.

Scores – A country or territory is awarded 0 to 4 points for each of 10 political rights indicators and 15 civil liberties indicators, which take the form of questions; a score of 0 represents the smallest degree of freedom and 4 the greatest degree of freedom. The political rights questions are grouped into three subcategories: Electoral Process (3 questions), Political Pluralism and Participation (4), and Functioning of Government (3). The civil liberties questions are grouped into four subcategories: Freedom of Expression and Belief (4 questions), Associational and Organizational Rights (3), Rule of Law (4), and Personal Autonomy and Individual Rights (4). The political rights section also contains two additional discretionary questions. For additional discretionary question A, a score of 1 to 4 may be added, as applicable, while for discretionary question B, a score of 1 to 4 may be subtracted, as applicable (the worse the situation, the more points may be subtracted). The highest score that can be awarded to the political rights checklist is 40 (or a total score of 4 for each of the 10 questions). The highest score that can be awarded to the civil liberties checklist is 60 (or a total score of 4 for each of the 15 questions). The scores from the previous edition are used as a benchmark for the current year under review. A score is typically changed only if there has been a real-world development during the year that warrants a decline or improvement (e.g., a crackdown on the media, the country's first free and fair elections), though gradual changes in conditions, in the absence of a signal event, are occasionally registered in the scores.

Political Rights and Civil Liberties Ratings – A country or territory is assigned two ratings (7 to 1)—one for political rights and one for civil liberties—based on its total scores for the political rights and civil liberties questions. Each rating of 1 through 7, with 1 representing the greatest degree of freedom and 7 the smallest degree of freedom, corresponds to a specific range of total scores (see tables 1 and 2).

Free, Partly Free, Not Free Status – The average of a country's or territory's political rights and civil liberties ratings is called the Freedom Rating, and it is this figure that determines the status of Free (1.0 to 2.5), Partly Free (3.0 to 5.0), or Not Free (5.5 to 7.0) (see table 3).

Trend Arrows – A country or territory may be assigned an upward or downward trend arrow to highlight developments of major significance or concern. These developments may include a positive or negative shift over multiple years, an especially notable change in a single year, or an important event in a country that is particularly influential in its region or the world. A trend arrow must be linked to a specific change or changes in score, and cannot be assigned if the country had no net change in score. Unlike in previous years, countries whose scores triggered a change in ratings or status could also be assigned a trend arrow in *Freedom in the World 2017*. Most score changes do not warrant trend arrows. Decisions on whether a country or territory should receive a trend arrow are made by Freedom House staff, after consultation with the analyst and expert advisers.

Electoral Democracy – *Freedom in the World* assigns the designation "electoral democracy" to countries that have met certain minimum standards for political rights; territories are not included in the list of electoral democracies. According to the methodology, an electoral democracy designation requires a score of 7 or better in the Electoral Process subcategory and an overall political rights score of 20 or better. Freedom House's term "electoral democracy" differs from "liberal democracy" in that the latter also implies the presence of a substantial array of civil liberties. In *Freedom in the World*, all Free countries can be considered both electoral and liberal democracies, while some Partly Free countries qualify as electoral, but not liberal, democracies.

RATINGS AND STATUS CHARACTERISTICS
Political Rights

1 – Countries and territories with a rating of 1 enjoy a wide range of political rights, including free and fair elections. Candidates who are elected actually rule, political parties are competitive, the opposition plays an important role and enjoys real power, and the interests of minority groups are well represented in politics and government.

2 - Countries and territories with a rating of 2 have slightly weaker political rights than those with a rating of 1 because of such factors as political corruption, limits on the functioning of political parties and opposition groups, and foreign or military influence on politics.

3, 4, 5 – Countries and territories with a rating of 3, 4, or 5 either moderately protect almost all political rights or strongly protect some political rights while neglecting others. The same factors that undermine freedom in countries with a rating of 2 may also weaken political rights in those with a rating of 3, 4, or 5, but to a greater extent at each successive rating.

6 – Countries and territories with a rating of 6 have very restricted political rights. They are ruled by one-party or military dictatorships, religious hierarchies, or autocrats. They may allow a few political rights, such as some representation or autonomy for minority groups, and a few are traditional monarchies that tolerate political discussion and accept public petitions.

7 – Countries and territories with a rating of 7 have few or no political rights because of severe government oppression, sometimes in combination with civil war. They may also lack an authoritative and functioning central government and suffer from extreme violence or rule by regional warlords.

Civil Liberties

1 – Countries and territories with a rating of 1 enjoy a wide range of civil liberties, including freedoms of expression, assembly, association, education, and religion. They have an established and generally fair legal system that ensures the rule of law (including an independent judiciary), allow free economic activity, and tend to strive for equality of opportunity for everyone, including women and minority groups.

2 – Countries and territories with a rating of 2 have slightly weaker civil liberties than those with a rating of 1 because of such factors as limits on media independence, restrictions on trade union activities, and discrimination against minority groups and women.

3, 4, 5 – Countries and territories with a rating of 3, 4, or 5 either moderately protect almost all civil liberties or strongly protect some civil liberties while neglecting others. The same factors that undermine freedom in countries with a rating of 2 may also weaken civil liberties in those with a rating of 3, 4, or 5, but to a greater extent at each successive rating.

6 – Countries and territories with a rating of 6 have very restricted civil liberties. They strongly limit the rights of expression and association and frequently hold political prisoners. They may allow a few civil liberties, such as some religious and social freedoms, some highly restricted private business activity, and some open and free private discussion.

7 – Countries and territories with a rating of 7 have few or no civil liberties. They allow virtually no freedom of expression or association, do not protect the rights of detainees and prisoners, and often control or dominate most economic activity.

The gap between a country's or territory's political rights and civil liberties ratings is rarely more than two points. Politically oppressive states typically do not allow a well-developed civil society, for example, and it is difficult, if not impossible, to maintain political freedoms in the absence of civil liberties like press freedom and the rule of law.

Because the designations of Free, Partly Free, and Not Free each cover a broad third of the available scores, countries or territories within any one category, especially those at either end of the range, can have quite different human rights situations. For example, those at the lowest end of the Free category (2 in political rights and 3 in civil liberties, or 3 in political rights and 2 in civil liberties) differ from those at the upper end of the Free group (1 for both political rights and civil liberties). Also, a designation of Free does not mean that a country or territory enjoys perfect freedom or lacks serious problems, only that it enjoys comparatively more freedom than those rated Partly Free or Not Free (and some others rated Free).

FREEDOM IN THE WORLD 2017
Checklist Questions

The bulleted subquestions are intended to provide guidance to the analysts regarding what issues are meant to be considered in scoring each checklist question. The analysts do not need to consider every subquestion during the scoring process, as the relevance of each varies from one place to another.

POLITICAL RIGHTS (0–40 POINTS)
A. ELECTORAL PROCESS (0–12 POINTS)
   1. Is the head of government or other chief national authority elected through free and fair elections?
   - Did established and reputable national and/or international election monitoring organizations judge the most recent elections for head of government to be free and fair? (*Note*: Heads of government chosen through various electoral frameworks, including direct elections for president, indirect elections for prime minister by parliament, and the electoral college system for electing presidents, are covered under this and the following subquestions. In cases of indirect elections for the head of government, the elections for the legislature that chose the head of government, as well as the selection process of the head of government himself, should be taken into consideration.)
   - Have there been undue, politically motivated delays in holding the most recent election for head of government?
   - Is the registration of voters and candidates conducted in an accurate, timely, transparent, and nondiscriminatory manner?
   - Can candidates make speeches, hold public meetings, and enjoy media access throughout the campaign free of intimidation?
   - Does voting take place by secret ballot or by equivalent free voting procedure?
   - Are voters able to vote for the candidate or party of their choice without undue pressure or intimidation?
   - Is the vote count transparent, and is it reported honestly with the official results made public? Can election monitors from independent groups and representing parties/candidates watch the counting of votes to ensure their honesty?
   - Is each person's vote given equivalent weight to those of other voters in order to ensure equal representation?
   - Has a democratically elected head of government who was chosen in the most recent election subsequently been overthrown in a violent coup? (*Note*: Although a peaceful, "velvet coup" may ultimately lead to a positive outcome— particularly if it replaces a head of government who was not freely and fairly elected—the new leader has not been freely and fairly elected and cannot be treated as such.)
   - In cases where elections for regional, provincial, or state governors and/or other subnational officials differ significantly in conduct from national elections, does

the conduct of the subnational elections reflect an opening toward improved political rights in the country, or, alternatively, a worsening of political rights?

2. **Are the national legislative representatives elected through free and fair elections?**
   - Did established and reputable domestic and/or international election monitoring organizations judge the most recent national legislative elections to be free and fair?
   - Have there been undue, politically motivated delays in holding the most recent national legislative election?
   - Is the registration of voters and candidates conducted in an accurate, timely, transparent, and nondiscriminatory manner?
   - Can candidates make speeches, hold public meetings, and enjoy media access throughout the campaign free of intimidation?
   - Does voting take place by secret ballot or by equivalent free voting procedure?
   - Are voters able to vote for the candidate or party of their choice without undue pressure or intimidation?
   - Is the vote count transparent, and is it reported honestly with the official results made public? Can election monitors from independent groups and representing parties/candidates watch the counting of votes to ensure their honesty?
   - Is each person's vote given equivalent weight to those of other voters in order to ensure equal representation?
   - Have the representatives of a democratically elected national legislature who were chosen in the most recent election subsequently been overthrown in a violent coup? (*Note*: Although a peaceful, "velvet coup" may ultimately lead to a positive outcome—particularly if it replaces a national legislature whose representatives were not freely and fairly elected—members of the new legislature have not been freely and fairly elected and cannot be treated as such.)
   - In cases where elections for subnational councils/parliaments differ significantly in conduct from national elections, does the conduct of the subnational elections reflect an opening toward improved political rights in the country, or, alternatively, a worsening of political rights?

3. **Are the electoral laws and framework fair?**
   - Is there a clear, detailed, and fair legislative framework for conducting elections? (*Note*: Changes to electoral laws should not be made immediately preceding an election if the ability of voters, candidates, or parties to fulfill their roles in the election is infringed.)
   - Are election commissions or other election authorities independent and free from government or other pressure and interference?
   - Is the composition of election commissions fair and balanced?
   - Do election commissions or other election authorities conduct their work in an effective and competent manner?
   - Do adult citizens enjoy universal and equal suffrage? (*Note*: Suffrage can be suspended or withdrawn for reasons of legal incapacity, such as mental incapacity or conviction of a serious criminal offense.)
   - Is the drawing of election districts conducted in a fair and nonpartisan manner, as opposed to gerrymandering for personal or partisan advantage?
   - Has the selection of a system for choosing legislative representatives (such as proportional versus majoritarian) been manipulated to advance certain political interests or to influence the electoral results?

B. POLITICAL PLURALISM AND PARTICIPATION (0–16 POINTS)

1. **Do the people have the right to organize in different political parties or other competitive political groupings of their choice, and is the system open to the rise and fall of these competing parties or groupings?**
   - Do political parties encounter undue legal or practical obstacles in their efforts to be formed and to operate, including onerous registration requirements, excessively large membership requirements, etc.?
   - Do parties face discriminatory or onerous restrictions in holding meetings, rallies, or other peaceful activities?
   - Are party members or leaders intimidated, harassed, arrested, imprisoned, or subjected to violent attacks as a result of their peaceful political activities?

2. **Is there a significant opposition vote and a realistic opportunity for the opposition to increase its support or gain power through elections?**
   - Are various legal/administrative restrictions selectively applied to opposition parties to prevent them from increasing their support base or successfully competing in elections?
   - Are there legitimate opposition forces in positions of authority, such as in the national legislature or in subnational governments?
   - Are opposition party members or leaders intimidated, harassed, arrested, imprisoned, or subjected to violent attacks as a result of their peaceful political activities?

3. **Are the people's political choices free from domination by the military, foreign powers, totalitarian parties, religious hierarchies, economic oligarchies, or any other powerful group?**
   - Do such groups offer bribes to voters and/or political figures in order to influence their political choices?
   - Do such groups intimidate, harass, or attack voters and/or political figures in order to influence their political choices?
   - Does the military control or enjoy a preponderant influence over government policy and activities, including in countries that nominally are under civilian control?
   - Do foreign governments control or enjoy a preponderant influence over government policy and activities by means including the presence of foreign military troops, the use of significant economic threats or sanctions, etc.?

4. **Do cultural, ethnic, religious, or other minority groups have full political rights and electoral opportunities?**
   - Do political parties of various ideological persuasions address issues of specific concern to minority groups?
   - Does the government inhibit the participation of minority groups in national or subnational political life through laws and/or practical obstacles?
   - Are political parties based on ethnicity, culture, or religion that espouse peaceful, democratic values legally permitted and de facto allowed to operate?

C. FUNCTIONING OF GOVERNMENT (0–12 POINTS)

1. **Do the freely elected head of government and national legislative representatives determine the policies of the government?**
   - Are the candidates who were elected freely and fairly duly installed in office?
   - Do other appointed or non–freely elected state actors interfere with or prevent freely elected representatives from adopting and implementing legislation and making meaningful policy decisions?

- Do nonstate actors, including criminal gangs, the military, and foreign governments, interfere with or prevent elected representatives from adopting and implementing legislation and making meaningful policy decisions?

2. **Is the government free from pervasive corruption?**
   - Has the government implemented effective anticorruption laws or programs to prevent, detect, and punish corruption among public officials, including conflict of interest?
   - Is the government free from excessive bureaucratic regulations, registration requirements, or other controls that increase opportunities for corruption?
   - Are there independent and effective auditing and investigative bodies that function without impediment or political pressure or influence?
   - Are allegations of corruption by government officials thoroughly investigated and prosecuted without prejudice, particularly against political opponents?
   - Are allegations of corruption given wide and extensive airing in the media?
   - Do whistle-blowers, anticorruption activists, investigators, and journalists enjoy legal protections that make them feel secure about reporting cases of bribery and corruption?
   - What was the latest Transparency International Corruption Perceptions Index score for this country?

3. **Is the government accountable to the electorate between elections, and does it operate with openness and transparency?**
   - Are civil society groups, interest groups, journalists, and other citizens able to comment on and influence pending policies or legislation?
   - Do citizens have the legal right and practical ability to obtain information about government operations and the means to petition government agencies for it?
   - Is the budget-making process subject to meaningful legislative review and public scrutiny?
   - Does the government publish detailed accounting expenditures in a timely fashion?
   - Does the state ensure transparency and effective competition in the awarding of government contracts?
   - Are the asset declarations of government officials open to public and media scrutiny and verification?

ADDITIONAL DISCRETIONARY POLITICAL RIGHTS QUESTIONS

A. **For traditional monarchies that have no parties or electoral process, does the system provide for genuine, meaningful consultation with the people, encourage public discussion of policy choices, and allow the right to petition the ruler? (0–4 points)**
   - Is there a non-elected legislature that advises the monarch on policy issues?
   - Are there formal mechanisms for individuals or civic groups to speak with or petition the monarch?
   - Does the monarch take petitions from the public under serious consideration?

B. **Is the government or occupying power deliberately changing the ethnic composition of a country or territory so as to destroy a culture or tip the political balance in favor of another group? (–4 to 0 points)**
   - Is the government providing economic or other incentives to certain people in order to change the ethnic composition of a region or regions?

- Is the government forcibly moving people in or out of certain areas in order to change the ethnic composition of those regions?
- Is the government arresting, imprisoning, or killing members of certain ethnic groups in order change the ethnic composition of a region or regions?

CIVIL LIBERTIES (0–60 POINTS)
D. FREEDOM OF EXPRESSION AND BELIEF (0–16 POINTS)
1. **Are there free and independent media and other forms of cultural expression? (*Note*: In cases where the media are state controlled but offer pluralistic points of view, the survey gives the system credit.)**
   - Are print, broadcast, and/or internet-based media directly or indirectly censored?
   - Is self-censorship among journalists common, especially when reporting on politically sensitive issues, including corruption or the activities of senior officials?
   - Are libel, blasphemy, or security laws used to punish journalists who scrutinize government officials and policies or other powerful entities through either onerous fines or imprisonment?
   - Is it a crime to insult the honor and dignity of the president and/or other government officials? How broad is the range of such prohibitions, and how vigorously are they enforced?
   - If media outlets are dependent on the government for their financial survival, does the government withhold funding in order to propagandize, primarily provide official points of view, and/or limit access by opposition parties and civic critics? Do powerful private actors engage in similar practices?
   - Does the government attempt to influence media content and access through means including politically motivated awarding of broadcast frequencies and newspaper registrations, unfair control and influence over printing facilities and distribution networks, selective distribution of advertising, onerous registration requirements, prohibitive tariffs, and bribery?
   - Are journalists threatened, arrested, imprisoned, beaten, or killed by government or nongovernmental actors for their legitimate journalistic activities, and if such cases occur, are they investigated and prosecuted fairly and expeditiously?
   - Are works of literature, art, music, or other forms of cultural expression censored or banned for political purposes?
2. **Are religious institutions and communities free to practice their faith and express themselves in public and private?**
   - Are registration requirements employed to impede the free functioning of religious institutions?
   - Are members of religious groups, including minority faiths and movements, harassed, fined, arrested, or beaten by the authorities for engaging in their religious practices?
   - Are religious practice and expression impeded by violence or harassment from nonstate actors?
   - Does the government appoint or otherwise influence the appointment of religious leaders?
   - Does the government control the production and distribution of religious books and other materials and the content of sermons?
   - Is the construction of religious buildings banned or restricted?

- Does the government place undue restrictions on religious education? Does the government require religious education?
- Are individuals free to eschew religious beliefs and practices in general?

3. **Is there academic freedom, and is the educational system free of extensive political indoctrination?**
   - Are teachers and professors free to pursue academic activities of a political and quasi-political nature without fear of physical violence or intimidation by state or nonstate actors?
   - Does the government pressure, strongly influence, or control the content of school curriculums for political purposes?
   - Are student associations that address issues of a political nature allowed to function freely?
   - Does the government, including through school administration or other officials, pressure students and/or teachers to support certain political figures or agendas, including pressuring them to attend political rallies or vote for certain candidates? Conversely, does the government, including through school administration or other officials, discourage or forbid students and/or teachers from supporting certain candidates and parties?

4. **Is there open and free private discussion?**
   - Are people able to engage in private discussions, particularly of a political nature (in places including restaurants, public transportation, and their homes) without fear of harassment or detention by the authorities or powerful nonstate actors?
   - Do users of personal online communications—including private e-mail, text messages, or personal blogs/social-media platform with a limited following— face legal penalties, harassment, or violence from the government or powerful nonstate actors in retaliation for critical remarks?
   - Does the government employ people or groups to engage in public surveillance and to report alleged antigovernment conversations to the authorities?

E. **ASSOCIATIONAL AND ORGANIZATIONAL RIGHTS (0–12 POINTS)**
   1. **Is there freedom of assembly, demonstration, and open public discussion?**
      - Are peaceful protests, particularly those of a political nature, banned or severely restricted?
      - Are the legal requirements to obtain permission to hold peaceful demonstrations particularly cumbersome and time consuming?
      - Are participants of peaceful demonstrations intimidated, arrested, or assaulted?
      - Are peaceful protesters detained by police in order to prevent them from engaging in such actions?

   2. **Is there freedom for nongovernmental organizations?** (*Note*: This includes civic organizations, interest groups, foundations, etc., with an emphasis on those engaged in human rights– and governance-related work.)
      - Are registration and other legal requirements for nongovernmental organizations particularly onerous and intended to prevent them from functioning freely?
      - Are laws related to the financing of nongovernmental organizations unduly complicated and cumbersome?
      - Are donors and funders of nongovernmental organizations free of government pressure?
      - Are members of nongovernmental organizations intimidated, arrested, imprisoned, or assaulted because of their work?

3. **Are there free trade unions and peasant organizations or equivalents, and is there effective collective bargaining? Are there free professional and other private organizations?**
   - Are trade unions allowed to be established and to operate free from government interference?
   - Are workers pressured by the government or employers to join or not to join certain trade unions, and do they face harassment, violence, or dismissal from their jobs if they do?
   - Are workers permitted to engage in strikes, and do members of unions face reprisals for engaging in peaceful strikes? (*Note*: This question may not apply to workers in essential government services or public safety jobs.)
   - Are unions able to bargain collectively with employers and able to negotiate collective bargaining agreements that are honored in practice?
   - For states with very small populations or primarily agriculturally-based economies that do not necessarily support the formation of trade unions, does the government allow for the establishment of peasant organizations or their equivalents? Is there legislation expressively forbidding the formation of trade unions?
   - Are professional organizations, including business associations, allowed to operate freely and without government interference?

F. RULE OF LAW (0–16 POINTS)

1. **Is there an independent judiciary?**
   - Is the judiciary subject to interference from the executive branch of government or from other political, economic, or religious influences?
   - Are judges appointed and dismissed in a fair and unbiased manner?
   - Do judges rule fairly and impartially, or do they commonly render verdicts that favor the government or particular interests, whether in return for bribes or other reasons?
   - Do executive, legislative, and other governmental authorities comply with judicial decisions, and are these decisions effectively enforced?
   - Do powerful private concerns comply with judicial decisions, and are decisions that run counter to the interests of powerful actors effectively enforced?

2. **Does the rule of law prevail in civil and criminal matters? Are police under direct civilian control?**
   - Are defendants' rights, including the presumption of innocence until proven guilty, protected?
   - Are detainees provided access to independent, competent legal counsel?
   - Are defendants given a fair, public, and timely hearing by a competent, independent, and impartial tribunal?
   - Are prosecutors independent of political control and influence?
   - Are prosecutors independent of powerful private interests, whether legal or illegal?
   - Is there effective and democratic civilian state control of law enforcement officials through the judicial, legislative, and executive branches?
   - Are law enforcement officials free from the influence of nonstate actors, including organized crime, powerful commercial interests, or other groups?

3. **Is there protection from political terror, unjustified imprisonment, exile, or torture, whether by groups that support or oppose the system? Is there freedom from war and insurgencies?**

- Do law enforcement officials make arbitrary arrests and detentions without warrants or fabricate or plant evidence on suspects?
- Do law enforcement officials beat detainees during arrest and interrogation or use excessive force or torture to extract confessions?
- Are conditions in pretrial facilities and prisons humane and respectful of the human dignity of inmates?
- Do citizens have the means of effective petition and redress when their rights are violated by state authorities?
- Is violent crime either against specific groups or within the general population widespread?
- Is the population subjected to physical harm, forced removal, or other acts of violence or terror due to civil conflict or war?

4. **Do laws, policies, and practices guarantee equal treatment of various segments of the population?**
   - Are members of various distinct groups—including ethnic and religious minorities, LGBT and intersex people, and the disabled—able to exercise effectively their human rights with full equality before the law?
   - Is violence against such groups widespread, and if so, are perpetrators brought to justice?
   - Do members of such groups face legal and/or de facto discrimination in areas including employment, education, and housing because of their identification with a particular group?
   - Do women enjoy full equality in law and in practice as compared to men?
   - Do noncitizens—including migrant workers and noncitizen immigrants—enjoy basic internationally recognized human rights, including the right not to be subjected to torture or other forms of ill-treatment, the right to due process of law, and the rights of freedom of association, expression, and religion?
   - Do the country's laws provide for the granting of asylum or refugee status in accordance with the 1951 UN Convention Relating to the Status of Refugees, its 1967 Protocol, and other regional treaties regarding refugees? Has the government established a system for providing protection to refugees, including against *refoulement* (the return of persons to a country where there is reason to believe they fear persecution)?

G. **PERSONAL AUTONOMY AND INDIVIDUAL RIGHTS (0–16 POINTS)**
   1. **Do individuals enjoy freedom of travel or choice of residence, employment, or institution of higher education?**
      - Are there restrictions on foreign travel, including the use of an exit visa system, which may be issued selectively?
      - Is permission required from the authorities or nonstate actors to move within the country?
      - Do state or nonstate actors determine or otherwise influence a person's type and place of employment?
      - Are bribes or other inducements needed to obtain the necessary documents to travel, change one's place of residence or employment, enter institutions of higher education, or advance in school?
   2. **Do individuals have the right to own property and establish private businesses? Is private business activity unduly influenced by government officials, the security forces, political parties/organizations, or organized crime?**

- Are people legally allowed to purchase and sell land and other property, and can they do so in practice without undue interference from the government or non-state actors?
- Does the government provide adequate and timely compensation to people whose property is expropriated under eminent domain laws?
- Are people legally allowed to establish and operate private businesses with a reasonable minimum of registration, licensing, and other requirements?
- Are bribes or other inducements needed to obtain the necessary legal documents to operate private businesses?
- Do private/nonstate actors, including criminal groups, seriously impede private business activities through such measures as extortion?

3. **Are there personal social freedoms, including gender equality, choice of marriage partners, and size of family?**
   - Is violence against women—including domestic violence, female genital mutilation, and rape—widespread, and are perpetrators brought to justice?
   - Is the trafficking of women and/or children abroad for prostitution widespread, and is the government taking adequate efforts to address the problem?
   - Do women face de jure and de facto discrimination in economic and social matters, including property and inheritance rights, divorce proceedings, and child custody matters?
   - Does the government directly or indirectly control choice of marriage partners and other personal relationships through means such as requiring large payments to marry certain individuals (e.g., foreign citizens), not enforcing laws against child marriage or dowry payments, restricting same-sex relationships, or criminalizing extramarital sex?
   - Does the government determine the number of children that a couple may have?
   - Does the government engage in state-sponsored religious/cultural/ethnic indoctrination and related restrictions on personal freedoms?
   - Do private institutions, including religious groups, unduly infringe on the rights of individuals, including choice of marriage partner, dress, gender expression, etc.?

4. **Is there equality of opportunity and the absence of economic exploitation?**
   - Does the government exert tight control over the economy, including through state ownership and the setting of prices and production quotas?
   - Do the economic benefits from large state industries, including the energy sector, benefit the general population or only a privileged few?
   - Do private interests exert undue influence on the economy through monopolistic practices, cartels, or illegal blacklists, boycotts, or discrimination?
   - Is entrance to institutions of higher education or the ability to obtain employment limited by widespread nepotism and the payment of bribes?
   - Are certain groups, including ethnic or religious minorities, less able to enjoy certain economic benefits than others? For example, are certain groups restricted from holding particular jobs, whether in the public or the private sector, because of de jure or de facto discrimination?
   - Do state or private employers exploit their workers through activities including unfairly withholding wages and permitting or forcing employees to work under unacceptably dangerous conditions, as well as through adult slave labor and child labor?

KEY TO SCORES, PR AND CL RATINGS, STATUS			
Table 1		Table 2	
Political Rights (PR)		Civil Liberties (CL)	
Total Scores	PR Rating	Total Scores	CL Rating
36–40	1	53–60	1
30–35	2	44–52	2
24–29	3	35–43	3
18–23	4	26–34	4
12–17	5	17–25	5
6–11	6	8–16	6
0–5*	7	0–7	7

Table 3	
Combined Average of the PR and CL Ratings (Freedom Rating)	Freedom Status
1.0 to 2.5	Free
3.0 to 5.0	Partly Free
5.5 to 7.0	Not Free

* It is possible for a country's or territory's total political rights score to be less than zero (between –1 and –4) if it receives mostly or all zeros for each of the 10 political rights questions *and* it receives a sufficiently negative score for political rights discretionary question B. In such a case, it would still receive a final political rights rating of 7.

Tables and Ratings

Independent Countries

Country	PR	CL	Freedom Status	Trend Arrow
Afghanistan	6	6	Not Free	
Albania*	3	3	Partly Free	
Algeria	6	5	Not Free	
Andorra*	1	1	Free	
Angola	6	6	Not Free	
Antigua and Barbuda*	2	2	Free	
Argentina*	2	2	Free	
Armenia	5	4	Partly Free	
Australia*	1	1	Free	
Austria*	1	1	Free	
Azerbaijan	7	6	Not Free	
Bahamas*	1	1	Free	
Bahrain	7	6	Not Free	
Bangladesh*	4	4	Partly Free	
Barbados*	1	1	Free	
Belarus	7	6	Not Free	
Belgium*	1	1	Free	
Belize*	1	2	Free	
Benin*	2	2	Free	
Bhutan*	3	4	Partly Free	
Bolivia*	3	3	Partly Free	
Bosnia and Herzegovina*	4	4 ▼	Partly Free	
Botswana*	3	2	Free	
Brazil*	2	2	Free	
Brunei	6	5	Not Free	
Bulgaria*	2	2	Free	
Burkina Faso*	4	3	Partly Free	
Burundi	7	6	Not Free	
Cambodia	6	5	Not Free	
Cameroon	6	6	Not Free	

Independent Countries

Country	PR	CL	Freedom Status	Trend Arrow
Afghanistan	6	6	Not Free	
Albania*	3	3	Partly Free	
Algeria	6	5	Not Free	
Andorra*	1	1	Free	
Angola	6	6	Not Free	
Antigua and Barbuda*	2	2	Free	
Argentina*	2	2	Free	
Armenia	5	4	Partly Free	
Australia*	1	1	Free	
Austria*	1	1	Free	
Azerbaijan	7	6	Not Free	
Bahamas*	1	1	Free	
Bahrain	7	6	Not Free	
Bangladesh*	4	4	Partly Free	
Barbados*	1	1	Free	
Belarus	7	6	Not Free	
Belgium*	1	1	Free	
Belize*	1	2	Free	
Benin*	2	2	Free	
Bhutan*	3	4	Partly Free	
Bolivia*	3	3	Partly Free	
Bosnia and Herzegovina*	4	4 ▼	Partly Free	
Botswana*	3	2	Free	
Brazil*	2	2	Free	
Brunei	6	5	Not Free	
Bulgaria*	2	2	Free	
Burkina Faso*	4	3	Partly Free	
Burundi	7	6	Not Free	
Cambodia	6	5	Not Free	
Cameroon	6	6	Not Free	

Country	PR	CL	Freedom Status	Trend Arrow
Canada*	1	1	Free	
Cape Verde*	1	1	Free	
Central African Republic	7	7	Not Free	
Chad	7	6	Not Free	
Chile*	1	1	Free	
China	7	6	Not Free	↓
Colombia*	3	3 ▲	Partly Free	↑
Comoros*	3	4	Partly Free	
Congo (Brazzaville)	7 ▼	5	Not Free	
Congo (Kinshasa)	7 ▼	6	Not Free	
Costa Rica*	1	1	Free	
Côte d'Ivoire*	4	4	Partly Free	
Croatia*	1	2	Free	
Cuba	7	6	Not Free	
Cyprus*	1	1	Free	
Czech Republic*	1	1	Free	
Denmark*	1	1	Free	
Djibouti	6	5	Not Free	
Dominica*	1	1	Free	
Dominican Republic*	3	3	Partly Free	
Ecuador*	3	4 ▼	Partly Free	
Egypt	6	5	Not Free	
El Salvador*	2	3	Free	
Equatorial Guinea	7	7	Not Free	
Eritrea	7	7	Not Free	
Estonia*	1	1	Free	
Ethiopia	7	6	Not Free	↓
Fiji*	3	4 ▼	Partly Free	
Finland*	1	1	Free	
France*	1	2 ▼	Free	
Gabon	6	5	Not Free	
The Gambia	6 ▲	6	Not Free	
Georgia*	3	3	Partly Free	
Germany*	1	1	Free	
Ghana*	1	2	Free	
Greece*	2	2	Free	
Grenada*	1	2	Free	

Country	PR	CL	Freedom Status	Trend Arrow
Guatemala*	4	4	Partly Free	
Guinea	5	5	Partly Free	
Guinea-Bissau	5	5	Partly Free	
Guyana*	2	3	Free	
Haiti	5	5	Partly Free	
Honduras	4	4	Partly Free	
Hungary*	3 ▼	2	Free	
Iceland*	1	1	Free	
India*	2	3	Free	
Indonesia*	2	4	Partly Free	
Iran	6	6	Not Free	
Iraq	5	6	Not Free	
Ireland*	1	1	Free	
Israel*	1	2	Free	
Italy*	1	1	Free	
Jamaica*	2	3	Free	
Japan*	1	1	Free	
Jordan	5 ▲	5	Partly Free ▲	
Kazakhstan	7 ▼	5	Not Free	
Kenya*	4	4	Partly Free	
Kiribati*	1	1	Free	
Kosovo*	3	4	Partly Free	
Kuwait	5	5	Partly Free	
Kyrgyzstan	5	5	Partly Free	
Laos	7	6	Not Free	
Latvia*	1 ▲	2	Free	
Lebanon	5	4	Partly Free	
Lesotho*	3	3	Partly Free	
Liberia*	3	4	Partly Free	
Libya	7 ▼	6	Not Free	
Liechtenstein*	2 ▼	1	Free	
Lithuania*	1	1	Free	
Luxembourg*	1	1	Free	
Macedonia	4	3	Partly Free	
Madagascar*	3	4	Partly Free	
Malawi*	3	3	Partly Free	
Malaysia	4	4	Partly Free	

Country	PR	CL	Freedom Status	Trend Arrow
Maldives	5 ▼	5	Partly Free	
Mali	5	4	Partly Free	
Malta*	1	1	Free	
Marshall Islands*	1	1	Free	
Mauritania	6	5	Not Free	
Mauritius*	1	2	Free	
Mexico*	3	3	Partly Free	
Micronesia*	1	1	Free	
Moldova*	3	3	Partly Free	
Monaco*	3 ▼	1	Free	
Mongolia*	1	2	Free	
Montenegro*	3	3	Partly Free	
Morocco	5	4	Partly Free	
Mozambique	4	4	Partly Free	↓
Myanmar	5 ▲	5	Partly Free ▲	
Namibia*	2	2	Free	
Nauru*	2	2	Free	
Nepal*	3	4	Partly Free	
Netherlands*	1	1	Free	
New Zealand*	1	1	Free	
Nicaragua	5 ▼	4 ▼	Partly Free	↓
Niger	4 ▼	4	Partly Free	
Nigeria*	3 ▲	5	Partly Free	
North Korea	7	7	Not Free	
Norway*	1	1	Free	
Oman	6	5	Not Free	
Pakistan*	4	5	Partly Free	
Palau*	1	1	Free	
Panama*	2	2	Free	
Papua New Guinea*	3 ▲	3	Partly Free	
Paraguay*	3	3	Partly Free	
Peru*	2	3	Free	
Philippines*	3	3	Partly Free	↓
Poland*	1	2 ▼	Free	↓
Portugal*	1	1	Free	
Qatar	6	5	Not Free	
Romania*	2	2	Free	

Country	PR	CL	Freedom Status	Trend Arrow
Russia	7 ▼	6	Not Free	
Rwanda	6	6	Not Free	
Saint Kitts and Nevis*	1 ▲	1	Free	
Saint Lucia*	1	1	Free	
Saint Vincent and the Grenadines*	1	1	Free	
Samoa*	2	2	Free	
San Marino*	1	1	Free	
São Tomé and Príncipe*	2	2	Free	
Saudi Arabia	7	7	Not Free	
Senegal*	2	2	Free	
Serbia*	3 ▼	2	Free	
Seychelles*	3	3	Partly Free	
Sierra Leone*	3	3	Partly Free	
Singapore	4	4	Partly Free	
Slovakia*	1	1	Free	
Slovenia*	1	1	Free	
Solomon Islands*	3	2 ▲	Free ▲	
Somalia	7	7	Not Free	
South Africa*	2	2	Free	
South Korea*	2	2	Free	
South Sudan	7	7 ▼	Not Free	↓
Spain*	1	1	Free	
Sri Lanka*	3 ▲	4	Partly Free	
Sudan	7	7	Not Free	
Suriname*	2	3	Free	
Swaziland	7	5	Not Free	
Sweden*	1	1	Free	
Switzerland*	1	1	Free	
Syria	7	7	Not Free	
Taiwan*	1	1 ▲	Free	
Tajikistan	7	6	Not Free	
Tanzania*	3	4	Partly Free	
Thailand	6	5	Not Free	
Timor-Leste*	3	3	Partly Free	
Togo	4	4	Partly Free	
Tonga*	2	2	Free	

Country	PR	CL	Freedom Status	Trend Arrow
Trinidad and Tobago*	2	2	Free	
Tunisia*	1	3	Free	
Turkey	4 ▼	5 ▼	Partly Free	↓
Turkmenistan	7	7	Not Free	
Tuvalu*	1	1	Free	
Uganda	6	5	Not Free	
Ukraine*	3	3	Partly Free	
United Arab Emirates	6	6	Not Free	
United Kingdom*	1	1	Free	
United States*	1	1	Free	
Uruguay*	1	1	Free	
Uzbekistan	7	7	Not Free	
Vanuatu*	2	2	Free	
Venezuela	6 ▼	5	Not Free ▼	
Vietnam	7	5	Not Free	
Yemen	7	6	Not Free	
Zambia	4 ▼	4	Partly Free	↓
Zimbabwe	5	5	Partly Free	

PR and CL stand for political rights and civil liberties, respectively; 1 represents the most free and 7 the least free rating.

▲ ▼ up or down indicates an improvement or decline in ratings or status since the last survey.

↑ ↓ up or down indicates a positive or negative trend.

* indicates a country's status as an electoral democracy.

NOTE: The ratings reflect global events from January 1, 2016, through December 31, 2016.

Territories

Territory	PR	CL	Freedom Status	Trend Arrow
Abkhazia	4	5	Partly Free	
Crimea	7	6	Not Free	
Gaza Strip	5	6	Not Free	
Hong Kong	5	2	Partly Free	↓
Indian Kashmir	4	4	Partly Free	
Nagorno-Karabakh	5	5	Partly Free	
Northern Cyprus	2	2	Free	
Pakistani Kashmir	6	5	Not Free	
Somaliland	5	5	Partly Free	
South Ossetia	7	6	Not Free	
Tibet	7	7	Not Free	
Transnistria	6	6	Not Free	
West Bank	7 ▼	5	Not Free	
Western Sahara	7	7	Not Free	

PR and CL stand for political rights and civil liberties, respectively; 1 represents the most free and 7 the least free rating.

▲ ▼ up or down indicates an improvement or decline in ratings or status since the last survey.

↑ ↓ up or down indicates a positive or negative trend.

NOTE: The ratings reflect global events from January 1, 2016, through December 31, 2016.

Combined Average Ratings—Independent Countries

FREE			
1.0	Latvia	Sierra Leone	Cambodia
Andorra	Liechtenstein	Timor-Leste	Djibouti
Australia	Mauritius	Ukraine	Egypt
Austria	Mongolia		Gabon
Bahamas	Poland	**3.5**	Iraq
Barbados		Bhutan	Mauritania
Belgium	**2.0**	Burkina Faso	Oman
Canada	Antigua and Barbuda	Comoros	Qatar
Cape Verde	Argentina	Ecuador	Thailand
Chile	Benin	Fiji	Uganda
Costa Rica	Brazil	Kosovo	Venezuela
Cyprus	Bulgaria	Liberia	
Czech Republic	Greece	Macedonia	**6.0**
Denmark	Monaco	Madagascar	Afghanistan
Dominica	Namibia	Nepal	Angola
Estonia	Nauru	Sri Lanka	Cameroon
Finland	Panama	Tanzania	Congo (Brazzaville)
France	Romania		Iran
Germany	Samoa	**4.0**	Kazakhstan
Iceland	São Tomé and	Bangladesh	Rwanda
Ireland	Príncipe	Bosnia and	Swaziland
Italy	Senegal	Herzegovina	The Gambia
Japan	South Africa	Côte d'Ivoire	United Arab Emirates
Kiribati	South Korea	Guatemala	Vietnam
Liechtenstein	Tonga	Honduras	
Lithuania	Trinidad and Tobago	Kenya	**6.5**
Luxembourg	Tunisia	Malaysia	Azerbaijan
Malta	Vanuatu	Mozambique	Bahrain
Marshall Islands		Niger	Belarus
Micronesia	**2.5**	Nigeria	Burundi
Netherlands	Botswana	Singapore	Chad
New Zealand	El Salvador	Togo	China
Norway	Guyana	Zambia	Congo (Kinshasa)
Palau	Hungary		Cuba
Poland	India	**4.5**	Ethiopia
Portugal	Jamaica	Armenia	Laos
Saint Lucia	Peru	Lebanon	Libya
Saint Vincent and the	Serbia	Mali	Russia
Grenadines	Solomon Islands	Morocco	Tajikistan
San Marino	Suriname	Nicaragua	Yemen
Slovakia		Pakistan	
Slovenia	**PARTLY FREE**	Turkey	**7.0**
Spain	**3.0**		Central African
Sweden	Albania	**5.0**	Republic
Switzerland	Bolivia	Guinea	Equatorial Guinea
Tuvalu	Colombia	Guinea-Bissau	Eritrea
United Kingdom	Dominican Republic	Haiti	North Korea
United States	Georgia	Jordan	Saudi Arabia
Uruguay	Indonesia	Kuwait	Somalia
	Lesotho	Kyrgyzstan	South Sudan
1.5	Malawi	Maldives	Sudan
Belize	Mexico	Myanmar	Syria
Croatia	Moldova	Zimbabwe	Turkmenistan
France	Montenegro		Uzbekistan
Ghana	Papua New Guinea	**NOT FREE**	
Grenada	Paraguay	**5.5**	
Israel	Philippines	Algeria	
	Seychelles	Brunei	

Combined Average Ratings—Territories

FREE
2.0
Northern Cyprus

PARTLY FREE
3.5
Hong Kong

4.0
Indian Kashmir

4.5
Abkhazia

5.0
Nagorno-Karabakh
Somaliland

NOT FREE
5.5
Pakistani Kashmir

6.0
Transnistria
West Bank

6.5
Crimea
Gaza Strip
South Ossetia

7.0
Tibet
Western Sahara

Electoral Democracies (123)

Albania	Grenada	Papua New Guinea
Andorra	Guatemala	Paraguay
Antigua and Barbuda	Guyana	Peru
Argentina	Hungary	Philippines
Australia	Iceland	Poland
Austria	India	Portugal
Bahamas	Indonesia	Romania
Bangladesh	Ireland	Samoa
Barbados	Israel	San Marino
Belgium	Italy	São Tomé and Príncipe
Belize	Jamaica	Senegal
Benin	Japan	Serbia
Bhutan	Kenya	Seychelles
Bolivia	Kiribati	Sierra Leone
Bosnia and Herzegovina	Kosovo	Slovakia
Botswana	Latvia	Slovenia
Brazil	Lesotho	Solomon Islands
Bulgaria	Liberia	South Africa
Burkina Faso	Liechtenstein	South Korea
Canada	Lithuania	Spain
Cape Verde	Luxembourg	Sri Lanka
Chile	Madagascar	St. Kitts and Nevis
Colombia	Malawi	St. Lucia
Comoros	Malta	St. Vincent and the
Costa Rica	Marshall Islands	Grenadines
Côte d'Ivoire	Mauritius	Suriname
Croatia	Mexico	Sweden
Cyprus	Micronesia	Switzerland
Czech Republic	Moldova	Taiwan
Denmark	Monaco	Tanzania
Dominica	Mongolia	Timor-Leste
Dominican Republic	Montenegro	Tonga
Ecuador	Namibia	Trinidad and Tobago
El Salvador	Nauru	Tunisia
Estonia	Nepal	Tuvalu
Fiji	Netherlands	Ukraine
Finland	New Zealand	United Kingdom
France	Nigeria	United States
Georgia	Norway	Uruguay
Germany	Pakistan	Vanuatu
Ghana	Palau	
Greece	Panama	

Contributors

ANALYSTS

Aalaa Abuzaakouk is a Middle East and North Africa analyst who works on Libya and Tunisia programs at the National Endowment for Democracy. Previously, she was a program officer with Freedom House's Middle East and North Africa team. She has contributed to *Freedom in the World*, *Freedom of the Press*, and *Voices in the Street*, Freedom House's special publication on social protests and freedom of assembly. She graduated from Georgetown University with a bachelor's degree in regional studies and a master's degree in Arab Studies. She served as a Middle East and North Africa analyst for *Freedom in the World*.

David Angeles is a program officer for Southeast Asia at the National Endowment for Democracy, a private, nonprofit foundation dedicated to the growth and strengthening of democratic institutions around the world. Previously, he worked in Thailand and Burma/Myanmar with various civil society and human rights groups. He received a master's degree in international affairs from the American University of Paris and a bachelor's degree in international studies from the University of North Carolina, Chapel Hill, where he was named a Truman Scholar. He served as an Asia-Pacific analyst for *Freedom in the World*.

Ignacio Arana Araya is a postdoctoral researcher at the Pontifical Catholic University of Chile and the editor of *Panoramas*, the scholarly platform of the Center for Latin American Studies at the University of Pittsburgh. His central line of research explores how the individual differences among presidents have an impact on relevant political phenomena, including institutional change and policy outcomes. His secondary line of research is the comparative study of institutions, with a focus on Latin America. His research has been published or is forthcoming in the *Journal of Law and Courts*, the *Journal of Legislative Studies*, *Latin American Politics and Society*, *Latin American Perspectives*, the *Global Encyclopedia of Public Administration*, *Bolivian Studies Journal*, and *Política*. He served as an Americas analyst for *Freedom in the World*.

Mokhtar Awad is a research fellow in the Program on Extremism at George Washington University's Center for Cyber and Homeland Security. He specializes in Islamist and Salafist groups in the Middle East. He has published analyses and conducted field research on Islamist groups and political dynamics in Tunisia, Jordan, Lebanon, Syria, and Egypt. Prior to joining the Program on Extremism, Awad worked as a research associate at the Center for American Progress, and before that he was a junior fellow in the Middle East Program at the Carnegie Endowment for International Peace. Awad's work has been published in *Foreign Policy*, the *Washington Post*, *Current Trends in Islamist Ideology*, and by the Carnegie Middle East Center, among other places. He served as a Middle East and North Africa analyst for *Freedom in the World*.

Oumar Ba is a PhD candidate in political science at the University of Florida and an assistant professor at Morehouse College, starting August 2017. He earned MA degrees in political science and African studies from Ohio University and the University of Florida, where he is affiliated with the Sahel Research Group. Oumar is also a contributing editor to the online magazine *Africa Is a Country*. He served as a sub-Saharan Africa analyst for *Freedom in the World*.

Angelita Baeyens is a programs director at Robert F. Kennedy Human Rights. She previously served at the United Nations as a political affairs officer in the Americas division of the UN Department of Political Affairs in New York, covering the Caribbean region. Baeyens also worked at the Inter-American Commission on Human Rights (IACHR) in Washington, D.C. in various capacities, including special assistant to the executive secretary and coordinator of the Rapporteurship on Human Rights Defenders of the IACHR. Baeyens has been an adjunct professor of law at Georgetown University Law Center since 2012. A dual Belgian and Colombian citizen, she holds a law degree from the University of Ibague, in Colombia, and an LLM in international human rights law from the University of Notre Dame. She served as an Americas analyst for *Freedom in the World*.

Cynthia Barrow-Giles is a senior lecturer in political science at the University of the West Indies at Cave Hill, Barbados, who served as deputy dean in the Faculty of Social Sciences and head of the Department of Government, Sociology, and Social Work. She has published books on issues of Caribbean sovereignty and development, women in Caribbean politics, and general elections and voting in the English-speaking Caribbean. She was a member of the St. Lucia constitutional reform commission, and has participated in a number of observation missions for the Organization of American States and the Commonwealth. She served as an Americas analyst for *Freedom in the World*.

Katherine Blue Carroll is an assistant professor and the director of the program in public policy studies at Vanderbilt University. She received her master's degree and PhD in politics from the University of Virginia. Her teaching and research interests include the comparative politics of the Middle East, political violence, and the U.S. military. Her work has appeared in *Middle East Policy* and the *Middle East Journal*. She served as a Middle East and North Africa analyst for *Freedom in the World*.

Mamadou Bodian holds a PhD in political science from the University of Florida. He is also the project coordinator for the Trans-Saharan Elections Project and a founding member of the Sahel Research Group. He has also been a senior researcher with the Islam Research Programme at the Embassy of the Netherlands in Senegal, a project sponsored by Leiden University and the Dutch Ministry of Foreign Affairs. His current research focuses on a comparative examination of elections and democracy in the Sahel, with special attention to Senegal, Mali, and Niger. He served as a sub-Saharan Africa analyst for *Freedom in the World*.

Alex Brockwehl is an MPA student at the Woodrow Wilson School of Public and International Affairs at Princeton University. Previously, he managed Freedom House projects in Latin America, which aim to support local civil society leaders and organizations in defending human rights. Alex writes frequently for the Freedom House blog, *Freedom at Issue*, and has been interviewed by various media outlets on regional human rights challenges and U.S. foreign policy. In 2013 he contributed to *Voices in the Streets,* a Freedom House special report on freedom of assembly rights and police responses to massive social protests. Prior to joining Freedom House, Alex worked as a fellow at the Yanapuma Foundation in Estero de Plátano, Ecuador, where he managed projects focused on secondary education, community development, and women's empowerment. He holds a bachelor of arts degree from Union College. He served as an Americas analyst for *Freedom in the World*.

Greg Brown is an adjunct professor at Georgetown University's Center for Australian, New Zealand, and Pacific Studies, and a senior analyst at CENTRA Technology, Inc., where he focuses on transnational and emerging national security issues. He has served as a consultant for the German Friedrich-Ebert-Stiftung (FES) foundation, as an editor for the Millennium Project's Global Challenges Program, and as an Australian National University Parliamentary Fellow. Brown's academic work in political demography, comparative migration policy, and diaspora politics has been highlighted in the *Economist*, the *Australian*, and the *New Zealand Herald*, and has been published in the *Georgetown Journal of International Affairs*, *Political Science*, and Australia's journal of demography, *People and Place*. He served as an Asia-Pacific analyst for *Freedom in the World*.

Nina Burbach is a former senior adviser to the Slovenian Ministry of Justice on international human rights issues. She holds a master's degree in international humanitarian law and human rights from the University of Geneva and a bachelor's degree in international law from the University of Ljubljana. She served as a Europe analyst for *Freedom in the World*.

Samlanchith Chanthavong is the senior program officer for Asia and global programs at the National Endowment for Democracy, where she manages grants to civil society organizations working to strengthen human rights, civic and political participation, and democratic governance. Previously, she worked on rule of law programs in Asia at the American Bar Association. She received a master's degree in international affairs from American University. She served as an Asia-Pacific analyst for *Freedom in the World*.

Kristian Coates Ulrichsen is a Baker Institute fellow for the Middle East. Working across the disciplines of political science, international relations, and international political economy, his research examines the changing position of Persian Gulf states in the global order, as well as the emergence of longer-term, nonmilitary challenges to regional security. His books include *Insecure Gulf: The End of Certainty and the Transition to the Post-Oil Era* and *Qatar and the Arab Spring*. His most recent book is entitled *The Gulf States in International Political Economy*. Coates Ulrichsen's articles have appeared in numerous academic journals, including *Global Policy* and the *Journal of Arabian Studies*, and he consults regularly on Gulf issues for the public and private sector around the world. Coates Ulrichsen holds a doctorate in history from the University of Cambridge. He served as a Middle East and North Africa analyst for *Freedom in the World*.

Douglas Coltart is a Zimbabwean human rights lawyer and consultant with experience working on democratic governance and elections in sub-Saharan Africa. He co-wrote a book on socioeconomic rights in Zimbabwe's constitution, and has served as a peer reviewer for one of southern Africa's leading journals. A recipient of a Konrad-Adenauer-Stiftung scholarship, he holds a law degree from the University of Cape Town and a bachelor's degree in southern African history from the same institution. He served as a sub-Saharan Africa analyst for *Freedom in the World*.

Julian Dierkes is an associate professor and the Keidanren Chair in Japanese Research at the University of British Columbia's Institute of Asian Research, where he coordinates the

Program on Inner Asia. His research has focused on history education and supplementary education in Japan, as well as contemporary Mongolia. He is the editor of *Change in Democratic Mongolia: Social Relations, Health, Mobile Pastoralism, and Mining*. He received a PhD in sociology from Princeton University. He served as an Asia-Pacific analyst for *Freedom in the World*.

Jake Dizard is a PhD candidate in political science at the University of Texas at Austin. He was previously the managing editor of *Countries at the Crossroads*, Freedom House's annual survey of democratic governance. His area of focus is Latin America, with a specific emphasis on the Andean region and Mexico. He received a master's degree from the Johns Hopkins University School of Advanced International Studies. He served as an Americas analyst for *Freedom in the World*.

Richard Downie is deputy director and a fellow of the Africa Program at the Center for Strategic and International Studies. Previously, he was a journalist for the British Broadcasting Corporation (BBC). He received a master's degree in international public policy from the Johns Hopkins University School of Advanced International Studies. He served as a sub-Saharan Africa analyst for *Freedom in the World*.

Maxim Edwards is a journalist and commissioning editor at oDR, openDemocracy's section on Russia and the post-Soviet world. He has a particular interest in the politics and societies of post-socialist Europe and Eurasia, with a focus on the South Caucasus. Max recently graduated from the University of Glasgow with an MA in Russian, Central, and Eastern European studies. He also worked as a research fellow with ECMI-Caucasus and CRRC-Armenia, investigating ethnic minorities and inter-ethnic relations in Armenia and Georgia. His work has appeared in places including openDemocracy, *Political Critique*, Al-Jazeera, *Al-Monitor*, *New Eastern Europe*, and the *Forward*, and he is now working on a series of essays about memory and European responses to the refugee crisis. He served as a Eurasia analyst for *Freedom in the World*.

Daniel Eizenga is a PhD candidate in the Department of Political Science and a research associate with the Sahel Research Group at the University of Florida. His area of focus is sub-Saharan Africa, specifically the Francophone African Sahel where he has conducted extensive research. He received a master's degree in political science from the University of Florida in 2013. He served as a sub-Saharan Africa analyst for *Freedom in the World*.

Brian Ernst is a senior program officer at the National Democratic Institute (NDI), focusing on improving governance in southern and eastern Africa. Brian previously served as a Peace Corps volunteer in Madagascar, and covers the Indian Ocean island nations for NDI. He received a master's degree in international security from the University of Denver and a bachelor's degree in political science from Vanderbilt University. He served as a sub-Saharan Africa analyst for *Freedom in the World*.

Golnaz Esfandiari is a senior correspondent with Radio Free Europe/Radio Liberty. Esfandiari's work focuses on political and social developments in Iran, and ties between Iran and the United States. Her work has appeared in and has been cited by publications including the *New Yorker*, the *New York Times*, the *Washington Post*, and *Foreign Policy*; she has also contributed to Freedom House's *Freedom of the Press* report. She served as a Middle East and North Africa analyst for *Freedom in the World*.

Annabella España-Nájera is an assistant professor of Chicano and Latin American Studies at California State University, Fresno. Her research interests include democratic institutions and democratization, representation, and parties and party systems in Latin America, with a special focus on Central America. She served as an Americas analyst for *Freedom in the World.*

Sarah J. Feuer, an expert on politics and religion in North Africa, is a Soref Fellow at the Washington Institute for Near East Policy. Feuer, who completed her doctorate in politics at Brandeis University's Crown Center for Middle East Studies in 2014, wrote her dissertation on the politics of religious education in Morocco and Tunisia. A book based on that research is due out by Cambridge University Press in 2017. Previously, she earned her MA in Middle Eastern history from Tel Aviv University and a BA in history and French literature at the University of Pennsylvania. She has extensive experience in the region, including stints living in Israel, Jordan, Morocco, and Tunisia. She served as a Middle East and North Africa analyst for *Freedom in the World.*

Jon Fraenkel is a professor of comparative politics in the School of History, Philosophy, Political Science and International Relations at Victoria University of Wellington, New Zealand. He was formerly a senior research fellow based at the Australian National University and the University of the South Pacific in Fiji. He is the Pacific correspondent for the *Economist.* His research focuses on the politics of the Pacific Islands region, institutional design in divided societies, electoral systems, political economy, and the economic history of Oceania. He served as an Asia-Pacific analyst for *Freedom in the World.*

Corinna-Barbara Francis is an independent consultant who works on project development, monitoring and evaluation, and capacity-building in support of Chinese NGOs and civil society activists. She is also a visiting research fellow at King's College London. Previously, she was a China researcher at Amnesty International headquarters in London, for ten years. She formerly held research and teaching positions at Brown University, the University of Michigan, and the University of Missouri and has been the recipient of numerous research grants, including a Fulbright-Hays research fellowship. She has published widely in academic journals on China's emerging civil society, student politics, and property rights, including in *Comparative Politics,* the *China Quarterly,* and *China Review International,* and has contributed to numerous co-authored books on China. She earned her PhD in Political Science from Columbia University and her BA from Yale University. She served as an Asia-Pacific analyst for *Freedom in the World.*

Julie George is an associate professor of political science at Queens College and the City University of New York Graduate Center. Her work addresses the intersection of state-building, democratization, and ethnic politics in postcommunist states. She is the author of *The Politics of Ethnic Separatism in Russia and Georgia.* Her work has appeared in *Electoral Studies, Post-Soviet Affairs,* and *Europe-Asia Studies,* and other outlets. She served as a Eurasia analyst for *Freedom in the World.*

Ana Pastor Gonzalez holds a journalism degree from the University of Navarra, in Spain, and has worked as a local and cultural journalist for different media companies. In 2015, she completed a master's degree in international relations from New York University. She served as a Europe analyst for *Freedom in the World.*

Alyssa Maraj Grahame is a PhD candidate in the Department of Political Science at the University of Massachusetts, Amherst. Her research focuses on the political economy of the 2008 financial crisis in Europe. Her work has been presented at conferences including American Political Science Association, Council for European Studies, and Western Political Science Association. She is presently completing a dissertation project titled "Democracy in Crisis: Social Mobilization against Financial Capital," which will be the basis for her first book. She served as a Europe analyst for *Freedom in the World.*

Shelby Grossman is a postdoctoral fellow at Stanford University's Center on Democracy, Development, and the Rule of Law. Her research focuses on the political economy of development. Her book project investigates the conditions under which private organizations will promote economic activity, focusing on informal markets in Lagos, Nigeria. She served as a sub-Saharan Africa analyst for *Freedom in the World.*

Liutauras Gudžinskas lectures on comparative politics at the Institute of International Relations and Political Science of Vilnius University. His main research interests are postcommunist transformation, Europeanization, and politics of the Baltic countries. Since 2013, Gudžinskas is also the editor-in-chief of the *Baltic Journal of Political Science*, and the president of the Lithuanian Political Science Association. In 2015, he was elected as General Secretary of Central European Political Science Association. He served as a Europe analyst for *Freedom in the World.*

Ted Henken is an associate professor in the Department of Sociology and Anthropology at Baruch College, City University of New York. He holds a joint appointment in Baruch's Black and Latino Studies department. He is president ex-officio of the Association for the Study of the Cuban Economy. He is the coauthor with Archibald Ritter of *Entrepreneurial Cuba: The Changing Policy Landscape*, coeditor with Miriam Celaya and Dimas Castellanos of *Cuba in Focus*, and author of *Cuba: A Global Studies Handbook*. He has published articles about Cuba in the journals *Human Geography*, *Current History*, *Nueva Sociedad*, *Cuban Studies*, *Latino Studies*, and *Latin American Research Review*, as well as in the *New York Times* and the blog of the Committee to Protect Journalists. He writes about contemporary Cuba on his blog, *El Yuma*. He received a PhD in Latin American studies from Tulane University in 2002. He has served as a consultant on Cuba for the Department of State and the White House and was an Americas analyst for *Freedom in the World.*

Franklin Hess is the coordinator of the Modern Greek Program at Indiana University and a senior lecturer at the Institute for European Studies. His scholarly work explores the economic, geopolitical, and geocultural contexts of modern Greece's cultural production. His other research interests include immigration and the cinematic representation of violence. He received a PhD in American studies from the University of Iowa, focusing on the influence of American television programming on Greek culture. He served as a Europe analyst for *Freedom in the World.*

Sylvana Habdank-Kolaczkowska is a political analyst and researcher specializing in postcommunist Europe. She has previously served as the director of *Nations in Transit*, Freedom House's annual report on democratic governance from Central Europe to Eurasia, and as the managing editor of the *Journal of Cold War Studies*, a peer-reviewed quarterly. She received a master's degree in Eastern European and Eurasian studies from Harvard University and a bachelor's in political science from the University of California, Berkeley. She writes reports on Central Europe for *Freedom of the Press* and served as a Europe analyst for *Freedom in the World.*

Ibrahim Yahaya Ibrahim is a PhD candidate in political science at the University of Florida, where he is also a research associate with the Sahel Research Group. His dissertation focuses on political contestations and religious discourse in the Sahel, with a particular emphasis on cases from Mali, Mauritania, and Niger. Ibrahim was a Fulbright grantee at the University of Florida from 2011 to 2013. He served as a sub-Saharan Africa analyst for *Freedom in the World.*

Rico Isaacs is a reader in politics at Oxford Brookes University. His research interests lie at the intersection of nation-building, democratization, and institutional development in post-Soviet states. He is the author of *Party System Formation in Kazakhstan: Between Formal and Informal Politics* (Routledge 2011) and has published on Central Asian politics in *Democratization, Europe-Asia Studies, Nationalities Papers, Contemporary Politics,* and *Electoral Studies,* among many other scholarly journals. He is the co-editor of *Nation-Building and Identity in the Post-Soviet Space: New Tools and Approaches* (Routledge 2016) and has a further two books forthcoming: *Film and Identity in Kazakhstan: Soviet and Post-Soviet Culture* (I.B. Tauris 2017) and *Politics: An Introduction, 3rd Edition* (Routledge 2017). He served as a Eurasia analyst for *Freedom in the World.*

Faysal Itani is a resident senior fellow with the Atlantic Council's Rafik Hariri Center for the Middle East, where he focuses primarily on the Syrian conflict and its regional impact. Itani has repeatedly briefed the U.S. government and its allies on the conflict in Syria and its effects on their interests. He has been widely published and quoted in prominent media outlets including the *New York Times, Time, Politico,* and the *Washington Post,* among other places. Itani holds a master's degree in strategic studies and international economics from the Johns Hopkins University School of Advanced International Studies, a certificate in public policy from Georgetown University, and a bachelor's degree in business from the American University of Beirut. He served as a Middle East and North Africa analyst for *Freedom in the World.*

Victoria Jennett is an independent consultant specializing in justice sector reform, anti-corruption, and the promotion of human rights. She has worked previously as a human rights adviser, as the chief of property in the Organization for Security and Co-operation in Europe Mission in Kosovo, and as a research analyst for Transparency International. She received her PhD in constitutional law and conflict transformation from the European University Institute in Florence, Italy, and is a British qualified lawyer who gained her bachelor of laws from King's College, London. She served as a Europe analyst for *Freedom in the World.*

Cara Jones received her PhD in political science and African studies from the University of Florida in 2013. She has published numerous articles on development and postconflict politics in Africa in academic, policy, and popular media. Now a development professional, she was an academic teacher-scholar for five years previously, in addition to a decade of work in the field. She served as a sub-Saharan Africa analyst for *Freedom in the World.*

Toby Craig Jones is an associate professor of history and the director of the Center for Middle Eastern Studies at Rutgers University, New Brunswick, New Jersey. He is the author of

Desert Kingdom: How Oil and Water Forged Modern Saudi Arabia and of *Running Dry: Essays on Energy and Environmental Crisis*, and is currently writing a book entitled *America's Oil Wars*. He is an editor of *Middle East Report* and has published widely, including in the *International Journal of Middle East Studies*, the *New York Times*, and *Foreign Affairs*. He received a PhD from Stanford University. He served as a Middle East and North Africa analyst for *Freedom in the World*.

Karin Deutsch Karlekar is the director of Free Expression at Risk Programs at PEN America. Prior to joining PEN, she served as director of Freedom House's *Freedom of the Press* project. As well as acting as an expert spokesperson on press freedom issues, she has developed index methodologies and conducted training sessions on press freedom, internet freedom, freedom of expression, and monitoring of dangerous speech; authored a number of special reports and academic papers; and conducted research, assessment, and advocacy missions to Nigeria, South Africa, Uganda, Zambia, Zimbabwe, Afghanistan, Indonesia, Pakistan, and Sri Lanka. She has also worked as an editor at the Economist Intelligence Unit and as a consultant to Human Rights Watch, and is currently a member of the governing council of the International Freedom of Expression Exchange (IFEX) network. She holds a PhD in Indian history from Cambridge University and a bachelor's degree from Vassar College. She served as an Asia-Pacific analyst for *Freedom in the World*.

Valery Kavaleuski holds a master's degree in foreign service from Georgetown University. As a former diplomat, he specialized in Belarus-U.S. political relations, as well as human rights and human trafficking issues with the UN agencies. He served as a Eurasia analyst for *Freedom in the World*.

Catherine Kelly has a PhD in government from Harvard University and is a Mellon/American Council of Learned Societies Public Fellow at the American Bar Association-Rule of Law Initiative in Washington, D.C. Substantively, she specializes in democracy, rule of law, and governance, and in program design, monitoring, and evaluation. Fluent in French and proficient in Wolof, she has done several years of field research. A former Fulbright Scholar and Foreign Language and Area Studies fellow, her work has appeared in the *Journal of Democracy* and *Electoral Studies*, and on the blogs of the *Washington Post*, the Council on Foreign Relations, and *Social Science Research Council*. She served as a sub-Saharan Africa analyst for *Freedom in the World*. The views expressed in the report are her personal views and not those of ABA ROLI.

Nicholas Kerr is an assistant professor of comparative politics in the Department of Political Science at the University of Alabama. His general research and teaching interests include African politics, democratization, electoral institutions, electoral integrity, and political corruption. In a current research project Nicholas explores the design and performance of electoral management bodies (EMBs) in Africa with emphasis on how political elites and citizens respond strategically to the autonomy and capacity of EMBs. Another research project examines the process through which citizens formulate their perceptions of election integrity. Specifically, he looks at how direct experiences with election management, electoral manipulation, and third-party actors influence citizens' attitudes toward election integrity. Nicholas has experience conducting qualitative fieldwork and organizing surveys in several African countries and his published work has appeared in *Electoral Studies*, *Governance*, the *Journal of Modern African Studies*, and *Political Research Quarterly*. He served as a sub-Saharan Africa analyst for *Freedom in the World*.

Niklas Kossow is a PhD candidate and communications officer at the European Research Centre for Anti-Corruption and State-Building in Berlin, focusing on the use of new media tools in anticorruption movements. He holds a bachelor's degree in European social and political studies from University College London, and a master's degree in public policy from the Hertie School of Governance. He previously worked as a volunteer fellow for Freedom House, an adviser for Transparency International, and a consultant for the UN Development Program and the World Wide Web Foundation. He served as a Europe analyst for *Freedom in the World.*

Paul Kubicek is a professor of political science and director of the International Studies Program at Oakland University. He is the author of numerous works on the European Union, democratization, and postcommunist and Turkish politics, which have appeared in journals including *Comparative Politics*, *Political Studies*, and *Political Science Quarterly*. His most recent book is *Political Islam and Democracy in the Muslim World*. He is the editor of *Turkish Studies*. He has taught in Ukraine, Turkey, and Austria, and was a Fulbright Scholar in Slovenia. He received a PhD in political science from the University of Michigan. He served as a Europe analyst for *Freedom in the World.*

Joshua Kurlantzick is a senior fellow for Southeast Asia at the Council on Foreign Relations. Previously, he was a scholar at the Carnegie Endowment for International Peace, where he focused on Southeast Asian politics and economics and China's relations with Southeast Asia. He is a longtime journalist whose articles have appeared in *Time*, the *New Republic*, the *Atlantic Monthly*, *Foreign Affairs*, and the *New Yorker*, among others. He is the author of the recently released book *State Capitalism: How the Return of Statism Is Transforming the World*. He served as an Asia-Pacific analyst for *Freedom in the World.*

Freja Landewall is a research associate with the Governance Group in Norway, and has broad experience from conducting analysis in both the private and public sectors. She holds a master's degree in democracy building and a bachelor's degree in political science, with a specialization in international and comparative politics. She served as a Europe analyst for *Freedom in the World.*

Astrid Larson is Director of Programs and Events at American Friends of the Louvre. She received a master's degree in international media and culture from the New School University. She has served as an analyst for Western Europe, sub-Saharan Africa, and the South Pacific for Freedom House's *Freedom of the Press* report. She served as a Europe analyst for *Freedom in the World.*

Joey Lee is the Asia Law and Justice Program director at the Leitner Center for International Law and Justice at Fordham Law School, where he leads research, advocacy, and capacity-building efforts to support strengthening of rule of law in Asia. He earned a juris doctor degree from Boston University and a master of laws degree from New York University. He served as an Asia-Pacific analyst for *Freedom in the World.*

Kelsey Lilley is associate director of the Atlantic Council's Africa Center, where she closely follows political, security, and economic developments on the continent. Kelsey was a Princeton in Africa Fellow with the International Rescue Committee, and she previously worked at the Africa Center for Strategic Studies at the National Defense University. She holds a bachelor's degree in political science from Davidson College. She served as a sub-Saharan Africa analyst for *Freedom in the World.*

Lone Lindholt holds a graduate degree in law and a PhD degree in international human rights law from the University of Copenhagen. She held for many years a position as senior analyst with the Danish Institute for Human Rights, and has authored and edited numerous publications in the field; undertaken teaching and lecturing in various human rights fields; and served as an expert in numerous development programs for the Institute in Africa, Asia, and the Middle East. In addition to serving an external examiner at several Danish universities, she is now an independent consultant and CEO of Lindholt Consult, as well as an internationally ICI-certified coach, specializing in human rights-related projects and program development and implementation, undertaking assignments in the field, and facilitating partner-driven processes relating to institutional and organizational development. She served as a Europe analyst for *Freedom in the World.*

Shahirah Mahmood recently received her doctorate in political science from the University of Wisconsin, Madison. Her work on Islam, democracy, and women's rights in Malaysia and Indonesia has been published in peer-reviewed journal articles, encyclopedia entries, and newspaper editorials. Her research expertise focuses on civil society activism, economic development, gender and politics, and Islam and politics. Shahirah was formerly a research analyst in Singapore at the Rajaratnam School of International Studies (Contemporary Islam Program) and covered the 2008 Malaysian general elections. She served as an Asia-Pacific analyst for *Freedom in the World.*

Philip Martin is a PhD Candidate in the Department of Political Science and the Security Studies Program at the Massachusetts Institute of Technology. His dissertation research examines the organization of armed movements and state formation in sub-Saharan Africa. He served as a sub-Saharan Africa analyst for *Freedom in the World.*

Aurelien Mondon is a senior lecturer in French and comparative politics at the University of Bath. His research focuses predominantly on elite discourse analysis and the mainstreaming of far right politics, particularly through the use of populism and racism. His recent projects include work on Islamophobia and abstention. His first monograph *A Populist Hegemony?: The Mainstreaming of the Extreme Right in France and Australia* was published in 2013. He is a regular contributor to the mainstream media and has written for CNN, *Newsweek*, openDemocracy, and the *Independent*, among others. He served as a Europe analyst for *Freedom in the World.*

Susana Moreira is an extractive-industries specialist at the World Bank. She received a PhD from the Johns Hopkins University School of Advanced International Studies, focusing on Chinese national oil companies' investment strategies in Latin America and sub-Saharan Africa. She is involved in several other research projects, including Coping with Crisis in African States and Sino-U.S. Energy Triangles. She served as a sub-Saharan Africa analyst for *Freedom in the World.*

Ben Morse is a PhD candidate in political science at the Massachusetts Institute for Technology. His research focuses on state-building and democratic governance in fragile states, with a particular emphasis on the relationship between political competition and state legitimation. He has conducted fieldwork in Liberia, Cote d'Ivoire, and Sierra Leone, and has worked on policy-focused research for Innovations for Poverty Action, the Norwegian Refugee Council, and the Government of Liberia. His work has been supported by the National Science Foundation, the International Growth Centre, and the Folke Bernadotte Academy. He served as a sub-Saharan Africa analyst for *Freedom in the World.*

Martijn Mos is a doctoral candidate at the Department of Government at Cornell University. His scholarly work focuses on the dynamics of shared understandings in international politics. He holds a master's degree in European politics and society from the University of Oxford, a master's degree in global history from the University of Vienna, and a bachelor's degree in liberal arts and sciences from Utrecht University. He served as a Europe and Americas analyst for *Freedom in the World.*

Jasmin Mujanović holds a PhD in political science from York University. His research focuses on postwar democratization processes in the former Yugoslavia and, more broadly, on the role of social movements as drivers of democratic reform in postwar and postauthoritarian states. His work has appeared in a number of scholarly publications, and he is a regular international affairs analyst whose commentary has appeared in the *New York Times*, the *Washington Post*, Al Jazeera, and openDemocracy, among other places. He served as a Europe analyst for *Freedom in the World.*

Joachim Nahem is the director of the Governance Group and senior adviser with the Norwegian Institute of International Affairs (NUPI). He has held multiple posts with the United Nations and has published broadly on governance metrics. He is a contributor to the recent publication *External Powers and the Arab Spring,* and is a board member for Care Norway. Nahem holds degrees from the School of Foreign Service at Georgetown University and the London School of Economics. He served as a Europe analyst for *Freedom in the World.*

Azra Naseem is a postdoctoral research fellow in the School of Law and Government at Dublin City University. She is the author of Dhivehi Sitee, a website providing analysis and commentary on political and social affairs of the Maldives. She served as an Asia-Pacific analyst for *Freedom in the World.*

Gareth Nellis is the Evidence in Governance and Politics postdoctoral fellow at the University of California, Berkeley. In 2016, he received his PhD in political science from Yale University, where he specialized in comparative politics, political economy, and modern South Asia. His research focuses on political parties, the origins and persistence of weakly institutionalized party systems, and the extent to which parties matter for key development outcomes. A second strand of work addresses the drivers of discrimination against internal migrants in fast-urbanizing settings. He served as an Asia-Pacific analyst for *Freedom in the World.*

Mooya Lynn Nyaundi is a staff attorney with the Justice Defenders Program at the American Bar Association Center for Human Rights, where she coordinates pro bono legal assistance for human rights defenders in sub-Saharan Africa. Prior to this, she was a senior civil and criminal litigation associate with the law firm Scanlen and Holderness in Harare, Zimbabwe. She holds an LLB degree from the University of Zimbabwe and an LLM degree in international legal studies from Georgetown University. She served as a sub-Saharan Africa analyst for *Freedom in the World.*

Alysson Akiko Oakley is a PhD candidate at the Johns Hopkins University School of Advanced International Studies (SAIS). Previously, she served as a senior adviser at the International Republican Institute and program director at the U.S.-Indonesia Society. She received a master's degree in international economics and Southeast Asian studies from SAIS and a bachelor's degree in international relations from Brown University. She served as an Asia-Pacific analyst for *Freedom in the World*.

Ken Opalo is an assistant professor at Georgetown University in the School of Foreign Service. His research interests include the political economy of development, elections and accountability, and institutional development, with a focus on African legislatures. Ken has had extensive work and research experience in 10 different countries in East, West, and Southern Africa. His work has been published in the *Journal of Democracy* and the *Journal of East African Studies*. He is currently working on a book manuscript titled *Institutions and Political Change: The Case of African Legislatures*, which examines the institutional development of African legislatures from the colonial period to the present. Ken holds a PhD degree in political science from Stanford University and a BA from Yale University. He served as a sub-Saharan Africa analyst for *Freedom in the World*.

Robert Orttung is research director at the George Washington University (GWU) Sustainability Collaborative and associate research professor of International Affairs at GWU's Elliott School of International Affairs. He is managing editor of *Demokratizatsiya: The Journal of Post-Soviet Democratization* and a coeditor of the *Russian Analytical Digest*. He received a PhD in political science from the University of California, Los Angeles. He served as a Eurasia analyst for *Freedom in the World*.

Chantal Pasquarello is an international human rights and development expert with nearly fifteen years of experience designing and implementing protection programs for at-risk populations, as well as education and humanitarian programs, with over eight years of field experience in Africa and Latin America. As an independent consultant, she has primarily supported human rights projects in Honduras, Colombia, and Mexico. She previously worked extensively on human rights and development, and on journalist protection issues, as deputy director for Freedom House's Mexico office and while leading Freedom House's emergency assistance program for activists and civil society organizations under threat. Prior to working with Freedom House, she coordinated the funding portfolio for the International Rescue Committee's largest country program in the Democratic Republic of Congo. While working with the Kenya National Commission on Human Rights in Nairobi, she developed human rights education trainings for police and government ministers and assisted in launching preelection human rights advocacy campaigns. She graduated with highest honors in international relations from Lafayette College and earned an MA in international affairs from Columbia University's School of International and Public Affairs (SIPA). She served as an Americas analyst for *Freedom in the World*.

Nicole Phillips is an adjunct professor at the University of California Hastings College of the Law, a law professor at the Université de la Foundation Dr. Aristide in Port-au-Prince, and staff attorney with the Institute for Justice and Democracy in Haiti. She serves as a member of the board of directors of Human Rights Advocates, a nongovernmental organization with consultative status to the United Nations, and has appeared before various UN bodies and the Inter-American Commission on Human Rights. She earned her bachelor's degree from the University of California, San Diego, in political science with a concentration in international relations, and her juris doctor degree from the University of San Francisco. She served as an Americas analyst for *Freedom in the World*.

Arch Puddington is the Distinguished Fellow for Democracy Studies at Freedom House and coeditor of *Freedom in the World*. He has written widely on American foreign policy, race relations, organized labor, and the history of the Cold War. He is the author of *Broadcasting Freedom: The Cold War Triumph of Radio Free Europe and Radio Liberty* and *Lane Kirkland: Champion of American Labor*. He received a bachelor's degree in English literature from the University of Missouri, Columbia. He served as an Americas analyst for *Freedom in the World*.

Tyson Roberts is a lecturer in political science and international studies at the University of California, Irvine. His research interests include authoritarian institutions, democratization, and international political economy. He has published in *Comparative Political Studies*, *Electoral Studies*, the *Journal of African Elections*, and the *Washington Post*'s Monkey Cage blog. He received a PhD in Political Science from the University of California, Los Angeles. He served as a sub-Saharan Africa analyst for *Freedom in the World*.

Eric Robinson is the associate director for Africa at the National Endowment for Democracy (NED). He has helped guide the NED's work in East, Horn, and Southern Africa for the past eight years and his academic and professional work for the past 20 years has had a special focus on the Horn of Africa. He received a master's degree in international relations, with a focus on conflict resolution, from Wayne State University, Detroit, and a bachelor's degree in political science from the University of Michigan, Ann Arbor. He served as a sub-Saharan Africa analyst for *Freedom in the World*.

Ryan Salzman is assistant professor of political science at Northern Kentucky University. His teaching and scholarship is focused on topics including Central American media, democratic behaviors, social media use, and creative placemaking. He has worked with Freedom House since 2014 on the *Freedom of the Press* and the *Freedom in the World* publications. He received his PhD in political science from the University of North Texas in 2011. He served as an Americas analyst for *Freedom in the World*.

Jean Scrimgeour is a public diplomacy and democratic governance specialist with experience working in the United States, the United Kingdom, and Southern Africa. Currently a global proposal development manager for Volunteer Services Overseas, Jean was formerly a parliamentary, political, and communications officer for the British High Commission in South Africa and trade, science, and innovation communications lead for the British Embassy in Washington, DC. Jean has masters's degree in conflict resolution in divided societies from King's College in London as a British Chevening Scholar and a bachelor of social science degree in law and politics in international relations from the University of Cape Town. She served as a sub-Saharan Africa analyst for *Freedom in the World*.

Michael Semple is a visiting research professor at Queen's University, Belfast Institute, for the Study of Conflict Transformation and Social Justice. He has practiced and written on humanitarian assistance and conflict resolution in Afghanistan and Pakistan. Since 2008 he has worked as a scholar and adviser on conflict resolution, with particular focus on the Afghan conflict. He has directly advised key policymakers concerning the conflict in

Afghanistan, particularly with regard to political engagement with the Taliban. He is currently researching the evolving rhetoric of the Taliban's armed struggle and the challenges facing militant jihadi groups evolving toward a political role. He served as an Asia-Pacific analyst for *Freedom in the World.*

Debbie Sharnak received her PhD from the University of Wisconsin, Madison, and teaches at New York University and Hunter College. Her research focuses on transitional justice and human rights discourse in the Southern Cone. She has worked at several organizations including the International Center for Transitional Justice, Public Action Research, and the New Media Advocacy Project. Her work has been published by *Foreign Policy*, the North American Congress on Latin America (NACLA), *Latin Correspondent*, *Diplomacy & Statecraft*, and in several edited volumes. Debbie was also a Fulbright Scholar in Uruguay. She served as an Americas analyst for *Freedom in the World.*

Dustin N. Sharp is an associate professor at the Kroc School of Peace Studies at the University of San Diego. He holds a juris doctor degree from Harvard Law School and a PhD from Leiden University. His research and teaching interests include international human rights law, transitional justice, and postconflict peacebuilding. Sharp previously worked for Human Rights Watch, where he was responsible for designing and implementing research and advocacy strategies in Francophone West Africa. He served as a sub-Saharan Africa analyst for *Freedom in the World.*

Elton Skendaj is a lecturer in the Department of Political Science at the University of Miami. His research focuses on how international and local actors can sustain peace and democracy in postwar societies. He has published a book with Cornell University Press and several articles in the *Global Governance* and *Problems of Postcommunism* journals. He has also worked professionally with international organizations and civil society organizations in Europe and the U.S. Skendaj holds a PhD in government from Cornell University, and has had research fellowships at the Woodrow Wilson International Center for scholars and the University of Notre Dame. He served as a Europe analyst for *Freedom in the World.*

Sheila A. Smith, an expert on Japanese politics and foreign policy, is senior fellow for Japan studies at the Council on Foreign Relations (CFR). She is the author of *Intimate Rivals: Japanese Domestic Politics and a Rising China* (Columbia University Press, 2015). She joined CFR from the East-West Center in 2007 and was a visiting scholar at Keio University in 2007–8 as part of the Abe Fellowship. Smith is vice chair of the U.S. advisers to the U.S.-Japan Conference on Cultural and Educational Exchange (CULCON) and serves on the advisory committee for the U.S.-Japan Network for the Future program of the Maureen and Mike Mansfield Foundation. She teaches as an adjunct professor at Georgetown University and serves on the board of its *Journal of Asian Affairs*. She earned her MA and PhD degrees from the Department of Political Science at Columbia University. She served as an Asia-Pacific analyst for *Freedom in the World.*

Amanda Snellinger is an affiliate scholar and lecturer in University of Washington's Jackson School of International Studies. She received her PhD in anthropology from Cornell University and did postdoctoral research at University of Oxford's School for Geography and the Environment. Her teaching and research interests include social and political mobility in South Asia through the lens of democratic and postconflict theory. Her work has appeared in *CounterPunch, Critical Asian Studies, Constellations: International Journal of Critical*

Democratic Theory, Cultural Anthropology, Current History, Modern Asian Studies, and *Political and Legal Anthropology Review.* She served as an Asia-Pacific analyst for *Freedom in the World.*

Natasha Borges Sugiyama is an associate professor of political science at the University of Wisconsin-Milwaukee. She received her PhD in government from the University of Texas at Austin. Her teaching interests include democratization, governance, and public policy in Latin America. Her research focuses on the politics of poverty relief, social sector reform, and human development in Brazil. She is author of *Diffusion of Good Government: Social Sector Reforms in Brazil* (University of Notre Dame Press, 2013). Her research has also been published in *American Political Science Review*, *Comparative Politics*, and *Perspectives on Politics*, among other journals. She served as an Americas analyst for *Freedom in the World.*

Natalie Sykes is a third-year law student at Columbia Law School. She earned her master's degree in human rights at the London School of Economics, and holds a bachelor's degree in foreign service from Georgetown University. A former intern at Freedom House, she has written for both *Freedom in the World* and *Freedom of the Press.* She served as an Americas analyst for *Freedom in the World.*

Paul Thissen is a PhD candidate in political science at the University of California, Berkeley. His research interests include governance in weakly institutionalized states and civil conflict, with a focus on sub-Saharan Africa. He has conducted research in Chad and Cameroon. His research has received support from the National Science Foundation and the United States Institute of Peace. In the 2015–16 academic year, he was a visiting researcher and instructor at the Université Adam Barka d'Abéché in Chad. He served as a sub-Saharan Africa analyst for *Freedom in the World.*

Luca Tomini is a lecturer in political science at the Université libre de Bruxelles (ULB) and guest professor at the University of Antwerp (Belgium). His main research interests cover transitions to democracy and democratization processes in a comparative perspective, including autocratization and democratic backsliding. He also works on the role of the European Union and its influence on the democratization of Central and Eastern Europe. He has recently published the book *Democratizing Central and Eastern Europe* (Routledge), and he is currently working on a new book titled *Why Democracies Collapse* (Routledge). In addition, he published with Palgrave Macmillan, and had articles in *Comparative European Politics*, *Europe-Asia Studies*, and *Journal of Contemporary Central and Eastern Europe.* He served as a Europe analyst for *Freedom in the World.*

Michael Toomey is a lecturer of political science at Wenzhou-Kean University in Wenzhou, China. He earned his master's degrees in international studies and European politics from University of Limerick and Lund University, respectively, and recently received his doctorate in global affairs from Rutgers University. He has contributed to *Freedom of the Press,* and served as a Europe analyst for *Freedom in the World.*

Jenny Town is the assistant director of the U.S.-Korea Institute at the Johns Hopkins University's School of Advanced International Studies. Previously, she worked for the Human Rights in North Korea Project at Freedom House. She received a master's degree from

Columbia University's School of International and Public Affairs, with a concentration in human rights. She served as an Asia-Pacific analyst for *Freedom in the World.*

Noah Tucker is the senior editor for Radio Free Europe/Radio Liberty's Uzbek service, *Ozodlik*, and an associate at George Washington University's Elliot School of International Affairs Central Asia Program (CAP). He was previously the lead researcher for the Central Asian Digital Islam Project launched with the University of Michigan Islamic Studies Program and CAP to explore the way social media is expanding the Islamic marketplace of ideas in Central Asia, and was the managing editor at Registan.net. As a research consultant, Noah worked on collaborative projects with government agencies and NGOs to identify the way social and religious groups affect political and security outcomes, and headed a team that tracks social media use by Uzbek violent extremist organizations and their effect on the Uzbek-language internet. He has worked on Central Asian issues since 2002— specializing in religion, national identity, ethnic conflict and social media—and received an MA from Harvard's Davis Center in Russian, East European, and Central Asian Studies in 2008. He has spent four and half years in the region, primarily in Uzbekistan, returned most recently for fieldwork on religious education and community-level antiviolence initiatives in southern Kyrgyzstan and the surrounding areas in 2016. He served as a Eurasia analyst for *Freedom in the World.*

Angela Vance is a senior program officer at the National Democratic Institute focusing on governance and advocacy issues in Africa. Previously, she served as a program officer at World Learning and was based in East Africa working for Pact, Save the Children, and Common Hope for Health. She holds a master's degree in conflict, security, and development from King's College London and a bachelor's degree in international relations from American University with a concentration in peace and conflict resolution. She served as a sub-Saharan Africa analyst for *Freedom in the World.*

Wouter Veenendaal is an assistant professor of political science at Leiden University, the Netherlands. His research focuses on politics and democracy in small states, and he has conducted field research in various microstates and small states around the world. Between 2014 and 2016, he worked as a postdoctoral researcher at the Royal Netherlands Institute of Southeast Asian and Caribbean Studies, where he studied politics in nonsovereign territories, with a particular focus on the Dutch Caribbean. In his current research project, which is funded by a grant of the Dutch National Science Foundation, he examines the causes of regime stability in small states. His research has been published in various journals in the field of comparative politics, and in 2017 his new book will be published by Oxford University Press. He served as a Europe analyst for *Freedom in the World.*

Anja Vojvodic is a PhD candidate at Rutgers University in New Brunswick, New Jersey. She studies women and politics, and comparative politics. Her interests include social movements in the Western Balkans, gender quota implementation in parliaments, and the substantive political representation of women and minority groups. Anja holds a master's degree in global affairs from New York University and a bachelor's degree in political science from Queens College. She was a United States Fulbright Scholar in Serbia from 2011–12. She served as a Europe analyst for *Freedom in the World.*

Gregory White is a professor of government at Smith College. Recently he is the author of *Climate Change and Migration: Borders and Security in a Warming World* and a coedited volume *North African Politics: Change and Continuity*. He is the recipient of a Mellon Foundation New Directions Fellowship, as well as Fulbright-IIE and Fulbright-Hays scholarships to Tunisia and Morocco, respectively. He is a co-editor of the *Journal of North African Studies*. He received a PhD from the University of Wisconsin, Madison. He served as a Middle East and North Africa analyst for *Freedom in the World*.

Raisa Wickrematunge is currently coeditor at Groundviews, a civic media initiative. Previously, she worked at Sri Lanka's national newspaper, the *Sunday Leader*, covering a variety of issues including politics, human rights, news, and features. She also has prior editorial experience as deputy chief subeditor and deputy features editor at the *Sunday Leader*. Raisa is a graduate of the University of Leicester, where she earned a MSc in marketing, and received a bachelor's degree in law from the University of London. She served as an Asia-Pacific analyst for *Freedom in the World*.

Mikayel Zolyan is a historian and political analyst. His interests include the South Caucasus and former USSR region, with a focus on such issues as democratization and nation-building in political movements and social activism, as well as issues of ethnicity, nationalism, and conflict. He served as a Eurasia analyst for *Freedom in the World*.

ADVISERS

Julio F. Carrión is an associate professor and associate chair of the Department of Political Science and International Relations at the University of Delaware.

Kathleen Collins is an associate professor in the Department of Political Science at the University of Minnesota in Minneapolis.

Javier Corrales is Dwight W. Morrow 1895 Professor of Political Science at Amherst College.

Tanya Domi is an adjunct professor at Columbia University's School of International and Public Affairs, an affiliate faculty member of the university's Harriman Institute, and a fellow at the Emerging Democracies Institute.

Tulia Falleti is the Class of 1965 Term associate professor of political science, director of the Latin American and Latino Studies Program, and senior fellow of the Leonard Davis Institute for Health Economics at the University of Pennsylvania.

Robert Lane Greene is an editor at the *Economist* in London, and a former adjunct assistant professor of global affairs at New York University.

Steven Heydemann is Janet W. Ketcham 1953 Professor and Director of Middle East Studies at Smith College, and a nonresident senior fellow at the Brookings Institution Center for Middle East Policy.

Melissa Labonte is an associate professor of political science and associate dean for strategic initiatives at the Graduate School of Arts and Sciences at Fordham University.

Thomas R. Lansner is an African affairs specialist who taught at Columbia University and Sciences Po Paris from 1994 to 2014, and is currently visiting faculty at Aga Khan University, Nairobi.

Adrienne LeBas is an associate professor of government at American University's School of Public Affairs.

Fabrice Lehoucq is professor of political science at the University of North Carolina Greensboro.

Peter Lewis is an associate professor and director of the African Studies Program at Johns Hopkins University's School of Advanced International Studies.

Adam Luedtke is an assistant professor of political science at City University of New York, Queensborough Community College.

Peter Mandaville is a professor of government and politics and director of the Ali Vural Ak Center for Islamic Studies at George Mason University.

Carl Minzner is a professor at Fordham Law School.

Alexander J. Motyl is a professor of political science at Rutgers University, Newark.

Andrew J. Nathan is the Class of 1919 Professor of Political Science at Columbia University.

Philip Oldenburg is a research scholar at Columbia University's South Asia Institute.

Tsveta Petrova is a fellow at the Harriman Institute, Columbia University.

Samer S. Shehata is an associate professor and Middle East studies program coordinator at the University of Oklahoma.

Scott Taylor is a professor at the School of Foreign Service and director of the African Studies Program at Georgetown University.

Bridget Welsh is a professor of political science at Ipek University, a senior research associate at the Center for East Asia Democratic Studies, National Taiwan University; a senior associate fellow of the Habibie Center; and a university fellow of Charles Darwin University.

Susanna Wing is an associate professor and chair of the political science department at Haverford College.

Selected Sources

PUBLICATIONS/BROADCASTS/BLOGS

ABC Color [Paraguay], www.abc.com.py
Africa Energy Intelligence,
    www.africaintelligence.com
African Arguments, africanarguments.org
African Elections Database, http://
    africanelections.tripod.com
Aftenposten [Norway], www.aftenposten.no
Agence France-Presse (AFP), www.afp.com
Al-Arab al-Yawm [Jordan]:
    www.alarabalyawm.net
Al-Arabiya, www.alarabiya.net
Al-Akhbar [Lebanon], www.al-akhbar.com
Al-Dustour [Egypt], www.addustour.com
Al-Jazeera America,
    www.america.aljazeera.com
allAfrica.com, www.allafrica.com
Al-Masry al-Youm [Egypt],
    www.almasryalyoum.com
Al-Ray Al-'am [Kuwait], www.alraialaam.com
Al-Quds al-Arabi, www.alquds.co.uk
Al-Thawra [Yemen], www.althawranews.net
Annual Review of Population Law (Harvard
    Law School), *www.hsph.harvard.edu/
    population*
Arab News [Saudi Arabia], www.arabnews.com
Asharq Alawsat, www.asharqalawsat.com
Asia Times, www.atimes.com
Associated Press (AP), www.ap.org
Awareness Times [Sierra Leone], www.news.sl
Balkan Insight, www.balkaninsight.com
The Baltic Times, www.baltictimes.com
Bangkok Post, www.bangkokpost.com
British Broadcasting Corporation (BBC),
    www.bbc.co.uk
BruDirect.com [Brunei], www.brudirect.com
Cameroon Tribune, www.cameroon-tribune.cm
Central News Agency [Taiwan], http://
    focustaiwan.tw
China Post, www.chinapost.com.tw
CIA World Factbook, www.cia.gov/cia/
    publications/factbook
Copenhagen Post [Denmark], www.cphpost.dk
Corriere della Sera [Italy], www.corriere.it
Czech News Agency, www.ceskenoviny.cz/
    news

Daily Excelsior [Indian Kashmir],
    www.dailyexcelsior.com
Daily Star [Lebanon], www.dailystar.com.lb
Danas [Serbia], www.danas.rs/danasrs/
    naslovna.1.html
Dani [Bosnia-Herzegovina], www.bhdani.com
Dawn [Pakistan], www.dawn.com
Der Spiegel [Germany], www.spiegel.de
Der Standard [Austria], www.derstandard.at
Deutsche Welle [Germany], www.dwelle.de
East Africa Standard [Kenya],
    www.eastandard.net
The Economist, www.economist.com
Ekho Moskvy [Russia], http://echo.msk.ru
El Mercurio [Chile], www.elmercurio.cl
El Pais [Uruguay], www.elpais.com.uy
El Tiempo [Colombia], www.eltiempo.com
El Universal [Venezuela], www.eluniversal.com
FBI Hate Crime Statistics, https://www.fbi.gov/
    about-us/investigate/civilrights/hate_crimes
Federated States of Micronesia Information
    Services, www.fsmpio.fm
Fiji Times Online, www.fijitimes.com
Financial Times, www.ft.com
Foreign Policy, www.foreignpolicy.com
France 24, www.france24.com
Global News Wire, www.lexis-nexis.com
The Guardian [Nigeria],
    www.ngrguardiannews.com
The Guardian [United Kingdom],
    www.guardian.co.uk
Gulf Daily News [Bahrain], www.gulf-daily-
    news.com
Haaretz [Israel], www.haaretz.com
Harakah Daily [Malaysia], http://
    bm.harakahdaily.net
Haveeru Daily [Maldives],
    www.haveeru.com.mv
Hindustan Times [India],
    www.hindustantimes.com
Hurriyet [Turkey], www.hurriyetdailynews.com
Iceland Review, www.icelandreview.com
The Independent [United Kingdom],
    www.independent.co.uk
Indian Express, www.indian-express.com
Inter Press Service, www.ips.org

IRIN news, www.irinnews.org
Irish Independent, http://www.independent.ie
Irish Times, http://www.irishtimes.com
Islands Business Magazine,
    www.islandsbusiness.com
Izvestia, www.izvestia.ru
Jadaliyya, www.jadaliyya.com
Jakarta Post, www.thejakartapost.com
Jamaica Gleaner, www.jamaica-gleaner.com
Jeune Afrique [France], www.jeuneafrique.com
Jordan Times, www.jordantimes.com
Journal of Democracy,
    www.journalofdemocracy.org
Jyllands-Posten [Denmark], www.jp.dk
Kashmir Times [Indian Kashmir],
    www.kashmirtimes.com
Kommersant [Russia], www.kommersant.ru
Kompas [Indonesia], www.kompas.com
Korea Times [South Korea], http://
    times.hankooki.com
Kuensel [Bhutan], www.kuenselonline.com
Kyiv Post, www.kyivpost.com
L'Informazione di San Marino,
    www.libertas.sm
La Nación [Argentina], www.lanacion.com.ar
La Presse de Tunisie [Tunisia], www.lapresse.tn
La Repubblica [Italy], www.repubblica.it
La Tercera [Chile], www.latercera.com
Latin American Regional Reports,
    www.latinnews.com
Le Faso [Burkina Faso], www.lefaso.net
Le Messager [Cameroon],
    quotidienlemessager.net
Le Monde [France], www.lemonde.fr
Le Quotidien [Senegal], www.lequotidien.sn
Le Temps [Switzerland], www.letemps.ch
Le Togolais [Togo], www.letogolais.com
The Local [Sweden], www.thelocal.se
L'Orient-Le Jour [Lebanon],
    www.lorientlejour.com
Mail & Guardian [South Africa], www.mg.co.za
Mada Masr, www.madamasr.com
Malaysiakini [Malaysia],
    www.malaysiakini.com
Maldives Independent, www.minivannews.com
Manila Times, www.manilatimes.net
Marianas Variety [Micronesia],
    www.mvariety.com
Matangi Tonga Magazine,
    www.matangitonga.to
The Messenger [Georgia],
    www.messenger.com.ge
Middle East Report, www.merip.org
Mongolia Focus, http://blogs.ubc.ca/mongolia

Moscow Times, www.themoscowtimes.com
Munhwa Ilbo [South Korea], www.munhwa.com
Nacional [Croatia], www.nacional.hr
The Namibian, www.namibian.com.na
The Nation [Thailand],
    www.nationmultimedia.com
The National [Papua New Guinea],
    www.thenational.com.pg
New Dawn [Liberia],
    www.thenewdawnliberia.com
New York Times, www.nytimes.com
New Zealand Herald, www.nzherald.co.nz
North Korea Economy Watch,
    www.nkeconwatch.com
Nyasa Times [Malawi], www.nyasatimes.com
O Globo [Brazil], www.oglobo.globo.com
Oman Arabic Daily, www.omandaily.com
Outlook [India], www.outlookindia.com
Pacific Islands Report, http://
    pidp.eastwestcenter.org/pireport
Página/12 [Argentina], www.pagina12.com.ar
Papua New Guinea Post-Courier,
    www.postcourier.com.pg
Philippine Daily Inquirer, www.inquirer.net
Phnom Penh Post, www.phnompenhpost.com
Politics.hu [Hungary], www.politics.hu
Politika [Serbia], www.politika.rs
Prague Post, *www.praguepost.com*
Radio Free Europe-Radio Liberty,
    www.rferl.org
Radio Okapi [Congo-Kinshasa],
    www.radioOkapi.net
Republika [Indonesia], www.republika.co.id
Rodong Sinmun [North Korea],
    www.rodong.rep.kp
Sahel Blog, http://sahelblog.wordpress.com
Semana [Colombia], www.semana.com
Slobodna Bosna [Bosnia-Herzegovina],
    www.slobodna-bosna.ba
SME [Slovakia], www.sme.sk
Somaliland Times, www.somalilandtimes.net
South China Morning Post [Hong Kong],
    www.scmp.com
Straits Times [Singapore],
    www.straitstimes.asia1.com.sg
Syria Comment, www.joshualandis.com
Taipei Times, www.taipeitimes.com
Tamilnet.com, www.tamilnet.com
The Telegraph [United Kingdom],
    www.telegraph.co.uk
Tico Times [Costa Rica], www.ticotimes.net
Times of Central Asia, www.times.kg
Trinidad Express, www.trinidadexpress.com

Union Patriótica de Cuba (UNPACU),
www.unpacu.org/acerca-de/sobre-unpacu
U.S. State Department Reports on Human
Rights Practices, www.state.gov/g/drl/rls/
hrrpt
U.S. State Department Reports on Human
Trafficking, www.state.gov/g/tip
U.S. State Department International Religious
Freedom Reports, www.state.gov/g/drl/irf
Voice of America, www.voa.gov
Wall Street Journal, www.wsj.com
Washington Post, www.washingtonpost.com
Xinhua News, www.xinhuanet.com
Yemen Times, www.yementimes.com
Zambia Reports, zambiareports.com

ORGANIZATIONS

Afghan Independent Human Rights
Commission, www.aihrc.org.af
Afrobarometer, www.afrobarometer.org
Alternative ASEAN Network on Burma,
www.altsean.org
American Bar Association Rule of Law
Initiative, www.abanet.org/rol
American Civil Liberties Union, www.aclu.org
Amnesty International, www.amnesty.org
Anti-Slavery International, www.antislavery.org
Arabic Network for Human Rights Information
(ANHRI), www.anhri.net
Asian Center for Human Rights [India],
www.achrweb.org
Assistance Association for Political Prisoners
[Burma], www.aappb.org
Balkan Human Rights Web,
www.greekhelsinki.gr
Belarusian Institute for Strategic Studies,
www.belinstitute.eu
Brookings Institution, www.brookings.edu
B'Tselem [Palestine], www.btselem.org
Cairo Institute for Human Rights,
www.cihrs.org
Carnegie Endowment for International Peace,
www.carnegieendowment.org
Center for Strategic and International Studies,
www.csis.org
Chatham House [United Kingdom],
www.chathamhouse.org
Committee for the Prevention of Torture,
www.cpt.coe.int
Committee to Protect Journalists, www.cpj.org
Council on Foreign Relations, www.cfr.org/
index.html

Ditshwanelo – Botswana Centre for Human
Rights, www.ditshwanelo.org.bw
Electoral Institute of Southern Africa,
www.eisa.org.za
European Roma Rights Center, www.errc.org
Extractive Industries Transparency Initiative,
www.eiti.org
Globe International [Mongolia],
www.globeinter.org.mn/old/en/index.php
Hong Kong Human Rights Monitor,
www.hkhrm.org.hk
Human Rights Commission of Pakistan,
www.hrcp-web.org
Human Rights Watch, www.hrw.org
Index on Censorship,
www.indexoncensorship.org
Indonesian Survey Institute, www.lsi.or.id
Institute for Democracy in Eastern Europe,
www.idee.org
Institute for War and Peace Reporting,
www.iwpr.net
Inter-American Press Association,
www.sipiapa.com
Internal Displacement Monitoring Center,
www.internal-displacement.org
International Campaign for Tibet,
www.savetibet.org
International Centre for Not-for-Profit Law:
NGO Law Monitor, www.icnl.org
International Crisis Group, www.crisisgroup.org
International Foundation for Electoral Systems,
www.ifes.org
International Freedom of Expression Exchange,
www.ifex.org
International Labour Organization, www.ilo.org
International Lesbian and Gay Association,
www.ilga.org
International Monetary Fund, www.imf.org
International Organization for Migration,
www.iom.int
Kashmir Study Group,
www.kashmirstudygroup.net
Korea Development Institute, www.kdi.re.kr
MADA_Palestinian Center for Development and
Media Freedoms, www.madacenter.org/
index.php?lang = 1
Media Institute of Southern Africa,
www.misa.org
Migrant Assistance Programme Thailand,
www.mapfoundationcm.org/eng
National Democratic Institute for International
Affairs, www.ndi.org
National Human Rights Commission of Korea,
www.humanrights.go.kr

National Peace Council of Sri Lanka,
www.peace-srilanka.org
National Society for Human Rights [Namibia],
www.nshr.org.na
Nicaragua Network, www.nicanet.org
Odhikar [Bangladesh], www.odhikar.org
Population Reference Bureau, www.prb.org
Reporters Sans Frontières, www.rsf.org
South African Human Rights Commission,
www.sahrc.org.za
South Asia Terrorism Portal [India],
www.satp.org

Transparency International,
www.transparency.org
Truth and Reconciliation Commission of
Liberia, www.trcofliberia.org
United Nations High Commissioner for
Refugees, www.unhcr.org
United Nations Office for the Coordination of
Humanitarian Affairs (OCHA), http://
unocha.org
World Bank, www.worldbank.org

Freedom House supports global freedom through comprehensive analysis, dedicated advocacy, and concrete assistance for democratic activists around the world.

Founded in 1941, Freedom House has long been a vigorous proponent of the right of all individuals to be free. Eleanor Roosevelt and Wendell Willkie served as Freedom House's first honorary co-chairpersons.

www.freedomhouse.org

Support the right of every individual to be free.
Donate now.